Child Development

A Cultural Approach

SECOND EDITION

Jeffrey Jensen Arnett
Clark University

Ashley E. Maynard
University of Hawai'i at Mānoa

PEARSON

Boston   Columbus   Indianapolis   New York City   San Francisco
Amsterdam   Cape Town   Dubai   London   Madrid   Milan   Paris   Montréal   Toronto
Delhi   Mexico City   São Paulo   Sydney   Hong Kong   Seoul   Singapore   Taipei   Tokyo

VP, Product Development: Dickson Musslewhite
Senior Acquisitions Editor: Amber Chow
Editorial Assistant: Stephany Harrington
Director, Content Strategy and Development: Brita Nordin
Senior Development Editor: Julie Swasey
Director, Project Management Services: Lisa Iarkowski
Project Team Lead: Denise Forlow
Project Manager: Barbara Mack
Program Team Lead: Amber Mackey
Program Manager: Cecilia Turner
Director of Field Marketing: Jonathan Cottrell
Senior Product Marketing Manager: Lindsey Prudhomme Gill
Executive Field Marketing Manager: Kate Stewart
Marketing Assistant, Field Marketing: Paige Patunas
Marketing Assistant, Product Marketing: Jessica Warren

Operations Manager: Mary Fischer
Operations Specialist: Carol Melville
Associate Director of Design: Blair Brown
Interior Design: Kathryn Foot
Cover Art Director: Maria Lange
Cover Design: Pentagram
Cover Art: Cover illustration by Alec Doherty, © Pearson Education, Inc.
Digital Studio Project Manager: Christopher Fegan
Digital Studio Project Manager: Elissa Senra-Sargent
Digital Studio Team Lead: Peggy Bliss
Full-Service Project Management and Composition: Integra Software Services Pvt. Ltd.
Printer/Binder: RR Donnelley/Kendallville
Cover Printer: Phoenix Color/Hagerstown

Acknowledgments of third party content appear on page C-1, which constitutes an extension of this copyright page.

Library of Congress Cataloging-in-Publication Data

Arnett, Jeffrey Jensen.
    Child development: a cultural approach/Jeffrey Arnett and Ashley Maynard.—Second edition.
    Revised edition of Child development, 2013.
    ISBN 9780134011899
    LCSH: Child development.   1. Child development—Cross-cultural studies.
    Child psychology.
    HQ767.9 .A75 2015
    305.231—dc23

                                                                        2015038745

10 9 8 7 6 5 4 3 2 1

Student Edition
ISBN-10:   0-13-401189-9
ISBN-13: 978-0-13-401189-9

Books a la Carte
ISBN-10:   0-13-422580-5
ISBN-13: 978-0-13-422580-7

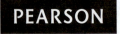

*To my mom, who loved it all,
from start to finish.*

—*Jeffrey Jensen Arnett*

I thank all my teachers, who taught me how to learn. I am especially grateful to Patricia Greenfield and Tom Weisner for helping me find my own path in the study of culture and development.

—Ashley E. Maynard

Contents

Preface

Welcome to *Child Development: A Cultural Approach.* For us, the most important motivation in writing this book was that we wanted to provide students with a portrayal of development that would cover the whole amazing range of human cultural diversity. As professors who have taught human development courses for years and were familiar with the available textbooks, we were struck by how narrow all of them seemed to be. They focused on human development in the United States as if it were the typical pattern for people everywhere, with only the occasional mention of people in other parts of the world. If you knew nothing about human development except what you read in a standard textbook, you would conclude that 95 percent of the human population must reside in the United States. Yet the United States is actually less than 5 percent of the world's population, and there is an immense range of patterns of human development in cultures around the globe, with most of those patterns strikingly different than the mainstream U.S. model. And, even within the United States, cultural diversity is much greater than what is found in the typical textbook.

So, in writing, we decided to take a cultural approach. We set out to portray child development as it takes place across all the different varieties of cultural patterns that people have devised in response to their local conditions and the creative inspiration of their imaginations. Our goal was to teach students to *think culturally*, so that when they apply child development to the work they do or to their own lives, they understand that there is, always and everywhere, a cultural basis to development. The cultural approach also includes learning how to critique research for the extent to which it does or does not take the cultural basis of development into account. We provide this kind of critique at numerous points throughout the book, with the intent that students will learn how to do it themselves by the time they reach the end.

We know from our experience as teachers that students find it fascinating to learn about the different forms that child development takes in various cultures, but there are also practical benefits to the cultural approach. It is more important than ever for students to have knowledge of the wider world because of the increasingly globalized economy and because so many problems, such as terrorism and climate change, cross borders. Whether they travel the globe or remain in their home towns, in a culturally diverse and globalized world, students will benefit from being able to apply the cultural approach and think culturally about development, whether in social interactions with friends and neighbors, or in their careers because they may have patients, students, or coworkers who come from different cultures.

The Chinese have an expression that loosely translates as "the frog in the well knows not of the great ocean," and it is often used as a cautionary reminder to look beyond our own experience and not to assume that what is true for ourselves is true for everyone else as well. We think all of us are like that frog, in a way (which is, in case you were wondering, why a frog is featured on the cover of this book). We've grown up in a certain cultural context. We've learned to think about life in a certain way. We've learned to think about development in a certain way. And most of us don't realize how broad and diverse our world really is. Our hope is that this book will help more students lift themselves out of the well and appreciate the wonderful diversity of child development.

The cultural approach makes this textbook much different from other child development textbooks, but there are other features that make this textbook distinct. This is the only major textbook to include a separate chapter on toddlerhood, the second and third years of life. Jeff had always been puzzled by the way other textbooks gloss over toddlerhood, usually including the second year of life as part of "infancy" and the third year of life as part of "early childhood." Yet any parent knows that years 2 and 3 are a lot different from what comes before or after, and Jeff remembered this well from his own experience as a father of twins. Infants cannot walk or talk, and once toddlers learn to do both in years 2 and 3, their experience of life—and their parents' experiences—change utterly. Toddlers are also different from older children, in that their ability for emotional self-regulation and their awareness of what is and is not acceptable behavior in their culture is much more limited.

This textbook is also set apart among major textbooks in that it includes an entire chapter on the stage of emerging adulthood. Emerging adulthood, roughly ages 18 to 25, is a new life stage that has arisen in developed countries over the past 50 years, as people have entered later into the commitments that structure adult life in most cultures: marriage, parenthood, and stable work. Jeff originally proposed the theory of emerging adulthood in 2000, and it has now become widely used in the social sciences. We think it is a fascinating and dynamic time of life, and we know students enjoy learning about it because many of them are in that life stage or about to enter it.

This textbook is somewhat shorter than most other texts on child development. There is one chapter devoted to each phase of child development through emerging adulthood, for a total of nine chapters. Each chapter is divided into three major sections, which correspond to the physical, the cognitive, and the emotional and social domains of development. This is an introductory textbook, and the goal is not to teach students everything there is to know about every aspect of child development, but to provide them with a foundation of knowledge on child development that hopefully will inspire them to learn more in other courses and throughout life.

What's New in the Second Edition?

Broader Emphasis on Cultural Diversity

New "Chapter Introduction" Videos begin each chapter and provide an overview of the developmental stage being covered. The videos feature Americans from diverse backgrounds discussing their lives, experiences, and the role that culture has played in their development or the development of their children.

WORLD, THE TRANSITION FROM EARLY CHILDHOOD TO MIDDLE CHILDHOOD IS RECOGNIZED AS AN IMPORTANT SHIFT IN CHILDREN'S DEVELOPMENT, WHEN THE CHILDREN BECOME CAPABLE OF GREATER COGNITIVE CHALLENGES AND PERSONAL RESPONSIBILITY (SAMEROFF & HAITH, 1996). In developing countries, middle childhood is often the age when children are first given important family duties, such as taking care of younger siblings, buying or selling goods, maintaining a fire, or caring for domestic animals (Gaskins, 2015; Weisner, 1996). According to Roy D'Andrade (1987), middle childhood is when children first show a grasp of **cultural models**, which are cognitive structures pertaining to common activities, for example buying something at the market, herding cattle, taking care of an infant, making bread, or delivering a message to a relative's house. Children in both developed and developing countries begin formal schooling in middle childhood, which includes cultural models of "listen to the teacher," "wait your turn," and "do

as early as toddlerhood, but during middle childhood their understanding of cultural models acquires greater complexity, so that they become capable of taking on a much broader range of tasks (Gaskins, 2015; Weisner, 1996). Children in middle childhood express an industriousness that makes them want to learn and take on new tasks.

Here as elsewhere in the human life span, how we experience a given stage of life depends greatly on cultural context. Children in all cultures become more capable of useful work in middle childhood, but the nature of their work varies greatly. For many children throughout human history it has been mainly farm work—tending the fields, herding the cows, and feeding the chickens. For today's children, it might be schoolwork or household work in developed countries, and any of a wide range of work in developing countries, from household work to factory work to feeding domestic animals. In this chapter we explore a wide range of cultural variations in children's experiences of middle childhood.

Watch CHAPTER INTRODUCTION: MIDDLE CHILDHOOD

Cultural Focus: Adolescent Conflict with Parents

In traditional cultures, it is rare for parents and adolescents to engage in the kind of frequent conflicts typical of parent–adolescent relationships in Western cultures (Larson et al., 2010). The role of parent carries greater authority in traditional cultures than in the West, and this makes it less likely that adolescents in such cultures will express disagreements and resentments toward their parents (Phinney et al., 2005). Even when they disagree with their parents, they are unlikely to express it because of their feelings of duty and respect (Phinney & Ong, 2002). Outside of the West, interdependence is a higher value than independence, not only during adolescence but throughout adulthood (Markus & Kitayama, 2010; Phinney et al., 2005). Just as a dramatic increase in autonomy during adolescence prepares Western adolescents for adult life in an individualistic culture, learning to submit to the authority

of one's parents prepares adolescents in traditional cultures for an adult life in which interdependence is among the highest values and each person has a clearly designated position in a family hierarchy.

In this video, adolescents from a variety of cultures are interviewed as they discuss their changing relationships with their parents as well as with their friends.

Review Question:

The narrator tells us that interdependence is valued in the Mexican village where one of the female teens is from. What are the economic reasons why interdependence might be more adaptive in this Mexican village than in the U.S. family also shown in the video?

Watch ADOLESCENT CONFLICT WITH PARENTS ACROSS CULTURES

Updated "Cultural Focus" Features highlight how culture impacts various aspects of development, such as breast-feeding practices, gross motor development, educational practices, and relationships with friends and family. Students read an overview of the topic, watch a cross-cultural video with footage from the United States, Mexico, and Botswana, and then answer a review question.

New emphasis on Weisner's ecocultural theory of development Children grow up in a remarkable diversity of settings that are marked by ecological and cultural features. Things like the subsistence patterns of parents, whether children work, whether children's play partners are relatives or other peers, and the role of fathers vary and impact the cultural pathways of development. Students read about this theory in Chapter 1 and then see references to it throughout the text.

Subsistence work cycle

The characteristics of the **subsistence work cycle** and the ecological and technological systems that produce it, including wage work, tending crops or animals, distance from the home, migration, and the like.

Health status and demographic characteristics

The **health status and demographic characteristics** of the community, including mortality risks, availability of health care, birth control, family size, and the like.

Community safety

Overall **community safety** other than health and mortality, such as dangers from motor vehicles, intra- and inter-community violence and warfare, and the like.

Division of labor

The **division of labor** by age and sex and perhaps other criteria like caste or race in childhood, adolescence, and adulthood, including the relative importance of various activities for subsistence and prestige.

Work that children are expected to do

The **work that children are expected to do** beginning as a toddler through adolescence.

Role of the father and older siblings

The **role of the father and older siblings** in child care as a special issue of nonmaternal child care. That is, how much do fathers and older siblings help with child care?

Children's play groups

The composition of **children's play groups** by age, sex, and kinship category (siblings, cousins, relatives, and non-relatives). That is, do children play mostly with relatives or non-relatives?

Figure 1.8 Weisner's Ecocultural Theory

Weisner's ecocultural theory of child development proposes that there are ecocultural niche features that affect a child's development. Here are a few examples.
SOURCE: Adapted from: Weisner, T. S. (1984).

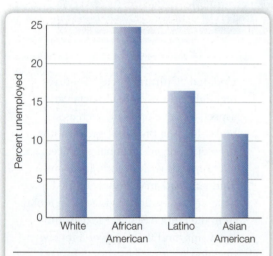

Figure 9.9 U.S. Unemployment Rates for Emerging Adults (Ages 16–24)

What explains the differences among ethnic groups?
SOURCE: Based on Bureau of Labor Statistics (2014)

New Research and Artwork have been incorporated to help students appreciate the diversity that exists within the United States, and understand the role of culture, ethnicity, socioeconomic status, and other factors in human development. In the later chapters, new sections have been added that examine the impact of globalization on cognitive change, gender roles, and political identity.

Expanded Coverage of Educational Issues

New "Education Focus" Features provide an in-depth view of educational issues from preschool through higher education. Topics include childcare options, preschool programs, achievement motivation, abstinence-only sex education programs, and study abroad programs. Updated research on education has also been incorporated throughout, including new sections on peer learning, educating children with special needs, and the transitions to middle school and high school.

Education Focus: How Does a Parent Choose Among the Many Kinds of Preschools?

When choosing a preschool, cost is a factor for many parents in many communities, but the philosophy of the program is also important to consider. Montessori, Reggio Emilia, and Waldorf are popular preschool programs, and each has a different philosophy.

The *Montessori* approach was developed by Maria Montessori in Rome in the early 1900s. Montessori programs are child-centered, with teachers serving as guides. The basic philosophy is that play is a child's work, meaning that play is central and important for development and that children ought to play the way adults generally spend time at work. The distinguishing feature of Montessori programs is that children learn at their own pace, choosing their own way through classroom centers and working at their own level. The tactile engagement of the child's senses and motor abilities is evident in a Montessori classroom. There are specially designed Montessori toys called *manipulatives* that are self-corrective; it is obvious to the child that he or she has assembled a puzzle correctly, for example, if the toy fits together, not because someone has demonstrated how to do it and then asks the child to parrot a response.

Children ages 3, 4, and 5 all learn in the same preschool classroom and in outdoor settings, when feasible. Children interact with others of different ages, and older children serve as observational models and helpers for the younger ones. This helpfulness can build self-efficacy because the older children feel a sense of accomplishment in aiding the younger ones. Montessori appeals to many parents because they believe the

In Montessori settings, children learn independently in different learning centers.

structure of the program encourages independent discovery in learning and solving tasks.

The *Reggio Emilia* approach is named for the Northern Italian town where it was developed in the 1940s after World War II. A schoolteacher named Lori Malaguzzi developed the approach with members of the community with the goal of helping children to become better citizens. The philosophy behind Reggio Emilia is that children should learn together by exploring.

In Reggio Emilia schools, children engage in projects based on their interests. For example, if children ask where a carrot comes from, the teacher encourages them to find out

Research Focus: The Daily Rhythms of Adolescents' Family Lives

Adolescent researchers have found the Experience Sampling Method (ESM) to be a helpful source of information on adolescents' social lives. The ESM involves having people wear beeper watches that randomly beep during the day so that people can record their thoughts, feelings, and behavior as events take place. Reed Larson and Maryse Richards are the two scholars who have done the most to apply the ESM to adolescents and their families.

In their classic book *Divergent Realities: The Emotional Lives of Mothers, Fathers, and Adolescents* (Larson & Richards, 1994), they described the results of their research on a sample of 483 American adolescents in 5th to 12th grades, and another sample of 55 5th to 8th graders and their parents. All were two-parent, White families. In each family, three family members (adolescent, mother, and father) were beeped at the same times, about 30 times per day between 7:30 in the morning and 9:30 at night, during the week of the study.

When beeped, adolescents and their parents paused from whatever they were doing and recorded a variety of information about where they were, whom they were with, what they were doing, and how they were feeling.

One striking finding of the study was that adolescents and their parents averaged only about an hour a day spent in shared activities, and their most common shared activity was watching television. The amount of time adolescents spent with their families dropped sharply between 5th and 12th grades. In turn, there was an increase from 5th to 9th grade in the amount of time adolescents spent alone in their bedrooms.

The study also revealed some interesting differences in mothers' and fathers' relationships with adolescents. The majority of mother–adolescent interactions were rated positively by both of

them, especially experiences such as talking together, going out together, and sharing a meal.

However, adolescents' negative feelings toward their mothers increased sharply from fifth to ninth grade, and their feelings of closeness to mothers decreased.

As for fathers, they tended to be only tenuously involved in their adolescents' lives. For most of the time they spent with their adolescents, the mother was there as well, and the mother tended to be more directly involved. Fathers averaged only 12 minutes per day alone with their adolescents, and 40 percent of this time was spent watching TV together.

The study showed that parents are often important influences on adolescents' emotional states. Adolescents brought home to the family their emotions from the rest of the day. If their parents were responsive and caring, adolescents' moods improved and their negative emotions were relieved. In contrast, if adolescents felt their parents were unavailable or unresponsive, their negative feelings became even worse. Even though adolescents spend less time with the parents than when they were younger, parents remain powerful influences in their lives.

Review Questions:

1. In the ESM studies of adolescents and their parents, adolescents have been found to have the most positive feelings when with _____ and the most negative feelings toward _____.
   a. Mothers; fathers
   b. Mothers; mothers
   c. Fathers; mothers
   d. Fathers; fathers

Increased Attention to Research Methodology

Updated "Research Focus" Features offer a detailed description of a research study, including its premises, methods, results, and limitations. New to this edition, each feature is available in both a traditional narrative format and as a sketch-art style video. Multiple-choice review questions appear at the end of the feature to ensure that students have a solid understanding of the research study and methodology.

Watch RESEARCH FOCUS: THE DAILY RHYTHMS OF ADOLESCENTS' FAMILY LIVES

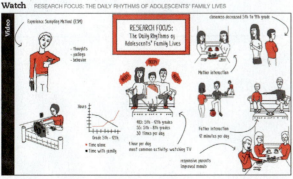

New Opportunities to Apply Knowledge

New "Career Focus" Videos are offered in every chapter, allowing students to learn about a wide variety of career paths. In the videos, career professionals describe their jobs and explain how a knowledge of child development and culture influence their work on a daily basis. More than 25 careers are profiled, including a genetic counselor, a pediatric nurse practitioner, a counselor, a middle school teacher, a dance instructor, and a family court judge.

Applying Your Knowledge as a Professional

The topics covered in this chapter apply to a wide variety of career professions. Watch these videos to learn how they apply to a birth doula and an instructor of maternity nursing.

Watch   CAREER FOCUS: BIRTH DOULA

Video

Samantha Huggins
Doula
Carriage House Birth

New "Critical Thinking Questions" encourage students to think more deeply and critically about a developmental topic. These questions appear in every major section and often focus on the role of culture in human development.

CRITICAL THINKING QUESTION

Are there any rituals in Western cultures that are comparable to the puberty rituals in traditional cultures? Should people in Western cultures recognize and mark the attainment of puberty more than they do now? If so, why, and how?

Teaching and Learning Aids

Learning Objectives

Learning objectives for each chapter are listed at the start of each section as well as alongside every section heading. Based on Bloom's taxonomy, these numbered objectives help students better organize and understand the material. The end-of-section summary is organized around these same objectives, as are all of the supplements and assessment material.

Neonatal Sleeping Patterns

LO 3.9 **Describe neonates' patterns of waking and sleeping, including how and why these patterns differ across cultures.**

Most neonates spend more time asleep than awake. The average for neonates is 16 to 17 hours of sleep a day, although there is great variation, from about 10 hours to about 21 (Peirano et al., 2003).

Section Summaries

Organized by learning objective, a summary now appears at the end of each major section.

Summary: Physical Development

LO 5.1 **Describe the typical changes in physical growth that take place in toddlerhood, and explain the harmful effects of nutritional deficiencies on growth.**

Toddlers' physical growth continues at a pace that is slightly reduced from infancy but is nevertheless faster than at any later time of life. Toddlers in developing countries often suffer protein and micronutrient deficiencies that impede their physical and cognitive development.

LO 5.2 **Describe the changes in brain development that take place during toddlerhood, and identify the two most common methods of measuring brain activity.**

The brain's synaptic density peaks at the end of toddlerhood, followed by many years of synaptic pruning. The two most common methods of measuring brain activity are the EEG and the fMRI.

LO 5.3 **Describe the advances in motor development that take place during toddlerhood.**

In their gross motor development, toddlers learn to walk, run, climb, and kick a ball. Toddlers in traditional cultures are often restricted in their movements to protect them from danger—especially cooking fires. Advances in fine motor development include holding a cup and building a tower of blocks. In their third year, toddlers may be able to brush their teeth, with some assistance.

LO 5.4 **Compare and contrast the process and timing of toilet training in developed countries and traditional cultures.**

Children vary widely in the timing of learning toilet training, but most are toilet trained by the end of toddlerhood. In traditional cultures, toddlers usually learn through observing and imitating older children.

LO 5.5 **Distinguish the weaning process early in infancy from weaning later in toddlerhood.**

When weaning takes place in the second or third year of life, toddlers often resist. Customs in traditional cultures for promoting weaning include sending the toddler to a relative's household for a while or coating the mother's breast with an unpleasant substance.

Chapter Quiz

A cumulative multiple-choice quiz appears at the end of every chapter to help students assess their comprehension of the material.

Chapter Quiz

1. The United States _____.
   a. is the developed country that will experience the steepest decline in population between now and 2050
   b. is one of the few developed countries that will experience an increase in population, largely as a result of immigration
   c. is expected to have approximately the same proportion of Latinos by 2050, but far fewer African Americans
   d. has a total fertility rate that is lower than most developed countries due to the availability of birth control

2. If a researcher wanted to measure the socioeconomic status (SES) of her adult participants, she would need to ask them about which of the following?
   a. Educational level   c. Religion
   b. Number of children   d. Ethnicity

3. Unlike early hominids, *Homo sapiens* had _____.
   a. a narrower pelvis
   b. a shorter period of dependency
   c. a slightly smaller brain
   d. smaller jaws

4. Which of the following best represents the impact of evolution on human development?
   a. Biologically, humans have changed drastically since the origin of *Homo sapiens*.
   b. Our development of bipedal locomotion is the most distinctive characteristic of our species.
   c. Cultures shape the raw material of biology into widely different paths throughout the life span.
   d. Instincts reduce humans' capacity for cultural learning more than they reduce animals' capacity for cultural learning.

   c. sees development as occurring in distinct stages
   d. ignores cognitive capacities at various points in childhood

9. The belief of many Americans in the value of individual freedom, as demonstrated in its capitalist economic system and its governmental system of representative democracy, reflects which system of Bronfenbrenner's theory?
   a. Exosystem   c. Microsystem
   b. Chronosystem   d. Macrosystem

10. The main tenet of ecocultural theory is that
    a. development occurs in stages
    b. development occurs because of the child's reaction to unconscious urges
    c. development happens in the context of everyday cultural activities
    d. all aspects of development are different all over the world

11. Where does the developmental life stage of emerging adulthood usually appear?
    a. In developed countries
    b. In traditional cultures
    c. In collectivistic cultures
    d. In developing countries

12. _____ generates hypotheses that can be tested in research.
    a. An unbiased sample
    b. A theory
    c. The research design
    d. The research method

13. In the famous case of Henrietta Lacks, an African American

REVEL™

Experience Designed for the Way Today's Students Read, Think, and Learn

When students are engaged deeply, they learn more effectively and perform better in their courses. This simple fact inspired the creation of REVEL: an immersive learning experience designed for the way today's students read, think, and learn. Built in collaboration with educators and students nationwide, REVEL is the newest, fully digital way to deliver respected Pearson content.

REVEL enlivens course content with media interactives and assessments—integrated directly within the authors' narrative—that provide opportunities for students to read about and practice course material in tandem. This immersive experience boosts student engagement, which leads to better understanding of concepts and improved performance throughout the course.

Learn More About REVEL

http://www.pearsonhighered.com/revel/

In developed countries, too, peer relations expand in toddlerhood, often in the form of some kind of group child care (Rubin et al., 2006). Research observing toddlers in these settings has found that their peer play interactions are more advanced than early studies had reported. One influential early study reported that toddlers engaged exclusively in *solitary play*, all by themselves, or *parallel play*, in which they would take part in the same activity but without acknowledging each other (Parten, 1932). However, more recent studies have found that toddlers engage in not only solitary and parallel play but in *simple social play*, where they talk to each other, smile, and give and receive toys, and even in *cooperative pretend play*, involving a shared fantasy such as pretending to be animals (Howes, 1996; Hughes & Dunn, 2007). Watch the video *Styles of Play* on the next page for examples of toddlers engaging in various types of play.

Watch STYLES OF PLAY

Video

Parallel Play

Furthermore, toddlers who know each other well tend to engage in more advanced forms of play than unacquainted toddlers do. In one study of toddlers attending the same child-care center, even young toddlers (16–17 months old) engaged in simple social play (Howes, 1985). By 24 months of age, half of the toddlers engaged in cooperative pretend play, and this kind of play was observed in all the toddlers between 30 and 36

The second edition includes integrated videos and media content throughout, allowing students to explore topics more deeply at the point of relevancy.

Revel also offers the ability for students to assess their content mastery by taking multiple-choice quizzes that offer instant feedback and by participating in a variety of writing assignments such as peer-reviewed questions and auto-graded assignments.

MyPsychLab™

MyPsychLab combines proven learning applications with powerful assessment to engage students, assess their learning, and help them succeed.

- **An individualized study plan for each student,** based on performance on chapter pre-tests, helps students focus on the specific topics where they need the most support. The personalized study plan arranges content from less complex thinking—like remembering and understanding—to more complex critical-thinking skills—like applying and analyzing—and is based on Bloom's taxonomy. Every level of the study plan provides a formative assessment quiz.
- **MyVirtualChild.** MyVirtualChild is an interactive simulation that allows students to play the role of a parent and raise their own virtual child. By making decisions about specific scenarios, students can raise their children from birth to age 18 and learn firsthand how their own decisions and other parenting actions affect their child over time.
- **Media assignments** for each chapter—including videos with assignable questions—feed directly into the gradebook, enabling instructors to track student progress automatically.
- **The Pearson eText** lets students access their textbook anytime and anywhere, and any way they want, including listening online.
- **The MyPsychLab Question Library** provides more than 1,000 test items in the form of Pre-Tests, Post-Tests, and Chapter Exams. These questions are parallel forms of questions found in the instructor test bank, ensuring that students using MyPsychLab for review and practice will find their tests to be of similar tone and difficulty, while protecting the integrity of the instructor test bank.

With assessment tied to every video, application, and chapter, students get immediate feedback, and instructors can see what their students know with just a few clicks. Instructors can also personalize MyPsychLab to meet the needs of their students.

Teaching and Learning Package

A textbook is but one component of a comprehensive learning package. The author team that prepared the teaching and learning package had as its goal to deliver the most comprehensive and integrated package on the market. All supplements were developed around the textbook's carefully constructed learning objectives. The authors are grateful to reviewers and focus group members who provided invaluable feedback and suggestions for improving various elements of the program.

TEST BANK Revised by Cara Bellwood (University of Hawai'i) and Michele Cantwell (University of Hawai'i) the Test Bank contains more than 1,200 questions, many of which were class-tested in multiple classes at both 2-year and 4-year institutions across the country prior to publication. Item analysis is provided for all class-tested items. All conceptual and applied multiple-choice questions include rationales for each correct answer and the key distracter. The item analysis helps instructors create balanced tests, whereas the rationales serve both as an added guarantee of quality and as a time-saver when students challenge the keyed answer for a specific item. Each chapter of the test bank includes a Total Assessment Guide, an easy-to-reference grid that organizes all test items by learning objective and question type.

The test bank comes with Pearson MyTest, a powerful test-generation program that helps instructors easily create and print quizzes and exams. Questions and tests can be authored online, allowing instructors ultimate flexibility and the ability to efficiently manage assessments wherever and whenever they want. Instructors can easily access existing questions and then edit, create, and store using simple drag-and-drop and Word-like controls. Data on each question provides information relevant to difficulty level and page number. In addition, each question maps to the text's major section and learning objective. For more information go to www.PearsonMyTest.com.

ENHANCED LECTURE POWERPOINT SLIDES WITH EMBEDDED VIDEOS Written by Marvin Tobias (St. Charles Community College), the Enhanced Lecture PowerPoints offer detailed outlines of key points for each chapter supported by selected visuals from the textbook, and include the videos from the human development video series featured in the text. Standard Lecture PowerPoints without embedded videos are also available. A separate *Art and Figure* version of these presentations contains all art from the textbook for which Pearson has been granted electronic permissions.

INSTRUCTOR'S MANUAL Written and compiled by Dorothy Marsil (Kennesaw State University), the Instructor's Manual includes suggestions for preparing for the course, sample syllabi, and current trends and strategies for successful teaching. Each chapter offers integrated teaching outlines and a list of the key terms for quick reference, and includes an extensive bank of lecture launchers, handouts, and activities, and suggestions for integrating third-party videos and web resources. Answers to the in-text features are provided. Detailed critical-thinking problems with accompanying rubrics were written by Diana Joy of the Community College of Denver. A set of questions for using MyVirtualChild with the cultural approach, written by Guyla Davis of Ouachita Baptist University, is also included. The electronic format features click-and-view hotlinks that allow instructors to quickly review or print any resource from a particular chapter. This tool saves prep work and helps you maximize your classroom time.

ACCESSING ALL RESOURCES For a list of all student resources available with *Child Development: A Cultural Approach*, second edition, go to www.mypearsonstore.com, enter the text ISBN (0134011899) and check out the "Everything That Goes with It" section under the book cover.

For access to all instructor supplements for *Child Development: A Cultural Approach*, second edition, go to www.pearsonhighered.com/irc and follow the directions to register (or log in if you already have a Pearson user name and password). Once you have registered and your status as an instructor is verified, you will be e-mailed a log-in name and password. Use your log-in name and password to access the catalog.

You can request hard copies of the supplements through your Pearson sales representative. If you do not know your sales representative, go to www.pearsonhighered.com/replocator and follow the directions. For technical support for any of your Pearson products, you and your students can contact http://247.pearsoned.com.

Acknowledgments

The second edition of this textbook has involved many talented and dedicated people. We are indebted to everyone who has contributed at each step of our writing of this book. We are especially grateful to Amber Chow, who has shown careful dedication and abundant enthusiasm for the study of culture and development and who has made this book and the related projects possible. Julie Swasey pored over drafts and provided gentle and insightful editing, the way a weaver finishes a beautiful tapestry, making sure every thread is in place. Thanks also go to Barbara Mack at Pearson and to Charles Fisher at Integra Software Services for coordinating all aspects of production. Debbie Coniglio, Joshua Johnson, Julie Tondreau, and Veronica Grupico filmed the wonderful new chapter introduction and career videos, under the direction of Ashley Maynard, as well as producing the new Research Focus videos. Katie Toulmin, Nick Kaufman, Howard Stern, and others at NKP Media, advised by Ashley Maynard and Bianca Dahl, filmed the fabulous Cultural Focus videos. Cecilia Turner, the Program Manager, oversaw all aspects of the program and its supplements package, and Pamela Weldin and Elissa Senra-Sargent, the Digital Media Project Managers, produced the MyPsychLab site and coordinated all aspects of digital media production. Lindsey Prudhomme Gill, Senior Product Marketing Manager, handled the marketing of the text and organized focus groups that provided valuable feedback on the Revel eText. Carly Bergey found the photos that do a great job of reflecting the cultural approach of the book. Kathryn Foot created the interior design and Pentagram created the cover design.

Finally, we would like to thank the hundreds of reviewers who reviewed chapters, sections, and other materials in the course of the development of the book. We benefited greatly from their suggestions and corrections, and now instructors and students reading the book will benefit, too.

—Jeff Arnett & Ashley Maynard

The Development of Child Development: A Cultural Approach

The textbook you hold in your hands is the product of the most extensive development effort this market has ever witnessed. *Child Development: A Cultural Approach* reflects the countless hours and extraordinary efforts of a team of authors, editors, and reviewers that shared a vision for not only a unique child development textbook but also the most comprehensive and integrated supplements program on the market. More than 200 manuscript reviewers provided invaluable feedback for making text as accessible and relevant to students as possible. Each chapter was also reviewed by a panel of subject matter experts to ensure accuracy and currency. Dozens of focus group participants helped guide every aspect of the program, from content coverage to the art style and design to the configuration of the supplements. In fact, some of those focus group participants were so invested in the project that they became members of the supplements author team themselves. Dozens of students compared the manuscript to their current textbooks and provided suggestions for improving the prose and design. We thank everyone who participated in ways great and small, and hope that you are as pleased with the finished product as we are!

INSTRUCTORS

Alabama
Sarah Luckadoo, *Jefferson State Community College*
Carroll Tingle, *University of Alabama*

Alaska
Karen Gibson, *University of Alaska Anchorage*

Arizona
Richard Detzel, *Arizona State University and Northern Arizona University*
Rosanne Dlugosz, *Scottsdale Community College*
Elaine Groppenbacher, *Chandler Gilbert Community College and Western International University*

Arkansas
Oscar Gomez, *Central Baptist College*

California
Laurel Anderson, *Palomar College*
Patricia Bellas, *Irvine Valley College*
Jennifer Briffa, *Merritt College*
Dianna Chiabotti, *Napa Valley College*
Bella DePaulo, *University of California, Santa Barbara*
Diana Deutsch, *Pierce College*
Ann Englert, *Cal Poly, Pomona*
Lenore Frigo, *Shasta College*
Juliana Fuqua, *Cal Poly Pomona*
Mary Garcia-Lemus, *Cal Poly San Luis Obispo*
Mary Gauvain, *University of California, Riverside*
Arthur Gonchar, *University of La Verne*
Brian Grossman, *San Jose State University*
Dani Hodge, *California State University, San Bernadino*
Richard Kandus, *Mt. San Jacinto College*
Denise Kennedy, *University of La Verne*

Jean Moylan, *California State University, Sacramento*

Deborah Muscari, *Gavilan College*

Wendy Orcajo, *Mt. San Jacinto College*

Jo Anne Pandey, *California State University, Northridge*

Melissa Paoloni, *Sacramento City College*

Michelle Pilati, *Rio Hondo College*

Laura Pirazzi, *San Jose State University*

Nicole Porter, *Modesto Junior College*

Wendy Sanders, *College of the Desert*

Emily Scott-Lowe, *Pepperdine University*

Jamie Shepherd, *Saddleback College*

Susan Siaw, *Cal Poly Pomona*

Valerie Singleton, *California State University, Chico*

April Taylor, *California State University, Northridge*

Hsing-chen Tung, *San Diego State University*

Leonor Vazquez, *California State University, Los Angeles*

Anthony Verive, *College of the Desert*

Curtis Visca, *Saddleback College*

Gina Wilson, *MiraCosta College*

Colorado

Silvia Sara Canetto, *Colorado State University*

Jessica Herrick, *Mesa State College*

Diana Joy, *Community College of Denver*

David MacPhee, *Colorado State University*

Peggy Norwood, *Community College of Aurora*

Jun Wang, *Colorado State University*

Connecticut

Carol LaLiberte, *Asnuntuck Community College*

Delaware

Allison Cassidy, *Delaware Technical Community College*

Florida

Maggie Anderson, *Valencia Community College*

Kathi Barrett, *Lake-Sumter Community College*

Norma Caltagirone, *Hillsborough Community College*

Diana Ciesko, *Valencia Community College*

Carol Connor, *Florida State University*

Sorah Dubitsky, *Florida International University*

Colleen Fawcett, *Palm Beach State College*

Christine Hughes, *University of Miami*

Shayn Lloyd, *Tallahassee Community College*

Haili Marotti, *Edison State Community College*

Madhavi Menon, *Nova Southeastern University*

Seth Schwartz, *University of Miami*

Anne Van Landingham, *Orlando Tech*

Lois Willoughby, *Miami Dade College*

Georgia

Jennie Dilworth, *Georgia Southern University*

Dorothy Marsil, *Kennesaw State University*

Valerie Misch, *Central Georgia Technical College*

Nicole Rossi, *Augusta State University*

Amy Skinner, *Gordon College*

Sharon Todd, *Southern Crescent Technical College*

Annette Wilson, *Armstrong Atlantic State University*

Hawai'i

Katherine Aumer, *Hawai'i Pacific University*

Illinois

Elbert Bolsen, *Columbia College*

Gregory Braswell, *Illinois State University*

Kelly Champion, *Northern Illinois University*

R.B. Church, *Northeastern Illinois University*

Carrie Dale, *Eastern Illinois University*

Joe Davis, *Chicago State University*

Carolyn Fallahi, *Waubonsee Community College*

Lisa Fozio-Thielk, *Waubonsee Community College*

Christine Grela, *McHenry County College*

Ericka Hamilton, *Moraine Valley Community College*

Lynnel Kiely, *Harold Washington College*

Kathy Kufskie, *Southwestern Illinois College*

Mikki Meadows, *Eastern Illinois University*

Michael Meyerhoff, *Columbia College*

Elizabeth Rellinger Zettler, *Illinois College*

Michelle Sherwood, *Eastern Illinois University*

Beth Venzke, *Concordia University Chicago*

Indiana

Kimberly Bays, *Ball State University*

Iowa

David Devonis, *Graceland University*

Kari Terzino, *Des Moines Area Community College*

Kansas

Jennifer Meehan Brennom, *Kirkwood Community College*

Joyce Frey, *Pratt Community College*

Shawn Haake, *Iowa Central Community College*

David P. Hurford, *Pittsburg State University*

Brenda Lohman, *Iowa State University*

Hira Nair, *Kansas City Kansas Community College*

James Rodgers, *Hawkeye Community College*

Kari Terzino, *Iowa State University*

Ruth Wallace, *Butler Community College*

Kentucky

Myra Bundy, *Eastern Kentucky University*

Janet Dean, *Asbury University*

April Grace, *Kentucky Community and Technical College System*

Louisiana

Kim Herrington, *Louisiana State University at Alexandria*

Eartha Johnson, *Dillard University*

Maine

Diane Lemay, *University of Maine at Augusta*

Elena Perrello, *The University of Maine and Husson University*

Ed Raymaker, *Eastern Maine Community College*

Candace Schulenburg, *Cape Cod Community College*

Alison Terry, *University of Maine, Farmington*

Maryland

Caitlin Faas, *Mount St. Mary's University*
Diane Finley, *University of Maryland University College*
Stacy Fruhling, *Anne Arundel Community College*
Carol Miller, *Anne Arundel Community College*
Gary Popoli, *Harford Community College*
Terry Portis, *Anne Arundel Community College*
Rachelle Tannenbaum, *Anne Arundel Community College*
Delaine Welch, *Frederick Community College*
Marlene Welch, *Carroll Community College*
Patricia Westerman, *Bowie State University*
Nicole Williams, *Anne Arundel Community College*

Massachusetts

Alfred Baptista, *Massasoit Community College*
Claire Ford, *Bridgewater State University*
Barbara Madden, *Fitchburg State University*
Kyla McKay-Dewald, *Bristol Community College*
Martha Pott, *Tufts University*
Candace J. Schulenburg, *Cape Cod Community College*
Margaret Vaughan, *University of Massachusetts Boston*
Marcia Weinstein, *Salem State University*
Phyllis Wentworth, *Bristol Community College*

Michigan

Laura C. Froyen, *Michigan State University*
Nancy Hartshorne, *Delta College*
H. Russell Searight, *Lake Superior State University*

Minnesota

Hope Doerner, *Minneapolis Community and Technical College*
Jarilyn Gess, *Minnesota State University Moorhead*
Dana Gross, *St. Olaf College*
Rodney Raasch, *Normandale Community College*
David Schieffer, *Minnesota West Community & Technical College*

Mississippi

Linda Fayard, *Mississippi Gulf Coast Community College*
Donna Carol Gainer, *Mississippi State University*
Myra Harville, *Holmes Community College*
Linda Morse, *Mississippi State University*
Lisa Thomas, *Mississippi College*

Missouri

Scott Brandhorst, *Southeast Missouri State University*
Sabrina Brinson, *Missouri State University*
Peter J. Green, *Maryville University*
Amy Kausler, *Jefferson College*
Michael Meehan, *Maryville University*
Bill Walkup, *Southwest Baptist University*

Nebraska

Elizabeth Brewer, *Metropolitan Community College*
Kim Glackin, *Metropolitan Community College*
Susan Nordstrom, *Wayne State College*
Brigette Ryalls, *University of Nebraska at Omaha*
Susan Sarver, *University of Nebraska-Lincoln*

Nevada

Bridget Walsh, *University of Nevada, Reno*

New Jersey

Christine Floether, *Centenary College*
Miriam Linver, *Montclair State University*
Stevie McKenna, *Rutgers University*
Melissa Sapio, *Montclair State University*
Wallace Smith, *Union County College*

New Mexico

Katherine Demitrakis, *Central New Mexico Community College*
Kourtney Vaillancourt, *New Mexico State University*

New York

Paul Anderer, *SUNY Canton*
Rachel Annunziato, *Fordham University*
Melissa Ghera, *St. John Fisher College*
Melody Goldman, *Brooklyn College*
Nancy Hughes, *Plattsburgh State University*
Sabrina Ismailer, *Hunter College*
Sybillyn Jennings, *Russell Sage College-The Sage Colleges*
Judith Kuppersmith, *College of Staten Island*
Jonathan Lang, *Borough of Manhattan Community College*
Joseph Lao, *Hunter College*
Randolph Manning, *Suffolk County Community College*
Leigh McCallen, *The Graduate Center, CUNY*
Steven McCloud, *Borough of Manhattan Community College*
Julie McIntyre, *The Sage Colleges*
Kristie Morris, *Rockland Community College*
Elisa Perram, *The Graduate Center, The City University of New York*
Monida R. Sylvia, *Le Moyne College*

North Carolina

Linda Aiken, *Southwestern Community College*
Margaret Annunziata, *Davidson County Community College*
Sharon Carter, *Davidson County Community College*
Paul Foos, *University of North Carolina, Charlotte*
Sherry Forrest, *Craven Community College*
Donna Henderson, *Wake Forest University*
Amy Holmes, *Davidson County Community College*
Jason McCoy, *Cape Fear Community College*
Andrew Supple, *University of North Carolina at Greensboro*
Karen Tinsley, *Guilford College*
Maureen Vandermaas-Peeler, *Elon University*

Ohio

Michelle Abraham, *Miami University, Hamilton*
Karen Corcoran, *Ohio University*
Amie Dunstan, *Lorain County Community College*
Lisa Green, *Baldwin Wallace College*
Jamie Harmount, *Ohio University, Chillicothe Campus*
James Jackson, *Clark State Community College*
James Jordan, *Lorain County Community College*
William Kimberlin, *Lorain County Community College*

Jennifer King-Cooper, *Sinclair Community College*
Carol Miller, *Sinclair Community College*
Michelle Slattery, *North Central State College*

Oklahoma
Matthew Brosi, *Oklahoma State University*
Melinda Burgess, *Southwestern Oklahoma State University*
Stephen Burgess, *Southwestern Oklahoma State University*
Yuthika Kim, *Oklahoma City Community College*
Gregory Parks, *Oklahoma City Community College*
John Phelan, *Western Oklahoma State College*

Oregon
Alishia Huntoon, *Oregon Institute of Technology*
Tara Vargas, *Lewis & Clark College*

Pennsylvania
Heather Bachman, *University of Pittsburgh*
Jason Baker, *Millersville University*
Melissa Calderon, *Community College of Allegheny County*
Nick Dominello, *Holy Family University*
Jaelyn Farris, *Penn State, Harrisburg*
Jyotsna Kalavar, *Penn State, New Kensington*
Martin Packer, *Duquesne University*

Rhode Island
Allison Butler, *Bryant University*
Clare Sartori, *University of Rhode Island*

South Carolina
Bill Fisk, *Clemson University*
Brantlee Haire, *Florence-Darlington Technical College*
Salvador Macias, *University of South Carolina Sumter*
Megan McIlreavy, *Coastal Carolina University*

South Dakota
Jennifer Kampmann, *South Dakota State University*
Rebecca Martin, *South Dakota State University*

Tennessee
Steve Bradshaw, *Richmont Graduate University*
Lee Ann Jolley, *Tennessee Tech University*
Marvin Lee, *Tennessee State University*
Clark McKinney, *Southwest Tennessee Community College*

Texas
Sarah Angulo, *Texas State University*
Terra Bartee, *Cisco College*
Wanda Clark, *South Plains College*
Trina Cowan, *Northwest Vista College*
Stephanie Ding, *Del Mar College*
Jim Francis, *San Jacinto College-South*
Robert Gates, *Cisco College*
Jerry Green, *Tarrant County College-Northeast Campus*
Heather Hill, *St. Mary's University*

Jerry Green, *Tarrant County College*
Gaye Hughes, *Austin Community College*
Hsin-hui Lin, *University of Houston, Victoria*
Jeffrey Liew, *Texas A&M University*
Catherine Perz, *University of Houston, Victoria*
Jean Raniseski, *Alvin Community College*
Elizabeth Rhoades, *University of Houston, Victoria*
Darla Rocha, *San Jacinto College*
Gaye Shook-Hughes, *Austin Community College*
Tyler Smith, *Baylor University*
Mario Tovar, *South Texas College*
Victoria Van Wie, *Lone Star College-CyFair*
Angela Williamson, *Tarrant County College*
Kim Wombles, *Cisco College*

Utah
Ann M. Berghout Austin, *Utah State University*
Thomas J. Farrer, *Brigham Young University*
Sam Hardy, *Brigham Young University*
Shirlene Law, *Utah State University*
Volkan Sahin, *Weber State University*
Julie Smart, *Utah State University*

Virginia
Christopher Arra, *Northern Virginia Community College-Woodbridge*
Geri M. Lotze, *Virginia Commonwealth University*
Stephan Prifti, *George Mason University*
Tresia Samani, *Rappahannock Community College*
Steve Wisecarver, *Lord Fairfax Community College*

Washington
Pamela Costa, *Tacoma Community College*
Dan Ferguson, *Walla Walla Community College*
Amy Kassler, *South Puget Sound Community College*
Staci Simmelink-Johnson, *Walla Walla Community College*

Washington, D.C.
Deborah Harris-O'Brien, *Trinity Washington University*

Wisconsin
Stacie Christian, *University of Wisconsin, Green Bay*
Ingrid Tiegel, *Carthage College*
Francesca Lopez, *Marquette University*

Wyoming
Ruth Doyle, *Casper College*

Australia
Laurie Chapin, *Victoria University*

Canada
Lillian Campbell, *Humber College*
Lauren Polvere, *Concordia University*

About the Authors

Jeffrey Jensen Arnett is a Research Professor in the Department of Psychology at Clark University in Worcester, Massachusetts. He received his Ph.D. in developmental psychology in 1986 from the University of Virginia, and did 3 years of postdoctoral work at the University of Chicago. From 1992 to 1998, he was Associate Professor in the Department of Human Development and Family Studies at the University of Missouri, where he taught a 300-student life-span development course every semester. In the fall of 2005, he was a Fulbright Scholar at the University of Copenhagen in Denmark.

His primary scholarly interest for the past 20 years has been in emerging adulthood. He coined the term, and he has conducted research on emerging adults concerning a wide variety of topics, involving several different ethnic groups in American society. He is the Founding President and Executive Director of the Society for the Study of Emerging Adulthood (SSEA; www.ssea.org). From 2005 to 2014 he was the editor of *the Journal of Adolescent Research* (JAR), and currently he is on the Editorial Board of *JAR* and five other journals. He has published many theoretical and research papers on emerging adulthood in peer-reviewed journals, as well as the books *Human Development: A Cultural Approach* (2016), *Adolescence and Emerging Adulthood: A Cultural Approach* (2015), and *Emerging Adulthood: The Winding Road from the Late Teens Through the Twenties* (2015).

He lives in Worcester, Massachusetts, with his wife Lene Jensen and their twins, Miles and Paris. For more information on Dr. Arnett and his research, see **www.jeffreyarnett.com**.

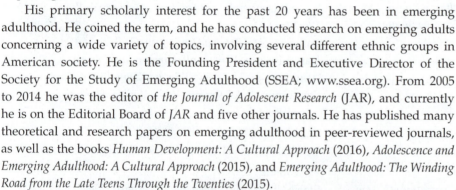

Ashley E. Maynard is Professor and Chair of the Department of Psychology at the University of Hawai'i at Mānoa, where she has been on the faculty since 2001. She received her Ph.D. in Psychology in 1999 from the University of California, Los Angeles (UCLA) and did two years of postdoctoral study in Anthropology and Cultural Psychology in the Department of Neuropsychiatry and Biobehavioral Sciences at UCLA. Ashley has taught approximately 4,000 students in courses ranging from Introductory Psychology to Lifespan Development at the graduate level.

Her primary research interest since 1995 has been the impact of cultural change at the macro level, such as economic and sociodemographic shifts, on socialization and cognition in childhood. She also studies the development of teaching in childhood and sibling interactions. She has worked with her students on research in Mexico, Costa Rica, and Hawai'i. She has won national awards for her research, including the James McKeen Cattell Award from the New York Academy of Sciences and the APA Division 7 (Developmental Psychology) Dissertation Award. She has published many articles on culture and human development in peer-reviewed journals, and in a volume she edited with Mary Martini *Learning in Cultural Context: Family, Peers, and School* (2005).

She lives, teaches, and writes in Honolulu, Hawai'i. For more information on Dr. Maynard and her research, please see **www.ashleymaynard.com**.

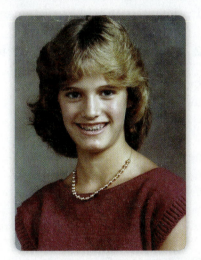

Chapter 1
A Cultural Approach to Child Development

THE CHINESE HAVE AN EXPRESSION FOR THE LIMITED WAY ALL OF US LEARN TO SEE THE WORLD: *jing di zhi wa*, meaning "frog in the bottom of a well." The expression comes from a fable about a frog that has lived its entire life in a small well. The frog assumes that its tiny world is all there is, and it has no idea of the true size of the world. It is only when a passing turtle tells the frog of the great ocean to the east that the frog realizes there is much more to the world than it had known.

All of us are like that frog. We grow up as members of a culture and learn, through direct and indirect teaching, to see the world from the perspective that becomes most familiar to us. Because the people around us usually share that perspective, we seldom have cause to question it. Like the frog, we rarely suspect how big and diverse our human species really is.

The goal of this book is to lift you out of the well, by taking a cultural approach to understanding **child development**, the ways people grow and change from conception through emerging adulthood. This means that the emphasis of the book is on how people develop as members of a culture. **Culture** is the total pattern of a group's customs, beliefs, art, and technology. In other words, a culture is a group's common way of life, passed on from one generation to the next, through language or other human forms of expression. From the day we are born, all of us experience our lives as members of a culture (sometimes more than one), and this profoundly influences how we develop, how we behave, how we see the world, and how we experience life.

Biology is important, too, of course, and at various points we will discuss the interaction between biological and cultural or social influences. However, human beings everywhere have essentially the same biological constitution, yet their paths through the life span are remarkably varied depending on the culture in which their development takes place.

Throughout this book, we'll explore child development from the perspectives of many different cultures around the world. We'll also learn to analyze and critique research based on whether it does or does not take culture into account. By the time you finish this book, you should be able to *think culturally*.

In the course of this book we will be your fellow frogs, your guides and companions as we rise together out of the well to gaze at the broad, diverse, remarkable cultural panorama of the human journey. The book will introduce you to many variations in child development and cultural practices you did not know about before, which may lead you to see your own development and your own cultural practices in a new light. You are about to encounter cultures with assumptions quite different from your own. This will enrich your awareness of the variety of human experiences and may allow you to draw from a wider range of options of how you wish to live.

In this chapter we set the stage for the rest of the book. The first section provides a broad summary of human life today around the world as well as an examination of how culture developed out of our evolutionary history. In the second section, we look at the history of conceptions of child development along with a cultural-developmental theory that will be the framework for this book. Finally, the third section provides an overview of child development as a scientific field.

Watch CHAPTER INTRODUCTION: A CULTURAL APPROACH TO CHILD DEVELOPMENT

Section 1   Child Development Today and Its Origins

Learning Objectives

1.1   Describe how the human population has changed over the past 10,000 years and distinguish between the demographic profiles of developed countries and developing countries

1.2   Define the term *socioeconomic status* (SES) and explain why SES, gender, and ethnicity are important aspects of child development within countries.

1.3   Trace the evolutionary origins of the human species and summarize the features of the first human cultures.

1.4   Apply information about human evolution to how child development takes place today.

CHILD DEVELOPMENT TODAY AND ITS ORIGINS: A Demographic Profile of Humanity Today

Because the goal of this book is to provide you with an understanding of how child development takes place in cultures all around the world, let's begin with a demographic profile of the world's human population in the early 21st century.

Population Growth and the Demographic Divide

LO 1.1   **Describe how the human population has changed over the past 10,000 years and distinguish between the demographic profiles of developed countries and developing countries.**

Perhaps the most striking demographic feature of the human population today is the sheer size of it. For most of history the total human population was fewer than 10 million people (McFalls, 2007). Women typically had from four to eight children, but most of the children died in infancy or childhood and never reached reproductive age. The human population began to increase notably around 10,000 years ago, with the development of agriculture and domestication of animals (Diamond, 1992).

Population growth in the millennia that followed was slow, and it was not until about 400 years ago that the world population reached 500 million people. Since that time, and especially in the past century, population growth has accelerated at an astonishing rate (see **Figure 1.1**). It took just 150 years for the human population to double from 500 million to 1 billion, passing that threshold around the year 1800. Then came the medical advances of the 20th century, and the elimination or sharp reduction of deadly diseases such as smallpox, typhus, diphtheria, and cholera. Subsequently, the human population reached 2 billion by 1930, then tripled to 6 billion by 1999. The 7-billion threshold was surpassed just 12 years later, in early 2011.

How high will the human population go? This is difficult to say, but most projections indicate it will rise to 10 billion by about 2090 and thereafter stabilize and perhaps

child development

way people grow and change from conception through emerging adulthood; includes people's biological, cognitive, psychological, and social functioning

culture

total pattern of a group's customs, beliefs, art, and technology, transmitted through language

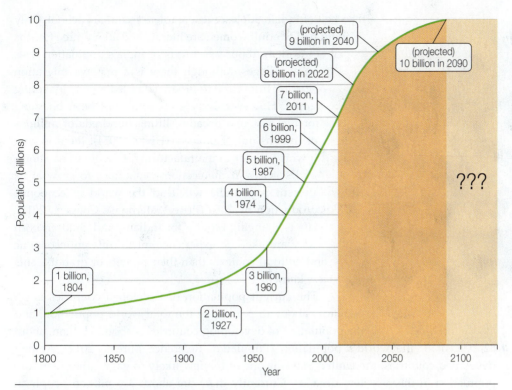

Figure 1.1 World Population Growth

What happened in recent human history to cause population to rise so dramatically?

SOURCE: Based on Population Reference Bureau (2014).

slightly decline. This forecast is based on the worldwide decline in birth rates that has taken place in recent years. The **total fertility rate (TFR)**, which is number of births per woman, worldwide is currently 2.5, which is substantially higher than 2.1, which is the *replacement rate* of a stable population. However, the TFR has been declining sharply for more than a decade and will decline to 2.1 by 2050 if current trends continue (Population Reference Bureau, 2014).

The population increase from now until 2090 will not take place equally around the world. On the contrary, there is a stark "global demographic divide" between the wealthy, economically developed countries that make up less than 20 percent of the world's population, and the economically developing countries that contain the majority of the world's population (Kent & Haub, 2005). Nearly all the population growth in the decades to come will take place in the economically developing countries. In contrast, nearly all wealthy countries are expected to decline in population during this period and beyond because they have fertility rates that are well below replacement rate.

For the purposes of this text, we'll use the term **developed countries** to refer to the most affluent countries in the world. Classifications of developed countries vary, but usually this designation includes the United States, Canada, Japan, South Korea, Australia, New Zealand, Chile, and nearly all the countries of Europe (Organization for Economic Cooperation and Development [OECD], 2014c). (The term *Western countries* is sometimes used to refer to most developed countries because they are in the Western hemisphere, except Japan and South Korea, which are considered Eastern countries.) For our discussion, developed countries will be contrasted with **developing countries**, which have less wealth than the developed countries but are experiencing rapid economic growth as they join the globalized economy. Many developing countries are changing rapidly today. For example, India is a developing country, and most of its people live on an income of less than two dollars a day (United Nations Development Program [UNDP], 2014). About half of Indian children are underweight and malnourished (World Bank, 2011). Less

total fertility rate (TFR)
in a population, the number of births per woman

developed countries
world's most economically developed and affluent countries, with the highest median levels of income and education

developing countries
countries that have lower levels of income and education than developed countries but are experiencing rapid economic growth

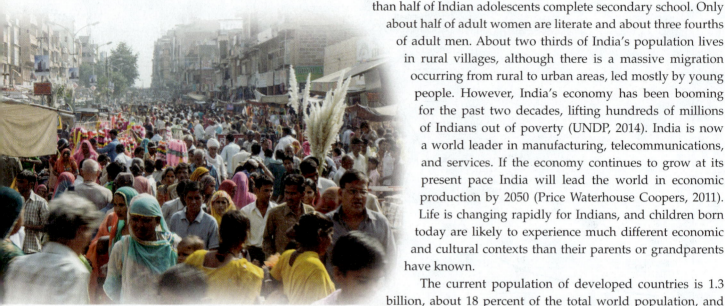

Nearly all the world population growth from now to 2050 will take place in developing countries. Pictured here is a busy street in Jodhpur, India.

than half of Indian adolescents complete secondary school. Only about half of adult women are literate and about three fourths of adult men. About two thirds of India's population lives in rural villages, although there is a massive migration occurring from rural to urban areas, led mostly by young people. However, India's economy has been booming for the past two decades, lifting hundreds of millions of Indians out of poverty (UNDP, 2014). India is now a world leader in manufacturing, telecommunications, and services. If the economy continues to grow at its present pace India will lead the world in economic production by 2050 (Price Waterhouse Coopers, 2011). Life is changing rapidly for Indians, and children born today are likely to experience much different economic and cultural contexts than their parents or grandparents have known.

The current population of developed countries is 1.3 billion, about 18 percent of the total world population, and the population of developing countries is about 6 billion, about 82 percent of the world's population (Population Reference Bureau, 2014). Among developed countries, the United States is one of the few likely to gain rather than lose population in the next few decades. Currently there are about 316 million people in the United States, but by 2050 there will be 400 million. Nearly all the other developed countries are expected to decline in population between now and 2050. The decline will be steepest in Japan, which is projected to drop from a current population of 120 million to just 97 million by 2050 as a result of a low fertility rate and virtually no immigration (Population Reference Bureau, 2014).

There are two reasons why the United States is following a different demographic path than most other developed countries. First, the United States has a TFR of 1.9, which is slightly below the replacement rate of 2.1 but still higher than the TFR in most other developed countries (Population Reference Bureau, 2014). Second, and more importantly, the United States allows more legal immigration than most other developed countries do, and there are millions of undocumented immigrants as well (Suarez-Orozco, 2015). The increase in population in the United States between now and 2050 will result entirely from immigration (Martin & Midgley, 2010). Both legal and undocumented immigrants to the United States come mainly from Mexico and Latin America, although many also come from Asia and other parts of the world. Consequently, as **Figure 1.2** shows, by 2050 the proportion of the U.S. population that is Latino is projected to rise from 16 to 30 percent. Canada, the United Kingdom, and Australia also have relatively open immigration policies, so they, too, may avoid the population decline that is projected for most developed countries (DeParle, 2010).

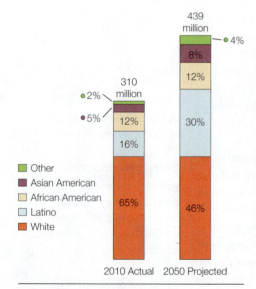

Figure 1.2 Projected Ethnic Changes in the U.S. Population to 2050

Which ethnic group is projected to change the most in the coming decades, and why?

SOURCE: Based on Kaiser Family Foundation (2013).

CRITICAL THINKING QUESTION

What kinds of public policy changes might be necessary in the United States between now and 2050 to adapt to nearly 100 million more immigrants and a rise in the proportion of Latinos to 30 percent?

The demographic contrast of developed countries compared to the rest of the world is stark not only with respect to population but also in other key areas, such as income and education (see **Map 1.1**). With respect to income, about 40 percent of the world's population lives on less than $2 per day, and

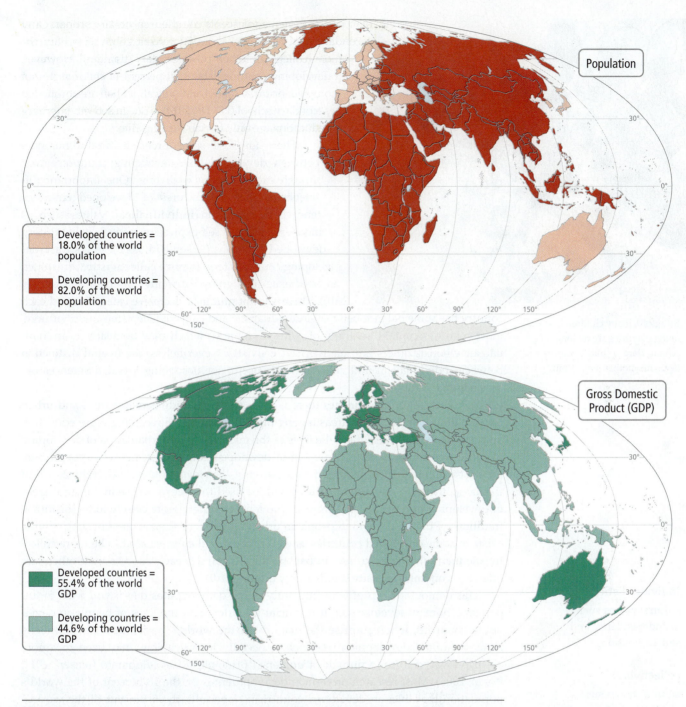

Population

Developed countries = 18.0% of the world population

Developing countries = 82.0% of the world population

Gross Domestic Product (GDP)

Developed countries = 55.4% of the world GDP

Developing countries = 44.6% of the world GDP

Map 1.1 Worldwide Variations in Population and Income Levels

Developed countries represent only 18 percent of the world population yet they are much wealthier than developing countries. At what point in its economic development should a developing country be reclassified as a developed country?

80 percent of the world's population lives on a family income of less than $6,000 per year (Population Reference Bureau, 2014). At one extreme are the developed countries, where 9 of 10 persons are in the top 20 percent of the global income distribution, and at the other extreme is southern Africa, where half of the population is in the bottom 20 percent of global income. Africa's economic growth has been strong for the past decade, but it remains the poorest region in the world (McKinsey Global Institute, 2010; UNDP, 2015).

A similar contrast between rich and poor countries exists regarding education. Your experience as a college student is a rare and privileged status in most of the world.

By age 10, many children in developing countries are no longer in school. Here, a child in Cameroon helps his mother make flour.

In developed countries, virtually all children obtain primary and secondary education, and about 50 percent go on to tertiary education (college or other postsecondary training). However, in developing countries about 20 percent of children do not complete primary school and only about half are enrolled in secondary school (UNDP, 2014). College and other tertiary education are only for the wealthy elite.

There are also some broad cultural differences between developed and developing countries, even though each category is diverse. One important difference is that the cultures of developed countries tend to be based on **individualistic** values such as independence and self-expression, especially in Western developed countries (Greenfield, 2005). In contrast, developing countries tend to prize **collectivistic** values such as obedience and group harmony (Sullivan & Cottone, 2010). These are not mutually exclusive categories and each country has some balance between individualistic and collectivistic values. Furthermore, most countries contain a variety of cultures, some of which may be relatively individualistic whereas others are relatively collectivistic. Nevertheless, the overall distinction between individualism and collectivism is useful for describing broad differences between human groups.

Within developing countries there is often a sharp divide between rural and urban areas, with people in urban areas having higher incomes and receiving more education and better medical care. Often, the lives of the middle-class in urban areas of developing countries resemble the lives of people in developed countries in many ways, yet they are much different than people in rural areas of their own countries (UNDP, 2014). In this book, the term **traditional cultures** will be used to refer to people in the rural areas of developing or developed countries, who tend to adhere more closely to the historical traditions of their culture than people in urban areas do. (The same kind of sharp divide exists in some developed countries as well.) Traditional cultures tend to be more collectivistic than other cultures are, in part because in rural areas close ties with others are often an economic necessity (Sullivan & Cottone, 2010).

This demographic profile of humanity today demonstrates that if you wish to understand human development, it is crucial to understand the lives of people in developing countries, who comprise the majority of the world's population. The tendency in most human development research, especially in psychology, has been to ignore or strip away culture in pursuit of universal principles of development (Jensen, 2011; Rozin, 2006). Most research on human development is on the 18 percent of the world's population that lives in developed countries—especially the 5 percent of the world's population that lives in the United States—because research requires money and developed countries can afford more of it than developing countries can (Arnett, 2008). This is changing, and over the past 50 years there has been increasing attention paid in psychology and other social science fields to the cultural context of human development (Jensen, 2015b; Shweder et al., 2011). By now, researchers have presented descriptions of human development in places all over the world, and researchers studying U.S. society have increased their attention to cultures within the United States that are outside of the White middle class.

Expanding our awareness of the other 95 percent of humanity also has many practical applications. Increasingly the world is approaching the *global village* that the social philosopher Marshall McLuhan (1960) forecast more than half a century ago. In recent decades there has been an acceleration in the process of **globalization**, which refers to the increasing connections between different parts of the world in trade, travel, migration, and communication (Arnett, 2002; Jensen et al., 2012; Hermans, 2015). Consequently,

individualistic
cultural values such as independence and self-expression

collectivistic
cultural values such as obedience and group harmony

traditional culture
a rural culture that adheres more closely to cultural traditions than people in urban areas; may be found in developing countries or rural areas of developed countries

globalization
increasing connections between different parts of the world in trade, travel, migration, and communication

wherever you live in the world, in the course of your personal and professional life you are likely to have many contacts with people of other cultures. Those of you going into the nursing profession may one day have patients who have a cultural background in various parts of Asia or South America. Those of you pursuing careers in education will likely teach students whose families emigrated from countries in Africa or Europe. Your coworkers, your neighbors, possibly even your friends and family members may include people from a variety of different cultural backgrounds. Through the Internet you may have contact with people all over the world, via e-mail, Facebook and other social media, YouTube, and new technologies to come. Thus, understanding the cultural approach to child development is likely to be useful in all aspects of life, helping you to communicate with and understand the perspectives of others in a diverse, globalized world. The video *Culture in Development* illustrates different people's understandings of culture, including individualism and collectivism.

Watch   CULTURE IN DEVELOPMENT

Variations Within Countries

LO 1.2   Define the term *socioeconomic status* (SES) and explain why SES, gender, and ethnicity are important aspects of child development within countries.

The contrast between developed countries and developing countries will be used often in this book, as a general way of drawing a contrast between child development in relatively rich and relatively poor countries. However, it should be noted that there is substantial variation within each of these categories. All developed countries are relatively wealthy, but child development in Japan is quite different from child development in France or Canada. All developing countries are less wealthy than developed countries, but child development in China is quite different than child development in Brazil or Nigeria. Throughout the book we will explore variations in child development within the broad categories of developed countries and developing countries.

Not only is there important variation in child development within each category of "developed" and "developing" countries, but there is additional variation within each country. Most countries today have a **majority culture** that sets most of the norms and standards and holds most of the positions of political, economic, intellectual, and media power. In addition, there may be many **microcultures** defined by ethnicity, religion, language, or other characteristics.

majority culture

within a country, the cultural group that sets most of the norms and standards and holds most of the positions of political, economic, intellectual, and media power

microculture

within a country, groups whose members share characteristics such as ethnicity, religion, or language

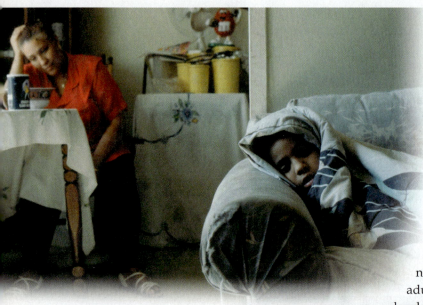

Within each country, SES is an influential context of human development. Here, a low-SES family in the United States.

Variations in child development also occur as a result of differences within countries in the settings and circumstances of individual lives. The settings and circumstances that contribute to variations in pathways of child development are called **contexts**. Contexts include environmental settings such as family, school, community, media, and culture, all of which will be discussed in this book. Three other important aspects of variation that will be highlighted are socioeconomic status, gender, and ethnicity.

The term **socioeconomic status (SES)** is often used to refer to a person's *social class*, which includes educational level, income level, and occupational status. For children and adolescents, because they have not yet reached the social-class level they will have as adults, SES is usually used in reference to their parents' levels of education, income, and occupation. In most countries, SES is highly important in shaping child development. It influences everything from the risk of infant mortality to the quality and duration of children's education to the kind of work adolescents or emerging adults do. Differences in SES are especially sharp in developing countries (UNDP, 2014). In a country such as India or Saudi Arabia or Peru, growing up as a member of the upper-class SES elite is different from growing up as a member of the relatively poor majority, in terms of access to resources such as health care and education. However, even in developed countries there are important SES differences in access to resources throughout the course of child development. For example, in the United States infant mortality is higher among low-SES families than among high-SES families, in part because low-SES mothers are less likely to receive prenatal care (Daniels et al., 2006).

Gender is a key factor in development throughout the life span, in every culture (Carroll & Wolpe, 2005; UNDP, 2014). The expectations cultures have for males and females are different from the time they are born (Hatfield & Rapson, 2005). However, the degree of the differences varies greatly among cultures. In most developed countries today, the differences are relatively blurred: Men and women hold many of the same jobs, wear many of the same clothes (e.g., jeans, T-shirts), and enjoy many of the same entertainments. If you have grown up in a developed country, you may be surprised to learn in the chapters to come how deep gender differences go in many other cultures. Nevertheless, gender-specific expectations exist in developed countries, too, as we will see.

Finally, **ethnicity** is a crucial part of child development. Ethnicity may include a variety of components, such as cultural origin, cultural traditions, race, religion, and language. Minority ethnic groups may arise as a consequence of immigration. There are also countries in which ethnic groups have a long-standing presence and may even have arrived before the majority culture. For example, Aboriginal peoples lived in Australia for many generations before the first European settlers arrived. Many African countries were constructed by European colonial powers in the 19th century and consist of people of a variety of ethnicities, each of whom has lived in their region for many generations. Often, ethnic minorities within countries have distinct cultural patterns that are different from those of the majority culture. For example, in the Canadian majority culture, premarital sex is common, but in the large Asian Canadian minority group, female virginity at marriage is still highly valued (Sears, 2012). In many developed countries, most of the ethnic minority groups have values that are less individualistic and more collectivistic than in the majority culture (Suarez-Orozco, 2015).

contexts

settings and circumstances that contribute to variations in pathways of human development, including SES, gender, and ethnicity, as well as family, school, community, media, and culture

socioeconomic status (SES)

person's social class, including educational level, income level, and occupational status

ethnicity

group identity that may include components such as cultural origin, cultural traditions, race, religion, and language

CHILD DEVELOPMENT TODAY AND ITS ORIGINS: The Origins of Human Diversity

Using a cultural approach to child development, we will see that humans are fabulously diverse in how they live. But how did this diversity arise? Humans are one species, so how did so many different ways of life develop from one biological origin? Let's take a brief tour now of human evolutionary history as a foundation for understanding the birth of culture and the historical context of individual child development today. For students who hold religious beliefs that may lead them to object to evolutionary theory, we understand that you may find this part of the book challenging, but it is nevertheless important to know about the theory of evolution and the evidence supporting it because this is the view of human origins accepted by virtually all scientists.

Evolution and the Birth of Culture

LO 1.3 **Trace the evolutionary origins of the human species and summarize the features of the first human cultures.**

Knowledge of our evolutionary and cultural past is important to understanding development today. We can trace the development of human culture across evolutionary time, beginning with our earliest hominid ancestors. In this history we see how features that were useful in adapting to and changing the environment became features that were critical in our survival. And many of these features persist in us today.

HUMAN ORIGINS To understand human origins, it is important to know a few basic principles of the theory of evolution first proposed by Charles Darwin in 1859 in his book *The Origin of Species*. At the heart of the theory of evolution is the proposition that species change through the process of **natural selection**. In natural selection, the young of any species are born with variations on a wide range of characteristics. Some may be relatively large and others relatively small, some relatively fast and others relatively slow, and so on. Among the young, those who will be most likely to survive until they can reproduce will be the ones whose variations are best adapted to their environment. The video *Natural Selection* has more detail on this process.

natural selection

evolutionary process in which the offspring best adapted to their environment survive to produce offspring of their own

Watch NATURAL SELECTION

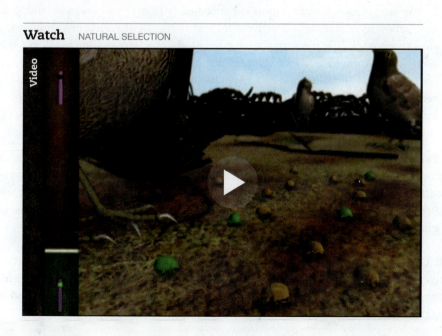

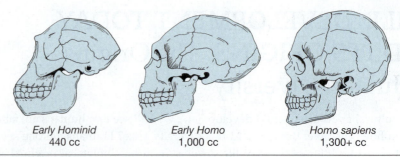

| Early Hominid | Early Homo | Homo sapiens |
| 440 cc | 1,000 cc | 1,300+ cc |

Figure 1.3 Changes in Brain Size in Early Humans

The mastery of fire by the early *Homo* species resulted in a sharp increase in brain size.

hominid

evolutionary line that led to modern humans

Homo sapiens

species of modern humans

hunter-gatherer

social and economic system in which economic life is based on hunting (mostly by males) and gathering edible plants (mostly by females)

Upper Paleolithic period

period of human history from 40,000 to 10,000 years ago, when distinct human cultures first developed

When did human evolution begin? According to evolutionary biologists, humans, chimpanzees, and gorillas had a common primate ancestor until 6 to 8 million years ago (Shreeve, 2010). At about that time, this common ancestor split into three paths, leading to the development of humans as well as to chimpanzees and gorillas. The evolutionary line that eventually led to humans is known as the **hominid** line. The primate ancestor we share with chimpanzees and gorillas lived in Africa, and so did the early hominids, as chimpanzees and gorillas do today.

By 200,000 years ago the early hominid species had evolved into our species, *Homo sapiens* (Shreeve, 2010; Wilson, 2012). During the millions of years of evolution that led to Homo sapiens, several characteristics developed that made us distinct from previous hominids and from other primates:

1. *Larger brain.* The most striking and important change during this period was the size of early *Homo*'s brain, which became more than twice as large as the brain of early hominids (see **Figure 1.3**; brain sizes are shown in cubic centimeters [cc]).
2. *Wider pelvis, females.* The female *Homo*'s pelvis became wider to allow the birth of bigger-brained babies.
3. *Longer dependency.* The larger brains of early *Homo* babies meant that babies were born less mature than they were for earlier hominids, resulting in a longer period of infant and childhood dependency.
4. *Development of tools.* Creating tools enhanced early *Homo*'s success in obtaining food. The earliest tools were apparently made by striking one stone against another to create a sharp edge. The tools may have been used for purposes such as slicing animal meat and whittling wood into sharp sticks for hunting.
5. *Control of fire.* Controlled use of fire enabled our early ancestors to cook food, and because cooked food is used much more efficiently by the body than raw food, this led to another burst in brain size (Wrangham, 2009). At the same time, the size of the teeth and jaws diminished because cooked food was easier to eat than raw food.

The long period of infant dependency may have made it difficult for early *Homo* mothers to travel for long distances to accompany the males on hunting or scavenging expeditions (Wrangham, 2009). So, a **hunter-gatherer** way of life developed, in which females remained in a relatively stable home base, caring for children and perhaps gathering edible plants in the local area, whereas males went out to hunt or scavenge.

THE ORIGIN OF CULTURES AND CIVILIZATIONS Physically, *Homo sapiens* has changed little from 200,000 years ago to the present. However, a dramatic change in the development of the human species took place during the **Upper Paleolithic period** from 40,000 to about 10,000 years ago (Ember et al., 2011; Wilson, 2012) (see **Figure 1.4**).

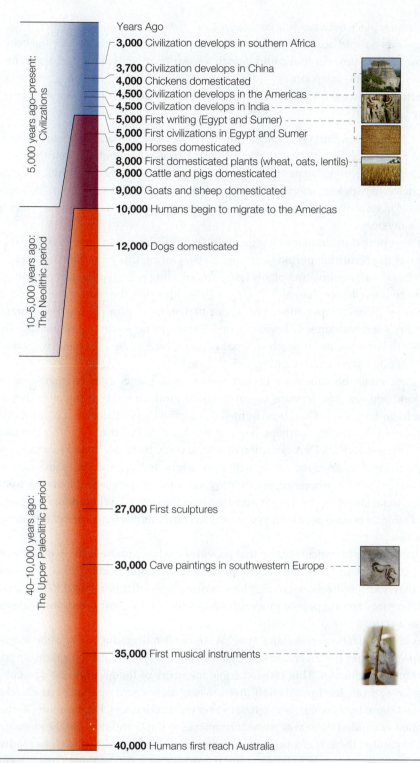

Figure 1.4 Key Changes in Human Species Development, Past 40,000 Years

For the first time, art appeared: musical instruments; paintings on cave walls; small ivory beads attached to clothes; decorative objects made from bone, antler, or shell; and human and animal figures carved from ivory or sculpted from clay.

Several other important changes mark the Upper Paleolithic, in addition to the sudden burst of artistic production:

- Humans began to bury their dead, sometimes including art objects in the graves.
- For the first time cultural differences developed between human groups, as reflected in their art and tools.

- Trade took place between human groups.
- There was a rapid acceleration in the development of tools, including the bow and arrow, a spear thrower that could launch a spear at an animal (or perhaps at human enemies), and the harpoon.
- The first boats were invented, allowing humans to reach and populate Australia and New Guinea.

Why this sudden burst of changes during the Upper Paleolithic, when there is no evidence for changes in the brain or body? Some researchers believe that this is when language first appeared (Diamond, 1992; Leakey, 1994). However, anatomical evidence of a capacity for spoken language is evident at least 300,000 years ago (Wrangham, 2009). So, for now the origin of the revolutionary changes of the Upper Paleolithic remains a mystery.

The next period of dramatic change, from 10,000 years ago to about 5,000 years ago, is known as the **Neolithic period** (Johnson, 2005). During this time, humans broadened their food sources by cultivating plants and domesticating animals. The key contributor to this advance was climate change. The Upper Paleolithic was the time of the last Ice Age, when average global temperatures were about 10 degrees Celsius (50 degrees Fahrenheit) below today's temperatures. Glaciers covered Europe as far south as present-day Berlin, and in North America, as far south as what is now Chicago. By the Neolithic period the climate was much warmer, resembling our climate today.

As the climate became warmer and wetter, new plants evolved that were good human food sources, and humans began to try to produce more of the ones they liked best. The huge animals that had been hunted during the Upper Paleolithic became extinct, perhaps from overhunting, perhaps because the animals failed to adapt to the climate changes (Diamond, 1992). Domestication of animals may have developed as a food source to replace the extinct animals. Along with agriculture and animal care came new tools: mortars and pestles for processing plants into food, and the spindle and loom for weaving cotton and wool into clothing. Larger, sturdier dwellings were built (and furniture such as beds and tables) because people stayed in settled communities longer to tend their plants and animals.

The final major historical change that provides the basis for how we live today began around 5,000 years ago with the development of **civilization** (Ridley, 2010). The characteristics that mark civilization include cities, writing, specialization into different kinds of work, differences among people in wealth and status, and a centralized political system known as a **state**.

Why did civilizations and states arise? As agricultural production became more efficient, especially after the invention of irrigation, not everyone in a cultural group had to work on food production. This allowed some members of the group to be concentrated in cities, away from food-production areas, where they could specialize as merchants, artists, musicians, bureaucrats, and religious and political leaders. Furthermore, as the use of irrigation expanded there was a need for a state to build and oversee the system, and as trade expanded there was a need for a state to build infrastructure such as roadways. Trade also connected people in larger cultural groups that could be united into a common state (Ridley, 2010).

Human Evolution and Child Development Today

LO 1.4 **Apply information about human evolution to how child development takes place today.**

What does this history of our development as a species tell us about child development today? First, it is important to recognize that how we develop today is based partly on our evolutionary history. We still share many characteristics with our hominid relatives and ancestors, such as a large brain compared to our body size, a relatively long period

Neolithic period

era of human history from 10,000 to 5,000 years ago, when animals and plants were first domesticated

civilization

form of human social life, beginning about 5,000 years ago, that includes cities, writing, occupational specialization, and states

state

centralized political system that is an essential feature of a civilization

of childhood dependence on adults before reaching maturity, and cooperative living in social groups. Researchers working in the field of **evolutionary psychology** claim that many other characteristics of child development are influenced by our evolutionary history, such as aggressiveness and mate selection (Crawford & Krebs, 2008). We will examine their claims in the course of the book.

A second important fact to note about our evolutionary history is that biologically we have changed little since the origin of *Homo sapiens* about 200,000 years ago, yet how we live has changed in astonishing ways (Ridley, 2010; Wilson, 2012). Although we are a species that originated in the grasslands and forests of Africa, now we live in every environment on earth, from mountains to deserts, from tropical jungles to the Arctic. Although we are a species that evolved to live in small groups of a few dozen people, now most of us live in cities with millions of other people. Although human females are capable of giving birth to at least eight children in the course of their reproductive lives, and probably did so through most of history, now most women have one, two, or three children—or perhaps none at all.

It is remarkable that an animal like us, which evolved in Africa adapted through natural selection to a hunting-and-gathering way of life, could have developed over the past 40,000 years an astonishing array of cultures, most of which bear little resemblance to our hunter-gatherer origins. Once we developed the large brain that is the most distinctive characteristic of our species, we became capable of altering our environments, so that it was no longer natural selection alone that would determine how we would live, but the cultures we created. As far as we can tell from the fossil record, all early hominids lived in the same way (Shreeve, 2010). Even different groups of early *Homo sapiens* seem to have lived more or less alike before the Upper Paleolithic period, as hunters and gatherers in small groups.

Today there are hundreds of different cultures around the world, all part of the human community but each with its distinctive way of life. There are wide cultural variations in how we live, such as how we care for infants, what we expect from children, and how we respond to the changes of puberty. As members of the species *Homo sapiens* we all share a similar biology, but cultures shape the raw material of biology into widely different paths through the life span.

It is also culture that makes us unique as a species. Other animals have evolved in ways that are adaptive for a particular set of environmental conditions. They can learn in the course of their lifetimes, certainly, but the scope of their learning is limited. When their environment changes, if their species is to survive it will do so not by learning new skills required by a new environment but through a process of natural selection that will enable those best-suited *genetically* to the new environmental conditions to survive long enough to reproduce, while the others do not.

In contrast, once humans developed the large brain we have now, it enabled us to survive in any environment by inventing and learning new skills and methods of survival and then passing them along to others as part of a cultural way of life. We can survive and thrive even in conditions that are vastly different from our environment of evolutionary adaptation because our capacity for cultural learning is so large and, compared to other animals, there is relatively little about us that is fixed by instinct.

evolutionary psychology
branch of psychology that examines how patterns of human functioning and behavior have resulted from adaptations to evolutionary conditions

Summary: Child Development Today and Its Origins

LO 1.1 **Describe how the human population has changed over the past 10,000 years and distinguish between the demographic profiles of developed countries and developing countries.**

The total human population was fewer than 10 million for most of history, but it rose from 2 billion in 1930 to 7 billion in 2011 and is expected to increase to 10 billion by 2090. Unlike most developed countries, the United States is projected to increase in population during the 21st century, primarily as a result of immigration. In general, cultural values are more individualistic in developed countries and more collectivistic in developing countries. Most people in developing countries are poor and live in rural areas, but these countries are experiencing rapid economic development and a massive migration to urban areas. Also, young people are receiving increasing levels of education as their countries become wealthier and enter the global economy.

LO 1.2 **Define the term *socioeconomic status* (SES) and explain why SES, gender, and ethnicity are important aspects of child development within countries.**

SES includes educational level, income level, and occupational status. It influences access to resources such as education and health care. Gender shapes expectations and opportunities in most cultures throughout life. Ethnicity often includes a distinct cultural identity.

LO 1.3 **Trace the evolutionary origins of the human species and summarize the features of the first human cultures.**

Natural selection results in species change because the young who are best adapted to the environment will be most likely to survive and reproduce. Humans arose from earlier hominids and developed distinctive characteristics such as large brains, long infancy, tool use, and control of fire. Our species, *Homo sapiens*, first appeared about 200,000 years ago.

The Upper Paleolithic period (40,000–10,000 years ago) is the first time human cultures became distinct from one another in their art and tools. During the Neolithic period (10,000–5,000 years ago), humans first domesticated plants and animals. The first civilizations around 5,000 years ago marked the origin of writing, specialized work, and a centralized state.

LO 1.4 **Apply information about human evolution to how child development takes place today.**

Humans are one species, but since the birth of culture, human groups have developed remarkably diverse ways of life. Our exceptionally large brain has allowed us to create cultural practices that enable us to live in a wide range of environments.

Section 2   Theories of Child Development

Learning Objectives

1.5 Summarize Freud's psychosexual theory and Erikson's psychosocial theory of child development and describe the main limitations of each.

1.6 Describe behaviorism, including the role of conditioning and the variation known as *social learning theory*.

1.7 Summarize the constructivist theories of Piaget and Vygotsky.

1.8 Describe the elements of the information-processing model of cognitive functioning.

1.9 Define the five systems of Bronfenbrenner's ecological framework.

1.10 Describe the main components of the ecocultural theory of Weisner and explain how it differs from stage theories.

1.11 Outline the cultural-developmental model that will be the structure of this book and describe the new life stage of emerging adulthood.

THEORIES OF CHILD DEVELOPMENT:
Classic Theories

People have been thinking about the ways that we change throughout life for a long time. Conceptions of childhood as a time that is different from adulthood are found in texts dating back 3,000 years ago. In the Indian *Dharmashastras*, the sacred law books of the Hindu religion, childhood was the time to be an apprentice, learning the skills necessary for adult life. Development from birth to age 25—roughly the span of time we are covering in this text—was not broken down into stages (Kakar, 1998; Rose, 2004).

A more fine-grained conception of childhood stages was proposed by Solon, a philosopher in ancient Greece about 2,500 years ago (Levinson, 1978). For Solon, early life was divided into 7-year segments

Ages 0–7: A stage of being "unripe."
Ages 7–14: Signs of approaching manhood "show in the bud."
Ages 14–21: His limbs are growing, his chin is "touched with fleecy down," and the bloom of his cheek is gone.
Ages 21–28: Now the young man "ripens to greatest completeness" physically, and "his worth becomes plain to see."

Although these conceptions of child development were written in widely different places and times, they share certain similarities. Both are ideal conceptions, a view of how we develop if all goes well: Preparation for life is made in youth. Furthermore, both view youth as a time of immaturity.

One important difference among these ancient conceptions of child development is that they have different ways of dividing up the life span, from just 4 stages in the *Dharmashastras* to 10 in the Ancient Greek conception. This is a useful reminder that for humans the life span is not really divided into clear and definite biologically based stages, the way an insect has stages of larva, juvenile, and adult. Instead, conceptions of child development are only partly biological—infants everywhere cannot walk or talk, adolescents everywhere experience puberty—and are also culturally and socially based, situated in a time and place.

The scientific study of child development has been around for a relatively short time, only about 120 years. During that time there have been a number of ways of conceptualizing child development. A good **theory** is a framework that presents a set of interconnected ideas in an original way and inspires further research. We will discuss nine of them: the psychosexual approach, the psychosocial approach, behaviorism and social learning approaches, Piaget's cognitive-developmental approach, Vygotsky's social constructivist approach, the information-processing approach, and ecological and ecocultural approaches. These theories set the framework for the research discussed in the rest of the text. The theories themselves are also interesting cultural artifacts. Consider that each theorist is a product of his or her cultural and historical context as you read about each theory.

Psychoanalytic Theories

LO 1.5 Summarize Freud's psychosexual theory and Erikson's psychosocial theory of child development and describe the main limitations of each.

Psychoanalytic approaches to human behavior examine the underlying psychological forces of human behavior, in particular the relationship between conscious and unconscious motivations. Development occurs through mastery of particular developmental challenges, and the growing person moves from one stage to the next.

FREUD'S PSYCHOSEXUAL THEORY The earliest scientific theory of child development was devised by Sigmund Freud (1856–1939), who was a physician in Vienna, Austria, in the late 19th century (Breger, 2000). Working with people suffering from various mental health problems, Freud concluded that a consistent theme across patients was that they seemed to have experienced some kind of traumatic event in childhood. The trauma then became buried in their unconscious minds, or *repressed*, and continued thereafter to shape their personality and their mental functioning even though they could no longer remember it.

In an effort to address their problems, Freud developed the first method of psychotherapy, which he called *psychoanalysis*. The purpose of psychoanalysis was to bring patients' repressed memories from the unconscious into consciousness, through having them discuss their dreams and their childhood experiences while guided by the psychoanalyst. According to Freud, just making the repressed memories conscious would be enough to heal the patient.

Freud's experiences as a psychoanalyst were the basis of his **psychosexual theory**. He believed that sexual desire was the driving force behind child development. Sexual desire arises from a part of the mind Freud called the *id*, and operates on the basis of the *pleasure principle*, meaning that it constantly seeks immediate and unrestrained satisfaction. However, from early in childhood, adults in the environment teach the child to develop a conscience, or *superego*, that restricts the satisfaction of desires and makes the child feel guilty for disobeying. At the same time as the superego develops, an *ego* also develops that serves as a mediator between id and superego. The ego operates on the *reality principle*, allowing the child to seek satisfaction within the constraints imposed by the superego.

For Freud, everything important in development happens before adulthood. In fact, Freud viewed the personality as complete by age 6. Although sexual desire is the driving force behind development throughout life in Freud's theory, the locus of the sexual drive shifts around the body during the course of early development (see **Table 1.1**). Infancy is the *oral stage*, when sexual sensations are concentrated in the mouth. Infants derive pleasure from sucking, chewing, and biting. The next stage, beginning at about a year

theory
framework that presents a set of interconnected ideas in an original way and inspires further research

psychosexual theory
Freud's theory proposing that sexual desire is the driving force behind development

Table 1.1 Freud's Psychosexual Stages

Age period	Psychosexual stage	Main features
Infancy	Oral	Sexual sensations centered on the mouth; pleasure derived from sucking, chewing, biting
Toddlerhood	Anal	Sexual sensations centered on the anus; high interest in feces; pleasure derived from elimination
Early childhood	Phallic	Sexual sensations move to genitals; sexual desire for other-sex parent and fear of same-sex parent
Middle childhood	Latency	Sexual desires repressed; focus on developing social and cognitive skills
Adolescence	Genital	Reemergence of sexual desire, now directed outside the family

and a half, is the *anal stage*, when sexual sensations are concentrated in the anus. Toddlers derive their greatest pleasure from the act of elimination and are fascinated by feces. The *phallic stage*, from about age 3 to 6, is the most important stage of all in Freud's theory. In this stage sexual sensations become located in the genitals, but the child's sexual desires are focused particularly on the other-sex parent. Freud proposed that all children experience an *Oedipus complex* in which they desire to displace their same-sex parent and enjoy sexual access to the other-sex parent, as Oedipus did in the famous Greek myth.

According to Freud, the Oedipus complex is resolved when the child, fearing that the same-sex parent will punish his or her incestuous desires, gives up those desires and instead identifies with the same-sex parent, seeking to become more similar to that parent. In Freud's theory this leads to the fourth stage of psychosexual development, the *latency stage*, lasting from about age 6 until puberty. During this period the child represses sexual desires and focuses the energy from those desires on learning social and intellectual skills.

The fifth and last stage in Freud's theory is the *genital stage*, from puberty onward. The sexual drive reemerges, but this time in a way approved by the superego, directed toward persons outside the family.

From our perspective today, it's easy to see plenty of gaping holes in psychosexual theory (Breger, 2000). Sexuality is certainly an important part of human development, but human behavior is complex and cannot be reduced to a single motive. Also, although his theory emphasizes the crucial importance of the first 6 years of life, Freud never studied children. His view of childhood was based on the retrospective accounts of patients who came to him for psychoanalysis, mainly upper-class women in Vienna. (Yet, ironically, his psychosexual theory emphasized boys' development and virtually ignored girls.) Nevertheless, Freud's psychosexual theory was the dominant view of development throughout the first half of the 20th century (Robins et al., 1999). Today, few people who study human development adhere to Freud's psychosexual theory, even among psychoanalysts (Grunbaum, 2006). It's important to notice how any theory, including Freud's, is a product of the culture and social setting, including the historical era, that the theorist lives and works in. We will see how the other theories that will carry us through the text are cultural products.

ERIKSON'S PSYCHOSOCIAL THEORY Even though Freud's theory was dominant in psychology for more than a half century, from the beginning many people objected to what they regarded as an excessive emphasis on the sexual drive as the basis for all development. Among the skeptics was Erik Erikson (1902–1994). Although he was trained as a psychoanalyst in Freud's circle in Vienna, he doubted the validity of Freud's psychosexual theory. Instead, Erikson proposed a theory of development with two crucial differences from Freud's theory. First, it was a **psychosocial theory**, in which the driving force behind development was not sexuality but the need to become integrated into the social and cultural environment. Second, Erikson viewed development as continuing throughout the life span, not as determined solely by the early years as in Freud's theory.

psychosocial theory
Erikson's theory that human development is driven by the need to become integrated into the social and cultural environment

Erik Erikson was the first to propose a life span theory of human development.

Infancy:
Trust vs. mistrust
Main developmental challenge
is to establish bond with
trusted caregiver

Toddlerhood:
Autonomy vs. shame and doubt
Main developmental challenge
is to develop a healthy sense
of self as distinct from others

Early Childhood:
Initiative vs. guilt
Main developmental challenge
is to initiate activities in a
purposeful way

Middle Childhood:
Industry vs. inferiority
Main developmental challenge
is to begin to learn knowledge
and skills of culture

Adolescence:
Identity vs. identity confusion
Main developmental challenge
is to develop a secure and
coherent identity

Early Adulthood:
Intimacy vs. isolation
Main developmental challenge
is to establish a committed,
long-term love relationship

Middle Adulthood:
Generativity vs. stagnation
Main developmental challenge
is to care for others and contribute
to well-being of the young

Late Adulthood:
Ego integrity vs. despair
Main developmental challenge
is to evaluate lifetime, accept
it as it is

Figure 1.5 Erikson's Eight Stages of Psychosocial Development

Erikson (1950) proposed a sequence of eight stages of development (see **Figure 1.5**). Each stage is characterized by a distinctive developmental challenge or "crisis" that the person must resolve. A successful resolution of the crisis prepares the person well for the next stage of development. However, a person who has difficulty with the crisis in one stage enters the next stage at high risk for being unsuccessful at that crisis as well. The stages build on each other, for better and for worse.

In the first stage of life, during infancy, the developmental challenge is *trust versus mistrust.* If the infant is loved and cared for, a sense of basic trust develops that the world is a good place and need not be feared. If not well-loved in infancy, the child learns to mistrust others and to doubt that life will be rewarding.

In the second stage, during toddlerhood, the developmental challenge is *autonomy versus shame and doubt.* During this stage the child develops a sense of self distinct from others. If the child is allowed some scope for making choices, a healthy sense of autonomy develops, but if there is excessive restraint or punishment, the child experiences shame and doubt.

In the third stage, during early childhood, the developmental challenge is *initiative versus guilt.* In this stage the child becomes capable of planning activities in a purposeful way. With encouragement of this new ability a sense of initiative develops, but if the child is discouraged and treated harshly then guilt is experienced.

The fourth stage, during middle to late childhood, is *industry versus inferiority.* In this stage children move out more into the world and begin to learn the knowledge and skills required by their culture. If a child is encouraged and taught well, a sense of industry develops that includes enthusiasm for learning and confidence in mastering the skills required. However, a child who is unsuccessful at learning what is demanded is likely to experience inferiority.

The fifth stage is adolescence, with the challenge of *identity versus identity confusion.* Adolescents must develop an awareness of who they are, what their capacities are, and what their place is within their culture. For those who are unable to achieve this, identity confusion results.

The sixth stage, *intimacy versus isolation,* takes place in early adulthood. In this stage, the challenge for young adults is to risk their newly formed identity by entering a committed intimate relationship, usually marriage. Those who are unable or unwilling to make themselves vulnerable end up isolated, without an intimate relationship.

The seventh stage, in middle adulthood, involves the challenge of *generativity versus stagnation.* The generative person in middle adulthood is focused on how to contribute to the well-being of the next generation, through providing for and caring for others. People who focus instead on their own needs at midlife end up in a state of stagnation.

Finally, in the eighth stage, late adulthood, the challenge is *ego integrity versus despair.* This is a stage of looking back and reflecting on how one's life has been experienced. The person who accepts what life has provided, good and bad parts alike, and concludes that it was a life well spent can be considered to have ego integrity. In contrast, the person who is filled with regrets and resentments at this stage of life experiences despair.

Erikson's psychosocial theory has endured better than Freud's psychosexual theory. Today, nearly all researchers who study human development would agree that development is lifelong, with important changes taking place at every phase of the life span (Baltes et al., 2006; Lerner, 2006; Jensen, 2015a). Similarly, nearly all researchers on human development today would agree with Erikson's emphasis on the social and cultural basis of development. However, not all of Erikson's proposed life stages have been accepted as valid or valuable. It is mainly his ideas about identity in adolescence and generativity in midlife that have inspired substantial interest and attention among researchers (Clark, 2010).

Behaviorism and Learning Theories

LO 1.6 **Describe behaviorism, including the role of conditioning and the variation known as *social learning theory*.**

Behaviorism arose in opposition to the psychoanalytic approach. Behaviorism is based on the idea that the study of development ought to be based on observable behavior— what a child actually does—rather than what a child thinks, feels, or imagines. Behaviorism is sometimes called *learning theory* because behaviorists believe that there are overarching laws that determine how children learn about the environment, and all behavior is learned step by step. Development occurs as children learn and gain new patterns of behavior.

In the first part of the 20th century, John Watson, an early proponent of behaviorism, believed that any behavior could be learned. He wrote:

> Give me a dozen healthy infants, well-formed, and my own specified world to bring them up in and I'll guarantee to take any one at random and train him to become any type of specialist I might selected—doctor, lawyer, artist, merchant, chief, and yes, even beggar-man and thief, regardless of his talents, penchants, tendencies, abilities, vocations, and race.
>
> Watson, 1924/1998, p. 82

CONDITIONING Conditioning is the fundamental learning process in behaviorism. A behavior is conditioned when specific types of experience make the behavior more or less probable. For example, in *classical conditioning*, a neutral stimulus is associated with a meaningful stimulus, and the person or animal undergoing conditioning gradually responds to the neutral stimulus with the same response as to the meaningful one. The most famous example of classical conditioning comes from Ivan Pavlov, who conditioned a dog to salivate at the presentation of a sound by associating the sound (neutral stimulus) with the presentation of food (meaningful stimulus).

In *operant conditioning*, learning is based on behavioral responses to stimuli in the environment (Skinner, 1953). Specifically, in operant conditioning, behavior is either more likely to occur or less likely to occur. Reinforcement always makes a behavior more likely to occur. In positive reinforcement, a behavior is encouraged by the presentation of the *reinforcer*, such as a gold star for good performance on an assignment. In negative reinforcement, a behavior is encouraged by the taking away of an *undesirable stimulus*, such as when your alarm stops when you press the snooze button. In these examples, the gold star is reinforcing studying and doing well on an assignment, and the alarm stopping is reinforcing your waking up and pressing the button.

Sometimes students learning this material confuse negative reinforcement with punishment. Punishment makes a behavior less likely. For instance, a child is grounded for swearing and learns not to swear again. Being grounded is a punishment because it is undesirable, and it is designed to influence the child not to swear again. The distinction between negative reinforcement and punishment can be tricky, however. For example, a punishment like spanking may function as a reinforcer for a child who is getting attention, even if it is uncomfortable. The child's undesirable behavior may be reinforced by the attention, and therefore more likely to recur, which is probably not what the parent desires.

Behaviorism is an important theory in child development. The theory's emphasis on observable behavior led to the careful study of what is learned, and how behaviors are learned. Even complex emotional patterns may have their roots in learning, rather than in unconscious drives or genetic blueprints. Furthermore, one aspect of behaviorism that is particularly useful for understanding child development is that behaviors that are learned can be unlearned. That is, behavior change is possible. Many teachers and parents use behaviorist techniques to teach children new behaviors, capitalizing on their social bonds to encourage children's learning and development.

SOCIAL LEARNING THEORY Strict proponents of behaviorism believed that *all* behavior came from learned responses, after instances of classical and operant conditioning. An important revision of behaviorism is *social learning theory*. In social learning, people and some animals learn through observation and imitation of other people—without direct reinforcement for themselves. People learn by watching others all the time as we interact with our families and friends, in schools and classes, and in other settings—even from watching advertisements and people in movies and television.

The central learning process in social learning is *modeling*, when a person observes and imitates the actions of others. In a famous set of studies known as the Bobo doll experiments, Bandura and colleagues (Bandura et al., 1961; Bandura et al., 1963) exposed young children to adult models acting either aggressively or non-aggressively with a Bobo doll. Children exposed to the aggressive model were more likely to imitate the aggressive behavior when left alone with the Bobo doll than children exposed to the non-aggressive model. Many activities are modeled for children, such as how to solve math problems, how to dance, or how to shave one's face. Modeling is not just simple imitation. People are more likely to repeat a behavior when the model is someone admired, powerful, nurturing, or familiar (Bandura, 1986).

Beyond the important concept of modeling, another way in which social learning theory has influenced the field of child development is the concept of *self-efficacy*, which is a feeling of self-confidence that comes with the belief that one has the ability to complete tasks and reach goals. The belief in one's self that comes along with self-efficacy is helpful in all kinds of settings, especially in schools, as we will see later in the text.

Scenes from Albert Bandura's classic Bobo doll experiment. Children exposed to the aggressive model were more likely to imitate the aggressive behavior when left alone with the Bobo doll than children exposed to the nonaggressive model.

Constructivist Theories

LO 1.7 Summarize the constructivist theories of Piaget and Vygotsky.

Constructivist theories posit that knowledge is not a copy of reality, but rather that children and other people actively construct reality in the mind as they interact with objects and others in the world. Piaget and Vygotsky were constructivists who were contemporaries from different cultures.

PIAGET'S COGNITIVE CONSTRUCTIVIST THEORY Unquestionably, the most influential theory of cognitive development from infancy through adolescence is the one developed by the Swiss psychologist Jean Piaget (pee-ah-ZHAY), who lived from 1896 to 1980. Piaget's observations convinced him that children of different ages think differently, and that changes in cognitive development proceed in distinct stages (Piaget, 1954).

Each stage of Piaget's theory involves a different way of thinking about the world. The idea of cognitive stages means that each person's cognitive abilities are organized into coherent **mental structures**; a person who is able to think within a particular stage in one aspect of life should be able to think using the abilities of that stage in other aspects of life as well. Because Piaget focused on how cognition changes with age, his approach (and the approach of those who have followed in his tradition) is known as the **cognitive-developmental approach**.

According to Piaget, the driving force behind development from one stage to the next is **maturation**, a biologically driven program of developmental change (Inhelder & Piaget, 1958; Piaget, 2002). Each of us has within our genes a prescription for cognitive development that prepares us for certain changes at certain ages. A reasonably normal environment is necessary for cognitive development to occur, but the effect of the environment is limited. You cannot teach a 1-year-old something that only a 4-year-old can learn, no matter how sophisticated your teaching techniques are. By the time the 1-year-old reaches age 4, the biological processes of maturation will make it easy to understand the world as a typical child of 4 years understands it, and no special teaching will be required.

Along with maturation, Piaget emphasized that cognitive development is driven by the child's efforts to understand and influence the surrounding environment (Demetriou & Ratopoulos, 2004; Piaget, 2002). Children actively construct their understanding of the world, rather than being merely the passive recipients of environmental influences. Piaget's view was in sharp contrast to the behaviorists (the leading theorists prior to Piaget), who viewed the environment as acting on the child through rewards and punishments rather than seeing the child as an active agent.

Piaget proposed that the child's construction of reality takes place through the use of **schemes**, which are cognitive structures for processing, organizing, and interpreting information. For infants, schemes are based on sensory and motor processes such as sucking and grasping, but after infancy, schemes become symbolic and representational, as words, ideas, concepts, and scripts for activity. For example, all nouns are schemes—*tree, chair, dog*—because thinking of these words evokes a cognitive structure that allows you to process, organize, and interpret information.

The process of cognitive development is one of continual adaptation to information coming in from the world. The two adaptive processes involved in the use of schemes are **assimilation** and **accommodation**. Assimilation and accommodation are used to equilibrate, or achieve balance in cognitive development. Assimilation occurs when *new information is altered to fit an existing scheme*. In contrast, accommodation entails *changing the scheme to adapt to the new information*. Assimilation and accommodation usually take place together in varying degrees; they are "two sides of the same cognitive coin" (Flavell et al., 2002, p. 5). For example, an infant who has been breast-feeding may use mostly assimilation and a slight degree of accommodation when learning to suck from the nipple on a bottle, but if sucking on a brush handle or a parent's finger the infant would be able

mental structure
in Piaget's theory of cognitive development, the cognitive systems that organize thinking into coherent patterns

cognitive-developmental approach
focus on how cognitive abilities change with age in stage sequence of development, pioneered by Piaget and since taken up by other researchers

maturation
concept that an innate, biologically based program is the driving force behind development

schemes
cognitive structures for processing, organizing, and interpreting information.

assimilation
cognitive process of altering new information to fit an existing scheme

accommodation
cognitive process of changing a scheme to adapt to new information

to use assimilation less and need to use accommodation more. The video *Assimilation and Accommodation* shows examples of each process.

Watch ASSIMILATION AND ACCOMMODATION

People of other ages, too, use both assimilation and accommodation whenever they are processing cognitive information. One example is right in front of you. In the course of reading this book, you will read things that sound familiar to you from your own experience, so that you can easily assimilate them to what you already know. Other information, especially the information from cultures other than your own, will be contrary to the schemes you have developed from living in your culture and will require you to use accommodation to expand your knowledge and understanding of child development.

CRITICAL THINKING QUESTION

Provide an example of something a 4-year-old child could learn easily but a 1-year-old child could not learn even with special teaching.

Piaget's theory is perhaps the most famous stage theory. Piaget and his collaborator Barbel Inhelder devised a theory of cognitive development to describe the stages that children's thinking passes through during their early years (Inhelder & Piaget, 1958; Piaget, 1972; see **Table 1.2**). The first 2 years of life Piaget termed the *sensorimotor stage*. Cognitive development in this stage involves learning how to coordinate the activities of the senses (such as watching an object as it moves across your field of vision) with motor activities (such as reaching out to grasp the object). During infancy, the two major cognitive achievements are the advance in sensorimotor development from reflex behavior to intentional action and the attainment of object permanence and representation.

These are marvelous cognitive achievements, and yet early childhood fascinated Piaget not only for what children of this age are able to do cognitively but also for the kinds of mistakes they make. In fact, Piaget termed the age period from 2 to 7 the

Table 1.2 Stages of Cognitive Development in Piaget's Theory

Ages	Stage	Characteristics
0–2	Sensorimotor	Capable of coordinating the activities of the senses with motor activities
2–7	Preoperational	Capable of symbolic representation, such as in language, but with limited ability to use mental operations
7–11	Concrete operations	Capable of using mental operations, but only in concrete, immediate experience; difficulty thinking hypothetically
11–15 and up	Formal operations	Capable of thinking logically and abstractly; capable of formulating hypotheses and testing them systematically; thinking is more complex; and can think about thinking (metacognition)

preoperational stage, emphasizing that children of this age were not yet able to perform mental *operations*, that is, cognitive procedures that follow certain logical rules. Piaget specified a number of areas of preoperational cognitive mistakes that are characteristic of early childhood, including conservation, egocentrism and animism, and classification.

Middle childhood is when children develop a better grasp of what the physical world is really like and what is and is not possible. Around age 7, children make an important cognitive advance toward becoming more systematic, planful, and logical thinkers. Piaget termed the cognitive stage from age 7 to 11 *concrete operations*. During this stage, children become capable of using mental operations, which allow them to organize and manipulate information mentally instead of relying on physical and sensory associations. According to Piaget, the advances of concrete operations are evident in new abilities for performing tasks of conservation, classification, and seriation.

The stage of *formal operations* begins at about age 11 and reaches completion somewhere between ages 15 and 20. Children in concrete operations can perform simple tasks that require logical and systematic thinking, but formal operations allows adolescents to reason about complex tasks and problems involving multiple variables. It also includes the development of abstract thinking, which allows adolescents to think about abstract ideas such as justice and time and gives them the ability to imagine a wide range of possible solutions to a problem, even if they have had no direct experience with the problem.

Overall, Piaget's cognitive-developmental theory has held up well over many decades. Many parts of it have been supported by research, and so far no other comprehensive theory has come along to replace it.

VYGOTSKY'S SOCIAL CONSTRUCTIVIST THEORY In recent years, the sociocultural theory has gained attention from scholars of child development. This approach is founded on the ideas of the Russian psychologist Lev Vygotsky (1896–1934). Vygotsky died of tuberculosis when he was just 37, and it took decades before his ideas about cognitive development were translated and recognized by scholars outside Russia. It is only in recent decades that his work has been widely influential among Western scholars, but his influence is increasing as interest in understanding the cultural basis of development continues to grow (Gardiner, 2001; Maynard & Martini, 2005; Segall et al., 1999).

Vygotsky's *social constructivist* theory is often referred to as a *sociocultural theory* because in his view cognitive development is always both a social and a cultural process (Daniels et al., 2007). It is social because children learn through interactions with others and require assistance from others in order to learn what they need to know. It is cultural because what children need to know is determined by the culture they live in. Vygotsky recognized that there are distinct cultural differences in the knowledge children must acquire—from agricultural skills in rural Asia, to caring for cattle in eastern Africa, to the verbal and scientific reasoning skills taught in Western schools. This is quite different from Piaget's theory, which emphasizes the child's interactions with the physical environment and views cognitive development as essentially the same across cultures. However, Vygotsky's theory is also considered a constructivist theory, in that he posited that the child takes in information from the environment to build knowledge in the mind, but that the knowledge is actively constructed in a social process with others. Unlike Piaget, Vygotsky emphasized the social contexts of development to a great extent.

Two of Vygotsky's most influential ideas are the zone of proximal development and scaffolding, both involving social interaction. The *zone of proximal development* is the difference between skills or tasks that children can accomplish alone and those they are capable of performing if guided by an adult or a more competent peer. According to Vygotsky, children learn best if the instruction they are provided is within the zone of proximal development, so that they need assistance at first but gradually become capable of performing the task on their own. For example, children learning a musical instrument may be lost or overwhelmed if learning entirely on their own but can make progress if guided by someone who already knows how to play the instrument.

In many cultural groups, children learn parts of cultural tasks before they do the tasks themselves.

Scaffolding is the degree of assistance provided to children in the zone of proximal development. According to Vygotsky's theory, scaffolding should gradually decrease as children become more competent at a task. When children begin learning a task, they require substantial instruction and involvement from an adult or more capable peer; but as they gain knowledge and skill, the teacher should gradually scale back the amount of direct instruction provided. For example, when infants and toddlers first learn language, parents' statements to them are usually simple, but they become more complex as children's language mastery grows (Capone & McGregor, 2005). Scaffolding can occur at any age, whenever there is someone who is learning a skill or gaining knowledge from someone else.

Scaffolding and the zone of proximal development underscore the social nature of learning in Vygotsky's theory. In his view, learning always takes place via a social process, through the interactions between someone who possesses knowledge and someone who is in the process of obtaining knowledge. The ideas of the zone of proximal development and scaffolding have been applied to all the stages of child development. Remember that scaffolding is an external structure—just like on the outside of a building—that makes it easier to accomplish a task. In infancy in many cultural groups, scaffolding of language development includes the simple grammar and word choice used in talk to babies. And, objects given to babies are appropriate for their physical and motor abilities. A baby can show the concept of "inside" by placing small blocks inside a larger tube. If an adult wishes to scaffold the baby's accomplishment of the task, the adult could simply angle the tube toward the baby to make it easier to insert the blocks. Scaffolding occurs when teachers break down tasks to make them easier for learners. For example, Vai tailors in Liberia would not just tell an apprentice to sew a pair of pants (Lave & Wenger, 1991). Apprentices would watch master tailors construct pants and then learn how to do so by first cutting legs of pants, and later learning how to attach the pant legs to waist bands, attaching zippers, and all the other aspects of tailoring pants. You can probably think of many examples of scaffolding in the course of your education—in school and out. In learning math, you first learned numbers, and later you learned arithmetic, algebra, and more advanced mathematical skills like trigonometry and calculus.

THEORIES OF CHILD DEVELOPMENT:
Recent Theories

The classic theories of child development are long-standing theories that many researchers still consider to be foundational to the study of child development. More recently, scholars who study child development have devised theories and frameworks to account for developmental change. Interestingly, in most of the more recent theories, there is a more explicit emphasis on the context of child development. Thus, these recent approaches are useful to our understanding of child development in cultural settings.

The Information-Processing Approach

LO 1.8   Describe the elements of the information-processing model of cognitive functioning.

The **information-processing approach** to understanding cognitive development is quite different from the theory offered by Piaget. Rather than viewing cognitive development

information-processing approach

approach to understanding cognitive functioning that focuses on cognitive processes that exist at all ages, rather than on viewing cognitive developing in terms of discontinuous stages

as *discontinuous*, that is, as separated into distinct stages, the way Piaget did, the information-processing approach views cognitive change as *continuous*, meaning gradual and steady. In this view, cognitive processes remain essentially the same over time (Halford, 2005). The focus is not on how mental structures and ways of thinking change with age but on the thinking processes that exist at all ages. In the information-processing approach, the focus is on how changes in attention, memory, connections in the mind, and outputs vary across development.

The original model for the information-processing approach was the computer (Hunt, 1989). Information-processing researchers and theorists have tried to break down human thinking into separate parts in the same way the functions of a computer are separated into capacities for *attention, processing*, and *memory*. In the case of the development of memory in infancy, for example, someone taking the information-processing approach would examine how infants draw their attention to the most relevant aspects of situations to be remembered, how they process the results of each trial, how they remember the results, and how they retrieve the results from previous trials to compare to the most recent trial. In this way the information-processing approach is a *componential approach* (Sternberg, 1983) because it involves breaking down the thinking process into its various components.

Recent models of information processing have moved away from a simple computer analogy and recognize that the brain is more complex than any computer (Ashcraft, 2009). Rather than occurring in a step-by-step fashion as in a computer, in humans the different components of thinking operate simultaneously, as **Figure 1.6** illustrates. Nevertheless, the focus of information processing remains on the components of the thinking process, especially attention and memory.

Information-processing theorists are thoughtful about the components of cognition that they are studying and how children at different ages understand those components. Attention and perception are aspects of sensory processing that are particularly important as babies first come to understand objects and the physical world. Infants have preferences for certain kinds of visual stimuli; they prefer things that have high contrast patterns and that move. In the course of the text, we will also see how the development of memory and of retrieval systems helps infants and older children develop ways of thinking and learning that help their cognitive development.

Some information-processing theorists have focused on the ways that contexts or cultures influence development, though a cultural approach is not a hallmark of this theoretical framework. In their clever study of early number naming and memory, Kevin Miller and his colleagues (1995) showed how the speed with which Chinese children could name numbers was related to the more obvious base-10 structure of number names in the Chinese language (the word for "eleven" is "ten one," the word for "twelve" is "ten two," and so on). Chinese children's faster naming was related to their earlier understanding of how numbers worked and more advanced memory for number terms, as compared to U.S. children learning to name numbers in English. By breaking down the overall question of differences between Chinese and U.S. children in early number development, Miller and colleagues show that the structure of number names in a given language may provide a basis for differences in mathematical performance.

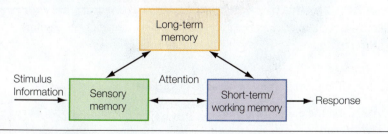

Figure 1.6 Information-Processing Model

The components of the model operate simultaneously.

Bronfenbrenner's Ecological Framework

LO 1.9   Define the **five systems of Bronfenbrenner's ecological framework.**

An important recent model of human development is Urie Bronfenbrenner's **ecological framework** (Bronfenbrenner, 1980, 2000, 2005; Bronfenbrenner & Morris, 1998). Unlike the theories proposed by Freud and Erikson, Bronfenbrenner doesn't consider stages of development. Instead, his framework focuses on the multiple influences that shape human development in the social environment.

Bronfenbrenner presented his framework as a reaction to what he viewed as an overemphasis in developmental psychology on the immediate environment, especially the mother–child relationship. The immediate environment is important, Bronfenbrenner acknowledged, but much more than this is involved in children's development. Bronfenbrenner's framework was intended to draw attention to the broader cultural environment that people experience as they develop, and to the ways the different levels of a person's environment interact. In later writings (Bronfenbrenner, 2000, 2005; Bronfenbrenner & Morris, 1998), Bronfenbrenner added a biological dimension to his framework and it is now sometimes called a *bioecological theory*, but the distinctive contribution of the model remains its portrayal of the cultural environment. Though many researchers in child development have found the framework useful, the framework has been criticized for not elaborating a theoretical core that accounts for the ways that the cultural-historical aspects of the settings of development (Worthman, 2010).

According to Bronfenbrenner, there are five key levels or *systems* that play a part in human development (see **Figure 1.7**):

ecological framework

Bronfenbrenner's theory that human development is shaped by five interrelated systems in the social environment

1. The *microsystem* is Bronfenbrenner's term for the immediate environment, the settings where people experience their daily lives. Microsystems in most cultures include relationships with each parent, with siblings, and perhaps with extended family; with peers and friends; with teachers; and with other adults (such as coaches, religious

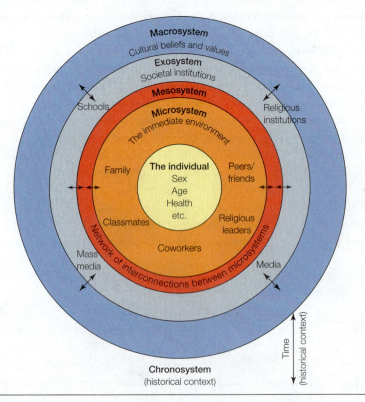

Figure 1.7 The Systems in Bronfenbrenner's Ecological Theory

How does this theory of human development differ from Freud's and Erikson's?

leaders, and employers). Bronfenbrenner emphasizes that the child is an *active* agent in the microsystems. For example, children are affected by their parents but children's behavior affects their parents as well; children are affected by their friends but they also make choices about whom to have as friends. The microsystem is where most research in developmental psychology has focused. Today, however, most developmental psychologists use the term *context* rather than microsystem to refer to immediate environmental settings and relationships.

2. The *mesosystem* is the network of interconnections between the various microsystems. For example, a child who is experiencing abusive treatment from parents may become difficult to handle in relationships with teachers; or, if a parent and child work together in a scouting troop, this is a mesosystem influence.

In countries such as Iran, the macrosystem is based on Islam, which influences all aspects of life.

3. The *exosystem* refers to the societal institutions that have indirect but potentially important influences on development. In Bronfenbrenner's theory, these institutions include schools, religious institutions, and media. For example, in Asian countries such as South Korea, competition to get into college is intense and depends chiefly on adolescents' performance on a national exam at the end of high school; consequently, the high school years are a period of extreme academic stress.

4. The *macrosystem* is the broad system of cultural beliefs and values, and the economic and governmental systems that are built on those beliefs and values. For example, in countries such as Iran and Saudi Arabia, cultural beliefs and values are based in the religion of Islam, and the economic and governmental systems of those countries are also based on the teachings of Islam. In contrast, in most developed countries, beliefs in the value of individual freedom are reflected in a free market economic system and in governmental systems of representative democracy.

5. Finally, the *chronosystem* refers to changes that occur in developmental circumstances over time, both with respect to individual development and to historical changes. For example, with respect to individual development, losing your job is a much different experience at 15 than it would be at 45; with respect to historical changes, the occupational opportunities open to young women in many countries today are much broader than they were for young women half a century ago.

There are many characteristics of Bronfenbrenner's ecological framework that make it important and useful. His framework recognizes the importance of historical contexts as influences on development, as we will see in this book. Also, Bronfenbrenner emphasized that children and adolescents are active participants in their development, not merely the passive recipients of external influences, and that will be stressed throughout this book as well.

Weisner's Ecocultural Theory

LO 1.10 Describe the main components of Weisner's ecocultural theory and explain how it differs from stage theories.

We have examined theories and a framework that take into account the individual child interacting in a cultural world, but none of the models presented so far provides a theoretical account of how the child engages in activities in cultural settings. Every child is growing up in a cultural setting that is affected by the surrounding environmental characteristics, like the land and the weather. People adapt to environments through their activities in them. To understand the cultural nature of development (Rogoff, 2003), we need a theoretical model that brings together cultural and ecological systems, with the related features that affect children and aspects of child development. Developmental researchers have long understood the child as an active agent in development (Piaget, 1929; Rogoff, 1990). Rogoff (1990), for example, discusses development as the process of the child's changing participation in activities. What is the child able to accomplish? How does the child participate in cultural activities? If development is the process of the child's increasing participation in activities that are important to the culture, how should we go about understanding children, activities, and cultures?

Thomas Weisner's (1996, 1997) **ecocultural theory** puts together aspects of the ecocultural (ecological-cultural) context with the different developmental states of the child and the settings where the child is involved in cultural activities (Gallimore et al., 1993). **Figure 1.8** shows a schematic representation of Weisner's ecocultural theory of child development. The ecocultural context includes ecocultural niche features that affect children and development. For example, it matters what the subsistence patterns of the parents are. What do the parents do every day to support the family? Are they farmers? Do they work in offices? What are the roles for women—who are usually primary caretakers of young children—in a given cultural group? Socioeconomic status matters because it shapes the kinds of subsistence patterns that parents engage in and the kinds of activities children are involved in. Children mature and develop as they increase their participation in cultural activities and practices. For example, infants might be held as they are a part of a family mealtime, and as they get older, they are able to feed themselves and become full participants in conversations at mealtimes. In some cultural groups, children might

ecocultural theory

theory that emphasizes ecological and cultural aspects of the activities and settings of development

---

Subsistence work cycle

The characteristics of the **subsistence work cycle** and the ecological and technological systems that produce it, including wage work, tending crops or animals, distance from the home, migration, and the like.

Health status and demographic characteristics

The **health status and demographic characteristics** of the community, including mortality risks, availability of health care, birth control, family size, and the like.

Community safety

Overall **community safety** other than health and mortality, such as dangers from motor vehicles, intra- and inter-community violence and warfare, and the like.

Division of labor

The **division of labor** by age and sex and perhaps other criteria like caste or race in childhood, adolescence, and adulthood, including the relative importance of various activities for subsistence and prestige.

Work that children are expected to do

The **work that children are expected to do** beginning as a toddler through adolescence.

Role of the father and older siblings

The **role of the father and older siblings** in child care as a special issue of nonmaternal child care. That is, how much do fathers and older siblings help with child care?

Children's play groups

The composition of **children's play groups** by age, sex, and kinship category (siblings, cousins, relatives, and non-relatives). That is, do children play mostly with relatives or non-relatives?

Figure 1.8 Weisner's Ecocultural Theory

Weisner's ecocultural theory of child development proposes that there are ecocultural niche features that affect a child's development. Here are a few examples.
SOURCE: Adapted from: Weisner, T. S. (1984).

become sibling caretakers and learn to feed younger children as they care for them. Even these mundane tasks, like eating a meal, carry messages about development and cultural values. The child's participation in day-to-day tasks in a cultural setting drive the child's development (Worthman, 2010). Over time, children become culture-bearing members of a group, and they pass on aspects of culture to others.

Weisner's theory shares some characteristics with Bronfenbrenner's framework. For example, Weisner (1984) proposes that there are ecocultural niche features that affect children, and these features exist on different levels similar to those found in Bronfenbrenner's framework. Some of the ecocultural niche features of Weisner's theory include the characteristics of the subsistence work cycle and the economic and techno-logical systems that produce it, the health status and demographic characteristics of the community, the division of labor by age and sex in childhood, adolescence, and adult-hood, parental sources of information concerning child health, nutrition, subsistence and child care, and measures of community change.

The features of the ecocultural niche have their effects on children and development through a unit of analysis known as the **activity setting** (Gallimore et al., 1993). There are five features of activity settings that are used in analyses of interactions that children engage in: the *personnel* present and available for children, *cultural goals and schemas* of activities, *motives and feelings* guiding action, *tasks* to be accomplished, and *normative scripts* for appropriate conduct. These features are basically the *who, what, when,* and *why* of activities. Who is participating? What are their motivations? Activity settings analysis can be used to understand development (Maynard et al., 2005). As children interact with others in settings, they develop the skills important in their cultures. We will see how the who, what, when, and why of activities provide information to the developing child about what is expected in a culture, and how this information is used to understand the variety of cultural pathways of development around the world.

A Cultural-Developmental Model for This Book

LO 1.11 Outline the cultural-developmental model that will be the structure of this book and describe the new life stage of emerging adulthood.

The structure of this book combines elements of Erikson's lifespan approach and Weisner's ecocultural approach. Today there is a widespread consensus among researchers and theorists that human development is lifelong and that important changes take place throughout the life span, as Erikson proposed (Baltes, 2006). There is also a consensus that there are multiple contextual factors that affect child development, in line with the ideas of Bronfenbrenner and Weisner. In addition, there are biological aspects of development, such as how contextual factors and engagement in activities affect biomarkers such as the production of stress and other hormones, and the functioning of our brains. The frame-work for this book will be a *cultural-developmental approach* to human development (Jensen, 2015a; Rogoff, 2003). This approach has its roots in the anthropological work of Margaret Mead (Mead, 1928; Mead & Macgregor, 1951), Ruth Benedict (1938), Beatrice and John Whiting (Whiting, 1963), Tom Weisner, and Richard Shweder (Stigler et al., 1990) and the psychological work of Lev Vygotsky, Jerome Bruner, Patricia Greenfield, and Michael Cole (Bruner, 1990; Greenfield & Bruner, 1966; Cole & Bruner, 1971; Cole, 1996; Greenfield, 1999; Vygotsky, 1978). According to this approach, it is crucial to recognize that throughout the life span, people live within cultural communities where they continuously interact and negotiate with others who convey cultural beliefs, skills, and knowledge. In the course of their development, people learn and respond to the ways of their culture, and become par-ticipants in shaping the culture's future. The biological basis of development is important in many ways, but it is culture that determines what we learn, what we aspire to become, and how we see ourselves in relation to the world. This is why, according to the cultur-al-developmental approach, it is necessary to study development across diverse cultures to

activity settings

framework for analysis of interactions that includes personnel, tasks, goals, motives, and scripts

People in developed countries often continue their education into their 20s.

have a full understanding of it. The approach also highlights that in today's globalizing world, cultural change can be quite rapid, and it is not uncommon for individuals to identify with more than one culture. Cultural change at a macro level also affects child development at a micro level; that is, socioeconomic or demographic changes that occur in the cultural setting affect the way a child develops in settings she is directly involved in, such as at home and school (Greenfield, 2009).

In this book, the stages of child development will be divided as follows:

- Prenatal development, from conception until birth
- Infancy, birth to age 12 months
- Toddlerhood, the 2nd and 3rd years of life, ages 12–36 months
- Early childhood, ages 3–6
- Middle childhood, ages 6–9
- Adolescence
- Emerging adulthood

You are probably familiar with all these stage terms, with the possible exception of *emerging adulthood*. **Emerging adulthood** is a new stage of life between adolescence and young adulthood that has appeared in recent decades, primarily in developed countries (Arnett, 2000, 2011, 2015a, b; Arnett & Schwab, 2014). The rise of this new life stage reflects the fact that most people in developed countries now continue their education into their 20s and enter marriage and parenthood in their late 20s or early 30s, rather than in their late teens or early 20s as was true half a century ago. Emerging adulthood is a life stage in which most people are not as dependent on their parents as they were in childhood and adolescence but have not yet made commitments to the stable roles in love and work that structure adult life for most people. This new life stage exists mainly in developed countries because for most people in developing countries, education still ends in adolescence and marriage and parenthood begin in the late teens or early 20s (Arnett, 2015a, b). However, emerging adulthood is becoming steadily more common in developing countries (Jensen et al., 2012; Manago, 2012).

Age ranges can be specified for the early stages, but the age ranges of later stages are more ambiguous and variable. Adolescence begins with the first evidence of puberty, but puberty may begin as early as age 9 or 10 or as late as age 15 or 16, depending on cultural conditions. Emerging adulthood exists in some cultures and not others, and consequently, responsibilities such as marriage and stable work may be taken on as early as the teens or as late as the early 30s.

Stages are a useful way of conceptualizing human development because they draw our attention to the distinctive features of each age period, which helps us understand how people change over time (Arnett & Tanner, 2009). Stages also help us understand how qualitative changes in development affect the ways that people interact in the world. A child who can understand that an object exists when it is out of sight has a qualitatively different idea of how the world works than an infant who believes the object has ceased to exist. Similarly, the things we understand in adulthood, and the ways we view things in the world, vary from the ways we understood things when we were teens, or when we were in elementary school. However, it should be kept in mind that for the most part, there are no sharp breaks between the stages, and it is possible to exhibit aspects of an earlier stage in a later stage of development. Although toddlerhood is different from early childhood in many important ways, we can observe that the typical 34-month-old is not sharply different than the typical 37-month-old; nothing magical or dramatic occurs at 36 months to mark the end of one stage and the beginning of the next. Similarly, nothing definite happens at a specific age to mark the end of early childhood and the beginning of middle childhood. However, scholars of human development generally regard the transition from middle childhood to adolescence as being marked by

emerging adulthood

new life stage in developed countries, lasting from the late teens through the twenties, in which people are gradually making their way toward taking on adult responsibilities in love and work

puberty—a discrete transition. This highlights an important distinction in child development: whether development is continuous or discrete. Some aspects of developmental change are *continuous*, such as the increase in height or weight across childhood. Other aspects are *discontinuous*, such as the shift from not being able to reproduce sexually to the being able to reproduce sexually—the hallmark of puberty.

Summary: Theories of Child Development

LO 1.5 **Summarize Freud's psychosexual theory and Erikson's psychosocial theory of child development and describe the main limitations of each.**

Freud's psychosexual theory of development emphasized the sexual drive as the primary motivator of human behavior. He proposed five stages of psychosexual development but believed that the early stages were crucial and that most of later development was determined by age 6.

Erikson proposed a psychosocial theory of development that emphasized social and cultural influences and proposed that important changes take place throughout the life span. In his theory of eight stages throughout the life span, each stage is characterized by a distinctive "crisis" with two possible resolutions, one healthy and one unhealthy.

LO 1.6 **Describe behaviorism, including the role of conditioning and the variation known as *social learning theory*.**

Behaviorism is the study of learning and behavior. Conditioning is the basic learning mechanism. In classical conditioning, responses are associated with stimuli. In operant conditioning, behavior is shaped by rewards and punishments. Social learning theory is based on people's ability to learn from and imitate models.

LO 1.7 **Summarize the constructivist theories of Piaget and Vygotsky.**

Maturation is the biologically based program of development. Piaget proposed that the child's construction of reality takes place through the use of schemes, which are cognitive structures for processing, organizing, and interpreting information. The two processes involved in the use of schemes are assimilation and accommodation. Assimilation occurs when new information is altered to fit an existing scheme. In contrast, accommodation entails changing the scheme to adapt to the new information. Unlike Piaget and most other cognitive theorists and researchers, Vygotsky emphasized the cultural basis of cognitive development in childhood. He proposed concepts such as scaffolding and the zone of proximal development to describe how children obtain cultural knowledge from adults.

LO 1.8 **Describe the elements of the information-processing model of cognitive functioning.**

In contrast to the cognitive-developmental approach initiated by Piaget, which divides cognitive development into distinct stages, the information-processing approach investigates the processes of cognitive functioning that occur at all ages. The focus is on the components of cognitive functioning, especially attention and memory.

LO 1.9 **Define the five systems of Bronfenbrenner's ecological framework.**

Bronfenbrenner's ecological framework emphasizes the different systems that interact in a person's development, including microsystems, the mesosystem, the exosystem, the macrosystem, and the chronosystem.

LO 1.10 **Describe the main components of the ecocultural theory of Weisner and explain how it differs from stage theories.**

Weisner's ecocultural theory emphasizes the influence of the ecological and cultural context and its features on the child's participation in activity settings that make up the daily routines of the child's life. It is not a stage model and instead emphasizes the multiple influences that shape child development in the ecological-cultural environment throughout life.

LO 1.11 **Outline the cultural-developmental model that will be the structure of this book and describe the new life stage of emerging adulthood.**

In the cultural-developmental approach, development is examined across cultures, and cultural change is taken into account. In this book development is divided into seven stages, from prenatal development through emerging adulthood. Most of the stages occur in all cultures, but emerging adulthood is a new life stage between adolescence and young adulthood that has become typical mainly in developed countries, although it is growing more common in developing countries. During emerging adulthood most people are less dependent on their parents but have not yet made commitments to the stable roles in love and work that structure adult life for most people.

Section 3   How We Study Child Development

Learning Objectives

1.12 Recall the five steps of the scientific method and the meanings and functions of hypotheses, sampling, and procedure in scientific research.

1.13 Describe some ethical standards for child development research.

1.14 Summarize the main methods used in research on child development.

1.15 Describe the major types of research designs used in child development research.

HOW WE STUDY CHILD DEVELOPMENT: The Scientific Method

The field of human development is based on scientific research and to understand the research presented in this book it is important for you to know the essential elements of how the scientific process works. Here we look at this process and how it is applied to the study of human development.

The Five Steps of the Scientific Method

LO 1.12 **Recall the five steps of the scientific method and the meanings and functions of hypotheses, sampling, and procedure in scientific research.**

In its classic form, the **scientific method** involves five basic steps: (1) identifying a question to be investigated, (2) forming a hypothesis, (3) choosing a research method and a research design, (4) collecting data to test the hypothesis, and (5) drawing conclusions that lead to new questions and new hypotheses. **Figure 1.9** summarizes these steps.

STEP 1: IDENTIFY A QUESTION OF SCIENTIFIC INTEREST Every scientific study begins with an idea (Machado & Silva, 2007). A researcher wants to find an answer to a question that can be addressed using scientific methods. For example, in research on human development the question might be "How do infants who breast-feed differ in their physical and social development from infants who bottle-feed?" or "How effective are the different ways of teaching children to read?" or "What are the most important determinants of risk-taking in adolescence?" The question of interest may be generated by a theory or previous research, or it may be something the researcher has noticed from personal observation or experience.

STEP 2: FORM A HYPOTHESIS In seeking to answer the question generated in Step 1, the researcher conducts a literature review and proposes one or more hypotheses. A **hypothesis** is the researcher's idea about one possible answer to the question of interest. For example, a researcher may be interested in the question "What happens to parents' marital satisfaction when their youngest child leaves home?" and propose the hypothesis "Marital satisfaction tends to improve because parents now have more time and energy

scientific method

process of scientific investigation, involving a series of steps from identifying a research question through forming a hypothesis, selecting research methods and designs, collecting and analyzing data, and drawing conclusions

hypothesis

in the scientific process, a researcher's idea about one possible answer to the question proposed for investigation

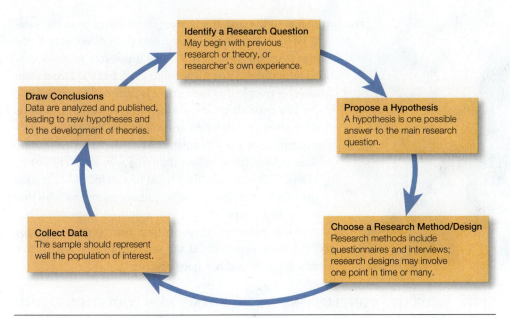

Figure 1.9 The Steps of the Scientific Method

for the marital relationship." The researcher would then design a study to test that hypothesis. The hypotheses of a study are crucial because they influence the sampling, research methods, research design, data analysis, and interpretation that follow.

STEP 3: CHOOSE A RESEARCH METHOD AND A RESEARCH DESIGN Once the hypothesis is proposed, the investigator must choose a research method and a research design (Salkind, 2011). The **research method** is the approach to investigating the hypothesis. For example, in developmental research two common research methods are questionnaires and interviews. The **research design** is the plan for when and how to collect the data for the study, for example the decision of whether to collect data at one time point or at more than one point. More detail on research methods and designs will be presented shortly.

STEP 4: COLLECT DATA TO TEST THE HYPOTHESIS After forming a hypothesis and choosing a research method and design, researchers who study human development seek to obtain a **sample**, which is a group of people who participate in a research study. The sample should represent the **population**, which is the entire category of people the sample represents. Suppose, for example, a researcher wants to study adolescents' attitudes toward contraception. Adolescents are the population, and the specific adolescents who participate in the study comprise the sample.

The goal in finding a sample is to seek out a sample that will be *representative* of the population of interest (Goodwin, 2009). To continue the example of a study of adolescents' attitudes toward contraceptive use, the waiting room of a clinic offering contraceptive services would probably not be a good place to look for a sample because the adolescents coming to such a clinic would be quite likely to have more favorable attitudes toward contraception than adolescents in general; otherwise, why would they be in a place that offers contraceptive services? If the population of interest is adolescents in general, it would be better to sample them through schools or through a telephone survey that selects households randomly from the community.

On the other hand, if a researcher is particularly interested in attitudes toward contraception among the population of adolescents who are already using or planning to use contraception, then a clinic offering contraceptive services would be a good place to find a sample. It depends on the population the researcher wishes to study and on the questions the researcher wishes to address. Again, the sample should be *representative* of

research method
in the scientific process, the approach to investigating the hypothesis

research design
plan for when and how to collect the data for a study

sample
subset of a population for which data are collected in a scientific study

population
in research, the entire category of people represented by a sample

If a sample of adolescents is obtained from a birth control clinic, what population does it represent?

the population of interest. If it is, then the findings from the sample will be *generalizable* to the population. In other words, the findings from the sample will make it possible to draw conclusions about not just the sample itself, but the larger population of people that the sample is intended to represent.

The **procedure** of the study is the way the study is conducted and the data are collected. One aspect of the procedure is the circumstances of the data collection. Researchers try to collect data in a way that will not be biased. For example, they must be careful not to phrase questions in an interview or questionnaire in a way that seems to lead people toward a desired response. They must also assure participants that their responses will be confidential, especially if the study concerns a sensitive topic such as sexual behavior or drug use.

STEP 5: DRAW CONCLUSIONS AND FORM NEW QUESTIONS AND HYPOTHESES Once the data for a study have been collected, statistical analyses are usually conducted to examine relationships between different parts of the data. Often, the analyses are determined by the hypotheses that generated the study. For example, a researcher studying relationships with parents in middle childhood may hypothesize, based on a theory or on past research, that children in this stage are closer to their mothers than to their fathers. The scientist will then test that hypothesis with a statistical analysis comparing the quality of children's relationships with mothers and with fathers.

Once the data are analyzed they must be interpreted. When scientists write up the results of their research for publication in a scientific journal, they interpret the results of the study in light of relevant theories and previous research. After researchers write an article describing the methods used, the results of the statistical analyses, and the interpretation of the results, they typically submit the manuscript for the article to a professional journal. The editor of the journal then sends the manuscript out for review by other researchers. In other words, the manuscript is **peer reviewed** for its scientific accuracy and credibility and for the importance of its contribution to the field. The editor typically relies on the reviews by the researchers' peers in deciding whether or not to accept the manuscript for publication. If the editor determines that the manuscript has passed the peer-review process successfully, the article is published in the journal. In addition to research articles, most journals publish occasional theoretical articles and review articles that integrate the findings from numerous other studies. Researchers studying human development also publish the results of their investigations in books, and often these books go through the peer-review process.

The results of research often lead to the development or modification of theories. Theories and research are intrinsically connected: A theory generates hypotheses that can be tested in research, and research leads to modifications of the theory, which generate further hypotheses and further research. There is no separate chapter on theories in this text because theories and research are intrinsically connected and should be presented together. Theories are presented in every chapter in relation to the research they have generated and the questions they have raised for future research.

Ethics in Child Development Research

LO 1.13 Describe some ethical standards for child development research.

Imagine that you were a child development researcher who was interested in language development, and you hypothesized that the number of words spoken to a toddler would influence the size of the toddler's vocabulary a year later. So, you designed a study in which families with toddlers were randomly assigned to two groups: In one

procedure

the way a study is conducted and the data are collected

peer-review

in scientific research, the system of having other scientists review a manuscript to judge its merits and worthiness for publication

group parents were trained to speak frequently to their toddlers, whereas in the other group the parents were given no instructions. Is this research design ethical?

Imagine that you were a human development researcher interested in the question of what makes some teenagers fight a lot with their parents, whereas others seem not to have conflicts. So, you proposed a study in which you invited mother-adolescent pairs to come into a laboratory situation, where they were provided with a list of possible areas of conflict and asked to pick one of them to discuss, while being filmed by the researchers. Is this research design ethical?

Imagine that you were a child development researcher who was working to develop a drug to enhance learning and memory in children. In experiments with rats the drug had been shown to enhance memory and learning, in that after receiving the drug, the rats had increased success in running mazes they had run before. However, the rats receiving the drug also died earlier than the rats in the control group. Would it be ethical to conduct a study on human children in which one group received the drug and another group did not?

These are the kinds of ethical issues that arise in the course of research on child development. To prevent ethical violations, most institutions that sponsor research, such as universities and research institutes, require proposals for research to be approved by an *institutional review board (IRB)*. IRBs are usually comprised of people who have research experience themselves and therefore can judge whether the research being proposed follows reasonable ethical guidelines. In addition to IRBs, professional organizations such as the Society for Research on Child Development (SRCD) often have a set of ethical guidelines for researchers.

The requirements of IRBs and the ethical guidelines of professional organizations usually include the following components (Fisher, 2003; Rosnow & Rosenthal, 2005):

1. *Protection from physical and psychological harm.* The most important consideration in human development research is that the people participating in the research will not be harmed by it.

2. *Informed consent before participation.* One standard ethical requirement of human development research is **informed consent**. Participants in any scientific study are supposed to be presented with a *consent form* before they participate (Salkind, 2011). Consent forms typically include information about who is conducting the study, what the purposes of the study are, what participation in the study involves, what risks (if any) are involved in participating, and what the person can expect to receive in return for participation. Consent forms also usually include a statement indicating that participation in the study is voluntary, and that people may withdraw from participation in the study at any time. For those younger than age 18, the consent of one of their parents is also usually required as part of a study's procedures.

3. *Confidentiality.* Researchers are ethically required to take steps to ensure that all information provided by participants in human development research is confidential, meaning that it will not be shared with anyone outside the immediate research group and any results from the research will not identify any of the participants by name.

4. *Deception and debriefing.* Sometimes developmental research involves deception. For example, a study might involve having children play a game but fix the game to ensure that they will lose because the objective of the study is to examine how children respond to losing a game. IRBs require researchers to show that the deception in the proposed study will cause no harm. Also, ethical guidelines require that participants in a study that involves deception must be *debriefed*, which means that following their participation they must be told the true purpose of the study and the reason for the deception.

informed consent

standard procedure in social scientific studies that entails informing potential participants of what their participation would involve, including any possible risks, and giving them the opportunity to agree to participate or not

CRITICAL THINKING QUESTION

Of the three hypothetical studies described in this module (i.e. toddlers' language development, parental conflict, and a drug to enhance learning and memory), which do you think would be likely to receive IRB approval and which not?

HOW WE STUDY CHILD DEVELOPMENT: Research Methods and Designs

Although all investigators of human development follow the scientific method in some form, there are many different ways of investigating research questions. Studies vary in the methods used and in their research designs.

Research Methods

LO 1.14 Summarize the main methods used in research on child development.

Researchers study child development in a variety of academic disciplines, including psychology, sociology, anthropology, education, social work, family studies, and medicine. They use various methods in their investigations, each of which has both strengths and limitations. We'll examine each of the major research methods next, then consider an issue that is important across methods, the question of reliability and validity.

QUESTIONNAIRES The most commonly used method in social science research is the questionnaire (Salkind, 2011). Usually, questionnaires have a *closed-question* format, which means that participants are provided with specific responses to choose from (Shaughnessy et al., 2011). Sometimes the questions have an *open-ended question* format, which means that participants are allowed to state their response following the question. One advantage of closed questions is that they make it possible to collect and analyze responses from a large number of people in a relatively short time. Everyone responds to the same questions with the same response options. For this reason, closed questions have often been used in large-scale surveys.

Although questionnaires are widely used in the study of child development, the use of questionnaires has certain limitations (Arnett, 2005a). When a closed-question format is used, the range of possible responses is already specified, and the participant must choose from the responses provided. The researcher tries to cover the responses that seem most plausible and most likely, but it is impossible in a few brief response options to do justice to the depth and diversity of human experience. For example, if a questionnaire contains an item such as "How close are you to your child? A. very close; B. somewhat close; C. not very close; D. not at all close," it is probably true that people who choose "very close" really are closer to their children than people who choose "not at all close." But this alone does not begin to capture the complexity of the parent-child relationship. Obviously, questionnaires may be difficult to use in research with young children.

INTERVIEWS Interviews are intended to provide the kind of individuality and complexity that questionnaires usually lack. An interview allows a researcher to hear people describe their lives in their own words, with all the uniqueness and richness that such descriptions make possible. Interviews also enable a researcher to know the whole person and see how the various parts of the person's life are intertwined. For example, an interview on an adolescent's family relationships might reveal how the adolescent's relationship with her mother is affected by her relationship with her father, and how the whole family has been affected by certain events—perhaps a family member's loss of a job, psychological problems, medical problems, or substance abuse.

Interviews provide **qualitative** data, as contrasted with the **quantitative** (numerical) data of questionnaires, and qualitative data can be interesting and informative. (Qualitative data are non-numerical and include not only interview data but also data from other non-numerical methods such as descriptive observations, video recordings, or

qualitative

data that is collected in nonnumerical form

quantitative

data that is collected in numerical form

photographs.) However, like questionnaires, interviews have limitations (Shaughnessy et al., 2011). Interviews may be difficult to conduct with children. And because interviews do not typically provide a range of specific responses the way questionnaires do, interview responses have to be coded according to some plan of classification. For example, if you asked emerging adults the interview question "What do you think makes a person an adult?" you might get a fascinating range of responses. However, to make sense of the data and present them in a scientific format, at some point you would have to code the responses into categories—legal markers, biological markers, character qualities, and so on. Only in this way would you be able to say something about the pattern of responses in your sample. Coding interview data takes time, effort, and money. This is one of the reasons far more studies are conducted using questionnaires than interviews.

Observations allow researchers to assess behavior directly rather than through self-report. Here, an infant's cognitive development is assessed.

OBSERVATIONS Another way researchers learn about child development is through *observations*. Studies using this method involve observing people and recording their behavior either on video or through written records. In some studies, the observations take place in the natural environment. For example, a study of aggressive behavior in children might involve observations on a school playground. In other studies, the observations take place in a laboratory setting. For example, many laboratory studies of attachments between toddlers and their parents have been conducted in which the parent leaves the room briefly and the toddler's behavior is observed while the parent is absent and when the parent returns. Whether in the natural environment or the laboratory, after the observations are completed the data are coded and analyzed. An important kind of observational research in child development is the study of *habituation*. Habituation is a simple learning mechanism in which an infant becomes used to a stimulus, indicating that they recognize it. Habituation is demonstrated when an infant who is exposed to a stimulus stops responding to it. For example, if a researcher shows the color red to an infant, the infant might look at the color for some period and then look away. If the infant is then shown the color green and the infant starts looking at the green stimulus, *dishabituation* has occurred, and this demonstrates that the infant can tell the difference between red and green. Habituation studies are done with infants because infants can't talk or explain what they're experiencing.

Observational methods have an advantage over questionnaires and interviews in that they involve actual behavior rather than self-reports of behavior. However, the disadvantage of observations is that the people being observed may be aware of the observer and this awareness may make their behavior different than it would be under normal conditions. For example, parents being observed in a laboratory setting with their children may be nicer to them than they would be at home.

ETHNOGRAPHIC RESEARCH Researchers have also learned about human development through **ethnographic research** (Jessor et al., 1996). In this method, researchers spend a considerable amount of time with the people they wish to study, often by actually living among them. Information gained in ethnographic research typically comes from researchers' observations, experiences, and informal conversations with the people they are studying. Ethnographic research is commonly used by anthropologists, often in

ethnographic research
research method that involves spending extensive time among the people being studied

Ethnographic research entails living or working closely among the people in the cultural group of interest. Here, the renowned anthropologist Margaret Mead talks to a mother in the Manus culture of Papua New Guinea.

studying non-Western cultural groups, but there are many compelling ethnographies of U.S. culture, including recent works that aim to help solve developmental problems (Lowe et al., 2006; Weisner, 2008). Anthropologists usually report the results of their research in an *ethnography*, which is a book that presents an anthropologist's observations of what life is like in a particular cultural setting.

The main advantage of the ethnographic method is that it allows the researcher to learn how people behave in their daily lives. Other methods capture only a slice or summary of people's lives, but the ethnographic method provides insights into the whole span of daily experience. The main disadvantage of the ethnographic method is that it requires a great deal of time, commitment, and sacrifice by the researcher. To engage in ethnographic work overseas means that researchers must give up their own lives for a period of time, from a few weeks to years, to live among the people whose lives they wish to understand. Ethnographic work in a researcher's own cultural setting also requires a large investment of time as the researcher becomes a participant-observer or conducts in-depth interviews with participants. Also, an ethnographic researcher is likely to form relationships with the people being studied, which may bias the interpretation of the results. However, consider that an ethnographer who invests time in getting to know research participants builds trust and likely has a deeper understanding of what is going on in the settings of child development than a researcher who merely invites participants into a lab setting for a brief experiment.

CASE STUDIES The case study method entails the detailed examination of the life of one person or a small number of persons. For more on this method, and an illustration from a famous study, see the *Research Focus: Darwin's Diary, A Case Study* feature.

Research Focus: Darwin's Diary, A Case Study

The case study method entails the detailed examination of the life of one person or a small number of persons. The advantage of a case study is in the detail and richness that is possible when only one or a few persons are being described. The disadvantage of the case study is that it is especially difficult to generalize the results to larger groups of people on the basis of only one or a few people's experiences.

Some of the most influential studies in the history of human development research were case studies. For example, Jean Piaget initially based his ideas about infants' cognitive development on his detailed observations of his own three children. Also, Charles Darwin recorded an extensive case study of the early years of his son Doddy.

Darwin is best known for his 1859 book *The Origin of Species*, which laid out his theory of evolution and dramatically changed how humans view themselves in relation to nature. However, 20 years before he published *The Origin of Species*, Darwin embarked on a different project.

He decided to keep a diary record of the development of his first child, Doddy. Already Darwin was intensely interested

in how and why animal species differ from one another. By keeping a careful record of Doddy's development, Darwin hoped to find evidence toward answering questions such as: "What is innate and what is learned?"; "What skills emerge in the first years of a child's life, and at what ages?"; and "How are human children different from other young primates?"

In his diary, Darwin recorded observations and insights concerning Doddy's cognitive, language, social, and moral development.

In observing Doddy's cognitive development, Darwin noted that it was at about 4 months of age that Doddy first became able to coordinate simple actions:

> Took my finger to his mouth & as usual could not get it back in, on account of his own hand being in the way; then he slipped his own back & so got my finger in.—This was not chance & therefore a kind of reasoning (p. 12).

Beginning to coordinate actions in this way was later recognized by psychological researchers as an important marker of early cognitive development.

With regard to social development, Darwin observed, as later researchers would, that Doddy's first smiles were the expression of internal states rather than being intended as communication. "When little under five weeks old, smiled but certainly not from pleasure" (p. 3). Over the course of the next months Darwin recorded how smiling changed from an expression of internal feelings to a social act directed toward others.

Darwin also noted Doddy's aggressive behavior. On one occasion when Doddy was 13 months old, he became angry when his nurse tried to take a piece of cake away from him: "He tried to slap her face, went scarlet, screamed & shook his head" (p. 29). Because Doddy had never been physically punished, Darwin concluded that this act of aggression must have been instinctive rather than learned.

Today the case study method is sometimes used in mental health research to describe a case that is unusual or that portrays the characteristics of a mental health issue in an especially vivid way. It is also used in combination with other methods, as a way of providing a sense of the whole of a person's life.

Review Questions:

1. Which of these was one of Darwin's goals in keeping a diary of his son Doddy's development?
   a. To see whether he preferred breast-feeding or bottle-feeding.
   b. To see how he responded to the family pets.
   c. To identify what was innate and what was learned.
   d. To give parents guidelines on how to soothe their crying children.

2. Which of these emotions did Doddy display vividly at age 13 months, according to Darwin's diary?
   a. Anger
   b. Sadness
   c. Curiosity
   d. Fear

Watch RESEARCH FOCUS: DARWIN'S DIARY, A CASE STUDY

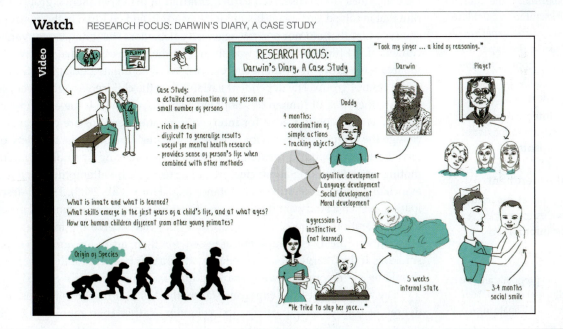

BIOLOGICAL MEASUREMENTS Biological changes are a central part of human development, so research may include biological measures in areas such as hormonal functioning, brain functioning, and the genetic basis of development. Some of this research involves assessing biological characteristics, such as hormone levels and markers of stress, and relating the results to data using other methods, such as questionnaires on aggressive behavior. Research on brain functioning often involves measuring brain activity during different kinds of behavior, like listening to music or solving a math problem. Research on genetics increasingly involves directly examining the structure of genes.

Biological methods have the advantage of providing precise measurements of many aspects of human functioning. They allow researchers to gain knowledge into how biological aspects of development are related to cognitive, social, and emotional functioning. However, biological methods tend to rely on expensive equipment. Also, although biological measurements can be precise, their relation to other aspects of functioning is often far from exact. For example, if levels of a certain hormone are positively associated with aggressive behavior, it may be that the hormone causes the aggressive behavior, or it could be that aggressive behavior causes levels of the hormone to rise. Methods in brain research yield data from monitoring the brain's electrical activity or recording images of the brain while it is engaged in various activities, but those data can be difficult to interpret (Gergen, 2011).

EXPERIMENTAL RESEARCH An approach used in many kinds of scientific research is the **experimental research method**. In the simplest form of this design, participants in the study are randomly assigned to either the *experimental group*, which receives a treatment of some kind, or the *control group*, which receives no treatment (Goodwin, 2009). Because participants were randomly assigned to either the experimental group or the control group, it can be reasonably assumed that the two groups did not differ before the experiment.

In an experiment there are independent variables and dependent variables. The **independent variable** is the variable that is different for the experimental group than for the control group. The **dependent variable** is the outcome that is measured to calculate the results of the experiment. For example, in the classic experiment by Albert Bandura and his colleagues (1961) discussed earlier, children in the experimental group were shown a film that involved aggressive behavior by an adult, and children in the control group were shown a film that did not portray aggressive behavior. The independent variable was the content of the film each group was shown. In the play session that followed, children in the treatment group were more aggressive toward an inflated doll ("Bobo") than children in the control group. The dependent variable was the children's aggressiveness.

Another area of human development research for which the experimental research method is commonly used is for **interventions**. Interventions are programs intended to change the attitudes or behavior of the participants. For example, a variety of programs have been developed to prevent adolescents from starting to smoke cigarettes, by promoting critical thinking about cigarette advertising or by attempting to change attitudes associating smoking with peer acceptance (e.g., Horn et al., 2005). The adolescents participating in such a study are randomly assigned to either the experimental group receiving the intervention or the control group that does not receive the intervention. After the intervention, the two groups are assessed for their attitudes and behavior regarding smoking. If the intervention worked, the attitudes or behavior of the experimental group should be less favorable toward smoking than those of the control group.

The advantage of the experimental method is that it allows the researcher a high degree of control over participants' behavior. Rather than monitoring behavior that occurs naturally, the researcher attempts to change the normal patterns of behavior by assigning some persons to an experimental group and some to a control group. This allows for a clearer and more definite measure of the effect of the experimental manipulation than is possible in normal life. However, the disadvantage of the experimental method is the flip side of the advantage: Because participants' behavior has been altered through experimental manipulation, it is difficult to say if the results would apply in normal life.

NATURAL EXPERIMENTS A **natural experiment** is a situation that exists naturally—in other words, the researcher does not control it—but that provides interesting scientific information to the perceptive observer (Goodwin, 2009). One natural experiment used frequently in human development research is adoption.

experimental research method

research method that entails comparing an *experimental group* that receives a treatment of some kind to a *control group* that receives no treatment

independent variable

in an experiment, the variable that is different for the experimental group than for the control group

dependent variable

in an experiment, the outcome that is measured to calculate the results of the experiment by comparing the experimental group to the control group

intervention

program intended to change the attitudes or behavior of the participants

natural experiment

situation that exists naturally but provides interesting scientific information

Intervention programs are one type of experimental research. Here, adolescents participate in an anti-drug use program.

Unlike in most families, children in adoptive families are raised by adults with whom they have no genetic relationship. Because one set of parents provide the child's genes and a different set of parents provide the environment, it is possible to examine the relative contributions of genes and environment to the child's development. Similarities between adoptive parents and adopted children are likely to be due to the environment provided by the parents because the parents and children are biologically unrelated. Similarities between adopted children and their biological parents are likely to be the result of genetics because the environment the children grew up in was not provided by the biological parents.

Natural experiments provide the advantage of allowing for exceptional insights into the relation between genes and the environment. However, they have disadvantages as well. Families who adopt children are not selected randomly but volunteer and go through an extensive screening process, which makes adoption studies difficult to generalize to biological families. Also, natural experiments tend to be rare and to occur unpredictably, and consequently such studies can only provide answers to a limited range of questions.

RELIABILITY AND VALIDITY In scientific research it is important that research methods have *reliability* and *validity*. **Reliability** refers to the consistency of measurements (Salkind, 2011). There are a variety of types of reliability, but in general, a method has high reliability if it obtains similar results on different occasions. For example, if a questionnaire asked girls in their senior year of high school to recall when their first menstrual period occurred, the questionnaire would be considered reliable if most of the girls answered the same on one occasion as they did when asked the question again 6 months later. Or, if teachers were interviewed about who is friends with whom in their classrooms, the measure would be reliable if the teachers' answers were the same in response to two different interviewers (Goodwin, 1995).

Validity refers to the truthfulness of a method (Shaughnessy et al., 2011). A method is valid if it *measures what it claims to measure*. For example, IQ tests are purported to measure intellectual abilities, but this claim is controversial. Critics claim that IQ tests are not valid (i.e., that they do not measure what they claim to measure). Notice that a measure is not necessarily valid even if it is reliable. It is widely agreed that IQ tests are reliable—people generally score about the same on one occasion as they do on another—but the validity of the tests is disputed. In general, validity is more difficult to establish than reliability. We will examine questions of reliability and validity throughout the text.

Take a moment to review **Table 1.3**, which lists the advantages and limitations of each of the research methods we have discussed.

reliability
in scientific research, the consistency of measurements across different occasions

validity
in scientific research, the extent to which a research method measures what it claims to measure

Table 1.3 Research Methods: Advantages and Limitations

Methods	Advantages	Limitations
Questionnaire	Large sample, quick data collection	Preset responses, no depth
Interview	Individuality and complexity	Time and effort of coding
Observations	Actual behavior, not self-report	Observation may affect behavior
Ethnographic research	Entire span of daily life	Researcher often lives among participants; possible bias
Case studies	Rich, detailed data	Difficult to generalize results
Biological measurements	Precise data	Expensive; relation to behavior may not be clear
Experiment	Control, identification of cause and effect	May not reflect real life
Natural experiment	Illuminate gene–environment relations	Unusual circumstances; rare

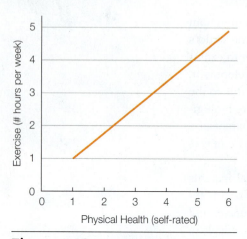

Figure 1.10 Physical Health and Exercise Are Correlated—But Which Causes Which?

Research Designs

LO 1.15 **Describe the major types of research designs used in child development research.**

In addition to choosing a research method, researchers must also choose a design for their study. Common research designs in the study of human development include cross-sectional and longitudinal designs (see **Table 1.4**).

CROSS-SECTIONAL RESEARCH The most common type of research design in the study of child development is **cross-sectional research**. In cross-sectional research, data are collected on a single occasion from people of different ages (Goodwin, 2009). Then, the researcher examines potential relations between variables in the data, based on the hypotheses of the study. For example, researchers may ask a sample of emerging adults to fill out a questionnaire reporting their physical health and how much they exercise, based on the hypothesis that exercising promotes better physical health. They then analyze the data to see if the amount of exercise is related to physical health (see **Figure 1.10** for a hypothetical illustration of this relationship).

Cross-sectional research has both strengths and weaknesses. The main strength is that these studies can be completed quickly and inexpensively. Data collection is done on one occasion, and the study is finished. This simplicity explains why cross-sectional research is so widely used among researchers.

However, there are weaknesses as well in the cross-sectional research design. Most importantly, cross-sectional research yields a *correlation* between variables, and correlations can be difficult to interpret. A **correlation** is a statistical relationship between two variables, such that knowing one of the variables makes it possible to predict the other. A *positive correlation* means that when one variable increases or decreases the other variable changes in the same direction; a *negative correlation* means that when one variable increases the other decreases. In the example just provided, the researcher may find a positive correlation between exercising and physical health. But does this mean that exercising causes better physical health, or that people with better physical health are more inclined to exercise? Based on cross-sectional research alone, there is no way to tell.

It is a basic statistical principle of scientific research that *correlation does not imply causation,* meaning that when two variables are correlated it is not possible to tell whether one variable caused the other. Nevertheless, this principle is frequently overlooked in research on human development. For example, there are hundreds of studies showing a correlation between parenting behaviors and children's functioning. Frequently this correlation has been interpreted as causation—parenting behaviors *cause* children to function in certain ways—but in fact the correlation alone does not show this (Pinker, 2002). It could be that children's characteristics cause parents to behave in certain ways, or it could be that the behavior of both parents and children is because of a third variable, such as SES or cultural context. We will explore this issue and other *correlation versus causation* questions in later chapters.

cross-sectional research

research design that involves collecting data on a single occasion

correlation

statistical relationship between two variables such that knowing one of the variables makes it possible to predict the other

Table 1.4 Research Designs: Advantages and Limitations

Method	Definition	Advantages	Limitations
Cross-sectional	Data collected at one time point	Quick and inexpensive	Correlations difficult to interpret
Longitudinal	Data collected at two or more time points	Monitors change over time	Time, expense, attrition
Cross-sequential	Data collected at two or more time points with the same participants, who are different ages at the outset of the study	Can detect differences related to chronological age and distinguish them from those related to cohort effects	Time, expense, attrition

LONGITUDINAL RESEARCH The limitations of cross-sectional research have led some researchers to use a **longitudinal research** design, in which the same people are followed over time and data are collected on two or more occasions. The length of longitudinal research designs varies widely, from a few weeks or months to years or even decades. Most longitudinal studies take place over a relatively short period, a year or less, but some studies have followed their samples over an entire lifetime, from infancy to old age (e.g., Friedman & Martin, 2011).

The great advantage of the longitudinal research design is that it allows researchers on human development to examine the question that is at the heart of the study of human development: "How do people change over time?" In addition, the longitudinal research design allows researchers to gain more insight into the question of correlation versus causation. For example, suppose a cross-sectional study of people in young, middle, and late adulthood shows a correlation between age and religiosity: The older people are, the more religious they report themselves to be (see **Figure 1.11** for a hypothetical illustration of this pattern). Does this mean that growing older causes people to become more religious? From a cross-sectional study, there is no way to tell; it could be that the culture has changed over the years, and that the older adults grew up in a more religious era than the younger adults did. This kind of explanation for age differences is called a **cohort effect**; people of different ages vary because they grew up in different *cohorts* or historical periods. However, if you could follow the younger adults into late adulthood using a longitudinal research design, you could see if they became more religious as they grew older. You could then draw more definite conclusions about whether or not aging leads to higher religiosity.

Longitudinal research designs have disadvantages as well. Most importantly, they take a great deal more time, money, and patience than a cross-sectional research design does. Researchers do not learn the outcome to the investigation of their hypothesis until weeks, months, or years later. Over time, it is inevitable that some people will drop out of a longitudinal study, for one reason or another—a process called *attrition*. Consequently, the sample the researcher has at Time 1 is likely to be different than the sample that remains at Time 2, 3, or 4, which limits the conclusions that can be drawn. In most studies, dropout is highest among people from low-SES groups, which means that the longer a longitudinal study goes on, the less likely it is to represent the SES range of the entire population.

CROSS-SEQUENTIAL RESEARCH There are positive aspects of cross-sectional and longitudinal research that compensate for the limitations in the other. Sometimes scientists combine the two approaches in a design called *cross-sequential research*. In this design, researchers study people in different age groups (a cross-sectional approach) and follow them

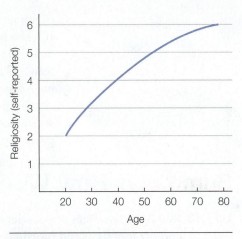

Figure 1.11 Religiosity Changes With Age—But Is It an Age Effect or a Cohort Effect?

longitudinal research

research design in which the same persons are followed over time and data are collected on two or more occasions

cohort effect

in scientific research, an explanation of group differences among people of different ages based on the fact that they grew up in different *cohorts* or historical periods

Longitudinal studies follow the same persons over time. Here, a U.S. girl is pictured in toddlerhood, early childhood, middle childhood, and adolescence.

over time (a longitudinal approach). A researcher might study children who are 4, 6, 8, and 10 years of age every 2 years. After 2 years, the 4-year-olds would be 6, and after 4 years, those same 4-year-olds would be 8. The main advantage of this design is that allows researchers to test whether differences are related to chronological age or to cohort effects. The main disadvantages are that it is expensive to follow people over time, and there is attrition.

Throughout this book, studies using a wide variety of research methods and research designs will be presented. For now, the methods and designs just described will provide you with an introduction to the approaches used most often.

Summary: How We Study Child Development

LO 1.12 **Recall the five steps of the scientific method and the meanings and functions of hypotheses, sampling, and procedure in scientific research.**

The scientific method entails five main steps: (1) identifying a research question, (2) forming a hypothesis, (3) choosing a research method and a research design, (4) collecting data, and (5) drawing conclusions that lead to new questions and new hypotheses.

LO 1.13 **Describe some ethical standards for child development research.**

Research on human development is required to follow ethical guidelines, which are laid out by professional organizations and enforced by IRBs. The main guidelines include protecting participants from physical or psychological harm, informed consent prior to participation, confidentiality, and debriefing after participation if deception was used.

LO 1.14 **Summarize the main methods used in research on child development.**

A variety of specific methods for data collection are used in the study of human development, ranging from questionnaires and interviews to ethnographic research to experiments. Each method has both strengths and weaknesses. Two important qualities in research methods are reliability (consistency of measurement) and validity (the accuracy of measurement in reflecting real life).

LO 1.15 **Describe the major types of research designs used in child development research.**

Common research designs include cross-sectional, longitudinal, and cross-sequential. Each design has both strengths and weaknesses.

Applying Your Knowledge as a Professional

The topics covered in this chapter apply to a wide variety of career professions. Watch these videos to learn how they apply to a developmental and evolutionary psychologist and professors of psychology and biology.

Watch CAREER FOCUS: PROFESSOR OF PSYCHOLOGY

LeaAnn Lucas, Ph.D.
Associate Professor, Psychology
Sinclair Community College

Chapter Quiz

1. The United States _____.

 a. is the developed country that will experience the steepest decline in population between now and 2050

 b. is one of the few developed countries that will experience an increase in population, largely as a result of immigration

 c. is expected to have approximately the same proportion of Latinos by 2050, but far fewer African Americans

 d. has a total fertility rate that is lower than most developed countries due to the availability of birth control

2. If a researcher wanted to measure the socioeconomic status (SES) of her adult participants, she would need to ask them about which of the following?

 a. Educational level   **c.** Religion

 b. Number of children   **d.** Ethnicity

3. Unlike early hominids, *Homo sapiens* had _____.

 a. a narrower pelvis

 b. a shorter period of dependency

 c. a slightly smaller brain

 d. smaller jaws

4. Which of the following best represents the impact of evolution on human development?

 a. Biologically, humans have changed drastically since the origin of *Homo sapiens*.

 b. Our development of bipedal locomotion is the most distinctive characteristic of our species.

 c. Cultures shape the raw material of biology into widely different paths throughout the life span.

 d. Instincts reduce humans' capacity for cultural learning more than they reduce animals' capacity for cultural learning.

5. According to Freud, _____ is the driving force behind human development.

 a. attachment to one's mother   **c.** cognitive development

 b. sexual desire   **d.** trust

6. A teacher would like for all students to complete all their homework before coming to class. One day, all students come to class having done all their work. How would the teacher positively reinforce the students' performance?

 a. give them all a voucher for a free cookie during lunch

 b. cancel the homework assignment for the next night

 c. drop the lowest homework grade

 d. do nothing. Students should come prepared anyway.

7. In Piagetian theory, a scheme is a:

 a. mental representation of knowledge that allows us to interpret and understand the world.

 b. process of taking in new information in the mind

 c. process of adjusting new information to old knowledge

 d. none of the above

8. The information-processing approach differs from Piaget's theory of cognitive development in that information processing:

 a. ignores developmental limitations at various points in childhood

 b. does not view children as active agents of their own cognitive development

 c. sees development as occurring in distinct stages

 d. ignores cognitive capacities at various points in childhood

9. The belief of many Americans in the value of individual freedom, as demonstrated in its capitalist economic system and its governmental system of representative democracy, reflects which system of Bronfenbrenner's theory?

 a. Exosystem   **c.** Microsystem

 b. Chronosystem   **d.** Macrosystem

10. The main tenet of ecocultural theory is that

 a. development occurs in stages

 b. development occurs because of the child's reaction to unconscious urges

 c. development happens in the context of everyday cultural activities

 d. all aspects of development are different all over the world

11. Where does the developmental life stage of emerging adulthood usually appear?

 a. In developed countries

 b. In traditional cultures

 c. In collectivistic cultures

 d. In developing countries

12. _____ generates hypotheses that can be tested in research.

 a. An unbiased sample

 b. A theory

 c. The research design

 d. The research method

13. In the famous case of Henrietta Lacks, an African American woman's cancer cells were removed from her cervix without her knowledge by a surgeon right before her death in 1951. Researchers wanted to study these cells to learn about the genes that cause cancer and those that suppress it. The ethical requirement of _____ would protect against this happening today.

 a. informed consent

 b. deception

 c. confidentiality

 d. generalizability of the findings

14. Which of the following statements is true regarding research methods?

 a. Qualitative data is considered unscientific among most researchers in the field of psychology.

 b. The strength of the case study approach is the ability to generalize the findings.

 c. The ethnographic method allows the researcher to learn how people behave in their daily lives.

 d. The most commonly used method in social science research is the open-ended interview.

15. Which of the following is a problem with cross-sectional research?

 a. Participants tend to drop out of the study.

 b. It tends to be more expensive to conduct than longitudinal research.

 c. It tends to be more time-consuming than longitudinal research.

 d. It yields a correlation, which may be difficult to interpret.

Chapter 2
Genetics and Prenatal Development

FOR MOTHERS-TO-BE WORLDWIDE, PREGNANCY IS OFTEN EXPERIENCED WITH A COMBINATION OF JOY, HOPE, AND FEAR. Yet here as in other aspects of development, the experience differs substantially depending on the economic and cultural context. For most women in rural areas of developing countries, there is little in the way of technology or medical care to promote the healthy development of the fetus. Instead, pregnant women often rely on folk beliefs, a midwife's years of experience, and social support from the extended family. For most women in developed countries, medical care and technological aids are available throughout pregnancy. Yet prospective mothers and fathers face formidable challenges in altering their lives to make room for the demands of raising a small child perhaps while continuing to pursue their careers.

Pregnancy is experienced in many different ways around the world, but everywhere it is a momentous event. In this chapter we examine the process of prenatal development, from its genetic beginnings until the final months of pregnancy. The first section of the chapter covers the basics of genetics and how a new human life begins. In the next section we examine prenatal development and prenatal care for both mother and baby to enhance the likelihood that all will go well. Sometimes problems arise in the course of pregnancy, so the final section of the chapter addresses prenatal complications as well as testing and counseling options.

Watch CHAPTER INTRODUCTION: GENETICS AND PRENATAL DEVELOPMENT

Section 1 Genetic Influences on Development

Learning Objectives

2.1 Distinguish between *genotype* and *phenotype* and identify the different forms of genetic inheritance.

2.2 Describe the sex chromosomes and identify what makes them different from other chromosomes.

2.3 Explain how behavior geneticists use heritability estimates and concordance rates in their research.

2.4 Describe how the concept of *epigenesis* frames gene–environment interactions, and connect epigenesis to the concept of *reaction range*.

2.5 Explain how the theory of genotype → environment effects casts new light on the old nature–nurture debate.

2.6 Outline the process of meiosis in the formation of reproductive cells.

2.7 Describe the process of fertilization and conception.

2.8 List the major causes of and treatments for infertility, and describe how infertility is viewed in different cultures.

GENETIC INFLUENCES ON DEVELOPMENT: Genetic Basics

In all organisms, humans included, individual development has a genetic beginning. To understand the role of genetics in human development, it is important to have a basic foundation of knowledge about genes and how they function.

Genotype and Phenotype

LO 2.1 **Distinguish between *genotype* and *phenotype* and identify the different forms of genetic inheritance.**

Nearly all cells in the human body contain 46 **chromosomes** in 23 pairs, with one chromosome in each pair inherited from the mother and the other inherited from the father (see **Figure 2.1**). The chromosomes are composed of complex molecules known as **DNA (deoxyribonucleic acid)** (see **Figure 2.2**). The DNA in the chromosomes is organized into segments called **genes**, which are the basic units of hereditary information. Genes contain paired sequences of chemicals called *nucleotides*, and these sequences comprise instructions for the functioning and replication of the cells. There are about 23,000 genes in our 46 chromosomes, the total human **genome**, with all together about 3 billion nucleotide pairs (International Human Genome Sequencing Consortium, 2004).

Not all 23,000 genes are expressed in the course of development. The totality of an individual's genes is the **genotype**, and the person's actual expressed characteristics are called the **phenotype**. In part, the difference between genotype and phenotype is a consequence of the person's environment. For example, if you were born with a genotype that included exceptional musical ability, this talent might never be developed if your environment

chromosome

sausage-shaped structure in the nucleus of cells, containing genes, which are paired, except in reproductive cells

DNA (deoxyriboynucleic acid)

long strand of cell material that stores and transfers genetic information in all life forms

gene

segment of DNA containing coded instructions for the growth and functioning of the organism

genome

entire store of an organism's hereditary information

genotype

organism's unique genetic inheritance

phenotype

organism's actual characteristics, derived from its genotype

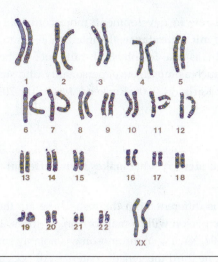

Figure 2.1 The Human Genome

The 46 chromosomes in the human genome are organized into 23 pairs. This is the genome of a female; in a male the 23rd pair would be XY rather than XX.

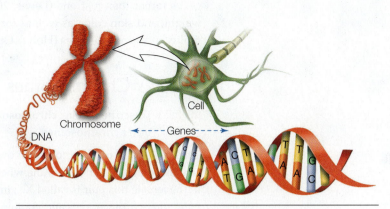

Figure 2.2 The Chemical Structure of DNA

DNA is composed of nucleotide pairs.

provided no access to musical instruments or musical instruction. Consequently, the musical ability present in your genotype would not be apparent in your phenotype.

Another aspect of genetic functioning that influences the relation between genotype and phenotype is **dominant–recessive inheritance** (Jones, 2006). On every pair of chromosomes there are two forms of each gene, one on the chromosome inherited from the mother and one on the chromosome inherited from the father. Each form of the gene is called an **allele**. On many of these pairs of alleles, dominant–recessive inheritance occurs. This means that only one of the two genes—the *dominant gene*—influences the phenotype, whereas the *recessive gene* does not, even though it is part of the genotype. For example, if you inherited a gene for curly hair from one parent and a gene for straight hair from the other, you would have curly hair because curly hair is dominant and straight hair is recessive. Recessive genes are expressed in the phenotype only when they are paired with another recessive gene. A clear pattern of dominant–recessive inheritance is evident only for traits determined by a single gene, which is not true of most traits, as we will see shortly. Some other examples of dominant and recessive characteristics are shown in **Table 2.1**.

Most characteristics in human development are not determined solely by a single pair of genes. Despite what you may have heard about the supposed existence of a "gay gene" or "religion gene" or "crime gene," no such specific genes have been found, nor are they likely to be (Pinker, 2004; "Special report on the human genome," 2010). Although

dominant–recessive inheritance

pattern of inheritance in which a pair of chromosomes contains one dominant and one recessive gene, but only the dominant gene is expressed in the phenotype

allele

on a pair of chromosomes, each of two forms of a gene

Table 2.1 Traits With Single-Gene Dominant–Recessive Inheritance

Dominant	Recessive
Curly hair	Straight hair
Dark hair	Blonde hair
Facial dimples	No dimples
Normal hearing	Deafness (some forms)
Normal vision	Nearsighted vision
Freckles	No freckles
Unattached ear lobe	Attached ear lobe
Can roll tongue in U-shape	Cannot roll tongue in U-shape

single gene pairs sometimes play a crucial role in development, more commonly the influence of genes is a consequence of **polygenic inheritance**, the interaction of multiple genes rather than just one (Lewis, 2005). This is true for physical traits such as height, weight, and skin color, as well as for traits such as intelligence, personality, and susceptibility to various diseases (Hoh & Ott, 2003; Karlsson, 2006; Rucker & McGuffin, 2010).

The Sex Chromosomes

LO 2.2 **Describe the sex chromosomes and identify what makes them different from other chromosomes.**

Of the 23 pairs of chromosomes, one pair is different from the rest. These are the **sex chromosomes**, which determine whether the person will be male or female (Jones, 2006). In the female this pair is called XX; in the male, XY. The Y chromosome is notably smaller than other chromosomes and contains only one third the genetic material. All eggs in the mother contain an X chromosome but sperm may carry either an X or a Y chromosome. So, it is the father's sperm that determines what the sex of the child will be. Ironically, people in many cultures mistakenly believe that the woman is responsible for the child's sex and blame her if she fails to have sons (DeLoache & Gottlieb, 2000; LeVine et al., 1994).

People in many cultures also have beliefs about how to predict the baby's sex (DeLoache & Gottlieb, 2000). Such beliefs demonstrate how important gender is to a child's future in most cultures, even before birth.

Many cultures have a bias in favor of boys, and the use of sex-selective abortion to achieve this is resulting in gender ratios skewed toward boys, especially in Asian cultures where this bias is especially pronounced (Abrejo et al., 2009). For more information on this, watch the video *A Preference for Sons*.

Watch A PREFERENCE FOR SONS

polygenic inheritance

expression of phenotypic characteristics as a result of the interaction of multiple genes

sex chromosomes

chromosomes that determine whether an organism is male (XY) or female (XX)

The sex of the developing organism also has biological consequences for prenatal development. Having only one X chromosome makes males more vulnerable than females to a variety of recessive disorders that are linked to the X chromosome (Narayanan & Warren, 2006). The reason for this is that if a female has one X chromosome that contains the recessive gene for a disorder, the disorder will not show up in her phenotype because the dominant gene on her other X chromosome will prevent it from being expressed.

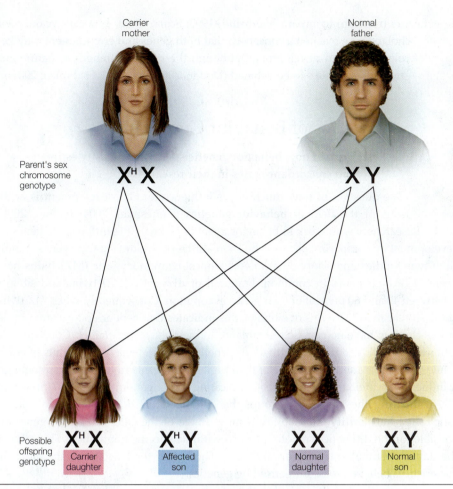

Figure 2.3 X-Linked Inheritance in Hemophilia

Why are males more vulnerable to recessive disorders carried on the X chromosome?

She will be a carrier of the disorder to the next generation but will not have the disorder herself. In contrast, if a male receives one X chromosome containing the recessive gene for a disorder, he will definitely have the disorder because he has no other X chromosome that may contain a dominant gene to block its expression. His Y chromosome cannot serve this function. An example of this pattern of **X-linked inheritance** is shown in **Figure 2.3** for hemophilia, a disorder in which the blood does not clot properly and the person may bleed to death from even a minor injury. Because of X-linked inheritance, males are at greater risk for a wide variety of genetically based problems, including learning disabilities and intellectual disability (Halpern, 2000; James et al., 2006).

GENETIC INFLUENCES ON DEVELOPMENT: Genes and the Environment

There is no doubt that genes have some influence on human development, but how much? Scholars have long debated the relative importance of genes and the environment in human development. In this **nature–nurture debate**, some scholars have claimed that development can be explained by genes (nature) and that environment matters little, whereas others have claimed that development depends mainly on environmental

X-linked inheritance

pattern of inheritance in which a recessive characteristic is expressed because it is carried on the male's X chromosome

nature–nurture debate

debate among scholars as to whether human development is influenced mainly by genes (nature) or environment (nurture)

MZ twins have the same genotype.

behavior genetics

field in the study of human development that aims to identify the extent to which genes influence behavior, primarily by comparing persons who share different amounts of their genes

monozygotic (MZ) twins

twins who have exactly the same genotype; also called *identical twins*

dizygotic (DZ) twins

twins that result when two ova are released by a female instead of one, and both are fertilized by sperm; also called *fraternal twins*

heritability

statistical estimate of the extent to which genes are responsible for the differences among persons within a specific population, with values ranging from 0 to 1.00

concordance rate

degree of similarity in phenotype among pairs of family members, expressed as a percentage

factors (nurture) (compare Baumrind, 1993; Scarr, 1993). In recent years, most scholars have reached a consensus that both genes and environment play key roles in human development, although the relative strength of nature and nurture continues to be debated (Dodge, 2007; Lerner, 2006; Pinker, 2004).

Principles of Behavior Genetics

LO 2.3 Explain how behavior geneticists use heritability estimates and concordance rates in their research.

The question of how much genes influence human development is at the heart of the field of **behavior genetics** (Gottesman, 2004; Plomin, 2009). Researchers who work in behavior genetics estimate the influence of genes on development by comparing people who share different amounts of their genes, mainly through twin studies and adoption studies. Identical or **monozygotic (MZ) twins** have 100 percent of their genes in common. Fraternal or **dizygotic (DZ) twins** and siblings have between 40 and 60 percent of their genes in common. Consequently, when MZ twins are more similar than DZ twins or siblings, this indicates that genetics play a strong role. Adoptive children have no genetic resemblance to their adoptive families. Consequently, adoption studies allow a researcher to study whether certain behaviors or traits of adoptive children are more similar to those of their biological parents (indicating a stronger genetic influence) or their adoptive families (indicating a stronger environmental influence).

By comparing these different groups, behavior geneticists are able to calculate a statistic called **heritability**. Heritability is an estimate of the extent to which genes are responsible for the differences among persons within a specific population. The value of the heritability estimate ranges from 0 to 1.00. The higher the heritability, the more the characteristic is believed to be influenced by genetics.

Behavior genetics has flourished in the past two decades, and heritability estimates have been calculated for a wide range of characteristics. For intelligence, heritability estimates for children and adolescents have been found to be about 0.50, meaning that about half the variation in their IQ scores has been attributed to genetic influences (Turkheimer et al., 2009). With regard to personality characteristics, heritability estimates range from 0.40 to 0.50 for a wide array of characteristics such as sociability, activity level, and even religiosity (Bouchard & McGue, 2003).

Heritability estimates have been criticized for giving a misleading impression of the influence of genetics on development (Collins et al., 2000; Rutter, 2002). According to the critics, to state that a trait is heritable implies that we know with precision how much genes contribute to its development, but this is not so. Heritability estimates are simply estimates based on comparisons of persons with different amounts of genetic material in common, not direct measures of the activity of genes. Heritability estimates are a measure not just of genetic influence but of *how much the environment allows the genes to be expressed.* In other words, heritability estimates measure phenotype rather than genotype.

This can be seen in the studies finding that heritability of intelligence increases from childhood to adulthood (McGue & Christensen, 2002). Obviously genes do not change during this time, but the environment changes to allow greater expression of genetic potentials, as children grow into adolescence and become increasingly able to choose their own environments (e.g., whom they will have as friends). Other studies find that heritability of intelligence is higher in middle-class families than in poor families (McCartney & Berry, 2009; Turkheimer et al., 2009). This is not because middle-class families have different kinds of genes than poor families do, but because the greater economic resources of middle-class families make it more likely that children's genotypic potential for intelligence will be expressed in their phenotype.

Another statistic of genetic influence used in behavior genetics is **concordance rate**. This is a percentage that indicates the degree of similarity in phenotype among pairs of family members. Concordance rates range from 0 to 100 percent. The higher the concordance rate, the more similar the two persons are.

In many studies, comparisons of concordance rates are made between MZ and DZ twins. When concordance rates are higher among MZ than DZ twins, this indicates that the basis for the trait is partly genetic. For example, concordance rates for schizophrenia, a severe mental disorder involving hallucinations and disordered patterns of thinking and behavior, are 50 percent for MZ twins and 18 percent for DZ twins (Insel, 2010). This means that when one MZ twin has schizophrenia, 50 percent of the time the other twin has schizophrenia as well. For DZ twins, when one twin has schizophrenia, the other twin has the disorder only 18 percent of the time. Adoption studies also sometimes use this statistic, comparing concordance rates between parents and adopted children, parents and biological children, and adoptive or biological siblings.

Gene–Environment Interactions: Epigenesis and Reaction Ranges

LO 2.4 **Describe how the concept of *epigenesis* frames gene–environment interactions, and connect epigenesis to the concept of *reaction range*.**

Studies of heritability show not only that genes influence development but also that the environment influences how genes are expressed. A related idea is **epigenesis**, which means that development results from the bidirectional interactions between genotype and environment (Gottlieb, 2004; Gottlieb & Lickliter, 2007). According to epigenetic theory, the expression of genes is affected by and responds constantly to environmental influences. Development is influenced by genes but not purely determined by them (Moffitt et al., 2006). Experience may result in some genes getting expressed and others not.

Here is an example of epigenesis. Girls normally begin menstruating around ages 11 to 16, toward the lower end of this range under healthy conditions and toward the higher end when nutrition is insufficient or the girl is suffering from medical problems (Neberich et al., 2010). Clearly it is part of the human-female genotype for menstruation to be initiated somewhere in this age range, with the timing influenced by environmental conditions. Furthermore, when girls' environmental conditions change, their menstrual patterns may also change. Girls who experience severe weight loss often stop menstruating (Roberto et al., 2008). If their nutritional intake improves, they begin menstruating again. This demonstrates a continuous interaction between genotype and environment, with menstruation being "turned on" genetically as part of puberty but "turned off" if environmental conditions are dire, then turned on again once the nutritional environment improves.

As this example illustrates, often when genes influence human development it is by establishing boundaries for environmental influences rather than specifying a precise characteristic. In other words, genes establish a **reaction range** of potential expression, and environment determines where a person's phenotype will fall within that range (McCartney & Berry, 2009). To take another example, height is known to be influenced by genes. You can probably tell this just by looking at your own height in relation to other members of your family. However, the genes for height simply establish the reaction range's upper and lower boundaries, and where a person's actual height ends up—the phenotype—is determined by environmental influences such as nutrition and disease.

Evidence for this is clear from the pattern of changes in height in societies around the world over the past century. In most Western countries,

epigenesis

in development, the continuous bidirectional interactions between genes and environment

reaction range

range of possible developmental paths established by genes; environment determines where development takes place within that range

Genes establish a reaction range for height, and environment determines where a person's height falls within that range. Here, sisters of the Hamer tribe in Ethiopia, a tribe known for being exceptionally tall.

average height rose steadily in the first half of the 20th century as nutrition and health care improved (Freedman et al., 2006). The genes of their populations could not have changed in just a generation or two; instead, the improving environment allowed them to reach a higher point in their genetic reaction range for height. In other countries, such as China and South Korea, improvements in nutrition and health care came later, in the second half of the 20th century, so increases in height in those countries have taken place only recently (Wang et al., 2010). However, people are unlikely ever to grow to be 10 or 20 feet tall. In recent decades in Western countries there has been little change in average height, indicating that the populations of these countries have reached the upper boundary of their reaction range for height.

Recently, scientists have explored the connections between stress and epigenetic effects. Stress during pregnancy can have negative effects on fetal development, including the development of the nervous system (Benoit, et al., 2015). Cognitive development of offspring may be affected by maternal stress during pregnancy (Dias, et al., 2015; Kleefstra, et al., 2014). Epigenetic effects also occur after birth. Early life stress is associated with genetic changes that may be precursors to psychiatric disorders later in life (Boku, et al., 2015). This evidence provides good motivation to help pregnant women and young children reduce their stress and develop coping mechanisms for stress. The video *Epigenetics* provides more information on this topic.

Watch EPIGENETICS

The Theory of Genotype → Environment Effects

LO 2.5 Explain how the theory of genotype → environment effects casts new light on the old nature–nurture debate.

One influential theory of behavior genetics is the **theory of genotype → environment effects** proposed by Sandra Scarr and Kathleen McCartney (Plomin, 2009; Scarr, 1993; Scarr & McCartney, 1983). According to this theory, both genotype and environment make essential contributions to human development. However, the relative strengths of genetics and the environment are difficult to unravel because our genes actually influence the kind of environment we experience. That is the reason for the arrow in the term *genotype → environment effects*. Based on our genotypes, we *create our own environments*, to a considerable extent.

theory of genotype → environment effects

theory proposing that genes influence the kind of environment we experience

THE THREE FORMS OF GENOTYPE → ENVIRONMENT EFFECTS These genotype → environment effects take three forms: passive, evocative, and active.

- **Passive genotype → environment effects** occur in biological families because *parents provide both genes and environment for their children.* This may seem obvious, but it has profound implications for how we think about development. Take this father–daughter example. Dad has been good at drawing things ever since he was a boy, and now he makes a living as a graphic artist. One of the first birthday presents he gives to his little girl is a set of crayons and colored pencils for drawing. As she grows up, he also teaches her a number of drawing skills as she seems ready to learn them. She goes to college and majors in architecture, then goes on to become an architect. It is easy to see how she became so good at drawing, given an environment that stimulated her drawing abilities so much—right?

When parents and children are similar, is the similarity as a result of genetics or environment?

Not so fast. It is true that Dad provided her with a stimulating environment, but he also provided her with half her genes. If there are any genes that contribute to drawing ability—such as genes for spatial reasoning and fine motor coordination—she may well have received those from Dad, too. The point is that in a biological family, it is difficult to separate genetic influences from environmental influences because *parents provide both,* and they are likely to provide an environment that reinforces the tendencies they have provided to their children through their genes.

So, you should be skeptical when you read studies that claim that parents' behavior is the cause of the characteristics of their biological children. Remember that correlation does not imply causation! Just because there is a *correlation* between the behavior of parents and the characteristics of their children does not mean the parents' behavior *caused* the children to have those characteristics. Maybe causation was involved, but in biological families it is difficult to tell. One good way to unravel this tangle is through adoption studies. These studies avoid the problem of passive genotype → environment effects because one set of parents provided the children's genes but a different set of parents provided the environment. We'll look at an extraordinary case of adoption in the *Research Focus: Twin Studies: The Story of Oskar and Jack* feature on the next page.

- **Evocative genotype → environment effects** occur when a person's inherited characteristics evoke responses from others in their environment. If you had a son who started reading at age 3 and seemed to love it, you might buy him more books. If you had a daughter who could sink 20-foot jump shots at age 12, you might arrange to send her to basketball camp. Did you ever baby-sit or work in a setting where there were many children? If so, you probably found that children differ in how sociable, cooperative, and obedient they are. In turn, you may have found that you responded differently to them, depending on their characteristics. This is what is meant by evocative genotype → environment effects—with the crucial addition of the assumption that characteristics such as reading ability, athletic ability, and sociability are at least partly based in genetics.
- **Active genotype → environment effects** occur when people seek out environments that correspond to their genotypic characteristics, a process called *niche-picking.* The child who is faster than her peers may be motivated to try out for a sports team; the adolescent with an ear for music may ask for piano lessons; the emerging adult for whom reading has always been slow and difficult may prefer to begin working

passive genotype → environment effects

in the theory of genotype → environment effects, the type that results from the fact that in a biological family, parents provide both genes and environment to their children

evocative genotype → environment effects

in the theory of genotype → environment effects, the type that results when a person's inherited characteristics evoke responses from others in the environment

active genotype → environment effects

in the theory of genotype → environment effects, the type that results when people seek out environments that correspond to their genotypic characteristics

full-time after high school rather than going to a college or university; in young adulthood a highly sociable person may seek a career that involves being around other people all day. The idea here is that people are drawn to environments that match their inherited abilities.

Research Focus: Twin Studies: The Story of Oskar and Jack

The interplay between genes and the environment is one of the most important, complex, and fascinating topics in the study of human development. One approach that has been helpful in unraveling these interactions is twin studies, especially research on twins separated early in life and raised in different environments. Studies of twins reared apart provide a good example of a natural experiment, which is something that occurs without the intervention of a researcher but can provide valuable scientific information.

The Minnesota Study of Twins Reared Apart, led by Thomas J. Bouchard, Jr., of the University of Minnesota, has been studying separated twins since 1979, and the results have been groundbreaking and sometimes astounding.

Among the most remarkable cases in the Minnesota study is the story of identical twins Oskar and Jack. They were born in Trinidad in 1933, but within 6 months their parents split up.

Oskar left for Germany with his Catholic mother, while Jack remained in Trinidad in the care of his Jewish father. Thus, unlike most separated twins, who at least remain within the same culture and country, Oskar and Jack grew up with the same genotype but with different cultures, different countries, and different religions.

Furthermore, Oskar migrated with his mother to Germany in 1933, the year the Nazis rose to power. And Jack was raised as a Jew, at a time when Jews were targeted for extermination by the Nazis.

In some ways, the twins' childhood family environments were similar—as in similarly miserable. Oskar's mother soon moved to Italy and left him in Germany in the care of his grandmother, who was stern and harsh. Jack's father alternated between ignoring him and beating him. Despite these similarities, their cultures were about as different as could be. Oskar was an enthusiastic member of the Hitler Youth, and he learned to despise Jews and to keep his own half-Jewish background hidden. Jack was raised as a Jew and at 16 was sent by his father to Israel to join the navy, where he met and married an American Jew. At age 21 he and his wife moved to the United States.

What were the results of this extraordinary natural experiment in the two men's adult development? The extensive data collected by the Minnesota team, which included a week of tests and interviews with the men as well as interviews with their family members and others close to them, indicated that they had highly similar adult personalities.

Both were described by themselves and others as short-tempered, demanding, and absent minded. In addition, they shared a remarkable range of unusual, quirky personal habits. Both read books from back to front, sneezed loudly in elevators, liked to wear rubber bands on their wrists, and wrapped tape around pens and pencils to get a better grip.

Watch RESEARCH FOCUS: TWIN STUDIES: THE STORY OF OSKAR AND JACK

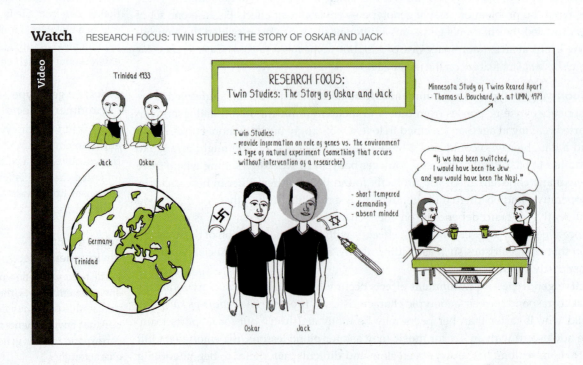

However, their cultural identities and worldviews were as far apart as one might imagine, given the vastly different cultures they grew up in. Oskar repented his membership in the Hitler Youth as an adult and lamented the Holocaust that had taken millions of Jewish lives under the Nazis, but he considered himself very German, and he and Jack disagreed vehemently over the responsibility and justification for bombings and other acts of war conducted during World War II.

Thus, despite all their similarities in personality because of their different cultural environments they ultimately had very different identities—starkly separate understandings of who they are and how they fit into the world around them. As Oskar told Jack when they met again in adulthood, "If we had been switched, I would have been the Jew and you would have been the Nazi."

Review Questions:

1. Studies of twins raised apart provide a good example of:
   a. Reliability but not validity
   b. Validity but not reliability
   c. Experimental research
   d. A natural experiment

2. Which of the following is *not* one of the ways that Oskar and Jack were similar?
   a. Both were absent-minded
   b. Both were short tempered
   c. Both had a strong Jewish faith
   d. Both read books from back to front

GENOTYPE → ENVIRONMENT EFFECTS OVER TIME The three types of genotype → environment effects operate throughout childhood, adolescence, and adulthood, but their relative balance changes over time (Scarr, 1993). In childhood, passive genotype → environment effects are especially pronounced, and active genotype → environment effects are relatively weak. This is because the younger a child is, the more parents control the daily environment the child experiences and the less autonomy the child has to seek out environmental influences outside the family.

However, the balance changes as children move through adolescence and into adulthood (Plomin, 2009). Parental control diminishes, so passive genotype → environment effects also diminish. Autonomy increases, so active genotype → environment effects also increase. In adulthood, passive genotype → environment effects fade entirely (except in cultures where persons continue to live with their parents even in adulthood), and active genotype → environment effects move to the forefront. Evocative genotype → environment effects remain relatively stable from childhood through adulthood.

CRITICAL THINKING QUESTION

Think of one of your abilities and describe how the various types of genotype → environment effects may have been involved in your development of that ability.

GENETIC INFLUENCES ON DEVELOPMENT: Genes and Individual Development

When does individual human development begin? The answer may surprise you. The process of forming a new human being actually begins long before sperm and egg are joined. Sperm and eggs themselves go through a process of development. In this section we look at the genetic basis of prenatal development, beginning with sperm and egg formation.

Sperm and Egg Formation

LO 2.6 **Outline the process of meiosis in the formation of reproductive cells.**

Most cells in the human body contain 46 chromosomes that reproduce by the process of **mitosis**, in which the chromosomes duplicate themselves and the cell divides to

mitosis

process of cell replication in which the chromosomes duplicate themselves and the cell divides into two cells, each with the same number of chromosomes as the original cell

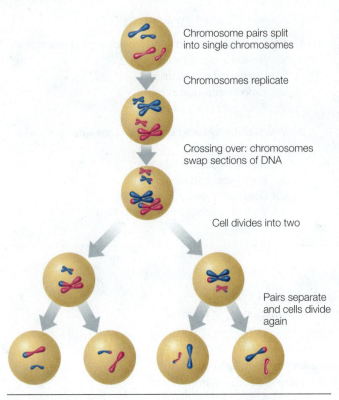

Chromosome pairs split into single chromosomes

Chromosomes replicate

Crossing over: chromosomes swap sections of DNA

Cell divides into two

Pairs separate and cells divide again

Figure 2.4 The Creation of Gametes Through Meiosis

How does meiosis differ from mitosis?

gametes

cells, distinctive to each sex, that are involved in reproduction (egg cells in the ovaries of the female and sperm in the testes of the male)

ovum

mature egg that develops in ovaries, about every 28 days in human females

meiosis

process by which gametes are generated, through separation and duplication of chromosome pairs, ending in four new gametes from the original cell, each with half the number of chromosomes of the original cell

cytoplasm

in an ovum, fluid that provides nutrients for the first 2 weeks of growth if the ovum is fertilized, until it reaches the uterus and begins drawing nutrients from the mother

become two cells, each containing the same number of chromosomes as the original cell (Pankow, 2008). The only cells in the human body that do not contain 46 chromosomes are the reproductive cells or **gametes**: the sperm in the male and the egg or **ovum** (plural, *ova*) in the female. Gametes form in the testes of the male and the ovaries of the female through a process that is a variation of mitosis called *meiosis* (see **Figure 2.4**). In **meiosis**, cells that begin with 23 pairs of chromosomes first split into 46 single chromosomes, then replicate themselves and split into two cells, each with 23 pairs of chromosomes like the original cell. So far the process is just like mitosis. But then the pairs separate into single chromosomes and split again, this time into gametes that have 23 unpaired chromosomes instead of the original 46. So, at the end of the process of meiosis, from the original cell in the testes or ovaries, four new cells have been created, each with 23 chromosomes.

There are some important sex differences in the process of meiosis (Jones, 2006). In males meiosis is completed before sperm are released, but in females the final stage of meiosis only takes place when and if the ovum is fertilized by a sperm (more on this shortly). Also, in males the outcome of meiosis is four viable sperm, whereas in females meiosis produces only one viable ovum along with three *polar bodies* that are not functional. The ovum hoards for itself a large quantity of **cytoplasm**, the fluid that will be the main source of nutrients in the early days after conception, whereas the polar bodies are left with little.

Did you ever think about why you are different from your brothers or sisters, even though both of you have 23 chromosomes each from mom and dad? Even parents of fraternal twins are constantly amazed at how different they are. Here's the explanation for sibling diversity. Something fascinating and remarkable happens at the outset of the process of meiosis. After the chromosomes first split and replicate but before the cell divides, pieces of genetic material are exchanged between the alleles in each pair, a process called **crossing over** (refer again to Figure 2.4). Crossing over mixes the combinations of genes in the chromosomes, so that genetic material that originated from the mother and father is rearranged in a virtually infinite number of ways (Pankow, 2008). Your parents could have had dozens, hundreds, even millions of children together (hypothetically!), and none of them would be exactly like you genetically (unless you have an identical twin).

Here is another interesting fact about the production of gametes. Upon reaching puberty, males begin producing millions of sperm each day. There are 100 to 300 million sperm in the typical male ejaculation (Johnson, 2008). In contrast, females have already produced all the ova they will ever have *while they are still in their own mothers' womb*. Because crossing over begins when ova are created, this means that the development of a unique genotype for each individual begins before the individual's mother is born!

Females are born with about 1 million ova, but this number diminishes to about 40,000 by the time they reach puberty, and about 400 of these will mature during a woman's childbearing years (Johnson, 2008; Moore & Persaud, 2003). Most women stop producing viable ova sometime in their 40s, but men produce sperm throughout their adult lives (although the quantity and quality of the sperm may decline with age) (Finn, 2001).

Conception

LO 2.7   **Describe the process of fertilization and conception.**

When sexual intercourse takes place between a man and a woman, many millions of sperm from the man begin making their way through the woman's reproductive organs—first into the vagina, then through the cervix, through the uterus, and up the fallopian tubes toward the ovaries. Hundreds of millions of sperm may seem like more than enough, but keep in mind that sperm are composed of a single cell, not much more than 23 chromosomes and a tail, so they are not exactly skilled at navigation. The distance from the vagina to the ovaries is vast for such a small object as a sperm. Furthermore, the woman's body responds to sperm as a foreign substance and begins killing them off immediately. Usually only a few hundred sperm make it up the fallopian tubes to where fertilization can take place (Jones, 2006).

Within the woman, there are two ovaries that release an ovum in alternating months. During the early part of the woman's cycle the ovum is maturing into a **follicle**. The follicle consists of the ovum plus other cells that surround it and provide nutrients. About 14 days into a woman's cycle, the mature follicle bursts and *ovulation* takes place as the ovum is released into the fallopian tube (see **Figure 2.5**). The ovum is 2,000 times larger than a sperm because it contains so much cytoplasm (Johnson, 2008). The cytoplasm will provide nutrients for the first 2 weeks of growth if the ovum is fertilized, until it reaches the uterus and begins drawing nutrients from the mother.

It is only during the first 24 hours after the ovum enters the fallopian tube that fertilization can occur. It takes sperm from a few hours to a whole day to travel up the fallopian tubes, so fertilization is most likely to take place if intercourse occurs on the day of ovulation or the two previous days (Wilcox et al., 1995). Sperm can live up to 5 days after entering the woman's body, but most do not last more than 2 days (Johnson, 2008).

When sperm reach the ovum they begin to penetrate the surface of the cell, aided by a chemical on the tip of the sperm that dissolves the ovum's membrane. Once the sperm penetrates the ovum's membrane, the head of the sperm detaches from the tail and continues toward the nucleus of the cell while the tail remains outside. The moment a sperm breaks through, a chemical change takes place in the membrane of the ovum that prevents any other sperm from getting in.

When the sperm head reaches the nucleus of the ovum, the final phase of meiosis is triggered in the ovum (Johnson, 2008). Fertilization takes place as the 23 chromosomes from the ovum pair up with the 23 chromosomes from the sperm and a new cell, the

crossing over

at the outset of meiosis, the exchange of genetic material between paired chromosomes

follicle

during the female reproductive cycle, the ovum plus other cells that surround the ovum and provide nutrients

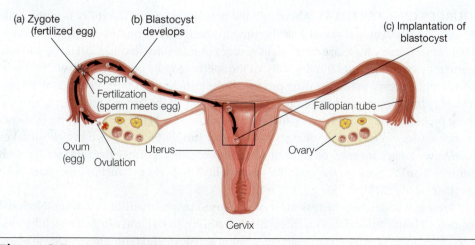

(a) Zygote (fertilized egg)

(b) Blastocyst develops

(c) Implantation of blastocyst

Sperm

Fertilization (sperm meets egg)

Fallopian tube

Ovum (egg)

Ovulation

Uterus

Ovary

Cervix

Figure 2.5 Ovulation Process

The two ovaries alternate ovulation in each monthly cycle.

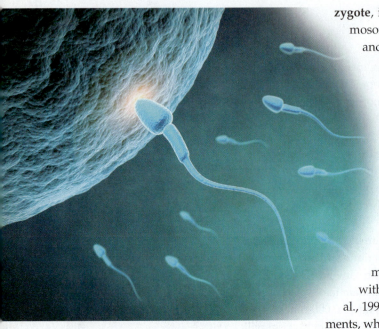

Fertilization can take place only in the first 24 hours after the ovum enters the fallopian tube.

zygote

following fertilization, the new cell formed from the union of sperm and ovum

infertility

inability to attain pregnancy after at least a year of regular sexual intercourse

zygote, is formed from the two gametes. The zygote's 46 paired chromosomes constitute the new organism's unique genotype, set once and for all at the moment of conception.

Although this is how conception usually takes place, there are occasional variations. One of the most common variations is that two ova are released by the woman instead of one, and both are fertilized by sperm, resulting in DZ twins (recall that DZ stands for *dizygotic*—two zygotes). This takes place overall about once in every 60 births, although there are substantial ethnic variations, ranging from 1 in every 25 births in Nigeria to 1 in every 700 births in Japan (Gall, 1996). In general, Asians have the lowest rates of DZ twins and Africans the highest (Mange & Mange, 1998). In addition to ethnic background, some of the factors that increase the likelihood of DZ twins are a family history of twins, age (older women are more likely to release two eggs at once), and nutrition (women with healthy diets are more likely to have DZ twins) (Bortolus et al., 1999). Today, another common cause of DZ twins is infertility treatments, which we will discuss in more detail shortly.

Twins can also result when a zygote that has just begun the process of cell division splits into two separate clusters of cells, creating MZ twins (recall that MZ stands for *monozygotic*—one zygote). MZ twins are less common than DZ twins, occurring about 1 in every 285 births (Zach et al., 2001). In contrast to DZ twins, MZ twins are not more common in some ethnic groups than others. They take place at the same frequency all around the world. Also unlike DZ twins, MZ twins do not run in families and are not predicted by age or nutrition.

Infertility

LO 2.8   List the major causes of and treatments for infertility, and describe how infertility is viewed in different cultures.

Most women of reproductive age (roughly ages 15–40) who have sexual intercourse on a regular basis will become pregnant within a year or two. However, for some couples becoming pregnant is more problematic. **Infertility** is defined as the inability to attain pregnancy after at least a year of regular sexual intercourse without contraception. Rates of infertility in the United States have been remarkably consistent over the past century at about 10 to 15 percent of couples (Johnson, 2008; Marsh & Ronner, 1996).

SOURCES OF INFERTILITY About half the time the source of infertility is in the male reproductive system and about half the time in the female reproductive system (Jones, 2006). Among men, there are three main sources of infertility (Jequier, 2011): (1) too few sperm may be produced; (2) the quality of the sperm may be poor, because of disease or defects in the sperm manufacturing process in the testicles; or, (3) the sperm may be low in *motility* (movement) and therefore unable to make it all the way up the fallopian tubes. These problems may be genetic or they may be caused by behavior such as drug abuse, alcohol abuse, or cigarette smoking. Or, they may simply be as a result of age—it takes three times longer for men older than 40 to impregnate a partner than it does for men younger than 25, because the quantity and quality of sperm production decreases with age (Patel et al., 2015).

Among women, infertility is most often caused by problems in ovulation (National Women's Health Information Center, 2011). Inability to ovulate can be caused by disease, or it can be because of drug abuse, alcohol abuse, or cigarette smoking, or to being extremely underweight or overweight. However, age is the most common cause of inability to ovulate (Maheshwari et al., 2008). As you learned, females are born with all the eggs they will ever have in their ovaries, and the quality of those eggs deteriorates gradually after puberty. Fertility decreases for women throughout their 20s and 30s but especially drops after age 40, when they become more likely to have menstrual cycles with no ovulation at all (see **Figure 2.6**).

INFERTILITY TREATMENTS We now know that men and women contribute equally to infertility. However, this knowledge is recent, coming only in about the past 50 years. For most of human history in most cultures, infertility has been regarded almost exclusively as a female problem, and women suffering from it were described not as infertile but as "barren" (Marsh & Ronner, 1996). In the West, for more than 2,000 years, from about the 4th century BCE to the 1800s, the reigning explanations for infertility were based on incorrect theories of how conception occurred. Thus, treatments were ineffective.

During the course of the 20th century, treatments for infertility became more scientifically based and technologically advanced. Today there are a variety of approaches. These methods are used by infertile couples as well as by gay and lesbian couples and by single women. A variety of related methods for overcoming infertility are grouped under the term **assisted reproductive technologies (ART)**, including artificial insemination, fertility drugs, and in vitro fertilization (IVF). ART methods are used in response to a wide variety of infertility problems in either the male or female reproductive system, or both (CDC, 2014).

The oldest effective treatment for infertility is **artificial insemination**, which involves injecting the man's sperm directly into the woman's uterus, timed to coincide with her ovulation (Schoolcraft, 2010). It was first developed in the 19th century when physicians believed the primary cause of infertility was a too-tight cervix (the opening between the vagina and the uterus). Today, artificial insemination most often occurs as *donor insemination*, in which a man other than the woman's husband or partner provides the sperm. Most often this approach is because of problems in the husband or partner's sperm production, but increasingly this procedure is chosen by lesbian couples or single women who wish to have a child. Artificial insemination is the simplest and most effective reproductive technology, with a success rate higher than 70 percent per trial (Wright et al., 2004).

If the primary problem is that the woman cannot ovulate properly, the most common approach is to stimulate ovulation through fertility drugs. The drugs mimic the activity of the hormones that normally provoke ovulation. Usually fertility drugs stimulate both the quality and the quantity of follicles in each cycle. More than half of the women who take the drugs become pregnant within six cycles (Schoolcraft, 2010).

Fertility drugs work for many women, but they also carry serious risks, including blood clots, kidney damage, and damage to the ovaries (Lauersen & Bouchez, 2000). The purpose of the drugs is to stimulate the development of follicles in the ovaries, but often more than one follicle develops, resulting in the release of two, three, or more ova. Consequently, use of fertility drugs produces high rates of multiple births, about 10 to 25 percent depending on the drug (Schoolcraft, 2010). Usually this means twins, but there is also the possibility of triplets or more. You may have seen magazine stories or television shows about multiple births of six, seven, or eight infants and how adorable they are, but the consequences of multiple births are often tragic. The more babies conceived at once, the higher the risk for miscarriages, premature birth, and serious developmental difficulties.

Figure 2.6 Fertility and Maternal Age

Why does fertility decline after the mid-20s?

assisted reproductive technologies (ART)

methods for overcoming infertility that include artificial insemination, fertility drugs, and IVF

artificial insemination

procedure of injecting sperm directly into the uterus

Multiple births often receive extensive media attention, but the consequences of such births are often tragic, with higher risks of miscarriages, premature birth, and serious developmental difficulties.

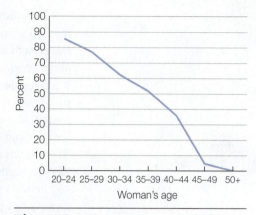

If fertility drugs are unsuccessful in achieving pregnancy, the next step in the ART method is **in vitro fertilization (IVF)**. In IVF, after fertility drugs are used to stimulate the growth of numerous follicles in the woman's ovaries, the ripe ova are then removed and combined with the man's sperm so that fertilization will take place. After a few days it is possible to tell which of the zygotes have developed and which have not, so the most promising two or three are placed into the woman's uterus in the hope that one will continue to develop. IVF success rates have steadily improved in recent years, and are currently about 40 percent per attempt for women younger than age 35 (Society for Assisted Reproductive Technology [SART], 2014). However, the success rate declines with age to 22 percent for women ages 38 to 40 and just 4 percent for women ages 42 and older.

Few people in developing countries have access to reproductive technologies like fertility drugs and IVF. Women may try herbal remedies provided by a midwife. Others may seek supernatural remedies (Leonard, 2002).

INFERTILITY WORLDWIDE Across cultures, most people wish to have children and infertility is experienced as a source of frustration and distress (Balen & Inhorn, 2002). However, there are definite cultural differences in how seriously infertility is viewed and how it is framed socially. In the individualistic West, infertile couples often experience a sense of sadness and loss. In one Swedish study, couples seeking infertility treatments felt frustration over missing out on a major focus of life, and they experienced a negative effect on their sexual relationship (Hjelmstedt et al., 1999). Other studies have found that infertility often creates strains in the marital relationship; but in the long run, about half of couples report that the experience of infertility made their relationship closer and stronger (Schmidt et al., 2005).

Outside the West, cultures tend to be more collectivistic, and the social consequences of infertility are even more profound. Infertility is often deeply stigmatized. This is especially true for women, who are usually blamed for the problem and for whom motherhood is essential to their identity and their place within the social world (Inhorn & Balen, 2002; Sembuya, 2010). In many cultures, infertility means much more than that the couple will miss out on the joys of raising a child. It may mean that there will be no one to continue the family tradition of remembering and worshipping the ancestors, a responsibility that often falls on the oldest son, especially in Asian and African cultures. It may also mean that the status of the wife is lowered in relation to her husband, her in-laws, and the community because infertility is viewed more as her failure than his. Even if she has a daughter, she may still be seen as inadequate if she fails to produce a son. This is misguided because biologically it is the father and not the mother who determines the sex of the child.

If infertility persists, it is viewed in many cultures as grounds for the husband to divorce his wife or take another wife. For example, in Vietnam it is generally accepted that if a man's wife is infertile he will attempt to have a child with another "wife," even though having more than one wife is actually illegal (Pashigian, 2002). In Cameroon, if a couple cannot conceive a child, the husband's family may encourage him to obtain a divorce and seek the return of the "bridewealth" his family paid to the wife's family when they married (Feldman-Savelsberg, 2002).

in vitro fertilization (IVF)
form of infertility treatment that involves using drugs to stimulate the growth of multiple follicles in the ovaries, removing the follicles and combining them with sperm, then transferring the most promising zygotes to the uterus

Summary: Genetic Influences on Development

LO 2.1 **Distinguish between *genotype* and *phenotype* and identify the different forms of genetic inheritance.**

There are 46 chromosomes in the human genome, organized into 23 pairs. The totality of an individual's genes is the genotype, and the person's actual characteristics are called the phenotype. Genotype and phenotype may be different as a result of dominant–recessive inheritance, incomplete dominance, and environmental influences. Most human characteristics are polygenic, meaning that they are influenced by multiple genes rather than just one.

LO 2.2 **Describe the sex chromosomes and identify what makes them different from other chromosomes.**

The sex chromosomes determine whether the person will be male or female. In the female this pair is called XX; in the male, XY. Having only one X chromosome makes males more vulnerable than females to a variety of recessive disorders that are linked to the X chromosome.

LO 2.3 **Explain how behavior geneticists use heritability estimates and concordance rates in their research.**

Heritability estimates indicate the degree to which a characteristic is believed to be influenced by genes within a specific population. Concordance rates indicate the degree of similarity between people with different amounts of their genes in common, for example MZ and DZ twins.

LO 2.4 **Describe how the concept of *epigenesis* frames gene–environment interactions, and connect epigenesis to the concept of *reaction range*.**

Epigenesis is the concept that development results from bidirectional interactions between genotype and environment. The concept of reaction range also involves gene-environment interactions because it means that genes set a range for development and environment determines where development falls within that range.

LO 2.5 **Explain how the theory of genotype → environment effects casts new light on the old nature–nurture debate.**

Rather than viewing nature and nurture as separate forces, this theory proposes that genes influence environments through three types of genotype → environment effects: passive (parents provide both genes and environment to their children); evocative (children evoke responses from those who care for them); and active (children seek out an environment that corresponds to their genotype). The three types of effects operate throughout the life span but their relative balance changes with time.

LO 2.6 **Outline the process of meiosis in the formation of reproductive cells.**

In meiosis, cells that begin with 23 pairs of chromosomes split and replicate repeatedly until they form four gametes, each with 23 individual chromosomes. In males the outcome of meiosis is four viable sperm, but in females meiosis produces only one viable ovum. Also, males produce millions of sperm daily beginning in puberty, whereas females produce all the eggs they will ever have while still in their mother's womb.

LO 2.7 **Describe the process of fertilization and conception.**

About 14 days into a woman's cycle an ovum is released into the fallopian tube. For the next 24 hours, fertilization can occur in which the 23 chromosomes from the ovum pair up with the 23 chromosomes from the sperm and a new cell, the zygote, is formed from the two gametes. The zygote's 46 paired chromosomes constitute the new organism's unique genotype, set at the moment of conception.

LO 2.8 **List the major causes of and treatments for infertility, and describe how infertility is viewed in different cultures.**

Male infertility may be caused by too few sperm, poor quality of sperm, or low motility of sperm. Female infertility is most often caused by problems in ovulation. Infertility in both men and women is often because of age, but it can also be genetic or caused by behavior such as drug abuse, alcohol abuse, or cigarette smoking. Treatments for infertility are termed *assisted reproductive technologies* (ART) and include artificial insemination, fertility drugs, and in vitro fertilization (IVF).

In developed countries, infertility often results in frustration and sadness, and presents a challenge to the couple's relationship, although it may ultimately make the relationship stronger. In developing countries, the woman is usually blamed for the infertility, and her social status is damaged.

Section 2 Prenatal Development and Prenatal Care

Learning Objectives

2.9 Describe the structures that form during the germinal period.

2.10 Outline the major milestones of the embryonic period.

2.11 Describe the major milestones of the fetal period and identify when viability occurs.

2.12 Compare and contrast prenatal care in traditional cultures and developed countries.

2.13 Identify the major teratogens in developing countries and developed countries.

PRENATAL DEVELOPMENT AND PRENATAL CARE: Prenatal Development

When sperm and ovum unite to become a zygote, a remarkable process is set in motion. If all goes well, about 9 months later a fully formed human being will be born. Now we look closely at this process, from conception to birth (summarized in **Figure 2.7**).

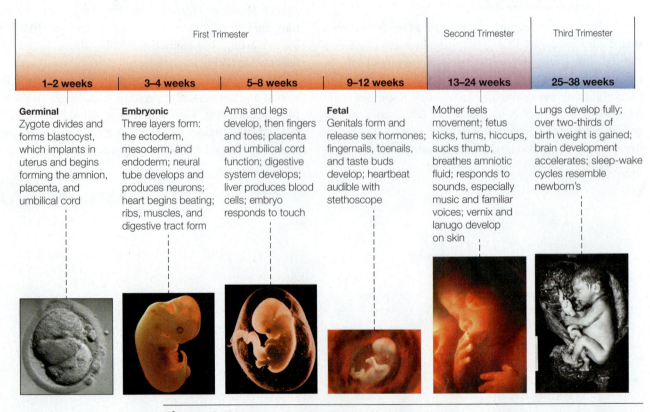

First Trimester				Second Trimester	Third Trimester
1–2 weeks	**3–4 weeks**	**5–8 weeks**	**9–12 weeks**	**13–24 weeks**	**25–38 weeks**
Germinal Zygote divides and forms blastocyst, which implants in uterus and begins forming the amnion, placenta, and umbilical cord	**Embryonic** Three layers form: the ectoderm, mesoderm, and endoderm; neural tube develops and produces neurons; heart begins beating; ribs, muscles, and digestive tract form	Arms and legs develop, then fingers and toes; placenta and umbilical cord function; digestive system develops; liver produces blood cells; embryo responds to touch	**Fetal** Genitals form and release sex hormones; fingernails, toenails, and taste buds develop; heartbeat audible with stethoscope	Mother feels movement; fetus kicks, turns, hiccups, sucks thumb, breathes amniotic fluid; responds to sounds, especially music and familiar voices; vernix and lanugo develop on skin	Lungs develop fully; over two-thirds of birth weight is gained; brain development accelerates; sleep-wake cycles resemble newborn's

Figure 2.7 Milestones of Prenatal Development

The Germinal Period (First 2 Weeks)

LO 2.9 **Describe the structures that form during the germinal period.**

The first 2 weeks after fertilization are called the **germinal period** (Jones, 2006). This is the period when the zygote travels down the fallopian tubes to the uterus and implants in the uterine wall. As it travels, it begins cell division and differentiation. The first cell division does not occur until 30 hours after conception, but after that, cell division takes place at a faster rate. By 1 week following conception there is a ball of about 100 cells known as a **blastocyst**. The blastocyst is divided into two layers. The outer layer of cells, called the **trophoblast**, will form the structures that provide protection and nourishment. The inner layer of cells, the **embryonic disk**, will become the embryo of the new organism.

During the second week after conception, implantation occurs as the blastocyst becomes firmly embedded into the lining of the uterus. Since the ovum was released from the ovary, the follicle from which it was released has been generating hormones that have caused the uterus to build up a bloody lining in preparation for receiving the blastocyst. Now the blastocyst is nourished by this blood.

The trophoblast begins to differentiate into several structures during this second week. Part of it forms a membrane, the **amnion**, which surrounds the developing organism and fills with fluid, helping to keep a steady temperature for the organism and protect it against the friction of the mother's movements (Johnson, 2008). In between the uterine wall and the embryonic disk a round structure, the **placenta**, begins to develop. The placenta will allow nutrients to pass from the mother to the developing organism and permit wastes to be removed. It also acts as a gatekeeper, protecting the developing organism from bacteria and wastes in the mother's blood, and it produces hormones that maintain the blood in the uterine lining and cause the mother's breasts to produce milk. An **umbilical cord** also begins to develop, connecting the placenta to the mother's uterus.

Implantation is the outcome of the germinal period if all goes well. However, it is estimated that more than half of blastocysts never implant successfully, usually as a result of chromosomal problems that have caused cell division to slow down or stop (Johnson, 2008). If implantation fails, the blastocyst will be eliminated from the woman's body along with the bloody uterine lining during her next menstrual period.

The Embryonic Period (Weeks 3–8)

LO 2.10 **Outline the major milestones of the embryonic period.**

During the germinal period the trophoblast differentiated faster than the embryonic disk, developing the structures to protect and nurture the organism during pregnancy. Now, differentiation occurs rapidly in the embryonic disk. Over the 6 weeks of the **embryonic period**, 3–8 weeks' **gestation** (the time elapsed since conception), nearly all the major organ systems are formed (Fleming, 2006).

During the first week of the embryonic period—the third week after conception—the embryonic disk forms three layers. The outer layer, the **ectoderm**, will become the skin, hair, nails, sensory organs, and nervous system. The middle layer, the **mesoderm**, will become the muscles, bones, reproductive system, and circulatory system. The inner layer, the **endoderm**, will become the digestive system and the respiratory system.

The nervous system develops first and fastest (Johnson, 2008). By the end of Week 3 (since conception), part of the ectoderm forms the **neural tube**, which will eventually become the spinal cord and brain. Once formed, the neural tube begins producing **neurons** (cells of the nervous system) in immense quantities, more than 250,000 per minute. In the fourth week the shape of the head becomes apparent, and the eyes, nose,

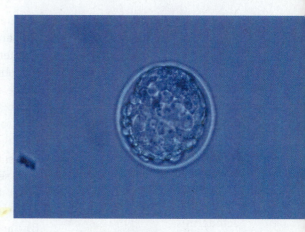

Cell division begins about 30 hours after conception.

germinal period

first 2 weeks after conception

blastocyst

ball of about 100 cells formed by about 1 week following conception

trophoblast

in the blastocyst, the outer layer of cells, which will go on to form structures that provide protection and nourishment to the embryo

embryonic disk

in the blastocyst, the inner layer of cells, which will go on to form the embryo

amnion

fluid-filled membrane that surrounds and protects the developing organism in the womb

placenta

in the womb, gatekeeper between mother and fetus, protecting the fetus from bacteria and wastes in the mother's blood, and producing hormones that maintain the blood in the uterine lining and cause the mother's breasts to produce milk

umbilical cord

structure connecting the placenta to the mother's uterus

mouth, and ears begin to form. The heart begins to beat during this week, and the ribs, muscles, and digestive tract appear. By the end of the fourth week the embryo is only one-quarter-inch long but already remarkably differentiated. Nevertheless, even an expert embryologist would have trouble at this point judging whether the embryo was to become a fish, a bird, or a mammal.

During Weeks 5–8, growth continues its rapid pace. Buds that will become the arms and legs appear in Week 5, developing webbed fingers and toes that lose their webbing by Week 8. The placenta and the umbilical cord become fully functional (Jones, 2006). The digestive system develops, and the liver begins producing blood cells. The heart develops separate chambers. The top of the neural tube continues to develop into the brain, but the bottom of it looks like a tail in Week 5, gradually shrinking to look more like a spinal cord by Week 8.

By the end of the eighth week, the embryo is just 1 inch (2½ centimeters) long and 1/30 of an ounce (1 g) in weight. Yet all the main body parts have formed, as have all of the main organs except the sex organs. Furthermore, the tiny embryo responds to touch, especially around its mouth, and it can move (Moore & Persaud, 2003). Now the embryo looks distinctly human (Johnson, 2008).

The Fetal Period (Week 9–Birth)

LO 2.11 Describe the major milestones of the fetal period and identify when viability occurs.

During the **fetal period**, lasting from 9 weeks after conception until birth, the organs continue to develop, and there is tremendous growth in sheer size, from 1/30 of an ounce in weight and 1 inch long at the beginning of the fetal period to an average (in developed countries) of 7½ pounds (3.4 kg) and 20 inches (51 cm) by birth.

By the end of the third month the genitals have formed. After forming, the genitals release hormones that influence the rest of prenatal development, including brain organization, body size, and activity level, with boys becoming on average somewhat larger and more active (Cameron, 2001). Also during the third month, fingernails, toenails, and taste buds begin to develop. The heart has developed enough so that the heartbeat can now be heard through a stethoscope.

After 3 months, the typical fetus weighs about 3 ounces and is 3 inches long. A good way to remember this is as "three times three"—3 months, 3 ounces, 3 inches. Or, you can think of it as 100 days, 100 grams, 100 millimeters. Prenatal development is divided into three 3-month periods called **trimesters**, and the end of the third month marks the end of the first trimester.

During the second trimester, the fetus becomes active and begins to respond to its environment (Henrichs et al., 2010). By the end of the fourth month the fetus's movements can be felt by the mother. Gradually over the course of the second trimester the activity of the fetus becomes more diverse. By the end of the second trimester it breathes amniotic fluid in and out; it kicks, turns, and hiccups; it even sucks its thumb. It also responds to sounds, including voices and music, showing a preference (indicated by increased heart rate) for familiar voices, especially the voice of the mother. A slimy white substance called **vernix** covers the skin, to protect it from chapping because of the amniotic fluid, and downy hair called *lanugo* helps the vernix stick to the skin. By birth the fetus usually sheds its lanugo, although sometimes babies are born with lanugo still on, then shed it in the early weeks of life.

By the end of the second trimester, 6 months after conception, the typical fetus is about 14 inches long (36 cm) and weighs about 2 pounds (0.9 kg). Although it seems well-developed in many aspects of its behavior, it is still questionable in its *viability*, meaning its ability to survive outside of the womb. Babies born before 22 weeks rarely survive, even with the most advanced technological assistance. Even at 26 weeks, near

embryonic period

weeks 3–8 of prenatal development

gestation

in prenatal development, elapsed time since conception

ectoderm

in the embryonic period, the outer layer of cells, which will eventually become the skin, hair, nails, sensory organs, and nervous system (brain and spinal cord)

mesoderm

in the embryonic period, the middle of the three cell layers, which will become the muscles, bones, reproductive system, and circulatory system

endoderm

in the embryonic period, the inner layer of cells, which will become the digestive system and the respiratory system

neural tube

in the embryonic period, the part of the ectoderm that will become the spinal cord and brain

neuron

cell of the nervous system

fetal period

in prenatal development, the period from Week 9 until birth

trimester

one of the three 3-month periods of prenatal development

vernix

at birth, babies are covered with this oily, cheesy substance, which protects their skin from chapping in the womb

the end of the second trimester, the survival rate is only 50 percent, and the survivors often have disabilities—14 percent have severe mental disabilities and 12 percent have cerebral palsy, which entails extensive physical and neurological disabilities (Lorenz et al., 1998). And this survival rate is only for babies that happen to be born in developed countries or in a wealthy family in a developing country. In most of the world, babies born before the end of the second trimester have no access to advanced medical care and will not survive (Organisation for Economic Co-operation and Development [OECD], 2009).

The main obstacle to viability at the beginning of the third trimester is the immaturity of the lungs. The lungs are the last major organ to become viable, and even a baby born in the seventh or early eighth month may need a respirator to breathe properly. Weight gain is also important. During the last trimester the typical fetus gains more than 5 pounds, and this additional weight helps it sustain life. Babies born weighing less than 5.5 pounds are at risk for a wide range of problems.

The brain is even less mature than the lungs in the third trimester, but its immaturity does not represent an obstacle to viability. Early brain immaturity was an evolutionary adaptation that enabled human beings to have an exceptionally large brain yet still fit through the birth canal. More than any other animal, humans are born with immature brains, which is why human babies are vulnerable and need parental care longer than other animals do. Nevertheless, more brain development occurs in the last 2 months of prenatal development than in any previous months. Neurons are created in vast numbers, up to 500,000 per minute, and the connections between them become increasingly elaborate (Gross, 2008).

By the third trimester, brain development has progressed to the point where, at 28 weeks, the sleep-wake cycles of the fetus are similar to those of a newborn infant. The fetus becomes increasingly aware of the external environment, especially in its ability to hear and remember sounds (James, 2010). In one study, mothers were asked to read Dr. Seuss's *The Cat in the Hat* to their fetuses every day during the last 6 weeks of pregnancy (DeCasper & Spence, 1986). After birth, the babies showed a preference for a recording of their mother reading *The Cat in the Hat*, by sucking on a plastic nipple to turn it on. They sucked harder to hear *The Cat and the Hat* than they did for recordings of their mothers reading similar rhyming stories they had not heard before. Fetuses respond to their internal environment as well. When the mother is highly stressed, the fetus's heart beats faster and its body movements increase (DiPietro et al., 2002).

PRENATAL DEVELOPMENT AND PRENATAL CARE: Prenatal Care

Because prenatal development carries risks for both mother and fetus, all cultures have developed customs and practices to try to promote a healthy outcome. First we look at some of the practices of prenatal care in traditional cultures, then we look at the scientific approach to prenatal care that has developed recently.

Variations in Prenatal Care

LO 2.12 **Compare and contrast prenatal care in traditional cultures and developed countries.**

All cultures have a store of advice about what a woman should and should not do during pregnancy (DeLoache & Gottlieb, 2000). What kind of guidelines or advice have you heard? You might ask your mother, your grandmother, and other mothers you know what advice they followed and where they obtained it.

Sometimes pregnancy advice seems practical and sensible. The practical advice reflects the collected wisdom that women pass down to each other over generations, based on their own experiences. Other times the advice may seem odd, especially to someone outside the given culture. Customs that seem peculiar to an outsider may arise because pregnancy is often perilous to both mother and fetus. Cultural groups sometimes develop their prenatal customs out of the intense desire to ensure that pregnancy will proceed successfully, but without the scientific knowledge that would make such control possible.

Here are a few examples. Among the Beng people of the West African nation of Ivory Coast, pregnant women are advised to avoid drinking palm wine during the early months of pregnancy (Gottlieb, 2000). This is wise practical advice drawn from the experience of women who drank alcohol during pregnancy, with unfortunate results. On the other hand, the mother-to-be is also advised to avoid eating meat from the bushbuck antelope while pregnant, and warned that if she does eat it, her baby may emerge from the womb striped like the antelope.

Thousands of miles away, on the Indonesian island of Bali, "hot" foods are to be avoided during pregnancy, including eggplant, mango, and octopus (Diener, 2000). Also, a pregnant mother should not accept food from someone who is viewed as spiritually impure, such as a menstruating woman or someone who has recently had a death in the family. Witches are believed to be especially attracted to the blood of a pregnant woman and her unborn child, so pregnant women are advised to obtain a magic charm and wear it on their belt or hang it on the gate of their yard, for protection.

Some of the examples of prenatal customs just provided may strike you as strange, but they are understandable as a human attempt to control events that are highly important but also mysterious.

Even in developed countries, which have a long scientific tradition, not much was known about prenatal care from a scientific perspective until recent decades. As recently as the middle of the 20th century, women in developed countries were being advised by their doctors to limit their weight gain during pregnancy to no more than 15 pounds (Murkoff & Mazel, 2008). By now, scientific studies have shown that women who have a healthy weight before becoming pregnant should typically gain 25 to 35 pounds during pregnancy, and women who gain less than 20 pounds are at risk for having babies who are preterm and low birth weight (Ehrenberg et al., 2003).

There are also risks of gaining too much weight during pregnancy. These risks may affect both the mother and her child (Restall et al., 2014). The expectant mother who gains too much weight may experience hypertension, preeclampsia, and diabetes (Chen et al., 2010). A larger fetus may make for a more difficult delivery, and that poses a higher risk of c-section. There is also a greater risk of the child becoming overweight later in life (Restall et al., 2014).

In other areas, too, an extensive body of scientific knowledge has accumulated on prenatal care in recent decades. One key conclusion of this research is that pregnant women should receive regular evaluations from a skilled health care worker, beginning as soon as possible after conception, to monitor the health of mother and fetus and ensure that the pregnancy is proceeding well. Babies born to mothers who received no prenatal care are more likely to have a low birth weight or to die than babies born to mothers who receive prenatal care (U.S. Department of Health and Human Services, 2015). Most women in developed countries have access to physicians, nurses, or certified midwives who can provide good prenatal care. However, some poor women may not have access to such care, especially in the United States. Groups such as migrant workers may not have access to adequate prenatal care, and special efforts to target women in these groups have resulted in increased prenatal care and better birth outcomes (Mazzurco, et al., 2014). Overall, the percentage of women in the United States who begin prenatal care in their first trimester varies greatly based on ethnicity and socioeconomic status, as shown in **Map 2.1**.

Pregnant women in developing countries are much less likely than those in developed countries to receive prenatal care from a skilled health care worker. The World Health

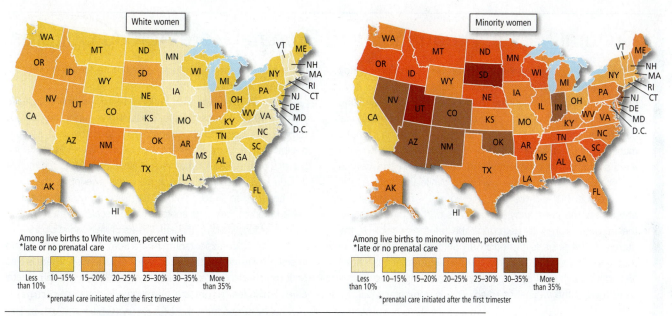

White women

Among live births to White women, percent with
*late or no prenatal care

| Less than 10% | 10–15% | 15–20% | 20–25% | 25–30% | 30–35% | More than 35% |

*prenatal care initiated after the first trimester

Minority women

Among live births to minority women, percent with
*late or no prenatal care

| Less than 10% | 10–15% | 15–20% | 20–25% | 25–30% | 30–35% | More than 35% |

*prenatal care initiated after the first trimester

Map 2.1 Ethnic Variations in Prenatal Care Within the United States

How does prenatal care differ for White women compared with other ethnic groups? What economic factors might account for these variations?

Organization's *Making Pregnancy Safer* program has focused on working with governments to set up programs that provide pregnant women with such care (World Health Organization [WHO], 2009). Currently 99 percent of maternal and infant deaths occur in developing countries—only 1 percent occur in developed countries—and the WHO program is focused on the 70 countries with the highest death rates, mostly in Africa and South Asia.

Guidelines for prenatal care focus mostly on three key areas: diet, exercise, and avoidance of potentially harmful influences called teratogens (see **Table 2.2**; WHO, 2009a).

CRITICAL THINKING QUESTION

Are there any beliefs in your culture about what a woman should eat or should avoid eating before or during pregnancy? Do the same beliefs apply to men during any point of the conception and gestation continuum?

Moderate exercise is part of good prenatal care.

Table 2.2 Essentials of Prenatal Care

Before Pregnancy

- Have a medical examination to ensure there are no diseases that may affect prenatal development. If not fully vaccinated, obtain vaccinations for diseases, such as rubella, that can damage prenatal development. (Vaccinations may be unsafe during pregnancy.)
- Avoid tobacco, alcohol, and other drugs, which may make it more difficult to become pregnant and are damaging to prenatal development.

During Pregnancy

- *Diet.* Maintain a balanced diet, including protein, grains, fruits, and vegetables. Avoid excessive fats and sugars and obtain sufficient iron and iodine. Gain between 25 and 35 pounds in total; avoid dieting as well as excessive weight gain. Women should also drink more fluids during pregnancy than they normally do because the fetus needs fluids for healthy development and a pregnant woman's body also requires more.
- *Exercise.* Engage in mild to moderate exercise regularly, including aerobic exercise, to stimulate circulatory system and muscles, as well as Kegel exercises to strengthen vaginal muscles. *Aerobic exercise*, such as walking, jogging, or swimming, stimulates the circulatory and muscular systems of a woman's body (Schmidt et al., 2006). However, it is important to avoid strenuous exercise and high-risk sports, such as long-distance running, contact sports, downhill skiing, waterskiing, and horseback riding.
- *Teratogens.* Avoid tobacco, alcohol, and other drugs. Avoid exposure to X-rays, hazardous chemicals, and infectious diseases.

Cultural Focus: Pregnancy and Prenatal Care Across Cultures

Although many cultures have folk beliefs about pregnancy that have no scientific or practical basis, most also have customs that provide genuine relief to pregnant women. One helpful method of prenatal care common in many traditional cultures is massage (Field, 2010; Jordan, 1994). The prenatal massage is usually performed by a **midwife** (a person who assists women in pregnancy and childbirth) in the course of her visits to the pregnant woman. While the massage is taking place, the midwife asks the woman various questions about how the pregnancy is going. As part of the massage, the midwife probes to determine the fetus's position in the uterus. If the fetus is turned in an unfavorable position, so that it would be likely to come out feet first rather than head first, the midwife will attempt an *inversion* to turn the fetus's head toward the vaginal opening. This is sometimes painful, but a head-first birth is much safer than a feet-first birth, for both baby and mother.

Prenatal massage has a long history in many cultures (Jordan, 1994). In recent years, it has also begun to be used by midwives, nurses, and physicians in developed countries. By now, a substantial amount of research has accumulated to support the benefits of massage for mother and fetus. Benefits to the mother include lower likelihood of back pain, less swelling of the joints, and better sleep (Field, 2004, 2010). Babies whose mothers received prenatal massage score higher on scales of their physical and social functioning in the early weeks of life (Field et al., 2006).

In this video expectant mothers from various countries are interviewed regarding their pregnancy experiences. There is also an interview with a Mayan midwife regarding her role in prenatal care. It includes her prenatal massage of a pregnant woman.

Watch PREGNANCY AND PRENATAL CARE ACROSS CULTURES

Video

Review Question:

What are the advantages of using a doctor or of using a midwife, as described in this video clip? What others can you think of?

Teratogens

LO 2.13 Identify the major teratogens in developing countries and developed countries.

midwife

person who assists in pregnant women's prenatal care and the birth process

teratogen

behavior, environment, or bodily condition that can have damaging influence on prenatal development

An essential part of good prenatal care is avoiding **teratogens**, which are behaviors, environmental effects (e.g., drugs and other chemicals, radiation), and bodily conditions that could be harmful to the developing organism (Haffner, 2007). Both the embryo and the fetus are vulnerable to a variety of teratogens. The embryonic period, especially, is a *critical period* for prenatal development, meaning that it is a period when teratogens can have an especially profound and enduring effect on later development, as **Figure 2.8** illustrates. This is because the embryonic period is when all the major organ systems are forming at a rapid rate. However, some teratogens can

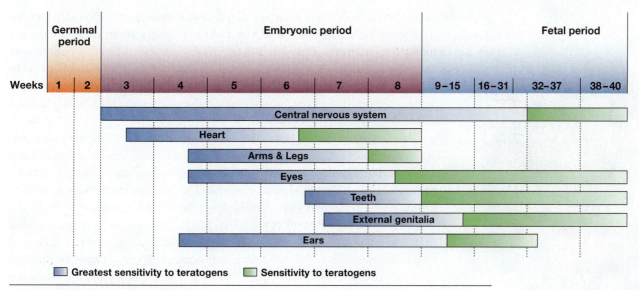

Figure 2.8 Timing of Teratogens

Vulnerability to teratogens is greatest in the embryonic period.
SOURCE: Based on Moore, 1974

do damage during the fetal period. Major teratogens include malnutrition, infectious diseases, alcohol, tobacco, and drugs. Other potential teratogens include environmental pollution, radiation, and severe maternal stress. Certain kinds of work are best avoided during pregnancy if they involve exposure to teratogens such as X-rays, hazardous chemicals, or infectious diseases.

Time of exposure, dosage and frequency of exposure to drugs and other chemicals, and genetic susceptibility all influence the extent of damage caused. The timing of exposure matters because specific teratogens may affect specific organs. Teratogens typically have their worst effects when those organs are developing. As you can see in Figure 2.8, the central nervous system may be affected any time during the embryonic and fetal periods because the central nervous system is developing the entire time. On the other hand, teratogens that affect the ears have their effects when the ears are developing, beginning in the fourth week and ending around week 32 (Moore, et al., 2011).

MALNUTRITION Probably the most common teratogen worldwide is malnutrition. Medical experts recommend that pregnant women who have a healthy weight before becoming pregnant gain 25 to 30 pounds, and that they eat a healthy, balanced diet of proteins, grains, fruit, and vegetables (Martin et al., 2002). However, 40 percent of the world's population lives on less than $2 a day, so you can imagine that most mothers who are part of that 40 percent receive a prenatal diet that falls far short of the ideal.

Furthermore, about half the world's population is rural, and the diet of people in rural areas often varies substantially depending on the time of year. They may eat fairly well during summer and fall when their crops provide food, but less well during winter and spring when fresh food is unavailable. Consequently, prenatal health may depend greatly on when the child was conceived.

Dramatic evidence of this effect has been shown in recent decades in China (Berry et al., 1999). In the 1980s China had the highest incidence in the world of two serious prenatal disorders, *anencephaly*, in which parts of the brain are missing or malformed, and *spina bifida*, which is an extreme distortion in the shape of the spinal column. It was discovered that in both of these disorders the main cause is a deficiency of folic acid, a nutrient found especially in fruits and vegetables. Furthermore, researchers observed that the traditional marriage period in China is January and February, and most couples try to conceive a child as soon after marriage as possible. Consequently, the early months of pregnancy typically take place in winter and early spring, when rural women are least likely to have fruits and vegetables as part of their diet. After this pattern was discovered, the Chinese government established a nationwide program to provide mothers with supplements of folic acid, and since that time the incidence of anencephaly and spina bifida has been sharply reduced (Centers for Disease Control and Prevention [CDC], 2011d).

Many other countries have also taken steps to reduce folic-acid deficiencies in pregnant mothers. After research established that folic acid was the key to preventing anencephaly and spina bifida, governments in many countries passed laws requiring folic acid to be added to grain products such as cereals, bread, pasta, flour, and rice. Almost immediately, the incidence of both disorders fell sharply (Honein et al., 2001). Medical authorities now recommend that women begin taking folic acid supplements and eating plenty of fruits and vegetables even when they are trying to become pregnant because the damage from lack of folic acid can take place in the early weeks of pregnancy, before the woman knows for sure that she is pregnant (de Villarreal et al., 2006).

Two other common nutritional deficiencies during pregnancy are iron and iodine. Iron-rich foods such as beef, duck, potatoes (including skin), spinach, and dried fruits are important for building the blood supply of mother and fetus. The World Health Organization (WHO) estimates that nearly one half of women worldwide are deficient in iron, placing them at risk for having preterm and low-birth-weight babies (WHO, 2009b). Even with a healthy diet including iron-rich foods, health authorities recommend an iron supplement from the 12th week of pregnancy onward.

Iodine is also crucial because low-iodine intake during pregnancy increases the risks of miscarriage, stillbirth, and abnormalities in fetal brain development. In developed countries salt has been iodized since the 1920s, so women receive adequate iodine as part of a normal diet. However, in developing countries most women do not use iodized salt and consequently they often experience iodine deficiencies. The WHO and other major health organizations have made a strong push recently to make iodine supplements available in developing countries.

INFECTIOUS DISEASES Infectious diseases are far more prevalent in developing countries than in developed countries (WHO, 2009a, b). Many of these diseases influence prenatal development. One of the most prevalent and serious is *rubella* (also known as *German measles*). The embryonic period is a critical period for exposure to rubella. More than half of infants whose mothers contract the illness during this period have severe problems including blindness, deafness, intellectual disability, and abnormalities of the heart, genitals, or intestinal system (Eberhart-Phillips et al., 1993). During the fetal period effects of rubella are less severe, but can include low birth weight, hearing problems, and skeletal defects (Brown & Susser, 2002). Since the late 1960s a vaccine given to children has made rubella rare in developed countries—girls retain the immunity into adulthood, when they become pregnant—but it remains widespread in developing countries where children are less likely to receive the vaccine (Plotkin et al., 1999; WHO, 2009a, b).

Another common infectious disease of prenatal development is **AIDS (acquired immune deficiency syndrome)**, a sexually transmitted infection (STI) caused by the human immunodeficiency virus (HIV), which damages the immune system. HIV/AIDS can be transmitted from mother to child during prenatal development through the blood, during birth, or through breast milk. HIV/AIDS damages brain development prenatally, and infants with HIV are unlikely to survive to adulthood unless they receive an expensive "cocktail" of medications rarely available in the developing countries where AIDS is most common. In developing countries mother–child transmission of HIV/AIDS has been dramatically reduced in recent years through three strategies: (1) effective medicines

Malnutrition is a common teratogen in developing countries. Pictured here is a pregnant woman in rural Zambia.

AIDS (acquired immune deficiency syndrome)

sexually transmitted infection caused by HIV, resulting in damage to the immune system

given to mothers before birth; (2) c-sections for mothers infected with AIDS; and (3) the use of infant formula in place of breast-feeding (WHO, 2010c). However, 95 percent of all HIV infections take place in Africa, and few African mothers or infants have access to the three strategies that are effective against HIV/AIDS.

ALCOHOL In developed countries, the teratogen that causes the most widespread damage to prenatal development is alcohol (Mattson et al., 2010; Sokol et al., 2003). Although it used to be believed that moderate alcohol use would cause no harm during pregnancy, recent research has shown that the only safe amount of alcohol for a pregnant woman is *none at all*. Even one or two drinks a few days a week puts the developing child at risk for lower height, weight, and head size at birth, and for lower intelligence and higher aggressiveness during childhood (Willford et al., 2004).

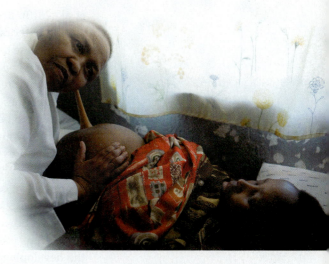

When mothers drink heavily during pregnancy, their infants are at risk for **fetal alcohol spectrum disorder (FASD)**, which includes facial deformities, heart problems, misshapen limbs, and a variety of cognitive problems such as intellectual disability and attention and memory deficits (Mattson et al., 2010). Infants born with FASD face a lifetime of trouble, and the more alcohol their mothers drank during pregnancy, the worse their problems are likely to be (Barr & Streissguth, 2001). In childhood and adolescence, their cognitive deficits make it difficult for them to succeed academically or socially in school (Korkman et al., 2003). Cognitive deficits in FASD have been linked to epigenetic effects (Bakoyiannis, et al., 2014; Kleiber, et al., 2014). In adolescence, FASD raises the risk of delinquency, alcohol and drug abuse, and depression and other mental health problems (Baer et al., 2003; Mattson et al., 2010). Rates of FASD are especially alarming, as high as 10 percent, in some American Indian and Canadian First Nations communities where alcoholism is prevalent (Caetano et al., 2006; Tough et al., 2007).

Pregnant women in developing countries who have AIDS rarely receive adequate medical treatment. Here, a woman is being treated at a clinic for HIV/AIDS patients in Lesotho.

NICOTINE Maternal cigarette smoking has a wide range of damaging effects on prenatal development. Women who smoke during pregnancy are at higher risk for miscarriage and premature birth, and smoking is the leading cause of low birth weight in developed countries (Espy et al., 2011). Maternal smoking raises the risks of health problems in infants, such as impaired heart functioning, difficulty breathing, and even death (Jaakkola & Gissler, 2004). Prenatal exposure to smoking predicts problems in childhood and adolescence, including poorer language skills, problems with attention and memory, and behavior problems (Cornelius et al., 2011; Sawnani et al., 2004).

Fathers' smoking is also a peril to prenatal development. The secondhand smoke from fathers' smoking leads to higher risks of low birth weight and childhood cancer (Ruckinger et al., 2010). Rates of smoking are generally higher in developed countries than in developing countries, but they are rising rapidly in developing countries around the world as their economies grow (WHO, 2011a).

DRUGS Alcohol and tobacco are the most common teratogens in developed countries, but other types of drugs also have a harmful effect on the developing child. Maternal use of recreational psychoactive drugs such as cocaine, heroin, and marijuana causes physical, cognitive, and behavioral problems in infants (Messinger & Lester, 2008; National Institute on Drug Abuse, 2001). Specifically, marijuana can affect the development of the brain and central nervous system, and it can retard the growth of the fetus (Gunn et al., 2015; Wu et al., 2011). The use of cocaine can result in low birth weight from slow growth of the fetus and premature labor as well as emotional reactivity from infancy through adolescence (Bridgett & Mayes, 2011; Eiden et al. 2007; Minnes et al., 2010). Like marijuana and cocaine, heroin can also slow fetal growth (Kaltenbach & Finnegan, 1989; Keegan

fetal alcohol spectrum disorder (FASD)

set of problems that occur as a consequence of high maternal alcohol use during pregnancy, including facial deformities, heart problems, misshapen limbs, and a variety of cognitive problems

et al., 2010). Babies born to mothers who used heroin during pregnancy go through a painful withdrawal and are usually given methadone to cope with the pain. It is helpful to have these babies room in with their mothers, rather than being in a separate nursery (Abrahams et al., 2007). It is best to avoid recreational drugs during pregnancy.

Certain prescription drugs can also cause harm. Even nonprescription drugs such as cold medicines can be damaging to prenatal development, so women who are pregnant or seeking to become pregnant should always check with their doctors about any medications they may be taking (Morgan et al., 2010). Among prescription drugs, Accutane, a drug used to treat severe acne, can cause devastating damage to major organs such as the brain and heart during embryonic development (Honein et al., 2001). Many women take selective serotonin reuptake inhibitors (SSRIs) for depression or anxiety, and some of these drugs (e.g., fluoxetine and paroxetine) have been found in some studies to cause heart and other abnormalities (Myles et al., 2013). However, many studies suggest that these drugs are safe overall (Casper, 2015). And, the effects of maternal depression on the developing fetus may be worse than the effects of any drugs that treat depression (Olivier et al., 2015). When it comes to any prescription or over-the-counter drugs, it is best to weigh potential risks and benefits in a discussion with a health provider.

Summary: Prenatal Development and Prenatal Care

LO 2.9 **Describe the structures that form during the germinal period.**

During the germinal period a ball of cells called the *blastocyst* forms and implants in the lining of the uterus. The blastocyst has two layers, the embryonic disk that will become the embryo of the new organism and the trophoblast that will form the supporting structures of the amnion, placenta, and umbilical cord.

LO 2.10 **Outline the major milestones of the embryonic period.**

During the embryonic period (3–8 weeks after conception) all the major organ systems are initially formed, except the sex organs. Rapid development of organs during this period makes it a critical period for the effects of teratogens.

LO 2.11 **Describe the major milestones of the fetal period and identify when viability occurs.**

During the fetal period (Week 9–birth) organ systems continue to develop and there is immense growth in size. Viability is rare before the third trimester because of the immaturity of the lungs. By 28 weeks the fetus has sleep-wake cycles similar to a newborn baby's and can remember and respond to sound, taste, and the mother's movements.

LO 2.12 **Compare and contrast prenatal care in traditional cultures and developed countries.**

In traditional cultures prenatal care often includes massage as well as folk knowledge that may or may not have practical consequences. For instance, many cultures advise pregnant women to avoid certain types of food. Essential elements of scientifically-based prenatal care include regular evaluations by a health care professional and guidelines concerning diet, exercise, and avoiding teratogens. Pregnant women are advised to gain 25 to 30 pounds in the course of pregnancy, and light to moderate exercise is encouraged.

LO 2.13 **Identify the major teratogens in developing countries and developed countries.**

The major teratogens are malnutrition and infectious diseases in developing countries and alcohol and tobacco in developed countries. The embryonic period is a critical period for prenatal development because all the major organ systems are forming at a rapid rate. However, some teratogens can do damage during the fetal period as well.

Section 3 Pregnancy Problems

 Learning Objectives

2.14 Explain how chromosomal disorders occur.

2.15 Describe causes and symptoms of some common genetic disorders.

2.16 Describe the three main techniques of prenatal diagnosis.

2.17 Explain who is likely to seek genetic counseling and for what purposes.

PREGNANCY PROBLEMS:
Chromosomal and Genetic Disorders

Most pregnancies proceed without major problems and end with the birth of a healthy infant. However, many things can go wrong in the course of prenatal development. In this section, we'll look at some common chromosomal disorders and genetic disorders.

Chromosomal Disorders

LO 2.14 Explain how chromosomal disorders occur.

In the course of the formation of the gametes during meiosis, sometimes errors take place and the chromosomes fail to divide properly. Consequently, instead of ending up with 46 chromosomes in each cell, the person has 45 or 47 (or even, in rare cases, 48 or 49), and problems occur. It is estimated that as many as half of all conceptions involve too many or too few chromosomes, but most of the zygotes that result either never begin to develop or are spontaneously aborted early in the pregnancy (Borgaonkar, 1997; Johnson, 2008). In 1 out of 200 live births, the child has a chromosomal disorder. There are two main types of chromosomal disorders: (1) those that involve the sex chromosomes and (2) those that take place on the 21st pair of chromosomes, resulting in a condition known as Down syndrome.

SEX CHROMOSOME DISORDERS The sex chromosomes are especially likely to be involved in chromosomal disorders. A person may have an extra X chromosome (resulting in XXX or XXY), or an extra Y chromosome (XYY), or may have only an X and no second sex chromosome. About 1 in every 500 infants has some type of sex chromosome disorder.

There are two common consequences of sex chromosome disorders (Batzer & Ravitsky, 2009). One is that the person has some type of cognitive deficit, such as intellectual disability (ranging from mild to severe), a learning disorder, or speech impairments. The other kind of problem is that the person has some abnormality in the development of the reproductive system at puberty, such as underdeveloped testes and penis in boys or no ovulation in girls. One of the functions of the sex chromosomes is to direct the production of the sex hormones, and having too few or too many sex chromosomes disrupts this process. However, treatment with hormone supplements is often effective in correcting the problem.

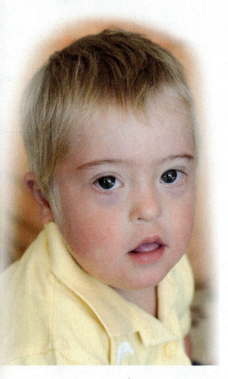

Persons with Down syndrome typically face a wide range of physical and cognitive problems.

DOWN SYNDROME When there is an extra chromosome on the 21st pair, the condition is known as **Down syndrome**, or *trisomy-21*. People with Down syndrome have distinct physical features, including a short, stocky build, an unusually flat face, a large tongue, and an extra fold of skin on the eyelids. They also have cognitive deficits, including intellectual disability and speech problems (Pennington et al., 2003). Many also have problems in their physical development, such as hearing impairments and heart defects.

Their social development varies widely. Some children with Down syndrome smile less readily than other persons and have difficulty making eye contact, but others are exceptionally happy and loving. Supportive and encouraging parents help children with Down syndrome develop more favorably (Hodapp et al., 2012; Sigman, 1999). Intervention programs in infancy and preschool have been shown to enhance their social, emotional, and motor skills (Carr, 2002; Hodapp et al., 2012). In adulthood, with adequate support many are able to hold a job that is highly structured and involves simple tasks.

People with Down syndrome age faster than other people (Berney, 2009). Their total brain volume begins to decrease as early as their 20s. Various physical ailments that may develop for other people in late adulthood begin to afflict people with Down syndrome in their 30s and 40s, including leukemia, cancer, Alzheimer's disease, and heart disease (Hassold & Patterson, 1999). As a result, their life expectancy is considerably lower than in the general population. However, with medical treatment most are able to live into at least their 50s or 60s (Hodapp et al., 2012).

PARENTAL AGE AND CHROMOSOMAL DISORDERS Children with chromosomal problems are almost always born to parents who have no disorder (Batzer & Ravitsky, 2009). Chromosomal problems occur not because the parents have an inherited problem that they pass on to their children, but usually because of the age of the parents, especially the mother. For example, the risk of Down syndrome rises with maternal age, from 1 in 1,900 births at age 20 to 1 in 30 births at age 45 (Meyers et al., 1997). The risk of chromosomal disorders is low for mothers in their 20s and rises only slightly in the 30s, but rises steeply after age 40 (see **Figure 2.9**; Umrigar et al., 2014).

Recall that a woman's gamete production takes place while she is still in the womb of her own mother. The older she gets, the longer the eggs have been in her ovaries. When conception takes place and the last part of meiosis is completed in the ovum, the older the woman, the greater the likelihood that the chromosomes will not separate properly because they have been suspended in that final stage of meiosis for so long. The father's sperm is the cause of the chromosomal disorder in 5 to 10 percent of cases, but it is unclear if the risk increases with the father's age (Crow, 2003; Fisch et al., 2003; Muller et al., 2000).

Genetic Disorders

LO 2.15 Describe causes and symptoms of some common genetic disorders.

Genetic disorders may be caused by incomplete dominance or by mutations. A common example of incomplete dominance is sickle-cell trait. Two common examples of genetic mutations are fragile X syndrome and phenylketonuria (PKU).

In **incomplete dominance** the phenotype is influenced primarily, but not exclusively, by the dominant gene. One example of incomplete dominance involves the sickle-cell trait that is common among black Africans and their descendants such as African Americans (see **Figure 2.10**). Most blood cells are shaped like a disk, but when a person inherits two recessive genes for the sickle-cell trait the blood cells become hook-shaped, like the blade of a sickle. This results in a condition called *sickle-cell anemia*, in which the sickle-shaped blood cells clog up the blood vessels and cause pain, susceptibility to disease, and early death. About 1 in 500 Africans (and African Americans) have this disorder, and it also occurs

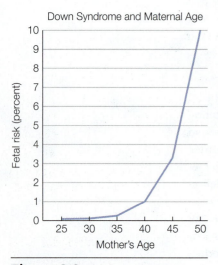

Down Syndrome and Maternal Age

Figure 2.9 Down Syndrome and Maternal Age

Why does the risk rise so steeply after age 40?

SOURCE: Based on Umrigar et al. (2014).

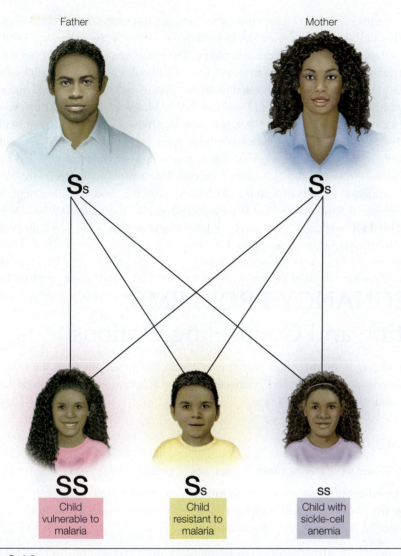

Figure 2.10 Incomplete Dominance in Sickle-Cell Inheritance

Two recessive genes for the sickle-cell trait results in sickle-cell anemia, but having one dominant and one recessive gene provides protection against malaria.

(less commonly) in people whose ancestors are from India or the Mediterranean region (Quinn et al., 2004).

However, if a person inherits only one recessive gene for the sickle-cell trait, along with a normal dominant gene, the dominance is incomplete, and a portion—but not all— of the person's blood cells will be sickle shaped. This portion is not large enough to cause sickle-cell anemia, but it is large enough to make the person resistant to malaria, a blood disease that is spread by mosquitoes. Malaria is often fatal, and even when it is not it can cause brain damage and other enduring health problems. It occurs worldwide in developing countries but is especially common in Africa, killing more than a million people a year. In many central African countries over 50 percent of children are affected (WHO, 2013).

This explains why the sickle-cell trait evolved especially among Africans. Because the effects of contracting malaria are so severe, in evolutionary terms it is an advantage genetically to have the sickle-cell trait to protect against malaria, even if it also raises the risk of sickle-cell anemia.

Other fairly common genetic disorders include fragile X syndrome and phenylketonuria (PKU). Fragile X syndrome, the most common inherited intellectual disability worldwide, is caused by genetic mutations on the X chromosome (Kanwal et al., 2015). It is also

Down syndrome

genetic disorder resulting from carrying an extra chromosome on the 21st pair

incomplete dominance

form of dominant–recessive inheritance in which the phenotype is influenced primarily by the dominant gene but also to some extent by the recessive gene

the most common genetic disorder associated with autism spectrum disorder (Dalton et al., 2008). Although the syndrome occurs in both males and females, males are more affected by the mutation and exhibit more symptoms. The majority of males have an intellectual disability, ranging from moderate to severe, but only about one third of females with fragile X exhibit intellectual delays. Intellectual problems tend to include difficulty paying attention and impulsiveness (Hagerman & Hagerman, 2002). Males tend to exhibit physical symptoms of a long face, large ears, flat feet, soft skin, and hyper-flexible joints. For females, the physical symptoms tend to be fewer and milder. There is no cure for fragile X syndrome.

PKU is a birth defect that causes the amino acid phenylalanine to build up in the body because people with PKU cannot process that amino acid effectively. Early, sustained treatment is usually effective and involves avoiding foods and drinks that contain phenylalanine. A low-protein diet is recommended into the teens and 20s (Nardecchia et al., 2015). Left untreated, PKU causes intellectual disability and poor information processing abilities (Weglage et al., 2013).

PREGNANCY PROBLEMS:
Testing and Counseling Options

Prenatal testing is an important part of monitoring the development of the fetus. In fact, some couples seek testing and counseling before attempting conception to know the risks or difficulties they might face.

Prenatal Diagnosis

LO 2.16 Describe the three main techniques of prenatal diagnosis.

In developed countries, a variety of techniques are available to monitor the growth and health of the fetus and detect prenatal problems. Common methods include ultrasound, amniocentesis, and chorionic villus sampling (CVS).

Ultrasound. In **ultrasound**, high-frequency sound waves are directed toward the uterus, and as they bounce off the fetus they are converted by computer into an image that can be viewed on a screen. Ultrasound technology has improved in recent years and the three- and four-dimensional (3D/4D) images are distinct enough to make it possible to measure the fetus's size and shape and to monitor its activities (Merz & Abramowicz, 2012). Studies have also found that viewing ultrasound images helps promote a feeling of parental involvement and attachment even before birth (Righetti et al., 2005).

Ultrasound is sometimes used to screen for Down syndrome, which can be detected 13 weeks into prenatal development (Reddy & Mennui, 2006). It is also used for pregnancies that involve multiple fetuses because these are high-risk pregnancies in which it is common for some of the fetuses to be developing less favorably than others. However, increasingly, ultrasound is used for normal pregnancies in developed countries, not just for those that are high risk (Merz & Abramowicz, 2012). It is cheap, easy, and safe, and it allows doctors to monitor fetal growth and gives parents the enjoyment of seeing the fetus as it is developing in the womb. It also allows parents to learn the sex of the child before birth, if they wish.

Amniocentesis. In **amniocentesis**, a long hollow needle is inserted into the pregnant woman's abdomen and, using the ultrasound image for guidance, a sample of the amniotic fluid is withdrawn from the placenta surrounding the fetus. This fluid contains

---

ultrasound

machine that uses sound waves to produce images of the fetus during pregnancy

amniocentesis

prenatal procedure in which a needle is used to withdraw amniotic fluid containing fetal cells from the placenta, allowing possible prenatal problems to be detected

Ultrasound allows medical professionals and parents to monitor prenatal development.

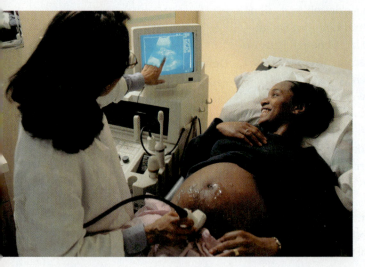

fetal cells sloughed off in the course of prenatal development, and the cells can be examined for information on the fetus's genotype. Amniocentesis is conducted 15 to 20 weeks into pregnancy. It is used only for women who are at risk for prenatal problems due to family history or age (35 or older) because it carries a small risk of triggering miscarriage. It can detect 40 different defects in fetal development with 100 percent accuracy (Brambati & Tului, 2005).

Chorionic villus sampling (CVS). Like amniocentesis, **chorionic villus sampling (CVS)** entails sampling and analyzing cells early in development to detect possible genetic problems. CVS takes place at 5 to 10 weeks into the pregnancy; the sample is obtained from the cells that are beginning to form the umbilical cord. Guided by ultrasound, a tube is inserted through the vagina and into the uterus to obtain the cell sample. CVS entails a slight but genuine risk of miscarriage or damage to the fetus, so it is used only when there is a family history of genetic abnormalities or the woman is age 35 or older (Brambati & Tului, 2005). It is 99 percent accurate in diagnosing genetic problems.

Genetic Counseling

LO 2.17 **Explain who is likely to seek genetic counseling and for what purposes.**

Even before pregnancy, couples whose family history places them at risk for having children with genetic disorders may seek *genetic counseling*, which involves analyzing the family history and genotypes of prospective parents to identify possible risks (Coughlin, 2009). Those with risks that merit genetic counseling include persons who have an inherited genetic condition or a close relative who has one; couples with a history of miscarriages or infertility; and older couples (women older than 35 and men older than 40) (Fransen et al., 2006). The decision to obtain genetic counseling may be difficult because the results may require the couple to make the choice between trying to become pregnant and risking that the child will have a genetic disorder, or deciding not to pursue pregnancy. However, the knowledge obtained from genetic counseling enables people to make an informed decision.

In the first step of genetic counseling, the counselor takes a comprehensive family history from each prospective parent, seeking to identify patterns that may indicate problematic recessive or X-linked genes. Then each partner provides a blood, skin, or urine sample that can be used to analyze their chromosomes to identify possible problems. With the information obtained from genetic counseling, the couple can then decide whether or not they wish to attempt pregnancy (Coughlin, 2009).

chorionic villus sampling (CVS)

prenatal technique for diagnosing genetic problems, involving taking a sample of cells at 5 to 10 weeks gestation by inserting a tube into the uterus

---

CRITICAL THINKING QUESTION

Do you think that genetic counseling will increase or decrease in the next 10 years? Provide reasons for your answer from an ecocultural point of view.

Summary: Pregnancy Problems

LO 2.14 **Explain how chromosomal disorders occur.**

Chromosomal disorders occur when the chromosomes fail to divide properly during meiosis. These disorders may involve the sex chromosomes or may take place on the 21st pair of chromosomes, resulting in a condition known as Down syndrome. Risks of chromosomal disorders rise with parental age.

LO 2.15 **Describe causes and symptoms of some common genetic disorders.**

Common genetic disorders include sickle-cell anemia fragile X syndrome, and phenylketonuria (PKU). Sickle-cell anemia is a genetic disorder that causes misshapen red blood cells that cannot process oxygen correctly. Sickle-cell trait is caused by incomplete dominance, in which the dominant gene exerts most, but not all, of the influence over genetic expression. Fragile X syndrome is caused by a mutation on the X chromosome, and it is the most common genetic disorder linked to intellectual disability. In PKU, individuals are unable to digest the amino acid phenylalanine.

LO 2.16 **Describe the three main techniques of prenatal diagnosis.**

Prenatal diagnosis may include ultrasound, amniocentesis, and chorionic villus sampling (CVS). Ultrasound carries no risks. The risks of amniocentesis and CVS should be discussed with a physician.

LO 2.17 **Explain who is likely to seek genetic counseling and for what purposes.**

Couples who may be at high risk for genetic disorders sometimes seek genetic counseling before attempting pregnancy. Information from family histories and blood, skin, or urine samples is used to help couples make family planning decisions.

Applying Your Knowledge as a Professional

The topics covered in this chapter apply to a wide variety of career professions. Watch these videos to learn how they apply to a reproductive endocrinologist, a genetic counselor, and a professor of microbiology.

Watch CAREER FOCUS: GENETIC COUNSELOR

Video

Elsa Reich, M.S.
Genetic Counselor
NYU Langone Medical Center

Chapter Quiz

1. The totality of an individual's genes is the _____.
   a. phenotype
   b. genotype
   c. allele
   d. dominant gene

2. Who has the greatest risk of developing hemophilia, which is an X-linked recessive disorder?
   a. A female who has one X chromosome that contains the gene for this disorder
   b. A male who has one X chromosome that contains the gene for this disorder
   c. Males and females with one X chromosome that contains the gene for the disorder will have equal risk.
   d. Only American Indians because of their unique genetic makeup

3. Which of the following questions would a behavior geneticist be most likely to ask?
   a. "Why are children in the same family so different from one another?"
   b. "Are preterm babies more likely to have learning difficulties during the school years?"
   c. "How can prenatal tests be used to detect Down syndrome?"
   d. "What effects does alcohol have on the developing organism?"

4. Why has there been little change in the average height in Western countries over the last few decades?

   a. The population has become overweight or obese, which negatively affects height.

   b. People in Western countries have been exposed to more diseases.

   c. People have reached the upper boundary of their reaction range for height.

   d. Evolutionary influences are causing all populations to decrease in height.

5. John is short for his age and is coordinated. Although exposed to a variety of activities, none has particularly interested him. His father, who used to wrestle when he was younger, signs John up for wrestling thinking this could be the perfect sport. He convinces John to give it a try and John goes on to become a champion wrestler. This is an example of _____.

   a. passive genotype → environment effects

   b. evocative genotype → environment effects

   c. active genotype → environment effects

   d. heritability

6. As a result of the process of crossing over _____.

   a. the risk of Down syndrome is increased

   b. boys are more likely to be born with a learning disability

   c. women are at increased risk for infertility

   d. each child born to a set of parents is genetically unique (with the exception of identical twins)

7. S. J. is most likely to have DZ twins if _____.

   a. she has Asian biological parents

   b. she is in her late teens

   c. she is concerned about gaining too much weight and severely restricts her calorie intake

   d. her mother had DZ twins

8. In the United States, about _____ percent of couples are infertile.

   a. 1–2

   b. 4–5

   c. 10–15

   d. 14–27

9. The germinal period lasts

   a. about 1 day

   b. about 3 days

   c. about 7 days

   d. about 14 days

10. During the embryonic period _____.

    a. the blastocyst forms

    b. the zygote is created

    c. the zygote attaches to the uterine wall

    d. the major organs develop

11. Saad, a baby born 6 weeks prematurely, is more at risk of not surviving than Nona, a baby who is full term, because Saad's _____ is(are) still immature.

    a. small intestines

    b. heart

    c. lungs

    d. spleen

12. Which is the following is true of good prenatal care?

    a. Exercise should be avoided.

    b. Tobacco, alcohol, and other drugs should be avoided.

    c. Women should drink fewer fluids than before pregnancy.

    d. Forty to 60 pounds should be gained.

13. K. L.'s baby was born blind, deaf, and with intellectual disability. It is most likely that during her pregnancy she _____.

    a. contracted AIDS

    b. had rubella

    c. had a severe nutritional deficiency

    d. ate foods that were too high in folic acid

14. A child who has an X0 chromosomal makeup (where 0 denotes a missing chromosome where there is supposed to be a 23rd pair) will most likely _____.

    a. be a male with Down syndrome

    b. be a female who will later experience problems in the development of the reproductive system

    c. be a typical female who will not experience cognitive or physical problems

    d. not survive past the age of 3

15. Keisha has inherited one recessive gene for the sickle-cell trait along with one normal dominant gene. As a result of this _____, she is resistant to malaria and does not have sickle-cell anemia.

    a. dominant-recessive inheritance

    b. incomplete dominance

    c. polygenic inheritance

    d. reaction range

16. Carissa has a family history of Down syndrome and is in her 5th week of pregnancy. She decides that she would like to find out as early as possible whether her unborn child has Down syndrome or any genetic abnormality. What test is she most likely to get?

    a. Fetal monitoring

    b. Ultrasound

    c. Amniocentesis

    d. Chorionic villus sampling

17. The first step of genetic counseling is that each prospective parent provides a _____.

    a. blood test

    b. comprehensive family history

    c. urine sample

    d. chorionic villus sampling

Chapter 3
Birth and the Newborn Child

ACROSS CULTURES, THE BIRTH OF A NEW HUMAN BEING IS REGARDED AS A JOYFUL EVENT, WORTHY OF CELEBRATION. At the same time, it is often a physically challenging and potentially perilous process, for both mother and child, especially when modern medical assistance is not available. In this chapter we will look at the birth process, followed by historical and cultural variations in birth beliefs and practices. We will then move on to examine the neonate's health and physical functioning. We'll close the chapter with a section on caring for the newborn that includes a discussion of breast feeding as well as social and emotional aspects of care.

Watch   CHAPTER INTRODUCTION: BIRTH AND THE NEWBORN CHILD

Section 1 Birth and Its Cultural Context

 Learning Objectives

3.1 Describe the three stages of the birth process.

3.2 Name two common types of birth complications and explain how they can be overcome by cesarean delivery.

3.3 Summarize the history of birth in the West from the 15th century to today.

3.4 Describe cultural variations in birth beliefs and identify who may assist with the birth.

3.5 Compare and contrast cultural practices and medical methods for easing the birth process.

BIRTH AND ITS CULTURAL CONTEXT: The Birth Process

All human beings are born into a cultural setting, and birth itself, although obviously biological, also brings with it cultural beliefs and practices. In this section we discuss three stages of the typical birth process and cesarean delivery.

Stages of the Birth Process

LO 3.1   **Describe the three stages of the birth process.**

Toward the end of pregnancy, hormonal changes take place that trigger the beginning of the birth process. Most importantly, the hormone **oxytocin** is released from the woman's pituitary gland. When the amount of oxytocin in the expectant mother's blood reaches a certain threshold level, her uterus begins to contract on a frequent and regular basis, and the birth process begins.

The birth process is generally divided into three stages: labor, delivery of the baby, and delivery of the placenta and umbilical cord, as shown in **Figure 3.1** (Mayo Clinic Staff, 2011). There is immense variability among women in the length and difficulty of this process, depending mostly on the size of the woman and the size of the baby, but in general it is longer and more difficult for women giving birth to their first child.

The first stage of the birth process, **labor**, is the longest and most taxing stage, averaging about 12 hours for first births and 6 hours for subsequent births (Lyon, 2007). During labor, contractions of the muscles in the uterus cause the woman's cervix to dilate (open) in preparation for the baby's exit. By the end of labor, the cervix has opened to about 10 centimeters (4½ inches). Contractions of the muscles of the uterus must occur with increasing intensity, frequency, and duration to dilate the cervix and move the fetus down the neck of the uterus and through the vagina. The contractions of the uterus are painful in the same way (and for the same reason) a cramp is painful. At their peak duration, contractions last 60 to 90 seconds.

oxytocin

hormone released by pituitary gland that causes labor to begin

labor

first stage of the birth process, in which the cervix dilates and the muscles of the uterus contract to push the fetus into the vagina toward the cervix

Stage 1: Labor	Stage 2: Delivery	Stage 3: Expelling of Placenta & Umbilical Cord
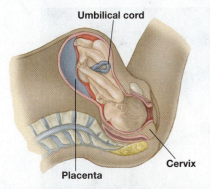	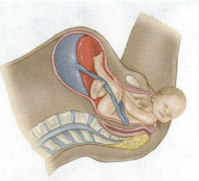	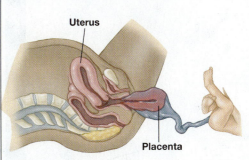
Contractions increase in duration, frequency, and intensity, causing the cervix to dilate.	The mother pushes, and the baby crowns and then exits the birth canal and enters the world.	Contractions continue as the placenta and umbilical cord are expelled.

Figure 3.1 The Three Stages of the Birth Process

Which stage is longest and most difficult?

The second stage of the birth process, **delivery,** usually takes a half hour to an hour, but again there is wide variation (Murkoff & Mazel, 2008). So far in the birth process there has been not much the expectant mother could do to influence it, other than bear the pain and discomfort as well as possible. Now, however, her efforts to push will help move the fetus through the cervix and out of the uterus. Contractions continue to help, too, but for most women the contractions are now less frequent, although they remain 60 to 90 seconds long. Usually the woman feels a tremendous urge to push during her contractions.

At last *crowning* occurs, meaning that the baby's head appears at the outer opening of the vagina. The woman often experiences a tingling or burning sensation at her vaginal opening as the baby crowns. At this point, if she is giving birth in a hospital she may be given an *episiotomy,* which is an incision to make the vaginal opening larger. The purpose of the episiotomy is to make the mother's vagina less likely to tear as the fetus's head comes out, and to shorten this part of the birth process by 15 to 30 minutes. However, critics of episiotomies say they are often unnecessary, and in response to such criticism the rate of episiotomies in the United States declined from about 90 percent in 1970 to just 16 percent in 2010 (Cassidy, 2006; Frankman et al., 2009; Leapfrog Group, 2014).

The delivery stage ends as the baby emerges from the vagina, but the birth process is not yet over. In this third and final stage, contractions continue as the placenta and umbilical cord are expelled from the uterus (Lyon, 2007). This process usually happens within a few minutes, at most a half hour. The contractions are mild and last about a minute each. Care must be taken that the entire placenta comes out. If it does not, the uterus will be unable to contract properly and the mother will continue to bleed, perhaps even to the point of threatening her life. Beginning to breast feed the newborn triggers contractions that help expel the placenta, and when advanced medical care is available the mother may be given an injection of synthetic oxytocin for the same purpose.

If the mother has had an episiotomy or her vagina has torn during delivery, she will be stitched up at this time. At this point, too, the umbilical cord must be cut and tied. There are many interesting cultural beliefs surrounding the cutting of the umbilical cord and the disposal of the placenta, as we will see later in the chapter.

The video *Labor and Delivery* on the next page shows excerpts from the delivery stage and the expelling of the placenta and umbilical cord, from a real birth.

delivery

second stage of the birth process, during which the fetus is pushed out of the cervix and through the birth canal

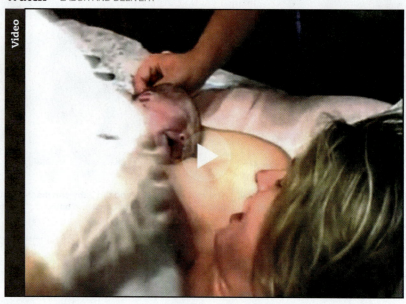

Watch   LABOR AND DELIVERY

Cesarean Delivery

LO 3.2   **Name two common types of birth complications and explain how they can be overcome by cesarean delivery.**

We have just examined the birth process as it occurs if all goes well, but there are often cases in which surgical interventions are necessary. Two of the most common birth complications are *failure to progress* and the *breech presentation* of the fetus.

"Failure to progress" means that the woman has begun the birth process but it is taking longer than normal. The woman may stimulate progress by walking around, taking a nap, or having an enema. She may also be given herbal medicines or synthetic oxytocin to stimulate her contractions.

Breech presentation is when the fetus is turned around so that the feet or buttocks are positioned to come first out of the birth canal, rather than the head. About 4 percent of fetuses present in the breech position (Martin et al., 2005). Breech births are dangerous to the baby because coming out feet- or buttocks-first can cause the umbilical cord to be constricted during delivery, potentially leading to insufficient oxygen and brain damage within minutes. Consequently, attempts are usually made to avoid a breech presentation. Midwives have long used their skills to massage the expectant mother's abdomen and turn the fetus from breech presentation to headfirst, but it must be done with extreme care to avoid tearing the placenta from the uterine wall. Today physicians in hospitals also seek to turn breech fetuses at about the 37th week of pregnancy. Doctors often use drugs to relax the muscles of the uterus as they attempt to turn the fetus with the massage (Hofmeyr, 2002).

If failure to progress takes place during delivery, or if a fetus in breech position cannot be turned successfully, or if other problems arise in the birth process, the woman may be given a **cesarean delivery, or c-section**. The c-section involves cutting open the mother's abdomen and retrieving the baby directly from the uterus. It is a safe procedure, although it takes women longer to heal from a cesarean than from a vaginal birth (Connolly & Sullivan, 2004). C-sections are generally safe for infants as well, and if the mother has a sexually transmitted infection, such as HIV or genital herpes, it is safer than a vaginal birth because it protects the infant from the risk of contracting the disease during the birth process. As **Map 3.1** shows, rates of c-sections vary widely among countries and do not seem to be related to world region or level of economic development

breech presentation

positioning of the fetus so that feet or buttocks, rather than the head, are positioned to come first out of the birth canal

cesarean delivery, or c-section

type of birth in which mother's abdomen is cut open and fetus is retrieved directly from the uterus

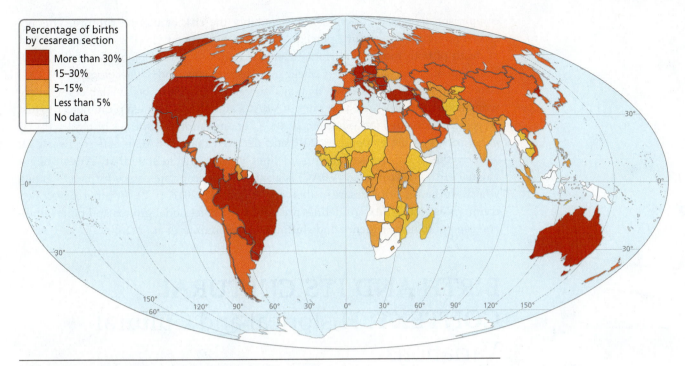

Map 3.1 Cesarean Section Rates, Selected Countries

Which countries have the highest rates of cesarean sections? What determines whether a country has high or low rates?

SOURCE: Based on WHO (2015)

Legend:
Percentage of births by cesarean section
- More than 30%
- 15–30%
- 5–15%
- Less than 5%
- No data

(World Health Organization [WHO], 2015). The World Health Organization (WHO) recommends that no country's c-section rate should exceed 15 percent (WHO, 2009a, b), but many countries exceed that rate, including the United States.

Critics of high c-section rates claim that they are performed far more than is necessary, and that they are often performed not so much to protect the mother and baby as to enrich doctors (c-sections are a type of surgery and thus cost far more than a vaginal birth). However, c-section rates are not substantially higher in countries that rely mostly on private medical insurance and where doctors get paid more for doing more c-sections (like the United States) than in countries like China, Italy, and Canada that have a national health care system that does not pay doctors per c-section (WHO, 2015). More likely, high rates of c-sections result from extreme caution by doctors seeking to avoid disaster during births.

Some of the countries that have the lowest rates of c-sections also have low rates of birth complications, which seems to indicate that many c-sections performed in other countries are unnecessary (WHO, 2015). Specifically, the countries that have the lowest rates of birth problems as well as the lowest rates of c-sections are the countries of northern Europe, where doctors and mothers alike share a cultural belief that birth should be natural and that technological intervention should take place only when absolutely necessary (Ravn, 2005). However, rates of c-sections are also low in countries like India and in most of Africa, where many people lack access to hospital facilities that could provide c-sections when necessary (WHO, 2015).

For women who have had a c-section, there is a possibility of having a vaginal birth with the next baby, a procedure known as a *vaginal birth after cesarean section* (VBAC); Shorten, 2010). As part of a more general movement in developed countries toward natural, less technological birth experiences, rates of VBAC rose in the 1980s and 1990s, and by the late 1990s about one fourth of U.S. women who had their first baby by c-section had a VBAC with their next baby (Roberts et al., 2007). However, evidence began to indicate that having a VBAC raised birth risks in several ways in comparison to repeat c-sections, most notably the risk of uterine rupture. This occurred rarely, in only about 1 percent of VBACs, but when it did it sometimes resulted in death of both mother and fetus from the mother's loss of blood (WebMD, 2011). Consequently, the American College of Obstetricians and Gynecologists (ACOG) issued guidelines advocating that an emergency c-section be available for every woman attempting VBAC, and rates of VBACs among U.S. women plummeted, to just 10 percent a decade later (Shorten, 2010). After an National Institutes of Health (NIH) panel reviewed the evidence in 2010 and declared that a VBAC is safe for nearly all women, the ACOG revised their guidelines in July 2010 to state that "Attempting a vaginal birth after cesarean (VBAC) is a safe and appropriate choice for most women who have had a prior cesarean delivery" (WebMD, 2011, p. 2). In other developed countries as well, VBAC guidelines are in flux as professional groups and policy makers respond to new evidence and shifting views (Foureur et al., 2010).

BIRTH AND ITS CULTURAL CONTEXT: Historical and Cultural Variations

Around 9 months after conception, if survival has been sustained through the amazing, dramatic, and sometimes hazardous events of the germinal, embryonic, and fetal periods, a child is born. Even for the child who has made it through those 9 months, the hazards are far from over. The birthing process is often difficult and sometimes fatal, to mother or child or both. Humans responded to this danger by developing cultural beliefs and practices intended to explain why labor is difficult and to alleviate the pain and enhance the safety of mother and child. Some of these beliefs and practices were surely helpful; others were indisputably harmful.

The Peculiar History of Birth in the West

LO 3.3   **Summarize the history of birth in the West from the 15th century to today.**

Given the perils of birth throughout human history one might assume that once modern scientific medicine developed, mothers and babies were safer than in the superstitious past. However, this is not quite how the story goes. On the contrary, as birth became "medical" the dangers for mothers and babies grew worse, not better, for *over a century*.

EARLY HISTORY: FROM MIDWIVES TO DOCTORS   In the West as in other cultures, most births throughout most of history were administered by midwives (Ehrenreich, 2010). The role of midwife was widely valued and respected. Most did their work for little or no pay, although families would often present them with a gift after the birth.

This began to change in the 15th century, as a witch-hunting fervor swept over Europe. Midwives became widely suspected of being witches, and many of them were put to death. After the witch-hunting fervor passed, midwifery revived, but to keep out any remaining witches, midwives were required to have licenses, issued by the Catholic church.

In the early 18th century a new challenge arose to the status of midwives. Medical schools were established throughout Europe, and the care and assistance of expectant mothers became a distinct field within medicine called **obstetrics**. By the 19th century it became increasingly common for doctors in the West to be called on to assist in births. Unfortunately, medical training at the time often included virtually nothing about childbirth. All the doctors-to-be were men, and in many medical schools it was considered improper for a man to see a woman's genitals under any circumstances. Consequently,

obstetrics

field of medicine that focuses on prenatal care and birth

medical students learned about assisting a birth only from reading books and attending lectures (Cassidy, 2006).

A major risk associated with childbirth in 19th century was the spread of disease. At the time, no one understood that it was necessary for doctors to wash their hands before examining a patient to avoid spreading infection. Consequently, hospitals became disease factories. Vast numbers of women died following childbirth from what was called *childbed fever* or *puerperal sepsis*. Records show that in many European and U.S. hospitals in the 19th century about 1 in 20 mothers died from childbed fever, and during occasional epidemics the rates were much higher (Nuland, 2003). Records from one Boston hospital in 1883 showed that 75 percent of mothers giving birth suffered from childbed fever, and 20 percent died from it (Cassidy, 2006).

In the early 20th century midwives still assisted at about 50 percent of births, but by 1930 this proportion had dwindled to 15 percent, and by 1973 to just 1 percent (Cassidy, 2006). In recent decades midwifery has seen a revival, and currently about 10 percent of births in the United States are assisted by midwives (MacDorman et al., 2010). Many now receive formal training and are certified and licensed as nurse-midwives, rather than simply learning their skills from an older midwife as in the past. In Europe, midwives are much more common than in the United States, especially in northern Europe. In Norway, for example, 96 percent of births are assisted by midwives (Cosminsky, 2003).

THE 20TH CENTURY: SLOW PROGRESS In obstetrics as in other branches of medicine, a more scientific basis of knowledge, care, and treatment developed during the 20th century. However, progress was slow. It was not until the 1940s that childbed fever was finally vanquished in the United States and Europe because it became standard for obstetricians to wash their hands and also wear rubber gloves in examining women. The development of antibiotics at this time cured the cases of childbed fever that did occur (Carter & Carter, 2005).

In some ways, obstetrical care of women grew still worse in the early 20th century. Episiotomies became more prevalent, and doctors increasingly used drugs to relieve mothers' pain during birth. A new drug method was developed that resulted in a condition that became known as *Twilight Sleep* (Cassidy, 2008). After being injected with narcotics (mainly morphine), a woman giving birth in Twilight Sleep became less inhibited, which helped her relax during her contractions and promoted dilation of her cervix. Women still felt pain—in fact, screaming and thrashing were so common in Twilight Sleep that women were often strapped in helmets and handcuffed to the birth bed—but afterward they remembered none of it, so as far as they were concerned, the birth had been painless and problem free. From the 1930s through the 1960s use of Twilight Sleep and other drug methods was standard practice in hospitals in Western countries, and women nearly always gave birth while heavily medicated (Cassidy, 2006). If you live in a Western country, ask your grandmother about it.

During the late 1960s a backlash began to develop against the medicalization of birth (Lyon, 2007). Critics claimed that medical procedures such as episiotomies and drugs were unnecessary and had been created by the medical profession mainly to make childbirth more profitable. These critics advocated **natural childbirth** as an alternative. Although this term was first proposed in the 1930s, it was only in the 1960s and the decades that followed that a variety of drug- and technology-free approaches to birth became popular, as part of more general trends toward greater rights for women, a greater push for consumer rights, and a growing interest in natural health practices (Thompson, 2005). Natural childbirth methods vary in their details, but all reject medical technologies and interventions as unhelpful to the birth process or even harmful. The premise is that a substantial amount of the pain women experience in childbirth is based on the anxiety created by fear of medical technologies and lack of understanding

natural childbirth
approach to childbirth that avoids medical technologies and interventions

In the mid-20th century birth in developed countries often took place in a condition of "Twilight Sleep," in which the mother was heavily medicated. Shown here is a 1946 photo of a new mother under sedation after giving birth in a London hospital.

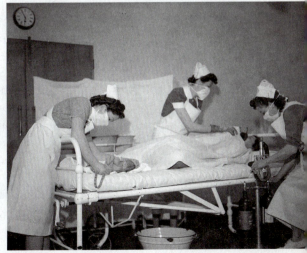

of the birth process. Consequently, natural childbirth includes classes in which the parents-to-be learn about the birth process. The remainder of the pain experienced in childbirth can be managed by relaxation and breathing techniques. Another important component of natural childbirth approaches is for the expectant mother to have the physical and emotional support of her husband or partner or others who could assist with the relaxation and breathing techniques.

No differences have been found in maternal and neonatal health outcomes between natural childbirth and medical methods, as long as the birth takes place in a health facility where medical intervention is available if necessary (Bergstrom et al., 2009). Most participants in natural childbirth methods report that it lowered their anxiety about the birth and made them feel that they were more knowledgeable about and more in control of the birth process (Westfall & Benoit, 2004). Natural childbirth methods remain popular today, especially in northern Europe (Ravn, 2005).

Although natural childbirth can enhance the birth experience for mothers, some studies have shown much higher rates of poor or fatal outcomes for women who have a "home birth." One large study of 13 million births in the United States found that the neonatal mortality rate (first 4 weeks) for babies born at home was 10 times higher than for babies born in a hospital setting (Grünebaum et al., 2014). Another analysis with the same sample concluded that babies born at home were 10 times as likely to have difficulty breathing shortly after birth, making them vulnerable to permanent brain damage (Grünebaum et al., 2013). As we have seen, babies' big heads in relation to the size of their mothers' pelvis makes birth in humans more perilous than it is in other species, so medical interventions can be necessary and may be life-saving. Home births are not recommended for women with high-risk pregnancies or preexisting medical conditions, and women are advised to have a plan for transfer to a medical facility, should complications arise. In African and south Asia, only about half of births take place in a health facility, and this is one reason for the high rates of neonatal mortality in these regions (UNICEF, 2014a). Worldwide, rates of neonatal mortality have declined steeply in recent decades, as more regions gain access to modern medical technologies.

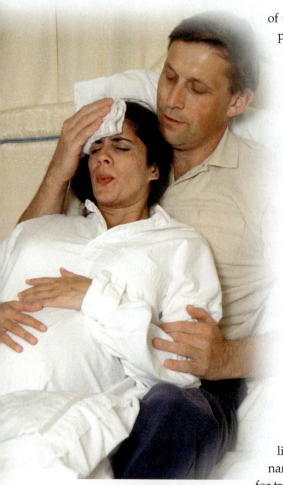

In natural childbirth, husbands or partners often assist with breathing techniques designed to manage the pain.

In developed countries today, the birth process is better than it has ever been before, for both mothers and babies. The natural childbirth movement has had many positive effects on how birth is assisted in mainstream medicine. Although most births in developed countries still take place in a hospital, birth has become less like an operation performed by a physician and more of a collaboration between doctors, nurses (often including nurse-midwives), and mothers. Some parents also choose to enlist the help of a *doula*, an experienced mentor and coach who provides physical, emotional, and informational support to the mother (Chen & Xu, 2013).

Fathers, partners, and other family members and friends are now often involved, too. Prior to the 1960s fathers were totally excluded from the birth, but by the late 1970s the majority of fathers in developed countries were present when their wives gave birth (Simkin, 2007). In general, the father's presence seems to benefit the mother during birth (Kainz et al., 2010). When fathers are present, mothers experience slightly shorter labor and express greater satisfaction with the birth experience (Hodnett et al., 2007). For fathers, being present at the birth evokes intense feelings of wonder and love (Erlandsson & Lindgren, 2009). However, some fathers also experience intense fears for the health and well-being of the mother and baby (Eriksson et al., 2007).

CRITICAL THINKING QUESTION

If you were pregnant or the partner of a pregnant woman, how "natural" would you want the childbirth to be, and why?

Cultural Variations in Birth Beliefs and Practices

LO 3.4 **Describe cultural variations in birth beliefs and identify who may assist with the birth.**

Cultural beliefs about birth are sometimes designed to protect mother and baby, and sometimes designed to isolate them and protect others. In most cultures, older women take the lead in assisting the birth, especially those designated as midwives.

BELIEFS AND RITUALS SURROUNDING BIRTH As noted at the outset of the chapter, across cultures a successful birth is marked with a joyful celebration (Newton & Newton, 2003). For example, among the Ila people of Zimbabwe, women attending the birth will shower praise on the woman having the baby. After the birth, her husband comes in to congratulate her, and other male relations also enter the hut to clasp her hand and provide her with gifts.

However, there are also cultural practices that frame birth and its aftermath with some degree of fear and wariness. Perhaps because birth is often dangerous, many traditional cultures have developed beliefs that giving birth puts a woman in a state of being spiritually unclean (Newton & Newton, 2003). In some cultures, birth must take place away from where most people reside, so that others will not be contaminated by it. For example, among the Arapesh of New Guinea, birth is allowed to take place only at the outskirts of the village, in a place reserved for other contaminating activities such as excretion and menstruation.

Many cultures have beliefs that the mother remains unclean long after the birth and must be kept away from others, for her own sake as well as theirs (Newton & Newton, 2003). In traditional Vietnam (but not today), the mother was to avoid going out for at least 30 days after birth, so as not to contaminate the rest of the village or endanger herself or her infant; even her husband could not enter her room but could only speak to her from outside the door. Some cultures have rituals for women to purify themselves after birth, and not just non-Western cultures. In the Bible, the 12th chapter of the book of Leviticus is devoted to ritual purification of women after childbirth, and until recent decades the Catholic church had a special ritual for new mothers to purify themselves.

Why would such beliefs develop? A frequent motivation for the development of cultural beliefs appears to be the desire for control (Jones & Kay, 2003). Birth is often fraught with pain and peril. Humans, faced with this unpleasant prospect, develop beliefs they hope will enable them to avoid, or at least minimize, the pain and peril. It is a comfort to believe that if certain rituals are performed, the mother, the baby, and everyone else will make it through the process unscathed.

The placenta is a component of the birth process that has often carried its own special cultural beliefs. Perhaps because delivery of the placenta is potentially dangerous, many cultures have developed beliefs that the placenta itself is potentially dangerous and must be disposed of properly so that no unpleasant consequences will result (Jones & Kay, 2003). Failure to do so is believed to carry consequences as minor as pimples on the baby or as major as the baby's death.

In some cultures the methods for disposing of the placenta are clear and simple: burial, burning, or throwing it in a river, or keeping it in a special place reserved for placentas. For example, among the Navajo, an American Indian culture, the custom was to bury the placenta in a sacred place to underscore the baby's bonds to the ancestral land (Selander, 2011). In other cultures, the traditions surrounding the placenta are more elaborate and involve beliefs that the placenta has a spirit or soul of its own. In these cultures, the placenta is not simply thrown away but given a proper burial similar to that given to a person. For example, in several parts of the world, including Ghana, Malaysia, and Indonesia, the placenta is treated as the baby's semihuman sibling (Cassidy, 2006). Following delivery, the midwife washes the placenta and buries it as she would a stillborn infant. In some cultures the burial includes prayers to the placenta imploring it not to harm the newborn child or the mother.

In developed countries the placenta is recognized as having special value as a source of hormones and nutrients. Hospitals give their placentas to researchers, or to cosmetic manufacturers who use them to make products such as hair conditioner (Jones & Kay, 2003). Some people in Western countries even advocate consuming part of the placenta because it is full of nutrients that can provide a boost to an exhausted new mother about to begin nursing. It also contains the hormone oxytocin, which helps prevent postpartum hemorrhage. Few human cultures have been found to have a custom of eating the placenta, although in some parts of the Philippines midwives add placental blood to a porridge intended to strengthen the new mother (Cassidy, 2006). Also, in traditional Chinese medicine dried placenta is sometimes used to stimulate maternal milk production (Tierra & Tierra, 1998).

WHO HELPS? Although there is great cultural variation in beliefs about birth, there is relatively little variation among traditional cultures in who assists with the birth. Almost always, the main assistants are older women (Bel & Bel, 2007). In one early study of birth practices in 60 traditional cultures, elderly women assisted in 58 of them (Ford, 1945). Rarely, men have been found to be the main birth attendants, such as in some parts of Mexico and the Philippines. More typically, all men are forbidden from even being present during birth, much less serving as the central helper (Newton & Newton, 2003). However, sometimes fathers assist by holding up the mother as she leans, stands, or squats to deliver the baby.

Although a variety of women are typically present with the mother at birth, especially her relatives, the women who are charged with managing the birth process usually have a special status as midwives. Midwives tend to be older women who have had children themselves but are now beyond childbearing age. They have direct experience with childbirth but no longer have young children to care for, so that they are available and able when called to duty.

There are a variety of ways a woman may become a midwife (Cosminsky, 2003). In some cultures, such as in Guatemala and the Ojibwa tribe of American Indians, she receives what she believes to be a supernatural calling in a dream or vision (Rogoff, 2011). In other cultures, the position of midwife is inherited from mother to daughter. Still other cultures allow women to volunteer to be midwives. Regardless of how she comes to the position, typically the woman who is to be a midwife spends several years in apprenticeship to a more experienced midwife before taking the lead in assisting with a birth. Through apprenticeship she learns basic principles of hygiene, methods to ease the birth, and practices for prenatal and postnatal care.

Cultures have varied widely in how they regard midwives. Most often, the midwife has a respected status in her culture, and is held in high regard for her knowledge and skills. Among the Zinacantec Maya of Mexico, for example, the midwife is given special gifts during prenatal visits with the expectant mother and when the baby is born. However, in some cultures midwives have been regarded with contempt or fear. In India, for example, midwives come from the *castes* (social status groups) that have the lowest status (Cosminsky, 2003). Birth is believed to be unclean and polluting, so only the lowest castes are deemed fit to be involved in it.

Today, in developed countries and increasingly in developing countries, birth usually takes place in a medical setting and is

Midwives are usually the main birth assistants in rural areas of developing countries. Here, a midwife attends to a pregnant woman in her Cambodian village home.

overseen by medical personnel, including an obstetrician and one or more nurses or nurse-midwives. In addition, the birth mother's husband or partner, mother, mother-in-law, or sisters may be present, but as sources of emotional support, not as assistants in the birth (da Motta et al., 2006).

Cultural Variations in Methods for Easing the Birth Process

LO 3.5   Compare and contrast cultural practices and medical methods for easing the birth process.

Midwives are often engaged in the prenatal assessment of the pregnancy and in the process of labor and delivery. When the pregnant woman begins to go into labor, the midwife is called, and the expectant mother's female relatives gather around her. Sometimes the midwife gives the mother-to-be medicine intended to ease the pain of labor and birth. Many cultures have used herbal medicines, but in the Ukraine, traditionally the first act of the midwife upon arriving at the home of a woman in labor was to give her a generous glass of whiskey (Newton & Newton, 2003). Expectant mothers may be fed special foods to strengthen them for the labor to come. In some cultures women are urged to lie quietly between contractions, but in others they are encouraged to walk around or even to exercise.

During the early part of labor, the midwife may use the intervals between contractions to explain to the expectant mother what is to come—how the contractions will occur more and more frequently, how the woman will eventually have to push the baby out, and what the woman's position should be during the birth (Bel & Bel, 2007). Sometimes the other women present add to the midwife's advice, describing or even demonstrating their own positioning when giving birth. As labor continues, often the midwife and other women present with the mother will urge her on during contractions with "birth talk," calling out encouragement and instructions, and sometimes even scolding her if she screams too loud or complains too much (Bergstrom et al., 2009, 2010).

The longer the labor, the more exhausted the mother and the greater the potential danger to mother and child. Consequently, cultures have created a wide variety of practices intended to speed it up. The most widespread approach, appearing in cultures in all parts of the world, is to use some kind of imagery or metaphor associated with opening up or expulsion (Bates & Turner, 2003). For example, in the Philippines a key (for "opening" the cervix) and a comb (for "untangling" the umbilical cord) are placed under the laboring woman's pillow. In other cultures, ropes are unknotted, bottles are uncorked, or animals are let out of their pens.

In some traditional cultures, the midwife calls on spiritual assistance from a *shaman*, a religious leader believed to have special powers and knowledge of the spirit world. Among the Cuna Indians, for example, according to traditional beliefs, difficult births are caused by the spirit of the womb, Muu, who may, for no apparent reason, decide to hold on to the fetus and prevent it from coming out (Lévi-Strauss, 1967). The shaman's job is to invoke magic that will release the fetus from Muu's grip, by singing a song that sends a spirit inside the womb to wage combat against Muu.

Do any of these traditional practices do any good to the woman suffering a difficult labor? Medically, obviously not, but be careful before you dismiss the effects of the shaman's song too easily. There is abundant evidence of the *placebo effect*, which means that sometimes if people believe something affects them, it does, just by virtue of the power of their belief. In the classic example, if people are given a sugar pill containing no medicine and told it is a pain reliever, many of them will report experiencing reduced pain (Balodis et al., 2011). It was not the sugar pill that reduced their pain but their belief that the pill would reduce their pain. In the case of the shaman assisting the birth, the mother may feel genuine relief, not only because of her belief in the shaman's song but also because of the emotional and social support the shaman's presence represents (Bates & Turner, 2003).

Emotional and social support help ease the birth for women in developed countries as well (da Motta et al., 2006). Here are some nonmedical strategies recommended by health professionals to ease the woman's discomfort during labor (Mayo Clinic Staff, 2011):

- Rock in a rocking chair.
- Breathe in a steady rhythm, fast or slow, depending on what is most comfortable.
- Take a warm shower or bath.
- Place a cool, damp cloth on the forehead.
- Take a walk, stopping to breathe through contractions.
- Have a massage between contractions.

Medical interventions are also common today in developed countries. Women in labor often receive an **epidural**, which involves the injection of an anesthetic drug into the spinal fluid to help them manage the pain while remaining alert (Vallejo et al., 2007). If administered in the correct dosage, an epidural allows enough feeling to remain so that the woman can push when the time comes, but sometimes synthetic oxytocin has to be administered because the epidural causes contractions to become sluggish. Rates of receiving epidurals for women having a vaginal birth vary widely in developed countries, for example 76 percent in the United States, 52 percent in Sweden, 45 percent in Canada, and 24 percent in New Zealand (Lane, 2009). The reasons for these variations are not clear.

Several technological developments have made the birth process safer for both mother and baby. **Electronic fetal monitoring (EFM)** tracks the fetus's heartbeat, either externally through the mother's abdomen or directly by running a wire through the cervix and placing a sensor on the fetus's scalp. In the United States, about 85 percent of births include EFM (Martin et al., 2005). Changes in the fetal heart rate may indicate distress and call for intervention. However, heart rate changes are not easy to interpret and do not necessarily indicate distress, so use of EFM may increase the rate of unnecessary c-sections (Thacker & Stroup, 2003). EFM is most useful in preterm or other high-risk deliveries, when fetal distress is most likely to occur.

An important part of the strategy for easing the birth process in many cultures is the physical position of the mother. In nearly all cultures some kind of upright position is used, most commonly kneeling or sitting, followed in prevalence by squatting or standing (Newton & Newton, 2003). In the Maya language of Tzotzil, the word for midwife literally means "the one who catches the baby," marking the upright position of delivery. Often a woman will lean back on a hammock or bed between contractions, but take a more upright position as birth becomes imminent. Lying flat was the most prevalent delivery position in developed countries during the 20th century, but it is rarely used in traditional cultures because it makes delivery more difficult by failing to make use of gravity. Today in developed countries many hospitals use a semisitting, half-reclining position (Murkoff & Mazel, 2008).

After birth, typically the baby is laid on the mother's abdomen until the placenta and umbilical cord are expelled from her uterus. Although there is often great joy and relief at the birth of the baby, the attention of the birth attendants and the mother is immediately directed toward delivering the placenta. A variety of strategies are used to promote the process, such as massage, medication, rituals involving opening or expelling, or attempts to make the woman sneeze or vomit (Cosminsky, 2003). Most common across cultures is the use of herbal medicines, administered as a tea or a douche (a liquid substance placed into the vagina). In developed countries, synthetic oxytocin may be used to promote contractions that will expel the placenta.

After the placenta is expelled, the umbilical cord is cut. Usually the cord is tied with thread, string, or plant fiber. In traditional cultures, some of the customs involved in cutting or treating the cord are unwittingly hazardous to the baby (Cosminsky, 2003). Tools used to cut the cord include bamboo, shell, broken glass, sickles, and razors, and they may not be clean, resulting in transmission of disease to the baby. Methods for treating the cut cord include, in one part of northern India, ash from burned cow dung mixed with dirt, which is now known to increase sharply the baby's risk of tetanus.

epidural
during birth process, injection of an anesthetic drug into the spinal fluid to help the mother manage the pain while also remaining alert

electronic fetal monitoring (EFM)
method that tracks the fetus's heartbeat, either externally through the mother's abdomen or directly by running a wire through the cervix and placing a sensor on the fetus's scalp

Summary: Birth and Its Cultural Context

LO 3.1 **Describe the three stages of the birth process.**

The three stages of the birth process are labor, delivery, and expelling of the placenta and umbilical cord. During labor, the contractions of the muscles in the uterus cause the mother's cervix to dilate in preparation for the baby's exit. By the end of labor, the cervix has opened to about 10 centimeters (4½ inches). During delivery, the woman pushes the fetus through the cervix and out of the uterus. In the final stage of the birth process, contractions continue as the placenta and umbilical cord are expelled.

LO 3.2 **Name two common types of birth complications and explain how they can be overcome by cesarean delivery.**

Cesarean-section is a method of delivery that is used to overcome birth complications. Two common birth complications are failure to progress, which occurs when the birth process is taking longer than normal, and the breech presentation of the fetus, which means the fetus is turned around so that the feet or buttocks are positioned to come first out of the birth canal. Today, c-section is generally safe for mothers and infants.

LO 3.3 **Summarize the history of birth in the West from the 15th century to today.**

Midwives have assisted in most births historically, but during the 15th century many were accused of being witches and were put to death. In the 18th and 19th centuries, birth became increasingly medical, but deadly infections were often spread to mothers by doctors with unclean hands. In the early 20th century the attempts to make birth safer were overzealous and overly medical, as birth was taken over by doctors and hospitals, with the maternal experience disregarded. In the past 50 years most of the West has moved toward a more reasonable middle ground, seeking to minimize medical intervention but making it available when necessary.

LO 3.4 **Describe cultural variations in birth beliefs and identify who may assist with the birth.**

Because birth is often dangerous, many traditional cultures have developed beliefs that childbirth puts a woman in a state of being spiritually unclean. The placenta is often disposed of carefully in traditional cultures because of beliefs that it is potentially dangerous or even semi-human. In most cultures, women giving birth are attended by female relatives and an older woman ("midwife" or similar title) who has experience assisting in the birth process.

LO 3.5 **Compare and contrast cultural practices and medical methods for easing the birth process.**

In traditional cultures, midwives ease birth pain through massage techniques, reassurance, and herbal medicines. In developed countries, an anesthetic drug called an *epidural* is often injected into a woman's spinal fluid to help manage the pain.

Section 2   The Neonate

Learning Objectives

3.6 Identify the features of the two major scales most often used to assess neonatal health.

3.7 Identify the neonatal classifications for low birth weight and describe the consequences and major treatments.

3.8 Describe the differences in maternal and neonatal mortality both within and between developed countries and developing countries.

3.9 Describe neonates' patterns of waking and sleeping, including how and why these patterns differ across cultures.

3.10 Describe the neonatal reflexes, including those that have a functional purpose and those that do not.

3.11 Describe the neonate's sensory abilities with respect to touch, taste and smell, hearing, and sight.

fontanels

soft spots on the skull between loosely joined pieces of the skull that shift during the birth process to assist passage through the birth canal

neonate

newborn baby, up to 4 weeks old

At birth, babies are covered with vernix, which protects their skin.

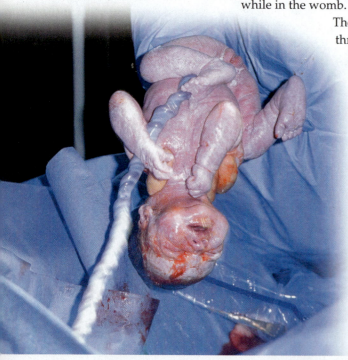

THE NEONATE: The Neonate's Health

Out comes baby at last, after 9 months or so inside the womb. If you were expecting cuddly and cute from the beginning, you may be in for a surprise. The baby may be covered with fine, fuzzy hair called *lanugo*, a vestige of our hairy primate ancestors. This hair will be shed after a few days, fortunately. The skin may also be coated all over with an oily, cheesy substance called *vernix*, which protected the skin from chapping while in the womb.

The head may be a bit misshapen as a consequence of being squeezed through the birth canal. One evolutionary solution to the problem of getting large-brained human fetuses out of the womb is that the skull of the infant's head is not yet fused into one bone. Instead, it is composed of several loosely joined pieces that can move around as necessary during the birth process. In between the pieces are two soft spots called **fontanels**, one on top and one toward the back of the head. It will take about 18 months before the pieces of the skull are firmly joined and the fontanels have disappeared.

It was only 9 months ago that sperm and ovum united to make a single cell, but by birth the newborn baby has 10 trillion cells! The typical newborn child, or **neonate**, is about 20 inches (50 centimeters) long and weighs about 7.5 pounds (3.4 kilograms). (The first 4 weeks of life comprise the *neonatal period*.) Neonates tend to lose about 10 percent of their weight in their first few days because they lose fluids and do not eat much (Verma et al., 2009). By the fifth day they start to regain this weight, and by the end of the second week most are back up to their birth weight.

Measuring Neonatal Health

LO 3.6   **Identify the features of the two major scales most often used to assess neonatal health.**

About half of all neonates have a yellowish look to their skin and eyeballs in the first few days of life. This condition, known as **neonatal jaundice**, is the result of the immaturity of the liver (Madlon-Kay, 2002). In most cases, neonatal jaundice disappears after a few days as the liver begins to function normally, but if it lasts more than a few days it should be treated, or it can result in brain damage (American Academy of Pediatrics [AAP], 2004). The most effective treatment is a simple one, *phototherapy*, which involves exposing the neonate to colored light; blue works best (AAP, 2004).

In the transition from the fetal environment to the outside world, the first few minutes are crucial. Especially important is for neonates to begin to breathe on their own, after months of obtaining their oxygen through their mothers' umbilical cord. Most neonates begin to breathe as soon as they are exposed to air, even before the umbilical cord is cut. However, if they do not, the consequences can become severe quickly. Deprivation of oxygen, a condition known as **anoxia**, results in swift and massive death of brain cells. If a neonate suffers anoxia for even a few minutes, the result can be permanent cognitive damage.

Because the transition from the fetal environment is crucial and occasionally problematic, methods have been developed for assessing neonatal health. In Western countries, two of the most widely used methods are the Apgar scale and the Brazelton Neonatal Behavioral Assessment Scale (NBAS).

THE APGAR SCALE The **Apgar scale** is named after its creator, the pediatrician Virginia Apgar (1953). The letters *APGAR* also correspond to the five subtests that comprise the scale: Appearance (color), Pulse (heart rate), Grimace (reflex irritability), Activity (muscle tone), and Respiration (breathing). The neonate is rated on each of these five subscales, receiving a score of 0, 1, or 2 (see **Table 3.1**), with the overall score ranging from 0–10. Neonates are rated twice, first about a minute after birth and then after 5 minutes because sometimes a neonate's condition can change quickly during this time, for better or worse.

A score of 7 to 10 means the neonate is in good to excellent condition. Scores in this range are received by over 98 percent of U.S. babies (Martin et al., 2003). If the score is from 4 to 6, anoxia is likely and the neonate is in need of assistance to begin breathing. If the score is 3 or below, the neonate is in life-threatening danger and immediate medical assistance is required. In addition to their usefulness immediately after birth, Apgar scores

neonatal jaundice

yellowish pallor common in the first few days of life due to immaturity of the liver

anoxia

deprivation of oxygen during birth process and soon after that can result in serious neurological damage within minutes

Apgar scale

neonatal assessment scale with five subtests: Appearance (color), Pulse (heart rate), Grimace (reflex irritability), Activity (muscle tone), and Respiration (breathing)

Table 3.1 The Apgar Scale

Total Score: 7–10 = Good to excellent condition; 4–6 = Requires assistance to breathe; 3 or below = Life-threatening danger

Subtest	0	1	2
Appearance (Body color)	Blue and pale	Body pink, but extremities blue	Entire body pink
Pulse (Heart rate)	Absent	Slow—less than 100 beats per minute	Fast—100–140 beats per minute
Grimace (Reflex irritability)	No response	Grimace	Coughing, sneezing, and crying
Activity (Muscle tone)	Limp and flaccid	Weak, inactive, but some flexion of extremities	Strong, active motion
Respiration (Breathing)	No breathing for more than 1 minute	Irregular and slow	Good breathing with normal crying

SOURCE: Based on Apgar (1953).

predict the neonate's risk of death in the first month of life, which can alert physicians that careful monitoring is necessary (Casey et al., 2001).

THE BRAZELTON SCALE Another widely used scale of neonatal functioning is the **Brazelton Neonatal Behavioral Assessment Scale (NBAS)**. The NBAS contains 27 items assessing *reflexes* (such as blinking), *physical states* (such as irritability and excitability), *responses to social stimulation*, and *central nervous system instability* (indicated by symptoms such as tremors). Based on these 27 items, the neonate receives an overall rating of "worrisome," "normal," or "superior" (Nugent & Brazelton, 2000; Nugent et al., 2009).

In contrast to the Apgar scale, which is administered immediately after birth, the NBAS is usually performed about a day after birth but can be given any time in the first 2 months. The NBAS most effectively predicts future development if it is given a day after birth and then about a week later. Neonates who are rated normal or superior at both points or who show a "recovery curve" from worrisome to normal or superior have good prospects for development over the next several years, whereas neonates who are worrisome at both points or go down from normal or superior to worrisome are at risk for early developmental problems (Ohgi et al., 2003).

For at-risk neonates as well as others, the NBAS can promote the development of the relationship between parents and their infants. In one study of Brazilian mothers, those who took part in an NBAS-guided discussion of their infants a few days after birth were more likely to smile, vocalize, and establish eye contact with their infants a month later, compared to mothers in a control group who received only general health care information (Wendland-Carro et al., 1999). In a U.S. study of full-term and preterm neonates, parents in both groups who participated in an NBAS program interacted more confidently with their babies than parents who did not take part in the program (Eiden & Reifman, 1996).

The NBAS has also been used in research to examine differences among neonates across cultures and how those differences interact with parenting practices (Nugent et al., 2009). For example, studies comparing Asian and White U.S. neonates on the NBAS have found that the Asian neonates tend to be calmer and less irritable (Muret-Wagstaff & Moore, 1989). This difference may be partly biological, but it also appears to be related to parenting differences. Asian mothers tended to respond quickly to neonates' distress and attempt to soothe them, whereas White mothers were more likely to let the neonates fuss for a while before tending to them. In another study, in Zambia, many of the neonates were born with low birth weights and were rated worrisome on the NBAS a day after birth (Brazelton et al., 1976). However, a week later most of the worrisome neonates had become normal or superior on the NBAS. The researchers attributed this change to the Zambian mothers' custom of carrying the baby close to their bodies during most of the day, providing soothing comfort as well as sensory stimulation.

Low Birth Weight

LO 3.7 Identify the neonatal classifications for low birth weight and describe the consequences and major treatments.

The weight of a baby at birth is one of the most important indicators of its prospects for survival and healthy development. Neonates are considered to have **low birth weight** if they are born weighing less than 5.5 pounds (2,500 grams). **Very low-birth-weight** neonates weigh less than 3.3 pounds (1,500 grams) at birth, and **extremely low-birth-weight** neonates weigh less than 2.2 pounds (1,000 grams) at birth. Some neonates with low birth weights are **preterm**, meaning that they were born 3 or more weeks earlier than the optimal 40 weeks after conception. Other low-birth-weight neonates are **small for date**, meaning that they weigh less than 90 percent of the average for other neonates who were born at the same *gestational age* (number of weeks since conception). Small-for-date neonates are especially at risk, with an infant death rate four times higher than preterm infants (Arcangeli et al., 2012).

Brazelton Neonatal Behavioral Assessment Scale (NBAS)

27-item scale of neonatal functioning with overall ratings "worrisome," "normal," and "superior"

low birth weight

term for neonates weighing less than 5.5 pounds (2,500 grams)

very low birth weight

term for neonates who weigh less than 3.3 pounds (1,500 grams) at birth

extremely low birth weight

term for neonates who weigh less than 2.2 pounds (1,000 grams) at birth

preterm

babies born at 37 weeks gestation or less

small for date

term applied to neonates who weigh less than 90 percent of other neonates who were born at the same gestational age

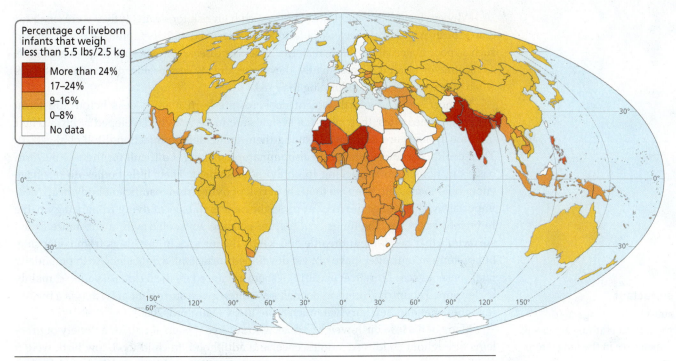

Map 3.2 Rates of Low Birth Weight Around the World

Why are rates so high in developing countries?

SOURCE: Based on UNICEF (2014a, b).

Rates of low-birth-weight neonates vary widely among world regions (UNICEF, 2014a, b). As **Map 3.2** shows, the overall rate worldwide is 15 percent. Asia and Africa have the highest rates, and Europe the lowest. The current rates in the United States (8 percent) and Canada (6 percent) are lower than in developing regions of the world but higher than in Europe. Within the United States, rates of low birth weight are rising and are about twice as high among African Americans as among other ethnic groups, for reasons that may include lower likelihood of good prenatal care and higher levels of stress (Casey Foundation, 2010; Giscombe & Lovel, 2005). Rates of low birthweight in the United States may be on the rise because of the correlated rise in pre-term births.

The causes of low birth weight also vary widely among world regions. In developing countries, the main cause is that mothers are frequently malnourished, in poor health, and receive little or no prenatal care. In developed countries, the primary cause of low birth weight is the mother's cigarette smoking (Rückinger et al., 2010a, b). Other contributors to low birth weight are multiple births (the more babies in the womb at once, the lower their birth weights), use of alcohol or other drugs during pregnancy, and young or old maternal age (younger than 17 or older than 40) (Gavin et al., 2011).

CONSEQUENCES OF LOW BIRTH WEIGHT Low-birth-weight babies are at high risk of death in their first year of life. Even in developed countries with advanced medical care, low birth weight is the second most common cause of death in infancy, next to genetic birth defects (Martin et al., 2005). Very low-birth-weight neonates and extremely low-birth-weight neonates are at especially high risk for early death (Tamaru et al., 2011). Even in the United States, which has the most advanced medical technology in the world, 24 percent of neonates who weigh less than 3.3 pounds die during their first year, compared to just 1 percent of those born at 3.3 to 5.5 pounds (Child Trends, 2014). In developing countries, where low birth weight is most common, deaths resulting from low birth weight contribute to higher overall rates of neonatal mortality.

Why are low-birth-weight neonates at such high risk for death? If they were small for date at birth, it was likely because of factors that interfered with their prenatal development, such as poor maternal nutrition, maternal illness or disease, or exposure to teratogens such as nicotine or alcohol. Consequently, they were already less healthy than other neonates when they were born, compounding their risk.

In most cases, low-birth-weight neonates are born many weeks before full term. For preterm neonates, their physical systems are inadequately developed at birth. Their immune systems are immature, leaving them vulnerable to infection (Stoll et al., 2004). Their central nervous systems are also immature, making it difficult for them to perform basic functions such as sucking to obtain nourishment. Their little bodies do not have enough fat to insulate them, so they are at risk of dying from insufficient body heat. Most importantly, their lungs are immature, so they are in danger of dying from being unable to breathe properly. The lungs of a mature neonate are coated with a substance called **surfactant** that helps them breathe and keeps the air sacs in the lungs from collapsing, but preterm infants often have not yet developed surfactant, a deficiency with potentially fatal consequences (Porath et al., 2011). Where advanced medical care is available, mainly in developed countries, preterm neonates are often given surfactant at birth (via a breathing tube), making their survival much more likely (Mugford, 2006).

Many of the low-birth-weight babies who survive remain at risk for a variety of problems throughout childhood, adolescence, and adulthood. In childhood, low birth weight predicts physical problems such as asthma and cognitive problems that include language delays and poor school performance (Davis, 2003; Marlow et al., 2005). In adolescence, low birth weight predicts relatively low intelligence-test scores and greater likelihood of repeating a grade (Martin et al., 2008). In adulthood, low birth weight predicts brain abnormalities, attention deficits, and low educational attainment (Fearon et al., 2004; Hofman et al., 2004; Strang-Karlsson et al., 2008).

The lower the birth weight, the worse the problems. Most neonates who weigh 3.3 to 5.5 pounds (1,500 to 2,500 grams) are likely to show no major impairments after a few years as long as they receive adequate nutrition and medical care, but neonates weighing less than 3.3 pounds, the very low-birth-weight and extremely low-birth-weight babies, are likely to have enduring problems in multiple respects (Child Trends, 2014; Davis, 2003). With an unusually healthy and enriched environment, some of the negative consequences of low birth weight can be avoided, even for very low-birth-weight babies (Doyle et al., 2004; Martin et al., 2008). However, in developed countries as well as in developing countries, low-birth-weight babies are most likely to be born to parents who have the fewest resources (UNICEF, 2014a, b; WHO, 2011).

surfactant

substance in lungs that promotes breathing and keeps the air sacs in the lungs from collapsing

kangaroo care

recommended care for preterm and low-birth-weight neonates, in which mothers or fathers are advised to place the baby skin-to-skin on their chests for 2 to 3 hours a day for the early weeks of life

Babies born with low birth weights are at risk for multiple problems. Unlike this neonate in Uganda, most low-birth-weight neonates in developing countries do not have access to advanced medical care.

TREATMENT FOR LOW-BIRTH-WEIGHT BABIES

What can be done for low-birth-weight babies? In developing countries, where few of them receive medical treatment, traditional methods of infant care are helpful. In many traditional cultures, young infants are strapped close to their mother's body for most of the time as she goes about her daily life (Small, 1998). In the West, this has been studied as a method called **kangaroo care**, in which mothers or fathers are advised to place their preterm newborns skin-to-skin on their chests for 2 to 3 hours a day during the early weeks of life (Warnock et al., 2010).

Research has shown that kangaroo care has highly beneficial effects on neonatal functioning. It helps newborns stabilize and regulate bodily functions such as heart rate, breathing, body temperature, and sleep–wake cycles (Ludington-Hoe, 2013; Reid, 2004). Preterm infants who receive kangaroo care are more likely to survive their first year, and they have longer periods of sleep, cry less, and gain weight faster than other preterm infants (Charpak et al., 2005; Kostandy et al., 2008). Mothers benefit as well. Kangaroo care gives them more confidence in caring for their tiny, vulnerable baby, which leads to more success in breast feeding (Feldman et al., 2003; Ludington-Hoe, 2013). The effects of kangaroo care on low-birth-weight babies are so well established that now it is used in more than three fourths of neonatal intensive care units in the United States, and nearly always with preterm neonates in northern Europe (Ludington-Hoe, 2013). An Italian study found that kangaroo care was practiced in two thirds of the neonatal intensive care units (de Vonderweid & Leonessa, 2009).

The other traditional method of infant care that is helpful for low-birth-weight babies is *infant massage*. This is a widespread custom in Asia, India, and Africa, not just for vulnerable babies, but for all of them (McClure, 2000). In the West, infant massage developed because low-birth-weight babies are often placed in an *isolette*, a covered, sterile chamber that provides oxygen and a controlled temperature. The isolette protects neonates from infection but also cuts them off from sensory and social stimulation. Infant massage, pioneered in the West by Tiffany Field and her colleagues (Field, 1998; Field et al., 2010), was intended to relieve the neonate's isolation.

Research has now established the effectiveness of massage in promoting the healthy development of low-birth-weight babies. Preterm neonates who receive three 15-minute massages a day in their first days of life gain weight faster than other preterm babies, and they are more active and alert (Field, 2001; Field et al., 2010). The massages work by triggering the release of hormones that promote weight gain, muscle development, and neurological development (Dieter et al., 2003; Ferber et al., 2002; Field et al., 2010). In the United States, 38 percent of hospitals practice massage in their neonatal intensive care units (Field et al., 2010).

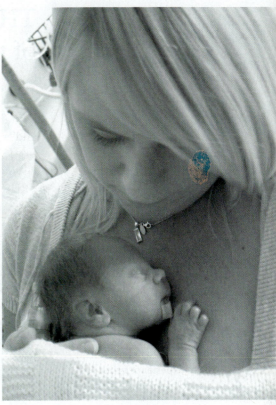

Kangaroo care has many benefits for low-birth-weight babies.

Neonatal and Maternal Mortality

LO 3.8   **Describe the differences in maternal and neonatal mortality both within and between developed countries and developing countries.**

As with rates of low birth weight, rates of infant and maternal mortality are vastly higher in developing countries than in developed countries. In much of the world, birth remains fraught with risk. However, there are some hopeful signs. Maternal mortality has decreased substantially in developing countries over the past 30 years because of improvements in nutrition and access to health care (Hogan et al., 2010; UNICEF, 2014a, b).

There is also substantial variation in neonatal and maternal mortality within developed countries, especially within the United States (UNICEF, 2014a, b). Infant mortality in the United States is about 1 in 170 overall, but it is lower for Whites (1/198) than for all other ethnic groups combined (1/115) and much lower than it is for African Americans (1/90) (National Vital Statistics Report, 2014). Variation in birth outcomes has been linked to income inequality in the United States and Japan (Fujiwara et al., 2013). Neonatal mortality is over twice as high for African Americans as for Whites primarily as a result of greater poverty and lower access to high-quality medical care among African Americans (CDC, 2014). However, neonatal mortality has dropped steeply across ethnic groups in the United States since 1980, by nearly half. Current rates among Latinos and Asian Americans are similar to those for Whites (CDC, 2014). In contrast, maternal mortality has been rising steadily since 1980, for reasons that are not clear (U.S. Bureau of the Census, 2010). Like neonatal mortality, maternal mortality is much higher among African Americans than in other ethnic groups, again because of socioeconomic issues.

THE NEONATE: Physical Functioning of the Neonate

Physical functioning in the first few weeks of life is different in some important ways when compared to the rest of life. Neonates sleep more and have a wider range of reflexes than the rest of us do. Their senses are mostly well developed at birth, although hearing and especially sight take some weeks to mature.

Neonatal Sleeping Patterns

LO 3.9 **Describe neonates' patterns of waking and sleeping, including how and why these patterns differ across cultures.**

rapid eye movement (REM) sleep

phase of the sleep cycle in which a person's eyes move back and forth rapidly under the eyelids; persons in REM sleep experience other physiological changes as well

Most neonates sleep 16 to 17 hours a day.

Most neonates spend more time asleep than awake. The average for neonates is 16 to 17 hours of sleep a day, although there is great variation, from about 10 hours to about 21 (Peirano et al., 2003).

Neonates not only sleep much of the time, the pattern and quality of their sleep is different than it will be later in infancy and beyond. Rather than sleeping 16 to 17 hours straight, they sleep for a few hours, wake up for awhile, sleep a few more hours, and wake up again. Their sleep–wake patterns are governed by when they get hungry, not whether it is light or dark outside (Davis et al., 2004). Of course, neonates' sleep–wake patterns do not fit very well with how most adults prefer to sleep, so parents are often sleep-deprived in the early weeks of their children's lives (Burnham et al., 2002). By about 4 months of age most infants have begun to sleep for longer periods, usually about 6 hours in a row at night, and their total sleep has declined to about 14 hours a day.

Another way that neonates' sleep is distinctive is that they spend an especially high proportion of their sleep in **rapid eye movement (REM) sleep**, so called because during this kind of sleep a person's eyes move back and forth rapidly under the eyelids. A person in REM sleep experiences other physiological changes as well, such as irregular heart rate and breathing and (in males) an erection. Adults spend about 20 percent of their sleep time in REM sleep, but neonates are in REM sleep about one half the time they are sleeping (Burnham et al., 2002). Furthermore, adults do not enter REM until about an hour after falling asleep, but neonates enter it almost immediately. By about 3 months of age, time spent in REM sleep has fallen to 40 percent, and infants no longer begin their sleep cycle with it.

In adults, REM sleep is the time when dreams take place. Are neonates dreaming during their extensive REM sleep periods? It is difficult to say, of course—they're not telling—but researchers in this area have generally concluded that the answer is no. Neonate's brain-wave patterns during REM sleep are different from the patterns of adults. For adults, REM brain waves look similar to waking brain waves, but for infants the REM brain waves are different than during either waking or non-REM sleep (Arditi-Babchuck et al., 2009). Researchers believe that for neonates, REM sleep stimulates brain development (McNamara & Sullivan, 2000). This seems to be supported by research showing that the percentage of REM sleep is even greater in fetuses than in neonates, and greater in preterm than in full-term neonates (Arditi-Babchuck et al., 2009; de Weerd & van den Bossche, 2003).

In addition to neonates' distinctive sleep patterns, they have a variety of other states of arousal that change frequently. When they are not sleeping, they may be alert but they may also be drowsy, dazed, fussing, or in a sleep–wake transition.

So far this description of neonates' sleep–wake patterns has been based on research in Western countries, but baby care is an area for which there is wide cultural variation that may influence sleep–wake patterns. In many traditional cultures, neonates and young infants are in physical contact with their mothers almost constantly, and this has important effects on the babies' states of arousal and sleep–wake patterns. For example, among the Kipsigis of Kenya, mothers strap their babies to their backs in the early months of life as they go about their daily work and social activities (Anders & Taylor, 1994; Super & Harkness, 2009). Swaddled cozily on Mom's back, the babies spend more time napping and dozing during the day than a baby in a developed country would. At night, Kipsigis babies are not placed in a separate room but sleep right alongside their mothers, so they are able to feed whenever they wish. Consequently, for the first year of life they rarely sleep more than 3 hours straight, day or night. In contrast, by 8 months of age American babies typically sleep about 8 hours at night without waking.

Neonatal Reflexes

LO 3.10 **Describe the neonatal reflexes, including those that have a functional purpose and those that do not.**

Looking at a newborn baby, you might think that it will be many months before it can do much, other than just lie there. Actually, though, neonates have a remarkable range of **reflexes**, which are automatic responses to certain kinds of stimulation. A total of 27 reflexes are present at birth or shortly after (Futagi et al., 2009). Some examples are shown in **Table 3.2** and in the video *Reflexes*.

reflex
automatic response to certain kinds of stimulation

Watch REFLEXES

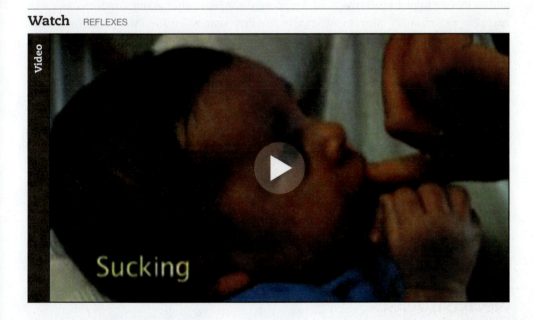

Sucking

Table 3.2 Neonatal Reflexes

Reflex	Stimulation	Response	Disappears by
Stepping	Hold baby under arms with feet touching floor	Makes stepping motions	2 months
Moro	Dip downward suddenly, or loud sound	Arch back, extend arms and legs outward, bring arms together swiftly	3 months
Babkin	Press and stroke both palms	Mouth opens, eyes close, head tilts forward	3 months
Sucking	Object or substance in mouth	Sucking	4 months
Rooting	Touch on cheek or mouth	Turn toward touch	4 months
Grasping	Object placed in palm	Hold tightly	4 months
Swimming	Baby is immersed in water	Holds breath, swims with arms and legs	4 months
Babinski	Stroke sole of foot	Foot twists in, toes fan out	8 months

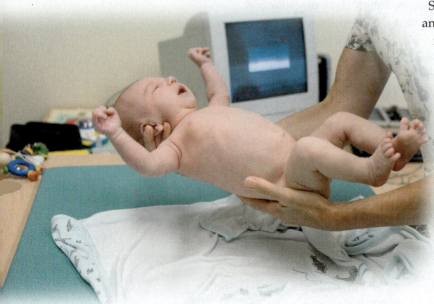

The Moro reflex is present at birth, but disappears by 3 months of age.

Some reflexes have clear survival value. Sucking and swallowing reflexes allow the neonate to obtain nourishment from the mother's breast. The **rooting reflex** helps neonates find the breast, because it causes them to turn their heads and open their mouths when touched on the cheek or the side of the mouth. The grasping reflex helps neonates hang on when something is placed in their palms. The **Moro reflex** serves a similar function, causing neonates to arch their backs, fling out their arms, and then bring their arms quickly together in an embrace, in response to a sensation of falling backward or a loud sound. Reflexes for coughing, gagging, sneezing, blinking, and shivering regulate neonates' sensory systems and help them avoid things in the environment that may be unhealthy.

Some reflexes are precursors of voluntary movements that will develop later. The stepping reflex can be observed about a month after birth, by holding an infant under the arms at a height that allows its feet to just touch the floor. Stepping disappears after about 2 months, but will reappear as voluntary movement later in the first year when the infant starts walking. The swimming reflex is one of the most surprising and remarkable. At about 1 month old, an infant placed face down in water will automatically hold its breath and begin making coordinated swimming movements. After 4 months this reflex has disappeared, and will become voluntary swimming movements only many years later.

Other reflexes have no apparent purpose, other than their obvious entertainment value. With the *Babkin reflex*, a neonate whose palms are firmly stroked will open its mouth, close its eyes, and tilt its head forward. With the *Babinski reflex*, when the sole of the neonate's foot is stroked, it will respond by twisting its foot inward as it fans out its toes (Singerman & Lee, 2008).

Most neonatal reflexes fade away after a few months because they are replaced by voluntary behavior. However, in the early weeks of life, reflexes serve as important indicators of normal development and healthy functioning (Schott & Rossor, 2003). Both the Apgar and the NBAS include items on reflex responses as an indirect measure of the neonate's neurological development.

Neonatal Senses

LO 3.11 Describe the neonate's sensory abilities with respect to touch, taste and smell, hearing, and sight.

The neonate's senses vary widely in how well developed they are at birth. Touch and taste are well developed, even in the womb, but sight does not mature until several months after birth. Let's look at each of the neonate's senses, from the most to the least developed.

TOUCH Touch is the earliest sense to develop. Even as early as 2 months gestation, the rooting reflex is present. By 7 months gestation, 2 months before a full-term birth, all the fetus's body parts respond to touch (Tyano et al., 2010). Most neonatal reflexes involve responses to touch.

Given that touch develops so early and is so advanced at birth, it is surprising that until recent decades, most physicians believed that neonates could not experience pain (Noia et al., 2008). In fact, surgery on neonates was usually performed without anesthetics. Physicians believed that even if neonates felt pain, they felt it only briefly,

rooting reflex

reflex that causes the neonate to turn its head and open its mouth when it is touched on the cheek or the side of the mouth; helps the neonate find the breast

Moro reflex

reflex in response to a sensation of falling backward or to a loud sound, in which the neonate arches its back, flings out its arms, and then brings its arms quickly together in an embrace

and they believed that the pain was less important than the danger of giving anesthetic medication to such a young child. This belief may have developed because neonates who experience pain (for example, boys who are circumcised) often either recover quickly and behave normally shortly afterward, or fall into a deep sleep immediately afterward, as a protective mechanism. Also, in response to some types of pain, such as being pricked on the heel, neonates take longer to respond (by several seconds) than they will a few months later (Tyano et al., 2010).

In recent years, research has established clearly that neonates feel pain. Their physiological reactions to pain are much like the reactions of people at other ages: their heart rates and blood pressure increase, their palms sweat, their muscles tense, and their pupils dilate (Warnock & Sandrin, 2004; Williams et al., 2009). They even have a specific kind of high-pitched, intense cry that indicates pain (Simons et al., 2003). Evidence also indicates that neonates who experience intense pain release stress hormones that interfere with sleep and feeding and heighten their sensitivity to later pain (Mitchell & Boss, 2002). For these reasons, physicians' organizations now recommend pain relief for neonates undergoing painful medical procedures (Noia et al., 2008). To minimize the dangers of anesthetics, nonmedical methods such as drinking sugar water can be used, or local rather than general anesthesia (Holsti & Grunau, 2010).

TASTE AND SMELL Like touch, taste is well developed even in the womb. The amniotic fluid that the fetus floats in has the flavor of whatever the mother has recently eaten, and neonates show a preference for the tastes and smells that were distinctive in the mother's diet in the days before birth (Schaal et al., 2000). In one study, when women drank carrot juice during pregnancy, their neonates were more likely to prefer the smell of carrots (Menella, 2000). Neonates exposed to the smell of their mother's amniotic fluid and another woman's amniotic fluid orient their attention to their mother's fluid (Marlier et al., 1998). In fact, neonates find the smell of their mother's amniotic fluid soothing, and cry less when it is present (Varendi et al., 1998).

In addition to showing an early preference for whatever is familiar from the womb, neonates have a variety of innate responses to tastes and smells. Like most children and adults, neonates prefer sweet tastes and smells over bitter or sour ones (Booth et al., 2010). If they smell or taste something bitter or sour, their noses crinkle up, their foreheads wrinkle, and their mouths show a displeased expression (Bartoshuk & Beauchamp, 1994). The video *Taste* shows neonates reacting to various tastes.

Watch TASTE

Preference for sweet tastes is present before birth. When an artificial sweetener is added to amniotic fluid, fetuses' swallowing becomes more frequent (Booth et al., 2010). After birth, preference for sweet tastes is demonstrated with a facial expression that looks like pleasure, and with a desire to consume more. As just noted, tasting something sweet can have a calming effect on neonates who are in pain. Preference for sweet tastes may be adaptive, because breast milk is slightly sweet (Porges et al., 1993). Enjoying the sweet taste of breast milk may make neonates more likely to nurse successfully.

In addition to their innate preferences, neonates quickly begin to discriminate smells after birth. At 2 days after birth, breast-feeding neonates show no difference in response between their mother's breast smell and the breast smell of another lactating mother, but by 4 days they orient more toward their mother's smell (Porter & Reiser, 2005).

HEARING Hearing is another sense that is quite well developed before birth because fetuses become familiar with their mother's voice and other sounds. After birth, they recognize distinctive sounds they heard in the womb. In the first few days of life, infants can turn their heads toward the source of a sound (Saffran et al., 2006).

Neonates have an innate sensitivity to human speech that is apparent from birth (Vouloumanos & Werker, 2004). Studies on this topic typically assess neonates' preferences by how vigorously they suck on a plastic nipple; the more frequently they suck, the stronger their preference for or attention to the sound. Using this method, studies have found that neonates prefer their mother's voice to other women's voices, and their mother's language to foreign languages (Vouloumanos et al., 2010). However, they show no preference for their father's voice over other male voices (Kisilevsky et al., 2003). This may be partly because they heard his voice less while in the womb, and partly because neonates generally prefer high-pitched voices over low-pitched voices.

Neonates and infants prefer sweet tastes to sour ones.

Neonates can distinguish small changes in speech sounds. In one study, neonates were given a special nipple that would produce a sound of a person saying "ba" every time they sucked on it (Aldridge et al., 2001). They sucked with enthusiasm for a minute or so, then their sucking pace slowed as they got used to the sound and perhaps bored with it. But when the sound changed to "ga," their sucking pace picked up, showing that they recognized the subtle change in the sound and responded to the novelty of it. Changes in neonate's sucking patterns show they also recognize the difference between two-syllable and three-syllable words, and between changes in emphasis such as when ma-*ma* changes to *ma*-ma (Sansavini et al., 1997).

In addition to their language sensitivity, neonates show a very early sensitivity to music (Levitin, 2007). At only a few days old, they respond when a series of musical notes changes from ascending to descending order (Trehub, 2001). After a few months, infants respond to a change in one note of a six-note melody, and to changes in musical keys (Trehub et al., 1985). One study even found that neonates preferred classical music over rock music (Spence & DeCasper, 1987).

Like language awareness, musical awareness begins prenatally. Neonates prefer songs their mother's sang to them during pregnancy to songs their mother sang to them for the first time after birth (Kisilevsky et al., 2003). Neonates' musical responses may simply reflect their familiarity with sounds they heard before birth, but it could also indicate an innate human responsiveness to music (Levitin, 2007). Music is frequently a part of human cultural rituals, and innate responsiveness to music may have served to enhance cohesiveness within human cultural groups.

Although neonates hear quite well in many respects, there are also some limitations to their hearing abilities that will improve over the first 2 years of life (Tharpe & Ashmead,

2001). One reason for these limitations is that it takes awhile after birth for the amniotic fluid to drain out of their ears. Another reason is that their hearing system is not physiologically mature until they are about 2 years old.

Neonates are unable to hear some soft sounds that adults can hear (Watkin, 2011). Overall, their hearing is better for high-pitched sounds than for midrange or low-pitched sounds (Aslin et al., 1998; Werner & Marean, 1996). They also have difficulty with **sound localization**, that is, with telling where a sound is coming from (Litovsky & Ashmead, 1997). In fact, their abilities for sound localization actually become worse for the first 2 months of life, but then improve rapidly and reach adult levels by 1 year old (Watkin, 2011).

Newborns' visual acuity is about 20/200, whereas expected adult vision is 20/20.

SIGHT Sight is the least developed of the neonate's senses (Atkinson, 2000). Newborns are legally blind. That is, they can make out objects or images that are close to their eyes, and their vision remains blurry. Several key structures of the eye are still immature at birth, specifically, (1) the muscles of the *lens*, which adjust the eyes' focus depending on the distance from the object; (2) the cells of the *retina*, the membrane in the back of the eye that collects visual information and converts it into a form that can be sent to the brain; (3) *cones*, which identify colors, and (4) the *optic nerve*, which transmits visual information from the retina to the brain.

At birth, neonates' vision is estimated to range from 20/200 to 20/600, which means that the clarity and accuracy of their perception of an object 20 feet away is comparable to a person with normal 20/20 vision looking at the same object from 200 to 600 feet away (Cavallini et al., 2002). Their visual acuity is best at a distance of 8 to 14 inches. Vision improves steadily as their eyes mature, and reaches 20/20 sometime in the second half of the first year. Their capacity for *binocular vision*, combining information from both eyes for perceiving depth and motion, is also limited at birth but matures quickly, by about 3 to 4 months old (Atkinson, 2000). Color vision matures at about the same pace. Neonates can distinguish between black, red, and white but not between white and other colors, probably because the cones are immature (Kellman & Arterberry, 2006). By 4 months old, infants are similar to adults in their perception of colors (Alexander & Hines, 2002; Delaney et al., 2000).

sound localization

perceptual ability for telling where a sound is coming from

Even newborns imitate some facial expressions of adults. Here, a newborn imitates the expression of developmental psychologist Andy Meltzoff.

Just as with taste and hearing, neonates show innate visual preferences (Colombo & Mitchell, 2009). ("Preference" is measured by how long they look at one visual stimulus compared to another. The longer they look, the more they are presumed to prefer the stimulus.) Even shortly after birth they prefer patterns to random designs, curved over straight lines, three-dimensional rather than two-dimensional objects, and colored over gray patterns. Above all, they prefer human faces over any other pattern (Pascalis & Kelly, 2009). This indicates that they are born with cells that are specialized to detect and prefer certain kinds of visual patterns (Csibra et al., 2000).

Neonates show a clear preference for images of human faces, and they also demonstrate the ability to use information from the facial expressions of others. Neonates can imitate live facial expressions from birth. In a classic study, psychologist Andy Meltzoff spent time hanging around maternity wards, waiting for babies to be born so that he could make faces at them. He tested neonates' ability to imitate a variety of facial expressions and found that infants as young as 2 hours old would reliably imitate a set of facial expressions (Meltzoff & Moore, 1983). More recently, researchers

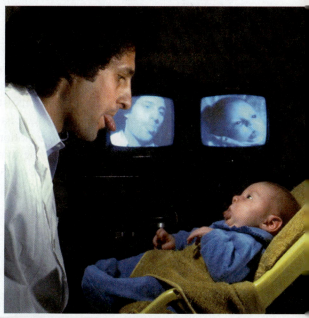

have identified *mirror neurons*, neurons found in humans and other species that fire when observing behavior in others. Mirror neurons appear to function from birth, as found in Meltzoff's study of neonatal imitation.

CRITICAL THINKING QUESTION

Given what you have learned here about neonate's sight preferences, how would you design a mobile for a newborn's room?

Summary: The Neonate

LO 3.6   Identify the features of the two major scales most often used to assess neonatal health.

Two of the most widely used methods of assessing neonatal health are the Apgar scale and the Brazelton Neonatal Behavioral Assessment Scale (NBAS). The Apgar scale, which is administered immediately after birth, assesses infants on five subtests with a total rating of 1 to 10. The NBAS, which is administered any time in the first 2 months, assigns infants an overall rating of "worrisome," "normal," or "superior."

LO 3.7   Identify the neonatal classifications for low birth weight and describe the consequences and major treatments.

Low-birth-weight neonates weigh less than 5.5 pounds and very low-birth-weight neonates weigh less than 3.3 pounds; extremely low-birth-weight babies weigh less than 2.2 pounds. Low birth weight is related to a variety of physical, cognitive, and behavioral problems, not just in infancy but throughout life. Close physical contact and infant massage can help ameliorate the problems.

LO 3.8   Describe the differences in maternal and neonatal mortality both within and between developed countries and developing countries.

In recent decades birth has become routinely safe and humane in developed countries, although there is considerable variation based on socioeconomic status and ethnicity. Childbirth remains highly dangerous in developing countries where little medical intervention is available, although mortality rates are decreasing due to recent improvements in nutrition and access to health care.

LO 3.9   Describe neonates' patterns of waking and sleeping, including how and why these patterns differ across cultures.

Neonates sleep an average of 16 to 17 hours a day (in segments of a few hours each), about 50 percent of it in REM sleep. By 4 months old the typical infant sleeps for 14 of every 24 hours, including about 6 hours straight at night, and the proportion of REM sleep declines to 40 percent. These patterns may vary across cultures due to differences in parenting practices such as how much time mothers spend holding their babies.

LO 3.10   Describe the neonatal reflexes, including those that have a functional purpose and those that do not.

There are 27 reflexes present at birth or shortly after, including some related to early survival (such as sucking and rooting) and others that have no apparent function (such as the *Babkin* and *Babinski* reflexes).

LO 3.11   Describe the neonate's sensory abilities with respect to touch, taste and smell, hearing, and sight.

Touch and taste develop prenatally to a large extent, and neonates' abilities are similar to adults'. Neonates quickly begin to discriminate smells after birth, showing a preference for the smell of their mother's breast. Hearing is also quite mature at birth, although neonates hear high-pitched sounds better than other sounds and their ability to localize sound does not mature until about 1 year old. Sight is the least developed of the senses at birth as a result of the physiological immaturity of the visual system, but it reaches maturity by the end of the first year.

Section 3 Caring for the Neonate

 Learning Objectives

3.12 Describe the cultural customs surrounding breast feeding across cultures and history.

3.13 Identify the advantages of breast feeding and where those advantages are largest.

3.14 Describe the pattern of neonates' crying and how soothing methods vary across cultures.

3.15 Describe the extent to which human mothers "bond" with their neonates and the extent to which this claim has been exaggerated.

3.16 Describe the reasons for postpartum depression and its consequences for children.

CARING FOR THE NEONATE:
Nutrition: Is Breast Best?

One of the most heavily researched topics regarding neonates is the question of how they should be fed. Specifically, attention has focused on whether breast feeding should be recommended for all children, and if so, for how long. Here we examine the evolutionary and historical basis of breast feeding, the evidence for its benefits, and the efforts to promote breast feeding in developing countries.

Historical and Cultural Perspectives on Breast Feeding

LO 3.12 Describe the cultural customs surrounding breast feeding across cultures and history.

Both mother and baby are biologically prepared for breast feeding. In the mother, the preparation begins well before birth. Early in pregnancy the mammary glands in her breasts expand greatly in size as milk-producing cells multiply and mature. By 4 months gestation the breasts are ready to produce milk. At birth, the mother's **let-down reflex** in her breasts causes milk to be released to the tip of her nipples whenever she hears the sound of her infant's cry, sees its open mouth, or even thinks about breast feeding (Walshaw, 2010).

Our closest primate relatives, chimpanzees, breast feed for about 4 years. In the human past, archaeological and historical evidence indicate that in most cultures infants were fed breast milk as their primary food for 2 to 3 years, followed by 2 to 3 more years of occasional nursing. There are also indications that breast feeding in the human past took place at frequent intervals. Among the !Kung San of Central Africa, a modern hunter-gatherer culture, infants feed about every 13 minutes, on average, during their first year of life (Sellen, 2001). In traditional cultures it is typical for infants to be bound to or close to their mothers almost constantly, day and night, allowing for frequent feeding. This has led anthropologists to conclude that this was probably the pattern for 99 percent of human history (Small, 1998).

let-down reflex

in females, a reflex that causes milk to be released to the tip of the nipples in response to the sound of an infant's cry, seeing its open mouth, or even thinking about breast feeding

Wet nursing has a long history in Europe. Here, a wet nurse is pictured with a baby in France in 1895.

Such frequent feeding is, of course, demanding on the mother, and many cultures have developed ways of easing this responsibility. One common way has been substituting mothers' milk with milk from other species, especially cows or goats, two species that are domesticated in many cultures and so readily available. Another way is **wet nursing**, which means hiring a lactating woman other than the mother to feed the infant. Wet nursing is a widespread custom as old as recorded human history. European records indicate that by the 1700s in some countries a majority of women employed a wet nurse to breast feed their babies (Fildes, 1995).

In the late 1800s, manufactured substitutes such as condensed milk and evaporated milk began to be developed and marketed in the West by large corporations such as Borden and Nestlé (Bryder, 2009). The corporations claimed that these milk substitutes were not only more convenient than breast milk but also cleaner and safer. Doctors were persuaded—thanks in part to generous payments from the corporations—and they in turn persuaded new mothers to use the milk substitutes. By the 1940s only 20 to 30 percent of babies in the United States were breast-fed, and the percentage stayed in this range until the 1970s (Small, 1998). By then, scientific evidence was accumulating that breast milk was far better than any substitute, and health organizations such as UNICEF and the World Health Organization (WHO) began to wage worldwide campaigns to promote breast feeding.

In recent years, rates of breast feeding have risen to over 70 percent in the United States and Canada because of government-sponsored campaigns touting the health benefits, and breast feeding has become nearly universal in northern Europe (CDC, 2014b; Ryan et al., 2006). In developed countries, the higher the mother's age, educational level, and socioeconomic status, the more likely she is to breast feed her infant (Schulze & Carlisle, 2010). Within the United States, rates of breast feeding are higher among Latinos (80 percent) and Whites (75 percent) than among African Americans (58 percent), but rates have risen across all ethnic groups in recent years (CDC, 2013b, 2014b). It should be noted that these rates are for *any duration* of breast feeding; across ethnic groups, less than half the neonates who breast feed initially are still breast feeding at age 6 months. Worldwide only about half of all infants are breast-fed even for a short time (UNICEF, 2014a, b).

Cultural Focus: Breast Feeding Practices Across Cultures

For nearly all of human history, until recent decades, breast feeding has been practiced in all cultures as the method of delivering nourishment in the early months of life. Neonates are ready for breast feeding as soon as they are born. The sucking and rooting reflexes are at their strongest 30 minutes after birth (Bryder, 2009). As noted previously, within a few days neonates recognize their mother's smell and the sound of her voice, which helps orient them for feeding.

Breast feeding not only provides nourishment, it soothes babies when they are distressed. Babies derive comfort from sucking on their mothers' breasts and from the closeness and warmth they experience during breast feeding, even when they are not hungry. Watch this video to see how mothers and expectant mothers in three countries view breast feeding.

Watch BREAST-FEEDING PRACTICES ACROSS CULTURES

Review Question:

Were you surprised to see that many of the women interviewed have similar reasons for breast feeding (regardless of their culture)? What are some of the benefits of breast feeding that they mentioned?

Benefits of Breast Feeding

LO 3.13 **Identify the advantages of breast feeding and where those advantages are largest.**

What benefits of breast feeding have been demonstrated by scientific research in recent decades? The list is a long one, and includes:

Disease protection. Breast milk contains antibodies and other substances that strengthen the baby's immune system, and breast feeding has been found to reduce the risk of a wide range of illnesses and diseases, such as diphtheria, pneumonia, ear infections, asthma, and diarrhea, among many others (American Academy of Pediatrics [AAP] Section on Breastfeeding, 2005; Godfrey & Meyers, 2009).

Cognitive development. Breast-fed infants tend to score higher than bottle-fed infants on measures of cognitive functioning, perhaps because the nutrients in breast milk promote early brain development (Kramer et al., 2008). This finding holds up even after controlling for many other factors such as parents' intelligence and education (Feldman & Eidelman, 2003). The benefits are mainly for infants who are preterm or low birth weight and consequently are at risk for cognitive difficulties (Ip et al., 2007; Schulze & Carlisle, 2010).

Reduced obesity. Breast feeding for at least 6 months reduces the likelihood of obesity in childhood (AAP Section on Breast-feeding, 2005; Shields et al., 2010). This is especially important in developed countries, where rates of obesity have risen dramatically in recent decades.

Better health in childhood and adulthood. In addition to protection from illnesses and disease early in life, breast feeding promotes long-term health in a variety of ways, such as promoting bone density, enhancing vision, and improving cardiovascular functioning (Gibson et al., 2000; Owen et al., 2002).

Mothers also benefit from breast feeding (Godfrey & Meyers, 2009). In the days following birth, breast feeding triggers the release of the hormone oxytocin, which reduces bleeding in the uterus and causes the uterus to return to its original size. Nursing the neonate also helps mothers return to their pre-pregnancy weight because it burns 500 to 1,000 calories per day. Nursing has long-term effects as well on mothers' health, strengthening their bones, and reducing their risk of ovarian and breast cancer even many years later (Ip et al., 2007). However, breast feeding has no influence on the emotional development of the infant or the social relationship between infant and mother (Schulze & Carlisle, 2010).

How long should mothers breast feed their infants? WHO recommends breast feeding for 2 years, with solid foods introduced to supplement breast milk at 6 months of age. Few women today breast feed for the recommended time (see **Map 3.3** on the next page).

However, even breast feeding for only a few days after birth provides important benefits for infants. The first milk the mother produces is **colostrum**, a thick, yellowish liquid that is extremely rich in protein and antibodies that strengthen the neonate's immune system (Napier & Meister, 2000). Colostrum is especially important for neonates to receive, but it lasts only a few days. Perhaps because of its odd appearance, colostrum is erroneously believed in many cultures to be bad for babies. For example, in India many mothers avoid giving colostrum to their babies, substituting it with a mix of butter and honey they believe is healthier (Small, 1998).

wet nursing

cultural practice, common in human history, of hiring a lactating woman other than the mother to feed the infant

colostrum

thick, yellowish liquid produced by mammalian mothers during the first days following birth, extremely rich in protein and antibodies that strengthen the baby's immune system

The benefits of breast feeding are especially important in developing countries, where risks to early development are higher. Here, a mother from the Desia Kondh tribe in India nurses her baby.

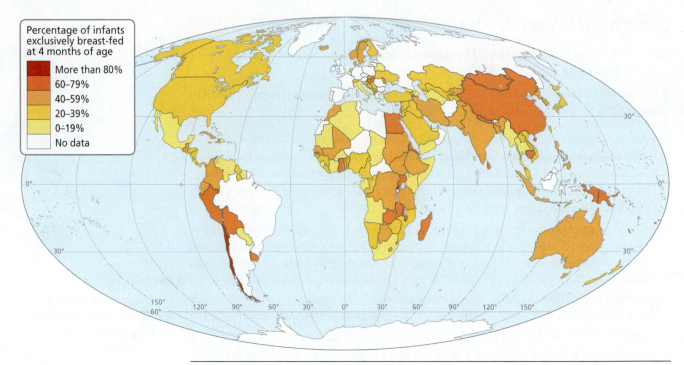

Map 3.3 Percentage of Infants Exclusively Breast-Fed at 4 Months of Age

Even in developed countries, where good health care is widely available, breast feeding provides advantages for infants and mothers. However, in developed countries the advantages of breast feeding are relatively small (Colen & Ramey, 2014), as we will see in the *Research Focus: Breast Feeding Benefits: Separating Correlation and Causation* feature. In contrast, breast feeding is crucial in developing countries, where risks of many diseases are higher and infants may not receive the vaccinations that are routine in developed countries. In developed countries, breast feeding helps infants avoid illnesses such as gastrointestinal infections, but in developing countries breast feeding can be literally a matter of life and death. UNICEF estimates that 1.5 million babies die each year in developing countries because they are bottle-fed rather than breast-fed (UNICEF, 2011). This is not only as a result of losing the advantages of breast feeding but also stems from making infant formula with unsafe water, as we will soon see in more detail.

If breast feeding is so important to infants' health, why don't more mothers nurse in the early months of their children's lives? Some women have difficulty with breast feeding, either because their infant cannot latch on properly (often a problem with low-birth-weight babies) or because they produce insufficient breast milk (Bryder, 2009). However, there are a number of practical obstacles as well. In developed countries, many mothers are employed outside the home, which makes breast feeding more difficult (but not impossible; some use a breast pump to make milk available in their absence). Breast feeding also makes it more difficult for fathers to take part in feeding (except via the pumped breast milk) and more challenging for fathers and mothers to share the care of the baby more or less equally, as many couples in developed countries would prefer (Genesoni & Tallandini, 2009; Wolf, 2007). When fathers are able to feed the neonate it helps mothers recover from the physical strain of giving birth (Simkin, 2007).

In developing countries, sometimes mothers have infectious diseases such as HIV/AIDS, tuberculosis, or West Nile virus that could be transmitted through breast milk, so they are advised not to breast feed (Centers for Disease Control & Prevention, 2002). However, only a small percentage of women have such diseases. A much larger contributor to low rates of breast feeding is that many mothers in developing countries have been deceived, by the marketing campaigns of corporations selling infant formula, into believing the formula is better for infants than breast milk is.

This is false. Infant formula today is better than the condensed or evaporated milk of a century ago, because it is fortified with many of the components that make breast milk healthy, but even the best infant formula today is not as good for infants as breast milk is. Worse yet, infant formula is typically mixed with water, and in many developing countries the available water is not purified and may contain disease. Consequently, not only do infants fed with formula miss out on the health benefits of breast milk, but they are also imperiled by the diseases that may be contained in the water mixed with the powdered formula.

In response to this situation, the WHO and UNICEF initiated a worldwide effort beginning in the early 1990s to promote breast feeding (UNICEF, 2011; WHO, 2000b). These organizations have attempted to educate women about the advantages of breast feeding for them and their infants. They have also worked with hospitals to implement programs to get breast feeding off to a good start in the first days of the neonate's life. In this "Baby-Friendly Hospital Initiative," hospital personnel educate mothers about breast feeding prior to the birth, help them with the first feeding shortly after birth, show them how to maintain lactation (milk flow), and organize them into breast feeding support groups (Merewood et al., 2005; Merten et al., 2005).

The WHO/UNICEF initiative has been successful, with rates of breast feeding increasing wherever it has been implemented (UNICEF, 2011). However, because most births in developing countries today take place in homes, most mothers are unlikely to come into contact with the Baby-Friendly Hospital Initiative. With only half of infants worldwide breast-fed for even a short time, clearly there remains much room for improvement.

CRITICAL THINKING QUESTION

Given that the benefits of breast feeding in developed countries are genuine but small, should public policies encourage or discourage more women to breast feed for longer? Consider the arguments that breast feeding makes returning to the workplace difficult for women and makes it hard for mothers and fathers to share the infant care equally.

Research Focus: Breast Feeding Benefits: Separating Correlation and Causation

Numerous studies have found benefits of breast feeding for children and mothers alike across a wide range of areas. In developing countries, breast feeding is crucial to infant health, because these populations receive little in the way of vaccines and other medical care to protect them from widespread diseases. But what about in developed countries? How much difference does breast feeding make to the long-term development of children?

In the most comprehensive summary analysis (also known as a meta-analysis) of breast-feeding studies yet conducted, Stanley Ip and colleagues (2007) screened over 9,000 studies and selected nearly 500 that met their criteria for valid research methods and design. The conclusions of their analysis of the results of the 500 studies generally support the conclusions stated in this chapter, that breast feeding is associated with a wide variety of benefits for infants and mothers.

However, the authors also warned that readers should not infer causality. Why not? Because most studies of breast-feeding benefits find a correlation between breast feeding and benefits, but correlation does not imply causation.

One reason to be skeptical of causation claims in studies of breast feeding is that breast-feeding status is based on self-selection, meaning that women choose to breast feed (or not), and those who choose to breast feed tend to be different in many ways than women who do not.

Most notably, the authors observed, women who breast feed generally have more education and higher IQs. Consequently, the differences between the two groups that are attributed to breast feeding may actually be due to their differences in education and IQ.

Education also tends to be connected to a lot of other aspects of mothers' lives, such as attention to prenatal care, access to health care resources, likelihood of having a stable partner, likelihood of smoking, and household income, among others. The correlation between breast feeding and babies' development could be explained by any combination of these differences.

So what can be done to find out accurately how much difference breast feeding makes in babies' and mothers' outcomes? Ethical standards would prohibit assigning new mothers into breast-feeding and non-breast-feeding groups. However, one study that was conducted by Canadian researcher Michael Kramer and his colleagues in Belarus in Eastern Europe approximated this design. The researchers gained the cooperation of 31 maternity hospitals and clinics and the study involved over 17,000 women who—note carefully—stated their intention to breast feed.

Kramer and colleagues randomly assigned the women into two groups, with one group receiving an intervention designed to promote and support breast feeding by providing women with advice, information, and instruction, whereas the women in the control group received no intervention.

The women and their babies were then followed up by Kramer and colleagues for the next 7 years (so far). Over the course of the first year, women in the intervention group were more likely to exclusively breast feed and babies in this group were less likely to have gastrointestinal infections. At age 6, the children in the intervention group had significantly higher IQs, by 6 points. This is especially notable because most studies on the cognitive effects of breast feeding find that no effects remain after controlling for education and other confounding variables, unless the children were born preterm or low birth weight. The result found by Kramer and colleagues seems to indicate a small but clear positive effect of breast feeding on children's cognitive development. Crucially, it shows causation rather than merely causation because moms and babies were randomly assigned to the two groups, and thus it can be assumed that they were more or less similar in all ways except their group assignment.

Review Questions:

1. Which of the following is *not* one of the characteristics that have been found to distinguish moms who breast feed from moms who do not, according to research studies summarized by Stanley Ip?
   a. Higher IQs
   b. More physically active during pregnancy
   c. More likely to have a stable partner
   d. More likely to receive prenatal care

2. What was the main finding of the Kramer study that separated moms into an intervention group provided with breast-feeding advice and instruction and a control group who did not receive the intervention, when the children were age 6?
   a. Children in the intervention group had more frequent illnesses.
   b. Children in the intervention group had closer attachments to their moms.
   c. Children in the intervention group had IQs that averaged 6 points higher.
   d. Children in the intervention group had IQs that averaged 16 points higher.

Watch   RESEARCH FOCUS: BREAST-FEEDING BENEFITS: SEPARATING CORRELATION AND CAUSATION

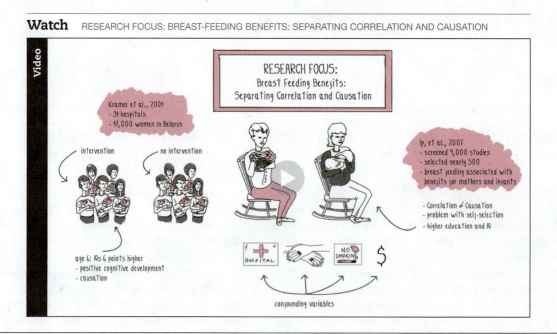

CARING FOR THE NEONATE: Social and Emotional Aspects of Neonatal Care

There are few events that change the life of an adult more than having a baby. Couples generally find the transition to parenting to be challenging in many ways. When a baby is born, the couple's familiar routines go out the window. The newborn demands to be fed, and has to be changed, dressed, walked, and included in the family's routines.

Neonates not only need protection and nutrition, they need social and emotional care as well. Here we look at neonates' crying patterns and the soothing methods that cultures have developed, and at the first social contacts between neonates and others, sometimes called *bonding*. In closing the chapter we examine the postpartum depression sometimes experienced by new mothers.

Crying and Soothing

LO 3.14 **Describe the pattern of neonates' crying and how soothing methods vary across cultures.**

Because human newborns are so immature and dependent in the early months of life, they need some way of signaling their needs to those who care for them, and their most frequent and effective signal is crying. Adults tend to find the crying of an infant hard to bear, so they have developed many creative ways of soothing them.

Across a variety of cultures with different infant-care practices, crying frequency follows what is known as the "crying curve" (Barr, 2009): stable for the first 3 weeks of life, rising steadily and reaching a peak by the end of the second month, then declining. **Figure 3.2** shows the pattern for U.S. infants. Sometimes crying has a clear source, but there is a lot of crying in the early months for no particular reason. This is important for parents to remember, because distress in neonates often triggers distress in those around them (Out et al., 2010). **Table 3.3** presents a way to remember the normal features of crying in the first 3 months of life.

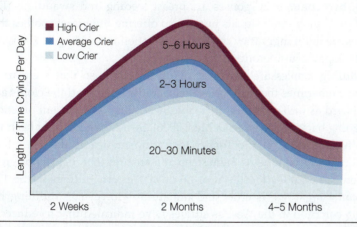

Figure 3.2 Daily Crying Duration in the Early Months

In their first months of life, infants often cry for no apparent reason.
SOURCE: Barr, 2009.

Table 3.3 Period of PURPLE Crying in the Early Months

A crying baby is difficult for others to bear, especially when the crying is frequent and does not appear to take place for an evident reason. Here is a way to remind parents and others of the normal features of crying in the early months of life.

P	Peak pattern	Crying peaks around age 2 months and then declines
U	Unpredictable	Crying in the early months often comes and goes unpredictably, for no apparent reason
R	Resistant to soothing	Crying may continue despite parents' best soothing efforts
P	Pain-like face	Crying babies may look like they are in pain even though they are not
L	Long lasting	Babies cry for longer in the early months, sometimes 30 to 40 minutes or more
E	Evening crying	Babies usually cry most in the afternoon and evening

The word *Period* means that the crying has a beginning and an end.
SOURCE: Barr, 2009 [see http://www.purplecrying.info/sections/index.php?sct=1&]

Although daily crying in the early months of life is consistent across cultures, there is wide variation in the *duration* and *intensity* of crying in infancy. Crying episodes are longer and more intense in cultures where infants are left on their own a lot and have relatively little time when they are being carried around. Four out of five U.S. infants have daily crying episodes in the early months of life of at least 15 minutes that do not have any apparent cause (Murkoff & Mazel, 2008). In contrast, infants in cultures where babies are held or carried around much of the day rarely have prolonged episodes of crying. For example, in a study comparing infants in South Korea and the United States, the U.S. infants cried for much longer periods, and this appeared to be explained by differences in parenting (Small, 1998). Korean infants spent much less of their time alone than U.S. infants did, Korean mothers carried their infants twice as long per day as the U.S. mothers did, and Korean mothers responded immediately to their infants' cries whereas U.S. mothers often let the infant cry it out.

The relation between parenting and infant crying has also been demonstrated experimentally. In one study, researchers divided U.S. mothers and their newborns into two equal groups (Hunziker & Barr, 1986). The mothers in Group A were asked to carry their babies for at least 3 hours a day, and mothers in Group B were not given any special instructions. Infants' mothers in both groups kept diaries of when and how long their babies cried. When the infants were 8 weeks old, the frequency of crying was the same in both groups, but the duration of crying was only about half as long for Group A, the babies who were held more often, as it was for Group B.

In traditional cultures babies are typically held for most of the day, either by their mothers or by another adult woman or an older sister. When neonates in traditional cultures cry, two common responses are breast feeding and swaddling (DeLoache & Gottlieb, 2000). Crying often signals hunger, so offering the breast soothes the baby, but even if babies are not hungry they can find consolation in suckling, in the same way that babies in developed countries are soothed by a pacifier.

In **swaddling**, babies are wrapped tightly in cloths so that their arms and legs cannot move. Sometimes the baby is laid on a cradle board and the cloths are wrapped around the board as well as around the baby. Swaddling is an ancient practice, with evidence of it going back 6,000 years (DeMeo, 2006). Swaddling has long been widely used in many cultures, from China to Turkey to South America, in the belief that neonates find it soothing and that it helps them sleep and ensures that their limbs grow properly (van Sleuwen et al., 2007). It fell out of favor in Western cultures in the 17th century, when it became regarded as cruel and unnatural. However, swaddling has recently become more common in the West as studies have indicated that it reduces crying and does not inhibit motor development (Thach, 2009). Indeed, babies may find swaddling soothing because it keeps them warm and decreases stimulation they get from moving their limbs through the air.

What else can parents and other caregivers do to soothe a crying neonate? First, of course, any apparent needs should be addressed, in case the baby is hungry, cold, tired, uncomfortable, injured, or needs a diaper change. For crying that has no apparent source, parents have devised a wide range of methods, such as (Eisenberg et al., 2011):

- Lifting baby up and holding to the shoulder
- Soothing repetitive movements such as rocking gently back and forth or riding in a car or stroller
- Soothing sounds such as singing, a fan or vacuum cleaner, or recordings of nature sounds like waves breaking on a beach
- A warm-water bath
- A pacifier or a finger to suck on
- Distraction, with some new sight or sound

swaddling

practice of infant care that involves wrapping an infant tightly in cloths or blankets

Swaddling babies to reduce crying spells is a long tradition in many cultures. Here, a Navajo baby in Arizona is swaddled to a traditional backboard.

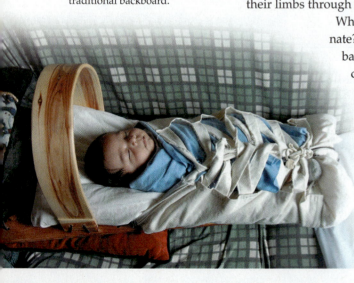

The common theme of these methods appears to be offering a new source of sensory stimulation, especially something gently repetitive. When Jeff's twins were neonates, he usually tried to soothe them by holding them to the shoulder or singing to them, but if those methods did not work their crying was almost always soothed by the gentle movements of the battery-operated infant seat he called their "wiggly chair." Parents with a crying neonate will often go to great lengths to make the crying stop, so there are many such items on the market today that promise to help parents achieve this goal. The video *Soothing Methods* shows some of the techniques used by parents and caregivers.

Watch SOOTHING METHODS

There is also the option of not responding to crying, until the infant stops. For decades, developmental psychologists have debated whether ignoring crying is a good or bad idea. Some argue that ignoring it is a good idea (unless of course the infant has a clear need for food or other care), because parents who respond will reinforce the infant's crying and thus make crying more likely the next time the infant wants attention (Crncec et al., 2010; Gewirtz, 1977; van IJzendoorn & Hubbard, 2000). Others argue that ignoring it is a bad idea, because infants whose cries are ignored will cry even more in order to get the attention they need (Bell & Ainsworth, 1972; Lohaus et al., 2004). Different studies have reported different findings, so all that can be concluded at this point is that responses to crying do not appear to be strongly related to infants' development (Alvarez, 2004; Hiscock & Jordan, 2004; Lewis & Ramsay, 1999).

About 1 in 10 Western babies have crying patterns of extreme duration, a condition known as **colic**. Babies are considered to be colicky if they fit the "rule of threes" (Barr, 2009): the crying goes on for more than 3 hours a day over more than 3 days at a time for more than 3 weeks. Colic usually begins in the second or third week of life and reaches its peak at 6 weeks, thereafter declining until it disappears at about 3 months of age (Barr & Gunnar, 2000; St. James-Roberts et al., 2003).

The causes of colic are unknown, but it exists primarily in Western cultures, where infants receive relatively little carrying time (Richman et al., 2010). Remedies for colic are also unknown. Babies with colic are inconsolable. None of the soothing methods described work with them. Fortunately, there appear to be no long-term effects of colic, in babies' physical, emotional, or social development (Barr, 2009; Murkoff& Mazel, 2008). However, this may be of little comfort to parents who must endure the persistent crying

colic
infant crying pattern in which the crying goes on for more than 3 hours a day over more than 3 days at a time for more than 3 weeks

of an inconsolable infant for many weeks. Colic is a risk factor for parents' maltreatment of their babies (Zeskind & Lester, 2001), so it is important for parents to seek help and support if they feel themselves reaching the breaking point.

Bonding: Myth and Truth

LO 3.15 **Describe the extent to which human mothers "bond" with their neonates and the extent to which this claim has been exaggerated.**

imprinting

instant and enduring bond to the first moving object seen after birth; common in birds

In some species, especially among birds such as geese, the first minutes after birth are a critical period for relations between mother and offspring. Geese form an instant and enduring bond to the first moving object they see, a phenomenon known as **imprinting**. Usually this first object is their mother, of course, and imprinting quickly to her promotes their survival because they will follow her everywhere she goes when they begin waddling around soon after birth. Konrad Lorenz (1957), who first identified the imprinting process, showed that geese would imprint to any moving object they saw soon after birth (including him—see photo).

Some physicians, learning of this research, applied it to humans and asserted that in humans, too, the first few minutes and hours after birth are critical to mother–infant **bonding** (Klaus & Kennell, 1976). Without contact with the mother shortly after birth, these physicians claimed, the baby's future development is jeopardized. However, when systematic research was done to test this hypothesis, it turned out not to be true (Lamb, 1994; Redshaw, 1997; Weinberg, 2004). Humans are not birds, and they are not at risk for later emotional and social problems if they do not bond with a caregiver in the first minutes, hours, or days after birth.

Nevertheless, this is a rare example of a false idea having good effects. As described previously, in developing countries the birth process had become overly medical by the 1950s and 1960s. Although bonding claims were false, the possibility that they were true

Goslings will imprint to the first moving object they see, which is usually—but not always—the mother goose. Here, the biologist Konrad Lorenz leads three goslings on a swim.

led hospitals all over the world to reexamine their policies of sedating the mother and separating mother and child immediately after birth (Lamb, 1994). Subsequently, during the 1970s and after, hospital policies changed so that mother, child, and even father could all be in close contact after the birth. This may not be necessary for the baby's successful later development, but there is no reason not to allow it, and it does alleviate parents' anxieties and promotes feelings of warmth and confidence in caring for their newborn child (Bergstrom et al., 2009).

Postpartum Depression

LO 3.16 **Describe the reasons for postpartum depression and its consequences for children.**

bonding

concept that in humans the first few minutes and hours after birth are critical to mother–infant relationships

postpartum depression

in parents with a new baby, feelings of sadness and anxiety so intense as to interfere with the ability to carry out simple daily tasks

Although the birth of a child is generally greeted with joy, some parents experience a difficult time emotionally in the early months of their baby's life. In one study of new mothers in 11 countries, **postpartum depression** was found at similar rates in all of them, about 10 percent (Oates et al., 2004). Postpartum depression is defined as a series of depressive episodes with mood symptoms first appearing in the 4 weeks following delivery (American Psychiatric Association, 2013).

In Western countries this condition was often seen as an illness requiring possible intervention of health professionals, whereas in non-Western countries social support from family members was relied upon for making it through. Studies in the United States and the United Kingdom report that about 4 percent of fathers also experience postpartum depression in the months following the birth of their child (Dennis, 2004; Ramchandani et al., 2005).

Low emotional states in mothers following birth may be the result of rapid hormonal changes, as the high concentrations of estrogen and progesterone in the mother's body return to normal levels. However, postpartum depression is deeper and more enduring. Feelings of sadness and anxiety become so intense that they interfere with the ability to carry out simple daily tasks. Other symptoms include extreme changes in appetite and difficulty sleeping. Postpartum depression often peaks about 4 weeks after childbirth—long after the mother's hormones would have returned to normal levels—and in 25 to 50 percent of mothers who experience postpartum depression it lasts 6 months or longer (Beck, 2002; Clay & Seehusen, 2004).

Why do some women and not others develop postpartum depression? Women are more at risk for postpartum depression if they have had previous episodes of major depression or if they have close family members who have experienced major depression (Bloch et al., 2006). This suggests that for postpartum depression, as for other forms of depression, some people may have a genetic vulnerability to becoming depressed when they experience intense life stresses. Women are also more likely to experience postpartum depression if they lack social support from a husband or partner (Iles et al., 2011). Thus, even if a mother has a genetic vulnerability to depression, it is unlikely to be expressed unless she also experiences a social and cultural context in which social support is lacking. For fathers, postpartum depression may result from the challenges of reconciling their personal and work-related needs with the demands of being a father (Genesoni & Tallandini, 2009; Ramchandani et al., 2005).

Across countries, about 10 percent of new mothers experience postpartum depression.

Mothers' and fathers' postpartum depression is related to children's developmental problems in infancy and beyond. Numerous studies of mothers with postpartum depression have found that their infants are more likely than other infants to be irritable, to have problems eating and sleeping, and to have difficulty forming attachments (Herrera et al., 2004; Martins & Griffin, 2000). In later development, the children are at risk for being withdrawn or displaying antisocial behavior (Nylen et al., 2006). Children of fathers with postpartum depression have been found to have similar risks for their development (Kane & Garber, 2004; Ramchandani et al., 2005).

Of course, all of these studies are subject to the research design problem of passive and evocative genotype → environment effects. That is, the children in these studies received not only their environment from their parents but also their genes, and it is difficult to tell whether the relation between their problems and their parents' depression is because of genetics or environment (the problem of passive genotype → environment effects). Also, the studies usually assume that the mother's depression affected the child, but it could also be that the mothers became depressed in part because their infant was especially irritable and difficult (evocative genotype → environment effects). However, observational studies of mothers with postpartum depression have found that they talk to and look at their infant less than other mothers, and that they also touch them less and smile less often at them (Righetti-Veltema et al., 2002). This suggests that the behavior of depressed mothers is different in ways that may affect infants, even if passive and evocative genotype → environment effects are also involved.

Treatment for postpartum depression typically includes psychotherapy to help the mother adjust (Guille et al., 2013; Miniati et al., 2014). A variety of antidepressants may be prescribed, but nursing women should discuss the use of antidepressants with their health care provider (Hantsoo et al., 2014; Sharma et al., 2015). Interestingly, exercise during pregnancy can help keep depressive symptoms at bay (Perales et al., 2015). And, postpartum exercise has been found in a number of studies to decrease symptoms of depression (Daley, 2009; Dritsa et al., 2009; Hahn-Holbrook & Haselton, 2014).

Summary: Caring for the Neonate

LO 3.12 Describe the cultural customs surrounding breast feeding across cultures and history.

In the human past, evidence indicates that in most cultures children were fed breast milk as their primary food for 2 to 3 years. To ease the burden of frequent feedings, the custom of wet nursing (hiring a lactating woman other than the mother to feed the infant) is a widespread custom as old as recorded human history. Using animal substitutes (cow's or goat's milk) also has a long history.

LO 3.13 Identify the advantages of breast feeding and where those advantages are largest.

Breast feeding is associated with protection from disease in infancy and better health in childhood and adulthood, healthy cognitive development, and reduced obesity. For mothers, breast feeding helps their bodies return to normal after pregnancy. The advantages are especially pronounced in developing countries. Nevertheless, worldwide only about half of all infants are breast-fed even for a short time.

LO 3.14 Describe the pattern of neonates' crying and how soothing methods vary across cultures.

Crying frequency rises steadily beginning at 3 weeks of age and reaches a peak by the end of the second month, then declines. This pattern is similar across cultures, but duration and intensity of crying are lower in cultures where babies are held or carried throughout much of the day and night.

LO 3.15 Describe the extent to which human mothers "bond" with their neonates and the extent to which this claim has been exaggerated.

Some physicians have claimed on the basis of animal studies that the first few minutes and hours after birth are critical to mother–infant "bonding." This has now been shown to be false, but the claims had the beneficial effect of changing hospital policies to allow more contact between mothers, fathers, and neonates.

LO 3.16 Describe the reasons for postpartum depression and its consequences for children.

Many mothers experience mood fluctuations in the days following birth as their hormones return to normal levels, but some mothers experience an extended period of postpartum depression, as do some fathers. The basis of postpartum depression appears to be a combination of genetic vulnerability to depression and a social and cultural context that does not provide enough social support.

Applying Your Knowledge as a Professional

The topics covered in this chapter apply to a wide variety of career professions. Watch these videos to learn how they apply to a birth doula and an instructor of maternity nursing.

Watch   CAREER FOCUS: BIRTH DOULA

Samantha Huggins
Doula
Carriage House Birth

Chapter Quiz

1. Juanita's cervix is 10 centimeters dilated, so she
   _____.
   a. is just beginning the labor stage
   b. requires an episiotomy.
   c. has completed labor and is ready to deliver the baby
   d. requires a C-section

2. C-sections _____.
   a. are performed when the baby is in the breech position and attempts to turn the baby into a head-first position have not been successful
   b. require the same recovery time as a vaginal birth if they are performed correctly
   c. have only been proven safe in the cases where there is a failure to progress
   d. are performed at equally small rates around the world because they are seen as a last resort

3. Which of the following is true about birthing practices?
   a. Recently, midwifery has seen a revival, and about 50 percent of births in the United States are assisted by midwifes.
   b. In the early 1900s, the intervention of doctors often made the birth process less dangerous because they now had better expertise and medical equipment.
   c. In the 1960s, doctors began administering drugs such as ether and chloroform, which offered pain relief without any side effects.
   d. Twilight Sleep was a drug method used in the early 20th century that promoted dilation of the cervix and resulted in mothers forgetting the events of birth.

4. In most cultures, _____ take the lead in assisting the birth.
   a. older men
   b. younger women
   c. older women
   d. religious figures

5. Surita is a midwife in a traditional culture. She is most likely to _____.
   a. have spent time as an apprentice to a more experienced midwife
   b. be childless, so that she is able to devote more time to this work
   c. be a young woman because she will be able to practice midwifery for longer than her older counterparts
   d. exclude other relatives from being present at the birth to reduce possible contamination

6. In developed countries, women in labor may be given _____ to help manage their pain.
   a. an epidural
   b. electronic fetal monitoring
   c. a placebo
   d. a douche

7. The five characteristics that are evaluated in the Apgar scale are _____.
   a. the Babinski, Moro, stepping, swimming, and grasping reflexes
   b. color, heart rate, reflex irritability, muscle tone, and breathing
   c. reaction to cuddling, startling, intelligence, vocal response, and visual response.
   d. sucking reflex, responses to social stimulation, and disease symptoms

8. Preterm babies are considered at risk because _____.
   a. their immune systems are immature
   b. they have too much surfactant in their lungs
   c. their bodies generate too much heat
   d. their gestational age is 40 weeks and that is still too early to perform basic functions, such as sucking

9. Which ethnic group in the United States has the highest rates of neonatal mortality?
   a. Whites
   b. African Americans
   c. Asian Americans
   d. Latinos

10. Compared to adults, neonates _____.
    a. spend a lower proportion of their sleep in REM
    b. enter REM sooner after falling asleep
    c. spend less time sleeping
    d. do not experience eye movements under the eyelids or brain-wave changes during REM sleep

11. Which of the following reflexes has no apparent survival value?
    a. Rooting reflex
    b. Moro reflex
    c. Babinski reflex
    d. Grasping reflex

12. The earliest sense to develop is _____.

    a. taste   **c.** vision

    b. touch   **d.** hearing

13. Breast feeding _____.

    a. is more common among women from low socioeconomic status groups

    b. increased in popularity as formulas came on to the market because the formulas were expensive and women worried about product quality

    c. is something both mother and baby are biologically prepared to do

    d. rates have stayed about the same in the United States since the 1940s

14. Which of the following statements about breast feeding is most accurate?

    a. Babies in developing countries are more at risk for health problems if their mothers do not breast feed them than are babies in developed countries.

    b. Breast feeding promotes better health in childhood, but does not have any influence on long-term health.

    c. Breast-fed babies are more likely than bottle-fed babies to become obese in childhood because they are used to eating on demand.

    d. The colostrum that mothers produce in the first weeks after birth can be dangerous to babies, so doctors advise using formula until the mother begins producing milk.

15. U.S. infants _____.

    a. are less likely to experience colic than are babies in non-Western cultures

    b. typically experience colic until they are about a year of age

    c. show the same frequency, intensity, and duration of crying as babies from all over the world

    d. have been found to cry more than babies from cultures where they are held or carried for much of the day

16. Which of the following statements about bonding is most accurate?

    a. There is a critical period for mother–child relations in all species.

    b. Imprinting is another name for the stepping reflex.

    c. In humans, if there is no contact with the mother shortly after birth, the baby's future development is at risk.

    d. Konrad Lorenz showed that following the first moving object after birth has survival value for geese.

17. Postpartum depression _____.

    a. is less common among women who have had previous episodes of major depression because they tend to seek preventive treatment

    b. is experienced by men as well as by women

    c. has a genetic component, and therefore has not been correlated with levels of social support

    d. has been linked with developmental outcomes for babies, but only among male babies

18. Symptoms of postpartum depression

    a. should not be treated with antidepressants

    b. are only found in developing countries

    c. can be decreased with exercise

    d. are not responsive to psychotherapy

Chapter 4
Infancy

MORE THAN IN OTHER LIFE STAGES, THE DAILY LIFE OF INFANTS IS SIMILAR EVERYWHERE IN SOME WAYS. In all cultures, infants have limited mobility and do not yet use language (the word *infant* means literally "without speech"), although they have a variety of ways of communicating. In all cultures, infants cannot do much for themselves and rely heavily on others for care and protection. However, even in infancy cultural variations are vast. In some cultures, infants are carried around for most of the day and breast feed often, whereas in others, they lay by themselves for a substantial proportion of the day—and night. In this chapter we will explore both cultural similarities and variations in infants' development. Beginning in this chapter and throughout the rest of the book (until the final chapter), the chapters will be divided into three major sections: physical development, cognitive development, and emotional and social development.

Watch CHAPTER INTRODUCTION: INFANCY

Video

Section 1   Physical Development

Learning Objectives

4.1 Describe how the infant's body changes in the first year, and explain the two basic principles of physical growth.

4.2 Identify the different parts of the brain, and describe how the brain changes in the first few years of life.

4.3 Describe how infant sleep changes in the course of the first year, and evaluate the risk factors for SIDS, including the research evidence regarding cosleeping.

4.4 Describe how infants' nutritional needs change during the first year of life, and identify the reasons for and consequences of malnutrition in infancy.

4.5 List the major causes and preventive methods of infant mortality, and describe some cultural approaches to protecting infants.

4.6 Describe the major changes during infancy in gross and fine motor development.

4.7 Describe how infants' sensory abilities develop in the first year.

PHYSICAL DEVELOPMENT:
Growth and Change in Infancy

We begin this section by examining physical growth (height and weight) and infant brain development. Then we'll examine changes in sleeping patterns, the dangers of SIDS, and cultural variations in where infants sleep (and with whom).

Growth Patterns

LO 4.1   **Describe how the infant's body changes in the first year, and explain the two basic principles of physical growth.**

Babies grow at a faster rate in their first year than at any later time of life (Adolph & Berger, 2005). Birth weight doubles by the time the infant is 5 months old and triples by the end of the first year, to about 22 pounds (10 kilograms) on average. If this rate of growth continued for the next 3 years, the average 4-year-old child would weigh 600 pounds! But the rate of weight gain decreases steeply after the first year.

Babies especially accumulate fat in the early months, which helps them maintain a constant body temperature. At 6 months, a well-nourished baby looks on the plump side, but by 1 year children lose much of their "baby fat," and the trend toward a lower fat-to-body weight ratio continues until puberty (Fomon & Nelson, 2002).

Height also increases dramatically in the first year, from about 20 inches (50 centimeters) to about 30 inches (75 cm), at the rate of about an inch per month. Unlike weight, growth in height in the first year is uneven, occurring in spurts rather than steadily. Studies that have monitored height closely have found that infants may grow very little for several days or even weeks, then spurt a half-inch in just a day or two (Lampl et al.,

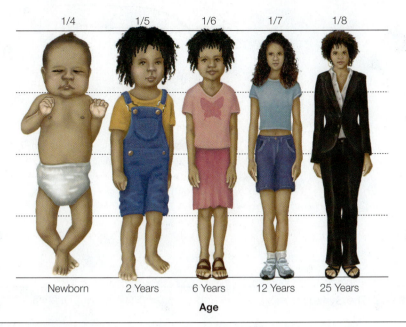

	1/4	1/5	1/6	1/7	1/8

| Newborn | 2 Years | 6 Years | 12 Years | 25 Years |

Age

Figure 4.1 The Cephalocaudal Principle of Body Growth

Growth begins with the head and then continues downward to the rest of the body.

2001). Girls tend to be shorter and lighter than boys, at birth and throughout childhood, until puberty when they briefly surpass boys in height (Geary, 2010).

Another way growth is uneven in infancy is that it tends to begin at the top, with the head, and then proceeds downward to the rest of the body (Adolph & Berger, 2005). This is called the **cephalocaudal principle** (*cephalocaudal* is Latin for "head to tail"). So, for example, the head is one-quarter of the neonate's body length, but only one eighth of an adult's (see **Figure 4.1**). In addition, growth proceeds from the middle of the body outward, which is the **proximodistal principle** (*proximodistal* is Latin for "near to far"). So, for example, the trunk and arms grow faster than the hands and fingers.

Brain Development

LO 4.2 **Identify the different parts of the brain, and describe how the brain changes in the first few years of life.**

Humans have relatively large brains at birth compared to other animals, thus making the birth process more painful and dangerous. But even though the human brain is relatively large at birth, it is also relatively immature (Johnson, 2001). We come out when we do because if we waited any longer, our brains would be too big for us ever to make it through the birth canal. Consequently, much of the basic brain development that takes place prenatally for other animals takes place in the first year for humans. Note, for example, that other animals are mobile at birth or within a few days or weeks, but humans cannot even crawl for about 6 months and cannot walk until the end of their first year.

Here we will look first at basics of infant brain growth, then at the specialized functions of different parts of the brain. Then we'll explore the special sensitivity of brain development during infancy.

BRAIN GROWTH During the second trimester of prenatal development neurons are produced at the astonishing rate of 250,000 per minute. The pace then slows considerably in the third trimester because the focus of development shifts to other organs and to overall size. After birth, the brain resumes its explosive

cephalocaudal principle

principle of biological development that growth tends to begin at the top, with the head, and then proceeds downward to the rest of the body

proximodistal principle

principle of biological development that growth proceeds from the middle of the body outward

Most babies are plump and have large heads in proportion to their bodies.

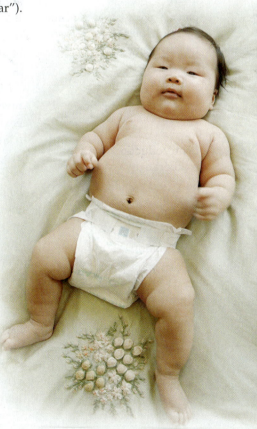

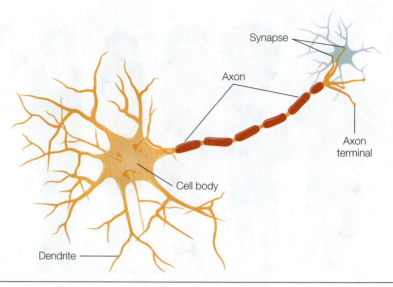

Figure 4.2 The Synapse

growth. The neonate's brain is about 25 percent the size of an adult's brain, but by age 2 it will reach 70 percent.

There are about 100 to 200 billion brain cells, or *neurons*, in the average infant brain (Kostovic & Vasung, 2009). Neurons differ from other cells in the body in that they are not directly connected to each other. Instead, they are separated by tiny gaps called *synapses*. Neurons communicate across the synapses by releasing chemicals called **neurotransmitters**. The **axon** of the neuron releases neurotransmitters, and the **dendrites** receive them (see **Figure 4.2**).

The brain growth that occurs in the first 2 years of life does not involve production of more and more neurons. In fact, the number of neurons in the brain drops by age 2 to about one half what it was at birth (de Haan & Johnson, 2003). There are two other ways that brain growth takes place during infancy. First, the dendritic connections between neurons multiply vastly, a process known as **overproduction** or **exuberance** (Kostovic et al., 2009). At birth the neurons have few interconnections, but by age 2 each neuron is connected to hundreds or even thousands of other cells. The greatest density of connections appears in toddlerhood. The second way the brain grows in infancy is through **myelination**, the process by which the axons become encased in a *myelin sheath*, an envelope of fatty material that increases the speed of communication between neurons (Gale et al., 2004). Myelination is especially active in the early years of life but continues at a slower rate until about age 30 (Taylor, 2006).

As neurons create vast networks of dendrites to connect to other neurons, a process begins that enhances the precision and efficiency of the connections. "Use it or lose it" is the principle that applies because dendritic connections that are used become stronger and faster and those that are unused wither away, in a process called **synaptic pruning** (Kostovic et al., 2009). If you were growing carrots in a backyard garden and you had planted thousands of seeds, how would you ensure that they would thrive? The best way would be to prune or pluck out the weaker shoots to allow the stronger ones more room and resources to grow on. This is what the brain does with synaptic pruning. Through synaptic pruning, the brain eliminates about one third of its synapses between early childhood and adolescence (Giedd et al., 2010).

BRAIN SPECIALIZATION Although the entire brain is composed of neurons, the neurons in different parts of the brain have specialized functions. Overall, the brain is divided into three major regions, the *hindbrain*, the *midbrain*, and the *forebrain*. Early in prenatal development, the neurons in these three regions begin to specialize. The hindbrain and

neurotransmitter

chemical that enables neurons to communicate across synapses

axon

part of a neuron that transmits electric impulses and releases neurotransmitters

dendrite

part of the neuron that receives neurotransmitters

overproduction or exuberance

burst in the production of dendritic connections between neurons

myelination

process of the growth of the myelin sheath around the axon of a neuron

synaptic pruning

process in brain development in which dendritic connections that are used become stronger and faster and those that are unused whither away

midbrain mature earliest and perform the basic biological functions necessary to life. They keep your lungs breathing, your heart beating, and your bodily movements balanced.

The forebrain is divided into two main parts, the *limbic system* and the *cerebral cortex*. The structures of the limbic system include the *hypothalamus*, the *thalamus*, and the *hippocampus*. The hypothalamus is small, about the size of a peanut, but plays a key role in monitoring and regulating our basic animal functions, including hunger, thirst, body temperature, sexual desire, and hormonal levels. The thalamus acts as a receiving and transfer center for sensory information from the body to the rest of the brain. The hippocampus is crucial in memory, especially the transfer of information from short-term to long-term memory.

The most distinctively human part of the brain is the outermost part of the forebrain, the **cerebral cortex**. This part of the human brain is far larger than in other animals. For example, adult humans weigh about as much as adult chimpanzees, but have a cerebral cortex three to four times larger (Wrangham, 2009). It accounts for 85 percent of the brain's total weight, and it is here that most of the brain's growth takes place after birth. The cerebral cortex is the basis of our distinctively human abilities, including the ability to speak and understand language, to solve complex problems, and to think in terms of concepts, ideas, and symbols.

The different parts of the cerebral cortex are specialized in two ways. First, the cerebral cortex is divided into two hemispheres, left and right, which are connected by a band of neural fibers called the *corpus callosum* that allows them to communicate. **Lateralization** is the term for the specialization of the two hemispheres. In general, the left hemisphere is specialized for language and for processing information in a sequential, step-by-step way (Harnad, 2012). The right hemisphere is specialized for spatial reasoning and for processing information in a holistic, integrative way. However, the specialization of the hemispheres should not be exaggerated because they work together in most aspects of language, emotion, and behavior. No one is mainly a "left-brain" or "right-brain" thinker.

The cerebral cortex is also specialized in that each hemisphere has four regions or lobes with distinct functions (see **Figure 4.3**). The *occipital lobes* at the rear of each hemisphere process visual information. The *temporal lobes* at the lower side of each hemisphere are involved in processing auditory information, including understanding

cerebral cortex

outer portion of the brain, containing four regions with distinct functions

lateralization

specialization of functions in the two hemispheres of the brain

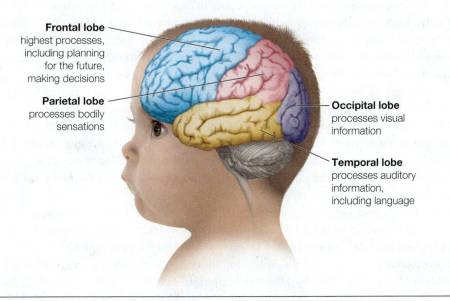

Figure 4.3 Lobes of the Brain

What are the distinct functions of each lobe?

spoken language. The *parietal lobes* above the temporal lobes process information from bodily sensations. The *frontal lobes* behind the forehead are the center of the most advanced human brain processes, including producing spoken language, planning for the future, and making decisions. With the lobes as with the hemispheres, it is important not to exaggerate the degree of specialization because more than one part of the brain is involved in most brain functions (Harnad, 2012; Knect et al., 2003).

THE PLASTICITY OF THE INFANT BRAIN Even before birth, the brain is well on its way toward specialization in the ways just described. However, in many ways the cerebral cortex of the neonate and the infant is still immature. Because the infant's brain is not as specialized as it will be later in development, it is high in **plasticity**, meaning that it is highly responsive to environmental circumstances.

The high plasticity of the infant brain makes it adaptable but also vulnerable (Gale et al., 2004). On the plus side, if a part of the brain is damaged in infancy as a result of an accident or disease, other parts of the brain can often take over the functions of the damaged portion, whereas this is less possible later in development once greater specialization has taken place. On the minus side, environmental deprivation can have permanent effects if it takes place in infancy, whereas later its effects would not be as profound or long lasting.

Brain plasticity is an example of phenotypic expression of the genotype. Remember that phenotype is the observable expression of genes that have interacted in an environment. There are also epigenetic aspects of brain development, such as the response to stress or stimulation. Based on the human genetic code, typical human babies anywhere in the world will develop similar basic brain functions such as vision, the ability to handle objects in the world, and some kind of bond with one or more caregivers. These basic functions have been characterized as **experience-expectant brain functions** (Greenough et al., 1987). From the simplest environment to the most complex, infant brain connections for these basic functions develop normally and in similar patterns, based on the brain's expectancy.

There are also **experience-dependent brain functions** that require specific experiences to develop and are more individual or idiosyncratic to each child (Greenough et al., 1987). For example, depending on the specific experiences an infant has, its brain may develop connections that other infants may not have. This is an example of phenotypic expression: genes for acquiring language help the infant acquire language, but the specific language an infant is exposed to, and the timing of input, will influence how synapses are formed. The process of forming new synapses in experience-dependent brain functions is in active response to specific stimuli. Children in some cultures may have the experiences for specific brain connections to develop, and others may not. For example, babies exposed to Hindi will make a categorical distinction between sounds that babies exposed to English will not, and the related connections in the brain will be different.

Although all typical infant brains expect to learn language (the experience-expectant function), the specific language and the number of words an infant hears will vary by cultural factors such as geographic location and socioeconomic status, and the brain function will be different (the experience-dependent function). In the United States, children in higher socioeconomic status (SES) families may hear 30 million more words by age 3 (Colker, n.d.), and this difference causes experience-dependent brain functions to vary. Specifically, children in lower SES households who hear fewer words show disparities in vocabulary and language-processing efficiency compared to children in higher SES households (Fernald et al., 2013). This disparity means that children in lower SES households often reach school with lower language skills (Hoff, 2013), which may set them up for lower academic achievement. Bolstering the early language input of children in lower SES households may help the long-term trajectories of these children in school. But it's not just words that matter. It's the opportunities to talk and the feedback that children get that help build vocabulary in interactions (Wasik & Hindman, 2015). Once again, we see how the ecocultural settings of development matter: the activities of people in the infant

plasticicty

degree to which development can be influenced by environmental circumstances

experience-expectant brain functions

brain functions that require basic, expectable experiences to develop in a normal pattern

experience-dependent brain functions

brain functions that only develop with particular experiences that may be idiosyncratic to a particular infant

environment, the tasks they accomplish, and the resources they have to do so are all part of the developmental pathways of children (Gallimore et al., 1993).

If the socioeconomic differences in the United States can be traced as a cause of lower vocabulary and verbal-processing efficiency as children from poor families enter school, you might imagine that more extreme deprivation might have an even greater impact on brain development. Imagine that, starting tomorrow, for 3 years you lived in conditions of great deprivation, with little food, little interaction with others, and nothing interesting to do. At the end of it, you might be hungry and not happy, but it is likely your weight would soon return to normal and your intellectual skills and abilities would be unaffected in the long run. This is what has usually happened to prisoners of war who have been subject to such grim conditions (Moore, 2010). Having already developed, adults are more resilient to this kind of deprivation.

If the same kind of deprivation had happened to you in the first 3 years of your life, the effects would have been much worse and more enduring. One demonstration of this comes from a horrible natural experiment that took place in Romania about 20 years ago. In the early 1990s, after Communist regimes fell in Eastern European countries, Western visitors to Romania were shocked at the conditions in the country's orphanages. Infants and young children in the orphanages had been given little in the way of nutrition and even less love, attention, and cognitive stimulation. They were kept in large, dim, bare rooms, attended by a small number of indifferent caregivers. In response to widespread outrage, the orphanages were soon closed and the children were adopted into homes in other countries, mostly in Canada and Great Britain.

The children had all been deprived, but they were adopted at different ages. Over the course of the next several years, it was possible to see how much difference the age at adoption made in their cognitive development (O'Connor et al., 2000; Rutter et al., 2004).

Age at adoption made an enormous difference. All the children recovered dramatically in physical size after a year or two in their new homes, but cognitive recovery depended strongly on age at adoption. As shown in **Figure 4.4**, by age 6, the Romanian children who had been adopted when they were younger than 6 months old were no different in their rate of cognitive impairment than British children adopted at the same age (Beckett et al., 2006). However, Romanian children adopted between 6 and 24 months of age had cognitive abilities significantly lower than the Romanian or British children adopted earlier, and Romanian children adopted at ages between 24 and 42 months of age had cognitive abilities that were lower still. This indicates that after about 6 months of age, the damage to the brain as a result of early deprivation often could not be entirely undone even by years of exposure to a more stimulating environment. Plasticity of the infant brain is high but diminishes steeply over the first few years of life. This demonstrates that the timing of experience in the ecocultural setting matters a whole lot early in development, and a shift to another ecocultural setting might not be able to undo early experience.

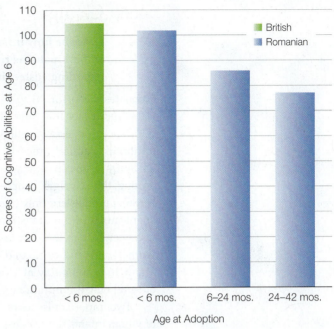

Figure 4.4 Romanian Adoptees' Cognitive Abilities, by Age of Adoption

The later the age of adoption, the lower their cognitive abilities.
SOURCE: Based on Beckett et al., 2006.

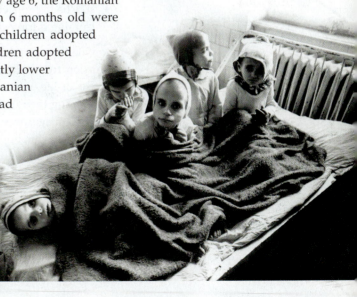

The cognitive recovery of adopted Romanian orphans depended greatly on the age at which they were adopted.

Sleep Changes

LO 4.3   Describe how infant sleep changes in the course of the first year, and evaluate the risk factors for SIDS, including the research evidence regarding cosleeping.

Neonates sleep for 16 to 17 hours a day in periods of a few hours, and are in REM sleep about half this time. By 3 to 4 months old, infants sleep for longer periods, up to 6 to 7 hours in a row at night, and REM sleep has declined to about 40 percent. By age 6 months, cultural practices influence how much infants sleep. U.S. infants sleep about 14 hours a day at this age, including daytime naps (Murkoff et al., 2009). However, among the Kipsigis people of Kenya studied by Charles Super and Sara Harkness (1986), infants slept only about 12 hours a day at 6 months of age, perhaps because they spent much of the day strapped to their mothers or an older sibling, and so expended less energy than U.S. infants do. Super and colleagues (1996) also studied infants in the Netherlands and compared their sleep patterns to U.S. infants. The Dutch infants slept about 16 hours a day at 6 months, 2 hours more than the Americans because of Dutch cultural beliefs emphasizing rest and early bedtimes for young children.

Two important issues of sleep in infancy are the risk of dying during sleep and the issue of whom infants should sleep with. For both issues, there are important cultural variations.

SUDDEN INFANT DEATH SYNDROME (SIDS) When infants are 2 to 4 months of age, they are at highest risk for **sudden infant death syndrome (SIDS)**. Infants who die of SIDS do not have any apparent illness or disorder, they simply fall asleep and never wake up. SIDS is the leading cause of death for infants 1 to 12 months of age in developed countries (OECD, 2014b). Infants of Asian descent are less likely to die of SIDS than those of European or African descent, and African American and American Indian infants are at especially high risk, with rates 4 to 6 times higher than White Americans (Pickett et al., 2005). The higher rates of SIDS among African Americans and American Indians are part of a larger pattern than begins with poorer prenatal care and continues with greater vulnerability in the first year of life.

Although deaths from SIDS have no clear cause, there are several factors known to put infants at risk (AAP Task Force on Sudden Infant Death Syndrome, 2011; Kinney & Thach, 2009), including:

- sleeping stomach-down instead of flat on the back;
- low birth weight and low Apgar score;
- having a mother who smoked during pregnancy or being around smoke during infancy;
- soft bedding, sleeping in an overheated room, or wearing two or more layers of clothing during sleep (most SIDS deaths take place in autumn and winter).

One theory is that babies' vulnerability to SIDS at 2 to 4 months of age reflects the transition from reflex behavior to intentional behavior (Lipsitt, 2003). For their first 2 months of life, when infants' breathing is blocked, a reflex causes them to shake their heads, bring their hands to their face, and push away the cause of the obstruction. After 2 months of age, once the reflex disappears, most babies are able to do this as intentional, learned behavior, but some are unable to make the transition, perhaps as a result in part of respiratory and muscular vulnerabilities. When these infants experience breathing difficulties during sleep, instead of being able to shake off the difficulty, they die.

One thing that is certain is that sleeping on the back instead of the stomach makes an enormous difference in lowering the risk of SIDS. In 1994, in response to growing research evidence of the risks of stomach-sleeping, pediatricians in the United States launched a major "BACK to Sleep" campaign to inform parents and health professionals of the importance of putting infants to sleep on their backs. Over the next decade, the prevalence of stomach-sleeping among U.S. infants declined from 70 to 20 percent and

sudden infant death syndrome (SIDS)

death within the first year of life resulting from unknown reasons, with no apparent illness or disorder

SIDS deaths declined by nearly one half (AAP Task Force on Sudden Infant Death Syndrome, 2011; National Center for Health Statistics, 2005). In response to similar campaigns in other countries, SIDS declined by 90 percent in the United Kingdom and by more than 50 percent in many other developed countries (see **Figure 4.5**; National Sudden and Unexpected Infant/Child Death & Pregnancy Loss Resource Center, 2010).

COSLEEPING: HELPFUL OR HARMFUL TO BABIES?

With whom should infants sleep? Should they sleep by themselves, in a crib or even a room of their own, or should they sleep alongside a parent or a sibling?

If you are a member of a Western cultural group, you may assume that it is better for infants to have their own crib and room within a few weeks after birth, so that they can learn to be independent and the parents can enjoy their marital intimacy without disruption (or without as much disruption, at least). Prominent pediatricians and health authorities in the United States and other Western countries warn against **cosleeping**, in which the infant sleeps in the same bed as the parents, arguing that it leads to excessive dependence by infants and can endanger the emotional health of infants or even lead to SIDS (American Academy of Pediatrics [AAP] Task Force on Infant Positioning and SIDS, 2000; AAP Task Force on Sudden Infant Death Syndrome, 2011; Spock & Needleman, 2004).

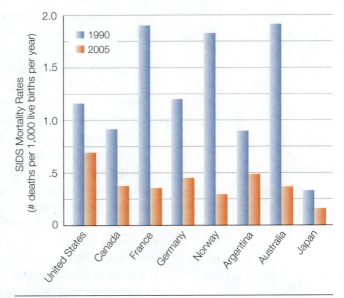

Figure 4.5 The Impact of Prevention Campaigns on SIDS Rates

Why did rates of SIDS decline so much over this period?

However, this is one of many issues in this book where what is normal and seems healthy and "natural" in Western countries is actually extremely unusual worldwide. Outside of the West, nearly all cultural groups have some form of cosleeping during infancy (Small, 2005). Many of the parents in these groups view the Western practice of nightly isolation of infants as "a form of child neglect or worse" (DeLoache & Gottlieb, 2000, pp. 16–17). They believe infants are highly vulnerable to injury, illness, and death, and that sleeping beside the mother is necessary to protect them. This arrangement also makes it easy for the infant to breast feed when necessary during the night, without disturbing others and arousing the mother only slightly. Typically, a child sleeps beside the mother until the next child is born, which is usually when the child is 2 to 4 years old. By looking around the world at these patterns, we see in the ecocultural setting that something that seems as simple and as taken for granted as who sleeps by whom is actually a cultural activity.

cosleeping

cultural practice in which infants and sometimes older children sleep with one or both parents

In most cultures, mothers and infants cosleep.

In a study comparing sleeping arrangements among Guatemalan Maya and White Americans, all the Mayan mothers coslept with their infants until the next child was born, whereupon the child would cosleep with the father or in a bed alongside the mother and the new baby (Morelli et al., 1992). The mothers explained that cosleeping helped promote a close parent–child attachment, highly valued in their collectivistic culture. The Mayan mothers were appalled when they learned that U.S. infants typically sleep alone and regarded this practice as cold and cruel. In contrast, few of the U.S. mothers coslept with their infants, explaining that they wanted the child to become independent and that cosleeping would foster a degree of dependency that would be emotionally unhealthy.

But it is not just in traditional cultures like the Guatemalan Maya that cosleeping is the norm. In Japan and South Korea, two of the most technologically advanced countries in the world, almost all infants cosleep with their mothers, and children continue to sleep with or near their mothers until puberty (Mindell et al., 2010). Like the Mayan mothers, Asian mothers justify their cosleeping practices on the basis of collectivistic values, explaining that this is one way for children to learn from an early age that they are closely tied to others in bonds of interdependence and mutual obligation.

Cultural customs regarding infant sleeping arrangements are a good example of a **custom complex**, that is, a distinctive cultural pattern of behavior that is based on underlying cultural beliefs. Cosleeping tends to reflect collectivistic beliefs, that members of the culture are closely bound to one another (Small, 1998). In contrast, having infants sleep alone tends to reflect an individualistic belief that each person should learn to be self-sufficient and not rely on others any more than necessary.

Parents in an individualistic culture may fear that cosleeping will make infants and children too dependent. However, children who cosleep with their parents in infancy are actually more self-reliant (e.g., able to dress themselves) and more socially independent (e.g., can make friends by themselves) than other children are (Keller & Goldberg, 2004).

What about the danger of SIDS? Don't cultures where cosleeping is the norm have high rates of SIDS, if cosleeping is a risk factor for SIDS as most U.S. pediatricians believe? On the contrary, SIDS is almost unknown in cultures where cosleeping is the norm (Hewlett & Roulette, 2014). In the United States, however, where most parents do not cosleep, rates of SIDS are among the highest in the world.

There appear to be several reasons for this pattern (McKenna & McDade, 2005). First, most parents and infants in cosleeping cultures sleep on relatively hard surfaces such as a mat on the floor or a futon, thus avoiding the soft bedding that is sometimes implicated in SIDS. Second, infants who cosleep breast feed more often and longer than infants who do not, and these frequent episodes of arousal in the course of the night make SIDS less likely. Third, cosleeping mothers tend to lay their infants on their backs to make the mother's breast more easily accessible for breast feeding. Thus back-sleeping developed as a widespread cultural practice for practical reasons long before research showed that it lessened the risk of SIDS.

Some cultures within the United States have a long tradition of infant cosleeping, as shown in the video *Cosleeping*. It is a common practice among African Americans and Latinos (Barajas et al., 2011; Milan et al., 2007). In the rural culture of the Appalachian Mountains children typically sleep alongside their parents for the first 2 years of life (Abbott, 1992). In many developed countries, the prevalence of cosleeping in infancy has grown in recent years as research has shown that it causes no emotional harm and may even be protective against SIDS (Mindell et al., 2010; Willinger et al., 2003). Cosleeping infants may be at risk for SIDS if their parents are obese or consume alcohol or other drugs before sleeping, but otherwise cosleeping is more often a protective factor than a risk factor for SIDS (McKenna & McDade, 2005).

custom complex

distinctive cultural pattern of behavior that reflects underlying cultural beliefs

Watch COSLEEPING

Video

What might cosleeping indicate about expectations for marital relations in a culture that practices it?

PHYSICAL DEVELOPMENT:
Infant Health

Infants' health depends a great deal on where they happened to be born, that is, on their cultural, economic, and social context. Here we look first at how nutritional needs change over the first year, then at the prevalence and effects of malnutrition. This will be followed by an examination of infant mortality rates and causes, immunizations, and cultural beliefs and practices to protect babies.

Nutritional Needs

LO 4.4   **Describe how infants' nutritional needs change during the first year of life, and identify the reasons for and consequences of malnutrition in infancy.**

Infants need a lot of food, and they need it often. In fact, during the first year of life nutritional energy needs are greater than at any other time of life, per pound of body weight (Vlaardingerbroek et al., 2009). Infants also need more fat in their diets than at any later point in life, to fuel the growth of their bodies and (especially) their brains.

INTRODUCTION OF SOLID FOODS The best way to obtain good high-fat nutrition during infancy is through breast milk. Infants also start eating some solid foods during the first year of life. Cultures vary widely in when they introduce solid food to infants, ranging from those that introduce it after just a few weeks of life to those that wait until the second half of the first year. Age 4 to 5 months is common for solid foods, in part because that is an age when infants can sit up with support and also the age when they often begin to show an interest in what others are eating (Small, 2005).

At 4 to 5 months old, infants still have a gag reflex that causes them to spit out any solid item that enters their mouths. Consequently, at first more food ends up on them than in them! The ability to chew and swallow does not develop until the second half of the first year (Napier & Meister, 2000).

In the West, pediatricians generally recommend introducing solid food during the fifth or sixth month of life (Seach et al., 2010). Usually the first solid food is rice cereal mixed with breast milk or formula, made thin when first introduced and gradually thickened as the baby becomes used to eating it (National Center for Education in Maternal and Child Health, 2002). A wider range of foods is introduced in the second half of the first year, but always soft foods that babies can easily eat and digest, such as pureed carrots or applesauce.

In traditional cultures, the first foods to be introduced have been mashed, pureed, or prechewed. For example, among the Balinese in Indonesia, even in the first weeks of life mothers give their babies soft prechewed foods such as bananas to supplement breast milk (Diener, 2000). In the course of the first year, the range of foods provided to the baby widens, but the mother typically chews the food first.

MALNUTRITION IN INFANCY Because infants have such great nutritional needs, and because their brains and bodies are growing at a faster rate than at any later time of life, the effects of malnutrition in infancy are especially severe and enduring. Infants are capable of thriving mainly on breast milk, along with a little solid food after the early months, so malnutrition in infancy is usually the result of the mother being unable or

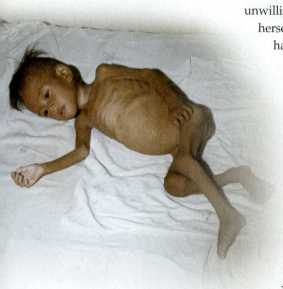

Infants with marasmus waste away from lack of nourishment.

unwilling to breast feed. Often the problem is that the mother is so ill or malnourished herself that she is unable to produce an adequate supply of breast milk. Or, she may have a disease that can be communicated through breast milk, such as tuberculosis or HIV, and she has been advised not to breast feed. She may also have been misled to believe that infant formula is better for her baby than breast milk, so she has stopped breast feeding and instead gives her infant the formula substitute, which may not be available in sufficient quantity. If the infant's mother has died—not unusual in the areas of the world where infant malnutrition is most common—there may be no one else who can breast feed the baby or otherwise provide adequate nutrition.

Malnutrition is a problem around the world, including in developed countries like the United States where most mothers are healthy. Government programs like WIC (the Special Supplemental Nutrition Program for Women, Infants and Children, first enacted in 1972) help provide nutritious foods to mothers of infants and children. WIC was first designed for breast-feeding women, but it was adjusted to include women who were feeding their infants with formula. Improving the WIC program's offerings helps improve women's diets, and leads to more breast feeding among poor women (Shafai et al., 2014). States and other locales, such as American Indian tribal areas, maintain lists of WIC-approved foods that mothers with infants may purchase with vouchers. The lists usually include items such as bread, pure fruit juice, milk, cereal, canned beans and fish, and eggs. WIC supplementation programs have been found to make a difference in children's later IQ and school performance (Hicks et al. 1982).

Malnourished infants are at risk for **marasmus**, a disease in which the body wastes away from lack of nutrients. The body stops growing, the muscles atrophy, the baby becomes increasingly lethargic, and eventually death results. Even among infants who survive, malnutrition impairs normal development for years to come (Galler et al., 2010; Nolan et al., 2002). However, studies in Guatemala and several other developing countries have found that nutritional supplements for infants in poor families have enduring beneficial effects on their physical, cognitive, and social development (Pollitt et al., 1996).

Infant Mortality

LO 4.5 List the major causes and preventive methods of infant mortality, and describe some cultural approaches to protecting infants.

The first year of life has always been a perilous period for the human species. Human females typically have a reproductive span of at least 20 years, from the late teens through the late 30s, and with regular sexual intercourse most would have at least three to seven children during that span. Yet, until recently in human history there was little increase in the total human population. This means that many children died before reaching reproductive age, and based on current patterns it seems likely that many of them died in infancy. Even now, worldwide, the first year of life has the highest risk of death of any period in the entire life span (UNICEF, 2014b).

CAUSES AND PREVENTION OF INFANT MORTALITY Most infant mortality takes place during the first month of life and is usually as a result of severe birth defects or low birth weight or is an indirect consequence of the death of the mother during childbirth (UNICEF, 2014b). As with neonatal mortality, rates of infant mortality are much higher in developing countries than in developed countries (see **Map 4.1**).

With regard to deaths beyond the first month but within the first year, in addition to deaths resulting from malnutrition, diseases are another major cause of infant mortality worldwide. Malaria, a blood disease spread by mosquitoes, is a major killer of infants, responsible for about 1 million infant deaths per year, mainly in Africa (Finkel, 2007a, b).

marasmus

disease in which the body wastes away from lack of nutrients

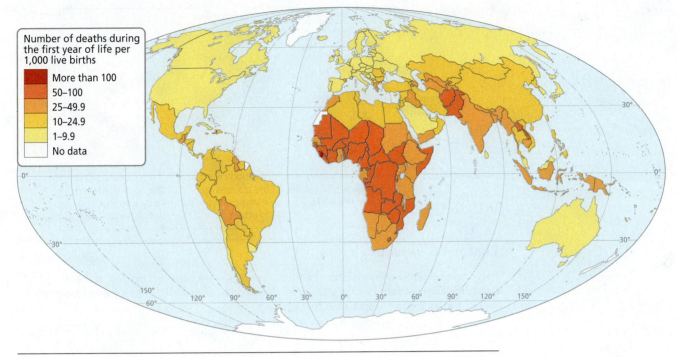

Map 4.1 Infant Mortality Rates Worldwide

How do infant mortality rates compare with neonatal mortality rates? What are some potential causes of the high infant mortality rates in developing countries?

SOURCE: Based on UNICEF (2014).

Dysentery, an illness of the digestive system, is also one of the top sources of infant mortality, especially in tropical regions in which dysentery bacteria thrive.

Overall, the number-one cause of infant mortality beyond the first month but within the first year is diarrhea (UNICEF, 2014b). Infants with diarrhea lose fluids and eventually die from dehydration if untreated. Diarrhea may be caused by a range of digestive illnesses and is often a consequence of bottle-feeding in unsanitary conditions. In developing countries, infants who bottle feed have a mortality rate five times higher than those who breast feed (Lamberti, et al. 2011), and many of the deaths are as a result of diarrhea caused by mixing formula powder with unclean water.

Diarrhea can be cured easily through simple, inexpensive **oral rehydration therapy (ORT)**. ORT involves having infants with diarrhea drink a solution of salt and glucose mixed with (clean) water. Since 1980 the World Health Organization (WHO) has led an international effort to reduce infant deaths through providing ORT, and the effort has reduced the worldwide rate of infant deaths as a result of diarrhea from 4.5 million per year to less than 2 million (Boschi-Pinto et al., 2009). However, the reason the rate is still as high as 2 million per year is that even now, in the parts of the world where infant diarrhea is most common, this simple, inexpensive remedy is often unavailable.

Although millions of infants worldwide die yearly from lack of adequate nutrition and medical care, in the past half-century, many diseases that formerly killed infants and young children have been reduced or even eliminated because of vaccines that provide immunization (see **Figure 4.6** on the next page). Smallpox has been eradicated, measles and polio have been eliminated in large regions of the world, and diphtheria, tetanus, and yellow fever have been greatly reduced in prevalence, all as a result of immunization programs (Population Reference Bureau, 2014).

Typically, children receive vaccinations for these diseases in the first or second year of life. However, there is a great deal of variability worldwide in how likely children are to be vaccinated. As of 2013, coverage for the major infant vaccines was about 70

oral rehydration therapy (ORT)

treatment for infant diarrhea that involves drinking a solution of salt and glucose mixed with clean water

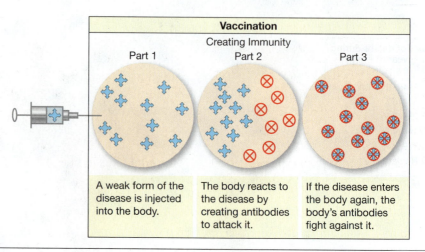

Figure 4.6 Vaccination

How a vaccine provides immunization. Part 1: A weak form of the disease is injected into the body; Part 2: The body reacts to the disease by creating antibodies to attack it; Part 3: If the disease enters the body again, the body's antibodies fight against it.

percent in Africa and South Asia, and more than 90 percent in Europe and the Americas (UNICEF, 2013). In recent years, a major effort to provide immunization to all children has been made by the World Health Organization (WHO), UNICEF, and private foundations, and the rate of immunization has been increasing, especially in Africa (UNICEF, 2013).

Although rumors have circulated that some vaccinations may actually cause harm to children, for example by triggering autism or causing SIDS, scientific studies have found no basis for these claims (CDC, 2010; Rodier, 2009). Unfortunately, some parents have been deceived by these claims and consequently refused to have their children vaccinated, which, ironically—and sadly—exposes their children and other people's children to the genuine danger of contracting infectious diseases. Recently, public health experts have determined that not vaccinating children today makes the risk of expected severity much greater for a non-vaccinated child (Fefferman & Naumova, 2015). Children who are not vaccinated may be exposed to the most severe possible outcomes should they contract diseases preventable by vaccines.

CULTURAL BELIEFS AND PRACTICES TO PROTECT INFANTS Perhaps the most striking feature of the infant's social environment in traditional cultures is the parents' acute awareness of infants' vulnerability and their resulting motive to do whatever they can to make the infant's survival most likely. The ecocultural practices of secluding infants in their early weeks, cosleeping with them, and constantly carrying them developed out of long and painful human experience with high infant mortality.

In cultures where medical remedies for infant illness are scarce, parents often resort to magical practices intended to protect their babies from disease and death. Observations today in places with little access to medical care offer many poignant examples of the cultural practices that have developed to try to protect infants. For example, the people of Bali, in Indonesia, believe that infants should

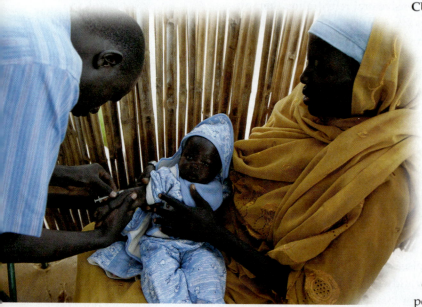

Increased prevalence of vaccinations in infancy has greatly reduced infant mortality worldwide. Here, an infant receives a vaccination in southern Sudan.

be treated like gods because they have just arrived from the spirit world, where the gods dwell (Diener, 2000). Consequently, infants should be held constantly and should never touch the ground out of respect for their godly status. If an infant dies, this is often interpreted as indicating that the infant was not shown the proper respect and so decided to return to the spirit world. Cultural explanations such as an infant's return to the spirit world are often ways of explaining high morality rates in certain cultural settings.

The Fulani people of West Africa believe that a sharp knife should always be kept near the baby to ward off the witches and evil spirits that may try to take its soul (Johnson, 2000). Compliments to the baby should be avoided at all costs because this may only make the baby seem more valuable and beautiful and so all the more attractive to the evil spirits. Instead, the Fulani people believe parents should give the infant an unattractive nickname such as "Cow Turd," so that the evil spirits will think the baby is not worth taking.

Finally, the Ifaluk of Micronesia believe that neonates should be covered with cloths in the weeks after birth to encourage sweating, which they believe helps babies grow properly (Le, 2000). Babies should be washed three times a day, morning, noon, and afternoon, but not in the evening, because evil spirits are out then. Any time babies are outside they should be covered with a cloth so that they will not be spied by evil spirits.

Many cultures resort to magic in an effort to protect their babies. Here, a baby from the Hamer Tribe of Ethiopia wears jewelry the mother has adorned her with to ward off disease.

PHYSICAL DEVELOPMENT: Motor and Sensory Development

One of the most striking features of human neonates is how little they are able to move around. Even if you hold neonates up, their heads flop to one side because their neck muscles are not yet strong enough to support their large heads. But over the course of the first year they develop from immobile to highly mobile, a dramatic change not just in their lives but in the lives of those who care for them. Sensory development in the first year is subtler, but advances take place, especially in the sense of sight.

Motor Development

LO 4.6   **Describe the major changes during infancy in gross and fine motor development.**

Over the first year of life remarkable advances take place in motor development. The changes occur in **gross motor development**, which includes balance and posture as well as whole-body movements such as crawling, and in **fine motor development**, which entails more finely tuned movements of the hands such as grasping and manipulating objects.

GROSS MOTOR DEVELOPMENT Ask a parent of an infant what's new, and it's quite likely you'll hear about some new milestone of gross motor development that has recently been achieved. "Emma can now sit up on her own without falling over!" or "Juan is suddenly crawling all over the house!" or "Maru took her first steps yesterday!" There are many achievements of gross motor development over the first year, including holding the head up without support, rolling over, sitting without support, crawling, standing, cruising (walking while holding on to something), and (for some) walking. Most children achieve these skills in this sequence, although sometimes the order of skills varies and sometimes children skip steps in the sequence. There is more variability in the timing of each milestone of gross motor development than in the sequence. As you

gross motor development

development of motor abilities including balance and posture as well as whole-body movements such as crawling

fine motor development

development of motor abilities involving finely tuned movements of the hands such as grasping and manipulating objects

can see in the video *Milestones of Gross Motor Development in Infancy*, for each milestone there is a normal range of variation of several months. Infants could reach the milestones anywhere within those ranges and still be developing normally.

Watch MILESTONES OF GROSS MOTOR DEVELOPMENT IN INFANCY

In many traditional cultures infants are strapped to their mothers' backs for most of the day. Here, a mother and infant are pictured in rural Vietnam.

How much of infants' gross motor development takes place as a result of an inborn, genetically based, individual timetable, and how much of it is because of experience and learning? As with most aspects of development, both genetics and environment are involved. Certainly the highly consistent sequence of gross motor milestones suggests a genetically based timetable. There is also evidence for genetic group differences, with infants of African heritage reaching most motor milestones earlier than other infants (Kelly et al., 2006). However, most developmental psychologists view gross motor development in infancy as a combination of the genetic timetable, the maturation of the brain, support and assistance from adults for developing the skill, and the child's own efforts to practice the skill (Adolf & Berger, 2006; Thelen, 2001).

Looking at infant gross motor development across cultures provides a vivid picture of how genetics and environment interact. In many traditional cultures it is a common practice for infants to be strapped onto their mothers' backs for most of the day, as the mothers go about their daily business of tending crops, preparing food, and other kinds of work (Pretorious et al., 2002; Super & Harkness, 2015). In some ecocultural settings a common infant-care practice in the first few months of life is swaddling. If infants are strapped to their mothers' backs or swaddled for most of the day, they receive little practice in developing gross motor skills. These restrictive practices are partly to free the mother to work, but cultures that swaddle infants also believe that swaddling protects the infant from sickness and other threats to health (DeLoache & Gottlieb, 2000). Swaddling beyond the early months of life is part of an ecocultural package of infant care that is meant to help ensure infant survival.

Even after they learn to crawl at about 6 months old and walk at about 1 year of age, infants in traditional cultures are restricted in their exercise of these new motor skills. If they are allowed to crawl around and explore they might wander into the cooking fire, or be trampled by livestock, or tumble off a cliff, or any number of other bad things, so it is viewed as best to keep them in someone's arms at all times. For example, among infants in the Gusii culture in Kenya, infants are held or carried 80 percent of the time their first 6 months, and 60 percent from 6 to 12 months, gradually declining to less than 10 percent by the end of the second year (LeVine et al., 1994).

In contrast, some cultures actively promote infants' gross motor development. For example, the Kipsigis people of Kenya begin encouraging gross motor skills from early on (Super & Harkness, 2009). When only 2 to 3 months old, infants are placed in shallow holes and kept upright by rolled blankets, months before they would be able to sit on their own. At about the same age, parents start encouraging their infants to practice walking by holding them up and bouncing their feet on the ground. Similarly, in Jamaica, mothers massage and stretch their babies' arms and legs beginning in early infancy to promote strength and growth, and like the Kipsigis, beginning at 2 to 3 months of age they help their babies practice walking (Hopkins & Westra, 1990). In some Western countries, pediatricians now recommend "tummy time" for infants, that is, placing them on their stomachs for a short period each day to encourage them to learn to push up, roll over, sit up, and stand (Iannelli, 2007). Tummy time is viewed as more important now than it was in the past because infants are now supposed to sleep on their backs to reduce the risk of SIDS and so spend less time on their stomachs.

How much does it matter, ultimately, if cultural practices hinder or promote infants' gross motor development? A little in the short run, perhaps, but not much in the long run. For the most part, infants in cultures where they are strapped to the mother's back or swaddled learn to crawl and walk at about the same age as infants in cultures that neither bind their infants nor make special efforts to support gross motor development (Adolph et al., 2010). One exception is the Ache people, a South American Indian culture (Kaplan & Dove, 1987). Ache mothers have extremely close contact with their infants, strapping, carrying, or holding them 93 percent of the time during the day and 100 percent of the night hours. Consequently, Ache children do not typically begin walking until about age 2, a year later than the norm across cultures. However, this appears to be partly because Ache infants enjoy being carried around so much that they often refuse to walk even after they are able! In any case, there is no difference in gross motor development by age 6 between Ache children and children in less restrictive cultures.

Infants in cultures where gross motor development is actively stimulated may develop slightly earlier than in cultures where parents make no special efforts. In a study comparing Jamaican immigrant infants in England with native-born English mothers, the Jamaican immigrant infants walked slightly earlier, evidently because their mothers encouraged them to walk and practiced with them, but the two groups were no different in when crawling began (Hopkins & Westra, 1990). In some African cultures that actively stimulate gross motor development, infants walk a few weeks earlier than children in the West (Adolph et al., 2010). Here again, however, by age 6 there are no differences in gross motor development between children in the cultures that promote early motor achievement and cultures that do not. Thus, it appears that cultural practices can slightly speed up or slow down the timetable for gross motor development in infancy, but the influence of the environment is relatively small and transient for this particular area of development.

FINE MOTOR DEVELOPMENT One of the evolutionary developments that makes humans anatomically distinctive among animals is the **opposable thumb**, that is, the position of our thumbs opposite our fingers. (Place your thumb now against your fingers and you will see what I mean.) The opposable thumb is the basis of fine motor development, the deft movements of our hands that enable us to make a tool, pick up a small object, or thread a needle. During the first year of life fine motor skills make considerable progress.

The principal milestones of fine motor development in infancy are reaching and grasping. Oddly, infants are better at reaching during the first month of life than they are at 2 months of age (Spencer et al., 2000). Neonates will extend their arms awkwardly toward an interesting object, an action called *prereaching*, although it is more like a swipe or a swing than a well-coordinated reach. By 2 months, however, prereaching no longer takes place

opposable thumb
position of the thumb apart from the fingers, unique to humans, that makes possible fine motor movements

By 9 to 12 months of age, infants are able to grasp small objects.

(Lee et al., 2008). Prereaching is a reflex that occurs in response to an object, and like many reflexes it disappears within the first months of life.

At about 3 months of age, reaching reappears, but in a more coordinated and accurate way than in the neonate. Reaching continues to develop over the course of the first year, becoming smoother, more direct, and more capable of adjusting to changes in the movement and position of the object (Berthier & Carrico, 2010).

Grasping is also a neonatal reflex, and this means it is not under intentional control (Schott & Rossor, 2003). Neonates will automatically grasp whatever is placed in their hands. Like reaching, grasping becomes smoother and more accurate during the first year, as infants learn to adjust the positions of their fingers and thumbs even before their hand reaches the object, and to adjust further once they grasp the object, in response to its size, shape, and weight (Daum et al., 2011). By the end of the first year, infants are able to grasp a spoon well enough to begin to feed themselves.

At the same time as infants' abilities for reaching and grasping are advancing, they are learning to coordinate the two. They use the combination to help them explore the environment around them. By 5 months of age, once they reach and grasp an object, they might hold it with one hand as they explore it with the other, or transfer it from one hand to the other (Keen, 2005).

Learning to coordinate reaching and grasping is the basis of further development of fine motor skills and an essential part of human motor functioning. However, during infancy it can also be a dangerous ability to have. Beginning at about 4 to 5 months, what is the first thing infants do with an object after reaching and grasping it? They put it in their mouths, of course—whether it is edible or not. (How this tendency somehow survived natural selection is a good question.) At this age they can mainly grasp objects that pose no danger because their grasping ability is not yet fine enough to enable them to grasp objects they could choke on. However, by 9 to 12 months of age infants learn the "pincer grasp" that allows them to hold a small object between their thumb and forefinger, such as a marble, a coin, or a crayon stub (Murkoff et al., 2003). This allows them to begin feeding themselves small pieces of food, but the tendency to

Cultural Focus: Infant Fine Motor Development Across Cultures

Fine motor development in infancy mainly involves learning how to reach and how to grasp, and then how to coordinate the two. Infants everywhere need to learn how to perform these simple but essential activities, and as you will see in this video, infants across countries show similarities in the development of their fine motor skills.

Review Question:

Can you think of any related skills that the pincer grasp might be a precursor for? What about skills related to grasping? In what ways would these primitive skills be important across cultures?

Watch INFANT FINE MOTOR DEVELOPMENT ACROSS CULTURES

Video

taste even the untasteable remains at this age, so others have to be especially vigilant in monitoring what infants reach, grasp, and place in their mouths.

Sensory Development

LO 4.7 Describe how infants' sensory abilities develop in the first year.

The senses vary in how developed they are at birth. Taste and touch are nearly mature, hearing is well-developed in most respects, and sight is the least mature of the senses. In this section, we review the development of hearing and sight in the infancy period.

HEARING AND VISION Hearing develops during the last trimester of fetal development and is mostly developed at birth. Over the course of the first year, infants can distinguish the sound categories and word boundaries in their native language (Kidd et al., 2014). However, infant attention, memory, and processing speed are limited, so they cannot encode all auditory aspects of a situation, let alone all the visual or social aspects. Some researchers have proposed that infants use **statistical learning** to encode and learn about the world, particularly the linguistic world (Saffran, 2003).

Sight develops rapidly after birth. Over the first couple months of life, experience in the world and rapid maturation of the visual cortex lead to an increased ability to make out different shapes and notice details. Young infants prefer to look at complex patterns, especially human faces, and they prefer moving faces to still faces (see **Figure 4.7**). More recently developed measures, such as eye tracking, have gone beyond looking times to examine how infants scan faces and social situations. The ability to extract the most relevant information from a face is something that develops over infancy. One-month-old infants tend to look at the periphery of faces, whereas 2-month-old infants tend to focus on the eyes (Maurer & Salapatek, 1976). From 4 to 8 months of age, hearing infants shift their attention from the eyes to the mouth as they are learning language (Lewkowicz & Hansen-Tift, 2012).

Typical infants' ability to see colors is present from birth, but their color vision improves over the first year of life (see **Figure 4.8**). Some infants are born color blind. Color-blindness is a result of the inability to see color and is typically manifested by the inability to differentiate red from green.

DEPTH PERCEPTION One important aspect of vision that develops during infancy is **depth perception**, which is the ability to discern the relative distance of objects in the

Figure 4.7 Visual Preferences in Infancy

Infants look longer at the face than they do at the jumbled face, and they look longer at the jumbled face than a less-complex image.

statistical learning

the ability to extract statistical regularities in information in the world

depth perception

ability to discern the relative distance of objects in the environment

Figure 4.8 Color Vision in Infancy

Infants have good color vision by about 5 months of age, although their color sensitivity is not as good as adults' color sensitivity.

Figure 4.9 The Visual Cliff Experiment

Infants' reluctance to cross the "visual cliff" shows their ability for depth perception.

environment (Kavšec, 2003). The key to depth perception is **binocular vision**, the ability to combine the images of each eye into one image. Because our two eyes are slightly apart on our faces, they have slightly different angles on the visual field before them, and combining these two angles into one image provides a perception of the depth or distance of the object. That is, it indicates the location of the object in relation to the observer and in relation to other objects in the visual field. Binocular vision begins to develop by about 3 months of age (Brown & Miracle, 2003; Slater et al., 2002).

Depth perception becomes especially important once babies become mobile. Once they begin to crawl and then walk they may run into things or fall off the edge of surfaces unless they can use depth perception to anticipate hazards.

This was first demonstrated in a classic experiment by Eleanor Gibson and James Walk (1960). Gibson's inspiration for the experiment was a recent trip to the Grand Canyon, where her fear that her young children would tumble over the edge inspired her to wonder when children develop an awareness of depth that allows them to avoid such mishaps. Back in the lab, she and Walk designed a clever experiment. They made a glass-covered table with a checkered pattern below the glass, but on one half of the table the checkered pattern was just below the surface whereas on the other half it was about two feet below, giving the appearance of a "visual cliff" in the middle of the table (see **Figure 4.9**).

The infants in the study (ages 6–14 months) were happy to crawl around on the "shallow" side of the cliff, but most would not cross over to the "deep" side, even when their mothers stood on the other side of it and beckoned them encouragingly. At first, these results were taken to show that they had learned depth perception.

Later results of studies of depth perception on the visual cliff showed the importance of disentangling depth perception from the emotional response of fear (Campos et al., 1970). Using concepts from the paradigm of habituation and the physical measure of heart rate, Campos and his colleagues found that infants as young as 2½ months can distinguish the deep and shallow sides of the visual cliff. Heart rate deceleration is a marker of orientation or interest that is reliable in even very young infants. Interestingly, when prelocomotor infants were lowered onto the deep side of the visual cliff, they showed heart rate deceleration, indicating that they could tell the difference between that side and the shallow side. However, they did not exhibit the emotional sign of fear. Fear in response to the deep side of the cliff appears to develop with crawling experience—a few months later, as Gibson and Walk had shown.

Campos and his colleagues concluded that the visual cliff would be useful to study infant perception as well as infant emotional development. Remember, researchers have had to use behavioral or physical measures to find out what infants know, rather than asking for a linguistic response that the infant, by definition, cannot give. Later work by Sorce, Emde, Campos, and Klilnnert (1985) showed that the mother's emotional response to the infant's behavior on the visual cliff influenced whether infants would crawl across the deep side. By about 12 months of age, infants use facial expressions of others to interpret situations. If a mother showed joy or interest at her 1-year-old's facial reference, the infant was more likely to cross over the deep side of the cliff than if

binocular vision
ability to combine the images of the two eyes into one image

the mother showed fear or sadness. This study is an example of how infant perceptual development proceeds with cognitive and social development.

INTERMODAL PERCEPTION   Studies of infants' sensory abilities typically try to isolate a single sense so that it can be studied without interference from the others, but of course, this is not how the senses function in real life. Shake a rattle in front of 6-month-old baby, and she sees it, hears it, reaches out and touches it, then tastes it, effortlessly coordinating all her senses at once. Speech perception typically involves perceiving through more than one sense at the same time—watching the lips of someone talking can help in understanding what they are saying.

The integration and coordination of sensory information is called **intermodal perception** (Lewkowitz & Lickliter, 2013). Even neonates possess a rudimentary form of this ability. When they hear a sound they look in the direction it came from, indicating coordination of auditory and visual responses. Over the course of the first year intermodal perception develops further. One-month-old infants recognize objects they have put in their mouths but have not seen before, indicating integration of touch and sight (Schweinle & Wilcox, 2004). Four-month-old infants look longer at a video of a puppet jumping up and down in time with music than at the same puppet when the jumping does not match the music, suggesting that the correspondence of visual and auditory stimuli appeals to them (Spelke, 1979). Six-month-old infants can match the approximate number of sounds they hear to the approximate number of sights they see, showing that infants compare numerical information across modalities (Feigenson, 2011).

The ability to understand people's emotions initially requires intermodal perception (Walker-Andrews, 1997). Interestingly, infants first use multimodal information, such as facial and vocal expressions together, to understand others' emotions. Later, they can recognize emotions from facial or vocal expressions alone.

Infants younger than 1 year of age have shown they can match facial and vocal expressions and body postures to emotions. For example, 6½-month-old infants can match static body postures to vocalizations (Zieber et al., 2014). By 8 months, infants can even match an unfamiliar person's face with the correct voice when the faces and voices vary on the basis of age and gender, indicating a developing ability to coordinate visual and auditory information (Patterson & Werker, 2002). Thus, the early development of intermodal perception helps infants learn about their physical and social world (Lewkowitz & Lickliter, 2013).

Recent developments in the measurement of brain function have shown that there are neural correlates of intermodal sensory activity. Specifically, evoked reaction potentials (ERPs) are used to measure neural responsiveness. When intersensory information is consistent, 5-month-old infants exhibit ERPs indicative of more efficient neural processing than when events presented provide no intersensory consistency (Reynolds et al., 2014).

intermodal perception
integration and coordination of information from the various senses

Summary: Physical Development

LO 4.1   **Describe how the infant's body changes in the first year, and explain the two basic principles of physical growth.**

The physical developments of infancy include a tripling of weight and an inch-per-month growth in height. The cephalocaudal principle means that physical growth tends to begin at the top, with the head, and then proceeds downward to the rest of the body. The proximodistal principle means that growth proceeds from the middle of the body outward.

LO 4.2   **Identify the different parts of the brain, and describe how the brain changes in the first few years of life.**

The brain is separated into two hemispheres connected by the corpus callosum, and each hemisphere has four lobes with distinct functions. Brain development in infancy is concentrated in the expansion of dendritic connections and myelination. Studies of infants and children exposed to extreme deprivation indicate that the brain is especially vulnerable in the first year of life.

LO 4.3 **Describe how infant sleep changes in the course of the first year, and evaluate the risk factors for SIDS, including the research evidence regarding cosleeping.**

Sleep needs decline during the first year. SIDS is most common at 2 to 4 months of age. Sleeping on the back rather than the stomach greatly reduces the risk of SIDS. In cultures where infants sleep alongside their mothers on a firm surface the risk of SIDS is very low. Historically and worldwide today, mother–infant cosleeping is far more common than putting babies to sleep in a room of their own.

LO 4.4 **Describe how infants' nutritional needs change during the first year of life, and identify the reasons for and consequences of malnutrition in infancy.**

The best way to obtain good high-fat nutrition during infancy is through breast milk. The timing of the introduction of solid food varies among cultures, from the first weeks of life to sometime in the second half of the first year. Malnutrition in infancy is usually as a result mainly of the mother being unable or unwilling to breast feed.

LO 4.5 **List the major causes and preventive methods of infant mortality, and describe some cultural approaches to protecting infants.**

Malnutrition is a common source of infant mortality, but the most common source is diarrhea. Diarrhea can be cured by oral rehydration therapy (ORT), though access to clean water makes this treatment unavailable in some parts of the world. The cultural practices of secluding infants in their early weeks, cosleeping with them, and constantly carrying them developed out of long and painful human experience with high infant mortality.

LO 4.6 **Describe the major changes during infancy in gross and fine motor development.**

Achievements in gross motor development in infancy include rolling over, crawling, and standing. Cultural practices restricting or encouraging gross motor development make a slight difference in the timing of gross motor achievements but little difference in the long run. Reaching and grasping are two of the fine motor milestones of the first year.

LO 4.7 **Describe how infants' sensory abilities develop in the first year.**

Increased adeptness at binocular vision around 3 months of age enables infants to develop depth perception during the first year. Infants also become better at intermodal perception or coordinating their senses.

Section 2   Cognitive Development

 Learning Objectives

4.8 Describe the first four sensorimotor substages of Piaget's theory.

4.9 Describe how the elements of the information-processing model of cognitive functioning change in infancy.

4.10 Describe the major scales used in measuring infant development, and explain how habituation assessments are used to predict later intelligence.

4.11 Evaluate the claim that educational media enhance infants' cognitive development.

4.12 Describe the course of language development over the first year of life.

4.13 Describe how cultures vary in their stimulation of language development.

COGNITIVE DEVELOPMENT:
Approaches to Understanding Cognitive Change

We begin this section with Piaget's sensorimotor stage, highlighting the development of the object concept. Then, we examine how the information processing aspects of attention and memory change during infancy.

Piaget's Sensorimotor Stage

LO 4.8   Describe the first four sensorimotor substages of Piaget's theory.

Piaget termed the first 2 years of life the **sensorimotor stage**. Cognitive change in this stage occurs as the infant learns how to coordinate sensory activities with motor activities. The two major cognitive achievements of infancy are the advance in sensorimotor development from reflex behavior to intentional action and the attainment of object permanence.

SUBSTAGES 1–4 According to Piaget, the sensorimotor stage can be divided into six substages (Piaget, 1952, 1954). The first four substages take place during the first year of life and will be described here. The last two sensorimotor stages develop in the second year and will be covered in Chapter 5 on toddlerhood.

> *Substage 1: Simple reflexes (0–1 month).* In this substage, cognitive activity is based mainly on the neonatal reflexes, such as sucking, rooting, and grasping. Reflexes are a type of scheme because they are a way of processing and organizing information. However, unlike most schemes, for which there is a balance of assimilation and accommodation, reflex schemes are weighted heavily toward assimilation because they do not adapt much in response to the environment.

> *Substage 2: First habits and primary circular reactions (1–4 months).* In this substage, infants' activities in relation to the world become based less on reflexes and more on

sensorimotor stage
in Piaget's theory, the first 2 years of cognitive development, which involves learning how to coordinate the activities of the senses with motor activities

the infants' purposeful behavior. Specifically, infants in this substage learn to repeat bodily movements that occurred initially by chance. For example, infants often discover how tasty their hands and fingers can be in this substage. Although moving their hands around randomly one ends up in their mouth and they begin sucking on it. Finding this sensation pleasurable, they repeat the movement, now intentionally. The movement is *primary* because it focuses on the infant's own body, and *circular* because once it is discovered it is repeated intentionally.

Substage 3: Secondary circular reactions (4–8 months). Like primary circular reactions, secondary circular reactions entail the repetition of movements that originally occurred by chance. The difference is that primary circular reactions involve activity that is restricted to the infant's own body, whereas secondary circular reactions involve activity in relation to the external world. For example, Piaget recorded how his daughter Lucienne accidentally kicked a mobile hanging over her crib. Delighted at the effect, she now repeated the behavior intentionally, over and over, each time squealing with laughter (Crain, 2000).

Substage 4: Coordination of secondary schemes (8–12 months). In this substage, for the first time the baby's actions begin not as accidents but as intentional, goal-directed behavior. Furthermore, rather than exercising one scheme at a time, the infant can now coordinate schemes. For example, at this age Piaget's son Laurent was able to move an object (Piaget's hand) out of the way to reach another object (a matchbox), thus coordinating three schemes: moving something aside, reaching, and grasping.

OBJECT PERMANENCE Another important cognitive advance in infancy is the initial understanding of **object permanence**. This is the awareness that objects (including people) continue to exist even when we are not in direct sensory or motor contact with them.

From his observations and simple experiments, Piaget concluded that infants have little understanding of object permanence for much of the first year of life (Piaget, 1952). When infants younger than 4 months drop an object, they do not look to see where it went. Piaget interpreted this as indicating that, to the infants, the object ceased to exist once they could not see or touch it. From 4 to 8 months, infants who drop an object will look briefly to see where it has gone, but only briefly, which Piaget interpreted as indicating that they are unsure whether the object still exists. If infants at this age are shown an interesting object—Piaget liked to use his pocket watch—and then the object is placed under a blanket, they will not lift up the blanket to look for it.

According to Piaget, it is only at 8 to 12 months that infants begin to show a developing awareness of object permanence. Now, when shown an interesting object that then disappears under a blanket, they will pick up the blanket to find it. However, their grasp of object permanence at this age is still rudimentary, as Piaget showed by making the task slightly more complicated. After an 8- to 12-month-old child successfully solved the object-under-the-blanket task several times, Piaget introduced a second blanket next to the first, showed the infant the object, and this time placed it under the second blanket. Infants at this age then looked for the object—but not under the second blanket, where they had just seen it hidden, but under the first blanket, where they had found it before!

Piaget called this the *A-not-B error*. The infants were used to finding the object under blanket A, so they continued to look under blanket A, not blanket B, even after they had seen the object hidden under blanket B. To Piaget, this error indicated that the infants believed that their own action of looking under blanket A was what had caused the object to reappear. They did not understand that the object continued to exist irrespective of their actions, so they did not yet fully grasp object permanence.

Limited understanding of object permanence could explain why infants love the game "peek-a-boo," in which adults cover their face with their hands or an object (such as a cloth), then suddenly reveal it. One study found that this game was played by adults and infants across a diverse range of cultures, including Brazil, Greece, India, Iran, Indonesia, South Korea, and South Africa (Fernald & O'Neill, 1993). Infants everywhere

object permanence
awareness that objects (including people) continue to exist even when we are not in direct sensory or motor contact with them

Cultural Focus: Object Permanence Across Cultures

Like the development of fine motor skills, the knowledge of object permanence is something that all young children need to learn to function in the world. In this video we see demonstrations of children at various ages being tested to see if they grasp the concept of object permanence or not. The children from many different cultures indicate that this is a universal concept.

Watch   OBJECT PERMANENCE ACROSS CULTURES

Review Question:

According to this video, object permanence is universal across cultures. Why would this be such an important concept for children to acquire?

delighted in the game, and across cultures there were developmental changes. In the early months, infants enjoyed the game but responded only when the other person's face reappeared. Beginning at about 5 months, babies would begin to smile and laugh even before the other person reappeared, indicating that they were anticipating the event. By 12 months old, infants would initiate the game themselves by holding a cloth up to the adult's face or putting it over their own. Perhaps infants everywhere love "peek-a-boo" because to them, given their limited understanding of object permanence, the other person's face seems to disappear when it is obscured, then suddenly, magically reappears.

There may be differences between children's understanding of object permanence and person permanence. Piaget thought that understanding person permanence preceded object permanence because children seemed to look for hidden people at an earlier age than they would look for objects (Piaget, 1937). But when tested in the lab under similar conditions, no differences between person permanence and object permanence have been found (Jackson et al., 1978). Perhaps the multimodal information from the social game of peek-a-boo helps infants understand that people continue to exist when they are hidden. And, obviously, the covering of the face while the body is still present is not a complete absence of the person.

EVALUATING PIAGET'S SENSORIMOTOR THEORY You may have noticed that some of the examples discussed previously involved Piaget's children. Actually, Piaget initially based his theory of sensorimotor development on his careful observations and experiments with his own three children, Laurent, Lucienne, and Jacqueline. It is remarkable—and it is a testimony to Piaget's brilliance—that a theory based on just three children within the same Swiss family became the reigning theory of infant cognitive development.

Even today, more than 70 years after he first proposed it, Piaget's theory of infant cognitive development remains influential. Like all good theories, it has inspired a wealth of research to test its assertions and implications. And, like even the best theories, it has been modified and altered on the basis of research (Morra et al., 2008).

In recent decades, methods of testing infants' cognitive abilities have become much more technologically advanced. Studies using these methods have generally concluded that Piaget's theory was correct in its overall description of infant cognitive development (Marcovitch et al., 2003). However, some critics argue that the theory may have underestimated infants' cognitive abilities, especially with regard to object permanence.

MOTOR COORDINATION AND MEMORY IN OBJECT PERMANENCE Infants' motor development occurs along with their cognitive development, so when they fail to look under a blanket for a hidden object, could it be they lack the motor coordination to search for the object rather than that they believe it is has disappeared? One line of research by Renée Baillargeon and colleagues has tested this hypothesis by using the *violation of expectations method*. This method is based on the assumption that infants will look longer at an event that has violated their expectations, and if they look longer at an event violating the rule of object permanence this indicates some understanding of object permanence, without requiring any motor movements. For example, at 5 to 6 months of age, infants will look longer when a toy they have seen hidden at one spot in a sandbox emerges from a different spot (Baillargeon, 2008; Newcombe & Huttenlocher, 2006). This seems to indicate an expectation that it should have emerged from the same spot, as a permanent object would. Even at 2 to 3 months of age, infants look longer at events that are physically impossible (Wang et al., 2005), perhaps showing a more advanced understanding of objects than Piaget would have predicted.

Using the violation of expectations method, Baillargeon (1987) conducted a clever experiment with 3½- and 4½-month-old infants. Infants were habituated to the movement of a drawbridge that turned on a hinge in a 180-degree arc. **Habituation** is the gradual decrease in attention to a stimulus after repeated presentations. It is a basic form of learning. For example, infants will look longer at a toy the first time it is presented than the fourth or fifth time. After habituation, a box was placed in the path of the drawbridge. Infants were then presented with two kinds of events. In the possible event, the drawbridge stopped upon hitting the box, thus occluding the box. In the impossible event, the drawbridge continued on the entire 180-degree path. When infants showed surprise and looked longer at the impossible event, Baillargeon concluded that the 4½-month-old infants and some of the 3½-month-old infants—those who were fast habituators understood that the box continued to exist and were thus surprised that the drawbridge would continue the full path (see **Figure 4.10**).

Remember, however, that the ways researchers find out what infants know cannot include verbal responses to questions. It can be difficult to infer the actual meaning of the findings rendered by nonverbal responses such as looking times. Susan Rivera and her colleagues (Rivera et al., 1997) conducted a test of the "drawbridge phenomenon" by varying whether a box was presented after habituation. Infants who were not presented with a box showed longer looking times when the drawbridge stopped at 112 degrees, where the box stopped in the condition where infants were presented with a box. The researchers concluded that infants prefer greater movement—the full 180-degree arc of the drawbridge rather than the 112-degree arc—rather than that the infants had attained the skill of object permanence.

Some critics of Piaget's sensorimotor theory argue that mistakes regarding object permanence may reflect memory development—an aspect of information processing—rather than a failure to understand the properties of objects. For example, with respect to the A-not-B error, the longer the delay between hiding the object under blanket B and the infant's attempts to find it, the higher the likelihood of making the error, suggesting that with a longer delay the infant may simply have forgotten where it was placed (Diamond, 1985). And, when presented with an array of three to six hiding places, rather than just two, infants tend to search for hidden objects reliably in the vicinity of the place where they had originally found the object, instead of randomly searching (Cummings & Bjork, 1983). The A-not-B error may be a memory problem related to deficits in information processing found in infancy.

CULTURE AND OBJECT PERMANENCE   Another criticism of Piaget's sensorimotor theory is cultural (Maynard, 2008). The theory was originally

habituation

gradual decrease in attention to a stimulus after repeated presentations

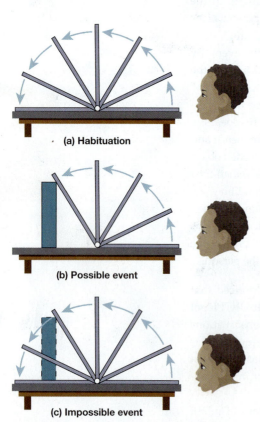

Figure 4.10 Baillargeon's Drawbridge Study

In Baillargeon's drawbridge study, the infant is habituated to a drawbridge turning on a hinge in a 180-degree arc. Then, a box is placed in the path of the drawbridge. In the possible event, the drawbridge hits the box and stops at about 120 degrees. In the impossible event, the drawbridge moves the full 180 degrees. Infants who know about the existence of the box express surprise and show longer looking times.

based on his own three Swiss children, and nearly all subsequent research has been on children in the West (Mistry & Saraswathi, 2003). However, one of the few non-Western studies of infants in Ivory Coast found that infants there reached the milestones of the sensorimotor stages earlier than Piaget had described (Dasen et al., 1978), perhaps because their parents encouraged them to develop motor skills.

Overall, however, Piaget's sensorimotor theory has held up well over many decades. Many parts of it have been supported by research, and so far no other comprehensive theory has come along to replace it. However, the information-processing approach described next views infant cognitive development quite differently.

The Information-Processing Approach

LO 4.9 **Describe how the elements of the information-processing model of cognitive functioning change in infancy.**

In Piagetian research, the focus is on how children's thinking changes across developmental stages. The idea of stages implies that we do not simply expand our cognitive capacity as we develop; our thinking actually undergoes qualitative changes that distinguish subsequent stages from the earlier ones. **Information-processing approaches** focus on the components of the thinking process, especially attention and memory. Let's look at how attention and memory develop during infancy.

ATTENTION Information processing begins with stimulus information that enters the senses, but much of what you see, hear, and touch is processed no further. For example, as you read this, there may be sounds in the environment, other sights in your visual field, and the feeling of your body in the seat where you are reading, but if you are focusing on what you are reading most of this information goes no further than sensory memory. The only information you proceed to process is the information on which you focus your attention.

In infants the study of attention has focused on habituation, the decrease in attention to a stimulus after lengthy or repeated presentation. A complementary concept, **dishabituation**, is the revival of attention when a new stimulus is presented following several presentations of a previous stimulus. For example, if you show infants a picture of the same face several times in a row, then show a new face, they will generally dishabituate to the new face; that is, they will pay more attention to it than to the "old" face. Habituation and dishabituation can be studied by monitoring infants' looking behavior, but infants rarely lay still for long even if they are paying attention to something, so two other methods have been frequently used: heart rate and sucking rate. Heart rate declines when a new stimulus is presented and gradually rises as habituation takes place. Infants suck on a pacifier more frequently when a new stimulus is presented and gradually decline in their sucking rate with habituation.

During the course of the first year of life, it takes less and less time for habituation to occur. When presented with a visual stimulus, neonates may take several minutes before they show signs of habituating (by changing their looking time, heart rate, or sucking rate). By 4 to 5 months old, habituation in a similar experiment takes only about 10 seconds, and by 7 to 8 months only a few seconds (Domsch et al., 2010; Kavšek & Bornstein, 2010). This appears to occur because infants become more efficient at perceiving and processing a stimulus.

Even when they are a few months old, infants of the same age vary in their rates of habituation, and these individual differences tend to be stable over time. Some infants are more efficient than others at processing information; consequently, they habituate more quickly. Infants who habituate relatively slowly appear to do so not because they are especially good at sustaining their attention but because they seem to get stuck on the stimulus and have difficulty disengaging from it. Speed of habituation predicts memory ability on other tasks in infancy, as well as later performance on intelligence tests (Courage et al., 2004; Rose et al., 2005).

information-processing approach

approach to understanding cognitive functioning that focuses on cognitive processes that exist at all ages, rather than on viewing cognitive development in terms of discontinuous stages

dishabituation

following habituation, the revival of attention when a new stimulus is presented

Joint attention develops by the end of the first year.

In the second half of the first year, infants' patterns of attention become increasingly social. They direct their attention not just to whatever sensations are most stimulating but to what the people around them are attending to, engaging in *joint attention*. By the end of the first year, they often notice what important people around them are paying attention to and will look or point in the same direction. One experiment showed that 10-month-old infants were less likely to look or point in the direction an adult was faced if the adult's eyes were closed or blindfolded, indicating that the infants were aware of the adults' attentional patterns and matched their own to them (Brooks & Meltzoff, 2005).

Joint attention is the basis not just of infants' information-processing development but of language and emotional communication (Van Hecke et al., 2007). This makes sense; one way infants and children learn new words is to observe what another person is doing or looking at when they use a word. Often this takes place during social interactions between infants and others, but it can also take place from infants observing where the attention of another person is directed. As we will see in more detail later in the chapter, not all cultures encourage verbal interactions with infants. A cultural analysis of this issue showed that in cultures where verbal interactions with adults are limited, infants and young children learn a great deal of their language by observing adults' language use and "listening in," that is, using joint attention to discern the meaning of words (Akhtar, 2005).

MEMORY Infants' memory abilities expand greatly during the first year of life, both for short-term and for long-term memory. One reflection of the development of short-term memory is their improvement in the object permanence task. As noted, object permanence is a test of short-term memory as well as a test of knowledge of the properties of objects. Memory studies using object permanence tasks show that the number of locations infants can remember and search to look for a hidden object increases sharply in the second half of the first year (Morra et al., 2008).

Long-term memory also improves notably over the course of the first year. In one experiment, researchers tied a string to the foot of infants 2 to 6 months old and taught them to move a mobile hanging above their cribs by kicking their foot (Rovee-Collier, 1999). The 2-month-old infants forgot the training within a week—they no longer kicked to make the mobile move when the string was tied to their legs—but the 6-month-old infants remembered it for about 3 weeks, demonstrating better long-term memories.

Further experiments showed an interesting distinction between *recognition memory* and *recall memory* (Hildreth et al., 2003). After the mobile-kicking trick appeared to be lost from the infants' memories, the researchers gave the infants a hint by making the mobile move. The infants *recognized* this clue and began kicking again to make the mobile move, up to a month later, even though they had been unable to *recall* the memory before being prompted. The older the infant was, the more effective the prompting. From infancy onward, recognition memory comes easier to us than recall memory (Flavell et al., 2002).

Infants and young children clearly learn a great deal, so why is it that later in our development we recall so little of what happened in our early years? Some researchers have proposed that long-term memories require language and a sense of self, but other animals also show this "infantile amnesia," so this cannot be the main explanation. Recently, memory researchers have proposed that the answer lies in the development of the hippocampus, part of the lower brain (Josselyn & Frankland, 2012). The hippocampus is immature at birth and adds neurons at a high rate in the early years of development. The addition of so many new neurons may interfere with the existing memory circuits, so that long-term memories cannot be formed until the production of neurons in the hippocampus declines in early childhood, as it becomes more fully developed.

COGNITIVE DEVELOPMENT:
Assessing Infant Development

Given the many remarkable changes in development that happen over the course of the first year, researchers have long been interested in evaluating infants to see if they are developing normally. There have also been efforts to improve infants' cognitive development through media stimulation.

Approaches to Assessing Development

LO 4.10 **Describe the major scales used in measuring infant development, and explain how habituation assessments are used to predict later intelligence.**

There are a variety of methods used to measure infant development, including the scales approach of Gesell and Bayley. More recently, assessments of infants' cognitive development have focused on information processing, especially habituation.

THE BAYLEY SCALES One approach to assessing infant development was pioneered by Arnold Gesell (1934, 1946). Gesell constructed an assessment of infant development that included four subscales: motor skills (such as sitting), language use, adaptive behavior (such as exploring a new object), and personal–social behavior (such as using a spoon). Following the model of intelligence tests, which produce an *intelligence quotient (IQ)* as an overall measure of mental abilities, Gesell combined the results of his assessment into a **developmental quotient (DQ)** as an overall measure of infants' developmental progress.

Gesell's scale for infants is no longer used, but his approach was continued by Nancy Bayley, who produced the **Bayley Scales of Infant Development**, now in their third edition, the Bayley-III (Bayley, 2005). The Bayley-III can assess development from age 3 months to age 3½ years. There are three main scales on the Bayley-III:

1. *Cognitive Scale.* This scale measures mental abilities such as attention and exploration. For example, at 6 months it assesses whether the baby looks at pictures in a book; at 23 to 25 months of age it assesses whether a child can match similar pictures.
2. *Language Scale.* This scale measures use and understanding of language. For example, at 17 to 19 months it assesses whether the child can identify objects in a picture, and at 38 to 42 months it assesses whether the child can name four colors.
3. *Motor Scale.* This scale measures fine and gross motor abilities, such as sitting alone for 30 seconds at 6 months, or hopping twice on one foot at 38 to 42 months.

As with Gesell's scales, the Bayley scales produce an overall DQ.

However, the Bayley scales do not predict later IQ or school performance well (Hack et al., 2005). If you look closely at the preceding examples, this should not be surprising because the Bayley scales measure quite different kinds of abilities than the verbal and spatial abilities that later IQ tests measure and that school work requires. (Let's face it, hopping on one foot is not likely to be predictive of school performance or any kind of work you are likely to do as an adult, unless you become a ballet dancer.) The only exception to this is at the lower extreme. An infant who scores very low on the Bayley scales may have serious developmental problems. Consequently, the Bayley scales are used mainly as a screening tool to identify infants who have serious problems in need of immediate attention, rather than as predictors of later development for children within the normal range.

INFORMATION-PROCESSING APPROACHES TO INFANT ASSESSMENT Efforts to predict later intelligence using information-processing approaches have shown greater promise. The focus of these approaches has been on habituation. As noted, infants vary in

developmental quotient (DQ)

in assessments of infant development, the overall score indicating developmental progress

Bayley Scales of Infant Development

widely used assessment of infant development from age 3 months to 3½ years

how long it takes them to habituate to a new stimulus, such as a sight or a sound. Some are "short-lookers" who habituate quickly, others are "long-lookers" who take more time and more presentations of the stimulus before they habituate. The shorter the habituation time, the more efficient the infant's information-processing abilities. They look for a shorter length of time because it takes them less time to take in and process information about the stimulus.

Longitudinal studies have found that short-lookers in infancy tend to have higher IQ scores later in development than long-lookers do (Cuevas & Bell, 2014; Kavšek, 2004; Rose et al., 2005). In one study, short-lookers in infancy had higher IQs and higher educational achievement when they were followed up 20 years later, in emerging adulthood (Fagan et al., 2007). Habituation assessments in infancy have also been found to be useful for identifying infants who have developmental problems (Kavšek & Bornstein, 2010). Furthermore, habituation assessments tend to be more reliable than assessments of DQ using the Bayley scales, that is, they are more likely to be consistent when measured across more than one occasion (Cuevas & Bell, 2014; Kavšek, 2004). The most recent version of the Bayley scales now includes a measure of habituation (Bayley, 2005), which may improve reliability and predictive validity above previous versions of the scale.

Can Media Enhance Cognitive Development? The Myth of "Baby Einstein"

LO 4.11 Evaluate the claim that educational media enhance infants' cognitive development.

In addition to efforts to assess infants' cognitive development, efforts have also been made to enhance it. One effort of this kind that has become popular in some developed countries is educational media products for infants.

In the early 1990s a study was published claiming that listening to the music of Mozart enhanced cognitive functioning (Rauscher et al., 1993). The study was conducted with university students, not babies, and the "effect" lasted only 10 minutes, and subsequent studies failed to replicate even a 10-minute effect (Rauscher, 2003). Nevertheless, the study received worldwide attention and inspired the creation of a vast range of educational media products claiming to promote infants' cognitive development.

Do they work? The answer appears to be no. Many studies investigating this question have concluded that educational media products have no positive effects on infants' cognitive development. In fact, one study of 8- to 16-month-old infants found that for every hour of "educational" DVDs viewed per day, the DVD viewers understood 8 to 16 *fewer* words than babies who watched no DVDs (Guernsey, 2007). The authors interpreted this surprising finding as a result that the DVD viewers may have spent less time interacting with the people around them. That is, they were watching DVDs instead of interacting socially, and the DVD watching did not compensate for the deficit in social interaction. Similar results were found in another study (DeLoache et al., 2010). Fortunately, national studies have found that only 10 percent of babies in the United States use educational media products (Rideout, 2013).

Babies probably don't learn a lot from television or DVDs because they don't know that video is a learning tool (Richert, et al., 2011). Babies also need parent–child interaction with television to learn (Barr et al., 2008). Barr (2010) has identified certain aspects of television that make it difficult for infants to retrieve encoded material. First, two-dimensional objects are smaller than three-dimensional objects and lack perceptual features that are present in three-dimensional objects. Second, the frame around the television does not match the real-life experience of objects. And, third, it is difficult for babies to transfer from one medium to another.

Educational media products for infants have not been demonstrated to enhance cognitive development.

These findings suggest that Piaget was right that children's cognitive maturity has its own innate timetable and that it is fruitless (and perhaps even detrimental) to try to hurry it along. So what can you do to promote infants' healthy cognitive development? Talk to them, read to them, respond to them—and be patient. They will grow up soon enough.

Researchers and parents alike have also wondered whether there were any *harmful* effects of media exposure in infancy. The results are mixed. Christakis et al. (2004) found that the number of hours of television exposure at ages 1 and 3 years was correlated with attention problems at age 7. However, Foster and Watkins (2010) reanalyzed the same data, controlling for mothers' achievement and family poverty, and found no correlation between television viewing hours and later attention problems. This means that the correlation found in the earlier study may have been a result of mothers' achievement or family poverty. Zimmerman et al. (2007) found that 8- to 16-month-old babies who watched DVDs created for that age range had worse language scores than babies who didn't watch DVDs. On the other hand, Schmidt et al. (2009) conducted a longitudinal study and found no association between early TV watching and language scores at 3 years of age.

Of course, TV and video are not the only media that babies use today. Babies are now also consumers of apps for mobile devices such as iPads. There is a growing industry of "baby apps." In an innovative study, Hourcade and colleagues (2015) analyzed YouTube videos of infants using tablet devices. They found that a majority of 12- to 17-month-old infants were capable of using tablets on their own. Recently, Hazrati and colleagues (2014) found in a large national sample in the United States that 94 percent of 6–month-old infants had media exposure, and 62.2 percent had tablet time. Interestingly, they found that younger and more educated mothers gave their children more screen time than did older and less-educated mothers. Although a mobile device may serve as a useful distraction for a parent trying to cook dinner or just keep an infant occupied, public health experts are concerned about long-term implications for the development of the visual system, later risk of obesity, attention deficit problems, and anxiety.

CRITICAL THINKING QUESTION

Discuss the ways that socioeconomic status plays a role in cognitive development.

COGNITIVE DEVELOPMENT:
The Beginnings of Language

According to the traditional beliefs of the Beng people of Ivory Coast (in Africa), in the spirit world all people understand all languages (Gottlieb, 2000). Babies have just come from the spirit world when they are born, so they understand whatever is said in any language. However, during the first year, memory of all other languages fades and babies come to understand only the language they hear around them. This is actually a pretty accurate summary of how babies' language development takes place in the course of the first year of life, as we will learn next. (See **Table 4.1** on the next page for the milestones of infant language development.)

First Sounds and Words

LO 4.12 Describe the course of language development over the first year of life.

Very early on, babies begin to make the sounds that will eventually develop into language (Waxman & Lidz, 2006). The video *Language Development* on the next page provides an overview of the progression of sounds. First is **cooing**, the "oo-ing" and "ah-ing" and

cooing

prelanguage "oo-ing" and "ah-ing," and gurgling sounds babies make beginning at about 2 months old

Table 4.1 Milestones of Infant Language Development

Age	Milestone
2 months	Cooing (preverbal and gurgling sounds)
4–10 months	Babbling (repetitive consonant–vowel combinations)
8–10 months	First gestures (such as "bye-bye")
10–12 months	Comprehension of words and simple sentences
12 months	First spoken word

NOTE: For each milestone there is a normal range, and babies who are somewhat later in reaching the milestones may nevertheless have normal language development.

gurgling sounds babies make beginning at about 2 months old. Often cooing takes place in interactions with others, but sometimes it takes place without interactions, as if babies are discovering their vocal apparatus and trying out the sounds it can make.

Watch LANGUAGE DEVELOPMENT

By about 4 to 6 months old, cooing develops into **babbling**, repetitive consonant–vowel combinations such as "ba-ba-ba" or "do-do-do-do." When Jeff's son Miles was 4 months old he repeated the sounds "ah-gee" so often that for a while his parents called him "Mr. Ah-Gee." Babbling is useful in language development because it exercises the vocal chords, and the baby gets experience in making different mouth shapes to make different sounds. Babbling appears to be universal among infants. In fact, babies the world over appear to babble with the same sounds initially, regardless of the language of their culture (Lee at al., 2010). However, after a couple of months, infants begin to babble in the sounds distinctive to their culture and cease to babble in sounds they have not heard used by the people around them. Deaf infants have a form of babbling, too, initially using their voices but also using their hands instead of sounds. If deaf infants are exposed to a signed language, their hand babbling has features of the signed language they are exposed to (van Beinum, 2008). By the time infants are about 10 or 11 months old, they stop babbling the sounds or signs of languages they are not exposed and only babble the sounds of the language or languages they are exposed to (Kuhl et al., 2014). Furthermore, by the time infants are about 9 months old, untrained

babbling

repetitive prelanguage consonant–vowel combinations such as "ba-ba-ba" or "do-do-do-do," made by infants universally beginning at about 6 months old listeners can distinguish whether a recording of babbling is from an infant raised amidst French, Arabic, or Chinese (Oller et al., 1997).

By around 8 to 10 months, infants begin to use gestures to communicate (Goldin-Meadow, 2009). They may lift their arms up to indicate they wish to be picked up, or point to an object they would like to have brought to them, or hold out an object to offer it to someone else, or wave bye-bye. Using gestures is a way of evoking behavior from others (for example, being picked up after lifting their arms in request), and also a way of evoking verbal responses from others (such as a spoken "bye-bye" in response to the infant's gestured bye-bye), at a time when infants still cannot produce words of their own.

Infants' first words usually are spoken a month or two before or after their first birthday. Typical first words in English include important people ("Mama," "Dada"), familiar animals ("dog"), moving objects ("car"), foods ("milk"), and greetings or farewells ("hi," "bye-bye") (Waxman & Lidz, 2006). Early words in other languages may show differences related to the input children are receiving. For example, in Mandarin- and Cantonese-learning infants, early words include fewer animal and object words than English-learning infants (Tardif et al., 2008).

Most infants can speak only a few words, at most, by the end of their first year, but they understand many more words than they can speak. In fact, at all ages, language *comprehension* (the words we understand) exceeds language *production* (the words we use), but the difference is especially striking and notable during infancy. Even as early as 4 months old, infants can recognize their own name (Mandel et al., 1995). By their first birthday, although infants can speak only a word or two they understand about 50 words (Menyuk et al., 1995).

The foundations of language comprehension are evident early, in the abilities of infants to recognize changes in language sounds (Werker & Fennell, 2009). To test this ability, researchers play a spoken sound repeatedly for an infant (for example, "ba, ba, ba, ba"), then change it slightly ("pa, pa, pa, pa"). If an infant looks in the direction of the sound when it changes, this is taken to indicate awareness of the change. Even when only a few weeks old, infants show this awareness (Saffran et al., 2006).

Furthermore, like babbling, discrimination of simple sounds appears to be universal at first, but becomes more specialized toward the end of the first year to the language of the infant's culture. In one study, U.S. and Japanese infants were compared at 6 and 12 months (Iverson et al., 2003). At 6 months, the U.S. and Japanese infants were equally responsive to the distinction between "ra" and "la," even though there are no "r" or "l" sounds in the Japanese language, so the Japanese infants would not have heard this distinction before. However, by 12 months old the U.S. infants could still recognize the "r" versus "l" distinction but the Japanese infants could not because their language skills were now more specialized to their own language.

What about babies learning more than one language? In many cultural groups, growing up bilingual is the norm. Babies with typical nervous systems will learn the languages they are exposed to, spoken or signed. Though babies can learn several languages at a time, most research on multilingual language development in infancy has been conducted with babies in bilingual contexts. Studies have found that babies developing bilingualism typically learn two languages at once without any obvious difficulties (Werker & Byers-Heinlein, 2008). They achieve early linguistic milestones in each of their languages at the same time as monolingual babies, they produce a substantial number of semantically corresponding words in each of their two languages from their very first words (or signs), and they mix languages (Kovács & Mehler, 2009, Petitto et al., 2001). On the whole, early perceptual sensitivities assist babies growing up bilingual in discriminating and separating their two languages even before they speak their first word. Bilingual babies are building representations of each of their languages in the first year of life.

Infant-Directed (ID) Speech

LO 4.13 **Describe how cultures vary in their stimulation of language development.**

Suppose you were to say to an adult, "Would you like something to eat?" How would you say it? Now imagine saying the same thing to an infant. Would you change how you said it? In many cultural settings, people speak in a special way to infants, called **infant-directed (ID) speech** (Bryant & Barrett, 2007). In ID speech, the pitch of the voice becomes higher than in normal speech, and the intonation is exaggerated. Grammar is simplified, and words and phrases are more likely to be repeated than in normal speech. Topics of ID speech often pertain to objects ("Look at the birdie! See the birdie?") or emotional communication ("What a good girl! You ate your applesauce!").

Why do people often use ID speech with infants? One reason is that the infants seem to like it. Even when ID speech is in a language they do not understand, infants show a preference for it by the time they are 4 months old, as indicated by paying greater attention to ID speech in an unfamiliar language than to non-ID speech in the same language (Singh, 2009). The video *Infant-Directed Speech* provides examples of parents using ID speech with their infants.

And why do infants like ID speech? One theory is that infants prefer it because it is more emotionally charged than other speech (Trainor et al., 2000). Also, at a time when language is still new to them, ID speech helps infants unravel language's mysteries. The exaggeration and repetition of words gives infants cues to their meaning (Soderstrom, 2007). By exaggerating the sounds used in making words, ID speech provides infants with information about the building blocks of speech they will use in the language of their culture (Kuhl, 2004). The exaggerations of ID speech also separate speech into specific words and phrases more clearly than normal speech does (Thiessen et al., 2005).

Adults in many cultures use infant-directed speech, with high pitch and exaggerated intonation.

infant-directed (ID) speech
special form of speech that adults in many cultures direct toward infants, in which the pitch of the voice becomes higher than in normal speech, the intonation is exaggerated, and words and phrases are repeated

Watch INFANT-DIRECTED SPEECH

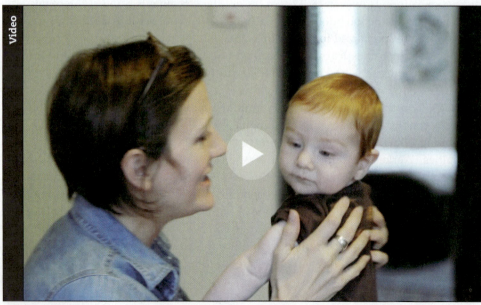

ID speech is common in Western cultural groups (Bryant & Barrett, 2007). Japanese studies have also found that ID speech is common (Mazuka et al., 2008). Outside the developed countries, however, there is more variability. Some traditional cultures use ID speech, such as the Fulani of West Africa, who say single words and phrases to their infants from their very first days of life in an effort to stimulate their language development (Johnson, 2000). However, in other traditional cultures parents do not use ID speech and make no special effort to speak to infants. For example, among the Gusii of Kenya, parents speak to infants substantially less than U.S. parents do (LeVine, 1994; Richman et al., 2010). The Gusii, like people in many traditional cultures, carry their infants around almost constantly and have a great deal of physical contact with them, including cosleeping at night, but they do not view it as necessary or useful to speak to infants. Similarly, the Ifaluk people of Micronesia believe there is no point in speaking to infants because they cannot understand what you say (Le, 2000). Nevertheless, despite receiving no ID speech, children in these cultures learn their language fluently within a few years, just as children in cultures with ID speech do.

Does this mean you do not need to speak to your own infants in your culture? Definitely not. In cultures such as the Gusii and the Ifaluk parents may not speak directly to their infants often, but infants are part of a language-rich environment all day long. Although no one speaks to infants directly, nor do they use the high-pitch and simple language seen in Western cultural settings, infants are surrounded by conversation from their mother, sister, and other relatives. Instead of spending the day with one parent and perhaps a sibling, as infants do in cultures where ID speech is common, infants in traditional cultures typically have many adults and children around them in the course of the day. Families are bigger, extended family members live either in the same household or nearby, and interactions with other community members are more common (Akhtar & Tomasello, 2000). Perhaps ID speech developed because, in the small nuclear families that are typical of developed countries today, without ID speech infants may have little other language stimulation. The success of children in traditional cultures in learning their languages despite having no ID speech shows that listening to others' conversations in a language-rich environment is also an effective way of acquiring a language (Akhtar, 2005).

Not only are there cultural differences in the ways that people talk to babies, but there are also gender differences as well because gender and how people of different genders relate are factors in ecocultural practices. Mothers and fathers talk to babies differently, and boys and girls are treated differently from one another. For example, even in the hospital delivery room, girls are often referred to with terms of endearment like "sweetie" or "pretty one," whereas boys are given more tough-sounding names that express the boy's ability to take action, like "tiger" or "big guy" (Maccoby, 1980; MacFarlane, 1977). Mothers tend to talk more to girls than they do to boys (Leaper et al., 1998; Maccoby, 1980). And, mothers tend to talk more with daughters and use more supportive speech than they do with sons (Leaper et al., 1998).

By the end of their first year, infants have laid an important foundation for language and can comprehend many words, but their language production is still limited. The real explosion in language development comes in the second year, so in the next chapter we will examine the origins and growth of language in greater detail.

Summary: Cognitive Development

LO 4.8 **Describe the first four sensorimotor substages of Piaget's theory.**

Substage 1 is based on neonatal reflexes; 2 is based more on purposeful behavior; 3 entails the repetition of movements that first occurred by chance; and 4 is based on intentional, goal-directed behavior. Object permanence has begun to develop by the end of infancy, but it is not complete until the end of the second year.

LO 4.9 **Describe how the elements of the information-processing model of cognitive functioning change in infancy.**

In contrast to the cognitive-developmental approach initiated by Piaget, which divides cognitive development into distinct stages, the information-processing approach investigates the processes of cognitive functioning that occur at all ages. The focus is on the components of cognitive functioning, especially attention and memory.

Infants pay more attention to a stimulus they have not seen before. Habituation develops more quickly during the course of the first year, and at any given age, quickness of habituation is positively related to later cognitive achievements. Increasingly during the first year, infants learn through joint attention with others.

Both short-term and long-term memory improve notably over the course of the first year, though recognition memory comes easier than recall memory, as it does at later ages.

LO 4.10 **Describe the major scales used in measuring infant development, and explain how habituation assessments are used to predict later intelligence.**

The Bayley scales are widely used to measure infants' development, but scores on the Bayley do not predict later cognitive development except for infants with serious deficits. Efforts to predict later intelligence using information processing approaches have shown greater promise. These assessments measure habituation by distinguishing between "short-lookers" and "long-lookers," with short-lookers higher in later intelligence.

LO 4.11 **Evaluate the claim that educational media enhance infants' cognitive development.**

Many studies investigating this question have concluded that educational media products have no effect on infants' cognitive development and may even be detrimental. Specifically, early use of media may be a risk factor for later obesity, attention issues, and anxiety.

LO 4.12 **Describe the course of language development over the first year of life.**

Infants begin cooing when about 2 months old. When they first begin to babble at about 6 months, infants use a wide range of sounds, but within a few months they more often make the sounds from the main language they hear around them. First words are usually spoken around the end of the first year; infants can already understand about 50 words by this time.

LO 4.13 **Describe how cultures vary in their stimulation of language development.**

Many cultures use infant-directed (ID) speech, and babies appear to enjoy hearing it. However, even in cultures that do not use ID speech children become adept users of language by the time they are a few years old.

Section 3   Emotional and Social Development

 ## Learning Objectives

4.14 Define *infant temperament* and its main dimensions.

4.15 Explain how the idea of goodness-of-fit pertains to temperament on both a family level and a cultural level.

4.16 Identify the primary emotions, and describe how they develop during infancy.

4.17 Describe infants' emotional perceptions and how their emotions become increasingly social over the first year.

4.18 List the main features of infants' social worlds across cultures.

4.19 Compare and contrast the two major theories of infants' social development.

EMOTIONAL AND SOCIAL DEVELOPMENT: Temperament

Have you had any experience in caring for infants, perhaps as a baby-sitter, older sibling, or parent? If so, you have probably observed that they differ from early on in how they respond to you and to the environment. Ask any parents of more than one child, and they will probably tell a similar tale (Reiss et al., 2000).

In the study of human development, these kinds of differences in emotionality are viewed as indicators of **temperament**. Temperament includes qualities such as activity level, soothability, emotionality, and sociability. You can think of temperament as the biologically based raw material of personality (Goldsmith, 2009; Rothbart et al., 2000).

temperament
innate responses to the physical and social environment, including qualities of activity level, irritability, soothability, emotional reactivity, and sociability

Conceptualizing Temperament

LO 4.14 Define *infant temperament* and its main dimensions.

Researchers on temperament believe that all infants are born with certain tendencies toward behavior and personality development and the environment then shapes those tendencies in the course of development. Let's look at ways of conceptualizing temperament, then at some of the challenges involved in measuring and studying it (see **Table 4.2** for a summary).

Temperament was originally proposed as a psychological concept by Alexander Thomas and Stella Chess, who in 1956 began the New York Longitudinal Study (NYLS). They asked parents to evaluate their babies on the basis of dimensions such as activity

Table 4.2 Dimensions of Temperament

Dimension	Description
Activity level	Frequency and intensity of gross motor activity
Attention span	Duration of attention to a single activity
Emotionality	Frequency and intensity of positive and negative emotional expression
Soothability	Responsiveness to attempts to soothe when distressed
Sociability	Degree of interest in others, positive or negative responses to social interactions
Adaptability	Adjustment to changes in routine
Quality of mood	General level of happy versus unhappy mood

level and adaptability, then classified the babies into three categories: easy, difficult, and slow-to-warm-up.

1. *Easy* babies (40 percent of the sample) were those whose moods were generally positive. They adapted well to new situations and were generally moderate rather than extreme in their emotional reactions.
2. *Difficult* babies (10 percent) did not adapt well to new situations, and their moods were intensely negative more frequently than other babies.
3. *Slow-to-warm-up* babies (15 percent) were notably low in activity level, reacted negatively to new situations, and had fewer positive or negative emotional extremes than other babies.

Temperament is difficult to assess in a research setting because infants' emotional states fluctuate so much.

By following these babies into adulthood in their longitudinal study, Thomas and Chess were able to show that temperament in infancy predicted later development in some respects (Chess & Thomas, 1984; Ramos et al., 2005; Thomas et al., 1968). The difficult babies in their study were at high risk for problems in childhood, such as aggressive behavior, anxiety, and social withdrawal. Slow-to-warm-up babies rarely seemed to have problems in early childhood, but once they entered school they were sometimes fearful and had problems academically and with peers because of their relatively slow responsiveness.

Perhaps you noticed that the three categories in the classic Thomas and Chess study only added up to 65 percent of the infants they studied. The other 35 percent could not be classified as easy, difficult, or slow-to-warm-up. It is clearly a problem to exclude 35 percent of infants, so other temperament researchers have avoided categories, instead rating all infants on the basis of temperamental traits.

Mary Rothbart and her colleagues have kept some of the Thomas and Chess temperament qualities, such as activity level and attention span, but they added several aspects of emotionality, measuring frequency and intensity of positive and negative emotions (Rothbart, 2004; Rothbart, 2011. Similarly, David Buss and Robert Plomin 1984) include some Thomas and Chess dimensions in their model, but add *sociability*, which refers to positive or negative responses to social interactions. Both models have been moderately successful in predicting children's later functioning from infant temperament (Buss, 1995; Rothbart & Bates, 2006). All three models of temperament face measurement challenges, as the *Research Focus: Measuring Temperament* feature shows, because infants' emotional states change so frequently.

Research Focus: Measuring Temperament

In 1956 Alexander Thomas and Stella Chess began the New York Longitudinal Study (NYLS), which assessed infant temperament by judging qualities such as activity level, adaptability, intensity of reactions, and quality of mood. The goal of the study was to see how infants' innate tendencies would be shaped into personality in the course of development through childhood and adolescence.

When Thomas and Chess began studying temperament, no biological measurements were available, so they used parents' reports of infants' behavior as the source of their temperament classifications. Even today, most studies of infant temperament are based on parents' reports.

There are some clear advantages to using parents' reports. After all, parents see their infants in many different situations on a daily basis over a long period of time. In contrast, a researcher who assesses temperament on the basis of the infants' performance on tasks administered in the laboratory sees the infant only on that one occasion. Because infants' states change so frequently, the researcher may assess infants as having a "difficult" temperament when in fact the infant is simply in a temporary state of distress—hungry, perhaps, or tired, or cold, or hot, or in need of a diaper change.

However, parents are not always accurate appraisers of their infants' behavior. For example, mothers who are depressed are more likely to rate their infants' temperament negatively, mothers' and fathers' ratings of their infants' temperament show only low to moderate levels of agreement, and parents tend to rate their twins or other siblings as less similar in temperament than researchers do, which suggests that parents may exaggerate the differences between their children.

Watch RESEARCH FOCUS: MEASURING TEMPERAMENT

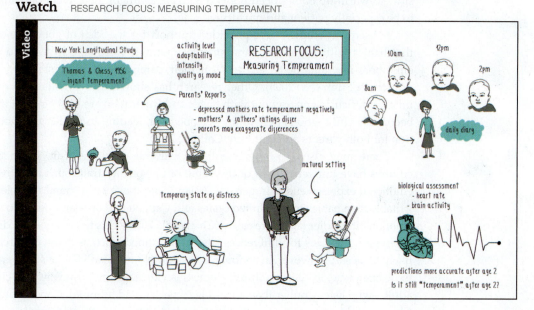

What are the options besides parents' reports? Thomas and Chess recommend that researchers observe infants' behavior in naturalistic settings (such as at home, or at the park) on several occasions, to avoid the problem of observing on just one occasion when the infant may have been in an unusually bad or good mood. Of course, this takes considerably more time and money than a simple parental questionnaire, and even a series of observations may not be as valid as the experiences parents accumulate over months of caring for their infants.

Another approach has been to have parents keep daily diaries of their infants' behavior (recording when they're sleeping, fussing, or crying). Reports using this method have been shown to correlate well with temperament ratings based on parental reports or performance on laboratory tasks.

Biological assessments of temperament are also useful since temperament is regarded as biologically based. One simple but effective biological measure of infant temperament is heart rate. Extremely shy children tend to have consistently high heart rates, and heart rates that show a greater increase in response to new stimulation such as new toys, new smells, or new people, compared to other children. Other biological assessments of temperament have been developed, including measures of brain activity.

Although infant temperament can predict later development to some extent, predictions are more accurate when assessments of temperament are made after age 2. Fussing, crying, and rapid changes in states are common in infancy across a wide range of infants. It is only after age 2 that children's moods and behavior settle into more stable patterns that predict later development. But can temperament still be assumed to be innate and biologically based once the environment has been experienced for 2 years or more?

Review Questions:

1. Although parents' reports are often used to evaluate infant temperament, a drawback of using parents' reports is that:
   a. Mothers' and fathers' reports are often inconsistent
   b. Parents tend to exaggerate the differences between their children
   c. Depressed mothers tend to rate their infants' temperaments more negatively
   d. All of the above

2. The most simple and effective biological measure of temperament is:
   a. Blood pressure
   b. Heart rate
   c. Brain-wave intensity
   d. Hormonal stability

Goodness-of-Fit

LO 4.15 **Explain how the idea of goodness-of-fit pertains to temperament on both a family level and a cultural level.**

All approaches to measuring temperament view it as the raw material of personality, which is then shaped by the environment. Thomas and Chess (1977) proposed the concept of **goodness-of-fit**, meaning that children develop best if there is a good fit between the temperament of the child and environmental demands. In their view, difficult and

goodness-of-fit
theoretical principle that children develop best if there is a good fit between the temperament of the child and environmental demands

slow-to-warm-up babies need parents who are aware of their temperaments and willing to be especially patient and nurturing.

Subsequent studies have provided support for the idea of goodness-of-fit, finding that babies with negative temperamental qualities were able to learn to control their emotional reactions better by age 3 if their parents were understanding and tolerant (Warren & Simmens, 2005). Other research has shown that parents who respond to an infant's difficult temperament with anger and frustration are likely to find that the infant becomes a child who is defiant and disobedient, leading to further conflict and frustration for both parents and children (Calkins, 2002).

There may also be something like a cultural goodness-of-fit, given that different cultures have different views of the value of personality traits such as activity level and emotional expressiveness. In general, Asian babies have been found to be less active and irritable than babies in the United States and Canada and appear to learn to regulate their emotionality earlier and more easily (Chen et al., 2005). This temperamental difference may be, in part, the basis for differences later in childhood, such as Asian children being more likely to be shy. However, in contrast to the North American view of shyness as a problem to be overcome, in Asian cultures, shyness is viewed more positively. The child—and the adult—who listens rather than speaks is respected and admired. Consequently, studies of Chinese children have shown that shyness is associated with academic success and being well liked by peers (Chen et al., 1995). Now that the culture and economy of China are changing so rapidly, there is some evidence that shyness is becoming less valued and related to poor rather than favorable adjustment in childhood (Chen, 2011; Chen et al., 2005). We'll cover more on this in later chapters. Interestingly, as ecocultural settings change, the values and practices within them also change. Culture is not static.

EMOTIONAL AND SOCIAL DEVELOPMENT: Infants' Emotions

Expressing and understanding emotions goes deep into our biological nature. As Charles Darwin observed in 1872 in *The Expression of Emotions in Man and Animals*, the strong similarity between emotional expressions in humans and other mammals indicates that human emotional expressions are part of a long evolutionary history. Tigers snarl, wolves growl, chimpanzees—and humans, too—bare their teeth and scream. Darwin also observed that emotional expressions were highly similar among humans in different cultures. Recent researchers have confirmed that people in various cultures can easily identify the emotions expressed in photographs of people from outside their culture (Ekman, 2003).

Primary Emotions

LO 4.16 Identify the primary emotions, and describe how they develop during infancy.

primary emotions
basic emotions, such as anger, sadness, fear, disgust, surprise, and happiness

secondary emotions
emotions that require social learning, such as embarrassment, shame, and guilt; also called *sociomoral emotions*

Infants are born with a limited range of emotions that become differentiated into a wider range in the course of the early years of life. Studies of emotional development distinguish between two broad classes of emotion (Lewis, 2008). **Primary emotions** are the most basic emotions, the ones we share with animals, such as anger, sadness, fear, disgust, surprise, and happiness. Primary emotions are all evident within the first year of life. **Secondary emotions** are emotions that require social learning, such as embarrassment, shame, and guilt. Secondary emotions are also called *sociomoral emotions* because infants are not born knowing what is embarrassing or shameful but have to learn this from their social environment. Secondary emotions develop mostly in the second year of life, so we will look at the development of primary emotions here and secondary emotions in Chapter 5.

Three primary emotions are evident in the early weeks of life: distress, interest, and pleasure (Lewis, 2002; 2008). Distress is evident in crying, of course, and we have seen in this chapter how infants' interest can be assessed from the first days of life by where they turn their attention. In our discussion of neonates we saw that they show a facial expression of pleasure when tasting a sweet substance. Gradually in the first months of life these three emotions become differentiated into other primary emotions: distress into anger, sadness, and fear; interest into surprise; and pleasure into happiness. (Disgust also appears early, but unlike distress, interest, and pleasure, it does not develop more complex forms.) Let's look at how each of the other primary emotions develops over the first year.

Anger develops over the course of the first year (Dodge et al., 2006; Lewis, 2010). In one study of infants at 1, 4, and 7 months of age, the babies' responses were observed as their forearms were held down so that they could not move them for a few minutes, a condition none of them liked much (Oster et al., 1992). The 1-month-old infants showed clear distress, but raters (who did not know the hypotheses of the study) did not classify their distress responses as anger. The 4-month-old infants were also distressed, but about half of them showed their distress in facial expressions that could be clearly identified as anger. By 7 months, nearly all the infants showed a definite anger response. Another study also observed the clear expression of anger in 7-month-old infants in response to having an attractive object taken away (Stenberg et al., 1983). As infants become capable of intentional behavior in the second half of the first year, their expressions of anger often occur when their intentions are thwarted (Izard & Ackerman, 2000).

Infants universally exhibit the primary emotions. Can you tell which primary emotion is represented in each photograph?

Sadness is rare in the first year of life, except for infants with depressed mothers. When mothers are depressed, by the time infants are 2 to 3 months old they, too, show facial expressions of sadness (Herrera et al., 2004). Could this be a case of passive genotype → environment interactions? Perhaps both infants and mothers have a genetic predisposition toward sadness in such families. This is something to consider, but in one study nondepressed mothers were instructed to look depressed in a 3-minute interaction with their infants (Cohn & Tronick, 1983). The infants responded with distress, suggesting that sad infants with depressed mothers are responding to their mothers' sadness rather than being genetically predisposed to sad emotional expressions.

Fear develops by 6 months of age (Gartstein et al., 2010). By then infants show facial expressions of fear, for example in response to a toy that moves toward them suddenly and unexpectedly (Buss & Goldsmith, 1998). Fear also becomes social at this age, as infants begin to show *stranger anxiety* in response to unfamiliar adults (Grossman et al., 2005). Stranger anxiety is a sign that the infant has begun to develop attachments to familiar persons.

Surprise, indicated by an open mouth and raised eyebrows, is first evident about halfway through the first year (Camras et al., 1996). It is most often elicited by something in the infant's perceptual world that violates expectations. For example, a toy such as a jack-in-the-box might elicit surprise, especially the first time the jack pops out.

Finally, the development of happiness is evident in changes in infants' smiles and laughter that take place during the early months. After a few weeks, infants begin to smile in response to certain kinds of sensory stimulation—after feeding, or while urinating, or while having their cheeks stroked (Murkoff et al., 2003). However, it is not until the second or third month of life that the first **social smile** appears, an expression of happiness in response to interacting with others (Fogel et al., 2006). The first laughs occur about a month after the first smiles (Nwokah et al., 1999). Beginning at this age, about 4 months old, both smiles and laughs can be elicited by social interactions or by sensory or perceptual events, such as tickling or kisses or games such as peek-a-boo (Fogel et al., 2006). By the end of the first year, infants have several different kinds of smiles that they show in response to different people and in different situations (Bolzani et al., 2002).

Infants' Emotional Perceptions

LO 4.17 Describe infants' emotional perceptions and how their emotions become increasingly social over the first year.

Infants not only communicate emotions from the first days of life, but they also perceive others' emotions. At just a few days old, neonates who hear another neonate cry often begin crying themselves, a phenomenon called **emotional contagion** (Geangu et al., 2010). This response shows that they recognize and respond to the cry as a signal of distress (Gazzaniga, 2008). Furthermore, they are more likely to cry in response to the cry of a fellow neonate than in response to an older infant's cry, a chimpanzee's cry, or a recording of their own cry, showing that they are remarkably perceptive at discriminating among cries.

At first, infants are better at perceiving emotions by hearing than by seeing. Remember, their auditory system is more developed than their visual system in the early weeks of life. When shown faces in the early weeks, neonates tend to look mainly at the boundaries and edges rather than at the internal features such as mouth and eyes that are most likely to express emotion. By 2 to 3 months old, infants' eyesight has improved substantially and they have begun to be able to discriminate between happy, sad, and angry faces (Haan & Matheson, 2009; Hunnius et al., 2011). To test this, researchers often use a habituation method, in which infants are presented with the same photograph of the same facial expression repeatedly until they no longer show any interest, that is, they become habituated. Then they are shown the same face with a different facial expression, and if they look longer at the new facial expression this is taken to indicate that they have noticed the difference.

Another interesting way of showing that infants perceive emotions is to show no emotion at all. By 2 to 3 months of age, when parents interacting with their infants are told by researchers to show no emotion for a time, the infants respond with distress (Adamson & Frick, 2003; Tronick, 2007). This method, known as the *still-face paradigm*, shows that infants quickly learn to expect certain emotional reactions from others, especially others who are familiar and important to them (Mesman et al., 2009).

More generally, infants' responses to the still-face paradigm demonstrate that from early on emotions are experienced through relations with others rather than originating only within the individual (Tronick, 2007). In the early weeks of life, infants have smiles that are stimulated by internal states and cries that may be as a result of being hungry, tired, or cold, but infants soon learn to discern others' emotions and adjust their own emotions in response. By the time they are just 2 to 3 months old, when infants vocalize or smile they expect the others they know and trust to respond in familiar ways, as they have in the past, which is why the still-face paradigm disturbs infants so much.

Another indicator of the development of emotional perception during the first year is in infants' abilities to match auditory and visual emotion. In studies on this topic, infants

social smile

expression of happiness in response to interacting with others, first appearing at 2 to 3 months of age

emotional contagion

in infants, crying in response to hearing another infant cry, evident beginning at just a few days old

are shown two photographs with markedly different emotions, such as happiness and sadness. Then a vocal recording is played, matching one of the facial emotions but not the other, and the infants' attention is monitored. By the time they are 7 months old, infants look more at the face that matches the emotion of the voice, showing that they expect the two to go together (Kahana-Kalman & Walker-Andrews, 2001; Soken & Pick, 1992).

Gradually over the first year, infants become more adept at observing others' emotional responses to ambiguous and uncertain situations and using that information to shape their own emotional responses. Known as **social referencing**, this is an important way that infants learn about the world around them. In studies testing social referencing abilities, typically a mother and infant in a laboratory situation are given an unfamiliar toy to play with, and the mother is instructed by the researchers to show positive or negative emotion in relation to the toy. Subsequently, the infant will generally play with the toy if the mother showed positive emotion toward it but avoid it if the mother's emotion was negative. This response appears by the time infants are about 9 to 10 months old (Schmitow & Stenberg, 2013). One recent study proposed that social referencing is the basis of the development of a sense of humor, which also first develops in the second half of the first year (Mireault et al., 2014). When parents smiled or laughed at an unexpected event, infants did, too.

EMOTIONAL AND SOCIAL DEVELOPMENT: The Social World of the Infant

The social world of the infant is a crucial part of understanding infant development because it affects every aspect of development, from physical and motor development to cognitive, emotional, and, of course, social development. Humans are built for social interactions and social relationships from day one.

Humans' social environments grow gradually more complex in the course of development as they enter new contexts such as school, community, and workplace. During infancy, social experience and social development occurs within a relatively small circle, a group of persons who are part of the infant's daily environment, and usually there is one person who provides the most love and care—typically, but not always, the mother. Here, let's look first at the broad cultural pattern of the infant's social world, then at two theories of infant social development.

Cultural Themes of Infant Social Life

LO 4.18 **List the main features of infants' social worlds across cultures.**

Although cultures vary in their customs of infant care, there are several themes that occur frequently across cultures. If we combine what scholars have learned from observing infants in a variety of different cultures today, along with what other scholars have learned from studying human evolutionary history and the history of human societies, a common picture of the social world of the infant emerges (DeLoache & Gottlieb, 2000; Friedlmeier et al., 2015; Leakey, 1994; LeVine, 1977; Levine et al., 1994; Richman et al., 2010; Small, 2005), characterized by the following features:

1. *Infants are with their mothers almost constantly during the early months of life.* Nearly all cultures have a period (usually 1–6 months) following birth when mother and infant do little but rest and recover from the birth together. After this rest period is over, the infant is typically strapped to the mother's back with a cloth as she goes back to her daily duties.

social referencing

term for process of becoming more adept at observing others' emotional responses to ambiguous and uncertain situations, and using that information to shape one's own emotional responses

Infants in many cultures are surrounded by adults all day, but cultures vary in how much the adults interact with infants. Here, two mothers and their babies are with other family members and friends in the Samburu culture of Kenya.

2. *After about 6 months, most daily infant care is done by older girls rather than the mother.* Once infants reach about 6 months old their care is delegated to older girls (usually 6 to 10 years old) so that the mother can devote her energy and attention to her work. Most often the girl is an older sister, but it could be any of a range of other people such as an older brother, cousin, grandmother, aunt, or a girl hired from outside the family. However, at night the infant sleeps with the mother.

3. *Infants are among many other people in the course of a day.* In addition to the mother and the caregiver who takes over at about age 6 months, infants are around many other people in the course of a day, such as siblings, aunts, cousins, grandparents, and neighbors.

4. *Infants are held or carried almost constantly.* In many traditional cultures, infants rarely touch the ground during their early months of life. This practice comes out of the belief that infants are highly vulnerable and must be shielded from dangers. Holding them close is a way of protecting them and also a way of keeping them comforted, quiet, and manageable.

5. *Fathers are usually remote or absent during the first year.* In most cultures only women are allowed to observe and assist at birth, and this exclusion of men often continues during the first year. Fathers are rarely involved in the direct care of infants, partly because mothers breast feed their infants frequently but also because care of infants is typically believed to be part of a woman's role but not a man's.

These features are still the dominant worldwide pattern in developing countries (Richman et al., 2010; Small, 2005), but the pattern in developed countries has become quite different over the past two centuries, especially in Western countries. The typical social environment for infants in developed countries is the "nuclear family" consisting of a mother, father (perhaps), and (perhaps) one sibling. Most infants in Western developed countries sleep in a separate room from the time they are born (Goldberg & Keller, 2007). Mother and infant are alone together for much of the time, and the infant may be left in a crib, stroller, or infant seat for a substantial proportion of the day (Baildum et al., 2000). Fathers in developed countries today are more involved than ever in infant care, although still not usually as much as mothers are (Hawkins et al., 2008).

Nevertheless, like infants in developing countries, infants in developed countries nearly always grow up to be capable of functioning well socially in their culture. They develop friendships with peers, they find adults outside the family with whom they form relationships, such as teachers, and they grow to adulthood and form work relationships and intimate relationships with persons outside the family, with most eventually starting a new family of their own. Clearly infants can develop well socially in a variety of cultural contexts. What seems to be crucial to infants' social development across cultures is to have at least one social relationship with someone who is devoted to their care, as we will see next.

CRITICAL THINKING QUESTION

Of the five features of the infant's social world described here, how many are similar to and how many are different from the ecocultural setting you are from? What do you think explains the differences?

The Foundation of Social Development: Two Theories

LO 4.19 Compare and contrast the two major theories of infants' social development.

The two most influential theories of infants' social development are by Erik Erikson and John Bowlby.

ERIKSON'S THEORY: TRUST VERSUS MISTRUST As introduced in Chapter 1, Erikson proposed an eight-stage theory of the life span, with a specific developmental challenge or "crisis" for each stage. For infancy, the central crisis in Erikson's theory is **trust versus mistrust** (Erikson, 1950). Erikson recognized how dependent infants are on others for their survival, and this dependence is at the heart of the idea of trust versus mistrust. Because they require others to provide for their needs, they must have someone who can be trusted to care for them and to be a reliable source of nourishment, warmth, love, and protection. Usually this caregiver is the mother, in most cultures, but it could also be a father, grandmother, older sister, or anyone else who provided love and care on a consistent basis. It is not the biological tie that is important but the emotional and social bond.

When infants have a caregiver who provides for them in these ways, they develop a basic trust in their social world. They come to believe that others will be trustworthy, and to believe that they themselves are worthy of love. However, if adequate love and care are lacking in the first year, infants may come to mistrust not only their first caregiver but others in their social world. They learn that they cannot count on the goodwill of others, and they may shrink from social relations in a world that seems harsh and unfriendly. This basic trust or mistrust lasts long beyond infancy. Remember, in Erikson's theory each stage builds on previous stages, for better or worse. Developing trust in infancy provides a strong foundation for all future social development, whereas developing mistrust is likely to be problematic not only in infancy but in future life stages.

BOWLBY'S ATTACHMENT THEORY Through most of the 20th century there was strong consensus that human infants become attached to their mothers because mothers provide them with food. Hunger is a distressing physical state, especially for babies, who are growing rapidly and need to be fed often. Mothers relieve this distressing state and provide the pleasure of feeding. Over time, infants come to associate the mother with the relief of distress and the experience of pleasure. This association becomes the basis for the love that infants feel for their mothers. This was the dominant view in psychology in the first half of the 20th century. However, around the middle of the 20th century, the British scholar John Bowlby (1969/1982) began to observe that many research findings were inconsistent with this consensus.

There were three findings that were especially notable to Bowlby. First, French psychiatrist René Spitz (1945) reported that infants raised in institutions suffered in their physical and emotional development, even if they were fed well. Spitz studied infants who entered an orphanage when they were 3 to 12 months old. Despite adequate physical care, the babies lost weight and seemed listless and passive, a condition Spitz called *anaclitic depression*. Spitz attributed the infants' condition to the fact that one nurse had to care for seven infants and spent little time with each except for feeding them and changing their diapers. (Anaclitic means "leaning upon," and Spitz chose this term because the infants had no one to lean upon.) The infants showed no sign of developing positive feelings toward the nurse, even though the nurse provided them with nourishment. Other studies of institutionalized infants reported similar results (Rutter, 1996).

The second set of findings that called feeding into question as the basis of the infant–mother bond involved primates, specifically rhesus monkeys. In a classic study, Harry Harlow (1958) placed baby monkeys in a cage with two kinds of artificial "mothers." One of the mothers was made of wire mesh, the other of soft terry cloth. Harlow found that even when he placed the feeding bottle in the wire mother, the baby monkeys spent almost all their time on the cloth

trust-versus-mistrust

in Erikson's psychosocial theory, the first stage of development, during infancy, in which the central crisis is the need to establish a stable attachment to a loving and nurturing caregiver

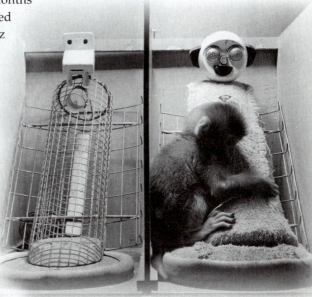

Harlow's studies showed that attachments were not based on nourishment. As shown here, the monkeys preferred the cloth "mother" even though the wire "mother" provided nourishment.

mother, going to the wire mother only to feed. Again, a simple link between feeding and emotional bonds seemed called into question.

The third set of findings noted by Bowlby proved the most important for his thinking. These findings came from the field of *ethology*, which, as we have noted, is the study of animal behavior. Ethologists reported that for some animals, the bond between newborns and their mothers was instantaneous and occurred immediately after birth. Konrad Lorenz (1965), a German ethologist, showed that newborn goslings would bond to the first moving object they saw after hatching and follow it closely, a phenomenon he called *imprinting* (see Chapter 3). To Lorenz and other ethologists, the foundation of the bond between the young of the species and their mothers was not nourishment but

stranger anxiety

fear in response to unfamiliar persons, usually evident in infants by age 6 months

Cultural Focus: Stranger Anxiety Across Cultures

Although infants can discriminate among the smells and voices of different people in their environment from early on, in their first months they can be held and cared for by a wide range of people, familiar as well as unfamiliar, without protesting. However, by about the middle of the first year of life, this begins to change. Gradually they become more selective, developing stronger preferences for familiar others who have cared for them, and **stranger anxiety** emerges in response to being approached, held, or even smiled at by people they do not recognize and trust. Stranger anxiety exists in a wide range of cultures beginning at about age 6 months and grows stronger in the months that follow (Super & Harkness, 1986). So, if an infant or toddler turns away, frowns, or bursts into tears in response to your friendly overtures, don't take it personally!

According to Bowlby (1969/1982), there is an evolutionary basis for the development of stranger anxiety at about age 6 months. This is the age when infants first become mobile, and learning to crawl allows them to begin to explore the environment but also carries the risk that they may crawl themselves into big trouble. Learning to stay close to familiar persons and avoid unfamiliar persons helps infants stay near those who will protect them and keep them safe. Consequently, stranger anxiety peaks at the outset of toddlerhood (about 12 months of age) across cultures (Kagan & Fox, 2006), although the degree of stranger anxiety varies depending on how much toddlers have experienced diverse caregivers.

Watch the *Stranger Anxiety Across Cultures* video to observe how children at different ages and from various cultures react to being approached by strangers and separated from their primary caregivers.

Watch STRANGER ANXIETY ACROSS CULTURES

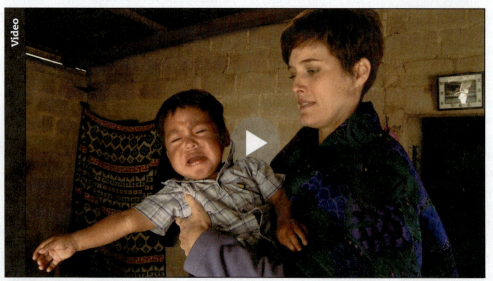

Review Question:

The clip here shows examples of separation and stranger anxiety. Discuss the difference between pure separation anxiety and the impact that including a stranger can have on a child's reaction.

protection. Imprinting to the mother would cause the young to stay close to her and thereby be protected from harm.

Considering these three sets of findings, Bowlby concluded that the emotional tie between children and their mothers was based on children's need for protection and care for many years. Thus, as Bowlby described it in his **attachment theory**, the *attachment* that develops between children and caring adults is an emotional bond that promotes the protection and survival of children during the years they are most vulnerable. The child's **primary attachment figure** is the person who is sought out when the child experiences some kind of distress or threat in the environment, such as hunger, pain, an unfamiliar person, or an unfamiliar setting. Usually the primary attachment figure is a parent, and is most often the mother because in nearly all cultures mothers are primarily the ones who are most involved in the care of infants. However, the primary attachment figure could also be the father, a grandparent, an older sister, or anyone else who is most involved in the infant's care. Separation from the primary attachment figure is experienced by the child as especially threatening, and the loss of the primary attachment figure is a catastrophe for children's development (Bowlby, 1980).

Although it promotes survival for children to stay close to caring adults, it also promotes survival for children to learn about the world around them. Consequently, under normal conditions young children use their primary attachment figure as a **secure base** from which to explore the surrounding environment (Bowlby, 1969/1982). If a threat appears in the environment, attachment behavior is activated and children seek direct physical contact with their attachment figure.

According to Bowlby, attachment develops gradually over the first 2 years of life, culminating in a *goal-corrected partnership* in which both persons use language to communicate about the child's needs and the primary attachment figure's responses. Over time, the child becomes steadily less dependent on the care and protection of the primary attachment figure. However, even into adulthood, people seek out their primary attachment figure for comfort during times of crisis.

COMPARING THE TWO THEORIES Both Erikson's and Bowlby's theories focused on the crucial importance of the infant's relationship with the primary caregiver. Like Erikson, Bowlby believed that the quality of this first important social relationship influenced emotional and social development not only in infancy but also in later stages of development. Like Erikson, Bowlby viewed trust as the key issue in the infant's first attachment to another person. In Bowlby's terms, if the primary caregiver is *sensitive* and *responsive* in caring for the infant, the infant will learn that others, too, can be trusted in social relationships. However, if these qualities are lacking in the primary caregiver, the infant will come to expect—in infancy and in later development—that others, too, may not be reliable social partners.

There are also important differences between the two theories. As we learned in Chapter 1, Erikson's psychosocial theory was a deliberate contrast to Freud's psychosexual theory. However, Bowlby's theory had quite different origins, in evolutionary theory and in research on mother–offspring relationships in animal species. Also, Bowlby's theory inspired methods for evaluating the infant–caregiver relationship that led to a research literature that now comprises thousands of studies (Cassidy & Shaver, 2008; Grossman et al., 2005; Morelli, 2015). Most of this research has been on toddlers rather than infants, so we will save a detailed analysis of it for the next chapter.

attachment theory
Bowlby's theory of emotional and social development, focusing on the crucial importance of the infant's relationship with the primary caregiver

primary attachment figure
person who is sought out when a child experiences some kind of distress or threat in the environment

secure base
role of primary attachment figure, allows child to explore world while seeking comfort when threats arise

Both Erikson and Bowlby viewed the first attachment relationship as crucial to future emotional and social development.

Summary: Emotional and Social Development

LO 4.14 Define *infant temperament* and its main dimensions.

Temperament includes qualities such as activity level, attention span, and emotionality. Thomas and Chess conceptualized temperament by classifying infants as easy, difficult, and slow-to-warm-up. Other theorists rate temperament on the basis of dimensions rather than categories. However, in all cases infant temperament is difficult to measure because of the frequent changes in infants' states.

LO 4.15 Explain how the idea of goodness-of-fit pertains to temperament on both a family level and a cultural level.

Goodness-of-fit means that children develop best if there is a "good fit" between the temperament of the child and environmental demands. It varies culturally, given that different cultures have different views of the value of personality traits such as emotional expressiveness.

LO 4.16 Identify the primary emotions, and describe how they develop during infancy.

The original primary emotions of distress, interest, and pleasure develop into anger, fear, surprise, and happiness within a few months after birth, but sadness tends to appear after infancy.

LO 4.17 Describe infants' emotional perceptions and how their emotions become increasingly social over the first year.

Infants are socially aware of others' emotions from the first days of life, and respond with distress to the distress of others. Toward the end of the first year they draw emotional cues from how others respond to ambiguous situations a process called social referencing.

LO 4.18 List the main features of infants' social worlds across cultures.

Infants are typically cared for by their mothers (in early months) and then by older siblings. They are surrounded by other people and held or carried often. In Western developed countries infants have a smaller social world and more time alone, but they also learn to function socially.

LO 4.19 Compare and contrast the two major theories of infants' social development.

The key to healthy social development, according to Erikson and Bowlby, is a strong, reliable attachment to a primary caregiver. The theories differ in their origins and Bowlby's theory has inspired thousands of studies.

Applying Your Knowledge as a Professional

The topics covered in this chapter apply to a wide variety of career professions. Watch these videos to learn how they apply to a pediatric nurse practitioner and a nanny.

Watch CAREER FOCUS: PEDIATRIC NURSE PRACTITIONER

Melinda Lando
Pediatric Nurse Practitioner

Chapter Quiz

1. Dayle goes to the doctor and expresses concern that her infant's head is too big for his body. The doctor tells her that this is normal because of _____.
   a. the fact that head size varies widely
   b. the cephalocaudal principle
   c. the proximodistal principle
   d. the fact that after infancy, growth slows down considerably

2. Tara and Paul adopted their baby daughter, Yet Kwai, from a Chinese orphanage 5 years ago. She was physically and emotionally deprived until they adopted her at age 2½. It is most likely that Yet Kwai _____.
   a. stayed underweight for much of her life
   b. had more cognitive impairment than she would have had if she had been adopted before 6 months of age
   c. will have greater brain plasticity later in development because of her nurturing environment
   d. will show no signs of cognitive impairment as a result of synaptic pruning

3. Sudden infant death syndrome (SIDS) is almost unknown in cultures where cosleeping is the norm because _____.
   a. babies tend to sleep with their parents on relatively hard surfaces
   b. parents tend to put cloth on both sides of their babies so they remain on their sides
   c. babies are less likely to be breast-fed and therefore parents are less likely to roll over on them
   d. babies are less likely to be aroused during the night in these quieter settings

4. Marasmus is _____.
   a. a disease common among malnourished women with HIV
   b. most common during childhood and contracted through breast milk
   c. an infant disease characterized by muscle atrophy and abnormal drowsiness
   d. a deadly disease resulting from contaminated water being used to dilute formula

5. Infant mortality is highest in:
   a. families that co-sleep.
   b. cultures in the developed world.
   c. cultures that vaccinate infants.
   d. cultures in the developing world.

6. Mahori was strapped to his mother's back for the first year of his life. Which of the following statements is true?
   a. Mahori's parents gave him extra "tummy time" to develop his muscles.
   b. Mahori's motor development will be similar to a U.S. child if they are compared during kindergarten.
   c. The sequence of his motor development will be different from that of babies in cultures where walking during infancy is actively encouraged.
   d. When it comes to Mahori's motor development, environment plays a stronger role than genetics.

7. The key to depth perception is _____.
   a. the development of the pincer grasp
   b. the development of intermodal perception
   c. being able to walk
   d. binocular vision

8. Maha begins rooting while being held by her mother's friend, who quickly passes Maha back to her mother to be breast-fed. Based on Piaget's sensorimotor substages, how old is Maha?
   a. 0–1 months
   b. 1–4 months
   c. 4–8 months
   d. 8–12 months

9. Critics of Piaget's sensorimotor theory argue that the likelihood of making the A-not-B error depends on the _____.
   a. sex of the child
   b. time of day the child is tested
   c. delay between hiding and searching
   d. color of the object

10. Speed of _____ is a good predictor of later memory and intelligence.
    a. habituation
    b. making the A-not-B error
    c. accommodation
    d. secondary circular reactions

11. From infancy onward, _____ memory comes easier to us than _____ memory.
    a. social, recognition
    b. recall, recognition
    c. recognition, recall
    d. infantile amnesia, recall

12. Scores on the Bayley Scales of Infant Development _____.

    a. are useful as a screening tool because those who score very low may have developmental problems

    b. are predictive of later IQ or school performance

    c. are no longer used because they are considered out of date

    d. are calculated for use with children ages 3 months to 9 years

13. Based on research, it would appear that educational media products _____.

    a. greatly accelerate the cognitive development of infants

    b. are used by almost 50 percent of babies in the United States

    c. have no effect on infants' cognitive development

    d. develop better attention spans in babies

14. Babbling _____.

    a. is found only in infants from the Western Hemisphere

    b. occurs only if the infant can hear

    c. develops before cooing

    d. is universal

15. Use of infant-directed speech _____.

    a. is less common outside the developed countries

    b. leads to slower development of language than the style of language typically spoken with adults

    c. involves speaking in a lower than normal tone and using less repetition than in normal speech

    d. has been shown to be less interesting to babies than normal speech; a reason why many parents do not use this type of "baby talk"

16. Temperament _____.

    a. has been measured using the same 19 components across various studies

    b. has only been assessed using cross-sectional methods

    c. is considered to have a biological basis

    d. has no bearing whatsoever on later development

17. Which of the following best illustrates a good fit between caregiver and child?

    a. An irritable baby who is reared by parents who are rigid and intolerant

    b. A "difficult" infant whose parents respond with anger and frustration

    c. A slow-to-warm-up baby whose parents are understanding and tolerant

    d. A baby with a tendency toward negative emotions whose parents try to overcome this by encouraging face-to-face interactions with others

18. The emotion that an infant would most likely display latest in development is _____.

    a. fear

    b. shame

    c. disgust

    d. anger

19. When mothers show negative emotions in relation to a toy in the laboratory, infants will avoid the toy, which illustrates _____.

    a. habituation

    b. social referencing

    c. the still-face paradigm

    d. goodness of fit

20. Which of the following is a common feature of infant social life in most cultures throughout history?

    a. Infants spend a lot of their day in the company of their fathers.

    b. Infants are cared for exclusively by the mothers until they become old enough to walk.

    c. Infants are often kept away from older adults so that they will be less vulnerable to the spread of disease.

    d. Infants are surrounded by others and carried or held almost constantly.

21. Erikson and Bowlby both view _____ as the key issue in an infant's attachment to others.

    a. nourishment

    b. trust

    c. age

    d. personality

Chapter 5
Toddlerhood

DEVELOPMENT DURING TODDLERHOOD, FROM 12 TO 36 MONTHS, RIVALS DEVELOPMENT DURING INFANCY FOR EVENTS OF DRAMA AND IMPORTANCE. On their first birthday most infants are barely able to walk without support; by their third birthday toddlers can run, jump, and climb stairs. On their first birthday infants speak only a handful of words; by their third birthday toddlers have achieved remarkable fluency in the language of their culture and are able to understand and speak about nearly any topic under the sun. On their first birthday infants have little in the way of emotional regulation and show their anger and their exuberance with equal unrestraint; by their third birthday, toddlers have begun to grasp well the moral worldview of their culture, and they exhibit the sociomoral emotions of guilt, embarrassment, and shame. On their first birthday the social world of most infants is limited to parents, siblings, and perhaps some extended family members; but by their third birthday toddlers' social world has greatly expanded. Anthropologist Margaret Mead (1930/2001) described the change from infancy to toddlerhood as going from being a "lap child," in almost constant physical contact with the mother, to being a "knee child" who is attached to the mother but also spends a lot of time in a wider social circle—especially with siblings and older children as part of a mixed-age play group.

Watch CHAPTER INTRODUCTION: TODDLERHOOD

Video

Section 1 Physical Development

Learning Objectives

5.1 Describe the typical changes in physical growth that take place in toddlerhood, and explain the harmful effects of nutritional deficiencies on growth.

5.2 Describe the changes in brain development that take place during toddlerhood, and identify the two most common methods of measuring brain activity.

5.3 Describe the advances in motor development that take place during toddlerhood.

5.4 Compare and contrast the process and timing of toilet training in developed countries and traditional cultures.

5.5 Distinguish the weaning process early in infancy from weaning later in toddlerhood.

PHYSICAL DEVELOPMENT: Growth and Change in Years 2 and 3

From 12 to 36 months, physical growth slows down from its blazing pace of the first year, but it remains more rapid than it will be at any later time of life. This is true for bodily growth as well as for brain development. Toddlerhood is also a time of dramatic advances in both gross and fine motor development.

Bodily Growth and Nutrition

LO 5.1 **Describe the typical changes in physical growth that take place in toddlerhood, and explain the harmful effects of nutritional deficiencies on growth.**

The growth of the body is swift and steady during the toddler years. **Figure 5.1** shows the changes in height and weight from birth to age 5, based on an international sample including children from Brazil, Ghana, India, Norway, Oman, and the United States (World Health Organization, 2006). Notice how growth is extremely rapid in the first year, then slows in pace during the toddler years and beyond. Throughout childhood the average boy is slightly taller and heavier than the average girl.

During toddlerhood, children lose the "baby fat" of infancy and become leaner as they become longer (Fomon & Nelson, 2002). They no longer need as much fat to keep their bodies at a constant temperature. Also, the head, which was one fourth of the neonate's length, is one fifth of the 2-year-old's height. The rest of the body will continue to grow faster than the head, and by adulthood the head will be one eighth the size of the whole body.

Toddlers in developing countries often do not grow as rapidly as toddlers in developed countries. Typically, at birth and for the first 6 months of life, rates of growth are similar in developed countries and developing countries (LeVine et al., 1994), because during the early months infants in most cultures rely mainly on breast milk or infant formula and eat little solid food. However, starting around 6 months of age, when they begin eating solid food as a larger part of their diet, children in developing countries receive less protein and begin to lag in their growth. According to the World Health Organization ([WHO], 2010), about one fourth of children worldwide have diets that are deficient in protein, nearly all of them in developing countries. By the time they reach their first birthday, the height and weight of average children in developing countries are comparable to the bottom 5 percent of children in developed countries, and this pattern continues through childhood into adulthood.

Protein deficiency not only limits the growth of children in developing countries but it makes them vulnerable to disease and early death. One outcome specific to toddlerhood is **kwashiorkor**, in which protein deficiency leads to a range of symptoms such as lethargy, irritability, and thinning hair (Medline, 2008). Often the body swells with water, especially the belly. Toddlers with kwashiorkor may be getting enough food in the form of starches such as rice, bread, or potatoes, but not enough protein. Kwashiorkor lowers the effectiveness of the immune system, making toddlers more vulnerable to disease, and over time can lead to coma followed by death. Improved protein intake can relieve the symptoms of kwashiorkor, but the damage to physical and cognitive development is likely to be permanent.

In addition to protein, toddlers need a diet that contains **micronutrients** such as iron, zinc, and vitamins A, B12, C, and D. Perhaps the most crucial micronutrient deficiency worldwide is iodine. About one third of the world's population has a dietary deficiency of iodine, especially in Africa

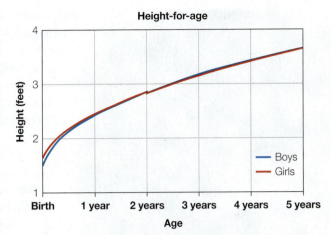

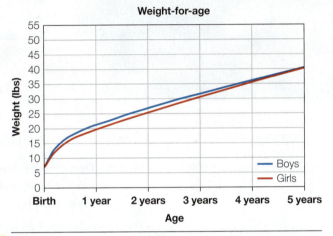

Figure 5.1 Growth Chart From Birth Through Age 5

Growth slows from infancy to toddlerhood but remains rapid.
SOURCE: Based on World Health Organization (2006)

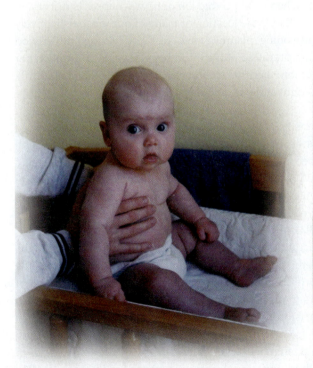

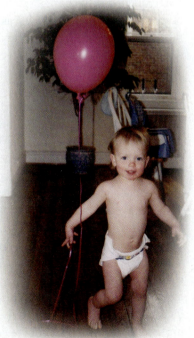

Toddlers lose a lot of their "baby fat" and often become leaner as they grow longer. This is Jeff's daughter Paris at 4 months and 18 months.

kwashiorkor

protein deficiency in childhood, leading to symptoms such as lethargy, irritability, thinning hair, and swollen body, which may be fatal if not treated

micronutrients

dietary ingredients essential to optimal physical growth, including iodine, iron, zinc, and vitamins A, B12, C, and D

Toddlers who do not receive enough protein in their diets sometimes suffer from kwashiorkor, as in this boy in Uganda.

and South Asia (Zimmermann et al., 2008). In young children a lack of iodine inhibits cognitive development, resulting in an estimated intelligence quotient (IQ) deficiency of 10 to 15 points, a substantial margin. Fortunately, adding iodine to a diet is simple—through iodized salt—and cheap, costing only a few cents per person per year. Unfortunately, one third of the world's children still lack this simple micronutrient. Some children in developed countries also lack sufficient micronutrients. One national study of toddlers in the United States found that iron deficiency prevalence rates were about 7 percent overall and were twice as high among Latino toddlers (12 percent) as among White or African American toddlers (both 6 percent; Brotanek et al., 2007). Iron deficiency makes toddlers tired and irritable.

Nutritional deficiencies can be found in developed countries as well, when toddlers do not consume a healthy diet. In the United States, French fries are the most common vegetable consumed by toddlers, and roughly one third of toddlers eat no fruits at all (Fox et al., 2004). It is important for parents to try to maintain toddlers' intake of orange and green vegetables after infancy, when children transition from baby food to more solid options (Deming et al., 2012).

Brain Development

LO 5.2 **Describe the changes in brain development that take place during toddlerhood, and identify the two most common methods of measuring brain activity.**

synaptic density

density of synapses among neurons in the brain; peaks around age 3

The brain continues its rapid growth during the toddler years, although it is not the production of new brain cells that marks early brain development. In fact, the brain has only about one half as many neurons at age 2 as it did at birth. What most distinguishes early brain development is the steep increase in **synaptic density**, the number of synaptic connections among neurons (Huttenlocher, 2002). These connections multiply immensely in the first 3 years, and toddlerhood is when peak production of new synapses is reached in the frontal lobes, the part of our brain that is the location of many of our most distinctively human cognitive qualities, such as reasoning, planning, and creativity. During toddlerhood new synapses in the frontal cortex are produced at the mind-boggling rate of 2 million per second, reaching a total by age 2 of more than 100 trillion (see **Figure 5.2**; Hill et al., 2010). The peak of synaptic density comes right at the end of toddlerhood, around the third birthday (Thompson & Nelson, 2001).

synaptic pruning

process of reducing number of connections between neurons so that they become more efficient

After the peak of synaptic density, a long process of **synaptic pruning** begins. In synaptic pruning, the connections between neurons become fewer but more efficient, with the synapses that are used becoming more developed, whereas unused synapses wither away. Synaptic pruning will remove about one third of synapses in the frontal cortex from early childhood to adolescence, and after a new burst of synaptic density in early adolescence the process of synaptic pruning will continue at a slower rate through adolescence and into adulthood (Blakemore, 2008).

electroencephalogram (EEG)

device that measures the electrical activity of the cerebral cortex, allowing researchers to measure overall activity of the cerebral cortex as well as activation of specific parts

Methods of assessing brain activity provide evidence of the rapid growth of the toddler brain. One widely used method, the **electroencephalogram (EEG)**, measures the electrical activity of the cerebral cortex. Every time a synapse fires it emits a tiny burst of electricity, which allows researchers to measure the overall activity of the cerebral cortex as well as activation of specific parts of it. EEG research on toddlers has found a sharp increase in overall cortical activity from 18 to 24 months (Bell & Wolfe, 2007), reflecting important advances in cognitive and language development that we will examine later in this chapter. Another common method, **functional magnetic resonance imaging (fMRI)**,

functional magnetic resonance imaging (fMRI)

method of monitoring brain activity in which a person lies inside a machine that uses a magnetic field to record changes in blood flow and oxygen use in the brain in response to different kinds of stimulation

requires a person to lie still inside a machine that uses a magnetic field to record changes

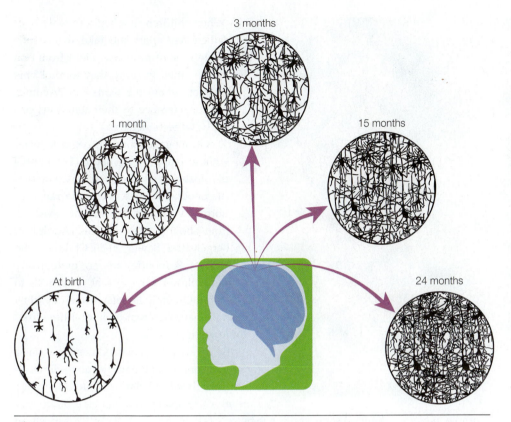

Figure 5.2 Changes in Synaptic Density From Birth to Age 2

Synaptic connections increase throughout the first 2 years, with the greatest density occurring at the end of toddlerhood.

It is not until after toddlerhood that most children can lie still long enough to have an fMRI.

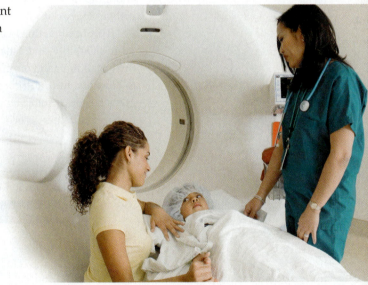

in blood flow and oxygen use in the brain in response to different kinds of stimulation, such as music. Unlike the EEG, an fMRI can detect activity in any part of the brain, not just the cerebral cortex. The fMRI method is not often used with toddlers, perhaps because they are too wiggly and incapable of restraining their movements. However, one study solved this problem by assessing toddlers (age 21 months) and 3-year-olds as they slept and found that toddlers showed greater frontal lobe activity in response to speech than the older children did, reflecting the brain's readiness for rapid language acquisition during the toddler period (Redcay et al., 2008).

Motor Development

LO 5.3 **Describe the advances in motor development that take place during toddlerhood.**

Toddlerhood is a time of dramatic advances in motor development. There are few physical advances more life changing than going from barely standing to walking, running, climbing, and jumping—and all this progress in gross motor development takes place during the toddler years. With regard to fine motor development, toddlers go from being able to place a small object inside a large object to holding a cup and building a tower of blocks.

GROSS MOTOR DEVELOPMENT: FROM TODDLING TO RUNNING, JUMPING, AND CLIMBING Next time you see a child about a year old trying to walk, observe

At 12 to 18 months of age, many toddlers can barely walk, but by their third year they can run and jump.

closely. When children first begin to walk they spread their feet apart and take small, stiff-legged steps, shifting their weight from one leg to the other. In short, they toddle! This is, in fact, where the word *toddler* comes from, in reference to their tentative, unsteady, wide-stance steps.

On average, children begin to walk without support at about 11 months old, just as they are about to enter toddlerhood; but there is a wide range of normal variation around this average, from about 9 to 17 months (Adolph & Berger, 2006; Bayley, 2005). Children who walk at 9 months are no more likely than children who walk at 17 months to become Olympic athletes some day, they simply have different biological time lines for learning to walk.

By 15 months most toddlers can stand (briefly) on one leg and have begun to climb, although once they have climbed onto something, they are much less skilled at climbing down. For example, most can climb up stairs at this age but not (safely) down. By 18 months most can run, although at first they run with the same stiff-legged, wide-stance posture as they use for walking. By 24 months they can kick a ball or throw a small object, and their running has become more flexible and fluid. At this age they can now go down the stairs that they earlier learned to climb up, and more: They can squat for minutes at a time, stand on tiptoes, and jump up and down. Small wonder toddlers move around so much, with so many new abilities to try out!

Through the third year, toddlers' gross motor skills continue to develop as they gain more flexibility and balance. They become better at using visual information to adjust their walking and running in response to changes in surfaces, so they become less likely to stumble and fall (Berger et al., 2005). **Table 5.1** summarizes the major milestones in gross motor development during toddlerhood. Interestingly, these motor milestones are rather similar across ecocultural settings.

Table 5.1 Milestones of Gross Motor Development in Toddlerhood

Age (Months)	Milestone
9–16	Stand alone
9–17	Walk without support
11–19	Stand on one leg
11–21	Climb onto chairs, beds, up stairs, etc.
13–17	Walk backward
14–22	Run
17–30	Jump in place
16–30	Walk on tiptoes
22–36	Walk up and down stairs

SOURCE: Based on Adolph & Berger (2006); Bayley (2005); Coovadia & Wittenberg (2004); Frankenburg et al. (1992); Murkoff (2011).

NOTE: The range shown is the age period at which 90 percent of toddlers achieve the milestone.

Cultural Focus: Gross Motor Development Across Cultures

The research just described is based on Western, mostly U.S. toddlers. What about toddlers in traditional cultures? Infants in traditional cultures are held or carried most of the time to keep them safe and secure. Toddlers in traditional cultures are allowed slightly more mobility—it is much harder to keep a toddler still than an infant—but they continue to be held and carried for about half their waking hours (LeVine, 1977; Morelli, 2015).

Nevertheless, they are equal to toddlers in developed countries in their gross motor skills (Greenfield & Keller, 2004). In fact, toddlers in Africa (as well as African Americans) tend to reach gross motor milestones earlier than toddlers of European backgrounds (Kelly et al., 2006).

The reason for restricting toddlers' movements is the same as for infants: to keep them safe and away from harm. In rural areas of traditional cultures fire is especially a danger because families often have a cooking fire burning perpetually—during the day for cooking meals, during the night for warmth. Other common potential dangers are falling off a cliff, falling into a lake or river, or being trampled by livestock. Holding and carrying toddlers for much of their waking hours makes mishaps less likely.

For similar safety reasons, parents in developed countries "baby proof" their homes once their children become mobile, removing sharp objects and other potential sources of harm (Cave, 2011). Parents of toddlers often place gates at the top of stairs to prevent the child from falling, add locks to cabinets containing sharp objects and household chemicals, install outlet

Watch   GROSS MOTOR DEVELOPMENT ACROSS CULTURES

Video

covers to prevent electrocution, and take other measures to protect against potential sources of harm or injury (Eisenberg et al., 2009).

To see how toddlers' gross motor development varies across and within cultural settings, watch the *Gross Motor Development Across Cultures* video.

Review Question:

Should parents be concerned if their child takes longer than other children to achieve a gross motor milestone, such as learning to walk? Why or why not?

FINE MOTOR DEVELOPMENT: FROM SCRIBBLING TO BUILDING WITH BLOCKS Toddler gains in fine motor development are not as revolutionary as their gains in gross motor development, but they are certainly substantial. Already at 12 months they have come a long way in the course of infancy and can hold an object in one hand while performing an action on it with the other; for example, they can hold a container with the right hand while placing rocks into it with the left hand (Y. P. Chen et al., 2010). At 12 months most have come to show a definite right- or left-hand preference for self-feeding, and over the next 6 months they try a variety of grips on their spoons until they find a grip they will use consistently (McCarty et al., 2001). During the first year of toddlerhood they also learn to hold a cup, scribble with a pencil or crayon, build a tower of three to four blocks, and turn the pages of a book (Murkoff, 2011).

The second year of toddlerhood, from the second to the third birthday, is marked by fewer major advances and more by extending the advances of the previous year. The block tower rises to 8 to 10 blocks, the scribbling becomes skillful enough to draw a semi-straight line, and an attempt to copy a circle may result in something that actually looks somewhat like a circle (Y. P. Chen et al., 2010). Toddlers in their third year of life can even begin to brush their teeth, with a little assistance. **Table 5.2** on the next page summarizes the major milestones in fine motor development during toddlerhood.

Toddlers become capable of eating with a spoon and show a right- or left-hand preference for self-feeding.

Table 5.2 Milestones of Fine Motor Development in Toddlerhood

Age (Months)	Milestone
7–15	Hold writing instrument (e.g., pencil, crayon)
8–16	Coordinate actions of both hands
10–19	Build tower of two blocks
10–21	Scribble vigorously
12–18	Feed self with spoon
15–23	Build tower of three to four blocks
20–28	Draw straight line on paper
24–32	Brush teeth
26–34	Build tower of 8–10 blocks
29–37	Copy circle

SOURCE: Based on Adolph & Berger (2006); Bayley (2005); Coovadia & Wittenberg (2004); Frankenburg et al. (1992); Murkoff (2011).

NOTE: The range shown is the age period at which 90 percent of toddlers achieve the milestone.

PHYSICAL DEVELOPMENT:
Socializing Physical Functions: Toilet Training and Weaning

Eating and eliminating wastes are two physical functions that humans share with other animals, but for humans these functions become socialized from an early age. Here we look at how toddlers become toilet trained and weaned.

Toilet Training

LO 5.4 **Compare and contrast the process and timing of toilet training in developed countries and traditional cultures.**

The toddler years are when most children first learn to control their urination and defecation and become "toilet trained." Expectations for exactly when during the toddler years this should happen have changed substantially over the past half-century in the United States (Blum et al., 2004). During the mid-20th century, pediatricians advocated early toilet training—the earlier the better—and in 1957 a study reported that 92 percent of U.S. toddlers were toilet trained by the time they were 18 months old (Goode, 1999). Gradually, pediatricians and parents concluded there was little reason to require toilet training so early, and in more recent studies only about 25 percent of toddlers were toilet trained by 18 months old and only about 60 percent by their third birthday (Barone et al., 2009; Schum et al., 2001). However, there are variations by social class. The more education parents have, the later their kids tend to be toilet trained (Horn et al., 2006).

Today, most U.S. pediatricians believe it is best to be patient with toddlers' progress toward toilet training and to time it according to when the toddler seems ready (American Academy of Pediatrics [AAP], 2001). Most toddlers show signs of readiness sometime between 18 and 30 months of age. Some key signs are

- staying "dry" for an hour or two during the day;
- regular bowel movements, occurring at about the same time each day;
- increased anticipation of the event, expressed through looks or words;
- directly asking to use the toilet or to wear underwear instead of a diaper.

Approaches to toilet training have changed in recent decades with experts now recommending a "child-centered" approach.

Although toilet training usually begins during the toddler years, it rarely happens overnight. Typically it is a process that continues over several weeks, months, or even years. The earlier toilet training begins, the longer it takes to complete it (Blum et al., 2004). After children are generally able to control urination and defecation, they may occasionally have an "accident" when they are especially tired, excited, or stressed (Murkoff, 2011). Even after children have ceased having accidents during the day, they may not have consistent control at night. For this reason, it is common for children to wear "training pants"—in between diapers and underwear—for a period after learning toilet training. Even at age 5, about one fourth of children have an occasional accident, usually at night (Fritz & Rockney, 2004).

Toddlers in developed countries usually have this process guided and supervised by parents, but for toddlers in traditional cultures, older siblings and other older children are often the guides. By age 2 or 3 most toddlers in traditional cultures spend the majority of their waking hours in groups with children of mixed ages, and they learn to become toilet trained from watching and imitating other children (Edwards et al., 2015; LeVine, 1994). Parents may be involved as well. For example, among the Ifaluk people on the Pacific Ocean islands of Micronesia, when toddlers reach about age 2 their parents encourage them to relieve themselves in the nearby lagoon, not in or near the house, and reprimand them if they fail to comply (Le, 2000). In Ashley's work with Maya people, she has seen that parents are also involved. The toddler indicates a need to relieve herself, and the parent may help by pulling down a young toddler's pants, or, if the child can do that herself, simply telling the child to go outside to the edge of the household compound.

CRITICAL THINKING QUESTION

How might a culture's values of individualism or collectivism influence toilet-training practices?

....

Weaning

LO 5.5 **Distinguish the weaning process early in infancy from weaning later in toddlerhood.**

Cultures vary widely in whether and how long mothers breast feed their children. However, based on what we know of human history and of practices today in traditional cultures, it is clear that breast feeding for 2 to 3 years has been the most typical human custom, until recently (Small, 1998).

If breast feeding takes place for only a few weeks or months during infancy, the transition from breast to bottle usually takes place fairly smoothly, especially if the bottle is introduced gradually (Murkoff & Mazel, 2008). However, the longer breast feeding continues into toddlerhood, the more challenging **weaning** becomes when the mother decides the time has come for the child to stop drinking breast milk. The toddler is much more socially aware than the infant, and much more capable of exercising intentional behavior. The toddler can also speak up, in a way the infant cannot, to make demands and protest prohibitions.

Consequently, most traditional cultures have customary practices for weaning toddlers from the breast. Often, the approach is gentle and gradual at first, but becomes harsher if the toddler resists. For example, in Bali (an island

weaning
cessation of breast feeding

Toddlers in traditional cultures often breast feed until they are about 2 years old. Here, a mother of a hill tribe in a village near Luang Prabang, Laos nurses her toddler.

that is part of Indonesia) parents feed their babies some solid food from the first few days of life and attempt gradual weaning beginning at about age 2. However, if the gradual approach does not work, mothers coat their breasts with bitter-tasting herbs (Diener, 2000). Similarly, toddlers in rural villages in Turkey are weaned at about age 2, but if they persist in trying to breast feed, the mother coats her breasts with tomato paste. The child usually cries and protests, but the method works without fail (Delaney, 2000).

Other cultures separate mother and toddler during weaning, so that the toddler will have no choice but to get used to life without breast feeding. Among the Fulani people of West Africa, toddlers are sent to their grandmother's household during weaning. If the toddler complains about not breast feeding, the grandmother may offer her own breast, but the toddler quickly loses interest on discovering that there is no milk in it (Johnson, 2000).

Summary: Physical Development

LO 5.1 **Describe the typical changes in physical growth that take place in toddlerhood, and explain the harmful effects of nutritional deficiencies on growth.**

Toddlers' physical growth continues at a pace that is slightly reduced from infancy but is nevertheless faster than at any later time of life. Toddlers in developing countries often suffer protein and micronutrient deficiencies that impede their physical and cognitive development.

LO 5.2 **Describe the changes in brain development that take place during toddlerhood, and identify the two most common methods of measuring brain activity.**

The brain's synaptic density peaks at the end of toddlerhood, followed by many years of synaptic pruning. The two most common methods of measuring brain activity are the EEG and the fMRI.

LO 5.3 **Describe the advances in motor development that take place during toddlerhood.**

In their gross motor development, toddlers learn to walk, run, climb, and kick a ball. Toddlers in traditional cultures are often restricted in their movements to protect them from danger—especially cooking fires. Advances in fine motor development include holding a cup and building a tower of blocks. In their third year, toddlers may be able to brush their teeth, with some assistance.

LO 5.4 **Compare and contrast the process and timing of toilet training in developed countries and traditional cultures.**

Children vary widely in the timing of learning toilet training, but most are toilet trained by the end of toddlerhood. In traditional cultures, toddlers usually learn through observing and imitating older children.

LO 5.5 **Distinguish the weaning process early in infancy from weaning later in toddlerhood.**

When weaning takes place in the second or third year of life, toddlers often resist. Customs in traditional cultures for promoting weaning include sending the toddler to a relative's household for a while or coating the mother's breast with an unpleasant substance.

Section 2 Cognitive Development

Learning Objectives

5.6 Outline the cognitive achievements of toddlerhood in Piaget's theory.

5.7 Explain Vygotsky's sociocultural theory of cognitive development and contrast it with Piaget's theory.

5.8 Summarize the evidence for the biological and evolutionary bases of language.

5.9 Describe the milestones in language development that take place during the toddler years.

5.10 Identify how parents' stimulation of toddlers' language varies across cultures, and evaluate how these variations relate to language development.

COGNITIVE DEVELOPMENT:
Cognitive Development Theories

In this section you will learn about Piaget's theory of cognitive development in toddlerhood. Also, you will read how Vygotsky's more cultural perspective on children's cognitive development applies to toddlerhood.

Cognitive Development in Toddlerhood: Piaget's Theory

LO 5.6   **Outline the cognitive achievements of toddlerhood in Piaget's theory.**

Piaget proposed that cognitive development during the first 2 years of life follows a sequence of six sensorimotor stages. During infancy the primary cognitive advance of the first four stages of sensorimotor development is from simple reflexes to intentional, coordinated behavior. Neonates have a wide range of reflexes and little intentional control over their behavior, but by the end of the first year infants have lost most of their reflexes and can perform intentional actions that combine schemes, such as moving one object aside to reach another. In the second year of life—during toddlerhood—the final two stages of sensorimotor development are completed.

SENSORIMOTOR STAGE 5: TERTIARY CIRCULAR REACTIONS Piaget called the fifth stage of sensorimotor development *tertiary circular reactions* (age 12–18 months). In this stage, toddlers intentionally try out different behaviors to see what the effects will be. In the previous stage, *secondary circular reactions*, the action first occurs by accident and then is intentionally repeated, but in tertiary circular reactions the action is intentional from the beginning. Like secondary circular reactions, tertiary circular reactions are circular because they are performed repeatedly.

For example, at 17 months Jeff's twins discovered how to flush the toilet, and one day they flushed and flushed and flushed until the flushing system broke and the water began overflowing. Jeff discovered this as he sat downstairs reading the newspaper and suddenly observed water whooshing out of the vents in the ceiling! He ran upstairs and there they were, standing in 3 inches of water, giggling with glee, absolutely delighted. Jeff said he didn't recall thinking of Piaget at that moment, but Piaget would have been pleased. To Piaget, in this stage toddlers become like little scientists, experimenting on the objects around them to learn more about how the world works. Jeff's twins certainly learned that day about what happens when you flush a toilet repeatedly.

SENSORIMOTOR STAGE 6: MENTAL REPRESENTATIONS The final stage of sensorimotor development, from 18 to 24 months, is the stage of **mental representations**. Now, instead of trying out a range of actions as in tertiary circular reactions, toddlers first think about the possibilities and select the action most likely to achieve the desired outcome. Piaget gave the example of his daughter Lucienne, who sought to obtain a small chain from inside the matchbox where her father had placed it. First she turned the box upside down; then she tried to jam her finger into it, but neither of these methods worked. She paused for a moment, holding the matchbox and considering it intently. Then she opened and closed her mouth, and suddenly slid back the cover of the matchbox to reveal the chain (Crain, 2000). To Piaget, opening and closing her mouth showed that she was pondering potential solutions, then mimicking the solution that had occurred to her.

Mental representation is a crucial milestone in cognitive development because it is the basis of the most important and most distinctly human cognitive abilities, including language. The words we use are mental representations of objects, people, actions, and ideas.

mental representations

Piaget's final stage of sensorimotor development in which toddlers first think about the range of possibilities and then select the action most likely to achieve the desired outcome

deferred imitation

ability to repeat actions observed at an earlier time

Toddlers' play is often based on deferred imitation. Here, a toddler in Peru offers a bottle to her doll.

OBJECT PERMANENCE IN TODDLERHOOD Object permanence also develops further during toddlerhood. By their first birthday infants will look for an object that they observe being hidden behind or under another object, but they still make the "A-not-B error." That is, if they find an object under blanket A, and then a second blanket B is added and they observe the object being hidden under blanket B, they nevertheless tend to look under blanket A, where they found the object the first time.

Toddlers learn to avoid the A-not-B error and search for the object where they last saw it hidden. However, even though the A-not-B error is less common in toddlerhood than in infancy, search errors happen occasionally on this task in toddlerhood and even into early childhood, up to ages 4 and 5 (Hood et al., 2003; Newcombe & Huttenlocher, 2006). But we can say with some confidence that toddlers have attained object permanence once they generally avoid the A-not-B error.

Object permanence is a major advance of cognitive development in toddlerhood, but it is not a distinctly human achievement. In fact, chimpanzees and human toddlers have equal success on object permanence tasks at age 2 (Call, 2001; Collier-Baker & Suddendorf, 2006). Understanding the permanence of the physical world is crucial to being able to function in that world, so it is not surprising that humans and nonhuman primates would share this fundamental ability (Brownell & Kopp, 2007).

DEFERRED IMITATION The ability for mental representation of actions also makes possible **deferred imitation**, which is the ability to repeat actions observed at an earlier time. Piaget's favorite example of deferred imitation involved his daughter Jacqueline, who witnessed another child exploding into an elaborate public tantrum and then repeated the tantrum herself at home the next day (Crain, 2000). Deferred imitation is a crucial ability for learning because it means that when we observe something important to know, we can repeat it later ourselves. Deferred imitation is a frequent part of toddlers' pretend play because they observe the actions of other children or adults—making a meal, feeding a baby, digging a hole—and then imitate those actions later in their play (Lillard, 2007).

Piaget proposed that deferred imitation begins at about 18 months, but subsequent research has shown that it develops much earlier than he had thought (Bauer, 2006). Deferred imitation of facial expressions has been reported as early as 6 weeks of age, when infants exposed to an unusual facial expression from an unfamiliar adult imitated it when the same adult appeared before them the next day (Meltzoff & Moore, 1994). At 6 months of age, infants can imitate a simple sequence of events a day later, such as taking off a puppet's glove and shaking it to ring a bell inside the glove (Barr et al., 2003).

However, if there is a longer delay, toddlers are more proficient at deferred imitation than infants are. In a series of studies, children 9, 13, and 20 months old were shown two-step sequences of events such as placing a car on a track to make a light go on, then pushing a rod to make the car run down a ramp (Bauer et al., 2000; 2001; 2003). After a 1-month interval, shown the same materials, fewer than half of the 9-month-olds could imitate the steps they had seen previously, compared with about two thirds of the 13-month-olds and nearly all the 20-month-olds. Other studies have shown that better deferred imitation among toddlers than among infants may be principally because of advances in the maturity of the brain. Specifically, the *hippocampus*, that part of the brain especially important in long-term memory encoding and recall, is still in a highly immature state of development during infancy but matures substantially during toddlerhood (Bauer et al., 2010; Liston & Kagan, 2002).

CATEGORIZATION Piaget also believed that mental representation in toddlerhood is the basis of categorization. Once we are able to represent an image of a house mentally, for example, we can understand the category "house" and understand that different houses are all part of that category. These categories, in turn, become the basis for language, because each noun and verb represents a category (Waxman, 2003). The word *truck* represents the category "truck" containing every possible variety of truck; the word *run* represents the category "run" containing all varieties of running, and so on.

Here, too, recent experiments seem to indicate that Piaget underestimated children's early abilities. Infants and toddlers are able to do more than he had thought. Even infants as young as a few months old have been shown to have a rudimentary understanding of categories. This can be demonstrated by their patterns of looking at a series of images. As we have seen, infants tend to look longer at images that are new or unfamiliar, and their attention to images is often used in research to infer what they know and do not know. In one study, 3- and 4-month-old infants were shown photographs of cats (Quinn et al., 1993). After a series of cat photos, the infants were shown two new photos, one of a cat and one of a dog. They looked longer at the dog photo, indicating that they had been using a category for "cat" and looked longer at the dog photo because it did not fit.

However, research has generally confirmed Piaget's insight that categorization becomes more advanced during toddlerhood (Bornstein & Arterberry, 2010). For example, one study compared children who were 9, 12, and 18 months old (Gopnik et al., 1999). The children were given four different toy horses and four different pencils. At 9 months, they played with the objects but made no effort to separate them into categories. At 12 months, some of the children would place the objects into categories and some would not. By 18 months, nearly all the children would systematically and deliberately separate the objects into a "horse" category and a "pencil" category.

By the time they are 2 years old, toddlers can go beyond the appearance of objects to categorize them on the basis of their functions or qualities. In a study demonstrating this ability, 2-year-olds were shown a machine and a collection of blocks that appeared to be identical (Gopnik et al., 1999). Then they were shown that two of the blocks made the machine light up when placed on it, whereas others did not. The researcher picked up one of the blocks that had made the machine light up and said, "This is a blicket. Can you show me the other blicket?" The 2-year-old children were able to choose the other block that had made the machine light go on, even though it looked the same as the blocks that had not had that effect. Although *blicket* was a nonsense word the toddlers had not heard before, they were able to understand that the category "blicket" was defined by causing the machine to light up. Can you see how this experiment also provides a good demonstration of how categorization is the basis of language?

Applying Vygotsky's Cultural Theory of Cognitive Development to Toddlerhood

LO 5.7   **Explain Vygotsky's sociocultural theory of cognitive development and contrast it with Piaget's theory.**

Although most studies of toddlers' cognitive development pay little attention to cultural context, Vygotsky's cultural theory of cognition has gained increased attention from scholars of human development. The **zone of proximal development** is the idea that the difference between what a child can accomplish with help and what she can accomplish alone indicates the child's current state of development and what the next developmental changes are likely to be.

As they learn in the zone of proximal development and have conversations with those guiding them, children begin to speak to themselves in a self-guiding and self-directing way, first aloud and then internally. Vygotsky called this **private speech** (Winsler et al., 2009). As children become more competent in what they are learning, they internalize their private speech and gradually decrease its use. Toddlerhood and early childhood are crucial periods in Vygotsky's theory because it is during these life stages that children are most likely to use private speech and make the transition from using it aloud to using it internally (Feigenbaum, 2002). However, private speech continues throughout life. In fact, Vygotsky believed that private speech was necessary to all higher order cognitive functioning. In recent years, studies have shown that adolescents and adults use private speech when solving tasks of diverse kinds (Medina et al., 2009).

Another key idea in Vygotsky's theory is **scaffolding**, which is characterized by the way more experienced people, usually parents or teachers, simplify tasks to make them easier for children to accomplish. It is easy to find many instances of scaffolding for toddlers. For example, toys are age-graded according to the ways that toddlers can handle them manually and the ways that they can understand them cognitively. Toddlers might play with large blocks, whereas children in middle childhood can handle tiny Lego pieces. Cognitively, toddlers enjoy sensorimotor toys that might bore older children. Watch the video *Scaffolding* to learn more.

zone of proximal development
difference between skills or tasks that children can accomplish alone and those they are capable of performing if guided by an adult or a more competent peer

private speech
in Vygotsky's theory, self-guiding and self-directing comments children make to themselves as they learn in the zone of proximal development

scaffolding
degree of assistance provided to the learner in the zone of proximal development, gradually decreasing as the learner's skills develop

Watch   SCAFFOLDING

One scholar who has been important in extending Vygotsky's theory is Barbara Rogoff (1990; 1995; 1998; 2003). Her idea of **guided participation** refers to the interaction between two people (often an adult and a child) as they participate in a culturally valued activity. The guidance is "the direction offered by cultural and social values, as well as social partners" (Rogoff, 1995, p. 142) as learning takes place. As an example of guided participation, Rogoff (2003) describes a toddler and caregiver in Taiwan "playing school" together. As part of the game, the caregiver teaches the toddler to stand up and bow down to the teacher at the beginning and end of class, thereby teaching not only the routine of the classroom but the cultural value of respect for teachers' authority. The teaching in guided participation may also be indirect. For example, from her research with the Mayan people of Guatemala, Rogoff (2003) describes how toddlers observe their mothers making tortillas and attempt to imitate them. Mothers give them a small piece of dough and help their efforts along by rolling the dough into a ball and starting the flattening process but otherwise do not provide explicit teaching, instead allowing toddlers to learn through observing and then attempting to imitate their mother's actions.

COGNITIVE DEVELOPMENT:
Language Development

Of all the qualities that distinguish humans from other animals, language may be the most important. Other species of animals have their own ways of communicating, but language allows humans to communicate about a vastly broader range of topics. Using language, humans can communicate about not just what is observable in the present, the way other animals might communicate about food or predators in their immediate environment, but about an infinite range of things beyond the present moment. With language we can also communicate not just about things that exist but about things that might exist, but also about things that we imagine. As linguist Derrick Bickerton remarks, "Only language could have broken through the prison of immediate experience in which every other creature is locked, releasing us into infinite freedoms of space and time" (Leakey, 1994, p. 119).

By the end of infancy most children can only speak a few words. It is during toddlerhood that language development has its most rapid and important advances. Toddlers go from speaking a few words at their first birthday to being fluent users of language by their third birthday. Let's examine the course of this remarkable achievement, looking first at the biological and evolutionary bases of language, then at specific language milestones of toddlerhood, and finally, at the cultural and social context of toddlers' language use.

The Biological and Evolutionary Bases of Language

LO 5.8   **Summarize the evidence for the biological and evolutionary bases of language.**

You may have heard that some primates have learned how to use language. Attempts to teach language to apes have a long history in the social sciences, going back more than a half-century. In the earliest attempts, researchers treated baby chimpanzees as closely as possible to how a human infant would be treated, having the chimpanzees live in the researcher's household as part of the family and making daily efforts to teach the chimps how to speak. Years of these efforts yielded nothing but the single word "mama"—and a badly disordered household. It turned out that chimpanzees, like other nonhuman primates, lack the vocal apparatus that makes human speech possible.

In the 1960s, researchers hit on the clever idea of teaching apes sign language. These attempts were much more successful. One famous chimpanzee, Washoe, learned to use

guided participation
teaching interaction between two people (often an adult and a child) as they participate in a culturally valued activity

Chimpanzees can learn to use some sign language in a limited way, but they lack the infinite generativity of human language.

about 100 signs, mostly involving requests for food (Small, 2001). She even learned to lie and to make jokes. However, she never learned to make original combinations of signs (with one possible exception, when she saw a duck for the first time and signed "water bird"). Mostly, Washoe and other primates who have learned sign language simply mimic the signs they have been taught by their human teachers. They lack the most important and distinctive feature of human language, which is **infinite generativity**, which is the ability to take the word symbols of a language and combine them in a virtually infinite number of new ways.

A variety of human biological characteristics indicate that we are a species built for language (Kenneally, 2007). First, humans have a unique vocal apparatus. We are able to make a much wider range of sounds than the other primates because, for us, the larynx is located lower in the throat, which creates a large sound chamber, the pharynx, above the vocal cords. We also have a relatively small and mobile tongue that can push the air coming past the larynx in various ways to make different sounds, and lips that are flexible enough to stop and start the passage of air.

Second, two areas in the left hemisphere of the human brain are specifically devoted to language functions (Nakano & Blumstein, 2004; Pizzamiglio et al., 2005). **Broca's area** in the left frontal lobe is specialized for language production, and **Wernicke's area** in the left temporal lobe is specialized for language comprehension (see **Figure 5.3**). If damage to one of these areas occurs in adulthood, the specialized language function of the area is also damaged; but if damage takes place in childhood, other areas of the brain can compensate—with compensation being greater the younger the brain injury takes place (Akshoomoff et al., 2002; Huttenlocher, 2002). In addition to Broca's and Wernicke's areas, many other regions of the brain contribute to language use (Dick et al., 2004). In fact, some linguists argue that the extraordinary size of the human brain in comparison to other species is mainly the result of the evolution of language (Pinker, 2004).

Third, genes for language development have recently been identified (Gazzaniga, 2008; Pinker, 2004). Because Broca's and Wernicke's areas have long been known to be part of normal brain anatomy, the genetic basis of language was clear. However, identifying the specific genes for language strengthens our knowledge of how deeply language is embedded in human species development.

Although modern humans are biologically equipped for language, our earliest ancestors were not. Early hominids had a larynx similar in placement to modern nonhuman primates, and so must have been incapable of language (Leakey, 1994). The placement of the larynx became notably lower beginning nearly 2 million years ago, and the earliest *Homo sapiens* 200,000 years ago had a vocal apparatus that was not much different from yours. Undoubtedly the development of language gave humans a substantial evolutionary advantage (Small, 2001). Language would have made it easier to communicate about the location of food sources and about how to make tools, which would in turn enhance survival. If your clan could craft a better spear, you would have a better

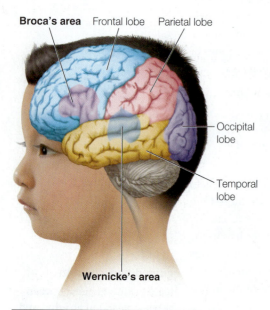

Figure 5.3 Brain Lobes Showing Broca's Area and Wernicke's Area

chance of killing the prey that would provide the necessary nourishment. If your group could construct a boat, you could potentially travel to new food sources if the local ones became depleted.

Many evolutionary biologists believe that language also conferred an evolutionary advantage because of its social function. During the course of human evolution, the size of human groups gradually increased (Leakey, 1994), leading to an increased need for communication that would allow them to function effectively. Because language abilities improved the efficiency of group functioning, groups that excelled in language would have been more likely than other groups to survive and reproduce. Within groups, too, using language effectively would have conferred an advantage in obtaining mates, food, and status, so natural selection would have favored language abilities in the course of human evolutionary history (Pinker, 2004).

The marvelous ability that young children have to learn the rules of their language is one more indication of the biological, evolutionary basis of language. A half-century ago, at a time when many psychologists were arguing that language has no biological origin and children learn it solely through imitation and parents' reinforcement, linguist Noam Chomsky (1957, 1969) protested that language is too complex to be learned in this way. Observing that all children learn the basic rules of grammar of their language at about the same age, 2 to 3 years old, Chomsky proposed that children are born with a **language acquisition device (LAD)** that enables them to perceive and grasp quickly the grammatical rules in the language around them. Today language researchers generally agree that language development is a biological potential that is then nurtured by social interaction, although there is still a lively debate about the nature of the biological foundation of language and the kinds of social stimulation needed to develop it (Hoff, 2009).

CRITICAL THINKING QUESTION

How, specifically, would language have conferred an evolutionary advantage to early humans in obtaining mates, food, and status?

Milestones of Toddler Language: From First Words to Fluency

LO 5.9   **Describe the milestones in language development that take place during the toddler years.**

Toddlers' advances in language begin slowly but then rise sharply, so that in less than 2 years they go from speaking a few words to being highly adept language users. Especially notable is the amazing burst of language development that occurs at 18 to 24 months.

TWELVE MONTHS TO 18 MONTHS: SLOW EXPANSION For the first 6 months of toddlerhood, language develops at a steady but slow pace. From 12 to 18 months old, toddlers learn to speak one to three new words a week, reaching a total of 10 words by 15 months old and 50 words by about 18 months old, on average, in U.S. studies (Bloom, 1998). There is a wide range of variability around these averages. Toddlers may speak their 10th word anywhere from 13 to 19 months old, and their 50th word anywhere from 14 to 24 months old, and still be considered within the normal range. Just as the timing of taking first steps has no relation to later athletic ability, timing of speaking the 1st, 10th, or 50th word has no relation to later verbal ability.

The first 50 words tend to be words that are part of toddlers' daily routines (Waxman & Lidz, 2006), and include mostly nouns in many languages:

- important people ("Mama," "Dada"),
- familiar animals ("dog," "kitty"),

infinite generativity

ability to take the word symbols of a language and combine them in a virtually infinite number of new ways

Broca's area

portion of the left frontal lobe of the human brain that is specialized for language production

Wernicke's area

portion of the left temporal lobe of the human brain that is specialized for language comprehension

language acquisition device (LAD)

according to Chomsky, innate feature of the brain that enables children to perceive and grasp quickly the grammatical rules in the language around them

- body parts ("hair," "tummy"),
- moving objects ("car," "truck"),
- foods ("milk," "cookie"),
- actions ("eat," "bath"),
- household items ("cup," "chair"),
- toys ("ball," "bear"),
- greetings or farewells ("hi," "bye-bye").

holophrase

single word that is used to represent a whole sentence

overextension

use of a single word to represent a variety of related objects

underextension

applying a general word to a specific object

fast mapping

learning and remembering a word for an object after just one time of being told what the object is called

Toddlers exhibit overextension when they use a single word (such as "raspberry") to represent a variety of related objects (such as strawberries and other red berries).

Toddlers first learn words they need to use in practical ways to communicate with the people around them, usually as part of shared activities. Often at this age they speak in partial words, for example "bah" for bird, "meh" for milk, or "na-na" for banana.

Toddlers' first words are influenced by the language they are learning. In English, nouns are primary, and toddlers learning English produce a lot of nouns among their first words. In languages that emphasize verbs, however, like Korean, verbs are more prominent among first words (Choi & Gopnik, 1995). Korean toddlers hear more verbs and produce more verbs in their early language development.

From 12 to 18 months most toddlers use one word at a time, but a single word can have varied meanings. Toddler's single words are called **holophrases**, meaning that for them a single word can be used to represent different forms of whole sentences (Flavell et al., 2002). For example, "cup" could mean "Fill my *cup* with juice," or "I dropped the *cup* on the floor," or "Hand me my *cup*, I can't reach it," or "Here, take this *cup*," depending on when and how and to whom it is said.

Another way toddlers make the most of their limited vocabulary is to have a single word represent a variety of related objects. This is called **overextension** (Bloom, 2000). For example, when the son of two language researchers learned the name of the furry family dog, Nunu, he applied it not only to the original Nunu but to all dogs, as well as to other fuzzy objects such as slippers, and even to a salad with a large black olive that apparently reminded him of Nunu's nose (de Villiers & de Villiers, 1978).

Toddlers also exhibit **underextension**, applying a general word to a specific object (Woodward & Markman, 1998). When Jeff was a child, his family had a cat named Kitty, who received that name because his brother was told that it was "the kitty," and began calling it Kitty, and the name stuck. He did not realize that *kitty* was the (slang) name for the larger category, "cats," but mistook it for the proper name of that particular cat.

Underextension often occurs in this way, with a toddler first applying a new word to a specific object, then learning later to apply it to a category of objects.

Here, as at all ages, *production* (speaking) lags behind *comprehension* (understanding) in language development. Although toddlers do not reach the 50-word milestone in production until about 18 months old, they usually achieve 50-word comprehension by about 13 months old (Menyuk et al., 1995). During toddlerhood, comprehension is a better predictor of later verbal intelligence than production is (Reznick et al., 1997).

EIGHTEEN MONTHS TO 24 MONTHS: THE NAMING EXPLOSION
After learning to speak words at a slow rate for the first half of their second year, toddlers' word production suddenly takes off from 18 to 24 months. The pace of learning new words doubles, from one to three words per week to five or six words per week (Kopp, 2003). This is known as the *naming explosion* or *vocabulary spurt* (Bloom et al., 1985; Goldfield & Reznick, 1990). After just one time of being told what an object is called, toddlers this age will learn it and remember it, a process called **fast mapping** (Gopnik et al., 1999; Markman & Jaswal, 2004). Fast mapping is not just as a result of memory but also of toddlers' ability to quickly infer the meaning of words based on how the word is used in a sentence and how it seems to be related to words they already know (Dixon et al., 2006). By their second birthday, toddlers have an average vocabulary of about 200 words (Dale & Goodman, 2005). This rapid pace of

learning and remembering words will continue for years, but it is especially striking at 18 to 24 months because this is when it begins (Ganger & Brent, 2004). Girls' vocabulary increases faster than boys' vocabulary during this period, initiating a gender difference in verbal abilities that will persist throughout childhood (Lovas, 2011).

Two of the most notable words toddlers learn during this period are *gone* and *no.* Using "gone" reflects their growing awareness of object permanence because it signifies that something has disappeared from view but still exists somewhere (Gopnik et al., 1999). Using "no" reflects their budding sense of self ("me," "my," and "mine" also begin to be used at this age). Saying "no" can be short for "You may want me to do to that, but I don't want to do it!" Of course, they also begin to hear "No!" more often around this age because their mobility and curiosity leads them to behavior that the adults around them may regard as dangerous or destructive (Kopp, 2003). During this 18- to 24-month period they also learn to name one or two colors, at least six body parts, and emotional states like "tired" and "mad" (Kopp, 2003; Murkoff, 2011).

Toward the end of the 18- to 24-month period, toddlers begin to combine spoken words for the first time. Their first word combinations are usually two words, in what is called **telegraphic speech** (Bloom, 1998; Brown, 1973; Edmonds, 2011). Telegraphic speech takes similar forms in a variety of languages, from English to German to Finnish to Samoan: "See doggie," "Big car," "My ball," "More cookie," or "Mommy gone" (Bochner & Jones, 2003; Slobin, 1972). Like a telegram in the old days, telegraphic speech strips away connecting words like *the* and *and*, getting right to the point with nouns, verbs, and modifiers.

An interesting feature of telegraphic speech is that it already shows an initial knowledge of syntax (word order). Toddlers learning English say "See doggie," not "Doggie see"; they say "My ball," not "Ball my." Similar to the one-word holophrases used previously, telegraphic speech implies more understanding of language than it states explicitly: "Big car" means "Look at the big car," "My ball" means "This is my ball," and so on.

Verbal production is the most striking advance of the 18- to 24-month period, but comprehension also advances notably as toddlers become faster and more efficient in processing words. In one series of experiments, toddlers 15 to 24 months old were shown pictures of two objects at a time while a recorded voice said "Where's the _____?" and named one of the objects (Fernald et al., 2006). At 15 months, toddlers waited until the whole word had been spoken before looking at the object the word referred to, but by 24 months they would shift their gaze even before the word had been completely spoken, for example looking at the shoe as soon as they heard the "sh" part spoken.

TWENTY-FOUR MONTHS TO 36 MONTHS: BECOMING ADEPT AT LANGUAGE

During the third year, toddlers continue to expand their speaking vocabulary at the same rapid pace that began at 18 to 24 months. They learn to use prepositions such as *under*, *over*, and *through* (Murkoff, 2011). They also use words that reflect a more complex understanding of categories. For example, they understand that a bear is not only a bear but also an animal (Kopp, 2003).

They continue to exhibit overextension and underextension, but with diminishing frequency as their vocabulary expands. They continue to use telegraphic speech as well, but now in three- and four-word statements ("Ball under bed!") rather than two words. Increasingly during the third year they begin to speak in short, complete sentences. At this age Jeff's son Miles would point to the moon and protest, "It's too high!" then look at his parents as if he expected them to do something about it.

By the end of the third year most toddlers are remarkably skilled language users (Maratsos, 1998). They can communicate with others about a wide range of topics. They can speak about events that are happening in the present as well as about past and future events. Toddlers raised in homes where Chinese is spoken have learned that raising or lowering the pitch of a word changes its meaning. French toddlers have learned how to

telegraphic speech
two-word phrases that strip away connecting words, such as *the* and *and*

make nasal sounds and say "Voilà!" and !Kung San toddlers in Botswana have learned how to click their tongues against various parts of their mouths to make the words of their language (Small, 2001). Although their pronunciation of words is not as precise as it will become later, by the time they reach age 3 most toddlers can speak clearly enough to make themselves understood about nearly anything they wish.

Furthermore, without any explicit instruction, by the end of the third year toddlers have learned the rules of their language, no matter how complex those rules may seem to someone who does not speak it. Consider this example (Slobin, 1972, 2014). In Turkish, the rules of syntax (word order) are different from English. In English, "The girl fed the dog" has quite a different meaning from "The dog fed the girl." The *subject* (girl) is supposed to go first, followed by the *verb* (fed) and then the *object* (dog). However, in Turkish the object is indicated not by the syntax but by attaching the suffix *u*. So, "The girl fed the dog-u" means the same as "The dog-u fed the girl." Turkish toddlers use the *u* rule correctly by their third year, just as English-speaking children learn the correct use of English syntax by their third year.

Toddlers' language mastery is evident not only in how well they use the rules of their language but in the mistakes they make. As they learn the grammar of their language, they make mistakes that reflect **overregularization**, which means applying grammatical rules even to words that are exceptions to the rule.

Here are two examples from English that illustrate overregularization. First, the plural of most English nouns can be obtained by adding *s* to the singular form, but there are irregular exceptions, such as "mice" as the plural of "mouse," and "feet" as the plural of "foot." In the third year, toddlers sometimes make mistakes with these kinds of words, saying "mouses" instead of "mice" and "foots" instead of "feet." Second, the rule for the past tense of an English verb is to add *ed* to the end, but there are irregular exceptions, such as "went" as the past tense of "go" and "threw" as the past tense of "throw." In the third year toddlers sometimes make mistakes with these exceptions, saying "Mommy *goed* to the store" or "I *throwed* the ball." However, it is a testament to toddlers' language mastery that even by the third year, mistakes of this kind are rare (Bochner & Jones, 2003).

Learning Language in a Social and Cultural Context

LO 5.10 **Identify how parents' stimulation of toddlers' language varies across cultures, and evaluate how these variations relate to language development.**

Humans are biologically built for learning language, but not for learning any specific language. There are more than 60,000 different human languages in the world (Small, 2001), but none of them comes preinscribed on our brains. Whatever language we learn must come from our social and cultural environment.

What kind of social environment do toddlers need to develop their language skills? In U.S. research, the focus has been on how parents foster language development in young children. In the United States and other developed countries, parents often read to their infants and toddlers, explaining the meaning of the words as they go along (Fitneva & Matsui, 2015). This is a way of preparing children for an economic future in which the ability to apprehend and use information will be crucial. Parents in the majority culture are more likely than parents in ethnic minority cultures to read to their toddlers, promoting an early advantage in verbal development that continues through the school years (Driessen et al., 2010).

Several studies have examined social-class differences in parents' language stimulation and how this is related to the pace of toddlers' language development. The higher the social class of the parents, the more likely they are to read to their toddlers (Fitneva & Matsui, 2015). Social-class status is also correlated with how much parents speak to their young children. For example, one study videotaped parent–child interactions in the homes of low-, middle-, and high-income families on several occasions, beginning

overregularization

applying grammatical rules even to words that are exceptions to the rule

when the children were 7 to 9 months old and continuing until they were about 30 months old (Hart & Risley, 1999, 2003). There were striking differences in how many words were spoken to children of different income levels (see **Figure 5.4**). Parents in high-income families talked the most to their children, averaging about 35 words a minute; parents in middle-income families talked to their children an average of about 20 words a minute; and parents of low-income families provided the least language stimulation, just 10 words per minute. By 30 months old there were substantial differences in the toddlers' vocabularies, averaging 766 words in the high-income families and just 357 words in the low-income families. A more recent study reached similar conclusions (Weisleder & Fernald, 2013).

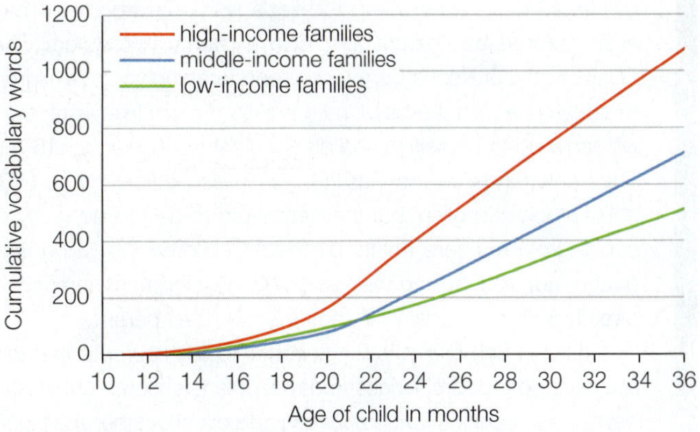

Of course, there is a research design problem in studies like this because parents provide not only the environment to their children but their genes; this is known as passive genotype–environment effects. In studies of parents and children in biological families, genes and environment are *confounded*, which means they are closely related and difficult to separate. However, in early childhood and beyond, the influence of teachers' language use on children's language development provides more definite evidence of an environmental effect because teachers and children have no genetic relationship (Huttenlocher, 2002).

However, given the concern with development in the early years and a hope to ensure success of all children, there has been a recent effort to improve the early language experiences of toddlers in low-income families. Some cities in the United States have developed programs to encourage parents to talk to children in ways that expand children's vocabulary and turn-taking skills (Talbot, 2015). A number of studies have shown that high-quality preschool programs for toddlers and older children have been found to improve learning and educational outcomes later in life (Dickinson et al., 2013).

Interventions to address parents' interactions with their children are not without criticism, however. Linguists and those who study multicultural education have asserted that there is no evidence that the number of words heard before age 3 years accounts for the academic differences across socioeconomic groups (Johnson, 2015). Researchers and those hoping to improve educational outcomes for children growing up in poor families should consider the language strengths that children from a variety of ecocultural backgrounds bring with them to school, and not treat linguistic minority ways of speaking as "impoverished" versions of English (Johnson, 2015).

Figure 5.4 Toddlers' Vocabulary by Income Group

Cumulative vocabulary by income group in the first 3 years of life.

Cultural Focus: Language Development Across Cultures

Although language development clearly has a biological basis, the cultural setting plays an important role as well. Because most research on language development is conducted in developed Western countries, an assumption of this research is that most toddler language use takes place in a parent–toddler dyad—just the two of them. This assumption may be true for the families being studied in developed countries, but the social environment that most toddlers experience worldwide is much different from this, and consequently their language environment differs as well.

Once they learn to walk and begin to talk, toddlers in most cultures spend most of their days not with their parents but in mixed-age groups of other children, including an older girl, often an older sister, who is mainly responsible for caring for them (Edwards et al., 2015). When toddlers are with their parents, usually many other people are around as well, such as siblings, extended family members, and neighbors. This makes for a language-rich environment because there is talking going on around them almost constantly, with so many people present. However, relatively little of this talk may be directed specifically at the toddler because there are so many other people around and because others may not see it as necessary to speak directly to toddlers to stimulate their language development (Fitneva & Matsui, 2015).

In fact, the others in a toddler's social environment may even see it as bad parenting to speak often with toddlers. The Gusii people of Kenya believe that encouraging young children to speak is a mistake because it makes it more likely that they will grow up to be selfish and disobedient (LeVine et al., 1994). Their children learn the Gusii language as proficiently as U.S. children learn English, but they learn it from being frequently in social groups where adults and older children are using language, not from having their language development stimulated directly in frequent daily interactions with their parents.

It is not only in rural cultures in developing countries that this approach to toddlers' language development is found, but also in developed countries that emphasize collectivistic rather than individualistic cultural beliefs. One study compared Japanese mothers and Canadian mothers in their interactions with their young children (Minami & McCabe, 1995). In Japanese culture, being talkative is considered impolite and undesirable, especially for males, because the Japanese believe it is better to blend in harmoniously with the group than to call attention to yourself (Markus & Kitayama, 2003; Rothbaum et al., 2001). Consequently, the Japanese mothers in the study often discouraged their children from talking, especially their boys. In contrast, the Canadian mothers encouraged their children to talk more, by asking them questions and suggesting they provide more details. This approach was interpreted by the researchers as being based on a belief system favoring the cultural values of individualism and self-expression.

Watch the *Language Development Across Cultures* video to see how parents from different cultural backgrounds communicate with their infants and toddlers and what parents do, if anything, to foster their child's language development.

Watch LANGUAGE DEVELOPMENT ACROSS CULTURES

Review Question:

Discuss the three factors mentioned in the clip that influence toddler language development. What are some additional factors that might also impact toddler language development?

Summary: Cognitive Development

LO 5.6 Outline the cognitive achievements of toddlerhood in Piaget's theory.

According to Piaget, the ability for mental representations develops in the second half of the second year and is the basis for important aspects of later cognitive functioning, including problem solving and language. Object permanence also reaches near-completion during this period. Deferred imitation and categorization also require mental representation.

LO 5.7 Explain Vygotsky's sociocultural theory of cognitive development and contrast it with Piaget's theory.

Unlike Piaget and most other cognitive theorists and researchers, Vygotsky emphasized the cultural basis of cognitive development in childhood. He proposed concepts such as *scaffolding* and the *zone of proximal development* to describe how children obtain cultural knowledge from adults.

LO 5.8 **Summarize the evidence for the biological and evolutionary bases of language.**

In humans the larynx is lower in the throat than it is in other primates, making spoken language possible. Humans also have areas in the brain specifically devoted to language functions. Anatomically the capacity for language appears to have first developed in early hominids 2 million years ago.

LO 5.9 **Describe the milestones in language development that take place during the toddler years.**

At 18 months, most toddlers speak about 50 words, usually in holophrases. By 24 months, most speak about 200 words and combine some words in telegraphic speech. By their third birthdays, most can easily use the language of their culture in full sentences.

LO 5.10 **Identify how parents' stimulation of toddlers' language varies across cultures and evaluate how these variations relate to language development.**

Cultures vary widely in how much they encourage toddlers' language development, from stimulating language use through direct interactions, to allowing toddlers to be present among conversing adults but otherwise not speaking to them much, to actually discouraging them from talking. Regardless of cultural practices, toddlers generally learn to use their language well by the time they reach age 3.

Section 3 Emotional and Social Development

 Learning Objectives

5.11 Describe how emotional development advances during toddlerhood, and identify the impact of culture on these changes.

5.12 Describe the changes in self-development that take place during toddlerhood.

5.13 Distinguish between *sex* and *gender*, and summarize the evidence for the biological basis of gender development.

5.14 Identify the four classifications of attachment according to the Strange Situation.

5.15 Identify the key factors influencing the quality of toddlers' attachment to their mothers, and explain what effect attachment quality has on development.

5.16 Compare and contrast the typical patterns of father involvement with infants and toddlers in traditional cultures and developed countries.

5.17 Describe relationships with siblings, peers, and friends during toddlerhood.

5.18 Identify the options for the care of toddlers and the effects of child care on toddlers.

5.19 Identify the characteristics of autism spectrum disorder (ASD), and recognize how it affects prospects for children as they grow to adulthood.

5.20 Identify the typical rates of television use in toddlerhood, and explain some consequences of toddlers' TV watching.

EMOTIONAL AND SOCIAL DEVELOPMENT: Emotional Development in Toddlerhood

All over the world, toddlerhood is the stage of life when we first learn how to regulate our emotions. As part of this process we learn emotions such as shame and guilt that reflect our responses to the expectations and requirements of others.

Toddlers' Emotions

LO 5.11 **Describe how emotional development advances during toddlerhood, and identify the impact of culture on these changes.**

As toddlers become more self-aware, they learn that the people in their cultural environment regard some behaviors as good and others as bad, some as right and some as wrong, and they learn to feel negative emotions when they do something defined as bad or wrong. They also begin to learn how to regulate their emotions.

EMOTIONAL SELF-REGULATION From the early months of life, infants tend to show how they feel. Happy or sad, hungry or mad, they let you know. Gradually during the first year, infants develop the rudiments of emotional regulation. They learn to turn their attention away from unpleasant stimulation (Axia et al., 1999). The people around them soothe their distress by cuddling and distracting them. In many cultures, frequent breast feeding is used as an emotional regulator, to quiet babies whenever they begin to fuss (DeLoache & Gottlieb, 2000; LeVine et al., 1994).

During toddlerhood, emotional self-regulation advances in four ways (Kopp, 1989; Miller, 2014; Thompson & Goodvin, 2007).

1. First, toddlers develop *behaviors* that can help them regulate their emotions. For example, toddlers who are frightened may run to a trusted adult or older sibling or cling to a comforting blanket or stuffed animal.

2. Second, toddlers use *language* to promote emotional self-regulation. As noted previously, from about 18 months old toddlers begin to use words to identify and talk about their emotions. Throughout toddlerhood and beyond, talking about feelings with others enhances children's understanding of their own and others' emotions, which in turn promotes their emotional self-regulation (Bugental & Grusec, 2006; Parke & Buriel, 2006).

3. Third, *external requirements* by others extend toddlers' capacities for emotional self-regulation. In toddlerhood, parents begin to convey and enforce rules that require emotional self-regulation: no hitting others no matter how angry you are, no jumping on the table no matter how happy you are, and so on (Calkins, 2012). Cultures vary in their requirements for emotional self-regulation, with collectivistic cultures such as China and Japan tending toward stiffer requirements than the more individualistic cultures of the West (Bornstein, 2006; Laible, 2004; Shweder et al., 2006).

4. Fourth and finally, emotional self-regulation in toddlerhood is promoted by the development of the *sociomoral emotions* (Brownell & Kopp, 2010). Becoming capable of guilt, shame, and embarrassment motivates toddlers to avoid these unpleasant emotional states. Because they may be admonished by others for expressing primary emotions too strongly (e.g., yelling angrily in a grocery store) or in the wrong context (e.g., laughing loudly in a quiet restaurant), they learn emotional self-regulation as part of an effort to win approval from others and avoid their disapproval. The sociomoral emotions are sometimes called *self-conscious* emotions because they involve having a sense of self. Once the child has a sense of self, the approval or disapproval of others matters and results in these new emotions.

If emotional self-regulation increases from infancy to toddlerhood, why is it toddlerhood that is associated with tantrums—and why is age 2 popularly known in some cultures as the "terrible twos"? Perhaps it is that for toddlers, abilities for emotional self-regulation increase but so do expectations for emotional control. Consequently, when they have the brief but intense outburst of anger, crying, and distress that constitutes a tantrum it is more noticed than the more frequent outbursts of infants (Calkins, 2012). Perhaps it is also that toddlers have a more developed sense of self, including the ability to protest with a tantrum when they don't get their way (Grolnick et al., 2006).

Another reason that cognitive gains in toddlerhood may result in tantrums in many cultures can be linked to Erikson's psychosocial theory of development. Remember that

Toddlers become capable of sociomoral emotions such as shame.

toddlerhood is the stage of **autonomy vs. shame and doubt**. For the 2-year-old child, there is a dawning awareness of what might be possible to accomplish, but the child lacks the cognitive skills to carry out the steps to reach many goals. Further, the limits placed on toddlers by parents and others in the environment may cause frustration and therefore a strong emotional reaction like a tantrum.

There is a cultural explanation as well. It is interesting to observe that in Western countries, such as the United States and the United Kingdom, it is widely accepted that toddlerhood tantrums are normal and even inevitable (Potegal & Davidson, 2003). One popular U.S. advice book for parents of toddlers asserts that "Tantrums are a fact of toddler life, a behavior that's virtually universal … turning little cherubs into little monsters" (Murkoff et al., 2003, p. 336). Yet outside the West, toddler tantrums are rarely mentioned, and toddlerhood is not seen as an age of "terrible" behavior. In African and Asian cultures, by the time toddlerhood is reached, children have already learned that they are expected to control their emotions and their behavior, and they exercise the control required of them (Holodynski, 2009; Miller, 2014; Fung, 2010). It appears that tantrums and the allegedly terrible twos are not "universal" after all, but a consequence of Western cultural beliefs in the value of self-expression, which children have already learned well by toddlerhood.

LEARNING THE SOCIOMORAL EMOTIONS Infants across cultures display a range of recognizable *primary emotions* from early in life, including anger, fear, and happiness. In toddlerhood new emotions appear, including guilt, shame, embarrassment, envy, and pride. These are known as *secondary emotions* because they develop later than the primary emotions, and they are based on the development of a sense of self and relating the self to others in their social environment (Cummings et al., 2010; Tracy & Robins, 2004). All toddlers have a capacity for developing secondary emotions, as indicated by the fact that these emotions appear across a wide range of cultures and are accompanied by characteristic body postures such as, for shame, lowering their eyes, bowing their heads, or covering their faces with their hands (Barrett & Nelson-Goens, 1997). However, what evokes the secondary emotions depends on what toddlers have been taught in their social and cultural environment.

The secondary emotions are called **sociomoral emotions** because they are evoked based on what the toddler has learned about culturally based standards of right and wrong (Brownell & Kopp, 2010; Mascolo & Fischer, 2007). When toddlers experience guilt, shame, or embarrassment, it is not just because they have made the cognitive comparison between what they have done and what others have expected of them. It is also because they have begun to learn to feel good when they conform to the expected standard and bad when they do not. Thus, by age 2 most toddlers have begun to develop a conscience, an internalized set of moral standards that guides their behavior and emotions (Kochanska, 2002; Thompson, 2006).

Another important sociomoral emotion that first develops in toddlerhood is **empathy**, the ability to understand and respond helpfully to another person's distress. Even neonates have an early form of empathy, as indicated by crying when they hear the cry of another infant. Throughout the first year, infants respond to the distress of others with distress of their own. However, true empathy requires an understanding of the self as separate from others, so it develops along with self-awareness in toddlerhood (Gopnik et al., 1999). It is only in the second and especially the third year that toddlers have enough of a developed self to understand the distress of others and respond, not by becoming distressed themselves but by helping other persons relieve their distress (Brownell et al., 2009). In one study, toddlers responded to a researcher's feigned distress by offering a hug, a comforting remark, or a favorite stuffed animal or blanket (Hoffman, 2000). This demonstrates the beginning of **prosocial behavior**, which is behavior intended to help or benefit others (Svetlova et al., 2010).

Although the triggers of the sociomoral emotions are learned from the social environment, there are probably some that are universal. Children everywhere seem to

autonomy vs. shame and doubt

the second stage in Erikson's theory, characterized by the child's learning to do things independently or becoming doubtful about his or her own abilities

sociomoral emotions

emotions evoked based on learned, culturally based standards of right and wrong; also called *secondary emotions*

empathy

ability to understand and respond helpfully to another person's distress

prosocial behavior

behavior intended to help or benefit others, including kindness, friendliness, and sharing

be taught not to hurt the people around them and not to damage or destroy things (Rogoff, 2003). However, even in toddlerhood there are cultural differences in how the sociomoral emotions are shaped. Cultural differences are especially sharp regarding the emotions of pride and shame, that is, in how good a person should feel about individual accomplishments and how quickly, easily, and often shame should be evoked. In Western countries, especially in the United States, pride is often viewed positively (Bellah et al., 1985; Twenge, 2006). Children are praised and encouraged to feel good about themselves for accomplishments such as hitting a ball, dancing in a show, or learning something new. Everybody on the soccer team gets a trophy, win or lose. Shame, in contrast, is applied with hesitation, as parents and others worry that shame may harm the development of children's self-esteem.

In most non-Western cultures, however, pride is seen as a greater danger than shame. In Japanese and Chinese cultures, for example, children are taught from early on not to call attention to themselves and not to display pride in response to personal success (Akimoto & Sanbonmatsu, 1999; Miller, 2014). For example, in one study of mothers' and 2½-year-olds' conversations about misbehavior in China and the United States, U.S. mothers tended to frame the misbehavior as an emotionally positive learning experience—"Now you know not to do that next time, don't you?"—to preserve their toddlers' self-esteem. In contrast, Chinese mothers cultivated shame in their toddlers by emphasizing the negative consequences and negative feelings of others that resulted from the misbehavior (Miller et al., 1997). To the Chinese mothers, teaching their toddlers shame was a way of teaching them to be considerate of others, and a way of preparing them to grow up in a collectivistic culture that emphasizes the value of consideration for others. Even an act such as correcting misbehavior is full of messages about how to be an appropriate member of a cultural group.

The Birth of the Self

LO 5.12 Describe the changes in self-development that take place during toddlerhood.

Even in the early weeks of life there is evidence that infants have the beginnings of a sense of self, a sense of being distinct from the external environment. Infants recognize the smell of their mother's breast and the sound of her voice after just a few days of life, indicating an awareness of a difference between their own smells and sounds and those of others. In the first month they display a stronger rooting reflex in response to another person touching their cheek than in response to their own hand performing the same movement (Rochat & Hespos, 1997). After a month or two they begin responding in interactions with others by smiling, moving, and vocalizing, thus showing an awareness of themselves and others as distinct social partners. By the middle of the first year they recognize and respond to their own name when it is spoken by others, indicating the beginning of a name-based identity. By the end of the first year, they search for hidden objects and examine objects and put them in their mouths, all behaviors showing an awareness of the distinction between themselves and the external world (Harter, 2006a, b; Thompson, 2006).

Although self-awareness begins to develop during infancy, it advances in important ways during toddlerhood. It is during the second and third years of life that children first demonstrate **self-recognition**. This was demonstrated in a classic experiment, known as the *rouge test*, in which toddlers were secretly dabbed on the nose with a red spot, then placed in front of a mirror (Lewis & Brooks-Gunn, 1979). Upon seeing the child with the red nose in the mirror, 9- and 12-month-old infants would reach out to touch the reflection as if it were someone else, but by 18 months most toddlers rubbed their own nose, recognizing the image as themselves.

The same test has been done with children in several cultures around the world to determine whether self-recognition is an ability that develops at the same time,

self-recognition

ability to recognize one's image in the mirror as one's self independent of cultural values and socialization. Kärtner and his colleagues (2012) tested self-recognition abilities among rural Nso people in Cameroon, rural and urban people in India, and urban people in Germany. The researchers had to make a methodological adjustment to the design; they used a pigment applied to the child's face to produce the highest contrast with the child's skin color. They found that children in Germany, where the development of autonomy is encouraged, developed self-recognition earlier than children in cultural groups where a more interdependent self is encouraged. The social cognitive skill of self-recognition is tied to the sociocultural context.

About the same time self-recognition first appears (as indicated in the rouge test) toddlers also begin to use personal pronouns for the first time ("I," "me," "mine"), and they begin to refer to themselves by their own names (Lewis & Ramsay, 2004; Pipp et al., 1987). These developments show that by the second half of their second year toddlers have the beginnings of **self-reflection**, the capacity to think about themselves as they would think about other persons and objects. Self-reflection enables toddlers to develop the sociomoral emotions described previously. As toddlers become more self-aware, they learn that the people in their cultural environment have expectations for how to behave and they learn to feel negative emotions when they do something defined as bad or wrong.

Once toddlers use personal pronouns and show self-awareness, they also demonstrate the ability to understand the emotions of others, even when those emotions differ from their own. Repacholi & Gopnik (1997) gave 14- and 18-month-old U.S. toddlers broccoli or crackers accompanied by statements that indicated the experimenter's preference ("Eww, yuck, I tasted the crackers/broccoli" or "Yum, I tasted the crackers/broccoli"). Then the experimenter asked the toddlers to give them what she wanted. The older children, but not the younger ones, were able to give the experimenter what she wanted regardless of whether the emotional information conflicted with the toddler's own desire. That is, even if the experimenter said, "Yum, I tasted the broccoli," and the toddler didn't like broccoli, the toddler would still give the experimenter the broccoli. Even at 18 months, toddlers are able to respond to a person's preference, even when it conflicts with their own.

Gender Identity and the Biology of Gender Development

LO 5.13 Distinguish between *sex* and *gender*, and summarize the evidence for the biological basis of gender development.

Another aspect of self-development that begins in toddlerhood is the formation of a **gender identity**. Between 18 and 30 months of age is when children first identify themselves and others as male or female (Kapadia & Gala, 2015). At age 2 they also apply gender terms like *boy* and *girl, woman* and *man* to others (Campbell et al., 2004; Raag, 2003).

Before proceeding further, let's clarify the difference between *sex* and *gender*. In general, social scientists use the term **sex** to refer to the biological status of being male or female. **Gender**, in contrast, refers to cultural categories such as "male" and "female" (Tobach, 2004). Use of the term *sex* implies that the characteristics of males and females have a biological basis. Use of the term *gender* implies that characteristics of males and females may be as a result of cultural and social beliefs, influences, and perceptions. For example, the fact that males are somewhat larger than females throughout life is a sex difference. However, the fact that girls in many cultures have longer hair than boys is a gender difference. The distinction between a sex difference and a gender difference is not always as clear as in these examples, as we will see in this and other chapters. The degree to which differences between males and females are biological or cultural is a subject of great importance and heated debate in the social sciences.

Even before toddlerhood, in all cultures people communicate gender expectations to boys and girls by dressing them differently, talking to them differently, and playing with

self-reflection
capacity to think about one's self as one would think about other persons and objects

gender identity
awareness of one's self as male or female

sex
biological status of being male or female

gender
cultural categories of "male" and "female"

them differently (Hatfield & Rapson, 2005). In a classic experimental study (Sidorowicz & Lunney, 1980), adults were asked to play with a 10-month-old infant they did not know. All adults played with the same infant, but some were told it was a girl, some were told it was a boy, and some were given no information about its sex. There were three toys to play with: a rubber football, a doll, and a teething ring. When the adults thought the child was male, 50 percent of the men and 80 percent of the women played with the child using the football. When they thought the child was female, 89 percent of the men and 73 percent of the women used the doll in play. Cultural scripts about gender can be quite powerful.

In the early years, it is mainly parents who convey cultural gender messages (Kapadia & Gala, 2015; Ruble et al., 2006). They give their children names, and usually the names are distinctively male or female. They dress boys differently from girls and provide them with different toys to play with (Bandura & Bussey, 2004). Toys are gender-specific *custom complexes*, representing distinctive cultural patterns of behavior that are based on underlying cultural beliefs. Toys for boys—such as guns, cars, and balls for playing sports—reflect the expectation that boys will be active, aggressive, and competitive. Toys for girls—such as dolls, jewelry, and playhouses—reflect the expectation that girls will be nurturing, cooperative, and attractive in appearance. Children readily learn cultural messages about gender roles in toddlerhood, and by early childhood they help enforce these roles with other children. However, gender development has a biological basis as well; *sex* and *gender* are intertwined. Let's look at the biological basis of gender development here, and then explore gender socialization in depth in Chapter 6.

Gender socialization begins early in all cultures.

GENDER AND BIOLOGY The cultural and social basis of gender development is well-substantiated. However, there is also a biological basis to gender development. To put this in terms of the distinction between sex and gender just described, sex differences sometimes underlie gender differences—but not always, as we shall see. There are three elements to the biological basis of gender development: evolutionary, ethological, and hormonal.

In the evolutionary view, males and females develop differently because over the course of many millennia of human evolution, different characteristics promoted survival for the two sexes (Buss, 2003). For males, survival was promoted by aggressiveness, competitiveness, and dominance. Males with these characteristics were more likely than their peers to outfight other males for scarce resources and more likely to gain sexual access to females. Consequently, they were more likely to reproduce, and through the process of natural selection, gradually these characteristics became a standard part of a male human being. The aggressiveness and competitiveness of boys in early childhood is an outcome of a long evolutionary history.

For human females, in contrast, over the course of many millennia of evolution, survival was promoted by being nurturing, cooperative, and emotionally responsive to others. Females with these characteristics were more likely than their peers to attract males who would protect them and provide for them. They needed males to protect them from other males because they would frequently be pregnant or caring for young children. Females with these qualities were also more likely to be effective at caring for children through the long period of vulnerability and dependency that is characteristic of the young of the human species. Consequently, their offspring were more likely to survive to reproductive age, and through natural selection, gradually these qualities became genetically, biologically based tendencies of the human female. The cooperativeness and emotional responsiveness of girls in early childhood is an outcome of a long evolutionary history.

Ethology, the study of animal behavior, also provides evidence of the biological basis of human gender differences. Many of the differences that exist among male and female humans are also true of our closest primate and mammalian relatives (Diamond, 1992; Pinker, 2004). Like human males, the males in those species closely related to us are also more aggressive, competitive, and dominant than females; and males who are highest in these qualities gain greater sexual access to females. Like human females, females in closely related species also are more nurturing and cooperative than males are, and they have primary responsibility for caring for young children. Like human children, the young of closely related species also play in same-sex groups. The similarity of sex-specific behavior across related species is strong evidence for a biological basis for human gender differences.

Hormonal evidence also supports the biological basis of human gender differences. Throughout life, beginning even prenatally, males and females differ in their hormonal balances, with males having more androgens and females more estrogens. In fact, males must receive a burst of androgens in their third month of prenatal development to develop into males. These hormonal differences influence human development and behavior. The strongest evidence for this is in studies of children who have hormonal abnormalities. Girls who were exposed to high levels of androgens in the womb are more likely than their peers to show male play behavior in early childhood, including playing with "male" toys like trucks and a preference for male playmates (Hines et al., 2004). Boys who were exposed to high levels of estrogens in the womb are more likely than their peers to show female play behavior in early childhood, including playing with "female" toys like dolls and a preference for female playmates (Knickmeyer & Baron-Cohen, 2006). In animal studies, too, females whose levels of prenatal androgen are increased experimentally show increased aggression and more active play than their animal peers, and less interest in caring for their offspring (Maccoby, 2002).

CRITICAL THINKING QUESTION

How is the case of children with hormonal abnormalities an example of a natural experiment? Are there any limitations to its validity as a natural experiment?

THE LIMITS OF BIOLOGY Taken together, the evidence from evolutionary theory, ethological research, and research on hormonal abnormalities makes a strong case for the biological basis of human gender differences. There is little doubt that gender differences are accentuated and reinforced by the socialization environment, in every culture. At the same time, there is little doubt that human males and females are biologically different and that these differences are evident in their development in toddlerhood and beyond, in all cultures.

However, there is good reason to be skeptical and wary of attributing all human gender differences mainly to biology (Kapadia & Gala, 2015). In the course of human history, especially in the last century, gender roles have changed dramatically, even though biologically we have not changed (Brumberg, 1997). It was only 100 years ago that women were excluded from higher education and from virtually all professions. It was widely believed, even among scientists—who were all male—that women were biologically incapable of strenuous intellectual work.

Today, women exceed men in university participation in most countries and are close to or equal to men in obtaining graduate degrees in medicine, law, business, and other fields (Arnett, 2015a, b). That fact should give us pause before we assert that the biological basis of children's gender differences today is indisputable. The changes in women's roles over the past century demonstrate the enormous influence that culture can have on the raw material of biology in human development. As cultures change, gender roles can change, even though the underlying biology of human development remains the same. Many male-female distinctions that were widely thought to be sex

ethology

study of animal behavior

differences have turned out to be gender differences after all. Gender is a social role that can change with changes in the ecocultural environment.

The other issue worth mentioning here is that when we speak of gender differences, we are comparing one-half of the human species to the other, more than 3.5 billion people to the other 3.5 billion persons. Even where there are gender differences, in early childhood and beyond, there are also many exceptions. To put it another way, the variability within each gender is usually much greater than the differences between the two genders, for most characteristics. Consequently, we should be careful not to let our perceptions of gender differences prejudge our estimations of the qualities or abilities of individual boys and girls or men and women.

EMOTIONAL AND SOCIAL DEVELOPMENT: Attachment Research

From infancy to toddlerhood, the social world expands. Across these two life stages, what remains crucial to social development is the relationship with one special person, usually but not always the mother, who provides love and care reliably. Attachment theory was first introduced in our discussion of infant social development. Here we examine the features of attachment theory in more detail, including ways of evaluating the quality of parent–child attachment and critiques of attachment theory.

Attachment and the Strange Situation

LO 5.14 **Identify the four classifications of attachment according to the Strange Situation.**

Research on attachment was pioneered by Mary Ainsworth (Ainsworth & Bell, 1969; Ainsworth et al., 1978). Ainsworth followed Bowlby's theory in viewing the child's attachment as being most evident in the response to separation from the primary attachment figure. To evoke children's attachment behavior, Ainsworth devised a laboratory procedure she called the **Strange Situation** (Ainsworth et al., 1978). The Strange Situation is a series of introductions, separations, and reunions involving the child, the mother, and an unfamiliar person (see **Figure 5.5** on the next page). It was devised for toddlers, ages 12 to 24 months because this is an age by which attachment has developed to a point where it can be assessed.

On the basis of toddlers' responses to the Strange Situation, four classifications of attachment were developed (Ainsworth et al., 1978; Ammaniti et al., 2005). The first three were proposed by Ainsworth, and the fourth was added by later researchers.

Secure attachment. Toddlers in this category use the mother as a secure base from which to explore, in the first part of the Strange Situation when only the mother and toddler are present. Upon separation, securely attached toddlers usually cry or vocalize in protest. When the mother returns, they greet her happily by smiling and going to her to be hugged and held.

Insecure–avoidant attachment. These toddlers show little or no interaction with the mother when she is present, and no response to the mother's departure or return. When these toddlers are picked up in the last episode of the Strange Situation, they may immediately seek to get down.

Insecure–resistant attachment. Toddlers classified as insecure–resistant are less likely than others to explore the toys when the mother is present, and they show greater distress when she leaves the room. When she returns, they show ambivalence, running to greet the mother in seeming relief but then pushing her away when she attempts to comfort or pick them up.

Strange Situation
laboratory assessment of attachment entailing a series of introductions, separations, and reunions involving the child, the mother, and an unfamiliar person

secure attachment
healthiest classification of parent–child attachment, in which the child uses the parent as a secure base from which to explore, protests when separated from parent, and is happy when the parent returns

insecure–avoidant attachment
classification of parent–child attachment in which there is relatively little interaction between them and the child shows little response to the parent's absence and may resist being picked up when the parent returns

insecure–resistant attachment
classification of parent–child attachment in which the child shows little exploratory behavior when the parent is present, great distress when the parent leaves the room, and ambivalence on the parent's return

Figure 5.5 The Strange Situation

The Strange Situation features a series of episodes in which (a) the mother leaves the room, (b) the toddler is alone with the stranger, and (c) the mother returns to the room and is reunited with the toddler. The eight episodes are designed to measure stranger anxiety, secure base behavior, and emotional attachment to the caregiver. Each episode lasts approximately 3 minutes.

disorganized–disoriented attachment

classification of parent–child attachment in which the child seems dazed and detached, with possible outbursts of anger, when the parent leaves the room, and exhibits fear on parent's return

Disorganized–disoriented attachment. Toddlers in this category show extremely unusual behavior in response to the Strange Situation (Ammaniti et al., 2005; van IJzendoorn et al., 1999; Padrón et al., 2014). They may seem dazed and detached when the mother leaves the room, but with outbursts of anger, and when the mother returns they may seem fearful. Some freeze their movements suddenly in odd postures. This kind of attachment is especially shown by toddlers who show other signs of serious problems, such as autism spectrum disorder or Down syndrome, and also by those who have suffered severe abuse or neglect.

Although attachment classification is based on behavior throughout the Strange Situation, Ainsworth viewed the toddler's reunion behavior as the best indicator of the quality of attachment (Ainsworth et al., 1978). Toddlers with secure attachments seemed delighted to see their mothers again after a separation and often sought physical contact with her, whereas toddlers with insecure attachments either responded little to her return (avoidant) or seemed both relieved and angry at her (resistant).

Quality of Attachment

LO 5.15 **Identify the key factors influencing the quality of toddlers' attachment to their mothers, and explain what effect attachment quality has on development.**

If toddlers differ in the quality of their attachments, what determines those differences? And what implications does attachment quality in toddlerhood have for later development?

DETERMINANTS OF ATTACHMENT QUALITY Ainsworth's early research indicated that about two thirds of toddlers had secure attachments to their mothers, with the remaining one third either insecure–avoidant or insecure–resistant (Ainsworth et al., 1978). Many other studies of U.S. and European children since then have found similar results (National Institute of Child Health and Development [NICHD] Early Child Care Research Network, 2006; van IJzendoorn & Sagi-Schwartz, 2008). Disorganized–disoriented attachment is rare.

But what determines the quality of toddlers' attachments to their mothers? In her early research, Ainsworth and her colleagues observed families in their homes, including the same mother–child pairs they later observed in the laboratory in the Strange Situation (Ainsworth, 1977). The home observations were extensive: every 3 weeks for 4 hours, from when the children were 3 weeks old to just past their first birthdays.

When considering the mother–child interactions in the home in relation to their behavior as observed in the Strange Situation, Ainsworth concluded that the quality of attachment was based mainly on how sensitive and responsive the mother was. To be *sensitive* means to be good at judging what the child needs at any given time. For example, sensitive mothers could tell when their children had had enough to eat, whereas others seemed to stop feeding while the children were still hungry or tried to keep feeding them after they seemed full. To be *responsive* means to be quick to assist or soothe the children when they need it. For example, responsive mothers would hug or pick up or talk soothingly when their children were distressed, whereas others would let them cry for a while before going to their assistance.

According to attachment theory, based on the degree of their mothers' sensitive and responsive behavior over the first year of life, children develop an *internal working model* of what to expect about her availability and supportiveness during times of need (Bowlby, 1969/1982, 1980; Bretherton & Munholland, 1999). Children with secure attachments have developed an internal working model of the mother as someone they can rely on to provide help and protection. Children with insecure attachments are unsure that the mother will come through when they need her. They have an internal working model of her as someone who is unpredictable and cannot always be trusted. One reason the Strange Situation is first assessed in toddlerhood rather than infancy is that it is only by toddlerhood that children are cognitively mature enough to have developed an internal working model of their primary attachment figure (Ainsworth et al., 1978; Bowlby, 1969/1982).

ATTACHMENT QUALITY AND LATER DEVELOPMENT According to Bowlby (1969/1982), the internal working model of the primary caregiver formed in infancy and toddlerhood is later applied to other relationships. Consequently, the attachment to the primary caregiver established in the first 2 years shapes expectations and interactions in relationships with others throughout life, from friends to teachers to romantic partners to one's own future children. Securely attached children are able to love and trust others because they could love and trust their primary caregiver in their early years. Insecurely attached children display hostility, indifference, or overdependence

Is early attachment the basis of all future love relationships?

on others in later relationships because they find it difficult to believe others will be worthy of their love and trust (Thompson, 1998).

This is a bold and intriguing claim. How well does it hold up in research? A number of longitudinal studies on attachment have by now followed samples from toddlerhood through adolescence or emerging adulthood, and they provide mixed support for the predictions of attachment theory. Some longitudinal studies show a relationship between attachment quality assessed in toddlerhood and later emotional and social development, but other studies do not (Egeland & Carlson, 2004; Fraley et al., 2013). The current view is that attachment quality in infancy and toddlerhood establishes tendencies and expectations that may then be modified by later experiences in childhood, adolescence, and beyond (McCarthy & Maughan, 2010; Thompson, 2008). To put this in terms of the theory, the internal working model established early may be modified substantially by later experiences. Only disorganized–disoriented attachment is highly predictive of later problems (Ammaniti et al., 2005; van IJzendoorn et al., 1999; Vondra & Barnett, 1999). Toddlers with this attachment classification exhibit high hostility and aggression in early and middle childhood, and are likely to have cognitive problems as well (Weinfeld et al., 2004). In adolescence and beyond, toddlers who had been classified as disorganized–disoriented are at higher risk for behavior problems and psychopathology (van IJzendoorn et al., 1999). However, this type of attachment is believed to be as a result of underlying biologically based problems in neurological development, not to the behavior of the primary caregiver (Barnett et al., 1999; Macfie et al., 2001).

CRITIQUES OF ATTACHMENT THEORY Attachment theory is undoubtedly one of the most influential theories of human development. It has generated hundreds of studies since Bowlby first articulated it more than 40 years ago (Atkinson & Goldberg, 2004; Cassidy & Shaver, 2010; Sroufe et al., 2005). However, it has also generated critiques that have pointed to limitations of the theory.

The "child effect" is one of the most common critiques of attachment theory. It claims the theory overstates the mother's influence and understates the child's influence on quality of attachment, in two related ways. First, it fails to recognize that children are born with different temperaments (Bakermans-Kranenburg et al., 2004). If, in the Strange Situation, a toddler is highly anxious when the mother leaves the room, then behaves aggressively by pushing her away when she returns, it could be the result of a difficult temperament, not of the mother's failure to be sufficiently sensitive and responsive (Atkinson et al., 1999; van IJzendoorn et al., 2004).

Second, in attachment theory the direction of influence is one way, from parents to children, but increasingly in recent decades researchers of human development have emphasized that parent–child relations are *reciprocal* or *bidirectional*. Parents influence their children, but children also influence their parents. For example, mothers of toddlers with a disorganized–disoriented attachment classification have been found to behave differently in the Strange Situation than other mothers. They may fail to respond when their toddlers become distressed, and may hold them at arm's length when picking them up, rather than comforting them by holding them close (Lyons-Ruth et al., 1999; van IJzendoorn et al., 1999). These mothers sometimes appear confused, frustrated, or impatient. This could be a failure to be sensitive and responsive, but it is also possible that the mothers are responding to the toddler's behavioral difficulties (Barnett et al., 1999). Most likely is that the mothers and disorganized–disoriented toddlers are influencing each other in a negative bidirectional cycle (Lyons-Ruth et al., 1999; Symons, 2001).

The other major critique of Bowlby's theory is cultural. In the decades of research since Bowlby proposed his theory, some researchers have concluded that children's attachments are "recognizably the same" across cultures (Cassidy & Shaver, 2010, p. xiii). However, other researchers have pointed to possible cultural biases in the theory.

Some aspects of attachment may be universal. In all cultures, infants and toddlers develop attachments to the people around them who provide loving, protective care (van IJzendoorn & Sagi-Schwartz, 2008). There is evidence that parents in many cultures have a common view of what constitutes a securely attached child. One study involved mothers of toddlers in six cultures: China, Columbia, Germany, Israel, Japan, and the United States (Posada et al., 1995). Across cultures, mothers described an "ideally secure" child in similar ways, as relying on the mother in times of need but also being willing to explore the surrounding world—in short, using her as a secure base from which to explore, much as described in attachment theory. Other studies involving multiple cultures have found that secure attachment is the most common classification in all cultures studied so far (van IJzendoorn & Sagi-Schwartz, 2008).

However, cultural variations have also been found (Morelli, 2015). Though Ainsworth did not intend for the Strange Situation to be carried abroad, researchers have used the paradigm outside the United States, with mixed results. One study compared Strange Situation results for toddlers in the United States, Japan, and several northern European countries (van IJzendoorn & Kroonenberg, 1988). In all countries, the majority of toddlers were found to be securely attached (see **Figure 5.6**). However, the U.S. and northern European toddlers were more likely than Japanese toddlers to be classified as insecure–avoidant. In contrast, insecure–resistant attachment was especially common among the Japanese toddlers, compared to toddlers in the other countries. These differences were attributed to cultural differences in typical patterns of care. Specifically, a U.S. and northern European cultural emphasis on early independence was deemed to make insecure–avoidant attachment more likely, whereas in Japan mothers are rarely apart from their children and encourage a high degree of dependency in children. Consequently, their toddlers may have found the Strange Situation more stressful than the European or U.S. toddlers did, making the insecure–resistant attachment classification more likely (Takahashi, 1986). This amplifies the point that methods may need to be adjusted to the local cultural setting in order to be valid.

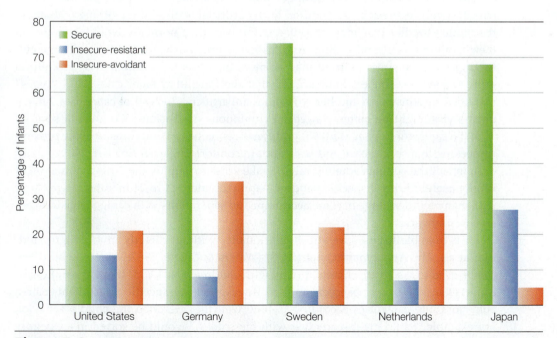

Figure 5.6 Cultural Variations in the Strange Situation

Across cultures, most toddlers exhibit secure attachment in response to the Strange Situation. In this study toddlers in Japan were more likely to be classified as insecure-resistant and less likely to be classified as insecure-avoidant than toddlers in other countries.

SOURCE: Based on van IJzendoorn & Kroonenberg (1988)

Mothers and children in Japan often have close relationships.

In traditional cultures, any kind of insecure attachment is probably rare (Morelli, 2015). Infants are soothed immediately at the first sign of distress, often with breast feeding. Toddlers are typically cared for by an older sister and also have frequent contact with the mother. However, as we have seen, weaning can be a major event in the lives of toddlers in traditional cultures, and it may have an influence on the security of attachment. In one of Ainsworth's (1977) earliest studies, on mother–child attachments in Uganda, she observed that toddlers in Uganda often changed in attachment after weaning, suddenly showing a sharp increase in insecurity, including "a remarkable increase in their fear of strangers" (p. 143).

In general, the traditional, non-Western norm of maternal care emphasizes interdependence and collectivism to a greater extent than is found in attachment theory (Morelli & Rothbaum, 2007; Rothbaum et al., 2000; Rothbaum & Morelli, 2005). Attachment theorists emphasize that sensitive and responsive maternal care should provide love and care while also encouraging self-expression and independence, but this is not an ideal found in all or even most cultures. For example, Rothbaum and colleagues (2007) describe the Japanese concept of *amae* (ah-mah-eh), which is a close, physical, indulgent relationship between the mother and her young child. This is the ideal in Japan, but to some attachment researchers it fits the description of the kind of mothering that promotes insecure–resistant attachment (George & Solomon, 1999). Also, attachment researchers describe how toddlers with secure attachments grow up to be children who are self-reliant, socially assertive, and have high self-esteem, but these traits are not viewed as virtues in all cultures (Rothbaum et al., 2000; Sullivan & Cottone, 2010).

Although it is clear that toddlers around the world develop bonds with caregivers to stay near a safe base, some researchers have criticized the Strange Situation as a way of measuring attachment. The Strange Situation is a laboratory paradigm that is contrived to induce stress in the toddler. In the artificial setting of the Strange Situation, the mother-toddler pair may not interact the way they normally would at home, in their familiar ecocultural setting. And, as noted previously, for toddlers in some cultural groups, the stress induced may be more than it is for toddlers in other cultural groups. Some researchers have argued that the four attachment categorical "types" identified by Ainsworth and her colleagues are artificial. Instead of categories, attachment styles might be better viewed on continuous dimensions, like overall security with the caregiver (Lay et al., 1995) or differences on behavioral measures like proximity seeking to a secure base and resistance to comfort (Fraley & Spieker, 2003). Lastly, even in cultural settings where it might make sense to employ the Strange Situation, it is only useful during a specific window—approximately 14 to 24 months of age. After that, many toddlers have become accustomed to separations with caregivers and exposure to strangers.

It is possible to measure attachment quality without directly involving the toddler at all. The Attachment Q-Set (AQS) (Waters & Deane, 1987; Waters et al., 1995) can be used to assess attachment quality with children ages 1 to 5. Using a set of cards, a parent or a trained observer sorts 90 descriptions of specific attachment-related behaviors into categories according to how well they describe the child's behavior. For example, "child greets caregiver with big smiles," would be sorted in a category ranging from "most like" to "least like" the child's behavior in the home setting. The Q-set can also be used to determine attachment "type," and results of the Q-set are usually correlated with the results of the Strange Situation paradigm (van IJzendoorn et al., 2004).

EMOTIONAL AND SOCIAL DEVELOPMENT: The Social World of the Toddler

In toddlerhood as in infancy, the social world includes ties to family, especially mothers and fathers. However, in toddlerhood relations with siblings, peers, and friends become more prominent. Many toddlers will find themselves in some kind of day care, as their parents return to work. Toddlerhood is also when symptoms of autism spectrum disorder first appears for some children, a serious disruption in their social development. Media use continues to be important in toddlerhood, especially television.

The Role of Fathers

LO 5.16 **Compare and contrast the typical patterns of father involvement with infants and toddlers in traditional cultures and developed countries.**

In nearly all cultures, mothers play a central role in the care of infants and toddlers (Shwalb & Shwalb, 2015). The first reason for this is biological. Because breast milk has usually been the main form of nourishment for human infants during the first half year, the mother tends to be the one who cares for the infant, more than anyone else. Consequently, by toddlerhood mothers are usually the primary attachment figure (Bowlby, 1969/1982; Cassidy & Shaver, 2010).

The second reason has a cultural basis. In most cultures through nearly all of human history, male and female gender roles have been separate and distinct (Gilmore, 1990; Hatfield & Rapson, 1996; Kapadia & Gala, 2015). In their adult roles, women have been expected to run the household and care for children, whereas men have been expected to protect and provide for the family (Arnett, 1998). In their leisure time women relax with children and other women, and men relax with other men (Gilmore, 1990). Consequently, in most cultures, historically, fathers have been on the periphery of the emotional lives of children.

FATHERS IN TRADITIONAL CULTURES Although fathers are rarely involved in daily child care in traditional cultures, they are part of the child's social environment in other ways. For example, in China the father's traditional role is provider and disciplinarian (Ho, 1987). Care and nurturance is left to the mother. In Latin America, too, the tradition is that the father provides for the family and has unquestioned authority over his children, although in many Latin American cultures this role coexists with warm, affectionate relations with his children (Halgunseth et al., 2006). Many cultures in Africa have a tradition of **polygyny**, meaning that men often have more than one wife (Westoff, 2003). (*Polygamy* is a more general term referring to having two or more spouses, regardless of whether they are wives or husbands.) Households are composed of each wife and her children, with the father either living separately or rotating among them. Here, too, his role is that of provider and disciplinarian, and the children are not usually emotionally close to him (Nsamenang, 1992). Polygyny has become less common in recent decades, but still occurs in about one third of marriages in sub-Saharan Africa (Riley Bove, 2009).

Although the most common cultural pattern worldwide is that fathers serve as providers but are otherwise remote from the emotional lives of infants and toddlers, there are some notable exceptions. Among the Manus people of New Guinea studied by Margaret Mead (1930/2001), during the first year of life the infant and mother are together almost constantly, and the father is involved only occasionally. However, once the child enters toddlerhood and begins to walk the father takes over most child care.

polygyny

cultural tradition in which men have more than one wife

The toddler sleeps with the father, plays with him, rides on his back, and goes along on his daily fishing expeditions. Later in childhood, if the parents quarrel and separate, the children often choose to stay with the father, indicating that by then he has become the primary attachment figure.

FATHERS IN DEVELOPED COUNTRIES In some ways, the role of fathers in developed countries today is in line with the pattern historically and in traditional societies. Across developed countries, fathers interact less with their infants and toddlers than mothers do, and provide less care such as bathing, feeding, dressing, and soothing (Chuang et al., 2004; Lamb & Lewis, 2010; Shwalb & Shwalb, 2015). In the United States, about one third of toddlers live with single mothers; nonresident fathers are less involved in care of their toddlers than fathers who live in the household, although involvement is greater among nonresident fathers who are African American or Latino than among Whites (Cabrera et al., 2008). When fathers do interact with their infants and toddlers, it tends to be in play rather than care, especially in physical, highly stimulating, rough-and-tumble play (Lamb & Lewis, 2010; Paquette, 2004). Dad is the one throwing the kids in the air and catching them, or wrestling with them, but usually he has not been the one feeding them applesauce or changing their diapers.

However, there is a definite trend toward greater father involvement, as gender roles have become more flexible and egalitarian in developed countries (Pleck, 2010). U.S. fathers have been found to spend about 85 percent as much time as mothers do in caring for their young children, and Canadian fathers about 75 percent (Lamb, 2010). Fathers are more likely to provide near-equal care for young children when the mother and father work similar numbers of hours outside the home, and when marital satisfaction is high (Lamb & Lewis, 2010; NICHD Early Child Care Network, 2000). Like the example of the Manus people, the findings of recent changes in fathers' care for young children in developed countries show that parenting is to a large extent a learned rather than innate behavioral pattern that can change as a culture changes.

Fathers in modern developed countries do more child care than they did in the past, but still not as much as mothers do.

The Wider Social World: Siblings, Peers, and Friends

LO 5.17 Describe relationships with siblings, peers, and friends during toddlerhood.

In studies of social development in toddlerhood, the focus has been on relations with parents, especially attachments to mothers. However, among the many ways toddlerhood is distinct from infancy is that the toddler's social world broadens to include a wider range of people, including siblings, peers, and friends.

SIBLINGS: YOUNGER AND OLDER We have seen already how important sibling relationships are for toddlers in traditional cultures, where an older sibling, usually a sister, often takes over the main responsibility for child care from the mother. Toddlers in these cultures most certainly develop an attachment to the older siblings who care for them, but from the limited evidence available, it appears to be a secondary attachment rather than the primary attachment (Ainsworth, 1977; LeVine et al., 1994). That is, under most conditions toddlers are content to be under the care of older siblings, but in times of crisis they want the care and comfort of their mothers.

In developed countries, too, studies show that toddlers have attachments to siblings (Shumaker et al., 2011). One study used an adaptation of the Strange Situation to examine U.S. toddlers' attachments to older siblings (Samuels, 1980). Two-year-old toddlers and their mothers were asked to come to the backyard of an unfamiliar home, sometimes with—and sometimes without—a 4-year-old sibling present. When no older sibling was present, the toddlers mostly responded to the mother's departure with distress and to her return with great relief, much as they do in the standard Strange Situation. However, when the older sibling was there along with the toddler, the toddler rarely showed distress when the mother left the backyard. The older sibling provided the emotional comfort and security of an attachment figure, making this outdoor Strange Situation less strange and intimidating.

A substantial amount of research on toddlers' relations with siblings has focused on how they respond to the birth of a younger sibling. Overall, their reaction tends to be negative (Boer et al., 2013). Often, following the birth of a younger sibling, toddlers' attachment to the mother changes from secure to insecure because they feel threatened by all the attention given to the new baby (Teti et al., 1996). Some toddlers display problems such as increased aggressiveness toward others or become increasingly whiny, demanding, and disobedient (Hughes & Dunn, 2007). They may regress in their progress toward toilet training or self-feeding. Sometimes mothers become less patient and responsive with their toddlers, under the stress of caring for both a toddler and a new baby (Dunn & Kendrick, 1982).

What can parents do to ease the transition for toddlers? Studies indicate that if mothers pay special attention to the toddler before the new baby arrives and explain the feelings and needs of the baby after the birth, toddlers respond more positively to their new sibling (Boer et al., 2013; Howe et al., 2001; Hughes & Dunn, 2007). However, the reality is that across cultures, conflict is more common with siblings than in any other relationship throughout childhood and adolescence.

What if the toddler is the younger sibling rather than the older sibling? Here there is both an upside and a downside. The upside is that once younger siblings are no longer infants but toddlers, and develop the ability to talk, walk, and share in pretend play, older siblings show less resentment and become much more interested in playing with them (Hughes & Dunn, 2007). By their second year of life, toddlers often imitate their older siblings and look to them for cues on what to do and how to do it (Barr & Hayne, 2003).

Toddlers often react negatively to the birth of a younger sibling.

The downside is that conflict rises as toddlers become increasingly capable of asserting their own interests and desires. In one study that followed toddlers and their older siblings from when the toddlers were 14 months old to when they were 24 months old, home observations showed that conflict increased steadily during this period and became more physical (Dunn & Munn, 1985). In another study, 15- to 23-month-old toddlers showed remarkably advanced abilities for annoying their older siblings (Dunn, 1988). For example, one toddler left a fight with an older sibling to go and destroy an object the older sibling cherished; another toddler ran to find a toy spider and pushed it in his older sibling's face, knowing the older sibling was afraid of spiders!

PEERS AND...FRIENDS? In most cultures, toddlerhood is a time of forming the first social relations outside the family. In traditional cultures, this usually means being part of a peer play group that may include siblings and cousins as well as other children (Gaskins, 2015). These play groups usually include children of a variety of ages, but toddlerhood is when children first come into the group after having been cared for during infancy mainly by the mother.

In developed countries, too, peer relations expand in toddlerhood, often in the form of some kind of group child care (Rubin et al., 2006). Research observing toddlers in these settings has found that their peer play interactions are more advanced than early studies had reported. One influential early study reported that toddlers engaged exclusively in *solitary play*, all by themselves, or *parallel play*, in which they would take part in the same activity but without acknowledging each other (Parten, 1932). However, more recent studies have found that toddlers engage in not only solitary and parallel play but in *simple social play*, where they talk to each other, smile, and give and receive toys, and even in *cooperative pretend play*, involving a shared fantasy such as pretending to be animals (Howes, 1996; Hughes & Dunn, 2007). Watch the video *Styles of Play* on the next page for examples of toddlers engaging in various types of play.

Watch STYLES OF PLAY

Parallel Play

Furthermore, toddlers who know each other well tend to engage in more advanced forms of play than unacquainted toddlers do. In one study of toddlers attending the same child-care center, even young toddlers (16–17 months old) engaged in simple social play (Howes, 1985). By 24 months of age, half of the toddlers engaged in cooperative pretend play, and this kind of play was observed in all the toddlers between 30 and 36 months old. This is a striking contrast to studies of social relations among unacquainted toddlers, which had found mainly solitary and parallel play, with cooperative pretend play not appearing until at least age 3 (Howes, 1996; Hughes & Dunn, 2007).

Clearly toddlers are capable of playing with each other in a variety of ways, but do they really form friendships? A substantial and growing body of research suggests they do (Goldman & Buysse, 2007). Their friendships appear to have many of the same features of friendships at other ages, such as companionship, mutual affection, and emotional closeness (Rubin et al., 2006). Even shortly after their first birthday, toddlers prefer some of their child-care or play-group peers over others and seek them out as companions when they are together (Shonkoff & Phillips, 2000). Like older children and even adults, toddlers choose each other as friends based partly on similarities, such as activity level and social skills (Rubin et al., 2006). Toddlers who become friends develop favorite games they play when together (Howes, 1996). Toddler friends share emotions more frequently with each other than they do with non-friends. They smile and laugh more, but also have more conflicts, although conflicts between toddler friends are milder and more quickly resolved than among non-friends (Ross & Lollis, 1989). Friendships do change in quality with age, as we will see in the chapters to come, but even in toddlerhood many of the features of friendship are evident.

Toddler friends smile and laugh more with each other than they do with non-friends. Here, three boys in South Africa share a laugh.

Child Care

LO 5.18 Identify the options for the care of toddlers and the effects of child care on toddlers.

Remember that the ecocultural setting includes all the personnel, the tasks that must be achieved, the resources available, and the subsistence or work patterns of everyone in a household and community. Because more than

60 percent of all mothers in the United States work outside the home (Pew Research Center, 2014), a high number of young children attend day care. The situation is similar in other developed countries. Most mothers have returned to work by the end of the child's first year, and so many toddlers are enrolled in some kind of day care. Options range from care by relatives, to family day care, where children are cared for in a home setting by a nonrelative who is paid for the service, to center day care, where children are cared for in specially designed settings. Whether parents choose family day care or center day care, there are characteristics of high-quality care that are shared across types of settings (NICHD, 2005a, b). The *Education Focus: How Do Parents Choose Among the Child-Care Options Available?* feature outlines some of the hallmarks of high-quality child care.

In many cases, children enter day care because parents need to work. The number of days of parental leave varies greatly across the developed world (Tanaka, 2005). Most developed countries use a formula for wage replacement for maternity leave, ranging from 50 to 60 percent, with the exceptions of the United States and South Korea, where there is unpaid maternity leave, and Australia, where there is no compulsory leave. Many European countries are known for being generous in their maternity and parental leave policies: New mothers may take time off before the birth of the child, and a number of weeks after the birth is typically required. Further, the leave is paid, and job security

Education Focus: How Do Parents Choose Among the Child-Care Options Available?

A variety of child care options exist to meet the needs of parents of toddlers, the majority of whom place their children in some kind of care outside the home. How does a parent decide which child-care option is best? Most states have requirements for both home and center day care settings to have a small teacher-to-child ratio, safety procedures, and health and hygiene practices, especially related to serving food. Parents should check to see if a home or center has been properly licensed, and whether it has National Association for the Education of Young Children (NAEYC) accreditation.

High-quality day care for toddlers has the following characteristics:

1. Sufficient and consistent attention to each toddler. A low caregiver-to-child ratio (such as two consistent caregivers and five toddlers) and, a small group of toddlers overall. Toddlers need familiar caregivers who provide warm and sensitive care.

2. Encouragement of language and sensorimotor development. Toddlers should be engaged in linguistic activities like songs, conversations, and all kinds of talk, along with toys that they can easily and safely manipulate. The setting should have a large enough designated space for children to move around, and an outdoor playground is ideal, weather permitting.

3. Proper attention to health and safety. Toddlers should be taught to engage in hygiene routines (such as hand-washing after toileting and before meals), and the setting should be designed to prevent accidents (such as providing safe toys that cannot be swallowed and providing materials that are safe for the age group).

4. Professional caregivers who are trained in child development. Although a natural interest is helpful in those who care for children, some understanding of child development is also beneficial, and specific training or coursework may be required in some states or communities. Child-care centers that employ caregivers who have degrees or certificates in early childhood education are considered to be of higher quality than those that employ noncredentialed caregivers. Related to providing consistent attention, as mentioned previously, turnover of caregivers should be low.

5. Warm and responsive caregivers. Caregivers should engage in discussions with toddlers, including joint problem-solving, rather than simply giving instructions. It is ideal when caregivers show genuine interest in helping children of the age group in their care.

Perhaps most importantly, parents should find a child-care setting where they feel comfortable leaving their child, and where the child seems comfortable. Parents should feel welcome to stop in at any time, to participate in their child's day. In other words, the child-care facility should have an open-door policy for parents. Parents should also ask for referrals and talk to other parents about their experiences at a given day care.

Survey Question:

If you could choose among any of these three kinds of care for your child, which would you choose?
A. Care by a family member
B. Home care (in the home of a non-relative)
C. Center care

Toddlers in high-quality child-care centers are as likely as children in home care to have secure attachments.

is ensured. In the United States, new parents may take up to 12 weeks of unpaid leave to care for a newborn or an adopted child. In Japan, companies are required to allow parental leave for a parent with a child younger than age 1, and shorter working hours are allowed for parents of preschool children. However, the leave is not usually paid; about half of Japanese companies provide paid parental leave, and only about half the female employees take advantage of the leave and return to work afterward.

Given that leave policies vary, the number of toddlers attending day care also varies. In Sweden, 46 percent of all 12- to 23-month-old children and 85.8 percent of all 24- to 35-month-old children attend daycare. In the United States, roughly 66 percent of toddlers attend some kind of day care. In Japan, it's not just leave policies that affect the use of day care; extremely low overall fertility rates mean that there aren't many children in day care. The government has an interest in building and subsidizing day care centers for toddlers and young children to encourage parents to have multiple children (Lee et al., 2015). In the developing world, day care for toddlers is extremely rare.

The effects of day care for toddlers are mostly positive, provided the day care is of high quality. High-quality day care supports children in developing social skills, emotional development, and intellectual outcomes like language skills and being ready for school (NICHD Early Child Care Research Network, 2000, 2001a, 2005b). On the other hand, low-quality day care is associated with much lower outcomes and the development of fewer skills. The *Research Focus: Early Child Care and Its Consequences* feature examines the impact of nonmaternal child care on toddlers' attachment.

Research Focus: Early Child Care and Its Consequences

The "NICHD Study of Early Child Care" began in 1991 with over 1,300 young children (from infancy through early childhood) at 10 sites around the United States.

The children and their families were followed longitudinally for 7 years (NICHD Early Child Care Research Network, 2005a, b). The sample was diverse in socioeconomic background, ethnicity, and geographical region. Multiple methods were used to assess the children and their families, including observations, interviews, questionnaires, and standardized tests.

Multiple aspects of the care children received were also assessed, including quantity, stability, quality, and type of care. A wide range of children's developmental domains were examined, including physical, social, emotional, cognitive, and language development.

There were many notable and illuminating findings in the study. About three fourths of the children in the study began nonmaternal child care by the age of 4 months. During infancy and toddlerhood most of this care was provided by relatives, but enrollment in child-care centers increased during toddlerhood, and beyond age 2 most children receiving nonmaternal care were in centers. Infants and toddlers averaged 33 hours a week in nonmaternal care. African American infants and toddlers experienced the highest number of hours per week of nonmaternal care and White infants and toddlers the lowest, with Latinos in between.

For infants and toddlers, the focus of the study was on how child-care arrangements might be related to attachment. The observations measured how sensitive and responsive caregivers were with the children, the two most important determinants of attachment quality according to attachment theory.

As measured by the Strange Situation, attachments to mothers were no different for toddlers receiving nonmaternal care than for toddlers receiving only maternal care. However, insecure attachments were more likely if the nonmaternal care was low in quality, for more than 10 hours per week, or if mothers were low in sensitivity.

This was an impressively ambitious and comprehensive study, but even this study has limitations. Most notably, the children were not randomly assigned into child-care groups. The choices about the care they received and how many hours per week they were in care were made by their parents, not the researchers. Consequently, the outcomes of the children's child-care experiences were interwoven with many other variables, such as parents' income, education, and ethnicity. This is an example of how social scientists are rarely able to create an ideal experimental situation in their research, but must usually take human behavior as they find it and do their best to unravel the daunting complexity of real life.

Watch RESEARCH FOCUS: EARLY CHILD CARE AND ITS CONSEQUENCES

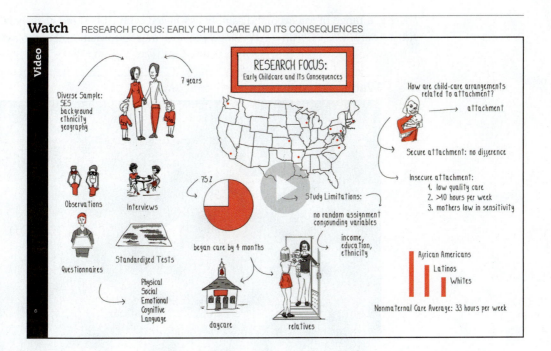

Review Questions:

1. Which of the following was *not* one of the research methods used in the study?
   a. questionnaires
   b. neurological exams
   c. interviews
   d. observations

2. Which of the following factors was related to insecure attachment in the toddlers?
   a. low-quality nonmaternal care
   b. greater than 10 hours a week in nonmaternal care
   c. low sensitivity in maternal care
   d. all of the above

Autism Spectrum Disorder: A Disruption in Social Development

LO 5.19 **Identify the characteristics of autism spectrum disorder (ASD), and recognize how it affects prospects for children as they grow to adulthood.**

In 1938, a well-known child psychiatrist received a visit from parents concerned about their little boy, Donald (Donovan & Zucker, 2010). According to the parents, even as a baby Donald had displayed "no apparent affection" (p. 85) for his parents and still did not. He never cried when separated from them or wished to be comforted by them. Nor did he seem interested in other adults or children, appearing to "live within himself" (p. 85) with no need for social relations. Furthermore, Donald's use of language was peculiar. He was often unresponsive to his parents' instructions and requests and did not even react to his own name. Yet certain unusual words captivated him and he would repeat them over and over again: *trumpet vine, business, chrysanthemum*. He enjoyed repetition not only of words but of behaviors, such as spinning round objects.

This description was the basis of the initial diagnosis of what became known as **autism spectrum disorder (ASD)**, which includes disorders that were formerly considered separate disorders called autism, Asperger's syndrome, and Pervasive Developmental Disorder-Not Otherwise Specified (PDD-NOS). The main features of the diagnosis of ASD are the same today as they were for Donald: (1) lack of interest in social relations, (2) abnormal language development, and (3) repetitive behavior (American Psychiatric Association, 2013). Many children with an autism spectrum disorder also prefer to have highly predictable routines and hate to have them disrupted. Some also have exceptional, isolated mental skills— Donald, for example, could multiply large numbers instantly in his head—but this is rare.

autism spectrum disorder

a range of developmental disorders marked by a lack of interest in social relations, abnormal language development, and repetitive behavior, appearing early in childhood

There is a range of intellectual disability associated with ASD (Lord & Bishop, 2010). The video *Against Odds: Children with Autism* provides more information about this disorder.

Watch AGAINST ODDS: CHILDREN WITH AUTISM

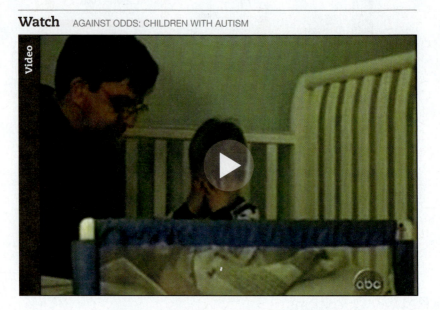

In the United States, 1 in 68 children (up from 1 in 2,500 25 years ago) fit the diagnostic criteria for ASD, meaning that they exhibit repetitive behavior and serious deficits in language development and social behavior (Centers for Disease Control and Prevention [CDC], 2014f). ASD occurs in all ethnic and socioeconomic groups, but it is five times more common among boys than girls. These rates are consistent across Asia, Europe, and North America, with some variation based on diagnostic criteria used (CDC, 2014). The origins of the disorder are unclear. It is believed to have a genetic basis, as evidence of abnormal brain development is present in the unusually large brains of children who will later develop symptoms of ASD (Hadjikhani et al., 2004). Various environmental causes for ASD have been proposed, from dietary contributors to toddlerhood vaccines, but none of them has been supported by research. Rates of ASD have increased sharply in recent decades in developed countries, but there is no consensus on the reasons for the increase (CDC, 2010). It may be that disorders once diagnosed as schizophrenia or mental retardation are now diagnosed as ASD because of increased awareness of the disorder (Donovan & Zucker, 2010). Physicians in many countries now routinely screen toddlers for the disorder, whereas they did not in the past (CDC, 2010).

Usually the diagnosis of ASD is made during toddlerhood, between 18 and 30 months of age (American Psychiatric Association, 2013). However, studies analyzing home videos of infants later diagnosed with ASD indicate that signs of the disorder are already present in infancy (Dawson et al., 1998; Werner et al., 2000). Even at 8 to 10 months old, infants with a more severe form of ASD show little or no evidence of normal social behaviors. They do not engage in joint attention with parents, or point to objects to show to others, or look at others, or respond to their own name. During infancy some of this behavior could be attributed to differences in temperament, but the diagnosis of ASD becomes more definite in toddlerhood with the failure to develop language skills during a period that is normally a time of dramatic advances. Many children with the more severe forms of ASD never develop language skills well enough to communicate about even basic needs, and the half who do develop some language skills are nevertheless impaired in their ability to communicate with others (Hale & Tager-Flusberg, 2005). Their social deficits compound their language deficits: Their lack of interest in others and lack of ability to understand others' perspectives makes it difficult for them to engage in the normal exchange of conversation that other people perform without effort, even in toddlerhood.

What happens to children with ASD when they grow up? The majority continue to live with parents, siblings, or other relatives (Donovan & Zucker, 2010). Some live in government-sponsored group homes, and in rare cases they are able to function at a high enough level to live alone, as Donald (now in his 70s) does. In some ways, ASD becomes more problematic in adulthood than in childhood because adults with severe ASD often lack emotional regulation as children with ASD do but are bigger and can cause more disruption. They also develop sexual desires, without the social knowledge of the appropriate expression of those desires. There is no cure for severe ASD and few effective treatments, but with help, many children and adults with severe ASD can learn some skills for daily living, such as wearing clean clothes, asking for directions (and then following them), and keeping track of money.

Toddlers with autism spectrum disorder have deficits in their social and language development. Here, a boy plays alone at a school for children with autism spectrum disorder in Beijing, China.

A growing number of individuals diagnosed with a mild form of ASD would have had formerly the diagnosis of Asperger's syndrome. Individuals with a mild form of ASD do not exhibit the cognitive or language delays found in severe forms of ASD. People with a mild form of ASD are usually diagnosed during the school years, and not in the toddler years, but what makes the diagnosis an ASD is that, looking back, symptoms were evident, if not pronounced. Individuals with mild forms of ASD can live independently and succeed in school and work functions. However, they may not pick up on social information, and they may be sensitive to touch—even a handshake may feel like a lot of painful stimulation (Willey, 2014).

Media Use in Toddlerhood

LO 5.20 Identify the typical rates of television use in toddlerhood, and explain some consequences of toddlers' TV watching.

Media use, especially watching television, is a typical part of daily life in most countries, even during toddlerhood. According to a national study in the United States, 58 percent of children younger than age 3 watch TV every day, and 30 percent even have a TV in their bedroom (Rideout & Hamel, 2006). African American and Latino toddlers watch more TV than toddlers in other ethnic groups, initiating a pattern of ethnic differences that will continue throughout life (Anand & Krosnick, 2005). Television dominates at all ages, but digital devices are increasingly popular, even among toddlers. A national survey in 2013 found that 38 percent of 2-year-olds in the United States had used digital devices such as iPhones or tablets (Rideout et al., 2013). There is now a vast range of "apps" (digital programs) for babies and toddlers, including educational apps, game apps, and art and music apps.

Most research on the effects of media use focus on television. Already in the second year of life, toddlers have begun to understand that the images on the TV screen are not real. In one study, 9-month-old infants and 14- and 19-month-old toddlers were shown a video in which a woman demonstrated how to play with a variety of toys for young children (Pierroutsakos & Troseth, 2003). The infants reached out to the screen and attempted to grasp, hit, or rub the toys, but the toddlers did not. However, other studies have shown that toddlers sometimes interact with televised images by talking to them, which suggests that for toddlers the television/reality boundary is not completely clear (Garrison & Christakis, 2005).

Television shows with prosocial themes can inspire prosocial behavior in toddlers.

How does TV-watching influence toddlers? Surveys indicate that a majority of U.S. parents fear that TV may harm their young children (Rideout et al., 2003; Woodward & Gridina, 2000). However, with television, as with other media we will examine in future chapters, the effects depend very much on the media content. In one U.S. study, one group of 2-year-olds was shown the TV show *Barney and Friends*, featuring a large, purple, talking dinosaur who encourages prosocial behavior such as kindness and sharing. This group was then compared in free play to another group of 2-year-olds who had not seen the show (Singer & Singer, 1998). The toddlers in the *Barney* group showed more prosocial behavior and less aggressiveness, along with a greater tendency to engage in symbolic play. In a national (U.S.) study, 70 percent of parents of children younger than age 3 reported that their toddlers had imitated positive behavior they had seen on television, such as sharing or helping, whereas only 27 percent had imitated aggressive behavior such as hitting or kicking (Rideout & Hamel, 2006).

Watch the video *Media Use in Infancy and Toddlerhood* to see examples from various families.

Watch MEDIA USE IN INFANCY AND TODDLERHOOD

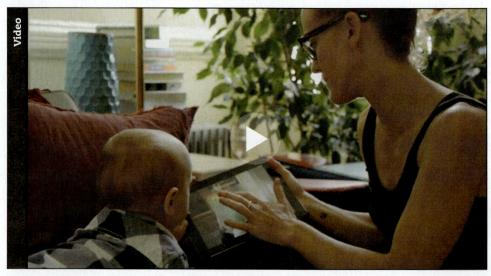

With regard to the effects of TV watching on cognitive development, evidence is mixed, with some studies indicating that watching TV helps toddlers expand their vocabularies and others reporting that it may be detrimental to language development (Courage & Setliff, 2009). Again, content matters. One study had parents report toddlers' TV-viewing patterns every 3 months from age 6 to 30 months, then assessed the toddlers' language development at 30 months (Linebarger & Walker, 2005). Watching educational programs such as *Dora the Explorer* resulted in greater vocabularies and higher expressive language scores than watching other programs did. Other studies have found that TV can inspire imaginative play among toddlers (Weber, 2006).

Even if TV sometimes inspires prosocial or creative behavior, a persistent concern about television use from toddlerhood onward is the **displacement effect**; that is, the fact that time spent watching TV is time not spent doing other activities such as reading or playing with other children (Weber, 2006). In 2001, the American Academy of Pediatrics recommended that children younger than 2 years old should not watch television at all, and children 2 years and older should be limited to no more than 2 hours of TV a day (American Academy of Pediatrics Committee on Public Education, 2001). The basis for

displacement effect

in media research, term for how media use occupies time that may have been spent on other activities

this recommendation was not that television content is damaging but that young children would benefit more from active learning through experiences such as play and conversations with others (Kirkorian et al., 2008). It should be added that in many households the television is on nearly all the time, and consequently even toddlers are exposed to TV content that is a long way from *Barney* (Rideout & Hamel, 2006).

Summary: Emotional and Social Development

LO 5.11 Describe how emotional development advances during toddlerhood, and identify the impact of culture on these changes.

Sociomoral emotions developing in toddlerhood include guilt, shame, embarrassment, envy, and pride. They are called *sociomoral emotions* because they indicate that toddlers have begun to learn the moral standards of their culture. Toddlers in Western cultures have occasional tantrums, perhaps because they have a more developed sense of intentionality than infants do and so are more likely to protest when thwarted. However, tantrums are rare outside the West where cultures place less emphasis on self-expression.

LO 5.12 Describe the changes in self-development that take place during toddlerhood.

The birth of the self in toddlerhood is indicated in the development of self-recognition and self-reflection. Toddlers begin to use personal pronouns such as "I" and "me" and to refer to themselves by name.

LO 5.13 Distinguish between *sex* and *gender*, and summarize the evidence for the biological basis of gender development.

Sex is the biological status of being male or female, whereas *gender* refers to the cultural categories of "male" and "female." Gender identity first develops during toddlerhood because children begin to identify themselves and others as male or female. The biological basis of gender is indicated in evolutionary theory, ethological studies, and hormonal studies. However, changes in male and female roles in recent times have shown that these roles can change dramatically over a relatively short time and therefore biological assumptions about gender should be viewed with skepticism.

LO 5.14 Identify the four classifications of attachment according to the Strange Situation.

In formulating attachment theory, Bowlby emphasized the evolutionary need for a person who would provide protection and care during the vulnerable early years of life. Ainsworth developed the Strange Situation to assess attachment quality, and concluded that it showed three distinct types of attachment: secure, insecure–avoidant, and insecure–resistant. Disorganized–disoriented is a fourth classification, added by later researchers.

LO 5.15 Identify the key factors influencing the quality of toddlers' attachment to their mothers, and explain what effect attachment quality has on development.

The quality of attachment is based mainly on how sensitive and responsive a mother is toward her child. Research indicates some relation between attachment quality in toddlerhood and later development but also shows that the internal working model established in toddlerhood can be modified by later experiences. Attachment quality is also influenced by infant temperament, and by reciprocal or bidirectional influences between parent and child.

LO 5.16 Compare and contrast the typical patterns of father involvement with infants and toddlers in traditional cultures and developed countries.

Fathers in traditional cultures usually serve as family providers but are remote from toddlers' emotional lives, although there are exceptions. Across cultures, fathers tend to provide less physical and emotional care than mothers, but this is changing as gender roles and work responsibilities change.

LO 5.17 Describe relationships with siblings, peers, and friends during toddlerhood.

Across cultures, toddlers often react negatively to the birth of a younger sibling. When toddlers themselves are the younger siblings, their older siblings enjoy playing with them more than when they were infants, but conflict tends to rise as toddlers become more capable of asserting their own desires. With friends, toddler play takes a variety of forms, including solitary play, parallel play, simple social play, and cooperative pretend play. Toddlers' friendships often have qualities similar to friendships at older ages, including companionship, mutual affection, and emotional closeness.

LO 5.18 Identify the options for the care of toddlers and the effects of child care on toddlers.

Care outside the home is a necessity for many parents in developed countries, who must return to work shortly after the birth or adoption of a child. Parental leave policies vary, and are most generous in Europe. The majority of toddlers in the developed world will experience some kind of care outside the home. Effects of high-quality day care are mostly positive, but low-quality care is associated with poor linguistic and academic outcomes.

LO 5.19 Identify the characteristics of autism spectrum disorder (ASD), and recognize how it affects prospects for children as they grow to adulthood.

ASD is a developmental disorder marked by a lack of interest in social relations, abnormal language development, and repetitive behavior. The social and language deficits of more severe forms of ASD make social and cognitive development problematic in childhood and beyond. People with a milder form of ASD, formerly known as Asperger's syndrome, do not have the cognitive or language delays found in severe ASD, and can go on to lead independent lives.

LO 5.20 Identify the typical rates of television use in toddlerhood and explain some consequences of toddlers' TV watching.

Toddlers in many countries watch TV every day. Television watching in toddlerhood may promote prosocial behavior if the TV content is prosocial, but there are concerns about the displacement effect, especially for children under 2 years old.

Applying Your Knowledge as a Professional

The topics covered in this chapter apply to a wide variety of career professions. Watch these videos to learn how they apply to a family dentist, a state legislator, and the director of a childcare and resource agency.

Watch CAREER FOCUS: FAMILY DENTIST

Sarah Hubert, DDS
Family Dentist
Williamsburg Dental Arts

Chapter Quiz

1. _____ is a potentially fatal condition specific to toddlerhood in which protein deficiency leads to varied symptoms such as swollen bellies, thinning hair, and lethargy.
   a. Marasmus
   b. Dysentery
   c. Sudden infant death syndrome
   d. Kwashiorkor

2. What most characterizes early brain development in toddlerhood is _____.
   a. the formation of the cerebral cortex
   b. the steep increase in synaptic density
   c. activity in the amygdala
   d. the production of new brain cells

3. Toddlers _____.
   a. who do not walk by 1 year are likely to have a gross motor problem
   b. in traditional cultures are equal to toddlers from Western cultures in the development of their gross motor skills
   c. can usually run before they can stand briefly on one leg
   d. show the same pace of gross motor development as fine motor development

4. In the West, _____.
   a. most children show signs of readiness for toilet training by their first birthday
   b. views on toilet training have remained the same over the last several decades
   c. children are toilet trained in a way that is nearly identical to their counterparts in traditional cultures
   d. a sign of being ready to begin toilet training is when the child can stay "dry" for an hour or two during the day

5. A toddler from a traditional culture would likely _____.

   a. experience some customary practice for being weaned

   b. be abruptly be weaned at age 1

   c. be given formula instead of breast milk

   d. still be breast feeding at age 5

6. When children generally avoid making the A-not-B error, they _____.

   a. show the ability to categorize

   b. have attained object permanence

   c. understand scaffolding

   d. use tertiary circular reactions

7. According to Vygotsky, _____ is required for cognitive development.

   a. social interaction

   b. formal education

   c. strong parent–child attachment

   d. emotional self-regulation

8. When it comes to learning language, the most significant difference between apes and humans is _____.

   a. the inability for apes to learn more than a few signs

   b. the faster pace of humans' sign language

   c. the inability of apes to generate word symbols in an infinite number of ways

   d. the inability of apes to make requests

9. Which is an example of overextension?

   a. A child saying, "He hitted me with a stick"

   b. A child saying, "The moon looks happy tonight"

   c. A child calling all dogs "Spot"

   d. A child saying "I no like peas"

10. Research on language development has shown that _____.

   a. social class status is correlated with how much parents speak to their young children

   b. genetics plays very little role in verbal ability

   c. language development in U.S. children is not linked to income level of parents

   d. maternal responsiveness to U.S. children's verbalizations has no impact on when children reach language milestones

11. Which emotion doesn't appear until toddlerhood?

   a. Anger

   b. Pride

   c. Fear

   d. Happiness

12. The capacity of toddlers to think about themselves as they would about other people and objects is _____.

   a. gender identity

   b. sex roles

   c. stranger anxiety

   d. self-reflection

13. When children can identify themselves and others as either male or female, they have developed _____.

   a. custom complexes

   b. gender identity

   c. gender stereotypes

   d. gender expectations

14. Which of the following best characterizes insecure-resistant attachment?

   a. a willingness to use the caregiver as a secure base to explore the environment

   b. a tendency to be self-centered

   c. acting both relieved and angry at a caregiver after seeing him or her again after separation

   d. a dependency on the mother for approval of all activities

15. Research has shown that a child with a(n) _____ attachment is most likely to have later problems such as hostility, psychopathology, and cognitive deficits.

   a. insecure–resistant

   b. insecure–avoidant

   c. disorganized–disoriented

   d. goal–corrected

16. Which of the following best describes attachment across cultures?

   a. Autonomy and independence are encouraged from an early age across cultures.

   b. In all cultures, infants and toddlers develop attachments to the people around them who provide loving, protective care.

   c. Insecure–resistant attachment is the most common classification in all cultures because many children find the Strange Situation to be stressful.

   d. Children from the United States and Japan tend to be classified the same way in studies employing the Strange Situation paradigm.

17. In developed countries, fathers would most likely be observed in which of the following activities with their infants or toddlers?

   a. Bathing

   b. Feeding

   c. Soothing

   d. Playing

18. During toddlerhood, _____.

   a. those who know each other well usually engage in solitary play rather than other forms of play

   b. friendships are based on companionship, mutual affection, and emotional closeness

   c. there seems to be no preference for play partners; they play equally with whatever children are present

   d. children are not yet capable of engaging in simply social play or cooperative pretend play

19. High-quality day care:

   a. is linked to positive social outcomes, but negative cognitive outcomes for children

   b. is linked to negative social outcomes, but positive cognitive outcomes for children

   c. is linked to negative social and cognitive outcomes for children

   d. is linked to positive social and cognitive outcomes for children

20. Which behavior would be most characteristic of a child who has been diagnosed with autism spectrum disorder?

   a. Preoccupation with talking to strangers

   b. Preoccupation with repetitive movements

   c. Preoccupation with looking at faces

   d. Preoccupation with pointing at objects until others look at them

21. Research on media has shown that _____.

   a. in the United States, it is rare to have a TV in a young child's bedroom

   b. children are only able to learn to model aggressive behaviors at this age because prosocial behaviors require more advanced cognitive development

   c. TV can inspire imaginative play among toddlers

   d. the displacement effect is no longer considered a major problem because of all the media options available

Chapter 6
Early Childhood

EARLY CHILDHOOD, FROM AGE 3 TO 6, IS A TIME OF IMPORTANT DEVELOPMENTAL CHANGES. Children in this age group improve dramatically in gross and fine motor skills, and they become more active physically and cognitively. In early childhood the cultural contexts of development expand in several important ways. Across ecocultural settings, children begin to learn culturally specific skills, through participation in daily tasks with their parents and siblings in some cultures or through participation in group care and preschool in other cultures. Their play comes to include pretend play, and the materials of their fantasy games are drawn from their cultural environment—toys or found household items made available to children. They become increasingly aware of their culture's differential gender expectations for boys and girls, and they develop an awareness of their culture's values and moral order. Many young children sleep alone in their own rooms, learning the cultural value of individualism. But even more young children sleep alongside others, learning that they are always intertwined with others in bonds of mutual support and obligation. We will explore all of these areas in the course of this chapter.

Watch CHAPTER INTRODUCTION: EARLY CHILDHOOD

Video

Section 1 Physical Development

 Learning Objectives

6.1 Describe the physical growth and change that takes place during early childhood.

6.2 Describe the changes in brain development that take place during early childhood and the aspects of brain development that explain "infantile" amnesia.

6.3 Identify the main nutritional deficiencies of early childhood.

6.4 Identify the primary sources of injury, illness, and mortality during early childhood in developed and developing countries.

6.5 Describe changes in gross and fine motor abilities during early childhood.

6.6 Describe the development of handedness and identify the consequences and cultural views of left-handedness.

PHYSICAL DEVELOPMENT: Growth From Age 3 to 6

The pace of bodily growth continues to decline in the period from toddlerhood to early childhood, as it did from infancy to toddlerhood. A variety of parts of the brain make crucial strides forward, although brain development still has a long way to go. Optimal growth in the body and the brain require adequate health and nutrition, which are lacking in much of the world during early childhood.

Bodily Growth

LO 6.1 **Describe the physical growth and change that takes place during early childhood.**

From ages 3 to 6 the typical U.S. child grows 2 to 3 inches (5–7 ½ cm) and adds 5 to 7 pounds (2.3–3.2 kg) per year. The typical 3-year-old is about 35 inches (89 cm) tall and weighs about 30 pounds (13.6 kg); the typical 6-year-old is about 45 inches (114 cm) tall and weighs about 45 pounds (20.4 kg). Throughout this period, boys are slightly taller and heavier than girls, although the average differences are small. Both boys and girls gain more in weight than in height during early childhood, but most add more muscle than fat. From toddlerhood to early childhood, most children lose their remaining "baby fat" and their bodily proportions become similar to those of adults.

In developing countries, average heights and weights in early childhood are considerably lower because of poorer nutrition and higher likelihood of childhood diseases. For example, the average 6-year-old child in Bangladesh is only as tall as the average 4-year-old child in Sweden (Leathers & Foster, 2004).

Within developing countries, too, differences in socioeconomic status influence gains in height and weight in early childhood. As noted in other chapters, economic differences tend to be large in developing countries; most have a relatively small middle and upper class and a large population of low-income people. Wealthier people have more access to nutritional foods, so their children are taller and weigh more than poorer children of the same age (UNICEF, 2014a). Given roughly equal levels of nutrition and health care, individual differences in height and weight gains during childhood are the result of genetics (Chambers et al., 2001).

By their third birthday, most children have a full set of 20 teeth (Murkoff, 2011). These are their *primary* or "baby" teeth that will be replaced by 32 permanent teeth in the course of childhood, beginning at about age 6. However, this replacement process takes place slowly, lasting until about age 14, so children use their baby teeth for up to 10 years and have to learn how to take care of them to prevent tooth decay.

In developed countries, children usually have their first visit to the dentist around age 3 (Bottenberg et al., 2008; Chi et al., 2011). Most children learn how to brush their teeth in early childhood, and in developed countries it is increasingly common for children's dental care to include fluoride rinses and sealants (plastic tooth coatings). Some countries and local areas also add fluoride to the water system, which greatly reduces children's rates of tooth decay. Nevertheless, about 40 percent of North American children have at least one dental cavity by age 5 (World Health Organization [WHO], 2008b), primarily because of inconsistent dental care and diets that are heavy in sugars and starches that cause cavities. Children in developing countries are less likely to have diets loaded with sugars and starches, but they are also less likely to have fluoride in their water systems and less likely to have access to regular dental care that would provide fluoride rinses and sealants. Overall, children in most developing countries have more tooth decay in early and middle childhood than children in developed countries do (WHO, 2008b).

Brain Development and "Infantile" Amnesia

LO 6.2   **Describe the changes in brain development that take place during early childhood and the aspects of brain development that explain "infantile" amnesia.**

The size of the brain continues to increase gradually during early childhood. At age 3 the brain is about 70 percent of its adult weight, and at age 6, about 90 percent (Bauer et al., 2009). In contrast, the average 6-year-old's body weight is less than 30 percent what it will be in adulthood, so the growth of the brain outpaces the rest of the body (Nihart, 1993).

The frontal lobes grow faster than the rest of the cerebral cortex during early childhood (Anderson & Jacobs, 2008; Blumenthal et al., 1999). Growth in the frontal lobes underlies the advances in emotional regulation, foresight, and planned behavior that take place during the preschool years (Diamond, 2004). Throughout the cerebral cortex, growth from age 3 to 15 takes place not gradually but in spurts within the different lobes, followed by periods of vigorous synaptic pruning (Hill et al., 2010).

During early childhood the number of neurons continues the decline that began in toddlerhood via synaptic pruning. The increase in brain size and weight during early childhood is as a result of an increase in dendritic connections between neurons and of myelination. Four parts of the brain are especially notable for their myelination during early childhood (see **Figure 6.1** on the next page).

In the **corpus callosum**, the band of neural fibers connecting the right and left hemispheres of the cerebral cortex, myelination peaks during early childhood, although it continues at a slower pace through adolescence. The corpus callosum allows for coordination of activity between the two hemispheres, so increased myelination of this area of the brain enhances the speed of functioning throughout the cerebral cortex.

Substantial myelination also takes place in early childhood in the **cerebellum**, a structure at the base of the brain involved in balance and motor movements. Increased

Young children in developing countries are often relatively small in stature, such as this child in Uganda.

corpus callosum

band of neural fibers connecting the two hemispheres of the brain

cerebellum

structure at the base of the brain involved in balance and motor movements

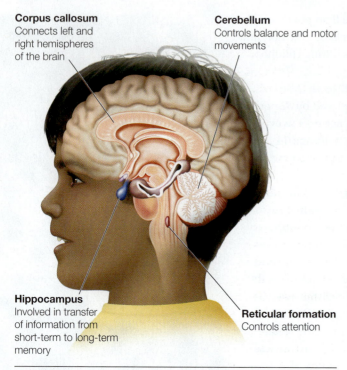

Corpus callosum
Connects left and right hemispheres of the brain

Cerebellum
Controls balance and motor movements

Hippocampus
Involved in transfer of information from short-term to long-term memory

Reticular formation
Controls attention

Figure 6.1 Brain Development in Early Childhood

In which structures is myelination completed by age 5?

myelination enhances connections between the cerebellum and the cerebral cortex. This change underlies the child's increasing abilities to jump, run, climb, and throw a ball.

In the **reticular formation**, a part of the brain involved in attention, myelination is completed by age 5, which helps explain the increase in attention span that takes place in the course of early childhood. For example, by age 4 or 5 most children could easily sit for 10 to 15 minutes in preschool while a story is read aloud, whereas most toddlers would be unable to sit still and pay attention for so long.

Similarly, myelination in the **hippocampus** is completed by age 5. The hippocampus is involved in the transfer of information from short-term to long-term memory, so the completion of myelination by age 5 may explain why *autobiographical memory* (memory for personal events and experiences) is limited before this age (Rolls, 2000). However, myelination in the hippocampus is gradual, and most adults can remember some autobiographical events that happened before age 5 (Howe et al., 2009). For example, in one study children who had been hospitalized for a medical emergency at age 2 to 3 were interviewed 5 years later (Peterson & Whalen, 2001). Even the children who were only 2 years old at the time of the injury recalled the main features of their hospital experience accurately 5 years later, although memory for details of the experience improved with age.

Other studies have found that many children and adults have autobiographical memories for events and experiences that happened as early as age 2 but remember little or nothing before this age (Courage & Cowan, 2009). The inability to remember anything before age 2 is known as **infantile amnesia**. One theory proposes that autobiographical memory before age 2 is limited because the awareness of self becomes stable at about 2 years of age and serves as a new organizer around which events can be encoded, stored, and retrieved in memory as personal, that is, as having happened "to me" (Howe et al., 2009). Another perspective proposes that the encoding of memories is promoted by language development because language allows us to tell ourselves a narrative of events and experiences; consequently, most autobiographical memory is encoded only after language development accelerates at age 2 (Newcombe et al., 2007).

Autobiographical memory may also be partly cultural. In a study comparing adults' autobiographical memories, British and (White) U.S. adults remembered more events before age 5 than Chinese adults did, and their earliest memory was 6 months earlier on average (Wang et al., 2004). The interpretation proposed by the authors was that the greater individualism of British and U.S. cultures promotes greater attention to individual experiences and consequently more and earlier autobiographical memories.

reticular formation

part of the lower brain, involved in attention

hippocampus

structure involved in transfer of information from short-term to long-term memory

infantile amnesia

inability to remember anything that happened before age 2

PHYSICAL DEVELOPMENT: Health and Safety in Early Childhood

By early childhood, children are not as vulnerable to health threats as they were in infancy and toddlerhood (UNICEF, 2014b). Nevertheless, there are many health and safety concerns associated with this period. Proper nutrition is essential to a child's healthy development, yet in developing countries the rates of malnutrition are alarmingly high. Children in developing countries remain vulnerable to some illnesses and diseases, and children worldwide are subject to high rates of injuries compared to other periods of the life course.

Eating Habits and Malnutrition

LO 6.3   **Identify the main nutritional deficiencies of early childhood.**

As the rate of physical growth slows down in early childhood, food consumption diminishes as well. Children may have some meals, or even some whole days, where they eat little. This can be alarming to parents, but it is nothing to worry about as long as it does not happen over an extended period and is not accompanied by symptoms that may indicate illness or disease. Appetites vary a lot from day to day in early childhood, and the 5-year-old who barely touched dinner one night may eat nearly as much as an adult the next night (Hursti, 1999).

Children generally learn to like whatever foods the adults in their environment like and provide for them. In India kids eat rice with spicy sauces, in Japan kids eat sushi, and in Mexico kids eat chili peppers. Nevertheless, a myth persists among many North American parents that kids in early childhood will only eat a small range of foods high in fat and sugar content, such as hamburgers, hot dogs, fried chicken, and macaroni and cheese (Zehle et al., 2007). This false belief then becomes a self-fulfilling prophecy because children who eat foods high in sugar and fat lose their taste for healthier foods (Black et al., 2002). The assumption that young children like only foods high in fat and sugar also leads parents to bribe their children to eat healthier foods—"If you eat three more bites of carrots, then you can have some ice cream"—which leads the children to view healthy foods as a trial and unhealthy foods as a reward (Birch et al., 2003). These cultural beliefs contribute to high rates of early childhood obesity in many developed countries, and this trend continues into middle childhood. In the United States, for example, 22.8 percent of children ages 3 to 5 are overweight or obese, but this is an instance where ethnic differences are important to uncover. As **Figure 6.2** shows, whereas rates of overweight are highest among White children, rates of obesity are highest among Latino children. The good news is that obesity is declining among young children overall, even though there are still problems with overweight and obesity in the overall population (Ogden et al., 2014). Public health

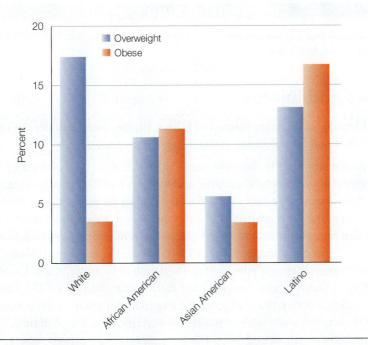

Figure 6.2 Rates of Overweight and Obesity in Early Childhood, by Ethnicity

Why might there be different rates of overweight and obesity across ethnic groups?

SOURCE: Based on Ogden et al., 2014

Many children in developed countries have nutritional deficiencies despite an abundance of food. Here, a child in London eats a fast-food meal that is high in fat and sugar.

campaigns to decrease overweight and obesity will be more effective if they specifically target ethnic groups in ways that fit with the cultural beliefs and practices.

Because young children in developed countries often eat too much of unhealthy foods and too little of healthy foods, many of them have specific nutritional deficiencies despite living in cultures where food is abundant. Calcium is the most common nutritional deficiency in the United States, with one third of U.S. 3-year-old children consuming less than the amount recommended by health authorities (Wagner & Greer, 2008). Calcium is especially important for the growth of bones and teeth and is found in foods such as beans, peas, broccoli, and dairy products (for example yogurt, milk, and cheese). Over the past 30 years, as children have consumed less milk and more soft drinks, calcium deficiencies in early childhood have become more common (Thacher & Clarke, 2011).

In developing countries, malnutrition is the norm rather than the exception. The World Health Organization (WHO) estimates that about 80 percent of children in developing countries lack sufficient food or essential nutrients (Van de Poel et al., 2008). The two most common types of nutritional deficiencies involve protein and iron. Lack of protein is experienced by about 25 percent of children younger than age 5 worldwide and can result in two fatal diseases, marasmus (in infancy) and kwashiorkor (in toddlerhood and early childhood). Iron deficiency, known as **anemia**, is experienced by the majority of children younger than age 5 in developing countries (WHO, 2008d). Anemia causes fatigue, irritability, and difficulty sustaining attention, which in turn lead to problems in cognitive and social development (Kaplan et al., 2007; Rao & Georgieff, 2001). Foods rich in iron include most meats, as well as vegetables such as potatoes, peas, and beets, and grains such as oatmeal and brown rice. Young children in developed countries may also experience anemia if they do not eat enough healthy foods (Brotanek et al., 2007).

CRITICAL THINKING QUESTION

Consider the foods that you typically see on the "Kid's Menu" in restaurants. How do these menus reflect cultural beliefs about food?

Illnesses and Injuries

LO 6.4 **Identify the primary sources of injury, illness, and mortality during early childhood in developed and developing countries.**

In developing countries, the causes of death in early childhood are usually illnesses and diseases, especially pneumonia, malaria, and measles (UNICEF, 2008). Because a lack of sufficient food reduces the effectiveness of the body's immune system, malnutrition is believed to be indirectly responsible for about half of early childhood deaths.

However, remarkable progress has been made in recent decades in reducing mortality in children younger than age 5. From 1960 to 2006, the number of deaths worldwide of children younger than age 5 declined from 20 million to under 10 million, even though the world's population more than doubled during that time (UNICEF, 2008). Progress has continued in recent years. As **Figure 6.3** illustrates, in many of the poorest countries in the world, younger-than-age-5 mortality rates fell by more than half from 1990 to 2012. The decline is the result of a variety of factors, especially improved food production in developing countries and increased prevalence of childhood vaccinations.

In developed countries, where most children receive vaccinations and have access to adequate food and medical care, life-threatening illnesses are rare, but minor illnesses are

anemia

dietary deficiency of iron that causes problems such as fatigue, irritability, and attention difficulties

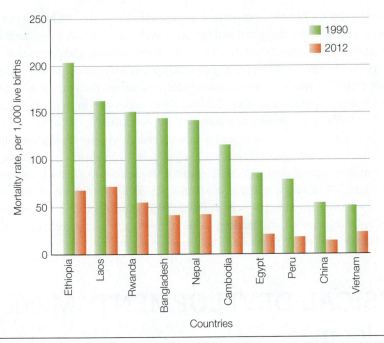

Figure 6.3 Reduction in Early Childhood Mortality Rates, Select Countries

SOURCE: Based on data from WHO; UN estimates

common in early childhood, with most children experiencing 7 to 10 per year (Kesson, 2007). Minor illnesses help build up the immune system, so that children experience them less frequently with age.

Do you remember becoming injured at all in early childhood? If you do, you are in good company. Most young children—and their parents—can count on spending a portion of their childhood nursing an injury; a minor "boo-boo" if they're lucky, but in some cases something more serious.

Young children have high activity levels and their motor development is advanced enough for them to be able to run, jump, and climb, but their cognitive development is not yet advanced enough for them to anticipate situations that might be dangerous. This combination leads to high rates of injuries in early childhood. In the United States each year, one third of children younger than age 10 become injured badly enough to receive medical attention (Field & Behrman, 2003). Boys are more likely than girls to become injured in early childhood, because their play tends to be rougher and more physically active. However, in developed countries, most of the injuries and deaths that take place in early childhood are not the result of high activity levels but of motor vehicle accidents (National Highway Traffic Safety Administration [NHTSA], 2015; Safe Kids Worldwide, 2013). Other common causes of injury and death in early childhood are drowning, falls, fire, and choking.

You might think that rates of injury and death as a result of accidents in early childhood would be lower in developing countries than in developed countries because people in developing countries are less likely to own the cars that are the predominant source of early childhood injury and death in developed countries. However, rates of early childhood injury and death resulting from accidents are actually higher in developing countries (WHO, 2008c). For example, rates of unintentional injury among 1- to 14-year-old children in South Africa are 5 times higher than

Deaths worldwide among children age 5 and younger have declined by more than half in the past 50 years, largely as a result of increased childhood vaccinations. Here, a Red Cross volunteer in El Salvador gives an oral vaccination to a 6-year-old boy.

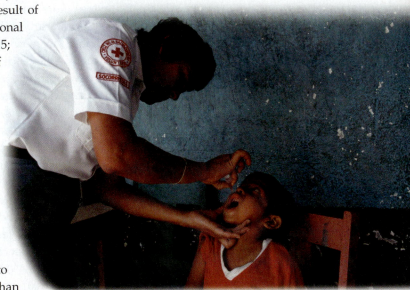

in developed countries; in Vietnam, rates are 4 times higher; and in China 3 times higher. This is as a result of more stringent safety codes in developed countries, such as requiring child seats in cars, strict building codes to prevent fires, and lifeguards in public swimming areas where drowning is a potential danger. An organization called Safe Kids Worldwide (2009) is working to advocate safety measures for young children in both developed and developing countries. It currently has chapters in 16 countries, including China, Brazil, India, and Canada, and is expanding steadily.

Despite the high rates of accidental injury among young children in developing countries, disease is a far greater danger. Only 3 percent of deaths of children younger than age 5 in developing countries are a result of injuries, and virtually all the other 97 percent are because of illness and disease (UNICEF, 2008). In contrast, even though rates of accidental injuries are much lower in developed countries than in developing countries, accidental injuries are the leading cause of death for young children in developed countries because so few of them die from illness or disease.

PHYSICAL DEVELOPMENT: Motor Development

One thing for certain about motor activity in early childhood is that there is a lot of it. Children of this age are frequently on the move, enjoying and extending the development of their new motor abilities.

Gross and Fine Motor Skills

LO 6.5 **Describe changes in gross and fine motor abilities during early childhood.**

In many ways, gross motor development in early childhood extends abilities that first appeared in toddlerhood. Toddlers can hop a step or two with both feet, but from age 3 to 6 young children learn to make more hops in a row and to hop on one foot. Toddlers can jump, but from age 3 to 6 children learn to jump farther from a standing position and to make a running jump. Toddlers begin to climb stairs, but age 3 to 6 is when children learn to climb stairs without support, alternating their feet. Toddlers can throw a ball, but from age 3 to 6, children learn to throw a ball farther and more accurately, and they become better at catching a ball, too. They also increase their running speed and their ability to stop suddenly or change direction. The video *Gross Motor Development in Early Childhood* provides more information on this topic. Gender differences in gross motor development appear in early childhood, with boys generally becoming better at skills emphasizing strength or size, such as jumping and throwing a ball, and girls becoming better at body-coordination skills, such as balancing on one foot (Cratty, 1986; Lung et al., 2011).

Fine motor development in early childhood involves a similar extension of skills that arose in toddlerhood, along with some new skills. As toddlers they could already pick up a small object using two fingers, but now they learn to do it more quickly and precisely. They could already hold a crayon and scribble on a piece of paper, but in early childhood they learn to draw something that is recognizable to others, such as a person, animal, or building. By age 6 they can even draw shapes such as a circle or triangle, and their first letters and some short words, perhaps including their own name. New fine motor skills learned in early childhood include putting on and removing their clothes, using scissors, and using a knife to cut soft food (Cratty, 1986; Piek et al., 2008). Their growing fine motor abilities allows children to learn to do many things their parents had been doing for them, such as putting on a coat or shoes and brushing their teeth.

In a classic study of the development of young children's drawing ability, Rhoda Kellogg (1959) analyzed 100,000 drawings from children around the world and came up

Watch GROSS MOTOR DEVELOPMENT IN EARLY CHILDHOOD

with a developmental sequence. In the first stage, children merely scribble. They make simple, random characters. In the second stage, children make basic forms with simple lines and shapes and some universal symbols, like the sun, waves, and rainbows. In the third stage, children's drawings are more pictorial. They elaborate on the forms in stage two and make symbolic representations of real people, like family members, and things in their worlds, like houses, trees, birds, and windows. At this stage, young children draw to really tell a story.

More recently, Heidi Keller and her colleagues have studied children's drawings in a number of cultures, including Germany, Turkey, and Cameroon (Gernhardt et al., 2013, 2014). Gernhardt, Rübeling, and Keller (2013) asked young children in Germany, Turkey, and Cameroon to draw pictures of themselves and their families. Even though the children had the same basic drawing abilities, expectable for their age group, the family drawings were different across the cultural settings. In Cameroon where the culture is more oriented toward relatedness with a large group of extended kin, particularly through the maternal kin, children drew their fathers less often, they drew more family members, and they also drew themselves more often next to a relative other than their nuclear family members or a non-relative. Interestingly, Cameroonian children differentiated family members much less than did the German and Turkish children. This highlights the Cameroonian emphasis on interrelatedness and the German and recent Turkish emphasis on individuality within the family.

Handedness

LO 6.6 **Describe the development of handedness and identify the consequences and cultural views of left-handedness.**

Once children begin drawing or writing in early childhood, they show a clear preference for using their right or left hand, but **handedness** appears long before early childhood. In fact, even prenatally, fetuses show a definite preference for sucking the thumb of their right or left hand, with 90 percent preferring the right thumb (Hepper et al., 2005). The same 90 percent proportion of right-handers continues into childhood and throughout adulthood in most cultures (Hinojosa et al., 2003).

If handedness appears so early, that must mean it is determined genetically, right? Actually, the evidence is mixed on this issue. Adopted children are more likely to resemble

handedness

preference for using either the right or left hand in gross and fine motor activities

Why have so many cultures regarded being left-handed as evil or dangerous?

their biological parents than their adoptive parents in their handedness, suggesting a genetic origin (Carter-Salzman, 1980). On the other hand (pun intended), identical twins are more likely than ordinary siblings to *differ* in handedness, even though identical twins share 100 percent of their genotype and other siblings only about 50 percent (Derom et al., 1996). Because this means that one identical twin will be left-handed and one will be right-handed, the experience in utero may influence handedness.

Culture is also a big part of the picture. Historically, many cultures have viewed left-handedness as dangerous and evil and have suppressed its development in children (Grimshaw & Wilson, 2013). In Western languages, the word *sinister* is derived from a Latin word meaning "on the left," and many paintings in Western art depict the devil as left-handed. In many Asian and Middle Eastern cultures, only the left hand is supposed to be used for wiping up after defecation, and all other activities are supposed to be done mainly with the right hand. In Africa, even today, using the left hand is suppressed in many cultures from childhood onward, and the prevalence of left-handedness in some African countries is as low as 1 percent, far lower than the 10 percent figure in cultures where left-handedness is tolerated (Provins, 1997).

Why do so many cultures regard left-handedness with such fear and contempt? Perhaps negative cultural beliefs about left-handedness developed because people noticed that left-handedness was associated with a greater likelihood of various problems. In early and middle childhood, left-handers are more likely to have problems learning to read and to have other verbal learning disabilities (Natsopoulos et al., 1998). This may have something to do with the fact that about one fourth of left-handers process language in both hemispheres rather than primarily in the left hemisphere (Knecht et al., 2000).

However, this explanation is not entirely convincing because left-handedness is associated not only with greater likelihood of some types of problems but also with excellence, and even genius, in certain fields. Left-handed children are more likely to show exceptional verbal and math abilities (Bower, 1985; Flannery & Leiderman, 1995). Left-handers are especially likely to have strong visual–spatial abilities, and consequently they are more likely than right-handers to become architects or artists (Grimshaw & Wilson, 2013). Some of the greatest artists in the Western tradition have been left-handed, including Leonardo da Vinci, Michelangelo, and Pablo Picasso (Schacter & Ransil, 1996). It is worth keeping in mind that the majority of left-handers are in the normal range in their cognitive development and show neither unusual problems nor unusual gifts. Hence the widespread cultural prejudice against left-handers remains mysterious.

Summary: Physical Development

LO 6.1   **Describe the physical growth and change that takes place during early childhood.**

The pace of physical development slows in early childhood. From ages 3 to 6 the typical American child grows 2 to 3 inches per year and adds 5 to 7 pounds. Average heights and weights in early childhood are considerably lower in developing countries because of inadequate nutrition and higher likelihood of childhood diseases.

LO 6.2 **Describe the changes in brain development that take place during early childhood and the aspects of brain development that explain "infantile" amnesia.**

The most notable changes in brain development during early childhood take place in the connections between neurons and in myelination. Most people experience infantile amnesia (the inability to remember anything before age 2) and have limited memory for personal events that happened before age 5, mainly as a result of the immaturity of the hippocampus.

LO 6.3 **Identify the main nutritional deficiencies of early childhood.**

About 80 percent of children in developing countries experience nutritional deficiencies, but a surprisingly high percentage of children in developed countries experience them as well. Calcium is the most common nutritional deficiency in the United States, whereas the two most common types of malnutrition in developing countries are lack of protein and lack of iron.

LO 6.4 **Identify the primary sources of injury, illness, and mortality during early childhood in developed and developing countries.**

Mortality rates in early childhood are much higher in developing countries than in developed countries, mainly as a result of the greater prevalence of infectious diseases, but have declined substantially in recent years. In developed countries, the most common cause of injury and death by far in early childhood is motor vehicle accidents.

LO 6.5 **Describe changes in gross and fine motor abilities during early childhood.**

From age 3 to 6, young children learn to: make more hops in a row and hop on one foot; jump farther from a standing position and make a running jump; climb stairs without support, alternating their feet; throw a ball farther and more accurately; become better at catching a ball; and increase their running speed and their ability to stop suddenly or change direction. In their fine motor development, children learn to pick up small objects more quickly and precisely, draw something that is recognizable to others, write their first letters and some short words, put on and remove their clothes, use scissors, and use a knife to cut soft food.

LO 6.6 **Describe the development of handedness and identify the consequences and cultural views of left-handedness.**

About 10 percent of children are left-handed. Being left-handed has been stigmatized in many cultures, perhaps because of its association with higher risk of developmental problems, but it is also associated with exceptional abilities.

Section 2 Cognitive Development

 Learning Objectives

6.7 Explain the features of Piaget's preoperational stage of cognitive development.

6.8 Explain the advances in information processing in early childhood.

6.9 Explain what "theory of mind" is and the evidence for how it develops during early childhood.

6.10 Identify the ways that cultural learning takes place in early childhood.

6.11 Identify the features that are most important in preschool quality and explain how they reflect cultural values.

6.12 Describe early intervention programs and their outcomes.

6.13 Explain how advances in vocabulary and grammar occur in early childhood.

6.14 Describe how children learn pragmatics in early childhood, and identify to what extent these social rules are culturally based.

COGNITIVE DEVELOPMENT: Theories of Cognitive Development

In the course of early childhood, children make many remarkable advances in their cognitive development. Several theoretical propositions shed light on these developments, including Piaget's preoperational stage; advances in information processing; "theory of mind," which examines how children think about the thoughts of others; and theories of cultural learning that emphasize the ways that young children gain the knowledge and skills of their culture. These theories complement each other to provide a comprehensive picture of cognitive development in early childhood.

Piaget's Preoperational Stage of Cognitive Development

LO 6.7 **Explain the features of Piaget's preoperational stage of cognitive development.**

In Piaget's theory, early childhood is a crucial turning point in children's cognitive development because this is when thinking becomes *representational* (Piaget, 1936/1952) meaning that children begin to internalize the images of their physical activities. During the first 2 years of life, the sensorimotor stage, thinking takes place primarily in association with sensorimotor activities such as reaching and grasping. Gradually toward the end of the sensorimotor period, in the second half of the second year, representational thought dawns, along with the ability to use language to represent thought.

However, it is during the latter part of toddlerhood and especially in early childhood that we become truly representational thinkers. Language requires the ability to represent the world symbolically, through words, and this is when language skills develop most dramatically. Once we can represent the world through language, we are freed from our momentary sensorimotor experience. With language we can represent not only the present but the past and the future, not only the world as we see it before us but the world as we previously experienced it and the world as it will be—the coming cold (or warm) season, a decline in the availability of food or water, and so on. We can even represent the world as it has never been, through mentally combining ideas—flying monkeys, talking trees, and people who have superhuman powers.

These are marvelous cognitive achievements, and yet early childhood fascinated Piaget not only for what children of this age are able to do cognitively but also for the kinds of mistakes they make. In fact, Piaget termed the age period from 2 to 7 the **preoperational stage**, emphasizing that children of this age were not yet able to perform mental *operations*, that is, cognitive procedures that follow certain logical rules. Piaget specified a number of areas of preoperational cognitive mistakes that are characteristic of early childhood, including conservation, egocentrism, and classification.

CONSERVATION According to Piaget, children in early childhood lack the ability to understand **conservation**, the principle that the amount of a physical substance remains the same even if its physical appearance changes. In his best known demonstration of this mistake, Piaget showed young children two identical glasses holding equal amounts of water and asked them if the two amounts of water were equal. The children typically answered "yes"; they were capable of understanding that much. Then Piaget poured the contents from one of the glasses into a taller, thinner glass, and asked the children again if the two amounts of water were equal. Now most of the children answered "no," failing to understand that the *amount* of water remained the same (was conserved) even though the *appearance* of the water changed. Piaget also demonstrated that children made this error with other substances besides water, as shown in the video *Conservation Tasks* and in **Figure 6.4** on the next page.

Watch CONSERVATION TASKS

Video

When Piaget tested young children on other kinds of conservation tasks (such as number, mass, and length), he found that their performance was similar to the conservation of volume task. What is it that all these tasks have in common? All the tasks involve reversible changes in appearance, but when children fail these tasks, they are focused on only one visible aspect of the problem at a time. These tasks highlight the hallmarks of preoperational thinking, according to Piaget: centration (on one aspect of a task), focusing on what is visible, static reasoning, and irreversibility.

preoperational stage

cognitive stage from ages 2 to 7 during which the child becomes capable of representing the world symbolically—for example, through the use of language—but is still limited in ability to use mental operations

conservation

mental ability to understand that the quantity of a substance or material remains the same even if its appearance changes

Type of Conservation	Modality	Change in Physical Appearance	Average Age Conservation Is Grasped
Number	Number of elements in a collection	Rearranging or dislocating elements	6–7 years
Substance (mass)	Amount of a malleable substance (e.g., clay or liquid)	Altering shape	7–8 years
Length	Length of a line or object	Altering shape or configuration	7–8 years
Area	Amount of surface covered by a set of plane figures	Rearranging the figures	8–9 years
Weight	Weight of an object	Altering shape	9–10 years
Volume	Volume of an object (in terms of water displacement)	Altering shape	14–15 years

Figure 6.4 Various Substances Used in Piaget's Conservation Task

What cognitive limitations in young children lead to mistakes in these tasks?

Piaget interpreted children's mistakes on conservation tasks as indicating four kinds of cognitive deficiencies. The first is **centration**, meaning that young children's thinking is *centered*, or focused, on one noticeable aspect of a cognitive problem to the exclusion of other important aspects. In the conservation-of-volume task, they notice the change in height as the water is poured into the taller glass but neglect to observe the change in width that takes place simultaneously.

Second, young children tend to focus on what is visible to them and are misled by appearances. Preoperational thinking is characterized by believing that "what you see is what you get (WYSIWYG)." In the conservation-of-number task shown at the top of Figure 6.4, when the spacing between the green dots is increased in one line, it may *look* like there are more green dots. Interestingly, even young children who can count the green dots in each line (and thus should realize the number is the same for each), often say that the line with more spacing has more green dots.

Third, preoperational children assume that the world stays the same as it is when they encounter it. Piaget called this **static reasoning**. For example, a 4-year-old child might be surprised and express protest when someone calls his mother, "Sylvie," saying,

centration

Piaget's term for young children's thinking as being centered, or focused, on one noticeable aspect of a cognitive problem to the exclusion of other important aspects

static reasoning

the assumption held by young children that things in the world are only one way and do not change

"She's not Sylvie. She's my mom." When things do change, young children believe they have changed suddenly and totally but can't explain why.

Fourth, thought in early childhood is characterized by **irreversibility**. Young children lack the ability to reverse an action mentally. When the water is poured from the original glass to the taller glass in the conservation task, anyone who can reverse that action mentally can see that the amount of water would be the same. Young children cannot perform the mental operation of reversibility, so they mistakenly believe the amount of water has changed.

Figure 6.5 Piaget's Three Mountains Task

How does performance on this task indicate egocentrism?

EGOCENTRISM Another cognitive limitation of the preoperational stage, in Piaget's view, is **egocentrism**, the inability to distinguish between your own perspective and another person's perspective. To demonstrate egocentrism, Piaget and his colleague Barbel Inhelder (1969) devised what they called the "three mountains task" (see **Figure 6.5**). In this task a child is shown a clay model of three different mountains of varying sizes, one with snow on top, one with a red cross, and one with a house. The child walks around the table to see what the mountain looks like from each side, then sits down while the experimenter moves a doll to different points around the table. At each of the doll's locations, the child is shown a series of photographs and asked which one indicates the doll's point of view. In the early years of the preoperational stage, children tend to pick the photo that matches their own perspective, not the doll's. Watch the video *Egocentrism Task* for another example of a research study on this topic.

Watch EGOCENTRISM TASK

irreversibility

lack of ability to reverse an action mentally

egocentrism

cognitive inability to distinguish between one's own perspective and another person's perspective

animism

tendency to attribute human thoughts and feelings to inanimate objects and forces

One aspect of egocentrism is **animism**, the tendency to attribute human thoughts and feelings to inanimate objects and forces. According to Piaget, when young children believe that the thunder is angry or the moon is following them, it reflects their animistic thinking. It also reflects their egocentrism, in that they are attributing the thoughts and feelings that they might have themselves to things that are inanimate.

Children's play with stuffed animals and dolls is a good example of animistic thinking. When they play with these toys, children frequently attribute human thoughts and feelings to them, often the thoughts and feelings they might have themselves. This is play, but it is a kind of play they take seriously. At age 5, Jeff's daughter Paris would sometimes "find" a stuffed puppy or kitten on their porch that she would treat as if it were a live animal that would now be her pet. If you humorously suggested that this might be an especially easy pet to care for, being stuffed—as Jeff made the mistake of doing one day—she took great offense and insisted it was a real animal. To her, at that moment, it was.

CLASSIFICATION Preoperational children also have limited skills in **classification**, according to Piaget, meaning that they have difficulty understanding that objects can be simultaneously part of more than one "class" or group. He demonstrated this by showing children a drawing of 4 blue flowers and 12 yellow flowers and asking, "Are there more yellow flowers, or more flowers?" In early childhood, children would typically answer "More yellow flowers," because they did not understand that yellow flowers could be part of the class "yellow flowers" and simultaneously part of the class "flowers."

Here, as with conservation, the cognitive limitations of centration and lack of reversibility are at the root of the error, in Piaget's view. Young children center on the fact that the yellow flowers are yellow, which leads them to overlook that the yellow flowers are also flowers. They also lack reversibility in that they cannot perform the mental operation of placing the yellow and blue flowers together into the "flowers" class and then moving them back into the "yellow flowers" and "blue flowers" classes, respectively.

EVALUATING PIAGET'S THEORY Piaget's theory of preoperational thought in early childhood has been challenged in the decades since he proposed it. The criticisms focus on two issues: claims that he underestimated children's cognitive capabilities and claims that development is more continuous and less stagelike than he proposed.

A number of studies over the past several decades have shown that children ages 2 to 7 are cognitively capable of more than Piaget recognized (Siegal, 2003). For example, regarding egocentrism, when the three mountains task is modified so that familiar objects are used instead of the three-mountain model, children give less egocentric responses (Newcombe & Huttenlocher, 2006). Studies using other methods also show that 2- to 7-year-old children are less egocentric than Piaget thought. Even toddlers show the beginnings of an ability to take others' perspectives, when they discern what they can do to annoy a sibling (Dunn, 1988). By age 4, children switch to shorter, simpler sentences when talking to toddlers or babies, showing a distinctly un-egocentric ability to take the perspective of the younger children (Bryant & Barrett, 2007).

Regarding Piaget's stage claims, research has shown that the development of cognitive skills in childhood is less stagelike and more continuous than Piaget believed (Bibok et al., 2009). Remember, Piaget's stage theory asserts that movement from one stage to another represents a wholesale cognitive shift, a change not just in specific cognitive skills but also in how children think. In this view, children ages 2 to 7 are incapable of performing mental operations and then in the next stage they become able to do so. However, research has generally shown that the ability to perform mental operations changes gradually over the course of childhood (Case, 1999).

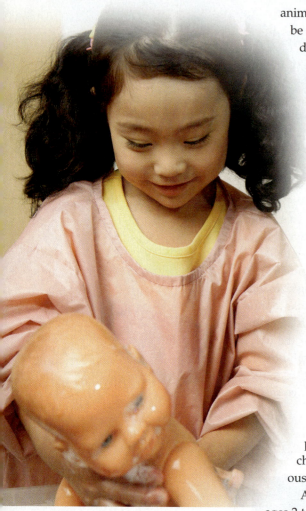

How does animism reflect young children's egocentrism?

classification

ability to understand that objects can be part of more than one cognitive group, for example an object can be classified with red objects as well as with round objects

executive function (EF)

mental processes and control over them, including working memory, controlling one's attention, cognitive flexibility, and self-regulation

Information Processing in Early Childhood: Attention, Memory, and Executive Function

LO 6.8 Explain the advances in information processing in early childhood.

Children's cognitive abilities develop to a large extent during early childhood as their attention spans, memory capacity, and executive function all increase. **Executive function (EF)**

generally refers to intentional control of mental processes, such as working memory, controlling one's attention, cognitive flexibility, and self-regulation (Zelazo et al., 2003). More complex EFs include problem solving, reasoning, and planning (Diamond & Lee, 2011). EFs predict math and reading performance throughout the school years (Gathercole et al., 2004).

Gains in EF abilities are related to brain development in early childhood, especially as areas of the brain continue to get more connected to each other than they were in infancy. Posner and colleagues (2014) have proposed that two attention systems in the brain—the orienting system and the executive system—are important in the development of EF. The orienting attention system works by controlling many other brain networks, such as the sensory systems, during infancy and early childhood. The executive attention system helps to resolve competing actions in tasks where there is conflict and a choice must be made. As these two attention systems get better connected to other parts of the brain, effortful control and self-regulation improve.

Working memory is memory for information that is currently the focus of one's attention. Working memory lasts about 10 to 15 seconds and is an essential EF component used in problem solving. Deficits in working memory have been linked to lower educational attainments (Gathercole & Alloway, 2008). Working memory capacity, and not IQ, has been found to be related to delayed measurements of learning in children with learning difficulties (Alloway, 2009) and those without any learning issues (Alloway et al., 2014). Interventions that target the exercise and improvement of working memory are therefore important in helping children become better learners (Holmes & Gathercole, 2014).

Understanding Thinking: The Development of "Theory of Mind"

LO 6.9 **Explain what "theory of mind" is and the evidence for how it develops during early childhood.**

Current research on cognitive development in early childhood includes many topics and areas that go beyond Piaget's theories. One popular area of research in recent years is **theory of mind**, the ability to understand thinking processes in one's self and others. Having a theory of mind means knowing that you have a mind, that other people have minds, and that minds do certain kinds of things. Minds think, dream, believe, desire, know, lie, deceive, and trick, among other things. Understanding how a theory of mind develops in young children tells us a lot about how cognition develops as children interact with others. Theory of mind is an aspect of development that reflects both cognitive and social skills. The child has to think about and take the perspective of himself or herself and others.

Understanding how others think is a challenge even for adults, but the beginnings of theory of mind appear early in infancy. Through behavior such as joint attention and the use of prelanguage vocalizations, infants show that they understand that others have mental states such as intentionality (Tomasello & Rakoczy, 2003). By age 2, as they begin to use language more, children show increasing recognition that others have thoughts and emotions that can be contrasted with their own (e.g., "That man is mad!" or "I like applesauce. Brother no like applesauce."). At age 2, children begin to use words that refer to mental processes, such as "think," "remember," and "pretend" (Flavell et al., 2002). By age 3, children know it is possible for them and others to imagine something that is not physically present (such as an ice cream cone). They can respond to an imaginary event as if it has really happened, and they realize that others can do the same (Andrews et al., 2003). This understanding becomes the basis of pretend play for many years to come.

However, there are limits to 3-year-olds' theory of mind, and crucial changes take place in the course of early childhood. They are better than 2-year-olds at understanding that others have thoughts and feelings that are different than their own, but they find it

theory of mind

ability to understand thinking processes in one's self and others

difficult to take others' perspectives. Perspective-taking ability advances considerably from age 3 to 6 (Callahan et al., 2005).

This change is vividly demonstrated in research involving *false-belief tasks*. The classic task for measuring understanding of false beliefs is the "Sally–Anne" task (see Baron-Cohen, et al., 1985). In this task (see **Figure 6.6**), a child is told the following story and presented with coordinated pictures or props, "Sally places her ball in a basket and goes out to play. While she is gone, Anne takes the ball from the basket and hides it in a box."

Figure 6.6 The "Sally–Anne" Task

The original Sally-Anne task was designed to measure whether young children understood certain aspects of the nature of beliefs—namely that beliefs come from certain sources and that beliefs can change.

The child is then asked where Sally will look for the hidden ball when she returns to play with it again. Most 3-year-old children answer erroneously that Sally will look for the ball in the new place, where Anne placed it. In contrast, by age 4 most children recognize that Sally will believe falsely that the ball is in the basket where she left it. The proportion of children answering correctly rises even more by age 5. A similar experiment, focusing on a doll named Maxi, yielded similar results.

The Sally–Anne task and other theory of mind tasks indicate some important changes in the thinking of young children as they develop across early childhood. Most 3-year-old children have a limited understanding of where knowledge comes from. But by age 4, most children understand that having knowledge about the locations of physical objects requires perceptual access to those objects. Further, most 3-year-old children do not understand that beliefs can change; they are more stuck on giving the "right answer," based on their own perceptions. Notice how this kind of thinking relates to the preoperational stage of Piaget: 3-year-old children are bound by a "what you see is what you get" mentality. If they see that an object is in a new place, their thinking about a situation seems to reflect a lack of flexibility in understanding how someone else might think about the same situation. In sum, not only is there a lack of understanding about the way knowledge works, but there is also a lack of understanding how beliefs can change based on new information and a lack of understanding how others might see the same situation if they have different knowledge.

Other kinds of theory of mind tasks also measure cognitive flexibility in understanding that others' desires and beliefs may be different from our own, that people can hide their emotions, and that seeing leads to knowing (knowledge access). In *diverse desires* tasks, the child must understand that people like and want different things—that others may not always want what we want. For example, a child chooses his own preferred food (cake or carrot) and then must predict the food choice of someone else with opposite preferences. In *diverse belief* tasks, the child must understand that different people can have different beliefs about something when both opinions might be true. For example, the child that says she believes that an animal is hiding in the bushes, who is told that another person believes the animal is hiding behind the house, must predict the search behavior of the person holding that different opinion. *Hidden emotions* tasks test the understanding that people may choose to hide what they really feel by showing an expression that doesn't match. For example, a boy being teased does not want to be called a "cry baby" by his friends. The child must say how the boy really feels and how he makes his face look. In tasks that measure the idea that *seeing leads to knowing*, the child who has seen a toy in a container must judge whether someone who hasn't seen inside the closed container will know what is in it. As children develop across early childhood, they come to understand all of these tasks. Wellman and Liu (2004) established these different kinds of skills as a theory of mind scale, which has been examined cross-culturally.

Theory of mind development has been linked to cultural values (Shahaeian et al., 2011) and to the number of siblings a child has (Peterson, 2000). If we recall the ecocultural model presented in Chapter 1, this makes sense. The values that people operate with influence the way that they think about situations and their behavior. In a collectivistic culture, children are more likely to acquire early the aspects of theory of mind that are related to respecting and cooperating with others. In an individualistic culture, children are more likely to acquire early the aspects of theory of mind that are related to acquiring knowledge for its own sake. Having more siblings is related to the personnel aspect of the ecocultural model: Having more siblings to negotiate with and keep track of may drive the earlier development of theory of mind skills.

In one cross-cultural study, Shahaeian and colleagues (2011) tested children in theory of mind development in Australia and Iran. Using the five kinds of theory of mind tasks outlined previously, they found a cross-cultural difference in the sequencing of the steps on the scale but not in the overall rates of mastering theory of mind. They linked some of their findings to cultural values. For example, the Iranian children understood knowledge access earlier than opinion diversity. The authors interpreted this to be in line with the collectivistic notions of filial piety and dispute avoidance prevalent in Iran. This indicates that while the pace and sequencing of the development of some aspects of theory of mind may be related to cultural values and practices, all typically developing children end up with similar theory of mind skills.

Interestingly, children with autism—noted for the characteristic lack of social connection between people with autism and others—have trouble understanding theory of mind and often cannot pass false-belief and related theory of mind tests. Children with autism spectrum disorders (ASDs) have trouble with various aspects of theory of mind behaviors, including language, EF, symbolic play, pragmatic conversational ability, and a number of academic functions like reading comprehension (Kimhi, 2014; Kimhi et al., 2014). These behaviors are sometimes linked to socio-emotional behaviors such as empathy. A recent study in Australia found that children with ASD exhibited less empathy than their peers without autism, but their empathic behavior was not related to theory of mind performance (Peterson, 2014). Researchers are still exploring the social and cognitive aspects of autism and its treatment.

Cultural Focus: Theory of Mind Across Cultures

In another theory of mind task, children are shown a box that appears to contain a kind of candy called "Smarties" and asked what they think is in the box (Gopnik & Astington, 1988). After they answer "candy" or "Smarties" they are shown that the box in fact contains pencils. Then they are asked what another person, who has not been shown the contents, will think is in the box. "Candy" or "Smarties" is the correct answer, showing theory of mind; "pencils" is incorrect. Most children in developed countries pass the test by the time they are 4 or 5 years old.

By age 6, nearly all children in developed countries solve false-belief tasks easily. In the video shown here, you will see that U.S. children make errors in the false-belief task at age 3 but answer correctly by age 5. However, in Mexico and Botswana, children continue to make mistakes at age 7. This could be because children in these cultures have not had preschool experiences that involved similar tasks. What other explanations could there be? What hypothesis would you propose, and how would you test it?

Review Question:

Can you think of any social interactions that may help or hinder a child in developing a theory of mind?

Watch THEORY OF MIND ACROSS CULTURES

Cultural Learning in Early Childhood

LO 6.10 Identify the ways that cultural learning takes place in early childhood.

In Piaget's depiction of cognitive development, the young child is like a solitary little scientist gradually mastering the concepts of conservation and classification and overcoming the errors of egocentrism and animism. Vygotsky's sociocultural theory of learning takes a much different approach, viewing cognitive development as a social and cultural process. Children learn not through their individual interactions with the environment but through the social process of guided participation, as they interact with a more knowledgeable member of the culture (often an older sibling or parent) in the course of daily activities.

Early childhood is a period when this kind of cultural learning comes to the fore (Gauvain & Nicolaides, 2015). More than in toddlerhood, young children have the capacity for learning culturally specific skills. Among the Tz'tujil Maya of Guatemala, a 5-year-old child can readily learn the skills involved in making tortillas, whereas a 2-year-old child would not have the necessary learning abilities, motor skills, or impulse control (Rogoff, 2003). In many cultures, the end of early childhood, ages 5 to 6, is the time when children are first given important responsibilities in the family for food preparation, child care, and animal care (LeVine & New, 2008). During early childhood they acquire the cultural learning necessary for these duties, sometimes through direct instruction but more often through observing and participating in adults' activities.

It is not only in traditional cultures that cultural learning takes place via guided participation. For example, a child in an economically developed country might help his parents prepare a grocery shopping list, and in the course of this process, learn culturally valued skills such as reading, using lists as tools for organization and planning, and calculating sums of money (Rogoff, 2003). Children in Western countries are also encouraged to speak up and hold conversations. For example, over dinner U.S. parents often ask their young children a series of questions ("What songs did you sing at preschool? What did you have for a snack?"), thereby preparing them for the question-and-answer structure of formal schooling they will enter in middle childhood (Martini, 1996). This is in contrast to cultures from Asia to northern Canada in which silence is valued, especially in children, and children who talk frequently are viewed as immature and low in intelligence (Rogoff, 2003).

Two factors make cultural learning in developed countries different from cultural learning in traditional cultures. One is that children in developed countries are often apart from their families for a substantial part of the day in a preschool or another group-care setting. Cultural learning takes place in the preschool setting, of course, but it is mostly a more direct kind of instruction (e.g., learning letters) rather than the cultural learning that takes place through guided participation in daily activities within the family. Second, the activities of adults in a complex economy are less accessible to children's learning than the activities that children learn through guided participation in traditional cultures, such as child care, tending animals, and food preparation. Most jobs in a complex economy require advanced skills of reading, analyzing information, and using technology, so there is a limit to which children can learn these skills through guided participation, especially in early childhood. However, the Vygotskian notion of learning by participating in activities with others is obvious in the learning settings of early childhood because children of this age are active and regularly engage with others in their environment.

How is cultural learning taking place here?

COGNITIVE DEVELOPMENT: Early Childhood Education

Traditionally in many cultures, formal schooling has started at about age 7. This is the age at which children have been viewed as first capable of learning the skills of reading, writing, and math. However, because the need to learn how to use words and numbers is so strong in the modern information-based economy, in many countries school now begins earlier than ever. In developed countries about three fourths of 3- to 5-year-old children are enrolled in group child care, preschool, or kindergarten (OECD, 2013). In developing countries, the percentages are lower but rising. In the United States, about half of the states now fund some type of preschool programs for 4-year-old children, usually focusing on children from low-income families. Nevertheless, preschool participation in the United States lags behind nearly all other developed countries (OECD, 2013).

The Importance of Quality in Early Childhood Education

LO 6.11 **Identify the features that are most important in preschool quality and explain how they reflect cultural values.**

What are the cognitive and social effects of attending preschool? For the most part, attending preschool is beneficial for young children (Campbell et al., 2002). Cognitive benefits of attending preschool include higher verbal skills and stronger performance on measures of memory and listening comprehension (Clarke-Stewart & Allhusen, 2002). Children from low-income families especially benefit cognitively from preschool (Love et al., 2013). They perform better on tests of school readiness than children of similar backgrounds who did not attend preschool.

There are also social benefits to attending preschool. Children who attend preschool are generally more independent and socially confident than children who remain home (National Institute of Child Health and Human Development [NICHD] Early Child Care Research Network, 2006). However, there appear to be social costs as well. Children attending preschool have been observed to be less compliant, less respectful toward adults, and more aggressive than other children (Jennings & Reingle, 2012). Furthermore, these negative social effects may endure long past preschool age. In one large national (U.S.) longitudinal study, children who attended preschool for more than 10 hours per week were more disruptive in class once they entered school, in follow-ups extending through 6th grade (NICHD Early Child Care Research Network, 2006).

Yet these findings concerning the overall positive or negative outcomes associated with preschool can be misleading. Preschool programs vary vastly in quality, and many studies have found that the quality of preschool child care is more important than simply the fact of whether children are in preschool or not (Clarke-Stewart & Allhusen, 2002; Maccoby & Lewis, 2003; NICHD Early Child Care Research Network, 2006). Also, cultural context matters. A recent national study in Norway found no relation between hours in preschool and aggression (Zachrisson et al., 2013).

DIFFERENT PRESCHOOL PROGRAMS What factors should parents consider when searching for a high-quality preschool experience for their children? There is a broad consensus among scholars of early childhood development that the most important features include the following (Lavzer & Goodson, 2006; National Association for the Education of Young Children [NAEYC], 2010; Vandell et al, 2005):

- *Education and training of teachers.* Unlike teachers at higher grade levels, preschool teachers often are not required to have education or credentials specific to early childhood education. Preschool teachers who have training in early childhood education provide a better social and cognitive environment.

- *Class size and child-to-teacher ratio.* Experts recommend no more than 20 children in a classroom, and a ratio of children to preschool teachers no higher than five to ten 3-year-old children per teacher or seven to ten 4-year-old children per teacher.
- *Age-appropriate materials and activities.* In early childhood, children learn more through active engagement with materials rather than through formal lessons or rote learning.
- *Teacher–child interactions.* Teachers should spend most of their time in interactions with the children rather than with each other. They should circulate among the children, asking questions, offering suggestions, and assisting them when necessary.

Notice that the criteria for high-quality preschools do not include intense academic instruction. Here again there is a broad consensus among early childhood scholars that preschool teaching should be based on *developmentally appropriate educational practice* (NAEYC, 2010). At the preschool age, this means that learning should involve exploring and discovering through relatively unstructured, hands-on experiences—learning about the physical world through playing in a water or sand area, for example, or learning new words through songs and nursery rhymes. Read the *Education Focus: How Does a Parent Choose Among the Many Kinds of Preschools?* feature for more on this topic.

Education Focus: How Does a Parent Choose Among the Many Kinds of Preschools?

When choosing a preschool, cost is a factor for many parents in many communities, but the philosophy of the program is also important to consider. Montessori, Reggio Emilia, and Waldorf are popular preschool programs, and each has a different philosophy.

The *Montessori* approach was developed by Maria Montessori in Rome in the early 1900s. Montessori programs are child-centered, with teachers serving as guides. The basic philosophy is that play is a child's work, meaning that play is central and important for development and that children ought to play the way adults generally spend time at work. The distinguishing feature of Montessori programs is that children learn at their own pace, choosing their own way through classroom centers and working at their own level. The tactile engagement of the child's senses and motor abilities is evident in a Montessori classroom. There are specially designed Montessori toys called *manipulatives* that are self-corrective; it is obvious to the child that he or she has assembled a puzzle correctly, for example, if the toy fits together, not because someone has demonstrated how to do it and then asks the child to parrot a response.

Children ages 3, 4, and 5 all learn in the same preschool classroom and in outdoor settings, when feasible. Children interact with others of different ages, and older children serve as observational models and helpers for the younger ones. This helpfulness can build self-efficacy because the older children feel a sense of accomplishment in aiding the younger ones. Montessori appeals to many parents because they believe the

In Montessori settings, children learn independently in different learning centers.

structure of the program encourages independent discovery in learning and solving tasks.

The *Reggio Emilia* approach is named for the Northern Italian town where it was developed in the 1940s after World War II. A schoolteacher named Lori Malaguzzi developed the approach with members of the community with the goal of helping children to become better citizens. The philosophy behind Reggio Emilia is that children should learn together by exploring.

In Reggio Emilia schools, children engage in projects based on their interests. For example, if children ask where a carrot comes from, the teacher encourages them to find out together. The class may then plant seeds for carrots and other garden plants, learning important pre-math and pre-reading concepts along the way. The teacher guides and supports the process of the children conducting cooperative projects together. Reggio Emilia programs document what children do with photos, videos, and teacher observations. Teachers and children review what they've done throughout the year. Children learn to work together and solve problems as they complete projects together. Parents who want their children to develop good citizenship skills may choose a Reggio Emilia preschool.

Waldorf is another popular form of education that also has a preschool model. Waldorf is a play-based approach that has a predictable structure, providing children with a dependable routine. For example, the days of the week correspond with baking or painting. The program emphasizes creative learning, reading, singing, and other activities. The Waldorf setting looks like a home. It is an inviting atmosphere, with natural materials and wooden toys.

Two things really set Waldorf apart from other schools: It does not use traditional grading systems, and it excludes all media in the curriculum. There are no computers, videos, or electronics in any Waldorf preschool. Children spend a lot of time outdoors in nature. Waldorf is characterized by individualism. Children are encouraged to develop their own curiosity and love of learning.

Of course, early childhood is generally a time of exploration, and there are many preschools that may blend aspects of these programs without officially ascribing to a specific philosophy. Many parents will want to visit preschools with their children to get a sense of which might be a good fit for an individual child.

Survey Question:

What kind of preschool would you prefer your child attend?
A. Montessori
B. Reggio Emilia
C. Waldorf
D. Any kind of high-quality preschool would be fine.

Research by developmental psychologist Angeline Lillard (2008; Lillard & Else-Quest, 2006) has demonstrated the effectiveness of the Montessori approach. Lillard compared two groups of 3- to 6-year-old children. One group of children had attended a Montessori preschool, and the other group attended other types of preschools. All the children in the non-Montessori group had originally applied to Montessori schools but were not able to enter because of space limitations, with admission determined by a random lottery. This was a crucial aspect of the study design; do you see why? If the researchers had simply compared children in Montessori schools with children in non-Montessori schools, any differences would have been difficult to interpret because there may have been many other differences between the families of children in the two types of schools (e.g., children in Montessori schools may have more-educated parents). Because the families of children in the non-Montessori schools had also applied to get their children into the Montessori schools, and selection among them was random via a lottery, it can be assumed that the family backgrounds of the children in the two groups were similar.

The children who attended Montessori preschools were more advanced in both cognitive and social development than the children who attended the other preschools. Cognitively, the Montessori children scored higher on tests of reading and math skills than the other children. Socially, in playground observations the Montessori children engaged more in cooperative play and less in rough, chaotic play such as wrestling. In sum, the Montessori approach appears to provide children with a setting that encourages self-initiated, active learning and thereby enhances cognitive and social development.

CULTURAL VARIATIONS IN PRESCHOOL Although attending preschool has become a typical experience among children in developed countries, there is great variation in how countries structure preschool and what they wish young children to learn. In most countries, parents hope for social benefits from preschool, but there is variation among countries in expectations of cognitive and academic benefits. In some countries, such as China and the United States, learning basic academic skills is one of the primary goals of having children attend preschool (Johnson et al., 2003; Tobin et al., 2009). In other countries, such as Japan and most European countries, learning academic skills is a low priority in preschool (Hayashi et al., 2009). Rather, preschool is mainly a time for learning social skills such as how to function as a member of a group.

Japan is of particular interest in this area because Japanese students have long been at or near the top of international comparisons in reading, math, and science from middle childhood through high school (National Center for Education Statistics [NCES], 2014). You might expect, then, that one reason for this success is that they begin academic instruction earlier than in other countries, but just the opposite turns out to be true. In one study of Japanese and U.S. parents and preschool teachers, only 2 percent of the Japanese listed "to give children a good start academically" as one of the top three reasons for young children to attend preschool (Tobin et al., 2009). In contrast, more than half the Americans named

Japanese preschools emphasize group play and cooperation.

this as one of the top three reasons. There was a similarly sharp contrast in response to the item "to give children the experience of being a member of the group." Sixty percent of Japanese endorsed this reason for preschool, compared to just 20 percent of the Americans.

Preschools in Japan teach nothing about reading and numbers. Instead, the focus is on group play, so that children will learn the values of cooperation and sharing. Preschool children wear identical uniforms, with different colors to indicate their classroom membership. They each have the same equipment, which they keep in identical drawers. Through being introduced to these cultural practices in preschool, children also learn collectivistic Japanese values.

KINDERGARTEN Many preschool and kindergarten classrooms in developed countries are influenced by Vygotsky's sociocultural approach, including the ideas of scaffolding and the zone of proximal development. The setting of the kindergarten classroom is one that is easy to look at through the lens of activity settings that we talked about in Chapter 1. The personnel of the classroom include specially trained teachers who understand the cognitive and emotional skills of kindergarten children. The tasks are designed to help children learn with guided help before they are able to accomplish more complex tasks on their own. The tasks are also designed to help children learn the routines of their cultural group, such as saying, "Good morning," putting one's things away in cubby-holes, and managing classroom duties, such as watering the class plants. The materials in the kindergarten class setting are specially designed for children and also reflect the Vygotskian notions of scaffolding and the zone of proximal development. For example, pencils and crayons may be larger so that little hands can manipulate them. Lined paper is designed with lines that are much farther apart than lines on regular notebook paper. Books and toys are specially sized and made simple for the age group. And the routine of the day reflects children's age and capabilities as well: Children learn, play, eat snacks, and they may take naps; some of which they won't be doing any more once they enter first grade, when the routines change. Once children reach first grade, the typical classroom, and the way that the teacher interacts with the children, shifts to a more academic, school-like setting that is designed for work rather than play.

All the special adaptations that we see in kindergarten help to get children ready for school. The support provided in kindergarten is important, and it helps children develop the emotional readiness to be in school. Emotional knowledge and regulation are important in success in first grade and beyond (Rhoades, et al., 2011).

Preschool as a Cognitive Intervention

LO 6.12 **Describe early intervention programs and their outcomes.**

One type of preschool experience that focuses intensively on cognitive development is the **early intervention program**. These are programs directed at young children who are at risk for later school problems because they come from low-income families. The goal of early intervention programs is to give these children extra cognitive stimulation in early childhood so that they will have a better opportunity to succeed once they enter school.

By far the largest early intervention program in the United States is Project Head Start. The program began in 1965 and is still going strong, with about 1 million U.S. children enrolled each year (Puma et al., 2010). The program provides 1 or 2 years of preschool, but it also includes other services. Children in the program receive free meals and health care. Parents receive health care as well as job-training services. Parents are also directly involved in the Head Start program, serving on councils that make policies for the centers and sometimes serving as teachers in the classroom. Canada has a similar program focusing on First Nations minority children who are often at risk for later school problems.

Do these programs work? The answer is not simple. The main goal of Head Start originally was to raise the intelligence of children from low-income backgrounds so that their academic performance would be enhanced once they entered school. Children in Head Start show a boost in IQ and academic achievement after their participation in the program, compared to children from similar backgrounds who did not take part, so in this respect, yes, the program worked. However, a consistent pattern in Head Start and many other early intervention programs is that the IQ and achievement gains fade within 2 or 3 years of entering elementary school (Barnett & Hustedt, 2005). This is not surprising in view of the fact that children in the program typically enter poorly funded, low-quality public schools after their Head Start experience, but nevertheless the fading of the initial gains was unexpected and fell short of the original goals of the program.

However, there have been some favorable results from the Head Start program, too (Brooks-Gunn, 2003; Resnick, 2010). Children who have participated in Head Start are less likely to be placed in special education or to repeat a grade. It should be kept in mind that Head Start is a program with a million children in tens of thousands of programs, and inevitably the programs vary in quality (Resnick, 2010; Zigler & Styfco, 2004). The more the mother is involved in the program, the more her child demonstrates benefits in terms of academic and social skills (Marcon, 1999).

Head Start was designed to serve children ages 4 to 6 and give them a "head start" in school readiness, but in the 1990s a new program, Early Head Start (EHS), was initiated for low-income families and their children from infancy up to age 3 (Raikes et al., 2010). The goal of this program was to see if greater effects on cognitive and social development could be obtained by beginning the intervention at an earlier age. Research has shown that by age 5 the EHS children exhibited better attention and fewer behavioral problems than children from similar families who were in a control group (Love et al., 2013). EHS moms benefitted, too, in their mental health and likelihood of employment. However, for children, being in EHS did not affect their early school achievement unless it was followed by preschool programs at ages 3 to 4.

Some small-scale, intensive early intervention programs have shown a broader range of enduring effects. One of the best known is the High Scope Preschool Project, a full-day, 2-year preschool program for children from low-income families (Schweinhart et al., 2004). The High Scope children showed the familiar pattern of an initial gain in IQ and academic achievement followed by a decline, but they demonstrated many other benefits of the program, compared to a control group. In adolescence, the girls were less likely to become pregnant and the boys were less likely to be arrested, and both boys and girls were more likely to graduate from high school and attend college (see **Figure 6.7**). At age 27, the High Scope participants were more likely to be married

early intervention program

program directed at young children who are at risk for later problems, intended to prevent problems from developing

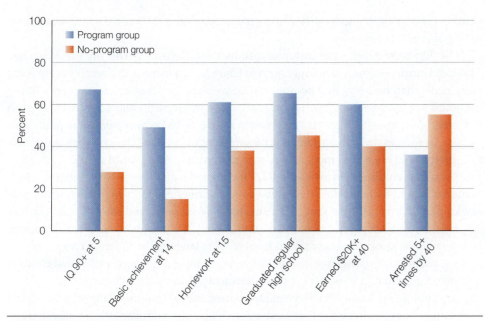

Figure 6.7 Major Findings of the High Scope Preschool Study

High Scope participants showed better academic performance, IQ scores, and earning potential and were less likely to be arrested later in life than other children.
SOURCE: Based on Schweinhart et al., 2005.

and to own their home, less likely to have spent time in prison, and their monthly income was higher. At age 40, High Scope participants still displayed benefits of the program in a wide range of areas, including income and family stability. This program shows that an intensive, high-quality early intervention program can have profound and lasting benefits.

COGNITIVE DEVELOPMENT:
Language Development

By age 3 children are remarkably adept at using language. Nevertheless, their language development from age 3 to 6 continues at a remarkable pace, in areas including vocabulary, grammar, and pragmatics.

Advances in Vocabulary and Grammar

LO 6.13 **Explain how advances in vocabulary and grammar occur in early childhood.**

Perhaps the most amazing advance in early childhood language is the growth in children's vocabulary. The average 3-year-old child has a vocabulary of about 1,000 words; by age 6, the average vocabulary has increased to more than 2,500 words (Bloom, 1998). This means they are adding words nearly every day (Clark, 1995).

How do they do it? Clearly children's brains are built for learning language, and early childhood is a **sensitive period** for language development, when the capacity for learning new words is especially pronounced (Pinker, 1994). Young children add new words to their vocabulary through a process known as *fast mapping* (Ganger & Brent, 2004; Swingley, 2010). This means that as young children learn new words they begin to form a mental map of interconnected sets of word categories. When they hear a word the first time they instantly connect it to one of these categories based on how the

sensitive period

in the course of development, a period when the capacity for learning in a specific area is especially pronounced

This is a fup.

Now there is another one.
There are two of them.
There are two _____.

Figure 6.8 Berko's
Language Study

This scenario is similar to the one posed to children in Berko's study. How do the results of Berko's study show young children's grasp of grammar?

SOURCE: Adapted from Berko, 1958.

word is used in a sentence and how it seems to be related to words they already know, to help discern its meaning.

The kinds of words children fast-map earliest depend partly on the language. Children learning Eastern languages such as Chinese, Japanese, and Korean tend to learn more verbs than nouns at first because sentences often emphasize verbs but only imply the nouns without speaking them (Kim et al., 2000). In contrast, children learning English and other Western languages fast-map nouns before verbs because nouns are prominent in these languages. In both Eastern and Western languages, modifiers (such as large, narrow, pretty, low) are added more slowly than nouns and verbs (Mintz, 2005).

As young children add new words to their vocabulary, they also continue to learn **grammar**, which is a language's distinctive system of rules. Some examples of rules include single/plural forms; past, present, and future tense; word order; and use of articles (such as "a" and "the") and prepositions (such as "under" and "by"). Without any formal training, young children grasp the grammatical rules of their language with few errors simply by hearing and using the language in daily interactions. By age 4, it is estimated that children use correct grammar in 90 percent of their statements (Guasti, 2000; Pinker, 1994).

But how do we know they have really learned the rules of their language? Couldn't they simply be repeating what they hear older children and adults say? In a classic study investigating this question, Jean Berko (1958) had young children respond to questions involving nonsense words such as *wug* (see **Figure 6.8** for a similar example). Although they had never heard the words before—Berko had made them up—the children were able to apply the grammar of English and use nouns in plural and possessive forms. This ability may be linked to the language acquisition device proposed by Chomsky (1969).

Pragmatics: Social and Cultural Rules of Language

LO 6.14 Describe how children learn pragmatics in early childhood, and identify to what extent these social rules are culturally based.

To use language effectively, children must learn not only vocabulary and grammar but the social rules or **pragmatics** for using language in interaction with others. Pragmatics guide us in knowing what to say—and what not to say—in a given social situation. For example, children learn to say "please" when asking for something and "thank you" when they receive something.

Children begin learning pragmatics even before they begin speaking, through gestures, for example when they wave "bye-bye" to someone when leaving. By the age of 2, they know the pragmatics of a basic conversation, including taking turns speaking (Pan & Snow, 1999). However, at this age they have not yet grasped the pragmatics of sustaining a conversation on one topic, and they tend to change topics rapidly as new things occur to them, without much awareness of the other person's perspective.

By age 4, children are more sensitive to the characteristics of their conversational partner and will adjust their speech accordingly. In one study using hand puppets, 4-year-old children used different kinds of speech when acting out different puppet roles (Anderson, 2000). When playing a socially dominant role such as teacher or doctor they used commands frequently, whereas when playing subordinate roles such as student or patient they spoke more politely.

The use of pragmatics represents not only social understanding but cultural knowledge. All cultures have their own rules for what kinds of speech can be used in what kinds of situations. For example, some cultures require children to address adults with respectful titles, such as "Mr." for adult men. Many cultures have words that are classified as "bad words" that are not supposed to be spoken, especially by children.

These are the kinds of pragmatics children learn in the course of early childhood, but while they are learning them there can be some embarrassing (and hilarious) moments for parents in some cultural groups along the way. Jeff recalls going through the check-out

grammar

a language's distinctive system of rules

pragmatics

social and cultural context of language that guides people as to what is appropriate to say and not to say in a given social situation

line in a grocery store with his daughter Paris, who was then 3 years old, and she said to the clerk, apropos of nothing, "When I grow to a mommy, I'm going to have a baby in my tummy!" Adults understand intuitively that young children lack a sense of pragmatics, so they tend to find such moments amusing rather than offensive. By middle childhood, most U.S. children learn when it is culturally appropriate to speak and when it is best to keep your thoughts to yourself. Ashley's experience with Mayan children indicates that they understand the pragmatics of "being seen and not heard" in early childhood. Mayan children don't blurt out such comments around adults.

How might the language used in this kind of play demonstrate a grasp of pragmatics?

Pragmatics and other aspects of language may be conveyed through reading practices. Although most 3- to 5-year-olds cannot yet read, it is a good practice for parents to read to their children. Exposing children to reading in early childhood can set them up for a lifelong love of books. Ashley remembers being read to regularly as a 4-year-old, and she could retell the story of *Chicken Little* while turning the pages (triggered by the illustrations). When parents and other caregivers read to children, it builds the habit of reading that can help children appreciate reading, and be ready for reading, when they get to school. Emergent literacy experiences from birth to age four lay the foundation for later literacy and academic achievement (Sloat et al., 2015). It is also a good idea for parents to read while their children look at or "read" books, fostering the habit of reading together. Having books in the household helps children think of reading as an important pastime, and this is useful for orienting them toward all the reading they will have to do to get through school. Not only do young children learn about language through these reading practices, they start to link written words with spoken language—the beginnings of literacy. However, it may be important for parents to make explicit links between the spoken and written words to ensure that children are not just paying attention to the pictures found in books designed for this age group (Phillips et al., 2008).

CRITICAL THINKING QUESTION

Can you think of examples of how pragmatics have changed in your culture compared to a century ago?

Summary: Cognitive Development

LO 6.7 Explain the features of Piaget's preoperational stage of cognitive development.

Piaget viewed the preoperational stage of cognitive development (ages 2–7) as prone to a variety of errors, including centration, lack of reversibility, egocentrism, and animism. In this stage children make mistakes in tasks of conservation and classification. Research has shown that Piaget underestimated the cognitive abilities of early childhood.

LO 6.8 Explain the advances in information processing in early childhood.

In the years from 3 to 6, children improve their executive function, which includes certain abilities and the capacity to control them, including working memory, attention,

cognitive flexibility, self-regulation, and problem solving. Better scores on executive function are related to better reading and math skills in early childhood, as well as to more positive outcomes later in school.

LO 6.9 Explain what "theory of mind" is and the evidence for how it develops during early childhood.

Theory of mind is the ability to understand thinking processes in one's self and others. By age 2, as they begin to use language more, children show increasing recognition that others have thoughts and emotions that can be contrasted with their own. By age 3, children know it is possible for them and others to imagine something that is not physically present, an understanding that becomes the basis of pretend play for many years to come. While 3-year-olds are better than 2-year-olds at understanding that others have thoughts and feelings that are different from their own, they still find it difficult to take others' perspectives. Perspective-taking ability advances considerably from age 3 to 6, as demonstrated by performance on false-belief tasks.

LO 6.10 Identify the ways that cultural learning takes place in early childhood.

A great deal of cultural learning takes place in early childhood through observing and working alongside parents or siblings, and in many cultures children begin to make important work contributions to the family during this stage. In developed countries, children also gain cultural learning in the preschool setting.

LO 6.11 Identify the features that are most important in preschool quality and explain how they reflect cultural values.

Children generally benefit cognitively from attending preschool, but the social effects of preschool are more mixed and in some ways negative. Key dimensions of high-quality preschool programs include education and training of teachers, class size and child-to-teacher ratio, age-appropriate materials and activities, and quality of teacher–child interactions.

U.S. and Chinese preschools often include academic preparation, but preschools in Japan focus more on group play, so that collectivistic Japanese values, such as cooperation and sharing, are reinforced.

LO 6.12 Describe early intervention programs and their outcomes.

Early intervention programs have often resulted in a rise in IQ that fades after a few years. Some early interventions via preschool have had long-term positive effects on children's development, but the effects depend greatly on the quality of the program.

LO 6.13 Explain how advances in vocabulary and grammar occur in early childhood.

Children's vocabularies expand immensely in early childhood, from about 1,000 words at age 3 to about 2,500 words at age 6, and they readily grasp the grammatical rules of their culture with few errors by age 4.

LO 6.14 Describe how children learn pragmatics in early childhood, and identify to what extent these social rules are culturally based.

Pragmatics guide us in knowing what to say—and what not to say—in a given social situation, and by age 4, children are sensitive to the characteristics of their conversational partner and will adjust their speech accordingly. All cultures have their own rules for what kinds of speech can be used in what kinds of situations.

Section 3 Emotional and Social Development

Learning Objectives

6.15 Identify advances in emotional understanding and self-regulation during early childhood.

6.16 Describe moral development in early childhood, including empathy, modeling, and morality as cultural learning.

6.17 Describe the roles that parents and peers play in gender socialization, and explain how gender schemas lead to self-socialization.

6.18 Describe the four types of parenting "styles," and identify the cultural limitations of this model.

6.19 Describe the main cultural variations in how parents discipline young children, and explain how cultural context influences children's responses to discipline.

6.20 Explain the progression of increasing independence across the social stages of infancy through early childhood.

6.21 Identify the most common features of sibling relationships worldwide, and describe how children with no siblings differ from other children.

6.22 Explain how the quality of friendships changes from toddlerhood to early childhood, and describe the role of play and aggression in young children's friendships.

6.23 Identify the rates and consequences of media use in early childhood.

EMOTIONAL AND SOCIAL DEVELOPMENT: Emotional Regulation and Gender Socialization

After the emotional volatility and intensity of the toddler years, children make great advances in emotional self-regulation in early childhood. Also notable in their emotional development during this time is increasing empathy and a greater grasp of the moral system of their culture, learned in part by modeling their behavior after the behavior of others who are important in their lives. With regard to gender development, early childhood is a life stage of great importance, with children gaining a fuller understanding of the gender roles and expectations of their culture and beginning to enforce those gender roles on others as well as on themselves.

Extreme expressions of emotion decrease in the course of early childhood, as effortful control develops.

Emotional Regulation

LO 6.15 Identify advances in emotional understanding and self-regulation during early childhood.

Early childhood is a time of great advances in emotional development, specifically in emotional understanding and self-regulation. With respect to emotional understanding, in the course of early childhood children become adept at understanding the sources of other people's expressed emotions (Eisenberg & Fabes, 2006). In studies that show children cards depicting expressed emotions, by age 5 children are usually accurate in explaining the emotions of the situation (e.g., "She's happy because she got a present," or "He's sad because his mom scolded him"). They are also adept at understanding how emotional states are the basis of subsequent actions; for example, an angry child is more likely to hit someone (Kagan & Hershkowitz, 2005).

Young children become more adept not only at understanding others' emotions but at controlling their own. In fact, **emotional self-regulation** is considered to be one of the major developmental tasks of early childhood (Grolnick et al., 2006). Developing emotional self-regulation is crucial to social relations because maintaining harmonious social relations often requires us to restrain our immediate impulses—to wait in line, to let others go first in a game or a conversation, or to take fewer pieces of candy than we really want. Across cultures, early childhood is a time when expectations for emotional self-regulation increase (Whiting & Edwards, 1988). From age 2 to 6, extremes of emotional expression such as temper tantrums, crying, and physical aggression decrease (Alink et al., 2006; Carlson, 2003). In the brain, the development of the frontal cortex promotes this process because this is the part of the brain most involved in emotional self-regulation (Bell & Wolfe, 2007).

Another key reason why emotional outbursts decline during early childhood is that children learn strategies for regulating their emotions (Grolnick et al., 2006). Experimental studies have identified the strategies that young children use when presented with an emotionally challenging situation, such as being given a disappointing prize after being led to expect an attractive prize (Eisenberg & Fabes, 2006). Some of the most effective strategies are leaving the situation; talking to themselves; redirecting their attention to a different activity; and seeking comfort from an attachment figure. These strategies are part of what researchers call *effortful control*, when children focus their attention on managing their emotions (Cipriano & Stifter, 2010). Parents can help young children develop effortful control, by providing emotional and physical comfort when their children are upset, by suggesting possible strategies for managing emotions, and by modeling effortful control themselves (Katz & Windecker-Nelson, 2004).

Children vary in their success at achieving emotional self-regulation in early childhood, depending both on their temperament and on the socialization provided by parents and others. Children who have problems of **undercontrol** in early childhood have inadequately developed emotional self-regulation. These children are at risk for **externalizing problems**, such as aggression and conflict with others, in early childhood and beyond (Cole et al., 2003). However, developing **overcontrol**, an excessive degree of self-regulation of emotions, is also problematic. This can lead to **internalizing problems**, such as anxiety and depression, in early childhood and beyond (Grolnick et al., 2006). Throughout life, internalizing problems is more common among females and externalizing problems is more common among males (Frick & Kimonis, 2008; Ollendick et al., 2008).

Successful emotional regulation means developing a level of effortful control that is between the two extremes. As Erikson (1950) noted in proposing that early childhood is the stage of **initiative vs. guilt**, children need to learn emotional control but without being so tightly regulated that they feel excess guilt and their ability to initiate activities

emotional self-regulation
ability to exercise control over one's emotions

undercontrol
trait of having inadequate emotional self-regulation

externalizing problems
problems that involve others, such as aggression

overcontrol
trait of having excessive emotional self-regulation

internalizing problems
problems that entail turning distress inward, toward the self, such as depression and anxiety

is undermined. But different cultures have different views of what the optimal level of emotional control is (Chen et al., 2007). Behavior that looks like undercontrol in one culture could be valued as a healthy expression of assertiveness in other countries like Italy, for example, at least for boys (Levine & New, 2008). Behavior that looks like overcontrol in one culture could be valued as the virtue of reticence in another culture (Chen et al., 2011; Rogoff, 2003).

Self-control in the form of delay of gratification is an aspect of self-regulation that has been linked to later developments. Children delay gratification when they stay on task in class, when they help with chores at home before going out to play, or any time they set aside their immediate desires to wait for a more valuable or sought after future experience. If you're thinking that this sounds a lot like EF, you're right. Delay of gratification is part of EF in that children have to focus on a goal, perhaps even distracting themselves by paying attention to something else other than the instant reward.

The most famous study of delay of gratification is the "marshmallow test" (Mischel et al., 1972). In the classic marshmallow study, Walter Mischel and his colleagues presented preschoolers with a marshmallow and a pretzel. The preschoolers were asked to point to the snack they preferred (most preferred the marshmallow), and then the experimenter said she was leaving. Then came the important point of the test: If the children could wait for the experimenter to come back, they could have the preferred snack. However, if at any time the children wanted the experimenter to come back, they could ring a bell, and the experimenter would come back, but the child would get the other snack (the one they did not prefer). Later, the marshmallow test was adapted, and children were given a marshmallow or other desirable snack and told if they could wait for the experimenter to return, they could have double the snack, but if they ate the marshmallow before the experimenter came back, that would be the only snack. The various marshmallow tests produced charming videos, to be sure, but more importantly, the results of these tests have been linked to later life skills and achievements. Children who could delay gratification by waiting for the experimenter to return to get a bigger reward were more likely to have positive outcomes on a number of variables later in life (Mischel, 2014). For example, those who delayed longer had higher ratings on social and cognitive function in adolescence and to get higher SAT scores. At ages 27 to 32, those who had waited longer as preschoolers were found to have pursued life goals more effectively, to have a lower body mass index, and to have better coping mechanisms for stress. It is clear that being able to put aside one's momentary desires to achieve goals is necessary for many positive developments across the life span.

In the original "marshmallow study," children displayed delay of gratification by not eating the marshmallow.

Moral Development

LO 6.16 Describe moral development in early childhood, including empathy, modeling, and morality as cultural learning.

The socio-moral emotions, such as guilt, shame, embarrassment, and pride, first appear in toddlerhood and are shaped by cultural standards. Toddlers feel guilt, shame, or embarrassment when they violate the expected standards for behavior in their social environment, and pride when they comply.

One socio-moral emotion that is especially important to moral development in early childhood is empathy. As we have seen, toddlers and even infants show indications of

initiative vs. guilt

in Erikson's lifespan theory, the early childhood stage in which the alternatives are learning to plan activities in a purposeful way, or being afflicted with excess guilt that undermines initiative

empathy, but the capacity for empathy develops further in early childhood (Eisenberg & Valiente, 2004). Children become better at perspective-taking and being able to understand how others think and feel makes them more empathic. Empathy promotes prosocial behavior such as being generous or helpful. It contributes to the moral understanding of principles such as avoiding harm and being fair because through empathy children understand how their behavior would make another person feel. As empathy increases, prosocial behavior increases over the course of early childhood (Eisenberg et al., 2006).

Moral development advances further in early childhood as children gain a more detailed and complex understanding of the rules and expectations of their culture (Jensen, 2015c). Toddlers know when others approve or disapprove of something they have done, and they usually respond with the appropriate socio-moral emotion. However, in early childhood there is greater awareness of the rule or expectation that evoked the approval or disapproval. Also, young children are more capable than toddlers of anticipating the potential consequences of their actions and avoiding behaviors that would be morally disapproved (Grolnick et al., 2006).

Young children do not inherently know the rules and expectations of their culture and must learn them, sometimes by unknowingly violating them and then observing the consequences in the responses of their parents and others. For example, one day when Jeff's twins were about 4 years old, they got into the laundry room in the basement and took cups of liquid detergent and spread it all over the basement furniture—sofa, table, loveseat, CD player—all of which were ruined! We don't think they had any intention or awareness of doing something wrong, although after their parents found out what they had done they knew from the response they should never do it again. And they never did.

A good example of cultural learning of morality can be found in the research of Richard Shweder, who has compared children, adolescents, and adults in India and the United States (2009; Shweder et al., 1990). Shweder has found that by about age 5, children already grasp the moral standards of their culture, and their views change little from childhood to adolescence to adulthood.

Shweder found that there are some similarities in moral views in early childhood in India and the United States, but also many differences. At age 5, children in both countries have learned that it is wrong to take others' property ("steal flowers from a neighbor's garden") or to inflict harm intentionally ("kick a dog sleeping on the side of the road"). However, young children also view many issues with a different moral perspective depending on whether they live in India or the United States. Young children in the United States view it as acceptable to eat beef, but young children in India view it as wrong. Young children in India view it as acceptable for more of a father's inheritance to go to his son than to his daughter, but young children in the United States view it as wrong. Young children in both cultures have the ability to understand their culture's moral rules, even though the moral rules they have learned by early childhood are quite different.

How do children learn moral rules so early in life? There are several ways. Sometimes moral rules are taught explicitly. The Ten Commandments of the Jewish and Christian religions are a good example of this. Sometimes morality is taught through stories. Barbara Rogoff (2003) gives examples of storytelling as moral instruction in a variety of cultures, including Canadian First Nations people, American Indians, and the Xhosa people of South Africa. Among the Xhosa (pronounced ZO-sa), it is usually the elders who tell the stories, but the stories have been told many times before, and even young children soon learn the stories and participate in the narrative.

Moral lessons are often communicated through stories. Here, a village elder tells children stories in Tanzania.

Describe a childhood story or fairy tale told in your culture that communicates a moral lesson.

Young children also learn morality through custom complexes (see Chapter 4). Remember, the essence of the custom complex is that every customary practice of a culture contains not just the customary practice itself but the underlying cultural beliefs, often including moral beliefs. Shweder (Shweder et al., 1990) gives an example of this kind of moral learning in India. Like people in many cultures, Indians believe that a woman's menstrual blood has potentially dangerous powers. Consequently, a menstruating woman is not supposed to cook food or sleep in the same bed as her husband. By the end of early childhood, Indian children have learned not just that a menstruating woman does not cook food or sleep with her husband (the cultural practice) but that it would be *wrong* for her to do so (the moral belief).

A variation on the custom complex can be found in U.S. research on *modeling*. Research extending over more than 30 years has shown that young children tend to model their behavior after the behavior of others they observe (Bandura, 1977; Bussey & Bandura, 2004). Most of this research has been experimental, involving situations in which children observe other children or adults behaving aggressively or kindly, selfishly or generously; then children's own behavior in a similar experimental situation is observed. Children are especially likely to model their behavior after another person if the other person's behavior is rewarded. Also, they are more likely to model their behavior after adults who are warm and responsive or who are viewed as having authority or prestige. According to modeling theory, after observing multiple occasions of others' behavior being rewarded or punished, children conclude that the rewarded behavior is morally desirable and the punished behavior is forbidden (Bandura, 2002). So, by observing behavior (and its consequences), they learn their culture's principles of moral conduct. As in the custom complex, culturally patterned behavior implies underlying moral beliefs.

In addition to grasping early their culture's moral principles, young children begin to display the rudiments of moral reasoning. By the age of 3 or 4, children are capable of making moral judgments that involve considerations of justice and fairness (Helwig, 2008). By age 4 they understand the difference between telling the truth and lying, and they believe it is wrong to tell lies even when the liar is not caught (Bussey, 1992). However, their moral reasoning tends to be rigid at this age. They are more likely than older children to state that stealing and lying are always wrong, without regard to the circumstances (Lourenco, 2003). Also, their moral judgments tend to be based more on fear of punishment than is the case for older children and adults (Gibbs, 2003). Their moral reasoning will become more complex with age, as we will see in later chapters.

Gender Development

LO 6.17 **Describe the roles that parents and peers play in gender socialization, and explain how gender schemas lead to self-socialization.**

In all cultures, gender is a fundamental organizing principle of social life. All cultures distinguish different roles and expectations for males and females, although the strictness of those roles and expectations varies widely. Some cultural groups highlight the differences between men and women, and other groups emphasize them very little. Of course, many other animals, including all our mammal relatives and certainly our primate cousins, have male–female differences in their typical patterns of behavior and development. What makes humans distinctive is that, unlike other animals, we require culture to tell us how males and females are supposed to behave.

GENDER IDENTITY AND GENDER SOCIALIZATION Early childhood is an especially important period with respect to gender development. Already at age 2, children attain *gender identity*, that is, they understand themselves as being either male or female (Ruble et al., 2006). However, in early childhood, gender issues intensify, as shown in the video *Gender Socialization*. By ages 3 to 4, children associate a variety of things with either males or females, including toys, games, clothes, household items, occupations, and even colors (Kapadia & Gala, 2015).

Watch   GENDER SOCIALIZATION

Furthermore, they are often adamant and rigid in their perceptions of maleness and femaleness, denying, for example, that it would be possible for a boy to wear a ponytail and still remain a boy, or for a girl to play roughly and still remain a girl (Blakemore, 2003)! One reason for their insistence on strict gender roles at this age may be cognitive. It is not until age 6 or 7 that children attain **gender constancy**, the understanding that maleness and femaleness are biological and cannot change (Ruble et al., 2006). Earlier, children may be so insistent about maintaining **gender roles** because they believe that changing external features like clothes or hair styles could result in a change in gender.

The similarity of children's gender roles and gender behavior across cultures is striking, and there is a biological basis to some gender differences. However, children in all cultures are also subject to gender socialization.

Parents play an active and early role in delivering cultural gender messages to their children (Liben et al., 2013; Ruble et al., 2006). They may give their children distinctively male or female names, dress them in gender-specific colors and styles, and provide them with cars or dolls to play with (Bandura & Bussey, 2004).

Parents' important role in gender socialization continues in early childhood. They continue to give their children the clothes and toys they believe are gender appropriate. They express approval when their children behave in gender-appropriate ways and disapproval when their children violate gender expectations (Kapadia & Gala, 2015). In conversations, parents sometimes communicate gender expectations directly (e.g., "Don't cry, you're not a little girl, are you?"). They also communicate indirectly, by approving or not contradicting their children's gender statements. ("Only boys can be doctors, Mommy.") Parents also provide models, through their own behavior, language, and appearance, of how males and females are supposed to be different in their culture (Bandura & Bussey, 2004).

gender constancy

understanding that maleness and femaleness are biological and cannot change

gender roles

cultural expectations for appearance and behavior specific to males or females

gender schema

gender-based cognitive structure for organizing and processing information, comprising expectations for males' and females' appearance and behavior

self-socialization

process by which people seek to maintain consistency between their gender schemas and their behavior

Fathers become especially important to gender socialization in early childhood and beyond. They tend to be more insistent about conformity to gender roles than mothers are, especially for boys (Lamb, 2010). They may not want their daughters to play rough-and-tumble games, but they are adamant that their boys not be "wimps." As we will see in later chapters, males' greater fear of violations of gender roles is something that continues throughout life in many cultures.

Peers also become a major source of gender socialization in early childhood. Once children learn gender roles and expectations, they apply them not only to themselves but to each other. They reinforce each other for gender-appropriate behavior, and reject peers who violate gender roles (Matlin, 2004; Ruble et al., 2006). Here, too, the expectations are stricter for boys than for girls (Liben et al., 2013). Boys who cry easily or who like to play with girls and engage in girls' games are likely to be ostracized by other boys (David et al., 2004).

GENDER SCHEMAS AND SELF-SOCIALIZATION As a result of gender socialization, from early childhood onward children use **gender schemas** as a way of understanding and interpreting the world around them. Recall that *scheme* is Piaget's term for a cognitive structure for organizing and processing information. (*Scheme* and *schema* are used interchangeably in psychology.) A gender schema is a gender-based cognitive structure for organizing and processing information (Martin & Ruble, 2004).

According to gender-schema theory, gender is one of our most important schemas from early childhood onward. By the time we reach the end of early childhood, on the basis of our socialization we have learned to categorize a wide range of activities, objects, and personality characteristics as "female" or "male." This includes not just the obvious—vaginas are female, penises are male—but many things that have no inherent "femaleness" or "maleness" but are nevertheless taught as possessing gender. Examples include the moon as "female" and the sun as "male" in traditional Chinese culture, or blue as a "boy color" and pink as a "girl color" (in Korea, pink is a "boy color," which illustrates how cultural these designations are).

Fathers tend to promote conformity to gender roles more than mothers do.

Gender schemas influence how we interpret the behavior of others and what we expect from them (Frawley, 2008). Gender schemas vary across ecocultural settings. However, in early childhood, children tend to believe that their own preferences are true for everyone of their gender (Liben et al., 2013). For example, a boy who dislikes peas may justify it by claiming "boys don't like peas." Young children also tend to remember in ways that reflect their gender schemas. In one study (Liben & Signorella, 1993), children who were shown pictures that violated typical gender roles (e.g., a woman driving a truck) tended to remember them in accordance with their gender schemas (a man, not a woman, driving the truck). Throughout life, we tend to notice information that fits within our gender schemas and ignore or dismiss information that is inconsistent with them (David et al., 2004).

Once children learn the gender roles of their culture, they may strive to conform to them. Here, girls in Cambodia attend a dance class.

Once young children possess gender schemas, they seek to maintain consistency between their schemas and their behavior, a process called **self-socialization**. Boys become quite insistent about doing things they regard as boy things and avoiding things that girls do; girls become equally intent on avoiding boy things and doing things they regard as appropriate for girls (Bandura & Bussey, 2004; Tobin et al., 2010). In this way, according to a prominent gender scholar, "cultural myths become self-fulfilling prophesies" (Bem, 1981, p. 355). By the end of early childhood, gender roles are enforced not only by socialization from others but by self-socialization because children strive to conform to the gender expectations they perceive in the culture around them.

EMOTIONAL AND SOCIAL DEVELOPMENT: Parenting

Parents are a key part of children's lives everywhere, but how parents view their role and their approaches to discipline and punishment vary widely. First, we look at an influential model of parenting "styles" based on U.S. parenting, then at more culturally based views of parenting.

Parenting "Styles"

LO 6.18 Describe the four types of parenting "styles," and identify the cultural limitations of this model.

Have you heard the joke about the man who, before he had any children, had five theories about how they should be raised? Ten years later he had five children and no theories.

Well, jokes aside, most parents do have ideas about how best to raise children, even after they have had children for awhile (Harkness et al., 2015; Tamis-Lamonda et al., 2008). In research, the investigation of this topic has often involved the study of **parenting styles**, that is, the practices that parents exhibit in relation to their children and their beliefs about those practices. This research originated in the United States and has involved mainly U.S. children and their parents, although it has now been applied in some other countries as well.

For more than 50 years, U.S. scholars have engaged in research on this topic, and the results have been quite consistent (Bornstein & Bradley, 2014; Collins & Laursen, 2004; Maccoby & Martin, 1983). Virtually all of the prominent scholars who have studied parenting have described it in terms of two dimensions: demandingness and responsiveness (also known by other terms such as *control* and *warmth*). Parental **demandingness** is the degree to which parents set down rules and expectations for behavior and require their children to comply with them. Parental **responsiveness** is the degree to which parents are sensitive to their children's needs and express love, warmth, and concern for them.

Various scholars have combined these two dimensions to describe different kinds of parenting styles. For many years, the best known and most widely used conception of parenting styles was the one articulated by Diana Baumrind (1968, 1971, 1991a, 1991b). Her research on middle-class White U.S. families, along with the research of other scholars inspired by her ideas, has identified four distinct parenting styles (Collins & Laursen, 2004; Maccoby & Martin, 1983; Steinberg, 2000; see **Table 6.1**).

Authoritative parents are high in demandingness and high in responsiveness. They set clear rules and expectations for their children. Furthermore, they make clear what the consequences will be if their children do not comply, and they make those consequences stick if necessary. However, authoritative parents do not simply "lay down the law" and then enforce it rigidly. A distinctive feature of authoritative parents is that they *explain* the reasons for their rules and expectations to their children, and they willingly engage in discussion with their children over issues of discipline, sometimes leading to negotiation and compromise. For example, a child who wants to eat a whole bag of candy would not simply be told "No!" by an authoritative parent but something like, "No, it wouldn't be healthy and it would be bad for your teeth." Authoritative parents are also loving and warm toward their children, and they respond to what their children need and desire. This can be characterized as a democratic way of parenting.

Authoritarian parents are high in demandingness but low in responsiveness. They require obedience

parenting styles
practices that parents exhibit in relation to their children and their beliefs about those practices

demandingness
degree to which parents set down rules and expectations for behavior and require their children to comply with them

responsiveness
degree to which parents are sensitive to their children's needs and express love, warmth, and concern for them

authoritative parents
in classifications of parenting styles, parents who are high in demandingness and high in responsiveness

authoritarian parents
in classifications of parenting styles, parents who are high in demandingness but low in responsiveness

Table 6.1 Parenting Styles and the Two Dimensions of Parenting

		Demandingness	
		High	**Low**
Responsiveness	**High**	Authoritative	Permissive
	Low	Authoritarian	Disengaged

from their children, and they punish disobedience without compromise. None of the verbal give-and-take common with authoritative parents is allowed by authoritarian parents. They expect their commands to be followed without dispute or dissent. To continue with the candy example, the authoritarian parent would respond to the child's request for a bag of candy simply by saying "No!" with no explanation. Also, authoritarian parents show little in the way of love or warmth toward their children. Their demandingness takes place without responsiveness, in a way that shows little emotional attachment and may even be hostile. This style of parenting is strict ("it's my way or the highway").

Permissive parents are low in demandingness and high in responsiveness. They have few clear expectations for their children's behavior, and they rarely discipline them. Instead, their emphasis is on responsiveness. They believe that children need love that is truly "unconditional." They may see discipline and control as having the potential to damage their children's healthy tendencies for developing creativity and expressing themselves however they wish. They provide their children with love and warmth and give them a great deal of freedom to do as they please. This parenting style appears "friendly," and permissive parents may describe themselves as wanting to be friends with their children.

Disengaged parents are low in both demandingness and responsiveness. Their goal may be to minimize the amount of time and emotion they devote to parenting. Thus, they require little of their children and rarely bother to correct their behavior or place clear limits on what they are allowed to do. They also express little in the way of love or concern for their children. They may seem to have little emotional attachment to them.

THE EFFECTS OF PARENTING STYLES ON CHILDREN A great deal of research has been conducted in the United States on how parenting styles influence children's development. A summary of the results is shown in **Table 6.2**. In general, authoritative parenting is associated with the most favorable outcomes, at least by U.S. standards. Children who have authoritative parents tend to be independent, self-assured, creative, and socially skilled (Baumrind, 1991a, 1991b; Collins & Larsen, 2004; Steinberg, 2000; Williams et al., 2009). They also tend to do well in school and to get along well with their peers and with adults (Hastings et al., 2007; Spera, 2005). Authoritative parenting helps children develop characteristics such as optimism and self-regulation that in turn have positive effects on a wide range of behaviors (Jackson et al., 2005; Purdie et al., 2004).

All the other parenting styles are associated with some negative outcomes for U.S. children, although the type of negative outcome varies depending on the specific parenting style (Baumrind, 1991a, 1991b; Snyder et al., 2005). Children with authoritarian parents tend to be less self-assured, less creative, and less socially adept than other children. Boys with authoritarian parents are more often aggressive and unruly, whereas girls are more often anxious and unhappy (Bornstein & Bradley, 2014; Russell et al., 2003). Children with permissive parents tend to be immature and lack self-control. Because they lack self-control, they have difficulty getting along with peers and teachers (Linver et al., 2002). Children with disengaged parents also tend to be impulsive. Partly as a consequence of their impulsiveness, and partly because disengaged parents do little to monitor their activities, children with disengaged parents tend to have higher rates of behavior problems (Pelaez et al., 2008).

permissive parents
in classifications of parenting styles, parents who are low in demandingness and high in responsiveness

disengaged parents
in classifications of parenting styles, parents who are low in both demandingness and responsiveness

Table 6.2 Outcomes Associated With Parenting Styles in White Middle-Class Families

Authoritative	Authoritarian	Permissive	Disengaged
Independent	Dependent	Irresponsible	Impulsive
Creative	Passive	Conforming	Behavior problems
Self-assured	Conforming	Immature	Early sex, drugs
Socially skilled			

How does the idea of reciprocal effects complicate claims of the effects of parenting styles?

A MORE COMPLEX PICTURE OF PARENTING EFFECTS Although parents undoubtedly affect their children profoundly by their parenting, the process is not nearly as simple as the cause-and-effect model just described. Sometimes discussions of parenting make it sound as though Parenting Style A automatically and inevitably produces Child Type X. However, enough research has taken place by now to indicate that the relationship between parenting styles and children's development is considerably more complex than that (Bornstein & Bradley, 2014; Lamb & Lewis, 2005; Parke & Buriel, 2006). Not only are children affected by their parents, but parents are also affected by their children. This principle is referred to by scholars as **reciprocal or bidirectional effects** between parents and children (Combs-Ronto et al., 2009).

Recall our discussion of evocative genotype → environment effects in Chapter 2. Children are not like billiard balls that head predictably in the direction they are propelled. They have personalities and desires of their own that they bring to the parent–child relationship. Thus, children may evoke certain behaviors from their parents. An especially aggressive child may evoke authoritarian parenting; perhaps the parents find that authoritative explanations of the rules are simply ignored, and their responsiveness diminishes as a result of the child's repeated disobedience and disruptiveness. An especially mild-tempered child may evoke permissive parenting because parents may see no point in laying down specific rules for a child who has no inclination to do anything wrong anyway.

Does this research discredit the claim that parenting styles influence children? No, but it does modify it. Parents certainly have beliefs about what is best for their children, and they try to express those beliefs through their parenting behavior (Alwin, 1988; Harkness et al., 2015; Way et al., 2007). However, parents' actual behavior is affected not only by what they believe is best but also by how their children behave toward them and respond to their parenting. Being an authoritative parent is easier if your child responds to your demandingness and responsiveness with compliance and love, and not so easy if your love is rejected and your rules and the reasons you provide for them are rejected. Parents whose efforts to persuade their children through reasoning and discussion fall on deaf ears may be tempted either to demand compliance (and become more authoritarian) or to give up trying (and become permissive or disengaged).

PARENTING STYLES IN OTHER CULTURES So far we have looked at the parenting styles research based mainly on White middle-class U.S. families. What does research in other cultures indicate about parenting and its effects in early childhood?

One important observation is how rare the authoritative parenting style is in non-Western cultures (Bornstein & Bradley, 2014; Harkness et al., 2015). Remember, a distinctive feature of authoritative parents is that they do not rely on the authority of the parental role to ensure that children comply with their commands and instructions. They do not simply declare the rules and expect to be obeyed. On the contrary, authoritative parents explain the reasons for what they want children to do and engage in discussion over the guidelines for their children's behavior (Baumrind, 1971, 1991a; Steinberg & Levine, 1997).

Outside of the West, however, this is an extremely rare way of parenting. In traditional cultures, parents expect that their authority will be obeyed, without question and without requiring an explanation (LeVine et al., 2008). This is true not only in nearly all developing countries but also in developed countries outside the West, most notably Asian countries such as Japan and South Korea (Tseng, 2004; Zhang & Fuligni, 2006). Asian cultures have a tradition of **filial piety**, meaning that children are expected to respect, obey, and revere their parents throughout life (Lieber et al., 2004). The role of parent carries greater inherent authority than it does in the West. Parents are not

reciprocal or bidirectional effects

in relations between two persons, the principle that each of them affects the other

filial piety

belief that children should respect, obey, and revere their parents throughout life; common in Asian cultures

supposed to provide reasons why they should be respected and obeyed. The simple fact that they are parents and their children are children is viewed as sufficient justification for their authority.

In Latin American cultures, too, the authority of parents is viewed as paramount. The Latino cultural belief system places a premium on the idea of *respeto*, which emphasizes respect for and obedience to parents and elders, especially the father (Cabrera & Garcia-Coll, 2004; Halgunseth et al., 2006; Harwood et al. 2002). The role of the parent is considered to be enough to command authority, without requiring that the parents explain their rules to their children. Another pillar of Latino cultural beliefs is *familismo*, which emphasizes the love, closeness, and mutual obligations of Latino family life (Halgunseth et al., 2006; Harwood et al., 2002).

Does this mean that the typical parenting style in non-Western cultures is authoritarian? No, although sometimes scholars have come to this erroneous conclusion. It would be more accurate to state that the parenting-styles model is a cultural model, rooted in the U.S. majority culture, and does not apply well to most other cultures. Of course, children everywhere need to have parents or other caregivers provide care for them in early childhood and beyond, and across cultures parents provide some combination of warmth and control. However, "responsiveness" is a distinctly U.S. kind of warmth, emphasizing praise and physical affection, and "demandingness" is a distinctly U.S. kind of control, emphasizing explanation and negotiation rather than the assertion of parental authority. Other cultures have their own culturally based forms of warmth and control, but across cultures, warmth rarely takes the U.S. form of praise, and control rarely takes the U.S. form of explanation and negotiation (Matsumoto & Yoo, 2006; Miller, 2004; Wang & Tamis-Lamonda, 2003).

Even within U.S. society, the authoritative style is mainly dominant among White, middle-class families (Bornstein & Bradley, 2014). Most U.S. minority cultures, including African Americans, Latinos, and Asian Americans, have been classified by researchers as "authoritarian," but this is inaccurate and results from applying to them a model that was based on the White majority culture (Chao & Tseng, 2002). In her work with Chinese immigrants to the United States, Ruth Chao (1994, 1996) found that Chinese mothers had a training model of parenting their children. Based on the Chinese value of *chiao shun*, which incorporates the idea of training, Chinese mothers had high expectations for their children, and the relationships were characterized by high control, or demandingness, and low warmth. However, these children knew that their mothers had their best interests at heart. That is, there was a level of trust that the mothers truly cared and knew what was best for the children. Each minority culture has its own distinctive form of warmth, but all tend to emphasize obeying parental authority rather than encouraging explanation and negotiation. Hence the U.S. model of parenting styles cannot really be applied to them.

Within cultures, parenting varies depending on the personalities of the parents, their goals for their children, and the characteristics of the children that evoke particular parenting responses. Overall, however, the dominant approach to parenting in a culture reflects certain things about the underlying cultural beliefs, such as the value of interdependence versus independence and the status of parental authority over children (Giles-Sims & Lockhart, 2005; Harkness et al., 2015; Hulei et al., 2006). The cultural context of parenting is so crucial that what looks like the same parental behavior in two different cultures can have two different effects, as we will see in the next section.

In most cultures, parents expect to be respected and obeyed without justifying their actions. Here, a mother and daughter in Japan.

familismo

cultural belief among Latinos that emphasizes the love, closeness, and mutual obligations among family members

Discipline and Punishment

LO 6.19 Describe the main cultural variations in how parents discipline young children, and explain how cultural context influences children's responses to discipline.

In many cultures, early childhood is when issues of discipline for disapproved of behavior first arise. As we have seen, it is common for cultures to be indulgent of infants and toddlers because they are seen to be too young to exercise much judgment or self-control. However, by early childhood children become more capable of emotional and behavioral self-regulation, and when they disobey or defy the authority of others they are believed to have enough understanding to know what they were doing and to be responsible for the consequences. For this reason, early childhood is usually the age when children are first disciplined for not following expectations or not doing what is required of them.

CULTURAL VARIATIONS IN DISCIPLINE All cultures require children to learn and follow cultural rules and expectations, and all cultures have some system of discipline for misbehavior. However, cultures vary widely in the nature of the discipline, and the consequences of discipline vary depending on the cultural beliefs that underlie the approach.

In Western cultures the approach to discipline in early childhood tends to emphasize the authoritative style of explaining the consequences of misbehavior and the reasons for discipline (Huang et al., 2009; Tamis-Lamonda et al., 2008). ("Michael, if you don't stop banging that toy against the floor I'm going to take it away! Okay, now I'm going to take it away until you can learn to play with it nicely.") Western parents also tend to use a lot of praise for compliant and obedient behavior, which is notable because the use of praise is rare in other cultures (LeVine et al., 2008; Whiting & Edwards, 1988). Discipline for misbehavior may involve taking away privileges or a **time out**, in which the child is required to sit still in a designated place for a brief period, usually only a few minutes (Morawska & Sanders, 2011). Little research has been conducted on the effectiveness of the time out under normal family circumstances, but it has been shown to be effective with young children who have behavioral problems (Everett et al., 2007; Fabiano et al., 2004).

In addition to using time out, parenting researchers recommend (1) explaining the reasons for discipline; (2) being consistent so that the consequences will be predictable to the child (and hence avoidable); and (3) exercising discipline at the time of the misbehavior (not later on) so that the connection will be clear (Klass et al., 2008). One popular approach suggests that if a parent's request to a young child is ignored or disobeyed, the parent counts a warning: "One-two-*three*," and if the request is not obeyed by "three" the child is then put in time out, 1 minute for each year of their age (Phelan, 2010).

Other cultures have different approaches to discipline. Japan provides an interesting example of a culture where shame and withdrawal of love is the core of discipline in early childhood. *Amae* is a Japanese word that describes the close attachment between mother and child (Rothbaum et al., 2007). During infancy, amae takes the form of an emotionally indulgent and physically close relationship between the Japanese mother and her baby. However, in toddlerhood and early childhood, a new element, shame and withdrawal of love, is added. Japanese mothers rarely respond to their children's misbehavior with loud reprimands or physical punishment. Instead, they express disappointment and withdraw their love temporarily. The child feels shame, which is a powerful inducement not to disobey again.

This system of early childhood socialization seems to work well in Japan because it is part of the ecocultural package of intense closeness to the mother. Japanese children have

"Time out" is a popular discipline strategy among middle-class U.S. parents.

time out

disciplinary strategy in which the child is required to sit still in a designated place for a brief period

low rates of behavioral problems, and high rates of academic achievement (Takahashi & Takeuchi, 2007). They grow up to be Japanese adults who have low rates of crime and social problems and high levels of economic productivity, making Japan one of the most stable and economically successful societies in the world.

However, the same parental behaviors appear to have a different, more negative effect in Western countries, illustrating that aspects of the entire ecocultural setting need to be considered together, rather than picking and choosing a specific practice out of context. Among U.S. researchers, parenting that uses shame and withdrawal of love has been described using the term **psychological control** (Barber, 2002). This kind of parenting has been found in U.S. studies to be related to negative outcomes in early childhood and beyond, including anxious, withdrawn, and aggressive behavior, as well as problems with peers (Barber et al., 2005; Silk et al., 2003). In Finland, too, a longitudinal study that began in early childhood found psychological control to predict negative outcomes in later childhood and adolescence, especially when psychological control was combined with physical affection, as it is in amae (Aunola & Nurmi, 2004).

What explains this difference? Why does amae appear to work well in Japan but not in the West? It is difficult to say, since this question has not been researched directly. However, the answer may be some kind of interaction between the parents' behavior and the cultural belief system. In Japan, amae fits neatly into a larger system of cultural beliefs about duty and obligations to others, especially to family. In the West, psychological control contrasts and perhaps collides with cultural beliefs about the value of thinking and behaving independently. It may be this friction between the parental practices and the cultural beliefs that results in negative outcomes, not the parental practices in themselves.

PHYSICAL PUNISHMENT AND ITS CONSEQUENCES Research on physical punishment (also known as **corporal punishment**) suggests a similar kind of interaction between parenting practices and cultural beliefs. Physical punishment of young children is common in most parts of the world (Curran et al., 2001; Levine & New, 2008). This approach to punishment has a long history. Most adults in most countries around the world remember experiencing physical punishment as children. Although most countries still allow parents to spank their young children, nearly all outlaw beatings and other harsh forms of physical punishment, which the historical record shows to have been quite common until about 100 years ago (Straus & Donnelly, 1994).

Is physical punishment damaging to young children, or is it a form of instruction that teaches them to respect and obey adults? Here, as with amae, the answer appears to be different depending on the cultural context. Many studies in the United States and Europe have been conducted on physical punishment of young children, and these studies have found a correlation between physical punishment and a wide range of antisocial behaviors in children, including telling lies, fighting with peers, and disobeying parents (Alaggia & Vine, 2006; Kazdin & Benjet, 2003). Furthermore, several longitudinal studies have reported that physical punishment in early childhood increases the likelihood of bullying and delinquency in adolescence and aggressive behavior (including spousal abuse) in adulthood (Ferguson, 2013). On the basis of these studies, some scholars have concluded that physical punishment in early childhood increases children's compliance in the short run but damages their moral and mental health in the long run (Amato & Fowler, 2002; Gershoff, 2002). The American Academy of Pediatrics and the American Psychological Association have made strong statements cautioning against spanking, and these professional organizations recommend *never* spanking a child.

However, studies that cast a wider cultural net report more complicated findings. In one ethnographic study, Helen Morton (1996) describes corporal punishment and physical aggression as part of the socialization of Tongan children. In Tonga, children are hit as punishment for misbehavior to socialize them to mind adults. Tongan children become well-trained members of their culture. Similarly, other studies of traditional cultures have found that many of the parents in these cultures use physical punishment on

psychological control
parenting strategy that uses shame and withdrawal of love to influence children's behavior

corporal punishment
physical punishment of children

young children, and the children nevertheless grow up to be well-behaved, productive, mentally healthy adults (Levine et al., 2008; Whiting & Edwards, 1988).

Like the findings regarding amae, the findings on physical punishment show the crucial role of cultural context in how young children respond to their parents' behavior. This cultural context makes the meaning and the consequences of physical punishment different in different cultural settings.

CHILD ABUSE AND NEGLECT Although there are wide cultural variations in discipline and punishment of young children, today there is a widespread view across cultures that children should not be physically harmed and that parents have a responsibility to provide for their children's physical and emotional needs (UNICEF, 2011). However, there are all kinds of parents in the world, and in all cultures there are some who fail to meet these basic requirements. **Child maltreatment** includes both the abuse and neglect of children, specifically:

- *Physical abuse*, which entails causing physical harm to a child, through hitting, kicking, biting, burning, or shaking the child;
- *Emotional abuse*, including ridicule and humiliation as well as behavior causing emotional trauma to children, such as locking them in a dark closet;
- *Sexual abuse*, meaning any kind of sexual contact with a minor; and
- *Neglect*, which is failure to meet children's basic needs of food, shelter, clothing, medical attention, and supervision.

Most research on the maltreatment of young children has focused on physical abuse. A variety of risk factors for physical abuse have been identified, involving characteristics of children as well as characteristics of parents. Young children are at risk for physical abuse if they are temperamentally difficult or if they are unusually aggressive or active and hence more difficult for parents to control (Li et al., 2010). Parental risk factors for physical abuse of children include poverty, unemployment, and single motherhood, all of which contribute to stress, which may in turn trigger abuse (Geeraert et al., 2004; Zielinski, 2009). Stepfathers are more likely to be abusive than biological fathers are, and child abuse is correlated with spouse abuse, suggesting that the abuser has a problem with anger management and self-control that is expressed in multiple ways (Asawa et al., 2008). Abusive parents often view their children as somehow deserving the abuse because of disobedience or because they are "no good" and will not respond to anything else (Bugental & Happaney, 2004). Parents who abuse their children were abused by their own parents in about one third of cases (Cicchetti & Toth, 1998).

Physical abuse is destructive to young children in a wide variety of ways. It impairs emotional self-development, including self-regulation, empathy, and self-concept (Haugaard & Hazen, 2004). It is damaging to the development of friendships and social skills because abused children find it difficult to trust others (Elliott et al., 2005). It also interferes with school performance because abused children are often low in academic motivation and have behavior problems in the classroom (Boden et al., 2007). Furthermore, children who are abused are at risk for later emotional, social, and academic problems in adolescence and beyond (Fergusson et al., 2008; Herrenkohl et al., 2004).

What can be done to help abused children? In most cultures, there is some kind of system that removes children from their parents' care when the parents are abusive. In traditional cultures, the system tends to be informal. Children with abusive parents may go to live with relatives with whom they have a more positive, less conflictual relationship (LeVine et al., 2008). In Western countries, it is more often the formal legal system that intervenes in cases of child abuse. A state agency investigates reports of abuse, and if the report is verified the child is removed from the home.

The agency may then place the child in **foster care**, in which adults approved by the agency take over the care of the child (Pew Commission on Foster Care, 2004). In the United States, about one fourth of children in foster care are placed with relatives

child maltreatment
abuse or neglect of children, including physical, emotional, or sexual abuse

foster care
for maltreated children, approach in which adults approved by a state agency take over the care of the child

through the formal system (Child Welfare Information Gateway, 2013). In addition, three times as many children are estimated to live with nonparental relatives without the intervention of an agency, similar to the informal system of traditional cultures. Sometimes children in foster care return home after a period, sometimes they are adopted by their foster family, and sometimes they "age out" of foster care when they turn age 18 (Smith, 2011). Children in foster care are at high risk for academic, social, and behavioral problems, especially if they experience multiple foster-home placements (Crum, 2010; Plant & Siegel, 2008; Vig et al., 2005).

Another alternative is for children to live in a *group home* staffed by the state agency that oversees child abuse and neglect cases (Dunn et al., 2010). Group homes are usually a temporary alternative until the child can be placed in foster care or with relatives (DeSena et al., 2005).

Programs have also been developed to prevent child maltreatment. In the United States, one notable program is the *Nurse–Family Partnership* (NFP), with sites in 22 states (U.S. Department of Health and Human Services [DHHS], 2005c). In this program, expectant mothers who have many of the risk factors for abuse receive regular home visits by a trained nurse for 2 years. The nurse provides information and advice about how to handle crises, how to manage children's behavior without physical punishment, and how to access community agencies that provide services for families (Olds, 2010). In a 15-year follow-up comparing families who participated in the NFP to other families with similar risks, the NFP group showed a 79 percent reduction in child abuse and neglect (Eckenrode et al., 2001).

EMOTIONAL AND SOCIAL DEVELOPMENT: The Child's Expanding Social World

Across cultures, the social world expands considerably in early childhood. Infants and toddlers need a great deal of care, nurturance, and supervision. And, as we have seen in the previous two chapters, infants and toddlers are usually kept in close proximity to someone who will provide this for them, usually the mother, sometimes in collaboration with a father, grandmother, aunt, or older sibling. However, in early childhood, children move further into the wider world.

Childhood Social Stages and Children's Increasing Independence

LO 6.20 Explain the progression of increasing independence across the social stages of infancy through early childhood.

Anthropologists Beatrice Whiting and John Whiting worked with many graduate students to build upon Mead's (1935) classifications of young children. In Mead's classification, children in this stage were characterized as "yard children," in that they had some independence from their mothers, but they stayed near the home. The Whiting group systematically observed and conducted interviews about child development in six different cultures: Nyansongo, a Gusii community in Kenya; the Rajputs of Khalapur, India; Taira, an Okinawan village; the Mixtecans of Juxtlahuaca, Mexico; Tarong, an Ilocos barrio in the Philippines; and the New Englanders of Orchard Town, United States (Whiting, 1966; Whiting & Whiting, 1975). Called the *Six Cultures Study*, the Whitings and their students were the first to undertake such a broad study using the same methods. Analyzing data from the Six Cultures Study and extending to an

Across cultures, children are given more autonomy and more responsibility in the course of early childhood. Here, a girl washes dishes outside her Guatemalan home.

additional six places, Whiting and Edwards (1988) studied children ages 2 to 10 in 12 different places around the world, including Africa, Asia, South America, and the United States. Their goal was to see what kinds of similarities and differences exist in the social worlds of children across cultures.

They found substantial similarities worldwide in how cultures socialize young children and structure their social environments. From birth to age 6, there is a gradual lessening of dependence on the mother and a gradual move into the social orbit of peers and older children. Like infants, children up to age 4 receive a great deal of nurturance from mothers and from older children. However, more is required of 3- to 4-year-old children than of infants. Most children are expected to stop breast-feeding by age 3 and to have less bodily contact with the mother. Parents and older children expect children to be toilet trained by age 3, and to have basic manners (such as waiting their turn) and perform minor chores. Older children exercise more dominance over 3- and 4-year-old children than over children from birth to 2, because, older than age of 3, children are perceived as better able to understand and follow commands.

Five- and 6-year-old children are allowed more freedom than younger children. These 5- and 6-year-old children spent a lot more time out of the home than do younger children: 20 percent of the time they are outside of their immediate home area doing errands or playing. However, most cultures share a view that children cannot reason very well until about age 6, and this limits how far a child of this age can be away from home or supervision.

The cultures studied by the Whitings and their students and colleagues were mostly in developing countries, but many of the same patterns apply in developed countries. Across countries and cultures, the social world expands in early childhood to include more time and more interactions with siblings, peers, and friends. In developed countries the media world expands as well, as children not only watch TV as they have from infancy, but many also begin to play electronic games as well.

Siblings and "Only Children"

LO 6.21 Identify the most common features of sibling relationships worldwide, and describe how children with no siblings differ from other children.

A gap of 2 to 4 years between children is common worldwide, traditionally. Consequently, it is often in early childhood that children experience the birth of a younger sibling.

How do young children respond to a baby brother or sister? In their study of 12 cultures, Whiting and Edwards (1988) found a great deal of variability on most issues, but in all 12 cultures jealousy was recognized as a common response to the birth of a younger sibling. From the outset, young children expressed love as well as jealousy toward their younger siblings. Like people of other ages, they enjoyed doting on the lap child. More recent U.S. studies show this same pattern of ambivalence toward younger siblings. Aggressive and hostile behavior is common, but so is helping, sharing, and teaching (Kramer & Kowal, 2005; Martin & Ross, 2005; Natsuaki et al., 2009).

Ambivalence continues with age, when there is a younger sibling in early childhood and an older sibling in middle childhood. Middle-childhood siblings care for and teach their younger siblings, but also command and dominate them, and sometimes physically punish them (Howe & Recchia, 2009; Pike et al., 2005; Volling, 2003). Younger siblings admire their older siblings and model their behavior after them, trying to learn to do what their older siblings can do, although sometimes resenting their authority. But even conflict between siblings can have positive effects. Studies indicate that young children with older siblings possess more advanced theory of mind understanding than children who have no older sibling (McAlister & Peterson, 2007; Randell & Peterson, 2009). One explanation of this is that, as siblings argue, compete, and cooperate they learn better how to understand the thinking of others and accept that others have a point of view that may be different than their own.

What about children who have no siblings? This has become an increasingly common condition over the past half century, as birth rates have fallen worldwide. In the United States, about 20 percent of children have no siblings. In some parts of Europe and Asia birth rates are just 1.1 to 1.4 children per woman, meaning that there are more children who do not have a sibling than do have one (Population Reference Bureau, 2014). What is it like to be an **only child**?

Having siblings is a mixed blessing, and having no siblings has mixed effects as well. In general, "only children" fare at least as well as children with siblings (Brody, 2004). Their self-esteem, social maturity, and intelligence tend to be somewhat higher than children with siblings, perhaps because they have more interactions with adults (Dunn, 2004). However, in U.S. studies they are somewhat less successful in social relations with peers, perhaps because children with siblings gain peerlike practice in social relations (Kitzmann et al., 2002).

Only children have been especially common in China in recent decades. Beginning in 1978, in response to fears of overpopulation, the Chinese government instituted a "one-child policy," making it illegal for parents to have more than one child without special government approval. There were fears that this policy would create a generation of "little emperors and empresses" who were overindulged and selfish, but those fears appear to be unfounded. Like only children in the United States, only children in China demonstrate several advantages over children with siblings, including higher cognitive development, higher emotional security, and higher likeability (Jiao et al.,1996; Wang & Fong, 2009; Yang et al., 1995). Unlike their U.S. counterparts, Chinese only children show no deficits in social skills or peer acceptance (Hart et al., 2003). One unexpected benefit of the one-child policy is that girls, who in Chinese tradition have been less favored than boys, have more opportunities in education than they did when they had to compete with brothers for family resources (Fong, 2002). China has recently loosened its one-child policy because of concerns that if the birth rate remains low the population may become too heavily weighted toward older people who are no longer working.

Because of its "one-child" policy, China today has many children without siblings.

Peers and Friends

LO 6.22 Explain how the quality of friendships changes from toddlerhood to early childhood, and describe the role of play and aggression in young children's friendships.

Children in early childhood are more capable than toddlers of understanding and describing what a friendship entails. They regard a friend as someone you like and who likes you, and as someone who plays with you and shares toys with you (Hartup & Abecassis, 2004). By age 5 or 6, they also understand that friendship is characterized

only child

child who has no siblings

by mutual trust and support, and that a friend is someone you can rely on over time (Bagwell & Schmidt, 2013).

Before proceeding further, it is important to distinguish between friends and peers. Friends are people with whom you develop a valued, mutual relationship. **Peers** are persons who share some aspect of their status in common, such as age. So, in social science research on human development, a child's peers are the same-age children who are part of the daily environment, such as the other children in the child's class at school. Some of those children may become the child's friends, others may not; a child's friends are usually peers, but not all peers become friends.

Across cultures, relations with both peers and friends tend to become more segregated by gender in the course of early childhood. Boys tend to have other boys as their peers and friends, and the social world of girls is populated mostly by other females. However, cultures differ substantially in the mix of ages in peer groups. A striking difference in early childhood peer relations between traditional cultures and Western cultures is that in the West, mixed-age peer play groups are relatively rare. By age 3 or 4, most children are in some kind of preschool setting for at least part of their typical week, and preschool classes are grouped by age. In contrast, children in traditional cultures often play in mixed-age groups that may include children in toddlerhood, early childhood, and middle childhood (LeVine and New, 2008).

Two of the most researched topics concerning peers and friends in early childhood are play and aggression.

peers

persons who share some aspect of their status in common, such as age

PLAY IN EARLY CHILDHOOD There are several distinct types of play, including solitary play, parallel play, simple social play, and cooperative pretend play. From toddlerhood through early childhood, solitary play and parallel play decline somewhat while simple social play and cooperative pretend play increase (Hughes & Dunn, 2007). Cooperative pretend play becomes more complex in the course of early childhood, as children's imaginations bloom and they become more creative and adept at using symbols, for example using a stick to represent a sword and a blanket over two chairs to represent a castle (Dyer & Moneta, 2006). Like toddlers, most young children display a variety of types of play, engaging in cooperative play for awhile and then making a transition to solitary play or parallel play (Robinson et al., 2003). The video *Development of Play Styles in Early Childhood* provides more on this topic.

Watch   DEVELOPMENT OF PLAY STYLES IN EARLY CHILDHOOD

In the course of early childhood and beyond, children become more sex-segregated in their play (Gaskins, 2015). In the 12-cultures study by Whiting and Edwards (1988), across cultures children played in same-sex groups 30 to 40 percent of the time at ages 2 to 3, rising to more than 90 percent of the time by age 11.

U.S. studies report similar results (Fabes et al., 2003). In one observational study, the percent of time playing in same-sex groups was 45 percent for 4-year-old children and 73 percent for 6-year-old children (Martin & Fabes, 2001). Furthermore, numerous studies have found that boys generally engage in high-activity, aggressive, competitive, "rough-and-tumble" play in their groups, whereas girls' play tends to be quieter, more cooperative, and more likely to involve fantasy and role playing (Ruble et al., 2006).

Children vary in their levels of sociability from infancy onward, and by early childhood there are distinct differences among children in how successful they are at using the social skills required for play in a group setting. Preschool social life rewards the bold, and children who are temperamentally inhibited spend a lot of their preschool time watching others play without taking part themselves (Coplan et al., 2004; Rubin et al., 2002). However, for some children it simply takes time to become accustomed to the preschool social environment. The more preschool experience children have, the more successful they are at taking part in social play (Dyer & Moneta, 2006). Sometimes children observe other children's play as a prelude to entering the play themselves (Lindsey & Colwell, 2003). Also, some children simply enjoy playing by themselves. They may spend more time than others in solitary play, but this could be an indication of an unusually lively and creative imagination rather than a sign of being withdrawn or rejected (Coplan et al., 2004). There are also cultural differences in how shyness in early childhood is regarded by peers, as you will see in *Research Focus: Shyness in China and Canada: Cultural Interpretations*.

Research Focus: Shyness in China and Canada: Cultural Interpretations

In studies of young children in the West, shyness has long been associated with negative characteristics such as anxiety, insecurity, and social incompetence. Shy children have been found to experience problems in their relations with peers and to be prone to negative self-perceptions and depression. Shyness in young children has been viewed by Western researchers as a problem to be cured.

But what about in other cultural contexts? Xinyin Chen, a developmental psychologist who grew up in China and now lives in Canada, hypothesized that shyness would have a different meaning in the Chinese cultural context, and set out to compare the consequences of shyness among Chinese and Canadian children (Chen et al., 2006).

In one study conducted by Chen and his colleagues, 4-year-old children in China and Canada were invited into a laboratory setting in groups of four and observed in two 15-minute free-play interactions.

Shy children were identified as those who spent the most time in onlooker behavior (watching the activities of others) or unoccupied behavior (wandering around the room alone or sitting alone doing nothing). Through this process, 50 of 200 Chinese children and 45 of 180 Canadian children were classified as shy. Although the proportion of shy children to non-shy children was

identical in the two countries, the responses shy children received from their peers were very different. When shy Canadian children made attempts to interact with their peers, the peers often reacted negatively (for instance, saying "No!" or "I won't do it") and rarely reacted positively with encouragement and support.

In contrast, peers of shy children in China responded much more positively when shy children initiated contact, often inviting them to play or allowing them to join a game. Overall, peers in Canada tended to be antagonistic or nonresponsive toward shy children, whereas in China, peers of shy children were more often supportive and cooperative.

However, Chen and his colleagues have been conducting research in China for over 20 years now, and they have recorded striking shifts in the social implications of shyness for young Chinese children over that time. Recent decades have been a period of dramatic social change in China, as the country has moved rapidly from a state-controlled Communist economy to a free-market economy. This transition has resulted in changes in values as well, with a decline in the traditional Chinese collectivistic values of duty, respect, and obligation, and a rise in individualistic values of self-assertion and independence.

The change in values has been reflected in Chen's research on peers' responses to shy Chinese children. In the

1990 sample Chen studied, shyness was positively associated with a variety of favorable aspects of adjustment, including peer acceptance, leadership, and academic achievement. However, by the time Chen repeated the study in 2002, the correlation had flipped.

Now shyness was associated with negative adjustment, including peer rejection and depression. In just a 12-year period, the cultural meaning of shyness had reversed. As Chen observed, "the extensive change toward the capitalistic system in the economic reform and the introduction of Western ideologies may have led to the decline in the adaptive value of shyness."

Review Quiz:

1. Studies of young Chinese children in the 1990s and a decade later showed that over that time period:
   a. prevalence of shyness increased due to economic upheaval.
   b. prevalence of aggressiveness increased during the transition to a market economy.
   c. shyness became less culturally valued.
   d. aggressiveness among girls rose substantially.

Watch   RESEARCH FOCUS: SHYNESS IN CHINA AND CANADA: CULTURAL INTERPRETATIONS

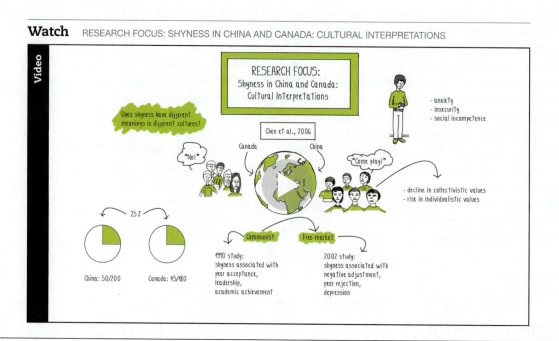

Play in early childhood is widespread across cultures, especially in the first years of this life stage (Gaskins, 2015). In one study comparing four cultural groups, in all four groups the 3-year-old children spent more time in play than in any other activity (Tudge et al., 2006). However, anthropologists have observed some cultures where play is rare even in early childhood, such as the Maya of Guatemala (Gaskins, 2000). In general, the more work parents have to do, the earlier they involve children in work and the less time children have for play (Rogoff, 2003). Nevertheless, in general, children in traditional cultures have some time for play. Often their play is structured and directed by the older children in the mixed-age peer group. Outside of the West, it is rare for children to play with adults (LeVine et al., 2008).

Sometimes children's play involves imitations of adult activity, such as going to the market (Rogoff, 2003; Roopnarine et al., 1994). Other times, play is purely for fun. For example, in India, young girls play a game that involves clapping hands in time to a song. They clap against each other's hands in a complex pattern as they sing, going faster and faster as the song proceeds. The song goes through 11 verses that describe a girl's likely course through life at each age, ending with turning into a spirit. In early childhood, girls learn first by observing and listening as the older girls play, then by gradually taking part in the clapping song themselves.

AGGRESSION Early childhood is an important time for the development of aggression. As young children move more into the world of peers, they encounter more competition for resources—toys, play companions, adult attention, the last cookie—and this competition sometimes leads to conflict and aggression (Rubin & Pepler, 2013).

Scholars distinguish between several different types of aggression (Underwood, 2003). **Instrumental aggression** is involved when a child wants something (toys, food, attention) and uses aggressive behavior or words to get it. A child may also exhibit signs of anger and intend to inflict pain or harm on others. This is known as **hostile aggression**. Instrumental and hostile aggression can each be expressed in several ways. *Physical aggression* includes hitting, kicking, pushing, or striking with an object. *Verbal aggression* is the use of words to hurt others, through yelling at them, calling them names, or hostile teasing. **Relational aggression** (or *social aggression*) may be direct or indirect and may involve damaging another person's relationships, reputation, or social status among peers through social exclusion and malicious gossip.

In most cultures, the proportion of same-gender play rises during early childhood. Here, young girls in India play a clapping game together.

Physical aggression among young children has been a target of a great deal of research. There is abundant evidence that physical aggression peaks in toddlerhood and early childhood (Alink et al., 2006). One top aggression researcher, Richard Tremblay (2002), summarized a wide range of longitudinal studies extending from infancy to adulthood, across many countries, and found a common pattern that physical aggression peaks at 24 to 42 months—the second year of toddlerhood and the first year of early childhood—then declines. Boys are consistently more physically aggressive than girls, in early childhood and throughout the life span.

However, there is a great deal of variation around this average pattern. Not all boys are aggressive in early childhood, and not all boys and girls show a decline in aggression after age 3. One national study in the United States followed the course of physical aggression in a longitudinal study of children from age 2 to 9 (NICHD Early Childhood Research Network, 2004). The researchers identified five different "trajectory groups" with regard to aggression. The largest group declined steeply in physical aggression from age 2 to 9. However, there were also two "low trajectory" groups that never showed much physical aggression, one "moderate trajectory" group that remained moderate, and one "high trajectory" group that remained high.

In general, individual differences in physical aggression remain stable across time. That is, children who rarely display physical aggression in early childhood are unlikely to display it in middle childhood and adolescence, and children who are especially aggressive in early childhood tend to be more aggressive than their peers in later periods as well (Brame et al., 2001; Lansford et al., 2006; Schaeffer et al., 2003; Vaillancourt et al., 2003). However, longitudinal studies show that parents who are especially patient, sensitive, and involved can reduce high aggression in early childhood to moderate aggression by middle childhood (NICHD Early Childhood Research Network, 2004; Rubin & Pepler, 2013). Early childhood is a crucial time for socializing physical aggression because when aggression is still high at the end of early childhood it is a strong predictor of later aggressive behavior in adolescence and adulthood (Loeber et al., 2005; Tremblay & Nagin, 2005).

Across cultures, aggression is frequently part of children's play in early and middle childhood, especially for boys (Edwards, 2005; Gaskins, 2015). Physical "rough-and-tumble" play such as wrestling is common among boys of the same age when they are brought together in school and playground settings (Scott & Panksepp, 2003). This aggressive play occurs in other mammals as well and is a way of establishing a dominance hierarchy (Hassett et al., 2008). Aggressive play establishes who is on top and who is not and in this way serves to avoid more serious aggression.

instrumental aggression
type of aggression when a child wants something and uses aggressive behavior or words to get it

hostile aggression
type of aggression that entails signs of anger and intent to inflict pain or harm on others

relational aggression
direct or indirect aggression and may involve damaging another person's relationships, reputation, or social status among peers

Physical aggression peaks in early childhood.

In contrast to physical aggression, verbal aggression rises across early childhood, at least in the Western countries where this research has been done (Dodge et al., 2006; Underwood, 2003). As children become more adept at using words, they grow capable of applying their verbal abilities to a wide range of purposes, including aggression. Also, verbal aggression becomes substituted for physical aggression across the years of early childhood as children learn that adults regard physical aggression toward peers as unacceptable and as children become more capable of restraining their physically aggressive impulses (Tremblay, 2000, 2002; Tremblay & Nagin, 2005).

Relational aggression also becomes more common in the course of early childhood (Crick et al., 2006). Like the increase in verbal aggression, the increase in relational aggression reflects children's growing cognitive and social understanding. They become more capable of understanding the complexities of social relationships and more aware of the ways that social weapons can be used to hurt others and gain social status. They learn that a punch on the shoulder does not hurt nearly as much, or last nearly as long, as the pain of being the only one not invited to a birthday party or being the subject of a nasty rumor (Murray-Close et al., 2007; Nelson et al., 2005). Verbal and relational aggression are slightly more common among girls than among boys in early childhood, but the differences are minor—much smaller than the gap between boys and girls in physical aggression (Underwood, 2003).

Media Use in Early Childhood

LO 6.23 Identify the rates and consequences of media use in early childhood.

Early childhood is a period when children's media world expands greatly, especially in developed countries. Many types of media use increase by early childhood (Lemish, 2007). Do you remember how old you were when you first started to watch TV? How about using a computer? Or playing a game on a handheld device? In 2011, a national sample of U.S. families were asked how old their children were when they first used different kinds of media in the household (Rideout, 2013). Results showed that:

- 89 percent had watched TV by 9 months
- 85 percent had watched DVDs or videotapes by 11 months
- 59 percent had used a computer by 3 ½ years
- 51 percent had played a game on a console by 3 years and 11 months
- 44 percent had played a game on a handheld device by 3 years and 11 months.

Total daily time devoted to media use is about 2 hours for U.S. children ages 2 to 8. The major types of media used in early childhood are television, electronic games, and recorded music.

THE NEGATIVE IMPACTS OF TELEVISION USE: VIOLENCE AND ADVERTISING
Television is popular with people all over the world, including young children. In early childhood, TV-viewing time per day varies from about 1 hour in the United States, Sweden, and Germany to about 3 hours in Hungary and Turkey (Hasebrink, 2007a; Rideout, 2013). In the United States, more than 40 percent of children ages 2 to 8 have a TV set in their bedroom (Rideout, 2013). The most popular shows among young children are the ones made especially for them, such as cartoons and educational shows like *Sesame Street* (Lemish, 2007; Rideout, 2013).

Although television is embraced everywhere for its entertainment value, many people have concerns about the effects of television, especially on children and especially with respect to violence. Content analyses have found that children's programs are even more violent than programs for adults. One study found that two thirds of all children's programs contained violence, and about half the violence took place in cartoons (Aikat, 2007). Violence was portrayed as funny about two thirds of the time, and in most cases the victims were not shown experiencing pain and the perpetrator of the violence was not punished.

What are the effects of witnessing so much TV violence on young children's development? More than five decades of research, including more than 300 studies using a variety of methods, has led to a strong consensus among scholars that watching TV violence increases children's aggression (Bushman & Chandler, 2007). The more aggressive children are, the more they like to watch TV violence, but TV violence inspires aggressive thoughts and behavior even in children who are not usually aggressive (Bushman & Huesmann, 2001). Experimental studies indicate that causation is involved, not just correlation. For example, in one early study, children in a preschool were randomly assigned to two groups (Steur et al., 1971). Over 11 days, one group watched violent cartoons, whereas the other group saw the same cartoons but with the violence removed. During playground observations following this 11-day experiment, children who had seen the violent cartoons were more likely than children in the nonviolent cartoon group to kick and hit their peers.

Young children ages 3 to 6 are believed to be especially vulnerable to the effects of TV violence (Bushman & Chandler, 2003). They are more likely than younger or older children to model their behavior after the behavior of others, including TV characters. Also, they are less likely than older children to have a clear understanding of the boundary between fantasy and reality, and so more likely to believe that what they witness on TV is real.

Another important effect of TV watching in early childhood concerns advertising. In the United States, the average child sees about 40,000 TV commercials each year, mostly for toys, cereal, candy, and fast food (Scheibe, 2007). Young children are especially susceptible to advertising because they are less aware of advertising intent than older children are. Most do not perceive a distinction between a program and an advertisement until about age 5 (Jennings, 2007). The more TV young children watch, the more they attempt to influence their parents to buy the advertised products (Valkenburg & Buijzen, 2007). Because most of the products children see advertised are unhealthy foods, concern has grown that TV advertising is one influence behind the growing international epidemic of obesity in children (Bergstrom, 2007a).

THE BENEFICIAL EFFECTS OF EDUCATIONAL TELEVISION TV has also been found to have some beneficial effects on young children. In recent decades, educational programs have been developed that are highly popular among young children. Perhaps most notable is the *Sesame Street* program, which is broadcast in 120 countries worldwide (Truglio, 2007). The content of the program is based on knowledge from developmental psychology of what will be most appealing to young children and most effective at teaching them the academic skills that will prepare them for school (Bergstrom, 2007b). Content is adapted to the culture in which the program is shown, for example addressing the stigma of AIDS in South Africa and promoting cross-cultural respect and understanding among children in the Middle East (Truglio, 2007).

Studies of *Sesame Street* and other programs have shown impressive positive effects on young children's development. In one study, viewing *Sesame Street* at ages 2 and 3 predicted higher scores at age 5 on tests of language development and math skills, even controlling for parents' education and income (Scantlin, 2007). In another study, children who viewed *Sesame Street* at age 5 were recontacted at ages 15 and 19 and were found to have higher grades in English, math, and science than children in the comparison group (Anderson et al., 2001). Studies of *Sesame Street* and other educational programs have shown the programs to have other positive effects as well, such as promoting imaginative play (Scantlin, 2007) and prosocial behavior such as cooperation (Bergstrom, 2007b).

Listening to recorded music is a common part of children's lives in developed countries.

ELECTRONIC GAMES AND MUSIC Although the focus of most media research concerning young children has been on television, other media are also important in their lives, notably electronic games and recorded music.

Television is now nearly universal, but playing electronic games usually depends on access to a computer, and computer access is much more variable across countries. In one international study, more than 60 percent of households in developed countries reported having a computer, but this percentage was much lower in other regions, including eastern Europe (25 percent), Latin America (about 10 percent), and Africa (about 5 percent) (Hasebrink, 2007b). In U.S. studies, 91 percent of 5- to 8-year-old children have used a computer, and average daily time playing electronic games is 9 minutes (Rideout, 2013).

Boys play electronic games more than girls do, overall, and the kinds of games they prefer differ, with boys preferring fighting and sports games and girls preferring adventure and learning games (Kubisch, 2007). These gender differences endure through childhood and adolescence, as we will see in later chapters. Electronic games can also be played on handheld devices and mobile phones, but access to these media tends to come in middle childhood and beyond.

Listening to recorded music is also part of the daily media diet of most children in developed countries. More than half of parents of young children report singing to or playing music for them each day (Kinnally, 2007). On average, children ages 2 to 8 listen to music for about 16 minutes per day. Children ages 3 to 5 listen mostly to children's songs, but by age 6 children pay more attention to popular music and start to recognize and prefer the latest "hit songs" of the day.

Music evokes a positive response even from infants, but early childhood is an especially important time for the development of responses to music (Kinnally, 2007). It is during early childhood that children first connect musical sounds with specific emotions, for example recognizing songs in major keys as happy and songs in minor keys as sad. By age 5, children show distinct preferences for music that is harmonious rather than dissonant and has a steady rather than erratic beat. There is little research on the effects of music on young children. Research on music's effects is concentrated on adolescence because of concerns about the effects of violent music on adolescent development, as we will see later in the book.

Summary: Emotional and Social Development

LO 6.15 Identify advances in emotional understanding and self-regulation during early childhood.

Early childhood is a key time for the development of emotional self-regulation because children improve at effortful control. Children also improve in their ability to understand the sources of others' emotions.

LO 6.16 Describe moral development in early childhood, including empathy, modeling, and morality as cultural learning.

The capacity for empathy increases in early childhood, which leads in turn to an increase in prosocial behavior. Children learn morality in part through modeling, that is, observing the behavior of others and its consequences. Early childhood is also a time when children begin to show a capacity for moral reasoning and demonstrate that they have learned the moral beliefs of their culture.

LO 6.17 Describe the roles that parents and peers play in gender socialization, and explain how gender schemas lead to self-socialization.

Children learn gender identity by age 2, but do not learn gender constancy until age 6 or 7. During early childhood they often become rigid in their views of gender roles. Parents are key agents of gender socialization, especially fathers, and conformity to gender roles is enforced by peers as well. Once young children possess gender schemas, they seek to maintain consistency between their schemas and their behavior, a process called *self-socialization*.

LO 6.18 Describe the four types of parenting "styles," and identify the cultural limitations of this model.

U.S. parenting research has emphasized the dimensions of demandingness and responsiveness, in combinations resulting in four categories of "parenting styles": authoritative, authoritarian, permissive, and disengaged. By U.S. standards, authoritative parenting is associated with the most favorable outcomes. The authoritative parenting style is rare in non-Western cultures because parents expect that their authority will be obeyed without question and without requiring an explanation.

LO 6.19 **Describe the main cultural variations in how parents discipline young children, and explain how cultural context influences children's responses to discipline.**

In Western cultures the approach to discipline in early childhood tends to emphasize the authoritative approach of explaining the consequences of misbehavior and the reasons for discipline, whereas outside of the West, the parental role has more authority and children are expected to obey. Physical punishment and "psychological control" have quite different effects on children depending on the cultural context.

LO 6.20 **Explain the progression of increasing independence across the social stages of infancy through early childhood.**

Children gradually decrease their dependence on others for care, and they increase independence and freedom as they develop physical, cognitive, and social skills.

LO 6.21 **Identify the most common features of sibling relationships worldwide, and describe how children with no siblings differ from other children.**

A combination of conflict along with helping and sharing between siblings is common worldwide in early childhood. "Only children" fare well compared to children with siblings.

LO 6.22 **Explain how the quality of friendships changes from toddlerhood to early childhood, and describe the role of play and aggression in young children's friendships.**

Children engage in cooperative pretend play more in early childhood than in toddlerhood. Physical aggression peaks in toddlerhood and the first year of early childhood, then declines as verbal aggression rises.

LO 6.23 **Identify the rates and consequences of media use in early childhood.**

In early childhood, TV-viewing time per day varies from about 1 to 3 hours across developed countries. Abundant evidence shows that violent television promotes aggressive behavior in young children. Early childhood is an especially important time for the development of responses to music because children learn to connect musical sounds with specific emotions.

Applying Your Knowledge as a Professional

The topics covered in this chapter apply to a wide variety of career professions. Watch these videos to learn how they apply to a paramedic and a dance instructor.

Watch   CAREER FOCUS: DANCE INSTRUCTOR

Sanoe Garcia
Dance Instructor

Chapter Quiz

1. Which of the following best describes the physical changes that take place during early childhood?

a. Both boys and girls gain more in weight than in height, but most add more muscle than fat.

b. Physical development occurs at a more rapid pace than it did in the first 3 years.

c. Girls are slightly taller and heavier than boys.

d. Cross-cultural comparisons have shown that only genetics play a role in individual differences in height and weight.

2. The limited memory for personal events and experiences before age 5 is probably as a result of incomplete myelination of the _____.

a. reticular formation

b. corpus callosum

c. cerebellum

d. hippocampus

3. The two most common types of nutritional deficiencies in developing countries are a lack of protein and _____.

a. marasmus

b. kwashiorkor

c. iron

d. calcium

4. Which of the following is true regarding illness and injury in early childhood?

a. Children become more vulnerable to health threats than they were in infancy.

b. Children eat more than they did in infancy or toddlerhood.

c. Children need less calcium than they did before.

d. Rates of injury and death from accidents are higher in developing countries than in developed countries.

5. How does motor development change between ages 3 and 6?

a. Children's fine motor skills become refined, but their gross motor skills remain the same as they were in toddlerhood.

b. Children's fine motor skills have been found to develop at the same rate all over the world.

c. Children develop the same motor skills at the same pace, regardless of gender.

d. Fine motor skill development allows children to become more independent by doing things, such as putting on a coat and using a knife to cut soft food.

6. Which of the following statements about handedness is most accurate?

a. The prevalence of left-handedness in some African countries is as low as 1 percent because using the left hand is suppressed.

b. Children first develop this tendency during the preschool years.

c. Children who are left-handed are often praised for their uniqueness in non-Western cultures.

d. There is no genetic component to handedness; it is based purely on one's environment.

7. A 5-year-old child draws a yellow sun in the upper corner of her paper complete with a smiley face and sunglasses. This is an example of _____.

a. sensorimotor thought

b. animism

c. gross motor skill refinement

d. centered thinking

8. Changes in executive function in early childhood include:

a. increases in attention but decreases in the speed of working memory

b. increases in working memory but decreases in attention

c. an increasing ability to self-regulate both cognitive and emotional processes

d. failing false-belief tests

9. Which of the following is true regarding theory of mind?

a. Children show a decrease in this ability from 4 to 6 years of age because they are becoming more independent.

b. It develops the same way in all cultures with spoken language.

c. It begins to develop, in rudimentary form, sometime in infancy.

d. A child who demonstrates theory of mind is not yet able to think about thinking.

10. Cultural learning skills, such as learning to set the table in a developed country or to help prepare food in a traditional culture, _____.

a. develop as part of a social and cultural process, according to Vygotsky

b. must be learned in the sensorimotor stage first or they never fully develop

c. cannot be appropriately acquired until early adolescence

d. usually develop best if they take place in a formal setting

11. As a parent of a 3-year-old child, you have visited several preschool programs to determine the one that will provide the highest-quality experience. Which of the following should be important in your decision about which preschool to pick, according to research?

a. The presence of formal lesson plans rather than play materials

b. Formal classrooms where the teacher sits in front and answers questions

c. No more than 10 students per teacher

d. A strong emphasis on rote learning

12. In Japan, _____.

a. learning academic skills is the number one goal of having children attend preschool

b. preschool is mainly a time for learning social skills

c. parents and preschool teachers list the same top reasons for young children to attend preschool as do their counterparts in the United States

d. individuality is stressed from the time children enter preschool as a way to encourage children to reach their full potential

13. A consistent pattern in early intervention programs such as Head Start is that the early gains in IQ and achievement _____.

   a. fade within 2 or 3 years of entering elementary school

   b. continue to increase throughout middle school

   c. continue but only for females

   d. continue throughout the life span

14. Young children's use of grammar _____.

   a. is entirely dependent on formal instruction in preschool

   b. develops more slowly in traditional cultures

   c. develops simply by hearing and using the language in daily interactions

   d. is mostly incorrect until age 6

15. When a 4-year-old child uses infant-directed speech when talking to her neighbor's new baby, this demonstrates _____.

   a. sensitive period   **c.** classification

   b. fast mapping   **d.** pragmatics

16. A key reason why emotional outbursts decline in early childhood is that children _____.

   a. learn strategies for regulating their emotions, in a practice known as *effortful control*

   b. have a more sophisticated theory of mind at this age

   c. at this age are no longer at risk for externalizing problems

   d. have learned the skill of over-controlling their emotions

17. Which of the following statements accurately describes moral development in early childhood?

   a. Children at this age are not yet able to experience empathy.

   b. Socio-emotional emotions such as shame and pride first appear.

   c. Perspective taking and being able to understand how others think and feel make children more empathic at this age.

   d. Young children inherently know the rules and expectations of their culture without needing to be taught.

18. The process by which people seek to maintain consistency between their gender schemas and their behavior is referred to as _____.

   a. gender identity   **c.** self-socialization

   b. gender constancy   **d.** self-regulation

19. Research on parenting has found that _____.

   a. the two main dimensions of parenting are demandingness and strictness

   b. children of permissive parents tend to do better in school than children of other parenting styles because they learn to think for themselves

   c. there are bidirectional effects between parents and their children

   d. the outcomes for children of authoritative parents are virtually identical to outcomes for children of permissive parents

20. Which of the following is the most accurate statement based on existing research?

   a. The typical parenting style in non-Western cultures is authoritarian.

   b. The U.S. model of parenting does not apply well to most other cultures.

   c. Providing explanations to their children is most common among non-Western parents who spend more time with their children than do U.S. parents.

   d. Permissive parenting would be most likely in cultures that have a tradition of filial piety.

21. The use of shame as a form of discipline _____.

   a. has resulted in positive outcomes in both the United States and Finland

   b. is referred to as psychological control by U.S. researchers

   c. is associated with high rates of behavior problems in Japanese children

   d. is universally accepted as the best method of discipline because it does not include physical punishment

22. Which of the following is false regarding stages of development?

   a. Older children exhibit more dominance over children who are two years old because very young children are easy to control.

   b. Children gradually take on more responsibility with household chores as they develop.

   c. Sibling caretaking is more prevalent in developing countries than in developed countries.

   d. In many cultures, children are given increased freedom from about the age of five or six.

23. Which of the following is true regarding siblings?

   a. A gap of 4 to 8 years between children is common in many cultures across the world.

   b. "Only children" are maladjusted, meaning they are more prone to depressive behavior disorders.

   c. Jealousy is a common response to the birth of a younger sibling across cultures.

   d. Research has shown that young children with older siblings have a less advanced theory of mind than those who are only children.

24. If you were a researcher observing play among 5-year-old children in the United States, what would you be most likely to observe?

   a. Boys playing with children from other kindergarten classes, rather than older boys

   b. Girls playing kickball with the boys (with the girls serving as referees to make sure the boys follow the rules)

   c. Boys engaging in cooperative, fantasy play

   d. The boys challenging the girls to a wrestling match

25. Watching TV during early childhood _____.

   a. has not been associated with any positive effects on development

   b. is a popular leisure activity all over the world

   c. has been correlated with aggressive thoughts and behaviors, but only among males who were already extremely aggressive before viewing

   d. has not been studied experimentally, and therefore no conclusions about causation can be made

Chapter 7
Middle Childhood

ACROSS ECOCULTURAL SETTINGS AROUND THE WORLD, THE TRANSITION FROM EARLY CHILDHOOD TO MIDDLE CHILDHOOD IS RECOGNIZED AS AN IMPORTANT SHIFT IN CHILDREN'S DEVELOPMENT, WHEN THEY BECOME CAPABLE OF GREATER COGNITIVE CHALLENGES AND PERSONAL RESPONSIBILITY (SAMEROFF & HAITH, 1996). In developing countries, middle childhood is often the age when children are first given important family duties, such as taking care of younger siblings, buying or selling goods, maintaining a fire, or caring for domestic animals (Gaskins, 2015; Weisner, 1996). According to Roy D'Andrade (1987), middle childhood is when children first show a grasp of **cultural models**, which are cognitive structures pertaining to common activities, for example buying something at the market, herding cattle, taking care of an infant, making bread, or delivering a message to a relative's house. Children in both developed and developing countries begin formal schooling in middle childhood, which includes cultural models of "listen to the teacher," "wait your turn," and "do your homework."

Children begin to grasp cultural models as early as toddlerhood, but during middle childhood their understanding of cultural models acquires greater complexity, so that they become capable of taking on a much broader range of tasks (Gaskins, 2015; Weisner, 1996). Children in middle childhood express an industriousness that makes them want to learn and take on new tasks.

Here as elsewhere in the human life span, how we experience a given stage of life depends greatly on cultural context. Children in all cultures become more capable of useful work in middle childhood, but the nature of their work varies greatly. For many children throughout human history it has been mainly farm work—tending the fields, herding the cows, and feeding the chickens. For today's children, it might be schoolwork or household work in developed countries, and any of a wide range of work in developing countries, from household work to factory work to feeding domestic animals. In this chapter we explore a wide range of cultural variations in children's experiences of middle childhood.

Watch CHAPTER INTRODUCTION: MIDDLE CHILDHOOD

Section 1 Physical Development

Learning Objectives

7.1 Identify the changes in physical and sensory development that take place during middle childhood.

7.2 Explain how motor development advances in middle childhood and how these advancements are related to new skills and participation in games and sports.

7.3 Describe the negative effects of both malnutrition and obesity on development, and identify the causes of obesity.

7.4 Explain why rates of illness and injury are relatively low in middle childhood, and why rates of asthma have risen.

PHYSICAL DEVELOPMENT: Growth in Middle Childhood

Middle childhood growth is not as rapid as at previous ages, but children continue to add height and weight. Some children become nearsighted during these years and need to start wearing glasses. Children's skills in motor development improve as they become more coordinated and gain strength.

cultural models

cognitive structures pertaining to common cultural activities

Middle childhood is the time of life when people are most likely to be slim.

Physical Growth and Sensory Development

LO 7.1 **Identify the changes in physical and sensory development that take place during middle childhood.**

In middle childhood, physical growth continues at a slow but steady pace, about 2 to 3 inches (5–8 cm) per year in height and about 5 to 7 pounds (2½–3 kg) per year in weight. On average, boys continue to be slightly taller and to weigh slightly more than girls. For both boys and girls, middle childhood is the time of life when they are mostly likely to be slim. Boys continue to have somewhat more muscle than girls do in middle childhood, and girls continue to have somewhat more body fat, so the average boy is stronger than the average girl. However, both boys and girls grow stronger during this stage. For example, the average 10-year-old child can throw a ball twice as far as the average 6-year-old child. Children run faster and longer, too, over the course of middle childhood, as lung capacity expands (Malina et al., 2004).

From age 6 to 12, children lose all 20 of their "primary teeth" and new, permanent teeth replace them. The two top front teeth are usually the first to go.

The permanent teeth are adult-sized teeth that do not grow much once they come in, giving children in middle childhood a toothy smile that sometimes looks a little too big for their mouths.

Sight and hearing both change in middle childhood, hearing usually for the better and sight more likely for the worse. Hearing often improves because the tube in the inner ear that is the site of ear infections in toddlerhood and early childhood has now matured and is longer and narrower than it was before (Bluestone & Klein, 2007). This structural change makes it less likely for fluid-containing bacteria to flow from the mouth to the ear, which in turn makes inner ear infections less likely.

With regard to sight, the incidence of **myopia**, also known as being *nearsighted*, rises sharply in middle childhood. This is a problem that is more likely to occur in developed countries than in developing countries. The more children read, write, and use computers, the more likely they are to develop myopia (Feldkamper & Schaeffel, 2003; Saw et al., 2002). Consequently, rates of myopia are highest in the developed countries where children are most likely to have access to books and computers. Myopia is also partly genetic because monozygotic (MZ) twins have a higher concordance rate than dizygotic (DZ) twins do (Pacella et al., 1999). About one fourth of children in developed countries need glasses by the end of middle childhood (Mutti et al., 2002).

Motor Development

LO 7.2   **Explain how motor development advances in middle childhood and how these advancements are related to new skills and participation in games and sports.**

Children advance in both gross and fine motor development during middle childhood, nearly reaching maturity in their fine motor abilities. Children become stronger and more agile, and as their gross motor skills develop, they spend more of their days in active play and organized sports. They also become capable of complex fine motor activities such as writing.

GROSS MOTOR DEVELOPMENT AND PHYSICAL ACTIVITY Watch a group of children on the playground of an elementary school, and you will see lots of activity. In one corner, a group of girls practices a dance routine one of them has learned from watching a TV show. In another, boys play four square, bouncing a ball into each other's square and attempting to defend their own by knocking the ball to someone else's square. In the middle, a group of boys and girls play tag, the perennial favorite.

In a variety of ways, gross motor development advances from early to middle childhood. Children's *balance* improves, allowing them to stay steady on a bike without training wheels or walk on a board across a river. They become *stronger*, so that they can jump higher and throw a ball farther. Their *coordination* advances so that they can perform movements in activities such as swimming and skating that require the synchronization of different body parts. They have greater *agility* so that they can move more quickly and precisely, for example when changing directions while playing soccer. Finally, their *reaction time* becomes faster, allowing them to respond rapidly to changing information, for example when hitting a tennis ball over the net or when catching or hitting a baseball (Kail, 2003). Increasing myelination of the *corpus callosum* connecting the two hemispheres of the brain accelerates reaction time in middle childhood for both gross motor and fine motor tasks (Roeder et al., 2008). Structures in the prefrontal cortex that control attention and cognition undergo significant changes in middle childhood (Posner & Rothbart, 2007), and these structures are important because they are used in motor activity as well. The video *Gross Motor Development in Middle Childhood* on the next page shows examples of these advances.

myopia

visual condition of being unable to see distant objects clearly; also known as being *nearsighted*

Watch   GROSS MOTOR DEVELOPMENT IN MIDDLE CHILDHOOD

Middle childhood is when children are most likely to be involved in organized sports.

As their gross motor development advances, children can enjoy a wide range of games and sports. All over the world, middle childhood is a time of playing physically active games with siblings and friends, from tag and hide-and-seek to soccer, cricket, baseball, and basketball. Most of their play is informal and takes place on the street or in a park or in the school yard when a few kids gather and decide to start a game (Kirchner, 2000). However, middle childhood is also the time when children are most likely to be involved in organized sports. For example, Little League baseball is played in 75 countries around the world during the middle childhood years. In the United States, 66 percent of boys and 52 percent of girls are involved in organized sports at least once between the ages of 5 and 18 (Statistic Brain, 2014). Although boys are slightly more likely than girls to play on sports teams in middle childhood, the rate of participation among girls has risen worldwide in recent decades, especially in sports such as soccer, swimming, gymnastics, and basketball.

Nevertheless, in the view of public health advocates, children do not get nearly as much gross motor activity as they should, leading to high rates of obesity, as we will see shortly. Middle childhood may be a time of great advancements in gross motor abilities, but physically active games and sports compete today with the electronic allurements of TV and computer games (Anderson & Butcher, 2006). In some places, schools are less likely than in the past to be a setting for physical activity. Physical activity is a domain where it is easy to see how socioeconomic status (SES) affects engagement in particular activity settings: In schools in lower SES areas, and for children in lower SES families, access to sports and other recreational activities may be limited. In the United States, the percentage of children involved in daily "physical education" programs during middle childhood decreased from 80 percent in 1969 to just 8 percent by 2005 (Centers for Disease Control and Prevention [CDC], 2006a). Health authorities recommend 60 minutes of physical activity a day for children ages 6 to 17, but few U.S. children get that much (see **http://www.cdc.gov/physicalactivity/everyone/guidelines/index.html**).

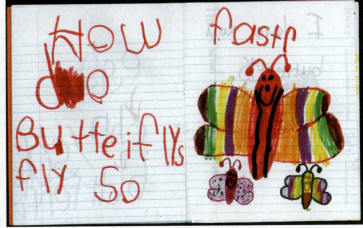

Figure 7.1 Change in Drawing Abilities from Early to Middle Childhood

Drawings become more realistic as fine motor development advances during middle childhood. Here are drawings that Jeff's daughter, Paris, made at ages 3 *(left)*, 5 *(right)*, and 7 *(bottom)*.

FINE MOTOR DEVELOPMENT Fine motor development also makes great advances from early childhood to middle childhood. Not many 3- or 4-year-old children can tie their shoes successfully, but nearly all 8- to 9-year-old children can. In Asian cultures, only about half of 4-year-old children can use chopsticks well enough to eat with them, but for children 6 years old and up it comes easily (Wong et al., 2002). In many developing countries, children become valuable as factory workers in middle childhood because of their abilities to perform intricate fine motor tasks such as weaving rugs (International Labor Organization [ILO], 2013).

Across cultures, advances in fine motor development are especially evident in two areas, drawing and writing. In early childhood, drawing skills are limited to crude depictions of two-dimensional figures. However, in the course of middle childhood children learn to indicate three-dimensional depth by overlapping objects and making near objects smaller than distant ones (Braine et al., 1993). They also learn to draw objects in greater detail and to adjust the size and relation of objects in a drawing so that they fit together into one coherent whole (see **Figure 7.1**; Case & Okamoto, 1996).

With regard to writing, in early childhood most children learn to write a few letters and numbers in rough form. In middle childhood, their skills greatly advance (Berninger et al., 2006). Even by age 6 most children are able to write the letters of the alphabet, their own names, and numbers from 1 to 10. In the course of the next several years, as their fine motor abilities develop, they are able to make their letters smaller and neater with more consistent height and spacing. By age 8 or 9 most children can learn to write in cursive. By the end of middle childhood their fine motor abilities have nearly reached adult maturity, whereas gross motor development will continue to advance for many years to come.

PHYSICAL DEVELOPMENT:
Health Issues

Middle childhood is an exceptionally healthy time of life. In this life stage, children become less vulnerable to the effects of malnutrition, and it is the time of life when they are least likely to be obese. However, obesity has become more prevalent in recent decades in developed countries, even in middle childhood. Asthma is also a health concern that impacts many children.

Malnutrition and Obesity

LO 7.3 Describe the negative effects of both malnutrition and obesity on development, and identify the causes of obesity.

By middle childhood, children have grown large enough that they are less vulnerable to the effects of malnutrition than they were previously. Even if they are deprived of food for a period of time, their bodies have enough resources to weather the deprivation without the effects being as severe as in prior life stages. Nevertheless, malnutrition can have enduring negative effects in middle childhood. Obesity also becomes a problem for many children in middle childhood, especially those in developed countries.

MALNUTRITION As we have seen in previous chapters, malnutrition in early development often results in illness, disease, or death. In middle childhood, bodies are stronger and more resilient, and immune systems are better developed. Nevertheless, malnutrition has effects in middle childhood as well. Even for children who survive early malnutrition, the damage to their physical and cognitive development accumulates by middle childhood (Liu et al., 2003).

A longitudinal study in Guatemala showed how nutrition in the early years contributes to cognitive and social functioning in middle childhood (Barrett & Frank, 1987). Children who were classified in early childhood as having "high nutrient levels" were more likely than children with "low nutrient levels" to explore new environments in middle childhood and to persist in a frustrating situation. They were also more energetic, less anxious, and showed more positive emotion. A more recent study, in Ghana, reported similar results, with children who experienced mild-to-moderate malnutrition in their early years demonstrating lower levels of cognitive development in middle childhood on standardized tests and in teacher ratings, compared to children who were not malnourished (Appoh & Krekling, 2004). The malnourished children were also more likely to be rated by teachers as anxious, sad, and withdrawn (Appoh, 2004).

Other studies in other countries have found similar results, with better-nourished children scoring higher than malnourished children on a wide range of cognitive and social measures in middle childhood (Grigorenko, 2003; Kitsao-Wekulo et al., 2013). However, there is a consensus that the sensitive period for long-term effects of malnutrition is from the second trimester of pregnancy through age 3 (Galler et al., 2005). Malnutrition that begins after age 3 does not appear to result in permanent cognitive or behavioral deficits.

body mass index (BMI)

measure of the ratio of weight to height

overweight

in children, defined as having a BMI higher than the 85th percentile for age

obesity

in children, defined as having a BMI higher than the 95th percentile for age

OBESITY Many children in developed countries have a different kind of nutritional problem: not too few calories but too many. Of all age groups in the life span, 6- to 10-year-old children have the lowest **body mass index (BMI)**, a measure of the ratio of weight to height (Gillaume & Lissau, 2002). Yet childhood rates of *overweight* and *obesity* have risen sharply worldwide in recent decades. **Figure 7.2** shows the increase in childhood obesity within the United States since the 1970s. Unlike the use of BMI figures for adults, there is no BMI cutoff for children. Instead, overweight and obesity are relative to the age group. For children, **overweight** means having a BMI more than the 85th percentile for age; **obesity** is a BMI higher than the 95th percentile for age (CDC, 2015). Across countries, rates of overweight and obesity are highest in the most affluent regions (North America

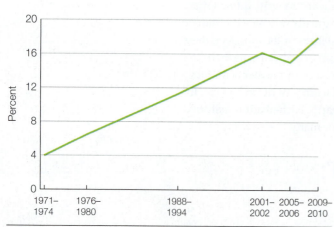

Figure 7.2 The Rise in Childhood Obesity, United States, Children Ages 6–11

SOURCE: Based on Fryar et al. (2012).

and Europe) and lowest in the poorest regions (Africa and Southeast Asia) (Wang & Lobstein, 2006). Rates across the United States are higher than in most other developed countries and are especially high in the least affluent ethnic minority groups, including African Americans and Latinos, as shown in **Figure 7.3** (Ogden et al., 2014).

A variety of changes have contributed to the rise in childhood obesity (Ogden et al., 2014). Most important is the change in diets. Over recent decades people have become less likely to prepare meals at home and more likely to buy meals away from home, especially "fast foods" such as hamburgers, french fries, and pizza that are high in fat content, and then they wash it down with soft drinks high in sugar content. This change reflects other social changes: Parents are less likely to prepare meals at home because they are more likely than in the past to be single parents or to be part of a dual-earner couple. Rates of overweight and obesity are rising in the populations of developing countries in part because their diets are becoming more like the diets of people in developed countries (Gu et al., 2005; Popkin, 2010).

Another contributor is television. Most children in most developed countries watch at least 2 hours of television a day (Rideout, 2013). In a longitudinal study that followed a sample of U.S. children from ages 4 to 11, TV watching predicted gains in body fat (Proctor et al., 2003). Specifically, children who watched at least 3 hours of TV a day gained 40 percent more body fat over the course of the study than children who watched less than 1½ hours a day. Other studies have shown that the more time children watch TV the less time they spend in physical exercise (Institute of Medicine of the National Academies, 2005; Williams, 2005). Watching TV also exposes children to numerous advertisements for high-fat, high-sugar foods, which they then lobby their parents to buy (Kelly et al., 2010). Rates of overweight and obesity are especially high among African American and Latino children in part because those are also the children that tend to watch the most TV per day (Rideout, 2013). The allure of the Internet and electronic games gives children additional reasons to stay inside rather than getting outside and playing active physical games (Anderson & Butcher, 2006).

Genetics also make a contribution to obesity. Concordance rates for obesity are higher among MZ twins than DZ twins. Adopted children tend to have BMIs that are closer to their biological parents than to their adoptive parents (Whitaker et al., 1997). Research has even identified a specific gene, called *FTO*, that sharply increases children's risk for obesity (Frayling et al., 2007). However, genetics cannot explain recent rises in obesity rates. Genetics provide only a risk for overweight and obesity, not a definite destiny.

A compelling demonstration of this comes from a naturalistic study of the Pima Indians in Arizona and Mexico (Gladwell, 1998). The Pima of Mexico live in a remote region and still maintain their traditional ways, including a traditional cultural diet that is high in vegetables and low in fats and sugars. In contrast, the Pima of Arizona have changed in recent decades and their diets have become more like the U.S. mainstream. Consequently, they have an average BMI that is 50 percent higher than their counterparts in Mexico, even though the two groups are similar genetically.

Obesity has both social and physical consequences for children. Being obese increases the likelihood that a child will be socially excluded and the object of ridicule by peers (Janssen et al., 2004; Puhl et al., 2010). Other children tend to associate obesity with undesirable traits such as being lazy, sloppy, ugly, and stupid

Figure 7.3 Childhood Obesity Rates in the United States, by Ethnicity

SOURCE: Based on Ogden et al. (2014).

Rates of obesity are rising in developing countries as diets become more like those in the developed world. This photo was taken in Mexico, which has one of the highest child obesity rates in the world.

(Tiggemann & Anesbury, 2000). By middle childhood obesity is a risk factor for a variety of emotional and behavioral problems (Puhl et al., 2010).

Physically, the consequences of obesity are equally serious. Even in middle childhood, obesity can result in diabetes, which can eventually lead to problems such as blindness, kidney failure, and stroke (Hannon et al., 2005; Ramchamdani, 2005). Obesity also proves hard to shake from childhood to adulthood. About 80 percent of obese children remain overweight as adults (Ogden et al., 2014; Oken & Lightdale, 2000). For adults, the range of health problems resulting from obesity is even greater—including high blood pressure, heart attack, and cancer—and more likely to be fatal (Ng et al., 2014).

What can be done to reverse the sharp increase in childhood obesity? One step is recognizing the problem. Perhaps because obese children tend to have obese parents, studies indicate that fewer than half of parents of obese children view their children as overweight (Jeffrey, 2004; Young-Hyman et al., 2003). Public policies have begun to address the problem of childhood obesity. In the United States, school lunches have been notoriously unhealthy for decades, but national standards have been recently revised to provide healthier school lunches that are lower in fats and sugars (Jalonick, 2010).

CRITICAL THINKING QUESTION

Why do you think overweight and obesity are most common among low-income U.S. ethnic groups even though, internationally, overweight and obesity are highest in the highest-income countries?

Illness and Injuries

LO 7.4 Explain why rates of illness and injury are relatively low in middle childhood, and why rates of asthma have risen.

Middle childhood is in many ways the safest, healthiest time of life. In both developed countries and developing countries, death rates are lower during middle childhood than at any other period of the life span (Hyder & Lunnen, 2009; National Center for Health Statistics [NCHS], 2009). In developed countries, by middle childhood nearly all children have been vaccinated against the diseases that may have been fatal in previous eras, such as smallpox, typhus, and diphtheria. In developing countries, an increasing proportion of children receive vaccinations in infancy, toddlerhood, and early childhood (World Health Organization [WHO], 2010c). Even children who do not receive vaccinations are less susceptible to fatal diseases in middle childhood than they were prior in their development. Their natural immune systems have become stronger, and their bodies are bigger, stronger, and more resilient.

In developed countries, even rates of minor illnesses have declined in middle childhood in recent decades because of public health policies. Over time, food production has become cleaner and safer, and food content more closely regulated by government agencies. The air and water have become cleaner in developed countries as a result of laws and restrictions by governments. For example, according to national U.S. studies, in 1978 nearly 30 percent of children ages 5 to 10 had dangerously elevated levels of lead in their blood, which can cause brain damage; by 2001, the rate had fallen to 1 percent (Centers for Disease Control and Prevention [CDC], 2005). This decline reflects government policies that eliminated lead from gasoline and household paint.

One exception to this trend toward healthier development in middle childhood is **asthma**, a chronic illness of the lungs characterized by wheezing, coughing, and shortness of breath. A person with asthma has periodic "asthma attacks" in which breathing is especially difficult (Israel, 2005). An asthma attack can be triggered by cold weather, exercise, illnesses, allergies, emotional stress, or for no clear reason (Akinbami & Schoendorf, 2002). Asthma attacks can be reduced through the use of medical injections and inhalers (Glauber et al., 2001; Yoos et al., 2006).

asthma

chronic illness of the lungs characterized by wheezing, coughing, and shortness of breath

Rates of asthma are highest in middle childhood and are increasing worldwide (Greenwood, 2011). Boys are at higher risk than girls, for reasons that are not clear (Federico & Liu, 2003). Other risk factors are low birth weight, having a parent who smokes, living in poverty, and obesity (Saha et al., 2005). Susceptibility to asthma is also transmitted genetically (Bosse & Hudson, 2007).

Why are rates of asthma higher now than in the past? The answer appears to be different for developed countries than for developing countries. In developed countries, common features of today's family households contribute to asthma, including carpets, hairy pets, and airtight windows (Tamay et al., 2007). There is also a "hygiene hypothesis" suggesting that high standards of cleanliness and sanitation expose children to fewer viruses and bacteria, and consequently they have fewer illnesses in their early years that would strengthen their immune systems and make them less susceptible to asthma (Tedeschi & Airaghi, 2006). In developing countries, air pollution has become worse as a result of increased industrialization, and air pollution can trigger asthma. One study in Mongolia compared people in rural and urban areas and found substantially higher rates of asthma in urban areas, as a result mainly of poorer air quality (Vinanen et al., 2007).

Middle childhood is when rates of asthma are highest. This Indian girl is using an inhaler to relieve the symptoms.

Rates of asthma are especially high among African American children because they often live in urban neighborhoods where the air quality is poor (Pearlman et al., 2006). African Americans also have especially high rates of risk factors for asthma such as low birth weight and obesity. However, one study found that among children with asthma, the families of African American children were more likely than White families to take steps to change the environment to reduce risk factors that can trigger asthma attacks, with steps including use of mattress covers, use of pillow covers, cigarette smoke avoidance, pet avoidance, and carpet removal (Roy & Wisnivesky, 2010).

Like illness rates, injury rates are relatively low in middle childhood (Hyder & Lunnen, 2011; U.S. Department of Health and Human Services, 2005c). Children in middle childhood are more agile than younger children and better at anticipating situations that may cause injury; compared to older children, they are kept closer to home and so are less likely to become involved in risky situations. The most common cause of injury in middle childhood is automobile accidents, followed by bicycle accidents (Safe Kids Worldwide, 2013). The use of bicycle helmets has become common in middle childhood in recent decades, and this practice has led to a sharp decrease in the number of head injuries experienced during these years (Miller et al., 2012).

Summary: Physical Development

LO 7.1 **Identify the changes in physical and sensory development that take place during middle childhood.**

In middle childhood physical growth continues at a slow but steady pace, about 2 to 3 inches (5–8 cm) per year in height and about 5 to 7 pounds (2½–3 kg) per year in weight. Children lose all 20 primary teeth and their permanent teeth begin to grow in. Ear health improves, but one fourth of children become nearsighted during middle childhood.

LO 7.2 **Explain how motor development advances in middle childhood and how these advancements are related to new skills and participation in games and sports.**

Children's gross motor skills improve in middle childhood as a result of improved balance, increased strength, better coordination, greater agility, and faster reaction time. As their gross motor development advances, children improve their performance in a wide range of games and sports, and many of them participate in organized sports.

Fine motor development reaches nearly an adult level at this age, and across cultures, advances are especially evident in two areas: drawing and writing. There are significant changes in areas of the prefrontal cortex that are important for motor development, in part because they are related to attention and control.

LO 7.3 **Describe the negative effects of both malnutrition and obesity on development, and identify the causes of obesity.**

Studies have shown that better-nourished children are more energetic, less anxious, show more positive emotion, and score higher than malnourished children on a wide range of cognitive measures in middle childhood. Across countries, rates of overweight and obesity are highest in the most affluent regions (North America and Europe) and lowest in the poorest regions (Africa and Southeast Asia). Obesity is a cultural phenomenon, and a variety of social and cultural changes have contributed to this problem, including diets with more fast food and high rates of television viewing. Genetics also make a contribution. Socially, being obese increases the likelihood that a child will be excluded and the object of ridicule by peers. Physically, obesity can result in diabetes in middle childhood, which eventually can lead to problems such as blindness, kidney failure, and stroke. Overweight and obesity are medical issues determined by a child's weight relative to his or her age group.

LO 7.4 **Explain why rates of illness and injury are relatively low in middle childhood, and why rates of asthma have risen.**

In both developed and developing countries, middle childhood is a time of unusually high physical well-being, with low rates of illnesses and diseases because of stronger immune systems, and the health of children has improved in recent years because of increased immunization rates and better public health policies. Rates of asthma have risen in developed countries as a result of carpets, pets, and airtight windows, and in developing countries because of worsening air pollution. Compared to younger children, children in middle childhood are more agile and better at anticipating situations that may cause injury.

Section 2   Cognitive Development

 ## Learning Objectives

7.5 Explain the major cognitive advances that occur during Piaget's concrete operations stage.

7.6 Describe how attention and memory change from early childhood to middle childhood.

7.7 Describe methods of conceptualizing and measuring intelligence, and identify genetic and environmental influences on intelligence.

7.8 Identify the advances in vocabulary, grammar, and pragmatics during middle childhood.

7.9 Explain the consequences for cognitive development of growing up bilingual.

7.10 Summarize the variations worldwide in school enrollment, socialization practices, and academic achievement during middle childhood.

7.11 Compare and contrast approaches to teaching reading and math skills in middle childhood, and describe the use of peer learning in the classroom.

7.12 Identify common disabilities in middle childhood, and explain the educational issues surrounding them.

COGNITIVE DEVELOPMENT: Theories of Cognitive Development

As we have seen in previous chapters, Piaget's approach and the information-processing approach offer two different but complementary ways of understanding cognitive development. First we examine Piaget's ideas about concrete operations, and then we discuss information processing advances in attention and memory.

Concrete Operations

LO 7.5   **Explain the major cognitive advances that occur during Piaget's concrete operations stage.**

If you grew up in a Western country, perhaps you believed in Santa Claus when you were a young child. According to the story, Santa Claus rides a sleigh borne by flying reindeer around the world on Christmas Eve, and at each house he comes down the chimney and delivers toys to all the good girls and boys. Do you remember when you stopped believing it? For most children, the story starts to seem far-fetched once they get to be 7 or 8 years old (Sameroff & Haith, 1996). How could one person make it all the way around the world in one night, even with flying reindeer? How could a large man make it down a narrow chimney, dragging a sack full of toys? And what if you don't have a chimney? The loss of belief in this myth reflects gains in cognitive development as children develop a more true-to-life understanding of the world.

Middle childhood is when children develop a better grasp of what the physical world is really like and what is and is not possible. Recall from Piaget's theory of cognitive development that early childhood is the preoperational stage. In Piaget's view, children ages 2 to 6 are most notable cognitively for what they *cannot* do—they cannot perform mental operations—and for the kinds of mistakes they make.

Around age 7, children make an important cognitive advance toward becoming more systematic, planful, and logical thinkers. Piaget termed the cognitive stage from age 7 to 11 **concrete operations**. During this stage, children become capable of using mental operations, which allow them to organize and manipulate information mentally instead of relying on physical and sensory associations. According to Piaget, the advances of concrete operations are evident in new abilities for performing tasks of conservation, classification, and seriation.

ADVANCES IN CONCRETE OPERATIONS After about age 6 or 7 children almost always succeed when performing tasks requiring an understanding of *conservation*. Conservation is a key milestone of cognitive development because it enables the child to perceive regularities and principles in the natural world, which is the basis of being able to think logically about how the world works.

A second important cognitive achievement of concrete operations is *classification*. Although in early childhood young children can sort objects or events that share common characteristics into the same class—*red, round, sweet, dog,* for example—and can also combine classes into more general categories—elephants and rabbits are both part of the larger class "animals"—they run into difficulty when a classification problem requires a mental operation. For example, in one experiment, Piaget showed a 5-year-old boy a drawing of 12 girls and 2 boys, and this exchange followed (Piaget, 1965, p. 167):

Piaget: Are there more girls or more children?
Boy: More girls.
Piaget: But aren't the girls children?
Boy: Yes.
Piaget: Then are there more children or more girls?
Boy: More girls.

Amusing, no doubt, at your age, but if you think about it, answering this question requires a fairly challenging mental operation, at least for a 5-year-old child. He must separate the girls and boys in the drawing into two classes (girls and boys), add them to form a larger class (children), and understand that the larger class (children) can be broken down again into each of its subclasses (girls and boys). Crucially, this must be done *mentally*. The number of girls can be compared to the number of boys visually, but comparing the number of children to the number of girls cannot, because girls are part of both categories. For this reason the 5-year-old child trips up on the problem, but by age 8 or 9 most children perform this mental operation easily. In another experiment, Piaget interviewed a 9-year-old boy, showing him a drawing of 12 yellow tulips, 3 red tulips, and 6 daisies:

Piaget: Which would make a bigger bunch, all the tulips or the yellow tulips?
Boy: All the tulips, of course. You'd be taking the yellow tulips as well.
Piaget: And which would be bigger, all the tulips or all the flowers?
Boy: All the flowers. If you take all the flowers, you take all the tulips, too.

(Adapted from Ginsburg & Opper, 1979, p. 123)

Seriation, the third achievement of concrete operations emphasized by Piaget, is the ability to arrange things in a logical order (e.g., shortest to longest, thinnest to thickest, lightest to darkest). Piaget found that preoperational children have an incomplete grasp of concepts such as *longer than* or *smaller than*. For example, when asked to arrange a set of sticks from shortest to longest, children in the preoperational age period would typically start with a short stick, then pick a long stick—but then pick another short

concrete operations

in Piaget's theory, the cognitive stage in which children become capable of using mental operations

seriation

ability to arrange things in a logical order, such as shortest to longest, thinnest to thickest, or lightest to darkest

stick, then another long stick, and so on. However, by age 7 most children can accurately arrange six to eight sticks by length. The video *Seriation* provides more examples of this.

Watch SERIATION

This kind of seriation task can be done visually—that is, it does not require a mental operation—but Piaget also found that during concrete operations children developed the ability to seriate mentally. Take this **transitive inference** problem, for example. If Julia is taller than Anna and Anna is taller than Lynn, is Julia taller than Lynn? To get this right, the child has to be able to order the heights mentally from tallest to shortest: Julia, Anna, Lynn. Piaget considered the achievement of this skill of performing mental operations to be a key part of learning to think logically and systematically.

EVALUATING PIAGET'S THEORY Research testing Piaget's theory has found that, for concrete operations as for the preoperational stage, children are capable of performing some tasks at an earlier age than Piaget had claimed (Marti & Rodriguez, 2012; Vilette, 2002). However, for Piaget it was not enough for a child to grasp *some* aspects of conservation, classification, and seriation to be considered a concrete operational thinker; the child had to have *complete* mastery of the tasks associated with the stage (Piaget, 1965). Thus, the difference between Piaget and his critics on this issue is more a matter of definition—"What qualifies a child as a concrete operational thinker?"—than of research findings. Piaget also claimed that teaching children the principles of concrete operations would not work because their grasp of the principles of the stage has to occur naturally as part of their interaction with their environment (Piaget, 1965). Here his critics appear to be right, with many studies showing that with training and instruction, children younger than age 7 can learn to perform the tasks of concrete operations and also understand the underlying principles well enough to apply them to new tasks (Marti & Rodriguez, 2012; Parameswaran, 2003).

Transporting Piaget's tasks across cultures shows that acquiring an understanding of concrete operations depends on exposure to similar tasks and materials. For example, in one study of 4- to 13-year-old children in the Mayan culture of Mexico and in Los Angeles, the children in Los Angeles performed better than the Mayan children on standard tests of concrete operations, whereas the Mayan children performed better on similar concrete operations tasks that involved materials used in weaving because these materials were familiar from their daily lives (Maynard & Greenfield, 2003).

transitive inference
the ability to detect an unspoken relationship between two facts

Information Processing

LO 7.6 **Describe how attention and memory change from early childhood to middle childhood.**

Ever try to play a board game with a 3-year-old child? If you do, it better be short and simple. By middle childhood, children can play a wide variety of board games that adults enjoy, too, because their powers of attention and memory have advanced. This is one reflection of how information processing improves during middle childhood. Because of increased myelination in the brain, especially of the corpus callosum connecting the two hemispheres, speed of processing information increases (Roeder et al., 2008). Consequently, the amount of time required to perform various tasks decreases in the course of middle childhood. Advances are also made in the two key areas of information processing: attention and memory.

ATTENTION In middle childhood, children become more capable of focusing their attention on relevant information and disregarding what is irrelevant, an ability termed **selective attention** (Goldberg et al., 2001; Janssen et al., 2014). For example, in one line of research, children of various ages were shown a series of cards, each containing one animal and one household item, and told to try and remember where the animal on each card was located (Hagen & Hale, 1973). Nothing was mentioned about the household items. Afterward, when asked about the location of the animals on each card, older children performed better than younger children. However, when asked how many of the household items they could remember, younger children performed better than older children. The older children were capable of focusing on the information they were told would be relevant, the location of the animals, and capable of ignoring the household items as irrelevant. In contrast, the poorer performance of the younger children in identifying the locations of the animals was partly as a result of being distracted by the household items.

MEMORY In early childhood, memory is often fleeting, as any parent can attest who has ever asked a 4-year-old child what happened to those nice new mittens he wore out to play that morning. Mittens? What mittens?

In middle childhood the capacity of *working memory*, which is memory for information currently the focus of your attention, enlarges. On memory tests for sequences of numbers, the length of the sequence recalled is just four numbers for the typical 7-year-old child, but for the typical 12-year-old child, it has increased to seven, equal to adults (Kail, 2003). More importantly, middle childhood is the period when children first learn to use **mnemonics** (memory strategies) such as rehearsal, organization, and elaboration.

Rehearsal, which involves repeating the information over and over, is a simple but effective mnemonic. You probably use it yourself, for example, when someone tells you a phone number and you are trying to remember it between the time you hear it and the time you use it. In a classic study, John Flavell and his colleagues (1966) showed how rehearsal emerges as a memory strategy in middle childhood. They outfitted children ages 5 and 10 with a space helmet with a dark visor and displayed seven pictures of familiar objects in front of them. Each child was told that the researcher was going to point to three objects that the child was to remember (in order), then pull down the space helmet visor so the child could not see for 15 seconds, and then lift the visor and ask the child to point to the three objects. During the 15-second delay, nearly all of the 10-year-old children, but only a few of the 5-year-old children, moved their lips or recited the names of the objects aloud, showing that they were using rehearsal. At each age, rehearsers recalled the objects much more accurately than non-rehearsers.

selective attention

ability to focus attention on relevant information and disregard what is irrelevant

mnemonics

memory strategies, such as rehearsal, organization, and elaboration

rehearsal

mnemonic that involves repeating the same information over and over

Organization—placing things into meaningful categories—is another effective memory strategy that is used more commonly in the course of middle childhood (Schneider, 2002). Studies typically test this ability by giving people a list of items to remember, for example, shoes, zebra, baseball, cow, tennis racket, dress, raccoon, soccer goal, hat. Numerous studies have shown that if children are given a list of items to remember, they are more likely to group them into categories—clothes, animals, sports items—in middle childhood than in early childhood (Sang et al., 2002). Organization is a highly effective memory strategy because each category serves as a *retrieval cue* for the items within the category, so that if the category can be remembered, all the items within the category are likely to be remembered as well (Schneider, 2002).

A third mnemonic that comes into greater use in middle childhood is **elaboration**, which involves transforming bits of information in a way that connects them and hence makes them easier to remember (Terry, 2003). One example of this is the standard way of teaching children the lines of the treble clef in music, EGBDF: *Every Good Boy Does Fine.* Or, if you were going to the grocery store and wanted to remember to buy butter, lettuce, apples, and milk, you could arrange the first letters of each of the items into one word, *BLAM*. The word *BLAM* serves as a retrieval cue for the items represented by each letter of the word.

Why do young chess masters remember chess configurations better than older novices do?

Although children are more likely to use organization and elaboration in middle childhood than in early childhood, even in middle childhood and beyond, relatively few people use memory strategies on a regular basis. Instead, they rely on more concrete, practical methods. In one study, children in kindergarten and first, third, and fifth grades were asked how they would remember to bring their ice skates to a party the next day (Kreutzer et al., 1975). At all three ages, children came up with sensible approaches such as putting the skates where they would be easy to see, writing themselves a note, and tying a string to their finger.

Another reason why memory improves from early childhood to middle childhood is that children's knowledge base expands, and the more you know, the easier it is to remember new information that is related to what you know. In a classic study illustrating this, 10-year-old chess masters and college student novice chess players were compared in their ability to remember configurations of pieces on a chess board (Chi, 1978). The 10-year-old chess masters performed far better than the college student novices, even though the college students were better at recalling a series of random numbers. In another study, 9- and 10-year-old children were separated into two groups, soccer "experts" and soccer "novices," and asked to try to remember lists of soccer items and nonsoccer items (Schneider & Bjorklund, 1992). The soccer experts remembered more items on the soccer list than on the nonsoccer list.

Middle childhood is not only a time of advances in memory abilities but of advances in understanding how memory works, or **metamemory**. Even by age 5 or 6, most children have some grasp of metamemory (Kvavilashvili & Ford, 2014). They recognize that it is easier to remember something that happened yesterday than something that happened long ago. They understand that short lists are easier to remember than long lists, and that familiar items are more easily remembered than unfamiliar items. However, their appraisal of their own memory abilities tends to be inflated. When children in early childhood and middle childhood were shown a series of 10 pictures and asked if they could remember all of them, more than half of the younger children but only a few older children claimed they could (none of them actually could!) (Flavell et al., 1970). In the course of middle childhood, children develop more accurate assessments of their memory abilities (Schneider & Pressley, 1997).

organization
mnemonic that involves placing things mentally into meaningful categories

elaboration
mnemonic that involves transforming bits of information in a way that connects them and hence makes them easier to remember

metamemory
understanding of how memory works

Intelligence and Intelligence Tests

LO 7.7 **Describe methods of conceptualizing and measuring intelligence, and identify genetic and environmental influences on intelligence.**

Both the Piagetian approach and the information-processing approach describe general patterns of cognitive development and functioning, intended to apply to all children. However, at any given age there are also *individual differences* among children in their cognitive functioning. Within any group of same-age children, some will perform relatively high in their cognitive functioning and some relatively low. Even in infancy, toddlerhood, and early childhood, individual differences in cognitive development are evident because children reach various cognitive milestones at different times, such as saying their first word. However, individual differences become more evident and more important in middle childhood, when children enter formal schooling and begin to be tested and evaluated on a regular basis.

In the study of human development, the examination of individual differences in cognitive development has focused mainly on measurements of **intelligence**. Definitions of intelligence vary, but it is generally understood to be a person's capacity for acquiring knowledge, reasoning, and solving problems (Sternberg, 2004). Intelligence tests usually provide an overall score of general intelligence as well as several subscores that reflect different aspects of intelligence.

Let us begin by looking at the characteristics of one of the most widely used intelligence tests, and follow with an exploration of the genetic and environmental sources of individual differences in intelligence. Then, we will consider two alternative ways of conceptualizing and measuring intelligence.

THE WECHSLER INTELLIGENCE TESTS The most widely used intelligence tests are the Wechsler scales, including the *Wechsler Intelligence Scale for Children (WISC-IV)* for ages 6 to 16 and the *Wechsler Adult Intelligence Scale (WAIS-IV)* for ages 16 and older.

The Wechsler scales consist of 11 subtests, of which 6 are verbal subtests and 5 are performance subtests. The results provide an overall **intelligence quotient,** or **IQ** score, which is calculated relative to the performance of other people of the same age, with 100 as the **median** score. The overall IQ can be broken down into a verbal IQ score, a performance IQ score, and scores for each of the 11 subtests. More detail on each of the subscales of the WISC-IV is provided in **Table 7.1**, so you can get an idea of what IQ tests really measure.

How accurate are the Wechsler IQ tests? IQ tests were originally developed to test children's abilities as they entered school, and IQ has proven to be a good predictor of children's school performance. One study of children in 46 countries found that across countries, IQ scores and school achievement scores were highly correlated (Lynn & Mikk, 2007). IQ scores are also quite good predictors of success in adulthood (Benbow & Lubinski, 2009).

However, IQ tests have been criticized on a variety of grounds. Critics have complained that IQ tests assess only a narrow range of abilities and miss some of the most important aspects of intelligence, such as creativity. IQ tests have also been attacked as culturally biased because some of the vocabulary and general knowledge items would be more familiar to someone who was part of the middle-class culture (Ogbu, 2002). However, attempts to develop "culture-fair" tests have found the same kinds of group differences as standard IQ tests have found (Johnson et al., 2008). It may not be possible to develop a culture-fair or culture-free IQ test because by the time people are able to take the tests (age 6) their cognitive development has already been shaped by living in a particular cultural and social environment. Although IQ tests aspire to test raw intellectual abilities, this would not really be possible unless everyone was exposed to essentially the same environment in the years before taking the test, which is obviously not the case. However, new approaches to studying intelligence have provided important insights into the relation between genetics and environment in performance on IQ tests, as we will discuss next.

intelligence

capacity for acquiring knowledge, reasoning, and solving problems

intelligence quotient (IQ)

score of mental ability as assessed by intelligence tests, calculated relative to the performance of other people the same age

median

in a distribution of data, the score that is precisely in the middle, with half the distribution lying above and half below

normal distribution

typical distribution of characteristics of a population, resembling a bell curve in which most cases fall near the middle and the proportions decrease at the low and high extremes

Table 7.1 The WISC-IV: Sample Items

Verbal Subtests	
Information	General knowledge questions, for example, "Who wrote *Huckleberry Finn*?"
Vocabulary	Give definitions, for example, "What does formulate mean?"
Similarities	Describe relationship between two things, for example, "In what ways are an apple and an orange alike?" and "In what ways are a book and a movie alike?"
Arithmetic	Verbal arithmetic problems, for example, "How many hours does it take to drive 140 miles at a rate of 30 miles per hour?"
Comprehension	Practical knowledge, for example, "Why is it important to use zip codes when you mail letters?"
Digit Span	Short-term memory test. Sequences of numbers of increasing length are recited, and the person is required to repeat them.
Performance Subtests	
	For all the performance tests, scores are based on speed as well as accuracy of response.
Picture arrangement	Cards depicting various activities are provided, and the person is required to place them in an order that tells a coherent story.
Picture completion	Cards are provided depicting an object or scene with something missing, and the person is required to point out what is missing (for example, a dog is shown with only three legs).
Matrix reasoning	Patterns are shown with one piece missing. The person chooses from five options the one that will fill in the missing piece accurately.
Block design	Blocks are provided with two sides all white, two sides all red, and two sides half red and half white. A card is shown with a geometrical pattern, and the person must arrange the blocks so that they match the pattern on the card.
Digit symbol	At top of sheet, numbers are shown with matching symbols. Below, sequences of symbols are given with an empty box below each symbol. The person must place the matching number in the box below each symbol.

INFLUENCES ON INTELLIGENCE IQ scores for a population-based sample usually fall into a **normal distribution**, or *bell curve*, in which most people are near the middle of the distribution and the proportions decrease at the low and high extremes, as shown in **Figure 7.4**. People with IQs less than 70 are classified as having **intellectual disability**, and those with IQs higher than 130 are classified as **gifted**. But what determines whether a person's score is low, high, or somewhere in the middle? Is intelligence mainly an inherited trait, or is it shaped mainly by the environment?

intellectual disability
level of cognitive abilities of persons who score 70 or less on IQ tests

gifted
in IQ test performance, persons who score 130 or higher

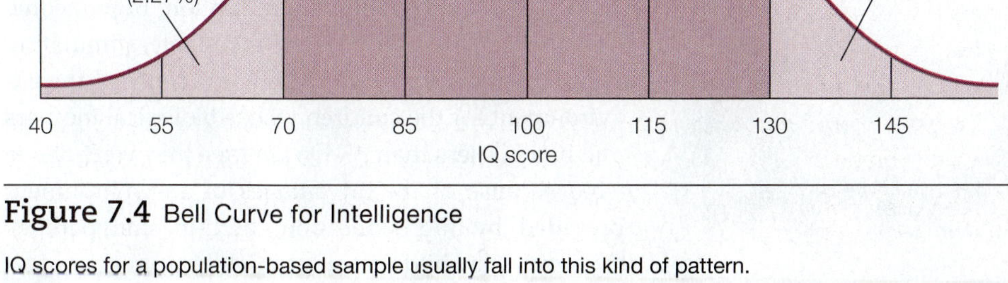

Figure 7.4 Bell Curve for Intelligence

IQ scores for a population-based sample usually fall into this kind of pattern.

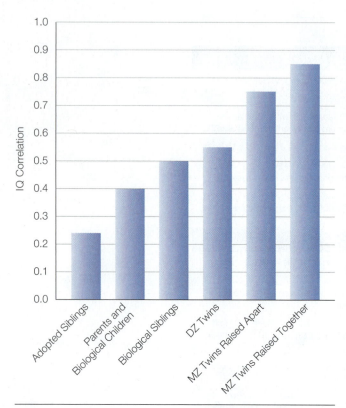

Figure 7.5 IQ and Genetics

The closer the genetic relationship, the higher the correlation in IQ.
SOURCE: Based on Brant et al. (2009).

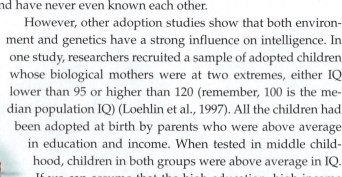

Identical twins have similar IQs, even when reared apart. Here, 6-year-old monozygotic twin sisters in Thailand smile for the camera.

Social scientists increasingly regard the old nature–nurture debate as sterile and obsolete. Nearly all accept that both genetics and environment are involved in development, including in the development of intelligence. A variety of new findings presented in the past 20 years provide insights into how genetics and environments interact and how both contribute to intelligence. Most of these studies use the natural experiments of adoption studies or twin studies to avoid the problem of passive genotype → environment effects. When parents provide both genetics and environment, as they do in most families, it is difficult to judge the relative contribution of each. Adoption and twin studies help unravel that tangle.

One important conclusion from adoption and twin studies is that the more two people in a family are alike genetically, the higher the correlation in their IQs (Brant et al., 2009). As shown in **Figure 7.5**, adopted siblings, who have none of their genotype in common, have a relatively low correlation for IQ, about 0.24. The environmental influence is apparent—ordinarily, the correlation between two genetically unrelated children would be zero—but limited. Parents and their biological children, who share half of their genotype in common, are correlated for IQ at about 0.40, slightly higher if they live together than if they live apart. The correlation for biological siblings is higher, about 0.50, and slightly higher still for DZ twins. Biological siblings and DZ twins share the same proportion of their genotype in common as parents and biological children do (again, about half), so the greater IQ similarity in DZ twins must be as a result of greater environmental similarity, from the womb onward. The highest IQ correlation of all, about 0.85, is among MZ twins, who have exactly the same genotype. Even when they are adopted by separate families and raised apart, the correlation in IQ scores of MZ twins is about 0.75 (Brant et al., 2009).

The results of these studies leave little doubt that genetics contribute strongly to IQ scores. It is especially striking that the correlation in IQ is much lower for adopted siblings, who have grown up in the same family and neighborhood and attended the same schools, than it is for MZ twins who have been raised separately and have never even known each other.

However, other adoption studies show that both environment and genetics have a strong influence on intelligence. In one study, researchers recruited a sample of adopted children whose biological mothers were at two extremes, either IQ lower than 95 or higher than 120 (remember, 100 is the median population IQ) (Loehlin et al., 1997). All the children had been adopted at birth by parents who were above average in education and income. When tested in middle childhood, children in both groups were above average in IQ. If we can assume that the high-education, high-income adoptive parents provided a healthy, stable, stimulating environment, this shows a strong influence of the environment for the children whose biological mothers all had IQs less than 95. On average they were above 100 because of the advantages of an environment provided by high-education, high-income parents. However, the children whose biological mothers had

IQs higher than 120 were significantly higher in IQ than the children whose biological mothers had IQs less than 95, even though children in both groups had an advantaged environment, which showed the substantial influence of genetics.

Taken together, the adoption and twin IQ studies show that both genetics and environment contribute to the development of intelligence. Specifically, every child has a genetically based *reaction range* for intelligence, meaning a range of possible developmental paths. With a healthy, stimulating environment, children reach the top of their reaction range for intelligence; with a poor, unhealthy, or chaotic environment, children are likely to develop a level of intelligence toward the bottom of the reaction range. There is both an upper and a lower limit to the reaction range. Even with an optimal environment, children with relatively low intellectual abilities are unlikely to develop superior intelligence; even with a subnormal environment, children with relatively high intellectual abilities are unlikely to end up well below average in IQ.

Recent research has revealed new insights into the intricate relations between genetics and environment in the development of intelligence. Specifically, research indicates that the influence of the environment on IQ is stronger for poor children than for children of affluent families (Nesbitt, 2009; Turkheimer et al., 2009). The less stimulating the environment, the less genetics influence IQ because children's potentials are suppressed in an unstimulating environment. In contrast, an affluent environment generally allows children to receive the cognitive stimulation necessary to reach the top of their reaction range for IQ.

One other highly important finding that attests to the importance of environmental influences on intelligence is that the median IQ score in Western countries rose dramatically in the course of the 20th century, a phenomenon known as the **Flynn effect**, named for the scholar who first noted it, James Flynn (1999, 2012). From 1932 to 1997 the median IQ score among children in the United States rose by 20 points (Howard, 2001). This is a huge difference. It means that a child whose IQ was average in 1932 would be way below average by today's standard. It means that half of children today would have scored at least 120 by 1932 scoring, placing them in the "superior intelligence" range, and about one fourth of children today would be considered by 1932 standards to have "very superior intelligence"—a classification actually held by only 3 percent of children in 1932 (Horton, 2001). As shown in **Figure 7.6**, similar results have been found in other countries as well (Flynn, 1999, 2012).

What explains the Flynn effect? The causes must be environmental, rather than genetic; the genes of the human population could not have changed so dramatically in such a short time. But what about the environment improved so much in the course of the 20th century that would explain such a dramatic rise in median IQ scores? Several possibilities have been identified (Rodgers & Wanstrom, 2007). Prenatal care is better now than in the early 20th century, and better prenatal care leads to better intellectual development, including higher IQs. Families are generally smaller now than in the early 20th century, and in general the fewer children in a family, the higher their IQs. It has even been suggested that the invention of television may be one of the sources of the Flynn effect. Although television and other media are often blamed for societal ills, there is good evidence that watching educational television enhances young children's intellectual development (Scantlin, 2007). Another possible explanation is that far more children attend preschool now than was true in 1932. Preschool enhances young children's intellectual development, whereas delays in starting school are related to lower IQ scores (Ceci & Williams, 1997).

An especially persuasive explanation has recently been proposed: the decline of infectious diseases (Eppig et al., 2010). Christopher Eppig and his colleagues note that the brain requires a great deal of the body's physical energy—87 percent in newborns, nearly half in 5-year-old children, and 25 percent in

Flynn effect

steep rise in the median IQ score in Western countries during the 20th century, named after James Flynn, who first identified it

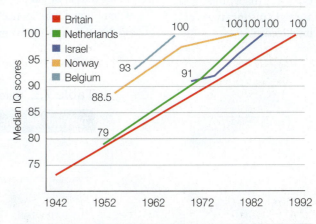

Figure 7.6 Flynn Effect

IQ scores rose across developed countries in the late 20th century.
SOURCE: Flynn (1999)

Figure 7.7 Inverse Relation Between IQ and Disease

Could this explain the Flynn effect?
SOURCE: Eppig et al. (2010)

adults. Infectious diseases compete for this energy by activating the body's immune system and interfering with the body's processing of food during years when the brain is growing and developing rapidly. If this explanation is true, there should be an inverse relationship between IQ and infectious disease rates, and this pattern was evident in the researchers' analysis of data from 113 countries (as shown in **Figure 7.7**). The higher a country's infectious disease burden, the lower the country's median IQ. Thus, the Flynn effect may have been primarily as a result of the elimination of major infectious diseases in developed countries. A Flynn effect of the future may be awaiting developing countries as they reduce and eliminate infectious diseases.

OTHER CONCEPTIONS OF INTELLIGENCE: GARDNER'S AND STERNBERG'S THEORIES IQ testing has dominated research on children's intellectual development for nearly a century. However, in recent decades alternative theories of intelligence have been proposed. These theories have sought to present a conception of intelligence that is much broader than the traditional one. Two of the most influential alternative theories of intelligence have been presented by Howard Gardner and Robert Sternberg.

Gardner's (1983, 2004) **theory of multiple intelligences** includes eight types of intelligence (see **Table 7.2**). In Gardner's view only two of them, *linguistic* and *logical–mathematical* intelligences, are evaluated by intelligence tests. The other intelligences are *spatial* (the ability to think three-dimensionally); *musical; bodily–kinesthetic* (the kind that athletes and dancers excel in); *naturalist* (ability for understanding natural phenomena); *interpersonal* (ability for understanding and interacting with others); and *intrapersonal* (self-understanding). As evidence for the existence of these different types of intelligence, Gardner argues that each involves distinct cognitive skills, that each can be destroyed by damage to a particular part of the brain, and that each appears in extremes in geniuses as well as in *idiots savant* (the French term for people who are low in general intelligence but possess an extraordinary ability in one specialized area).

Gardner argues that schools should give more attention to the development of all eight kinds of intelligence and design programs that would be tailored to each child's individual profile of intelligences. He has proposed methods for assessing different intelligences, such as measuring musical intelligence by having people attempt to sing a song, play an instrument, or orchestrate a melody (Gardner, 1999, 2011). However, thus far neither Gardner nor others have developed reliable and valid methods for analyzing the intelligences he proposes. Gardner has also been criticized for extending the boundaries of intelligence too widely. When an adolescent displays exceptional musical ability, is this an indication of musical "intelligence" or simply of musical talent? Gardner himself has been critical of the concept of "emotional intelligence" proposed by Daniel Goleman and others (Goleman, 1997), arguing that the capacity to empathize and cooperate with others is better viewed as "emotional

theory of multiple intelligences

Gardner's theory that there are eight distinct types of intelligence

Table 7.2 Gardner's Theory of Multiple Intelligences

Type of Intelligence	Description
Linguistic	Ability to use language
Musical	Ability to compose or perform music
Logical–mathematical	Ability to think logically and to solve mathematical problems
Spatial	Ability to understand how objects are oriented in space
Bodily–kinesthetic	Speed, agility, and gross motor control
Interpersonal	Sensitivity to others and understanding motivation of others
Intrapersonal	Understanding of one's emotions and how they guide actions
Naturalist	Ability to recognize the patterns found in nature

sensitivity" rather than intelligence (Gardner, 1999). However, Gardner is vulnerable to a similar criticism for proposing "interpersonal" and "intrapersonal" intelligences. Gardner (2011) is continuing to develop his theory and methods to assess it.

CRITICAL THINKING QUESTION

Do you agree that all the mental abilities described by Gardner are different types of intelligence? If not, which types would you remove? Are there other types you would add?

Sternberg's (1983, 1988, 2002, 2003, 2005) **triarchic theory of intelligence** includes three distinct but related forms of intelligence. *Analytical intelligence* is Sternberg's term for the kind of intelligence that IQ tests measure, which involves acquiring, storing, analyzing, and retrieving information. *Creative intelligence* involves the ability to combine information in original ways to produce new insights, ideas, and problem-solving strategies. *Practical intelligence* is the ability to apply information to the kinds of problems faced in everyday life, including the capacity to evaluate social situations. Sternberg has conducted extensive research to develop tests of intelligence that measure the three types of intelligence he proposes. These tests involve solving problems, applying knowledge, and developing creative strategies. Sternberg's research on Americans has demonstrated that each person has a different profile on the three intelligences that can be assessed (Sternberg, 2005, 2007). He proposes that the three components are universal and contribute to intelligent performance in all cultures (Sternberg, 2005), but so far the theory has been tested little outside the United States. Neither Sternberg's nor Gardner's tests are widely used among psychologists, in part because they take longer to administer and score than standard IQ tests do.

The underlying issue in judging alternative theories of intelligence is the question of how intelligence should be defined. If intelligence is defined simply as the mental abilities required to succeed in school, the traditional approach to conceptualizing and measuring intelligence is generally successful. However, if one wishes to define intelligence more broadly, as the entire range of human mental abilities, the traditional approach may be seen as too narrow, and an approach such as Gardner's or Sternberg's may be preferred. For a thoughtful perspective on how differently cultures may conceptualize intelligence, see the video *Robert Sternberg on Cultural Influences*.

Is musical ability a type of intelligence?

triarchic theory of intelligence

Sternberg's theory that there are three distinct but related forms of intelligence

Watch ROBERT STERNBERG ON CULTURAL INFLUENCES

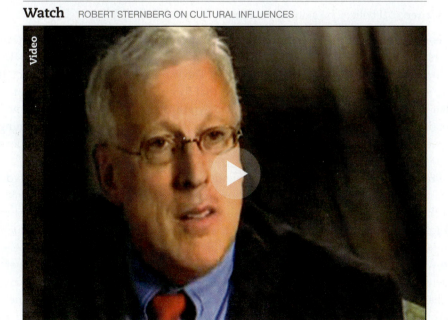

COGNITIVE DEVELOPMENT:
Language Development

In middle childhood, advances in language development may not be as noticeable as in the earliest years of life, but they are nevertheless dramatic. There are important advances in vocabulary, grammar, and pragmatics. Bilingual children face special challenges in language development but also benefit in some ways.

Vocabulary, Grammar, and Pragmatics

LO 7.8 **Identify the advances in vocabulary, grammar, and pragmatics during middle childhood.**

Once they enter formal school at age 5 to 7 and begin reading, children's vocabulary expands as never before because they pick up new words not just from conversations but also from books. At age 6 the average child knows about 10,000 words, but by age 10 or 11 this sum has increased fourfold, to about 40,000 (Fitneva & Matsui, 2015). Part of this growth comes from children's growing abilities to understand the different forms words can take. A child who learns the meaning of *calculate* will also now understand *calculating, calculated, calculation*, and *miscalculate* (Anglin, 1993).

The grammar of children's language use becomes more complex in middle childhood. For example, they are more likely than younger children to use *conditional sentences* such as "If you let me play with that toy, I'll share my lunch with you."

Another important aspect of language that improves in middle childhood is *pragmatics*, the social context and conventions of language. Even in early childhood children have begun to understand pragmatics. For example, they realize that what people say is not always just what they mean, and that interpretation is required. They understand that "How many times do I have to tell you not to feed the dog off your plate?" is not really a math question. However, in middle childhood the understanding of pragmatics grows substantially (Ishihara, 2014). This can be seen vividly in children's use of humor. A substantial amount of humor in middle childhood involves violating the expectations set by pragmatics. For example, here is an old joke that made Jeff's son Miles howl with laughter when he first learned it at age 8:

> **Man:** "Waiter, what's that fly doing in my soup?"
> **Waiter:** "I believe he's doing the backstroke, sir."

For this to be funny, you have to understand pragmatics. Specifically, you have to understand that by asking "What's that fly doing in my soup?" the man means "What are you going to do about that disgusting fly?" The waiter, a bit slow on his pragmatics, interprets the man to mean, "What activity is that fly engaged in?" What makes it funny is that your understanding of pragmatics leads you to expect the first response, and the second response comes as a surprise. By substituting the expected pragmatic meaning of the question with an unexpected meaning, the joke creates a humorous effect (at least if you are 8 years old).

Pragmatics are always culturally grounded, which is one reason why jokes don't travel well between cultures. To know the pragmatics of a language, you have to know well the culture of the people using the language. For example, many languages have two forms of the word *you*, one form used when there is a close attachment (such as with family and close friends) and the other used with unfamiliar persons and persons with whom there is a professional but not personal relationship (such as employers or students). Knowing when and with whom to use each form of you requires extensive familiarity not just with the language but also with the cultural norms for using the two forms in the appropriate social contexts.

Bilingualism and Second-Language Learning

LO 7.9 **Explain the consequences for cognitive development of growing up bilingual.**

An increasing number of children around the world grow up knowing two languages; that is, they are **bilingual**. There are two main reasons for this trend. First, with increased migration between countries, children are more likely to be exposed early to two languages, one spoken at home and one spoken with friends, teachers, and others outside the home. Second, school systems increasingly seek to teach children a second language to enhance their ability to participate in the global economy. Because the United States is the most influential country in the world economy, English is the most-common second language for children around the world. For example, in China all children now begin learning English in primary school (Chang, 2008). There are many bilingual families living within the United States as well because of the large number of immigrants that have come to the United States in recent decades, and they speak a variety of languages (see **Map 7.1**).

As we have seen in previous chapters, children are marvelously well-suited to learning a language. But what happens when they try to learn two languages? Does learning two languages enhance their language development or impede it?

For the most part, becoming bilingual is favorable to language development. When children learn two languages, they usually become adept at using both (Baker, 2011; Ishihara, 2014). Learning a secondary language does not interfere cognitively with mastering the primary language (Lessow-Hurley, 2005). One minor problem that does arise is that in early childhood there is sometimes a tendency to intermix the syntax of the two languages. For example, in Spanish dropping the subject in a sentence is grammatically correct, as in *no quiero ir.* However, if a child who is bilingual in Spanish applies this rule to English it comes out as *no want go*, which is not correct. By middle childhood, children can easily keep their two languages separate, although they may intentionally import some words from one language when speaking in the other, to create

bilingual

capable of using two languages

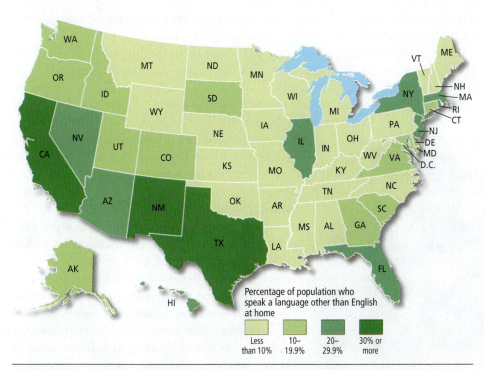

Map 7.1 Speaking a Language Other Than English at Home

Which states have the highest percentage of families who speak a language other than English at home? How might this relate to the ethnic diversity that exists within these states?

"Spanglish" (a blend of Spanish and English) or "Chinglish" (a blend of Chinese and English), for example.

When children learn their second language after already becoming fluent in a first language, it takes longer to master the second language, usually 3 to 5 years (Baker, 2011; Hakuta, 1999). Even so, learning a second language comes much easier in early and middle childhood than it does at later ages. For example, in one study, adults who had immigrated to the United States from China or Korea at various ages were tested on their grammatical knowledge of English (Johnson & Newport, 1991). The participants who had arrived in the United States in early or middle childhood scored as well on the test as native English speakers, but beyond middle childhood, the older the age at immigration, the less the person's grammatical knowledge. Other studies have shown that beyond the age of about 12 it is difficult for people to learn to speak a new language without a noticeable accent (Birdsong, 2006). Clearly, children have a biological readiness for learning a new language that adults lack, but the decline in this ability is gradual and steady from childhood to adulthood.

Becoming bilingual has a variety of benefits. Children who are bilingual have better **metalinguistic skills** than single-language children, meaning that they have greater awareness of the underlying structure of language (Schwartz et al., 2008). In one early study (Oren, 1981), researchers compared bilingual and single-language children ages 4 to 5 on metalanguage skills by instructing them to use nonsense words for familiar objects (e.g., *dimp* for dog, *wug* for car) and by asking them questions about the implications of changing object labels (if we call a dog a cow, does it give milk?). The bilingual children were consistently better than the single-language children in metalanguage understanding. Specifically, they were better at applying grammatical rules to nonsense words (one *wug*, two *wugs*) and at understanding that words are symbols for objects (calling a dog a cow won't make it give milk). Other studies have confirmed that bilingual children are better than single-language children at detecting mistakes in grammar and meaning (Baker, 2011; Bialystok, 1993, 1997). Bilingual children also score higher on more general measures of cognitive ability, such as analytical reasoning, cognitive flexibility, and cognitive complexity, indicating that becoming bilingual also has general cognitive benefits (Bialystok, 1999, 2001; Swanson et al., 2004).

In the United States, there is an ongoing debate about whether bilingual education is better for learning than English immersion for English-language learners (ELLs). In bilingual education, children can use the language skills they come to school with to engage with the activities of the school setting. ELLs in bilingual education tend to perform better and feel more competent (Jost, 2009). On the other hand, it is difficult for some school districts to hire bilingual teachers, and English immersion is a politically mandated practice in some states (Jost, 2009). Unfortunately, there is an ongoing achievement gap for ELLs in both formats.

In some countries, such as India, many children are not just bilingual but **multilingual**. Indian children first learn their local language, of which there are over a thousand across India (MacKenzie, 2009). Then they learn Hindi, which is the official national language, and many also learn English as well, to participate in the global economy. Studies indicate that by middle childhood, Indian children exposed to multiple languages use their different languages effectively in different contexts (Bhargava & Mendiratta, 2006). However, language diversity can be an obstacle to learning for children who come to school

metalinguistic skills

in the understanding of language, skills that reflect awareness of the underlying structure of language

multilingual

capable of using three or more languages

Many Indian children learn several languages.

knowing only their local language and are then faced with a school curriculum that is entirely in a new and unfamiliar language (MacKenzie, 2009). Currently, some Indian schools are changing their curriculum in the early school years to the local language before introducing Hindi or English, but others are emphasizing English from the outset of schooling in an effort to prepare children for participation in the global economy.

COGNITIVE DEVELOPMENT: School in Middle Childhood

In most of the world today, the daily lives of children in middle childhood are oriented around school. School is where they begin to gain the cognitive skills, especially in reading and math, that will enable them to participate economically in adult life.

School Experiences and Achievement

LO 7.10 Summarize the variations worldwide in school enrollment, socialization practices, and academic achievement during middle childhood.

Many developmental psychologists refer to children in middle childhood as "school-age children," as if going to school is a natural, universal, and inevitable part of children's development once they reach the age of 6 or 7. However, attending school has been a typical part of children's lives in most countries only for less than 200 years.

Today, going to school has become a typical part of middle childhood, but it still is not universal, as **Figure 7.8** shows (UNICEF, 2014b). In most developing countries, about 18 percent of children ages 6 to 10 do not attend primary school, and in sub-Saharan Africa, 23 percent of boys and 21 percent of girls ages 6 to 10 do not attend. However, in all developing countries, primary school enrollment has risen steeply in recent decades.

CULTURAL VARIATIONS IN EDUCATION Schooling is on the rise around the world as the result of economic development and efforts by the United Nations and governments to encourage families to send their children to school. In Mexico, for example, 87 percent of children now complete their primary education compared to 46.6 percent in 1980 (Welti, 2002). Rates in Africa are increasing as well. Just a few years ago, only about half of the school-age children in sub-Saharan African attended school (UNESCO, 2008); now the figure is closer to 75 percent (UNICEF, 2014b). As the graph in Figure 7.8 shows, schooling rates are lower in developing countries than in developed countries. Therefore, it is important to consider specific countries within regions when interpreting schooling rates, which will vary greatly by a country's economy.

Interestingly, the activity setting of school is quite similar around the world, across different ecocultural settings. If you visited any school setting around the world, you would be likely to find similar personnel, activities, tasks, and goals. Of course, the resources for education vary significantly, and the lack of resources may be related to outcomes and achievement.

There are also differences in values related to schooling, particularly across the United States and Asian countries. A great deal of research has focused on comparisons

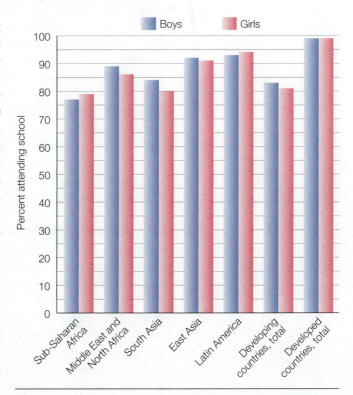

Figure 7.8 Primary School Attendance in World Regions

Attending primary school is common but not universal worldwide.

SOURCE: Based on UNICEF (2014)

Children in many Asian countries are required to wear school uniforms. How is the requirement of wearing school uniforms a custom complex?

between schools in the United States and in Asian countries such as Japan, China, and South Korea. These Asian countries have cultural traditions going back more than two millennia emphasizing the importance and value of education, and the traditions remain strong today. High standards are applied to all children because people in these countries believe that educational success is derived mainly from hard work and any child can succeed who tries hard enough (Stevenson et al., 2000; Sun et al., 2013). The same beliefs are characteristic of Asian American families (Fuligni et al., 2005). In contrast, most other Americans tend to believe that educational success is mainly the result of innate ability, so when a child does poorly they tend to believe there is not much that can be done. Another difference is that Asian children tend to view academic striving as something they do not just for themselves but as a moral obligation to their families (Sun et al., 2013). In contrast, U.S. children tend to view academic achievement as a mark of individual success. Individual choice is also a factor in U.S. education. There are many options for school formats in the United States: private and public schools, including charter schools and magnet schools (such as for arts or industry training), and home schooling.

Several features of Asian schools reflect collectivistic cultural beliefs emphasizing obedience and cooperation. Children are required to wear uniforms, a classic *custom complex* underscoring diminished individuality and emphasizing conformity to the group. Children are also required to help to maintain the cleanliness and order of the school, emphasizing the collectivistic cultural value of contributing to the well-being of the community. Furthermore, children often work in groups, with students who have mastered a concept instructing those who have yet to grasp it (Shapiro & Azuma, 2004). In contrast, children in U.S. schools typically do not wear uniforms (except in some private schools), are not required to help with school maintenance, and spend more time working alone (Stevenson & Zusho, 2002).

There are other important differences between the United States and Asian countries in the structure of the school day and year. Asian children spend more time on a typical school day learning academic subjects than U.S. children do; Americans spend only about half as much of their school time in academic activities as children in China and Japan do, and spend more school time in art, music, and sports (Shapiro & Azuma, 2004). Both the school day and the school year are longer in Asian countries. The school year in the United States is 180 days, compared to 220 in South Korea and 245 in China (Luckie, 2010).

ACADEMIC PERFORMANCE How are these differences in school socialization and structure related to children's academic performance? In recent years, several excellent cross-national studies of academic performance have been conducted at regular intervals, including the Progress in International Reading Literacy Study (PIRLS) and the Trends in International Mathematics and Science Study (TIMSS). On the basis of these results, it appears that academic performance in fourth grade is related mainly to countries' economic development rather than to differences in cultural beliefs and (consequently) in educational practices (Aud, et al., 2013). The highest-performing countries have widely varying educational approaches, but they all have high levels of economic development. As a result, they are most able to afford the resources that contribute to high academic performance, from good prenatal care to high-quality preschools to well-funded primary schools.

Within countries as well, the economic background of the family makes a great difference in children's academic performance. This is especially true in the United States, where schools are funded mostly on the basis of local property taxes rather than by the national government. As a result, the rich get richer, and the poor get poorer: schools in the poorest areas have the least amount of resources to provide for children coming from poor families, whereas schools in the most affluent areas have the most resources, and the children attending those schools, who are mainly from affluent families, reap the benefits. Not surprisingly, given this system, children from low-income families generally score worse than children from high-income families on tests of academic achievement (NCES, 2013). Similarly, the wealthiest U.S. states have the highest school achievement test scores, and the poorest states have the lowest scores.

Cultural Focus: School and Education in Middle Childhood Across Cultures

Attending primary school has become a near-universal experience of middle childhood. However, in many developing countries, the change to a school-oriented daily life in middle childhood has been swift (Gaskins, 2015). For example, in Guatemala, Barbara Rogoff has been conducting ethnographic research in the same village for more than 30 years. Over the course of just one generation, children's experiences were transformed (Rogoff et al., 2005). For example, not a single village girl today has learned weaving, even though nearly all of their mothers (87 percent) weaved as girls. For boys, the percentage who helped care for younger children dropped from 53 percent to 7 percent in just one generation. The percentage of boys helping with farm work also dropped from 57 percent in the parents' generation to just 36 percent in the current generation. Because they now spend most of the day in school, girls no longer learn weaving, and boys are no longer available for farm work.

The change in children's focus from work to school was reflected in the change in their aspirations. In the parents' generation, few expected as children to continue education past Grade 6; for today's children, about three fourths expect to go beyond Grade 6, and more than half expect to go beyond Grade 12. Both boys and girls today envisioned a wider range of future occupations than their parents could have imagined, including accountant, teacher, pastor, and doctor.

Across cultural settings, all primary schools teach children reading, writing, and math, but there are many variations in how children are taught and in what is expected of them, as you will see in this video.

Until recently, boys were more likely than girls to attend primary school. School attendance requires school fees in many countries, and some poor families would use their extremely limited resources for the boys' education. Girls were often kept home because it was believed that boys' education would be of greater benefit to the family. However, in recent years this gender difference has disappeared, and boys and girls are now equally likely to obtain primary education (UNICEF, 2014a). In this video, a Mexican girl observes that in her village, girls are more likely than boys to attend schools because boys are more often required to work to help the family.

Review Question:

What common educational themes do you see among the individuals in this video?

Watch SCHOOL AND EDUCATION IN MIDDLE CHILDHOOD ACROSS CULTURES

Education Focus: Achievement Motivation in School

Why are you interested in studying for the next exam? Is it so that you will learn the material because it is interesting to you? Or is it because you want to get a good grade on the test? Doing something because it is internally rewarding is called **intrinsic motivation**. Striving for an external reward or to avoid an external punishment is **extrinsic motivation**. An important theory of motivation, *self-determination theory*, proposes that people are motivated intrinsically to behave in effective and healthy ways (Ryan & Deci, 2000). Children may be intrinsically motivated to achieve in school because learning is interesting and feels good. Or they may be extrinsically motivated to get a good grade or avoid a bad grade. Learning involves effort and requires attention, effort, persistence, and dealing with not understanding or getting something right the first time (Stipek, 2011), and children must be motivated to learn and to study. Offering an external reward for learning that is already rewarding can actually diminish motivation. Thus, it is important for teachers to motivate children to learn intrinsically and to avoid overdoing the external rewards (Ryan & Weinstein, 2009).

Motivation in school is related to how one thinks about intelligence as one grapples to learn a new subject or skill. Children who think that intelligence is a fixed trait may give up easily if they fail at a new task. Children who believe that intelligence is malleable are more likely to keep trying at a difficult task. Self-efficacy is the belief that one can change one's habits and behavior to succeed. Children with a sense of self-efficacy change their study habits or their study environment to succeed in school.

Motivation for learning also has some cultural variations. In some cultures, such as in the United States, teachers and children tend to think that success in learning is related to *intelligence*, and they think of intelligence as a fixed trait in individuals. In other cultures, such as in Japan, teachers and children tend to think that success in learning is related to *effort*, and they think of intelligence as malleable, and much less important (Stevenson & Lee, 1990). The mantra of a Japanese teacher would be, "Everyone can learn if they try. If you have trouble learning, keep trying, and you will learn." Imagine the implications for this if a child is trying to learn something new and can't get it the first time. The child is likely to try again, and the teacher is likely to encourage the child to keep trying different strategies and not give up.

Survey Question:

Do you think elementary school students today are motivated more by intrinsic or extrinsic rewards?
A. Intrinsic rewards
B. Extrinsic rewards

Learning the Cognitive Skills of School

LO 7.11 Compare and contrast approaches to teaching reading and math skills in middle childhood, and describe the use of peer learning in the classroom.

In most cultures, middle childhood is when children first focus on academic skills in school, such as learning how to read and how to do math. However, there are variations in the timing and methods of teaching these skills, both within and between cultures. We'll also examine the use of peer learning in the classroom.

APPROACHES TO READING Children learn language with remarkable proficiency without being explicitly taught or instructed, just from being around others who use the language and interacting with them. However, when they reach middle childhood, children must learn a whole new way of processing language, via reading, and for most children learning to read takes direct instruction. Learning to read is a relatively new development in human history. Until about 200 years ago, most people were illiterate all their lives. For example, in the United States in 1800, only about half of army recruits were even able to sign their own names on the enlistment documents (Rogoff et al., 2005). Because most human economic activity involved simple agriculture or hunting or fishing, learning to read was unnecessary for most people. They could learn what they needed to know from observing others and working alongside them, through guided participation. Today, of course, in a globalized, information-based economy, learning to read is an essential skill for most economic activity, across cultures. Consequently, children almost everywhere learn to read, usually beginning around age 6 or 7, when they enter school.

Think for a moment about the cognitive skills reading requires, so that you can appreciate how complex and challenging it is. To read, you have to recognize that letters are

intrinsic motivation

motivation to engage in behavior that is driven by internal rewards

extrinsic motivation

motivation to engage in behavior that is driven by external rewards or avoidance of punishment

symbols of sounds, and then match a speech sound to each letter or letter combination. You have to know the meanings of whole words—one or two at first, then dozens, then hundreds, and eventually many thousands. As you read a sentence, you have to keep the meanings of individual words or combinations of words in working memory while you continue to read the rest of the sentence. At the end of the sentence, you must put all the word and phrase meanings together into a coherent meaning for the sentence as a whole. Then you have to combine sentences into paragraphs and derive meanings of paragraphs from the relations between the sentences; then combine paragraphs for still larger meanings; and so on.

By now this process no doubt comes naturally to you, after so many years of reading. We perform the complex cognitive tasks of reading automatically after reading for some years, without thinking about the components that go into it. But what is the best way to teach children who are first learning to read? Two major approaches have emerged in educational research over the years. The **phonics approach** advocates teaching children by breaking down words into their component sounds, called *phonics*, then putting the phonics together into words (Gray et al., 2007). Reading in this approach involves learning gradually more complex units: phonics, then single words, then short sentences, then somewhat longer sentences, and so on. After mastering their phonics and being able to read simple words and sentences, children begin to read longer materials such as poems and stories.

The other major approach to teaching reading is the **whole-language approach** (Donat, 2006). In this view, the emphasis should be on the meaning of written language in whole passages, rather than breaking down each word into its smallest components. This approach advocates teaching children to read using complete written material, such as poems, stories, and lists of related items. Children are encouraged to guess at the meaning of words they do not know, based on the context of the word within the written material. In this view, if the material is coherent and interesting, children will be motivated to learn and remember the meanings of words they do not know.

Which approach works best? Each side has advocates, but evidence is substantial that the phonics approach is more effective at teaching children who are first learning to read (Beck & Beck, 2013). Children who have fallen behind in their reading progress using other methods improve substantially when taught with the phonics approach (Shaywitz et al., 2004; Xue & Meisels, 2004). However, once children have begun to read they can also benefit from supplementing phonics instruction with the whole-language approach, with its emphasis on the larger meanings of written language and on using material from school subjects such as history and science to teach reading as well (Pressley et al., 2002; Silva & Martins, 2003).

LEARNING MATH SKILLS There has been far more research on the development of reading than on the development of math skills (Berch & Mazzocco, 2007). Nevertheless, some interesting aspects of math development have been discovered. One is that even some nonhuman animals have a primitive awareness of **numeracy**, which means understanding the meaning of numbers, just as *literacy* means understanding the meaning of written words (Posner & Rothbart, 2007). Rats can be taught to discriminate between a two-tone and an eight-tone sequence, even when the sequences are matched in total duration. Monkeys can learn that the numbers 0 through 9 represent different quantities of rewards. In human infants the beginning of numeracy appears surprisingly early. When they are just 6 weeks old, if they are shown a toy behind a screen and see a second toy added, when the screen is then lowered they look longer and appear more surprised if one or three toys are revealed rather than the two toys they expected.

From toddlerhood through middle childhood, the development of math skills follows a path parallel to the development of language and readings skills (Doherty & Landells, 2006). Children begin to count around age 2, the same age at which their language development accelerates dramatically. They begin to be able to do simple

phonics approach

method of teaching reading that advocates breaking down words into their component sounds, called *phonics*, then putting the phonics together into words

whole-language approach

method of teaching reading in which the emphasis is on the meaning of written language in whole passages, rather than breaking down words into their smallest components

numeracy

understanding of the meaning of numbers

Street children may learn math from the transactions involving the objects they sell. Here, a boy sells candy in a park in Rio de Janeiro, Brazil.

addition and subtraction around age 5, about the same age they often learn to read their first words. In the course of middle childhood, as they become more adept readers, they typically advance in their math skills, moving from addition and subtraction to multiplication and division, and increasing their speed of processing in response to math problems (Posner & Rothbart, 2007). Children who have problems learning to read frequently have problems mastering early math skills as well.

Cultural groups vary in their timing and approach to teaching math skills to children, with consequences for the pace of children's learning. One study compared 5-year-old children in China, Finland, and England (Aunio et al., 2008). The children in China scored highest, with children in Finland second, and the English children third. The authors related these variations to cultural differences in how math is taught and promoted. Children in China learn math beginning in preschool, and there is a strong cultural emphasis on math as an important basis of future learning and success. In contrast, English preschools usually make little attempt to teach children math skills, in the belief that they are not ready to learn math until they enter formal schooling. In the United States, the current "math wars" is a debate among educators about whether "skill-and-drill" and memorizations are better than a "whole math" constructivist approach, which focuses more on concepts.

Most children learn math skills one way or another within school, but sometimes math skills can be learned effectively in a practical setting. In a study of Brazilian street children, Geoffrey Saxe (2002) found that in selling candy they worked out complex calculations of prices and profits. Some had attended school and some had not, and the ones who had been to school were more advanced in some math skills but not in the skills necessary for them to succeed in their candy selling on the street.

GLOBALIZATION AND COGNITIVE CHANGE Globalization includes processes like modernization of communities, health care systems, and education, as well as the extending reach of media and communication. As ecocultural settings change globally, cognition and cognitive development also change (Gauvain & Munroe, 2012; Greenfield, 2009). In one study that examined globalization and cognitive change, Maynard and colleagues (Maynard et al., 2015) studied three generations of Mayan children—in 1969, 1991, and 2012. Their study was informed by Greenfield's (2009) theory that societies are changing in the same direction—from small-scale communities toward more complex, less face-to-face, more money-oriented societies. With these changes come changes in ecocultural settings that affect children, like school.

Greenfield's theory states that whatever variable is changing the most will have the biggest effect on development. And Maynard and colleagues found just that. From the first to second generation, the variable changing the most was involvement in the money economy, and that was the variable most related to changes in cognitive development, namely abstract representation and the ability to deal with novelty (both of which are skills emphasized in commerce and in school). From the second to third generation, it was increases in schooling that were related to those changes in cognitive development; commerce had become the norm and was no longer having the main effect as a driver of change.

Changes in the money economy were also the subject of research by Saxe (2008; Saxe & Esmonde, 2005), who worked with Oksapmin people in Papua New Guinea. Saxe found that the traditional number system that involved using body parts to count (starting on one hand, going up the arm, across the face, and down the other hand) had changed. The Oksapmin developed a system for indicating multiples of amounts or sets. The change was related to involvement in the cash economy, which had made this kind of math and linguistic form necessary.

Global change has become the rule. Industrialization and modernization are forces that will continue to occur, and it is important that we understand how children's development is shaped by changes in ecocultural settings.

PEER LEARNING IN THE CLASSROOM Think about what it takes to teach someone something. To teach someone well, you have to know what they know and don't know. And you have to set up tasks and break them down in ways that can help learners accomplish tasks you are teaching them. Teaching is a skill that you have probably taken for granted as something that people "just know how to do," but some theorists believe teaching is a cognitive and social skill that develops (Maynard, 2002; Strauss, et al., 2002). Though four-year-old children are capable of teaching others simple tasks (Davis-Unger & Carlson, 2008), the perspective-taking and theory of mind skills that children develop during early childhood become much sharper and can be applied in teaching others in middle childhood. The ability to break down tasks, provide careful feedback, and guide the learning of another child becomes clear and focused during middle childhood (Maynard, 2002).

Children's teaching skills can be applied when children become peer tutors. Peer-tutoring programs tend to use either a Piagetian model or a Vygotskian model. In the Piagetian models, lessons are provided that stimulate cognitive conflict and resolution with the help of the tutor. The Vygotskian models emphasize co-construction of the solution by the tutor and the learner together (Thurston & Topping, 2007). Increasingly, teaching as a developing cognition in childhood is being considered in teacher education programs (Strauss, 2005).

Educating Children With Special Needs

LO 7.12 **Identify common disabilities in middle childhood, and explain the educational issues surrounding them.**

Attention-deficit/hyperactivity disorder (ADHD) and learning disabilities, including dyslexia, are common disabilities first identified in middle childhood. The timing of identification is usually because there is a mismatch between what is expected in the school setting and what children with these disabilities are capable of doing relative to that setting.

CHILDHOOD DISABILITIES Childhood disabilities like ADHD and learning difficulties are an impediment to adjustment in school. Efforts to understand and remedy these issues are informed by research.

ADHD Being able to maintain attention becomes especially important once children enter school at about age 6 or 7 because the school setting requires children to pay attention to their teachers' instructions. Children with especially notable difficulties in maintaining attention may be diagnosed with **attention-deficit/hyperactivity disorder (ADHD)**, which includes problems of inattention, hyperactivity, and impulsiveness. Children with ADHD have difficulty following instructions and waiting their turn. In the United States, it is estimated that 7 percent of children ages 4 to 10 are diagnosed with ADHD (National Resource Center on ADHD, 2014). Boys are over twice as likely as girls to have ADHD. The diagnosis is usually made by a pediatrician after evaluation of the child and consultation with parents and teachers (Sax & Kautz, 2003). Watch the video *A Boy Talks About Having ADHD* on the next page for a child's perspective on the disorder.

In the United States, nearly 9 of 10 children and adolescents diagnosed with ADHD receive Ritalin or other medications to suppress their hyperactivity and help them concentrate better (Kaplan et al., 2004). Medications are often effective in controlling the symptoms of ADHD, with 70 percent of children showing improvements in academic performance and peer relations (Prasad et al., 2013). However, there are concerns about side effects, including slower physical growth and higher risk of depression (Reeves & Schweitzer, 2004). Behavioral therapies are also effective, and the combination of medication and behavioral therapy is more effective than either treatment alone (American Academy of Pediatrics, 2005; Hoza et al., 2008).

**attention-deficit/
hyperactivity disorder
(ADHD)**

diagnosis that includes problems of inattention, hyperactivity, and impulsiveness

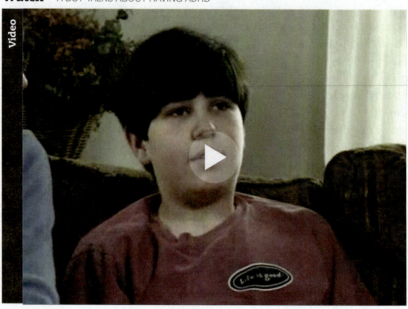

Watch A BOY TALKS ABOUT HAVING ADHD

dyslexia

learning disability that includes difficulty sounding out letters, difficulty learning to spell words, and a tendency to misperceive the order of letters in words

learning disability

cognitive disorder that impedes the development of learning a specific skill such as reading or math

individual education plan (IEP)

plan developed by a teacher with a parent to help a child with special needs adjust to the school setting

least restrictive environment (LRE)

requirement that students with disabilities must have the opportunity to be educated with nondisabled peers to the extent possible

inclusion

educational practice where children with special needs learn in the main classroom with nondisabled children

Although most research on ADHD has taken place in the United States, one large study of ADHD was completed in Europe, involving more than 1,500 children and adolescents (ages 6–18) in 10 countries (Rotheberger et al., 2006). In this Attention-deficit/hyperactivity Disorder Observational Research in Europe (ADORE) study, pediatricians and child psychiatrists across Europe collected observational data on children and adolescents at seven time points over 2 years, with data including diagnosis, treatment, and outcomes. Parents also participated, and their assessments showed high agreement with the assessments of the pediatricians and child psychiatrists.

Like the U.S. studies, ADORE found higher rates of ADHD among boys than among girls, but the ratios varied widely among countries, from 3:1 to 16:1 (Novik et al., 2006). Symptoms of ADHD were similar among boys and girls, but girls with ADHD were more likely than boys to have additional emotional problems and to be bullied by their peers, whereas ADHD boys were more likely than girls to have conduct problems. For both boys and girls, having ADHD resulted in frequent problems in their relations with peers, teachers, and parents (Coghill et al., 2006). Parents reported frequent stresses and strains because of children's ADHD behavior, including disruptions of family activities and worries about the future (Riley et al., 2006). In contrast to the U.S. approach of relying heavily on Ritalin and other medications, the European approaches to treatment were diverse: medications (25 percent), psychotherapy (19 percent), combination of medications and psychotherapy (25 percent), other therapy (10 percent), and no treatment (21 percent) (Preuss et al., 2006).

Learning Disabilities Although learning to read is cognitively challenging, most children become able readers by Grade 3 (Popp, 2005). However, some children find learning to read unusually difficult. One condition that interferes with learning to read is **dyslexia**, which includes difficulty sounding out letters, difficulty learning to spell words, and a tendency to misperceive the order of letters in words (Snowling, 2004; Spafford & Grosser, 2005). Dyslexia is one of the most-common types of **learning disabilities**, which are cognitive disorders that impede the development of learning a specific skill such as reading or math. As with other learning disabilities, children with dyslexia are not necessarily any less intelligent than other children; their cognitive problem is specific to the skill of reading. The causes of dyslexia are not known, but boys are about three times as likely as girls to have the disability, suggesting a genetic link to the Y chromosome (Hensler et al.,

2010; Vidyasagar, 2004). Another learning disability is *dyscalculia*, which is difficulty in making arithmetical calculations—an impediment to learning math.

SPECIAL EDUCATION Approximately 13 percent of children in U.S. public schools are receiving services under the federal Individuals with Disabilities Education Act (IDEA) (U.S. Department of Education, 2012). Individualized instruction can help children with special needs adjust to school and develop better learning strategies. **Individual education plans (IEPs)** are developed by a teacher with a parent to help the child with special needs adjust to the school setting. The goal is to keep as many children in school as possible. The IDEA also stipulates that students with disabilities must have the opportunity to be educated with nondisabled peers to the extent possible. This is known as the **least restrictive environment (LRE)**.

Before 1960, children with special needs typically did not attend school. Today, many children with special needs are *mainstreamed*, meaning that they are educated in a regular class. Some schools have special resource rooms, where children with special needs are pulled out of class to work with a teacher individually. Other schools may use **inclusion**, where children with special needs are assigned special skills teachers to help them learn in the main classroom alongside other children. In some school districts, children with special needs could have skills trainers for reading, math, social and emotional skills, and motor planning, among others. Although it is still up to parents to determine where their children will be educated, school districts have come a long way in helping children with special needs develop cognitive and social skills.

Children with special needs are often included in regular classrooms with the help of special learning aids.

Summary: Cognitive Development

LO 7.5   Explain the major cognitive advances that occur during Piaget's concrete operations stage.

According to Piaget, children progress from the preoperational stage to the stage of concrete operations during middle childhood because they learn to think more systematically and scientifically about how the world works and avoid cognitive errors. Cognitive advances during this stage include the ability to understand conservation, improved classification skills, and the understanding of seriation.

LO 7.6   Describe how attention and memory change from early childhood to middle childhood.

In middle childhood, children become more capable of focusing their attention on relevant information and disregarding what is irrelevant. Middle childhood is the period when children first learn to use memory strategies such as rehearsal, organization, and elaboration.

LO 7.7   Describe methods of conceptualizing and measuring intelligence, and identify genetic and environmental influences on intelligence.

Intelligence testing first becomes a reliable predictor of later development in middle childhood. Critics have complained, however, that IQ tests assess only a narrow range of abilities, and miss some of the most important aspects of intelligence, such as creativity. There is a strong genetic component to intelligence. However, as with many traits, there is a reaction range where genes interact with environmental influences. Average IQ scores have risen substantially over the 20th century. In recent decades, alternative theories of intelligence have sought to present a conception of intelligence that is much broader than the traditional one. Gardner's theory of multiple intelligences proposes eight types of intelligence, whereas Sternberg's triarchic theory proposes three, but neither theorist has been able to develop an effective way of assessing the intelligences they proposed.

LO 7.8   Identify the advances in vocabulary, grammar, and pragmatics during middle childhood.

Language development continues apace with massive additions to children's vocabularies once they learn to read.

There is a fourfold increase in children's vocabularies between the ages of 6 and 10 or 11, and the grammar of children's language use becomes more complex. Their understanding of pragmatics also grows substantially during middle childhood, which can be seen vividly in children's use and appreciation of humor.

LO 7.9 Explain the consequences for cognitive development of growing up bilingual.

Becoming bilingual is beneficial, most notably in the development of metalinguistic knowledge. The difficulty of learning a second language increases with age.

LO 7.10 Summarize the variations worldwide in school enrollment, socialization practices, and academic achievement during middle childhood.

Attending school is a relatively recent historical development in children's lives, and even today 18 percent of children in developing countries do not attend primary school. School has important influences on children's social development because it separates children from the world of adults and places them among same-age peers. It also makes them less of an economic asset to their parents. Schools vary widely around the world depending on cultural beliefs about how children should learn, but it is economic development, not school philosophy, that mainly determines children's performance on international tests of academic performance.

LO 7.11 Compare and contrast approaches to teaching reading and math skills in middle childhood, and describe the use of peer learning in the classroom.

In middle childhood, children must learn a new way of processing language, via reading, and for most children learning to read takes direct instruction. Phonics appears to be the most effective approach to teaching children to read. Most children learn math skills within school, but sometimes math skills can be learned effectively in a practical setting. Because of children's developing teaching skills, peer tutoring may be an effective learning activity in the classroom.

LO 7.12 Identify common disabilities in middle childhood, and explain the educational issues surrounding them.

ADHD and learning disabilities like dyslexia are often first identified in middle childhood because of children's participation in school settings. Children with ADHD may learn skills to control their attention and behavior to perform better in school. Ritalin is a highly prescribed medication that is effective in treating the symptoms of ADHD for many children. Special education for children with disabilities focuses on inclusion, so that all children may receive the benefits of the typical classroom environment to the extent possible.

Section 3 Emotional and Social Development

 Learning Objectives

7.13 Describe how emotional self-regulation and emotional understanding advance by middle childhood.

7.14 Summarize how self-concept and self-esteem change in middle childhood, and identify cultural influences on conceptions of the self.

7.15 Describe how beliefs and behavior regarding gender change in middle childhood.

7.16 Explain the distinctive features of family relations in middle childhood, and describe the consequences of parental divorce and remarriage.

7.17 Explain the main basis of friendships in middle childhood, and describe the four categories of peer social status and the dynamics between bullies and victims.

7.18 Describe the kinds of work children do in middle childhood, and explain why work patterns differ between developed and developing countries.

7.19 Summarize the rates of daily TV watching among children worldwide, and describe the positive and negative effects of television, especially the hazards related to TV violence.

EMOTIONAL AND SOCIAL DEVELOPMENT: Emotional and Self-Development

Children advance in their emotional self-regulation in middle childhood and experience relatively few emotional extremes. They grow in their self-understanding, and their self-esteem is generally high, although it depends on cultural context. They grow in their understanding of gender roles, too, but in some respects they become more rigid about those roles.

Smooth Sailing: Advances in Emotional Self-Regulation

LO 7.13 Describe how emotional self-regulation and emotional understanding advance by middle childhood.

Middle childhood is in some ways a golden age emotionally, a time of high well-being and relatively low volatility. In infancy, toddlerhood, and even early childhood, there are many emotional highs, but plenty of emotional lows, too. Outbursts of crying and anger are fairly frequent in the early years of life, but by middle childhood the frequency of such negative emotions has declined substantially (Shipman et al., 2003). Children develop ways of managing stress. Negative emotions will rise again in adolescence, but during middle childhood most days are free of any negative emotional extremes.

One valuable source of information about emotions in middle childhood is research using the **Experience Sampling Method (ESM)** pioneered by Reed Larson and his colleagues (Larson & Richards, 1994; Larson et al., 2002; Richards et al., 2002). The ESM involves having people wear wristwatch beepers that randomly beep during the day so that people can record their thoughts, feelings, and behavior. Each time they are "beeped," participants rate the degree to which they currently feel happy to unhappy, cheerful to irritable, and friendly to angry, as well as how hurried, tired, and competitive they are feeling.

The overall conclusion of ESM research with regard to middle childhood is that it is time of remarkable contentment and emotional stability (Larson & Richards, 1994). When beeped, children in middle childhood report being "very happy" 28 percent of the time, a far higher percentage than for adolescents or adults. Children at this age mostly have "quite enjoyable lives" in which they "bask in a kind of naïve happiness" (Larson & Richards, 1994, p. 85). Sure, they are sad or angry occasionally, but it is almost always because of something concrete and immediate such as getting scolded by a parent or losing a game, "events that pass quickly and are forgotten" (p. 85).

Emotional self-regulation improves from early childhood to middle childhood in part because the environment requires it (Geldhof et al., 2010). Middle childhood is often a time of moving into new contexts: primary school, civic organizations (such as the Boy Scouts and Girl Scouts), sports teams, and music groups. All of these contexts make demands for emotional self-regulation. Children are required to do what they are told (whether they feel like it or not), to wait their turn, and to cooperate with others. Expressions of emotional extremes are disruptive to the functioning of the group and are discouraged. Most children are capable of meeting these demands by middle childhood.

Emotional understanding also advances from early to middle childhood. Children become better able to understand both their own and others' emotions. They become aware that they can experience two contradictory emotions at once, an emotional state known as **ambivalence**; for example being both happy (because my team won the game) and sad (because my best friend was on the losing team) (Pons et al., 2003). They also learn how to conceal their emotions intentionally (Saarni, 1999). This allows them to show a socially acceptable emotion such as gratitude when, for example, they open a birthday present they didn't really want. In Asian cultures, children in middle childhood learn the concept of "face," which means showing to others the appropriate and expected emotion regardless of how you actually feel (Han, 2011).

In the same way that children become able to suppress or conceal their own true emotions, they come to understand that other people may display emotional expressions that do not indicate what they actually feel (Saarni, 1999). Children's understanding of others' emotions is also reflected in increased capacity for empathy (Goldstein & Winner, 2012; Hoffman, 2000). By middle childhood, children become better cognitively at perspective-taking and the ability to understand how others view events fosters the ability to understand how they feel, too.

Middle childhood is also a time when children become capable of managing stress. Modern life is full of stressors, even for children. In the developed world, children manage a variety of stresses like homework, and many children have busy schedules after school. Mary Gauvain and her colleagues have related planning and stress management

Middle childhood is an exceptionally happy time of life.

Experience Sampling Method (ESM)

research method that involves having people wear beepers, usually for a period of 1 week; when they are beeped at random times during the day, they record a variety of characteristics of their experience at that moment

ambivalence

emotional state of experiencing two contradictory emotions at once

to executive function (Perez & Gauvain, 2009, 2010). They found that children's adaptive emotional functioning in response to goals was related to better school performance. Through socialization, parents may help children develop the emotional management skills to deal with stress.

Self-Understanding

LO 7.14   Summarize how self-concept and self-esteem change in middle childhood, and identify cultural influences on conceptions of the self.

Sociologist George Herbert Mead (1934) made a distinction between what he called the *I-self* (how we believe others view us) and the *me-self* (how we view ourselves). Both the I-self and the me-self change in important ways in middle childhood. We discuss the me-self first, then the I-self, and then we look at the cultural basis of conceptions of the self.

SELF-CONCEPT Our **self-concept**, that is, how we view and evaluate ourselves, changes during middle childhood from the external to the internal and from the physical to the psychological (Lerner et al., 2005; Marsh & Ayotte, 2003; Rosenberg, 1979). Up until the age of 7 or 8, most children describe themselves mainly in terms of external, concrete, physical characteristics. ("My name is Mona. I'm 7 years old. I have brown eyes and short black hair. I have two little brothers.") They may mention specific possessions ("I have a red bicycle.") and activities they enjoy ("I like to dance." "I like to play sports."). In the course of middle childhood, they add more internal, psychological, personality-related traits to their self-descriptions ("I'm shy." "I'm friendly." "I try to be helpful."). They may also mention characteristics that are *not me* ("I don't like art." "I'm not very good at math."). Toward the end of middle childhood their descriptions become more complex because they recognize that they may be different on different occasions (Harter, 2003) ("Mostly I'm easy to get along with, but sometimes I lose my temper.").

Another important change in self-concept in middle childhood is that children engage in more accurate **social comparison**, in which they compare themselves to others (Guest, 2007). A 6-year-old child might describe himself by saying, "I'm really good at math," whereas a 9-year-old child might say "I'm better than most kids at math, although there are a couple of kids in my class who are a little better." These social comparisons reflect advances in the cognitive ability of seriation, discussed previously. In the same way that children learn how to arrange sticks accurately from shortest to tallest in middle childhood, they also learn to rank themselves more accurately in abilities relative to other children. The age grading of schools promotes social comparisons because it places children in a setting where they spend most of a typical day around other children their age. Teachers compare them to one another by giving them grades, and they notice who is relatively good and relatively not so good at reading, math, and so on.

Self-concept can be influenced not only by age but by social context. In a multicultural society like the United States, the views of the majority culture can influence how children in minority cultures think

self-concept
person's perception and evaluation of himself or herself

social comparison
how persons view themselves in relation to others with regard to status, abilities, or achievements

In middle childhood, children become more accurate in comparing themselves to others.

about themselves. One classic study in the 1940s found that when African American and White children in middle childhood were given a choice of two dolls to play with, one White and one Black, even most of the Black children chose the White doll (Clark & Clark, 1947). Furthermore, children of both groups tended to choose the White doll as the "good" doll and the Black doll as the "bad" doll. Even recent studies continue to show that children often view dark skin as "bad" and white skin as "good" (Byrd, 2012).

SELF-ESTEEM Self-esteem is a person's overall sense of worth and well-being. A great deal has been written and discussed about self-esteem in U.S. society in the past 50 years. Even among Western countries, Americans value high self-esteem to a greater extent than people in other countries, and the gap between the United States and non-Western countries in this respect is especially great. For example, in traditional Japanese culture, self-criticism is a virtue and high self-esteem is a character problem (Heine et al., 1999). The belief in the value of high self-esteem is part of U.S. individualism (Bellah et al., 1985; Rychlak, 2003).

Self-esteem declines slightly in the transition from early childhood to middle childhood because children enter a school environment in which social comparisons are a daily experience (Lerner et al., 2005; Wigfield et al., 1997). The decline is mild and simply reflects children's more realistic appraisal of their abilities as they compare themselves to others and are rated by teachers. For the rest of middle childhood, overall self-esteem is high for most children, reflecting the generally positive emotional states mentioned previously. In Western countries, having low self-esteem in middle childhood is related to anxiety, depression, and antisocial behavior (Robins et al., 2002).

An important change in self-esteem in middle childhood is that it becomes more differentiated. In addition to overall self-esteem, children have self-concepts for several specific areas, including academic competence, social competence, athletic competence, and physical appearance (Harter, 2012; Marsh & Ayotte, 2003). Within each of these areas, self-concept is differentiated into subareas. For example, children may see themselves as good at baseball but not basketball, while also having an overall high or low evaluation of their athletic competence.

Children combine their different areas of self-concept into an overall level of self-esteem. For most children and adolescents, physical appearance is the strongest contributor to overall self-esteem (Harter, 2012; Klomsten et al., 2004). However, in other areas, children's self-concept contributes to overall self-esteem only if they value doing well in that area. For example, a child may be no good at sports but not care about sports, in which case low athletic self-concept would have no effect on overall self-esteem.

CULTURE AND THE SELF The conception of the self that children have by middle childhood varies substantially among cultures. In discussing cultural differences in conceptions of the self scholars typically distinguish between the *independent self* promoted by individualistic cultures and the *interdependent self* promoted by collectivistic cultures (Cross & Gore, 2003; Markus & Kitayama, 1991; Shweder et al., 2006). Cultures that promote an independent, individualistic self also promote and encourage reflection about the self. In such cultures it is seen as a good thing to think about yourself, to consider who you are as an independent person, and to think highly of yourself (within certain limits, of course—no culture values selfishness or egocentrism). Americans are especially known for their individualism and their focus on self-oriented issues. It was an American who first invented the term *self-esteem* (William James, in the late 19th century), and the United States continues to be known to the rest of the world as a place where the independent self is valued and promoted (Green et al., 2005; Triandis, 1995).

self-esteem

person's overall sense of worth and well-being

However, not all cultures look at the self in this way or value the self to the same extent. In collectivistic cultures, an interdependent conception of the self prevails (Markus & Kitayama 2010). In these cultures, the interests of the group—the family, the kinship group, the ethnic group, the nation, the religious institution—are supposed to come first, before the needs of the individual. This means that it is not necessarily a good thing, in these cultures, to think highly of yourself. People who think highly of themselves, who possess a high level of self-esteem, threaten the harmony of the group because they may be inclined to pursue their personal interests regardless of the interests of the groups to which they belong.

Cultural variations in views of the self influence approaches to parenting. Parents in most places and times have been more worried that their children would become too selfish than that they would have low self-esteem. As a result, parents have discouraged self-inflation as part of family socialization (Harkness et al., 2015; LeVine et al., 2008). However, this kind of parenting works differently if it is part of a cultural norm rather than an exception within a culture. For example, children from Asian cultures are discouraged from valuing the self highly, yet they generally have high levels of academic performance and low levels of psychological problems (Markus & Kitayama, 2010). In contrast, children within the U.S. majority culture who are exposed to parenting that is critical and negative show negative effects such as depression and poor academic performance (Bender et al., 2007; DeHart et al., 2006). It may be that children in Asian cultures learn to expect criticism if they show signs of high self-esteem, and they see this as normal in comparison to other children, whereas U.S. children learn to expect frequent praise, and hence they suffer more if their parents are more critical than the parents of their peers (Rudy & Grusec, 2006).

It should be added that most cultures are not purely either independent or interdependent in their conceptions of the self, but have elements of each (Killen & Wainryb, 2000). Also, with globalization, many cultures that have a tradition of interdependence are changing toward a more independent view of the self (Arnett, 2002b, 2011).

Gender Development

LO 7.15 Describe how beliefs and behavior regarding gender change in middle childhood.

Cultural beliefs about gender become well established by the end of early childhood, and gender roles become even more sharply divided during middle childhood. In traditional cultures, the daily activities of men and women are different, and the activities of boys and girls become more differentiated in middle childhood as they begin to take part in their parents' work. In the human past, men have been responsible for hunting, fishing, caring for domestic animals, and fighting off animal and human attackers (Gilmore, 1990). Women have been responsible for caring for young children, tending the crops, food preparation, and running the household (Shlegel & Barry, 1991). This pattern still prevails in many developing countries (Gaskins, 2015). During middle childhood, boys increasingly learn to do what men do and girls increasingly learn to do what women do.

Boys and girls not only learn gender-specific tasks in middle childhood, but they are also socialized to develop personality characteristics that enhance performance on those tasks: independence and toughness, for boys, and nurturance and compliance for girls. In an early study of 110 traditional cultures, boys and girls were socialized to develop these gender-specific traits in virtually all cultures (Barry et al., 1957). More recent analyses of gender socialization in traditional cultures have

In developing countries, the kinds of work children and adults do is often divided strictly by gender. Here, a girl in Mozambique helps prepare cassava, a local food.

Why are interactions between boys and girls often quasi-romantic and antagonistic in middle childhood?

found that these patterns persist (Banerjee, 2005; Kapadia & Gala, 2015; LeVine, 2008).

In modern developed countries, too, children's gender attitudes and behavior become more stereotyped in middle childhood. Children increasingly view personality traits as associated with one gender or the other rather than both. Traits such as "gentle" and "dependent" become increasingly viewed as feminine, and traits such as "ambitious" and "dominant" become increasingly viewed as masculine (Best, 2001; Heyman & Legare, 2004). Both boys and girls come to see occupations they associate with men (such as firefighter or astronomer) as having higher status than occupations they associate with women (such as nurse or librarian) (Liben et al., 2001; Weisgram et al., 2010). Furthermore, children increasingly perceive some school subjects as boys' areas (such as math and science) and others as girls' areas (such as reading and art) (Guay et al., 2010). Teachers may bring gender biases into the classroom, perhaps unknowingly, in ways that influence children's perceptions of what areas are gender-appropriate for them (Sadker & Sadker, 1994). Accordingly, boys come to feel more competent than girls at math and science and girls come to feel more competent than boys at verbal skills—even when they have equal abilities in these areas (Hong et al., 2003).

Socially, children become even more gender-segregated in their play groups in middle childhood than they were in early childhood. In traditional cultures, gender-segregated play is a consequence of the gender-specific work boys and girls are doing by middle childhood. In the 12-culture analysis by Whiting and Edwards (1988; see Chapter 6), same-gender play groups rose from a proportion of 30 and 40 percent at ages 2 to 3 to more than 90 percent by ages 8 to 11. However, the same pattern is true in developed countries, where boys and girls are in the same schools engaged in the same daily activities (McHale et al., 2003). When boys' and girls' play groups do interact in middle childhood, it tends to be in a manner that is at once quasi-romantic and antagonistic, such as playing a game in which the girls chase the boys, or tossing mild insults at each other, like the one Jeff's daughter Paris came home chanting one day at age 7:

> GIRLS go to COllege to get more KNOWledge.
> BOYS go to JUpiter to get more STUpider.

Thorne (1993) calls this kind of gender play "border work" and sees its function as clarifying gender boundaries during middle childhood. It can also be seen as the first tentative step toward the romantic relations that will develop in adolescence.

In terms of their gender self-perceptions, boys and girls head in different directions in middle childhood (Banerjee, 2005; Kapadia & Gala, 2015). Boys increasingly describe themselves in terms of "masculine" traits. They become more likely to avoid activities that might be considered feminine, because their peers become increasingly intolerant of anything that threatens to cross gender boundaries (Blakemore, 2003). In contrast, girls become more likely to attribute masculine characteristics such as "forceful" and "self-reliant" to themselves in the course of middle childhood. They do not become less likely to describe themselves as having "feminine" traits such as "warm" and "compassionate," but they add masculine traits to their self-perceptions. Similarly, they become more likely during middle childhood to consider future occupations usually associated with men, whereas boys become less likely to consider future occupations associated with women (Gaskins, 2015; Liben & Bigler, 2002).

EMOTIONAL AND SOCIAL DEVELOPMENT: The Social and Cultural Contexts of Middle Childhood

There is both continuity and change in social contexts from early to middle childhood. Nearly all children remain within a family context, although the composition of the family may change in some cultures because of parents' divorce or remarriage. A new social context is added because children in nearly all cultures begin formal schooling when they enter this life stage. For children in developing countries today, middle childhood may also mean entering a work setting such as a factory. In all countries, media have become an important socialization context, especially television.

Family Relations

LO 7.16 **Explain the distinctive features of family relations in middle childhood, and describe the consequences of parental divorce and remarriage.**

Middle childhood represents a key turning point in family relations. Up until that time, children in all cultures need, and receive, a great deal of care and supervision, from parents and older siblings and sometimes from extended family members. They lack sufficient emotional and behavioral self-regulation to be on their own for even a short period of time. However, in middle childhood they become much more capable of going about their daily activities without constant monitoring and control by others. From early childhood to middle childhood, parents and children move away from direct parental control and toward **coregulation**, in which parents provide broad guidelines for behavior but children are capable of a substantial amount of independent, self-directed behavior (Calkins, 2012; Maccoby, 1984; McHale et al., 2003). Parents continue to provide assistance and instruction, and they continue to know where their children are and what they are doing nearly all the time, but there is less need for direct, moment-to-moment monitoring.

This pattern applies across cultures. In developed countries, studies have shown that children spend substantially less time with their parents in middle childhood than in early childhood (Parke, 2004). Children respond more to parents' rules and reasoning because of advances in cognitive development and self-regulation, and parents in turn use more explanation and less physical punishment (Collins et al., 2002; Parke, 2004). Parents begin to give their children simple daily chores such as making their own beds in the morning and setting the table for dinner.

In traditional cultures, parents and children also move toward coregulation in middle childhood. Children have learned family rules and routines by middle childhood and will often carry out their family duties without having to be told or urged by their parents (Gaskins, 2015; Weisner, 1996). Also, children are allowed to play and explore further from home once they reach middle childhood (Whiting & Edwards, 1988). Boys are allowed more of this freedom than girls are, in part because girls are assigned more daily responsibilities in middle childhood. However, girls are also allowed more scope for independent activity in middle childhood. For example, in the Mexican village described by Beverly Chinas (1992), when they reach middle childhood girls have responsibility for going to the village market each day to sell the tortillas they and their mothers have made that morning. By middle childhood they are capable of going to the market without an adult to monitor them, and they are also capable of making the monetary calculations required in selling the tortillas and providing change.

Sibling relationships also change in middle childhood (Bryant, 2014). Children with an older sibling often benefit from the sibling's help with academic, peer, and parent

coregulation

relationship between parents and children in which parents provide broad guidelines for behavior but children are capable of a substantial amount of independent, self-directed behavior

Siblings often benefit from having each other as companions.

issues (Brody, 2004). Both older and young siblings benefit from mutual companionship and assistance. However, at least among U.S. children, sibling conflict peaks in middle childhood (Cole & Kerns, 2001). In one study that recorded episodes of conflict between siblings, the average frequency of conflict was once every 20 minutes they were together (Kramer et al., 1999). The most-common source of conflict is personal possessions (McGuire et al., 2000). Sibling conflict is especially high when one sibling perceives the other as receiving more affection and material resources from the parents (Dunn, 2004). Other factors contributing to sibling conflict are family financial stress and parents' marital conflict (Jenkins et al., 2003).

DIVERSE FAMILY FORMS Children worldwide grow up in a wide variety of family environments. Some children have parents who are married, whereas others are in single-parent, divorced, or step-families; some children are raised by heterosexual parents whereas others are raised by gay or lesbian parents; and still others live with extended family members or in multigenerational families. Some are adopted or live with relatives other than their parents. **Figure 7.9** shows the distribution of family patterns in the United States.

Gay couples are now allowed to adopt children in some U.S. states and some European countries, and lesbian couples often adopt children or become artificially inseminated. In the latest U.S. census, more than 20 percent of gay couples and one third of lesbian couples were living with children, a dramatic increase over the past 20 years (U.S. Bureau of the Census, 2010). The video *A Family with Two Fathers* describes the adoption process for one such family. Studies of the children of gay and lesbian couples have found that they are highly similar to other children (Goldberg, 2010; Patterson, 2002). In adolescence nearly all are heterosexual, despite the homosexual model their parents provide (Hyde & DeLamater, 2005).

Over the past 50 years, it has become increasingly common in some countries for children to be born to a single mother. The United States is one of the countries where the increase has been greatest. Single motherhood has increased among both Whites and African Americans, but is highest among African Americans; more than 70 percent of African American children are born to a single mother (U.S. Bureau of the Census, 2010). Rates of single motherhood are also high in northern Europe (Ruggeri & Bird, 2014). However, it is more likely in northern Europe than in the United States for the father to be in the home as well, even though the mother and father may not be married. If we combine those children born to single mothers with those living with a single parent as a result of divorce, fewer than half of U.S. children live with both biological parents throughout their entire childhood.

What are the consequences of growing up with in a single-parent household? Because there is only one parent to carry out household responsibilities such as cooking and cleaning, children in single-parent households often contribute a great deal to the functioning of the family, much like children in traditional cultures. However, the most important consequence of growing up in a single-parent family is that it greatly

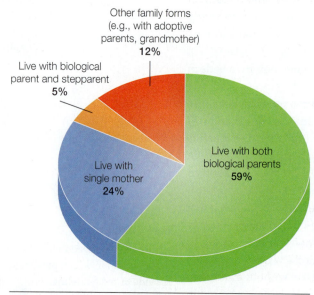

Other family forms (e.g., with adoptive parents, grandmother) 12%

Live with biological parent and stepparent 5%

Live with single mother 24%

Live with both biological parents 59%

Figure 7.9 Family Patterns in the United States through Middle Childhood

In the United States, there is great variation in family living patterns.

Watch A FAMILY WITH TWO FATHERS

increases the likelihood of growing up in poverty, and growing up in poverty, in turn, has a range of negative effects on children (Harvey & Fine, 2004). Children in single-parent families generally are at higher risk for behavior problems and low school achievement when compared to their peers in two-parent families (Ricciuti, 2004).

Single-parent families are diverse, and many children who grow up in single-parent families function very well. When the mother makes enough money so the family is not in poverty, children in single-parent families function as well as children in two-parent families (Lipman et al., 2002). Single-father families are relatively rare, but children with a single father are no different than their peers in middle childhood in regard to social and academic functioning (Amato, 2000). It should also be noted that having a single parent does not always mean there is only one adult in the household. In many African American families, the grandmother is highly involved and provides child care, household help, and financial support to the single mother (Crowther & Rodrigues, 2003). In about one fourth of families with an African American single mother, the grandmother also lives in the household (Kelch-Oliver, 2011).

Poverty is common in single-parent families.

CHILDREN'S RESPONSES TO DIVORCE Rates of divorce have risen dramatically over the past half-century in the United States, Canada, and northern Europe. Currently, close to half of children in many of these countries experience their parents' divorce by the time they reach middle childhood. In contrast, divorce remains rare in southern Europe and in non-Western countries.

How do children respond to their parents' divorce? A wealth of U.S. and European research has addressed this question, including several excellent longitudinal studies. Overall, children respond negatively in a variety of ways, especially boys and especially in the first 2 years following divorce (Amato & Anthony, 2014). Children display increases in both externalizing problems (such as unruly behavior and conflict with mothers, siblings, peers, and teachers) and internalizing problems (such as depressed mood, anxieties, phobias, and sleep disturbances) (Clarke-Stewart & Brentano, 2006). Their school performance also declines (Amato & Boyd, 2013). If the divorce takes place during early childhood, children often blame themselves, but by middle childhood most children are less egocentric and more capable of understanding that their parents may have reasons for divorcing that have nothing to do with them (Hetherington & Kelly, 2002). In the video *Pam: Divorced Mother of Nine-Year-Old*, a woman describes the impact that her divorce has had on her daughter.

Watch PAM: DIVORCED MOTHER OF NINE-YEAR-OLD

In one renowned longitudinal study of divorces that took place when the children were in middle childhood, the researchers classified 25 percent of the children in divorced families as having severe emotional or behavioral problems, compared to 10 percent of children in two-parent nondivorced families (Hetherington & Kelly, 2002). The low point for most children came 1 year after divorce. After that point, most children gradually improved in functioning, and by 2 years post-divorce, girls were mostly back to normal. However, boys' problems were still evident even 5 years after divorce. Problems continue for some children into adolescence, and new consequences appear.

Not all children react negatively to divorce. Even if 25 percent have severe problems, that leaves 75 percent who do not. What factors influence how a divorce will affect children? Increasingly researchers have focused on **family process**, that is, the quality of the relationships between family members before, during, and after the divorce. In all families, whether divorced or not, parental conflict is linked to children's emotional and behavioral problems (Kelly & Emery, 2003). When parents divorce with minimal conflict, or when parents are able to keep their conflicts private, children show far fewer problems (Amato & Anthony, 2014). If divorce results in a transition from a high-conflict household to a low-conflict household, children's functioning often improves rather than deteriorates (Davies et al., 2002).

Another aspect of family process is children's relationship to the mother after divorce. Mothers often struggle in numerous ways following divorce (Wallerstein & Johnson-Reitz, 2004). In addition to the emotional stress of the divorce and conflict with ex-husbands, they now have full responsibility for household tasks and child care. There is increased financial stress, with the father's income no longer coming directly into the household. Most countries have laws requiring fathers to contribute to the care of their children after leaving the household, but despite these laws mothers often receive less than full child support from their ex-husbands (Children's Defense Fund, 2005; Statistics

family process

quality of the relationships between family members

Canada, 2012). Given this pile-up of stresses, it is not surprising that the mother's parenting often takes a turn for the worse in the aftermath of divorce, becoming less warm, less consistent, and more punitive (Hetherington & Kelly, 2002).

Relationships between boys and their mothers are especially likely to go downhill after divorce. Mothers and boys sometimes become sucked into a **coercive cycle** following divorce, in which boys' less-compliant behavior evokes harsh responses from mothers, which in turn makes boys even more resistant to their mothers' control, evoking even harsher responses, and so on (Patterson, 2002). However, when the mother is able to maintain a healthy balance of warmth and control despite the stresses, her children's response to divorce is likely to be less severe (Leon, 2003).

Family processes involving fathers are also important in the aftermath of divorce. In about 90 percent of cases (across countries) mothers retain custody of the children, so the father leaves the household and the children no longer see him on a daily basis. They may stay with him every weekend or every other weekend, and perhaps see him one evening during the week, in addition to talking to him on the phone. Now fathers must get used to taking care of the children on their own, without mothers present, and children must get used to two households that may have different sets of rules. For most children, contact with the father diminishes over time, and only 35 to 40 percent of children in mother-custody families still have at least weekly contact with their fathers within a few years of the divorce (Kelly, 2003). When the father remarries, as most do, his contact with children from the first marriage declines steeply (Dunn, 2002). However, when fathers remain involved and loving, children have fewer postdivorce problems (Dunn et al., 2004 Finley & Schwartz, 2010).

In recent decades, **divorce mediation** has developed as a way of minimizing the damage to children that may take place as a result of heightened parental conflict during and after divorce (Emery et al., 2005; Sbarra & Emery, 2008). In divorce mediation, a professional mediator meets with divorcing parents to help them negotiate an agreement that both will find acceptable. Research has shown that mediation can settle a large percentage of cases otherwise headed for court and lead to better functioning in children following divorce and to improved relationships between divorced parents and their children, even 12 years after the settlement (Emery et al., 2005).

Relationships between mothers and sons sometimes go downhill following divorce.

OUT OF THE FRYING PAN: CHILDREN'S RESPONSES TO REMARRIAGE Most adults who divorce remarry. Consequently, most children who experience their parents' divorce spend part of their childhood in a stepfamily. Because mothers retain custody of the children in about 90 percent of divorces, most stepfamilies involve the entrance of a stepfather into the family. Stepmothers, too, may become part of children's lives.

You might expect that the entrance of a second earner would be a positive development in most cases, given the economic problems that face most split families following divorce. Low income is a problem, particularly for single mothers, and when a stepfather comes into the family this usually means a rise in overall family income. Mothers' stress over handling all the household and child-care responsibilities is a problem, and after a stepfather enters the family he can share some of the load. Mothers' emotional well-being is a problem, and her well-being is typically enhanced by remarriage, at least initially (Visher et al., 2003). If mothers' lives improve in all these ways, their children's lives must improve, too, right?

Unfortunately, no. Frequently, children take a turn for the worse once a stepfather enters the family. Compared to children in nondivorced families, children in stepfamilies have lower academic achievement, lower self-esteem, and greater behavioral problems (Coleman et al., 2000; Nicholson et al., 2008). According to one estimate, about 20 percent of children in stepfamilies have serious problems in at least one aspect of functioning in middle childhood, compared to 10 percent of their peers in nondivorced families (Hetherington & Kelly, 2002). Girls respond more negatively than boys to remarriage, a reversal of their responses

coercive cycle

pattern in relations between parents and children in which children's disobedient behavior evokes harsh responses from parents, which in turn makes children even more resistant to parental control, evoking even harsher responses

divorce mediation

arrangement in which a professional mediator meets with divorcing parents to help them negotiate an agreement that both will find acceptable

to divorce (Bray, 1999). If the stepfather also has children of his own that he brings into the household, making a *blended stepfamily*, the outcomes for children are even worse than in other stepfamilies (Becker et al., 2013).

There are a number of reasons for children's negative responses to remarriage. First, remarriage represents another disruption that requires adjustment, usually at a point when the family had begun to stabilize following the earlier disruption of divorce (Hetherington & Stanley-Hagan, 2002). Second, stepfathers may be perceived by children as coming in between them and their mothers, especially by girls, who may have become closer to their mothers following divorce (Bray, 1999). Third, and perhaps most importantly, children may resent and resist their stepfathers' attempts to exercise authority and discipline (Robertson, 2008). Stepfathers may be attempting to support the mother in parenting and to fulfill the family role of father, but children may refuse to regard him as a "real" father and may in fact regard him as taking their biological father's rightful place (Weaver & Coleman, 2010). When asked to draw their families, many children in stepfamilies literally leave their stepfathers out of the picture (Stafford, 2004).

However, it is important to add that here, as elsewhere, family process counts for as much as family structure. Many stepfathers and stepchildren form harmonious, close relationships (Becker et al., 2013; Coleman et al., 2000). The likelihood of this outcome is enhanced if the stepfather is warm and open to his stepchildren and does not immediately try to assert authority (Visher et al., 2003). Also, the younger the children are, the more open they tend to be to accepting the stepfather (Jeynes, 2007). The likelihood of conflict between stepfathers and stepchildren increases with the children's age, from early childhood to middle childhood and again from middle childhood to adolescence (Hetherington & Kelly, 2002).

Friends and Peers

LO 7.17 Explain the main basis of friendships in middle childhood, and describe the four categories of peer social status and the dynamics between bullies and victims.

Friends rise in importance from early childhood to middle childhood because greater freedom of movement allows children to visit and play with friends. Also, the entrance into formal schooling takes children away from the family social environment and places them in an environment where they spend a substantial amount of most days around many other children of similar age. Daily contact between children makes it possible for them to develop close friendships.

In this discussion of friends and peers we will first examine the characteristics of friendships in middle childhood, and then look at popularity and bullying in peer groups.

MAKING FRIENDS Why do children become friends with some peers but not others? An abundance of research over several decades has shown that the main basis of friendship is similarity, not just during middle childhood but at all ages (Rubin et al., 2008). People tend to prefer being around others who are like themselves, a principle called **selective association** (Popp et al., 2008). We have already seen how gender is an especially important basis of selective association in middle childhood. Boys tend to play with boys and girls with girls, more than at either younger or older ages. Other important criteria for selective association in middle childhood are sociability, aggression, and academic orientation (Hartup, 1996). Sociable kids are attracted to each other as friends, as are shy kids; aggressive kids tend to form friendships with each other, as do kids who refrain from aggression; kids who care a lot about school tend to become friends, and so do kids who dislike school.

In middle childhood, shared activities are still an important part of friendships, but now trust, too, becomes important. Children name fewer of their peers as friends, and friendships last longer, often several years (Rose & Asher, 1999). Your friends are kids who

selective association

in social relations, the principle that people tend to prefer being around others who are like themselves not only like to do things you like to do, but also whom you can rely on to be nice to you almost all the time and whom you can trust with information you would not reveal to just anyone. In one study of children in Grades 3 to 6, the expectation that a friend would keep a secret increased from 25 percent to 72 percent across that age span among girls; among boys the increase came later and did not rise as high (Azmitia et al., 1998). This finding reflects a more general gender difference found in many other studies, that girls prize trust in middle childhood friendships more than boys do, and that boys' friendships focus more on shared activities, although for both genders trust is more important in middle childhood than in early childhood (Rubin et al., 2008). As trust becomes more important to friendships in middle childhood, breaches of trust (such as breaking a promise or failing to provide help when needed) also become the main reason for ending friendships (Hartup & Abecassis, 2004).

Trust becomes more important to friendships in middle childhood.

PLAYING WITH FRIENDS Even though trust becomes a more important part of friendship in middle childhood, friends continue to enjoy playing together in shared activities. As in early childhood, simple social play and cooperative pretend play continue in middle childhood. For example, children might play with dolls or action figures together, or they might pretend to be superheroes or animals.

What is new about play in middle childhood is that it becomes more complex and more rule based. Children in early childhood may play with action figures, but in middle childhood there may be elaborate rules about the powers and limitations of the characters. For example, in the early 21st century, Japanese games involving Pokemon action figures became popular in middle childhood play worldwide, especially among boys (Ogletree et al., 2004; Simmons, 2014). These games involve characters with an elaborate range of powers and provide children with the enjoyment of competition and mastering complex information and rules. In early childhood the information about the characters would be too abundant and the rules too complex for children to follow, but by middle childhood this cognitive challenge is exciting and pleasurable.

In addition to games such as Pokemon, many of the games with rules that children play in middle childhood are more cognitively challenging than the games younger children play. Card games and board games become popular, and often these games require children to count, remember, and plan strategies. Middle childhood is also a time when many children develop an interest in hobbies such as collecting certain types of objects (e.g., coins, dolls) or constructing and building things (such as with LEGO toys, a Danish invention that is popular around the world in middle childhood). These hobbies also provide enjoyable cognitive challenges of organizing and planning (McHale et al., 2001). Recently, electronic games have become a highly popular type of game in middle childhood, and these games also present substantial cognitive challenges (Olson et al., 2008).

Although the complexity and cognitive challenges of play in middle childhood distinguish it from play in early childhood, children continue to enjoy simple games as well (Manning, 1998). According to cross-cultural studies, games such as tag and hide-and-seek are popular all over the world in middle childhood (Edwards, 2000). Children also play simple games that are drawn from their local environment, such as the herding games played by boys in Kenya in the course of caring for cattle.

Middle childhood games also reflect children's advances in gross motor development. As children develop greater physical agility and skill in middle childhood, their games with rules include various sports that require greater physical challenges than their early childhood games did. As noted previously, in many countries middle childhood is the time when children first join organized teams to play sports such as soccer, baseball, or basketball. Many children also play sports in games they organize themselves, often including discussions of the rules of the game (Davies, 2004).

POPULARITY AND UNPOPULARITY In addition to having friendships, children are also part of a larger social world of peers, especially once they enter primary school. Schools are usually age graded, which means that students at a given grade level tend to be the same age. When children are in a social environment with children of different ages, age is a key determinant of **social status**, in that older children tend to have more authority than younger children. However, when all children are about the same age, they find other ways of establishing who is high in social status and who is low. Based on children's ratings of who they like or dislike among their peers, researchers have described four categories of social status (Cillessen & Mayeux, 2004; Rubin et al., 2008):

social status

within a group, the degree of power, authority, and influence that each person has in the view of the others

- *Popular children* are the ones who are most often rated as "liked" and rarely rated as "disliked."
- *Rejected children* are most often disliked and rarely liked by other children. Usually, rejected children are disliked mainly for being overly aggressive, but in about 10 to 20 percent of cases rejected children are shy and withdrawn (Hymel et al., 2004; Sandstrom & Zakriski, 2004). Boys are more likely than girls to be rejected.

Cultural Focus: Friendships and Peer Relationships in Middle Childhood Across Cultures

Although selective association is an important basis of friendship at all ages, over the course of childhood friendships change in other ways. An important change from early to middle childhood is in the relative balance of activities and trust (Rubin et al., 2008). Friendships in early childhood are based mainly on shared activities. Your friends are the kids who like to do the same things you like to do. Consequently, young children usually claim they have lots of friends, and their friends are more or less interchangeable. If you like to ride bikes, whoever is available to ride bikes with you is your friend. When they describe their friends, young children talk mainly about their shared activities (Damon, 1983; Rubin et al., 2008). In this video, children in three cultures talk about their friendships.

Review Question:

Many of those interviewed discuss how friendships in middle childhood are often same gender. Why do you feel this self-segregation takes place?

Watch FRIENDSHIPS AND PEER RELATIONSHIPS IN MIDDLE CHILDHOOD ACROSS CULTURES

Video

- *Neglected children* are rarely mentioned as either liked or disliked; other children have trouble remembering who they are. Girls are more likely than boys to be neglected.
- *Controversial children* are liked by some children but disliked by others. They may be aggressive at times but friendly at other times.

About two thirds of children in U.S. samples fall into one of these categories in middle childhood, according to most studies (Wentzel, 2003). The rest are rated in mixed ways by other children and are classified by researchers as "average."

What characteristics determine a child's social status? Abundant research indicates that the strongest influence on popularity is **social skills** such as being friendly, helpful, cooperative, and considerate (Caravita & Cillessen, 2012; Chan et al., 2000). Children with social skills are good at perspective-taking; consequently they are good at understanding and responding to other children's needs and interests (Cassidy et al., 2003). Other important influences on popularity are intelligence, physical appearance, and (for boys) athletic ability (McHale et al., 2003). Despite the stereotype of the "nerd" or "geek" as a kid who is unpopular for being smart, in general, intelligence enhances popularity in middle childhood. "Nerds" and "geeks" are unpopular because they lack social skills, not because of their intelligence.

Rejected children are usually more aggressive than other children, and their aggressiveness leads to conflicts (Coie, 2004). They tend to be impulsive and have difficulty controlling their emotional reactions, which disrupts group activities, to the annoyance of their peers. In addition to this lack of self-control, their lack of social skills and social understanding leads to conflict with others. According to Kenneth Dodge (2008), who has done decades of research on this topic, rejected children often fail in their **social information processing (SIP)**. That is, they tend to interpret their peers' behavior as hostile even when it is not, and they tend to blame others when there is conflict.

For rejected children who are withdrawn rather than aggressive, the basis of their rejection is less clear. They may be shy and even fearful of other children, but these characteristics are also found often in neglected children. What distinguishes between rejected-withdrawn and neglected children? Rejected-withdrawn children are more likely to have internalizing problems such as low self-esteem and anxiety. In contrast, neglected children are usually quite well-adjusted (Wentzel, 2003). They may not engage in social interactions with peers as frequently as other children do, but they usually have social skills equal to average children, are not unhappy, and report having friends.

Controversial children often have good social skills, as popular children do, but they are also high in aggressiveness, like rejected children (DeRosier & Thomas, 2003). Their social skills make them popular with some children, and their aggressiveness makes them unpopular with others. They may be adept at forming alliances with some children and excluding others. Sometimes they defy adult authority in ways their peers admire but do not dare to emulate (Vaillancourt & Hymel, 2006).

Social status is related to other aspects of children's development, in middle childhood and beyond, especially for rejected children. Because other children exclude them from their play and they have few or no friends, rejected children often feel lonely and they dislike going to school (Buhs & Ladd, 2001). Their aggressiveness and impulsiveness cause problems in their other social relationships, not just with peers, and they have higher rates of conflict with parents and teachers than other children do (Coie, 2004). According to longitudinal studies, being rejected in middle childhood is predictive of later conduct problems in adolescence and emerging adulthood (Caravita & Cillessen, 2012; Miller-Johnson et al., 2003). This does not necessarily mean that being rejected causes later problems; rather, it may indicate that the aggressiveness that inspires rejection from peers in middle childhood often continues at later ages and causes problems that take other forms. Nevertheless, being rejected by peers makes it more difficult for children to develop the social skills that would allow them to overcome a tendency toward aggressiveness.

social skills
behaviors that include being friendly, helpful, cooperative, and considerate

social information processing (SIP)
in social encounters, evaluations of others' intentions, motivations, and behavior

Because rejected children are at risk for a downward spiral of problems in their social relationships, psychologists have developed interventions to try to ameliorate their low social status. Some of these interventions focus on social skills, training rejected children how to initiate friendly interactions with their peers (Asher & Rose, 1997). Other programs focus on social information processing and seek to teach rejected children to avoid jumping to the conclusion that their peers' intentions toward them are negative (Li et al., 2013). As part of the intervention, rejected children may be asked to role play hypothetical situations with peers or watch a recording of peer interactions with an instructor and talk about why the peers in the video acted as they did (Ladd et al., 2004). These programs have often shown success in the short term, improving rejected children's social understanding and the quality of their peer interactions, but it is unknown whether the gains from the programs are deep enough to result in enduring improvements in rejected children's peer relations.

CRITICAL THINKING QUESTION

Which of these categories of social status do you believe applied best to you in middle childhood: popular, rejected, neglected, controversial, or average? Do you believe your social status at that life stage has influenced your later development, or not?

BULLIES AND VICTIMS An extreme form of peer rejection is **bullying**. Bullying is defined by researchers as having three components (Olweus, 2000; Wolak et al., 2007): *aggression* (physical or verbal); *repetition* (not just one incident but a pattern over time); and *power imbalance* (the bully has higher peer status than the victim). The prevalence of bullying rises through middle childhood and peaks in early adolescence, then declines substantially by late adolescence (Pepler et al., 2006). Bullying is an international phenomenon, observed in many countries in Europe (Dijkstra et al., 2008; Eslea et al., 2004; Gini et al., 2008), Asia (Ando et al., 2005; Hokoda et al., 2006; Kanetsuna et al., 2006), and North America (Espelage & Swearer, 2004; Pepler et al., 2008; Volk et al., 2006). Estimates vary depending on age and country, but overall about 20 percent of children are victims of bullies at some point during middle childhood. Boys are more often bullies as well as victims (Berger, 2007). Boys bully using both physical and verbal aggression, but girls can be bullies, too, most often using verbal methods (Pepler et al., 2004; Rigby, 2004).

There are two general types of bullies in middle childhood. Some are rejected children who are bully victims; that is, they are bullied by children who are higher in status and they in turn look for lower-status victims to bully (Kochenderfer-Ladd, 2003). Bully victims often come from families where the parents are harsh or even physically abusive (Schwartz et al., 2001). Other bullies are controversial children who may have high peer status for their physical appearance, athletic abilities, or social skills, but who are also resented and feared for their bullying behavior toward some children (Vaillancourt et al., 2003). Bullies of both types tend to have a problem controlling their aggressive behavior toward others, not just toward peers but also in their other relationships, during middle childhood and beyond (Olweus, 2000). Bullies are also at higher risk than other children for depression (Fekkes et al., 2004; Ireland & Archer, 2004).

Victims of bullying are most often rejected-withdrawn children who are low in self-esteem and social skills (Champion et al., 2003). Because they have few friends, they often have no allies when bullies begin victimizing them (Goldbaum et al., 2003). They cry easily in response to bullying, which makes other children regard them as weak and vulnerable and deepens their rejection. Compared to other children, victims of bullying are more likely to be depressed and lonely (Baldry & Farrington, 2004; Rigby, 2004). Their low moods and loneliness may be

bullying

pattern of maltreatment of peers, including aggression; repetition; and power imbalance

The prevalence of bullying rises through middle childhood across countries.

partly a response to being bullied, but these are also characteristics that may make bullies regard them as easy targets.

How do other children respond when they witness one of their peers being bullied? One study observed U.S. children in Grades 1 to 6 on playgrounds and recorded bullying episodes (Hawkins et al., 2001). Other children intervened to help a victim about half the time, and when they did the bullies usually backed off. However, a study in Finland found that in 20 to 30 percent of bullying episodes, peers actually encouraged bullies and sometimes even joined in against the victim (Salmivalli & Voeten, 2004).

What are some good ways to treat or stop bullying? Dan Olweus and his colleagues have developed an anti-bulling intervention program (the Olweus Bullying Prevention Program (OBPP, Olweus & Limber, 2010) that has been used around the world. The OBPP includes components at the community, school, classroom, and individual levels. For example, in the community, there should be anti-bullying messages and school-community partnerships. At the school level, a committee should be formed, and parents are encouraged to get involved. In the classroom, rules against bullying should be posted, and weekly meetings with the class are encouraged. At the individual level, students should be supervised, and staff should intervene when they see bullying.

Work

LO 7.18 Describe the kinds of work children do in middle childhood, and explain why work patterns differ between developed and developing countries.

Increasingly in the course of middle childhood, Ashley came up with ways to earn money. Beginning at about age 10, she worked as a baby-sitter or did extra chores like raking leaves or washing hard-to-reach windows by climbing on the roof. Erik Erikson (1950), whose life span theory we have been discussing in each chapter, called middle childhood the stage of **industry versus inferiority**, when children become capable of doing useful work as well as their own self-directed projects, unless the adults around them are too critical of their efforts, leading them to develop a sense of inferiority instead. This part of Erikson's theory has received little research. However, it is possible to see some verification of it in the way children across cultures are regarded as more capable than they were in early childhood and in the way they are often given important work responsibilities (Gaskins, 2015; Rogoff, 2003).

In developing countries, the work that children do in middle childhood is a serious and sometimes perilous contribution to the family. In most developed countries, it is illegal to employ children in middle childhood (United Nations Development Programme [UNDP], 2010). However, in a large proportion of the world, middle childhood is the time when productive work begins. Children who do not attend school are usually working, often for their families on a farm or family business, but sometimes in industrial settings. With the globalization of the world economy, many large companies have moved much of their manufacturing to developing countries, where labor costs are cheaper. Cheapest of all is the labor of children. Before middle childhood, children are too immature and lacking in self-regulation to be useful in manufacturing. Their gross and fine motor skills are limited, their attention wanders too much, and they are too erratic in their behavior and their emotions. However, by age 6 or 7 children have the motor skills, the cognitive skills, and the emotional and behavioral self-regulation to be excellent workers at many jobs.

The International Labor Organization (ILO) has estimated that about 73 million children ages 5 to 11 are employed worldwide, which is about 9 percent of the total population of children in that age group, and 95 percent of working children are in developing countries (ILO, 2013). A substantial proportion of children work in Latin America, Asia, and the Middle East/North Africa, but the greatest number of child workers is found in sub-Saharan Africa. Agricultural work is the most common form of child employment, usually on commercial farms or plantations, often working alongside parents but

industry versus inferiority

Erikson's middle childhood stage, in which the alternatives are to learn to work effectively with cultural materials or, if adults are too critical, develop a sense of being incapable of working effectively

Children in developing countries often work long hours in poor conditions by middle childhood. Here, a young boy works in a factory in Bangladesh.

for only one third to one half the pay (ILO, 2013). Children can quickly master the skills needed to plant, tend, and harvest agricultural products.

In addition, many children in these countries work in factories and shops where they perform labor such as weaving carpets, sewing clothes, gluing shoes, curing leather, and polishing gems. The working conditions are often miserable—crowded garment factories where the doors are locked and children (and adults) work 14-hour shifts, small poorly lit huts where they sit at a loom weaving carpets for hours on end, glass factories where the temperatures are unbearably hot and children carry rods of molten glass from one station to another (ILO, 2004). Other children work in cities in a wide variety of jobs, including in domestic service, at grocery shops, in tea stalls, and delivering messages and packages.

If children's work is so often difficult and dangerous, why do parents allow their children to work, and why do governments not outlaw child labor? For parents, the simple answer is that they need the money. Billions of people worldwide are very poor. Poor families in developing countries often depend on children's contributions to the family income for basic necessities such as food and clothing. Children's work may be difficult and dangerous, but so is the work of adults; often, parents and children work in the same factories. As for governments, nearly all countries do have laws prohibiting child labor, but some developing countries do not enforce them because of bribes from the companies employing the children or because they do not wish to incur the wrath of parents who need their children's income (Chaudary & Sharma, 2007).

Although the exploitation of children's labor in developing countries is widespread and often harsh, signs of positive changes can be seen. According to the International Labor Organization, the number of child laborers ages 5 to 11 is rapidly declining (ILO, 2013). This decline has taken place because the issue of child labor has received increased attention from the world media, governments, and international organizations such as the ILO and the United Nations Children's Fund (UNICEF). Furthermore, legislative action has been taken in many countries to raise the number of years children are legally required to attend school and to enforce the often-ignored laws against employing children younger than their mid-teens. Amid such signs of progress, it remains true that millions of children work in unhealthy conditions all around the world (ILO, 2013).

Media Use

LO 7.19 Summarize the rates of daily TV watching among children worldwide, and describe the positive and negative effects of television, especially the hazards related to TV violence.

Media use is a part of daily life for most children even in early childhood. Rates of media use remain about the same from early to middle childhood, except that time playing electronic games daily goes up, as shown in **Figure 7.10** (Rideout, 2013). Although many new media forms have appeared in the past decade, such as social media, television remains the most-used media form among children, at about an hour a day. By middle childhood about one fourth of children's media use involves **media multitasking**, the simultaneous use of more than one media form, such as playing an electronic game while watching TV (Warren, 2007).

Media forms and media content within each form are highly diverse, so it would be a mistake to characterize media use in childhood as solely positive or negative. There is a big difference between watching *Clifford the Big Red Dog* on TV and watching a highly violent movie or TV show; children who play on prosocial websites like *Webkinz* or *Club*

media multitasking

simultaneous use of more than one media form, such as playing an electronic game while watching TV

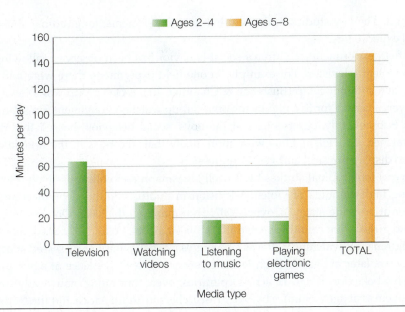

Figure 7.10 Media Use in Early and Middle Childhood
SOURCE: Based on Rideout (2013).

Penguin can be expected to respond differently than children who play violent electronic games like *Quake* or *Mortal Kombat*.

In general, media research on middle childhood has focused on the question of negative effects, as it has at other ages, but positive effects have also been noted. With regard to television, one analysis of 34 studies found that prosocial content in children's television shows had positive effects on four areas of children's functioning: altruism, positive social interactions, self-control, and combating negative stereotypes (Kotler, 2007). Furthermore, the positive effect of prosocial content was found to be equal to or greater than the negative effects of violent content. The Internet has been shown to be a valuable resource for children to learn about a wide range of topics, in school projects or just for enjoyment (Foehr, 2007; Van Evra, 2007). Much of children's media use is simply harmless fun, such as listening to music, playing nonviolent electronic games, and watching children's television shows.

The consequences of media use depend partly on whether children are light, moderate, or heavy media users (Van Evra, 2007). Light to moderate media use is generally harmless and can even be positive, especially if the media content is educational, prosocial, or at least nonviolent. In contrast, heavy media use is associated with a variety of problems in middle childhood, including obesity, anxiety, poor school performance, and social isolation. It is difficult to tell whether heavy media use is a cause or consequence of these problems; perhaps it is both.

Of all the problems associated with media use in middle childhood, aggression has been studied most extensively, specifically the effects of violent television on children's aggressiveness. It is estimated that the average child in the United States witnesses 200,000 acts of violence on television by age 18, including 16,000 murders (Aikat, 2007). The violence is not just on adults' programs that children watch along with their parents. On the contrary, an analysis of programming for children ages 5 to 10 on eight TV networks found that the programs depicted an average of eight acts of violence per hour, *higher* than the rate on shows for adults (Fyfe, 2006).

With such high rates of violence in the television shows that children watch most, many parents and scholars have expressed concern about the possibility that television violence causes aggression in children. Although early childhood is considered to be the life stage of greatest vulnerability to the effects of media violence, some of the most important studies linking media violence to children's aggression have focused on middle childhood. The key studies have included field experiments, longitudinal studies, and natural experiments.

In field experiments, children's social behavior has been observed following exposure to violent television. For example, in one field experiment, there were two groups of boys at a summer camp (Bushman & Chandler, 2007). One group was shown violent films every evening for five nights; the other group watched nonviolent films during this period. Subsequently, observations of the boys' social behavior showed that the boys who watched the violent films were more likely than the boys in the nonviolent film group to display physical and verbal aggression.

Several longitudinal studies by Rowell Huesmann and colleagues have shown that watching high amounts of violent television in middle childhood predicts aggressive behavior at later life stages (Coyne, 2007; Huesmann et al., 2003). One study involved boys and girls in five countries: Australia, Finland, Israel, Poland, and the United States. The children's TV-watching patterns and aggressive behavior were assessed at age 6 and then 5 years later at age 11. High levels of exposure to TV violence at age 6 predicted aggressive behavior at age 11 across countries, even controlling statistically for initial aggressiveness at age 6. Studies by other researchers in South Africa and the Netherlands have reported similar results (Coyne, 2007).

Huesmann's longitudinal study in the United States extends even further into the life span (Huesmann et al., 1984, 2003). Television-viewing patterns and aggressive behavior were assessed in middle childhood (age 8) and again at ages 19 and 30. A correlation was found at age 8 between aggressiveness and watching violent TV, not surprisingly. But watching violent TV at age 8 also predicted aggressive behavior in boys at age 19, and by age 30 the men who had watched high amounts of violent TV at age 8 were more likely to be arrested, more likely to have traffic violations, and more likely to abuse their children. As in the other longitudinal studies by Huesmann and colleagues, the results predicting aggressive behavior at ages 19 and 30 were sustained even when aggressiveness at age 8 was controlled statistically. So, it was not simply that aggressive persons liked to watch violent television at all three ages, but that aggressive 8-year-old children who watched high levels of TV violence were more likely to be aggressive at later ages than similarly aggressive 8-year-old children who watched lower levels of TV violence.

Perhaps the most persuasive evidence that watching television causes aggression in children comes from a natural experiment in a Canadian town. This natural experiment is the subject of the *Research Focus: TV or Not TV?* feature.

In sum, there is good reason for concern about the effects of violent media content in middle childhood. However, it should be kept in mind that media can have positive effects as well. The focus of media research is generally on the negative effects, in middle childhood as in other life stages; but with nonviolent content, and if used in moderation, media use can be a positive and enjoyable part of childhood (Van Evra, 2007).

Research Focus: TV or Not TV?

Researchers on human development are limited in the methods they can use because they have to take into account ethical issues concerning the rights and well-being of the people they involve in their studies. For instance, the environments of human beings cannot be changed and manipulated in the same way as those of animals, especially if the change would involve a condition that is potentially unhealthy or dangerous.

One way that researchers can obtain information about human development despite this restriction is to look for opportunities for a natural experiment. A natural experiment is a condition that takes place without the researcher's manipulation or involvement, but that nevertheless provides important information to the perceptive observer.

One human development topic for which natural experiments have been available is the effect of television on children's behavior. Television use spread all over the world with remarkable speed after it was invented in the 1940s, but there are still parts of the world that do not have television or have received it only recently.

In the early 1980s, a group of Canadian researchers, led by Tannis MacBeth, observed that there were areas of Canada that still did not have TV, although it was spreading rapidly. They decided to take advantage of this natural experiment to observe children's behavior before and after the introduction of TV.

Three towns were included in the study: "Notel" (as the researchers dubbed it), which had no television at the beginning of the study, "Unitel," which had one television channel, and "Multitel," with multiple channels. The focus of the study was on middle childhood, grades 1 to 5. In each grade, five boys and five girls were randomly selected in each town for participation in the study.

Each child's behavior was recorded by a trained observer for 21 one-minute periods over a period of 2 weeks across different times of day and different settings (for instance, school and home). The observers focused on aggressive behavior, using a checklist of 14 physically aggressive behaviors (such as hits, pushes, bites) and 9 verbally aggressive behaviors (such as mocking, curses, and threats). Neither children, nor parents, nor teachers were aware that the study focused on aggressive behavior or television.

In addition to the observations, the researchers obtained peer and teacher ratings of children's aggressiveness.

The ratings and observations took place just before the introduction of TV to Notel and then 2 years later, after Notel had obtained TV reception. The same children were included in the study at Time 1 and Time 2.

The results of the study showed clearly that the introduction of television caused children in Notel to become more aggressive. Children in Notel increased their rates of both physical and verbal aggression from Time 1 to Time 2, whereas there was no change for children in Unitel or Multitel. The increase in aggression in Notel occurred for both boys and girls. In all three towns at Time 2, the more TV children watched, the more aggressive they were.

This natural experiment provides persuasive evidence that the relation between TV watching and aggressiveness in children involves not only correlation but causation. It would not be ethical to place children into a "TV" condition and a "Not TV" condition—especially with what we now know about TV's potential effects—but making use of the natural experiment taking place in Notel, Unitel, and Multitel allowed the researchers to obtain important results about the effects of television on children's behavior.

Review Question:

1. The finding of greater aggression in Notel after the introduction of TV can best be interpreted as:
   a. Correlation but not causation
   b. Causation because levels of aggression were assessed before and after the introduction of TV
   c. Neither correlation nor causation, because children's behavior in Notel did not change once TV was introduced
   d. None of the above

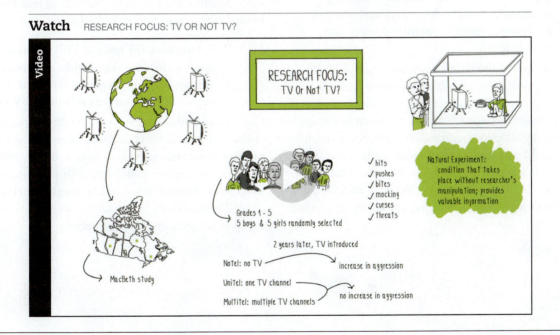

Watch RESEARCH FOCUS: TV OR NOT TV?

Summary: Emotional and Social Development

LO 7.13 Describe how emotional self-regulation and emotional understanding advance by middle childhood.

Emotionally, middle childhood is generally a time of exceptional stability and contentment as emotional self-regulation becomes firmly established and emotional understanding advances. Increased involvement in contexts outside the family, such as school and sports teams, requires higher levels of emotional self-regulation. Middle childhood is a time when children learn to manage stress.

LO 7.14 **Summarize how self-concept and self-esteem change in middle childhood, and identify cultural influences on conceptions of the self**

Children's self-understanding becomes more complex in middle childhood, and they engage in more social comparison once they enter school. Their overall self-concepts are based on their self-concepts in specific areas that are important to them, which for most children includes physical appearance. In discussing cultural differences in conceptions of the self scholars typically distinguish between the *independent self* promoted by individualistic cultures and the *interdependent self* promoted by collectivistic cultures. High self-esteem is encouraged in individualistic cultures but discouraged in collectivistic cultures.

LO 7.15 **Describe how beliefs and behavior regarding gender change in middle childhood.**

Children's tasks and play become more gender-segregated in middle childhood, and their views of gender roles become more sharply defined. In traditional cultures boys and girls do separate kinds of work in middle childhood, but playing in gender-specific groups takes place across cultures.

LO 7.16 **Explain the distinctive features of family relations in middle childhood, and describe the consequences of parental divorce and remarriage.**

Children become more independent during middle childhood as they and their parents move toward coregulation rather than parental dominance and control. Conflict with siblings peaks at this age. Divorce has become increasingly common in developed countries, and children (especially boys) respond negatively to divorce, particularly when it includes high conflict between parents. Parents' remarriage is also experienced negatively in middle childhood, even though it often improves the family's economic situation.

LO 7.17 **Explain the main basis of friendships in middle childhood, and describe the four categories of peer social status and the dynamics between bullies and victims.**

Similarity is important as the basis of friendship in middle childhood, as it is at other ages. Trust also becomes important in middle childhood friendships. Children's play becomes more complex and rule-based in this stage. Popularity and unpopularity become prominent in peer relations once children develop the capacity for seriation and spend a considerable part of their day in age-graded schools. Rejected children have the greatest problems in peer relations and the poorest long-term prospects for social development, mainly because of their aggressiveness. Bullying is a worldwide problem in middle childhood peer relations.

LO 7.18 **Describe the kinds of work children do in middle childhood, and explain why work patterns differ between developed and developing countries.**

About 73 million children in developing countries perform paid work by the time they reach middle childhood, in a wide variety of jobs ranging from agricultural work to factory work. Children in developing countries work more than children in developed countries in middle childhood because their contribution to the family income is needed.

LO 7.19 **Summarize the rates of daily TV watching among children worldwide, and describe the positive and negative effects of television, especially the hazards related to TV violence.**

Children's media use stays about the same from early childhood to middle childhood, except for a rise in time playing electronic games. A causal link between media violence and aggression in middle childhood has been established through field studies, longitudinal studies, and natural experiments. Prosocial TV content promotes qualities such as altruism and self-control.

Applying Your Knowledge as a Professional

The topics covered in this chapter apply to a wide variety of career professions. Watch these videos to learn how they apply to a counselor, a zoo director, and a court-appointed special advocate for children.

Watch CAREER FOCUS: ZOO DIRECTOR

Thane Maynard
Director of Cincinnati Zoo & Botanical Garden

Chapter Quiz

1. Which best describes sensory changes during middle childhood?

  a. Hearing problems increase because of higher rates of ear infections.

  b. The incidence of myopia increases.

  c. Vision and hearing both improve dramatically.

  d. Rates of farsightedness increase while myopia decreases.

2. In middle childhood, _____.

  a. girls are more likely than their male counterparts to be on a sports team because they are more collaborative

  b. children are more likely to be involved in organized sports than they were when they were younger

  c. children are less coordinated than they were in early childhood because they are going through an awkward phase

  d. children have a slower reaction time than they did early in childhood because they are less impulsive

3. By the end of middle childhood _____.

  a. fine motor development has nearly reached adult maturity

  b. children's drawings look about the same as they did in early childhood in terms of level of detail

  c. improvements in fine motor skills are seen primarily among children who were educated in a formal school setting

  d. most children are just beginning to learn to tie their shoes

4. Rates of overweight and obesity _____.

  a. are lowest in the most affluent regions of the world, such as North America and Europe

  b. are lowest among African American females compared to all other ethnic groups in the United States

  c. are lower among Latinos and American Indians than among European Americans

  d. are rising worldwide

5. In developed countries _____.

  a. rates of lead poisoning in children have fallen over the last several decades

  b. middle childhood is one of the least safe and healthy times of life because of children's increased need for independence

  c. the most-common cause of injury is poisoning

  d. asthma rates are at their lowest point in decades

6. When capable of concrete operational thought, children _____.

  a. still have great difficulty with seriation tasks, such as arranging items from shortest to longest

  b. can organize and manipulate information mentally

  c. can reason about abstractions

  d. are likely to be misled by appearances

7. _____, a memory strategy in which things are placed into meaningful categories, is more commonly used in middle childhood.

 a. Organization

 b. Rehearsal

 c. Elaboration

 d. Selective attention

8. The Wechsler Intelligence Scale for Children (WISC-IV) _____.

 a. is the most widely used intelligence test for children

 b. has been criticized for focusing too much on creativity and not enough on core skills of reading and writing

 c. has both math and performance subtests

 d. has only been predictive of the future outcomes of gifted children

9. Compared to younger children, those in middle childhood _____.

 a. use less complex grammar, but longer sentences

 b. are more serious and therefore have more difficulty understanding the punch lines in jokes

 c. are more likely to realize that what people say is not always what they mean

 d. are less likely to use conditional sentences (e.g., If you do this, I will do that…) because they know that it may be interpreted negatively

10. Compared to single-language children, those who are bilingual _____.

 a. are behind in metalinguistic skills

 b. have better metalinguistic skills

 c. are worse at detecting mistakes in grammar

 d. score lower on general measures of cognitive ability

11. Compared to Asian students, U.S. schoolchildren _____.

 a. spend more time studying art and music

 b. work in groups and help teach one another difficult concepts

 c. have a longer school year

 d. care about the maintenance of their schools

12. Research on reading and math skills _____.

 a. has only been conducted in the United States and Canada

 b. has shown that numeracy doesn't develop in humans until the second year

 c. has shown that the whole-language approach is more effective than the phonics approach for children who are first learning to read

 d. has found that even some nonhuman animals have a primitive awareness of numeracy

13. In the United States, _____children have the highest rates of ADHD.

 a. Asian American

 b. female

 c. male

 d. African American

14. During middle childhood, _____.

 a. children learn how to conceal their emotions and show socially acceptable emotions

 b. children tend to be less happy than they were in early childhood because they engage in more social comparison

 c. children experience less emotional stability than they did at early stages in development because they are changing social contexts more often

 d. children's emotions become more intense, so they are not yet able to conceal their true feelings

15. A 9-year-old boy from a collectivistic culture, such as Japan, would be most likely to describe himself as _____.

   a. really good at math

   b. shy

   c. a son

   d. funny as can be

16. In terms of gender development, during middle childhood _____.

   a. children increasingly view personality traits as associated with one gender or the other

   b. play groups become less gender-segregated than they were in early childhood

   c. gender roles become less rigid than earlier in life

   d. play groups become less gender-segregated in developed countries only

17. Which of the following best illustrates coregulation?

   a. Siblings negotiate a conflict without resorting to physical aggression.

   b. A child is able to prepare himself breakfast, provided that he follow his parents' rules and not use the stove.

   c. A child counts to three and tells himself to calm down after getting angry at his brother.

   d. A child describes himself in relation to others.

18. Sam is unpopular and has trouble making friends. He is aggressive and just last week started a fight by punching a boy who disagreed with him. Which of the following is most likely the case? Sam is a(n) _____ child.

   a. neglected

   b. rejected

   c. controversial

   d. average

19. Child labor _____.

   a. has declined worldwide in the last decade

   b. is most common in Mexico and Hawaii

   c. is considered legal in most countries

   d. is difficult to monitor because no international labor organizations exist

20. Media use in middle childhood _____.

   a. has not been associated with any positive outcomes

   b. has only been studied with male participants

   c. has been associated with a number of negative outcomes later in development

   d. has been linked with aggression only in the United States

Chapter 8
Adolescence

ADOLESCENCE IS A TIME OF DRAMATIC CHANGES. The physical changes are the most obvious because the body goes through puberty. However, there are other dramatic changes as well, in family relations, peer relations, sexuality, and media use. Adolescents also change in how they think and talk about the world around them.

Adolescence is a cultural construction, not simply a biological phenomenon or an age range. *Puberty*—the set of biological changes involved in reaching physical and sexual maturity—is universal, and the same biological changes take place in puberty for young people everywhere, although with differences in timing and in cultural meanings, as we shall see. But adolescence is more than the events and processes of puberty. **Adolescence** is a period of the life span between the time puberty begins and the time adult status is approached, when young people are preparing to take on the roles and responsibilities of adulthood in their culture. To say that adolescence is culturally constructed means that cultures vary in how they define adult status and in the content of the adult roles and responsibilities adolescents are learning to fulfill. Almost all cultural groups have some kind of adolescence, but the length, content, and daily experiences of adolescence vary greatly among cultures (Larson et al., 2010). There is no definite age when adolescence begins or ends, but it usually begins after age 10 and ends by age 20, so it comprises most of the second decade of life. Among the Zinacantec Mayans with whom Ashley works, adolescence has lengthened from a year or two to the more typical 6 years, and emerging adulthood is a new stage that some young people experience as they explore identities and options.

There are two broad cultural forms that adolescence takes today. In developed countries, adolescents begin puberty early in the second decade of life, usually around age 10 or 11. They spend most of their days in school with their peers. Outside of school, too, they spend most of their leisure time with other persons their age—friends and romantic partners. A substantial proportion of their daily lives involves media use, including mobile phones, electronic games, television, and recorded music.

But there is another cultural form of adolescence that is prevalent in most of the developing world, including Africa, Asia, and South America. In this kind of adolescence, a typical day is spent not mostly with peers in school but with family members, working (Schlegel, 2010; Schlegel & Barry, 2015). Girls spend most of their time with their mothers and other adult women, learning the skills and knowledge necessary to fulfill the roles for women in their culture. Boys spend most of their time with adult men, learning to do what men in their culture are required to do, but they are allowed more time with friends than adolescent girls are. Some adolescent boys and girls in developing countries go to school, but for others school is something they left behind by the end of childhood.

We will discuss both of these forms of adolescence in the course of this chapter, and the many variations that exist within each form. We will also discuss the ways that the traditional cultural forms of adolescence are changing with exposure to industrialization and globalization.

Watch   CHAPTER INTRODUCTION: ADOLESCENCE

Video

Section 1 Physical Development

 Learning Objectives

8.1 List the physical changes that begin puberty, and summarize the surprising changes in brain development during adolescence.

8.2 Describe the normative timing of pubertal events, cultural variations, and how being early or late influences emotional and social development.

8.3 Identify the main gender differences in puberty rituals worldwide.

8.4 Describe the prevalence, symptoms, and treatment of eating disorders.

8.5 Classify adolescent substance use into four categories.

PHYSICAL DEVELOPMENT:
Biological Changes of Puberty

Adolescence begins with the first notable changes of puberty, and in the course of puberty the body is transformed in many ways and reaches the capacity for sexual reproduction. Many changes take place, and they are often dramatic. After growing at a more or less steady rate through childhood, at some time early in the second decade of life children begin a remarkable metamorphosis that includes a growth spurt, the appearance of pubic hair and underarm hair, changes in body shape, breast development and menstruation in girls, the appearance of facial hair in boys, and much more. The changes can be exciting and joyful, but adolescents experience them with other emotions as well—fear, surprise, annoyance, and anxiety. New research reveals some surprising findings in brain development, too, as we will see.

The Physical Changes of Puberty

LO 8.1 **List the physical changes that begin puberty, and summarize the surprising changes in brain development during adolescence.**

The word *puberty* is derived from the Latin word *pubescere*, which means "to grow hairy." This fits; during puberty hair sprouts in a lot of places where it had not been before! But adolescents do a lot more during puberty than grow hairy. **Puberty** entails a biological revolution that dramatically changes the adolescent's anatomy, physiology, and physical appearance. By the time adolescents reach the end of their second decade of life they look much different than before puberty, their bodies function much differently, and they are biologically prepared for sexual reproduction.

HORMONAL CHANGES During middle childhood the proportion of fat in the body gradually increases, and once a threshold level is reached a series of chemical events is triggered beginning in the *hypothalamus*, a bean-sized structure located in the lower part of the brain (Shalatin & Philip, 2003). These events start a cascading process of the release of **hormones**, chemicals, produced in the body or given synthetically, that regulate physiological function, that cause puberty to occur. The pituitary gland (known as the "master" gland) releases growth hormone, which stimulates the adrenal glands. Known as the HPA

---

adolescence

period of the life span between the time puberty begins and the time adult status is approached, when young people are preparing to take on the roles and responsibilities of adulthood in their culture

puberty

changes in physiology, anatomy, and physical functioning that develop a person into a mature adult biologically and prepare the body for sexual reproduction

hormones

chemicals, produced in the body or given synthetically, that regulate physiological function

estrogens

sex hormones that have especially high levels in females from puberty onward and are mostly responsible for female primary and secondary sex characteristics

Puberty transforms physical appearance. These photos show the same boy at age 11 and age 15.

axis, the hypothalamus-pituitary-adrenal connection causes the secretion of a number of hormones, including sex hormones (see **Figure 8.1** on the next page). Another pituitary function that begins in adolescence is the production of gonadotropin-releasing hormone, which causes the gonads—ovaries in girls and testes in boys—to increase their production of sex hormones. Known as the HPG axis, the link from the hypothalamus to the pituitary to the gonads is a parallel route for regulating sex hormones in the body (refer again to Figure 8.1). There are two classes of sex hormones, the **estrogens** and the **androgens**. With respect to pubertal development, the most important estrogen is **estradiol** and the most important androgen is **testosterone** (Shirtcliff et al., 2009).

Estradiol and testosterone are produced in both males and females, and throughout childhood the levels of these hormones are about the same in boys and girls (Money, 1980). However, once puberty begins, the balance changes dramatically (see **Figure 8.2** on page 351).

By the mid-teens, estradiol production is about 8 times as high in females as it was before puberty, but only about twice as high in males (Susman & Rogol, 2004). In contrast, testosterone production in males is about 20 times as high by the mid-teens as it was before puberty, but in females it is only about 4 times as high. These hormonal increases lead to the other bodily changes of puberty, the primary and secondary sex characteristics.

PRIMARY AND SECONDARY SEX CHARACTERISTICS Two kinds of changes take place in the body in response to increased sex hormones during puberty. **Primary sex characteristics** are directly related to reproduction: specifically, the production of ova (eggs) in females and sperm in males. **Secondary sex characteristics** are the other bodily changes resulting from the rise in sex hormones during puberty, not including the changes related directly to reproduction. These include the development of breasts and a tendency toward higher body fat in females and facial hair and relatively less body fat in males.

The development of ova and sperm takes place quite differently. Females are born with all the eggs they will ever have, and they have about 40,000 eggs in their ovaries at the time they reach puberty. Once a girl reaches **menarche** (her first menstrual period) and begins having menstrual cycles, one egg develops into a mature egg, or *ovum*, every 28 days or so. Females release about 400 ova in the course of their reproductive lives.

In contrast, males have no sperm in their testes when they are born, and they do not produce any until they reach puberty. However, beginning with their first ejaculation (called

androgens

sex hormones that have especially high levels in males from puberty onward and are mostly responsible for male primary and secondary sex characteristics

estradiol

the estrogen most important in pubertal development among girls

testosterone

the androgen most important in pubertal development among boys

primary sex characteristics

production of eggs (ova) and sperm and the development of the sex organs

secondary sex characteristics

bodily changes of puberty not directly related to reproduction

menarche

first menstrual period

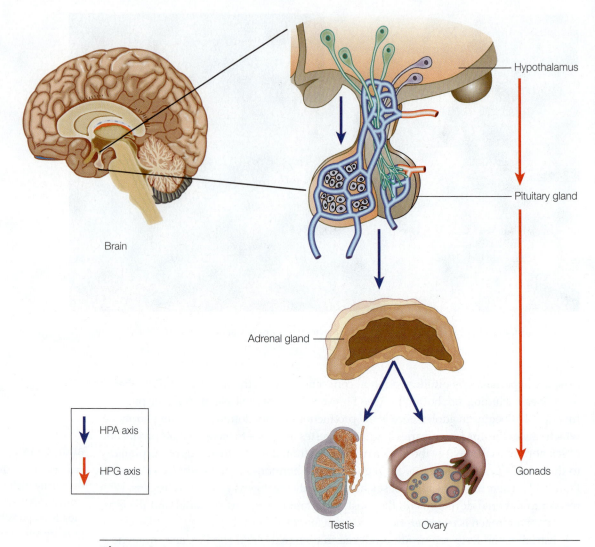

↓ (blue arrow)	HPA axis
↓ (red arrow)	HPG axis

Figure 8.1 The HPA and HPG Axes

Representation of the hypothalamic-pituitary-adrenal and the hypothalamic-pituitary-gonadal hormonal paths.

spermarche), males produce sperm in astonishing quantities. There are between 100 and 300 million sperm in the typical male ejaculation, which means that the average male produces millions of sperm every day. If you are a man, you will probably produce more than a million sperm during the time you read this chapter—even if you are a fast reader!

The secondary sex characteristics are many and varied, ranging from the growth of pubic hair to a lowering of the voice to increased production of skin oils and sweat. A summary of the major primary and secondary sex characteristics and when they develop is shown in **Figure 8.3**.

BRAIN DEVELOPMENT In addition to the hormonal changes and development of primary and secondary sex characteristics, there are important neurological changes taking place during adolescence. In recent years, there has been a surge of research on neurological development in adolescence and emerging adulthood (Casey et al., 2008; Giedd, 2008; Taber-Thomas & Perez-Edgar, 2015). Some of the findings from this new research have been surprising and have overturned previous views of brain development in adolescence.

It has long been known that by age 6 the brain is already 95 percent of its adult size. However, when it comes to brain development, size is not everything. Equally if not

spermarche

beginning of development of sperm in boys' testicles at puberty

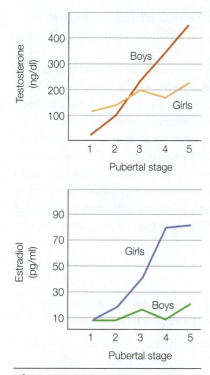

Figure 8.2 Hormonal Changes in Puberty

Girls and boys follow different hormonal paths at this life stage.

SOURCE: Nottelmann et al. (1987)

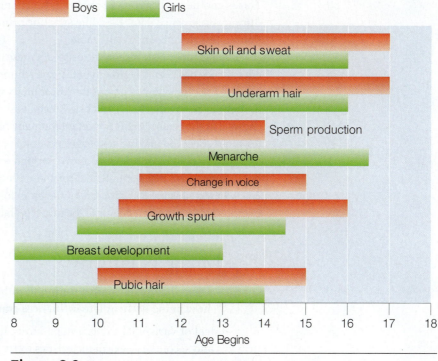

Figure 8.3 Timing of the Physical Changes of Puberty

SOURCE: Based on Goldstein (1976); Chumlea et al. (2003)

more important are the synaptic connections between the neurons. Now scientists have learned that a sharp increase in synaptic connections occurs around the time puberty begins, ages 10 to 12, a process called *overproduction* or *exuberance*. Previous studies had shown that overproduction occurs during prenatal development and through the first three years of life, but now it turns out that overproduction occurs in early adolescence as well (Giedd, 2008). Overproduction of synaptic connections occurs in many parts of the brain during adolescence but is especially concentrated in the frontal lobes (Keating, 2004). The frontal lobes are involved in most of the higher functions of the brain, such as planning ahead, solving problems, and making moral judgments.

The findings about overproduction in early adolescence are surprising and fascinating, but equally fascinating is what follows. Overproduction peaks at about age 11 or 12, but obviously that is not when our cognitive abilities peak. In the years that follow a massive amount of *synaptic pruning* takes place, in which the overproduction of synapses is whittled down considerably—synapses that are used remain, whereas those that are not used wither away. In fact, between the ages of 12 and 20 the average brain loses 7 to 10 percent of its volume through synaptic pruning (Giedd et al., 2012). Research using functional magnetic resonance imaging (fMRI) methods, shows that synaptic pruning is especially rapid in adolescents with high intelligence (Shaw et al., 2006). Synaptic pruning allows the brain to work more efficiently, as brain pathways become more specialized. However, as the brain specializes in this way it also becomes less flexible and less amenable to change.

Myelination is another important process of neurological growth in adolescence. Myelin is a blanket of fat wrapped around the main part of the neuron, and it serves the function of keeping the brain's electrical signals on one path and increases their speed. Like overproduction, myelination was previously thought to be finished prior to puberty but has now been found to continue through the teens (Giedd, 2008; Sowell et al., 2002).

This is another indication of how brain functioning is becoming faster and more efficient during adolescence. However, like synaptic pruning, myelination also makes brain functioning less flexible and changeable.

Finally, one last recent surprise for researchers studying brain development in adolescence has been the growth of the cerebellum. This is perhaps the biggest surprise of all because the cerebellum is part of the lower brain, well beneath the cortex, and has long been thought to be involved only in basic functions such as movement. Now, however, research shows that the cerebellum is important for many higher functions as well, such as mathematics, music, decision making, and even social skills and understanding humor. It also turns out that the cerebellum continues to grow through adolescence and well into emerging adulthood, suggesting that the potential for these functions continues to grow as well (Strauch, 2005). In fact, it is the last structure of the brain to stop growing, not completing its phase of overproduction and pruning until the mid-20s (Taber-Thomas & Perez-Edgar, 2015).

The Timing of Puberty

LO 8.2 Describe the normative timing of pubertal events, cultural variations, and how being early or late influences emotional and social development.

A great deal of variability exists among individuals in the timing of the development of primary and secondary sex characteristics (refer back to Figure 8.3). For example, among girls, underarm hair could begin to appear as early as age 10 or as late as age 16; among boys, the change in voice could begin as early as age 11 or as late as age 15. Overall, girls begin puberty 2 years earlier than boys, on average (Archibald et al., 2003).

The norms in Figure 8.3 are for White American and British adolescents, who have been studied extensively in this area for many decades, but three studies demonstrate the variations that may exist in other groups. Among the Kikuyu, a culture in Kenya, boys show the first physical changes of puberty *before* their female peers, a reversal of the Western pattern (Worthman, 1987). In a study of Chinese girls, researchers found that pubic hair began to develop in most girls about 2 years after the development of breast buds, and only a few months before menarche, whereas in the Western pattern girls develop pubic hair much earlier (Lee et al., 1963). Also, in a U.S. study (Herman-Giddens et al., 1997; Herman-Giddens et al., 2001), many African American girls were found to begin developing breast buds and pubic hair considerably earlier than White girls. At age 8, nearly 50 percent of the African American girls had begun to develop breasts or pubic hair or both, compared with just 15 percent of the White girls. This was true even though African American and White girls were similar in their ages of menarche. Similarly, pubic hair and genital development began earlier for African American boys than for White boys. Studies such as these indicate that it is important to investigate further cultural differences in the rates, timing, and order of pubertal events.

Given a similar cultural environment, variation in the order and timing of pubertal events among adolescents appears to be as a result of genetics. The more similar two people are genetically, the more similar they tend to be in the timing of their pubertal events, with identical twins the most similar of all (Ge et al., 2007; Marshall, 1978). However, when cultural environments vary, the timing of puberty also varies, as we shall see next.

Boys in Kenya reach puberty before girls do, contrary to the pattern in the West.

CULTURE AND THE TIMING OF PUBERTY
Culture includes a group's technologies, and technologies include food production and medical care. The age at which puberty begins is strongly

influenced by the extent to which food production provides adequate nutrition and medical care protects health throughout childhood (Alsaker & Flammer, 2006; Eveleth & Tanner, 1990).

Persuasive evidence for the influence of technologies on pubertal timing comes from historical records showing a steady decrease in the average age of menarche in Western countries from the mid-19th to the late-20th centuries, as shown in **Figure 8.4**. This downward pattern in the age of menarche, known as a **secular trend**, has occurred in every Western country for which records exist (Sørensen et al., 2012). Menarche is not a perfect indicator of the initiation of puberty; the first outward signs of puberty appear much earlier for most girls, and of course menarche does not apply to boys. However, menarche is a good indicator of when other events have begun in girls, and it is a reasonable assumption that if the downward trend in the age of puberty has occurred for girls, it has occurred for boys as well. Menarche is also the only aspect of pubertal development for which we have records going back so many decades. Scholars believe that the downward trend in the age of menarche is a result of improvements in nutrition and medical care that have taken place during the past 150 years (Archibald et al., 2003; Bullough, 1981). As the inset to Figure 8.4 shows, age of menarche has been unchanged since about 1970 because access to adequate nutrition and medical care has become widespread in developed countries.

Further evidence of the role of nutrition and medical care in pubertal timing comes from cultural comparisons in the present. The average age of menarche is lowest in developed countries (currently about 12.5 years old), where adequacy of nutrition and medical care is highest (Eveleth & Tanner, 1990; McDowell et al., 2007; Sørensen et al., 2012). In contrast, menarche takes place at an average age as high as 15 in developing countries, where nutrition may be limited and medical care is often rare or nonexistent (Eveleth & Tanner, 1990). In countries that have undergone rapid economic development in recent decades, such as China and South Korea, a corresponding decline in the average age of menarche has been recorded (Graham et al., 1999; Park et al., 1999). Note that these comparisons are correlational. No one has proven experimentally that better nutrition and medical care *cause* earlier puberty, though the inference that these are causes makes a lot of sense based on what we know about biology and reproduction.

SOCIAL AND PERSONAL RESPONSES TO PUBERTAL TIMING Think back for a moment to when you were passing through puberty. What were your most memorable pubertal events? How did you respond to those events, and how did the people around

secular trend
change in the characteristics of a population over time

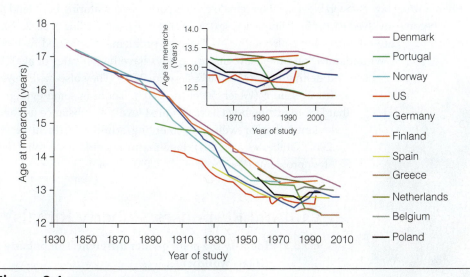

Figure 8.4 The Secular Trend in Age of Menarche

Why did age of reaching menarche decline?
SOURCE: Sørensen et al (2012)

you respond? Jeff loved to sing at that age, and he remembers going from soprano at age 13—the only boy in a sea of girls—to second bass by age 15. He reached puberty quite a bit later than most of his peers. Ashley remembers the tremendous curiosity that girls her age had about menstruation.

Social and personal responses to puberty are intertwined because how adolescents respond to reaching puberty depends in part on how others respond to them. In developed countries, social and personal responses may depend on whether adolescents reach puberty relatively early or relatively late compared with their peers. When adolescents spend time in school on most days, surrounded by peers, they become acutely aware of how their maturation compares to others'.

A great deal of research has been conducted on early versus late maturation among adolescents in the West, especially in the United States, extending back over a half-century. The results are complex: They differ depending on gender, and the short-term effects of maturing early or late appear to differ from the long-term effects.

Research consistently shows that the effects of early maturation are usually negative for girls. Findings from a variety of Western countries concur that early-maturing girls are at risk for numerous problems, including depressed mood, negative body image, eating disorders, substance use, delinquency, aggressive behavior, school problems, and conflict with parents (Harden & Mendle, 2012; Lynne et al., 2007; Westling et al., 2008). Early maturation is a problem for girls in part because it leads to a shorter and heavier appearance, which is a disadvantage in cultures that value slimness in females. It can also be troublesome because their early physical development draws the attention of older boys, who then introduce them to an older group of friends and to substance use, delinquency, and early sexual activity (Lynne et al., 2007; Westling et al., 2008). Studies of the long-term effects of early maturation for girls are mixed, with some finding that the effects diminish by the late teens and others finding negative effects well into emerging adulthood (Graber et al., 2004; Posner, 2006; Weichold et al., 2003).

In contrast to girls, the effects of early maturation for boys are positive in some ways and negative in others (Mendle & Ferrero, 2012). Early-maturing boys tend to have more favorable body images and higher popularity than other boys (Graber et al., 1997; Weichold et al., 2003). The earlier development of facial hair, lowered voice, and other secondary sex characteristics may make early-maturing boys more attractive to girls. Early-maturing boys may also have a long-term advantage. One study that followed early-maturing adolescent boys 40 years later found that they had achieved greater success in their careers and had higher marital satisfaction than later-maturing boys (Taga et al., 2006). However, not everything about being an early-maturing boy is favorable. Like their female counterparts, early-maturing boys tend to become involved earlier in delinquency, sex, and substance use (Westling et al., 2008).

Late-maturing boys also show evidence of problems. Compared to boys who mature "on time," late-maturing boys have higher rates of alcohol use and delinquency (Mendle & Ferrero, 2012). They also have lower grades in school (Weichold et al., 2003). There is some evidence that late-maturing boys have elevated levels of substance use and deviant behavior well into emerging adulthood (Biehl et al., 2007; Graber et al., 2004). Late-maturing girls have relatively few problems (Weichold et al., 2003).

Early-maturing girls are at high risk for problems, in part because they attract the interest of older boys.

Cultural Responses: Puberty Rituals

LO 8.3   Identify the main gender differences in puberty rituals worldwide.

Does your culture have any formal way of marking the entrance from childhood to adolescence? Have you ever participated in or witnessed a bar mitzvah or bat mitzvah, the Catholic ritual of confirmation, or the *quinceañera* that takes place at age 15 for girls in Latin American cultures? These are examples of **puberty rituals** that have developed in many cultures to mark the departure from childhood and the entrance into adolescence. Puberty rituals are especially common in traditional cultures. Alice Schlegel and Herbert Barry (1991) analyzed information on adolescent development across 186 traditional cultures and reported that 68 percent had a puberty ritual for boys, 79 percent for girls (Schlegel & Barry, 1991). Puberty rituals reflect the goals and values for men and women in the ecocultural settings where they occur.

For girls, menarche is the pubertal event that is most often marked by ritual (Schlegel & Barry, 2015). In fact, in many cultures menarche initiates a monthly ritual related to menstruation that lasts throughout a woman's reproductive life. It is remarkably common for cultures to have strong beliefs concerning the power of menstrual blood. Such beliefs are not universal, but they have been common in all parts of the world, in a wide variety of cultures. Menstrual blood is often believed to present a danger to the growth and life of crops, to the health of livestock, to the likelihood of success among hunters, and to the health and well-being of other people, particularly the menstruating woman's husband (Buckley & Gottlieb, 1988; Marván & Trujillo, 2010). Consequently, the behavior and movement of menstruating women are often restricted in many domains, including food preparation and consumption, social activities, religious practices, bathing, school attendance, and sexual activities (Crumbley, 2006; Mensch et al., 1998). Menarche is often believed to possess special power, perhaps because it is a girl's first menstruation, so the restrictions imposed may be even more elaborate and extensive (Yeung et al., 2005).

Traditional puberty rituals for males do not focus on a particular biological event comparable to menarche for females, but the rites for males nevertheless share some common characteristics. Typically, they require the young man to display courage, strength, and endurance (Gilmore, 1990; Schlegel & Barry, 2015). Daily life in traditional cultures often demands these capacities from young men in warfare, hunting, fishing, and other tasks. Thus, the rituals could be interpreted as letting them know what will be required of them as adult men and testing whether they will be up to adulthood's challenges.

In the past, rituals for boys were often violent, requiring boys to submit to and sometimes engage in bloodletting of various kinds. For example, among the Amhara of Ethiopia, boys were forced to take part in whipping contests in which they faced off and lacerated each other's faces and bodies (LeVine, 1966).

Although these rituals may sound cruel if you have grown up in the West, adults of these cultures believed that the rituals were necessary for boys to make the passage out of childhood toward manhood and to be ready to face life's challenges. In all these cultures, however, the rituals have declined in frequency or disappeared altogether in recent decades as a consequence of globalization (Schlegel, 2010; Schlegel & Barry, 2015). Because traditional cultures are changing rapidly in response to globalization, the traditional puberty rituals no longer seem relevant to the futures that young people anticipate. However, public circumcision for boys is still maintained as a puberty ritual in many African cultures (Vincent, 2008).

Female circumcision in adolescence, which involves cutting or altering the genitals, also remains common in Africa, with rates of more than 70 percent in many countries and greater than 90 percent in Mali, Egypt, Somalia, and Djibouti (Baron & Denmark, 2006; Chibber et al., 2011). The physical consequences of circumcision are much more severe for girls than for boys. Typically, a great deal of bleeding occurs, and the possibility of infection is high.

puberty ritual
formal custom developed in many cultures to mark the departure from childhood and the entrance into adolescence

Public circumcision for boys at puberty is still practiced in some African cultures. Here, three Masai adolescents from Tanzania celebrate their successful completion of the ritual.

Afterward many girls have chronic pain whenever they menstruate or urinate, and their risks of urinary infections and childbirth complications are heightened (Eldin, 2009). Critics have termed it *female genital mutilation* (FGM) and have waged an international campaign against it (Odeku et al., 2009). Nevertheless, it remains viewed in many African cultures as necessary for a young woman to be an acceptable marriage partner (Baron & Denmark, 2006).

CRITICAL THINKING QUESTION

Are there any rituals in Western cultures that are comparable to the puberty rituals in traditional cultures? Should people in Western cultures recognize and mark the attainment of puberty more than they do now? If so, why, and how?

PHYSICAL DEVELOPMENT: Health Issues in Adolescence

Like middle childhood, adolescence is a life stage when physical health is generally good. The immune system functions more effectively in middle childhood and adolescence than previously in development, so susceptibility to infectious diseases is lower. Diseases that will become more common later in adulthood, such as heart disease and cancer, are rare during adolescence. However, unlike middle childhood, adolescence is a time when problems arise not from physical functioning but from behavior. Two common problems of adolescence are eating disorders and substance use.

Eating Disorders

LO 8.4 **Describe the prevalence, symptoms, and treatment of eating disorders.**

For many adolescents, changes in the way they think about their bodies are accompanied by changes in the way they think about food. Girls, in particular, pay more attention to the food they eat once they reach adolescence, and worry more about eating too much and getting fat (Nichter, 2001). Sixty percent of U.S. adolescent girls and 30 percent of boys believe they weigh too much, even though only 15 percent of girls and 16 percent of boys are actually overweight by medical standards (Centers for Disease Control and Prevention [CDC], 2008). This dissatisfaction exists far more often among girls than among boys (Gray et al., 2011). Boys are much less likely to believe they are overweight, and much more likely to be satisfied with their bodies.

These perceptions can lead adolescents to exhibit eating disordered behavior, including fasting for 24 hours or more, use of diet products, purging, and use of laxatives to control weight. According to a national U.S. study, about 20 percent of U.S. adolescent girls and 10 percent of boys in Grades 9 to 12 report engaging in eating disordered behavior in the past 30 days (CDC, 2009). Similar findings have been reported in other Western countries. In a national study of German 11- to 17-year-old adolescents, one third of girls and 15 percent of boys reported symptoms of eating disorders (Herpetz-Dahlmann et al., 2008). In Finland, a large study of 14- to 15-year-old adolescents found eating disordered behavior among 24 percent of girls and 16 percent of boys (Hautala et al., 2008).

The two most common eating disorders are **anorexia nervosa** (intentional self-starvation) and **bulimia** (binge eating combined with purging [intentional vomiting]). About 0.3 percent of U.S. adolescents have anorexia nervosa and about 0.9 percent have bulimia (Swanson et al., 2011). Nearly all (90 percent) of eating disorders occur among females. Most cases of eating disorders have their onset among females in their teens and early 20s (Smink et al., 2012).

anorexia nervosa

eating disorder characterized by intentional self-starvation

bulimia

eating disorder characterized by episodes of binge eating followed by purging (self-induced vomiting)

Anorexia is characterized by four primary symptoms:

1. inability to maintain body weight at least 85 percent of normal for height;
2. fear of weight gain;
3. lack of menstruation; and
4. distorted body image.

One of the most striking symptoms of anorexia is the cognitive distortion of body image (Striegel-Moore & Franko, 2006). Young women with anorexia sincerely believe themselves to be too fat, even when they have become so thin that their lives are threatened. Standing in front of a mirror with them and pointing out how emaciated they look does no good—the person with anorexia looks in the mirror and sees a fat person, no matter how thin she is. The video *Anorexia Nervosa: Tamora* provides an example of this.

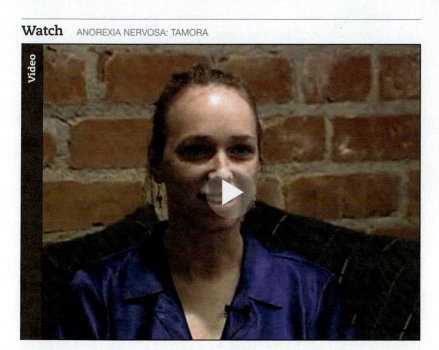

Watch   ANOREXIA NERVOSA: TAMORA

Like those with anorexia, persons with bulimia have strong fears that their bodies will become big and fat (Bowers et al., 2003). They engage in binge eating, which means eating a large amount of food in a short time. Then they purge themselves; that is, they use laxatives or induce vomiting to get rid of the food they have just eaten during a binge episode. People with bulimia often suffer damage to their teeth from repeated vomiting (because stomach acids erode tooth enamel). Unlike those with anorexia, persons with bulimia typically maintain a normal weight because they have more or less normal eating patterns in between their episodes of bingeing and purging (Striegel-Moore & Franko, 2006). Another difference from anorexia is that persons with bulimia do not regard their eating patterns as normal. They view themselves as having a problem and often hate themselves in the aftermath of their binge episodes.

Self-starvation among young women has a long history in Western countries (Vandereycken & van Deth, 1994). Today, eating disorders are most common in cultures that emphasize slimness as part of the female physical ideal, especially Western countries (Latzer et al., 2011; Walcott et al., 2003). Presented with a cultural ideal that portrays the ideal female body as slim, at a time when their bodies are biologically tending to become less slim and more rounded, many adolescent girls feel distressed at the changes taking place in their body shape, and they attempt to resist or at least modify those changes. Young women who have an eating disorder are at higher risk for other internalizing disorders, such as depression and anxiety disorders (Swanson et al., 2011; Swinbourne & Touyz,

2007). Eating disordered behavior is also related to substance use, especially cigarette smoking and binge drinking (Pisetsky et al., 2008). Within the United States, eating disorders are more common among White women than among women of other ethnic groups, probably because of a greater cultural value on female slimness.

Although mainly a Western problem, eating disorders are increasing in parts of the world that are becoming more Westernized. For example, on the island nation of Fiji, traditionally the ideal body type for women was round and curvy. However, television was first introduced in 1995, mostly with programming from the United States and other Western countries, and subsequently the incidence of eating disorders rose substantially (Becker et al., 2007). Interviews with adolescent girls on Fiji showed that they admired the Western television characters and wanted to look like them, and that this goal in turn led to higher incidence of negative body image, preoccupation with weight, and purging behavior to control weight (Becker, 2004).

The success of treating anorexia and bulimia through hospitalization, medication, or psychotherapy is limited (Bulik et al., 2007; Grilo & Mitchell, 2010). About two thirds of people treated for anorexia in hospital programs improve, but one third remain chronically ill despite treatment (Steinhausen et al., 2003). Similarly, although treatments for bulimia are successful in about 50 percent of cases, there are repeated relapses in the other 50 percent of cases, and recovery is often slow (Smink et al., 2012). Adolescents and emerging adults with a history of eating disorders often continue to show significant impairments in mental and physical health, self-image, and social functioning even after their eating disorder has faded (Berkman et al., 2007; Striegel-Moore et al., 2003). About 10 percent of those with anorexia eventually die from starvation or from physical problems caused by their weight loss, one of the highest mortality rates of any psychiatric disorder (Smink et al., 2012).

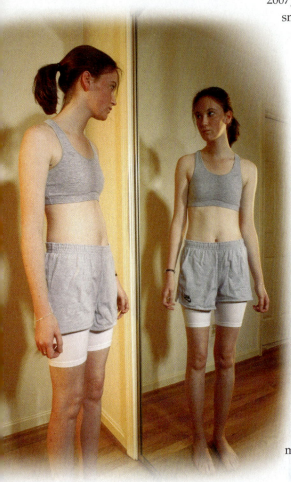

Young women with anorexia nervosa often see themselves as too fat even when they are so thin their lives are at risk.

Substance Use

LO 8.5   Classify adolescent substance use into four categories.

In U.S. society, substance use is rare before adolescence but fairly common by the end of secondary school (Johnston et al., 2014). In 2013, according to national Monitoring the Future (MTF) data, 39 percent of U.S. high school seniors used alcohol and 26 percent reported binge drinking—consuming five or more alcoholic drinks in a row—at least once in the past month. Cigarette use (at least once in the past 30 days) was reported by 16 percent of high school seniors in 2013. Rates of marijuana use were actually higher than for cigarette smoking: 23 percent of high school seniors reported using marijuana in the past month in the 2013 MTF survey. In general, substance use in adolescence is highest among American Indians, followed by White and Latino adolescents, with African American and Asian American adolescents lowest (Shih et al., 2010). Other than alcohol, cigarettes, and marijuana, substance use is uncommon among U.S. adolescents.

How do the current rates of substance use in adolescence and emerging adulthood compare with previous decades? Because the MTF studies go back to 1975, there are excellent data on this question for U.S. adolescents over more than three decades (Johnston et al., 2014). Rates of most types of substance use (past month) among adolescents in 12th grade declined from the late 1970s to the early 1990s, rose through the rest of the 1990s, then declined further over the past decade. Alcohol use declined from about 70 percent in 1975 to 39 percent in 2013. Cigarette smoking declined from nearly 40 percent in 1975 to 16 percent in 2013. Marijuana use declined from a peak of 37 percent in 1978 to 23 percent in 2013. Use of amphetamines peaked at 15 percent in 1981 and declined to 4 percent by 2013. During this period, an increasing proportion of young people defined themselves as "straight-edge," meaning that they abstain from all substance use (Kuhn,

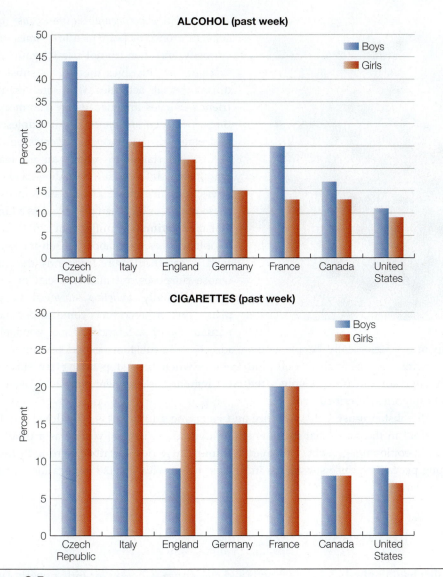

Figure 8.5 Substance Use in Western Countries

Why are rates of alcohol and cigarette use low in the United States and Canada?

SOURCE: Based on World Health Organization (2012)

2010). The reasons for this shift away from substance use are not clear, but it is likely that an intensive government-funded public campaign against teenage substance use during this period contributed to the decline.

Rates of substance use in adolescence vary across Western countries. A study by the World Health Organization (WHO) investigated use of alcohol and cigarettes among 15-year-old adolescents in 41 Western countries (WHO, 2012). A summary of the results is shown in **Figure 8.5**.

Rates of cigarette smoking are lower among adolescents in the United States and Canada than in Europe, most likely because governments in the United States and Canada have waged large-scale public health campaigns against smoking, whereas European countries have not. Cigarette smoking among young people is of particular concern because in the long run smoking is the source of more illness and mortality than all illegal drugs combined, and because the majority of persons who smoke begin in their early teens (Johnston et al., 2014).

Young people use substances for a variety of purposes, which can be classified as experimental, social, medicinal, and addictive (Weiner, 1992). Young people who

Rates of smoking in adolescence are higher in Europe than in the United States and Canada. Here, young adolescents in Germany light up.

self-medication

use of substances to relieve unpleasant emotional states

take part in *experimental substance use* try a substance once or perhaps a few times out of curiosity and then do not use it again. *Social substance use* involves the use of substances during social activities with one or more friends. Parties and dances are common settings for social substance use in adolescence and emerging adulthood. *Medicinal substance use* is undertaken to relieve an unpleasant emotional state such as sadness, anxiety, stress, or loneliness. Using substances for these purposes has been described as a kind of **self-medication** (Reimuller et al., 2011). Young people who use substances for self-medication tend to use them more frequently than those whose purposes are mainly social or experimental. Finally, *addictive substance use* takes place when a person has come to depend on regular use of substances to feel good physically or psychologically. People who are addicted to a substance experience withdrawal symptoms such as high anxiety and tremors when they stop taking the substance. Addictive substance use involves the most regular and frequent substance use of the four categories described here.

All substance use in adolescence and emerging adulthood is considered "problem behavior" in the sense that it is something that adults generally view as a problem if young people engage in it. However, the four categories described here indicate that young people may use substances in diverse ways, with diverse implications for their development.

Summary: Physical Development

LO 8.1 **List the physical changes that begin puberty, and summarize the surprising changes in brain development during adolescence.**

Increases in sex hormones lead to the development of primary and secondary sex characteristics. Recent findings in brain research show that the adolescent brain develops in some surprising ways, including a burst of overproduction (followed by synaptic pruning) and increased myelination.

LO 8.2 **Describe the normative timing of pubertal events, cultural variations, and how being early or late influences emotional and social development.**

The timing of pubertal events is determined partly by genes, but puberty generally begins earlier in cultures with adequate nutrition and medical care. Early-maturing girls are at risk for a wide variety of problems, in part because they draw the attention of older boys.

LO 8.3 **Identify the main gender differences in puberty rituals worldwide.**

Most traditional cultures mark puberty with a community ritual. For boys, puberty rituals often entail tests of

strength and endurance, whereas for girls puberty rituals center around menarche.

LO 8.4 **Describe the prevalence, symptoms, and treatment of eating disorders.**

Eating disorders are most prevalent in adolescence and emerging adulthood, and occur mainly among females. Prevalence of symptoms is higher than full-blown disorders; in some Western countries one third of girls report eating disordered behavior such as fasting for more than 24 hours and using laxatives to control weight. Treatments for eating disorders have had limited success.

LO 8.5 **Classify adolescent substance use into four categories.**

Adolescents' substance use can be classified as experimental, social, medicinal, or addictive. Adolescents whose substance use is addictive experience withdrawal symptoms when they reduce or stop their use of the substance.

Section 2 Cognitive Development

 Learning Objectives

8.6 Explain the features of hypothetical-deductive reasoning, and identify critiques of Piaget's theory of formal operations.

8.7 Summarize the major changes in attention and memory that take place from middle childhood to adolescence.

8.8 Define the *imaginary audience* and the *personal fable*, and explain how they reflect egocentrism in adolescence.

8.9 Produce an example of the zone of proximal development and scaffolding involving adolescents.

8.10 Describe why the transition to secondary schools may be challenging for adolescents, and identify some factors influencing high school graduation and dropout rates.

8.11 Compare and contrast the secondary education systems and academic performance of developed countries and developing countries.

8.12 Summarize the typical forms of adolescent work in developing countries and developed countries, and name the features of apprenticeships in Europe.

COGNITIVE DEVELOPMENT:
Adolescent Cognition

In adolescence, as at previous life stages, Piaget's theory of cognitive development has been influential but has also been questioned and critiqued. Research using the information-processing approach documents the advances in memory and attention that occur in adolescence. Cognitive approaches have also been applied to social topics, investigating how adolescents view themselves and others.

Piaget's Theory of Formal Operations

LO 8.6 **Explain the features of hypothetical-deductive reasoning, and identify critiques of Piaget's theory of formal operations.**

According to Piaget (1972), the stage of **formal operations** begins at about age 11 and reaches completion somewhere between ages 15 and 20. Children in concrete operations can perform simple tasks that require logical and systematic thinking, but formal operations allows adolescents to reason about complex tasks and problems involving multiple variables. It also includes the development of abstract thinking, which allows adolescents to think about abstract ideas such as justice and time and gives them the ability to imagine a wide range of possible solutions to a problem, even if they have had no direct experience with the problem.

HYPOTHETICAL-DEDUCTIVE REASONING The stage of formal operations involves the development of **hypothetical-deductive reasoning**, which is the ability to think

formal operations

in Piaget's theory, cognitive stage beginning at age 11 in which people learn to think systematically about possibilities and hypotheses

hypothetical-deductive reasoning

Piaget's term for the process of applying scientific thinking to cognitive tasks

Figure 8.6 Pendulum Problem

How does performance on this task test formal operations?

scientifically and apply the rigor of the scientific method to cognitive tasks. To demonstrate this new ability, let us look at one of the tasks Piaget used to test whether a child has progressed from concrete to formal operations, the *pendulum problem* (Inhelder & Piaget, 1958). In this task, illustrated in **Figure 8.6**, children and adolescents are shown a pendulum (consisting of a weight hanging from a string and then set in motion) and asked to try to figure out what determines the speed at which the pendulum sways from side to side. Is it the heaviness of the weight? The length of the string? The height from which the weight is dropped? The force with which it is dropped? They are given various weights and various lengths of string to use in their deliberations.

Children in concrete operations tend to approach the problem with random attempts, often changing more than one variable at a time. They may try the heaviest weight on the longest string dropped from medium height with medium force, then a medium weight on the smallest string dropped from medium height with less force. When the speed of the pendulum changes, it remains difficult for them to say what caused the change because they altered more than one variable at a time. If they happen to arrive at the right answer—it's the length of the string—they find it difficult to explain why. For Piaget, this is the crucial point. Cognitive advances at each stage are reflected not just in the answers children devise for problems, but in their explanations for how they arrived at the solution.

It is only with formal operations that we become able to find the right answer to a problem like this and to understand and explain why it is the right answer. The formal operational thinker approaches the pendulum problem by using the kind of hypothetical thinking involved in a scientific experiment. "Let's see, it could be weight; let me try changing the weight while keeping everything else the same. No, that's not it; same speed. Maybe it's length; if I change the length while keeping everything else the same, that seems to make a difference; it goes faster with a shorter string. But let me try height, too; no change; then force; no change there, either. So it's length, and only length, that makes the difference." Thus, the formal operational thinker changes one variable while holding the others constant and tests the different possibilities systematically. Through this process the formal operational thinker arrives at an answer that not only is correct but can also be defended and explained.

CRITIQUES OF PIAGET'S THEORY OF FORMAL OPERATIONS Formal operations is the part of Piaget's theory that has been critiqued the most and that has been found to require the most modifications (Keating, 2004; Marti & Rodriguez, 2012). The limitations of Piaget's theory of formal operations fall into two related categories: individual differences in the attainment of formal operations, and the cultural basis of adolescent cognitive development.

Piaget asserted that people develop through the same stages at about the same ages (Inhelder & Piaget, 1958). Every 8-year-old child is in the stage of concrete operations; every 15-year-old adolescent should be a formal operational thinker. Furthermore, Piaget's idea of stages means that 15-year-old teens should reason in formal operations in all aspects of their lives because the same mental structure should be applied no matter what the nature of the problem (Keating, 2004).

Abundant research indicates decisively that these claims were inaccurate, especially for formal operations (Kuhn, 2008). In adolescence and even in adulthood, a great range of individual differences exists in the extent to which people use formal operations. Some adolescents and adults use formal operations over a wide range of situations;

others use it selectively; still others appear to use it rarely or not at all. On any given Piagetian task of formal operations, the success rate among late adolescents and adults is only 40 to 60 percent, depending on the task and on individual factors such as educational background (Keating, 2004; Lawson & Wollman, 2003). Furthermore, even people who demonstrate the capacity for formal operations tend to use it selectively for problems and situations in which they have the most experience and knowledge (Flavell et al., 2002). For example, an adolescent with experience working on cars may find it easy to apply principles of formal operations in that area but have difficulty performing classroom tasks that require formal operations. Adolescents who have had courses in math and science are more likely than other adolescents to exhibit formal operational thought (Keating, 2004; Lawson & Wollman, 2003).

In what ways might hunting seals require formal operations?

Questions have also been raised about the extent to which cultural groups differ in whether their members reach formal operations at all. By the early 1970s numerous studies indicated that cultures varied widely in the prevalence with which their members displayed an understanding of formal operations on the kinds of tasks that Piaget and others had used to measure it, and many researchers concluded that in some cultures formal operational thought does not develop, particularly in cultures that do not have formal schooling that includes training in the scientific method (Cole, 1996). More recent research suggests that people in many cultures use reasoning that could be called formal operational, provided that they are using materials and tasks familiar to them and relevant to their daily lives (Matusov & Hayes, 2000). There is widespread support among scholars for the view that the stage of formal operations constitutes a universal human potential but it takes different forms across cultures depending on the kinds of problems people encounter in their daily lives (Cole, 1996).

For example, adolescent boys in the Inuit culture of the Canadian Arctic traditionally learn how to hunt seals (Condon, 1990; Grigorenko et al., 2004). To become successful, a boy would have to think through the components involved in a hunt and test his knowledge of hunting through experience. If he were unsuccessful on a particular outing, he would have to ask himself why. Was it because of the location he chose? The equipment he took along? The tracking method he used? Or were there other causes? On the next hunt he might alter one or more of these factors to see if his success improved. This would be hypothetical-deductive reasoning, altering and testing different variables to arrive at the solution to a problem. However, in every culture there is likely to be considerable variation in the extent to which adolescents and adults display formal operational thought, from persons who display it in a wide variety of circumstances to persons who display it little or not at all.

It is clear that cognitive development is an adaptation to ecocultural conditions. Piaget's theory of formal operations has inspired a great deal of research on adolescents' cognitive development in different cultures. However, information processing research shows other types of gains in cognitive development from childhood to adolescence.

Information Processing: Selective Attention and Advances in Memory

LO 8.7 Summarize the major changes in attention and memory that take place from middle childhood to adolescence.

Attention and memory are the two keys to cognition in the information-processing approach, and in both areas distinctive forms of cognitive development sprout in adolescence. Adolescents become more proficient in executive function. Specifically, they are better at both selective and divided attention, they become better at using memory strategies, and they develop further skills in metacognition.

Are you able to read a textbook while someone else in the same room is watching television? Are you able to have a conversation at a party where music and other conversations are blaring loudly all around you? These are tasks that require *selective attention*, the ability to focus on relevant information while screening out information that is irrelevant (Hahn et al., 2009). Adolescents tend to be better than younger children at tasks that require selective attention, and emerging adults are generally better than adolescents (Sinha & Goel, 2012). Adolescents are also more adept than younger children at tasks that require **divided attention**—reading a book and listening to music at the same time, for example—but even for adolescents, divided attention may result in less efficient learning than if attention were focused entirely on one thing. One study found that watching TV interfered with adolescents' homework performance but listening to music did not (Pool et al., 2003).

Memory also improves in adolescence, especially long-term memory. Adolescents are more likely than younger children to use *mnemonic devices* (memory strategies), such as organizing information into coherent patterns (Schneider, 2010). Think of what you do, for example, when you sit down to read a textbook chapter. You probably have various organizational strategies you have developed over the years (if you do not, you would be wise to develop some), such as writing a chapter outline, organizing information into categories, focusing on key terms, and so on. By planning your reading in these ways, you remember (and learn) more effectively.

Another way long-term memory improves in adolescence is that adolescents have more experience and more knowledge than children do, and these advantages enhance the effectiveness of long-term memory (Keating, 1990, 2004). Having more knowledge helps you learn new information and store it in long-term memory. This is a key difference between short- and long-term memory. The capacity of short-term memory is limited, so the more information you have in there already, the less effectively you can add new information to it. With long-term memory, however, the capacity is essentially unlimited, and the more you know the easier it is to learn new information because you can relate it to what you already know.

Cognitive development in adolescence also includes the development of **metacognition**, which is the capacity to think about thinking. This advance includes the ability to think about not only your own thoughts but also the thoughts of others. Adolescents are generally better at metacognition than younger children are. Adolescents have greater skill in understanding where their thoughts come from and how to manage their attention and memory, through mnemonics or other memory devices. Part of metacognition involves taking the perspectives of others, based on what others know and don't know or what others see or don't see, and adolescents may have difficulty with this at first.

Social Cognition: The Imaginary Audience and the Personal Fable

LO 8.8 Define the *imaginary audience* and the *personal fable*, and explain how they reflect egocentrism in adolescence.

The difficulty in distinguishing their thinking about their own thoughts from their thinking about the thoughts of others, results in a distinctive kind of **adolescent egocentrism**. Ideas about adolescent egocentrism were first put forward by Piaget (1967) and were developed further by David Elkind (1967, 1985; Alberts et al., 2007). According to Elkind, adolescent egocentrism has two aspects, the imaginary audience and the personal fable.

THE IMAGINARY AUDIENCE The **imaginary audience** results from adolescents' limited capacity to distinguish between their thinking about themselves and their thinking

divided attention

ability to focus on more than one task at a time

metacognition

capacity to think about thinking

adolescent egocentrism

type of egocentrism in which adolescents have difficulty distinguishing their thinking about their own thoughts from their thinking about the thoughts of others

imaginary audience

belief that others are acutely aware of and attentive to one's appearance and behavior

about the thoughts of others. Because they think about themselves so much and are so acutely aware of how they might appear to others, they conclude that others must also be thinking about them a great deal. Because they exaggerate the extent to which others think about them, they imagine a rapt audience for their appearance and behavior.

The imaginary audience makes adolescents much more self-conscious than they were in middle childhood, as shown in the video *Imaginary Audience*. Do you remember waking up in seventh or eighth grade with a pimple on your forehead, or discovering a mustard stain on your pants and wondering how long it had been there, or saying something in class that made everybody laugh (even though you didn't intend it to be funny)? Of course, experiences like these are not much fun as an adult, either. But they tend to be worse in adolescence, because the imaginary audience makes it seem as though "everybody" knows about your humiliation and will remember it for a long, long time.

Watch IMAGINARY AUDIENCE

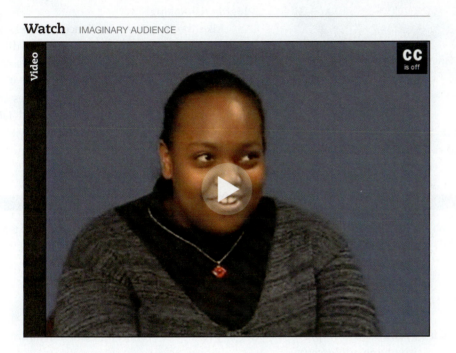

The imaginary audience is not something that simply disappears when adolescence ends. Adults are egocentric, too, to some extent. Adults, too, imagine (and sometimes exaggerate) an audience for their behavior. It is just that this tendency is stronger in adolescence, when the capacity for distinguishing between our own perspective and the perspective of others is less developed (Alberts et al., 2007).

THE PERSONAL FABLE According to Elkind (1967, 1985), the belief in an imaginary audience that is highly conscious of how you look and act leads to the belief that there must be something special, something unique, about you. Adolescents' belief in the uniqueness of their personal experiences and their personal destiny is known as the **personal fable**.

The personal fable can be the source of adolescent anguish, when it makes them feel that "no one understands me" because no one can share their unique experience (Elkind, 1978). It can be the source of high hopes, too, because adolescents imagine their unique personal destiny leading to the fulfillment of their dreams to be a rock musician, a professional athlete, a famous actor, or simply successful in the field of their choice. It can also contribute to risky behavior by some adolescents whose sense of uniqueness leads them to believe that adverse consequences from behavior such as unprotected sex or drunk driving "won't happen to me." According to research by Elkind and his colleagues, personal fable scores increase from early to mid-adolescence and are correlated with

personal fable

belief in one's personal uniqueness, often including a sense of invulnerability to the consequences of taking risks

The personal fable can lead adolescents to believe that negative consequences from taking risks "won't happen to me."

participation in risk behaviors (Alberts et al., 2007). Some aspects of the personal fable may be positive, however, including the idea that adolescents might explore more or try new things because they believe they are capable of greatness. However, some adolescents may have a heightened perception of risk and err on the side of caution (Mills et al., 2008). It is important to understand how adolescents are thinking about risky behavior in order to help them make decisions (Reyna et al., 2011). The intervention for an adolescent who is overly cautious would be different than the intervention for an adolescent who is more highly risk-taking.

Like the imaginary audience, the personal fable diminishes with age, but it never disappears entirely for most of us. Even most adults like to think there is something special, if not unique, about their personal experiences and their personal destiny. But the personal fable tends to be stronger in adolescence than at later ages because with age our experiences and conversations with others lead us to an awareness that our thoughts and feelings are not as exceptional as we once might have believed (Elkind, 1978; Martin & Sokol, 2011).

CRITICAL THINKING QUESTION

Do you think most people your age have outgrown adolescent egocentrism? Give examples of the imaginary audience and the personal fable that you have witnessed among your peers or experienced yourself.

Culture and Cognition

LO 8.9 **Produce an example of the zone of proximal development and scaffolding involving adolescents.**

As noted in previous chapters, two of Vygotsky's most influential ideas are scaffolding and the zone of proximal development. The zone of proximal development is the difference between skills or tasks a person can accomplish alone and those they are capable of doing if guided by a more experienced person. Scaffolding refers to the degree of assistance provided in the zone of proximal development. In Vygotsky's view, learning always takes place via a social process, through the interactions between someone who possesses knowledge and someone who is in the process of obtaining it.

Scaffolding and the zone of proximal development continue to apply during adolescence, when the skills necessary for adult work are being learned. An example can be found in research on weaving skills among male adolescents in the Dioula culture in Ivory Coast, on the western coast of Africa (Tanon, 1994). An important part of the Dioula economy is making and selling large handmade cloths with elaborate designs. The training of weavers begins when they are ages 10 to 12 and continues for several years. Boys grow up watching their fathers weave, but it is in early adolescence that they begin learning weaving skills themselves. Teaching takes place through scaffolding: The boy attempts a simple weaving pattern, the father corrects his mistakes, and the boy tries again. When the boy gets it right, the father gives him a more complex pattern, thus raising the upper boundary of the zone of proximal development so that the boy continues to be challenged and his skills continue to improve. As the boy becomes more competent at weaving, the scaffolding provided by the father diminishes. Eventually the boy gets his own loom, but he continues to consult with his father for several years before he can weave entirely by himself.

As this example illustrates, learning in adolescence is always a cultural process, in which adolescents are acquiring the skills and knowledge that will be useful in their culture. Increasingly, the skills and knowledge of the global economy involve the ability to use information technology such as computers and the Internet. In most countries, the highest paying jobs require these kinds of skills. However, as the example of the Dioula illustrates, in developing countries the most necessary skills and knowledge are often those involved in making things the family can use or that other people will want to buy (Larson et al., 2010).

It is not only skills for work that are scaffolded or modeled for adolescents. Correct social behaviors may be trained in a zone of proximal development as well. For example, Schlegel (2011) found that German adolescents join a *Verein*, or club, where they interact with adults in informal settings. There is a Verein for a variety of activities, such as sports, singing, gardening, or intellectual pursuits like history or literature. Adolescents typically join a Verein around age 15 or 16. In the context of the Verein, 16-year-old adolescents, who may drink alcohol legally in Germany, can join the adults in drinking alcohol. The Verein is a cultural setting where adolescents learn to drink in moderation—an important skill to have to avoid taking risks like drinking and driving, unsafe sexual activities, or consuming to the point of being out of control or falling ill.

COGNITIVE DEVELOPMENT:
Education and Work

Their cognitive advances prepare adolescents for new forms of school and work, especially as they enter secondary school, where the demands are greater and the social environment is often less supportive. In developing countries, young people often engage in adult work by adolescence, and in developed countries they may take part-time jobs or apprenticeships that introduce them to the adult world of work.

Secondary Education in the United States

LO 8.10 Describe why the transition to secondary schools may be challenging for adolescents, and identify some factors influencing high school graduation and dropout rates.

Education in adolescence centers around **secondary schools** (middle schools and high schools). The transition to secondary school may be difficult because adolescents have to learn to manage their schedules, and the social and academic pressures may increase.

MIDDLE SCHOOL The transition from elementary school to middle school is challenging for adolescents. Middle school in the United States usually covers grades sixth through eighth, but this may vary. The transition to middle school usually means moving from a small, personalized classroom setting to a larger setting where a student has not one teacher but five or six or more. It also means moving into a setting where the academic work is at a higher level and grades are suddenly viewed as a more serious measure of academic attainment than they may have been in primary school.

These changes in school experience can add to early adolescents' anxieties and school-related stress. A longitudinal study of more than 1,500 adolescents found a steady decline from the beginning of sixth grade to the end of eighth grade in students' perceptions of teacher support, autonomy in the classroom, and clarity of school rules and regulations (Way et al., 2007). These declines were in turn related to declines in psychological well-being

secondary school

school attended during adolescence, after primary school

and increases in behavior problems. However, there were also benefits from the transition to secondary school. One study found that seventh-grade adolescents made more positive than negative comments about the transition to middle school, with positive comments about topics such as peer relationships (more people to "hang around" with), academics (greater diversity of classes available), and independence (Berndt & Mekos, 1995).

HIGH SCHOOL In the United States, high school usually covers Grades 9 to 12. The ecocultural setting of high school includes teachers who are qualified to teach more advanced courses in their topic areas, and the goal is preparing adolescents for college, the workplace, or both. Frank Levy (a scholar on education) and Richard Murnane (an economist) have researched the job skills needed to succeed in the workplace (Levy & Murnane, 2004; Levy & Murnane, 2012; Murnane & Levy, 1997). Levy and Murnane conducted observations in a variety of factories and offices to gain information about the kinds of jobs now available to high school graduates and the kinds of skills required for those jobs. They focused not on routine jobs that require little skill and pay low wages but also on the most promising new jobs available to high school graduates in the changing economy, jobs that offer the promise of career development and middle-class wages. They concluded that six basic skills are necessary for success at these new jobs:

1. reading at a ninth-grade level or higher;
2. doing math at a ninth-grade level or higher;
3. solving semi-structured problems;
4. communicating orally and in writing;
5. using a computer for word processing and other tasks;
6. collaborating in diverse groups.

The good news is that all six of what Levy and Murnane call the *new basic skills* could be taught to adolescents by the time they leave high school. The bad news is that many U.S. adolescents currently graduate from high school without learning them adequately. Levy and Murnane focused on reading and math skills because those are the skills on which the most data are available. They concluded that the data reveal a distressing picture: close to half of all 17-year-old adolescents cannot read or do math at the level needed to succeed at the new jobs. The half who do have these skills are also the half who are most likely to go to college rather than seeking full-time work after high school. More recently, Levy and Murnane (2012) focused on the growing importance of computer skills, again concluding that high schools are failing to provide adolescents with the knowledge they need to succeed in the new economy.

Of course, this does not mean that the current situation cannot be changed. There is certainly no reason that high schools could not be expected to require that students master the new basic skills by the time they graduate. The results of Levy and Murnane's research suggest that it may be wise for administrators of high schools and job-training programs to revise their curricula to fit the requirements of the new information- and technology-based economy.

However, even with a revised curriculum available, if you are a member of an ethnic minority in a developed country and your family has a low income, your chances of finishing secondary school may be substantially lower than in the majority culture (NCES, 2014). In the United States, high school graduation rates vary widely by ethnic group, as **Figure 8.7** shows (NCES, 2014). African American, American Indian, and Latino adolescents are particularly at risk for not finishing high school and suffering difficult consequences in the labor market (Wimer & Bloom, 2014). Though the achievement gap across ethnic groups is closing between White and Black children, Black and Hispanic children still lag behind their peers in a number of measures of academic success (Duncan & Magnuson, 2011; Snyder & Dillow, 2010). The high dropout rate for Latino students is partly explained by economic reasons: Latino students leave high school in high numbers to work to help their families (Batalova & Fix, n.d.).

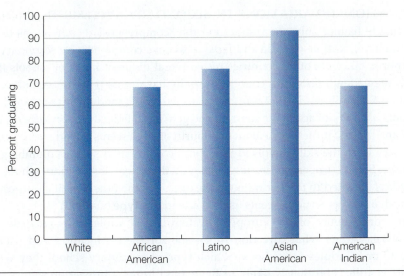

Figure 8.7 U.S. High School Completion Rate by Ethnic Group
SOURCE: Based on NCES (2014)

Secondary Education Worldwide

LO 8.11 Compare and contrast the secondary education systems and academic performance of developed countries and developing countries.

There is a great deal of diversity worldwide in the kinds of secondary schools that adolescents attend. World regions also vary in how likely adolescents are to attend secondary school at all. There is an especially sharp contrast between developed countries and developing countries. Virtually all adolescents are enrolled in secondary school in developed countries. In contrast, in many developing countries only about 50 percent of adolescents attend secondary school (UNESCO, 2014; see **Map 8.1**).

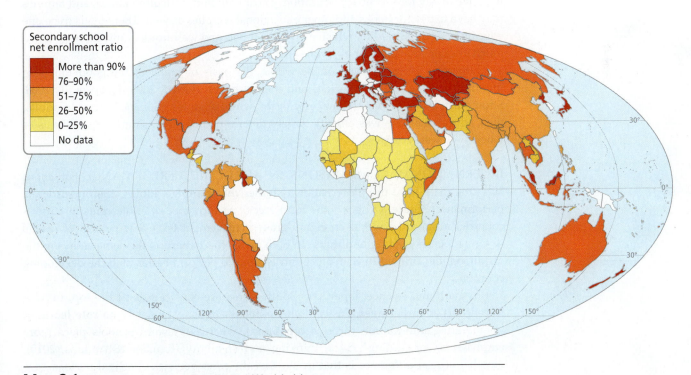

Map 8.1 Secondary School Enrollment Worldwide

Which countries have the highest enrollment rates for secondary education? Which are the lowest? What cultural and economic factors might explain these variations?

INTERNATIONAL VARIATIONS IN SECONDARY SYSTEMS The United States is unusual in having only one institution—the "comprehensive" school—as the source of secondary education. Canada and Japan also have comprehensive secondary schools as the norm, but most other countries have several different kinds of schools that adolescents may attend. European countries usually have three types of secondary schools (Hamilton & Hamilton, 2006). About half of adolescents attend a *college-preparatory school* that offers a variety of academic courses. The goal is general education rather than training for any specific profession. About one fourth of adolescents attend a *vocational school*, where they learn the skills involved in a specific occupation such as plumbing or auto mechanics. Some European countries also have a third type of secondary school, a *professional school*, devoted to teacher training, the arts, or some other specific purpose. About one fourth of European adolescents usually attend this type of school.

One consequence of the European system is that adolescents must decide at a relatively early age what direction to pursue for their education and occupation. At age 15 or 16 adolescents choose which type of secondary school they will enter, and this is a decision that is likely to have an enormous impact on the rest of their lives. Usually the decision is made by adolescents in conference with their parents and teachers, based on adolescents' interests as well as on their school performance (Motola et al., 1998). Although adolescents sometimes change schools after a year or two, and adolescents who attend a vocational school sometimes attend university, these switches are rare.

In contrast to developed countries, where attending secondary school is virtually universal for adolescents and the schools are well funded, in developing countries secondary education is often difficult to obtain and relatively few adolescents stay in school until graduation. A number of common themes recur in accounts of secondary education in developing countries (Lloyd, 2005; Lloyd et al., 2008). All developing countries have seen rising rates of enrollment in recent decades (UNESCO, 2014). That's about where the good news ends. Many of the schools are poorly funded and overcrowded. Many countries have too few teachers, and the teachers are insufficiently trained. Often families have to pay for secondary education, a cost they find difficult to afford, and families may have to pay for books and other educational supplies as well. There tends to be one education for the elite—in exclusive private schools and well-funded universities—and a much inferior education for everyone else.

Education is, in all parts of the world, the basis of many of the good things in life, from income level to physical and mental health (Lloyd, 2005; Lloyd et al., 2008; Stromquist, 2007). Yet for the majority of the world's adolescents and emerging adults, their educational fate was already largely determined at birth, simply on the basis of where they were born.

INTERNATIONAL COMPARISONS IN ACADEMIC PERFORMANCE For about 30 years, there have been international studies that compare adolescents on academic performance. **Figure 8.8** shows the most recent performance of adolescents in various countries around the world on eighth-grade achievement tests. The pattern of results is similar across reading and math. In both areas, the pattern is the same as in middle childhood: the affluent developed countries tend to perform better than the developing countries.

In math and science, Japan and South Korea are consistently at the top. In adolescence as at earlier ages, Eastern schools focus almost exclusively on **rote learning** (memorizing information through repetition), whereas Western schools place more emphasis on promoting critical thinking and creativity (Kember & Watkins, 2010). Another crucial difference is that in the East the consequences of school performance in adolescence are much more serious and enduring. Adolescents in Japan and South Korea have to take entrance exams for both high school and college. These two exams have a great influence on young people's occupational fate for the rest of their lives,

rote learning

learning by memorization and repetition

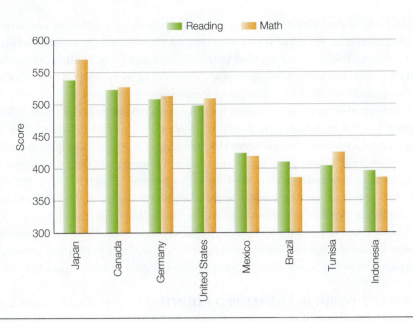

Figure 8.8 International Performance in Reading and Math, Eighth Grade

What explains why Japan scores highest?

SOURCE: Based on NCES (2014)

because in Asian countries, obtaining a job is based primarily on the status of the schools a person has attended. To prepare for the entrance exams, adolescents in Eastern countries are pressed by parents and teachers to apply themselves seriously at school and in their homework. In addition, from middle childhood through adolescence many of them attend "cram schools" after school or receive instruction from private tutors (Takahashi & Takeuchi, 2007).

With longer school days, a longer school year, cram schools, and private tutors, Eastern adolescents have far less time for after-school leisure and informal socializing with friends than U.S. adolescents do (Chaudhary & Sharma, 2012). In recent decades some Asian countries have reduced the length of the school day and cut the number of school days per week from six to five, but the average school day remains long and cram schools remain the norm (Takahashi & Takeuchi, 2007).

Work

LO 8.12 Summarize the typical forms of adolescent work in developing countries and developed countries, and name the features of apprenticeships in Europe.

Adolescents' new physical, cognitive, and social abilities make them valuable as potential workers all around the world. However, the kind of work they do varies sharply between developing countries and developed countries.

ADOLESCENT WORK IN DEVELOPING COUNTRIES For children in developing countries, work often begins long before adolescence. Within the family, from early childhood onward, children begin to contribute to the work required in daily life, helping with tasks such as cleaning, cooking, gathering firewood, and caring for younger siblings. By middle childhood, many of them work in factory settings, where they do jobs such as weaving rugs and polishing gems (International Labor Organization [ILO], 2013). They also work on farms and in domestic service, and some sell goods on the street.

Adolescents in developing countries often do the same types of difficult, dangerous, and poorly paid work as younger children do, but one type of work that usually begins in adolescence is prostitution. Estimates of the number of adolescent sex workers in developing countries vary, but it is widely agreed that adolescent prostitution is a pervasive problem, especially in Asia, and within Asia especially in Thailand (Basu & Chau, 2007; ILO, 2002). Of course, adolescent sex workers exist in developed countries as well, but the problem is much more widespread in developing countries.

Adolescent girls in these countries become sex workers in several ways. Some are kidnapped and taken to a separate country. Isolated in a country where they are not citizens and where they do not know the language, they are highly vulnerable and dependent on their kidnappers. Some are rural adolescent girls who are promised jobs in restaurants or domestic service, then forced to become prostitutes once the recruiter takes them to their urban destination. Sometimes parents sell the girls into prostitution, out of desperate poverty or simply out of the desire for more consumer goods (ILO, 2004). A large proportion of the customers in Asian brothels are Western tourists, leading the United States and several European countries to pass laws permitting prosecution of their citizens for sexually exploiting young adolescent girls in other countries.

ADOLESCENT WORK IN DEVELOPED COUNTRIES What do you remember about your jobs in adolescence, if you worked at that time? Both Jeff and Ashley had jobs as adolescents as restaurant workers. Jeff cooked hamburgers and washed dishes, and Ashley was a hostess. Both used the money they earned for their own enjoyment. Likewise, for most adolescents in developed countries, work is usually not done as part of contributing to family survival but as a way of supporting an active leisure life. About 80 percent of adolescents in the United States and Canada hold at least one part-time job by the end of high school (Lee & Staff, 2007). Very little of the money they earn goes to their family's living expenses or saving for their future education. For the most part, the money goes toward purchases for themselves, here and now: stylish clothes, music, car payments and gas, concert tickets, movies, eating out—and alcohol, cigarettes, and other drugs (Greenberger & Steinberg, 1986; Mortimer, 2013). Adolescents in ethnic minority groups are more likely to contribute to their families (Fuligni, 2011; Mortimer, 2003), and some even leave high school to support the family.

Unlike in developing countries, the work done by adolescents in developed countries does little to prepare them for the kind of work they are likely to be doing as adults. For example, the majority of jobs held by U.S. and Canadian adolescents in high school involve restaurant work or retail sales (Mortimer, 2013; Staff et al., 2004). Consequently, few adolescents see their high school jobs as the basis for a future career (Mortimer et al., 2008).

Not only does working part-time appear to do adolescents little good in developed countries, but it can also be harmful to their development in a variety of ways. The amount of time worked per week is a crucial variable. Most studies find that up to 10 hours a week working at a part-time job has little effect on adolescents' development. However, beyond 10 hours a week problems arise, and beyond 20 hours a week the problems become considerably worse.

Beyond 10 hours a week, the more adolescents work the lower their grades, the less time they spend on homework, the more they cut class, the more they cheat on their schoolwork, the less committed they are to school, and the lower their educational aspirations (Marsh & Kleitman, 2005). Similarly, reports of psychological symptoms jump sharply for adolescents working more than 10 hours a week and continue to rise among adolescents working 20 hours a week or more (Lee & Staff, 2007; Mortimer, 2013). Canadian research reports that when adolescents take on demanding jobs, they reduce their sleep by an hour per night and eliminate nearly all sports activities (Sears, 2012). Adolescents who work are also more likely to use alcohol, cigarettes, and other drugs, especially if they work more than 10 hours a week (Bachman et al., 2003; Longest & Shanahan, 2007; Wu et al., 2003). A national study of adolescents in Finland also found numerous negative effects of working more than 20 hours a week (Kuovonen & Kivivuori, 2001).

Although working part-time is related to a variety of negative outcomes, a case can also be made in favor of adolescent work, as long as it is 10 hours a week or less. Adolescents see many benefits from their work, such as learning responsibility, how to manage money, social skills, and how to organize their time (Aronson et al., 1996; Mortimer, 2013). More than 40 percent believe that their jobs have helped them develop new occupational skills, in contrast to the portrayal of adolescent work as involving nothing but dreary tasks (although we might note that 40 percent, although substantial, is still a minority).

APPRENTICESHIPS IN EUROPE Although most employment in adolescence in the United States and Canada has little relation to later jobs, many European countries have a long tradition of apprenticeships that provides excellent preparation for adult occupations. In an **apprenticeship**, an adolescent "novice" serves under contract to a "master" who has substantial experience in a profession, and through working under the master the novice learns the skills required (Hamilton & Hamilton, 2000; Hamilton & Hamilton, 2006; Vazsonyi & Snider, 2008). Although apprenticeships originally began centuries ago in craft professions such as carpentry and blacksmithing, today they are undertaken to prepare for a wide range of professions, from auto mechanics and carpenters to police officers, computer technicians, and child-care workers (Fuller et al., 2005). Apprenticeships are especially common in central and northern Europe. For example, more than 60 percent of adolescents in Germany and Switzerland participate in apprenticeships (Dolphin & Lanning, 2011).

Common features of apprenticeship programs are (Hamilton & Hamilton, 2006):

- entry at age 16, with the apprenticeship lasting 2 to 3 years;
- continued part-time schooling while in the apprenticeship, with the school curriculum closely connected to the training received in the apprenticeship;
- training that takes place in the workplace, under real working conditions; and
- preparation for a career in a respected profession that provides an adequate income.

This kind of program requires close coordination between schools and employers, so that what adolescents learn at school will complement and reinforce what is being learned in their apprenticeship. This means that schools consult employers with respect to the skills required in the workplace, and employers make opportunities available for adolescent apprentices. In Europe, the employers see this as worth their trouble because apprenticeships provide them with a reliable supply of well-qualified entry-level employees (Dustmann & Schoenberg, 2008).

Apprenticeships are common in Europe. These adolescents are apprenticing at a German power plant company.

apprenticeship

an arrangement, common in Europe, in which an adolescent "novice" serves under contract to a "master" who has substantial experience in a profession, and through working under the master, learns the skills required to enter the profession

Summary: Cognitive Development

LO 8.6 **Explain the features of hypothetical-deductive reasoning, and identify critiques of Piaget's theory of formal operations.**

Hypothetical-deductive reasoning entails the ability to test solutions to a problem systematically, altering one variable while holding the others constant. The pendulum problem is one way Piaget tested the attainment of formal operations.

Piaget proposed that when adolescents reach formal operations they use it for all cognitive activities; however, research has shown that both adolescents and adults tend to use formal operations in some areas of their lives but not in others. Piaget also proposed that formal operations is a universal stage of cognitive development, but its prevalence appears to vary across cultures as measured by standard tasks, although it may be used in the course of culturally specific daily activities.

LO 8.7 **Summarize the major changes in attention and memory that take place from middle childhood to adolescence.**

Information-processing abilities improve in adolescence, with the notable additions of selective attention, divided attention, and use of mnemonic devices.

LO 8.8 **Define the *imaginary audience* and the *personal fable*, and explain how they reflect egocentrism in adolescence.**

The imaginary audience is the exaggerated belief that others are paying intense attention to one's appearance and behavior. The personal fable is the belief that there is something special and unique about one's personal destiny. The imaginary audience results from adolescents' egocentric inability to distinguish their thoughts about themselves from their thoughts about others' thoughts.

LO 8.9 **Produce an example of the zone of proximal development and scaffolding involving adolescents.**

Scaffolding and the zone of proximal development are evident in adolescence, when the skills necessary for adult work are being learned. For example, male adolescents in the Dioula culture in Ivory Coast are first taught simple weaving patterns but learn increasingly complex patterns as their skills improve in response to correction and instruction by their fathers, until they can weave entirely by themselves.

LO 8.10 **Describe why the transition to secondary schools may be challenging for adolescents, and identify some factors influencing high school graduation and dropout rates.**

The transition to secondary school may be challenging for adolescents because they are allowed increased independence and choice, and some may have trouble focusing. High school graduation and dropout rates are influenced by factors such as socioeconomic status, parenting, and whether adolescents also work at jobs for money.

LO 8.11 **Compare and contrast the secondary education systems and academic performance of developed countries and developing countries.**

The United States, Canada, and Japan have a comprehensive high school, but most other countries have at least three different types of secondary school. Academic performance is generally higher in developed countries than in developing countries, but highest of all in Asian developed countries, where pressure to excel is high.

LO 8.12 **Summarize the typical forms of adolescent work in developing countries and developed countries, and name the features of apprenticeships in Europe.**

Adolescents' work is often hard and perilous in developing countries, and in some countries adolescent girls are forced into prostitution. In developed countries, working more than 10 hours per week interferes with adolescents' school performance, sleep, and psychological health. In some European countries, apprenticeships are available, in which adolescents spend part of their time in school and part of their time in the workplace receiving direct occupational training.

Section 3 Emotional and Social Development

Learning Objectives

8.13 Summarize the results of the ESM studies with respect to adolescent emotionality.

8.14 Describe how self-conceptions change during adolescence.

8.15 Discriminate between Kohlberg's theory of moral development and Jensen's worldviews theory.

8.16 Describe the cultural variations in religious beliefs during adolescence as well as the sources and outcomes of religiosity within cultures.

8.17 Summarize the cultural variations in adolescents' relationships with parents, siblings, and extended family.

8.18 Describe cultural variations in adolescents' relationships with friends, and characterize their interactions with peers.

8.19 Identify cultural variations in adolescent love and sexuality, including variations in adolescent pregnancy and contraceptive use.

8.20 Explain the function of media use in adolescents' lives, and apply the Media Practice Model to the playing of electronic games.

8.21 Summarize the explanations for why age and crime are so strongly correlated, and describe the multisystemic approach to combating delinquency.

8.22 Identify the different types and rates of depression, and summarize the most effective treatments.

8.23 Define *resilience*, and name the protective factors that are related to resilience in adolescence.

EMOTIONAL AND SOCIAL DEVELOPMENT: Emotional and Self-Development

Adolescence has long been regarded as a time of emotional volatility, and here we'll look at the history of views on this topic as well as current research. Issues of self-concept and self-esteem are also at the forefront of adolescent development, partly because of advances in cognitive development. Gender issues are prominent as well, because adolescence involves reaching sexual maturity.

Emotionality in Adolescence: Storm and Stress?

LO 8.13 **Summarize the results of the ESM studies with respect to adolescent emotionality.**

One of the most ancient and enduring observations of adolescence is that it is a time of heightened emotions (Arnett, 1999). More than 2,000 years ago, the Greek philosopher Aristotle observed that youth "are heated by Nature as drunken men by wine." About 250 years ago, the French philosopher Jean-Jacques Rousseau made a similar observation: "As the roaring of the waves precedes the tempest, so the murmur of rising passions announces the tumultuous change" of puberty and adolescence. Around the same time that Rousseau was writing, a type of German literature was developing that became known as *"sturm und drang"* literature—German for "storm and stress." In these stories, young people in their teens and early 20s experienced extreme emotions of angst, sadness, and romantic passion.

What does contemporary research tell us about the validity of these historical and popular views of adolescent emotionality? Probably the best source of data on this question is research using the Experience Sampling Method (ESM), which involves having people wear wristwatch beepers and then beeping them randomly during the day so that they can record their thoughts, feelings, and behavior (Csikszentmihalyi & Larson, 1984; Larson & Csikszentmihalyi, 2014; Schneider, 2006). ESM studies have also been conducted with younger children and adults, so if we compare the patterns of emotions reported by the different groups, we can get a good sense of whether adolescence is a stage of more extremes of emotions than middle childhood or adulthood.

The results indicate that adolescence in the United States is often a time of emotional volatility (Larson & Csikszentmihalyi, 2014; Larson et al., 1980; Larson & Richards, 1994). U.S. adolescents report feeling "self-conscious" and "embarrassed" two to three times more often than their parents and are also more likely than their parents to feel awkward, lonely, nervous, and ignored. Adolescents are also moodier when compared to younger children. Comparing preadolescent fifth graders to adolescent eighth graders, Reed Larson and Maryse Richards (1994) describe the emotional "fall from grace" that occurs during that time, as the proportion of time experienced as "very happy" declines by 50 percent, and similar declines take place in reports of feeling "great," "proud," and "in control." The result is an overall "deflation of childhood happiness" (p. 85) as childhood ends and adolescence begins.

How do emotional states change during the course of adolescence? Larson and Richards assessed their original ESM sample of 5th to 8th graders 4 years later, in 9th to 12th grades (Larson et al., 2002). As **Figure 8.9** shows, they found that there was a decline in average emotional states with age.

What about other cultures? Is adolescent emotionality especially a U.S. phenomenon, or does it take place in other cultures as well? There is limited evidence to answer this question. However, in one study ESM was used with adolescents and their parents in India (Verma & Larson, 1999). The results indicated that, in India as in the United States, adolescents reported more extremes of emotion than their parents did.

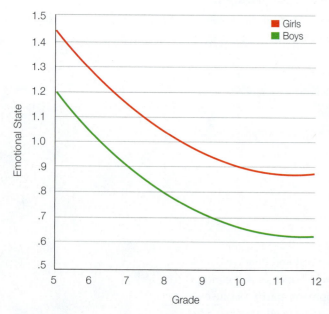

Figure 8.9 Change in Emotional States During Adolescence

Average emotional state becomes steadily more negative in the course of adolescence.

SOURCE: Larson et al. (2002)

Self-Development

LO 8.14 **Describe how self-conceptions change during adolescence.**

Self-conceptions become more complex in adolescence as a result of advances in cognitive development. Self-esteem also becomes more complex, but overall self-esteem declines in early adolescence before rising in late adolescence and emerging adulthood.

SELF-UNDERSTANDING AND SELF-CONCEPT Self-conceptions in adolescence become more complex and more abstract. One aspect of the complexity of adolescents' self-conceptions is that they can distinguish between an **actual self** and **possible selves** (Markus & Nurius, 1986; Oyserman & Fryberg, 2006; Whitty, 2002). The actual self is your self-conception, and possible selves are the different people you imagine you could become in the future depending on your choices and experiences. Scholars distinguish two kinds of possible selves, an ideal self and a feared self (Chalk et al., 2005). The **ideal self** is the person the adolescent would like to be (for example, an adolescent may have an ideal of becoming highly popular with peers or highly successful in athletics or music). The **feared self** is the person the adolescent dreads becoming (for example, an adolescent might fear becoming an alcoholic, or fear becoming like a disgraced relative or friend). Both kinds of possible selves require adolescents to think abstractly. That is, possible selves exist only as abstractions, as *ideas* in the adolescent's mind.

The capacity for thinking about an actual, an ideal, and a feared self is a cognitive achievement, but this capacity may be troubling in some respects. If you can imagine an ideal self, you can also become aware of the discrepancy between your actual self and your ideal self, between what you are and what you wish you were. If the discrepancy is large enough, it can result in feelings of failure, inadequacy, and depression. Studies have found that the size of the discrepancy between the actual and ideal self is related to depressed mood in both adolescents and emerging adults (Moretti & Wiebe, 1999; Papadakis et al., 2006). Furthermore, the discrepancy between the actual and the ideal self is greater in mid-adolescence than in either early or late adolescence (Ferguson et al., 2010). This helps explain why rates of depressed mood rise from early adolescence to mid-adolescence, as we will see in more detail later in the chapter.

A related aspect of the increasing complexity of self-conceptions is that adolescents become aware of times when they are exhibiting a **false self**, which is a self they present to others while realizing that it does not represent what they are actually thinking and feeling (Harter et al., 1997; Weir & Jose, 2010). With whom would you think adolescents would be most likely to exhibit their false selves—friends, parents, or potential romantic partners? Research indicates that adolescents are most likely to put on their false selves with potential romantic partners, and least likely with their close friends; parents are in between (Harter, 2006a, b; Sippola et al., 2007). Most adolescents indicate that they sometimes dislike putting on a false self, but many also say that some degree of false self behavior is acceptable and even desirable, to impress someone or to conceal aspects of the self they do not want others to see.

SELF-ESTEEM Several longitudinal studies show that self-esteem declines in early adolescence, then rises through late adolescence and emerging adulthood (Harter, 2012; Robins & Trzesniewski, 2005). There are a number of reasons why self-esteem might follow this developmental pattern. The "imaginary audience" that we have discussed as part of adolescents' cognitive development can make them self-conscious in a way that decreases their self-esteem (Elkind, 1967, 1985). That is, as adolescents develop the capacity to imagine that others are especially conscious of how they look and what they say and how they act, they may suspect or fear that others are judging them harshly.

actual self
person's perception of the self as it is, contrasted with the possible self

possible self
person's conceptions of the self as it potentially may be; may include both an ideal self and a feared self

ideal self
person one would like to be

feared self
person one imagines it is possible to become but dreads becoming

false self
self a person may present to others while realizing that it does not represent what he or she is actually thinking and feeling

Adolescents are most likely to use a false self with dating partners.

And they may be right. Adolescents in Western cultures tend to value the opinion of their peers highly, especially on day-to-day issues such as how they are dressed and what they say in social situations (Berndt, 1996). Also, their peers have developed new cognitive capacities for sarcasm and ridicule, which tend to be dispensed freely toward any peer who seems odd or awkward or uncool (Eder, 1995; Rosenbloom & Way, 2004). So, the combination of greater self-consciousness about evaluations by peers and peers' potentially harsh evaluations contributes to declines in self-esteem in early adolescence. Self-esteem rises in late adolescence and emerging adulthood as peers' evaluations become less important (Berndt, 1986; Robins & Trzesniewski, 2005).

As scholars have studied self-esteem, they have concluded that it has many aspects in addition to overall self-esteem. Multiple aspects of adolescent self-esteem have been investigated by Susan Harter (1990a, 1990b, 2006a, b, 2012). Her *Self-Perception Profile for Adolescents* distinguishes the following eight domains of adolescent self-concept:

- Scholastic competence
- Social acceptance
- Athletic competence
- Physical appearance
- Job competence
- Romantic appeal
- Behavioral conduct
- Close friendship

In addition to the eight subscales on specific domains of self-concept, Harter's scale also contains a subscale for global (overall) self-esteem. Her research indicates that adolescents do not need to have a positive self-image in all domains to have high global self-esteem. Each domain of self-concept influences global self-esteem only to the extent that the adolescent views that domain as important. For example, some adolescents may view themselves as having low scholastic competence, but that would only influence their global self-esteem if it was important to them to do well in school.

Nevertheless, some domains of self-concept are more important than others to most adolescents. Research by Harter and others has found that physical appearance is most strongly related to global self-esteem, followed by social acceptance from peers (DuBois et al., 1996; Harter, 2012; Shapka & Keating, 2005). Adolescent girls are more likely than boys to emphasize physical appearance as a basis for self-esteem. Because girls tend to evaluate their physical appearance negatively, and because physical appearance is at the heart of their global self-esteem, girls' self-esteem tends to be lower than boys' during adolescence (Robins & Trzesniewski, 2005; Shapka & Keating, 2005).

GENDER Gender is related not only to self-esteem but to many other aspects of self-development in adolescence. Adolescents may feel pressure to conform to culturally prescribed gender roles, although this may be changing as a result of globalization.

Gender Intensification in Adolescence Psychologists John Hill and Mary Ellen Lynch (1983; Lynch 1991) proposed that adolescence is a particularly important time in gender socialization, especially for girls. According to their **gender-intensification hypothesis**, psychological and behavioral differences between males and females become more pronounced in the transition from childhood to adolescence because of intensified socialization pressures to conform to culturally prescribed gender roles. Hill and Lynch (1983) believe that it is this intensified socialization pressure, rather than the biological changes of puberty, that results in increased differences between males and females as adolescence progresses. Furthermore, they argue that the intensity of gender socialization in adolescence is greater for females than for males, and that this is reflected in a variety of ways in adolescent girls' development. In the United States, many adolescent girls feel pressure to fit an idealized and standardized cultural norm of slimness and beauty. For

gender-intensification hypothesis

hypothesis that psychological and behavioral differences between males and females become more pronounced at adolescence because of intensified socialization pressures to conform to culturally prescribed gender roles

an illustration of how girls in the United States respond to gender intensification, view the *Body Image in Adolescent Girls* video.

Watch BODY IMAGE IN ADOLESCENT GIRLS

Since Hill and Lynch (1983) proposed this hypothesis, other studies have been presented that support it (Galambos, 2004; Shanahan et al., 2007; Priess & Lindberg, 2014). In one study, boys and girls filled out a questionnaire on gender identity each year in sixth, seventh, and eighth grades (Galambos et al., 1990). Over this 2-year period, girls' self-descriptions became more "feminine" (e.g., gentle, affectionate) and boys' self-descriptions became more "masculine" (e.g., tough, aggressive). However, in contrast to Hill and Lynch's (1983) claim that gender intensification is strongest for girls, the pattern in this study was especially strong for boys and masculinity. A more recent study found that gender stereotypes were embraced more by adolescents than by younger children, for both boys and girls (Rowley et al., 2007). Another study found that increased conformity to gender roles during early adolescence took place primarily for adolescents whose parents valued traditional gender roles (Crouter et al., 1995).

Gender intensification is often considerably stronger in traditional cultures than in the West. One striking difference in gender expectations in traditional cultures is that for boys manhood is something that has to be *achieved*, whereas girls reach womanhood inevitably, mainly through their biological changes (Leavitt, 1998; Lindsay & Miescher, 2003). It is true that girls are required to demonstrate various skills and character qualities before they can be said to have reached womanhood. However, in most traditional cultures womanhood is seen as something that girls attain naturally during adolescence, and their readiness for womanhood is viewed as indisputably marked when they reach menarche. Adolescent boys have no comparable biological marker of readiness for manhood. For them, the attainment of manhood is often fraught with peril and carries a definite and formidable possibility of failure.

So, what must an adolescent boy in traditional cultures do to achieve manhood and escape the stigma of being viewed as a failed man? The anthropologist David Gilmore (1990) examined this question in traditional cultures around the world and concluded that an adolescent boy must demonstrate three capacities before he can be considered a man: *provide, protect,* and *procreate.* He must *provide* in the sense that he must demonstrate that he has developed skills that are economically useful and that will enable him to support the wife and children he is likely to have as an adult man. For example, if what adult men

mainly do is fish, the adolescent boy must demonstrate that he has learned the skills involved in fishing adequately enough to provide for a family. Second, he must *protect*, in the sense that he must show that he can contribute to the protection of his family, kinship group, tribe, and other groups to which he belongs, from attacks by human enemies or animal predators. He learns this by acquiring the skills of warfare and the capacity to use weapons. Conflict between human groups has been a fact of life in most cultures throughout human history, so this is a pervasive requirement. Finally, he must learn to *procreate*, in the sense that he must gain some degree of sexual experience before marriage. This is not so he can demonstrate his sexual attractiveness but simply so that he can demonstrate that in marriage he will be able to perform sexually well enough to produce children.

Learning to provide for a family economically is a traditional part of the male gender role. Here, an Egyptian father and son fish together on the Nile River.

Globalization and Shifting Gender Roles   Although gender intensification has historically been stronger in traditional cultures than in developed countries, it is important to note that gender roles may change over time. Studies of globalization are finding a tendency toward greater gender equality. For example, Adriana Manago compared Zincantec Mayan adolescents who had been to high school with those who had not. High school—a recent institution in these adolescents' hometown of Zinacantán—affords opportunities for teenage boys and girls to interact together in ways and in settings that are far different from traditional practices. Manago (2015) found similarities and differences in the ways that girls and boys saw the changes in gender roles that were occurring in the community. Both girls and boys in high school tended to emphasize equivalent and chosen gender roles, rather than complementary and ascribed roles. There were also differences in the ways that girls and boys saw the new gender role possibilities. Girls thought the opportunities for expanded gender roles for females were favorable, but they perceived some risks in negotiating cross-sex relations. Boys lamented the loss of the female homemaker role, but thought favorably of new opportunities for intimacy in cross-sex relations. School is one factor in the trends of globalization. Other things that come with the possibility of attending high school, such as the financial ability to stay in school and not go to work, are important factors as well in the shifts toward equal roles.

EMOTIONAL AND SOCIAL DEVELOPMENT: Cultural Beliefs: Morality and Religion

As we have seen, cognitive development in adolescence entails a greater capacity for abstract and complex thinking. This capacity is applied not only to scientific and practical problems but also to cultural beliefs, most notably in the areas of moral and religious development.

Moral Development

LO 8.15   **Discriminate between Kohlberg's theory of moral development and Jensen's worldviews theory.**

For most of the past half-century, moral development was viewed as following a universal pattern, grounded in cognitive development. However, more recently, moral development has been argued to be fundamentally rooted in cultural beliefs. First we look at a theory of universal moral development, then at a cultural theory.

KOHLBERG'S THEORY OF MORAL DEVELOPMENT Lawrence Kohlberg (1958) presented an influential theory of moral development that dominated research on this topic for several decades. Kohlberg viewed moral development as based on cognitive development and believed that moral thinking changes in predictable ways as cognitive abilities develop, regardless of culture. He presented people with hypothetical moral dilemmas and had them indicate what behavior they believed was right or wrong in that situation, and why.

Kohlberg began his research by studying the moral judgments of 72 boys ages 10, 13, and 16 from middle-class and working-class families in the Chicago area (Kohlberg, 1958). He presented the boys with a series of fictional dilemmas, each of which was constructed to elicit their moral reasoning. For example, in one dilemma, a man must decide whether or not to steal a drug he cannot afford, to save his dying wife.

To Kohlberg, what was crucial for understanding the level of people's moral development was not whether they concluded that the actions of the persons in the dilemma were right or wrong but how they explained their conclusions; his focus was on adolescents' *moral reasoning*, not moral evaluations of right and wrong or their moral behavior. Kohlberg (1976) developed a system for classifying moral reasoning into three levels of moral development, as follows:

Level 1: **Preconventional reasoning**. At this level, moral reasoning is based on perceptions of the likelihood of external rewards and punishments. What is right is what avoids punishment or results in rewards.

Level 2: **Conventional reasoning**. At this level, moral reasoning is less egocentric and the person advocates the value of conforming to the moral expectations of others. What is right is whatever agrees with the rules established by tradition and by authorities.

Level 3: **Postconventional reasoning**. Moral reasoning at this level is based on the person's own independent judgments rather than on what others view as wrong or right. What is right is derived from the person's perception of objective, universal principles rather than being based on the needs of the individual (as in Level 1) or the standards of the group (as in Level 2).

Kohlberg followed his initial group of adolescent boys over the next 20 years (Colby et al., 1983), interviewing them every 3 or 4 years, and he and his colleagues also conducted numerous other studies on moral reasoning in adolescence and adulthood. The results verified Kohlberg's theory of moral development in two ways:

- The stage of moral reasoning tended to increase with age. However, even after 20 years, when all of the original participants were in their 30s, few of them had proceeded to Level 3 (Colby et al., 1983).
- Moral development proceeded in the predicted way, in the sense that the participants did not drop from a higher level to a lower level but proceeded from one level to the next highest over time.

Kohlberg's goal was to propose a universal theory of moral development, a theory that would apply to people in all cultures. One reason he used hypothetical moral dilemmas rather than having people talk about moral issues they had confronted in real life was that he believed that the culture-specific and person-specific *content* of moral reasoning is not important to understanding moral development. According to Kohlberg, what matters is the *structure* of moral reasoning, not the content. In other words, what matters is *how* people make their moral judgments, not whether they view certain acts as right or wrong.

preconventional reasoning
first level in Kohlberg's theory of moral development, in which moral reasoning is based on perceptions of the likelihood of external rewards and punishments

conventional reasoning
second level in Kohlberg's theory of moral development, in which moral reasoning is based on the expectations of others

postconventional reasoning
third level in Kohlberg's theory of moral development, in which moral reasoning is based on the individual's own independent judgments rather than on what others view as wrong or right

CULTURE AND MORAL DEVELOPMENT: THE WORLDVIEWS THEORY Does Kohlberg's theory of moral development apply universally, as he intended? Research based on Kohlberg's theory has included cross-cultural studies in countries all over the world, such as Turkey, Japan, Taiwan, Kenya, Israel, and India (Gibbs et al., 2007; Snarey, 1985). Many of these studies have focused on moral development in adolescence and emerging adulthood. In general, the studies confirm Kohlberg's hypothesis that moral development as classified by his coding system progresses with age. Also, as in the U.S. studies, participants in longitudinal studies in other cultures have rarely been found to regress to an earlier stage.

Nevertheless, Kohlberg's claims of a universal theory of moral development have been challenged, most notably by cultural psychologist Richard Shweder (2003; Shweder et al., 1990; Shweder et al., 2006). Shweder argued that it is impossible to understand moral development unless you understand the cultural worldview that underlies it. In contrast to Kohlberg, Shweder proposed that the *content* of people's moral reasoning, including their views of right and wrong, is at the heart of moral development and cannot simply be ignored.

Shweder and his colleagues have presented an alternative to Kohlberg's theory of moral development (Shweder et al., 1997). The new theory has been developed mostly by a former student of Shweder's, Lene Jensen (1997a, 1997b, 2008, 2011, 2015a, b, c). According to Jensen, the ultimate basis of morality is a person's **worldview**. A worldview is a set of cultural beliefs that explain what it means to be human, how human relations should be conducted, and how human problems should be addressed. Worldviews provide the basis for *moral reasoning* (explanations for why a behavior is right or wrong). The outcome of moral reasoning is *moral evaluations* (judgments as to whether a behavior is right or wrong), which in turn prescribe *moral behaviors.* Moral behaviors reinforce worldviews. An illustration of the worldviews theory is shown in **Figure 8.10**.

In her research, Jensen codes people's responses to moral issues according to three types of "ethics" based on different worldviews.

worldview

set of cultural beliefs that explain what it means to be human, how human relations should be conducted, and how human problems should be addressed

- The *Ethic of Autonomy* defines the individual as the primary moral authority. Individuals are viewed as having a right to do as they wish so long as their behavior does not harm others.
- The *Ethic of Community* defines individuals as members of social groups to which they have commitments and obligations. In this ethic, the responsibilities of roles in the family, community, and other groups are the basis of one's moral judgments.
- The *Ethic of Divinity* defines the individual as a spiritual entity, subject to the prescriptions of a divine authority. This ethic includes moral views based on traditional religious authorities and religious texts (e.g., the Bible, the Koran).

Several recent studies using the three ethics have focused on adolescents. For example, a study in India found that adolescents used more Autonomy than their parents did, whereas the parents used Community more; use of Divinity was rare in both groups (Kapadia & Bhangaokar, 2015). A U.S. study compared children, adolescents, and adults, and found that adolescents as well as adults used less Autonomy and more Community than children did (Jensen, 2015a, b, c). A study in Finland found that most adolescents used a combination of Autonomy and Community in their moral reasoning, but for conservatively religious adolescents, Divinity was used most often (Vainio, 2015). Research using the three ethics has

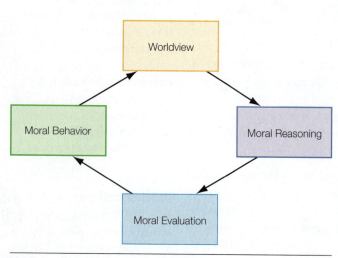

Figure 8.10 Worldviews Theory

How is this theory different from Kohlberg's?

SOURCE: Based on Jensen (2008)

only begun, and it remains to be seen how their use changes in different cultures throughout the life span (Jensen, 2011).

Religious Beliefs

LO 8.16 Describe the cultural variations in religious beliefs during adolescence as well as the sources and outcomes of religiosity within cultures.

Table 8.1 Religious Beliefs of U.S. Adolescents

Believe in God or a universal spirit	84%
Pray at least once a week	65%
Religion important in daily life	51%
Believe in the existence of angels	63%
Attend religious services at least twice a month	52%
Involved in a church youth group	38%

SOURCE: Based on Smith & Denton (2005)

Like moral development, the development of religious beliefs reaches a critical point in adolescence because adolescence is a time when the abstract ideas involved in religious beliefs can first be fully grasped. In general, adolescents and emerging adults in developed countries are less religious than their counterparts in developing countries. Developed countries tend to be highly **secular**, which means based on nonreligious beliefs and values. In every developed country, religion has gradually faded in its influence over the past two centuries (Bellah et al., 1985; Watson, 2014). Religious beliefs and practices are especially low among adolescents in Europe. For example, in Belgium only 8 percent of 18-year-old citizens attend religious services at least once a month (Goossens & Luyckx, 2007). In Spain, traditionally a highly Catholic country, only 18 percent of adolescents attend church regularly (Gibbons & Stiles, 2004).

Americans are more religious than people in virtually any other developed country, and this is reflected in the lives of U.S. adolescents (see **Table 8.1**; Smith & Denton, 2005). However, religion has a lower priority for most of them than many other parts of their lives, including school, friendships, media, and work. Furthermore, the religious beliefs of U.S. adolescents tend not to follow traditional doctrines, and they often know little about the doctrine of the religion they claim to follow. Instead, they tend to believe that religious faith is about how to be a good person and feel happy (Smith & Denton, 2005).

Many U.S. adolescents are religious, but many others are not. What explains differences among adolescents in their religiosity? Family characteristics are one important influence (Smith & Denton, 2005). Adolescents are more likely to embrace the importance of religion when their parents talk about religious issues and participate in religious activities (King et al., 2002; Layton et al., 2011). Adolescents are less likely to be religious when their parents disagree with each other about religious beliefs, and when their parents are divorced (Smith & Denton, 2005). Ethnicity is another factor. In U.S. society religious faith and religious practices tend to be stronger among African Americans than among Whites (Chatters et al., 2008).

The relatively high rate of religiosity among African American adolescents helps explain why they have such low rates of alcohol and drug use (Stevens-Watkins & Rostosky, 2010). However, it is not only among minority groups that religiosity is associated with favorable adolescent outcomes. Across U.S. cultural groups, adolescents who are more religious report less depression and lower rates of premarital sex, drug use, and delinquent behavior (Kerestes et al., 2004; Smith & Denton, 2005). The protective value of religious involvement is especially strong for adolescents living in the worst neighborhoods (Bridges & Moore, 2002). Religious adolescents tend to have better relationships with their parents (Smith & Denton, 2005; Wilcox, 2008). Also, adolescents who value religion are more likely than other adolescents to perform volunteer service in their community (Hart & Atkins, 2004; Youniss et al., 1999). In other cultures, too, religious involvement has been found to be related to a variety of positive outcomes, for example among Indonesian Muslim adolescents (French et al., 2008).

secular

based on nonreligious beliefs and values

African American adolescents are often highly religious.

EMOTIONAL AND SOCIAL DEVELOPMENT: The Social and Cultural Contexts of Adolescence

Like younger children, adolescents typically remain within the family, and most of them also attend school. However, social contexts of peers, romantic relations, work, and media often have greater prominence in adolescence than previously. Also, for some adolescents, certain types of problems develop that were rare in previous life stages.

Family Relationships

LO 8.17 **Summarize the cultural variations in adolescents' relationships with parents, siblings, and extended family.**

The family is a key part of the daily social context of adolescents in all cultures, but in most cultures there are also profound changes in family relations from middle childhood to adolescence. Perhaps the most notable change is the decline in the amount of time spent with family members, as described in the *Research Focus: The Daily Rhythms of Adolescents' Family Lives* feature. When adolescents do spend time with their parents, conflict is more frequent than in middle childhood, as we will see next.

CONFLICT WITH PARENTS Numerous studies have shown that adolescents and their parents agree on many of their beliefs and values, and typically they have a great deal of love and respect for one another (Kağitçibaşi & Yalin, 2015; Moore et al., 2002; Smetana, 2005). Nevertheless, studies in Western countries also indicate that conflict with parents increases sharply in early adolescence, compared with middle childhood, and remains high for several years before declining in late adolescence (Dworkin & Larson, 2001; Kağitçibaşi & Yalin, 2015; Laursen et al., 1998).

Figure 8.11 shows the increase in conflict from middle childhood to adolescence, from a longitudinal study that observed U.S. mothers and sons in videotaped interactions on five occasions over 8 years (Granic et al., 2003). A Canadian study found that 40 percent of adolescents reported arguments with their parents at least once a week (Sears, 2012). Conflict in adolescence is especially frequent and intense between mothers and daughters (Collins & Laursen, 2004). By mid-adolescence, conflict with parents tends to become somewhat less frequent but more intense before declining substantially in late adolescence (Laursen et al., 1998).

There are several reasons why conflict with parents often rises during adolescence. First, adolescence entails reaching sexual maturity, which means that sexual issues may be a source of conflict in a way they would not have been in childhood (Arnett, 1999). Early-maturing adolescents tend to have more conflict with parents than adolescents who mature "on time," perhaps because sexual issues arise earlier (Collins & Laursen, 2004). Second, advances in cognitive development make it possible for adolescents to rebut their parents' reasoning about rules and restrictions more effectively than they could have earlier. Third, and most importantly, in many cultures adolescence is a time of gaining greater independence from the family. Although parents and adolescents in these cultures usually share the same goal that the adolescent will eventually become a self-sufficient adult, they often disagree about the pace of adolescents' growing **autonomy** (Daddis & Smetana, 2006; Smetana, 2005).

autonomy

quality of being independent and self-sufficient, capable of thinking for one's self

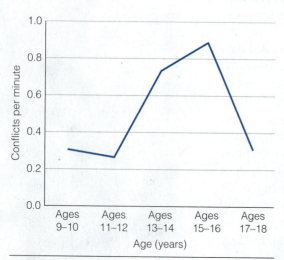

Figure 8.11 Parental Conflict in Adolescence

Why does conflict peak in the mid-teens?

SOURCE: Granic et al. (2003)

Research Focus: The Daily Rhythms of Adolescents' Family Lives

Adolescent researchers have found the Experience Sampling Method (ESM) to be a helpful source of information on adolescents' social lives. The ESM involves having people wear beeper watches that randomly beep during the day so that people can record their thoughts, feelings, and behavior as events take place. Reed Larson and Maryse Richards are the two scholars who have done the most to apply the ESM to adolescents and their families.

In their classic book *Divergent Realities: The Emotional Lives of Mothers, Fathers, and Adolescents* (Larson & Richards, 1994), they described the results of their research on a sample of 483 American adolescents in 5th to 12th grades, and another sample of 55 5th to 8th graders and their parents. All were two-parent, White families. In each family, three family members (adolescent, mother, and father) were beeped at the same times, about 30 times per day between 7:30 in the morning and 9:30 at night, during the week of the study.

When beeped, adolescents and their parents paused from whatever they were doing and recorded a variety of information about where they were, whom they were with, what they were doing, and how they were feeling.

One striking finding of the study was that adolescents and their parents averaged only about an hour a day spent in shared activities, and their most common shared activity was watching television. The amount of time adolescents spent with their families dropped sharply between 5th and 12th grades. In turn, there was an increase from 5th to 9th grade in the amount of time adolescents spent alone in their bedrooms.

The study also revealed some interesting differences in mothers' and fathers' relationships with adolescents. The majority of mother–adolescent interactions were rated positively by both of them, especially experiences such as talking together, going out together, and sharing a meal.

However, adolescents' negative feelings toward their mothers increased sharply from fifth to ninth grade, and their feelings of closeness to mothers decreased.

As for fathers, they tended to be only tenuously involved in their adolescents' lives. For most of the time they spent with their adolescents, the mother was there as well, and the mother tended to be more directly involved. Fathers averaged only 12 minutes per day alone with their adolescents, and 40 percent of this time was spent watching TV together.

The study showed that parents are often important influences on adolescents' emotional states. Adolescents brought home to the family their emotions from the rest of the day. If their parents were responsive and caring, adolescents' moods improved and their negative emotions were relieved. In contrast, if adolescents felt their parents were unavailable or unresponsive, their negative feelings became even worse. Even though adolescents spend less time with the parents than when they were younger, parents remain powerful influences in their lives.

Review Questions:

1. In the ESM studies of adolescents and their parents, adolescents have been found to have the most positive feelings when with _____ and the most negative feelings toward _____.
   a. Mothers; fathers
   b. Mothers; mothers
   c. Fathers; mothers
   d. Fathers; fathers

Watch   RESEARCH FOCUS: THE DAILY RHYTHMS OF ADOLESCENTS' FAMILY LIVES

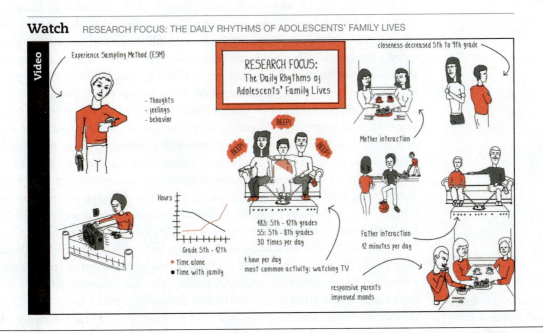

Why does conflict with parents rise from middle childhood to adolescence?

Parents may have concerns about adolescents' safety with respect to sexuality, automobile driving, and substance use, and so restrict adolescents' behavior in an effort to protect them from risks (Arnett, 1999). Adolescents expect to be able to make their own decisions in these areas and resent their parents' restrictions, so conflict results.

Some parents engage in **parental monitoring**, which is when parents keep track of adolescents' whereabouts, activities, and friends. Some parents may track their children's cell phone activity and locations, and some read their children's email or diaries, whereas others just ask their adolescent children questions about these areas. Some adolescents experience monitoring as privacy invasion, and this may have consequences for the parent-child relationship. In a 3-year longitudinal study of Dutch adolescents, Hawk and colleagues (2009) found that when adolescents perceived privacy invasion, they shared less with their parents over time. Furthermore, adolescents may have conflict with parents in the process of negotiating privacy issues, and the conflict may be a way for adolescents to manage privacy boundaries. In another study, Hawk and colleagues (2013) found a similar pattern and concluded that privacy invasion may be counterproductive because adolescents may increase their secrecy to maintain privacy.

However, not all cultures value and encourage increased autonomy in adolescence, as you will see in the *Cultural Focus: Adolescent Conflict with Parents Across Cultures* feature.

SIBLING AND EXTENDED-FAMILY RELATIONS For about 80 percent of U.S. adolescents, and similar proportions in other developed countries, the family system also includes relationships with at least one sibling (U.S. Bureau of the Census, 2009). The proportion of families with siblings is even higher in developing countries, where birth rates tend to be higher and families with only one child are rare (Population Reference Bureau, 2014).

How did you get along with your siblings when you were in adolescence? In the United States, sibling rivalry is a source of conflict in adolescence. Across cultures, siblings may not have rivalry, but they may still experience conflict as they learn each other's boundaries. In studies that compare adolescents' relationships with siblings to relationships with parents, grandparents, teachers, and friends, adolescents report more frequent conflicts with their siblings than with anyone else (Campione-Barr & Smetana, 2010). Common sources of conflict include teasing, possessions (e.g., borrowing a sibling's clothes without permission), responsibility for chores, name-calling, invasions of privacy, and perceived unequal treatment by parents (Noller, 2005; Updegraff et al., 2005). However, even though adolescents tend to have more conflicts with siblings than in their other relationships, conflict with siblings is lower in adolescence than at younger ages (Brody, 2004; Noller, 2005). From childhood to adolescence, relationships with siblings become less emotionally intense, mainly because adolescents gradually spend less time with their siblings (Hetherington et al., 1999).

Adolescents in traditional cultures often have responsibility for caring for young siblings. In Schlegel and Barry's (1991) analysis of adolescence in traditional cultures, more than 80 percent of adolescent boys and girls had frequent responsibility for caring for younger siblings. This responsibility promotes conflict between siblings, but also close attachments. Time together, and closeness, is especially high between siblings of the same gender, mainly because in traditional cultures, daily activities are often separated

parental monitoring

actions parents take to keep track of their children's behavior and whereabouts

Cultural Focus: Adolescent Conflict With Parents Across Cultures

In traditional cultures, it is rare for parents and adolescents to engage in the kind of frequent conflicts typical of parent–adolescent relationships in Western cultures (Larson et al., 2010). The role of parent carries greater authority in traditional cultures than in the West, and this makes it less likely that adolescents in such cultures will express disagreements and resentments toward their parents (Phinney et al., 2005). Even when they disagree with their parents, they are unlikely to express it because of their feelings of duty and respect (Phinney & Ong, 2002). Outside of the West, interdependence is a higher value than independence, not only during adolescence but throughout adulthood (Markus & Kitayama, 2010; Phinney et al., 2005). Just as a dramatic increase in autonomy during adolescence prepares Western adolescents for adult life in an individualistic culture, learning to submit to the authority of one's parents prepares adolescents in traditional cultures for an adult life in which interdependence is among the highest values and each person has a clearly designated position in a family hierarchy.

In this video, adolescents from a variety of cultures are interviewed as they discuss their changing relationships with their parents as well as with their friends.

Review Question:

The narrator tells us that interdependence is valued in the Mexican village where one of the female teens is from. What are the economic reasons why interdependence might be more adaptive in this Mexican village than in the U.S. family also shown in the video?

Watch ADOLESCENT CONFLICT WITH PARENTS ACROSS CULTURES

by gender. Close relationships between siblings are also common in African American families, in part because many African American families are headed by single mothers who rely on older siblings to help with child care (Brody et al., 2003).

Adolescents in traditional cultures also tend to be close to their extended family members. In these cultures children often grow up in a household that includes not only their parents and siblings but also grandparents, and often uncles, aunts, and cousins as well. These living arrangements promote closeness between adolescents and their extended family. In Schlegel and Barry's (1991) cross-cultural analysis, daily contact was as high with grandparents as with parents for adolescents in traditional cultures, and adolescents were usually even closer to their grandparents than to their parents. Perhaps this is because parents typically exercise authority over adolescents, which may add ambivalence to adolescents' relationships with their parents, whereas grandparents are less likely to exercise authority and may focus more on nurturing and supporting adolescents.

Extended family members are also important figures in the lives of adolescents in Western majority cultures. About 80 percent of U.S. adolescents list at least one member of their extended family among the people most important to them, and closeness to grandparents is positively related to adolescents' well-being (Ruiz & Silverstein, 2007). However, in the U.S. majority culture adolescents' contact with extended family members is relatively infrequent, in part because extended family members often live many miles away. When extended family members live within the household or nearby, as is often the case in African American, Latino, and Asian American families, adolescents' closeness to them tends to resemble the pattern in traditional cultures (Fuligni et al., 1999; Suarez-Orozco & Suarez-Orozco, 1996; Oberlander et al., 2007).

Peers and Friends

LO 8.18 **Describe cultural variations in adolescents' relationships with friends, and characterize their interactions with peers.**

As time spent with family decreases from middle childhood to adolescence, time spent with friends increases, in most cultures. Friends also become increasingly important in adolescents' emotional lives. In adolescence, as at other ages, friends choose one another primarily because of similarities in characteristics such as age, gender, ethnic group, personality, and leisure interests (Popp et al., 2008). As shown in the video *Peer Pressure: Tim*, adolescence is also a time of increasing peer pressure.

Watch PEER PRESSURE: TIM

FRIENDSHIPS: CULTURAL THEMES AND VARIATIONS Although family ties remain important in the lives of adolescents, friends become preferred in some ways. Adolescents indicate that they depend more on friends than on their parents or siblings for companionship and intimacy (French et al., 2001; Nickerson & Nagle, 2005; Updegraff et al., 2002). Friends become the source of adolescents' happiest experiences, the people with whom they feel most comfortable, and the persons they feel they can talk to most openly (French, 2015; Richards et al., 2002; Youniss & Smollar, 1985).

European studies comparing relationships with parents and friends show a pattern similar to U.S. studies. For example, a study of Dutch adolescents (ages 15–19) asked them who they rely on to communicate about themselves, including their personal feelings, sorrows, and secrets (Bois-Reymond & Ravesloot, 1996). Nearly half of the adolescents named their best friend or their romantic partner, whereas just 20 percent named one or both parents (only 3 percent their fathers). Another Dutch study found that 82 percent of adolescents named spending free time with friends as their favorite activity (Meeus, 2007). Studies in other European countries confirm that adolescents tend to be happiest when with their friends and that they tend to turn to their friends for advice and information on social relationships and leisure, although they come to parents for advice about education and career plans (Hurrelmann, 1996).

As noted previously, adolescence in traditional cultures often entails less involvement with family and greater involvement with peers for boys but not for girls. However, for boys as well as girls, the social and emotional balance between friends and family remains tilted more toward family for adolescents in developing countries than it does in the West. For example, in India, adolescents tend to spend their leisure time with family rather than friends, not because they are required to do so but because of collectivistic Indian cultural values and because they enjoy their time with family (Chaudhary & Sharma, 2012; Larson et al., 2000). Among Brazilian adolescents, emotional support is higher from parents than friends (Van Horn & Cunegatto, 2000). In a study comparing adolescents in Indonesia and the United States, Indonesian adolescents rated their family members higher and their friends lower on companionship and enjoyment, compared to U.S. adolescents (French et al., 2001). Nevertheless, friends were the primary source of intimacy in both countries. Thus, it may be that adolescents in developing countries remain close to their families even as they also develop greater closeness to their friends during adolescence, whereas in the West closeness to family diminishes as closeness to friends grows.

Adolescents in Western cultures tend to be happiest when with friends.

THE IMPORTANCE OF INTIMACY Probably the most important feature of adolescent friendships is intimacy. **Intimacy** is the degree to which two people share personal knowledge, thoughts, and feelings. Adolescent friends confide hopes and fears, and help each other understand what is going on with their parents, their teachers, and peers to a far greater degree than younger children do.

When adolescents are asked what they would want a friend to be like or how they can tell that someone is their friend, they tend to mention intimate features of the relationship (Berndt, 1996; Radmacher & Azmitia, 2006). They state, for example, that a friend is someone who understands you, someone you can share your problems with, someone who will listen when you have something important to say (Bauminger et al., 2008; Way, 2004). Younger children are less likely to mention these kinds of features and more likely to stress shared activities—we both like to play basketball, we ride bikes together, we play computer games, and so on. There are consistent gender differences in the intimacy of adolescent friendships, with girls tending to have more intimate friendships than boys do (Bauminger et al., 2008). Girls spend more time than boys talking to their friends, and they place a higher value on talking together as a component of their friendships (Apter, 1990; Youniss & Smollar, 1985). Girls also rate their friendships as higher in affection, helpfulness, and nurturance, compared with boys' ratings of their friendships (Bokhorst et al., 2010). And girls are more likely than boys to say they trust and feel close to their friends (Shulman et al., 1997). In contrast, even in adolescence, boys are more likely to emphasize shared activities as the basis of friendship, such as sports or hobbies (Radmacher & Azmitia, 2006).

intimacy

degree to which two people share personal knowledge, thoughts, and feelings

Cliques are often formed around shared activities. Here, South African adolescents enjoy a game of soccer.

Nevertheless, intimacy does become more important to boys' friendships in adolescence, even if not to the same extent as for girls. In one study of African American, Latino, and Asian American boys from poor and working-class families, Niobe Way (2004) reported themes of intimacy that involved sharing secrets, protecting one another physically and emotionally, and disclosing feelings about family and friends.

CLIQUES AND CROWDS So far we have focused on close friendships. Now we turn to larger groups of friends and peers. Scholars generally make a distinction between two types of adolescent social groups, cliques and crowds. **Cliques** are small groups of friends who know each other well, do things together, and form a regular social group (Brown & Braun, 2013). Cliques have no precise size—3 to 12 is a rough range—but they are small enough so that all the members of the clique feel they know each other well and they think of themselves as a cohesive group. Sometimes cliques are defined by distinctive shared activities—for example, working on cars, playing music, playing basketball—and sometimes simply by shared friendship (a group of friends who eat lunch together every day, for example).

Crowds, in contrast, are larger, reputation-based groups of adolescents who are not necessarily friends and may not spend much time together (Brown et al., 2008; Brown & Braun, 2013; Horn, 2003). A review of 44 studies on adolescent crowds concluded that five major types of crowds are found in many schools (Susman et al., 2007):

- Elites (aka Populars, Preppies). The crowd recognized as having the highest social status in the school.
- Athletes (aka Jocks). Sports-oriented students, usually members of at least one sports team.
- Academics (aka Brains, Nerds, Geeks). Known for striving for good grades and for being socially inept.
- Deviants (aka Druggies, Burnouts). Alienated from the school social environment, suspected by other students of using illicit drugs and engaging in other risky activities.
- Others (aka Normals, Nobodies). Students who do not stand out in any particular way, neither positively nor negatively; mostly ignored by other students.

Crowds mainly serve the function of helping adolescents to locate themselves and others within the secondary school social structure. In other words, crowds help adolescents to define their own identities and the identities of others. Knowing that others think of you as a "Brain" has implications for your identity—it means you are the kind of person who likes school, does well in school, and perhaps has more success in school than in social situations. Thinking of someone else as a "Druggie" tells you something about that person (whether it is accurate or not)—he or she uses drugs, of course, probably dresses unconventionally, and does not seem to care much about school.

BULLYING At the age of 15, Phoebe Prince immigrated to the United States from Ireland with her family. She liked her new school at first and made friends, but then a popular boy took an interest in her, and she dated him a few times. Other girls who were interested in the boy began to harass her aggressively, calling her names in school and sending vicious e-mail messages spreading false rumors about her. Friendless and persecuted in and out of school, she sank deeper and deeper into despair and finally committed suicide, to the horror of her family and her community.

clique

small group of friends who know each other well, do things together, and form a regular social group

crowd

large, reputation-based group of adolescents

This shocking true-life example shows how serious the consequences of bullying in adolescence can be. Bullying is common in middle childhood, but the prevalence of bullying rises through middle childhood and peaks in early adolescence, then declines substantially by late adolescence (Pepler et al., 2006). Bullying is an international phenomenon, observed in many countries in Europe (Dijkstra et al., 2008; Gini et al., 2008), Asia (Ando et al., 2005; Hokoda et al., 2006), and North America (Pepler et al., 2008; Volk et al., 2006). In a landmark study of bullying among more than 100,000 adolescents ages 11 to 15 in 28 countries around the world, self-reported prevalence rates of being a victim of bullying ranged from 6 percent among girls in Sweden to 41 percent among boys in Lithuania, with rates in most countries in the 10 to 20 percent range (Due et al., 2005). Across countries, in this study and many others, boys are consistently more likely than girls to be bullies as well as victims.

Bullying has a variety of negative effects on adolescents' development. In the 28-country study of adolescent bullying just mentioned, victims of bullying reported higher rates of a wide range of problems, including physical symptoms such as headaches, backaches, and difficulty sleeping, as well as psychological symptoms such as loneliness, helplessness, anxiety, and unhappiness (Due et al., 2005). Not only victims but also bullies are at high risk for problems (Klomek et al., 2007). A Canadian study of bullying that surveyed adolescents for 7 years beginning at ages 10 to 14 found that bullies reported more psychological problems and more problems in their relationships with parents and peers than non-bullies did (Pepler et al., 2008).

A recent variation on bullying is **cyberbullying** (also called electronic bullying), which involves bullying behavior via social media (such as Facebook), e-mail, or mobile phones (Kowalski et al., 2012; Valkenberg & Peter, 2011). A Swedish study of 12- to 20-year-olds found an age pattern of cyberbullying similar to what has been found in studies of "traditional" bullying, with the highest rates in early adolescence and a decline through late adolescence and emerging adulthood (Slonje & Smith, 2008). In a study of nearly 4,000 adolescents in Grades 6 to 8 in the United States, 11 percent reported being victims of a cyberbullying incident at least once in the past 2 months; 7 percent indicated that they had been cyberbullies as well as victims during this time period; and 4 percent reported committing a cyberbullying incident (Kowalski & Limber, 2007). Notably, half of the victims did not know the bully's identity, a key difference between cyberbullying and other bullying. However, cyberbullying usually involves only a single incident, so it does not involve the repetition required in the standard definition of traditional bullying, and might be better termed *online harassment* (Wolak et al., 2007).

What does it take to stand up to a bully? It is important to try to understand what factors affect the willingness of youth to stand up to a bully—whether as individuals being bullied or as defenders of victims. In a study in Finland, Pöyhönen, et al. (2010) found that cognitive, emotional, and interpersonal factors all play a role in whether an adolescent will defend a victim of bullying. Having empathy is a factor, as is having social status. Children who were more popular felt more self-efficacy in standing up to bullies.

Romantic Relationships and Adolescent Sexuality

LO 8.19 Identify cultural variations in adolescent love and sexuality, including variations in adolescent pregnancy and contraceptive use.

Puberty means reaching sexual maturity. Consequently, adolescence is when sexual feelings begin to stir and—in many cultures, but not all—sexual behavior is initiated. First we look at love, then at sex.

ROMANTIC RELATIONSHIPS The prevalence of involvement in romantic relationships increases gradually over the course of adolescence. According to a study in the

cyberbullying

bullying via electronic means, mainly through the Internet

In the West most adolescents have a romantic partner at some point in their teens.

permissive culture

culture that encourages and expects sexual activity from their adolescents

semirestrictive culture

culture that has prohibitions on premarital adolescent sex, but the prohibitions are not strongly enforced and are easily evaded

restrictive culture

culture that places strong prohibitions on adolescent sexual activity before marriage

United States called the National Study of Adolescent Health, the percentage of adolescents reporting a current romantic relationship rises from 17 percent in 7th grade to 32 percent in 9th grade to 44 percent in 11th grade (Furman & Hand, 2006). By 11th grade, 80 percent of adolescents had experienced a romantic relationship at some point, even if they did not have one currently. Adolescents with an Asian cultural background tend to have their first romantic relationship later than adolescents with a European, African American, or Latino cultural background, because of Asian cultural beliefs that discourage early involvement in romantic relationships and encourage minimal or no sexual involvement before marriage (Connolly & McIsaac, 2011; Regan et al., 2004).

Though adolescents around the world appear to experience romantic love (Jankowiak & Fischer, 1992), in many cultural groups adolescents do not date. In most cultures throughout most of history, marriages have been arranged by parents, with little regard for the passionate desires of their children. Romantic love as the basis for marriage is a fairly new cultural idea (Hatfield & Rapson, 2005).

ADOLESCENT SEXUALITY Even though adolescents in all cultures go through similar biological processes in reaching sexual maturity, cultures vary enormously in how they view adolescent sexuality. Variations among countries in sexual behavior during adolescence is primarily as a result of variations in cultural beliefs about the acceptability (or not) of premarital sex. The best framework for understanding this variation among countries remains a book that is now more than 60 years old, *Patterns of Sexual Behavior,* by Clellan Ford and Frank Beach (1951). These two anthropologists compiled information about sexuality from more than 200 cultures. On the basis of their analysis they described three types of cultural approaches to adolescent sexuality: *permissive, semirestrictive,* and *restrictive.*

Permissive cultures tolerate and even encourage adolescent sexuality. Most of the countries of northern Europe today would fall into this category. Adolescents in these countries usually begin an active sexual life in their late teens, and parents often allow them to have a boyfriend or girlfriend spend the night (Trost, 2012). In Sweden, for example, most adolescents are sexually active around age 15 (Edgardh, 2002).

Semirestrictive cultures have prohibitions on premarital adolescent sex. However, in these cultures the formal prohibitions are not strongly enforced and are easily evaded. Adults in these cultures tend to ignore evidence of premarital sexual behavior as long as young people are fairly discreet. Most developed countries today would fall into this category, including the United States, Canada, and most of Europe (Regnerus & Uecker, 2011). In the United States, the average age of first sexual intercourse is 17 (Guttmacher Institute, 2014).

Restrictive cultures place strong prohibitions on adolescent sexual activity before marriage. The prohibition on premarital sex is enforced through strong social norms and by keeping boys and girls separated through adolescence. Young people in Asia and South America tend to disapprove strongly of premarital sex, reflecting the view they have been taught by their cultures (Regan et al., 2004). In Mexico, *marianismo* is a cultural ideal that women have a sacred duty to be chaste and self-sacrificing (Gil & Vasquez, 1996). Mexican adolescent girls are encouraged by marianismo to maintain their chastity until marriage. However, despite this cultural ideal, rates of adolescent sexual intercourse are fairly high in Mexico, especially in rural areas (Arceo-Gomez & Campos-Vazquez, 2014).

In some countries, the restrictiveness of the taboo on premarital sex even includes the threat of physical punishment and public shaming. A number of Middle Eastern countries take this approach, including Algeria, Syria, and Saudi Arabia. Premarital female virginity is a matter of not only the girl's honor but the honor of her family, and if she is known to lose her virginity before marriage, the males of her family may punish her, beat her, or even kill her (Dorjee et al., 2013). Although many cultures also value male premarital chastity, no culture punishes male premarital sex with such severity.

CRITICAL THINKING QUESTION

Is there a gender double standard for adolescent sexuality in your culture? Provide some examples to support your answer.

ADOLESCENT PREGNANCY AND CONTRACEPTIVE USE Although cultures vary in how they view adolescent sex, nearly everywhere in the world premarital pregnancy in adolescence is viewed as undesirable. Two types of countries have low rates of premarital pregnancy: those that are permissive about adolescent sex and those that are restrictive. Northern European countries such as Denmark, Sweden, and the Netherlands have low rates of adolescent pregnancy because they are permissive about adolescent sex (Avery & Lazdane, 2008). There are explicit safe-sex campaigns in the media. Adolescents have easy access to all types of contraception. Parents accept that their children will become sexually active by their late teens (Trost, 2012).

At the other end of the spectrum, restrictive countries such as Japan, South Korea, and Morocco strictly forbid adolescent sex (Davis & Davis, 2012; Dorjee et al., 2013; Hatfield & Rapson, 2005). Adolescents in these countries are strongly discouraged even from dating until they are well into emerging adulthood and are seriously looking for a marriage partner. It is rare for an adolescent boy and girl even to spend time alone together, much less have sex. Some adolescents follow the call of nature anyway and violate the taboo, but violations are rare because the taboo is so strong and the shame of being exposed for breaking it is so great.

The United States has a higher rate of teenage pregnancy than any other developed country (Sedgh, et al, 2015), as **Figure 8.12** illustrates. The main reason U.S. adolescents have high rates of teenage pregnancy may be that there is no clear cultural message regarding adolescent sexuality (Males, 2010). The semirestrictive view of adolescent sexuality prevails: Adolescent sex is not strictly forbidden, but neither is it widely accepted. As a consequence, most U.S. adolescents have sexual intercourse at some time before they reach the end of their teens, but often those who are sexually active are not comfortable enough with their sexuality to acknowledge that they are having sex and to prepare for it responsibly by obtaining and using contraception. However, rates of teen pregnancy in the United States have declined steeply in the past two decades, especially among African Americans (Males, 2011). This may be because the threat of HIV/AIDS has made it more acceptable in the United States to talk to adolescents about sex and contraception and to provide them with sex education through the schools. However, recent increases in abstinence-only programs are a threat to teen health and pregnancy rates, as we discuss in the *Education Focus: Sex Education: A Public Health Endeavor* feature on the next page.

sexual orientation

a person's tendencies of sexual attraction

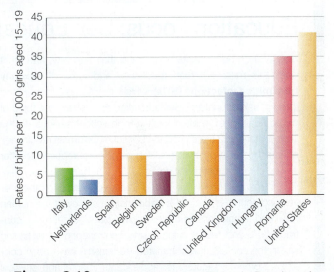

Figure 8.12 Teenage Pregnancy Rates in Developed Countries

Why are rates so high in the United States?
SOURCE: Based on World Health Organization (2010)

SEXUAL ORIENTATION Adolescence is when most people first become fully aware of their **sexual orientation**, meaning their tendencies of sexual attraction. There are many gender roles and sexual orientations, and they may be fluid throughout adolescence as part of the identity search. In U.S. society, 2 percent of adolescents self-identify as lesbian, gay, bisexual, or transgender (LGBT) (Savin-Williams & Joyner, 2014).

Why are rates of adolescent pregnancy especially high in the United States?

In the past in Western cultures, and still today in many of the world's cultures, most people would keep this knowledge to themselves all their lives because they would be stigmatized and persecuted if they disclosed the truth. Today in most Western cultures, however, LGBTs commonly engage in a process of **coming out**, which involves a person's recognizing his or her own sexual identity and then disclosing the truth to friends, family, and others (Flowers & Buston, 2001; Savin-Williams, 2001). Awareness of an LGBT sexual identity usually begins in early adolescence, with disclosure to others coming in late adolescence or emerging adulthood (Floyd & Bakeman, 2006).

Given the pervasiveness of **homophobia** (fear and hatred of homosexuals) that exists in many societies, coming to the realization of an LGBT identity can be traumatic for many adolescents. Lesbian, gay, or bisexual adolescents are often the targets of bullying when peers learn of their sexual identity (Mishna et al., 2009). Many parents respond with dismay or even anger when they learn that their adolescents are lesbian, gay, bisexual, or transgender. When parents reject LGBT adolescents after learning of their sexual identity, the consequences are dire. One study found that LGBT adolescents who experienced parental rejection were eight times more likely to report having attempted suicide, six times more likely to report high levels of depression, three times more likely to use illegal drugs, and three times more likely to have had unprotected sex than LGBT adolescents whose parents were more accepting of their sexual orientation (Ryan, 2009).

Nevertheless, in recent years there has been a noticeable change in Western attitudes toward LGBTs, constituting "a dramatic cultural shift" toward more favorable and tolerant perceptions, according to Ritch Savin-Williams (2005), a prominent researcher on LGBT adolescents. Savin-Williams notes changes in popular culture, such as favorable portrayals of LGBTs in television, movies, and popular songs. Notably, the average age of coming out has declined in recent decades, from 21 in the 1970s to 16 in the present, perhaps because of growing acceptance of homosexuality (Savin-Williams & Joyner, 2014). The United States and several European countries now allow same-sex marriages, another sign that people in the West are becoming more accepting of variations in sexual orientation.

Education Focus: Sex Education: A Public Health Endeavor

How well do adolescents understand their sexuality, and what does this mean for teen pregnancy and rates of **sexually transmitted infections (STIs)**, which are infections transmitted through sexual contact? Sex education or "sex ed" is a topic of public health that is often dealt with in school settings. In the United States, 22 states and the District of Columbia require sex ed in schools. In other states, schools are not required to offer sex ed curricula, but many do.

In many states in the United States as well as in other developed countries, sex ed is traditionally a survey of the human male and female reproductive systems, pubertal changes, contraception, and relationships. Using contraception and having sex in the context of a committed relationship have been considered protective factors for adolescents' mental and physical health, and most sex ed courses include information about these topics. Sex ed classes typically have also included discussions of what to say when you don't want to have sex and ideas for intimacy that do not include sexual contact (like holding hands or snuggling with clothes on). Sex ed curricula that discuss sexuality and contraception have been found to increase knowledge about the emotional and health-related issues of sexuality, including knowledge of and more positive attitudes toward contraception (Abdullah et al., 2003). Sex ed curricula are cost effective in that they decrease teen pregnancy and STIs (Kivela et al., 2014).

Sex ed has taken a distinctly political turn in recent years. In the United States, influence from the federal government after the year 2000 led to the growth of abstinence-only sex ed programs (Gusrang & Cheng, 2010). Although abstinence was always a part of the sex ed curriculum, abstinence-only approaches have been increasingly popular in a number of states and in other countries, such as in South Africa (Francis & DePalma, 2014). In abstinence-only approaches, adolescents do not learn about contraceptives. This is based on the ideas that "if we tell them about it, they will do it" and that sexual activity is something that should be avoided (usually until marriage). How effective have these programs been at decreasing teen pregnancy?

The United States has the highest teen pregnancy rate of any developed country, and abstinence-only programs have been found to increase teen pregnancy rates in White and African American teens (Yang & Gaydos, 2010). Even though more teens are sexually active in permissive cultures, teens in those places have access to and use contraceptives when they have sex (Trost, 2012). Thus, the teen pregnancy rate is lower.

Abstinence is certainly a respectable choice. Although it is possible that abstinence-only approaches might be improved (Jones & Biddlecom, 2011), approaches that include information about contraception and STIs and ways for adolescents to discuss these issues with potential partners have been found to be more effective at achieving the public health goals of safe and healthy sexuality among teens (Mabray & Laubauve, 2002; Smylie, et al., 2008).

Survey Question:

At what age would you like your children to learn about contraception?
a. Around age 10
b. Around age 12
c. Around age 16
d. I would not like my children to learn about contraception.

Media Use

LO 8.20   Explain the function of media use in adolescents' lives, and apply the Media Practice Model to the playing of electronic games.

Now that Jeff's twins are adolescents, media use has become an important part of their daily lives. Jeff's son Miles loves his iPad, and uses it daily for everything from researching school assignments to playing electronic games to monitoring the latest sports news. For Jeff's daughter Paris, recorded music is her primary media use. She loves to sing along with everything from Taylor Swift to opera.

No account of adolescent development would be complete without a description of the media they use. Recorded music, television, movies, magazines, electronic games, mobile phones, and the Internet are part of the daily environment for nearly all adolescents currently growing up in developed countries (and increasingly in developing countries as well). There is a dramatic increase in media use from middle childhood to early adolescence, especially electronic games, the Internet, and social media. A national U.S. study found that adolescents use social media for about 8 hours a day (Rideout et al., 2010). About one fourth of their media use involves multiple media—listening to music while playing an electronic game, for example, or reading a magazine while watching TV (which is increasingly done via the Internet on a computer or on a mobile device).

A MODEL OF ADOLESCENTS' MEDIA USES Spending 8 hours a day on anything means that it is a big part of your life, and many concerns have been expressed about adolescents' media use (Arnett, 2007a). Although claims are often made about the harmful effects of media on adolescents, their media use is more complex than simple cause and effect. A helpful model of the functions media play in the lives of adolescents has been presented by Jane Brown and her colleagues (Brown, 2006; Brown et al., 2002; Steele, 2006). An illustration of their *Media Practice Model* is shown in **Figure 8.13** on the next page.

As the figure shows, the model proposes that adolescents' media use is active in a number of ways. Adolescents do not all have the same media preferences. Rather, each adolescent's identity motivates the *selection* of media products. Paying attention to certain media products leads to *interaction* with those products, meaning that the products are evaluated and interpreted. Then adolescents engage in *application* of the media content they have chosen. They may incorporate this content into their identities—for example, adolescents who respond to cigarette advertisements by taking up smoking—or they may resist the content—for example, adolescents who respond to cigarette advertisements by rejecting them as false and misleading. Their developing identity then motivates new media selections, and so on. This model reminds us that adolescents actively

coming out

for homosexuals, the process of acknowledging their homosexuality and then disclosing the truth to their friends, family, and others

homophobia

fear and hatred of homosexuals

STI (sexually transmitted infection)

infection transmitted through sexual contact

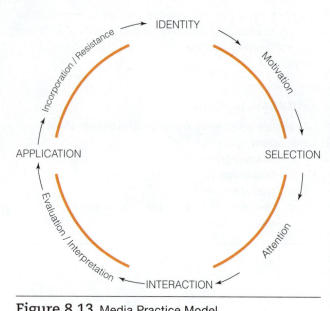

IDENTITY

Incorporation / Resistance

Motivation

APPLICATION

SELECTION

Evaluation / Interpretation

Attention

INTERACTION

Figure 8.13 Media Practice Model

In this model, identity is the main motivator of media use.

SOURCE: Brown et al. (2002), p. 9

select the media they use, and they respond to media content in diverse ways depending on how they interpret it and how it relates to them personally.

Adolescents use media for many different purposes, but as with younger children, the focus of research has been on negative effects. In the following discussion, we examine electronic games, which have been the target of some of these concerns. We also examine the use of mobile phones and social media, the use of which is on the rise among adolescents.

ELECTRONIC GAMES A relatively new type of media use among adolescents is electronic games, usually played on a computer or a handheld device. This form of media use has quickly become popular among adolescents, especially boys (Rideout et al., 2013). In a study of middle school students in the United States (Olson et al., 2007), 94 percent reported having played electronic games during the preceding 6 months. Of those who played electronic games, one third of boys and 11 percent of girls said they played nearly every day.

The majority of adolescents' favorite electronic games involve violence (Gentile, 2011). Many studies have examined the relation between violent electronic games and aggressiveness (Anderson et al., 2007; Brake, 2006; Funk et al., 2005; Gentile, 2011). One study asked boys themselves about the effects of playing violent electronic games (Olson et al., 2008). The interviews showed that the boys (ages 12–14) used electronic games to experience fantasies of power and fame and to explore what they perceived to be exciting new situations. The boys enjoyed the social aspect of electronic game playing, in playing with friends and talking about the games with friends. The boys also said they used electronic games to work through feelings of anger or stress and that playing the games had a cathartic effect on these negative feelings. They did not believe that playing violent electronic games affected them negatively.

It seems likely that with electronic games, as with other violent media, there is a wide range of individual differences in responses, with young people who are already at risk for violent behavior being most likely to be affected by the games, as well as most likely to be attracted to them (Funk, 2003; Slater et al., 2003; Unsworth et al., 2007). With electronic games as with television, violent content may rarely provoke violent behavior, but it more often influences social attitudes. For example, playing violent electronic games has been found to lower empathy and raise the acceptability of violent responses to social situations (Anderson, 2004; Funk, 2005; Funk et al., 2004; Gentile, 2011).

SOCIAL MEDIA AND MOBILE PHONES Lenhart and colleagues (2010) found that Internet use is almost ubiquitous among adolescents: 93 percent of adolescents ages 12 to 17 go online. The two main reasons adolescents go online are to visit a social networking site (73 percent), like Facebook, or to get news about current events and politics (62 percent). Older adolescents—especially girls—are more likely to use Twitter than younger adolescents.

Three quarters of adolescents have a cell phone (Madden et al., 2013). Sometimes parents purchase the cell phone for adolescents so that they can monitor their whereabouts, but adolescents use their phones mostly for the Internet and texting their friends. Texting is wildly popular among teens, and they prefer to text with one another rather than use the phone, email, or a face-to-face visit (Ling et al., 2014). Rideout and colleagues (2010) found that U.S. adolescents in grades 7 through 12 spend 1.5 hours per day texting. A study of Japanese adolescents found that they used their mobile phones much more often for text messaging than for talking (Kamibeppu & Sugiura, 2005). More than half of those who owned a mobile phone sent at least 10 text messages a day to their friends. Similar rates have been found in Western developed countries (Axelsson, 2010).

There are safety issues associated with social media and mobile phone usage. High levels of Internet and mobile phone usage have been linked to higher rates of depression among adolescents, and it is recommended that parents discuss household rules for managing the use of the Internet and mobile devices (Bickham et al., 2015). Texting while driving is a serious problem that many states are addressing through laws prohibiting the use of any mobile devices while operating a vehicle (Raymond, 2014). And, cyberbullying and sexting are other threats to the well-being of adolescents that parents, educators, and lawmakers are attempting to address (Srinivas et al., 2011).

EMOTIONAL AND SOCIAL DEVELOPMENT: Problems and Resilience

After the relatively calm period of middle childhood, a variety of types of problems rise in prevalence during adolescence, including crime and delinquency and depressed mood. However, most adolescents make it through this life stage without serious problems, and many adolescents exhibit resilience in the face of difficult conditions.

Crime and Delinquency

LO 8.21 Summarize the explanations for why age and crime are so strongly correlated, and describe the multisystemic approach to combating delinquency.

Rates of crime begin rising in the mid-teens and peak at about age 18, then decline steadily. The great majority of crimes are committed by young people—mostly males—who are between the ages of 12 and 25 (Craig & Piquero, 2014). In the West, this finding is remarkably consistent over a period of greater than 150 years. **Figure 8.14** on the next page shows the age–crime relationship at two points, one in the 1840s and one relatively recent. At any point before, after, or in between these times, in most countries, the pattern would look very similar (Craig & Piquero, 2014; Wilson & Herrnstein, 1985). Adolescents and emerging adults are not only more likely than children or adults to commit crimes but also more likely to be the victims of crimes.

What explains the strong and consistent relationship between age and crime? One theory suggests that the key to explaining the age–crime relationship is that adolescents and emerging adults combine increased independence from parents and other adult authorities with increased time with peers and increased orientation toward peers (Wilson & Herrnstein, 1985). A consistent finding of research on crime is that crimes committed by young people in their teens and early 20s usually take place in a group, in contrast to the solitary crimes typical of adult offenders (Dishion & Dodge, 2005). Crime is an activity that in some adolescent cliques is encouraged and admired (Dishion et al., 1999). However, this theory does not explain why it is mainly boys who commit crimes, and why girls, who also become more independent from parents and more peer-oriented in adolescence, rarely do.

Most surveys find that over three-fourths of adolescent boys commit at least one criminal act sometime before the age of 20 (Loebert & Burke, 2011; Moffitt, 2003). However, there are obvious differences between committing one or two acts of minor crime—vandalism or underage drinking, for example—and committing crimes frequently over a long period, including more serious crimes such as rape and assault. Ten percent of

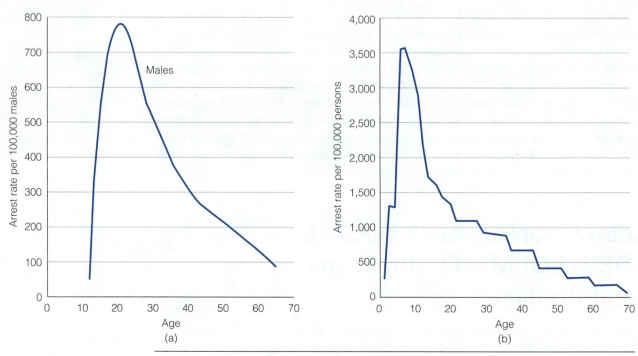

Figure 8.14 Age–Crime Relationship in (a) 1842 and (b) 1992

Why does crime peak in the late teens?
SOURCE: Gottfredson & Hirschi (1990), p. 125; Osgood (2009)

young men commit more than two thirds of all offenses (Craig & Piquero, 2014). What are the differences between adolescents who commit an occasional minor violation of the law and adolescents who are at risk for more serious, long-term criminal behavior?

Terrie Moffitt (2003, 2007) has proposed a provocative theory in which she distinguishes between *adolescence-limited* delinquency and *life-course-persistent* delinquency. In Moffitt's view, these are two distinct types of delinquency, each with different motivations and different sources. However, the two types may be hard to distinguish from one another in adolescence, when criminal offenses are more common than in childhood or adulthood. The way to tell them apart, according to Moffitt, is to look at behavior before adolescence.

Life-course-persistent delinquents (LCPDs) show a pattern of problems from birth onward. Moffitt believes their problems originate in neuropsychological deficits that are evident in a difficult temperament in infancy and a high likelihood of attention-deficit/hyperactivity disorder (ADHD) and learning disabilities in childhood; all of these are more common among boys than girls. Children with these problems are also more likely than other children to grow up in a high-risk environment (e.g., low-income family, single parent), with parents who have a variety of problems of their own. Consequently, their neurological deficits tend to be made worse rather than better by their environments. When they reach adolescence, children with the combination of neurological deficits and a high-risk environment are highly prone to engage in criminal activity. Furthermore, they tend to continue their criminal activity long after adolescence has ended, well into adulthood.

The **adolescence-limited delinquents (ALDs)** follow a much different pattern. They show no signs of problems in infancy or childhood, and few of them engage in any criminal activity after their mid-20s. It is just during adolescence—actually, adolescence and emerging adulthood, ages 12 to 25—that they have a period of occasional criminal activity, breaking the law with behavior such as vandalism, theft, and use of illegal drugs.

Parents and the peer group play a role in rates of delinquency among adolescents. Adolescents who select friends who engage in delinquent acts will tend to engage in

life-course-persistent delinquent (LCPD)

delinquent who shows a pattern of problems from birth onward and whose problems continue into adulthood

adolescent-limited delinquent (ALD)

delinquent who shows no evidence of problems before adolescence and whose delinquent behavior in adolescence is temporary

more delinquent acts themselves (O'Donnell, 2003). Parental monitoring may mediate some of this risk by encouraging adolescents to select friends who abstain from criminal acts (O'Donnell et al., 2012). In a European sample, Tilton-Weaver and colleagues (2013) found that parental monitoring reduced the selection of delinquent peers among older adolescents. For early adolescents, parental monitoring reduced friendships with delinquent peers, but only for those adolescents who did not feel overcontrolled by parents. For those who felt overcontrolled by parental monitoring, parental rules increased the likelihood of selecting a delinquent friend. However, having no parental monitoring would be risky for adolescents who hang out with a peer group that engages in delinquent acts.

In addition to the activity settings issues of who the adolescent hangs out with and how parents monitor adolescents' activities, there are maturational issues as well. The brain is still a long way from maturity during adolescence. Does the immaturity of the brain help explain why rates of delinquency and some other types of risky behavior are higher in adolescence than at younger ages? This theory has been proposed by researchers who claim that neurological studies show that the brain's frontal lobe areas in charge of judgment and impulse control are not mature until at least the mid-20s; consequently, during adolescence behavior is governed more by emotions and less by reason than in later years (Steinberg, 2010). However, other researchers dispute this conclusion. Some studies have found that the brain development of adolescents who engage in risky behavior is actually *more* mature in some ways than in their less-risk-prone peers (Engelmann et al., 2012). Others point out that rates of most types of risky behavior continue to increase into the early 20s; brain development also advances during this time, so immaturity of the brain cannot explain the increase in risky behavior during these years (Males, 2010). It should also be noted that boys and girls are highly similar in brain development during adolescence, yet boys commit far more crimes.

Delinquency has often proven to be resistant to change in adolescence, but one successful approach has been to intervene at several levels, including the home, the school, and the neighborhood. This is known as the *multisystemic approach* (Borduin et al., 2003; Henggeler, 2011). Programs based on this approach include parent training, job training and vocational counseling, and the development of neighborhood activities such as youth centers and athletic leagues. The goal is to direct the energy of delinquents into more socially constructive directions. The multisystemic approach has now been adopted by youth agencies all over the world (Henggeler, 2011; Schoenwald et al., 2008). As **Figure 8.15** illustrates, programs using this approach have been shown to be effective in reducing arrests and out-of-home placements among delinquents (Henggeler et al., 2007; Ogden & Amlund-Hagen, 2006). Furthermore, multisystemic programs have been found to be cheaper than other programs, primarily because they reduce the amount of time that delinquent adolescents spend in foster homes and detention centers (Alexander, 2001).

Depression

LO 8.22 Identify the different types and rates of depression, and summarize the most effective treatments.

Do you remember feeling sad at times during your teen years? As we have seen, studies of adolescents' emotional lives have found that they experience sadness and other negative emotions much more frequently than younger children or adults do.

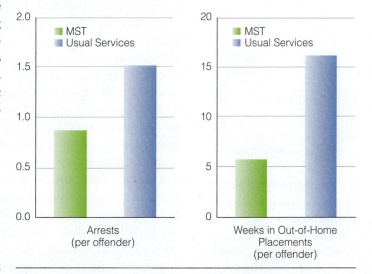

Figure 8.15 Multisystemic Approach to Delinquency

Why is MST more effective than other types of interventions for delinquency?

SOURCE: Alexander (2001), p. 42

Psychologists make distinctions between different levels of depression. **Depressed mood** is a term for a temporary period of sadness, without any related symptoms. The most serious form of depression is **major depressive disorder**, which includes a more enduring period of sadness along with other symptoms such as frequent crying, fatigue, feelings of worthlessness, and feeling guilty, lonely, or worried. Major depressive disorder may also include symptoms such as difficulty sleeping and changes in appetite (American Psychiatric Association [APA], 2013).

Rates of major depressive disorder among adolescents range in various studies from 3 to 7 percent (Cheung et al., 2005; Compas et al., 1993; Thapar et al., 2012), which is about the same rate found in studies of adults. However, rates of depressed mood are substantially higher. For example, one longitudinal study found that the rate of depressed mood for Dutch adolescents at age 11 was 27 percent for girls and 21 percent for boys, rising by age 19 to 37 percent for girls and 23 percent for boys (Bennik et al., 2013). The most common causes of depressed mood tend to be common experiences among adolescents: conflict with friends or family members, disappointment or rejection in love, and poor performance in school (Costello et al., 2008; Larson & Richards, 1994).

One of the strongest risk factors for all types of depression in adolescence and beyond is simply being female (Thapar et al., 2012). A variety of explanations have been proposed. Some scholars have suggested that body image concerns provoke depression. There is substantial evidence that adolescent girls who have a poor body image are more likely than other girls to be depressed (Graber et al., 2004; Marcotte et al., 2002; Wichstrom et al., 1999). Also, when faced with the beginning of a depressed mood, boys (and men) are more likely to distract themselves (and forget about it), whereas girls (and women) have a greater tendency to **ruminate** on their depressed feelings and thereby amplify them (Jose & Brown, 2008; Nolen-Hoeksema et al., 2008). Adolescent girls are more likely than adolescent boys to devote their thoughts and feelings to their personal relationships, and these relationships can be a source of distress and sadness (Bakker et al., 2010; Conway et al., 2011).

For adolescents, as for adults, the two main types of treatment for depression are antidepressant medications and psychotherapy. Recent studies indicate that newly developed antidepressants such as Prozac are highly effective in treating adolescent depression (Bostic et al., 2005; Brent, 2004; Cohen et al., 2004; Thapar et al., 2012). The combination of the newest medications and psychotherapy appear to be the most effective approach to treating adolescent depression. In one recent major study of 12- to 17-year-old adolescents at 13 sites across the United States who had been diagnosed with major depression, 71 percent of the adolescents who received both Prozac and psychotherapy experienced an improvement in their symptoms (Treatment for Adolescents with Depression Study Team, 2004, 2007). Improvement rates for the other groups were 61 percent for Prozac alone, 43 percent for psychotherapy alone, and 35 percent for the placebo group. However, some research has raised concerns that use of antidepressants with adolescents may provoke suicidal thoughts and behavior (Bridge et al., 2007). Other research contradicts this finding, so currently it is advised that adolescents who are on antidepressant medications should be monitored closely (Thapar et al., 2012).

Tragically, suicide is the third highest cause of death among young people ages 10 to 24 (CDC, 2015). Suicide affects some groups more than others. Boys are more likely to die from suicide attempts than girls, and American Indian and Latino adolescents have the highest rates of suicide (CDC, 2015). Cultural identity is an issue associated with depression for some young people; it is important for indigenous people and for those with immigrant status to maintain continuity in the self as well as in ties to their native cultures (Chandler, 2001). Among First Nations adolescents in Canada, efforts to promote the resilience and continuation of cultural practices are associated with reductions in suicide (Chandler et al., 2003). Other suicide prevention efforts include looking for warning signs and intervening with help. Warning signs of suicide include talking about wanting to die or to kill oneself, looking for a way to kill oneself, talking about feeling hopeless

depressed mood

enduring period of sadness, without any other related symptoms of depression

major depressive disorder

clinical diagnosis that includes a range of specific symptoms such as depressed mood, appetite disturbances, sleeping disturbances, and fatigue

ruminate

to think persistently about bad feelings and experiences

or having no reason to live, depressed mood, sleeping too little or too much, feeling withdrawn or isolated, or displaying extreme mood swings. Suicide hotlines are reachable by phone in many communities in the United States, and there is a National Suicide Prevention Lifeline (1-800-273-8255) that is open 24 hours a day and 7 days a week.

Resilience in Adolescence

LO 8.23   Define *resilience*, and name the protective factors that are related to resilience in adolescence.

The source of adolescent problems can often be traced to risk factors, such as poverty, poor family relationships, abusive or neglectful parenting, and inadequate schools. However, there are many adolescents who face dire conditions like these yet manage to adapt and function well. **Resilience** is the term for this phenomenon, defined as "good outcomes in spite of serious threats to adaptation and development" (Masten, 2001, p. 228). Sometimes "good outcomes" are measured as notable academic or social achievements, sometimes as psychological traits such as high well-being or self-esteem, and sometimes as the absence of notable problems. Young people who are resilient are not necessarily high achievers who have some kind of extraordinary ability. More often they display what resilience researcher Ann Masten calls the "ordinary magic" of being able to function reasonably well despite being faced with unusually difficult circumstances (Masten, 2001, p. 227).

Resilience is promoted by **protective factors** that enable adolescents to overcome the risk factors in their lives (Rafaelli & Iturbide, 2015). Some of the most important protective factors identified in resilience research are high intelligence, physical attractiveness, parenting that provides an effective balance of warmth and control, and a caring adult "mentor" outside the family. For example, high intelligence may allow an adolescent to perform well academically despite going to a low-quality school and living in a disorderly household (Masten et al., 2006). Effective parenting may help an adolescent have a positive self-image and avoid antisocial behavior despite growing up in poverty and living in a rough neighborhood (Brody & Flor, 1998). A mentor may foster high academic goals and good future planning in an adolescent whose family life is characterized by abuse or neglect (Rhodes & DuBois, 2008).

One classic study followed a group of infants from birth through adolescence (Werner & Smith, 1982, 1992, 2001). It is known as the Kaua`i (Ka-WA-ee) study, after the Hawaiian island where the study took place. The Kaua`i study focused on a high-risk group of children who had four or more risk factors by age 2, such as problems in physical development, parents' marital conflict, parental drug abuse, low maternal education, and poverty. Out of this group, there was a resilient subgroup that showed good social and academic functioning and few behavior problems by ages 10 to 18. Compared with their less resilient peers, adolescents in the resilient group were found to benefit from several protective factors, including one well-functioning parent, higher intelligence, and higher physical attractiveness.

More recent studies have supported the Kaua`i findings but also broadened the range of protective factors (Masten, 2007, 2014). *Religiosity* has become recognized as an especially important protective factor. Adolescents who have a strong religious faith are less likely to have problems such as substance abuse, even when they have grown up in a high-risk environment (Howard et al., 2007; Wallace et al., 2007).

resilience

overcoming adverse environmental circumstances and achieving healthy development despite those circumstances

protective factors

characteristics of young people that are related to lower likelihood of problems despite experiencing high-risk circumstances

A mentor can be a source of resilience for adolescents at risk for problems. Here, an adolescent girl and her mentor discuss homework together at an after-school mentoring program in New Orleans.

Summary: Emotional and Social Development

LO 8.13 **Summarize the results of the ESM studies with respect to adolescent emotionality.**

Experience Sampling Method (ESM) studies show greater mood swings in adolescence than in middle childhood or adulthood. Also, there is a decline in overall emotional state from 5th grade through 12th grade.

LO 8.14 **Describe how self-conceptions change during adolescence.**

Self-development in adolescence is complex and may include an ideal self, a possible self, a feared self, and a false self along with an actual self. Overall self-esteem often declines in early adolescence, especially for girls. Self-concept includes a variety of aspects in adolescence, but overall self-concept is strongly influenced by self-perceptions of physical attractiveness. Adolescence is a time of gender intensification, as young people become more aware of the gender expectations of their culture. Boys in many cultures risk becoming a failed man unless they learn to provide, protect, and procreate. Girls are generally believed to reach womanhood when they reach menarche.

LO 8.15 **Discriminate between Kohlberg's theory of moral development and Jensen's worldviews theory.**

Kohlberg proposed three universal levels of moral reasoning: preconventional, conventional, and postconventional. According to Jensen, morality develops in culturally diverse ways based on Ethics of Autonomy, Community, and Divinity.

LO 8.16 **Describe the cultural variations in religious beliefs during adolescence as well as the sources and outcomes of religiosity within cultures.**

U.S. adolescents are more religious than adolescents in other developed countries. In general, higher religiosity is related to a variety of positive features of adolescents' development, such as better relationships with parents and lower rates of substance use.

LO 8.17 **Summarize the cultural variations in adolescents' relationships with parents, siblings, and extended family.**

Adolescence is a time of increased conflict with parents in cultures that promote autonomy. Sibling conflict is not as high in adolescence as in earlier life stages, but adolescents have more conflict with siblings than in any of their other relationships. Relations with grandparents tend to be close and positive worldwide.

LO 8.18 **Describe cultural variations in adolescents' relationships with friends, and characterize their interactions with peers.**

In most cultures, adolescents spend less time with family and more time with friends than they did in middle childhood. Intimacy is more important in adolescent friendships than at earlier ages. Adolescents also have groups of friends, or "cliques," and see their peers as falling into "crowds." Bullying is more common in adolescence than at other ages.

LO 8.19 **Identify cultural variations in adolescent love and sexuality, including variations in adolescent pregnancy and contraceptive use.**

Cultures vary widely in their tolerance of adolescent sexuality, from permissive to semi-restrictive to restrictive. Rates of adolescent pregnancy are lowest in cultures that are highly accepting of adolescent sexuality and in those that strictly forbid it. U.S. adolescents have high rates of adolescent pregnancy mainly as a result of the mixed cultural messages they receive about adolescent sexuality.

LO 8.20 **Explain the function of media use in adolescents' lives, and apply the Media Practice Model to the playing of electronic games.**

Adolescents are avid users of a wide range of media, from television and music to electronic games and mobile phones. Concern has been expressed about the potential negative effects of playing electronic games, mainly focusing on aggressive behavior and attitudes, but positive effects have been found in areas such as mood regulation. Texting is hugely popular among adolescents, who prefer to text with their friends rather than call or email them.

LO 8.21 **Summarize the explanations for why age and crime are so strongly correlated, and describe the multisystemic approach to combating delinquency.**

According to one theory, age and crime are highly correlated because adolescents are more independent from parents than at earlier ages and also more peer-oriented. Parental monitoring can help adolescents select an appropriate peer group to avoid engaging in delinquent behavior. The multisystemic approach entails intervening at several levels, including home, school, and neighborhood.

LO 8.22 **Identify the different types and rates of depression, and summarize the most effective treatments.**

Depressed mood involves a relatively brief period of sadness, whereas major depression entails a more enduring period of sadness combined with a variety of other symptoms, such as disruptions in patterns of sleeping and eating. Although major depression is rare in adolescence, depressed mood is common, especially among adolescent girls. The most effective approach to treating adolescent depression combines the newest medications and psychotherapy. Suicide is a leading cause of death among young people, and suicide prevention efforts include education about warning signs and letting adolescents know about options for help.

LO 8.23 Define *resilience*, and name the protective factors that are related to resilience in adolescence.

Resilience means functioning well despite adverse circumstances. Some of the protective factors promoting resilience in adolescence are high intelligence, a good relationship with a parent or mentor, and physical attractiveness.

Applying Your Knowledge as a Professional

The topics covered in this chapter apply to a wide variety of career professions. Watch these videos to learn how they apply to a middle school teacher, a high school teacher and coach, a family court judge, and the head of a residential facility for teenage mothers.

Watch CAREER FOCUS: MIDDLE SCHOOL TEACHER

Video

Terra Spears
Middle school teacher

Chapter Quiz

1. The most important estrogen is estradiol and the most important androgen is _____.

   a. human growth hormone   **c.** leptin

   b. testosterone   **d.** insulin

2. Which of the following best describes pubertal timing?

   a. The average age of menarche is much later today than it was in earlier generations.

   b. Menarche takes place as late as age 15 in some developing countries because of lack of proper nutrition and medical care.

   c. The timing of puberty has no effect on adolescent boys.

   d. The effects of early maturation are generally positive for girls.

3. Puberty rituals _____.

   a. developed to mark the departure from adolescence into emerging adulthood

   b. are only carried out for females and are most often related to menstruation

   c. are declining in many cultures as a consequence of globalization

   d. focus on a particular biological event across all cultures

4. In the United States, girls _____.
   a. who have an eating disorder are also more likely than other females to be depressed
   b. with bulimia are usually about 20 percent overweight
   c. who are Asian American are more likely to have eating disorders than are those in other ethnic groups
   d. are more likely than boys to be satisfied with their bodies

5. The substance use of an adolescent who drinks alcohol to relieve feelings of sadness and loneliness would be classified as _____.
   a. social substance use
   b. medicinal substance use
   c. experimental substance use
   d. addictive substance use

6. Compared to the concrete thinking abilities displayed in childhood, the ability to reason in adolescence _____.
   a. uses the hypothetical thinking involved in a scientific experiment
   b. involves more random attempts at problem solving as they persist longer
   c. differs quantitatively, but not qualitatively
   d. is not significantly different

7. Which of the following best represents the research on formal operational thinking across cultures?
   a. Formal operational thinking takes the same form, regardless of culture.
   b. Individuals in collectivistic cultures take much longer to develop formal operations.
   c. Formal operational thinking only exists in developed countries.
   d. The way that formal operational thinking is manifested is likely different across different cultures.

8. Compared to his 7-year-old brother, a 14-year-old adolescent will have an easier time reading a book and listening to music at the same time because he's more adept at _____.
   a. using mnemonic devices consistently
   b. tasks that require divided attention
   c. tasks that require transfer of information from sensory memory to short-term memory
   d. maximizing his metamemory

9. Compared to his brother in college, Jonah is more likely to think that if he starts smoking marijuana, he will be able to quit when he wants to and nothing bad will happen. This way of thinking demonstrates _____.
   a. the personal fable
   b. the imaginary audience
   c. selective attention
   d. hypothetical reasoning

10. After learning to knit a simple scarf with her grandmother's guidance, Alexis began to knit a sweater while on break from college. She went over to her grandmother's once when she had a question. By the time Alexis had to go back to school, she had nearly finished the sweater. She finished the sweater a few weeks later while she was back at college, needing only one Skype session to help her. After finishing the sweater, her grandmother mailed her a pattern so she can knit a handbag. This illustrates _____.
   a. selective attention
   b. synaptic pruning
   c. scaffolding
   d. hypothetical-deductive reasoning

11. According to Levy & Murnane, which of the following is one of the *new basic skills* that should be taught during high school?
   a. solving semistructured problems
   b. building a website
   c. familiarity with computer programming languages
   d. fluency in a foreign language

12. Compared to schools in the United States, those in Eastern countries _____.
   a. have a shorter school day
   b. are all sex-segregated
   c. focus almost exclusively on rote learning
   d. place a greater emphasis on creativity

13. Adolescents in developed countries who work part-time _____.
   a. are less likely to use drugs and alcohol than their nonworking counterparts
   b. have higher grades in school than other students
   c. usually contribute the majority of their earnings to support the household income
   d. do not typically see their high school jobs as the basis for a future career

14. A developmental psychologist would most likely use the Experience Sampling Method (ESM) to _____.
   a. evaluate the strength of cohort differences
   b. examine changes in emotions at various time points
   c. examine how different environmental experiences affect brain development
   d. determine whether behavioral differences between males and females become more pronounced in the transition from childhood to adolescence

15. Adolescents are most likely to exhibit their false selves with _____.
   a. close friends
   b. dating partners
   c. acquaintances
   d. parents

16. In traditional cultures, girls reach womanhood mainly through _____.

    a. their achievements

    b. the same means that males reach manhood

    c. their biological changes

    d. protecting their young

17. Research on Kohlberg's stages of moral development has shown that _____.

    a. the stage of moral reasoning achieved tends to increase with age

    b. over time, people regress to an earlier stage of moral reasoning

    c. people often skip stages and advance to the highest stage in adulthood

    d. the majority of people reach Stage 5: community right and individual rights orientation

18. Religiosity in adolescence is _____.

    a. usually lowest among African Americans

    b. associated with lower rates of delinquency

    c. highest in European and Asian countries

    d. the same regardless of if adolscents' parents are married or divorced

19. In Western countries, conflict with parents _____.

    a. remains constant during adolescence

    b. steadily increases until the end of emerging adulthood

    c. declines in late adolescence

    d. is highest during middle childhood

20. Who comprises the source of adolescents' happiest experiences?

    a. Friends

    b. Parents

    c. Extended family

    d. Siblings

21. On the basis of anthropological evidence, the United States would be considered a(n) _____culture in terms of its cultural beliefs about the acceptability (or not) of premarital sex.

    a. permissive

    b. authoritarian

    c. semirestrictive

    d. restrictive

22. Research on the media use of adolescents _____.

    a. has found that only females report that they enjoy the social aspect of gaming

    b. has found that adolescents in industrialized countries use media for about 2 hours every day

    c. has focused primarily on the benefits, such as increasing problem-solving ability and strategizing

    d. has shown that the content of electronic games is related to their emotional responses

23. Which of the following best describes the relationships between age and crime?

    a. Adolescents are less likely than adults to commit crimes because they do not have enough opportunity to do so.

    b. Adolescents are less likely to be the victims of crime than are children or adults.

    c. Adolescents are likely to commit crimes alone because they worry about their reputation if they get caught.

    d. A small percentage of adolescents commit the majority of crimes.

24. Which of the following statements about depression is most accurate?

    a. Rates of major depressive disorder are higher among adolescents than rates of depressed mood.

    b. Psychotherapy alone was as effective in treating adolescent depression as psychotherapy combined with medication.

    c. Rates of depressed mood rise substantially from middle childhood to adolescence.

    d. Boys are more likely than girls to show increases in depressed mood during adolescence.

25. Research on resilience has shown that _____.

    a. bouncing back from adversity requires a high level of achievement and extraordinary abilities

    b. high intelligence characterizes many individuals who are considered resilient

    c. as a group, girls are more resilient than boys

    d. parenting has no influence on resilience

Chapter 9
Emerging Adulthood

THE LIVES OF YOUNG PEOPLE HAVE CHANGED DRAMATICALLY IN RECENT YEARS. For many young people in the developed world, the years after adolescence are a time of further exploration. They may attend college, but drop out after a couple years, in part because they are not sure what they want to study. They often work in jobs that they don't intend to do long-term. And, they are often unsure about love. They may live with significant others, but they don't feel pressure to get married. Even across international boundaries, many young people are taking longer to develop their interests and identities, exploring options in education, work, and love before committing.

This is a different pattern than that experienced a generation or two ago. The lives of young people all over the world have changed dramatically over the past half-century. This chapter is about the new life stage of *emerging adulthood* that has developed as a consequence of those changes.

Watch   CHAPTER INTRODUCTION: EMERGING ADULTHOOD

Section 1   Physical Development

Learning Objectives

9.1 Name the five developmental features distinctive to emerging adulthood.

9.2 Describe some of the ways emerging adulthood varies among cultures.

9.3 Name the indicators that emerging adulthood is a period of peak physical functioning.

9.4 Summarize college students' sleep patterns and the main elements of sleep hygiene.

9.5 Explain why young drivers have the highest rates of crashes, and name the most effective approach to reducing those rates.

9.6 Explain why rates of substance use peak in the early 20s and then decline.

PHYSICAL DEVELOPMENT:
The Emergence of Emerging Adulthood

Before we examine the changes in physical development that occur in emerging adulthood, let's begin with a closer look at the origins of this new life stage. Traditionally, theories of human development described a stage of adolescence followed by a stage of young adulthood (Erikson, 1950). The transition to young adulthood was assumed to be marked by entry to adult roles, specifically marriage, parenthood, and stable work. For most people, entry into these roles took place around the age of 20 or shortly thereafter. By their early 20s, most people had formed the stable structure of an adult life.

However, traditional stage models no longer fit the pattern of development that most people experience, especially in developed countries. The 20s are not a time of settling into a stable occupational path but a time of exceptional instability in work because the completion of education and training is followed by multiple job changes, for most people. Similarly, most people marry and become parents in their late 20s or early 30s rather than in their early 20s. Shifts in the ecocultural setting, especially in opportunities and values, have shifted the way that people develop and the length of time that it takes many to feel they have reached full adulthood.

As a consequence of these changes, it is increasingly recognized among scholars in human development that a new life stage has developed between adolescence and young adulthood. Rather than making the transition from adolescence to young adulthood quickly at around age 20, most people in developed countries experience a stage of *emerging adulthood* from their late teens to at least their mid-20s, before entering a more stable young adulthood at around age 30 (Arnett, 2004, 2007a, b, 2011). "Thirty is the new 20," as a popular U.S. saying puts it.

Five Features

LO 9.1   Name the five developmental features distinctive to emerging adulthood.

Perhaps the most obvious indicator of the emergence of emerging adulthood as a normative life stage in developed countries is the rise in the ages of entering marriage and parenthood. As recently as 1960 the median age of marriage in most developed countries was in the early 20s, around 21 for women and 23 for men (Douglass, 2005). Now the median age of marriage is 27 in the United States (as **Figure 9.1** shows), and close to 30 in most other developed countries (Arnett, 2015a, b). Age at entering parenthood followed a similar rise.

But why the dramatic rise in the typical ages of entering marriage and parenthood? Four revolutionary changes took place in the 1960s and 1970s that laid the foundation for the new life stage of emerging adulthood: the Technology Revolution, the Sexual Revolution, the Women's Movement, and the Youth Movement (Arnett, 2015a, b).

By the Technology Revolution, we refer to the shift from a manufacturing economy to a service economy requiring information and technology skills. To accommodate this shift, participation in *tertiary education* (any education or training past high school) in the United States has risen in all groups in recent decades, although it varies by ethnic group, as **Figure 9.2** shows (Arnett, 2011). Most young people wait until they have finished school before they start thinking seriously about making adult commitments such as marriage and parenthood, and for many of them this means postponing those commitments until at least their late 20s.

The Sexual Revolution, sparked by the invention of the birth control pill in 1964, was another important contributor. Widespread use of "the Pill," in combination with less stringent standards of sexual morality after the sexual revolution of the 1960s and early 1970s, meant that young people no longer had to enter marriage to have a stable sexual relationship (Arnett, 2015a, b). Now most young people have a series of sexual relationships before entering marriage, and there is widespread tolerance for premarital sex in the context of a committed, loving relationship. The values of the culture have shifted.

The Women's Movement of the 1960s and 1970s vastly expanded the opportunities available to young women (Arnett, 2015a, b). In the 1950s and early 1960s, relatively few women attended college and the range of occupations open to them was severely restricted—secretary, waitress, teacher, nurse, perhaps a few others. Even these occupations were supposed to be temporary for young women—a precursor to finding a husband and having children. Today, in nearly every developed country, girls excel over boys at every level of education from grade school through graduate school. Young women's occupational possibilities are now virtually unlimited. With so many options open to them, and with so little pressure on them to marry in their early 20s, the lives of young women in developed countries today have changed almost beyond recognition from what they were 50 years ago. Like young men, they typically spend the years from the late teens through at least the mid-20s trying out various possible options before making definite choices.

The fourth major change of the 1960s and 1970s was the Youth Movement, which denigrated adulthood and exalted being, acting, and feeling young. As a consequence of the Youth Movement, there has been a profound change in how young people view the meaning and value of becoming an adult and entering adult roles of spouse, parent, and employee. Young people of the 1950s were eager to enter adulthood and "settle down" (Modell, 1989). The young people of today, in contrast, see adulthood and its obligations in quite a different light. In

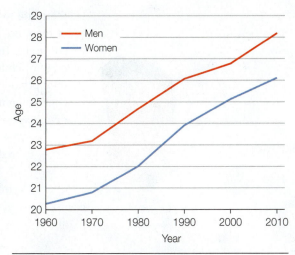

Figure 9.1 The Rise in Age of Marriage Since 1960, United States

SOURCE: Based on U.S. Bureau of the Census (2004, 2010).

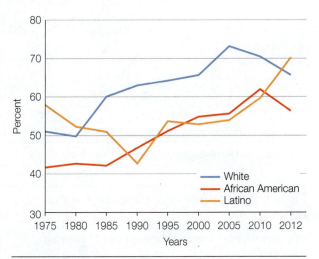

Figure 9.2 The Rise in Tertiary Education, United States

their late teens and early 20s, marriage, home, and children are seen by most of them not as achievements to be pursued but as perils to be avoided (Arnett, 2015a, b). It is not that they reject the prospect of marriage, home, and (one or two) children—eventually. It is just that, in their late teens and early 20s, they ponder these obligations and think, "yes, but *not yet.*" Adulthood and its commitments offer security and stability, but also represent the end of independence, spontaneity, and a sense of wide-open possibility.

What are the main features of emerging adulthood? What makes it distinct from the adolescence that precedes it and the young adulthood that follows it? There are five characteristics that distinguish emerging adulthood from other age periods (Arnett, 2004, 2006, 2015a, b; Reifman et al., 2006). Emerging adulthood is

1. the age of identity explorations;
2. the age of instability;
3. the self-focused age;
4. the age of feeling in-between; and
5. the age of possibilities.

Today in developed countries, young women exceed young men in educational attainment and have a wide range of opportunities in the workplace that they did not have before.

All of these features begin to develop before emerging adulthood and continue to develop afterward, but it is during emerging adulthood that they reach their peak (Reifman et al., 2006).

Perhaps the most distinctive characteristic of emerging adulthood is that it is the *age of identity explorations*. This means that it is an age when people explore various possibilities in love and work as they move toward making enduring choices. Through trying out these different possibilities they develop a more definite identity, that is, an understanding of who they are, what their capabilities and limitations are, what their beliefs and values are, and how they fit into the society around them. Erik Erikson (1950), who was the first to develop the idea of identity, asserted that it is mainly an issue in adolescence, but that was more than 50 years ago, and today it is mainly in emerging adulthood that identity explorations take place (Arnett, 2000, 2004, 2005b, 2015a, b; Schwartz, 2005).

The explorations of emerging adulthood also make it the *age of instability*. As they explore different possibilities in love and work, emerging adults' lives are often unstable. A good illustration of this is in how often they move from one residence to another. As **Figure 9.3** shows, rates of residential change in American society are much higher at ages 18 to 29 than at any other period of life. This is a reflection of the explorations going on in emerging adults' lives. Some move out of their parents' household for the first time in their late teens to attend a residential college, others move out simply to be independent (Goldscheider & Goldscheider, 1999). They may move again when they drop out of college or when they graduate. They may cohabit with a romantic partner, then move out when the relationship ends. Some move to another part of the country or the world to study or work. For nearly half of U.S. emerging adults, their residential changes include moving back in with their parents at least once (Sassler et al., 2008). In countries where emerging adults remain home rather than moving out, such as in most of southern Europe, they may nevertheless experience instability in education, work, and love relationships (Douglass, 2005, 2007; Iacovou, 2011).

Emerging adulthood is also a *self-focused age*, which is a time in between adolescents' reliance on parents and young

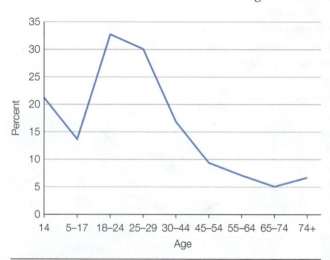

Figure 9.3 Rate of Residential Change in Past Year, United States

Why does the rate of residential change peak in emerging adulthood?

SOURCE: U.S. Bureau of the Census (2011)

adults' long-term commitments in love and work. During these years, emerging adults focus on themselves as they develop the knowledge, skills, and self-understanding they will need for adult life. In the course of emerging adulthood they learn to make independent decisions small and large, about everything from what to have for dinner to whether to marry their current partner.

Being self-focused does not mean being selfish, and emerging adults are generally less egocentric than adolescents and more capable of taking the perspectives of others (Arnett, 2004; Lapsley & Woodbury, 2015). The goal of being self-focused is learning to stand alone as a self-sufficient person, but emerging adults do not see self-sufficiency as a permanent state. Rather, they view it as a necessary step before committing themselves to lasting relationships with others, in love and work.

Another distinctive feature of emerging adulthood is that it is an *age of feeling in-between*, no longer an adolescent but not fully an adult. When asked, "Do you feel that you have reached adulthood?" the majority of emerging adults respond neither "yes" nor "no" but with the ambiguous "in some ways yes, in some ways no" (Arnett, 1997, 1998, 2001, 2003, 2004; Arnett & Schwab, 2012; Nelson & Luster, 2015). As **Figure 9.4** shows, it is only when people reach their late 20s that a clear majority feel they have reached adulthood. Most emerging adults have the subjective feeling of being in a transitional period of life, on the way to adulthood but not there yet. This "in-between" feeling in emerging adulthood has been found in a wide range of countries, including Argentina (Facio & Micocci, 2003), Israel (Mayseless & Scharf, 2003), the Czech Republic (Macek et al., 2007), China (Nelson et al., 2004), and Austria (Sirsch et al., 2009). It is interesting that there are developmental consistencies across such different ecocultural settings.

The 20s are the decade of life when people are most likely to change residence.

Finally, emerging adulthood is the *age of possibilities*, when many different futures remain possible, when little about a person's direction in life has been decided for certain. It tends to be an age of high hopes, in part because few of their dreams have been tested in the fires of real life. In one national survey of 18- to 29-year-old adults in the United States, nearly all—89 percent—agreed with the statement "I am confident that eventually I will get to where I want to be in life" (Arnett & Schwab, 2012). This optimism in emerging adulthood has been found in other countries as well, such as China (Nelson & Chen, 2007).

Emerging adulthood is also the age of possibilities because it is a time that holds the potential for dramatic changes. For those who have come from a troubled family, this is their chance to try to straighten the parts of themselves that have become twisted. No longer dependent on their parents, no longer subject to their parents' problems on a daily basis, they may be able to make independent decisions—perhaps to move to a different area or go to college—that turn their lives in a dramatically different direction (Arnett, 2004; Masten et al., 2006). Even for those who have come from families that are relatively happy and healthy, emerging adulthood is an opportunity to transform themselves so that they are not merely made in their parents' images but have made independent decisions about what kind of person they wish to be and how they wish to live. For this limited window of time—7, perhaps 10 years—the fulfillment of all their hopes seems possible, because for most people the range of their choices for how to live is greater than it has ever been before and greater than it will ever be again.

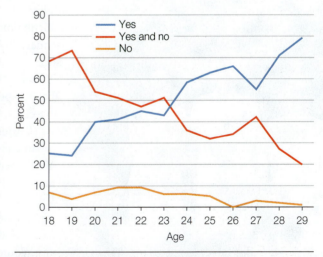

Figure 9.4 Do You Feel You Have Reached Adulthood?

Emerging adults often feel adult in some ways but not others.
SOURCE: Based on Arnett (2015).

The Cultural Context of Emerging Adulthood

LO 9.2 **Describe some of the ways emerging adulthood varies among cultures.**

Emerging adulthood exists as a life stage across developed countries, but the forms it takes vary by world region (Arnett, 2011). Europe is the region where emerging adulthood is longest and most leisurely. The median age of entering marriage and parenthood is around 30 in most European countries (Douglass, 2007; Moreno Mínguez et al., 2012). Europe today is the location of the most affluent, generous, egalitarian societies in the world—in fact, in human history (Arnett, 2007). Governments pay for tertiary education, assist young people in finding jobs, and provide generous unemployment benefits for those who cannot find work. In northern Europe, many governments also provide housing support. Emerging adults in European societies make the most of these advantages.

The experience of emerging adulthood in Asian developed countries is markedly different than in Europe. Europe has a long history of individualism, dating back at least 500 years, and today's emerging adults represent that legacy in their focus on self-development and leisure. In contrast, Asian cultures have a shared history emphasizing collectivism and family obligations. Although Asian cultures have become more individualistic in recent decades as a consequence of globalization, the legacy of collectivism persists in the lives of emerging adults. They pursue identity explorations and self-development during emerging adulthood, like their American and European counterparts, but within narrower boundaries set by their sense of obligations to others, especially their parents (Phinney & Baldelomar, 2011). For example, in their views of the most important criteria for becoming an adult, emerging adults in the United States and Europe consistently rank *financial independence* among the most important markers of adulthood. In contrast, emerging adults with an Asian cultural background especially emphasize *capable of supporting parents financially* as among the most important criteria (Arnett, 2003; Nelson et al., 2004; Zhong & Arnett, 2014). This sense of family obligation may curtail their identity explorations in emerging adulthood to some extent, as they pay more heed to their parents' wishes about what they should study and what job they should take and where they should live than emerging adults do in the West.

Within countries as well as between countries, emerging adulthood takes many different forms, just as we have seen for adolescence and childhood. About half of emerging adults in developed countries obtain tertiary education and training, but that leaves half who do not, and their experience of emerging adulthood is much different. Specifically, they are likely to have a much more difficult time finding a decent job in an economy that rewards educational credentials. There are other important differences across countries and cultures, such as in the degree of tolerance for premarital sex and cohabitation, as we will see later in the chapter. Thus, there is not just one emerging adulthood that is experienced worldwide, but many emerging adulthoods with distinctive cultural characteristics (Arnett, 2011).

Currently in developing countries, there tends to be a split between urban and rural areas in whether emerging adulthood is experienced at all. Young people in urban areas of countries such as China, India, and Mexico are more likely to experience emerging adulthood, because they marry later, have children later, obtain more education, and have a greater range of occupational and recreational opportunities than young people in rural areas have (Manago, 2012; Nelson & Chen, 2007; Zhong & Arnett, 2014). In contrast, young people in rural areas of developing countries often receive minimal schooling, marry early, and have little choice of occupation aside from agricultural work. However, as choices for future possibilities in work and love increase, even young people in rural areas in countries such as Mexico are more likely to take the time to explore options before settling down (Manago, 2012). Shifts in cultural settings influence development (Greenfield, 2009).

In Asian countries such as Japan, emerging adults feel an obligation to take care of their parents.

Cultural Focus: The Features of Emerging Adulthood

Emerging adulthood is not a universal period of human development but a period that exists under certain conditions that have occurred only quite recently and only in some cultures. As we have seen, what is mainly required for emerging adulthood to exist is a relatively high median age of entering marriage and parenthood, in the late 20s or beyond. Postponing marriage and parenthood until the late 20s allows the late teens and most of the 20s to be devoted to other activities, such as the identity explorations just described. So, emerging adulthood

exists today mainly in developed countries, including Europe, the United States, Canada, Australia, and New Zealand, along with Asian countries such as Japan and South Korea (Arnett, 2011). However, emerging adulthood is emerging in urban areas of developing countries such as Brazil, Chile, India, and Mexico (Galambos & Martínez, 2007; Manago, 2012; Zhong & Arnett, 2014).

This video shows interviews with individuals from various cultures regarding the features of emerging adulthood.

Watch   THE FEATURES OF EMERGING ADULTHOOD

Review Question:

Emerging adulthood is described as an "unstable" time in one's life. Based on this video, why would this be an accurate description?

Given these trends, emerging adulthood is likely to become more pervasive worldwide in the decades to come, with the increasing globalization of the world economy (Arnett, 2011). Participation in tertiary education is rising in developing countries, as are median marriage ages, especially in the urban middle class. These changes open up the possibility for the spread of emerging adulthood in developing countries. It seems possible that by the end of the 21st century emerging adulthood will be a normative period for young people worldwide, although it is likely to continue to vary in length and content both within and between countries.

PHYSICAL DEVELOPMENT: Physical Changes of Emerging Adulthood

Physical maturity is reached in many ways by the end of adolescence. By age 18, people reach their full height. Puberty is over, and a degree of sexual maturity has been attained that is sufficient to allow for reproduction. However, strength and endurance continue to grow into the 20s for most people, and illness rates are especially low as the immune system reaches peak effectiveness. On the other hand, health risks continue to loom in some areas, most notably automobile accidents and substance abuse.

The Peak of Physical Functioning

LO 9.3   **Name the indicators that emerging adulthood is a period of peak physical functioning.**

Do you enjoy watching the Olympics? Have you noticed that nearly all the athletes in the Olympics are ages 18 to 29? Emerging adulthood is the life stage of peak physical functioning, when the body is at its zenith of health, strength, and vigor. Physical stamina is often measured in terms of *maximum oxygen uptake,* or **VO2 max**, which reflects the ability of the body to take in oxygen and transport it to various organs. VO2 max peaks in the early 20s (Whaley, 2007). Similarly, **cardiac output**, the quantity of blood flow from the heart, peaks at age 25 (Lakatta, 1990; Parker et al., 2007). Reaction time is also faster in the early 20s than at any other time of life. Studies of grip strength among men show the same pattern, with a peak in the 20s followed by a steady decline (Aldwin & Spiro, 2006). The strength of the bones increases during this time as well. Even after maximum height is attained in the late teens, the bones continue to grow in density, and peak bone mass is reached in the 20s (Zumwalt, 2008).

It is not only the Olympics that demonstrate that emerging adulthood is a stage of exceptional physical functioning in terms of peak performances in athletic activity. Several studies have been conducted to determine the ages when athletes produce their best performances (Ericsson, 1990; Schultz & Curnow, 1988; Stones & Kozma, 1996; Tanaka & Seals, 2003). The peak ages have been found to vary depending on the sport, with swimmers youngest (the late teens) and golfers oldest (the early 30s). However, for most sports the peak age of performance comes during the 20s.

Emerging adulthood is also the period of the life span with the least susceptibility to physical illnesses (Braveman et al., 2011; Gans, 1990). Emerging adults are no longer vulnerable to the illnesses and diseases of childhood, and with rare exceptions they are not yet vulnerable to diseases such as cancer and heart disease that rise in prevalence later in adulthood. Because the immune system is at its most effective during emerging adulthood, the late teens and early 20s are the years of fewest hospital stays and fewest days spent sick in bed at home.

In many ways, then, emerging adulthood is an exceptionally healthy time of life. However, this is not the whole story. The lifestyles of many emerging adults often include a variety of factors that undermine health, such as poor nutrition, lack of sleep, and the high stress of trying to juggle school and work or multiple jobs (Braveman et al., 2011; Ma et al., 2002; Steptoe & Wardle, 2001). Longitudinal studies in the United States and Finland have found that physical activity, sports participation, and exercise decline from adolescence through emerging adulthood (Gordon-Larsen et al., 2004; Telama et al., 2005). These lifestyle factors often make emerging adults feel tired, weak, and depleted, despite their bodies' potential for optimal health. Furthermore, in many countries the late teens and early 20s are the years of highest incidence of a variety of types of injury, death, and disease because of behavior (Arnett, 2015a, b). The areas of heightened risk in emerging adulthood include automobile accidents and substance abuse, as we'll see shortly. The risks associated with sexual activity, including sexually transmitted infections (STIs), will be explored later in the chapter.

Sleep Patterns and Deficits

LO 9.4   **Summarize college students' sleep patterns and the main elements of sleep hygiene.**

How are you sleeping these days? If you are reading this, you are probably a college student, and if you are a college student your

VO2 max

ability of the body to take in oxygen and transport it to various organs; also called *maximum oxygen uptake*

cardiac output

quantity of blood flow from the heart

Emerging adulthood is a time of peak physical functioning. The swimmer Michael Phelps won a record seven gold medals at the 2008 Olympic games, at the age of 23, but has found it difficult to stay on top now that he has entered his 30s.

sleep pattern is probably not ideal—far from it. Nearly all research on sleep in emerging adulthood has focused on college students in developed countries. According to this research, college students' sleep patterns are distinctive in ways that undermine their cognitive functioning and their emotional well-being. College students are more than twice as likely as other adults to report the symptoms of *delayed sleep phase syndrome* (Brown et al., 2002). This syndrome entails a pattern of sleeping far longer on weekends and holidays than on school or work days, which leads to poor academic and job performance as well as excessive sleepiness during school and work days. College students tend to accumulate a *sleep debt* during the week as they sleep less than they need, then they try to make up their lost sleep when they have time off, with negative consequences for their cognitive and emotional functioning (Regestein et al., 2010).

College students' self-reports of their sleep patterns indicate that problems are common. Two-thirds of students report occasional sleep problems and about one fourth report frequent severe sleep disturbances such as insomnia (Buboltz et al., 2002). Sleep disturbances are in turn related to a wide variety of problems, such as depression and anxiety (Millman, 2005). Poor sleeping habits also cause cognitive deficits in attention, memory, and critical thinking.

One reason college students and other emerging adults often have sleep problems is that the daily routines of their lives are set mostly by older adults who are likely to have different sleep preferences than they do. Sleep researchers have established that people vary in their **morningness** and **eveningness**, that is, their preference for either going to bed early and waking up early (morningness) or going to bed late and waking up late (eveningness). Furthermore, these preferences change with age as a result of hormonal changes that are part of normal physical development, specifically, levels of *growth hormone*. One massive study of more than 55,000 Europeans from childhood through late adulthood concluded that children tend toward morningness, but in the course of adolescence and the early part of emerging adulthood the balance shifts toward eveningness, with the peak of eveningness coming at about ages 20 to 21 (slightly earlier for women than for men) (Roenneberg et al., 2007). After ages 20 to 21, the balance shifts again toward morningness for the remainder of the life span. Other studies have found similar relations between age and sleep preferences (Brown et al., 2002). So, your 60-year-old professors may schedule their classes for 8:00 or 8:30 in the morning because that is a time of day when they feel alert and ready to go, whereas if you are in your early 20s that may well be a time of day when you feel like something scraped off the bottom of the garbage can.

However, it is not just physiological changes that contribute to college students' sleep disturbances, but also lifestyle factors, such as partying until late at night or waiting until the day before an exam to begin studying seriously. Have you ever stayed up all night long to study for an exam or to complete a paper due the next day? Among U.S. college students this feat, known as an "all-nighter," is quite common. In one study of students at a 4-year liberal arts college, 60 percent had pulled at least one all-nighter since coming to college (Thacher, 2008). Those who had pulled an all-nighter tended to have a greater preference for eveningness and had poorer overall academic achievement. Another study of all-nighters found that students who stayed up all night before exams self-rated their exam performance as better than students who slept 8 hours, but their actual performance turned out to be much worse (Pilcher & Waters, 1997).

Sleep experts recommend the following practices to promote *sleep hygiene* (Brown et al., 2002; Horne, 2014):

- waking at the same time each day;
- getting regular exercise;
- taking late-afternoon naps;
- limiting caffeine intake;
- avoiding excessive alcohol intake.

morningness

preference for going to bed early and waking up early

eveningness

preference for going to bed late and waking up late

Most emerging adults tend toward eveningness, not morningness.

This may seem like common sense advice, but the actual behavior of many students contradicts these suggestions. Many drink coffee frequently during the day to stay alert, not realizing that frequent caffeine use will make it more difficult for them to sleep that night. Many believe that they can compensate for getting little sleep during the week by making it up during weekends and holidays, but this is precisely the delayed sleep phase syndrome, just discussed, that constitutes disrupted sleep. And of course, many drink alcohol excessively, with sleep hygiene the last thing on their minds.

PHYSICAL DEVELOPMENT:
Risk Behavior and Health Issues

When Jeff was 21 years old, during the summer between his junior and senior years of college, he was hungry for adventure, so he decided to take a hitchhiking trip across the United States. He stuck out his thumb down the street from his house in Michigan and proceeded to hitchhike 8,000 miles, from Michigan west to Seattle, down to Los Angeles, then all the way home again via Las Vegas. It was an adventure, all right, and in most ways a good one. For decades afterward he kept in touch with an elderly couple he met on that trip, who were remarkably kind to him.

It strikes us today that hitchhiking is probably not a good idea—to say the least—but the risks Jeff took in emerging adulthood are not unique. Emerging adulthood is a time of life when many types of risk behavior reach their peak prevalence (Arnett, 2000, 2015a, b). Unlike children and adolescents, emerging adults do not have their parents monitoring their behavior and setting rules for them, at least not nearly to the same extent. Unlike older adults, many emerging adults do not have the daily responsibilities of long-term commitments to a partner and children and to a long-term employer to restrain their behavior. Because emerging adulthood is the low point of **social control**—the restraints on behavior imposed by social obligations and relationships—individuals are more likely to take certain kinds of risks (Arnett, 2005a; Hirschi, 2002). (Nobody could stop Jeff from taking that hitchhiking trip, although his mom certainly tried.) Not all emerging adults take risks of course, but risk behavior of some kinds is more common at this time than at other age periods. Here we examine automobile driving and substance use.

Injuries and Fatalities: Automobile Accidents

LO 9.5   **Explain why young drivers have the highest rates of crashes, and name the most effective approach to reducing those rates.**

Across developed countries, the most serious threat to the lives and health of adolescents and emerging adults comes from automobile driving (Patton et al., 2009). In the United States, young people—especially males—ages 16 to 24 have the highest rates of automobile accidents, injuries, and fatalities of any age group (see **Figure 9.5**; National Highway Traffic Safety Administration [NHTSA], 2014). In other developed countries, a higher minimum driving age (usually 18) and less access to automobiles have made rates of accidents and fatalities among young people substantially lower than in the United States, but motor vehicle injuries are the leading cause of death during emerging adulthood in those countries as well (Pan et al., 2007; Twisk & Stacey, 2007).

What is responsible for these grim statistics? Is it young drivers' inexperience or their risky driving behavior? Inexperience certainly plays a large role. Rates of accidents

social control

restraints on behavior imposed by social obligations and relationships and fatalities are extremely high in the early months of driving, but fall dramatically by 1 year after licensure (McNight & Peck, 2002; Valentine et al., 2013). Studies that have attempted to disentangle experience and age in young drivers have generally concluded that inexperience is partly responsible for young drivers' accidents and fatalities.

However, studies have also concluded that inexperience is not the only factor involved. Equally important is the way young people drive and the kinds of risks they take (Valentine & Williams, 2013). Compared to older drivers, young drivers (especially males) are more likely to drive at excessive speeds, follow other vehicles too closely, violate traffic signs and signals, take more risks in lane changing and passing other vehicles, allow too little time to merge, and fail to yield to pedestrians (Bina et al., 2006; Williams & Ferguson, 2002). They are also more likely than older drivers to report driving under the influence of alcohol. Drivers ages 21 to 24 involved in fatal accidents are more likely to have been intoxicated at the time of the accident than persons in any other age group (NHTSA, 2014). Nearly half of U.S. college students report driving while intoxicated within the past year (Clapp et al., 2005; Glassman et al., 2010). Young people are also less likely than older drivers to wear seat belts, and in serious car crashes, occupants not wearing seat belts are twice as likely to be killed and three times as likely to be injured, compared to those wearing seat belts (NHTSA, 2011).

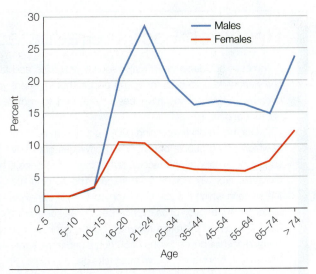

Figure 9.5 Rates of Car Fatalities by Age

Why are rates so high at ages 16–24?
SOURCE: Based on NHTSA (2014)

💬 I love to drive fast, but after awhile driving fast just wasn't doing it any more. So I started driving without the lights on [at night], going about ninety on country roads. I even got a friend to do it. We'd go cruising down country roads, turn off the lights, and just fly. It was incredible. We'd go as fast as we could, [and] at night, with no lights it feels like you're just flying."

—Nick, age 23 (in Arnett, 1996, p. 79)

What else leads to crashes among young drivers? Young drivers are more likely than older drivers to believe their friends would approve of risky driving behavior such as speeding, closely following another vehicle, and passing another car in risky circumstances (Chen et al., 2007; U.S. Department of Transportation, 1995). Driver characteristics matter, too. Personality characteristics such as sensation seeking and aggressiveness promote risky driving and subsequent crashes, and these characteristics tend to be highest in young male drivers (Shope & Bingham, 2008). This explains why car insurance rates are highest for that group.

What can be done to reduce the rates of automobile accidents and fatalities among young drivers? Parental involvement and monitoring of adolescents' driving behavior has been shown to be especially important in the early months of driving, and interventions to increase parental involvement can be effective (Simons-Morton et al., 2002; Simons-Morton et al., 2006; Simons-Morton, 2007; Simons-Morton et al., 2008). However, by far the most effective approach is a program of restricted driving privileges called **graduated driver licensing (GDL)**. GDL is a government program in which young people obtain driving privileges gradually, contingent on a safe driving record, rather than all at once. GDL programs allow young people to obtain driving experience under conditions that limit the likelihood of crashes by restricting the circumstances under which novices can drive (Foss, 2007; Williams et al., 2012).

graduated driver licensing (GDL)

government program in which young people obtain driving privileges gradually, contingent on a safe driving record, rather than all at once

Research Focus: Graduated Driver Licensing

Automobile accidents are a major source of injuries and fatalities worldwide, especially for young people, but in recent years effective public policies have been developed to reduce the number of deaths.

Graduated driver licensing (GDL) is a government program in which young people obtain driving privileges gradually, contingent on a safe driving record, rather than all at once. These programs typically include three stages. The learning license is the stage in which the young person obtains driving experience under the supervision of an experienced driver. For example, the GDL program in California requires young people to complete learning-license driver training of 50 hours under the supervision of a parent, of which 10 hours must take place at night.

The second stage is a period of restricted license driving. In this stage young drivers are allowed to drive unsupervised, but with tighter restrictions than those that apply to adults. The restrictions are based on research revealing the factors that are most likely to place young drivers at risk for crashes. For example, in some states GDL programs include driving curfews, which prohibit young drivers from driving late at night except for a specific purpose such as going to and from work. There are also prohibitions against driving with teenage passengers when no adults are present, requirements for seat belt use, and a "zero tolerance" rule for alcohol use. Recently, most American states have also passed laws against any cell phone use for novice drivers, including both calling and texting.

Watch RESEARCH FOCUS: GRADUATED DRIVER LICENSING

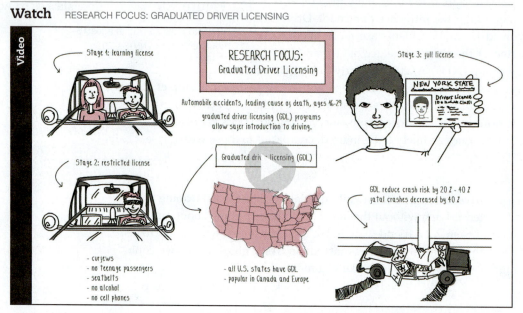

In the restricted stage, any violations of these restrictions may result in a suspended license. It is only after the GDL period has passed—usually no more than one year—that a young person obtains a full license and has the same driving privileges as adults.

What have research studies shown regarding the effectiveness of GDL programs? Numerous studies in the past decade have shown GDL programs to be the most effective way to reduce automobile accidents among young drivers. One summary review (or meta-analysis) of 21 studies conducted by Jean Shope in 2007 concluded that GDL programs consistently reduce young drivers' crash risk by 20 percent to 40 percent. Driving curfews in particular have been found to reduce young people's crash involvement dramatically. Fatal crashes among 16-year-old drivers in the United States decreased by 40 percent in the past decade, and this improvement is attributed mainly to GDL programs.

Legislators in many states have responded to this evidence by passing more of these programs. All 50 American states now have some kind of GDL program, a dramatic rise over the past 20 years. Graduated driver license programs have also been instituted in Canada and are becoming more common in European countries. Research indicates that these laws work

in part by making it easier for parents to enforce restrictions on their adolescents' driving behavior. Across developed countries, automobile accidents remain the number-one cause of death in the teens and 20s, but effective GDL programs have dramatically reduced the number of deaths in recent decades.

Review Questions:

1. Which of the following is *not* one of the typical components of a GDL program?
   a. Driving curfew
   b. No more than two teenage passengers
   c. Mandatory seat belt use
   d. Zero tolerance for alcohol

2. Which of the following has been the consequence of widespread adoption of GDL programs?
   a. Injuries among teens have declined, but not fatalities
   b. Most teens have found ways to avoid the regulations
   c. Auto fatalities among 16-year-olds have sharply declined
   d. Girls' driving habits have changed but boys' have not

Substance Use and Abuse

LO 9.6   **Explain why rates of substance use peak in the early 20s and then decline.**

Many types of substance use reach their peak in emerging adulthood. The national Monitoring the Future study, which has followed several U.S. cohorts from high school through middle age, shows that substance use of all kinds rises through the late teens and peaks in the early 20s before declining in the late 20s. **Figure 9.6** shows the pattern for marijuana use and **binge drinking** (consuming five or more drinks in a row for men, four in a row for women) (Bachman et al., 2008). Substance use, especially alcohol use, is higher among college students than among emerging adults who do not attend college (Core Institute, 2013). It also tends to be somewhat higher among men than among women.

Some evidence shows that substance use is also high among emerging adults in other developed countries. A study of Spanish adults reported that among 18- to 24-year-old adults, rates of binge drinking in the past 30 days were 31 percent for men and 18 percent for women, far higher than in any other age group (Valencia-Martín et al., 2007). A peak in binge drinking in emerging adulthood has been found in other European countries as well (Kuntsche et al., 2004). Among female college students in Scotland, most regarded binge drinking as "harmless fun" (Guise & Gill, 2007). However, binge drinking and other types of substance use in emerging adulthood are related to a wide variety of negative consequences, from fatal car crashes to unintended pregnancy to criminal activity to physical fights, in both Europe and the United States (Jochman & Fromme, 2010; Plant et al., 2010).

What explains the higher rates of substance use among emerging adults? Wayne Osgood has proposed a useful answer to this question. Osgood (2009; Osgood et al.,

binge drinking

consuming five or more drinks in a row for men, four in a row for women

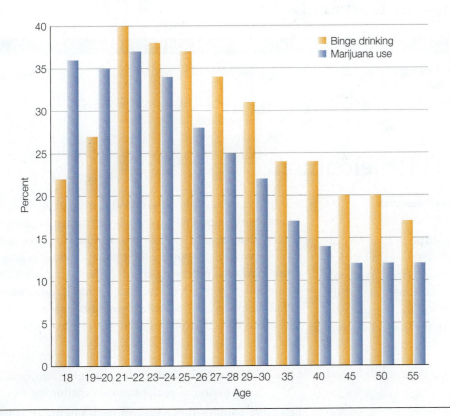

Figure 9.6 Marijuana Use and Binge Drinking in Emerging Adulthood

Rates of most kinds of substance use peak in the early 20s.

SOURCE: Based on Johnston et al. (2014)

Unstructured socializing is often the setting for risk behaviors such as substance use. –

unstructured socializing

socializing with friends without any specific goal or activity; includes behavior such as riding around in a car for fun, going to parties, visiting friends informally, and going out with friends

2005; Osgood et al., 1996) borrows from a sociological theory that explains all deviance on the basis of *propensity* and *opportunity*. People behave deviantly when they have a combination of sufficient propensity (that is, motivation for behaving deviantly) along with sufficient opportunity. In his explanation, Osgood especially focuses on the high degree of opportunity that emerging adults have for engaging in substance use and other deviant behavior, as a result of spending a high proportion of their time in unstructured socializing.

Osgood uses the term **unstructured socializing** to include behavior such as riding around in a car for fun, going to parties, visiting friends informally, and going out with friends. Unstructured socializing is highest in the late teens and early 20s and, emerging adults who are highest in unstructured socializing are also highest in use of alcohol and marijuana (Osgood et al., 2005; Osgood et al., 1996). Rates of most types of substance use are especially high among emerging adults who are college students because they have so many opportunities for unstructured socializing.

Osgood and others have found that the relationship between unstructured socializing and deviance holds not only for substance use but for other types of risk behavior such as crime and dangerous driving (Haynie & Osgood, 2005; Maimon & Browning, 2010). Furthermore, the relationship between unstructured socializing and deviance holds for both genders, a variety of ethnic groups, and across a wide range of developed and developing countries. Research also shows that substance use and other types of risk behavior decline in the mid- to late 20s, as role transitions such as marriage, parenthood, and full-time work cause a sharp decline in unstructured socializing (Johnston et al., 2014; Patrick et al., 2011).

CRITICAL THINKING QUESTION

Besides unstructured socializing, what other factors might contribute to substance use in emerging adulthood?

....

Summary: Physical Development

LO 9.1   Name the five developmental features distinctive to emerging adulthood.

The rise of emerging adulthood was due to four revolutions that began in the 1960s and 1970s: the Technological Revolution, the Sexual Revolution, the Women's Movement, and the Youth Movement. Emerging adulthood is the age of identity explorations, the age of instability, the self-focused age, the age of feeling in-between, and the age of possibilities.

LO 9.2   Describe some of the ways emerging adulthood varies among cultures.

Emerging adulthood is longest in Europe, where education often lasts well into the 20s and the median age of

entering marriage and parenthood is around 30. In Asian countries, emerging adults balance their identity explorations with a sense of obligation to family. They seek to become capable of supporting their parents, which is seen as a key marker of becoming an adult. Emerging adulthood is rare but growing in developing countries, especially in urban areas, or in areas where young people are able to take more time to explore options in identity, work, and love.

LO 9.3   Name the indicators that emerging adulthood is a period of peak physical functioning.

Emerging adulthood is a time of peak physical functioning as indicated in measures such as VO2 max and grip strength. However, many emerging adults feel less than optimally healthy and energetic due to lifestyle factors such as poor nutrition and the strain of balancing school and work obligations.

LO 9.4   Summarize college students' sleep patterns and the main elements of sleep hygiene.

College students' sleep patterns are often irregular and disrupted, so that they accumulate a large sleep debt during the week and then try to compensate on weekends. Part of the problem is that they tend toward eveningness in their 20s, whereas the older adults who set emerging adults' work and class schedules tend toward morningness. Good sleep hygiene includes waking up at the same time each day, getting regular exercise, and limiting caffeine and alcohol consumption.

LO 9.5   Explain why young drivers have the highest rates of crashes, and name the most effective approach to reducing those rates.

Rates of automobile fatalities are high in adolescence and emerging adulthood because of a combination of inexperience and risky driving behaviors, but have been reduced substantially by GDL programs.

LO 9.6   Explain why rates of substance use peak in the early 20s and then decline.

Substance use rates peak in the early 20s primarily because this is when social control is lowest and unstructured socializing is highest. The decline in substance use in the late 20s and beyond is primarily as a result of taking on new social roles such as spouse and parent, which provide new sources of social control.

Section 2   Cognitive Development

Learning Objectives

9.7 Describe how growing abilities of pragmatism allow emerging adults to become better at addressing real-life problems.

9.8 Outline the development of reflective judgment in Perry's theory.

9.9 Name the various long-term benefits of tertiary education.

9.10 Describe the transition from school to full-time work, and explain why unemployment rates among emerging adults are higher than for older adults.

COGNITIVE DEVELOPMENT:
Postformal Thought

In Piaget's theory, formal operations is the culmination of cognitive development. Once formal operations is fully attained, by age 20 at the latest, cognitive maturation is complete. However, like many aspects of Piaget's theory of formal operations, this view has been altered by research. In fact, research indicates that cognitive development often continues in important ways during emerging adulthood. This is probably because the prefrontal cortex is not fully mature until the early 20s (Steinberg, 2011). Furthermore, changes in the socio-emotional areas of the brain change the way late adolescents and emerging adults make judgments (Steinberg, 2008). Some theorists have proposed a kind of cognitive development beyond formal operations, known as **postformal thought** (Malott, 2011; Sinnott, 2014). Two of the most notable aspects of postformal thinking in emerging adulthood concern advances in pragmatism and reflective judgment.

Pragmatism

LO 9.7   **Describe how growing abilities of pragmatism allow emerging adults to become better at addressing real-life problems.**

Pragmatism involves adapting logical thinking to the practical constraints of real-life situations. Theories of postformal thought emphasizing pragmatism have been developed by several scholars (Basseches, 1984; Basseches, 1989; Labouvie-Vief, 1998, 2006; Labouvie-Vief & Diehl, 2002; Sinnott, 2014). The theories have in common an emphasis that the problems faced in normal adult life often contain complexities and inconsistencies that cannot be addressed with the logic of formal operations.

According to Gisela Labouvie-Vief (1982; 1990; 1998; 2006), cognitive development in emerging adulthood is distinguished from adolescent thinking by a greater recognition and incorporation of practical limitations to logical thinking. In this view, adolescents exaggerate the extent to which logical thinking will be effective in real life. In contrast, emerging adulthood brings a growing awareness of how social influences and factors specific to a given situation must be taken into account in approaching most of life's problems.

For example, in one study Labouvie-Vief (1990) presented adolescents and emerging adults with stories and asked them to predict what they thought would happen. One story described a man who was a heavy drinker, especially at parties. His wife had warned him that if he came home drunk one more time, she would leave him and take the children. Some time later he went to an office party and came home drunk. What would she do?

postformal thought

according to some theorists, the stage of cognitive development that follows formal operations and includes advances in pragmatism and reflective judgment

pragmatism

theory of cognitive development proposing that postformal thinking involves adapting logical thinking to the practical constraints of real-life situations

Labouvie-Vief found that adolescents tended to respond strictly in terms of the logic of formal operations: She said she would leave if he came home drunk once more, he came home drunk, therefore she will leave. In contrast, emerging adults considered many possible dimensions of the situation. Did he apologize and beg her not to leave? Did she really mean it when she said she would leave him? Has she considered the possible effects on the children? Rather than relying strictly on logic and assuming an outcome of definite wrong and right answers, the emerging adults tended to be postformal thinkers in the sense that they realized that the problems of real life often involve a great deal of complexity and ambiguity. However, Labouvie-Vief (2006) emphasizes that with postformal thinking, as with formal thinking, not everyone continues to move to higher levels of cognitive complexity, and many people continue to apply earlier, more concrete thinking in emerging adulthood and beyond.

A similar theory of cognitive development in emerging adulthood has been presented by Michael Basseches (1984; 1989). Like Labouvie-Vief, Basseches (1984) views cognitive development in emerging adulthood as involving a recognition that formal logic can rarely be applied to the problems most people face in their daily lives. **Dialectical thought** is Basseches's term for the kind of thinking that develops in emerging adulthood, involving a growing awareness that problems often have no clear solution and two opposing strategies or points of view may each have some merit (Basseches, 1984). For example, people may have to decide whether to quit a job they dislike without knowing whether their next job will be more satisfying.

Some cultures may promote dialectical thinking more than others. Chinese culture traditionally promotes dialectical thought, by advocating an approach to knowledge that strives to reconcile contradictions and combine opposing perspectives by seeking a middle ground (Peng & Nisbett, 1999). In contrast, the U.S. approach tends to apply logic in a way that polarizes contradictory perspectives in an effort to determine which is correct.

To support this theory, one team of researchers conducted studies comparing Chinese and U.S. college students (Peng & Nisbett, 1999). They found that the Chinese students were more likely than the Americans to prefer dialectical proverbs containing contradictions. In addition, when two apparently contradictory propositions were presented, the Americans tended to embrace one and reject the other, whereas the Chinese students were moderately accepting of both propositions, seeking to reconcile them.

Reflective Judgment

LO 9.8   Outline the development of reflective judgment in Perry's theory.

Reflective judgment, another cognitive quality that has been found to develop in emerging adulthood, is the capacity to evaluate the accuracy and logical coherence of evidence and arguments. An influential theory of the development of reflective judgment in emerging adulthood was proposed by William Perry (1970/1999), who based his theory on his studies of college students in their late teens and early 20s. According to Perry (1970/1999), adolescents and first-year college students tend to engage in *dualistic thinking*, which means they often see situations and issues in polarized terms—an act is either right or wrong, with no in-between; a statement is either true or false, regardless of the nuances or the situation to which it is being applied. In this sense, they lack reflective judgment. However, reflective judgment begins to develop for most people around age 20. First a stage of *multiple thinking* begins, in which young people come to believe that there are two or more legitimate views of every issue, and that it can be difficult to justify one position as the only true or accurate one. In this stage people tend to value all points of view equally, even to the extent of asserting that it is impossible to make any judgments about whether one point of view is more valid than another.

Next, according to Perry, multiple thinking develops into *relativism*. Like people in the stage of multiple thinking, relativists are able to recognize the legitimacy of

dialectical thought

according to Basseches, a kind of thinking in emerging adulthood that involves a growing awareness that problems often have no clear solution and two opposing strategies or points of view may each have some merit

reflective judgment

capacity to evaluate the accuracy and logical coherence of evidence and arguments, theorized to develop during emerging adulthood

competing points of view. However, rather than denying that one view could be more persuasive than another, relativists attempt to evaluate the merits of competing views. Finally, by the end of their college years, many young people reach a stage of *commitment*, in which they commit themselves to a worldview they believe to be the most valid, while being open to reevaluating their views if new evidence is presented to them.

Research on reflective judgment indicates that significant gains may take place in emerging adulthood (King & Kitchener, 2015; Kitchener et al., 2006; Pascarella & Terenzini, 1991). However, the gains that take place in emerging adulthood appear to be due more to education than to maturation—that is, people who pursue a college education during emerging adulthood show greater advances in reflective judgment than people who do not. Also, Perry and his colleagues acknowledged that the development of reflective judgment is likely to be more common in a culture that values pluralism and whose educational system promotes tolerance of diverse points of view (Perry, 1970/1999). However, thus far little cross-cultural research has taken place on reflective judgment.

COGNITIVE DEVELOPMENT: Education and Work

As mentioned at the outset of the chapter, one of the changes of recent decades that has led to the development of a new life stage of emerging adulthood is increasing participation in higher education. Emerging adults tend to look for jobs that help them along a career path.

Tertiary Education: College, University, and Training Programs

LO 9.9   **Name the various long-term benefits of tertiary education.**

As **Map 9.1** shows, a majority of emerging adults across a wide range of developed countries now obtain **tertiary education**, which includes any kind of education or training program beyond secondary school. This has been a remarkably rapid historical change. One hundred years ago, few young people—less than 10 percent—obtained tertiary education in any developed country; in fact, the majority did not even attend secondary school. Those who did attend college or university were mostly men. Historically, women were deemed to be cognitively inferior to men and therefore not worthy of higher education. A hundred years later, tertiary education is now a normative experience, and in most countries women are more likely than men to obtain it (Arnett, 2015a, b).

Tertiary education is perhaps most relaxed and undemanding in Japan. You may find this surprising, because, Japanese secondary schools are exceptionally demanding and competition to get into the best universities is fierce (Fackler, 2007). Beyond college and university, the Japanese workplace is notoriously demanding as well, requiring long hours and mandatory after-hours socializing. For the Japanese, their time of leisure and fun comes during their college years. Once they enter college, grades matter little and standards for performance are relaxed. Instead, they have "four years of university-sanctioned leisure to think and explore" (Rohlen, 1983, p. 168; Fackler, 2007). Japanese college students spend a great deal of time walking around the city and hanging out together. Average homework time for Japanese college students is half the homework time of middle school or high school students (Takahashi & Takeuchi, 2007). For most Japanese, this brief period in emerging adulthood is the only time in their lives, from childhood until retirement, that they are allowed to enjoy extensive hours of leisure.

The European tertiary education system, which had traditionally lasted an average of 6 years and culminated in an advanced degree, has changed recently to match the

tertiary education

education or training beyond secondary school

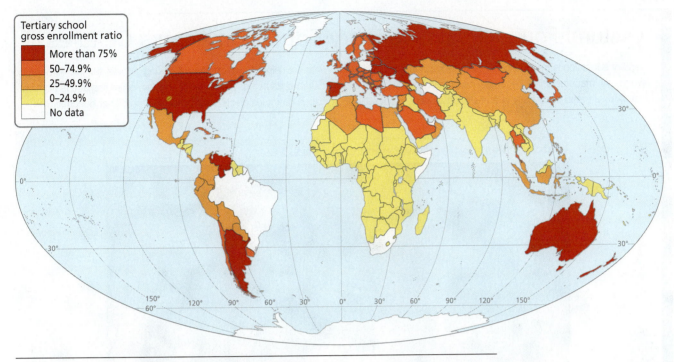

Map 9.1 Worldwide Enrollment in Tertiary Education

Which countries have the highest and lowest enrollment rates for higher education? How do these rates compare to the enrollment rates for secondary school (as shown in Map 8.1)? What economic and cultural factors might explain these variations?

SOURCE: Based on UNESCO (2013)

U.S. system, with separate bachelor's, master's, and doctoral degrees. This was done to shorten the time European emerging adults spend in university, and to promote the development of coordinated programs between European and U.S. universities. It also reflects the growing globalization of education.

For most young Americans, tertiary education takes longer now than it did two or three decades ago. Currently, it takes an average of 6 years for students to obtain a "4-year" degree. Furthermore, only 57 percent of students who enter a 4-year college or university have graduated 6 years later (National Center for Education Statistics, 2014).

A number of factors explain why it takes students longer to graduate and nearly half never graduate at all. Some students prefer to extend their college years to switch majors, add a minor field of study, or take advantage of internship programs or study-abroad programs. However, financial concerns are the main reason that a 4-year degree is so elusive for many emerging adults (Arnett & Schwab, 2012). Tuition rates have increased to a shocking extent and were over *four times higher* (even taking into account inflation) in 2013 than they were in 1982 in both public and private colleges and universities (NCES, 2014). Financial aid has also shifted markedly from grants to loans, which has led many students to work long hours while attending college to avoid accruing excessive debt before they graduate. African Americans especially struggle to fund their college educations, as **Figure 9.7** illustrates, and lack of money is one of the key reasons why they are less likely to obtain a college degree than Whites or Asian Americans are (McDonough & Calderone, 2006).

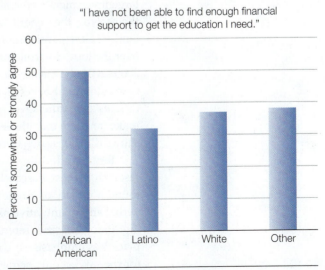

Figure 9.7 Ethnicity and College Affordability

SOURCE: Based on Arnett & Schwab (2012).

Cultural Focus: Postsecondary Education Across Cultures

Tertiary education is becoming increasingly important around the world, as manufacturing becomes more mechanized and the new jobs created are mostly in areas such as health, education, and business, which require young people to gain knowledge and skills in these areas. In this video, emerging adults from various countries discuss their thoughts on higher education.

Watch POSTSECONDARY EDUCATION ACROSS CULTURES

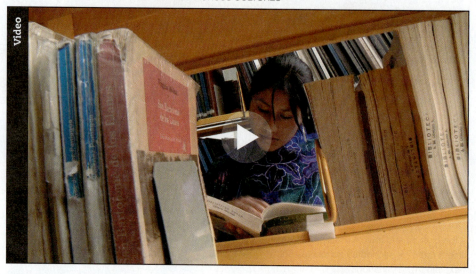

Review Question:

Compare and contrast at least two of the individuals interviewed in this video regarding their views on higher education.

Is tertiary education worth the time and money it requires? It is certainly a substantial investment, but the benefits of tertiary education are great. For societies, an educated population is a key to economic growth in a world economy that is increasingly based on information, technology, and services. This is why countries are willing to make such a large investment in the tertiary education of their emerging adults. For emerging adults themselves, the benefits are also clear. Emerging adults who obtain tertiary education tend to have considerably higher earnings, occupational status, and career attainment over the long run, compared to those who do not attend college (NCES, 2014; Pascarella, 2005, 2006; Schneider & Stevenson, 1999). Those students who opt to study abroad reap additional benefits, as discussed in the *Education Focus: Study Abroad and Global Citizenship* feature. Over a lifetime of working, Americans with a college degree or more make far more than those who only obtain a high school education or less, as **Figure 9.8** shows (Pew Research Center, 2014).

Tertiary education has multiple benefits in addition to increased earnings. In their research, Ernest Pascarella and Patrick Terenzini (1991; Pascarella, 2005, 2006) have found a variety of intellectual benefits from attending college, in areas such as general verbal and quantitative skills, oral and written communication skills, and critical thinking. Pascarella and Terenzini also find that in the course of the college years students place less emphasis on college as a way to a better job and more emphasis on learning for the sake of enhancing their intellectual and personal growth. Nonacademic benefits include a more distinct identity and becoming more confident socially. Students who have attended college become less dogmatic, less authoritarian, and less ethnocentric

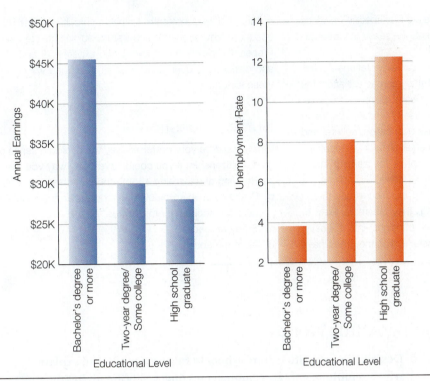

Figure 9.8 "The College Bonus" Showing Economic Benefits of Tertiary Education
SOURCE: Based on Pew Research Center (2014).

in their political and social views. Their self-concepts and psychological well-being improve. This wide range of benefits holds up even after taking into account factors such as age, gender, precollege abilities, and family social class background.

CRITICAL THINKING QUESTION

How does the way that a country structures its tertiary education system reflect its cultural values, if at all?

Education Focus: Study Abroad and Global Citizenship

Study abroad has become quite popular in recent years. The number of U.S. students going abroad to study more than doubled from 1999 to 2014, from about 130,000 to 289,000 (Institute of International Education, 2014). Most universities offer a study abroad option, and there are a couple dozen countries represented across programs. Many U.S. students visit countries in Europe, Latin America, and Asia, though some go to Australia and Africa as well. There are short-term and long-term programs. Shorter programs last a few weeks and might involve an intensive study of a foreign language, for example. Longer programs may last a regular term (semester or quarter) or a whole year. Many campuses have an office dedicated to study abroad, whereas other campuses have these options through student services.

What kinds of skills do students develop when they study abroad? There are individual skills, knowledge, and abilities, such as second language proficiency and intercultural competence. Students who have gone on study abroad are more likely than the general student population to pursue graduate degrees. And, students return from study abroad invigorated about their majors. There are nonacademic benefits as well. Study abroad helps to open the consciousness of many students to other ways of being in the world, reducing cultural biases. Going on study abroad shows initiative and independence that a lot of employers think is indicative of career skills. There is also the possibility of fostering a sense of global citizenship, which would mean developing a sense of collective responsibility and action.

Berlin (2015) measured three factors related to global citizenship in a population of students who had gone on study broad: Social responsibility, global competence, and global civic engagement are all part of a sense of global citizenship. In survey research and interviews, Berlin found that students who studied abroad scored higher on a global citizenship scale than students who did not. However, there are four specific practices and factors that made the development of a sense of global citizenship more likely.

First, students' motivation, goals, and expectations are important. What they want to get out of study abroad will affect the experiences they seek and what they learn. Second, students' perceptions of the host culture, the sense of what it was like to be an outsider, and perceptions of their own nation, culture, and values will also shape any developmental shifts in perceptions and insights they gain. Third, the contexts for learning inside and outside the classroom matter for students. If students get a chance to live with a host family and experience day-to-day life outside a typical university setting, they are more likely to get a real sense of the culture and more insights into it. Lastly, it is important for students to understand that they may have culture shock upon reentry to their own cultures, and there is a need for them to reflect on how study abroad affected their lives. Preparation before the study abroad experience, and journaling and discussions during and after study abroad will help with all these factors.

Survey Question:

What would be your preferred way to develop a sense of global citizenship, if you could have it any way you wanted?
a. Reading and learning about other cultures
b. Doing a service project in my hometown for people in a different socioeconomic status
c. Study abroad
d. All of the above

Finding Adult Work

LO 9.10 **Describe the transition from school to full-time work, and explain why unemployment rates among emerging adults are higher than for older adults.**

The kinds of work adolescents do—waiting tables, washing dishes, mowing lawns, sales clerking, and the like—are generally viewed as temporary and transient, not as forming the basis of a long-term career (Mortimer, 2004, 2013). Most emerging adults, in contrast, are looking for a job that will turn into a career, something that will not only bring in a paycheck but provide personal fulfillment (Arnett, 2015a, b; Taylor, 2005).

Work in emerging adulthood focuses on identity questions: What do I really want to *do*? What am I best at? What do I enjoy the most? How do my abilities and desires fit in with the kinds of opportunities that are available to me? In asking themselves what kind of work they want to do, emerging adults are also asking themselves what kind of person they are. In the course of emerging adulthood, as they try out various jobs, they begin to answer their identity questions, and they develop a better sense of what work suits them best.

THE TRANSITION TO WORK What career did you imagine for yourself when you were 15 years old? At 15 Jeff thought he would probably go into law, then politics. At the same age, Ashley thought she would become a child therapist or a pediatrician. Jeff knew nothing about developmental psychology until after he graduated college and Ashley didn't take a developmental psychology class until she was a third-year undergraduate. We never imagined that we would one day become academic psychologists and writers.

Many adolescents have an idea, in high school, of what kind of career they want to go into (Schneider & Stevenson, 1999). Often that idea dissolves in the course of emerging adulthood because they develop a clearer identity and discover that their high school aspiration does not align with it. In place of their high school notions many emerging adults seek *identity-based work*, something they enjoy and really want to do (Arnett, 2015a, b; Vaughan, 2005). Watch the video *Looking for Identity-Based Work* for more information.

For most U.S. emerging adults the road to a stable, long-term job is long, with many brief, low-paying, dreary jobs along the way. The average American holds eight different jobs between the ages of 18 and 30 (U.S. Department of Labor, 2012).

Watch LOOKING FOR IDENTITY-BASED WORK

Some emerging adults engage in systematic exploration as they look for a career path that they wish to settle into for the long term. But for many others, *exploration* is a bit too lofty a word to describe their work history during their late teens and early 20s. Many emerging adults express a sense that they did not really choose their current job, they just one day found themselves in it. In Jeff's interviews with emerging adults, "I just fell into it" is a frequently used phrase when they describe how they found their current job (Arnett, 2015a, b). Yet even the meandering process of trying various jobs often serves the function of helping emerging adults sort out what kind of work they want to do.

Although at least half of young people in developed countries now obtain tertiary education in some form, a substantial proportion of emerging adults finish their education after secondary school and enter the workplace. What are the work prospects like for these emerging adults, and how successfully are they able to make the transition from school to the workplace?

For the most part, they struggle to find work that pays enough to live on, much less the identity-based work that is the ideal for many emerging adults. Because the economy in developed countries has shifted from manufacturing to information, technology, and services over the past half-century, tertiary education is more import-

Today, high-paying manufacturing jobs are scarce in developed countries.

ant than ever in obtaining jobs that pay well. Those who lack the training, knowledge, and credentials conferred by tertiary education are at a great disadvantage in the modern economy. Their rates of unemployment are about three times as high as for people who have obtained a college degree (OECD, 2014d). This may be because a high number of high school graduates do not have the necessary skills to succeed at the kinds of jobs required in our technology- and information-based economy (Levy & Murnane, 2012).

UNEMPLOYMENT Although most young people in developed countries are able to find a job once they leave high school or college, this is not true for all of them. In both Europe and the United States, the unemployment rate for emerging adults is consistently *twice as high* as for

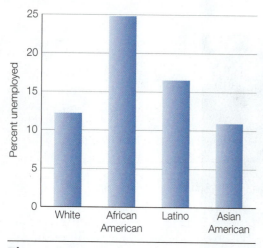

Figure 9.9 U.S. Unemployment Rates for Emerging Adults (Ages 16–24)

What explains the differences among ethnic groups?

SOURCE: Based on Bureau of Labor Statistics (2014)

unemployment

work status of adults who are not in school, are not working, and are looking for a job

Unemployment rates in emerging adulthood are especially high among African Americans and Latinos. Here, young African Americans seek opportunities at a job fair.

adults beyond age 25 (OECD, 2014d). In both Europe and the United States, unemployment has been found to be associated with higher risk for depression, especially for emerging adults who lack strong parental support (Bjarnason & Sigurdardottir, 2003; Hämäläinen et al., 2005; Mossakowski, 2009).

To say that someone is unemployed does not just mean that the person does not have a job. A large proportion of young people in their late teens and early 20s are attending high school or college, but they are not classified as unemployed because school is considered to be the focus of their efforts, not work. People whose time is mainly devoted to caring for their own children also would not be classified as unemployed. **Unemployment** applies only to people who are not in school, are not working, and are looking for a job.

This status applies to a substantial proportion of young people in the United States. **Figure 9.9** shows the unemployment rates for young people in their late teens and early 20s. As you can see from the figure, unemployment is especially concentrated among African American and Latino emerging adults. Also, unemployment is extremely high among young people who drop out of high school. More than *half* of high school dropouts ages 18 to 21 are unemployed (NCES, 2014).

What explains the high rates of unemployment among minority groups? This was not always the case. Consider that in 1954, the teenage unemployment rate for African Americans was only slightly higher than for Whites—16.5 percent for African Americans, lower than it is today, and 12 percent for Whites (Quillian, 2003). To a large extent, the explanation for the change lies in shifting employment patterns in the U.S. economy. Over the past several decades, as the economy has become more strongly focused on information and technology rather than manufacturing, the number of jobs available to unskilled workers has diminished sharply (Levy & Murnane, 2012). The days are gone in the United States when stable, high-paying jobs were plentiful in settings such as automobile factories and steel mills. Today, most of the new jobs, and certainly the best jobs, require people to have at least a minimal level of information skills such as basic math knowledge and the ability to use a computer.

Those skills come from education, and young African Americans and Latinos tend to obtain less education than young Whites or Asian Americans (Hamilton & Hamilton, 2006; NCES, 2014). Without educational credentials, gaining access to jobs in the new economy is difficult.

Summary: Cognitive Development

LO 9.7 **Describe how growing abilities of pragmatism allow emerging adults to become better at addressing real-life problems.**

In contrast to the thinking of formal operations, which emphasizes scientific approaches to problems, pragmatism recognizes that the problems people confront in their daily lives are often complex and ambiguous and do not submit to definite answers.

LO 9.8 **Outline the development of reflective judgment in Perry's theory.**

William Perry found that college students' reflective judgment develops through stages of dualistic thinking, multiple thinking, relativism, and commitment, but other research indicates this pattern is due more to education than to maturation.

LO 9.9 **Name the various long-term benefits of tertiary education.**

Participation in tertiary education has risen dramatically in recent decades. A majority of emerging adults now obtain tertiary education in most developed countries, with women consistently attaining higher educational achievement than men. Countries vary greatly in their tertiary education systems, with Europe the most structured and Japan the least.

Tertiary education has been shown to have many benefits, occupationally and financially, as well as personally. Benefits include greater earnings and better verbal and quantitative skills, as well as nonacademic benefits such as developing a clearer identity and more definite values.

LO 9.10 **Describe the transition from school to full-time work, and explain why unemployment rates among emerging adults are higher than for older adults.**

Emerging adults tend to seek identity-based work that fits their abilities and interests. In developed countries the best jobs require tertiary education, and emerging adults often struggle in the job market because they lack basic skills as well as educational credentials. Across developed countries, unemployment peaks in emerging adulthood. In the United States, unemployment is especially high among African Americans and Latinos, because they are more likely to lack educational credentials.

Section 3   Emotional and Social Development

Learning Objectives

9.11   Describe the course of self-esteem from adolescence through emerging adulthood, and explain the reasons for this pattern.

9.12   Describe the various forms identity development can take in emerging adulthood, and consider patterns of cultural and ethnic identity.

9.13   Summarize findings from research on gender stereotypes among college students.

9.14   Summarize Smith and Snell's description of the religious beliefs and practices of U.S. emerging adults.

9.15   Explain why emerging adults have often been at the forefront of political movements rather than conventional politics.

9.16   Describe patterns of home-leaving in the United States and Europe and how this transition influences relations with parents.

9.17   Describe the role of intimacy in emerging adults' friendships and the most common activities of emerging adult friends.

9.18   Explain how romantic relationships and sexual behavior change during emerging adulthood.

9.19   Explain how emerging adults use the Internet to maintain social contacts.

EMOTIONAL AND SOCIAL DEVELOPMENT: Emotional and Self-Development

Emerging adulthood is a period when emotional and self-development turn more favorable in a variety of ways. After declining in adolescence, self-esteem now rises steadily. Identity development advances and reaches fruition in some ways, as young people move toward making enduring choices in love and work. Gender issues are confronted in new ways as emerging adults enter the workplace and encounter occupational gender expectations and sometimes gender stereotypes.

Self-Esteem

LO 9.11   **Describe the course of self-esteem from adolescence through emerging adulthood, and explain the reasons for this pattern.**

Think for a moment: how is your self-esteem today different from your self-esteem as an adolescent? As described in the previous chapter, self-esteem often declines during early adolescence. However, for most people it rises during emerging adulthood (Galambos et al., 2006; McLean & Breen, 2015). **Figure 9.10** shows this pattern.

There are a number of reasons why self-esteem increases during emerging adulthood. Physical appearance is important to adolescents' self-esteem, but by emerging adulthood most people have passed through the awkward changes of puberty and may be more comfortable with how they look. Also, feeling accepted and approved by parents contributes to self-esteem, and from adolescence to emerging adulthood, relationships with parents generally improve, while conflict diminishes (Arnett, 2015a, b; Fingerman & Yahurin, 2015; Galambos et al., 2006). Peers and friends are also important to self-esteem, and entering emerging adulthood means leaving the social pressure cooker of secondary school, where peer evaluations are a part of daily life and can be harsh (Gavin & Furman, 1989; Pascoe, 2007).

Also, reaching emerging adulthood usually means having more control over the social contexts of everyday life, which makes it possible for emerging adults to seek out the contexts they prefer and avoid the contexts they find disagreeable, in a way that adolescents cannot. For example, adolescents who dislike school and do poorly have little choice but to attend school, where poor grades may repeatedly undermine their self-esteem. However, emerging adults can leave school and instead engage in full-time work that they may find more gratifying and enjoyable, thus enhancing their self-esteem.

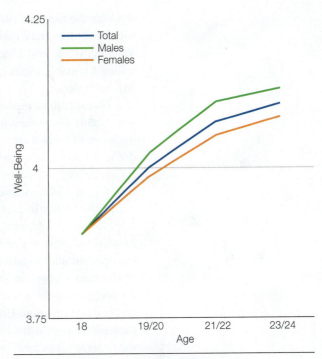

Figure 9.10 Changes in Self-Esteem

Why does self-esteem rise during the emerging adult years?
SOURCE: Johnston, L. D., O'Malley, P. M., & Bachman, J. G. (2003)

Identity Development

LO 9.12 Describe the various forms identity development can take in emerging adulthood, and consider patterns of cultural and ethnic identity.

As noted previously, a key feature of emerging adulthood is that it is the age of identity explorations. Emerging adulthood is when most people move toward making definite, long-term choices in love and work. Making these choices often involves thinking about who you are, where you want your life to go, what you believe in, and how your life fits into the world around you. During this time, explorations are made into various aspects of identity, especially love and work, culminating in commitments that set the foundation for adult life.

It is now generally accepted among scholars that emerging adulthood is the life stage when many of the most important steps in identity development take place (Côté, 2006; Luyckx, 2006; Schacter, 2005; Schwartz, 2015). However, for most of the history of research on identity, the focus was on adolescence. This focus was due mainly to Erik Erikson's influence, as we will explain shortly, but it is also because adolescence was formerly the life stage when the main choices in love and work were made. We'll first consider Erikson's theory and traditional research on identity development in adolescence and then discuss the more recent turn to identity development in emerging adulthood.

ERIK ERIKSON'S THEORY In Erikson's (1950) theory of development, each stage of life has a central crisis, and in adolescence the crisis is **identity versus identity confusion**. The healthy path in adolescence involves establishing a clear and definite sense of who you are and how you fit into the world around you. The unhealthy alternative is identity confusion, which is a failure to form a stable and secure identity. Identity formation involves reflecting on what your traits, abilities, and interests are, then sifting

identity versus identity confusion

in Erikson's theory, the crisis of adolescence, with two alternative paths, establishing a clear and definite identity, or experiencing identity confusion, which is a failure to form a stable and secure identity through the range of life choices available in your culture, trying out various possibilities, and ultimately making commitments. The key areas in which identity is formed are love, work, and ideology (beliefs and values) (Erikson, 1968). In Erikson's view, a failure to establish commitments in these areas by the end of adolescence reflects identity confusion.

There are three elements essential to developing an identity according to Erikson. First, adolescents assess their own abilities and interests. By this age, most people have a growing sense of what their strengths and weaknesses are and what they most and least enjoy doing. Second, adolescents reflect on the *identifications* they have accumulated in childhood (Erikson, 1968). Children *identify* with their parents and other loved ones as they grow up—that is, children love and admire them and want to be like them. Thus, adolescents create an identity in part by modeling themselves after parents, friends, and others they have loved in childhood, not simply by imitating them but by integrating parts of their loved ones' behavior and attitudes into their own personality. Third, adolescents assess the opportunities available to them in their society. Many dream of a fabulous career in sports, music, or entertainment (Schneider, 2009), yet there are relatively few opportunities for people to make a living in these areas. Sometimes opportunities are restricted as a result of discrimination. Until fairly recently, women were discouraged or even barred from professions such as medicine and law. Today, ethnic minorities in many societies find that the doors to many professions are barred to them. In every society, adolescents need to take into account not only what they would like to do but what adults will allow them to do.

Erikson's most influential interpreter has been James Marcia (Marcia, 1966, 1980, 1989, 1999, 2010; Marcia & Carpendale, 2004). Marcia constructed a measure called the Identity Status Interview that classified adolescents into one of four identity statuses: *diffusion, moratorium, foreclosure,* or *achievement*. This system of four categories, known as the **identity status model**, has also been used by scholars who have constructed questionnaires to investigate identity development rather than using Marcia's interview (e.g., Adams, 1999; Benson et al., 1992; Grotevant & Adams, 1984; Kroger, 2007).

As shown in **Table 9.1**, each of these classifications involves a different combination of exploration and commitment. Erikson (1968) used the term *identity crisis* to describe the process through which young people construct their identity, but Marcia and other current scholars prefer the term *exploration* (Kroger, 2007; Marcia & Carpendale, 2004; Waterman, 2007). "Crisis" implies that the process inherently involves anguish and struggle, whereas "exploration" implies a more positive investigation of possibilities.

Diffusion is an identity status that combines no exploration with no commitment. For adolescents in a state of identity diffusion, no commitments have been made among the choices available to them. Furthermore, no exploration is taking place. The person in this status is not seriously attempting to sort through potential choices and make enduring commitments.

Moratorium involves exploration but no commitment. This is a status of actively trying out different personal, occupational, and ideological possibilities. Different possibilities are being sifted through, with some being discarded and some selected, for adolescents to be able to determine which of the available possibilities are best suited to them.

Adolescents who are in the *foreclosure* status have not experimented with a range of possibilities but have nevertheless committed themselves to certain choices—commitment, but no exploration. This is often a result of their parents' strong influence. Marcia and most other scholars tend to see exploration as a necessary part of forming a healthy identity, and therefore see foreclosure as unhealthy. This is an issue we will discuss further shortly.

Finally, the classification that combines exploration and commitment is *achievement*. Identity achievement is the status of young people who have made definite personal, occupational, and ideological choices. By definition, identity achievement is preceded by a period of identity moratorium in which exploration takes place. If commitment

identity status model

model for researching Erikson's theory of identity development, classifying identity development into four categories: diffusion, foreclosure, moratorium, or achievement

Table 9.1 The Four Identity Statuses

		Commitment	
		Yes	**No**
Exploration	**Yes**	Achievement	Moratorium
	No	Foreclosure	Diffusion

takes place without exploration, it is considered identity foreclosure rather than identity achievement.

Although Erikson designated adolescence as the stage of the identity crisis, and research using Marcia's model has mostly focused on adolescence, studies indicate that it takes longer than scholars had expected to reach identity achievement, and in fact for most young people this status is reached—if at all—in emerging adulthood or beyond rather than in adolescence. Studies that have compared adolescents from ages 12 through 18 have found that although the proportion of adolescents in the diffusion category decreases with age and the proportion of adolescents in the achievement category increases, even by early emerging adulthood less than half are classified as having reached identity achievement (Kroger, 2003; Meeus et al., 1999; van Hoof, 1999; Waterman, 1999).

Studies of college students find that progress toward identity achievement also takes place during the college years, but mainly in the specific area of occupational identity rather than for identity more generally (Waterman, 1992). Some studies indicate that identity achievement may come faster for emerging adults who do not attend college, perhaps because the college environment tends to be a place where young people's ideas about themselves are challenged and they are encouraged to question previously held ideas (Lytle et al., 1997; Munro & Adams, 1997). However, for noncollege emerging adults as well, the majority has not reached identity achievement by age 21 (Kroger et al., 2010; Waterman, 1999).

Even 50 years ago, Erikson observed that identity formation was taking longer and longer for young people in developed countries. He commented on the "prolonged adolescence" that was becoming increasingly common in such countries and how this was leading to a prolonged period of identity formation, "during which the young adult through free role experimentation may find a niche in some section of his society" (1968, p. 156). Considering the changes that have taken place since he made this observation in the 1960s, including much later ages of marriage and parenthood and longer education, Erikson's observation applies to far more young people today than it did then (Schwartz et al., 2014). Indeed, the conception of emerging adulthood as a distinct period of life is based to a considerable extent on the fact that, over recent decades, the late teens and early 20s have become a period of "free role experimentation" for an increasing proportion of young people (Arnett, 2000, 2004, 2015a, b). The achievement of an adult identity comes later, compared with previous generations because many emerging adults use the years of their late teens and 20s for identity explorations in love, work, and ideology.

CULTURE AND IDENTITY Most of the research inspired by Erikson's theory has taken place among White middle-class adolescents in the United States, Canada, and Europe (Schwartz et al., 2014). What can we say about identity development among adolescents and emerging adults in other cultures? One observation that can be made is that although Erikson sought to ground his theory in historical and cultural context (Erikson, 1950, 1968; Kroger, 2002), his discussion of identity development nevertheless assumes an independent self that is allowed to make free choices in love, work, and ideology. The focus of Erikson's identity theory is on how young people develop an understanding of themselves as unique individuals. However, as we have discussed in earlier chapters, this conception of the self is distinctively Western and is historically recent (Markus & Kitiyama, 1991; Shweder et al., 2006). In most cultures, until recently, the self has been understood as *interdependent*, defined in relation to others, rather than as independent. Even today, Erikson's assertions of the prominence of identity issues in adolescence may apply more to modern Western adolescents than to adolescents

In most cultures through history, young people have been expected to believe what their parents believe, not to decide on their own beliefs. Here, a young Israeli man prays.

in other cultures. For example, explorations in love are clearly limited or even nonexistent in cultures in which dating is not allowed and marriages are either arranged by parents or strongly influenced by them. Explorations in work are limited in cultures where the economy is simple and offers only a limited range of choices.

Limitations on explorations in both love and work tend to be narrower for girls in developing countries than they are for boys. With regard to love, some degree of sexual experimentation is encouraged for adolescent boys in most cultures, but for girls sexual experimentation is more likely to be restricted or forbidden (Schlegel, 2010). With regard to work, in most traditional cultures today and for most of human history in every culture, adolescent girls have been designated by their cultures for the roles of wife and mother, and these were essentially the only choices open to them.

In terms of ideology, too, a psychosocial moratorium has been the exception in human cultures rather than the standard. In most cultures, young people have been expected to grow up to believe what adults teach them to believe, without questioning it. It is only in recent history, and mainly in Western developed countries, that these expectations have changed, and that it has come to be seen as desirable for adolescents and emerging adults to think for themselves, decide on their own beliefs, and make their life choices independently (Arnett, 1998; Bellah et al., 1985).

Another identity issue that has important cultural dimensions is how globalization influences identity, especially for adolescents and emerging adults (Arnett, 2002; 2011). Because of globalization, more young people around the world now develop a **bicultural identity**, with one part of their identity rooted in their local culture, whereas another part stems from an awareness of their relation to the global culture. For example, India has a growing, vigorous high-tech economic sector, led largely by young people. However, even the better-educated young people, who have become full-fledged members of the global economy, still mostly prefer to have an arranged marriage, in accordance with Indian tradition (Chaudhary & Sharma, 2012). They also generally expect to care for their parents in old age, again in accordance with Indian tradition. Thus, they have one identity for participating in the global economy and succeeding in the fast-paced world of high technology, and another identity, rooted in Indian tradition, that they maintain with respect to their families and their personal lives.

ETHNIC IDENTITY In addition to the complex identity issues that arise as a consequence of globalization, many people experience the challenge of growing up as a member of an ethnic minority group. In fact, more people than ever experience this challenge, as worldwide immigration has climbed to unprecedented levels in recent decades (Berry et al., 2006; Phinney, 2006).

Like other identity issues, issues of ethnic identity come to the forefront in adolescence and continue to grow in importance into emerging adulthood (Pahl & Way, 2006; Syed & Mitchell, 2015). As part of their growing cognitive capacity for self-reflection, adolescents and emerging adults who are members of ethnic minorities are likely to have a sharpened awareness of what it means for them to be a member of their minority group. Bicultural identities such as *African American*, *Chinese Canadian*, and *Turkish Dutch* take on a new meaning, as adolescents and emerging adults can now think about what these terms mean and how the term for their ethnic group applies to themselves. Also, as a consequence of their growing capacity to think about what others think about them, adolescents and emerging adults become more acutely aware of the prejudices and stereotypes about their ethnic group that others may hold.

For emerging adults, ethnic identity issues are likely to take on a greater prominence as they enter new social contexts such as college and the workplace, and as they meet a broader range of people from different ethnic backgrounds (Phinney, 2006). As children and adolescents they may have been mostly around people of their own ethnic group, but emerging adulthood is likely to take them into new contexts with greater ethnic diversity, sharpening their awareness of their ethnic identity (Syed & Azmitia, 2010). For example,

bicultural identity

identity with two distinct facets, for example one for the local culture and one for the global culture, or one within one's ethnic group and one for others

when you entered your college environment it is likely that you came into contact with persons from a greater variety of ethnic backgrounds than you had known previously.

Because adolescents and emerging adults who are members of ethnic minorities have to confront ethnic identity issues, their identity development is likely to be more complex than for those who are part of the majority culture (Phinney, 2000, 2006; Syed & Mitchell, 2015). Consider, for example, identity development in the area of love. Love—along with dating and sex—is an area where cultural conflicts are especially likely to come up for adolescents and emerging adults who are members of ethnic minorities. For example, part of identity development in the U.S. majority culture means trying out different possibilities in love by forming emotionally intimate relationships with different people and gaining sexual experience. However, this model is in sharp conflict with the values of certain U.S. ethnic minority groups. In most Asian American groups, for example, recreational dating is disapproved of and sexual experimentation before marriage is taboo—especially for females (Qin, 2009; Talbani & Hasanali, 2000). Young people in Asian American ethnic groups face a challenge in reconciling the values of their ethnic group on such issues with the values of the majority culture, to which they are inevitably exposed through school, the media, and peers.

How, then, does identity development take place for young people who are members of minority groups within Western societies? To what extent do they develop an identity that reflects the values of the majority culture, and to what extent do they retain the values of their minority group? One scholar who has done extensive work on these questions among American minorities is Jean Phinney (Phinney, 1990, 2000, 2006, 2010; Phinney & Devich-Navarro, 1997). On the basis of her research, Phinney has concluded that young people who are members of minority groups have four different ways of responding to their awareness of their ethnicity (see **Table 9.2**).

Assimilation is the option that involves leaving behind the ways of one's ethnic group and adopting the values and way of life of the majority culture. This is the path that is reflected in the idea that a society is a "melting pot" that blends people of diverse origins into one national culture. *Marginality* involves rejecting one's culture of origin but also feeling rejected by the majority culture. Some young people may feel little identification with the culture of their parents and grandparents, nor do they feel accepted and integrated into the larger society. *Separation* is the approach that involves associating only with members of one's own ethnic group and rejecting the ways of the majority culture. *Biculturalism* involves developing a dual identity, one based in the ethnic group of origin and one based in the majority culture. Being bicultural means moving back and forth between the ethnic culture and the majority culture, and alternating identities as appropriate to the situation.

Which of these identity statuses is most common among ethnic minorities? Although ethnic identity is potentially most prominent in emerging adulthood (Phinney, 2006),

Table 9.2 Four Ethnic Identity Statuses

		Identification with Ethnic Group	
		High	**Low**
Identification with Majority Culture	**High**	Bicultural	Assimilated
	Low	Separated	Marginal

Examples:

Assimilation: "I don't really think of myself as Asian American, just as American."

Separation: "I am not part of two cultures. I am just Black."

Marginality: "When I'm with my Indian friends, I feel White, and when I'm with my White friends, I feel Indian. I don't really feel like I belong with either of them."

Biculturalism: "Being both Mexican and American means having the best of both worlds. You have different strengths you can draw from in different situations."

SOURCE: Based on Phinney & Devich-Navarro (1997)

Biculturalism means developing a dual identity, one for the ethnic culture and one for the majority culture.

most research thus far has taken place on adolescents. The bicultural status is the most common status among Mexican Americans and Asian Americans, as well as among some European minority groups such as Turkish adolescents in the Netherlands (Neto, 2002; Rotheram-Borus, 1990; Phinney, Dupont, et al., 1994; Verkuyten, 2002). However, separation is the most common ethnic identity status among African American adolescents, and marginality is pervasive among American Indian adolescents. Of course, each ethnic group is diverse and contains adolescents with a variety of different ethnic identity statuses. Adolescents tend to be more aware of their ethnic identity when they are in a context where they are in the minority. For example, in one study, Latino adolescents attending a predominately non-Latino school reported significantly higher levels of ethnic identity than adolescents in a predominately Latino or a balanced Latino/non-Latino school (Umaña-Taylor, 2005).

Is ethnic identity related to other aspects of development in adolescence and emerging adulthood? Some studies have found that adolescents who are bicultural or assimilated have higher self-esteem (e.g., Farver et al., 2002). Furthermore, several studies have found that having a strong ethnic identity is related to a variety of other favorable aspects of development, such as overall well-being, academic achievement, and lower rates of risk behavior (Giang & Wittig, 2006; St. Louis & Liem, 2005; Syed & Mitchell, 2015; Yasui et al., 2004).

Gender Development: Cultural Beliefs and Stereotypes

LO 9.13 Summarize findings from research on gender stereotypes among college students.

Emerging adulthood is an important time for gender development because this is the life stage when many people become involved full time in the workplace. Consequently, they may encounter more vividly during this stage their society's beliefs about gender in relation to occupational roles and aspirations.

What sort of cultural beliefs about gender exist for adolescents and emerging adults currently growing up in U.S. society? Given the differential gender socialization that people in U.S. society experience in childhood and adolescence, it should not be surprising to find that by the time they reach emerging adulthood, they have different expectations for males and females (Norona et al., 2015). Most research on gender expectations in adulthood has been conducted by social psychologists, and because social psychologists often use college undergraduates as their research participants, much of this research pertains to emerging adults' views of gender. Social psychologists have especially focused on gender stereotypes. A **stereotype** occurs when people believe others possess certain characteristics simply as a result of being a member of a particular group. Gender stereotypes, then, attribute certain characteristics to others on the basis of whether they are male or female (Kite et al., 2008).

One area of particular interest with regard to emerging adulthood is research on college students' gender stereotypes involving work and roles at home. Generally, this research indicates that college students often evaluate women's work performance less favorably than men's. Studies in the United States and Canada indicate that college students' attitudes are changing (Gere & Helwig, 2012), but some stereotypes persist. In one classic study, college women were asked to evaluate the quality of several articles supposedly written by professionals in a variety of fields (Goldberg, 1968). Some of the

stereotype

belief that others possess certain characteristics simply as a result of being a member of a particular group

articles were in stereotypically female fields such as dietetics, some were in stereotypically male fields such as city planning, and some were in gender-neutral fields. There were two identical versions of each article, one supposedly written by, for example, "John McKay" and the other written by "Joan McKay." The results indicated that the women rated the articles more highly when they thought a man was the author. Even articles in the "female" fields were judged as better when written by a man. Other studies have found similar results with samples of both male and female college students (Cejka & Eagly, 1999; Paludi & Strayer, 1985). Recent studies have continued to find strong gender stereotypes related to work (Cabrera et al., 2009; Johnson et al., 2008; White & White, 2006). Although not all studies have found a tendency for men's work to be evaluated more favorably, when differences are found they tend to favor men.

Would you assume a female mechanic would be less competent than a male mechanic? Gender stereotypes related to work remain strong.

One study reported that gender stereotypes can be especially harsh for persons who have high status in gender-incongruent occupations, for example a woman who has become head of an engineering department (Brescoll et al., 2010). College students were asked to read vignettes describing a leader's successful performance or mistakes in gender-congruent or gender-incongruent professions, then evaluate the leader's competence. Leaders who made mistakes in gender-incongruent professions were rated as lowest in competence.

Gender-related evaluations may also depend on the age of the evaluator. One study compared males who were early adolescents, late adolescents, or college students (Lobel et al., 2004). Participants were given a description of either an average or outstanding male election candidate behaving gender-stereotypically or counter-stereotypically and were asked to indicate their personal election choice, to estimate the likelihood that others would choose each candidate, and to speculate how successful the candidate would be if he were elected. Adolescents were more likely than the emerging adult college students to favor the gender-stereotypical candidate. No differences were found between the two stages of adolescence. This suggests that gender stereotypes may wane from adolescence to emerging adulthood.

EMOTIONAL AND SOCIAL DEVELOPMENT: Cultural Beliefs

Children and adolescents learn the cultural beliefs distinctive to their culture, and by emerging adulthood they have developed a worldview composed of these beliefs. However, beliefs continue to develop during emerging adulthood and beyond. In emerging adulthood there are notable developments in religious and political beliefs and behavior.

Religious Development

LO 9.14 **Summarize Smith and Snell's description of the religious beliefs and practices of U.S. emerging adults.**

A landmark study by Christian Smith and Patricia Snell went into greater depth and detail than previous studies on religious development among American emerging adults (Smith & Snell, 2010). The study included survey data on more than 2,500 emerging adults (ages 18–23) in 37 states; 250 participants were interviewed. Most of the emerging adults in the study had been included in Smith's previous study of adolescents' religious development 5 years prior.

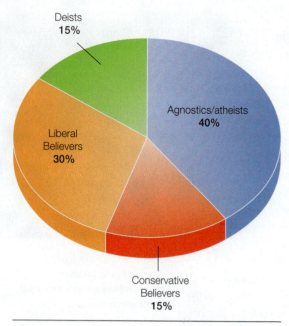

Figure 9.11 The Four Categories of Religious Beliefs

Overall, there was a decline in religiosity from adolescence to emerging adulthood, both in behavior and in beliefs. Only about 30 percent of emerging adults attended religious services at least once a month; over half attended only a few times a year or less. Beliefs were stronger than behavior; 44 percent reported that religious faith is "very" or "extremely" important in their lives, and 75 percent reported believing in God. Nevertheless, these percentages were lower than they had been in adolescence.

Just as in adolescence, in emerging adulthood religious beliefs were highly individualized. Few emerging adults accepted a standard religious doctrine; instead, they adopted a make-your-own approach to their religious beliefs, constructed partly from what they had learned from their parents but also from many other sources. Consequently, religious denomination did not hold much meaning for most of them. They could state they were "Catholic" or "Presbyterian" or "Jewish" without actually believing much of what is stated in the traditional doctrine of that faith and without participating in it. In fact, 38 percent of "Protestants" and 35 percent of "Catholics" reported that they *never* attend religious services. This individualized approach to religion led to great religious diversity in emerging adulthood, which can be classified into four categories, listed here from least to most religious: agnostics/atheists, deists, liberal believers, and conservative believers (see **Figure 9.11**).

Just as in adolescence, religious faith in emerging adulthood tends to be associated with a variety of positive characteristics. Smith and Snell (2010) found religious belief and participation among emerging adults to be related to higher well-being and lower rates of participation in a variety of types of risk behavior. Another study, comparing African American and White emerging adults, reported that African Americans were more likely to cope with stress by relying on their religious beliefs, and in turn they experienced fewer anxiety symptoms than White emerging adults did (Chapman & Steger, 2010). This is consistent with studies in other age periods showing that African Americans tend to be more religious than Whites are (Dilworth-Anderson et al., 2007).

Political Development

LO 9.15 Explain why emerging adults have often been at the forefront of political movements rather than conventional politics.

In most countries, 18 is the age when people first receive the right to vote, so political development might be expected to be an important issue in emerging adulthood. However, political involvement tends to be very low among emerging adults (Núñez & Flanagan, 2015). In Europe, as well as in Canada and the United States, emerging adults' political participation is strikingly low by conventional measures such as voting rates and involvement in political parties (Barrio et al., 2007; Botcheva et al., 2007; Meeus, 2007; Sears et al., 2007). Emerging adults tend to have lower political participation not only in comparison to adults, but also in comparison to previous generations of young people. They tend to be skeptical of the motivations of politicians, and to see the activities of political parties as irrelevant to their lives. One study of young people in eight European countries found that low levels of trust in political authorities and political systems were consistent from adolescence through emerging adulthood (Hooghe & Wilkenfeld, 2008).

However, the rejection of conventional politics should not be construed as a lack of interest in improving the state of their communities, their societies, and the world. On the contrary, emerging adults in many countries are more likely than older adults to be involved in organizations devoted to particular issues, such as environmental protection and efforts against war and racism (Goossens & Luyckx, 2007; Meeus, 2007; Núñez & Flanagan, 2015). In one nationwide survey of college freshmen in the United States, only 28 percent said they were interested in politics, but 81 percent had done volunteer work, and 45 percent had participated in a political demonstration (Kellogg, 2001). Emerging adulthood is also the time when people in the United States are mostly likely to devote a year or two of their lives to volunteer programs such as the Peace Corps, Americorps, and Teach for America (Arnett, 2015a, b). Often frustrated by conventional political processes, emerging adults choose instead to direct their energies toward specific areas of importance to them, where they believe they are more likely to see genuine progress.

EMERGING ADULTS AND POLITICAL MOVEMENTS Furthermore, emerging adults have often been involved in movements at the political extremes, including protests, revolutionary movements, and terrorism. The leaders of politically extreme groups are usually in midlife or later, but many of their most zealous followers are often emerging adults. There are many recent historical examples of this. The Cultural Revolution that took place in China from 1966 to 1975 and involved massive destruction and violence toward anyone deemed to be a threat to the "purity" of Chinese communism was instigated by Chairman Mao and his wife Jiang Ching, but it was carried out almost entirely by fervent Chinese emerging adults (MacFarquhar & Schoenhals, 2006). Terrorist attacks by Muslim extremists against Western (especially U.S.) targets—most notably the attacks of September 11, 2001—have been planned by older men but executed almost entirely by young men in the 18- to 29-age range (Sen & Samad, 2007).

These examples involve destruction and violence, but emerging adults have also been prominent in peaceful political movements. For example, when the collapse of communism began in eastern Europe in 1989, it was initiated by emerging adults through strikes, demonstrations, and the formation of new youth-oriented political parties (Botcheva et al., 2007; Flanagan & Botcheva, 1999; Macek, 2007). Recent protests against governments in the Middle East have also involved emerging adults more than any other age group (Barber, 2013).

Why are emerging adults especially likely to be involved in extreme political movements? One reason is that they have fewer social ties and obligations than people in other age periods (Arnett, 2005a). Children and adolescents can be restrained from involvement by their parents. Young, middle, and older adults can be deterred from involvement by their commitments to others who depend on them, especially a spouse and children. However, emerging adulthood is a time when social commitments and social control are at their low point. Emerging adults have more freedom than people at other age periods, and this freedom allows some of them to become involved in extreme political movements.

Another possibility is that their involvement is identity-related. As we have seen, one aspect of identity explorations is ideology or worldview (Arnett, 2015a, b; Erikson, 1968). Emerging adulthood is a time when people are looking for an ideological framework for explaining the world, and some emerging adults may be attracted to the definite answers provided by extreme political movements. Embracing an extreme political ideology may relieve the discomfort that can accompany the uncertainty and doubt of ideological explorations. Still, these explanations raise the question, since only a small minority of emerging adults are involved in these extreme movements: why them and not the others?

GLOBALIZATION AND POLITICAL IDENTITY
Globalization brings changes in ecocultural settings that

Emerging adults have often been at the forefront of political movements. Here, emerging adults participate in anti-government protests in Tahrir Square in Cairo, Egypt. Demonstrations such as this led to the peaceful overthrow of the government in 2011.

include opportunities for education, work, and social interaction. For emerging adults, globalization has also brought new opportunities for civic engagement, including political action (Jensen et al., 2012). How does globalization increase the likelihood that emerging adults will be more likely to be involved in these movements? Easy access to media and a worldview that frames emerging adults as independent and having their own wherewithal to change the world are part of the answer. The recent "Arab Spring" and events in Egypt's Tahrir Square were instigated by emerging adults, in large part because of their use of social media like Facebook, Twitter, and YouTube. What are the factors of globalization that appeal to emerging adults and affect their participation in political movements? Increases in communication, especially via the Internet, have had a major impact. Not only are people able to communicate with each other almost instantaneously, but they are also able to communicate with thousands or even millions of people at a time. With the mobility of people in education, work, and through migration, people are exposed to different ideas and possibilities about how to live in the world. There have also been shifts in values toward democracy, capitalism, and a sense that youth have the ability to make changes in their environments or situations (Jensen et al., 2012). Some consequences of all these factors include bicultural or even multicultural identity, and perhaps the development of a sense of the self as a "global citizen."

EMOTIONAL AND SOCIAL DEVELOPMENT: The Social and Cultural Contexts of Emerging Adulthood

Emerging adulthood is a life stage in which sociocultural contexts change in some profound and dramatic ways. After living within a family context from infancy through adolescence, emerging adults in many countries move out of their parents' household, diminishing their parents' influence and giving them more control over their daily lives. Friends are highly important, especially for emerging adults who are currently without a romantic relationship. Romantic relationships take on new importance, as intimacy deepens and emerging adults move toward making an enduring commitment to a love partner. Media remain a source of entertainment and enjoyment, especially new media such as the Internet and mobile phones.

Family Relationships

LO 9.16 Describe patterns of home-leaving in the United States and Europe and how this transition influences relations with parents.

In most Western majority cultures, most young people move out of their parents' home sometime during emerging adulthood. The most common reasons for leaving home stated by emerging adults are going to college, cohabiting with a partner, or simply the desire for independence (Goldscheider & Goldscheider, 1999; Seiffge-Krenke, 2009).

Typically, relationships between parents and emerging adults improve once the young person leaves home. In this case, at least, absence makes the heart grow fonder. Numerous studies have confirmed that emerging adults report greater closeness and fewer negative feelings toward their parents after moving out (Aquilino, 2006; Arnett & Schwab, 2012, 2013; Fingerman & Yahirun, 2015). Furthermore, emerging adults who move out tend to get along better with their parents than those who remain at home. For example, in one study of 21-year-old adults, those who had moved at least an hour away (by car) from their parents reported the highest levels of closeness to their parents and valued their parents' opinions most highly (Dubas & Petersen, 1996). Emerging adults who remained at home had the poorest relations with their parents, and those who had moved out but remained within an hour's drive were in between the other two groups.

What explains these patterns? Some scholars have suggested that leaving home leads young people to appreciate their parents more (Arnett, 2015a, b; Katchadourian & Boli, 1985). Another factor may be that it is easier to be fond of someone you no longer live with. Once emerging adults move out, they no longer experience the day-to-day friction with their parents that inevitably results from living with others. They can now control the frequency and timing of their interactions with their parents in a way they could not when they were living with them. They can visit their parents for the weekend, for a holiday, or for dinner, enjoy the time together, and still maintain full control over their daily lives. As a 24-year-old woman in Jeff's research put it, "I don't have to talk to them when I don't want to, and when I want to, I can" (Arnett, 2004, p. 49).

African American emerging adults often live at home with their families.

In the United States, although most emerging adults move out of their parents' home in their late teens, a substantial proportion (more than one third) stay home through their early 20s (Arnett & Schwab, 2012). Staying at home is more common among Latinos, African Americans, and Asian Americans than among White Americans. The reason for this is sometimes economic, especially for Latinos and African Americans, who have high rates of unemployment in emerging adulthood (Ayres, 2013). However, another important reason appears to be the greater emphasis on family closeness and interdependence in minority cultures, and less emphasis on being independent as a value in itself. For example, one emerging adult in Jeff's research (Arnett, 2004) lived with her Chinese American mother and Mexican American father throughout her college years at the University of California–Berkeley. She enjoyed the way staying home allowed her to remain in close contact with them. "I loved living at home. I respect my parents a lot, so being home with them was actually one of the things I liked to do most," she said. "Plus, it was free!" (Arnett, 2004, p. 54). For Latinos and Asian Americans, an additional reason for staying home is specific to young women, and concerns the high value placed on virginity before marriage.

About 40 percent of U.S. emerging adults "return to the nest" to live at least once after they leave (Arnett & Schwab, 2012). There are many reasons why emerging adults sometimes move home again (Goldscheider & Goldscheider, 1999). For those who left home for college, moving back home may be a way of bridging their transition to post-college life after they graduate or drop out. It gives them a chance to decide what to do next, be it graduate school, a job near home, or a job farther away. For those who left home for independence, some may feel that the glow of independence dims after a while as the freedom of doing what they want when they want becomes outweighed by the burden of taking care of a household and paying all their own bills. An early divorce or a period of military service are other reasons emerging adults give for returning home (Goldscheider & Goldscheider, 1999). Under these circumstances, too, coming home may be attractive to young people as a transition period, a chance to get back on their feet before they venture again into the world.

There are a number of possible outcomes when emerging adults move back home (Arnett, 2015a, b; Arnett & Schwab, 2013). For some, the return home is welcome and the transition is managed easily. A successful transition home is more likely if parents recognize the change in their children's maturity and treat them as adults rather than adolescents. For others, however, the return home is a bumpy transition. Parents may have

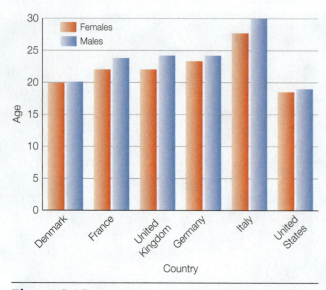

Figure 9.12 Median Age of Leaving Home in Europe Versus the United States

SOURCE: Based on Iacovov (2011)

come to enjoy having the nest all to themselves, without children to provide for and feel responsible for. Emerging adults may find it difficult to have parents monitoring them daily again, after a period when they had grown used to managing their own lives. Emerging adults may experience ambivalence when they move back home. They are grateful for the support their parents provide, even as they resent returning to the subordinate role of a dependent child. Perhaps because of this ambivalence, the return home tends to be brief, with two thirds of emerging adults moving out again within 1 year (Aquilino, 2006).

In European countries, emerging adults tend to live with their parents longer than in the United States, especially in southern and eastern Europe (Douglass, 2005, 2007; Kins et al., 2009). **Figure 9.12** shows the patterns in various European countries, as compared to the United States (Iacovov, 2011). There are a number of practical reasons why European emerging adults stay home longer. European university students are more likely than U.S. students to continue to live at home while they attend university. European emerging adults who do not attend university may have difficulty finding or affording an apartment of their own. However, also important are European cultural values that emphasize mutual support within the family while also allowing young people substantial autonomy. Italy provides a good case in point (Chisholm & Hurrelman, 1995; Krause, 2005). Ninety-four percent of Italians aged 15 to 24 live with their parents, the highest percentage in the European Union (EU), and many of them continue to live with their parents even into their late 20s and early 30s (Bonino & Cattelino, 2012). However, only 8 percent of them view their living arrangements as a problem—the lowest percentage among EU countries. Many European emerging adults remain at home contentedly through their early 20s, by choice rather than necessity.

There is more to the changes in relationships with parents from adolescence to emerging adulthood than simply the effects of moving out, staying home, or moving back in. Emerging adults also grow in their ability to understand their parents (Arnett, 2015a, b). Adolescence is in some ways an egocentric period, and adolescents often have difficulty taking their parents' perspectives. They sometimes evaluate their parents harshly, magnifying their deficiencies and becoming easily irritated by their imperfections. As emerging adults mature and begin to feel more adult themselves, they become more capable of understanding how their parents look at things. They come to see their parents as persons and begin to realize that their parents, like themselves, have a mix of qualities, merits as well as faults.

Friendships

LO 9.17 Describe the role of intimacy in emerging adults' friendships and the most common activities of emerging adult friends.

In a number of ways, friendships may be especially important in emerging adulthood (Barry et al., 2014). The majority of emerging adults move away from home and so lose the daily social support they may have received from their parents and siblings. Even for the ones who return home or remain home, they may rely less on their parents for social support as they strive toward becoming self-sufficient and making their own decisions (Arnett, 2015a, b). Consequently, they may turn more to friends than to parents for companionship and support.

As we have seen, intimacy becomes more important to friendships in adolescence than it had been in middle childhood, and that trend may continue into emerging adulthood. In one study (Radmacher & Azmitia, 2006), early adolescents (ages 12–13) and emerging adults (ages 18–20) described a time when they felt especially close to a friend. Emerging adults' accounts contained more self-disclosure and fewer shared activities, compared to early adolescents. Among the emerging adults (but not the early adolescents) there was a gender difference. Self-disclosure promoted emotional closeness for young women, whereas for young men shared activities were usually the basis of feeling emotional closeness.

What kinds of things do emerging adults do with their friends? Much of their time together is unstructured socializing (described previously in the chapter), in activities such as visiting each other informally and going out together. Some drink alcohol or use drugs together, and as we have seen, unstructured socializing and substance use often take place together (Osgood, 2009). Emerging adults also participate in media-related activities together, such as watching TV or playing electronic games (Brown, 2006). Many enjoy playing sports or exercising together (Malebo et al., 2007). Overall, leisure activities with friends decline steadily in the course of the 20s as emerging adults form close romantic relationships and begin to enter adult responsibilities such as stable work, marriage, and parenthood (Osgood, 2009).

CRITICAL THINKING QUESTION

What are some other reasons why leisure activities with friends might decline in the course of emerging adulthood, other than those mentioned here?

Love and Sexuality

LO 9.18 **Explain how romantic relationships and sexual behavior change during emerging adulthood.**

Emerging adulthood is a time of gradually building the structure of an adult life in love and work. In many cultures, explorations in love are part of this process, as emerging adults experience a series of romantic and sexual relationships in the course of deciding on a long-term partner.

IN SEARCH OF A SOUL MATE: FINDING A ROMANTIC PARTNER A key part of emerging adulthood involves moving away from one's family, not just geographically but socially and emotionally, and toward a new love partner, in marriage or another long-term romantic partnership. Jennifer Tanner (Tanner, 2006, 2015) calls this process "recentering." For children and adolescents, the center of their emotional lives is within their family, with their parents and siblings. For adults, the center of their emotional lives is usually with a new family constellation, mainly a romantic partner, and usually children as well. Emerging adulthood is when the change takes place, as the center of emotional life is transferred from the original family to a long-term romantic partner. Parents and siblings remain important, of course. As we have seen, relations with them even improve in many ways. But the center of emotional life usually moves to a romantic partner.

When they talk about what they are looking for in a romantic partner, emerging adults around the world mention a wide variety of ideal qualities (Gibbons & Stiles, 2004; Hatfield & Rapson, 2005). Sometimes these are qualities of the person, the individual: intelligent, attractive, or funny. But most often they mention interpersonal qualities, qualities a person brings to a relationship, such as kind, caring, loving, and trustworthy. Emerging adults hope to find someone who will treat them well and who will be capable of an intimate, mutually loving, durable relationship.

How do emerging adults find romantic partners? The increase in online dating sites like Match.com, grindr, and pinkcupid, as well as applications such as OkCupid and

Tinder reflects the widespread use of the internet for finding a partner. A recent Pew study found that 11 percent of Americans have used a dating site (Smith & Duggan, n.d.). Facebook is also used to find partners, and "relationship status" updates on Facebook reflect the prevailing use of technology in emerging adults' romantic partnerships (Fox & Warber, 2013).

In romantic relationships as in friendships, intimacy becomes more important in emerging adulthood than it had been in adolescence (Shulman & Connolly, 2014). One study investigated views of the functions of love relationships among early adolescents (6th grade), late adolescents (11th grade), and college students (Roscoe et al., 1987). The early and late adolescents both considered recreation to be the most important function, followed by intimacy, and then status. In contrast, for the college students intimacy ranked highest, followed by companionship, with recreation a bit lower, and status much lower. A more recent study reported similar results (Montgomery, 2005).

In addition to looking for intimacy, emerging adults also seek a romantic partner who will be like themselves in many ways (Shulman & Connolly, 2015). Opposites rarely attract; on the contrary, birds of a feather flock together. A long line of studies has established that emerging adults, like people of other ages, tend to have romantic relationships with people who are similar to themselves in characteristics such as personality, intelligence, social class, ethnic background, religious beliefs, and physical attractiveness (Furman & Simon, 2008; Markey & Markey, 2007). Scholars attribute this to what they call *consensual validation*, which means that people like to find in others a match, or *consensus*, with their own characteristics. Finding this consensus reaffirms, or *validates*, their own way of looking at the world. The more similar your love partner is to you, the more likely you are to reaffirm each other, and the less likely you are to have conflicts that spring from having different views and preferences.

COHABITATION For many emerging adults in the West, the next step after forming an exclusive, enduring relationship with a romantic partner is not marriage but moving in together. In the United States and Canada, as well as in northern European countries, **cohabitation** before marriage is now experienced by at least two-thirds of emerging adults (Manning, 2013). The percentage is highest in the Scandinavian countries, where nearly all young people cohabit before marriage (Syltevik, 2010). Cohabitation tends to be brief and unstable for young Americans. One study found that half of cohabiting relationships lasted less than a year, and only 1 in 10 couples were together 5 years later (Bumpass & Liu, 2000). In contrast, cohabiting couples in European countries tend to stay together as long as married couples (Hacker, 2002; Hymowitz et al., 2013).

However, in Europe there are distinct differences in cohabitation between north and south (Kiernan, 2002, 2004). Emerging adults in southern Europe are considerably less likely than their counterparts in the north to cohabit; most emerging adults in southern Europe live at home until marriage (Douglass, 2005), especially females. Perhaps because of the Catholic religious tradition in the south, cohabitation carries a moral stigma there that it does not have in the north. Cohabitation is also rare in Asian cultures, most of which have a long tradition of sexual conservatism and virginity at marriage.

Young people choose to cohabit sometimes for practical reasons—two together can live more cheaply than two separately—and sometimes because they wish to enhance the likelihood that when they marry, it will last. Indeed, in a national (U.S.) survey of 20- to 29-year-old adults, 62 percent agreed that "Living together with someone before marriage is a good way to avoid eventual divorce" (Popenoe & Whitehead, 2001). Emerging adults from divorced families are especially likely to cohabit, because they are especially determined to avoid their parents' fate (Cunningham & Thornton, 2007).

Although living together before marriage is motivated partly by the fear of divorce, the divorce rate is about the same for couples who cohabit and those who do not (Manning, 2013). This may be because cohabiting couples become used to living together

cohabitation

unmarried romantic partners living together

while maintaining separate lives in many ways, especially financially, so that they are unprepared for the compromises required by marriage. Also, even before entering cohabitation, emerging adults who cohabit tend to be different from emerging adults who do not, in ways that are related to higher risk of divorce—less religious, more skeptical of the institution of marriage, and more accepting of divorce (Hymowitz et al., 2013). However, one analysis concluded that cohabitation itself increases the risk of divorce because it leads some couples who are not compatible to marry anyway, out of "the inertia of cohabitation" (Stanley et al., 2006).

SEXUALITY In their sexual behavior as in other aspects of their lives, there is a great deal of diversity among emerging adults. The most common pattern among U.S. 18- to 23-year-old adults is to have had one partner in the past year (Lefkowitz, 2006; Regnerus & Uecker, 2011). However, emerging adults are more likely than adults in older age groups to have had either more or fewer sexual partners. About one third of 18- to- 23-year-old adults report having had two or more partners in the past year, but about one fourth report having had sex not at all in the past year (Regnerus & Uecker, 2011). At the beginning of emerging adulthood, age 18, about half of Americans have had intercourse at least once, and by age 25 nearly all emerging adults have had intercourse at least once, but those who have their first episode of intercourse relatively late tend to be "active abstainers" rather than "accidental abstainers" (Lefkowitz, 2006). That is, they remain virgins longer because they have chosen to wait rather than because they had no opportunity for sex. Common reasons for abstaining are fear of pregnancy, fear of sexually-transmitted infections (STIs), religious or moral beliefs, and the feeling one has not yet met the right person (Lefkowitz et al., 2004; Sprecher & Regan, 1996).

Sexual behavior in emerging adulthood most commonly takes place in the context of a close romantic relationship (Regnerus & Uecker, 2011). However, emerging adults are more likely than adults in older age groups to engage in recreational sex or "hooking up." Various studies indicate that about one fourth of sexual episodes among U.S. emerging adults takes place outside of a romantic partnership (Claxton & van Dulmen, 2015). Within U.S. ethnic groups, African American emerging adults are most likely to report casual sexual experiences, and Asian American emerging adults least likely (Regnerus & Uecker, 2011). Male emerging adults are more likely than females to have sexual attitudes that favor recreational sex. They tend to be more likely than females to be willing to have intercourse with someone they have known for only a few hours, to have sex with two different partners in the same day, and to have sex with someone they do not love (Knox et al., 2001).

Frequently, episodes of hooking up are fueled by alcohol. In various studies, from one fourth to one half of emerging adults report having consumed alcohol before their most recent sexual encounter (Lefkowitz, 2006), and emerging adults who drink often are more likely than others to have had multiple sexual partners (Regnerus & Uecker, 2011). The college environment is especially conducive to hooking up because it brings together so many emerging adults in a common setting that includes frequent social events that involve alcohol use.

Most U.S. emerging adults are quite responsible about contraceptive use, although certainly not all of them. Only about 10 percent of sexually active emerging adults report never using contraception, but an additional 35 percent of them report inconsistent or ineffective contraceptive use (Regnerus & Uecker, 2011). As a romantic relationship develops between emerging adults, they often move from condom use to oral contraceptives because they believe sex feels better without a condom or because

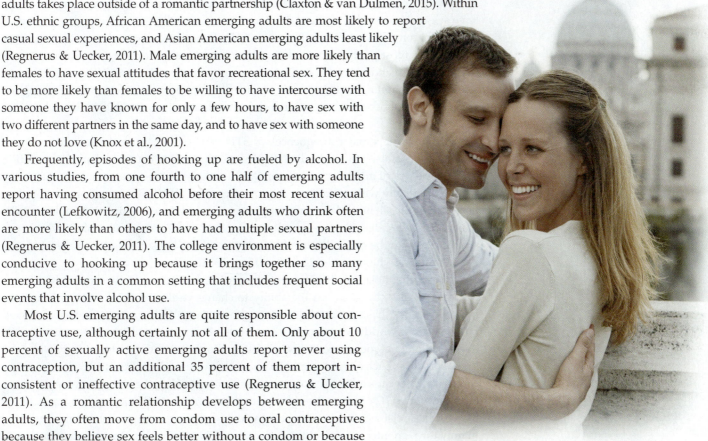

Premarital sex in emerging adulthood is accepted in some cultures and forbidden in others.

switching to oral contraceptives signifies a deeper level of trust and commitment (Hammer et al., 1996; Lefkowitz, 2006). A deeper commitment may mean that couples who used condoms switch to another form of contraception because they are less worried about STIs (Manlove et al., 2014).

Surveys have been conducted in numerous countries that demonstrate the wide variability in cultural approaches to premarital sexuality around the world (Hatfield & Rapson, 2005). Rates of premarital sex are somewhat lower in the countries of South America, although the large differences in reported premarital sex by male and female adolescents in countries such as Brazil and Chile suggest that males exaggerate their sexual activity or females underreport theirs (or both). Finally, premarital sex is least common in Asian and Middle Eastern countries, where the emphasis on female virginity before marriage is still very strong (Davis & Davis, 2012).

SEXUALLY TRANSMITTED INFECTIONS Emerging adults in Western countries may view sex as a normal and enjoyable part of life, but that does not mean it is unproblematic. The long period between the initiation of sexual activity in adolescence and the entry into marriage in young adulthood typically includes sex with a series of romantic partners as well as occasional episodes of hooking up, and in the course of these years unintended pregnancies are not unusual. Although responsible contraceptive use is the norm among emerging adults, inconsistent and ineffective use of contraception is common enough to make emerging adulthood the age period when both abortion and nonmarital childbirth are most common, across many countries (Claxton & van Dulmen, 2015; Hymowitz et al., 2013).

Emerging adulthood is also the peak period for sexually transmitted infections (STIs), including chlamydia, human papilloma virus (HPV), herpes simplex virus 2 (HSV-2), and HIV/AIDS. One half of STIs in the United States occur in people who are ages 15 to 24 (Centers for Disease Control [CDC], 2013c). Rates of STIs are higher in emerging adulthood than in any other life stage, in both the United States and Europe (Lehtinen et al., 2006).

Why are emerging adults particularly at risk for STIs? Although few emerging adults have sex with numerous partners, hooking up occasionally with a temporary partner is quite common (Claxton & van Dulmen, 2015). Even if sex takes place in a committed relationship, most youthful love relationships do not endure for long and partners eventually break up and move on. In this way, young people gain experience with love and sex and see what it is like to be involved with different people. Unfortunately, having sex with a variety of people, even within a series of relationships, carries with it a substantial risk for STIs.

The symptoms and consequences of STIs vary widely, from the merely annoying (pubic lice or "crabs") to the deadly (HIV/AIDS). Some STIs, such as chlamydia and HPV, increase the risk of infertility for women (Mills et al., 2006). Fortunately, chlamydia can be treated effectively with antibiotics. Also, a vaccine for HPV is now available, and public health advocates in many Western countries are vigorously promoting that adolescents be vaccinated before they become sexually active (Kahn, 2007; Woodhall et al., 2007). Herpes simplex 2 cannot be cured, but medications can relieve the symptoms and speed up the healing process when an episode occurs (King, 2005).

One of the most deadly diseases, HIV/AIDS, has proven to be extremely difficult to treat, because the virus has the ability to change itself and thus render medications ineffective. AIDS has been most devastating in southern Africa, where 10 of every 11 new HIV infections worldwide take place (see **Map 9.2**). Incidence of new HIV infections has decreased among young people worldwide in the past decade, due to a decline in risky sexual practices such as having multiple sexual partners (UNAIDS, 2010).

In recent years effective drug treatments for slowing the progress of AIDS have been developed. The cost of these drug treatments was initially extremely high, but now the cost has declined and the drugs are widely available even in developing countries, mainly through international aid organizations (UNAIDS, 2010). Prevention programs to

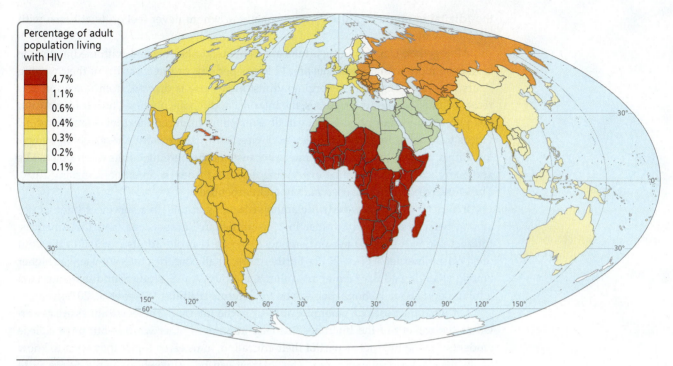

Map 9.2 HIV Population Worldwide, by Region

Which regions have the highest population of adults living with HIV? How might you explain these variations?

SOURCE: Based on UNAIDS, GAP Report (2014)

reduce HIV risk among emerging adults have now been conducted in many developing countries, and have been successful in changing young people's behavior to reduce their HIV risk (Ngongo et al., 2012).

Studies of risk-taking in sexual behavior in cultural groups within the United States reveal some similarities and some differences across ethnic groups. STI rates among ethnic minority youth ages 16 to 24 are 8 to 21 times higher than the rates for Whites in the same age group (Hock-Long et al., 2012). Latina and African American women present the highest rates of HPV (Tsubokura et al., 2008). Interestingly, however, regardless of ethnic group, college-age emerging adults are rather inconsistent in their condom use; they tend to use condoms only about 20 percent of the time, regardless of ethnic background (Thomas et al., 2015). There are also variations across ethnic groups in the ways that emerging adults experience perceived stigma of STIs, with Latina women perceiving higher stigma. And, the effectiveness of different kinds of interventions appears to vary across ethnic groups. African American emerging adult women tend to benefit the most from discourse skills training related to asking their male partners to use condoms (Jemmott et al., 2005). Skills training may prove effective for other ethnic groups as well. Researchers engaging in public health campaigns for decreasing STIs call for examination of cultural and geographic differences and suggest that we modify programs to account for cultural variations.

Media Use

LO 9.19 Explain how emerging adults use the Internet to maintain social contacts.

Media are a big part of the lives of today's emerging adults. They have grown up in a time of extraordinary innovation in the way media products are delivered and consumed (Coyne et al., 2015). Educator and writer Marc Prensky (2010) calls them "digital natives," entirely at home in the digital world from infancy onward, in contrast to the "digital immigrants," their parents, many of whom never feel quite at home with all the new media

All together, U.S. emerging adults are estimated to be engaged with media of some kind even more than adolescents are: 12 hours per day, or three fourths of their waking hours (Coyne et al., 2015). Emerging adults' media use is diverse, from television and recorded music to electronic games, the Internet, and mobile phones—which are now not just phones but smart phones that can do everything from send text messages to record videos to surf the Internet (Hundley & Shyles, 2010). There is little research on emerging adults' uses of television and music because most emerging adults do not own TVs and many take pride in getting everything they need from the Internet (Konstam, 2015). Therefore, research has focused mainly on Internet use.

Internet use is high worldwide among emerging adults. In a survey of Internet use among persons ages 18 and older in 13 countries in Europe, Asia, and the Americas, Internet use was over 80 percent among 18- to 24-year-old adults in all countries but one (World Internet Project, 2013). Furthermore, in all countries Internet use was higher among emerging adults than in any other age group. A U.S. study found that emerging adults spend about 3½ hours per day on the Internet (Padilla-Walker et al., 2010).

For what purposes do emerging adults use the Internet? The possibilities are as varied as the content of the Internet—virtually infinite, in other words—but most college students use the Internet as part of their education, to research topics they need to know about for courses (Selwyn, 2008). The Internet can be extremely valuable as a way to find information, but like other media forms, its effects can be negative at the extremes of use. One study of college students in the United Kingdom found a negative correlation between grade performance and hours per week spent online (Englander et al., 2010). Another study, of Chinese college students in eight universities, found that heavy Internet use (more than 15 hours a week) was related to poorer academic performance, as well as to symptoms of depression (Huang et al., 2009). The Internet is also sometimes misused for the purposes of academic cheating, for example downloading answers on a digital device during an exam (Mastin et al., 2009; Stephens et al., 2007).

The use of the Internet for social-networking is highly popular among emerging adults. Facebook—developed by and for college students—is by far the most popular social-networking web site, surpassing one billion members worldwide in 2012. Among 18- to 29-year-old adults in the United States, nearly 90 percent use social-networking web sites (as shown in **Figure 9.13**), the same rate as for teens and nearly twice the rate for persons age 30 and older (Duggan & Brenner, 2013). Other social networking applications like Instagram, Snapchat, and Twitter are quite popular among emerging adults.

Social-networking profiles are an arena for identity presentation and reflect the prominence of identity issues in emerging adulthood (Davis, 2010). That is, users make choices about how to present themselves on social networking sites, and their choices reflect their perceptions of who they are and how they want others to perceive them. For adolescents as well as emerging adults, social networking sites allow a space for "identity play," in which they try out different ways of presenting themselves in the course of deciding who they really are (Mazur & Kozarian, 2010).

Having a profile also allows users to maintain and expand their social networks. Emerging adults use the sites mainly to keep in touch with old friends and current friends and to make new ones (Ellison et al., 2007; Raacke & Bonds-Raacke, 2008). This function is especially important in emerging adulthood because emerging adults often leave home and the network of friends they formed in secondary school. Furthermore, emerging adults frequently change educational settings, jobs, and residences. Social-networking sites allow

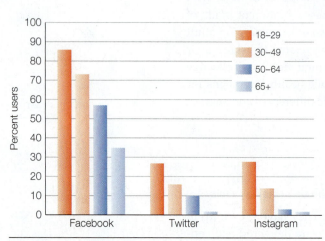

Figure 9.13 Social Media Use by Age

SOURCE: Based on Duggan & Brenner (2013).

them to keep in contact with the friends they leave behind as they move through emerging adulthood, and to make new friends in each new place (Subrahmanyam et al., 2008).

Increasingly, emerging adults may feel a kind of **parasocial attachment**—a one-way bond that an individual feels with others who may be on television (Cole & Leets, 1998) or on the Internet. These parasocial attachments are like the bonds that individuals feel with others in their day-to-day lives, except that the relationship is almost always entirely imagined. YouTube is increasingly popular site for building online communities among emerging adults that appears to result in the feelings of parasocial attachments. YouTubers post videos of themselves and others comment and engage in discussions about the posts. Sometimes YouTubers also engage online with their community, but not always. Emerging adults have reported positive feelings of warmth, caring, and loyalty for the YouTubers they follow (Cantwell, 2015).

Another common use of the Internet among emerging adults is to gain access to pornography. Although pornographic magazines and movies have existed for a long time, the invention of the Internet has made pornographic material much easier to obtain. In fact, of all the many uses of the Internet, the number-one use is accessing pornography, as measured by number of hits, number of web sites, or the amount of money spent (Young, 2008).

MOBILE PHONES Like the Internet, the pervasiveness and popularity of mobile phones has skyrocketed in the past decade, and like the Internet, mobile phones are especially popular among adolescents and emerging adults. For example, mobile phones are used by more than 90 percent of 18- to 24-year-old adults in Sweden (Axelsson, 2010). In the United States, 93 percent of 18- to 19-year-old adults own a mobile phone, a higher rate than in any other age group (Lenhart, 2010). Mobile phones are used by young people not only for calling someone and talking the way other phones have long been used, but also for text messaging. One U.S. study found that 18- to 29-year-old adults report sending and receiving more texts per day than any older age group (Taylor & Keeter, 2010).

Mobile phones resemble e-mail and social-networking web sites as a way for adolescents and emerging adults to remain in contact with each other when they are apart, virtually all day long. The social worlds of young people are no longer neatly divided into time with family and time with friends or at school. Rather, the new media allow the world of friends to be a nearly constant presence in their lives. The limited evidence so far indicates that young people enjoy the way the new media allow them to keep in touch with their friends. In one study in Italy, adolescents reported many of their happiest moments took place while communicating with friends on the Internet or using their mobile phones (Bassi & Antonella, 2004). A study of emerging adults in Sweden reported that they were in contact with friends and family throughout the day via texting (Axelsson, 2010). In a national study of U.S. 18- to 29-year-old adults, 51 percent agreed that "I rely a lot on the support I get from family and friends through e-mail, texting, and social networking web sites" (Arnett & Schwab, 2012).

Emerging adults who have moved out of their parents' household often use their mobile phones to keep in contact with their parents. In one study of U.S. college students, the students sent an average of 13 text messages a week to their parents (Hofer & Moore, 2010). Students valued texting as a way to keep in touch with their parents as they went about their busy days at school, allowing for parental support while also giving them room to run their own lives.

parasocial attachment
a one-way bond that an individual feels with others who may be on television or on the Internet

Texting allows emerging adults to keep in contact with family and friends all day long.

Cultural Focus: Media Use in Emerging Adulthood Across Cultures

All over the world, electronic media have become a big part of the daily lives of emerging adults. They use media to learn, to keep in contact with the people they care about, and to find new people who share their interests. In this video, emerging adults from various countries are interviewed about their media and technology use.

Watch   MEDIA USE IN EMERGING ADULTHOOD ACROSS CULTURES

Video

Review Question:

The U.S. emerging adult interviewed in this video mentions a heavy reliance on Facebook as a "tool" to stay connected. What are some other positive uses of Facebook and other social media? What are some negative aspects of social media use?

Summary: Emotional and Social Development

LO 9.11   Describe the course of self-esteem from adolescence through emerging adulthood, and explain the reasons for this pattern.

Self-esteem often rises for emerging adults because they have moved beyond some of the difficult issues of adolescence and they have more control over their lives.

LO 9.12   Describe the various forms identity development can take in emerging adulthood, and consider patterns of cultural and ethnic identity.

In the identity status model, James Marcia proposed four categories of identity development: diffusion, moratorium, foreclosure, and achievement. Research indicates that for most people identity achievement is not reached until emerging adulthood or beyond. Cultures influence identity development by the extent to which they allow or restrict their young people's opportunities to make choices in love and work. Today, globalization often influences the cultural context of identity development, resulting in bicultural

identities. For members of ethnic minorities, there are a variety of possible forms their ethnic identity may take, including assimilation, marginality, separation, and biculturalism.

LO 9.13   Summarize findings from research on gender stereotypes among college students.

Beliefs about gender roles have become less restrictive in U.S. society over the last half-century. However, gender stereotypes persist in occupational roles, in the expectations for men and women to perform different kinds of jobs, and in less favorable evaluations of women's work performance.

LO 9.14   Summarize Smith and Snell's description of the religious beliefs and practices of U.S. emerging adults.

Religious beliefs and practices decline in emerging adulthood, reaching their lowest point in the life span. Emerging adults tend to hold highly individualized religious beliefs rather than adhering to a traditional doctrine.

LO 9.15 **Explain why emerging adults have often been at the forefront of political movements rather than conventional politics.**

Political participation is low in emerging adulthood with respect to conventional measures such as voting. However, emerging adults are more likely than older adults to engage in volunteer work and to join extreme political movements because their ideological identity search and their lack of binding social commitments.

LO 9.16 **Describe patterns of home-leaving in the United States and Europe and how this transition influences relations with parents.**

Emerging adults in the United States and northern Europe usually move out of their parents' household at age 19 or 20 to live on their own or with a friend or romantic partner. In southern Europe, emerging adults usually remain at home for longer but enjoy doing so. Relations with parents often improve as emerging adults become better at taking their parents' perspectives.

LO 9.17 **Describe the role of intimacy in emerging adults' friendships and the most common activities of emerging adult friends.**

Friends are important to emerging adults, especially to those without a current romantic partner, and intimacy is more important to their friendships than it is in childhood or adolescence. Common activities among friends include unstructured socializing, which may involve alcohol use and media use. Activities with friends decline steadily during the 20s as emerging adults form stable romantic partnerships.

LO 9.18 **Explain how romantic relationships and sexual behavior change during emerging adulthood.**

Today's emerging adults often seek a "soul mate" who provides an ideal fit with their own identity. Cohabitation is now normative in most Western countries. In northern Europe cohabitation relationships are as enduring as marriages, but in the United States they typically dissolve within a year or two. Worldwide, emerging adults' premarital sexual behavior varies greatly across countries and cultures. STIs are more common in emerging adulthood than in any other age group, including chlamydia, HPV, herpes, and HIV/AIDS.

LO 9.19 **Explain how emerging adults use the Internet to maintain social contacts.**

Today's emerging adults are "digital natives," having grown up with the Internet, and they eagerly adopt new technologies such as mobile phones. Many emerging adults use the Internet for social networking.

Applying Your Knowledge as a Professional

The topics covered in this chapter apply to a wide variety of career professions. Watch these videos to learn how they apply to a director of career services, professor of sociology, director of a nonprofit for human trafficking victims, and a life science instructor.

Watch   CAREER FOCUS: DIRECTOR OF CAREER SERVICES

Video

Jason Eckert
Director, Career Services
University of Dayton

Chapter Quiz

1. In emerging adulthood, _____.
   a. rates of residential change in U.S. society are much higher at ages 18 to 29 than at any other period of life
   b. there is a sense of optimism about being able to "get where I want to be in life" among those from individualistic cultures, but not for those from collectivistic cultures
   c. the focus on self-exploration means that individuals are more egocentric than their adolescent counterparts
   d. the feeling "in-between" is unique to those in the United States and Canada because emerging adults in other cultures tend to remain at home, rather than moving out

2. Emerging adults who live in _____ would emphasize becoming capable of supporting parents financially as among the most important criteria for becoming an adult.
   a. Canada
   b. Japan
   c. the United States
   d. Europe

3. Which of the following is true of emerging adults' health?
   a. Most emerging adults experience an increased susceptibility to physical illness due to the increased stressors associated with this developmental period.
   b. For most sports, the peak age of performance comes during adolescence, and athletic abilities begin to decline in the early twenties.
   c. During emerging adulthood the immune system is weak.
   d. The heart is strong during emerging adulthood and reaction time is faster than at any other time of life.

4. Which of the following statements best summarizes the current research on sleep patterns of emerging adults?
   a. The research showing delayed sleep phase syndrome and sleep debt is based almost exclusively on low-income emerging adults who work full-time, rather than attending college.
   b. The preference of being a morning person versus a night person changes with age due to increased levels of cortisol.
   c. Sleep debt has negative consequences for both cognitive and emotional functioning.
   d. Students who stayed up all night before exams thought they did worse than their peers who got a full night's sleep.

5. Researchers who study young drivers have found that _____.
   a. increased parental monitoring does not reduce automobile accidents because adolescents spend so much time with their friends
   b. graduated driver licensing (GDL) is an excellent approach to reducing automobile accidents
   c. inexperience is the only factor found to be significantly correlated with accidents and fatalities
   d. the best way to reduce car accidents and fatalities is for parents to encourage their children to gain more experience driving with their friends who have taken driver's education and who will serve as role models for safe driving

6. Binge drinking _____.
   a. peaks in emerging adulthood in the United States, but not in Europe where adolescents are often allowed to drink alcohol with their meals
   b. has not been studied longitudinally because of the difficulty getting IRB approval to ask about alcohol use among high school students
   c. is highest among single mothers in their early 20s who do not go to college
   d. is more likely among emerging adults than those in other age groups because they spend more time in unstructured socializing

7. Dialectical thought _____.
   a. relies strictly on emotion in solving real-life problems
   b. has been found to characterize emerging adults in individualistic cultures more than those in collectivistic cultures
   c. refers to the need for explaining human actions in terms of logical principles
   d. involves the growing awareness that problems often have no clear-cut solutions

8. Reflective judgment _____.
   a. is a synonym for dualism
   b. increases over time for all emerging adults as a result of maturation, regardless of their educational background or the skills required in their job
   c. is more likely to characterize students in their first year of college than those in their senior year because first-year college students are more open to new ideas
   d. is more likely to develop in cultures that value pluralism

9. An emerging adult from _____ would be most likely to express the following sentiment upon first entering college: "In many ways, college is easier than high school; it's a relief to spend less time on homework and to have more time to explore my options."
   a. Canada
   b. Japan
   c. the United States
   d. Germany

10. Most emerging adults:
    a. continue to work in the kinds of jobs they did as teenagers
    b. will find one career and stick with it throughout their lives
    c. find a job on a career path, but switch jobs several times throughout emerging adulthood
    d. are unemployed

11. For most people, self-esteem _____.
    a. rises during emerging adulthood
    b. declines during emerging adulthood
    c. stays about the same as it was in adolescence
    d. declines during the first half of emerging adulthood and increases in later emerging adulthood

12. Which of the following ethnic identify statuses involves rejecting one's culture of origin but also feeling rejected by the majority culture?

   a. Assimilation
   b. Marginality
   c. Separation
   d. Biculturalism

13. Which of the following is true of gender-related evaluations of work?

   a. Generally, research indicates that college students often evaluate women's work performance more favorably than men's.
   b. College students evaluate work done by someone of their own gender higher than work done by someone of the opposite gender.
   c. Some studies have found that evaluations can be especially harsh when a person's behavior violates stereotypical gender expectations.
   d. Gender-related evaluations do not depend on characteristics of the evaluators, such as their age.

14. Which of the following best describes religious beliefs in emerging adulthood?

   a. There is an overall decline in religious behavior, but not religious beliefs from adolescence to emerging adulthood.
   b. Emerging adults are not tolerant of religious differences.
   c. In emerging adulthood, religious beliefs are highly individualized.
   d. Emerging adults place great emphasis on the religious doctrine of their faith.

15. Which of the following is true of emerging adults' political beliefs?

   a. Unlike their counterparts in Canada or Western Europe, emerging adults' political participation is very low in the United States.
   b. Emerging adults tend to see the activities of political parties as highly relevant to their lives.
   c. Emerging adults tend to be skeptical of the motivations of politicians.
   d. Emerging adults tend to have higher conventional political participation compared to previous generations of young people.

16. _____ are most likely to be living on their own rather than with their parents in their early 20s.

   a. Latinos
   b. African Americans
   c. White Americans
   d. Asian Americans

17. Leisure activities with friends _____.

   a. decline steadily in the course of the 20s
   b. decline for women, but not for men, in the course of the 20s
   c. increase slightly in the course of the 20s
   d. stay at about the same level in the course of the twenties as they were during adolescence

18. Male emerging adults are more likely than females to _____.

   a. have negative attitudes toward recreational sex
   b. suffer severe punishments if they have premarital sex
   c. be willing to have intercourse with someone they have known for only a few hours
   d. have sex only in the context of a close romantic relationship

19. Based on current research, which is a true statement about media use in emerging adulthood?

   a. In all countries, Internet use is higher among adolescents than among emerging adults because increased responsibilities among emerging adults reduce time they can spend online.
   b. Social networking profiles are a way for individuals to express their identity.
   c. Most emerging adults prefer face-to-face interactions to social contact via the Internet, and therefore the use of social networking has decreased in the past few years as the novelty has worn off.
   d. Cross-cultural research has shown that more women than men view pornography on the Internet.

Glossary

accommodation   cognitive process of changing a scheme to adapt to new information

active genotype → environment effects   in the theory of genotype → environment effects, the type that results when people seek out environments that correspond to their genotypic characteristics

activity settings   framework for analysis of interactions that includes personnel, tasks, goals, motives, and scripts

actual self   person's perception of the self as it is, contrasted with the possible self

adolescence   period of the life span between the time puberty begins and the time adult status is approached, when young people are preparing to take on the roles and responsibilities of adulthood in their culture

adolescent egocentrism   type of egocentrism in which adolescents have difficulty distinguishing their thinking about their own thoughts from their thinking about the thoughts of others

adolescent-limited delinquent (ALD)   delinquent who shows no evidence of problems before adolescence and whose delinquent behavior in adolescence is temporary

AIDS (acquired immune deficiency syndrome)   sexually transmitted infection caused by HIV, resulting in damage to the immune system

allele   on a pair of chromosomes, each of two forms of a gene

ambivalence   emotional state of experiencing two contradictory emotions at once

amniocentesis   prenatal procedure in which a needle is used to withdraw amniotic fluid containing fetal cells from the placenta, allowing possible prenatal problems to be detected

amnion   fluid-filled membrane that surrounds and protects the developing organism in the womb

androgens   sex hormones that have especially high levels in males from puberty onward and are mostly responsible for male primary and secondary sex characteristics

anemia   dietary deficiency of iron that causes problems such as fatigue, irritability, and attention difficulties

animism   tendency to attribute human thoughts and feelings to inanimate objects and forces

anorexia nervosa   eating disorder characterized by intentional self-starvation

anoxia   deprivation of oxygen during birth process and soon after that can result in serious neurological damage within minutes

Apgar scale   neonatal assessment scale with five subtests: Appearance (color), Pulse (heart rate), Grimace (reflex irritability), Activity (muscle tone), and Respiration (breathing)

apprenticeship   an arrangement, common in Europe, in which an adolescent "novice" serves under contract to a "master" who has substantial experience in a profession, and through working under the master, learns the skills required to enter the profession

artificial insemination   procedure of injecting sperm directly into the uterus

assimilation   cognitive process of altering new information to fit an existing scheme

assisted reproductive technologies (ART)   methods for overcoming infertility that include artificial insemination, fertility drugs, and IVF

asthma   chronic illness of the lungs characterized by wheezing, coughing, and shortness of breath

attachment theory   Bowlby's theory of emotional and social development, focusing on the crucial importance of the infant's relationship with the primary caregiver

attention-deficit/hyperactivity disorder (ADHD)   diagnosis that includes problems of inattention, hyperactivity, and impulsiveness

authoritarian parents   in classifications of parenting styles, parents who are high in demandingness but low in responsiveness

authoritative parents   in classifications of parenting styles, parents who are high in demandingness and high in responsiveness

autism spectrum disorder (ASD)   a range of developmental disorders marked by a lack of interest in social relations, abnormal language development, and repetitive behavior, appearing early in childhood

autonomy   quality of being independent and self-sufficient, capable of thinking for one's self

autonomy vs. shame and doubt   the second stage in Erikson's theory, characterized by the child's learning to do things independently or becoming doubtful about his or her own abilities

axon   part of a neuron that transmits electric impulses and releases neurotransmitters

babbling   repetitive prelanguage consonant–vowel combinations such as "ba-ba-ba" or "do-do-do-do," made by infants universally beginning at about 6 months old

Bayley Scales of Infant Development   widely used assessment of infant development from age 3 months to 3½ years

behavior genetics   field in the study of human development that aims to identify the extent to which genes influence behavior, primarily by comparing persons who share different amounts of their genes

bicultural identity   identity with two distinct facets, for example one for the local culture and one for the global culture, or one within one's ethnic group and one for others

bilingual   capable of using two languages

binge drinking   consuming five or more drinks in a row for men, four in a row for women

binocular vision   ability to combine the images of the two eyes into one image

blastocyst   ball of about 100 cells formed by about 1 week following conception

body mass index (BMI)   measure of the ratio of weight to height

bonding   concept that in humans the first few minutes and hours after birth are critical to mother–infant relationships

Brazelton Neonatal Behavioral Assessment Scale (NBAS)   27-item scale of neonatal functioning with overall ratings "worrisome," "normal," and "superior"

breech presentation   positioning of the fetus so that feet or buttocks, rather than the head, are positioned to come first out of the birth canal

Broca's area   portion of the left frontal lobe of the human brain that is specialized for language production

bulimia   eating disorder characterized by episodes of binge eating followed by purging (self-induced vomiting)

bullying   pattern of maltreatment of peers, including aggression; repetition; and power imbalance

cardiac output   quantity of blood flow from the heart

centration   Piaget's term for young children's thinking as being centered, or focused, on one noticeable aspect of a cognitive problem to the exclusion of other important aspects

cephalocaudal principle   principle of biological development that growth tends to begin at the top, with the head, and then proceeds downward to the rest of the body

cerebellum   structure at the base of the brain involved in balance and motor movements

cerebral cortex   outer portion of the brain, containing four regions with distinct functions

cesarean delivery, or c-section   type of birth in which mother's abdomen is cut open and fetus is retrieved directly from the uterus

child development   way people grow and change from conception through emerging adulthood; includes people's biological, cognitive, psychological, and social functioning

child maltreatment   abuse or neglect of children, including physical, emotional, or sexual abuse

chorionic villus sampling (CVS)   prenatal technique for diagnosing genetic problems, involving taking a sample of cells at 5 to 10 weeks gestation by inserting a tube into the uterus

chromosome   sausage-shaped structure in the nucleus of cells, containing genes, which are paired, except in reproductive cells

civilization   form of human social life, beginning about 5,000 years ago, that includes cities, writing, occupational specialization, and states

classification   ability to understand that objects can be part of more than one cognitive group, for example an object can be classified with red objects as well as with round objects

clique   small group of friends who know each other well, do things together, and form a regular social group

coercive cycle   pattern in relations between parents and children in which children's disobedient behavior evokes harsh responses from parents, which in turn makes children even more resistant to parental control, evoking even harsher responses

cognitive-developmental approach   focus on how cognitive abilities change with age in stage sequence of development, pioneered by Piaget and since taken up by other researchers

cohabitation   unmarried romantic partners living together

cohort effect   in scientific research, an explanation of group differences among people of different ages based on the fact that they grew up in different cohorts or historical periods

colic   infant crying pattern in which the crying goes on for more than 3 hours a day over more than 3 days at a time for more than 3 weeks

collectivistic   cultural values such as obedience and group harmony

colostrum   thick, yellowish liquid produced by mammalian mothers during the first days following birth, extremely rich in protein and antibodies that strengthen the baby's immune system

coming out   for homosexuals, the process of acknowledging their homosexuality and then disclosing the truth to their friends, family, and others

concordance rate   degree of similarity in phenotype among pairs of family members, expressed as a percentage

concrete operations   in Piaget's theory, the cognitive stage in which children become capable of using mental operations

conservation   mental ability to understand that the quantity of a substance or material remains the same even if its appearance changes

contexts   settings and circumstances that contribute to variations in pathways of human development, including SES, gender, and ethnicity, as well as family, school, community, media, and culture

conventional reasoning   second level in Kohlberg's theory of moral development, in which moral reasoning is based on the expectations of others

cooing   prelanguage "oo-ing" and "ah-ing," and gurgling sounds babies make beginning at about 2 months old

coregulation   relationship between parents and children in which parents provide broad guidelines for behavior but children are capable of a substantial amount of independent, self-directed behavior

corporal punishment   physical punishment of children

corpus callosum   band of neural fibers connecting the two hemispheres of the brain

correlation   statistical relationship between two variables such that knowing one of the variables makes it possible to predict the other

cosleeping   cultural practice in which infants and sometimes older children sleep with one or both parents

crossing over   at the outset of meiosis, the exchange of genetic material between paired chromosomes

cross-sectional research   research design that involves collecting data on a single occasion

crowd   large, reputation-based group of adolescents

cultural models   cognitive structures pertaining to common cultural activities

culture   total pattern of a group's customs, beliefs, art, and technology, transmitted through language

custom complex   distinctive cultural pattern of behavior that reflects underlying cultural beliefs

cyberbullying   bullying via electronic means, mainly through the Internet

cytoplasm   in an ovum, fluid that provides nutrients for the first 2 weeks of growth if the ovum is fertilized, until it reaches the uterus and begins drawing nutrients from the mother

deferred imitation   ability to repeat actions observed at an earlier time

delivery   second stage of the birth process, during which the fetus is pushed out of the cervix and through the birth canal

demandingness   degree to which parents set down rules and expectations for behavior and require their children to comply with them

dendrite   part of the neuron that receives neurotransmitters

dependent variable   in an experiment, the outcome that is measured to calculate the results of the experiment by comparing the experimental group to the control group

depressed mood   enduring period of sadness, without any other related symptoms of depression

depth perception   ability to discern the relative distance of objects in the environment

developed countries   world's most economically developed and affluent countries, with the highest median levels of income and education

developing countries   countries that have lower levels of income and education than developed countries but are experiencing rapid economic growth

developmental quotient (DQ)   in assessments of infant development, the overall score indicating developmental progress

dialectical thought   according to Basseches, a kind of thinking in emerging adulthood that involves a growing awareness that problems often have no clear solution and two opposing strategies or points of view may each have some merit

disengaged parents   in classifications of parenting styles, parents who are low in both demandingness and responsiveness

dishabituation   following habituation, the revival of attention when a new stimulus is presented

disorganized–disoriented attachment classification of parent–child attachment in which the child seems dazed and detached, with possible outbursts of anger, when the parent leaves the room, and exhibits fear on parent's return

displacement effect in media research, term for how media use occupies time that may have been spent on other activities

divided attention ability to focus on more than one task at a time

divorce mediation arrangement in which a professional mediator meets with divorcing parents to help them negotiate an agreement that both will find acceptable

dizygotic (DZ) twins twins that result when two ova are released by a female instead of one, and both are fertilized by sperm; also called *fraternal twins*

DNA (deoxyriboynucleic acid) long strand of cell material that stores and transfers genetic information in all life forms

dominant–recessive inheritance pattern of inheritance in which a pair of chromosomes contains one dominant and one recessive gene, but only the dominant gene is expressed in the phenotype

Down syndrome genetic disorder resulting from carrying an extra chromosome on the 21st pair

dyslexia learning disability that includes difficulty sounding out letters, difficulty learning to spell words, and a tendency to misperceive the order of letters in words

early intervention program program directed at young children who are at risk for later problems, intended to prevent problems from developing

ecocultural theory theory that emphasizes ecological and cultural aspects of the activities and settings of development

ecological framework Bronfenbrenner's theory that human development is shaped by five interrelated systems in the social environment

ectoderm in the embryonic period, the outer layer of cells, which will eventually become the skin, hair, nails, sensory organs, and nervous system (brain and spinal cord)

egocentrism cognitive inability to distinguish between one's own perspective and another person's perspective

elaboration mnemonic that involves transforming bits of information in a way that connects them and hence makes them easier to remember

electroencephalogram (EEG) device that measures the electrical activity of the cerebral cortex, allowing researchers to measure overall activity of the cerebral cortex as well as activation of specific parts

electronic fetal monitoring (EFM) method that tracks the fetus's heartbeat, either externally through the mother's abdomen or directly by running a wire through the cervix and placing a sensor on the fetus's scalp

embryonic disk in the blastocyst, the inner layer of cells, which will go on to form the embryo

embryonic period weeks 3–8 of prenatal development

emerging adulthood new life stage in developed countries, lasting from the late teens through the twenties, in which people are gradually making their way toward taking on adult responsibilities in love and work

emotional contagion in infants, crying in response to hearing another infant cry, evident beginning at just a few days old

emotional self-regulation ability to exercise control over one's emotions

empathy ability to understand and respond helpfully to another person's distress

endoderm in the embryonic period, the inner layer of cells, which will become the digestive system and the respiratory system

epidural during birth process, injection of an anesthetic drug into the spinal fluid to help the mother manage the pain while also remaining alert

epigenesis in development, the continuous bidirectional interactions between genes and environment

estradiol the estrogen most important in pubertal development among girls

estrogens sex hormones that have especially high levels in females from puberty onward and are mostly responsible for female primary and secondary sex characteristics

ethnicity group identity that may include components such as cultural origin, cultural traditions, race, religion, and language

ethnographic research research method that involves spending extensive time among the people being studied

ethology study of animal behavior

eveningness preference for going to bed late and waking up late

evocative genotype → environment effects in the theory of genotype → environment effects, the type that results when a person's inherited characteristics evoke responses from others in the environment

evolutionary psychology branch of psychology that examines how patterns of human functioning and behavior have resulted from adaptations to evolutionary conditions

executive function (EF) mental processes and control over them, including working memory, controlling one's attention, cognitive flexibility, and self-regulation

Experience Sampling Method (ESM) research method that involves having people wear beepers, usually for a period of 1 week; when they are beeped at random times during the day, they record a variety of characteristics of their experience at that moment

experimental research method research method that entails comparing an *experimental group* that receives a treatment of some kind to a *control group* that receives no treatment

experience-dependent brain functions brain functions that only develop with particular experiences that may be idiosyncratic to a particular infant

experience-expectant brain functions brain functions that require basic, expectable experiences to develop in a normal pattern

externalizing problems problems that involve others, such as aggression

extremely low birth weight term for neonates who weigh less than 2.2 pounds (1,000 grams) at birth

extrinsic motivation motivation to engage in behavior that is driven by external rewards or avoidance of punishment

false self self a person may present to others while realizing that it does not represent what he or she is actually thinking and feeling

familismo cultural belief among Latinos that emphasizes the love, closeness, and mutual obligations among family members

family process quality of the relationships between family members

fast mapping learning and remembering a word for an object after just one time of being told what the object is called

feared self person one imagines it is possible to become but dreads becoming

fetal alcohol spectrum disorder (FASD) set of problems that occur as a consequence of high maternal alcohol use during pregnancy, including facial deformities, heart problems, misshapen limbs, and a variety of cognitive problems

fetal period in prenatal development, the period from week 9 until birth

filial piety belief that children should respect, obey, and revere their parents throughout life; common in Asian cultures

fine motor development development of motor abilities involving finely tuned movements of the hands such as grasping and manipulating objects

Flynn effect steep rise in the median IQ score in Western countries during the 20th century, named after James Flynn, who first identified it

follicle during the female reproductive cycle, the ovum plus other cells that surround the ovum and provide nutrients

fontanels soft spots on the skull between loosely joined pieces of the skull that shift during the birth process to assist passage through the birth canal

formal operations in Piaget's theory, cognitive stage beginning at age 11 in which people learn to think systematically about possibilities and hypotheses

foster care for maltreated children, approach in which adults approved by a state agency take over the care of the child

functional magnetic resonance imaging (fMRI) method of monitoring brain activity in which a person lies inside a machine that uses a magnetic field to record changes in blood flow and oxygen use in the brain in response to different kinds of stimulation

gametes cells, distinctive to each sex, that are involved in reproduction (egg cells in the ovaries of the female and sperm in the testes of the male)

gender cultural categories of "male" and "female"

gender constancy understanding that maleness and femaleness are biological and cannot change

gender identity awareness of one's self as male or female

gender roles cultural expectations for appearance and behavior specific to males or females

gender schema gender-based cognitive structure for organizing and processing information, comprising expectations for males' and females' appearance and behavior

gender-intensification hypothesis hypothesis that psychological and behavioral differences between males and females become more pronounced at adolescence because of intensified socialization pressures to conform to culturally prescribed gender roles

gene segment of DNA containing coded instructions for the growth and functioning of the organism

genome entire store of an organism's hereditary information

genotype organism's unique genetic inheritance

germinal period first 2 weeks after conception

gestation in prenatal development, elapsed time since conception

gifted in IQ test performance, persons who score 130 or higher

globalization increasing connections between different parts of the world in trade, travel, migration, and communication

goodness-of-fit theoretical principle that children develop best if there is a good fit between the temperament of the child and environmental demands

graduated driver licensing (GDL) government program in which young people obtain driving privileges gradually, contingent on a safe driving record, rather than all at once

grammar a language's distinctive system of rules

gross motor development development of motor abilities including balance and posture as well as whole-body movements such as crawling

guided participation teaching interaction between two people (often an adult and a child) as they participate in a culturally valued activity

habituation gradual decrease in attention to a stimulus after repeated presentations

handedness preference for using either the right or left hand in gross and fine motor activities

heritability statistical estimate of the extent to which genes are responsible for the differences among persons within a specific population, with values ranging from 0 to 1.00

hippocampus structure involved in transfer of information from short-term to long-term memory

holophrase single word that is used to represent a whole sentence

Homo sapiens species of modern humans

homophobia fear and hatred of homosexuals

hominid evolutionary line that led to modern humans

hormones chemicals, produced in the body or given synthetically, that regulate physiological function

hostile aggression type of aggression that entails signs of anger and intent to inflict pain or harm on others

hunter-gatherer social and economic system in which economic life is based on hunting (mostly by males) and gathering edible plants (mostly by females)

hypothesis in the scientific process, a researcher's idea about one possible answer to the question proposed for investigation

hypothetical-deductive reasoning Piaget's term for the process of applying scientific thinking to cognitive tasks

ideal self person one would like to be

identity status model model for researching Erikson's theory of identity development, classifying identity development into four categories: diffusion, foreclosure, moratorium, or achievement

identity versus identity confusion in Erikson's theory, the crisis of adolescence, with two alternative paths, establishing a clear and definite identity, or experiencing identity confusion, which is a failure to form a stable and secure identity

imaginary audience belief that others are acutely aware of and attentive to one's appearance and behavior

imprinting instant and enduring bond to the first moving object seen after birth; common in birds

in vitro fertilization (IVF) form of infertility treatment that involves using drugs to stimulate the growth of multiple follicles in the ovaries, removing the follicles and combining them with sperm, then transferring the most promising zygotes to the uterus

inclusion educational practice where children with special needs learn in the main classroom with nondisabled children

incomplete dominance form of dominant–recessive inheritance in which the phenotype is influenced primarily by the dominant gene but also to some extent by the recessive gene

independent variable in an experiment, the variable that is different for the experimental group than for the control group

individual education plans (IEPs) plans developed by a teacher with a parent to help a child with special needs adjust to the school setting

individualistic cultural values such as independence and self-expression

industry versus inferiority Erikson's middle childhood stage, in which the alternatives are to learn to work effectively with cultural materials or, if adults are too critical, develop a sense of being incapable of working effectively

infant-directed (ID) speech special form of speech that adults in many cultures direct toward infants, in which the pitch of the voice becomes higher than in normal speech, the intonation is exaggerated, and words and phrases are repeated

infantile amnesia inability to remember anything that happened before age 2

infertility inability to attain pregnancy after at least a year of regular sexual intercourse

infinite generativity ability to take the word symbols of a language and combine them in a virtually infinite number of new ways

information-processing approach approach to understanding cognitive functioning that focuses on cognitive processes that exist at all ages, rather than on viewing cognitive developing in terms of discontinuous stages

informed consent standard procedure in social scientific studies that entails informing potential participants of what their participation would involve, including any possible risks, and giving them the opportunity to agree to participate or not

initiative vs. guilt in Erikson's lifespan theory, the early childhood stage in which the alternatives are learning to plan activities in a purposeful way, or being afflicted with excess guilt that undermines initiative

insecure–avoidant attachment classification of parent–child attachment in which there is relatively little interaction between them and the child shows little response to the parent's absence and may resist being picked up when the parent returns

insecure–resistant attachment classification of parent–child attachment in which the child shows little exploratory behavior when the parent is present, great distress when the parent leaves the room, and ambivalence on the parent's return

instrumental aggression type of aggression when a child wants something and uses aggressive behavior or words to get it

intellectual disability level of cognitive abilities of persons who score 70 or less on IQ tests

intelligence capacity for acquiring knowledge, reasoning, and solving problems

intelligence quotient (IQ) score of mental ability as assessed by intelligence tests, calculated relative to the performance of other people the same age

intermodal perception integration and coordination of information from the various senses

internalizing problems problems that entail turning distress inward, toward the self, such as depression and anxiety

intervention program intended to change the attitudes or behavior of the participants

intimacy degree to which two people share personal knowledge, thoughts, and feelings

intrinsic motivation motivation to engage in behavior that is driven by internal rewards

irreversibility lack of ability to reverse an action mentally

kangaroo care recommended care for preterm and low-birth-weight neonates, in which mothers or fathers are advised to place the baby skin-to-skin on their chests for 2 to 3 hours a day for the early weeks of life

kwashiorkor protein deficiency in childhood, leading to symptoms such as lethargy, irritability, thinning hair, and swollen body, which may be fatal if not treated

labor first stage of the birth process, in which the cervix dilates and the muscles of the uterus contract to push the fetus into the vagina toward the cervix

language acquisition device (LAD) according to Chomsky, innate feature of the brain that enables children to perceive and grasp quickly the grammatical rules in the language around them

lateralization specialization of functions in the two hemispheres of the brain

learning disability cognitive disorder that impedes the development of learning a specific skill such as reading or math

least restrictive environment (LRE) requirement that students with disabilities must have the opportunity to be educated with nondisabled peers to the extent possible

let-down reflex in females, a reflex that causes milk to be released to the tip of the nipples in response to the sound of an infant's cry, seeing its open mouth, or even thinking about breast feeding

life-course-persistent delinquent (LCPD) delinquent who shows a pattern of problems from birth onward and whose problems continue into adulthood

longitudinal research research design in which the same persons are followed over time and data are collected on two or more occasions

low birth weight term for neonates weighing less than 5.5 pounds (2,500 grams)

major depressive disorder clinical diagnosis that includes a range of specific symptoms such as depressed mood, appetite disturbances, sleeping disturbances, and fatigue

majority culture within a country, the cultural group that sets most of the norms and standards and holds most of the positions of political, economic, intellectual, and media power

marasmus disease in which the body wastes away from lack of nutrients

maturation concept that an innate, biologically based program is the driving force behind development

media multitasking simultaneous use of more than one media form, such as playing an electronic game while watching TV

median in a distribution of data, the score that is precisely in the middle, with half the distribution lying above and half below

meiosis process by which gametes are generated, through separation and duplication of chromosome pairs, ending in four new gametes from the original cell, each with half the number of chromosomes of the original cell

menarche first menstrual period

mental representations Piaget's final stage of sensorimotor development in which toddlers first think about the range of possibilities and then select the action most likely to achieve the desired outcome

mental structure in Piaget's theory of cognitive development, the cognitive systems that organize thinking into coherent patterns

mesoderm in the embryonic period, the middle of the three cell layers, which will become the muscles, bones, reproductive system, and circulatory system

metacognition capacity to think about thinking

metalinguistic skills in the understanding of language, skills that reflect awareness of the underlying structure of language

metamemory understanding of how memory works

microculture within a country, groups whose members share characteristics such as ethnicity, religion, or language

micronutrients dietary ingredients essential to optimal physical growth, including iodine, iron, zinc, and vitamins A, B12, C, and D

midwife person who assists in pregnant women's prenatal care and the birth process

mitosis process of cell replication in which the chromosomes duplicate themselves and the cell divides into two cells, each with the same number of chromosomes as the original cell

mnemonics memory strategies, such as rehearsal, organization, and elaboration

monozygotic (MZ) twins twins who have exactly the same genotype; also called *identical twins*

morningness   preference for going to bed early and waking up early

Moro reflex   reflex in response to a sensation of falling backward or to a loud sound, in which the neonate arches its back, flings out its arms, and then brings its arms quickly together in an embrace

multilingual   capable of using three or more languages

myelination   process of the growth of the myelin sheath around the axon of a neuron

myopia   visual condition of being unable to see distant objects clearly; also known as being *nearsighted*

natural childbirth   approach to childbirth that avoids medical technologies and interventions

natural experiment   situation that exists naturally but provides interesting scientific information

natural selection   evolutionary process in which the offspring best adapted to their environment survive to produce offspring of their own

nature–nurture debate   debate among scholars as to whether human development is influenced mainly by genes (nature) or environment (nurture)

neonatal jaundice   yellowish pallor common in the first few days of life due to immaturity of the liver

neonate   newborn baby, up to 4 weeks old

Neolithic period   era of human history from 10,000 to 5,000 years ago, when animals and plants were first domesticated

neural tube   in the embryonic period, the part of the ectoderm that will become the spinal cord and brain

neuron   cell of the nervous system

neurotransmitter   chemical that enables neurons to communicate across synapses

normal distribution   typical distribution of characteristics of a population, resembling a bell curve in which most cases fall near the middle and the proportions decrease at the low and high extremes

numeracy   understanding of the meaning of numbers

object permanence   awareness that objects (including people) continue to exist even when we are not in direct sensory or motor contact with them

obesity   in children, defined as having a BMI higher than the 95th percentile for age

obstetrics   field of medicine that focuses on prenatal care and birth

only child   child who has no siblings

opposable thumb   position of the thumb apart from the fingers, unique to humans, that makes possible fine motor movements

oral rehydration therapy (ORT)   treatment for infant diarrhea that involves drinking a solution of salt and glucose mixed with clean water

organization   mnemonic that involves placing things mentally into meaningful categories

overcontrol   trait of having excessive emotional self-regulation

overextension   use of a single word to represent a variety of related objects

overproduction or exuberance   burst in the production of dendritic connections between neurons

overregularization   applying grammatical rules even to words that are exceptions to the rule

overweight   in children, defined as having a BMI higher than the 85th percentile for age

ovum   mature egg that develops in ovaries, about every 28 days in human females

oxytocin   hormone released by pituitary gland that causes labor to begin

parasocial attachment   a one-way bond that an individual feels with others who may be on television

parental monitoring   actions parents take to keep track of their children's behavior and whereabouts

parenting styles   practices that parents exhibit in relation to their children and their beliefs about those practices

passive genotype → environment effects   in the theory of genotype → environment effects, the type that results from the fact that in a biological family, parents provide both genes and environment to their children

peer-review   in scientific research, the system of having other scientists review a manuscript to judge its merits and worthiness for publication

peers   persons who share some aspect of their status in common, such as age

permissive culture   culture that encourages and expects sexual activity from their adolescents

permissive parents   in classifications of parenting styles, parents who are low in demandingness and high in responsiveness

personal fable   belief in one's personal uniqueness, often including a sense of invulnerability to the consequences of taking risks

phenotype   organism's actual characteristics, derived from its genotype

phonics approach   method of teaching reading that advocates breaking down words into their component sounds, called *phonics*, then putting the phonics together into words

placenta   in the womb, gatekeeper between mother and fetus, protecting the fetus from bacteria and wastes in the mother's blood, and producing hormones that maintain the blood in the uterine lining and cause the mother's breasts to produce milk

plasticicty   degree to which development can be influenced by environmental circumstances

polygenic inheritance   expression of phenotypic characteristics as a result of the interaction of multiple genes

polygyny   cultural tradition in which men have more than one wife

population   in research, the entire category of people represented by a sample

possible self   person's conceptions of the self as it potentially may be; may include both an ideal self and a feared self

postconventional reasoning   third level in Kohlberg's theory of moral development, in which moral reasoning is based on the individual's own independent judgments rather than on what others view as wrong or right

postformal thought   according to some theorists, the stage of cognitive development that follows formal operations and includes advances in pragmatism and reflective judgment

postpartum depression   in parents with a new baby, feelings of sadness and anxiety so intense as to interfere with the ability to carry out simple daily tasks

pragmatics   social and cultural context of language that guides people as to what is appropriate to say and not to say in a given social situation

pragmatism   theory of cognitive development proposing that postformal thinking involves adapting logical thinking to the practical constraints of real-life situations

preconventional reasoning   first level in Kohlberg's theory of moral development, in which moral reasoning is based on perceptions of the likelihood of external rewards and punishments

preoperational stage   cognitive stage from age 2 to 7 during which the child becomes capable of representing the world symbolically—for example, through the use of language—but is still limited in ability to use mental operations

preterm babies born at 37 weeks gestation or less

primary attachment figure person who is sought out when a child experiences some kind of distress or threat in the environment

primary emotions basic emotions, such as anger, sadness, fear, disgust, surprise, and happiness

primary sex characteristics production of eggs (ova) and sperm and the development of the sex organs

private speech in Vygotsky's theory, self-guiding and self-directing comments children make to themselves as they learn in the zone of proximal development

procedure the way a study is conducted and the data are collected

prosocial behavior behavior intended to help or benefit others, including kindness, friendliness, and sharing

protective factors characteristics of young people that are related to lower likelihood of problems despite experiencing high-risk circumstances

proximodistal principle principle of biological development that growth proceeds from the middle of the body outward

psychological control parenting strategy that uses shame and withdrawal of love to influence children's behavior

psychosexual theory Freud's theory proposing that sexual desire is the driving force behind development

psychosocial theory Erikson's theory that human development is driven by the need to become integrated into the social and cultural environment

puberty changes in physiology, anatomy, and physical functioning that develop a person into a mature adult biologically and prepare the body for sexual reproduction

puberty ritual formal custom developed in many cultures to mark the departure from childhood and the entrance into adolescence

qualitative data that is collected in nonnumerical form

quantitative data that is collected in numerical form

rapid eye movement (REM) sleep phase of the sleep cycle in which a person's eyes move back and forth rapidly under the eyelids; persons in REM sleep experience other physiological changes as well

reaction range range of possible developmental paths established by genes; environment determines where development takes place within that range

reciprocal or bidirectional effects in relations between two persons, the principle that each of them affects the other

reflective judgment capacity to evaluate the accuracy and logical coherence of evidence and arguments, theorized to develop during emerging adulthood

reflex automatic response to certain kinds of stimulation

rehearsal mnemonic that involves repeating the same information over and over

relational aggression direct or indirect aggression and may involve damaging another person's relationships, reputation, or social status among peers

reliability in scientific research, the consistency of measurements across different occasions

research design plan for when and how to collect the data for a study

research method in the scientific process, the approach to investigating the hypothesis

resilience overcoming adverse environmental circumstances and achieving healthy development despite those circumstances

responsiveness degree to which parents are sensitive to their children's needs and express love, warmth, and concern for them

restrictive culture culture that places strong prohibitions on adolescent sexual activity before marriage

reticular formation part of the lower brain, involved in attention

rooting reflex reflex that causes the neonate to turn its head and open its mouth when it is touched on the cheek or the side of the mouth; helps the neonate find the breast

rote learning learning by memorization and repetition

ruminate to think persistently about bad feelings and experiences

sample subset of a population for which data are collected in a scientific study

scaffolding degree of assistance provided to the learner in the zone of proximal development, gradually decreasing as the learner's skills develop

schemes cognitive structures for processing, organizing, and interpreting information.

scientific method process of scientific investigation, involving a series of steps from identifying a research question through forming a hypothesis, selecting research methods and designs, collecting and analyzing data, and drawing conclusions

secondary emotions emotions that require social learning, such as embarrassment, shame, and guilt; also called sociomoral emotions

secondary school school attended during adolescence, after primary school

secondary sex characteristics bodily changes of puberty not directly related to reproduction

secular based on nonreligious beliefs and values

secular trend change in the characteristics of a population over time

secure attachment healthiest classification of parent–child attachment, in which the child uses the parent as a secure base from which to explore, protests when separated from parent, and is happy when the parent returns

secure base role of primary attachment figure, allows child to explore world while seeking comfort when threats arise

selective association in social relations, the principle that people tend to prefer being around others who are like themselves

selective attention ability to focus attention on relevant information and disregard what is irrelevant

self-concept person's perception and evaluation of himself or herself

self-esteem person's overall sense of worth and well-being

self-medication use of substances to relieve unpleasant emotional states

self-recognition ability to recognize one's image in the mirror as one's self

self-reflection capacity to think about one's self as one would think about other persons and objects

self-socialization process by which people seek to maintain consistency between their gender schemas and their behavior

semirestrictive culture culture that has prohibitions on premarital adolescent sex, but the prohibitions are not strongly enforced and are easily evaded

sensitive period in the course of development, a period when the capacity for learning in a specific area is especially pronounced

sensorimotor stage in Piaget's theory, the first 2 years of cognitive development, which involves learning how to coordinate the activities of the senses with motor activities

seriation ability to arrange things in a logical order, such as shortest to longest, thinnest to thickest, or lightest to darkest

sex biological status of being male or female

sex chromosomes chromosomes that determine whether an organism is male (XY) or female (XX)

sexual orientation a person's tendencies of sexual attraction

sexually transmitted infection (STI) infection transmitted through sexual contact

small for date term applied to neonates who weigh less than 90 percent of other neonates who were born at the same gestational age

social comparison how persons view themselves in relation to others with regard to status, abilities, or achievements

social control restraints on behavior imposed by social obligations and relationships

social referencing term for process of becoming more adept at observing others' emotional responses to ambiguous and uncertain situations, and using that information to shape one's own emotional responses

social skills behaviors that include being friendly, helpful, cooperative, and considerate

social smile expression of happiness in response to interacting with others, first appearing at age 2 to 3 months of age

social status within a group, the degree of power, authority, and influence that each person has in the view of the others

social information processing (SIP) in social encounters, evaluations of others' intentions, motivations, and behavior

socioeconomic status (SES) person's social class, including educational level, income level, and occupational status

sociomoral emotions emotions evoked based on learned, culturally based standards of right and wrong; also called secondary emotions

sound localization perceptual ability for telling where a sound is coming from

spermarche beginning of development of sperm in boys' testicles at puberty

state centralized political system that is an essential feature of a civilization

static reasoning the assumption held by young children that things in the world are only one way and do not change

statistical learning the ability to extract statistical regularities in information in the world

stereotype belief that others possess certain characteristics simply as a result of being a member of a particular group

Strange Situation laboratory assessment of attachment entailing a series of introductions, separations, and reunions involving the child, the mother, and an unfamiliar person

stranger anxiety fear in response to unfamiliar persons, usually evident in infants by age 6 months

sudden infant death syndrome (SIDS) death within the first year of life resulting from unknown reasons, with no apparent illness or disorder

surfactant substance in lungs that promotes breathing and keeps the air sacs in the lungs from collapsing

swaddling practice of infant care that involves wrapping an infant tightly in cloths or blankets

synaptic density density of synapses among neurons in the brain; peaks around age 3

synaptic pruning Process of reducing number of connections between neurons so that they become more efficient; process in

brain development in which dendritic connections that are used become stronger and faster and those that are unused wither away

telegraphic speech two-word phrases that strip away connecting words, such as the and and

temperament innate responses to the physical and social environment, including qualities of activity level, irritability, soothability, emotional reactivity, and sociability

teratogen behavior, environment, or bodily condition that can have damaging influence on prenatal development

tertiary education education or training beyond secondary school

testosterone the androgen most important in pubertal development among boys

theory framework that presents a set of interconnected ideas in an original way and inspires further research

theory of genotype → environment effects theory proposing that genes influence the kind of environment we experience

theory of mind ability to understand thinking processes in one's self and others

theory of multiple intelligences Gardner's theory that there are eight distinct types of intelligence

time out disciplinary strategy in which the child is required to sit still in a designated place for a brief period

total fertility rate (TFR) in a population, the number of births per woman

traditional culture a rural culture that adheres more closely to cultural traditions than people in urban areas; may be found in developing countries or rural areas of developed countries

transitive inference the ability to detect an unspoken relationship between two facts

triarchic theory of intelligence Sternberg's theory that there are three distinct but related forms of intelligence

trimester one of the three 3-month periods of prenatal development

trophoblast in the blastocyst, the outer layer of cells, which will go on to form structures that provide protection and nourishment to the embryo

trust-versus-mistrust in Erikson's psychosocial theory, the first stage of development, during infancy, in which the central crisis is the need to establish a stable attachment to a loving and nurturing caregiver

ultrasound machine that uses sound waves to produce images of the fetus during pregnancy

umbilical cord structure connecting the placenta to the mother's uterus

undercontrol trait of having inadequate emotional self-regulation

underextension applying a general word to a specific object

unemployment work status of adults who are not in school, are not working, and are looking for a job

unstructured socializing socializing with friends without any specific goal or activity; includes behavior such as riding around in a car for fun, going to parties, visiting friends informally, and going out with friends

Upper Paleolithic period period of human history from 40,000 to 10,000 years ago, when distinct human cultures first developed

validity in scientific research, the extent to which a research method measures what it claims to measure

vernix at birth, babies are covered with this oily, cheesy substance, which protects their skin from chapping in the womb

very low birth weight term for neonates who weigh less than 3.3 pounds (1,500 grams) at birth

VO2 max ability of the body to take in oxygen and transport it to various organs; also called *maximum oxygen uptake*

weaning cessation of breast feeding

Wernicke's area portion of the left temporal lobe of the human brain that is specialized for language comprehension

wet nursing cultural practice, common in human history, of hiring a lactating woman other than the mother to feed the infant

whole-language approach method of teaching reading in which the emphasis is on the meaning of written language in whole passages, rather than breaking down words into their smallest components

worldview set of cultural beliefs that explain what it means to be human, how human relations should be conducted, and how human problems should be addressed

X-linked inheritance pattern of inheritance in which a recessive characteristic is expressed because it is carried on the male's X chromosome

zone of proximal development difference between skills or tasks that children can accomplish alone and those they are capable of performing if guided by an adult or a more competent peer

zygote following fertilization, the new cell formed from the union of sperm and ovum

References

A special report on the human genome. (2010). *The Economist*. Retrieved from http://www.economist.com/node/16349358.

Abbott, S. (1992). Holding on and pushing away: Comparative perspectives on an eastern Kentucky child-rearing practice. *Ethos, 20*, 33–65.

Abdullah, A. S. M., Ming, C. Y., Seng, C. K., Ping, C. Y., Fai, C. K., Wing. F. Y., Man, H. W., Kei, H. B., Mun, W. Y., & Yee, W. M. (2003). Effects of a brief sexual education intervention of the knowledge and attitudes of Chinese public school students. *Journal of HIV/AIDS Prevention & Education for Adolescents & Children, 5*(3–4), 129–149. http://doi.org/10.1300/J129v05n03_07.

Abrahams, R. R., Kelly, S. A., Payne, S., Thiessen, P. N., Mackintosh, J., & Janssen, P. A. (2007). Rooming-in compared with standard care for newborns of mothers using methadone or heroin. *Canadian Family Physician, 53*(10), 1722–1730.

Abrejo, F. G., Shaikh, B. T., & Rizvi, N. (2009). And they kill me, only because I am a girl…a review of sex-selective abortions in South Asia. *European Journal of Contraception and Reproductive Health Care, 14*, 10–16.

Adams, G. R. (1999). *The objective measure of ego identity status: A manual on test theory and construction*. Guelph, Ontario, Canada: Author.

Adamson, L., & Frick, J. (2003). The still face: A history of a shared experimental paradigm. *Infancy, 4*, 451–473.

Adolph, K. E., & Berger, S. E. (2005). Physical and motor development. In M. H. Bornstein & M. E. Lamb (Eds.), *Developmental science: An advanced textbook* (5th ed., pp. 223–281). Mahwah, NJ: Lawrence Erlbaum.

Adolph, K. E., & Berger, S. E. (2006). Motor development. In W. Damon & R. Lerner (Series Eds.), & D. Kuhn & R. Siegler (Vol. Eds.), *Handbook of child psychology: Vol. 2. Cognition, perception and language* (6th ed., pp. 161–213). New York, NY: Wiley.

Adolph, K. E., Karasik, L. B., & Tamis-Lemonda, C. S. (2010). Motor skill. In M. H. Bornstein (Ed.), *Handbook of cultural developmental science* (pp. 61–88). New York, NY: Psychology Press.

Aikat, D. (2007). Violence, extent and responses to. In J. J. Arnett (Ed.), *Encyclopedia of children, adolescents, and the media* (Vol. 2, pp. 852–854). Thousand Oaks, CA: Sage.

Ainsworth, M. D. S. (1977). Infant development and mother–infant interaction among Ganda and American families. In P. H. Leiderman, S. R. Tulkin, & A. Rosenfeld (Eds.), *Culture and infancy: Variations in the human experience* (pp. 119–149). New York, NY: Academic Press.

Ainsworth, M. D. S., & Bell, S. M. (1969). Some contemporary patterns of mother–infant interaction in the feeding situation. In A. Ambrose (Ed.), *Stimulation in early infancy* (pp. 133–170). London, UK: Academic Press.

Ainsworth, M. D. S., Behar, M. C., Waters, E., & Wall, S. (1978). *Patterns of attachment: A psychological study of the strange situation*. Oxford, UK: Erlbaum.

Akhtar, N. (2005). Is joint attention necessary for early language learning? In B. D. Homer & C. S. Tamis-LeMonda (Eds.), *The development of social cognition and communication* (pp. 165–179). Mahwah, NJ: Lawrence Erlbaum.

Akhtar, N., & Tomasello, M. (2000). The social nature of words and word learning. In R. M. Golinkoff, K. Hirsh-Pasek, L. Bloom, L. B. Smith, A. L. Woodward, & N. Akhtar (Eds.), *Becoming a word learner: A debate on lexical acquisition* (pp. 115–135). New York, NY: Oxford University Press.

Akimoto, S. A., & Sanbonmatsu, D. M. (1999). Differences in self-effacing behavior between European and Japanese Americans: Effect on competence evaluations. *Journal of Cross-Cultural Psychology, 30*, 159–177.

Akinbami, L. J., & Schoendorf, K. C. (2002). Trends in childhood asthma: Prevalence, health care utilization, and mortality. *Pediatrics, 110*, 315–22.

Akshoomoff, N. A., Feroleto, C. C., Doyle, R. E., & Stiles, J. (2002). The impact of early unilateral brain injury on perceptual organization and visual memory. *Neuropsychologia, 40*, 539–561.

Alaggia, R., & Vine, C. (Eds.). (2006). *Cruel but not unusual: Violence in Canadian families*. Waterloo, Ontario, Canada: Wilfrid Laurier University Press.

Alberts, A., Elkind, D., & Ginsberg, S. (2007). The personal fable and risk-taking in early adolescence. *Journal of Youth and Adolescence, 36*, 71–76.

Aldridge, M. A., Stillman, R. D., & Bower, T. G. R. (2001). Newborn categorization of vowel-like sounds. *Developmental Science, 4*, 220–232.

Aldwin, C. M., & Spiro, A. III (2006). *Health, behavior, and optimal aging: A life span developmental perspective*. San Diego, CA: Academic Press.

Alexander, B. (2001, June). Radical idea serves youth, saves money. *Youth Today*, pp. 1, 42–44.

Alexander, G. M., & Hines, M. (2002). Sex differences in response to children's toys in nonhuman primates. *Evolution and Human Behavior, 23*, 467–479.

Alink, L. R. A., Mesman, J., van Zeijl, J., Stolk, M. N., Juffer, F., Koot, H. M.,…van IJzendoorn, M. H. (2006). The early childhood aggression curve: Development of physical aggression in 10- to 50-month-old children. *Child Development, 77*, 954–966.

Alloway, T. P. (2009). Working memory, but not IQ, predicts subsequent learning in children with learning difficulties. *European Journal of Psychological Assessment, 25*(2), 92–98. http://doi.org/10.1027/1015-5759.25.2.92.

Alloway, T. P., Alloway, R. G., & Wootan, S. (2014). Home sweet home: Does where you live matter to working memory and other cognitive skills? *Journal of Experimental Child Psychology, 124*, 124–131.

Alsaker, F. D., & Flammer, A. (2006). Pubertal maturation. In S. Jackson & L. Goossens (Eds.), *Handbook of adolescent development* (pp. 30–50). New York, NY: Psychology Press.

Alvarez, M. (2004). Caregiving and early infant crying in a Danish community. *Journal of Developmental and Behavioral Pediatrics, 25*, 91–98.

Alwin, D. F. (1988). From obedience to autonomy: Changes in traits desired in children, 1928–1978. *Public Opinion Quarterly, 52*, 33–52.

Amato, P. R. (2000). Diversity within single-parent families. In D. H. Demo, K. R. Allen, & M. A. Fine (Eds.), *Handbook of family diversity* (pp. 149–172). New York, NY: Oxford University Press.

Amato, P. R., & Anthony, C. J. (2014). Estimating the effects of parental divorce and death with fixed effects models. *Journal of Marriage and Family, 76*(2), 370–386.

Amato, P. R., & Boyd, L. M. (2013). Children and divorce in world perspective. Contemporary Issues in Family Studies: *Global Perspectives on Partnerships, Parenting and Support in a Changing World*, 227–243.

Amato, P. R., & Fowler, F. (2002). Parenting practices, child adjustment, and family diversity. *Journal of Marriage and the Family, 64*, 703–716.

American Academy of Pediatrics (AAP). (2001). *Toilet training*. Available: www.aap.org/family./toil.htm/

American Academy of Pediatrics (AAP). (2004). Management of hyperbilirubinemia in the newborn infant 35 or more weeks of gestation. *Pediatrics, 114,* 297–316. doi: 10.1542/peds.114.1.297.

American Academy of Pediatrics (AAP). (2005). Breastfeeding and the use of human milk: Policy statement. *Pediatrics, 115,* 496–506.

American Academy of Pediatrics Committee on Public Education. (2001). Children, adolescents, and television. *Pediatrics, 107,* 423–426.

American Academy of Pediatrics (AAP) Subcommittee on Attention-Deficit Hyperactivity Disorder. (2005). Treatment of attention-deficit hyperactivity disorder. *Pediatrics, 115,* e749–e757.

American Academy of Pediatrics (AAP) Task Force on Infant Positioning and SIDS (AAPTFIPS). (2000). Changing concepts of sudden infant death syndrome. *Pediatrics, 105,* 650–656.

American Academy of Pediatrics (AAP) Task Force on Sudden Infant Death Syndrome. (2011). SIDS and other sleep-related infant deaths: Expansion of recommendations for a safe infant sleeping environment. *Pediatrics, 128,* e1341–e1367.

American Psychiatric Association (APA). (2013). *Diagnostic and statistical manual of mental disorders* (5th ed.). Arlington, VA: American Psychiatric Association.

Ammaniti, M. A. S. S. I. M. O., Speranza, A. M., & Fedele, S. I. L. V. I. A. (2005). Attachment in infancy and in early and late childhood. *Attachment in middle childhood,* 115–136.

Anand, S., & Krosnick, J. A. (2005). Demographic predictors of media use among infants, toddlers, and preschoolers. *American Behavioral Scientist, 48*(5), 539–561.

Anders, T. F., & Taylor, T. (1994). Babies and their sleep environment. *Children's Environments, 11,* 123–134.

Anderson, C. A. (2004). An update on the effects of playing violent video games. *Journal of Adolescence, 27,* 113–122.

Anderson, C. A., Gentile, D. A., & Buckley, K. E. (2007). *Violent video game effects on children and adolescents: Theory, research, and public policy.* New York, NY: Oxford University Press.

Anderson, C. M. (2000). The persistence of polygyny as an adaptive response to poverty and oppression in apartheid South Africa. *Cross-cultural research, 34,* 99–112.

Anderson, D. R., Huston, A. C., Schmitt, K., Linebarger, D. L., & Wright, J. C. (2001). Early childhood viewing and adolescent behavior: The recontact study. *Monographs of the Society for Research in Child Development, 66*(1, Serial No. 264).

Anderson, P., & Butcher, K. (2006). Childhood obesity: Trends and potential causes. *The Future of Children, 16,* 19–45.

Anderson, V., & Jacobs, R. (Eds.). (2008). *Executive functions and the frontal lobes: A lifespan perspective.* Philadelphia, PA: Taylor & Francis.

Ando, M., Asakura, T., & Simons-Morton, B. (2005). Psychosocial influences in physical, verbal and indirect bullying among Japanese early adolescents. *Journal of Early Adolescence, 25,* 268–297.

Andrews, G., Halford, G., & Bunch, K. (2003). Theory of mind and relational complexity. *Child Development, 74,* 1476–1499.

Anglin, J. M. (1993). Vocabulary development: A morphological analysis. *Monographs of the Society for Research in Child Development, 58*(10, Serial No. 238).

Apgar, V. (1953). A proposal for a new method of evaluation of the newborn infant. *Current Researches in Anesthesia and Analgesia,* July–August, 260–267.

Appoh, L. Y. (2004). Consequences of early malnutrition for subsequent social and emotional behaviour of children in Ghana. *Journal of Psychology in Africa; South of the Sahara, the Caribbean, and Afro-Latin America, 14,* 87–94.

Appoh, L. Y., & Krekling, S. (2004). Effects of early childhood malnutrition on cognitive performance of Ghanaian children. *Journal of Psychology in Africa; South of the Sahara, the Caribbean, and Afro-Latin America, 14,* 1–7.

Apter, T. (1990). *Altered loves: Mothers and daughters during adolescence.* New York, NY: St. Martin's.

Aquilino, W. S. (2006). Family relationships and support systems in emerging adulthood. In J. J. Arnett & J. Tanner (Eds.), *Coming of age in the 21st century: The lives and contexts of emerging adults* (pp. 193–218). Washington, DC: American Psychological Association.

Arcangeli, T., Thilaganathan, B., Hooper, R., Khan, K. S., & Bhide, A. (2012). Neurodevelopmental delay in small babies at term: A systematic review. *Ultrasound in Obstetrics & Gynecology, 40,* 267–275.

Archibald, A. B., Graber, J. A., & Brooks-Gunn, J. (2003). Pubertal processes and physiological growth in adolescence. In G. Adams & M. Berzonsky (Eds.), *Blackwell handbook of adolescence.* Malden, MA: Blackwell.

Arditi-Babchuk, H., Eidelman, A. I., & Feldman, R. (2009). Rapid eye movement (REM) in premature neonates and developmental outcome at 6 months. *Infant Behavior & Development, 32,* 27–32.

Arceo-Gomez, E. O., & Campos-Vazquez, R. M. (2014). Teenage pregnancy in Mexico: Evolution and consequences. *Latin American Journal of Economics, 51*(1), 109–146. http://doi.org/10.7764/LAJE.51.1.109.

Arnett, J. J. (1996). *Metalheads: Heavy metal music and adolescent alienation.* Boulder, CO: Westview Press.

Arnett, J. J. (1997). Young people's conceptions of the transition to adulthood. *Youth & Society, 29,* 1–23.

Arnett, J. J. (1998). Learning to stand alone: The contemporary American transition to adulthood in cultural and historical context. *Human Development, 41,* 295–315.

Arnett, J. J. (1999). Adolescent storm and stress, reconsidered. *American Psychologist, 54,* 317–326.

Arnett, J. J. (2000). Emerging adulthood: A theory of development from the late teens through the twenties. *American Psychologist, 55,* 469–480.

Arnett, J. J. (2001). Conceptions of the transition to adulthood: Perspectives from adolescence to midlife. *Journal of Adult Development, 8,* 133–143.

Arnett, J. J. (2002a). Adolescents in Western countries in the 21st century: Vast opportunities—for all? In B. B. Brown, R. W. Larson, & T. S. Saraswathi (Eds.), *The world's youth: Adolescence in eight regions of the globe* (pp. 307–343). New York, NY: Cambridge University Press.

Arnett, J. J. (2002b). The psychology of globalization. *American Psychologist, 57,* 774–483.

Arnett, J. J. (2003). Conceptions of the transition to adulthood among emerging adults in American ethnic groups. *New Directions in Child and Adolescent Development, 100,* 63–75.

Arnett, J. J. (2004). *Emerging adulthood: The winding road from the late teens through the twenties.* New York: Oxford University Press.

Arnett, J. J. (2005a). The Vitality Criterion: A new standard of publication for *Journal of Adolescent Research. Journal of Adolescent Research, 20,* 3–7.

Arnett, J. J. (2005b). The developmental context of substance use in emerging adulthood. *Journal of Drug Issues, 35,* 235–253.

Arnett, J. J. (2006). G. Stanley Hall's adolescence: Brilliance and nonsense. *History of Psychology, 9,* 186–197.

Arnett, J. J. (2007a). Introduction. In J. J. Arnett (Ed.), *Encyclopedia of children, adolescents, and the media, Volume 1: A-K* (pp. xxxv-xxxvi). Thousand Oaks, CA: Sage.

Arnett, J. J. (2007b). The long and leisurely route: Coming of age in Europe today. *Current History, 106,* 130–136.

Arnett, J. J. (2008). The neglected 95%: Why American psychology needs to become less American. *American Psychologist, 63,* 602–614.

Arnett, J. J. (2011). Emerging adulthood(s): The cultural psychology of a new life stage. In L. A. Jensen (Ed.), *Bridging cultural and developmental psychology: New syntheses in theory, research, and policy.* New York, NY: Oxford University Press.

Arnett, J. J. (2015a). *Emerging adulthood: The winding road from the late teens through the twenties* (2nd ed.). New York, NY: Oxford University Press.

Arnett, J. J. (2015b). The cultural psychology of emerging adulthood. In L. A. Jensen (Ed.), *Oxford handbook of human development and culture.* New York, NY: Oxford University Press.

Arnett, J. J., & Schwab, J. (2012). *The Clark University Poll of Emerging Adults: Thriving, struggling, and hopeful.* Worcester, MA: Clark University. Retrieved from http://www.clarku.edu/clark-poll-emerging-adults/.

Arnett, J. J., & Schwab, J. (2013). *Parents and their grown kids: Harmony, support, and (occasional) conflict.* Worcester, MA: Clark University. Retrieved from http://www.clarku.edu/clark-poll-emerging-adults/.

Arnett, J. J., & Schwab, J. (2014). *Beyond emerging adulthood: The Clark University Poll of Established Adults.* Worcester, MA: Clark University. Retrieved from http://www.clarku.edu/clark-poll-emerging-adults/.

Arnett, J. J., & Tanner, J. L. (2009). Toward a cultural-developmental stage theory of the life course. In K. McCartney & R. Weisberg (Eds.), *Development and experience: A festschrift in honor of Sandra Wood Scarr* (pp. 17–38). New York, NY: Taylor & Francis.

Aronson, P. J., Mortimer, J. T., Zierman, C., & Hacker, M. (1996). Adolescents, work, and family: *An intergenerational developmental analyses. Understanding families*, 6, 25–62.

Asawa, L. E., Hansen, D. J., & Flood, M. F. (2008). Early childhood intervention programs: Opportunities and challenges for preventing child maltreatment. *Education and Treatment of Children*, 31, 73–110.

Ashcraft, M. H. (2009). *Cognition.* Upper Saddle River, NJ: Prentice Hall.

Asher, S. R., & Rose, A. J. (1997). Promoting children's social–emotional adjustment with peers. In P. Salovey & D. J. Sluyter (Eds.), *Emotional development and emotional intelligence* (pp. 193–195). New York, NY: Basic Books.

Aslin, R. N., Jusczyk, P. W., & Pisoni, D. B. (1998). Speech and auditory processing during infancy: Constraints on and precursors to language. In W. Damon (Ed.), *Handbook of child psychology* (5th ed., Vol. 2). New York, NY: Wiley.

Atkinson, J. (2000). *The developing visual brain.* Oxford, UK: Oxford University Press.

Atkinson, L., & Goldberg, S. (Eds.). (2004). *Attachment issues in psychopathology and intervention.* Mahwah, NJ: Erlbaum.

Atkinson, L., Chisholm, V. C., Scott, B., Goldberg, S., Vaughn, B. E., Blackwell, J., Dickens, S., & Tam, F. (1999). Maternal sensitivity, child functional level, and attachment in Down syndrome. *Monographs of the Society for Research in Child Development*, 64, 45–66.

Aud, S., Wilkinson-Flicker, S., Kristapovich, P., Rathbun, A., Wang, X., & Zhang, J. (2013). *The Condition of Education 2013* (NCES 2013-037). U.S. Department of Education, National Center for Education Statistics. Washington, DC. Retrieved from http://nces.ed.gov/pubsearch.

Aunio, P., Aubrey, C., Godfrey, R., Pan, Y., & Liu, Y. (2008). Children's early numeracy in England, Finland and People's Republic of China. *International Journal of Early Years Education*, 16, 203–221.

Aunola, K., & Nurmi, J.-E. (2004). Maternal affection moderates the impact of psychological control on a child's mathematical performance. *Developmental Psychology*, 40, 965–978.

Avery, L., & Lazdane, G. (2008). What do we know about sexual and reproductive health among adolescents in Europe? *European Journal of Contraception and Reproductive Health*, 13, 58–70.

Axia, G., Bonichini, S., & Benini, F. (1999). Attention and reaction to distress in infancy: A longitudinal study. *Developmental Psychology*, 35, 500–504.

Axelsson, A.-S. (2010). Perpetual and personal: Swedish youth adults and their use of mobile phones. *New Media & Society*, 12, 35–54.

Azmitia, M., Kamprath, N., & Linnet, J. (1998). Intimacy and conflict: The dynamics of boys' and girls' friendships during middle childhood and early adolescence. In L. Meyer, H. Park, M. Gront-Scheyer, I. Schwartz, & B. Harry (Eds.), *Making friends: The influences of culture and development* (pp. 171–189). Baltimore, MD: Brookes Publishing.

Bachman, J. G., O'Malley, P. M., Schulenberg, J. E., Johnston, L. D., Freedman-Doan, P., & Messersmith, E. E. (2008). *The education-drug use connection: How successes and failures in school relate to adolescent smoking, drinking, drug use, and delinquency.* New York, NY: Lawrence Erlbaum.

Bachman, J. G., Safron, D. J., Sy, S. R., & Schulenberg, J. E. (2003). Wishing to work: New perspectives on how adolescents' part-time work intensity is linked to educational engagement, substance use, and other problem behaviors. *International Journal of Behavioral Development*, 27, 301–315.

Baer, J. S., Sampson, P. D., Barr, H. M., Connor, P. D., & Streissguth, A. P. (2003). A 21-year longitudinal analysis of the effects of prenatal alcohol exposure on young adult drinking. *Archives of General Psychiatry*, 60, 377–385.

Bagwell, C. L., & Schmidt, M. E. (2013). Friendships in childhood and adolescence. Guilford Press.

Baillargeon, R. (1987). Object permanence in 3½- and 4½-month-old infants. *Child Development*, 23(5), 655–664.

Baillargeon, R. (2008). Innate ideas revisited: For a principle of persistence in infants' physical reasoning. *Perspectives on Psychological Science*, 3(Special issue: From philosophical thinking to psychological empiricism), 2–13.

Baker, C. (2011). *Foundations of bilingual education and bilingualism* (5th ed.). New York, NY: Multilingual Matters.

Bakermans-Kranenburg, M. J., van Uzendoorn, M. H., Bokhorst, C. L., & Schuengel, C. (2004). The importance of shared environment in infant–father attachment: A behavioral genetic study of the attachment q-sort. *Journal of Family Psychology*, 18, 545–549.

Bakker, M. P., Ormel, J., Verhulst, F. C., & Oldehinkel, A. J. (2010). Peer stressors and gender differences in adolescents' mental health: the TRAILS study. *Journal of Adolescent Health*, 46(5), 444–450.

Bakoyiannis, I., Gkioka, E., Pergialiotis, V., Mastroleon, I., Prodromidou, A., Vlachos, G. D., & Perrea, D. (2014). Fetal alcohol spectrum disorders and cognitive functions of young children. *Reviews in the Neurosciences*, 25(5), 631–639.

Baldry, A. C., & Farrington, D. P. (2004). Evaluation of an intervention program for the reduction of bullying and victimization in schools. *Aggressive Behavior*, 30, 1–15.

Balen, F. v., & Inhorn, M. C. (2002). Interpreting infertility: A view from the social sciences. In M. C. Inhorn & F. v. Balen, *Infertility around the globe: New thinking on childlessness, gender, and reproductive technologies* (pp. 3–32). Berkeley, CA: University of California Press.

Balodis, I. M., Wynne-Edwards, K. E., & Olmstead, M. C. (2011). The stress-response-dampening effects of placebo. *Hormones and Behavior*, 59, 465–472.

Baltes, P. B., Lindenberger, U., & Staudinger, U. M. (2006). Life span theory in developmental psychology. In W. Damon & R. M. Lerner (Eds.), *Handbook of child psychology* (Vol. 1., pp. 569–664). New York, NY: Wiley.

Bandura, A. (1977). *Social learning theory.* Englewood Cliffs, NJ: Prentice-Hall.

Bandura, A. (1986). *Social foundations of thought and action: A social cognitive theory.* Englewood Cliffs, NJ: Prentice-Hall.

Bandura, A. (2002). Social cognitive theory in cultural context. *Applied Psychology: An International Review*, 51(Special Issue), 269–290.

Bandura, A., & Bussey, K. (2004). On broadening the cognitive, motivational, and sociostructural scope of theorizing about gender development and functioning: Comments on Martin, Buble and Szkrybalo (2002). *Psychological Bulletin*, 130, 691–701.

Bandura, A., Ross, D., & Ross, S. A. (1961). The transmission of aggression through imitation of aggressive models. *Journal of Abnormal and Social Psychology*, 63, 575–582.

Bandura, A., Ross, D., & Ross, S. A. (1963). Imitation of film-mediated aggressive models. *The Journal of Abnormal and Social Psychology, 66*(1), 3–11.

Banerjee, R. (2005). Gender identity and the development of gender roles. In S. Ding & K. Littleton (Eds.), *Children's personal and social development* (pp. 142–179). Malden, MA: Blackwell.

Barajas, R. G., Martin, A., Brooks-Gunn, J., & Hale, L. (2011). Mother-child bed-sharing in toddlerhood and cognitive and behavioral outcomes. *Pediatrics,128*(2), e339–e347.

Barber, B. K. (Ed.). (2002). *Intrusive parenting: How psychological control affects children and adolescents*. Washington, D.C: American Psychological Association.

Barber, B. K. (2013). Annual Research Review: The experience of youth with political conflict–challenging notions of resilience and encouraging research refinement. *Journal of Child Psychology and Psychiatry, 54*(4), 461–473.

Barber, B. K., Stolz, H. E., & Olsen, J. A. (2005). Parental support, psychological control, and behavioral control: Assessing relevance across time, culture, and method: IV. Assessing relevance across time: U.S. analyses and results. *Monographs of the Society for Research in Child Development, 70*(4).

Barnett, D., Ganiban, J., & Cicchetti, D. (1999). Maltreatment, negative expressivity, and the development of type D attachments from 12 to 24 months of age. *Monographs of the Society for Research in Child Development, 64*, 97–118.

Barnett, W. S., & Hustedt, J. T. (2005). Head Start's lasting benefits. *Infants and Young Children, 18*, 16–24.

Baron, E. M., & Denmark, F. L. (2006). An exploration of female genital mutilation. In F. L. Denmark, H. H. Krauss, E. Halpern, & J. A. Sechzer (Eds.), *Violence and exploitation against women and girls* (pp. 339–355). Malden, MA: Blackwell.

Baron-Cohen, S., Leslie, A.M., & Frith, U. (1985). Does the autistic child have a "theory of mind"? *Cognition, 21*(1), 37–46.

Barone, J. G., Jasutkar, N., & Schneider, D. (2009). Later toilet training is associated with urge incontinence in children. *Journal of pediatric urology, 5*(6), 458–461.

Barr, H. M., & Streissguth, A. P. (2001). Identifying maternal self-reported alcohol use associated with Fetal Alcohol Spectrum Disorders. *Alcoholism: Clinical and Experimental Research, 25*, 283–287.

Barr, R. (2010). Transfer of learning between 2D and 3D sources during infancy: Informing theory and practice. *Developmental Review, 30*(2), 128–154. doi:10.1016/j.dr.2010.03.001.

Barr, R., & Hayne, H. (2003). It's not what you know, it's who you know: Older siblings facilitate imitation during infancy. *Child Development, 70*, 1067–1081.

Barr, R., Marrott, H., & Rovee-Collier, C. (2003). The role of sensory preconditioning in memory retrieval by preverbal infants. *Learning and Behavior, 31*, 111–123.

Barr, R., Zack, E., Garcia, A., & Muentener, P. (2008). Infants' attention and responsiveness to television increases with prior exposure and parental interaction. *Infancy, 13*(1), 30–56. doi:10.1080/15250000701779378.

Barr, R. G. (2009). The phenomena of early infant crying and colic. Paper presented at the Centre for Community and Child Health, Melbourne, Australia, March 2.

Barr, R. G., & Gunnar, M. (2000). Colic: The "transient responsivity" hypothesis. In R. G. Barr, B. Hopkins, & J. A. Green (Eds.), *Crying as a sign, a symptom, and a signal* (pp. 41–66). Cambridge, UK: Cambridge University Press.

Barrett, D. E., & Frank, D. A. (1987). *The effects of undernutrition on children's behavior*. New York, NY: Gordon & Breach.

Barrett, K. C., & Nelson-Goens, G. C. (1997). Emotion communication and the development of the social emotions. *New Directions for Child Development, 77*, 69–88.

Barrio, C., Morena, A., & Linaza, J. L. (2007). Spain. In J. J. Arnett, R. Ahmed, B. Nsamenang, T. S. Saraswathi, & R. Silbereisen (Eds.), *International encyclopedia of adolescence*. New York, NY: Routledge.

Barry, C. M., & Christofferson, J. L. (2014). The Role of Peer Relationships in Emerging Adults' Religiousness and Spirituality. *Emerging Adults' Religiousness and Spirituality: Meaning-Making in an Age of Transition*, 76–92.

Barry, H. III, Bacon, M. K., & Child I. L. (1957). A cross-cultural survey of some sex differences in socialization. *Journal of Abnormal Social Psychology, 55*, 327–332.

Bartoshuk, L. M., & Beauchamp, G. K. (1994). Chemical senses. *Annual Review of Psychology, 45*, 419–449.

Basseches, M. (1984). *Dialectical thinking and adult development*. Norwood, NJ: Ablex.

Basseches, M. (1989). Dialectical thinking as an organized whole: Comments on Irwin and Kramer. In M. L. Commons, J. D. Sinnott, F. A. Richards, & C. Armon (Eds.), *Adult development, Vol. 1: Comparisons and applications of developmental models* (pp. 161–178). New York, NY: Praeger.

Bassi, M., & Antonella, D. F. (2004). Adolescence and the changing context of optimal experience in time: Italy 1986–2000. *Journal of Happiness Studies, 5*, 155–179.

Basu, A. K., & Chau, N. H. (2007). An exploration of the worst forms of child labor: Is redemption a viable option? In K. A. Appiah & M. Bunzl (Eds.), *Buying freedom: The ethics of economics of slave redemption* (pp. 37–76). Princeton, NJ: Princeton University Press.

Batalova, J., & Fix, M. (n.d.). Up for grabs: The gains and prospects of first- and second-generation young Adults. Retrieved May 25, 2015, from http://www.migrationpolicy.org/research/prospects-first-second-generation-young-adults-up-for-grabs.

Bates, B., & Turner, A. N. (2003). Imagery and symbolism in the birth practices of traditional cultures. In L. Dundes (Ed.), *The manner born: Birth rites in cross-cultural perspective* (pp. 85–97). Walnut Creek, CA: AltaMira Press.

Batzer, F. R., & Ravitsky, V. (2009). Preimplantation genetic diagnosis: Ethical considerations. In V. Ravitsky, A. Fiester, & A. L. Caplan (Eds.), *The Penn Center guide to bioethics* (pp. 339–354). New York, NY: Springer.

Bauer, P. J. (2006). Event memory. In W. Damon & R. Lerner (Eds.), *Handbook of child psychology: Vol. 2. Cognition, perception and language* (6th ed., pp. 373–425). New York, NY: Wiley.

Bauer, P. J., San Souci, P., & Pathman, T. (2010). Infant memory. *Wiley Interdisciplinary Reviews: Cognitive Science, 1*, 267–277.

Bauer, P. J., Wenner, J. A., Dropik, P. I., & Wewerka, S. S. (2000). Parameters of remembering and forgetting in the transition from infancy to early childhood. *Monographs of the Society for Research in Child Development, 65*, 1–204.

Bauer, P. J., Wiebe, S. A., Carver, L. J., Waters, J. M., & Nelson, C. A. (2003). Developments in long-term explicit memory late in the first year of life: Behavioral and electrophysiological indices. *Psychological Science, 14*, 629–635.

Bauer, P. J., Wiebe, S. A., Waters, J. M., & Banston, S. K. (2001). Reexposure breeds recall: Effects of experience on 9-month olds' ordered recall. *Journal of Experimental Child Psychology, 80*, 174–200.

Bauer, P. M., Hanson, J. L., Pierson, R. K., Davidson, R. J., & Pollak, S. D. (2009). Cerebellar volume and cognitive functioning in children who experienced early deprivation. *Biological Psychiatry, 66*, 1100–1106.

Bauminger, N., Finzi-Dottan, R., Chason, S., & Har-Even, D. (2008). Intimacy in adolescent friendship: The roles of attachment, coherence, and self-disclosure. *Journal of Social and Personal Relationships, 25*, 409–428.

Baumrind, D. (1968). Authoritative vs. authoritarian parental control. *Adolescence, 3*, 255–272.

Baumrind, D. (1971). Current patterns of parental authority. *Developmental Psychology Monograph, 4* (No. 1, Pt. 2).

Baumrind, D. (1991a). Effective parenting during the early adolescent transition. In P. A. Cowan & E. M. Hetherington (Ed.), *Advances in family research* (Vol. 2, pp. 111–163). Hillsdale, NJ: Erlbaum.

Baumrind, D. (1991b). The influence of parenting style on adolescent competence and drug use. *Journal of Early Adolescence, 11*, 56–95.

Baumrind, D. (1993). The average expectable environment is not enough: A response to Scarr. *Child Development, 64*, 1299–1317.

Bayley, N. (2005). *Bayley Scales of Infant and Toddler Development, Third Edition* (Bayley-III). San Antonio, TX: Harcourt Assessment.

Beck, C. T. (2002). Theoretical perspectives on postpartum depression and their treatment implications. *American Journal of Maternal/Child Nursing, 27*, 282–287.

Beck, I. L., & Beck, M. E. (2013). *Making sense of phonics, Second Edition: The hows and whys edition.* New York, NY: Guilford Press.

Becker, A. E. (2004). Television, disordered eating, and young women in Fiji: Negotiating body image and identity during rapid social change. *Culture, Medicine, and Psychiatry, 28*, 533–559.

Becker, A. E., Fay, K., Gilman, S. E., & Striegel-Moore, R. (2007). Facets of acculturation and their diverse relations to body shape concern in Fiji. *International Journal of Eating Disorders, 40*, 42–50.

Becker, O. A., Salzburger, V., Lois, N., & Nauck, B. (2013). What narrows the stepgap? Closeness between parents and adult (step) children in Germany. *Journal of Marriage and Family, 75*(5), 1130–1148.

Beckett, C., Maughan, B., Rutter, M., Castle, J., Colvert, E., Groothues, C.,... Sonuga-Barke, E. J. S. (2006). Do the effects of early severe deprivation on cognition persist into early adolescence? Findings from the English and Romanian adoptees study. *Child Development, 77*, 696–711.

Bel, A., & Bel, B. (2007). Birth attendants: Between the devil and the deep blue sea. In B. Bel, J. Brouwer, B. T. Das, V. Parthasarathi, & G. Poitevin (Eds.), *Communication processes 2: The social and the symbolic* (pp. 353–385). Thousand Oaks, CA: Sage.

Bell, M. A., & Wolfe, C. D. (2007). The cognitive neuroscience of early socioemotional development. In C. A. Brownell & C. B. Kopp (Eds.), *Socioemotional development in the toddler years: Transitions and transformations* (pp. 345–369). New York, NY: Guilford Press.

Bell, S. M., & Ainsworth, M. D. S. (1972). Infant crying and maternal responsiveness. *Child Development, 43*, 1171–1190.

Bellah, R. N., Madsen, R., Sullivan, W. M., Swidler, A., & Tipton, S. M. (1985). *Habits of the heart: Individualism and commitment in American life.* New York, NY: Harper & Row.

Bem, S. L. (1981). Gender schema theory: A cognitive account of sex-typing. *Psychological Review, 88*, 354–364.

Benbow, C. P., & Lubinski, D. (2009). Extending Sandra Scarr's ideas about development to the longitudinal study of intellectually precocious youth. In K. McCartney & R. A. Weinberg (Eds.), *Experience and development: A festschrift in honor of Sandra Wood Scarr* (pp. 231–252). New York, NY: Psychology Press.

Bender, H. L., Allen, J. P., McElhaney, K. B., Antonishak, J., Moore, C. M., Kelly, H. O., & Davis, S. M. (2007). Use of harsh physical discipline and developmental outcomes in adolescence. *Development and Psychopathology, 19*, 227–242.

Benedict, R. (1938). Continuities and discontinuities in cultural conditioning. *Psychiatry: Journal for the Study of Interpersonal Processes, 2*, 161–167.

Bennik, E. C., Nederhof, E., Ormel, J., & Oldehinkel, A. J. (2013). Anhedonia and depressed mood in adolescence: Course, stability, and reciprocal relation in the TRAILS study. *European Child & Adolescent Psychiatry, 1–8.*

Benoit, J. D., Rakic, P., & Frick, K. M. (2015). Prenatal stress induces spatial memory deficits and epigenetic changes in the hippocampus indicative of heterochromatin formation and reduced gene expression. *Behavioural Brain Research, 281, 1–8.* http://dx.doi.org.eres.library.manoa.hawaii.edu/10.1016/j.bbr.2014.12.001.

Benson, M., Harris, P., & Rogers, C. (1992). Identity consequences of attachment to mothers and fathers among late adolescents. *Journal of Research on Adolescents, 2*, 187–204.

Berch, D., & Mazzocco, M. (2007). Why is math so hard for some children? *The nature and origins of mathematical learning difficulties and disabilities.* Baltimore, MD: Paul H. Brookes.

Berger, K. S. (2007). Update on bullying at school: Science forgotten? *Developmental Review, 27*, 90–126.

Berger, S. E., Adolph, K. E., & Lobo, S. A. (2005). Out of the toolbox: Toddlers differentiate wobbly and wooden handrails. *Child Development, 76*, 1294–1307.

Bergstrom, A. (2007a). Food advertising, international. In J. J. Arnett (Ed.), *Encyclopedia of children, adolescents, and the media* (pp. 347–348). Thousand Oaks, CA: Sage.

Bergstrom, A. (2007b). Cartoons, educational. In J. J. Arnett (Ed.), *Encyclopedia of children, adolescents, and the media* (pp. 137–140). Thousand Oaks, CA: Sage.

Bergström, L., Richards, L., Morse, J. M., & Roberts, J. (2010). How caregivers manage pain and distress in second-stage labor. *Journal of Midwifery & Women's Health, 55*, 38–45.

Bergström, M., Kieler, H., & Waldenström, U. (2009). Effects of natural childbirth preparation versus standard antenatal education on epidural rates, experience of childbirth and parental stress in mothers and fathers: A randomised controlled multicentre trial. BJOG: *An International Journal of Obstetrics & Gynaecology 116*, 1167–1176.

Berkman, N. D., Lohr, K. N., & Bulik, C. M. (2007). Outcomes of eating disorders: A systematic review of the literature. *International Journal of Eating Disorders, 40*, 293–309.

Berko, J. (1958). The child's learning of English morphology. *Word, 14*, 150–177.

Berlin, J. (2015). *Is intercultural competence enough? Study abroad and global citizenship.* Unpublished dissertation. University of Hawaii.

Berndt, T. J. (1996). Transitions in friendship and friends' influence. In J. A. Graber, J. Brooks-Gunn, & A. C. Petersen (Eds.), *Transitions through adolescence: Interpersonal domains and context* (pp. 57–84). Mahwah, NJ: Erlbaum.

Berndt, T. J., & Mekos, D. (1995). Adolescents' perceptions of the stressful and desirable aspects of the transition to junior high school. *Journal of Research on Adolescence, 5*(1), 123–142.

Berney, T. (2009). Ageing in Down Syndrome. In G. O'Brien, & L. Rosenbloom (Eds.), *Developmental disability and ageing* (pp. 31–38). London, UK: Mac Keith Press.

Berninger, V. W., Abbott, R. D., Jones, J., Wolf, B. J., Gould, L., Anderson-Youngstrom, M.,...Apel, K. (2006). Early development of language by hand: Composing, reading, listening, and speaking connections; three letter-writing modes; and fast mapping in spelling. *Developmental Neuropsychology, 29* (Special issue on writing), 61–92.

Berry, J. W., Phinney, J. S., Sam, D. L., & Vedder, P. (Eds.). (2006). *Immigrant youth in cultural transition: Acculturation, identity, and adaptation across national contexts.* Mahwah, NJ: Lawrence Erlbaum.

Berry, R. J., Li, Z., Erickson, J. D., Li, S., Moore, C. A., Wang, H.,... Correa, A. (1999). Prevention of neural-tube defects with folic acid in China. *New England Journal of Medicine, 341*, 1485–1490.

Berthier, N. E., & Carrico, R. L. (2010). Visual information and object size in infant reaching. *Infant Behavior and Development, 33*, 555–566.

Best, D. L. (2001). Gender concepts: Convergence in cross-cultural research and methodologies. *Cross-cultural Research: The Journal of Comparative Social Science, 35*, 23–43.

Bhargava, S., & Mendiratta, A. (2006). Understanding language patterns of multilingual children (8–10 years) belonging to high socio-economic class. *Social Science International, 22*, 148–158.

Bialystok, E. (1993). Metalinguistic awareness: The development of children's representations in language. In C. Pratt & A. Garton (Eds.), *Systems of representation in children* (pp. 211–233). London, UK: Wiley.

Bialystok, E. (1997). Effects of bilingualism and biliteracy on children's emerging concepts of print. *Developmental Psychology, 33*, 429–440.

Bialystok, E. (1999). Cognitive complexity and attentional control in the bilingual mind. *Child Development, 70*, 636–644.

Bialystok, E. (2001). *Bilingualism in development: Language, literacy, and cognition*. New York, NY: Cambridge University Press.

Bibok, M. B., Müller, U., & Carpendale, J. I. M. (2009). Childhood. In U. Müller, J. I. M. Carpendale, & L. Smith (Eds.), *The Cambridge companion to Piaget* (pp. 229–254). New York, NY: Cambridge University Press.

Bickham, D. S., Hswen, Y., & Rich, M. (2015). Media use and depression: Exposure, household rules, and symptoms among young adolescents in the USA. *International Journal of Public Health, 60*(2), 147–155. http://doi.org/10.1007/s00038-014-0647-6.

Biehl, M. C., Natsuaki, M. N., & Ge, X. (2007). The influence of pubertal timing on alcohol use and heavy drinking trajectories. *Journal of Youth and Adolescence, 36*, 153–167.

Bina, M., Graziano, F., & Bonino, S. (2006). Risky driving and lifestyles in adolescence. *Accident Analysis & Prevention, 38*, 472–481.

Birch, L. L., Fisher, J. O., & Davison, K. K. (2003). Learning to overeat: Maternal use of restrictive feeding practices promotes girls' eating in the absence of hunger. *American Journal of Clinical Nutrition, 78*, 215–220.

Birdsong, D. (2006). Age and second language acquisition and processing: A selective overview. *Language Learning, 56* (Suppl. s1), 9–49.

Bjarnason, T., & Sigurdardottir, T. J. (2003). Psychological distress during unemployment and beyond: Social support and material deprivation among youth in six Northern European counties. *Social Science & Medicine, 56*, 973–985.

Black, R. E., Williams, S. M., Jones, I. E., & Goulding, A. (2002). Children who avoid drinking cow milk have lower dietary calcium intakes and poor bone health. *American Journal of Clinical Nutrition, 76*, 675–680.

Blakemore, J. E. O. (2003). Children's beliefs about violating gender norms: Boys shouldn't look like girls, and girls shouldn't act like boys. *Sex Roles, 48*, 411–419.

Blakemore, S-J. (2008). The social brain in adolescence. *Nature Reviews Neuroscience, 9*, 267–277.

Bloch, M., Klein, E., Koren, D., & Rotenberg, N. (2006). Risk factors for early postpartum depressive symptoms. *General Hospital Psychiatry, 28*, 3–8.

Bloom, L. (1998). Language acquisition in its developmental context. In W. Damon (Ed.), & D. Kuhn & R. S. Siegler (Vol. Eds.), *Handbook of Child Psychology* (5th ed.): *Vol. 2. Cognition, perception and language* (pp. 309–370). New York, NY: Wiley.

Bloom, L., Lifter, K., & Broughton, J. (1985). The convergence of early cognition and language in the second year of life: Problems in conceptualization and measurement. In M. Barrett (Ed.), *Single word speech* (pp. 149–181). New York, NY: Wiley.

Bloom, P. (2000). *How children learn the meanings of words*. Cambridge, MA: MIT Press.

Bluestone, C. D., & Klein, J. O. (2007). *Otitis media in infants and children*. New York, NY: Decker.

Blum, N. J., Taubman, B., & Nemeth, N. (2004). Why is toilet training occurring at older ages? A study of factors associated with later training. *Journal of Pediatrics, 145*, 107–111.

Blumenthal, J., Jeffries, N. O., Castellanos, F. X., Liu, H., Zijdenbos, A., Paus, T.,... Giedd, J. N. (1999). Brain development during childhood and adolescence: A longitudinal MRI study. *Nature Neuroscience, 10*, 861–863.

Bochner, S., & Jones, J. (2003). Augmentative and alternative forms of communication as stepping stones to speech. *Child Language Development: Learning to Talk, Second Edition*, 143–156.

Boden, J. M., Horwood, L. J., & Fergusson, D. M. (2007). Exposure to childhood sexual and physical abuse and subsequent educational achievement outcomes. *Child Abuse and Neglect, 31*, 1101–1114.

Boer, F., Goedhardt, A. W., & Treffers, P. D. A. (2013). Siblings and their parents. In F. Boer, J. Dunn, & J. F. Dunn (Eds.), *Children's sibling relationships: Developmental and clinical issues* (pp. 41–54). New York, NY: Wiley.

Bois-Reymond, M., & Ravesloot, J. (1996). The roles of parents and peers in the sexual and relational socialization of adolescents. In K. Hurrelmann & S. Hamilton (Eds.), *Social problems and social contexts in adolescence: Perspectives across boundaries* (pp. 175–197). Hawthorne, NY: Aldine de Gruyter.

Bokhorst, C. L., Sumpter, S. R., & Westenberg, P. M. (2010). Social support from parents, friends, classmates, and teachers in children and adolescents aged 9 to 18 years: Who is perceived as most supportive. *Social Development 19*(2), 417–426. doi: 10.1111/j.1467-9507.2009.00540.x.

Boku, S., Toda, H., Nakagawa, S., Kato, A., Inoue, T., Koyama, T., Hiroi, N., & Kusumi, I. (2015). Neonatal maternal separation alters the capacity of adult neural precursor cells to differentiate into neurons via methylation of retinoic acid receptor gene promoter. *Biological Psychiatry, 77*(4), 335–344. http://dx.doi.org.eres.library.manoa.hawaii.edu/10.1016/j.biopsych.2014.07.008.

Bolzani, L. H., Messinger, D. S., Yale, M., & Dondi, M. (2002). Smiling in infancy. In M. H. Abel (Ed.), *An empirical reflection on the smile* (pp. 111–136). Lewiston, NY: Edwin Mellen Press.

Bonino, S., & Cattelino, E. (2012). Italy. In J. J. Arnett (Ed.), *Adolescent psychology around the world*. New York, NY: Taylor & Francis.

Booth, D. A., Higgs, S., Schneider, J., & Klinkenberg, I. (2010). Learned liking versus inborn delight: Can sweetness give sensual pleasure or is it just motivating? *Psychological Science, 21*, 1656–1663.

Borduin, C. M., Schaeffer, C. M., & Ronis, S. T. (2003). Multisystemic treatment of serious antisocial behavior in adolescents. In C. A. Essau (Ed.), *Conduct and oppositional defiant disorders: Epidemiology, risk factors, and treatment* (pp. 299–318). Mahwah, NJ: Lawrence Erlbaum.

Borgaonkar, D. S. (1997). Chromosomal variation in man: A catalog of chromosomal variants and anomalies (8th ed.). New York, NY: Wiley.

Bornstein, M. H. (2006). Parenting science and practice. In W. Damon & R. Lerner (Eds.), & K. A. Renninger & L. E. Sigel (Vol. Eds.), *Handbook of child psychology: Vol. 4. Child psychology in practice* (6th ed., pp. 893–949). New York, NY: Wiley.

Bornstein, M. H., & Arterberry, M. E. (2010). The development of object categorization in young children: Hierarchical inclusiveness, age, perceptual attribute, and group versus individual analyses. *Developmental Psychology, 46*, 350–365. doi: 10.1037/a0018411

Bornstein, M. H., & Bradley, R. H. (2014). *Socioeconomic status, parenting, and child development*. New York, NY: Routledge.

Bortolus, R., Parazzini, F., Chatenoud, L., Benzi, G., Bianchi, M. M., & Marini, A. (1999). The epidemiology of multiple births. *Human Reproduction Update, 5*, 179–187.

Boschi-Pinto, C., Lanata, C. F., & Black, R. E. (2009). The global burden of childhood diarrhea. *Maternal and Child Health, 3*, 225–243.

Bosse, Y., & Hudson, T. J. (2007). Toward a comprehensive set of asthma susceptibility genes. *Annual Review of Medicine, 58*, 171–184.

Bostic, J. Q., Rubin, D. H., Prince, J., & Schlozman, S. (2005). Treatment of depression in children and adolescents. *Journal of Psychiatric Practice, 11*, 141–154.

Botcheva, L., Kalchev, P., & Leiderman, P. H. (2007). Bulgaria. In J. J. Arnett, R. Ahmed, B. Nsamenang, T. S. Saraswathi, & R. Silbereisen (Eds.), *International encyclopedia of adolescence*. (pp. 108–120). New York, NY: Routledge.

Bottenberg, P., Van Melkebeke, L, Louckx, F., & Vandenplas, Y. (2008). Knowledge of Flemish paediatricians about children's oral health—Results of a survey. *Acta Paediatrica, 97*, 959–963.

Bouchard, T. J., & McGue, M. (2003). Genetic and environmental influences on human psychological differences. *Journal of Neurobiology, 54*, 4–45.

Bower, B. (1985). The left hand of math and verbal talent. *Science News, 127*, 263.

Bowers, W. A., Evans, K., LeGrange, D., & Andersen, A. E. (2003). Treatment of adolescent eating disorders. In M. A. Reinecke & F. M. Dattilio (Eds.), *Cognitive therapy with children and adolescents: A casebook for clinical practice* (2nd ed., pp. 247–280). New York, NY: Guilford Press.

Bowlby, J. (1969/1982). *Attachment and loss: Vol. 1. Attachment.* (2nd ed.). New York, NY: Basic Books.

Bowlby, J. (1980). *Attachment and loss: Vol. 3. Loss: Sadness and depression.* New York, NY: Basic Books.

Braine, L. G., Schauble, L., Kugelmass, S., & Winter, A. (1993). Representation of depth by children: Spatial strategies and lateral biases. *Developmental Psychology, 29,* 466–479.

Brake, D. (2006). Electronic games, effects. In J. J. Arnett (Ed.), *Encyclopedia of children, adolescents, and the media.* Thousand Oaks, CA: Sage.

Brambati, B., & Tului, L. (2005). Chronic villus sampling and amniocentesis. *Current Opinion in Obstetrics and Gynecology, 17,* 197–201.

Brame, B., Nagin, D. S., & Tremblay, R. E. (2001). Developmental trajectories of physical aggression from school entry to late adolescence. *Journal of Child Psychology and Psychiatry, 42,* 503–512.

Brant, A. M., Haberstick, B. C., Corley, R. P., Wadsworth, S. J., DeFries, J. C., & Hewitt, J. K. (2009). The development etiology of high IQ. *Behavior Genetics, 39,* 393–405.

Braveman, P., Egerter, S., & Williams, D. R. (2011). The social determinants of health: Coming of age. *Annual Review of Public Health, 32,* 381–398.

Bray, J. H. (1999). From marriage to remarriage and beyond: Findings from the Developmental Issues in Stepfamilies Research Project. In E. M. Hetherington (Ed.), *Coping with divorce, single parenting, and remarriage: A risk and resiliency perspective* (pp. 295–319). Mahwah, NJ: Erlbaum.

Brazelton, T. B., Koslowski, B., & Tronick, E. (1976). Neonatal behavior among urban Zambians and Americans. *Journal of the American Academy of Child Psychiatry, 15,* 97–107.

Breger, L. (2000). *Freud: Darkness in the midst of vision.* New York, NY: Wiley & Sons.

Brent, D. A. (2004). Antidepressants and pediatric depression: The risk of doing nothing. *New England Journal of Medicine, 35,* 1598–1601.

Brescoll, V. L., Dawson, E., & Uhlmann, E. L. (2010). Hard won and easily lost: The fragile status of leaders in gender-stereotype incongruent occupations. *Psychological Science, 21,* 1640–1642.

Bretherton, I., & Munholland, K. (1999). Internal working models in attachment relationships: A construct revisited. In J. Cassidy & P. R. Shaver (Eds.), *Handbook of attachment: Theory, research, and clinical applications* (pp. 89–111). New York, NY: Guilford Press.

Bridge, J. A., Yengar, S., Salary, C. B., et al. (2007). Clinical response and risk for reported suicidal ideation and suicide attempts in pediatric antidepressant treatment: A meta-analysis of randomized controlled trials. *JAMA, 63,* 332–339.

Bridges, L., & Moore, K. (2002). Religious involvement and children's well-being: What research tells us (and what it doesn't). *Child Trends Research Brief.* Washington, DC: Author. Available: www.childtrends.org

Bridgett, D. J., & Mayes, L. C. (2011). Development of inhibitory control among prenatally cocaine exposed and non-cocaine exposed youths from late childhood to early adolescence: The effects of gender and risk and subsequent aggressive behavior. *Neurotoxicology and Teratology, 33*(1), 47–60. http://doi.org/10.1016/j.ntt.2010.08.002.

Brody, G. (2004). Siblings' direct and indirect contributions to child development. *Current Directions in Psychological Science, 13,* 124–126.

Brody, G. H., & Flor, D. L. (1998). Maternal resources, parenting practices, and child competence in rural, single-parent African American families. *Child Development, 69,* 803–816.

Brody, G. H., Kim, S., Murry, V. M., & Brown, A. C. (2003). Longitudinal direct and indirect pathways linking older sibling competence to the development of young sibling competence. *Developmental Psychology, 39,* 618–628.

Bronfenbrenner, U. (1980). *The ecology of human development.* Cambridge, MA: Harvard University Press.

Bronfenbrenner, U. (2000). Ecological theory: In A. Kazdin (Ed.), *Encyclopedia of psychology.* Washington, DC: American Psychological Association.

Bronfenbrenner, U. (Ed.). (2005). *Making human beings human: Bioecological perspectives on human development.* Thousand Oaks, CA: Sage.

Bronfenbrenner, U., & Morris, P. A. (1998). The ecology of developmental processes. In W. Damon (Series Ed.) and R. Lerner (Vol. Ed.), *Handbook of child psychology, Vol. 1: Theoretical models of human development* (pp. 993–1028). New York, NY: Wiley.

Brooks, R., & Meltzoff, A. N. (2005). The development of gaze following and its relation to language. *Developmental Science, 8,* 535–543.

Brooks-Gunn, J. (2003). Do you believe in magic? What we can expect from early childhood intervention programs. *Social Policy Report of the Society for Research in Child Development, 17,* 3–14.

Brotanek, J. M., Gosz, J., & Weitzman, M. (2007). Iron deficiency in early childhood in the United States: Risk factors and racial/ethnic disparities. *Pediatrics, 120,* 568–575.

Brown, A. M., & Miracle, J. A. (2003). Early binocular vision in human infants: Limitations on the generality of the Superposition Hypothesis. *Vision Research, 43,* 1563–1574.

Brown, A. S., & Susser, E. S. (2002). In utero infection and adult schizophrenia. *Mental Retardation and Developmental Disabilities Research Reviews, 8,* 51–57.

Brown, B. B., & Braun, M. T. (2013). Peer relations. In *Research, applications, and interventions for children and adolescents* (pp. 149–164). Netherlands: Springer.

Brown, B. B., Herman, M., Hamm, J. V., & Heck, D. K. (2008). Ethnicity and image: Correlates of crowd affiliation among ethnic minority youth. *Child Development, 79,* 529–546.

Brown, J. D. (2006). Emerging adults in a media-saturated world. In J. J. Arnett & J. Tanner (Eds.), *Coming of age in the 21st century: The lives and contexts of emerging adults* (pp. 279–299). Washington, DC: American Psychological Association.

Brown, J. D., Steele, J., & Walsh-Childers, K. (Eds.). (2002). *Sexual teens, sexual media.* Mahwah, NJ: Erlbaum.

Brown, R. (1973). *A first language: The early stages.* Cambridge, MA: Harvard University Press.

Brownell, C. A., & Kopp, C. B. (2007). *Socioemotional development in the toddler years.* New York, NY: Guilford.

Brownell, C. A., Svetlova, M., & Nichols, S. (2009). To share or not to share: When do toddlers respond to another's needs? *Infancy, 14*(1): 117–130.

Brumberg, J. J. (1997). *The body project: An intimate history of American girls.* New York, NY: Random House.

Bruner, J. (1990). Culture and human development: A new look. *Human Development, 33*(6), 344–355.

Bryant, B. E. (2014). Sibling relationships in middle childhood. In M. E. Lamb & B. Sutton-Smith (Eds.), *Sibling relationships: Their nature and significance across the lifespan* (pp. 87–122). London, England: Routledge.

Bryant, G. A., & Barrett, H. C. (2007). Recognizing intentions in infant-directed speech: Evidence for universals. *Psychological Science, 18,* 746–751.

Bryder, L. (2009). From breast to bottle: a history of modern infant feeding. *Endeavour 33,* 54–59.

Buboltz, W. C., Soper, B., Brown, F., & Jenkins, S. (2002). Treatment approaches for sleep difficulties in college students. *Counseling Psychology Quarterly, 15,* 229–237.

Buckley, T., & Gottlieb, A. (1988). *Blood magic: The anthropology of menstruation.* Berkeley, CA: University of California Press.

Bugental, D. B., & Grusec, J. E. (2006). Socialization processes. In N. Eisenberg, W. Damon, & R. M. Lerner (Eds.), *Handbook of child psychology: Vol. 3. Social, emotional, and personality development* (6th ed., pp. 366–428, xxiv, 1128). Hoboken, NJ: John Wiley & Sons.

Bugental, D. B., & Happaney, K. (2004). Predicting infant maltreatment in low-income families: The interactive effects of maternal attributions and child status at birth. *Developmental Psychology, 40*, 234–243.

Buhs, E. S., & Ladd, G. W. (2001). Peer rejection as antecedent of young children's school adjustment: An examination of mediating processes. *Developmental Psychology, 37*, 550–560.

Bulik, C. M., Berkman, N. D., Brownley, K. A., Sedway, L. A., & Lohr, K. N. (2007). Anorexia nervosa treatment: A systematic review of randomized controlled trials. *International Journal of Eating Disorders, 40*, 310–320.

Bullough, V. L. (1981). Comments on Mosher's "Three dimensions of depth involvement in human sexual response." *Journal of Sex Research, 17*, 177–178.

Bumpass, L., & Liu, H. H. (2000, March). Trends in cohabitation and implications for children's family contexts in the United States. *Population Studies, 54*, 29–41.

Burnham, M., Goodlin-Jones, B., & Gaylor, E. (2002). Nighttime sleep–wake patterns and self–soothing from birth to one year of age: A longitudinal intervention study. *Journal of Child Psychology & Psychiatry & Allied Disciplines, 43*, 713–725.

Bushman, B. J., & Chandler, J. J. (2007). Violence, effects of. In J. J. Arnett (Ed.), *Encyclopedia of children, adolescents, and the media* (Vol. 2, pp. 847–850). Thousand Oaks, CA: Sage.

Bushman, B. J., & Huesmann, L. R. (2001). Effects of televised violence on aggression. In D. G. Singer & J. L. Singer (Eds.), *Handbook of children and the media* (pp. 223–254). Thousand Oaks, CA: Sage.

Buss, A. H. (1995). *Personality, temperament, social behavior, and the self.* Boston, MA: Allyn & Bacon.

Buss, D. M. (2003). *The evolution of desire: Strategies of human mating* (Revised Ed.). New York, NY: Basic Books

Buss, K. A., & Goldsmith, H. H. (1998). Fear and anger regulation in infancy: Effects on the temporal dynamics of affective expression. *Child Development, 69*, 359–374.

Buss, K. A., & Plomin, R. (1984). *Temperament: Early developing personality traits.* Hillsdale, NJ: Erlbaum.

Bussey, K. (1992). Lying and truthfulness: Children's definitions, standards, and evaluative reactions. *Child Development, 63*, 129–137.

Bussey, K., & Bandura, A. (2004). Social cognitive theory of gender development and functioning. In A. H. Eagly, A. Beall, & R. Sternberg (Eds.), *The psychology of gender* (2nd ed., pp. 92–119). New York, NY: Guilford.

Byrd, C. M. (2012). The measurement of racial/ethnic identity in children a critical review. *Journal of Black Psychology, 38*(1), 3–31.

Cabrera, N. J., & Garcia-Coll, C. (2004). Latino fathers: Uncharted territory in need of much exploration. In M. E. Lamb (Ed.), *The role of the father in child development* (4th ed., pp. 98–120). Hoboken, NJ: Wiley.

Cabrera, N. J., Ryan, R. M., Mitchell, S. J., Shannon, J. D., & Tamis-LeMonda, C. T. (2008). Low-income nonresident father involvement with their toddlers: Variation by Fathers' race and ethnicity. *Journal of Family Psychology, 22*(4), 643–651. doi:10.1037/0893-3200.22.3.643.

Cabrera, S. F., Sauer, S. J., & Thomas-Hunt, M. C. (2009). The evolving manager stereotype: The effects of industry gender typing on performance expectations for leaders and their teams. *Psychology of Women Quarterly, 33*, 419–428.

Caetano, R., Ramisetty-Mikler, S., Floyd, L. R., & McGrath, C. (2006). The epidemiology of drinking among women of child-bearing age. *Alcoholism: Clinical and Experimental Research, 30*, 1023–1030.

Calkins, S. (2012). Caregiving as coregulation: Psychobiological processes and child functioning. In A. Booth, S. M. McHale, & N. Landale (Eds.), *Biosocial foundations of family processes* (pp. 49 59). New York, NY: Springer.

Calkins, S. D. (2002). Does aversive behavior during toddlerhood matter? The effects of difficult temperament on maternal perceptions and behavior. *Child Development, 67*, 523–540.

Call, J. (2001). Object permanence in orangutans, chimpanzees, and children. *Journal of Comparative Psychology, 115*, 159–171.

Callahan, C. M., Boustani, M. A., Unverzagt, F. W., Austrom, M. G., Damush, T. M., Perkins, et al. (2006). Effectiveness of collaborative care for older adults with Alzheimer disease in primary care: A randomized controlled trial. *JAMA: Journal of the American Medical Association, 295*, 2148–2157.

Cameron, J. L. (2001). Effects of sex hormones on brain development. In C. A. Nelson & M. Luciana (Eds.), *Handbook of developmental cognitive neuroscience* (pp. 59–78).

Campbell, A., Shirley, L., & Candy, J. (2004). A longitudinal study of gender-related cognition and behavior. *Developmental Science, 7*, 1–9.

Campbell, E., Ramey, C., & Pungello, E. (2002). Early childhood education: Young adult outcomes from the Abecedarian Project. *Applied Developmental Science, 6*, 42–57.

Campione-Barr, N., & Smetana, J. G. (2010). "Who said you could wear my sweater?" Adolescent siblings' conflicts and associations with relationship quality. *Child Development, 81*, 464–471.

Capone, N. C., & McGregor, K. K. (2005). The effect of semantic representation on toddlers' word retrieval. *Journal of Speech, Language, and Hearing Research, 48*, 1468–1480.

Campos, J. J., Langer, A., & Krowitz, A. (1970). Cardiac responses on the visual cliff in prelocomotor human infants. *Science, 170*, 196–197.

Camras, L. A., Lambrecht, L., & Michel, G. F. (1996). Infant "surprise" expressions as coordinative motor structures. *Journal of Nonverbal Behavior, 20*, 183–195.

Cantwell, M. N., and Maynard, A. E. (2015). Growing up YouTube: Cultural values and identity among emerging adults on YouTube. Manuscript submitted for publication.

Caravita, S., & Cillessen, A. H. (2012). Agentic or communal? Associations between interpersonal goals, popularity, and bullying in middle childhood and early adolescence. *Social development, 21*(2), 376–395.

Carlson, S. M. (2003). Executive function in context: Development, measurement, theory and experience. *Monographs of the Society for Research in Child Development, 68*(3, Serial No. 274), 138–151.

Carr, J. (2002). Down syndrome. In P. Howlin & O. Udwin (Eds.), *Outcomes in neurodevelopmental and genetic disorders* (pp. 169–197). New York, NY: Cambridge University Press.

Carroll, J. L., & Wolpe, P. R. (2005). *Sexuality now: Embracing diversity.* Belmont, CA: Wadsworth.

Carter, K. C., & Carter, B. R. (2005). *Childbed fever. A scientific biography of Ignaz Semmelweis.* Edison, NJ: Transaction.

Carter-Saltzman, L. (1980). Biological and sociocultural effects on handedness: Comparison between biological and adoptive families. *Science, 209*, 1263–1265.

Case, R. (1999). Conceptual development in the child and the field: A personal view of the Piagetian legacy. In E. K. Skolnick, K. Nelson, S. A. Gelman, & P. H. Miller (Eds.), *Conceptual Development.* Mahwah, NJ: Erlbaum.

Case, R., & Okamato, Y. (Eds.). (1996). The role of central conceptual structures in the development of children's thought. *Monographs of the Society for Research in Child Development, 61* (1–2, Serial No. 246).

Casey Foundation (2010). *2010 Kids Count data book.* Baltimore, MD: Annie E. Casey Foundation.

Casey, B. J., Getz, S., & Galvan, A. (2008). The adolescent brain. *Developmental Review, 28*, 62–77.

Casey, B. M., McIntire, D. D., & Leveno, K. J. (2001). The continuing value of Apgar score for the assessment of the newborn infants. *New England Journal of Medicine, 344*, 467–471.

Casper, R. C. (2015). Use of selective serotonin reuptake inhibitor antidepressants in pregnancy does carry risks, but the risks are small. *The Journal of Nervous and Mental Disease, 203*(3), 167–169. http://doi.org/10.1097/NMD.0000000000000258.

Cassidy, J., & Shaver, P. R. (2008). *Handbook of attachment: Theory, research, and clinical applications.* New York, NY: Guilford.

Cassidy, J., & Shaver, P. R. (2010). *Handbook of attachment: Theory, research, and clinical applications* (2nd ed.). New York, NY: Guilford.

Cassidy, K. W., Werner, R. S., Rourke, M., Zubernis, L. S., & Balaraman, G. (2003). The relationship between psychological understanding and positive social behaviors. *Social Development, 12,* 198–221.

Cassidy, T. (2006). *Birth: The surprising history of how we are born.* New York, NY: Atlantic Monthly Press.

Cavallini, A., Fazzi, E., & Viviani, V. (2002). Visual acuity in the first two years of life in healthy term newborns: An experience with the Teller Acuity Cards. *Functional Neurology: New Trends in Adaptive & Behavioral Disorders, 17,* 87–92.

Cave, S. (2011). *Baby to toddler month by month.* New York: Hay House, Inc.

Ceci, S. J., & Williams, W. M. (1997). Schooling, intelligence, and income. *American Psychologist, 52*(10), 1051–1058. http://doi.org/10.1037/0003-066X.52.10.1051.

Cejka, M. A., & Eagly, A. H. (1999). Gender-stereotypic images of occupations correspond to the sex segregation of employment. *Personality and Social Psychology Bulletin, 25,* 413–423.

Centers for Disease Control and Prevention (CDC) (2002). Infant mortality and low birth weight among Black and White infants: United States, 1980–2000. *Morbidity & Mortality Weekly Report, 51,* 589–592.

Centers for Disease Control and Prevention (CDC) (2005). Blood lead levels: United States, 1999–2002. *Morbidity & Mortality Weekly Report, 54,* 513–516.

Centers for Disease Control and Prevention (CDC) (2006a). School health policies and programs study (SHPPS). *Journal of School Health.* 2007; 27(8).

Centers for Disease Control and Prevention (CDC). (2009). National Center for Health Statistics (NCHS). National Health and Nutrition Examination Survey Data. Hyattsville, MD: U.S. Department of Health and Human Services, Centers for Disease Control and Prevention, 2005–2008.

Centers for Disease Control and Prevention (CDC) (2010e). *Sudden Infant Death Syndrome (SIDS) and infant vaccines.* Retrieved from http://www.cdc.gov/vaccinesafety/Concerns/sids_faq.html

Centers for Disease Control (CDC). (2010f). *U.S. Obesity Trends: Trends by State 1985–2009.* Atlanta, GA: Author.

Centers for Disease Control (CDC). (2011d). *Spina bifida fact sheet.* Retrieved from http://www.cdc.gov/ncbddd/spinabifida/documents/spina–bifida- fact-sheet1209.pdf

Centers for Disease Control and Prevention (CDC). (2014). National Vital Statistics Report (NVSR) *"Deaths: Final Data for 2013."* The complete version of this report (NVSR Volume 64, Number 2).

Centers for Disease Control and Prevention (CDC). (2015a). Defining childhood obesity. http://www.cdc.gov/obesity/childhood/defining.html Retrieved July 4, 2015.

Centers for Disease Control and Prevention (CDC). (2015b). Suicide prevention. http://www.cdc.gov/violenceprevention/pub/youth_suicide.html Retrieved May 25, 2015.

Centers for Disease Control and Prevention, American Society for Reproductive Medicine, Society for Assisted Reproductive Technology. (2014). 2012 Assisted Reproductive Technology National Summary Report. Atlanta (GA): US Dept of Health and Human Services.

Chalk, L. M., Meara, N. M., Day, J. D., & Davis, K. L. (2005). Occupational possible selves: Fears and aspirations of college women. *Journal of Career Assessment, 13,* 188–203.

Chambers, M. L., Hewitt, J. K., Schmitz, S., Corley, R. P., & Fulker, D. W. (2001). Height, weight, and body mass index. In R. N. Emde & J. K. Hewitt (Eds.), *Infancy to early childhood:*

Genetic and environmental influences on developmental change (pp. 292–306). New York, NY: Oxford University Press.

Champion, K. M., Vernberg, E. M., & Shipman, K. (2003). Non-bullying victims of bullies: Aggression, social skills, and friendship characteristics. *Journal of Applied Developmental Psychology, 24,* 535–551.

Chan, D., Ramey, S., Ramey, C., & Schmitt, N. (2000). Modeling intraindividual changes in children's social skills at home and at school: A multivariate latent growth approach to understanding between-settings differences in children's social skill development. *Multivariate Behavioral Research, 35,* 365–396.

Chandler, M. J. (2001). The time of our lives: Self-continuity in native and non-native youth. In H. W. Reese & R. Kail (Eds.), *Advances in child development and behavior* (pp. 175–221). San Diego, CA, US: Academic Press.

Chandler, M. J., Lalonde, C. E., Sokol, B. W., & Hallett, D. (2003). Personal persistence, identity development, and suicide: A study of Native and non-Native North American adolescents. *Monographs of the Society for Research in Child Development, 68*(2), vii–130.

Chang, L. (2008). Factory girls: *From village to city in a changing China.* New York, NY: Spiegel & Grau.

Chao, R. K. (1994). Beyond parental control and authoritarian parenting style: Understanding Chinese parenting through the cultural notion of training. *Child Development, 65*(4), 1111–1119.

Chao, R. K. (1996). Chinese and European American mothers' beliefs about the role of parenting in children's school success. *Journal of Cross-Cultural Psychology, 27*(4), 403–423.

Chao, R., & Tseng, V. (2002). Parenting of Asians. In M. H. Bornstein (Ed.), *Handbook of parenting, Vol. 4: Social conditions and applied parenting* (pp. 59–93). Mahwah, NJ: Erlbaum.

Chapman, L. K., & Steger, M. F. (2010). Race and religion: Differential prediction of anxiety symptoms by religious coping in African American and European American young adults. *Depression and Anxiety, 27*(3), 316–322.

Charpak, N., Ruiz-Pelaez, J. G., & Figueroa, Z. (2005). Influence of feeding patterns and other factors on early somatic growth of healthy, preterm infants in home-based kangaroo mother care: A cohort study. *Journal of Pediatric Gastroenterology and Nutrition, 41,* 430–437.

Chatters, L. M., Taylor, R. J., Bullard, K. M., & Jackson, J. S. (2008). Spirituality and subjective religiosity among African Americans, Caribbean Blacks, and non-Hispanic Whites. *Journal for the Scientific Study of Religion,* 725–737.

Chaudhary, N., & Sharma, N. (2007). India. In J. J. Arnett (Ed.), *International encyclopedia of adolescence* (pp. 442–459). New York, NY: Routledge.

Chaudhary, N., & Sharma, P. (2012). India. In J. J. Arnett (Ed.), *Adolescent psychology around the world.* New York, NY: Taylor & Francis.

Chen, H., & Xu, L. (2013). Observation on efficacy of whole range Doula delivery combined with labor analgesia in process of spontaneous delivery. *Journal of Clinical Medicine in Practice, 12,* 044.

Chen, X. (2011). Culture, peer relationships, and human development. In L. A. Jensen (Ed.), *Bridging cultural and developmental approaches to psychology* (pp. 92–111). New York, NY: Oxford University Press.

Chen, X., Cen, G., Li, D., & He, Y. (2005). Social functioning and adjustment in Chinese children: The imprint of historical time. *Child Development, 76,* 182–195.

Chen, X., Rubin K. H., & Li, Z. (1995). Social functioning and adjustment in Chinese children: A longitudinal study. *Developmental Psychology, 31,* 531–539.

Chen, X., Wang, L., & Cao, R. (2011). Shyness-Sensitivity and Unsociability in Rural Chinese Children: Relations With Social, School, and Psychological Adjustment. *Child development, 82*(5), 1531–1543.

Chen, X., Wang, L., & DeSouza, A. (2007). Temperament, socioemotional functioning, and peer relationships in Chinese and North American children. In X. Chen, D. C. French, & B. H. Schneider

(Eds.), *Peer relationships in cultural context* (pp. 123–146). New York, NY: Cambridge University Press.

Chen, Y. P., Keen, R., Rosander, K., & Von Hofsten, C. (2010). Movement planning reflects skill level and age changes in toddlers. *Child development, 81*(6), 1846–1858.

Chen, Z., Du, J., Shao, L., Zheng, L., Wu, M., Ai, M., & Zhang, Y. (2010). Prepregnancy body mass index, gestational weight gain, and pregnancy outcomes in China. *International Journal of Gynecology & Obstetrics, 109*(1), 41–44. http://doi.org/10.1016/j.ijgo.2009.10.015.

Chess, S., & Thomas, A. (1984). *Origins and evolution of behavior disorders*. New York, NY: Brunner/Mazel.

Cheung, A. H., Emslie, G. J., & Mayes, T. (2005). Review of the efficacy and safety of antidepressants in youth depression. *Journal of Child Psychology & Psychiatry*, 735–754.

Chi, D. L., Momany, E. T., Neff, J., Jones, M. P., Warren, J. J., Slayton, R. L.,…Damiano, P. C. (2011). Impact of chronic condition status and the severity on the time of first dental visit for newly Medicaid-enrolled children in Iowa. *Health Services Research, 46*, 572–595.

Chi, M. T. (1978). Knowledge structures and memory development. In R. S. Siegler (Ed.), *Children's thinking: What develops?* (pp. 73–96). Hillsdale, NJ: Erlbaum.

Chibber, R., El-saleh, E., & El harmi, J. (2011). Female circumcision: Obstetrical and psychological sequelae continues unabated in the 21st century. *Journal of Maternal-Fetal and Neonatal Medicine 24*(6), 833–836.

Child Trends (2014). *Low and very low birth weight infants*. Child Trends Data Bank. Retrieved from http://www.childtrends.org/?indicators=low-and-very-low-birthweight-infants.

Child Welfare Information Gateway (2013). *Foster care statistics*. Retrieved from https://www.childwelfare.gov/pubs/factsheets/foster.pdf#page=1&view=Key Findings.

Children's Defense Fund (2005). *State of America's children*. Washington, DC: Author.

Chinas, L. (1992). *The Isthmus Zapotecs: A matrifocal culture of Mexico*. New York, NY: Harcourt Brace Jovanovich College Publishers.

Chisholm, L., & Hurrelmann, K. (1995). Adolescence in modern Europe: Pluralized transition patterns and their implications for personal and social risks. *Journal of Adolescence, 18*, 129–158.

Choi, S., & Gopnik, A. (1995). Early acquisition of verbs in Korean: A cross-linguistic study. *Journal of Child Language, 22*(3), 497–529. http://doi.org/10.1017/S0305000900009934.

Chomsky, N. (1957). *Syntax structures*. The Hague: Mouton and Co.

Chomsky, N. (1969). *Aspects of the theory of syntax*. Cambridge, MA: MIT press.

Christakis, D. A., Zimmerman, F. J., DiGiuseppe, D. L., & McCarty, C. A. (2004). Early Television Exposure and Subsequent Attentional Problems in Children. *Pediatrics, 113*(4), 708–713.

Chuang, M. E., Lamb, C. P., & Hwang, C. P. (2004). Internal reliability, temporal stability, and correlates of individual differences in parental involvement: A 15-year longitudinal study in Sweden. In R. D. Day & M. E. Lamb (Eds.), *Conceptualizing and measuring father involvement* (pp. 129–148). Mahwah, NJ: Erlbaum.

Chumlea, W. C., Schubert, C. M., Roche, A. F., Kulin, H. E., Lee, P. A., Himes, J. H. & Sun, S. S. (2003) Age at menarche and racial comparisons in US girls. *Pediatrics, 111*, 110–113.

Cicchetti, D., & Toth, S. L. (1998). Perspectives on research and practice in developmental psychology. In W. Damon (Series Ed.) & I. E. Sigel & K. A. Renninger (Vol. Eds.), *Handbook of child psychology* (Vol. 4) (pp. 479–583). New York, NY: Wiley.

Cillessen, A. H. N., & Mayeux, L. (2004). From censure to reinforcement: Developmental changes in the association between aggression and social status. *Child Development, 75*, 147–163.

Cipriano, E. A., & Stifter, C. A. (2010). Predicting preschool effortful control from toddler temperament and parenting behaviour. *Journal of Applied Developmental Psychology, 31*, 221–230.

Clapp, J. D., Johnson, M., Voas, R. B., Lange, J. E., Shillington, A., & Russell, C. (2005). Reducing DUI among U.S. college students: Results of an environmental prevention trial. *Addiction, 100*, 327–334.

Clark, E. V. (1995). The lexicon and syntax. In J. L. Miller & P. D. Eimas (Eds.), *Speech, language, and communication* (pp. 303–337). San Diego, CA: Academic Press.

Clark, J. J. (2010). Life as a source of theory: Erik Erikson's contributions, boundaries, and marginalities. In T. W. Miller (Ed.), *Handbook of stressful transitions across the lifespan* (pp. 59–83). New York, NY: Springer.

Clark, K.B., & Clark, M.P. (1947). Racial identification and preference in negro children. *Readings in Social Psychology*, 602–611.

Clarke-Stewart, A., & Brentano, C. (2006). *Divorce: Causes and consequences*. New Haven, CT: Yale University Press.

Clarke-Stewart, K., & Allhusen, V. (2002). Nonparental caregiving. In M. Born- stein (Ed.), *Handbook of parenting: Vol. 3: Being and becoming a parent* (2nd ed., pp. 215–252). Mahwah, NJ: Lawrence Erlbaum Associates.

Claxton, S.E., & van Dulmen, M.H. (2015). Casual sexual relationships and experiences. In J. J. Arnett (Ed.), *Oxford handbook of emerging adulthood*. New York: Oxford University Press.

Clay, E. C. & Seehusen, D. A. (2004). A review of postpartum depression for the primary care physician. *Southern Medical Journal, 97*, 157–162.

Coghill, D., Spiel, G., Baldursson, G., Döpfner, M., Lorenzo, M. J., Ralston, S. J., & Rothenberger, A., & ADORE Study Group (2006). Which factors impact on clinician-rated impairment in children with ADHD? *European Child & Adolescent Psychiatry, 15* (Suppl. 1), I30–I37.

Cohen, D., Gerardin, P., Mazet, P., Purper-Ouakil, D., & Flament, M. F. (2004). Pharmacological treatment of adolescent major depression. *Journal of Child and Adolescent Psychopharmacology, 14*, 19–31.

Cohn, J. F., & Tronick, E. Z. (1983). Three-month-old infants' reaction to stimulated maternal depression. *Child Development, 23*, 185–193.

Coie, J. (2004). The impact of negative social experiences on the development of antisocial behavior. In J. B. Kupersmidt & K. A. Dodge (Eds.), *Children's peer relations: From the development to intervention*. Washington, DC: American Psychological Association.

Colby, A., Kohlberg, L., Gibbs, J., & Lieberman, M. (1983). A longitudinal study of moral judgment. *Monographs of the Society for Research in Child Development, 48*(1–2).

Cole, A., & Kerns, K. A. (2001). Perceptions of sibling qualities and activities in early adolescents. *Journal of Early Adolescence, 21*, 204–226.

Cole, M. (1996). *Cultural psychology: A once and future discipline*. Cambridge, MA: Harvard University Press.

Cole, M., & Bruner, J. S. (1971). Cultural differences and inferences about psychological processes. *American Psychologist, 26*(10), 867.

Cole, P. M., Teti, L. O., & Zahn-Waxler, C. (2003). Mutual emotion regulation and the stability of conduct problems between preschool and early school age. *Development and Psychopathology, 15*, 1–18.

Cole, T., & Leets, L. (1998). Linguistic masking devices and intergroup behavior further evidence of an intergroup linguistic bias. *Journal of Language and Social Psychology, 17*(3), 348–371.

Coleman, M., Ganong, L., & Fine, M. (2000). Reinvestigating remarriage: Another decade of progress. *Journal of Marriage and the Family, 62*, 1288–1307.

Colen, C.G., & Ramey, D.M. (2014). Is breast truly best? Estimating the effects of breastfeeding on long-term child health and well being in the United States using sibling comparisons. *Social Science Medicine, 109*, 55–65.

Colker, L. J. (n.d.). The word gap: The early years make a difference. *Teaching Young Children, 7*(3). Washington, DC: National Association for the Education of Young Children.

Collier-Baker, E., & Suddendorf, T. (2006). Do chimpanzees and 2-year-old children understand double invisible displacement? *Journal of Comparative Psychology, 120*, 89–97.

Collins, W. A., & Laursen, B. (2004). Parent–adolescent relationships and influences. In R. M. Lerner & L. Steinberg (Eds.), *Handbook of adolescent psychology* (2nd ed., pp. 331–361).

Collins, W. A., Maccoby, E. E., Steinberg, L., Hetherington, E. M., & Bornstein, M. H. (2000). Contemporary research on parenting: The case for nature and nurture. *American Psychologist, 55*, 218–232.

Collins, W. A., Madsen, S. D., & Susman-Stillman, A. (2002). Parenting during middle childhood. In M. H. Bornstein (Ed.), *Handbook of parenting: Vol. 1* (2nd ed., pp. 73–101). Mahwah, NJ: Erlbaum.

Colombo, J., & Mitchell, D. W. (2009). Infant visual habituation. *Neurobiology of Learning and Memory, 92*, 225–234.

Combs-Ronto, L. A., Olson, S. L., Lunkenheimer, E. S., & Sameroff, A. J. (2009). Interactions between maternal parenting and children's early disruptive behaviour: Bidirectional associations across the transition from preschool to school entry. *Journal of Abnormal Child Psychology, 37*, 1151–1163.

Compas, B. E., Ey, S., & Grant, K. E. (1993). Taxonomy, assessment, and diagnosis of depression during adolescence. *Psychological Bulletin, 114*, 323–344.

Condon, R. (1990). The rise of adolescence: Change and life stage dilemmas in the central Canadian arctic. *Human Organization, 49(3)*, pp. 266–279.

Connolly, J., & McIsaac, C. (2011). Romantic relationships in adolescence. In M. K. Underwood & J. H. Rosen (Eds.), *Social development: Relationships in infancy, childhood, and adolescence*, 180–206. New York, NY: Guilford.

Connolly, M., & Sullivan, D. (2004). *The essential c-section guide: Pain control, healing at home, getting your body back, and everything else you need to know about a cesarean birth.* New York, NY: Broadway Books.

Conway, C. C., Rancourt, D., Adelman, C. B., Burk, W. J., & Prinstein, M. J. (2011). Depression socialization within friendship groups at the transition to adolescence: The roles of gender and group centrality as moderators of peer influence. *Journal of abnormal psychology, 120(4)*, 857.

Coovadia, H. M., & Wittenberg, D. F. (Eds.) (2004). *Pediatrics and child health: A manual for health professionals in developing countries.* (5th ed.). New York, NY: Oxford University Press.

Coplan, R. J., Prakash, K., O'Neil, K., & Arner, M. (2004). Do you "want" to play? Distinguishing between conflicted shyness and social disinterest in early childhood. *Developmental Psychology, 40*, 244–258.

Core Institute (2013). Executive summary, Core Alcohol and Drug Survey-Long Form. Retrieved from http://core.siu.edu/_common/documents/report0911.pdf.

Cornelius, M. D., Day, N. L., De Genna, N. M., Goldschmidt, L., Leech, S. L., & Willford, J. A. (2011). Effects of prenatal cigarette smoke exposure on neurobehavioral outcomes in 10-year-old children of adolescent mothers. *Neurotoxicology and Teratology, 33*, 137–144.

Cosminsky, S. (2003). Cross-cultural perspectives on midwifery. In L. Dundes (Ed.), *The manner born: Birth rites in cross-cultural perspective* (pp. 69–84). Walnut Creek, CA: AltaMira Press.

Costello, D. M., Swendsen, J., Rose, J. S., & Dierker, L. C. (2008). Risk and protective factors associated with trajectories of depressed mood from adolescence to early adulthood. *Journal of Consulting and Clinical Psychology, 76*, 173–183.

Côté, J. (2006). Emerging adulthood as an institutionalized moratorium: Risks and benefits to identity formation. In J. J. Arnett & J. L. Tanner (Eds.), *Emerging adults in America: Coming of age in the 21st century* (pp. 85–116). Washington, DC: American Psychological Association Press.

Coughlin, C. R. (2009). Prenatal choices: Genetic counseling for variable genetic diseases. In V. Ravitsky, A. Fiester, A. L. Caplan (Eds.), *The Penn Center guide to bioethics* (pp. 415–424). New York, NY: Springer.

Courage, M., & Cowan, N. (Eds.). (2009). *The development of memory in infancy and childhood* (2nd ed.). New York, NY: Psychology Press.

Courage, M. L., & Setliff, A. E. (2009). Debating the impact of television and video material on very young children: Attention, learning, and the developing brain. *Child Development Perspectives, 3(1)*, 72–78.

Courage, M. L., Howe, M. L., & Squires, S. E. (2004). Individual differences in 3.5 month olds' visual attention: What do they predict at 1 year? *Infant Behavior and Development, 127*, 19–30.

Coyne, S. (2007). Violence, longitudinal studies of. In J. J. Arnett (Ed.), *Encyclopedia of children, adolescents, and the media* (Vol. 2, pp. 859–860). Thousand Oaks, CA: Sage.

Coyne, S. M., Padilla-Walker, L. M., & Howard, E. (2015). Media uses in emerging adulthood. In J. J. Arnett (Ed.), *Oxford handbook of emerging adulthood.* New York, NY: Oxford University Press.

Craig, J. M., & Piquero, A. R. (2014). Crime and punishment in emerging adulthood. In J. J. Arnett (Ed.), *Oxford handbook of emerging adulthood.* New York, NY: Oxford University Press.

Crain, W. (2000). *Theories of development: Concepts and applications.* Upper Saddle River, NJ: Prentice Hall.

Cratty, B. J. (1986). *Perceptual and motor development in infants and children* (3rd ed.). Englewood Cliffs, NJ: Prentice-Hall.

Crawford, C., & Krebs, D. (2008). *Foundations of evolutionary psychology.* New York, NY: Lawrence Erlbaum.

Crick, N. R., Ostrov, J. M., Burr, J. E., Cullerton-Sen, C., Jansen-Yeh, E., & Ralston, P. (2006). A longitudinal study of relational and physical aggression in preschool. *Journal of Applied Developmental Psychology, 27*, 254–268.

Crncec, R., Matthey, S., & Nemeth, D. (2010). Infant sleep problems and emotional health: A review of two behavioural approaches. *Journal of Reproductive and Infant Psychology, 28*, 44–54.

Cross, S. E., & Gore, J. S. (2003). Cultural models of the self. In E. S. Cross, S. J. Gore, & R. M. Leary (Eds.), *Handbook of self and identity* (pp. 536–564). New York, NY: Guilford Press.

Crouter, A. C., Manke, B. A., & McHale, S. M. (1995). The family context of gender intensification in early adolescence. *Child Development, 66*, 317–329.

Crow, J. F. (2003). There's something curious about parental–age effects. *Science, 301*, 606–607.

Crowther, M., & Rodriguez, R. (2003). A stress and coping model of custodial grandparenting among African Americans. In B. Hayslip & I. Patrick (Eds.), *Working with custodial grandparents* (pp. 145–162). New York, NY: Springer.

Crum, W. (2010). Foster parent parenting characteristics that lead to increased placement stability or disruption. *Children and Youth Services Review, 32*, 185–190.

Crumbley, D. H. (2006). "Power in the blood": Menstrual taboos and women's power in an African Instituted Church. In R. M. Griffith & B. D. Savage, *Women and religion in the African diaspora: Knowledge, power, and performance* (pp. 81–97). Baltimore, MD: Johns Hopkins University Press.

Csibra, G., Davis, G., Spratling, M. W., & Johnson, M. H. (2000). Gamma oscillations and object processing in the infant brain. *Science, 290*, 1582–1585.

Csikszentmihalyi, M., & Larson, R. W. (1984). *Being adolescent: Conflict and growth in the teenage years.* New York, NY: Basic Books.

Cuevas, K., & Bell, M. A. (2014). Infant attention and early childhood executive function. *Child Development, 85*, 397–404. doi: 10.1111/cdev.12126.

Cummings, E. M., & Bjork, E. L. (1983). Search behavior on multi-choice hiding tasks: Evidence for an objective conception of space in infancy. *International Journal of Behavioral Development, 6(1)*, 71–87. doi:10.1177/016502548300600105.

Cummings, E. M., George, M. R., & Kouros, C. D. (2010). Emotional development. In I. B. Weiner & W. B. Craighead (Eds.), *Corsini encyclopedia of psychology* (pp. 1–2). New York, NY: Wiley.

Cunningham, M., & Thorton, A. (2007). Direct and indirect influences of parents' marital instability on children's attitudes toward cohabitation in young adulthood. *Journal of Divorce & Remarriage, 46*, 125–143.

Curran, K., DuCette, J., Eisenstein, J., & Hyman, I. A. (2001, August). *Statistical analysis of the cross-cultural data: The third year*. Paper presented at the meeting of the American Psychological Association, San Francisco, CA.

D'Andrade, R. (1987). A folk model of the mind. In D. Holland & N. Quinn (Eds.), *Cultural models in language and thought* (pp. 112–148). New York, NY: Cambridge University Press.

da Motta, C. C. L., Naziri, D., & Rinne, C. (2006). The Influence of emotional support during childbirth: A clinical study. *Journal of Prenatal & Perinatal Psychology & Health, 20*, 325–341.

Daddis, C., & Smetana, J. (2005). Middle-class African American families' expectations for adolescents' behavioural autonomy. *International Journal of Behavioral Development, 29*, 371–381.

Dale, P. S., & Goodman, J. C. (2005). Commonality and individual differences in vocabulary growth. In M. Tomasello & D. I. Slobin (Eds.), *Beyond nature–nurture: Essays in honor of Elizabeth Bates* (pp. 41–78). Mahwah, NJ: Erlbaum.

Daley, A., Jolly, K., & MacArthur, C. (2009). The effectiveness of exercise in the management of post-natal depression: Systematic review and meta-analysis. *Family Practice, 26*(2), 154–162. http://doi.org/10.1093/fampra/cmn101.

Dalton, K. M., Holsen, L., Abbeduto, L., & Davidson, R. J. (2008). Brain function and gaze fixation during facial-emotion processing in fragile X and autism. *Autism Research: Official Journal of the International Society for Autism Research, 1*(4), 231–239. http://doi.org/10.1002/aur.32.

Damon, W. (1983). *Social and personality development*. New York, NY: Norton.

Daniels, H., Cole, M., & Wertsch, J. V. (Eds.). (2007). *The Cambridge companion to Vygotsky*. London: Cambridge University Press.

Daniels, P., Godfrey, F. N., & Mayberry, R. (2006). Barriers to prenatal care among Black women of low socioeconomic status. *American Journal of Health Behavior, 30*, 188–198.

Darwin, C. (1872). *The expression of the emotions in man and animals*. New York, NY: D. Appleton.

Dasen, P., Inhelder, B., Lavalle, M., & Retschitzki, J. (1978). *Naissance de l'intelligence chez l'enfant Baoule de Cote d'Ivorie*. Berne: Hans Huber.

Daum, M. M., Prinz, W., & Aschersleben, G. (2011). Perception and production of object-related grasping in 6-month-olds. *Journal of experimental child psychology, 108*(4), 810–818.

David, B., Grace, D., & Ryan, M. K. (2004). The gender wars: A self-categorization perspective on the development of gender identity. In M. Bennett & S. Fabio (Eds.), *The development of the social self* (pp. 135–157). East Sussex, UK: Psychology Press.

Davies, P. T., Harold, G. T., Goeke-Morey, M. C., & Cummings, E. M. (2002). Child emotional security and interparental conflict. *Monography of the Society for Research in Child Development, 67*(3, Serial No. 270).

Davies, R. (2004). New understandings of parental grief. *Journal of Advanced Nursing, 46*, 506–513.

Davis, D. W. (2003). Cognitive outcomes in school-age children born prematurely. *Neonatal Network, 22*, 27–38.

Davis, K. (2010). Coming of age online: The developmental underpinnings of girls' blogs. *Journal of Adolescent Research, 25*, 145–171.

Davis, K. F., Parker, K. P., & Montgomery, G. L. (2004). Sleep in infants and young children. Part I: Normal sleep. *Journal of Pediatric Health Care, 18*, 65–71.

Davis, S., & Davis, D. (2012). Morocco. In J. J. Arnett (Ed.), *Adolescent Psychology Around the World*. New York, NY: Taylor & Francis.

Davis-Unger, A. C., & Carlson, S. M. (2008). Children's teaching skills: The role of theory of mind and executive function. *Mind, Brain, and Education, 3*, 128–135.

Dawson, G., Meltzoff, A. N., Osterling, J., Rinaldi, J., & Brown, E. (1998). Children with autism fail to orient to naturally occurring social stimuli. *Journal of Autism & Developmental Disorders, 28*, 479–485.

de Haan, M., & Johnson, M. H. (2003). Mechanisms and theories of brain development. In M. de Haan & M. H. Johnson (Eds.), *The cognitive neuroscience of development* (pp. 1–18). Hove, UK: Psychology Press.

de Villarreal, L. E. M., Arredondo, P., Hernández, R., & Villarreal, J. Z. (2006). Weekly administration of folic acid and epidemiology of neural tube defects. *Maternal and Child Health Journal, 10*, 397–401.

de Villiers, P. A., & de Villiers, J. G. (1978). *Language acquisition*. Cambridge, MA: Harvard University Press.

de Vonderweid, U., & Leonessa, M. (2009). Family centered neonatal care. *Early Human Development, 85*, S37–S38.

De Weerd, A. W., & van den Bossche, A. S. (2003). The development of sleep during the first months of life. *Sleep Medicine Reviews, 7*, 179–191.

DeCasper, A. J., & Spence, M. J. (1986). Prenatal maternal speech influences newborns' perception of speech sounds. *Infant Behavior and Development, 9*, 133–150.

DeHart, T., Pelham, B., & Tennen, H. (2006). What lies beneath: Parenting style and implicit self–esteem. *Journal of Experimental Social Psychology, 42*, 1–17.

Delaney, C. (2000). Making babies in a Turkish village. In J. DeLoache & A. Gottlieb (Eds.), *A world of babies: Imagined childcare guides for seven societies* (pp. 117–144). New York, NY: Cambridge University Press.

Delaney, S. M., Dobson, V., Harvey, E. M., Mohan, K. M., Weidenbacher, H. J., & Leber, N. R. (2000). Stimulus motion increases measured visual field extent in children 3.5 to 30 months of age. *Optometry & Vision Science, 77*(2), 82–89.

DeLoache, J., & Gottlieb, A. (2000). *A world of babies: Imagined childcare guides for seven societies*. New York, NY: Cambridge University Press.

DeLoache, J. S., Chiong, C., Sherman, K., Islam, N., Vanderborght, M., Troseth, G. L., …O'Doherty, K. (2010). Do babies learn from baby media? *Psychological Science, 21*, 1570–1574.

DeMeo, J. (2006). *Saharasia: The 4000 bce origins of child abuse, sex-repression, warfare and social violence, in the deserts of the old world* (Revised 2nd ed.). El Cerrito, CA: Natural Energy Works.

Demetriou, A., & Raftopoulos, A. (Eds.). (2004). *Cognitive developmental change: Theories, models and measurement*. New York, NY: Cambridge University Press.

Deming, D. M., Reidy, K. C., Briefel, R. R., Fox, M. K., & Condon, E. (2012). The Feeding Infants and Toddlers Study (FITS) 2008: Dramatic changes in the amount and quality of vegetables in the diet occur after the first year of life. *The FASEB Journal, 26*, 374.4.

Dennis, C. L. (2004). Can we identify mothers at risk for postpartum depression in the immediate postpartum period using the Edinburgh Postnatal Depression Scale? *Journal of Affective Disorders, 78*, 163–169.

DeParle, J. (2010, June 27). A world on the move. *The New York Times*, pp. WK1, 4.

Derom, C., Thiery, E., Vlientinck, R., Loos, R., & Derom, R. (1996). Handedness in twins according to zygosity and chorion type: A preliminary report. *Behavior Genetics, 26*, 407–408.

DeRosier, M. E., & Thomas, J. M. (2003). Strengthening sociometric prediction: Scientific advances in the assessment of children's peer relations. *Child Development, 75*, 1379–1392.

DeSena, A. D., Murphy, R. A., Douglas-Palumberi, H., Blau, G., Kelly, B., Horwitz, S. M., & Kaufman, J. (2005). SAFE homes: Is it worth the cost? An evaluation of a group home permanency planning program for children who first enter out-of-home care. *Child Abuse and Neglect, 29*, 627–643.

Diamond, A. (2004). Normal development of prefrontal cortex from birth to young adulthood: Cognitive functions, anatomy, and biochemistry. In D. T. Stuff & R. T. Knight (Eds.), *Principles of frontal lobe function* (pp. 466–503). New York, NY: Oxford University Press.

Diamond, A., & Lee, K. (2011). Interventions shown to aid executive function development in children 4 to 12 years old. *Science, 333*(6045): 959–964. doi: 10.1126/science.1204529.

Diamond, A. D. (1985). Development of the ability to use recall to guide action, as indicated by infants' performance on AB. *Child Development, 56,* 868–883.

Diamond, J. (1992). *The third chimpanzee: The evolution and future of the human animal.* New York, NY: Harper Perennial.

Dias, B. G., Maddox, S. A., Klengel, T., & Ressler, K. J. (2015). Epigenetic mechanisms underlying learning and the inheritance of learned behaviors. *Trends in Neurosciences, 38*(2), 96–107. doi:10.1016/j.tins.2014.12.003.

Dick, F., Dronkers, N. F., Pizzamiglio, L., Saygin, A. P., Small, S. L., & Wilson, S. (2004). Language and the brain. In M. Tomasello & D. I. Slobin (Eds.), *Beyond nature–nurture: Essays in honor of Elizabeth Bates* (pp. 237–260). Mahwah, NH: Erlbaum.

Dickinson, D. K., McCabe, A., & Essex, M. J. (2013). A window of opportunity we must open to all: The case for preschool with high-quality support for language and literacy. In D. K. Dickinson & S. B. Neuman (Eds.), *Handbook of Early Literacy Research,* 2nd ed. (pp. 11–28). New York, NY: Guilford Press.

Diener, M. (2000). Gifts from gods: A Balinese guide to early child rearing. In J. DeLoache & A. Gottlieb (Eds.), *A world of babies: Imagined childcare guides for seven societies* (pp. 91–116). New York, NY: Cambridge University Press.

Dieter, J. N., Field, T., Hernandez-Reif, M., Emory, E. K., & Redzepi, M. (2003). Stable preterm infants gain more weight and sleep less after five days of massage therapy. *Journal of Pediatric Psychology, 28*(6), 403–411.

Dijkstra, J. K., Lidenberg, S., & Veenstra, R. (2008). Beyond the class norm: Bullying behavior of popular adolescents and its relation to peer acceptance and rejection. *Journal of Abnormal Child Psychology, 36,* 1289–1299.

Dilworth-Anderson, Boswell, G., & Cohen, M. D. (2007). Spiritual and religious coping values and beliefs among African American caregivers: A qualitative study. *Journal of Applied Gerontology, 26,* 355–369.

DiPietro, J., Hilton, S., Hawkins, M., Costigan, K., & Pressman, E. (2002). Maternal stress and affect influence fetal neurobehavioral development. *Developmental Psychology, 38,* 659–668.

Dishion, T. J., & Dodge, K. A. (2005). Peer contagion in interventions for children and adolescents: Moving towards an understanding of the ecology and dynamics of change. *Journal of Abnormal Child Psychology, 33,* 395–400.

Dishion, T. J., McCord, J., & Poulin, F. (1999). When interventions harm: Groups and problem behavior. *American Psychologist, 54,* 755–764.

Dixon Jr, W. E., Salley, B. J., & Clements, A. D. (2006). Temperament, distraction, and learning in toddlerhood. *Infant Behavior and Development, 29*(3), 342–357.

Dodge, K. A. (2007). The nature–nurture debate and public policy. In G. W. Ladd (Ed.), *Appraising the human developmental sciences: Essays in honor of Merrill-Palmer Quarterly* (pp. 262–271). Detroit, MI: Wayne State University Press.

Dodge, K. A. (2008). Framing public policy and prevention of chronic violence in American youths. *American Psychologist, 63,* 573–590.

Dodge, K. A., Coie, J.D., & Lynam, D. (2006). Aggression and antisocial behavior in youth. In W. Damon & R. Lerner (Eds.), & N. Eisenberg (Vol. Ed.), *Handbook of child psychology: Vol. 3. Social, emotional and personality development* (6th ed., pp. 719–788). New York, NY: Wiley.

Doherty, I., & Landells, J. (2006). Literacy and numeracy. In J. Clegg & J. Ginsborg (Eds.), *Language and social disadvantage: Theory into practice* (pp. 44–58). Hoboken, NJ: John Wiley & Sons.

Dolphin, T., & Lanning, T. (Eds.) (2011). *Rethinking apprenticeships.* London, England: Institute for Public Policy Research.

Domsch, H., Lohaus, A., & Thomas, H. (2010). Infant attention, heart rate, and looking time during habituation/dishabituation. *Infant Behavior & Development, 33,* 321–329.

Donat, D. (2006). Reading their way: A balanced approach that increases achievement. *Reading & Writing Quarterly: Overcoming Learning Difficulties, 22,* 305–323.

Donovan, J., & Zucker, C. (2010, October). Autism's first child. *The Atlantic,* pp. 78–90.

Dorjee, T., Baig, N., & Ting-Toomey, S. (2013). A social ecological perspective on understanding "honor killing": An intercultural moral dilemma. *Journal of Intercultural Communication Research, 42*(1), 1–21.

Douglass, C. B. (2005). *Barren states: The population "implosion" in Europe.* New York, NY: Berg.

Douglass, C. B. (2007). From duty to desire: Emerging adulthood in Europe and its consequences. *Child Development Perspectives, 1,* 101–108.

Doyle, L. W., Faber, B., Callanan, C., Ford, G. W., & Davis, N. M. (2004). Extremely low birth weight and body size in early adulthood. *Archives of Disorders in Childhood, 89,* 347–350.

Driessen, R., Leyendecker, B., Schölmerich, A., & Harwood, R. (2010). Everyday experiences of 18- to 36-month-old children from migrant families: The influence of host culture and migration experience. *Early Child Development and Care, 180,* 1143–1163.

Dritsa, M., Dupuis, G., Lowensteyn, I., & Da Costa, D. (2009). Effects of home-based exercise on fatigue in postpartum depressed women: Who is more likely to benefit and why? *Journal of Psychosomatic Research, 67*(2), 159–163. http://doi.org/10.1016/j.jpsychores.2009.01.010.

Dubas, J. S., & Petersen, A. (1991). A longitudinal investigation of adolescents' changing perceptions of pubertal timing. *Developmental Psychology, 27,* 580–586.

DuBois, D., Felner, R., Brand, S., Phillip, R., & Lease, A. (1996). Early adolescent self-esteem: A developmental–ecological framework and assessment strategy. *Journal of Research on Adolescence, 6,* 543–579.

Due, P., Holstein, B. E., Lunch, J., Diderichsen, F., Gabhain, S. N., Scheidt, P., & Currie, C. (2005). The health behavior in school-aged children bullying working group. *European Journal of Public Health, 15,* 128–132.

Duggan, M., & Brenner, J. (2013). *The demographics of social media users.* Washington, DC: Pew Research Center.

Duncan, G. J., & Magnuson, K. (2011). The nature and impact of early achievement skills, attention skills, and behavior problems. In G. J. Duncan & R. J. Murnane (Eds.), *Whither opportunity? Rising inequality, schools, and children's life chances* (pp. 47–70). New York, NY: Russell Sage Foundation.

Dunn, D. M., Culhane, S. E., & Taussig, H. N. (2010). Children's appraisals of their experiences in out-of-home care. *Children and Youth Services Reviews, 32,* 1324–1330.

Dunn, J. (1988). *The beginnings of social understanding.* Cambridge, MA: Harvard University Press.

Dunn, J. (2002). The adjustment of children in stepfamilies: Lessons from community studies. *Child and Adolescent Mental Health, 7,* 154–161.

Dunn, J. (2004). Sibling relationships. In P. K. Smith & C. H. Hart (Eds.), *Handbook of childhood social development* (pp. 223–237). Malden, MA: Blackwell.

Dunn, J., & Kendrick, C. (1982). *Siblings: Love, envy, and understanding.* London, UK: Grant McIntyre.

Dunn, J., & Munn, P. (1985). Becoming a family member: Family conflict and the development of social understanding in the second year. *Child Development, 56,* 480–492.

Dustmann, C., & Schoenberg, U. (2008). Why does the German apprenticeship system work? In K. U. Mayer & H. Solga (Eds.), *Skill information: Interdisciplinary and cross-national perspective* (p. 85–108). New York, NY: Cambridge University Press.

Dworkin, J. B., & Larson, R. (2001). Age trends in the experience of family discord in single-mother families across adolescence. *Journal of Adolescence, 24,* 529–534.

Dyer, S., & Moneta, G. (2006). Frequency of parallel, associative and cooperative play in British children of different socioeconomic status. *Social Behavior and Personality, 34,* 587–592.

Eberhart-Phillips, J. E., Frederick, P. D., & Baron, R. C. (1993). Measles in pregnancy: A descriptive study of 58 cases. *Obstetrics and Gynecology, 82,* 797–801.

Eckenrode, J., Zielinski, D., Smith, E., Marcynyszyn, L. A., Henderson, C. R., Jr., & Kitzman, H. (2001). Child maltreatment and the early onset of problem behaviors: Can a program of nurse home visitation break the link? *Development and Psychopathology, 13,* 873–890.

Eder, D. (1995). *School talk: Gender and adolescent culture.* New Brunswick, NJ: Rutgers University Press.

Edgardh, K. (2002). Adolescent sexual health in Sweden. *Sexually Transmitted Infections, 78*(5), 352–356.

Edmonds, L. (2011). Telegraphic speech. In J. Kreutzer, J. DeLuca, & B. Kaplan (Eds.), *Encyclopedia of clinical neuropsychology.* New York, NY: Springer.

Edwards, C. P. (2000). Children's play in cross-cultural perspective: A new look at the Six Cultures study. *Cross-Cultural Research: The Journal of Comparative Social Science, 34,* 318–338.

Edwards, C. P. (2005). Children's play in cross-cultural perspective: A new look at the "six cultures" study. In F. F. McMahon, D. E. Lytle, & B. Sutton-Smith (Eds.), *Play: An interdisciplinary synthesis* (pp. 81–96). Lanham, MD: University Press of America.

Edwards, C. P., Ren, L., & Brown, J. (2015). Early contexts of learning: Family and community socialization during infancy and toddlerhood. In L. A. Jensen (Ed.), *Oxford handbook of human development and culture.* (pp. 165–181). New York, NY: Oxford University Press.

Egeland, B., & Carlson, B. (2004). Attachment and psychopathology. In L. Atkinson & S. Goldberg (Eds.), *Attachment issues in psychopathology and intervention* (pp. 27–48). Mahwah, NJ: Erlbaum.

Ehrenberg, H. M., Dierker, L., Milluzzi, C., & Mercer, B. M. (2003). Low maternal weight, failure to thrive in pregnancy, and adverse pregnancy outcomes. *American Journal of Obstetrics and Gynecology, 189,* 1726–1730.

Ehrenreich, B. (2010). *Witches, midwives, and nurses: A history of women healers.* New York, NY: Feminist Press.

Eiden, R. D., & Reifman, A. (1996). Effects of Brazelton demonstrations on later parenting: A meta-analysis. *Journal of Pediatric Psychology, 21,* 857–868.

Eiden, R. D., Foote, A., & Schuetze, P. (2007). Maternal cocaine use and care-giving status: Group differences in caregiver and infant risk variables. *Addictive Behaviors, 32,* 465–476.

Eisenberg, A., Murkoff, H., & Hathaway, S. (2009). *What to expect the toddler years.* New York, NY: Workman Publishing.

Eisenberg, N., & Fabes, R. A. (2006). Emotion regulation and children's socioemotional competence. In L. Balter & C. S. Tamis-LeMonda (Eds.), *Child psychology: A handbook of contemporary issues* (2nd ed., pp. 357–381). New York, NY: Psychology Press.

Eisenberg, N. & Valiente, C. (2004). Empathy-related responding: Moral, social and socialization correlates. In A. G. Miller (Ed.), *Social psychology of good and evil.* New York, NY: Guilford Press.

Eisenberg, N., Zhou, Q, Liew, J., Champion, C., & Pidada, S. U. (2006). Emotion, emotion-regulated regulation, and social functioning. In X. Chen, D. C. French, & B. H. Schneider (Eds.), *Peer relationships in cultural context* (pp. 170–199). New York, NY: Cambridge University Press.

Ekman, P. (2003). *Emotions revealed.* New York, NY: Times Books.

Eldin, A. S. (2009). Female mutilation. In P. S. Chandra, H. Herrman, J. Fisher, M. Kastrup, U. Niaz, M. B. Rondón, & A. Okasha (Eds.), *Contemporary topics in women's mental health: Global perspectives in a changing society* (pp. 485–498). Hoboken, NJ: Wiley & Sons.

Elkind, D. (1967). Egocentrism in adolescence. *Child Development, 38,* 1025–1034.

Elkind, D. (1978). Understanding the young adolescent. *Adolescence, 13,* 127–134.

Elkind, D. (1985). Egocentrism redux. *Developmental Review, 5,* 218–226.

Elliott, G. C., Cunningham, S. M., Linder, M., Colangelo, M., & Gross, M. (2005). Child physical abuse and self-perceived social isolation among adolescents. *Journal of Interpersonal Violence, 20,* 1663–1684.

Ellison, N. C., Steinfield, C., & Lampe, C. (2007). The benefits of Facebook "friends": Social capital and college students' use of online social network sites. *Journal of Computer-Mediated Communication, 12,* 1143–1168.

Ember, C. R., Ember, M., & Peregrine, P. N. (2011). *Anthropology* (13th edition). New York, NY: Pearson.

Emery, R. E., Sbarra, D., & Grover, T. (2005). Divorce mediation: Research and reflections. *Family Court Review, 43,* 22–37.

Engelmann, J. B., Moore, S., Capra, C. M., & Berns, G. S. (2012). Differential neurobiological effects of expert advice on risky choice in adolescents and adults. *Social cognitive and affective neuroscience, 7*(5), 557–567.

Englander, F., Terregrossa, R. A., & Wang, Z. (2010). Internet use among college students: Tool or toy? *Educational Review, 62,* 85–96.

Eppig, C., Fincher, C. L., & Thornhill, R. (2010). Parasite prevalence and the worldwide distribution of cognitive ability. *Proceedings of the Royal Society B, 277,* 3801–3808.

Ericsson, K. A. (1990). Peak performance and age: An examination of peak performance in sports. In P. Baltes & M. M. Baltes (Eds.), *Successful aging* (pp. 164–196). Cambridge, MA: Cambridge University Press.

Erikson, E. H. (1950). *Childhood and society.* New York, NY: Norton.

Erikson, E. H. (1968). *Identity: Youth and crisis.* New York, NY: Norton.

Eriksson, C., Hamberg, K., & Salander, P. (2007). Men's experiences of intense fear related to childbirth investigated in a Swedish qualitative study. *Journal of Men's Health & Gender, 4,* 409–418.

Erlandsson, K., & Lindgren, H. (2009). From belonging to belonging through a blessed moment of love for a child—The birth of a child from the fathers' perspective. *Journal of Men's Health,* 338–344.

Eslea, M., Menesini, E., Morita, Y., O'Moore, M., Mora-Nerchan, J. A., Pereira, B., & Smith, P. K. (2004). Friendship and loneliness among bullies and victims: Data from seven countries. *Aggressive Behavior, 30,* 71–83.

Espelage, D. L., & Swearer, S. M. (2004). *Bullying in American schools.* Mahwah, NJ: Lawrence Erlbaum.

Espy, K. A., Fang, H., Johnson, C., Stopp, C., Wiebe, S. A., & Respass, J. (2011). Prenatal tobacco exposure: Developmental outcomes in the neonatal period. *Developmental Psychology, 47,* 153–169.

Eveleth, P. B., & Tanner, J. M. (1990). *Worldwide variation in human growth.* Cambridge, MA: Cambridge University Press.

Everett, G. E., Olmi, D. J., Edwards, R. P., Tingstrom, D. H., Sterling-Turner, H. E. & Christ, T. J. (2007). An empirical investigation of time-out with and without escape extinction to treat escape-maintained noncompliance. *Behavior Modification, 31,* 412–434.

Fabes, R. A., Martin, C. L., & Hanish, L. D. (2003). Young children's play qualities in same-, other-, and mixed-sex peer groups. *Child Development, 74,* 921–932.

Fabiano, G. A., Pelham, Jr., W. E., Manos, M. J., Gnagy, E. M., Chronis, A. M., Onvango, A. N.,...Swain, S. (2004). An evaluation of three time-out procedures for children with attention deficit/hyperactivity disorder. *Behavior Therapy, 35,* 449–469.

Facio, A., & Micocci, F. (2003). Emerging adulthood in Argentina. In J. J. Arnett & N. Galambos (Eds.), *New Directions in Child and Adolescent Development, 100,* 21–31.

Fackler, M. (2007, June 22). As Japan ages, universities struggle to fill classrooms. *The New York Times,* p. A3.

Fagan, J. F., Holland, C. R., & Wheeler, K. (2007). The prediction, from infancy, of adult IQ and achievement. *Intelligence, 35,* 225–231.

Farver, J. A., Bhadha, B. R., & Narang, S. K. (2002). Acculturation and psychological functioning in Asian Indian adolescents. *Social Development, 11,* 11–29.

Fearon, P., O'Connell, P., Frangou, S., Aquino, P., Nosarti, C., Allin, M.,… Murray, R. (2004). Brain volumes in adult survivors of very low birth weight: A sibling–controlled study. *Pediatrics, 114,* 367–371.

Federico, M. J., & Liu, A. H. (2003). Overcoming childhood asthma disparities of the inner-city poor. *Pediatric Clinics of North America, 50,* 655–675.

Fefferman, N. H., & Naumova, E. N. (2015). Dangers of vaccine refusal near the herd immunity threshold: a modelling study. *The Lancet. Infectious Diseases.* http://doi.org/10.1016/S1473-3099(15)00053-5.

Feigenbaum, P. (2002). Private speech: Cornerstone of Vygotsky's theory of the development of higher psychological processes. *Voices within Vygotsky's non-classical psychology: Past, present, future, 161–174.*

Feigenson, L. (2011). Predicting sights from sounds: 6-month old infants' intermodal numerical abilities. *Journal of Experimental Child Psychology, 110*(3), 347–361.

Fekkes, M., Pijpers, F. I., & Verloove-Vanhorick, S. P. (2004). Bullying behavior and associations with psychosomatic complaints and depression in victims. *Journal of Pediatrics, 144,* 17–22.

Feldkamper, M., & Schaeffel, F. (2003). Interactions of genes and environment in myopia. *Developmental Opthalmology, 37,* 34–49.

Feldman, R., & Eidelman, A. I. (2003). Skin-to-skin contact (kangaroo care) accelerates autonomic and neurobehavioral maturation in preterm infants. *Developmental Medicine and Child Neurology, 45,* 274–281.

Feldman, R., Weller, A., Sirota, L., & Eidelman, A. I. (2003). Testing a family intervention hypothesis: The contribution of mother–infant skin-to-skin (kangaroo care) to family interaction, proximity, and touch. *Journal of Family Psychology, 17,* 94–107.

Feldman-Salverlsberg, P. (2002). Is infertility an unrecognized public health and population problem? The view from the Cameroon grassfields. In M. C. Inhorn & F. van Balen (Eds.), *Infertility around the globe: New thinking on childlessness, gender, and reproductive technologies* (pp. 215–231). Berkeley: University of California Press.

Ferber, S. G., Kuint, J., Weller, A., Feldman, S. D., Arbel, E., & Kohelet, D. (2002). Massage therapy by mothers and trained professionals enhances weight gain in preterm infants. *Early Human Development, 67,* 37–45.

Ferguson, C. J. (2013). Spanking, corporal punishment and negative long-term outcomes: *A meta-analytic review of longitudinal studies. Clinical Psychology Review, 33*(1), 196–208.

Fergusson, D. M., Boden, J. M., & Horwood, L. J. (2008). Exposure to childhood sexual and physical abuse and adjustment in early adulthood. *Child Abuse and Neglect, 32,* 607–619.

Ferguson, G. M., Hafen, C. A., & Laursen, B. (2010). Adolescent psychological and academic adjustment as a function of discrepancies between actual and ideal self-perceptions. *Journal of Youth and Adolescence, 39,* 1485–1497.

Fernald, A., & O'Neill, D. K. (1993). Peekaboo across cultures: How mothers and infants play with voices, faces, and expectations. In K. MacDonald (Ed.), *Parent–child play* (pp. 259–285). Albany: State University of New York Press.

Fernald, A., Marchman, V. A., & Weisleder, A. (2013). SES differences in language processing skill and vocabulary are evident at 18 months. *Developmental Science, 16*(2), 234–248. http://doi.org/10.1111/desc.12019.

Fernald, A., Perfors, A., & Marchman, V. A. (2006). Picking up speed in understanding: Speech processing efficiency and vocabulary growth across the 2nd year. *Developmental Psychology, 42,* 98–116.

Field, M. J., & Behrman, R. E. (Eds.) (2003). *When children die.* Washington, DC: National Academies Press.

Field, T. (2010). Pregnancy and labor massage. *Expert Reviews in Obstetrics & Gynecology, 5,* 177–181.

Field, T. M. (1998). Massage therapy effects. *American Psychologist, 53,* 1270–1281.

Field, T. M. (2001). Massage therapy facilitates weight gain in preterm infants. *Current Directions in Psychological Science, 10,* 51–55.

Field, T. M. (2004). Massage therapy effects on depressed pregnant women. *Journal of Psychosomatic Obstetrics and Gynaecology, 25,* 115–122.

Field, T., Diego, M., & Hernandez-Reif, M. (2010). Preterm infant massage therapy: A review. *Infant Behavior and Development, 33,* 115–124.

Field, T., Hernandez-Reif, M., & Diego, M. (2006). Newborns of depressed mothers who received moderate versus light pressure massage during therapy. *Infant Behavior and Development, 29,* 54–58.

Fildes, V. (1995). The culture and biology of breastfeeding: An historical review of Western Europe. In P. Stuart-Macadam & K. A. Dettwyler (Eds.), *Breastfeeding: Biocultural perspectives* (pp. 101–131). Hawthorne, NY: Aldein de Gruyter.

Fingerman, K.L., & Yahirun, J.J. (2015). Family relationships. In J. J. Arnett (Ed.), *Oxford Handbook of Emerging Adulthood.* New York: Oxford University Press.

Finkel, M. (2007a). Bedlam in the blood: Malaria. *National Geographic,* July, 32–67.

Finkel, M. (2007b). Stopping a global killer. *National Geographic Magazine.* Retrieved from http://ngm.nationalgeographic.com/2007/07/malaria/finkel-text.

Finley, G. E., & Schwartz, S. J. (2010). The divided world of the child: Divorce and long-term psychosocial adjustment. *Family Court Review, 48,* 516–527.

Finn, C. A. (2001). Reproductive ageing and the menopause. *International Journal of Developmental Biology, 45,* 613–617.

Fisch, H., Hyun, G., Golden, R., Hensle, T. W., Olsson, C. A., & Liberson, G. L. (2003). The influence of paternal age on Down syndrome. *Journal of Urology, 169,* 2275–2278.

Fisher, C. B. (2003). A goodness–of–fit ethic for child assent to nonbeneficial research. *The American Journal of Bioethics, 3,* 27–28.

Fitneva, S., & Matsui, T. (2015). The emergence and development of language across cultures. In L. A. Jensen (Ed.), *Oxford handbook of human development and culture: An interdisciplinary perspective.* New York, NY: Oxford University Press.

Flanagan, C., & Botcheva, L. (1999). Adolescents' preference for their homeland and other countries. In F. D. Alsaker & A. Flammer (Eds.), *The adolescent experience: European and American adolescents in the 1990s* (pp. 131–144). Mahwah, NJ: Erlbaum.

Flannery, K. A., & Liederman, J. (1995). Is there really a syndrome involving the co-occurrence of neurodevelopmental disorder, talent, non–right handedness and immune disorder among children? *Cortex, 31,* 503–515.

Flavell, J. H., Beach, D. R., & Chinsky, J. M. (1966). Spontaneous verbal rehearsal in a memory task as a function of age. *Child Development, 37,* 283–299.

Flavell, J. H., Friedrichs, A., & Hoyt, J. (1970). Developmental changes in memorization process. *Cognitive Psychology, 1,* 324–340.

Flavell, J. H., Miller, P. H., & Miller, S. A. (2002). *Cognitive development* (4th ed.). Upper Saddle River, NJ: Prentice Hall.

Fleming, T. P. (2006). The periconceptional and embryonic period. In P. Gluckman, & M. Hanson (Eds.), *Developmental origins of health and disease* (pp. 51–61). New York, NY: Cambridge University Press.

Flowers, P., & Buston, K. (2001). "I was terrified of being different": Exploring gay men's accounts of growing up in a heterosexist society. *Journal of Adolescence, 24,* 51–66.

Floyd, F., & Bakeman, R. (2006). Coming-out across the life course: Implications of age and historical context. *Archives of Sexual Behavior, 35,* 287–297.

Flynn, J. R. (1999). The discovery of IQ gains over time. *American Psychologist, 54,* 5–20.

Flynn, J. R. (2012). Are we getting smarter? Rising IQ in the twenty-first century. Cambridge, England: Cambridge University Press.

Foehr, U. (2007). Computer use, age differences in. In J. J. Arnett (Ed.), *Encyclopedia of children, adolescents, and the media, Vol. 1* (pp. 202–204). Thousand Oaks, CA: Sage.

Fogel, A., Hsu, H., Nelson-Goens, G. C., Shapiro, A. F., & Secrist, C. (2006). Effects of normal and perturbed social play on the duration and amplitude of different types of infant smiles. *Developmental Psychology, 42,* 459–473.

Fomon, S. J., & Nelson, S. E. (2002). Body composition of the male and female reference infants. *Annual Review of Nutrition, 22,* 1–17.

Fong, V. L. (2002). China's one-child policy and the empowerment of urban daughters. *American Anthropologist, 104,* 1098–1109.

Ford, C., & Beach, F. (1951). *Patterns of sexual behavior.* New York, NY: Harper & Row.

Ford, C. S. (1945). *A comparative study of human reproduction.* New Haven, CT: Yale University Press.

Foss, R. D. (2007). Improving graduated driver licensing systems: A conceptual approach and its implications. *Journal of Safety Research, 38,* 185–192.

Foster, E. M., & Watkins, S. (2010). The value of reanalysis: TV viewing and attention problems. *Child Development, 81*(1), 368–375.

Foureur, M., Ryan, C. L., Nicholl, M., & Homer, C. (2010). Inconsistent evidence: Analysis of six national guidelines for vaginal birth after cesarean section. *Birth: Issues in Perinatal Care, 37,* 3–10.

Fox, J., & Warber, K. M. (2013). Romantic relationship development in the age of Facebook: An exploratory study of emerging adults' perceptions, motives, and behaviors. *CyberPsychology, Behavior & Social Networking, 16*(1), 3–7. http://doi.org/10.1089/cyber.2012.0288.

Fox, M. K., Pac, S., Devaney, B., & Jankowski, L. (2004). Feeding infants and toddlers study: What foods are infants and toddlers eating? *American Dietetic Association Journal, 104* (Suppl.), S22–S30.

Fraley, R. C., & Spieker, S. J. (2003). Are infant attachment patterns continuously or categorically distributed? A taxometric analysis of strange situation behavior. *Developmental Psychology, 39*(3), 387–404. http://doi.org/10.1037/0012-1649.39.3.387.

Fraley, R. C., Roisman, G. I., Booth-LaForce, C., Owen, M. T., & Holland, A. S. (2013). Interpersonal and genetic origins of adult attachment styles: A longitudinal study from infancy to early adulthood. *Journal of Personality and Social Psychology, 104,* 817–838. doi: 10.1037/a0031435.

Francis, D. A., & DePalma, R. (2014). Teacher perspectives on abstinence and safe sex education in South Africa. *Sex Education: Sexuality, Society and Learning, 14(1),* 81–94.

Frankenburg, W. K., Dodds, J., Archer, P., Shapiro, H., & Bresnick, B. (1992). The Denver II: A major revision and restandardization of the Denver Developmental Screening Test. *Pediatrics, 89,* 91–97.

Frankman, E. A., Wang, L., Bunker, C. H., & Lowder, J. L. (2009). Episiotomy in the United States: Has anything changed? *American Journal of Obstetrics and Gynecology, 537,* e1–e7.

Fransen, M., Meertens, R., & Schrander-Stumpel, C. (2006). Communication and risk presentation in genetic counseling: Development of a checklist. *Patient Education and Counseling, 61,* 126–133.

Frawley, T. J. (2008). Gender schema and prejudicial recall: How children misremember, fabricate, and distort gendered picture book information. *Journal of Research in Childhood Education, 22,* 291–303.

Frayling, T. M., Timpson, N. J., Weedon, M. N., Zeggini, E., Freathy, R. M., Lindgren, C. M.,…McCarthy, M. I. (2007). A common variant in the FTO gene is associated with body mass index and predisposes children and adult obesity. *Science, 316,* 889–894.

Freedman, D. S., Khan, L. K., Serdula, M. K., Ogden, C. L., & Dietz, W. H. (2006). Racial and ethnic differences in secular trends for childhood BMI, weight, and height. *Obesity,* 301–308.

French, D. (2015). Cultural templates of adolescent friendships. In L. A. Jensen (Ed.), *Oxford handbook of human development and culture: An interdisciplinary perspective.* New York, NY: Oxford University Press.

French, D. C., Eisenberg, N., Vaughan, J., Purwono, U., & Suryanti, T. A. (2008). Religious involvement and the social competence and adjustment of Indonesian Muslim adolescents. *Developmental Psychology, 44,* 597–611.

French, D. C., Rianasari, J. M., Piadada, S., Nelwan, P., & Buhrmester, D. (2001). Social support of Indonesian and U.S. children and adolescents by family members and friends. *Merrill-Palmer Quarterly, 47,* 377–394.

Frick, P. J., & Kimonis, E. R. (2005). Externalizing disorders of childhood and adolescence. In E. J. Maddux & A. B. Winstead (Eds.), *Psychopathology: Foundations for a contemporary understanding* (pp. 325–351). Mahwah, NJ: Lawrence.

Friedlmeier, W., Corapci, F., & Benga, O. (2015). Early emotional development in cultural perspective. In L. A. Jensen (Ed.), *Oxford handbook of human development and culture: An interdisciplinary perspective.* New York, NY: Oxford University Press.

Friedman, H. S., & Martin, L. R. (2011). *The longevity project.* New York, NY: Penguin.

Fritz, G., & Rockney, R. (2004). Summary of the practice parameter for the assessment and treatment of children and adolescents with enuresis. *Work Group on Quality Issues: Journal of the American Academy of Child & Adolescent Psychiatry, 43,* 123–125.

Fryar, C. D., Carroll, M. D., & Ogden, C. L. (2012). Prevalence of obesity among children and adolescents: United States, Trends 1963–1965 Through 2009–2010. Prevention. Retrieved from http://www.cdc.gov/nchs/data/hestat/obesity_child_09_10/obesity_child_09_10.pdf.

Fujiwara, T., Ito, J., & Kawachi, I. (2013). Income inequality, parental socioeconomic status, and birth outcomes in Japan. *American Journal of Epidemiology, 177*(10), 1042–1052. doi:10.1093/aje/kws355.

Fuligni, A., Tseng, V., & Lam, M. (1999). Attitudes toward family obligation among American adolescents with Asian, Latin American, and European backgrounds. *Child Development, 70,* 1030–1044.

Fuligni, A. J., Witkow, M., & Garcia, C. (2005). Ethnic identity and the academic adjustment of adolescents from Mexican, Chinese, and European backgrounds. *Developmental Psychology, 41*(5), 799–811.

Fuligni, A. J. (2011). Social identity, motivation, and well being among adolescents from Asian and Latin American backgrounds. In G. Carlo, L. J. Crockett, & M. A. Carranza (Eds.), *Health disparities in youth and families: Research and applications* (pp. 97–120). New York, NY: Springer.

Fuller, A., Beck, V., & Unwin, L. (2005). The gendered nature of apprenticeship: Employers' and young peoples' perspectives. *Education & Training, 47,* 298–311.

Fung, H. (2010). Cultural psychological perspectives on social development in childhood. *The Wiley-Blackwell handbook of childhood social development.* New York, NY: Wiley.

Funk, J. B. (2003). Violent video games: Who's at risk? In D. Ravitch & J. P. Viteritti (Eds.), *Kid stuff: Marketing sex and violence to America's children* (pp. 168–192). Baltimore, MD: Johns Hopkins University Press.

Funk, J. B. (2005). Children's exposure to violent video games and desensitization to violence. *Child & Adolescent Psychiatric Clinics of North America, 14,* 387–404.

Funk J. B., Baldacci H. B., Pasold T., & Baumgardner J. (2004). Violence exposure in real-life, video games, television, movies, and the internet: Is there desensitization? *Journal of Adolescence, 27,* 23–39.

Furman, W., & Hand, L. S. (2006). The slippery nature of romantic relationships: Issues in definition and differentiation. In A. C. Crouter & A. Booth (Eds.), *Romance and sex in adolescence and emerging adulthood: Risks and opportunities* (pp. 171–178). The Penn State University family issues symposia series. Mahwah, NJ: Lawrence Erlbaum.

Furman, W., & Simon, V. A. (2008). Homophily in adolescent romantic relationships. In M. J. Prinstein & K. A. Dodge (Eds.), *Understanding peer influence in children and adolescents* (pp. 203–224). New York, NY: Guilford.

Futagi, Y., Toribe, Y., & Suzuki, Y. (2009). Neurological assessment of early infants. *Current Pediatric Reviews, 5*, 65–70.

Fyfe, K. (2006). Wolves in sheep's clothing: A content analysis of children's television. Retrieved from http://wwww.parentstelevision.org/.

Galambos, N. L. (2004). Gender and gender role development in adolescence. In R. Lerner & L. Steinberg (Eds.), *Handbook of adolescent psychology*. New York, NY: Wiley.

Galambos, N. L., Barker, E. T., & Krahn, H. J. (2006). Depression, anger, and self-esteem in emerging adulthood: Seven-year trajectories. *Developmental Psychology, 42*, 350–365.

Galambos, N. L., & Martínez, M. L. (2007). Poised for emerging adulthood in Latin America: A pleasure for the privileged. *Child Development Perspectives, 1*, 109–114.

Galambos, N. L., Almeida, D., & Petersen, A. (1990). Masculinity, femininity, and sex role attitudes in early adolescence: Exploring gender intensification. *Child Development, 61*, 1905–1914.

Gale, C. R., Godfrey, K. M., Law, C. M., Martyn, C. N., & O'Callaghan, F. J. (2004). Critical periods of brain growth and cognitive function in children. *Brain: A Journal of Neurology, 127*, 321–329.

Gall, S. (Ed.). (1996). *Multiple pregnancy and delivery*. St. Louis, MO: Mosby.

Galler, J. R., Bryce, C. P., Waber, D., Hock, R. S., Exner, N., Eaglesfield, D.,… Harrison, R. (2010). Early childhood malnutrition predicts depressive symptoms at ages 11–17. *Journal of Child Psychology and Psychiatry, 51*, 789–798.

Galler, J. R., Waber, D., Harrison, R., & Ramsey, F. (2005). Behavioral effects of childhood malnutrition. *The American Journal of Psychiatry, 162*, 1760–1761.

Gallimore, R., Goldenberg, C., & T. Weisner. (1993). The social construction and subjective reality of activity settings: Implications for community psychology. *American Journal of Community Psychology 21*(4), 537–559.

Ganger, J., & Brent, M. R. (2004). Reexamining the vocabulary spurt. *Developmental Psychology, 40*, 621–632.

Gans, J. (1990). *America's adolescents: How healthy are they?* Chicago, IL: American Medical Association.

Gardiner, H. W. (2001). Child and adolescent development: Cross-cultural perspectives. In L. L. Adler & U. P. Gielen (Eds.), *Cross-cultural topics in psychology* (pp. 63–79). Westport, CT: Praeger.

Gardner, H. (1983). *Frames of mind*. New York, NY: Basic Books.

Gardner, H. (1999). Who owns intelligence? *Atlantic Monthly, 283*, 67–76.

Gardner, H. (2004). *Frames of mind: The theory of multiple intelligences*. New York, NY: Basic Books.

Gardner, H. (2011). Multiple intelligences: The first thirty years. *Harvard Graduate School of Education*.

Garrison, M. M., & Christakis, D. A. (2005). *A teacher in the living room? Educational media for babies, toddlers and preschoolers*. Menlo Park, CA: The Henry J. Kaiser Family Foundation.

Gartstein, M. A., Slobodskaya, H. R., Zylicz, P. O., Gosztyla, D., & Nakagawa, A. (2010). A cross-cultural evaluation of temperament: Japan, USA, Poland and Russia. *International Journal of Psychology and Psychological Therapy, 10*(1), 55–75.

Gaskins, S. (2000). Children's daily activities in a Mayan village: A culturally grounded description. *Cross-Cultural Research, 34*, 375–389.

Gaskins, S. (2015). Childhood practices across cultures: Play and household work. In L. A. Jensen (Ed.), *Oxford handbook of human development and culture: An interdisciplinary perspective*. New York, NY: Oxford University Press.

Gathercole, S. E., & Alloway, T. P. (2008). Working memory and classroom learning. In S. K. Thurman & C. A. Fiorello (Eds.), *Applied cognitive research in K–3 classrooms*. (Vol. xi, pp. 17–40). New York, NY, US: Routledge/Taylor & Francis Group.

Gathercole, S. E., Pickering, S. J., Knight, C., & Stegmann, Z. (2004). *Working memory skills and educational attainment: Evidence from national curriculum assessments at 7 and 14 years of age. Applied Cognitive Psychology, 18*(1), 1–16.

Gauvain, M., & Munroe, R. L. (2012). Cultural change, human activity, and cognitive development. *Human Development, 55*(4), 205–228. http://doi.org/10.1159/000339451.

Gauvain, M., & Nicolaides, C. (2015). Cognition in childhood across cultures. In L. A. Jensen (Ed.), *Oxford handbook of human development and culture: An interdisciplinary perspective*. New York, NY: Oxford University Press.

Gavin, A. R., Hill, K. G., Hawkins, J. D., & Maas, C. (2011). The role of maternal early-life and later-life risk factors on offspring low birth weight: Findings from a three-generational study. *Journal of Adolescent Health, 49*, 166–171.

Gavin, L., & Furman, W. (1989). Age differences in adolescents' perceptions of their peer groups. *Developmental Psychology, 25*, 827–834.

Gazzaniga, M. (2008). *Human: The science behind what makes us unique*. New York, NY: Ecco.

Ge, X., Natsuaki, M. N., Neiderhiser, J. M., & Reiss, D. (2007). Genetic and environmental influences on pubertal timing: Results from two national sibling studies. *Journal of Research on Adolescence, 17*, 767–788.

Geangu, E., Benga, O., Stahl, D., & Striano, T. (2010). Contagious crying beyond the first days of life. *Infant Behavior & Development, 33*, 279–288.

Geary, D. C. (2010). *Male, female: The evolution of human sex differences* (2nd ed.). Washington, DC: American Psychological Association.

Geeraert, L., Van den Noortgate, W., Grietens, H., & Onghena, P. (2004). The effects of early prevention programs for families with young children at risk for physical child abuse and neglect: A meta-analysis. *Child Maltreatment, 9*, 277–291.

Geldhof, G. J., Little, T. D., & Columbo, J. (2010). Self-regulation across the lifespan. *Handbook of lifespan development*. II: 5. New York, NY: Wiley.

Genesoni, L., & Tallandini, M. A. (2009). Men's psychological transition to fatherhood: An analysis of the literature, 1989–2008. *Birth: Issues in Perinatal Care, 36*, 305–318.

Gentile, D. (2011). The multiple dimensions of violent video game effects. *Child Development Perspectives 5*, 75–81. doi: 10.1111/j.1750-8606.2011.00159.x.

George, C., & Solomon, J. (1999). Attachment and caregiving: The caregiving behavioural system. In J. Cassidy & P. R. Shaver (Eds.), *Handbook of attachment: Theory, research, and clinical applications* (pp. 649–670). New York, NY: Guilford Press.

Gere, J., & Helwig, C. C. (2012). Young adults' attitudes and reasoning about gender roles in the family context. *Psychology of Women Quarterly, 36*(3), 301–313. http://doi.org/10.1177/0361684312444272.

Gergen, K. (2011). The acculturated brain. *Theory and Psychology, 20*, 1–20.

Gernhardt, A., Rübeling, H., & Keller, H. (2013). "This is my family": Differences in children's family drawings across cultures. *Journal of Cross-Cultural Psychology, 44*(7) 1166–1183.

Gernhardt, A., Rübeling, H., & Keller, H. (2014). Self- and family-conceptions of Turkish migrant, native German, and native Turkish children: A comparison of children's drawings. *International Journal of Intercultural Relations, 40*, 154–166. http://doi.org/10.1016/j.ijintrel.2013.12.005.

Gershoff, E. T. (2002). Corporal punishment by parents and associated child behaviors and experiences: A meta-analytic and theoretical review. *Psychological Bulletin, 128,* 539–579.

Gesell, A. (1946). The ontogenesis of infant behaviour. In L. Carmichael (Ed.), *Manual of child psychology* (pp. 295–331). Hoboken, NJ: Wiley.

Gesell, A. L. (1934). *Infancy and human growth.* New York, NY: Macmillan.

Gewirtz, J. (1977). Maternal responding and the conditioning of infant crying: Directions of influence within the attachment–acquisition process. In B. C. Etzel, J. M. LeBlanc, & D. M. Baer (Eds.), *New developments in behavioral research* (pp. 31–57). Hillsdale, NJ: Lawrence Erlbaum.

Giang, M. T., & Wittig, M. A. (2006). Implications of adolescents' acculturation strategies for personal and collective self-esteem. *Cultural Diversity and Ethnic Minority Psychology, 12,* 725–739.

Gibbons, J. L., & Stiles, D. A. (2004). *The thoughts of youth: An international perspective on adolescents' ideal persons.* Greenwich, CT: IAP Information Age.

Gibbs, J. C. (2003). *Moral development and reality: Beyond the theories of Kohlberg and Hoffman.* Thousand Oaks, CA: Sage.

Gibbs, J. C., Basinger, K. S., Grime, R. L., & Snarey, J. R. (2007). Moral judgment development across cultures: Revisiting Kohlberg's universality claims. *Developmental Review, 27,* 443–500.

Gibson, E. J., & Walk, R. D. (1960). The "visual cliff." *Scientific American, 202,* 64–71.

Gibson, J. H., Harries, M., Mitchell, A., Godfrey, R., Lunt, M., & Reeve, J. (2000). Determinants of bone density and prevalence of osteopenia among female runners in their second to seventh decades of age. *Bone, 26,* 591–598.

Giedd, J. N. (2008). The teen brain: Insights from neuroimaging. *Journal of Adolescent Health, 42,* 335–343.

Giedd, J. N., Raznahan, A., Mills, K. L., & Lenroot, R. K. (2012). Review: magnetic resonance imaging of male/female differences in human adolescent brain anatomy. *Biol Sex Differ, 3*(1), 19.

Giedd, J. N., Stockman, M., Weddle, C., Liverpool, M., Alexander-Bloch, A., et al. (2010). Anatomic magnetic resonance imaging of the developing child and adolescent brain: The effects of genetic variation. *Neuropsychology Review, 20,* 349–361.

Gil, R. M. & Vazquez, C. I. (1996). *The Maria paradox.* New York, NY: The Berkeley Publishing Group.

Giles-Sims, J., & Lockhart, C. (2005). Culturally shaped patterns of disciplining children. *Journal of Family Issues, 26,* 196–218.

Gilmore, D. (1990). *Manhood in the making: Cultural concepts of masculinity.* New Haven, CT: Yale University Press.

Gini, G., Albierto, P., Benelli, B., & Altoe, G. (2008). Determinants of adolescents' active defending and passive bystanding behavior in bullying. *Journal of Adolescence, 31,* 93–105.

Ginsburg, H. P., & Opper, S. (1979). *Piaget's theory of intellectual development.* Englewood Cliffs, NJ: Prentice Hall.

Giscombé, C. L., & Lobel, M. (2005). Explaining disproportionately high rates of adverse birth outcomes among African Americans: The impact of stress, racism, and related factors in pregnancy. *Psychological Bulletin, 131,* 662–683.

Gladwell, M. (1998, February 2). The Pima paradox. *The New Yorker,* pp. 44–57.

Glassman, T. J., Dodd, V., Miller, E. M., & Braun, R. E. (2010). Preventing high-risk drinking among college students: A social marketing case study. *Social Marketing Quarterly, 16,* 92–110.

Glauber, J. H., Farber, H. J., & Homer, C. J. (2001). Asthma clinical pathways: Toward what end? *Pediatrics, 107,* 590–592.

Godfrey, J. R., & Meyers, D. (2009). Toward optimal health: Maternal benefits on breastfeeding. *Journal of Women's Health, 18,* 1307–1310.

Goldbaum, S., Craig, W. M., Pepler, D., & Connolly, J. (2003). Developmental trajectories of victimization: Identifying risk and protective factors. *Journal of Applied School Psychology, 19,* 139–156.

Goldberg, A. E. (2010). *Lesbian and gay parents and their children.* Washington, DC: American Psychological Association.

Goldberg, W. A. & Keller, M. A. (2007). Parent–infant co-sleeping: why the interest and concern? *Infant and Child Development, 16*(4), 331–339.

Goldberg, M. C., Maurer, D., & Lewis, T. L. (2001). Developmental changes in attention: The effects of endogenous cueing and of distracters. *Developmental Science, 4,* 209–219.

Goldberg, P. H. (1968). Are women prejudiced against women? *Transaction, 5,* 28–30.

Goldfield, B. A., & Reznick, J. S. (1990). Early lexical acquisition: Rate, content and the vocabulary spurt. *Journal of Child Language, 17,* 171–183.

Goldin-Meadow, S. (2009). Using the hands to study how children learn language. In J. Colombo, L. Freund, & P. McCardle (Eds.), *Infant pathways to language: Methods, models, and research disorders* (pp. 195–210). New York, NY: Psychology Press.

Goldman, B. D., & Buysse, V. (2007). Friendships in very young children. In *Contemporary perspectives on socialization and social development in early childhood education,* 165–192. New York: IAP.

Goldscheider, F., & Goldscheider, C. (1999). *The changing transition to adulthood: Leaving and returning home.* Thousand Oaks, CA: Sage.

Goldsmith, H. H. (2009). Genetics of emotional development. In R. J. Davidson, K. R. Scherer, & H. H. Goldsmith (Eds.), *Handbook of affective sciences* (pp. 300–319). New York, NY: Oxford University Press.

Goldstein, T. R., & Winner, E. (2012). Enhancing empathy and theory of mind. *Journal of Cognition and Development, 13*(1), 19–37.

Goleman, D. (1997). *Emotional intelligence.* New York, NY: Bantam.

Goode, E. (1999, May 20). Study finds TV trims Fiji girls' body image and eating habits. *The New York Times,* p. A1.

Goodwin, C. J. (2009). *Research in psychology: Methods and design.* New York, NY: Wiley.

Goossens, L., & Luyckx, K. (2007). Belgium. In J. J. Arnett, U. Gielen, R. Ahmed, B. Nsamenang, T. S. Saraswathi, & R. Silbereisen (Eds.), *International encyclopedia of adolescence* (pp. 64–76). New York, NY: Routledge.

Gopnik, A., & Astington, J. W. (1998). Children's understanding of representational change and its relation to the understanding of false belief and the appearance–reality distinction. *Child Development, 59,* 26–37.

Gopnik, A., Meltzoff, A. N., & Kuhl, P. K. (1999). *The scientist in the crib: Minds, brains, and how children learn.* New York, NY: William Morrow.

Gordon-Larsen, P., Nelson, M. C., & Popkin, B. M. (2004). Longitudinal physical activity and sedentary behavior trends: Adolescence to adulthood. *American Journal of Preventative Medicine, 27,* 277–283.

Gottesman, I. I. (2004). Postscript: Eyewitness to maturation. In L. E. DiLalla (Ed.), *Behavior genetics principles.* Washington, DC: American Psychological Association.

Gottlieb, A. (2000). Luring your child into this life: A Beng path for infant care. In J. DeLoache & A. Gottlieb (Eds.), *A world of babies: Imagined childcare guides for seven societies* (pp. 55–89). New York, NY: Cambridge University Press.

Gottlieb, G. (2004). Normally occurring environmental and behavioral influences on gene activity. In C. G. Coll, E. L. Bearer, & R. M. Lerner (Eds.), *Nature and nature: The complex interplay of genetic and environmental influences on human behavior and development* (pp. 85–106). Mahwah, NJ: Erlbaum.

Gottlieb, G., & Lickliter, R. (2007) Probabilistic epigenesis. *Developmental Science, 10,* 1–11.

Graber, J. A., Lewinsohn, P. M., Seeley, J. R., & Brooks-Gunn, J. (1997). Is psychopathology associated with the timing of pubertal development? *Journal of the American Academy of Child and Adolescent Psychiatry, 36,* 1768–1776.

Graber, J. A., Seeley, J. R., Brooks-Gunn, J., & Lewinsohn, P. M. (2004). Is pubertal timing associated with psychopathology in young adulthood? *Journal of the American Academy of Child & Adolescent Psychiatry, 43,* 718–726.

Graham, M. J., Larsen, U., & Xu, X. (1999). Secular trend in age of menarche in China: A case study of two rural counties in Anhui province. *Journal of Biosocial Science, 31,* 257–267.

Granic, I., Dishion, T. J., & Hollerstein, T. (2003). The family ecology of adolescence: A dynamic systems perspective on normative development. In G. R. Adams & M. D. Berzonsky (Eds.), *Blackwell handbook of adolescence* (pp. 60–91). Malden, MA: Blackwell.

Gray, C., Ferguson, J., Behan, S., Dunbar, C., Dunn, J., & Mitchell, D. (2007). Developing young readers through the linguistic phonics approach. *International Journal of Early Years Education, 15,* 15–33.

Gray, W. N., Simon, S. L., Janicke, D. M., & Dumont-Driscoll, M. (2011). Moderators of weight-based stigmatization among youth who are overweight and non-overweight: The role of gender, race, and body dissatisfaction. *Journal of Developmental & Behavioral Pediatrics, 32*(2), 110–116.

Green, E. G. T., Deschamps, J.-C., & Paez, D. (2005). Variation of individualism and collectivism within and between 20 countries: A typological analysis. *Journal of Cross-Cultural Psychology, 36,* 321–339.

Greenberger, E., & Steinberg, L. (1986). *When teenagers work: The psychological social costs of adolescent employment.* New York, NY: Basic Books.

Greenfield, P. M. (1999). Cultural change and human development. *New Directions for Child and Adolescent Development, 83,* 37–59.

Greenfield, P. M. (2005). Paradigms of cultural thought. In K. J. Holyoak, & R. G. Morrison (Eds.), *The Cambridge Handbook of Thinking and Reasoning* (pp. 663–682). New York, NY: Cambridge University Press.

Greenfield, P. M. (2009). Linking social change and developmental change: shifting pathways of human development. *Developmental Psychology, 45*(2), 401.

Greenfield, P. M., & Bruner, J. S. (1966). Culture and cognitive growth. *International Journal of Psychology, 1*(2), 89–107.

Greenfield, P. M., & Keller, H. (2004). Cultural psychology. *Encyclopedia of applied psychology, 1,* 545–554.

Greenough, W. T., Black, J. E., & Wallace, C. S. (1987). Experience and brain development. *Child Development, 58*(3), 539–559. http://doi.org/10.2307/1130197.

Greenwood, V. (2011). Why are asthma rates soaring? *Scientific American,* March 22. Retrieved from http://www.scientificamerican.com/article/why-are-asthma-rates-soaring/.

Grigorenko, E. (2003). Intraindividual fluctuations in intellectual functioning: Selected links between nutrition and the mind. In R. Sternberg & J. Lautrey (Eds.), *Models of intelligence: International perspectives.* Washington, DC: American Psychological Association.

Grigorenko, E. L., Lipka, J., Meier, E., Mohatt, G., Sternberg, R. J., & Yanez, E. (2004). Academic and practical intelligence: A case study of the Yup'ik in Alaska. *Learning and Individual Differences, 14,* 183–207.

Grilo, C. M., & Mitchell, J. E. (Eds.). (2010). *The treatment of eating disorders: A clinical handbook.* New York, NY: Guilford.

Grimshaw, G. S., & Wilson, M. S. (2013). A sinister plot? Facts, beliefs, and stereotypes about the left-handed personality. *Laterality: Asymmetries of Body, Brain and Cognition, 18,* 135–151.

Grolnick, W. S., McMenamy, J. M., & Kurowski, C. O. (2006). Emotional self-regulation in infancy and toddlerhood. In L. Balter & C. S. Tamis-Lamonda (Eds.), *Child psychology: A book of contemporary issues* (pp. 3–25). New York, NY: Psychology Press.

Gross, D. (2008). *Infancy (3rd ed.)* Upper Saddle River, NJ: Prentice Hall.

Grossman, K. E., Grossman, K., & Waters, E. (Eds.). (2005). *Attachment from infancy to adulthood: The major longitudinal studies.* New York, NY: Guilford.

Grotevant, H. D., & Adams, G. R. (1984). Development of an objective measure to assess ego identity in adolescence: Validation and replication. *Journal of Youth and Adolescence, 13,* 419–438.

Grunbaum, A. (2006). Is Sigmund Freud's psychoanalytic edifice relevant to the 21st century? *Psychoanalytic Psychology, 23,* 257–284.

Grünebaum, A., et al. (2013). Apgar score of 0 at 5 minutes and neonatal seizures or serious neurologic dysfunction in relation to birth setting. *American Journal of Obstetrics and Gynecology, 323,* e1–e6.

Grünebaum, A., et al. (2014). Early and total neonatal mortality in relation to birth setting in the United States, 2006-09. *American Journal of Obstetrics and Gynecology, 324.* doi: 10.1016/j.ajog.2014.03.047.

Gu, D., Reynolds, K., Wu, N., Chen, J., Duan, X., Reynolds, R. F., et al. (InterASIA Collaborative Group). (2005). Prevalence of the metabolic syndrome and overweight among adults in China. *Lancet, 365,* 1398–1405.

Guasti, M. T. (2000). An excursion into interrogatives in early English and Italian. In M. A. Friedemann & L. Rizzi (Eds.), *The acquisition of syntax* (pp. 105–128). Harlow, England: Longman.

Guay, F., Chanal, J., Ratelle, C. F., Marsh, H. W., Larose, S., & Boivin, M. (2010). Intrinsic, identified, and controlled types of motivation for school subjects in young elementary school children. *British Journal of Educational Psychology, 80,* 711–735.

Guernsey, L. (2007). *Into the minds of babes: How screen time affects children from birth to age 5.* New York, NY: Perseus.

Guest, A. M. (2007). Cultures of childhood and psychosocial characteristics: Self-esteem and social comparison in two distinct communities. *Ethos, 35,* 1–32.

Guillaume, M., & Lissau, I. (2002). Epidemiology. In W. Burniat, T. Cole, I. Lissau, & E. M. E. Poskitt (Eds.), *Child and adolescent obesity: Causes and consequences, prevention and management* (pp. 28–49). Cambridge, MA: Cambridge University Press.

Guille, C., Newman, R., Fryml, L. D., Lifton, C. K., & Epperson, C. N. (2013). Management of postpartum depression. *Journal of Midwifery & Women's Health, 58*(6), 643–653. doi: 10.1111/jmwh.12104.

Guise, J. M. F., & Gill, J. S. (2007). "Binge drinking? It's good, it's harmless fun": A discourse analysis of female undergraduate drinking in Scotland. *Health Education Research, 22,* 895–906.

Gunn, J. K., Rosales, C. B., Center, K. E., Nuñez, A. V., Gibson, S. J., & Ehiri, J. E. (2015). The effects of prenatal cannabis exposure on fetal development and pregnancy outcomes: a protocol. *BMJ open, 5*(3), e007227.

Gusrang, J., & Cheng, S. (2010). Comparing government influences and community involvements on abstinence only programs in 1999 and 2004: An examination of policy shift. *American Journal of Sexuality Education, 5,* 240–267.

Guttmacher Institute. (2014). American teens' sexual and reproductive health. http://www.guttmacher.org/pubs/FB-ATSRH.html Accessed May 25, 2015.

Haan, M. D., & Matheson, A. (2009). The development and neural bases of processing emotion in faces and voices. In M. d. H. & M. R. Gunnar, *Handbook of developmental social neuroscience* (pp. 107–121). New York, NY: Guilford.

Hack, M., Taylor, G., Drotar, D., Schluchter, M., Cartar, L., Wilson-Costello, D.,… Morrow, M. (2005). Poor predictive validity of the Bayley Scales of Infant Development for cognitive function of extremely low birth weight children at school age. *Pediatrics, 116,* 333–341.

Hacker, J. (2002). *The divided welfare state: The battle over public and private social benefits in the United States.* New York, NY: Cambridge University Press.

Hadjikhani, N., Chabris, C. F., Joseph, R. M., Clark, J., McGrath, L., Aharon, L.,…Harris, G. J. (2004). Early visual cortex organization in autism: An fMRI study. *Neuroreport: For Rapid Communication of Neuroscience Research, 15,* 267–270.

Haffner, W. H. J. (2007). Development before birth. In M. L. Batshaw, L. Pellegrino, & N. J. Roizen (Eds.), *Children with disabilities* (pp. 23–33). Baltimore, MD: Paul H Brookes.

Hagen, J., & Hale, G. (1973). The development of attention in children. In A. Pick (Ed.), *Minnesota symposium on child psychology* (Vol. 7, pp. 117–140). Minneapolis, MN: University of Minnesota Press.

Hagerman, R. J., & Hagerman, P. J. (2002). *Fragile X Syndrome: Diagnosis, treatment, and Research.* New York, NY: Taylor & Francis.

Hahn, B., Ross, T. J., Wolkenberg, F. A., Shakleya, D. M., Huestis, M. A., & Stein, E. A. (2009). Performance effects of nicotine during selective attention, divided attention, and simple stimulus detection: An fMRI study. *Cerebral Cortex, 19,* 1990–2000.

Hahn-Holbrook, J., & Haselton, M. (2014). Is postpartum depression a disease of modern civilization? *Current Directions in Psychological Science, 23*(6), 395–400. http://doi.org/10.1177/0963721414547736.

Hakuta, K. (1999). The debate on bilingual education. *Developmental and Behavioral Pediatrics, 20,* 36–37.

Hale, C. M., & Tager-Flusberg, H. (2005). Social communication with children with autism: The relationship between theory of mind and discourse development. *Autism, 9,* 157–178.

Halford, G. S. (2005). Development of thinking. In K. J. Holyoak & Robert G. Morrison (Eds.), *The Cambridge handbook of thinking and reasoning* (pp. 529–558). New York, NY: Cambridge University Press.

Halgunseth, L. C., Ispa, J. M., & Rudy, D. (2006). Parental control in Latino families: An integrated review of the literature. *Child Development, 77,* 1282–1297.

Halpern, D. F. (2000). *Sex differences in cognitive abilities* (3rd ed.). Mahwah, NJ: Lawrence Erlbaum.

Hämäläinen, J., Poikolainen, K., Isometsa, E., Kaprio, J., Heikkinen, M., Lindermman, S., & Aro, H. (2005). Major depressive episode related to long unemployment and frequent alcohol intoxication. *Nordic Journal of Psychiatry, 59,* 486–491.

Hamilton, S. F., & Hamilton, M. A. (2000). Research, intervention, and social change: Improving adolescents' career opportunities. In L. J. Crockett & R. K. Silbereisen (Eds.), *Negotiating adolescence in times of social change* (pp. 267–283). New York, NY: Cambridge University Press.

Hamilton, S., & Hamilton, M. A. (2006). School, work, and emerging adulthood. In J. J. Arnett & J. L. Tanner (Eds.), *Coming of age in the 21st century: The lives and contexts of emerging adults* (pp. 257–277). Washington, DC: American Psychological Association.

Hammer, J. C., Fisher, J. D., Fitzgerald, P., & Fisher, W. A. (1996). When two heads aren't better than one: AIDS risk behavior in college-age couples. *Journal of Applied Social Psychology, 26,* 375–397.

Han, C. (2011). Embitterment in Asia: Losing face, inequality, and alienation under historical and modern perspectives. In M. Linden & A. Maercker (Eds.), *Embitterment: Societal, psychological, and clinical perspectives* (pp. 168–176). New York, NY: Springer.

Hannon, T. S., Rao, G., & Arslanian, S. A. (2005). Childhood obesity and Type 2 diabetes mellitus. *Pediatrics, 116,* 473–480.

Hantsoo, L., Ward-O'Brien, D., Czarkowski, K. A., Gueorguieva, R., Price, L. H., & Neill, C. (2014). A randomized, placebo-controlled, double-blind trial of sertraline for postpartum depression. *Psychopharmacology, 231*(5), 939–948. http://doi.org/10.1007/s00213-013-3316-1.

Harden, K. P., & Mendle, J. (2012). Gene-environment interplay in the association between pubertal timing and delinquency in adolescent girls. *Journal of Abnormal Psychology, 121*(1), 73.

Harkness, S., Mavridis, C. J., Liu, J. J., & Super, C. (2015). Parental ethnotheories and the development of family relationships in early and middle childhood. In L. A. Jensen (Ed.), *Oxford handbook of human development and culture: An interdisciplinary perspective.* New York, NY: Oxford University Press.

Harnad, S. (2012). *Lateralization in the nervous system.* New York, NY: Academic Press.

Harris, G. (2002). *Grandparenting: How to meet its responsibilities.* Los Angeles: The Americas Group.

Hart, B., & Risley, T. R. (1999). *The social world of children learning to talk.* Baltimore, MD: Paul H. Brookes.

Hart, B., & Risley, T. R. (2003). The early catastrophe: The 30 million word gap by age 3. *American Educator, 27*(1), 4–9.

Hart, C. H., Newell, L. D., & Olsen, S. F. (2003). Parenting skills and social-communicative competence in childhood. In J. O. Greene & B. R. Burleson (Eds.), *Handbook of communication and social interaction skills* (pp. 753–797). Mahwah, NJ: Erlbaum.

Hart, D., & Atkins, R. (2004). Religious participation and the development of moral identity in adolescence. In T. A. Thorkildsen & H. J. Walberg (Eds.), *Nurturing morality* (pp. 157–172). New York, NY: Kluwer.

Harter, S. (1990a). Processes underlying adolescent self-concept formation. In R. Montemayor, G. R. Adams, & T. P. Gullotta (Eds.), *From childhood to adolescence: A transitional period?* Newbury Park, CA: Sage.

Harter, S. (1990b). Self and identity development. In S. S. Feldman & G. R. Elliott (Eds.), *At the threshold: The developing adolescent* (pp. 352–387). Cambridge, MA: Harvard University Press.

Harter, S. (2003). The development of self-representations during childhood and adolescence. In M. R. Leary & J. P. Tangney (Eds.), *Handbook of self and identity* (pp. 610–642). New York, NY: Guilford.

Harter, S. (2006a). The development of self-esteem. In M. H. Kernis (Ed.), *Self-esteem issues and answers: A sourcebook of current perspectives* (pp. 144–150). New York, NY: Psychology Press.

Harter, S. (2006b). The self. In W. Damon & R. Lerner (Eds.), & N. Eisenberg (Vol. Ed.), *Handbook of child psychology: Vol. 3. Social, emotional and personality development* (6th ed., pp. 505–570). New York, NY: Wiley.

Harter, S. (2012). The construction of the self: *Developmental and sociocultural foundations.* New York: Guilford.

Harter, S., Waters, P. L., & Whitesell, N. R. (1997). Lack of voice as a manifestation of false-self behavior among adolescents: The school setting as a stage upon which the drama of authenticity is enacted. *Educational Psychologist, 32,* 153–173.

Hartup, W. W. (1996). The company they keep: Friendships and their developmental significance. *Child Development, 67,* 1–13.

Hartup, W. W., & Abecassis, M. (2004). Friends and enemies. In P. K Smith & C. H. Hart (Eds.), *Blackwell handbook of childhood social development* (pp. 285–306). Malden, MA: Blackwell.

Harvey, J. H., & Fine, M. A. (2004). *Children of divorce: Stories of loss and growth.* Mahwah, NJ: Lawrence Erlbaum Associates.

Harwood, R., Leyendecker, B., Carlson, V., Asencio, M., & Miller, A. (2002). Parenting among Latino families in the U.S. In M. H. Bornstein (Ed.), *Handbook of parenting, Vol. 4. Social conditions and applied parenting* (2nd ed., pp. 21–46). Mahwah, NJ: Erlbaum.

Hasebrink, U. (2007a). Computer use, international. In J. J. Arnett (Ed.), *Encyclopedia of children, adolescents, and the media* (pp. 207–210). Thousand Oaks, CA: Sage.

Hasebrink, U. (2007b). Television, international viewing patterns and. In J. J. Arnett (Ed.), *Encyclopedia of children, adolescents, and the media* (pp. 808–810). Thousand Oaks, CA: Sage.

Hassett, J. M., Siebert, E. R., & Wallen, K. (2008). Sex differences in rhesus monkey toy preference parallel those of children. *Hormones and Behavior, 54,* 359–364.

Hassold, T. J., & Patterson, D. (Eds.) (1999). *Down syndrome: A promising future, together.* New York, NY: Wiley-Liss.

Hastings, P. D., McShane, K. E., Parker, R., & Ladha, F. (2007). Ready to make nice: Parental socialization of young sons' and daughters' prosocial behaviors with peers. *The Journal of Genetic Psychology: Research and Theory on Human Development, 168,* 177–200.

Hatfield, E., & Rapson, R. L. (2005). *Love and sex: Cross-cultural perspectives* (2nd edition). Boston, MA: Allyn & Bacon.

Hatfield, E., & Rapson, R. L. (1996). *Love and sex: Cross-cultural perspectives.* Boston, MA: Allyn & Bacon.

Hatfield, E., & Rapson, R. L. (2005). *Love and sex: Cross-cultural perspectives* (2nd edition). Boston, MA: Allyn & Bacon.

Haugaard, J. L., & Hazan, C. (2004). Recognizing and treating uncommon behavioral and emotional disorders in children and adolescents who have been severely maltreated: Reactive attachment disorder. *Child Maltreatment, 9,* 154–160.

Hautala, L. A., Junnila, J., Helenius, H., Vaananen, A.-M., Liuksila, P.-R., Raiha, H., et al. (2008). Towards understanding gender differences in disordered eating among adolescents. *Journal of Clinical Nursing, 17,* 1803–1813.

Hawk, S. T., Keijsers, L., Frijns, T., Hale III, W. W., Branje, S., & Meeus, W. (2013). "I still haven't found what I'm looking for": Parental privacy invasion predicts reduced parental knowledge. *Developmental Psychology, 49*(7), 1286–1298. http://doi.org/10.1037/a0029484.

Hawk, S. T., Keijsers, L., Hale III, W. W., & Meeus, W. (2009). Mind your own business! Longitudinal relations between perceived privacy invasion and adolescent-parent conflict. *Journal of Family Psychology, 23*(4), 511–520. http://doi.org/10.1037/a0015426.

Hawkins, A. J., Lovejoy, K. R., Holmes, E. K., Blanchard, V. L., & Fawcett, E. (2008). Increasing fathers' involvement in child care with a couple-focused intervention during the transition to parenthood. *Family Relations, 57*(1), 49–59.

Hawkins, D. L., Pepler, D. J., & Craig, W. M. (2001). Naturalistic observations of peer intervention in bullying. *Social Development, 10,* 512–527.

Hayashi, A., Karasawa, M., & Tobin, J. (2009). The Japanese preschool's pedagogy of feeling: Cultural strategies for supporting young children's emotional development. *Ethos, 37,* 32–49.

Haynie, D. L., & Osgood, D. W. (2005). Reconsidering peers and delinquency: How do peers matter? *Social Forces, 84,* 1109–1130.

Hazrati, S., Klein, E., Huddleston, K. C., De La Cruz, F., Fuller, A., Donnelly, K., Wong, W., & Niederhuber, J. E. (2014). Baby apps: Media exposure in infants. Presented at the 142nd APHA Annual Meeting and Exposition (November 15 - November 19, 2014), APHA. Retrieved from https://apha.confex.com/apha/142am/webprogram/Paper310733.html.

Heine, S. H., Lehman, D. R., Markus, H. R., & Kitayama, S. (1999). Is there a universal need for positive self-regard? *Psychological Review, 106,* 766–794.

Helwig, C. C. (2008). The moral judgment of the child reevaluated: Heteronomy, early morality, and reasoning about social justice and inequalities. In C. Wainryb, J. G. Smetana, & E. Turiel (Eds.), *Social development, social inequalities, and social justice* (pp. 27–51). New York, NY: Taylor & Francis Group.

Henggeler, S. W. (2011). Efficacy studies to large-scale transport: The development and validation of multisystemic therapy programs. *Annual Review of Clinical Psychology 7,* 351–381.

Henggeler, S. W., Sheidow, A. J., & Lee, T. (2007). Multisystemic treatment of serious clinical problems in youths and their families. In D. W. Springer & A. R. Roberts (Eds.), *Handbook of forensic mental health with victims and offenders: Assessment, treatments, and research* (pp. 315–345). New York, NY: Springer.

Henrichs, J., Schenk, J. J., Barendregt, C. S., Schmidt, H. G., Steegers, E. A. P., Hofman, A., . . . Tiemeier, H. (2010). Fetal growth from mid- to late pregnancy is associated with infant development: The Generation R study. *Developmental Medicine & Child Neurology, 52,* 644–651.

Hensler, B. A., Schatschneider, C., Taylor, J., & Wagner, R. K. (2010). Behavioral genetic approach to the study of dyslexia. *Journal of Developmental and Behavioral Pediatrics, 31* (Special Issue: The genetics and genomics of childhood neurodevelopmental disorders: An update), 525–532.

Hepper, P. G., Wells, D. L., & Lynch, C. (2005). Prenatal thumb sucking is related to postnatal handedness. *Neuropsychologia, 43,* 313–315.

Herman-Giddens, M., Slora, E., Wasserman, R., Bourdony, C., Bhapkar, M., Koch, G., & Hasemeier, C. (1997). Secondary sexual characteristics and menses in young girls seen in office practice: A study from the Pediatric Research in Office Settings Network. *Pediatrics, 88,* 505–512.

Herman-Giddens, M., Wang, L., & Koch, G. (2001). Secondary sexual characteristics in boys. *Archives of Pediatrics and Adolescent Medicine, 155,* 1022–1028.

Hermans, H. (2015). Human development in today's globalizing world: Implications for self and identity. In L. A. Jensen (Ed.), *Oxford handbook of human development and culture.* New York, NY: Oxford University Press.

Herpetz-Dahlmann, B., Wille, N., Holling, J., Vloet, T. D., Ravens-Sieberer, U. [BELLA study group (Germany)]. (2008). Disordered eating behavior and attitudes, associated psychopathology and health-related quality of life: Results of the BELLA study. *European Child & Adolescent Psychiatry, 17*(Suppl. 1), 82–91.

Herrenkohl, T. I., Mason, W. A., Kosterman, R., Lengua, L. J., Hawkins, J. D., & Abbott, R. D. (2004). Pathways from physical childhood abuse to partner violence in young adulthood. *Violence and Victims, 19,* 123–136.

Herrera, E., Reissland, N., & Shepherd, J. (2004). Maternal touch and maternal child-directed speech: Effects of depressed mood in the postnatal period. *Journal of Affective Disorders, 81,* 29–39.

Hetherington, E. M., & Kelly, J. (2002) *For better or worse: Divorce reconsidered.* New York, NY: Norton.

Hetherington, E. M., & Stanley-Hagan, M. (2002). Parenting in divorced and remarried families. In M. H. Bornstein (Ed.), *Handbook of parenting* (pp. 287–299). Mahwah, NJ: Erlbaum.

Hetherington, E. M., Henderson, S., & Reiss, D. (1999). Adolescent siblings in stepfamilies: Family functioning and adolescent adjustment. *Monographs of the Society for Research in Child Development, 64*(4).

Hewlett, B. S., & Roulette, J. W. (2014). Cosleeping beyond infancy: Culture, ecology, and evolutionary biology of bed-sharing among Aka foragers and Ngandu farmers in central Africa. In D. Narvaez et al., (Eds.), *Ancestral landscapes in human evolution: Culture, childrearing, and social well-being.* New York, NY: Oxford University Press.

Heyman, G. D., & Legare, C. H. (2004). Children's beliefs about gender differences in the academic and social domains. *Sex Roles, 50,* 227–239.

Hicks, L. E., Langham, R. A., & Takenaka, J. (1982). Cognitive and health measures following early nutritional supplementation: a sibling study. *American Journal of Public Health, 72*(10), 1110–1118.

Hildreth, K., Sweeney, B., & Rovee-Collier, C. (2003). Differential memory-preserving effects of reminders at 6 months. *Journal of Experimental Child Psychology, 84,* 41–62.

Hill, J., Inder, T., Neil, J., Dierker, D., Harwell, J., & Van Essen, D. (2010). Similar patterns of cortical expansion during human development and evolution. *Proceedings of the National Academy of Sciences, 107,* 13135–13140.

Hill, J., & Lynch, M. (1983). The intensification of gender-related role expectations during early adolescence. In J. Brooks-Gunn & A. Petersen (Eds.), *Girls at puberty: Biological and psychosocial perspectives* (pp. 201–228). New York, NY: Plenum.

Hines, M., Brook, C., & Conway, G. S. (2004). Androgen and psychosexual development: Core gender identity, sexual orientation, and recalled childhood gender role behavior in women and men with congenital adrenal hyperplasia (CAH). *Journal of Sex Research, 41*(1), 75–81.

Hinojosa, T., Sheu, C.-F., & Michael, G. F. (2003). Infant hand-use preference for grasping objects contributes to the development of a hand-use preference for manipulating objects. *Developmental Psychobiology, 43*, 328–334.

Hirschi, T. (2002). *Causes of delinquency*. Piscataway, NJ: Transaction.

Hiscock, H., & Jordan, B. (2004). Problem crying in infancy. *Medical Journal of Australia, 181*, 507–512.

Hjelmsedt, A., Andersson, L., Skoog-Svanberg, A., Bergh, T., Boivin, J., & Collins, A. (1999). Gender differences in psychological reactions to infertility among couples seeking IVF- and ICSI-treatment. *Acta Obstet Gynecol Scand, 78*, 42–48.

Ho, D. Y. F. (1987). Fatherhood in Chinese culture. In M. E. Lamb (Ed.), *The father's role: Cross-cultural perspectives* (pp. 227–245). Hillsdale, NJ: Erlbaum.

Hock-Long L, Henry-Moss D, Carter M, Hatfield-Timajchy K, Erickson PI, Cassidy A, Chittams J. (2012). Condom use with serious and casual heterosexual partners: Findings from a community venue-based survey of young adults. *AIDS and Behavior, 17*(3), 900-913.

Hodapp, R. M., Burke, M. M., & Urdano, R. C. (2012). What's age got to do with it? Implications of maternal age on families of offspring with Down syndrome. In R. M. Hodapp (Ed.), *International review of research in developmental disabilities* (pp. 111–143). New York, NY: Academic Press.

Hodnett, E. D., Gates, S., Hofmeyr, G. J., & Sakala, C. (2007). Continuous support for women during childbirth. *Cochrane Database of Systematic Reviews, 3*.

Hofer, K., & Moore, A. S. (2010). *The iconnected parent: Staying close to your kids in college (and beyond) while letting them grow up*. New York, NY: Free Press.

Hoff, E. (2009). *Language development*. Belmont, CA: Wadsworth.

Hoff, E. (2013). Interpreting the early language trajectories of children from low SES and language minority homes: Implications for closing achievement gaps. *Developmental Psychology, 49*(1), 4–14.

Hofman, P. L., Regan, F., Jackson, W. E., Jefferies, C., Knight, D. B., Robinson, E. M., & Cutfield, W. S. (2004). Premature birth and later insulin resistance. *New England Journal of Medicine, 351*, 2179–2186.

Hoffman, M. L. (2000). *Empathy and moral development*. New York, NY: Cambridge University Press.

Hofmeyr, G. J. (2002). Interventions to help external cephalic version for breech presentation at term. *Cochrane Database of Systematic Reviews, 2*, CD000184.

Hogan, M. C., Foreman, K. J., Naghavi, M., Ahn, S. Y., Wang, M., Makela, S. M.,...Murray, C. J. L. (2010). Maternal mortality for 181 countries, 1980–2008: A systematic analysis of progress toward Millennium Development Goal 5. *The Lancet, 375*, 1–15.

Hoh, J., & Ott, J. (2003). Mathematical multi-locus approaches to localizing complex human trait genes. *Nature Reviews Genetics, 4*, 701–709.

Hokoda, A., Lu, H.-H., A., & Angeles, M. (2006). School bullying in Taiwanese adolescents. *Journal of Emotional Abuse, 64*, 69–90.

Holmes, J., & Gathercole, S. E. (2014). Taking working memory training from the laboratory into schools. *Educational Psychology, 34*(4), 440–450.

Holodynski, M. (2009). Milestones and mechanisms of emotional development. *In Emotions as bio-cultural processes* (pp. 139–163). Springer US.

Holsti, L., & Grunau, R. E. (2010). Considerations for using sucrose to reduce procedural pain in preterm infants. *Pediatrics, 125*, 1042–1049.

Honein, M. A., Paulozzi, L. J., Mathews, T. J., Erickson, J. D., & Wong, L. C. (2001). Impact of folic acid fortification of the U.S. food supply on the occurrence of neural tube defects. *The Journal of American Medical Association, 285*, 2981–2986.

Hong, Z.-R., Veach, P. M., & Lawrenz, F. (2003). An investigation of the gender stereotyped thinking of Taiwanese secondary school boys and girls. *Sex Roles, 48*, 495–504.

Hood, B., Cole-Davies, V., & Dias, M. (2003). Looking and search measures of object knowledge in preschool children. *Developmental Psychology, 39*, 61–70.

Hooghe, M., & Wilkenfeld, B. (2008). The stability of political attitudes and behaviors across adolescence and early adulthood: A comparison of survey data on adolescents and young adults in eight countries. *Journal of Youth and Adolescence, 37*, 155–167.

Hopkins, B., & Westra, T. (1990). Motor development, maternal expectations and the role of handling. *Infant Behavior and Development, 13*, 117–122.

Horn, I. B., Brenner, R., Rao, M., & Cheng, T. L. (2006). Beliefs about the appropriate age for initiating toilet training: are there racial and socioeconomic differences?. *The Journal of Pediatrics, 149*(2), 165–168.

Horn, K., Dino, G., Kalsekar, I., & Mody, R. (2005). The impact of Not on Tobacco on teen smoking cessation: End-program evaluation results, 1998–2003. *Journal of Adolescent Research, 20*, 640–661.

Horn, S. (2003). Adolescents' reasoning about exclusion from social groups. *Developmental Psychology, 39*, 71–84.

Horne, J. (2014). Sleep hygiene: Exercise and other "do's and don'ts." *Sleep Medicine*.

Horton, D. M. (2001). The disappearing bell curve. *Journal of Secondary Gifted Education, 12*, 185–188.

Hourcade, J. P., Mascher, S. L., Wu, D., & Pantoja, L. (2015). Look, my baby is using an iPad! An analysis of YouTube videos of infants and toddlers using tablets. In *Proceedings of the 33rd Annual ACM Conference on Human Factors in Computing Systems* (pp. 1915–1924). New York, NY, USA: ACM. http://doi.org/10.1145/2702123.2702266.

Howard, K. S., Carothers, S. S., Smith, L. E., & Akai, C. E. (2007). Overcoming the odds: Protective factors in the lives of children. In J. G. Borkowski, J. R. Farris, T. L. Whitman, S. S. Carothers, K. Weed, & D. A. Keogh (Eds.), *Risk and resilience: Adolescent mothers and their children grow up* (pp. 205–232). Mahwah, NJ: Lawrence Erlbaum.

Howard, R. W. (2001). Searching the real world for signs of rising population intelligence. *Personality & Individual Differences, 30*, 1039–1058.

Howe, M. L., Courage, M. L., Rooksby, M. (2009). The genesis and development of autobiographical memory. In M. L. Courage & N. Cowan (Eds.), *The development of memory in infancy and childhood* (2nd ed., pp. 177–196). New York, NY: Psychology Press.

Howe, N., & Recchia, H. (2009). Individual differences in sibling teaching in early and middle childhood. *Early Education and Development, 20*, 174–197.

Howe, N., Aquan-Assee, J., & Bukowski, W. M. (2001). Predicting sibling relations over time: Synchrony between maternal management styles and sibling relationship quality. *Merrill-Palmer Quarterly, 47*, 121–141.

Howes, C. (1985). Sharing fantasy: Social pretend play in toddlers. *Child Development, 56*(5), 1253–1258.

Howes, C. (1996). The earliest friendships. In W. M. Bukowski, A. F. Newcomb, & W. W. Hartup (Eds.), *The company they keep: Friendship in childhood and adolescence* (pp. 66–86). Boston, MA: Cambridge University Press.

Hoza, B., Kaiser, N., & Hurt, E. S. (2008). Evidence-based treatments for attention-deficit/hyperactivity disorder (ADHD). In G. Ric, T. D. Elkin, & M. C. Robers (Eds.), *Handbook of evidence-based therapies for children and adolescents: Bridging science and practice. Issues in clinical child psychology* (pp. 197–219). New York, NY: Springer.

Huang, R. L., Lu, Z., Liu, J. J., You, Y. M., Pan, Z. Q., Wei, Z.,... Wang, Z. Z. (2009). Features and predictors of problematic Internet use in Chinese college students. *Behaviour & Information Technology, 28*, 485–490.

Huesmann, L. R., Eron, L. D., Lefkowitz, M. M., & Walder, L. O. (1984). Stability of aggression over time and generations. *Developmental Psychology, 20*, 1120–1134.

Huesmann, L. R., Moise-Titus, J., Podolski, C., & Eron, L. D. (2003). Longitudinal relations between children's exposure to TV violence and their aggressiveness in young adulthood, 1977–1992. *Developmental Psychology, 39*, 201–221.

Hughes, C., & Dunn, J. (2007). Children's relationships with other children. In C. A. Brownell & C. B. Kopp (Eds.), *Socioemotional development in the toddler years* (pp. 177–200). New York, NY: Guilford.

Hulei, E., Zevenbergen, A., & Jacobs, S. (2006). Discipline behaviors of Chinese American and European American mothers. *Journal of Psychology: Interdisciplinary and Appeal, 140*, 459–475.

Hundley, H. L., & Shyles, L. (2010). U.S. teenagers' perceptions and awareness of digital technology: A focus group approach. *New Media & Society, 12*, 417–433.

Hunnius, S., de Wit, T. C. J., Vrins, S., & von Hofsten, C. (2011). Facing threat: Infants' and adults' visual scanning of faces with neutral, happy, sad, angry, and fearful emotional expressions. *Cognition and Emotion, 25*, 193–205.

Hunt, E. (1989). Cognitive science: Definition, status, and questions. *Annual Review of Psychology, 40*, 603–629.

Hunziker, U. A., & Barr, R. G. (1986). Increased carrying reduces infant crying: A randomized controlled trial. *Pediatrics, 77*, 641–648.

Hurrelmann, K. (1996). The social world of adolescents: A sociological perspective. In K. Hurrelmann & S. Hamilton (Eds.), *Social problems and social contexts in adolescence: Perspectives across boundaries* (pp. 39–62). Hawthorne, NY: Aldine de Gruyter.

Hursti, U. K. (1999). Factors influencing children's food choice. *Annals of Medicine, 31*, 26–32.

Huttenlocher, P. R. (2002). *Neural plasticity: The effects of environment on the development of the cerebral cortex*. Cambridge, MA: Harvard University Press.

Hyde, J. S., & DeLamater, J. D. (2004). *Understanding human sexuality* (9th ed.). Boston, MA: McGraw Hill.

Hyde, J. S., & DeLamater, J. D. (2005). *Understanding human sexuality* (8th ed., Rev.).

Hyder, A. A., & Lunnen, J. (2009). Reduction of childhood mortality through millennium, development goal 4. *BMJ, 342*.

Hymel, S., McDougall, P., & Renshaw, P. (2004). Peer acceptance/rejection. In P. K. Smith & C. H. Hart (Eds.), *Blackwell handbook of childhood social development* (pp. 265–284). Malden, MA: Blackwell.

Hymowitz, K., Carroll, J. S., Wilcox, W. B., & Kaye, K. (2013). *Knot yet: The benefits and costs of delayed marriage in America*. Charlottesville, VA: National Marriage Project.

Iacovou, M. (2011). *Leaving home: Independence, togetherness, and income in Europe*. New York, NY: United Nations Population Division. Retrieved from http://www.un.org/en/development/desa/population/publications/pdf/expert/2011-10_Iacovou_Expert-paper.pdf.

Iannelli, V. I. (2007). *Tummy time: Infants*. About.com Guide. Retrieved from http://pediatrics.about.com/od/infants/a/0607_tummy_time.htm.

Iles, J., Slade, P., & Spiby, H. (2011). Posttraumatic stress symptoms and postpartum depression in couples after childbirth: The role of partner support and attachment. *Journal of Anxiety Disorders, 25*, 520–530.

Inhelder, B., & Piaget, J. (1958). *The growth of logical thinking from childhood to adolescence*. New York, NY: Basic Books.

Insel, T. (2010). Rethinking schizophrenia. *Nature, 468*, 187–193.

Institute of International Education. (2014). *Open Doors 2014: Report on International Educational Exchange*. Washington, DC: Author.

Institute of Medicine of the National Academies (2005). *Preventing childhood obesity: Health in the balance*. Washington, DC.

International Genome Sequencing Consortium. (2004). Finishing euchromatic sequence of the human genome. *Nature, 431*, 931–945.

International Labor Organization (ILO). (2002). *A future without child labour*. New York, NY: Author.

International Labour Organization (ILO) (2004). *Investing in every child. An economic study of the costs and benefits of eliminating child labour*. New York, NY: Author.

International Labour Organization (ILO). (2013). *Marking progress against child labour: Global estimates and trends 2000–2012*. Geneva, Switzerland: Author.

Ip, S., Chung, M., Raman, G., Chew, P., Magula, N., DeVine, D., . . . Lau, J. (2007). *Breastfeeding and maternal and infant health outcomes in developed countries. Evidence Report/Technology Assessment No. 153*. Rockville, MD: Agency for Healthcare Research and Quality.

Ireland, J. L., & Archer, N. (2004). Association between measures of aggression and bullying among juvenile young offenders. *Aggressive Behavior, 30*, 29–42.

Ishihara, N. (2014). Is it rude language? Children learning pragmatics through visual narrative. *TESL Canada Journal, 30*(7), 135.

Israel, E. (2005). Introduction: The rise of the age of individualism—variability in the pathobiology, response to treatment, and treatment outcomes in asthma. *Journal of Allergy and Clinical Immunology, 115*, S525.

Iverson, R., Kuhl, P. K., Akahane-Yamada, R., Diesch, E., Tohkura, Y., & Kettermann, A. (2003). A perceptual interference account of acquisition difficulties for non-native phonemes. *Cognition, 87*, B47–B57.

Izard, C. E., & Ackerman, B. P. (2000). Motivational, organizational, and regulatory functions of discrete emotions. In M. Lewis & J. M. Haviland-Jones (Eds.), *Handbook of emotions*, (2nd ed., pp. 253–264). New York, NY: Guilford.

Jaakkola, J. J., & Gissler, M. (2004). Maternal smoking in pregnancy, fetal development, and childhood asthma. *American Journal of Public Health, 94*, 136–140.

Jackson, E., Campos, J. J., & Fischer, K. W. (1978). The question of decalage between object permanence and person permanence. *Developmental Psychology, 14*(1), 1–10. doi:10.1037/0012-1649.14.1.1.

Jackson, L. M., Pratt, M. W., Hunsberger, B., & Pancer, S. M. (2005). Optimism as a mediator of the relation between perceived parental authoritativeness and adjustment among adolescents: Finding the sunny side of the street. *Social Development, 14*, 273–304.

Jalonick, M. C. (2010, December 13). Obama signs historic school lunch nutrition bill. Retrieved from http://www.salon.com/food/feature/2010/12/13/us_obama_child_nutrition.

James, C., Hadley, D. W., Holtzman, N. A., & Winkelstein, J. A. (2006). How does the mode of inheritance of a genetic condition influence families? A study of guilt, blame, stigma, and understanding of inheritance and reproductive risks in families with X-linked and autosomal recessive diseases. *Genetics in Medicine, 8*, 234–242.

James, D. K. (2010). Fetal learning: A critical review. *Infant and Child Development, 19*, 45–54.

Jankowiak, W. R., & Fischer, E. F. (1992). A cross-cultural perspective on romantic love. *Ethology, 31*, 149–155.

Janssen, I., Katzmarzyk, P. T., Ross, R., Leon, A. S., Skinner, J. S., Rao, D. C., Wilmore, J. H., . . . Bouchard, C. (2004). Fitness alters the associations of BMI and waist circumference with total and abdominal fat. *Obesity Research, 12*, 525–537.

Janssen, M., et al. (2014). A short physical activity break from cognitive tasks increases selective attention in primary school children aged 10-11. *Mental Health and Physical Activity, 7*, 129–134.

Jeffrey, J. (2004, November). Parents often blind to their kids' weight. *British Medical Journal Online*. Retrieved from content.health.msn.com/content/article/97/104292.htm.

Jenkins, J. M., Rabash, J., & O'Connor, T. G. (2003). The role of the shared family context in differential parenting. *Developmental Psychology, 39*, 99–113.

Jennings, N. (2007). Advertising, viewer age and. In J. J. Arnett (Ed.), *Encyclopedia of children, adolescents, and the media* (pp. 55–57). Thousand Oaks, CA: Sage.

Jennings, W. G., & Reingle, J. M. (2012). On the number and shape of developmental/life-course violence, aggression, and delinquency trajectories: A state-of-the-art review. *Journal of Criminal Justice, 40*, 472–489.

Jensen, L. A. (1997a). Culture wars: American moral divisions across the adult life span. *Journal of Adult Development, 4*, 107–121.

Jensen, L. A. (1997b). Different worldviews, different morals: America's culture war divide. *Human Development, 40*, 325–344.

Jensen, L. A. (2008). Coming of age in a multicultural world: Globalization and adolescent cultural identity formation. In D. L. Browning (Ed.), *Adolescent identities: A collection of readings* (pp. 3–17). New York, NY: Analytic Press.

Jensen, L. A. (Ed.). (2011). *Bridging cultural and developmental psychology.* New York, NY: Oxford University Press.

Jensen, L. A. (2015a). Cultural-developmental scholarship for a global world: An introduction. In L. A. Jensen (Ed.), *Oxford handbook of human development and culture.* (pp. 3–13). New York, NY: Oxford University Press.

Jensen, L. A. (2015b). *Moral development in a global world: Research from a cultural-developmental perspective.* New York, NY: Cambridge University Press.

Jensen, L. A. (2015c). Moral reasoning: Developmental emergence and life course pathways among cultures. In L. A. Jensen (Ed.), *Oxford handbook of human development and culture: An interdisciplinary perspective.* (pp. 23–254). New York, NY: Oxford University Press.

Jensen, L. A., Arnett, J. J., & McKenzie, J. (2012). Globalization and cultural identity development in adolescence and emerging adulthood. In S. J. Schwartz, K. Luyckx, & V. L. Vignoles (Eds.), *Handbook of identity theory and research* (pp. 285–301). New York, NY: Springer Publishing Company.

Jemmott, J. B., III, Jemmott, L. S., Braverman, P. K., Fong, G. T. (2005) HIV/STD risk reduction interventions for African American and Latino adolescent girls at an adolescent medicine clinic: A randomized controlled trial. *Archives of Pediatrics and Adolescent Medicine, 159*(5), 440–449.

Jequier, A. (2011). *Male infertility: A clinical guide.* New York, NY: Cambridge University Press.

Jessor, R., Colby, A., & Shweder, R. A. (1996). *Ethnography and human development: Context and meaning in social inquiry.* Chicago, IL: University of Chicago Press.

Jeynes, W. (2007). The impact of parental remarriage on children: A metaanalysis. *Marriage & Family Review, 40*, 75–102.

Jiao, S., Ji, G., & Jing, Q. (1996). Cognitive development of Chinese urban only children and children with siblings. *Child Development, 67*, 387–395.

Jochman, K. A., & Fromme, K. (2010). Maturing out of substance use: The other side of etiology. In L. Scheier (Ed.), *Handbook of drug use etiology: Theory, methods, and empirical findings* (pp. 565–578). Washington, DC: American Psychological Association.

Johnson, D. J., Jaeger, E., Randolph, S. M., Cauce, A. M., Ward, J. & National Institute of Child Health and Human Development: Early Child Care Research Network. (2003). Studying the effects of early child care experiences on the development of children of color in the United States: Toward a more inclusive research agenda. *Child Development, 74*, 1227–1244.

Johnson, D. M. (2005). Mind, brain, and the upper Paleolithic. In C. E. Erneling & D. M. Johnson (Eds.), *The mind as a scientific object: Between brain and culture* (pp. 499–510). New York, NY: Oxford University Press.

Johnson, E. J. (2015). "Debunking the 'language gap.'" *Journal for Multicultural Education, 9*(1), 42–50.

Johnson, J. S., & Newport, E. L. (1991). Critical period effects on universal properties of language: The status of subjacency in the acquisition of a second language. *Cognition, 39*, 215–258.

Johnson, M. C. (2000). The view from the Wuro: A guide to child rearing for Fulani parents. In J. DeLoache & A. Gottlieb (Eds.), *A world of babies: Imagined childcare guides for seven societies* (pp. 171–198). New York, NY: Cambridge University Press.

Johnson, M. D. (2008). *Human biology: Concepts and current issues.* Upper Saddle River, NJ: Prentice Hall.

Johnson, M. H. (2001). Functional brain development in humans. *Nature Reviews Neuroscience, 2*, 475–483.

Johnson, S. K., Murphy, S. R., Zewdie, S., & Reichard, R. J. (2008). The strong, sensitive type: Effects of gender stereotypes and leadership prototypes on the evaluation of male and female leaders. *Organizational Behavior and Human Decision Processes, 106*, 39–60.

Johnston, L. D., O'Malley, P. M., Bachman, J. G., Schulenberg, J. E. & Miech, R. A. (2014). Monitoring the Future national survey results on drug use, 1975–2013: Volume 2, College students and adults ages 19–55. Ann Arbor, MI: Institute for Social Research, University of Michigan.

Jones, E., & Kay, M. A. (2003). The cultural anthropology of the placenta. In L. Dundes (Ed.), *The manner born: Birth rites in cross-cultural perspective* (pp. 101–116). Walnut Creek, CA: AltaMira Press.

Jones, R. E. (2006). *Human reproductive biology.* New York, NY: Academic Press.

Jones, R. K., & Biddlecom, A. E. (2011). Exposure to and views of information about sexual abstinence among older teens. *American Journal of Sexuality Education, 6*(4), 381–395.

Jordan, B. (1994). *Birth in four cultures.* Long Grove, IL: Westland.

Jose, P. E., & Brown, I. (2008). When does the gender difference in rumination begin? Gender and age differences in the use of rumination by adolescents. *Journal of Youth and Adolescence, 37*(2), 180–192.

Josselyn, S. A., & Frankland, P. W. (2012). Infantile amnesia: A neurogenic hypothesis. *Learning & Memory, 19*(9), 423–433.

Jost, K. (2009). Bilingual Education vs. English Immersion: Which is better for students with limited English? *CQ Researcher, 19*(43), 1029–1052

Kagan, J., & Fox, N. A. (2006). Biology, culture, and temperamental biases. In W. Damon & R. Lerner (Eds.), & N. Eisenberg (Vol. Ed.), *Handbook of child psychology: Vol. 3. Social, emotional, and personality development* (6th ed., pp. 167–225). New York, NY: Wiley.

Kagan, J., & Herschkowitz, E. C. (2005). *Young mind in a growing brain.* Mahwah, NJ: Erlbaum.

Kağıtçıbaşi, C., & Yalin, C. (2015). Family in adolescence: Relatedness and cutonomy across cultures. In L. A. Jensen (Ed.), *Oxford handbook of human development and culture: An interdisciplinary perspective.* New York, NY: Oxford University Press.

Kahana-Kalman, R., & Walker-Andrews, A. S. (2001). The role of person familiarity in young infants' perception of emotional expressions. *Child Development, 72*, 352–369.

Kahn, J. A. (2007). Maximizing the potential public health impact of HPV vaccines: A focus on parents. *Journal of Adolescent Health, 20*, 101–103.

Kail, R. V. (2003). Information processing and memory. In M. H. Bornstein, L. Davidson, C. L. M. Keyes, K. A. Moore, and the Center for Child Well-Being (Eds.), *Well-being: Positive development across the life course* (pp. 269–280). Mahwah, NJ: Erlbaum.

Kainz, G., Eliasson, M., & von Post, I. (2010). The child's father, an important person for the mother's well–being during the childbirth: A hermeneutic study. *Health Care for Women International, 31*, 621–635.

Kaiser Family Foundation (2013). *Distribution of U.S. population by race and ethnicity, 2010 and 2050.* Retrieved from http://kaiserfamilyfoundation.files.wordpress.com/2013/03/distribution-of-u-s population-by-raceethnicity-2010-and-2050-disparities.png.

Kakar, S. (1998). The search for the middle age in India. In R. A. Shweder (Ed.), *Welcome to middle age! (and other cultural fictions)* (pp. 75–98). Chicago, IL: University of Chicago Press.

Kaltenbach, K. A., & Finnegan, L. P. (1989). Prenatal narcotic exposure: perinatal and developmental effects. *Neurotoxicology, 10*(3), 597–604.

Kamibeppu, K., & Sugiura, H. (2005). Impact of the mobile phone on junior high-school students' friendships in the Tokyo metropolitan area. *Cyber Psychology & Behavior, 8,* 121–130.

Kane, P., & Garber, J. (2004). The relations among depression in fathers, children's psychopathology, and father–child conflict: A meta-analysis. *Child Psychology Review, 24,* 339–360.

Kanetsuna, T., Smith, P., & Morita, Y. (2006). Coping with bullying at school: Children's recommended strategies and attitudes to school-based intervention in England and Japan. *Aggressive Behavior, 32,* 570–580.

Kanwal, M., Alyas, S., Afzal, M., Mansoor, A., Abbasi, R., Tassone, F.,... Mazhar, K. (2015). Molecular diagnosis of fragile x syndrome in subjects with intellectual disability of unknown origin: implications of its prevalence in regional Pakistan. *PloS One, 10*(4), e0122213. DOI: http://doi.org/10.1371/journal.pone.0122213.

Kapadia, S., & Bhangaokar, R. (2015). An Indian moral worldview: Developmental patterns in adolescents and adults. In L. A. Jensen (Ed.), *Moral development in a global world: Research from a cultural-developmental perspective.* New York, NY: Cambridge University Press.

Kapadia, S., & Gala, J. (2015). Gender across cultures: Sex and socialization in childhood. In L. A. Jensen (Ed.), *Oxford handbook of human development and culture: An interdisciplinary perspective.* New York, NY: Oxford University Press.

Kaplan, B. J., Crawford, S. G., Field, C. J., Simpson, J., & Steven, A. (2007). Vitamins, minerals, and mood. *Psychological Bulletin, 133,* 747–760.

Kaplan, H., & Dove, H. (1987). Infant development among the Ache of Eastern Paraguay. *Developmental Psychology, 23,* 190–198.

Kaplan, S., Heiligenstein, J., West, S., Busner, J., Hardor, D., Dittmann, R.,... Wernicke, J. E. (2004). Efficacy and safety of atomoxetine in childhood attention deficit/hyperactivity disorder with comorbidity oppositional defiant disorder. *Journal of Attention Disorders, 8,* 45–52.

Karlsson, J. L. (2006). Specific genes for intelligence. In L. V. Wesley (Ed.), *Intelligence: New research* (pp. 23–46). Hauppauge, NY: Nova Science.

Kärtner, J., Keller, H., Chaudhary, N., & Yovsi, R. D. (2012). The development of mirror self-recognition in different sociocultural contexts. *Monographs of the Society for Research in Child Development, 77*(4), vii–viii, 1–87.

Katchadourian, H., & Boli, J. (1985). *Careerism and intellectualism among college students.* San Francisco, CA: Jossey-Bass.

Katz, L. F., & Windecker-Nelson, B. (2004). Parental meta-emotion philosophy in families with conduct-problem children: Links with peer relations. *Journal of Abnormal Child Psychology, 32,* 385–398.

Kavšek, M. (2003). Development of depth and object perception in infancy. In G. Schwarzer & H. Leder (Eds.), *The development of face processing* (pp. 35–52). Ashland, OH: Hogrefe & Huber.

Kavšek, M. (2004). Predicting later IQ from infant visual habituation and dishabituation: A meta-analysis. *Journal of Applied Developmental Psychology, 25,* 369–393.

Kavšek, M., & Bornstein, M. H. (2010). Visual habituation and dishabituation in preterm infants: A review and meta-analysis. *Research in Developmental Disabilities, 31,* 951–975.

Kazdin, A. E., & Benjet, C. (2003). Spanking children: Evidence and issues. *Current Directions in Psychological Science, 12,* 99–103.

Keating, D. (1990). Adolescent thinking. In S. Feldman & G. Elliott (Eds.), *At the threshold: The developing adolescent* (pp. 54–89). Cambridge, MA: Harvard University Press.

Keating, D. (2004). Cognitive and brain development. In L. Steinberg & R. M. Lerner (Eds.), *Handbook of adolescent psychology* (2nd ed., pp. 45–84). New York, NY: Wiley.

Keegan, J., Parva, M., Finnegan, M., Gerson, A., & Belden, M. (2010). Addiction in pregnancy. *Journal of Addictive Diseases, 29*(2), 175–191. DOI: http://doi.org/10.1080/10550881003684723.

Keen, R. (2005). Using perceptual representations to guide reaching and looking. In J. J. Reiser, J. J. Lockman, & C. A. Nelson (Eds.), *Action as an organizer of learning and development: Minnesota Symposia on Child Psychology* (Vol. 33, pp. 301–322). Mahwah, NJ: Erlbaum.

Keller, M. A., & Goldberg, W. A. (2004). Co–sleeping: Help or hindrance for young children's independence? *Infant and Child Development, 13,* 369–388.

Kellman, P. J., & Arterberry, M. E. (2006). Infant visual perception. In W. Damon & R. Lerner (Eds.), & D. Kuhn & R. Siegler (Vol. Eds.), *Handbook of child psychology: Vol. 2. Cognition, perception, and language* (6th ed., pp. 109–160). New York, NY: Wiley.

Kellogg, A. (2001, January). Looking inward, freshmen care less about politics and more about money. *Chronicle of Higher Education,* A47–A49.

Kellogg, R. (1959). *What children scribble and why.* Palo Alto, CA: N-P Publications.

Kelly, B., Halford, J. C. G., Boyland, E. J., Chapman, K., Bautista-Castaño, I., Berg, C., et al. (2010). Television food advertising to children: A global perspective. *American Journal of Public Health, 100,* 1730–1736.

Kelly, J. B. (2003). Changing perspectives on children's adjustment following divorce: A view from the United States. *Childhood: A Global Journal of Child Research, 10,* 237–254.

Kelly, J. B., & Emery, R. E. (2003). Children's adjustment following divorce: Risk and resilience perspectives. *Family Relations, 52,* 352–362.

Kelly, Y., Nazroo, J., Sacker, A., & Schoon, I. (2006). Ethnic differences in achievement of developmental milestones by 9 months of age: The Millennium Cohort Study. *Developmental Medicine & Child Neurology, 48,* 825–830.

Kelch-Oliver, K. (2011). The experiences of African American grandmothers in grandparent–headed families. *The Family Journal, 19,* 73–82.

Kember, D., & Watkins, D. (2010). Approaches to learning and teaching by the Chinese. In M. Harris (Ed.), *The Oxford handbook of Chinese psychology* (pp. 169–185). New York, NY: Oxford University Press.

Kenneally, C. (2007). *The first words: The search for the origins of language.* New York, NY: Viking.

Kent, M. M., & Haub, C. (2005). Global demographic divide. *Population Bulletin, 60,* 1–24.

Kerestes, M., Youniss, J., & Metz, E. (2004). Longitudinal patterns of religious perspective and civic integration. *Applied Developmental Science, 8,* 39–46.

Kesson, A. M. (2007). Respiratory virus infections. *Paediatric Respiratory Reviews, 8,* 240–248.

Kidd, C., Piantadosi, S. T., & Aslin, R. N. (2014). The Goldilocks Effect in infant auditory attention. *Child Development, 85*(5), 1795–1804. doi:10.1111/cdev.12263.

Kiernan, K. (2002). Cohabitation in Western Europe: Trends, issues, and implications. In A. Booth & A. C. Crouter (Eds.), *Just living together: Implications of cohabitation on families, children, and social policy* (pp. 3–31). Mahwah, NJ: Lawrence Erlbaum.

Kiernan, K. (2004). Cohabitation and divorce across nations and generations. In P. L. Chase-Lansdale, K. Kiernan, & R. J. Friedman (Eds.), *Human development across lives and generations: The potential for change* (pp. 139–170). New York, NY: Cambridge University Press.

Killen, M., & Wainryb, C. (2000). Independence and interdependence in diverse cultural contexts. In S. Harkness, C. Raeff, & C. M. Super (Eds.), *Variability in the social construction of the child* (pp. 5–21). San Francisco, CA: Jossey-Bass.

Kim, M., McGregor, K. K., & Thompson, C. K. (2000). Early lexical development in English- and Korean-speaking children: Language-general and language-specific patterns. *Journal of Child Language, 27,* 225–254.

Kimhi, Y. (2014). Theory of mind abilities and deficits in autism spectrum disorders. *Topics in Language Disorders, 34*(4), 329–343.

Kimhi, Y., Shoam-Kugelmas, D., Agam Ben-Artzi, G., Ben-Moshe, I., & Bauminger-Zviely, N. (2014). Theory of mind and executive function in preschoolers with typical development versus intellectually able preschoolers with autismspectrum disorder. *Journal of Autism and Developmental Disorders, 44*(9), 2341–2354.

King, B. M. (2005). *Human sexuality today* (5th ed.). Upper Saddle River, NJ: Prentice Hall.

King, P. E., Furrow, J. L., & Roth, N. (2002). The influence of families and peers on adolescent religiousness. *Journal of Psychology and Christianity, 21,* 109–120.

King, P. M., & Kitchener, K. S. (2015). Cognitive development in the emerging adult: The emergence of complex cognitive skills. In J. J. Arnett (Ed.), *Oxford handbook of emerging adulthood.* New York, NY: Oxford University Press.

Kinnally, W. (2007). Music listening, age effects on. In J. J. Arnett (Ed.), *Encyclopedia of children, adolescents, and the media* (pp. 585–586). Thousand Oaks, CA: Sage.

Kinney, H. C., & Thach, B. T. (2009). Medical progress: The sudden infant death syndrome. *The New England Journal of Medicine, 361,* 795–805.

Kins, E., Beyers, W., Soenens, B., & Vansteenkiste, M. (2009). Patterns of home leaving and subjective well-being in emerging adulthood: The role of motivational processes and parental autonomy support. *Developmental Psychology, 45,* 1416–1429.

Kirchner, G. (2000). *Children's games from around the world.* Boston, MA: Allyn & Bacon.

Kirkorian, H. L., Wartella, E. A., & Anderson, D. R. (2008). Media and young children's learning. *The Future of Children, 18*(1), 39–61.

Kisilevsky, B. S., Hains, S. M., Lee, K., Xic, X., Huang, H., Ye, H. H., Zhang, K., & Wang, Z. (2003). Effects of experience on fetal voice recognition. *Psychological Science, 14,* 220–224.

Kitchener, K. S., King, P. M., & DeLuca, S. (2006). Development of reflective judgment in adulthood. In C. Hoare (Ed), *Handbook of adult development and learning* (pp. 73–98). New York, NY: Oxford University Press.

Kite, M. E., Deaux, K., & Hines, E. (2008). Gender stereotypes. In F. L. Denmark & M. A. Paludi (Eds.), *Psychology of women: A handbook of issues and theories* (2nd ed., pp. 205–236). Westport, CT: Praeger.

Kitsao-Wekulo, P., Holding, P., Taylor, G. H., Abubakar, A., Kvalsvig, J., & Connolly, K. (2013). Nutrition as an important mediator of the impact of background variables on outcomes in middle childhood. *Frontiers in Human Neuroscience, 7,* 713.

Kitzmann, K. M., Cohen, R., & Lockwood, R. L. (2002). Are only children missing out? Comparison of the peer-related social competence of only children and siblings. *Journal of Social and Personal Relationships, 19,* 299–316.

Kivela, J., Haldre, K., Part, K., Ketting, E., & Baltussen, R. (2014). Impact and cost-effectiveness analysis of the national school-based sexuality education programme in Estonia. *Sex Education, 14*(1), 1–13. http://doi.org/10.1080/14681811.2013.813386.

Klass, C. S. (2008). *The home visitor's guidebook: Promoting optimal parent and child development* (3rd ed.). Baltimore, MD: Paul H. Brookes.

Klaus, M. H., & Kennell, J. H. (1976). *Maternal–infant bonding: The impact of early separation or loss on family development.* St. Louis, MO: Mosby.

Kleefstra, T., Schenck, A., Kramer, J. M., & van Bokhoven, H. (2014). The genetics of cognitive epigenetics. *Neuropharmacology, 80,* 83–94. http://dx.doi.org.eres.library.manoa.hawaii.edu/10.1016/j.neuropharm.2013.12.025.

Kleiber, M. L., Laufer, B. I., Stringer, R. L., & Singh, S. M. (2014). Third trimester-equivalent ethanol exposure is characterized by an acute cellular stress response and an ontogenetic disruption of genes critical for synaptic establishment and function in mice. *Developmental Neuroscience, 36*(6), 499–519.

Klomek, A. B., Marrocco, F., Kleinman, M., Schonfeld, I. S., & Gould, M. S. (2007). Bullying, depression, and suicidality in adolescents. *Journal of the American Academy of Child & Adolescent Psychiatry, 46,* 40–49.

Klomsten, A. T., Skaalvik, E. M., & Espnes, G. A. (2004). Physical self-concept and sports: Do gender differences exist? *Sex Roles, 50,* 119–127.

Knecht, S., Drager, B., Deppe, M., Bobe, L., Lohmann, H., Floel, A., . . . Henningsen, H. (2000). Handedness and hemispheric language dominance in healthy humans. *Brain, 135,* 2512–2518.

Knect, S., Jansen, A., Frank, A., van Randenborgh, J., Sommer, J., Kanowski, M., & Heinze, H. J. (2003). How atypical is atypical language dominance? *Neuroimage, 18,* 917–927.

Knickmeyer, C. R., & Baron-Cohen, S. (2006). Fetal testosterone and sex differences. *Early human development, 82*(12), 755–760.

Knox, D., Sturdivant, L., & Zusman, M. E. (2001). College student attitudes toward sexual intimacy. *College Student Journal, 35,* 241–243.

Kochanska, G. (2002). Mutually responsive orientation between mothers and their young children: A context for the early development of conscience. *Current Directions in Psychological Science, 11,* 191–195.

Kochenderfer-Ladd, B. (2003). Identification of aggressive and asocial victims and the stability of their peer victimization. *Merrill-Palmer Quarterly, 49,* 401–425.

Kohlberg, L. (1958). *The development of modes of moral thinking and choice in the years 10 to 16.* Unpublished doctoral dissertation. University of Chicago.

Kohlberg, L. (1976). Moral stages and moralization: The cognitive-developmental approach. *Moral development and behavior: Theory, research, and social issues,* 31–53.

Konstam, V. (2015). The virtual life alongside: Technology and the emerging and young adult. In *Emerging and Young Adulthood* (pp. 51–66). Springer International Publishing. Retrieved from http://link.springer.com/chapter/10.1007/978-3-319-11301-2_4.

Kopp, C. B. (1989). Regulation of distress and negative emotions: A developmental view. *Developmental Psychology, 25,* 343–354.

Kopp, C. B. (2003). *Baby steps: A guide to your child's social, physical, mental, and emotional development in the first two years.* New York, NY: Owl.

Korkman, M., Kettunen, S., & Autti-Rämö, I. (2003). Neurocognitive impairment in early adolescence following prenatal alcohol exposure of varying duration. *Child Neuropsychology, 9*(2), 117–128.

Kostandy, R. R., Ludington-Hoe, S. M., Cong, X., Abouelfettoh, A., Bronson, C., Stankus, A., & Jarrell, J. R. (2008). Kangaroo care (skin contact) reduces crying response to pain in preterm neonates: Pilot results. *Pain Management Nursing, 9,* 55–65.

Kotler, J. (2007). Television, prosocial content and. In J. J. Arnett (Ed.), *Encyclopedia of children, adolescents, and the media, Vol. 2* (pp. 817–819). Thousand Oaks, CA: Sage.

Kostovic, I., & Vasung, L. (2009). Insights from in vitro magnetic resonance imaging of cerebral development. *Seminars in Perinatology, 33,* 220–233.

Kouvonen, A., & Kivivuori, J. (2001). Part-time jobs, delinquency and victimization among Finnish adolescents. *Journal of Scandinavian Studies in Criminology and Crime Prevention, 2*(2), 191–212.

Kovács, Á. M., & Mehler, J. (2009). Cognitive gains in 7-month-old bilingual infants. *Proceedings of the National Academy of Sciences, 106*(16), 6556–6560. doi:10.1073/pnas.0811323106.

Kowalski, R. M., & Limber, S. P. (2007). Electronic bullying among middle school students. *Journal of Adolescent Health, 41*, S22–S30.

Kowalski, R. M., Limber, S., Limber, S. P., & Agatston, P. W. (2012). *Cyberbullying: Bullying in the digital age.* New York, NY: John Wiley & Sons.

Kramer, L., & Kowal, A. K. (2005). Sibling relationship quality from birth to adolescence: The enduring contributions of friends. *Journal of Family Psychology, 19* (Special issue: Sibling Relationship Contributions to Individual and Family Well-Being), 503–511.

Kramer, L., Perozynski, L., & Chung, T. (1999). Parental responses to sibling conflict: The effects of development and parent gender. *Child Development, 70*, 1401–1414.

Kramer, M. S., Aboud, F., Mironova, E., Vanilovich, I., Platt, R. W., Matush, L.,…Promotion of Breastfeeding Intervention Trial (PROBIT) Study Group (2008). Breastfeeding and child cognitive development: New evidence from a large randomized trial. *Archives of General Psychiatry, 65*, 578–584.

Krause, E. L. (2005). *A crisis of births: Population politics and family-making in Italy.* Belmont, CA: Wadsworth.

Kreutzer, M., Leonard, C., & Flavell, J. H. (1975). An interview study of children's knowledge about memory. *Monographs of the Society for Research in Child Development, 40*(1, Serial No. 159).

Kroger, J. (2002). Commentary on "Feminist perspectives on Erikson's theory: Their relevance for contemporary identity development research." *Identity, 2*, 257–266.

Kroger, J. (2003). Identity development during adolescence. In G. Adams & M. Berzonsky (Eds.), *Blackwell handbook of adolescence* (pp. 205–225). Malden, MA: Blackwell.

Kroger, J. (2007). *Identity development: Adolescence through adulthood* (2nd ed.). Thousand Oaks, CA: Sage.

Kroger, J., Martinussen, M., & Marcia, J. E. (2010). Identity status change during adolescence and young adulthood: A meta-analysis. *Journal of Adolescence, 33*, 683–698.

Kubisch, S. (2007). Electronic games, age and. In J. J. Arnett (Ed.), *Encyclopedia of children, adolescents, and the media* (pp. 264–265). Thousand Oaks, CA: Sage.

Kuhl, P. K. (2004). Early language acquisition: Cracking the speech code. *Nature Reviews Neuroscience, 5*, 831–843.

Kuhl, P. K., Ramírez, R. R., Bosseler, A., Lin, J.-F. L., & Imada, T. (2014). Infants' brain responses to speech suggest analysis by synthesis. *Proceedings of the National Academy of Sciences, 111*(31), 11238–11245. doi:10.1073/pnas.1410963111.

Kuhn, D. (2008). Formal operations from a twenty-first century perspective. *Human Development, 51* (Special issue: Celebrating a Legacy of Theory with New Directions for Research on Human Development), 48–55.

Kuhn, G. (Ed.). (2010) *Sober living for the revolution: Hardcore punk, straight-edge, and radical politics.* Oakland, CA: PM Press.

Kuntsche, E., Rehm, J., & Gmel, G. (2004). Characteristics of binge drinkers in Europe. *Social Science & Medicine, 59*, 113–127.

Kvavilashvili, L., & Ford, R. M. (2014). Metamemory prediction accuracy for simple prospective and retrospective memory tasks in 5-year-old children. *Journal of Experimental Psychology, 127*, 65–81.

Labouvie-Vief, G. (1982). Dynamic development and mature autonomy: A theoretical prologue. *Human Development, 25*, 161–191.

Labouvie-Vief, G. (1990). Modes of knowledge and the organization of development. In M. L. Commons, J. D. Sinnott, F. A. Richards, & C. Armon (Eds.), *Models and methods in the study of adolescent and adult thought* (pp. 43–62). New York, NY: Praeger.

Labouvie-Vief, G. (1998). Cognitive-emotional integration in adulthood. In K. W. Schaie & M. P. Lawton (Eds.), *Annual review of gerontology and geriatrics, Vol. 17: Focus on emotion and adult development* (pp. 206–237). New York, NY: Springer.

Labouvie-Vief, G. (2006). Emerging structures of adult thought. In J. J. Arnett & J. Tanner (Eds.), *Emerging adults in America: Coming of age in the 21st century* (pp. 59–84). Washington, DC: American Psychological Association.

Labouvie-Vief, G., & Diehl, M. (2002). Cognitive complexity and cognitive-affective integration: Related or separate domains of adult development? *Psychology and Aging, 15*, 490–594.

Ladd, G. W., Buhs, E., & Troop, W. (2004). School adjustment and social skills training. In P. K. Smith & C. H. Hart (Eds.), *Blackwell handbook of childhood social development* (pp. 394–416). Malden, MA: Blackwell.

Laible, D. (2004). Mother–child discourse in two contexts: Links with child temperament, attachment security and socioemotional competence. *Developmental Psychology, 40*, 979–992.

Lakatta, E. G. (1990). Heart and circulation. In E. L. Schneider & J. W. Rowe (Eds.), *Handbook of the biology of aging* (3rd ed., pp. 181–217). San Diego, CA: Academic Press.

Lamb, M. E. (1994). Infant care practices and the application of knowledge. In C. B. Fisher & R. M. Lerner (Eds.), *Applied developmental psychology* (pp. 23–45). New York, NY: McGraw-Hill.

Lamb, M. E. (2010). *The role of the father in child development.* New York, NY: Wiley.

Lamb, M. E., & Lewis, C. (2005). The role of parent–child relationships in child development. In M. H. Bornstein & M. E. Lamb (Eds.), *Developmental psychology* (5th ed., pp. 429–468). Mahwah, NJ: Erlbaum.

Lamb, M. E., & Lewis, C. (2010). The role and significance of father-child relationships in two-parent families. In M. E. Lamb (Ed.), *The role of the father in child development* (pp. 94–153). New York, NY: Wiley.

Lamberti, L. M., Walker, C. L. F., Noiman, A., Victora, C., & Black, R. E. (2011). Breastfeeding and the risk for diarrhea morbidity and mortality. *BMC public health, 11*(Suppl 3), S15.

Lampl, M., Johnson, M. L., & Frongillo, E. A., Jr. (2001). Mixed distribution analysis identifies saltation and stasis growth. *Annals of Human Biology, 28*, 403–411.

Lane, B. (2009). *Epidural rates in the U.S. and around the world: How many mothers choose to use an epidural to provide pain relief?* Retrieved from http://www.suite101.com/content/epidural-for-labor-a168170.

Lansford, J. E., Malone, P. S., Dodge, K. A., Crozier, J. C., Pettit, G. S., & Bates, J. E. (2006). A 12-year prospective study of patterns of social information processing problems and externalizing behaviors. *Journal of Abnormal Child Psychology, 34*, 715–724.

Lapsley, D., & Woodbury, R. D. (2015). Social cognitive development in emerging adulthood. In J. J. Arnett (Ed.), *Oxford handbook of emerging adulthood.* New York, NY: Oxford University Press.

Larson, R., & Csikszentmihalyi, M. (2014). The Experience Sampling Method. In M. Csikszentmihalyi, *Flow and Positive Psychology* (pp. 21–34). New York, NY: Springer.

Larson, R., & Richards, M. H. (1994). *Divergent realities: The emotional lives of mothers, fathers, and adolescents.* New York, NY: Basic Books.

Larson, R., Verman, S., & Dwokin, J. (2000, March). Adolescence without family disengagement: The daily family lives of Indian middle-class teenagers. Paper presented at the biennial meeting of the Society for Research on Adolescence, Chicago, IL.

Larson, R. W., Csikszentmihalyi, M., & Graef, R. (1980). Mood variability and the psycho-social adjustment of adolescents. *Journal of Youth & Adolescence, 9*, 469–490.

Larson, R. W., Moneta, G., Richards, M. H., & Wilson, S. (2002). Continuity, stability, and change in daily emotional experience across adolescence. *Child Development, 73*, 1151–1165.

Larson, R. W., Wilson, S., & Rickman, A. (2010). Globalization, societal change, and adolescence across the world. In R. Lerner & L. Steinberg (Eds.), *Handbook of adolescent psychology* (3rd ed., pp. 590–622). Hoboken, NJ: John Wiley & Sons.

Latzer, Y., Merrick, J., & Stein, D. (2011). *Understanding eating disorders: Integrating culture, psychology and biology.* New York, NY: Nova Science.

Lauersen, N. H., & Bouchez, C. (2000). *Getting pregnant: What you need to know right now*. New York, NY: Fireside.

Laursen, B., Coy, K. C., & Collins, W. A. (1998). Reconsidering changes in parent–child conflict across adolescence: A meta-analysis. *Child Development, 69*, 817–832.

Lave, J., & Wenger, E. (1991). *Situated learning: Legitimate peripheral participation*. New York: Cambridge University Press.

Lavzer, J. L., & Goodson, B. D. (2006). The "quality" of early care and education settings: Definitional and measurement issues. *Evaluation Review, 30*, 556–576.

Lawson, A. E., & Wollman, W. T. (2003). Encouraging the transition from concrete to formal operations: An experiment. *Journal of Research in Science Teaching, 40*(Suppl.), S33–S50.

Lay, K., Waters, E., & Posada, G., & Ridgeway, D. (1995). Attachment security, affect regulation,and defensive responses to mood induction. In Waters, E., Vaughn, B., Posada, G., & Kondo-Ikemura, K. (Eds.) *Culture, caregiving, and cognition: Perspectives on secure base phenomena and attachment working models. Monographs of the Society for Research in Child Development, 60*, (Serial No. 244, 2–3), 179–198.

Layton, E., Dollahite, D. C., & Hardy, S. A. (2011). Anchors of religious commitment in adolescents. *Journal of Adolescent Research, 26*, 381–413.

Le, H. N. (2000). Never leave your little one alone: Raising an Ifaluk child. In J. DeLoache & A. Gottlieb (Eds.), *A world of babies: Imagined childcare guides for seven societies* (pp. 199–222). New York, NY: Cambridge University Press.

Leakey, R. (1994). *The origins of humankind*. New York, NY: Basic Books.

Leaper, C., Anderson, K. J., & Sanders, P. (1998). Moderators of gender effects on parents' talk to their children: A meta-analysis. *Developmental Psychology, 34*(1): 3–27.

Leapfrog Group. (2014). *Fact sheet: Maternity care*. New York, NY: Author.

Leathers, H. D., & Foster, P. (2004). *The world food problem: Tackling causes of undernutrition in the third world*. Boulder, CO: Lynne Rienner Publishers.

Leavitt, S. C. (1998). The Bikhet mystique: Masculine identity and patterns of rebellion among Bumbita adolescent males. In G. Herdt & S. C. Leavitt (Eds.), *Adolescence in Pacific island societies* (pp. 173–194). Pittsburgh, PA: University of Pittsburgh Press.

Lee, H. M., Bhat, A., Scholz, J. P., & Galloway, J. C. (2008). Toy-oriented changes during early arm movements: IV: Shoulder-elbow coordination. *Infant Behavior and Development, 31*, 447–469.

Lee, J. C., & Staff, J. (2007). When work matters: The varying impact of work intensity on high school dropouts. *Sociology of Education, 80*, 158–178.

Lee, M. M. C., Chang, K. S. F., & Chan, M. M. C. (1963). Sexual maturation of Chinese girls in Hong Kong. *Pediatrics, 32*, 389–398.

Lee, S. A. S., Davis, B., & MacNeilage, P. (2010). Universal production patterns and ambient language influences in babbling: A cross-linguistic study of Korean- and English-learning infants. *Journal of Child Language, 37*, 293–318.

Lee, S-H., Ogawa, N., & Matsukura, R. (2015). The effects of daycare center use on marital fertility in Japan. In N. Ogawa & I. H. Shah (Eds.), *Low Fertility and Reproductive Health in East Asia. International Studies in Population* (Volume 11, pp. 59–73). New York, NY: Springer.

Lefkowitz, E. S., & Gillen, M. M. (2006). "Sex is just a normal part of life": Sexuality in emerging adulthood. In J. J. Arnett & J. L. Tanner (Eds.), *Emerging adults in America: Coming of age in the 21st century* (pp. 235–255). Washington, DC: American Psychological Association.

Lefkowitz, E. S., Gillen, M. M., Shearer, C. L., & Boone, T. L. (2004). Religiosity, sexual behaviors, and sexual attitudes during emerging adulthood. *Journal of Sex Research, 41*, 150–159.

Lehtinen, M., Paavonen, J., & Apter, D. (2006). Preventing common sexually transmitted infections in adolescents: Time for rethinking. *The European Journal of Contraception and Reproductive Health Care, 11*, 247–249.

Lemish, D. (2007). *Children and television: A global perspective*. Oxford, UK: Blackwell.

Lenhart, A., Purcell, K., Smith, A., & Zickuhr, K. (2010). *Social media and mobile Internet use among teens and young adults*. Washington, DC: Pew Research Center.

Leon, K. (2003). Risk and protective factors in young children's adjustment to parental divorce: A review of the research. *Family Relations, 52*, 258–270.

Leonard, L. (2002). Problematizing fertility: "Scientific" accounts and Chadian women's narratives. In M. C. Inhorn & F. van Balen (Eds.), *Infertility around the globe: New thinking on childlessness, gender, and reproductive technologies* (pp. 193–213). Berkeley, CA: University of California Press.

Lerner, R. M. (2006). Developmental science, developmental systems, and contemporary theories of human development. In W. Damon & R. M. Lerner (Eds.), *Handbook of child psychology, Vol. 1: Theoretical models of human development* (5th ed., pp. 1–17). New York, NY: Wiley.

Lerner, R. M., Theokas, C., & Jelicic, H. (2005). Youth as active agents in their own positive development: A developmental systems perspective. In W. Greve, L. Rothermund, & D. Wentura, *The adaptive self: Personal continuity and intentional self-development* (pp. 31–47). Göttingen, Germany: Hogrefe & Huber.

Lessow-Hurley, J. (2005). *The foundations of dual language instruction* (4th ed.). Boston, MA: Allyn & Bacon.

Lévi-Strauss, C. (1967). *The scope of anthropology*, trans. Sherry Ortner Paul and Robert A. Paul. London, UK: Jonathan Cape.

LeVine, D. N. (1966). The concept of masculinity in Ethiopian culture. *International Journal of Social Psychiatry, 12*, 17–23.

LeVine, R. A. (1977). Child rearing as cultural adaptation. In P. H. Leiderman, S. R. Tulkin, & A. Rosenfeld (Eds.), *Culture and infancy: Variations in the human experience* (pp. 15–27). New York, NY: Academic Press.

LeVine, R. A. (1994). *Child care and culture*. Cambridge, UK: Cambridge University Press.

LeVine, R. A., & New, R. S. (Eds.). (2008). *Anthropology and child development: A cross-cultural reader*. Malden, MA: Blackwell.

LeVine, R. A., Dixon, S., LeVine, S., Richman, A., Leiderman, P. H., Keefer, C. H., & Brazelton, T. B. (1994). *Childcare and culture: Lessons from Africa*. New York, NY: Cambridge University Press.

Levinson, D. J. (1978). *The seasons of a man's life*. New York, NY: Knopf.

Levitin, D. (2007). *This is your brain on music*. New York, NY: Plume.

Levy, F., & Murnane, R. (2004). *The new division of labor: How computers are creating the next job market*. Princeton, NJ: Princeton University Press.

Lewis, M. (2002). Early emotional development. In A. Slater & M. Lewis (Eds.), *Introduction to infant development* (pp. 216–232). New York, NY: Oxford University Press.

Lewis, M. (2008). The emergence of human emotions. In L. F. Barrett, J. M. Haviland-Jones, & M. Lewis (Eds.), *Handbook of emotions* (3rd ed., pp. 304–319). New York, NY: Guilford Press.

Lewis, M. (2010). The development of anger. In M. Potegal, G. Stemmler, & C. Spielberger (Eds.), *International handbook of anger: Constituent and concomitant biological, psychological, and social processes* (pp. 177–191). New York, NY: Springer.

Lewis, M., & Brooks-Gunn, J. (1979). *Social cognition and the acquisition of self*. New York, NY: Plenum.

Lewis, M., & Ramsay, D. S. (1999). Effect of maternal soothing and infant stress response. *Child Development, 70*, 11–20.

Lewis, M., & Ramsay, D. S. (2004). Development of self-recognition, personal pronoun use, and pretend play during the 2nd year. *Child Development, 75*, 1821–1831.

Lewis, R. (2005). *Human genetics* (6th ed.). New York, NY: McGraw-Hill.

Lewkowicz, D. J., & Hansen-Tift, A. M. (2012). Infants deploy selective attention to the mouth of a talking face when learning speech. *Proceedings of the National Academy of Sciences of the United States of America, 109*(5), 1431–1436.

Lewkowitz, D. J., & Lickliter, R. (2013). *The development of intersensory perception.* New York, NY: Psychology Press.

Li, F., Godinet, M. T., & Arnsberger, P. (2010). Protective factors among families with children at risk of maltreatment: Follow up to early school years. *Children and Youth Services Review, 33,* 139–148.

Li, J., Fraser, M. W., & Wike, T. L. (2013). Promoting social competence and preventing childhood aggression: A framework for applying social information processing theory in intervention research. *Aggression and Violent Behavior, 18*(3), 357–364.

Liben, L. S., & Bigler, R. S. (2002). The developmental course of gender differentiation: Conceptualizing, measuring, and evaluating constructs and pathways. *Monographs of the Society for Research in Child Development, 6*(4, Series. No. 271).

Liben, L. S., Bigler, R. S., & Hilliard, L. J. (2013). Gender Development. Societal Contexts of Child Development: *Pathways of Influence and Implications for Practice and Policy, 3.*

Liben, L. S., & Signorella, M. L. (1993). Gender-schematic processing in children: The role of initial interpretation of stimuli. *Developmental Psychology, 29,* 141–149.

Liben, L. S., Bigler, R. S., & Krogh, H. R. (2001). Pink and blue collar jobs: Children's adjustments of job status and job aspirations in relation to sex of worker. *Journal of Experimental Child Psychology, 79,* 346–363.

Lieber, E., Nihira, K., & Mink, I. T. (2004). Filial piety, modernization, and the challenges of raising children for Chinese immigrants: Quantitative and qualitative evidence. *Ethos, 32,* 324–347.

Lillard, A. S. (2007). Pretend play in toddlers. In C. A. Brownell & C. B. Kopp (Eds.), *Socioemotional development in the toddler years* (pp. 149–176). New York, NY: Guilford.

Lillard, A. S. (2008). *Montessori: The science behind the genius.* New York, NY: Oxford University Press.

Lillard, A. S. & Else-Quest, N. (2006). Evaluating Montessori education. *Science, 313,* 1893–1894.

Lindsay, L. A., & Miescher, S. F. (Eds.). (2003). *Men and masculinities in modern Africa.* Portsmouth, NH: Heinemann.

Lindsey, E., & Colwell, M. (2003). Preschooler's emotional competence: Links to pretend and physical play. *Child Study Journal, 33,* 39–52.

Linebarger, D. L., & Walker, D. (2005). Infants' and toddlers' television viewing and language outcomes. *American Behavioral Scientist, 48*(5), 624–645.

Ling, R., Bertel, T. F., & Sundsøy, P. R. (2012). The socio-demographics of texting: An analysis of traffic data. *New Media & Society, 14*(2), 281–298. http://doi.org/10.1177/1461444811412711.

Linver, M. R., Brooks-Gunn, J., & Kohen, D. E. (2002). Family processes as pathways from income to young children's development. *Developmental Psychology, 38,* 719–734.

Lipman, E. L., Boyle, M. H., Dooley, M. D., & Offord, D. R. (2002). Child well-being in single-mother families. *Journal of the American Academy of Child and Adolescent Psychiatry, 41,* 75–82.

Lipsitt, L. P. (2003). Crib death: A biobehavioral phenomenon? *Psychological Science, 12,* 164–170.

Liston, C., & Kagan, J. (2002). Brain development: Memory enhancement in early childhood. *Nature, 419*(6910), 896–896.

Litovsky, R. Y., & Ashmead, D. H. (1997). Development of binatural and spatial hearing in infants and children. In R. H. Gilkey & T. R. Anderson (Eds.), *Binaural and spatial hearing in real and virtual environments* (pp. 571–592). Mahwah, NJ: Erlbaum.

Liu, J., Raine, A., Venables, P. H., Dalais, C., & Mednick, S. A. (2003). Malnutrition at age 3 years and lower cognitive ability at age 11 years. *Archives of Paediatric and Adolescent Medicine, 157,* 593–600.

Lloyd, C. (Ed.). (2005). *Growing up global: The changing transitions to adulthood in developing countries.* Washington, DC: National Research Council and Institute of Medicine.

Lloyd, C. B., Grant, M., & Ritchie, A. (2008). Gender differences in time use among adolescents in developing countries: Implications of rising school enrollment rates. *Journal of Research on Adolescence, 18,* 99–120.

Lobel, T. E., Nov-Krispin, N., Schiller, D., Lobel, O., & Feldman, A. (2004). Perceptions of social status, sexual orientation, and value dissimilarity. Gender discriminatory behavior during adolescence and young adulthood: A developmental analysis. *Journal of Youth & Adolescence, 33,* 535–546.

Loeber, R., & Burke, J. D. (2011). Developmental pathways in juvenile externalizing and internalizing problems. *Journal of Research on Adolescence, 21,* 34–46.

Loeber, R., Lacourse, E., & Homish, D. L. (2005). Homicide, violence, and developmental trajectories. In R. E. Tremblay, W. W. Hartup, & J. Archer (Eds.), *Developmental origins of aggression* (pp. 202–222). New York, NY: Guilford Press.

Loehlin, J. C., Horn, J. M., & Willerman, L. (1997). Heredity, environment, and IQ in the Texas Adoption Project. In R. J. Sternberg & E. L. Grigrenko (Eds.), *Intelligence, heredity, and environment* (pp. 105–125). New York, NY: Cambridge University Press.

Lohaus, A., Keller, H., Ball, J., Voelker, S., & Elben, C. (2004). Maternal sensitivity in interactions with three- and 12-month-old infants: Stability, structural composition, and developmental consequences. *Infant and Child Development, 13,* 235–252.

Longest, K. C., & Shanahan, M. J. (2007). Adolescent work intensity and substance use: The meditational and moderational roles of parenting. *Journal of Marriage & Family, 69,* 703–720.

Lord, C., & Bishop, S. L. (2010). Autism spectrum disorders. *Social Policy Report, 24*(2), 3–16.

Lorenz, J. M., Wooliever, D. E., Jetton, J. R., & Paneth, N. (1998). A quantitative review of mortality and developmental disability in extremely premature newborns. *Archives of Pediatric Medicine, 152,* 425–435.

Lorenz, K. (1957). Companionship in bird life. In C. Scholler (Ed.), *Instinctive behavior: The development of a modern concept* (pp. 83–128). New York, NY: International Universities Press.

Lourenco, O. (2003). Making sense of Turiel's dispute with Kohlberg: The case of the child's moral competence. *New Ideas in Psychology, 21,* 43–68.

Lovas, G. S. (2011). Gender and patterns of language development in mother-toddler and father-toddler dyads. *First language, 31*(1), 83–108.

Love, J. M., Chazan-Cohen, R., Raikes, H., & Brooks-Gunn, J. (2013). What makes a difference: Early Head Start evaluation findings in a developmental context. *Monographs of the Society for Research in Child Development, 78*(1), vii–viii.

Lowe, E. D., Weisner, T. S., & Yoshikawa, H. (2006). *Making it work: Low-wage employment, family life, and child development.* New York, NY: Russell Sage Foundation.

Luckie, M. (2010). School year around the world. Retrieved from http://californiawatch.org/k-12/how-long-school-year compare-california-world.

Ludington-Hoe, S. M. (2013). Kangaroo care as neonatal therapy. *Newborn and Infant Nursing Reviews, 13,* 73. doi: 10.1053/j.nainr.2013.03.004.

Lung, F.-W., Chiang, T.-L., Lin, S.-J., Feng, J.-Y., Chen, P.-F., Shu, B.-C. (2011). Gender differences of children's developmental trajectory from 6 to 60 months in the Taiwan Birth Cohort Pilot Study. *Research in Developmental Disabilities, 32,* 100–106.

Luyckx, K. (2006). *Identity formation in emerging adulthood: Developmental trajectories, antecedents, and consequences.* Dissertation, Catholic University, Leuven, Belgium.

Lynch, M. E. (1991). Gender intensification. In R. M. Lerner, A. C. Petersen, & J. Brooks-Gunn (Eds.), *Encyclopedia of adolescence* (Vol. 1). New York, NY: Garland.

Lynn, R., & Mikk, J. (2007). National differences in intelligence and educational attainment. *Intelligence, 35,* 115–121.

Lynne, S. D., Graber, J. A., Nichols, T. R., Brooks-Gunn, J., & Botvin, G. J. (2007). Links between pubertal timing, peer influences, and externalizing behaviors among urban students followed through middle school. *Journal of Adolescent Health, 40,* e7–e13.

Lyon, E. (2007). *The big book of birth.* New York, NY: Plume.

Lyons-Ruth, K., Bronfman, E., & Parsons, E. (1999). Maternal frightened, frightening, or atypical behavior and disorganized infant attachment patterns. *Monographs of the Society for Research in Child Development, 64*(3, Serial No. 258), 67–96.

Lytle, L. J., Bakken, L., & Romig, C. (1997). Adolescent female identity development. *Sex Roles, 37,* 175–185.

Ma, J., Betts, N. M., Horacek, T., Georgiou, C., White, A., & Nitzke, S. (2002). The importance of decisional balance and self-efficacy in relation to stages of change for fruit and vegetable intakes by young adults. *American Journal of Health Promotion, 16,* 157–166.

Mabray, D., & Labauve, B. J. (2002). A multidimensional approach to sexual education. *Sex Education: Sexuality, Society and Learning, 2*(1), 31–44.

Maccoby, E. (1980). *Social development.* San Diego, CA: Harcourt Brace Jovanovich.

Maccoby, E., & Martin, J. (1983). Socialization in the context of the family: Parent–child interaction. In P. H. Mussen (Ed.) & E. M. Hetherington (Vol. Ed.), *Handbook of child psychology. Vol. 4: Socialization, personality, and social development* (4th ed., pp. 1–101). New York, NY: Wiley.

Maccoby, E. E. (1984). Socialization and developmental change. *Child Development, 55,* 317–328.

Maccoby, E. E. (2002). Gender and group process: A developmental perspective. *Current Directions in Psychological Science, 11,* 54–57.

Maccoby, E. E., & Lewis, C. C. (2003). Less day care or different day care? *Child Development, 76,* 1069–1075.

MacDorman, M. F., Menacker, F., & Declercq, E. (2010). Trends and characteristics of home and other out-of-hospital births in the United States, 1990–2006. *National Vital Statistics Reports, 58,* 1–14, 16.

Macek, P. (2007). Czech Republic. In J. J. Arnett (Ed.), *International encyclopedia of adolescence* (pp. 206–219). New York, NY: Routledge.

Macek, P., Bejcek, J., & Vanickova, J. (2007). Contemporary Czech emerging adults: Generation growing up in the period of social changes. *Journal of Adolescent Research, 22,* 444–475.

MacFarlane, A. (1977). *The psychology of childbirth.* Cambridge, MA: Harvard University Press.

MacFarquhar, R., & Schoenhals, J. (2006). *Mao's last revolution.* Cambridge, MA: Harvard University Press.

Macfie, J., Cicchetti, D., & Toth, S. L. (2001). The development of dissociation in maltreated preschool-aged children, *Development and Psychopathology, 13,* 233–254.

Machado, A., & Silva, F. J. (2007). Toward a richer view of the scientific method: The role of conceptual analysis. *American Psychologist, 62,* 671–681.

MacKenzie, P. J. (2009). Mother tongue first multilingual education among the tribal communities in India. *International Journal of Bilingual Education and Bilingualism, 12,* 369–385.

Madden, M.; Lenhart, A.; Duggan, M. (2013). *Teens and Technology.* Washington, DC: Pew Research Center.

Madlon-Kay, D. J. (2002). Maternal assessment of neonatal jaundice after hospital discharge. *The Journal of Family Practice, 51,* 445–448.

Maheshwari, A., Hamilton, M., & Bhattacharya, S. (2008). Effect of female age on the diagnostic categories of infertility. *Human Reproduction, 23,* 538–542.

Maimon, D., & Browning, C. R. (2010). Unstructured socializing, collective efficacy, and violent behavior among urban youth. *Criminology: An Interdisciplinary Journal, 48,* 443–474.

Malebo, A., van Eeden, C., & Wissing, M. P. (2007). Sport participation, psychological well-being, and psychosocial development in a group of young black adults. *South African Journal of Psychology, 37,* 188–206.

Males, M. (2010). Is jumping off the roof always a bad idea? A rejoinder on risk taking and the adolescent brain. *Journal of Adolescent Research, 25,* 48–63.

Malina, R. M., Bouchard, C., & Bar-Or, O. (2004). *Growth, maturation and physical activity* (2nd ed.). Champaign, IL: Human Kinetics.

Malott, C. S. (2011). What is postformal psychology? Toward a theory of critical complexity. In C. S. Malott (Ed.), *Critical pedagogy and cognition* (pp. 97–111). Netherlands: Springer.

Manago, A. M. (2012). The new emerging adult in Chiapas, Mexico perceptions of traditional values and value change among first-generation Maya University students. *Journal of Adolescent Research, 27*(6), 663–713.

Manago, A. M. (2015). Values for gender roles and relations among high school and non-high school adolescents in a Maya community in Chiapas, Mexico. *International Journal of Psychology, 50*(1), 20–28. http://doi.org/10.1002/ijop.12126.

Mandel, D. R., Lusczyk, P. W., & Pisoni, D. B. (1995). Infants' recognition of the sound patterns of their own names. *Psychological Science, 6,* 314–317.

Mange, E. J., & Mange, A. P. (1998). *Basic human genetics* (2nd ed.). Sunderland, MA: Sinauer Associates.

Manlove, J., Welti, K., Wildsmith, E., & Barry, M. (2014). Relationship types and contraceptive use within young adult dating relationships. *Perspectives on Sexual and Reproductive Health, 46*(1), 41–50. http://doi.org/10.1363/46e0514.

Manning, M. L. (1998). Play development from ages eight to twelve. In D. P. Fromberg & D. Bergen, *Play from birth to twelve and beyond* (pp. 154–161). London, UK: Garland Publishing.

Manning, W. D. (2013). *Trends in cohabitation: Over twenty years of change, 1987–2010.* (FP-13-12). National Center for Family & Marriage Research. Retrieved from http://ncfmr.bgsu.edu/pdf/family_profiles/file130944.pdf.

Maratsos, M. (1998). The acquisition of grammar. In W. Damon (Ed.), & D. Kuhn & R. S. Siegler (Vol. Eds.), *Handbook of child psychology* (5th ed.): *Vol. 2.Cognition, perception and language* (pp. 421–466). New York, NY: Wiley.

Marcia, J. (1966). Development and validation of ego identity status. *Journal of Personality and Social Psychology, 3,* 551–558.

Marcia, J. (1980). Identity in adolescence. In J. Adelson (Ed.), *Handbook of adolescent Psychology* (pp. 159–187). New York, NY: Wiley.

Marcia, J. (1989). Identity and intervention. *Journal of Adolescence, 12,* 401–410.

Marcia, J. E. (1999). Representational thought in ego identity, psychotherapy, and psychosocial developmental theory. In I. E. Siegel (Ed.), *Development of mental representation: Theories and applications* (pp. 391–414). Mahwah, NJ: Erlbaum.

Marcia, J. E. (2010). Life transitions and stress in the context of psychosocial development. In T. W. Miller (Ed.), *Handbook of stressful transitions across the lifespan* (pp. 19–34). New York, NY: Springer.

Marcia, J. E., & Carpendale, J. I. (2004). Identity: Does thinking make it so? *Changing conceptions of psychological life,* 113–126.

Marcon, R. A. (1999). Positive relationships between parent–school involvement and public school inner-city preschoolers' development and academic performance. *School Psychology Review, 28,* 395–412.

Marcotte, D., Fortin, L., Potvin, P., & Papillon, M. (2002). Gender differences in depressive symptoms during adolescence: Role of gender-typed characteristics, self-esteem, body image, stressful life events, and pubertal status. *Journal of Emotional and Behavioral Disorders, 10,* 29–42.

Marcovitch, S., Zelazo, P., & Schmuckler, M. (2003). The effect of the number of A trials on performance on the A-not-B task. *Infancy*, *3*, 519–529.

Markey, P. M., & Markey, C. N. (2007). Romantic ideals, romantic obtainment, and relationship experiences: The complementarity of interpersonal traits among romantic partners. *Journal of Social and Personal Relationships*, *24*, 517–533.

Markman, E. M., & Jaswal, V. K. (2004). Acquiring and using a grammatical form class: Lessons from the proper-count distinction. *Weaving a lexicon*, 371–409.

Markus, H., & Kitayama, S. (1991). Culture and the self: Implications for cognition, emotion, and motivation. *Psychological Review*, *98*, 224–253.

Markus, H., & Nurius, R. (1986). Possible selves. *American Psychologist*, *41*, 954–969.

Markus, H. R., & Kitayama, S. (2003). Culture, self, and the reality of the social. *Psychological Inquiry*, *14*, 277–283.

Markus, H. R., & Kitayama, S. (2010). Cultures and selves: A cycle of mutual constitution. *Perspectives on Psychological Science*, *5*(4), 420–430.

Marlier, L., Schaal, B., & Soussignan, R. (1998). Neonatal responsiveness to the odor of amniotic and lacteal fluids: A test of perinatal chemosensory continuity. *Child Development*, *69*, 611–623.

Marlow, N., Wolke, D., Bracewell, M. A., & Samara, M. (2005). Neurologic and developmental disability at six years of age after extremely preterm births. *New England Journal of Medicine*, *352*, 9–19.

Marsh, H. W., & Ayotte, V. (2003). Do multiple dimensions of self-concept become more differentiated with age? The differential distinctiveness hypothesis. *Journal of Educational Psychology*, *95*, 687–706.

Marsh, H., & Kleitman, S. (2005). Consequences of employment during high school: Character building, subversion of academic goals, or a threshold? *American Educational Research Journal*, *42*, 331–369.

Marsh, M., & Ronner, W. (1996). *The empty cradle: Infertility in America from colonial times to the present*. Baltimore, MD: Johns Hopkins University Press.

Marshall, W. (1978). Puberty. In F. Falkner & J. Tanner (Eds.), *Human growth* (Vol. 2). (pp. 141–181). New York, NY: Plenum.

Marti, E., & Rodriguez, C. (Eds.) (2012). *After Piaget*. New York, NY: Transaction Publishers.

Martin, A., Brooks-Gunn, J., Klebanov, P., Buka, S., & McCormick, M. (2008). Long-term maternal effects of early childhood intervention: Findings from the Infant Health and Development Program (IHDP). *Journal of Applied Developmental Psychology*, *29*, 101–117.

Martin, C. K., & Fabes, R. A. (2001). The stability and consequences of young children's same-sex peer interactions. *Developmental Psychology*, *37*, 431–446.

Martin, C. L., & Ruble, D. (2004). Children's search for gender cues: Cognitive perspectives on gender development. *Current Directions in Psychological Science*, *13*, 67–70.

Martin, J., & Sokol, B. (2011). Generalized others and imaginary audiences: A neo-Meadian approach to adolescent egocentrism. *New Ideas in Psychology*, *29*(3), 364–375.

Martin, J. A., Hamilton, B. E., Sutton, P. D., Ventura, S. J., Menacker, F., & Munson, M. L. (2003). Births: Final data for 2002. *National Vital Statistics Reports*, *52*(10). Hyattsville, Maryland: National Center for Health Statistics.

Martin, J. A., Hamilton, B. E., Sutton, P. D., Ventura, S. J., Menacker, F., & Munson, M. L (2005). Births: Final data for 2003. *National Vital Statistics Reports*, *54*, 1–116.

Martin, J. A., Park, M. M., & Sutton, P. D. (2002). Births: Preliminary data for 2001. *National Vital Statistics Reports*, *50*(10). Hyattsville, MD: National Center for Health Statistics.

Martin, J. L, & Ross, H. S. (2005). Sibling aggression: Sex differences and parents' reactions. *International Journal of Behavioral Development*, *29*, 129–138.

Martin, P., & Midgley, E. (2010). *Immigration in America, 2010*. Washington, DC: Population Reference Bureau.

Martin, T. C., Bell, P., & Ogunbiyi, O. (2007). Comparison of general anaesthesia and spinal anaesthesia for caesarean section in Antigua and Barbuda. *West Indian Medical Journal*, *56*(4), 330–333.

Martini, M. (1996). "What's new?" at the dinner table: Family dynamics during mealtimes in two cultural groups in Hawaii. *Early Development and Parenting*, *5*, 23–24.

Martins, C., & Gaffan, E. A. (2000). Effects of maternal depression on patterns of infant–mother attachment: A meta-analytic investigation. *Journal of Child Psychology and Psychiatry*, *41*, 737–746.

Marván, M. L., & Trujillo, P. (2010). Menstrual socialization, beliefs, and attitudes concerning menstruation in rural and urban Mexican women. *Health Care for Women International*, *31*, 53–67.

Mascolo, M. F., & Fischer, K. W. (2007). The codevelopment of self and sociomoral emotions during the toddler years. In C. A. Brownell & C. B. Kopp (Eds.), *Socioemotional development in the toddler years* (pp. 66–99). New York, NY: Guilford.

Masten, A. S. (2001). Ordinary magic: Resilience processes in development. *American psychologist*, *56*(3), 227.

Masten, A. S. (2007). Competence, resilience, and development in adolescence: Clues for prevention science. In D. Romer & E. F. Walker (Eds.), *Adolescent psychopathology and the developing brain: Integrating brain and prevention science* (pp. 31–52). New York, NY: Oxford University Press.

Masten, A. S. (2014). Global perspectives on resilience in children and youth. *Child Development*, *85*(1), 6–20.

Masten, A. S., Obradovic, J., & Burt, K. B. (2006). Resilience in embracing emerging adulthood: Developmental perspectives on continuity and transformation. In J. J. Arnett & J. L. Tanner (Eds.), *Emerging adults in America: Coming of age in the 21st century* (pp. 173–190). Washington, DC: American Psychological Association.

Mastin, D. F., Peszka, J., & Lilly, D. R. (2009). Online academic integrity. *Teaching of Psychology*, *36*(3), 174–178.

Matlin, M. W. (2004). *The psychology of women* (5th ed.). Belmont, CA: Wadsworth.

Matsumoto, D., & Yoo, S. H. (2006). Toward a new generation of cross-cultural research. *Perspectives on Psychological Science*, *1*, 234–250.

Mattson, S. N., Roesch, S. C., Fagerlund, Å., Autti-Rämö, I., Jones, K. L., May, P. A., Adnams, C. M., Konovalova, V., Riley, E. P., & CIFASD. (2010). Toward a neurobehavioral profile of fetal alcohol spectrum disorders. *Alcoholism: Clinical and Experimental Research*, *34*, 1640–1650.

Matusov, E., & Hayes, R. (2000). Sociocultural critique of Piaget and Vygotsky. *New Ideas in Psychology*, *18*, 215–239.

Maurer, D., & Salapatek, P. (1976). Developmental changes in the scanning of faces by young infants. *Child Development*, *47*(2), 523–527. doi:10.2307/1128813.

Maynard, A. E. (2002). Cultural teaching: The development of teaching skills in Zinacantec Maya sibling interactions. *Child Development*, *73*(3), 969–982.

Maynard, A. E. (2008). What we thought we knew and how we came to know it: Four decades of cross-cultural research from a Piagetian point of view. *Human Development*, *51* (Special issue: Celebrating a legacy of theory with new directions for research on human development), 56–65.

Maynard, A. E., & Greenfield, P. M. (2003). Implicit cognitive development in cultural tools and children: Lessons from Maya Mexico. *Cognitive Development*, *18*(Special Issue: The sociocultural construction of implicit knowledge), 485–510.

Maynard, A. E., & Martini, M. I. (Eds.). (2005). *Learning in cultural context: Family, peers, and school.* New York, NY: Kluwer.

Maynard, A. E., Greenfield, P. M., & Childs, C. P. (2015). Developmental effects of economic and educational change: Cognitive representation in three generations across 43 years in a Maya community. *International Journal of Psychology, 50,* 12–19.

Mayo Clinic Staff. (2011). *Stages of Labor: Baby, it's time!* Retrieved from http://www.mayoclinic.com/health/stages-of-labor/PR00106/NSECTIONGROUP=2.

Mayseless, O., & Scharf, M. (2003). What does it mean to be an adult? The Israeli experience. In J. J. Arnett & N. Galambos (Eds.), *New directions in child and adolescent development* (Vol. 100, pp. 5–20). San Francisco, CA: Jossey-Bass.

Mazuka, R., Kondo, T., & Hayashi, A. (2008). Japanese mothers' use of specialized vocabulary in infant-directed speech: Infant-directed vocabulary in Japanese. In N. Masataka (Ed.), *The origins of language: Unraveling evolutionary forces* (pp. 39–58). New York, NY: Springer.

Mazur, E., & Kozarian, L. (2010). Self-presentation and interaction in blogs of adolescents and young emerging adults. *Journal of Adolescent Research, 25,* 124–144.

Mazzurco, J., Zhang, S. F., Hernandez, N., & Fernandez, M. I. (2014). Female farmworkers' access to and experiences with prenatal care in South Florida. *Journal of Women's Health Care, 3*(167), 2167–2420.

McAlister, A., & Peterson, C. (2007). A longitudinal study of child siblings and theory of mind development. *Cognitive Development, 22,* 258–270.

McCarthy, G., & Maughan, B. (2010). Negative childhood experiences and adult love relationships: The role of internal working models of attachment. *Attachment & human development, 12*(5), 445–461.

McCartney, K., & Berry, D. (2009). Whether the environment matters more for children in poverty. In K. McCartney and R. A. Weinberg (Eds.), *Experience and development: A festschrift in honor of Sandra Wood Scarr* (pp. 99–124). New York, NY: Psychology Press.

McCarty, M. E., Clifton, R. K., & Collard, R. R. (2001). The beginnings of tool use by infants and toddlers. *Infancy, 2*(2), 233–256.

McClure, V. S. (2000). *Infant massage—Revised Edition: A handbook for loving parents.* New York, NY: Bantam.

McDonough, P. M., & Calderone, S. (2006). The meaning of money: Perceptual differences between college counselors and low-income families about college costs and financial aid. *American Behavioral Scientist, 49,* 1703–1718.

McDowell, M. A., Brody, D. J., & Hughes, J. P. (2007). Has age at menarche changed? Results from the National Health and Nutrition Examination Survey (NHANES) 1999–2004. *Journal of Adolescent Health, 40,* 227–231.

McFalls, J. A. (2007). Population: A lively introduction. *Population Bulletin, 62,* 1–31.

McGue, M., & Christensen, K. (2002). The heritability of level and rate-of-change in cognitive functioning in Danish twins aged 70 years and older. *Experimental Aging Research, 28,* 435–451.

McGuire, S., Manke, B., Eftekhari, A., & Dunn, J. (2000). Children's perceptions of sibling conflict during middle childhood: Issues and sibling (Dis)similarity. *Social Development, 9,* 173–190.

McHale, S. M., Crouter, A. C., & Tucker, C. J. (2001). Free-time activities in middle childhood: Links with adjustment in early adolescence. *Child Development, 72,* 1764–1778.

McHale, S., Dariotis, J., & Kauh, T. (2003). Social development and social relationships in middle childhood. In R. Lerner & M. Easterbrooks (Eds.), *Handbook of psychology: Developmental psychology* (Vol. 6., pp. 241–265). New York, NY: John Wiley & Sons.

McKenna, J. J., & McDade, T. (2005). Why babies should never sleep alone: A review of the co-sleeping controversy in relation to SIDS, bed-sharing, and breastfeeding. *Paediatric Respiratory Reviews, 6,* 134–152.

McKinsey Global Institute. (2010). *Lions on the move: The progress and potential of Africa's economies.* Washington, DC: Author.

McKnight, A. J., & Peck, R. C. (2002). Graduated licensing: What works? *Injury Prevention, 8*(Suppl. 2), ii32–ii38.

McLean, K. C., & Breen, A. V. (2015). Selves in a world of stories during emerging adulthood. In J. J. Arnett (Ed.), *Oxford handbook of emerging adulthood.* New York, NY: Oxford University Press.

McLuhan, M. (1960). *The Gutenberg galaxy.* Toronto, Canada: University of Toronto Press.

McNamara, F., & Sullivan, C. E. (2000). Obstructive sleep apnea in infants. *Journal of Pediatrics, 136,* 318–323.

Mead, G. H. (1934). *Mind, self, and society.* Chicago, IL: University of Chicago Press.

Mead, M. (1928). *Coming of age in Samoa: A psychological study of primitive youth for Western civilization.* New York, NY: Morrow.

Mead, M. (1935). *Sex and Temperament in Three Primitive Societies.* New York, NY: William Morrow.

Mead, M. (1930/2001). *Growing up in New Guinea.* New York, NY: Anchor.

Mead, M., & Macgregor, F. C. (1951). *Growth and culture: A photographic study of Balinese childhood.* Oxford, UK: Putnam.

Medina, J., Ojeda-Aciego, M., & Ruiz-Calviño, J. (2009). Formal concept analysis via multi-adjoint concept lattices. *Fuzzy Sets and Systems, 160*(2), 130–144.

Medline (2008). Kwashiorkor. *Medline Plus medical encyclopedia.* Available: http://www.nlm.nih.gov/MEDLINEPLUS/ency/article/001604.htm.

Meeus, W. (2007). Netherlands. In J. J. Arnett, R. Ahmed, B. Nsamenang, T. S. Saraswathi, & R. Silbereisen (Eds.), *International encyclopedia of adolescence* (pp. 666–680). New York, NY: Routledge.

Meeus, W., Iedema, J., Helsen, M., & Vollebergh, W. (1999). Patterns of adolescent identity development: Review of literature and longitudinal analysis. *Developmental Review, 19,* 419–461.

Meltzoff, A. N., & Moore, M. K. (1983). Newborn infants imitate adult facial gestures. *Child Development, 54*(3), 702–709. doi:10.2307/1130058.

Meltzoff, A. N., & Moore, M. K. (1994). Imitation, memory, and the representation of persons. *Infant Behavior and Development, 17,* 83–99.

Mendle, J., & Ferrero, J. (2012). Detrimental psychological outcomes associated with pubertal timing in adolescent boys. *Developmental Review, 32*(1), 49–66.

Menella, J. (2000, June). The psychology of eating. Paper presented at the annual meeting of the American Psychological Society, Miami, FL.

Mensch, B. S., Bruce, J., & Greene, M. E. (1998). *The uncharted passage: Girls' adolescence in the developing world.* New York, NY: Population Council.

Menyuk, P., Liebergott, J., & Schultz, M. (1995). *Early language development in full-term and premature infants.* Hillsdale, NJ: Erlbaum.

Merewood, A., Mehta, S. D., Chamberlain, L. B., Phillipp, B. L., & Bauchner, H. (2005). Breastfeeding rates in U.S. baby-friendly hospitals: Results of a national survey. *Pediatrics, 116,* 628–634.

Merten, S., Dratva, J., & Achermann-Liebrich, U. (2005). Do baby-friendly hospitals influence breastfeeding duration on a national level? *Pediatrics, 116,* c702–c708.

Merz, E., & Abramowicz, J. (2012). 3D/4D ultrasound in prenatal diagnosis: Is it time for routine use? *Clinical Obstetrics & Gynecology, 55,* 336–351.

Mesman, J., van IJzendoorn, M. H., & Bakermans-Kranenburg, M. J. (2009). The many faces of the Still-Face Paradigm: A review and meta-analysis. *Developmental Review, 29,* 120–162.

Messinger, D. S., & Lester, B. M. (2008). Prenatal substance exposure and human development. In A. Fogel, B. J. King, & S. G. Shanker (Eds.), *Human development in the 21st century: Visionary policy ideas from systems scientists* (pp. 225–232). Bethesda, MD: Council on Human Development.

Meyers, C., Adam, R., Dungan, J., & Prenger, V. (1997). Aneuploidy in twin gestations: When is maternal age advanced? *Obstetrics and Gynecology, 89,* 248–251.

Milan, S., Snow, S., & Belay, S. (2007). The context of preschool children's sleep: Racial/ethnic differences in sleep locations, routines, and concerns. *Journal of Family Psychology, 21*(Special issue: *Carpe noctem:* Sleep and family processes), 20–28.

Miller, J. G. (2004). The cultural deep structure of psychological theories of social development. In R. J. Sternberg & E. L. Grigorenko (Eds.), *Culture and competence: Contexts of life success* (pp. 111–138). Washington, DC: American Psychological Association.

Miller, K. F., Smith, C. M., Zhu, J., & Zhang, H. (1995). Preschool origins of cross-national differences in mathematical competence: The role of number-naming systems. *Psychological Science, 6*(1), 56–60.

Miller, P. J. (2014). Placing discursive practices front and center: A sociocultural approach to the study of early socialization. In C. Wainryb & H. E. Recchia (Eds.), *Talking about right and wrong: Parent-child conversations as contexts for moral development* (pp. 416–447). New York, NY: Cambridge University Press.

Miller, P. J., Wiley, A. R., Fung, H., & Liang, C.-H. (1997). Personal storytelling as a medium of socialization in Chinese and American families. *Child Development, 68,* 557–568.

Miller, T. R., Finkelstein, A. E., Zaloshnja, E., & Hendrie, D. (2012). The cost of child and adolescent injuries and savings from prevention. In K. Liller (Ed.), *Injury prevention for children and adolescents* (pp. 21–81). Washington, DC: American Public Health Association.

Miller-Johnson, S., Costanzo, P. R., Cole, J. D., Rose, M. R., & Browne, D. C. (2003). Peer social structure and risk-taking behaviour among African American early adolescents. *Journal of Youth & Adolescence, 32,* 375–384.

Millman, R. P. (2005). Excessive sleepiness in adolescents and young adults: Causes, consequences, and treatment strategies. *Pediatrics, 115,* 1774–1786.

Mills, B., Reyna, V. F., & Estrada, S. (2008). Explaining contradictory relations between risk perception and risk taking. *Psychological Science, 19*(5), 429–433. http://doi.org/10.1111/j.1467-9280.2008.02104.x.

Mills, N., Daker-White, G., Graham, A., Campbell, R., & The Chlamydia Screening Studies (ClaSS) Group. (2006). Population screening for *Chlamydia trachomatis* infection in the UK: A qualitative study of the experiences of those screened. *Family Practice, 23,* 550–557.

Minami, M., & McCabe, A. (1995). Rice balls and bear hunts: Japanese and North American family narrative patterns. *Journal of Child Language, 22,* 423–445.

Mindell, J. A., Sadeh, A., Kohyama, J., & How, T. H. (2010). Parental behaviors and sleep outcomes in infants and toddlers: A cross cultural comparison. *Sleep Medicine, 11,* 393–399.

Miniati, M., Callari, A., Calugi, S., Rucci, P., Savino, M., Mauri, M., & Dell'Osso, L. (2014). Interpersonal psychotherapy for postpartum depression: a systematic review. *Archives of Women's Mental Health, 17*(4), 257–268. http://doi.org/10.1007/s00737-014-0442-7.

Minnes, S., Singer, L. T., Kirchner, H. L., Short, E., Lewis, B., Satayathum, S., & Queh, D. (2010). The effects of prenatal cocaine-exposure on problem behavior in children 4–10 years. *Neurotoxicology and Teratology, 32*(4), 443–451. http://doi.org/10.1016/j.ntt.2010.03.005.

Mintz, T. H. (2005). Linguistic and conceptual influences on adjective acquisition in 24- and 36-month-olds. *Developmental Psychology, 41,* 17–29.

Mireault, G. C., Crockenberg, S. C., Sparrow, J. E., Pettinato, C. A., Woodard, K. C., & Malzac, K. (2014). Social looking, social referencing, and humor perception in 6- and 12-month-old infants. *Infant Behavior and Development, 37,* 536–545.

Mischel, W. (2014). *The Marshmallow Test: Mastering self-control.* New York, NY: Little, Brown and Co.

Mischel, W., Ebbesen, E. B., & Raskoff Zeiss, A. (1972). Cognitive and attentional mechanisms in delay of gratification. *Journal of Personality and Social Psychology, 21*(2), 204–218. doi:10.1037/h0032198.

Mishna, F., Newman, P. A., Daley, A., & Solomon, S. (2009). Bullying of lesbian and gay youth: A qualitative investigation. *British Journal of Social Work, 39,* 1598–1614.

Mistry, J., & Saraswathi, T. (2003). The cultural context of child development. In R. Lerner & M. Easterbrooks (Eds.), *Handbook of psychology: Developmental psychology* (Vol. 6, pp. 267–291). New York, NY: John Wiley & Sons.

Mitchell, A., & Boss, B. J. (2002). Adverse effects of pain on the nervous systems of newborns and young children: A review of the literature. *Journal of Neuroscience and Nursing, 34,* 228–235.

Modell, J. (1989). *Into one's own: From youth to adulthood in the United States, 1920–1975.* Berkeley: University of California Press.

Moffitt, T. E. (2003). Life-course-persistent and adolescence-limited antisocial behavior: A 10-year research review and a research agenda. In B. B. Lahey & T. E. Moffitt (Eds.), *Causes of conduct disorder and juvenile delinquency* (pp. 49–75). New York, NY: Guilford.

Moffitt, T. E., (2006). Life–course–persistent versus adolescence–limited antisocial behavior. In D. J. Cohen & D. Cicchetti (Eds.), *Developmental psychopathology, Vol. 3: Risk, order, and adaption* (2nd ed., pp. 570–598). Hoboken, NJ: Wiley.

Moffitt, T. E. (2007). A review of research on the taxonomy of life-course persistent versus adolescence-limited antisocial behavior. In D. J. Flannery, A. T. Vazsonyi, & I. D. Waldman (Eds.), *The Cambridge handbook of violent behavior and aggression* (pp. 49–74). New York, NY: Cambridge University Press.

Money, J. (1980). *Love and love sickness: The science of sex, gender difference, and pair-bonding.* Baltimore, MD: Johns Hopkins University Press.

Montgomery, M. J. (2005). Psychosocial intimacy and identity: From early adolescence to emerging adulthood. *Journal of Adolescent Research, 20,* 346–374.

Moore, J. L. (2010). The neuropsychological functioning of prisoners of war following repatriation. In C. H. Kennedy & J. L. Moore (Eds.), *Military neuropsychology* (pp. 267–295). New York, NY: Springer.

Moore, K. A., Chalk, R., Scarpa, J., & Vandivere, S. (2002, August). Family strengths: Often overlooked, but real. *Child Trends Research Brief,* 1–8.

Moore, K. L. (1974). *Before we are born: Basic embryology and birth defects.* Philadelphia, PA: Saunders.

Moore, K. L., & Persaud, T. V. N. (2003). *Before we are born* (6th ed.). Philadelphia, PA: Saunders.

Moore, K. L., Persaud, T. V. N., & Torchia, M. G. (2011). *The developing human.* New York, NY: Elsevier Health Sciences.

Morawska, A., & Sanders, M. (2011). Parental use of time out revisited: A useful or harmful parenting strategy? *Journal of Child and Family Studies, 20,* 1–8.

Morelli, G. (2015). The evolution of attachment theory and cultures of human attachment in infancy and early childhood. In L. A. Jensen (Ed.), *Oxford handbook of human development and culture.* (pp. 149–164). New York, NY: Oxford University Press.

Morelli, G., Rogoff, B., Oppenheim, D., & Goldsmith, D. (1992). Cultural variation in infants' sleeping arrangements: Question of independence. *Developmental Psychology, 39,* 604–613.

Morelli, G., & Rothbaum, F. (2007). Situating the child in context: Attachment relationships and self-regulation in different cultures. In S. Kitayama & D. Cohen (Eds.), *Handbook of cultural psychology* (pp. 500–527). New York, NY: Guilford Press.

Moreno Mínguez, A., López Peláez, A., & Sánchez-Cabezudo, S. S. (2012). *The transition to adulthood in Spain: Economic crisis and late emancipation.* Barcelona, Spain: La Caixa Foundation.

Moretti, M. M., & Wiebe, V. J. (1999). Self-discrepancy in adolescence: Own and parental standpoints on the self. *Merrill-Palmer Quarterly, 45,* 624–649.

Morgan, M. A., Cragan, J. D., Goldenberg, R. L., Rasmussen, S. A., & Schulkin, J. (2010). Management of prescription and nonprescription drug use during pregnancy. *Journal of Maternal–Fetal and Neonatal Medicine, 23,* 813–819.

Morra, S., Gobbo, C., Marini, Z., & Sheese, R. (2008). *Cognitive development: Neo–Piagetian perspectives.* New York, NY: Taylor & Francis.

Mortimer, J. (2013). Work and its positive and negative effects on youth's psychosocial development. *Health and Safety of Young Workers, 66*–79.

Mortimer, J. T. (2003). *Working and growing up in America.* Cambridge, MA: Harvard University Press.

Mortimer, J. T., Vuolo, M., Staff, J., Wakefield, S., & Xie, W. (2008). Tracing the timing of "career" acquisition in a contemporary youth cohort. *Work and Occupations, 35,* 44–84.

Morton, H., (1996). *Becoming Tongan: An ethnography of childhood.* Honolulu: University of Hawaii Press.

Mossakowski, K. N. (2009). The influence of past unemployment duration on symptoms of depression among young women and men in the United States. *American Journal of Public Health, 99*(10), 1826–1832.

Motola, M., Sinisalo, P., & Guichard, J. (1998). Social habitus and future plans. In J. Nurmi (Ed.), *Adolescents, cultures, and conflicts* (pp. 43–73). New York, NY: Garland.

Mugford, M. (2006). Cost effectiveness of prevention and treatment of neonatal respiratory distress (RDS) with exogenous surfactant: What has changed in the last three decades? *Early Human Development, 82,* 105–115.

Muller, F., Rebiff, M., Taillandier, A., Qury, J. F., & Mornet, E. (2000). Parental origin of the extra chromosome in prenatally diagnosed fetal trisomy. *Human Genetics, 106,* 340–344.

Munro, G., & Adams, G. R. (1977). Ego-identity formation in college students and working youth. *Developmental Psychology, 13,* 523–524.

Muret-Wagstaff, S., & Moore, S. G. (1989). The Hmong in America: Infant behavior and rearing practices. In J. K. Nugent, B. M. Lester, & T. B. Brazelton (Eds.), *Biology, culture, and development* (Vol. 1, pp. 319–339). Norwood, NJ: Ablex.

Murkoff, H. (2011). *What to expect the second year.* New York, NY: Workman.

Murkoff, H., & Mazel, S. (2008). *What to expect when you're expecting.* New York, NY: Workman.

Murkoff, H., Eisenberg, A., & Hathaway, S. (2009). *What to expect the first year.* New York, NY: Workman.

Murkoff, H. E., Eisenberg, A., Mazel, S., & Hathaway, S. E. (2003). *What to expect the first year* (2nd ed.). New York, NY: Workman.

Murnane, R. J., & Levy, F. (1997). *Teaching the new basic skills: Principles for educating children to thrive in a changing economy.* New York, NY: Free Press.

Murray-Close, D., Ostrov, J., & Crick, N. (2007). A short-term longitudinal study of growth and relational aggression during middle childhood: Associations with gender, friendship, intimacy, and internalizing problems. *Development and Psychopathology, 19,* 187–203.

Mutti, D. O., Mitchell, G. L., Moeschberger, M. L., Jones, L. A., & Zadnik, K. (2002). Parental myopia, near work, school achievement, and children's refractive error. *Investigative Ophthalmology and Visual Science, 43,* 3633–3640.

Myles, N., Newall, H., Ward, H., & Large, M. (2013). Systematic meta-analysis of individual selective serotonin reuptake inhibitor medications and congenital malformations. *The Australian and New Zealand Journal of Psychiatry, 47*(11), 1002–1012. http://doi.org/10.1177/0004867413492219.

Nakano, H., & Blumstein, S. E. (2004). Deficits in thematic processes in Broca's and Wernicke's aphasia. *Brain and Language, 88,* 96–107.

Napier, K., & Meister, K. (2000). *Growing healthy kids: A parents' guide to infant and child nutrition.* New York, NY: American Council on Science and Heath.

Narayanan, U., & Warren, S. T. (2006). Neurobiology of related disorders: Fragile X syndrome. In S. O. Moldin & J. L. R. Rubenstein, *Understanding autism: From basic neuroscience to treatment* (pp. 113–131). Washington, DC: Taylor Francis.

Nardecchia, F., Manti, F., Chiarotti, F., Carducci, C., Carducci, C., & Leuzzi, V. (2015). Neurocognitive and neuroimaging outcome of early treated young adult PKU patients: A longitudinal study. *Molecular Genetics and Metabolism.* http://doi.org/10.1016/j.ymgme.2015.04.003.

National Association for the Education of Young Children. (2010). *2010 NAEYC Standards for Initial and Advanced Early Childhood Professional Preparation Programs.* Washington, DC: Author.

National Center for Education in Maternal and Child Health. (2002). *Bright futures in practice: Nutrition pocket guide.* Washington, DC: Georgetown University.

National Center for Education Statistics. (2014). *The condition of education, 2014.* Washington, DC: U. S. Department of Education. Available: www.nces.gov.

National Center for Health Statistics. (2005). *Health, United States, 2005. With chartbook on trends in the health of Americans.* Hyattsville, MD: Author.

National Center for Health Statistics. (2009). *Health, United States, 2009.* Hyattsville, MD: Prevention.

National Center for Statistics and Analysis. (2015). *Children: 2013 data.* (Traffic Safety Facts. Report No. DOT HS 812 154). Washington, DC: National Highway Traffic Safety Administration.

National Highway Traffic Safety Administration. (2014). *Traffic safety facts.* Washington, DC: U.S. Department of Transportation.

National Institute of Child Health Development (NICHD). (2005a). *Child care and child development: Results from the NICHD study of early child care and youth development.* New York, NY: Guilford Press.

National Institute of Drug Abuse. (2001). *Marijuana.* Washington, DC: National Institutes of Health.

National Resource Center on ADHD. (2014). *Statistical prevalence of ADHD.* Retrieved from http://www.help4adhd.org/about/statistics.

National Sudden and Unexpected Infant/Child Death & Pregnancy Loss Resource Center. (2010). *Statistics overview.* Retrieved from http://sidcenter.org/Statistics.html.

National Vital Statistics Report. (2014). *Deaths: Final data for 2012.* NVSR Volume 63, Number 9. Hyattsville, MD: Author.

National Women's Health Information Center. (2011). *Infertility.* Retrieved from http://www.womenshealth.gov/faq/infertility.cfm#f.

Natsopoulos, D., Kiosseoglou, G., Xeroxmeritou, A., & Alevriadou, A. (1998). Do the hands talk on the mind's behalf? Differences in language between left- and right-handed children. *Brain and Language, 64,* 182–214.

Natsuaki, M. N., Ge, X., Reiss, D., & Neiderhiser, J. M. (2009). Aggressive behavior between siblings and the development of externalizing problems: Evidence from a genetically sensitive study. *Developmental Psychology, 45,* 1009–1018.

Neberich, W., Penke, L., Lenhart, J., & Asendorph, J. B. (2010). Family of origin, age at menarche, and reproductive strategies: A test of four evolutionary–developmental models. *European Journal of Developmental Psychology, 7*, 153–177.

Nelson, D. A., Robinson, C. C., & Hart, C. H. (2005). Relational and physical aggression of preschool-age children: Peer status linkages across informants. *Early Education and Development, 16*, 115–139.

Nelson, L. J., & Chen, X. (2007). Emerging adulthood in China: The role of social and cultural factors. *Child Development Perspectives, 1*, 86–91.

Nelson, L. J., & Luster, S. S. (2015). "Adulthood" by whose definition? The complexity of emerging adults' conceptions of adulthood. In J. J. Arnett (Ed.), *Oxford handbook of emerging adulthood.* New York, NY: Oxford University Press.

Nelson, L. J., Badger, S., & Wu, B. (2004). The influence of culture in emerging adulthood: Perspectives of Chinese college students. *International Journal of Behavioral Development, 28*, 26–36.

Nesbitt, R. E. (2009). *Intelligence and how to get it: Why schools and cultures matter.* New York, NY: Norton.

Neto, F. (2002). Acculturation strategies among adolescents from immigrant families in Portugal. *International Journal of Intercultural Relations, 26*, 17–38.

Newcombe, N. S., Lloyd, M. E., & Ratliff, K. R. (2007). Development of episodic and autobiographical memory: A cognitive neuroscience perspective. In R. V. Kail (Ed.), *Advances in child development and behavior* (Vol. 35, pp. 37–85). San Diego, CA: Elsevier Academic Press.

Newcombe, N., & Huttenlocher, J. (2006). Development of spatial cognition. In W. Damon & R. Lerner (Eds.), & D. Kuhn & R. Siegler (Vol. Eds.), *Handbook of child psychology: Vol. 2. Cognition, perception and language* (6th ed., pp. 734–776). New York, NY: Wiley.

Newton, N., & Newton, M. (2003). Childbirth in cross–cultural perspective. In L. Dundes (Ed.), *The manner born: Birth rites in cross–cultural perspective* (pp. 9–32). Walnut Creek, CA: AltaMira.

Ng, M., Fleming, T., Robinson, M., Graetz, N., Margono, C., Mullany, E. C.,... Gakidou, E. (2014). Global, regional, and national prevalence of overweight and obesity in children and adults during 1980–2013: A systematic analysis of the Global Burden of Disease Study 2013. *The Lancet 309.* doi: 10.1016/S0140-6736(14)60460-8.

Ngongo, P. B., Priddy, F., Park, H., Becker, J., Bender, B., Fast, P.,...& Mebrahtu, T. (2012). Developing standards of care for HIV prevention research in developing countries—A case study of 10 research centers in Eastern and Southern Africa. *AIDS Care, 24*(10), 1277–1289.

NICHD Early Child Care Research Network. (2000). The relation of child care to cognitive and language development. *Child Development, 71*, 960–980.

NICHD Early Child Care Research Network. (2001). Child care and children's peer interactions at 24 and 36 months: The NICHD study of early child care. *Child Development, 72*, 1478–1500.

NICHD Early Child Care Research Network. (2005b). Early child care and children's development in the primary grades: Results from the NICHD Study of Early Child Care. *American Educational Research Journal, 43*, 537–570.

NICHD Early Child Care Research Network. (2004). Trajectories of physical aggression from toddlerhood to middle childhood. *Monographs of the Society for Research in Child Development, 69* (Serial No. 278), vii–129.

NICHD Early Child Care Research Network. (2006). Infant-mother attachment classification: Risk and protection in relation to changing maternal caregiving quality. *Developmental Psychology, 42*, 38–58.

Nicholson, J. M., Sanders, M. R., Halford, W. K., Phillips, M., & Whitton, S. W. (2008). The prevention and treatment of children's adjustment problems in stepfamilies. In J. Pryor (Ed.), *The international handbook of stepfamilies: Policy and practice in legal, research, and clinical environments* (pp. 485–521). Hoboken, NJ: John Wiley & Sons.

Nichter, M. (2001). *Fat talk: What girls and their parents say about dieting.* Cambridge, MA: Harvard University Press.

Nickerson, A. B., & Nagle, R. J. (2005). Parent and peer attachment in late childhood and early adolescence. *Journal of Early Adolescence, 25*, 223–249.

Nihart, M. A. (1993). Growth and development of the brain. *Journal of Child and Adolescent Psychiatric and Mental Health Nursing, 6*, 39–40.

Noia, G., Cesari, E., Ligato, M. S., Visconti, D., Tintoni, M., Mappa, I.,...Caruso, A. (2008). Pain in the fetus. *Neonatal Pain, 2*, 45–55.

Nolan, K., Schell, L. M., Stark, A. D., & Gomez, M. I. (2002). Longitudinal study of energy and nutrient intakes for infants from low-income, urban families. *Public Health Nutrition, 5*, 405–412.

Nolen-Hoeksema, S., Wisco, B. E., & Lyubomirsky, S. (2008). Rethinking rumination. *Perspectives on psychological science, 3*(5), 400–424.

Noller, P. (2005). Sibling relationships in adolescence: Learning and growing together. *Personal Relationships, 12*, 1–22.

Norona, J. C., Preddy, T. M., & Welsh, D. P. (2015). How gender shapes emerging adulthood. In J. J. Arnett (Ed.), *Oxford handbook of emerging adulthood.* New York, NY: Oxford University Press.

Nottelmann, E. D., Susman, E. J., Dorn, L. D., Inoff-Germain, G., Loriaux, D. L., Cutler, G. B., & Chrousos, G. P. (1987). Developmental processes in early adolescence: Relations among chronologic age, pubertal stage, height, weight, and serum levels of gonadotropins, sex steroids, and adrenal androgens. *Journal of Adolescent Health Care, 8*(3), 246–260.

Novik, T. S., Hervas, A., Ralston, S. J., Dalsgaard, S., Rodrigues Pereira, R., Lorenzo, M. J., & ADORE Study Group. (2006). Influence of gender on attention deficit/hyperactivity disorder in Europe—ADORE. *European Child & Adolescent Psychiatry, 15*(Suppl. 1), 5–24.

Nsamengnang, B. A. (1992). Perceptions of parenting among the Nso of Cameroon. *Father–child relations: Cultural and biosocial contexts* (pp. 321–344). New York, NY: De Gruyter.

Nugent, K. J., Petrauskas, B. J., & Brazelton, T. B. (Eds.). (2009). *The newborn as a person: Enabling healthy infant development worldwide.* Hoboken, NJ: John Wiley & Sons.

Nugent, K., & Brazelton, T. B. (2000). Preventive infant mental health: Uses of the Brazelton scale. In J. D. Osofsky & H. E. Fitzgerald (Eds.), *WAIMH Handbook of infant mental health* (Vol. 2). New York, NY: Wiley.

Nuland, S. B. (2003). *The doctor's plague: Germs, childbed fever, and the strange story of Ignac Semmelweis.* New York, NY: Norton.

Núñez, J., & Flanagan, C. (2015). Political beliefs and civic engagement in emerging adulthood. In J. J. Arnett (Ed.), *Oxford handbook of emerging adulthood.* New York, NY: Oxford University Press.

Nwokah, E. E., Hsu, H., Davies, P., & Fogel, A. (1999). The integration of laughter and speech in vocal communication: A dynamic systems perspective. *Journal of Speech and Hearing Research, 42*, 880–894.

Nylen, K., Moran, T., Franklin, C., & O'Hara, M. (2006). Maternal depression: A review of relevant treatment approaches for mothers and infants. *Infant Mental Health Journal, 27*, 327–343.

O'Connor, T. G., Rutter, M., Beckett, C., Keaveney, L., Dreppner, J. M., & the English and Romanian Adoptees Study Team. (2000). The effects of global severe privation on cognitive competence: Extension and longitudinal follow-up. *Child Development, 71*, 376–390.

Oates, M. R., Cox, J. L., Neema, S., Asten, P., Glangeaud-Freudenthal, N., Figueiredo, B.,...TCS–PND Group. (2004). Postnatal depression across countries and cultures: A qualitative study. *British Journal of Psychiatry, 184*, s10–s16.

Oberlander, S. E., Black, M. M., & Starr, R. H., Jr. (2007). African American adolescent mothers and grandmothers: A multigenerational approach to parenting. *American Journal of Community Psychology, 39*, 37–46.

Odeku, K., Rembe, S., & Anwo, J. (2009). Female genital mutilation: A human rights perspective. *Journal of Psychology in Africa, 19*(Special issue: Violence against children in Africa), 55–62.

OECD. (2009). *Health at a glance 2009: OECD indicators.* Author.

OECD. (2013). *Education at a glance: Indicators and annexes.* Retrieved from http://www.oecd.org/edu/educationataglance2013-indicatorsandannexes.htm#ChapterC.

OECD. (2014a). Infant mortality. Family database, Social Policy Division. Retrieved from www.oecd.org/social/family/database.

OECD. (2014b). *OECD Statextracts: Labor Force Statistics by sex and age.* Retrieved from http://stats.oecd.org/Index.aspx?DatasetCode=LFS_SEXAGE_I_R.

O'Donnell, C. R. (Ed.) (2003). *Culture, peers, and delinquency.* New York: Haworth Press.

O'Donnell, P., Richards, M., Pearce, S., & Romero, E. (2012). Gender differences in monitoring and deviant peers as predictors of delinquent behavior among low-income urban African American youth. *The Journal of Early Adolescence, 32*(3), 431–459.

Ogbu, J. U. (2002). Cultural amplifiers of intelligence: IQ and minority status in cross-cultural perspective. In J. M. Fish (Ed.), *Race and intelligence: Separating science from myth* (pp. 241–278). Mahwah, NJ: Erlbaum.

Ogden, C. L., Carroll, M. D., Kit, B. K., & Flegal, K. M. (2014). Prevalence of childhood and adult obesity. *JAMA 311*, 806–814.

Ogden, T., & Amlund-Hagen, K. (2006). Multisystemic treatment of serious behavior problems in youth: Sustainability of therapy effectiveness two years after intake. *Child and Adolescent Mental Health, 11*, 142–149.

Ogletree, S. M., Martinez, C. N., Turner, T. R., & Mason, M. (2004). Pokémon: Exploring the role of gender. *Sex Roles, 50*(11–12), 851–859.

Ohgi, S., Arisawa, K., Takahashi, T., Kusomoto, T., Goto, Y. & Saito, A.T. (2003). Neonatal behavioral assessment scale as a predictor of later developmental disabilities of low birth-weight and/or premature infants. *Brain Development, 25*, 313–321.

Oken, E., & Lightdale, J. R. (2000). Updates in pediatric nutrition. *Current Opinion in Pediatrics, 12*, 282–290.

Olds, D. L. (2010). The nurse–family partnership: From trials to practice. In A. J. Reynolds, A. J. Rolnick, M. M. Englund, & J. A. Temple (Eds.), *Childhood programs and practices in the first decade of life: A human capital integration* (pp. 49–75). New York, NY: Cambridge University Press.

Olivier, J. D. A., Åkerud, H., & Sundström Poromaa, I. (2015). Antenatal depression and antidepressants during pregnancy: Unraveling the complex interactions for the offspring. *European Journal of Pharmacology, 753*, 257–262. http://doi.org/10.1016/j.ejphar.2014.07.049.

Ollendick, T. H., Shortt, A. L., & Sander, J. B. (2008). Internalizing disorders in children and adolescents. In J. E. Maddux & B. A. Winstead (Eds.), *Psychopathology: Foundations for a contemporary understanding* (2nd ed., pp. 375–399). New York, NY: Routledge.

Oller, D. K., Eilers, R. E., Urbano, R., & Cobo-Lewis, A. B. (1997). Development of precursors to speech in infants exposed to two languages. *Journal of Child Language, 24*, 407–425.

Olson, C. K., Kutner, L. A., & Warner, D. E. (2008). The role of violent video game content in adolescent development: Boys' perspectives. *Journal of Adolescent Research, 23*, 55–75.

Olson, C. K., Kutner, L. A., Warner, D. E., Almerigi, J., Baer, L., Nicholi, A. M., & Beresin, E. V. (2007). Factors correlated with violent video game use by adolescent boys and girls. *Journal of Adolescent Health, 41*, 77–83.

Olweus, D. (2000). Bullying. In A. E. Kazdin (Ed.), *Encyclopedia of psychology* (Vol. 1, pp. 487–489). Washington, DC: American Psychological Association.

Olweus, D., & Limber, S. P. (2010). Bullying in school: Evaluation and dissemination of the Olweus Bullying Prevention Program. *American Journal of Orthopsychiatry, 80*(1), 124–134. http://doi.org/10.1111/j.1939-0025.2010.01015.x.

Oquendo, M. A., Ellis, S. P., Greenwald, S., Malone, K. M., Weissman, M. M., & Mann, J. J. (2014). Ethnic and sex differences in suicide rates relative to major depression in the United States. *American Journal of Psychiatry, 158*, 1652–1658.

Oren, D. L. (1981). Cognitive advantages of bilingual children related to labeling ability. *The Journal of Educational Research*, 163–169.

Osgood, D. W. (2009). *Illegal behavior: A presentation to the Committee on the Science of Adolescence of the National Academies.* Washington, DC.

Osgood, D. W., Anderson, A. L., & Shaffer, J. N. (2005). Unstructured leisure in the afterschool hours. In L. J. Mahoney, R. W. Larson, & J. S. Eccles (Eds.), *Organized activities as contexts of development: Extracurricular activities, after-school and community programs* (pp. 45–64). Mahwah, NJ: Lawrence Erlbaum.

Osgood, D. W., Wilson, J. K., Bachman, J. G., O'Malley, P. M., & Johnston, L. D. (1996). Routine activities and individual deviant behavior. *American Sociological Review, 61*, 635–655.

Oster, H., Hegley, D., & Nagel, L. (1992). Adult judgments and fine-grained analysis of infant facial expressions: Testing the validity of a priori coding formulas. *Developmental Psychology, 28*, 1115–1131.

Out, D., Pieper, S., Bakermans-Kranenburg, M. J., Zeskind, P. S., & van IJzendoorn, M. H. (2010). Intended sensitive and harsh caregiving responses to infant crying: The role of cry pitch and perceived urgency in an adult twin sample. *Child Abuse & Neglect, 34*, 863–873.

Owen, C. G., Whincup, P. H., Odoki, K., Gilg, J. A. & Cook, D. G. (2002). Infant feeding and blood cholesterol: A study in adolescents and a systematic review. *Pediatrics, 110*, 597–608.

Oyserman, D., & Fryberg, S. (2006). The possible selves of diverse adolescents: Content and function across gender, race and national origin. In C. Dunkel & J. Kerpelman (Eds.), *Possible selves: Theory, research and applications* (pp. 17–39). Hauppauge, NY: Nova Science.

Pacella, R., McLellan, M., Grice, K., Del Bono, E. A., Wiggs, J. L., & Gwiazda, J. E. (1999). Role of genetic factors in the etiology of juvenile-onset myopia based on the longitudinal study of refractive error. *Optometry and Vision Science, 76*, 381–386.

Padilla-Walker, L. M., Nelson, L. J., Carroll, J. S., & Jensen, A. C. (2010). More than a just a game: Video game and Internet use during emerging adulthood. *Journal of Youth and Adolescence, 39*, 103–113.

Padrón, E., Carlson, E. A., & Sroufe, L. A. (2014). Frightened versus not frightened disorganized infant attachment: Newborn characteristics and maternal caregiving. *American Journal of Orthopsychiatry, 84*, 201–208.

Pahl, K., & Way, N. (2006). Longitudinal trajectories of ethnic identity among urban Black and Latino adolescents. *Child Development, 77*, 1403–1415.

Paludi, M. A., & Strayer, L. A. (1985). What's in an author's name? Differential evaluations of performance as a function of author's name. *Sex Roles, 12*, 353–362.

Pan, B. A., & Snow, C. E. (1999). The development of conversation and discourse skills. In M. Barrett (Ed.), *The development of language* (pp. 229–249). Hove, UK: Psychology Press.

Pan, S. Y., Desmueles, M., Morrison, H., Semenciw, R., Ugnat, A.-M., Thompson, W., & Mao, Y. (2007). Adolescent injury deaths and hospitalization in Canada: Magnitude and temporal trends (1979–2003). *Journal of Adolescent Health, 41*, 84–92.

Pankow, L. J. (2008). Genetic theory. In B. A. Thyer, K. M. Sowers, & C. N. Dulmus (Eds.), *Comprehensive handbook of social work and social welfare: Vol. 2. Human behavior in the social environment* (pp. 327–353). Hoboken, NJ: John Wiley & Sons.

Papadakis, A. A., Prince, R. P., Jones, N. P., & Strauman, T. J. (2006). Self-regulation, rumination, and vulnerability to depression in adolescent girls. *Development and Psychopathology, 18*, 815–829.

Paquette, D. (2004). Theorizing the father–child relationship: Mechanisms and developmental outcomes. *Human Development, 47*, 193–219.

Parameswaran, G. (2003). Age, gender, and training in children's performance of Piaget's horizontality task. *Educational Studies, 29*, 307–319.

Park, S. H., Shim, Y. K., Kim, H. S., & Eun, B. L. (1999). Age and seasonal distribution of menarche in Korean girls. *Journal of Adolescent Health, 25*, 97.

Parke, R. D. (2004). Development in the family. *Annual Review of Psychology, 55*, 363–399.

Parke, R. D., & Buriel, R. (2006). Socialization in the family: Ethnic and ecological perspectives. In W. Damon & R. Lerner (Eds.), & N. Eisenberg (Vol. Ed.), *Handbook of child psychology: Vol. 3. Social, emotional and personality development* (6th ed., pp. 429–504). New York, NY: Wiley.

Parker, E. D., Schmitz, K. H., Jacobs, D. R., Jr., Dengel, D. R., & Schreiner, P. J. (2007). Physical activity in young adults and incident hypertension over 15 years of follow-up: The CARDIA study. *American Journal of Public Health, 97*, 703–709.

Parten, M. (1932). Social play among preschool children. *Journal of Abnormal Social Psychology, 27*, 243–269.

Pascalis, O., & Kelly, D. J. (2009). The origins of face processing in humans: Phylogeny and ontogeny. *Perspectives on Psychological Science, 4*, 200–209.

Pascarella, E. T. (2005). Cognitive impacts of the first year of college. In R. S. Feldman (Ed.), *Improving the first year of college: Research and practice* (pp. 111–140). Mahwah, NJ: Lawrence Erlbaum.

Pascarella, E. T. (2006). How college affects students: Ten directions for future research. *Journal of College Student Development, 47*, 508–520.

Pascarella, E., & Terenzini, P. (1991). *How college affects students: Findings and insights from twenty years of research.* San Francisco, CA: Jossey-Bass.

Pascoe, C. J. (2007). *Dude, you're a fag: Masculinity and sexuality in high school.* Berkeley, CA: University of California Press.

Pashigian, M. J. (2002). Conceiving the happy family: Infertility and marital politics in northern Vietnam. In M.C. Inhorn & F. van Balen (Eds.), *Infertility around the globe: New thinking on childlessness, gender, and reproductive technologies* (pp. 134–150). Berkeley, CA: University of California Press.

Patel, D. P., Brant, W. O., Myers, J. B., Zhang, C., Presson, A. P., Johnstone, E. B., . Dorais, J. A., Aston, K. I., Carrell, D. T., & Hotaling, J. M. (2015). Sperm concentration is poorly associated with hypoandrogenism in infertile men. *Urology, 85*(5), 1062–1067.

Patrick, M. E., Schulenberg, J. E., O'Malley, P. M., Johnston, L. D., & Bachman, J. G. (2011). Adolescents' reported reasons for alcohol and marijuana use as predictors of substance use and problems in adulthood. *Journal of studies on alcohol and drugs, 72*(1), 106.

Patterson, G. R. (2002). The early development of coercive family process. In J. B Reid, G. R. Patterson, & J. Snyder (Eds.), *Antisocial behavior in children and adolescents: A developmental analysis and model for intervention* (pp. 25–44). Washington, DC: American Psychological Association.

Patterson, M. L., & Werker, J. F. (2002). Infants' ability to match dynamic phonetic and gender information in the face and voice. *Journal of Experimental Child Psychology, 81*, 93–115.

Patton, G. C., Coffey, C., Sawyer, S. M., Viner, R. M., Haller, D. M., Bose, K., Vos, T., Ferguson, J., & Matthers, C. D. (2009). Global patterns of mortality in young people: A systematic analysis of population health data. *Lancet, 374*, 881–892.

Pearlman, D., Zierler, S., Meersman, S., Kim, H., Viner-Brown, S., & Caron, C. (2006). Race disparities in childhood asthma: Does where you live matter? *Journal of the National Medical Association, 98*, 239–247.

Peirano, P., Algarin, C., & Uauy, R. (2003). Sleep–wake states and their regulatory mechanism throughout early human development. *Journal of Pediatrics, 143*(Suppl.), S70–S79.

Pelaez, M., Field, T., Pickens, J. N., & Hart, S. (2008). Disengaged and authoritarian parenting behavior of depressed mothers with their toddlers. *Infant Behavior and Development, 31*, 145–148.

Peng, K., & Nisbett, R. E. (1999). Culture, dialectics, and reasoning about contradiction. *American Psychologist, 54*, 741–754.

Pennington, B. F., Moon, J., Edgin, J., Stedron, J., & Nadel, L. (2003). The neuropsychology of Down syndrome: Evidence for hippocampal dysfunction. *Child Development, 74*, 75–93.

Pepler, D., Craig, W., Yuile, A., & Connolly, J. (2004). Girls who bully: A developmental and relational perspective. In M. Putallaz & K. L. Bierman (Eds.), *Aggression, antisocial behavior, and violence among girls: A developmental perspective* (pp. 90–109). New York, NY: Guilford.

Pepler, D. J., Craig, W. M., Connolly, J. A., Yuile, A., McMaster, L., & Jiang, D. (2006). A developmental perspective on bullying. *Aggressive Behavior, 32*, 376–384.

Pepler, D. J., Jiang, D., Craig, W. M., & Connolly, J. A. (2008). Developmental trajectories of bullying and associated factors. *Child Development, 79*, 325–338.

Perales, M., Refoyo, I., Coteron, J., Bacchi, M., & Barakat, R. (2015). Exercise during pregnancy attenuates prenatal depression: A randomized controlled trial. *Evaluation & the Health Professions, 38*(1), 59–72. http://doi.org/10.1177/0163278714533566.

Perez, S. M., & Gauvain, M. (2009). Mother–child planning, child emotional functioning, and children's transition to first grade. *Child Development, 80*, 776–791.

Perez, S. M., & Gauvain, M. (2010). Emotional contributions to the development of executive functions in the family context. In Sokol, B. W., Müller, U., & Carpendale, J. I. M., Young, A. R., & Iarocci, G. (Eds.), *Self and social regulation: Social interaction and the development of social understanding and executive functions.* (pp. 358–385). New York, NY: Oxford University Press.

Perry, W. G. (1970/1999). *Forms of ethical and intellectual development in the college years: A scheme.* San Francisco, CA: Jossey-Bass.

Peterson, C. (2014). Theory of mind understanding and empathic behavior in children with autismspectrum disorders. *International Journal of Developmental Neuroscience, 39*, 16–21.

Peterson, C., & Whalen, N. (2001). Five years later: Children's memory for medical emergencies. *Applied Cognitive Psychology, 15*(Special issue: Trauma, stress, and autobiographical memory), S7–S24.

Peterson, C. C. (2000). Influence of siblings' perspectives on theory of mind. *Cognitive Development, 15*, 435–455.

Petitto, L. A., Katerelos, M., Levy, B. G., Gauna, K., Tréault, K., & Ferraro, V. (2001). Bilingual signed and spoken language acquisition from birth: implications for the mechanisms underlying early bilingual language acquisition. *Journal of Child Language, 28*(02), 453–496. doi:10.1017/S0305000901004718.

Pew Research Center (2014). Pew research center analysis of March Current Population Survey Integrated Public Use Microdata Series (IPUMS-CPS), 1968–2013.

Pew Research Center. (2014). *The rising cost of not going to college.* Retrieved from http://www.pewsocialtrends.org/2014/02/11/the-rising-cost-of-not-going-to-college/.

Pew Commission on Children in Foster Care. (2004). *Safety, permanence and well-being for children in foster care*. Retrieved from: http://pewfostercare.org/research/docs/FinalReport.pdf.

Phelan, T. W. (2010). *1-2-3 magic: Effective discipline for children 2-12*. New York, NY: Child Management.

Phillips, L. M., Norris, S. P., & Anderson, J. (2008). Unlocking the door: Is parents' reading to children the key to early literacy development? *Canadian Psychology/Psychologie canadienne, 49*(2), 82–88.

Phinney, J. S. (1990). Ethnic identity in adolescents and adults: A review of research. *Psychological Bulletin, 108*, 499–514.

Phinney, J. S. (2000). *Identity formation among U.S. ethnic adolescents from collectivist cultures*. Paper presented at the biennial meeting of the Society of Research on Adolescence, Chicago, IL.

Phinney, J. S. (2006). Ethnic identity in emerging adulthood. In J. J. Arnett & J. L. Tanner (Eds.), *Emerging adults in America: Coming of age in the 21st century* (pp. 117–134). Washington, DC: American Psychological Association.

Phinney, J. S. (2010). Multigroup Ethnic Identity Measure (MEIM). In *Encyclopedia of Cross-Cultural School Psychology* (pp. 642–643). Springer US.

Phinney, J. S., & Baldelomar, O. A. (2011). Identity development in multiple cultural contexts. In L. A. Jensen (Ed.), *Bridging cultural and developmental psychology: New syntheses in theory, research and policy* (pp. 161–186). New York, NY: Oxford University Press.

Phinney, J. S., & Devich-Navarro, M. (1997). Variation in bicultural identification among African American and Mexican American adolescents. *Journal of Research on Adolescence, 7*, 3–32.

Phinney, J. S., & Ong, A. D. (2002). Adolescent–parent disagreement and life satisfaction in families from Vietnamese and European American backgrounds. *International Journal of Behavioral Development, 26*, 556–561.

Phinney, J. S., DuPont, S., Espinosa, A., Revill, J., & Sanders, K. (1994). Ethnic identity and American identification among ethnic minority adolescents. In A. M. Bouvy, F. J. R. van de Vijver, P. Boski, & P. Schmitz (Eds.), *Journeys into cross-cultural psychology* (pp. 167–183). Amsterdam: Swets & Zeitlinger.

Phinney, J. S., Kim-Jo, T., Osorio, S., & Vilhjalmsdottir, P. (2005). Autonomy and relatedness in adolescent-parent disagreements: Ethnic and developmental factors. *Journal of Adolescent Research, 20*, 8–39.

Piaget, J. (1929). *The child's conception of the world*. London, UK: Routledge & Kegan Paul, Ltd.

Piaget, J. (1936/1952). *The origins of intelligence in children*. New York, NY: Norton.

Piaget, J. (1937/1954). *The construction of reality in the child*. New York, NY: Basic Books.

Piaget, J. (1954). *The construction of reality in the child*. New York, NY: Basic Books.

Piaget, J. (1965). *The moral judgment of the child*. New York, NY: Free Press.

Piaget, J. (1967). *Six psychological studies*. New York, NY: Random House.

Piaget, J. (1972). Intellectual evolution from adolescence to adulthood. *Human Development, 15*, 1–12.

Piaget, J. (2002). The epigenetic system and the development of cognitive functions. In R. O. Gilmore, Mark H. Johnson, & Yuko Munakata (Eds.), *Brain development and cognition: A reader* (2nd ed., pp. 29–35). Malden: Blackwell.

Piaget, J., & Inhelder, B. (1969). *The child's conception of space* (F. J. Langdon & J. L. Lunger, Trans.). New York, NY: W. W. Norton.

Pickett, K. E., Luo, Y., & Lauderdale, D. S. (2005). Widening social inequalities in risk for sudden infant death syndrome. *American Journal of Public Health, 95*(11), 1976.

Piek, J. P., Dawson, L., Smith, L., & Gasson, N. (2008). The role of early fine and gross motor development on later motor and cognitive ability. *Human Movement Science, 27*, 668–681.

Pierroutsakos, S. L., & Troseth, G. L. (2003). Video verite: Infants' manual investigation of objects on video. *Infant Behavior & Development, 26*, 183–199.

Pike, A., Coldwell, J., & Dunn, J. F. (2005). Sibling relationships in early/middle childhood: Links with individual adjustment. *Journal of Family Psychology, 19*, 523–532.

Pilcher, J. J., & Walters, A. S. (1997). How sleep deprivation affects psychological variables related to college students' cognitive performance. *Journal of American College Health, 46*, 121–126.

Pinker, S. (1994). *The language instinct*. New York, NY: Williams Morrow.

Pinker, S. (2004). *The blank slate: The modern denial of human nature*. New York, NY: Penguin.

Pipp, S., Fischer, K. W., & Jennings, S. (1987). Acquisition of self- and mother knowledge in infancy. *Developmental Psychology, 23*, 86–96.

Pinker, S. (2002). *The blank slate*. New York, NY: Viking.

Pisetsky, E. M., Chao, Y. M., Dierker, L. C., May, A. M., & Striegel-Moore, R. H. (2008). Disordered eating and substance use in high school students: Results from the Youth Risk Behavior Surveillance System. *International Journal of Eating Disorders, 41*, 464–470.

Pizzamiglio, A. P., Saygin, S. L., Small, S., & Wilson, S. (2005). Language and the brain. In M. Tomasello & D. A. Slobin (Eds.), *Beyond nature-nurture* (pp. 237–260). Mahwah, NJ: Erlbaum.

Plant, M., Miller, P., Plant, M., Gmel, G., Kuntsche, S., Bergmark, K., . . . Vidal, A. (2010). The social consequences of binge drinking among 24- to 32-year-olds in six European countries. *Substance Use & Misuse, 45*, 528–542.

Plant, R. W., & Siegel, L. (2008). Children in foster care: Prevention and treatment of mental health problems. In T. P. Gullotta & G. M. Blau (Eds.), *Family influences on childhood behavior and development: Evidence-based prevention and treatment approaches* (pp. 209–230). New York, NY: Routledge.

Pleck, J. H. (2010). Paternal involvement: Revised conceptualization and theoretical linkages to child outcomes. In M. E. Lamb (Ed.), *The role of the father in child development* (pp. 58–93). New York, NY: Wiley.

Plomin, R. (2009). The nature of nurture. In K. McCartney and R. A. Weinberg (Eds.), *Experience and development: A festschrift in honor of Sandra Wood Scarr* (pp. 61–80). New York, NY: Psychology Press.

Plotkin, S. A., Katz, M., & Cordero, J. F. (1999). The eradication of rubella. *JAMA: Journal of the American Medical Association, 306*, 343–450.

Pollitt, E., Golub, M., Gorman, K., Gratham-McGregor, S., Levitsky, D., Schurch, B., . . . Wachs, T. (1996). A reconceptualization of the effects of undernutrition on children's biological, psychosocial, and behavioral development. *Social Policy Report, 10*, 1–28.

Pons, F., Lawson, J., Harris, P. L., & de Rosnay, M. (2003). Individual differences in children's emotion understanding: Effects of age and language. *Scandinavian Journal of Psychology, 44*, 347–353.

Pool, M. M., Koolstra, C. M., & van der Voort, T. H. A. (2003). The impact of background radio and television on high school students' homework performance. *Journal of Communication, 53*, 74–87.

Popenoe, D., & Whitehead, B. D. (2001). *The state of our unions, 2001: The social health of marriage in America*. Report of the National Marriage Project, Rutgers, New Brunswick, NJ. Available: http://marriage.rutgers.edu.

Popkin, B. M. (2010). Recent dynamics suggest selected countries catching up to US obesity. *The American journal of clinical nutrition, 91*(1), 284S–288S.

Popp, D., Lauren, B., Kerr, M., Stattin, H., & Burk, W. K. (2008). Modeling homophily over time with an actor–partner independence model. *Developmental Psychology, 44,* 1028–1039.

Popp, M. S. (2005). *Teaching language and literacy in elementary classrooms.* Mahwah, NJ: Erlbaum.

Population Reference Bureau. (2014). *World population data sheet, 2014.* Washington, DC: Author.

Porath, M., Korp, L., Wendrich, D., Dlugay, V., Roth, B., & Kribs, A. (2011). Surfactant in spontaneous breathing with nCPAP: Neurodevelopmental outcome at early school age of infants = 27 weeks. *Acta Paediatrica, 100,* 352–359.

Porges, S. W., & Lispitt, L. P. (1993). Neonatal responsivity to gustatory stimulation: The gustatory–vagal hypothesis. *Infant Behavior & Development, 16,* 487–494.

Porter, R. H., & Rieser, J. J. (2005). Retention of olfactory memories by newborn infants. In R. T. Mason, P. M. LeMaster, & D. Müller-Schwarze (Eds.), *Chemical Signals in Vertebrates* (pp. 300–307). New York, NY: Springer.

Posada, G., Gao, Y., Wu, F., Posada, R., Tascon, M., Schoelmerich, A.,… Synnevaag, B. (1995). The secure-base phenomenon across cultures: Children's behavior, mothers' preferences, and experts' concepts. *Monographs of the Society for Research in Child Development, 60,* 27–48.

Posner, M. I., & Rothbart, M. K. (2007). Numeracy. In M. I. Posner & M. K. Rothbart, *Educating the human brain* (pp. 173–187). Washington, DC: American Psychological Association.

Posner, M. I., Rothbart, M. K., Sheese, B. E., & Voelker, P. (2014). Developing attention: Behavioral and brain mechanisms. *Advances in Neuroscience,* 2014, e405094. http://doi.org/10.1155/2014/405094.

Posner, R. B. (2006). Early menarche: A review of research on trends in timing, racial differences, etiology and psychosocial consequences. *Sex Roles, 54,* 315–322.

Potegal, M., & Davison, R. J. (2003). Temper tantrums in young children, 1: Behavioral composition. *Journal of Developmental & Behavioral Pediatrics, 24,* 140–147.

Pöyhönen, V., Juvonen, J., & Salmivalli, C. (2010). What does it take to stand up for the victim of bullying? The interplay between personal and social factors. *Merrill-Palmer Quarterly, 56*(2). Retrieved from http://digitalcommons.wayne.edu/mpq/vol56/iss2/4.

Prasad, V., Brogan, E., Mulvaney, C., Grainge, M., Stanton, W., & Sayal, K. (2013). How effective are drug treatments for children with ADHD at improving on-task behaviour and academic achievement in the school classroom? A systematic review and meta-analysis. *European child & adolescent psychiatry, 22*(4), 203–216.

Prensky, M. R. (2010). *Teaching digital natives: Partnering for real learning.* Corwin Press.

Pressley, M., Wharton-McDonald, R., Raphael, L. M., Bogner, K., & Roehrig, A. (2002). Exemplary first-grade teaching. In B. M. Taylor & P. D. Pearson (Eds.), *Teaching reading: Effective schools, accomplished teachers* (pp. 73–88). Mahwah, NJ: Erlbaum.

Pretorius, E., Naude, H., & Van Vuuren, C. J. (2002). Can cultural behavior have a negative impact on the development of visual integration pathways? *Early Child Development and Care, 123,* 173–181.

Preuss, U., Ralston, S. J., Baldursson, G., Falissard, B., Lorenzo, M. J., Rodrigues Pereira, R.,…ADORE Study Group. (2006). Study design, baseline patient characteristics and intervention in a cross-cultural framework: Results from the ADORE study. *European Child & Adolescent Psychiatry, 15*(Suppl. 1), 4–19.

Price Waterhouse Coopers. (2011). *The accelerating shift of global economic power: Challenges and opportunities.* Retrieved from http://www.pwc.com/en_GX/gx/world-2050/pdf/world-in-2050-jan-2011.pdf.

Priess, H. A., & Lindberg, S. A. (2014). Gender intensification. In R. Levesque (Ed.), *Encyclopedia of Adolescence* (pp. 1135–1142). New York, NY: Springer.

Proctor, M. H., Moore, L. L., Gao, D., Cupples, L. A., Bradlee, M. L., Hood, M. Y., & Ellison, R. C. (2003). Television viewing and change in body fat from preschool to early adolescence: The Framingham Children's Study. *International Journal of Obesity, 27,* 827–833.

Provins, K. A. (1997). Handedness and speech: A critical reappraisal of the role of genetic and environmental factors in the cerebral lateralization of function. *Psychological Review, 104,* 554–571.

Puhl, R. M., Heuer, C. A., & Brownell, K. D. (2010). Stigma and social consequences of obesity. In P.G. Kopelman, I.D. Caterson, & W.H. Dietz (Eds.), *Clinical obesity in adults and children* (pp. 25–40). New York, NY: Wiley.

Puma, M., Bell, S., Cook, R., Heid, C., Shapiro, G., Broene, P., Jenkins, F., Fletcher, P., Quinn, L., Friedman, J., Ciarico, J., Rohacek, M., Adams, G., & Spier, E. (2010). Head Start Impact Study. Final Report. Administration for Children & Families. Washington, DC: US Department of Health and Human Services.

Purdie, N., Carroll, A., & Roche, L. (2004). Parenting and adolescent self-regulation. *Journal of Adolescence, 27,* 663–676.

Qin, D. B. (2009). Being "good" or being "popular": Gender and ethnic identity negotiations of Chinese immigrant adolescents. *Journal of Adolescent Research, 24,* 37–66.

Quillian, L. (2003). The decline of male employment in low income Black neighborhoods, 1950–1990. *Social Science Research, 32,* 220–250.

Quinn, C. T., Rogers, Z. R., & Buchanan, G. R. (2004). Survival of children with sickle cell disease. *Blood, 103,* 4023–4027.

Quinn, P. C., Eimas, P. D., & Rosenkranz, S. L. (1993). Evidence for representations of perceptually similar natural categories by 3-month-old and 4-month-old infants. *Perception, 22,* 463–475.

Raacke, J., & Bonds-Raacke, J. (2008). MySpace and Facebook: Applying the uses and gratifications theory to exploring friend-networking sites. *CyberPsychology & Behavior, 11,* 169–174.

Raag, T. (2003). Racism, gender identities and young children: Social relations in a multi-ethnic, inner-city primary school. *Archives of Sexual Behavior, 32,* 392–393.

Radmacher, K., & Azmitia, M. (2006). Are there gendered pathways to intimacy in early adolescents' and emerging adults' friendships? *Journal of Adolescent Research, 21,* 415–448.

Rafaelli, M., & Iturbide, M. (2015). Adolescence risks and resiliences across cultures. In L. A. Jensen (Ed.), *Oxford handbook of human development and culture: An interdisciplinary perspective.* (pp. 341–354). New York, NY: Oxford University Press.

Raikes, H. H., Chazan-Cohen, R., Love, J. M., & Brooks-Gunn, J. (2010). Early Head Start impacts at age 3 and a description of the age 5 follow-up study. In A. J. Reynolds, A. J. Rolnick, & M. M. Englund (Eds.), *Childhood programs and practices in the first decade of life: A human capital integration* (pp. 99–118). New York, NY: Cambridge University Press.

Ramchandani, P., Stein, A., Evans, J., O'Connor, T. G., & the ALSPAC Study Team. (2005). Paternal depression in the postnatal period and child development: A prospective population study. *Lancet, 365,* 2201–2205.

Ramos, M. C., Guerin, D. W., Gottfried, A. W., Bathurst, K., & Oliver, P. H. (2005). Family conflict and children's behavior problems: The moderating role of child temperament. *Structural Equation Modeling, 12,* 278–298.

Randell, A. C., & Peterson, C. C. (2009). Affective qualities of sibling disputes, mothers' conflict attitudes, and children's theory of mind development. *Social Development, 18,* 857–874.

Rao, R., & Georgieff, M. K. (2001). Neonatal iron nutrition. *Seminars in Neonatology, 6,* 425–435.

Rauscher, F. H. (2003). Can music instruction affect children's cognitive development? *ERIC Digest, EDO-PS-03-12.*

Rauscher, F. H., Shaw, G. L., & Ky, K. N. (1993). Listening to Mozart enhances spatial-temporal reasoning: Towards a neurophysiological basis. *Neuroscience Letters, 185,* 44–47.

Ravn, M. N. (2005). A matter of free choice? Some structural and cultural influences on the decision to have or not to have children in Norway. In C. B. Douglas (Ed.), *Barren states: The population "implosion" in Europe* (pp. 29–47). New York, NY: Berg.

Raymond, C. (2014). Driver distraction: A perennial but preventable public health threat to adolescents. *Journal of Adolescent Health, 54*(5, Suppl), S3–S5. http://doi.org/10.1016/j.jadohealth.2014.02.015.

Reynolds, G. D., Bahrick, L. E., Lickliter, R., & Guy, M. W. (2014). Neural correlates of intersensory processing in 5-month-old infants. *Developmental Psychobiology, 56*(3), 355–372.

Redcay, E., Haist, F., & Courchesne, E. (2008). Functional neuroimaging of speech perception during a pivotal period in language acquisition. *Developmental science, 11*(2), 237–252.

Reddy, U. M., & Mennuti, M. T. (2006). Incorporating first-trimester Down syndrome studies into prenatal screening. *Obstetrics and Gynecology, 107,* 167–173.

Redshaw, M. E. (1997). Mothers of babies requiring special care: Attitudes and experiences. *Journal of Reproductive & Infant Psychology, 15,* 109–120.

Reeves, G., & Schweitzer, J. (2004). Pharmacological management of attention deficit hyperactivity disorder. *Expert Opinions in Pharmacotherapy, 5,* 1313–1320.

Regan, P. C., Durvasula, R., Howell, L., Ureno, O., & Rea, M. (2004). Gender, ethnicity, and the developmental timing of the first sexual and romantic experiences. *Social Behavior & Personality, 32,* 667–676.

Regestein, Q., Natarajan, V., Pavlova, M., Kawasaki, S., Gleason, R., & Koff, E. (2010). Sleep debt and depression in female college students. *Psychiatry research, 176*(1), 34–39.

Regev, R. H., Lusky, A., Dolfin, T., Litmanovitz, I., Arnon, S., Reichman, B., & Israel Neonatal Network. (2003). Excess mortality and morbidity among small-for-gestational-age premature infants: a population-based study. *The Journal of pediatrics, 143*(2), 186–191.

Regnerus, M., & Uecker, J. (2011). *Premarital sex in America: How young Americans meet, mate, and think about marrying.* New York, NY: Oxford University Press.

Reid, C. (2004). Kangaroo care. *Neonatal Network, 23,* 53.

Reifman, A., Arnett, J. J., & Colwell, M. J. (2006). Emerging adulthood: Theory, assessment, and application. *Journal of Youth Development, 1,* 1–12.

Reimuller, A., Shadur, J., & Hussong, A. M. (2011). Parental social support as a moderator of self-medication in adolescents. *Addictive Behaviors, 36,* 203–208.

Reiss, D., Neiderhiser, J., Hetherington, E. M., & Plomin, R. (2000). The relationship code: Deciphering genetic and social influences on adolescent development. Cambridge, MA: Harvard University Press.

Repacholi, B. M., & Gopnik, A. (1997). Early reasoning about desires: Evidence from 14- and 18-month-olds. *Developmental Psychology, 33*(1), 12–21.

Resnick, G. (2010). Project Head Start: Quality and links to child outcomes. In A. J. Reynolds, A. J. Rolnick, M. M. Englund, & J. A. Temple (Eds.), *Childhood programs and practices in the first decade of life: A human capital integration* (pp. 121–156). New York, NY: Cambridge University Press.

Restall, A., Taylor, R. S., Thompson, J. M. D., Flower, D., Dekker, G. A., Kenny, L. C., … McCowan, L. M. E. (2014). Risk factors for excessive gestational weight gain in a healthy, nulliparous cohort. *Journal of Obesity,* e148391. http://doi.org/10.1155/2014/148391.

Reyna, V. F., Estrada, S. M., DeMarinis, J. A., Myers, R. M., Stanisz, J. M., & Mills, B. A. (2011). Neurobiological and memory models of risky decision making in adolescents versus young adults. *Journal of Experimental Psychology: Learning, Memory, and Cognition, 37*(5), 1125–1142. http://doi.org/10.1037/a0023943.

Reznick, J. S., Corley, R., & Robinson, J. (1997). A longitudinal study of intelligence in the second year. *Monographs of the Society for Research in Child Development, 62,* 1–154.

Rhoades, B. L., Warren, H. K., Domitrovich, C. E., & Greenberg, M. T. (2011). Examining the link between preschool social–emotional competence and first grade academic achievement: The role of attention skills. *Early Childhood Research Quarterly, 26*(2), 182–191. http://doi.org/10.1016/j.ecresq.2010.07.003.

Rhodes, J. R., & DuBois, D. L. (2008). Mentoring relationships and programs for youth. *Current Directions in Psychological Science, 17,* 254–258.

Ricciuti, H. N. (2004). Single parenthood, achievement, and problem behavior in White, Black, and Hispanic children. *Journal of Educational Research, 97,* 196–206.

Richards, M. H., Crowe, P. A., Larson, R., & Swarr, A. (2002). Developmental patterns and gender differences in the experience of peer companionship in adolescence. *Child Development, 69,* 154–163.

Richert, R. A., Robb, M. B., & Smith, E. I. (2011). Media as social partners: The social nature of young children's learning from screen media. *Child Development, 82*(1), 82–95. doi:10.1111/j.1467-8624.2010.01542.x.

Richman, A. L., Miller, P. M., & LeVine, R. A. (2010). Cultural and educational variations in maternal responsiveness. In R. A. LeVine (Ed.), *Psychological anthropology: A reader on self in culture* (pp. 181–192). Malden, MA: Wiley-Blackwell.

Rideout, V. (2013). *Zero to eight: Children's use of media in America, 2013.* Washington, DC: Common Sense Media.

Rideout, V. J., Foehr, U. G., & Roberts, D. F. (2010). *Generation M$_2$: Media in the lives of 8-18 year-olds.* Kaiser Family Foundation.

Rideout, V. J., & Hamel, E. (2006). *The media family: Electronic media in the lives of infants, toddlers, preschoolers, and their parents.* Menlo Park, CA: The Henry J. Kaiser Family Foundation.

Rideout, V. J., Vandewater, E. A., & Wartella, E. A. (2003). *Zero to six: Electronic media in the lives of infants, toddlers and preschoolers.* Menlo Park, CA: The Henry J. Kaiser Family Foundation.

Ridley, M. (2010). *The rational optimist: How prosperity evolves.* New York, NY: Harper.

Rigby, K. (2004). Bullying in childhood. In P. K. Smith & C. H. Hart (Eds.), *Blackwell handbook of childhood social development.* Malden, MA: Blackwell.

Righetti, P. L., Dell'Avanzo, M., Grigio, M., & Nicolini, U. (2005). Maternal/paternal antenatal attachment and fourth–dimensional ultrasound technique: A preliminary report. *British Journal of Psychology, 96,* 129–137.

Righetti-Veltema, M., Conne-Perreard, E., Bousquest, A., & Manzano, J. (2002). Postpartum depression and mother–infant relationship at 3 months old. *Journal of Affective Disorders, 70,* 291–306.

Riley, A. W., Lyman, L. M., Spiel, G., Döpfner, M., Lorenzo, M. J., Ralston, S. J., & ADORE Study Group. (2006). The Family Strain Index (FSI). Reliability, validity, and factor structure of a brief questionnaire for families of children with ADHD. *European Child & Adolescent Psychiatry, 15*(Suppl. 1), 72–78.

Riley Bove, C. V. (2009). Polygyny and women's health in sub-Saharan Africa. *Social Science & Medicine, 68,* 21–29.

Rivera, S. M., Wakeley, A., & Langer, J. (1999). The drawbridge phenomenon: Representational reasoning or perceptual preference? *Developmental Psychology, 35*(2), 427–435.

Roberto, C. A., Steinglass, J., Mayer, L. E. S., Attia, E., & Walsh, B. T. (2008). The clinical significance of amenorrhea as a diagnostic criterion for anorexia nervosa. *International Journal of Eating Disorders, 41*, 559–563.

Roberts, R. G., Deutchman, M., King, V. J., Fryer, G. E., & Miyoshi, T. J. (2007). Changing policies on vaginal birth after cesarean: Impact on access. *Birth: Issues in Perinatal Care, 34*, 316–322.

Robertson, J. (2008). Stepfathers in families. In J. Pryor (Ed.), *The international handbook of stepfamilies: Policy and practice in legal, research, and clinical environments* (pp. 125–150). Hoboken, NJ: John Wiley & Sons.

Robins, R. W., & Trzesniewski, K. H. (2005). Self-esteem development across the lifespan. *Current Directions in Psychological Science, 14*, 158–162.

Robins, R. W., Gosling, S. D. & Craik, K. H. (1999). An empirical analysis of trends in psychology. *American Psychologist, 54*, 117–128.

Robins, R. W., Trzesniewski, K. H., Tracey, J. L., Potter, J., & Gosling, S. D. (2002). Age differences in self-esteem from age 9 to 90. *Psychology and Aging, 17*, 423–434.

Robinson, C. C., Anderson, G. T., Porter, C. L., Hart, C. H., & Wouden-Miller, M. (2003). Sequential transition patterns of preschoolers' social interactions during child-initiated play: Is parallel-aware play a bi-directional bridge to other play states? *Early Childhood Research Quarterly, 18*, 3–21.

Rochat, P., & Hespos, S. J. (1997). Differential rooting responses by neonates: Evidence for an early sense of self. *Early Development and Parenting, 6*, 105–112.

Rodgers, J. L., & Wanstrom, L. (2007). Identification of a Flynn Effect in the NLSY: Moving from the center to the boundaries. *Intelligence, 35*, 187–196.

Rodier, P. M. (2009). *Science under attack: Vaccines and autism.* Berkeley, CA: University of California Press.

Roeder, M. B., Mahone, E. M., Larson, J. G., Mostofsky, S., Cutting, L. E., Goldberg, M. C., & Denckla, M. B. (2008). Left–right differences on timed motor examination in children. *Child Neuropsychology, 14*, 249–262.

Roenneberg, T., Kuehnle, T., Juda, M., Kantermann, T., Allebrandt, K., Gordijn, M., & Merrow, M. (2007). Epidemiology of the human circadian clock. *Sleep Medicine Reviews, 11*, 429–438.

Rogoff, B. (1990). *Apprenticeship in thinking: Cognitive development in social context.* New York, NY: Oxford University Press.

Rogoff, B. (1995). Observing sociocultural activities on three planes: Participatory appropriation, guided participation, and apprenticeship. In J. V. Wertsch, P. del Rio, & A. Alvarez (Eds.), *Sociocultural studies of the mind* (pp. 273–294). New York, NY: Cambridge University Press.

Rogoff, B. (1998). Cognition as a collaborative process. In D. Kuhn & R. S. Siegler (Eds.), *Handbook of child psychology: Vol. 2. Cognition, perception, and language* (5th ed., pp. 679–744). New York, NY: Wiley.

Rogoff, B. (2003). *The cultural nature of human development.* New York, NY: Oxford University Press.

Rogoff, B. (2011). *Developing destinies: A Mayan midwife and town.* New York, NY: Oxford University Press.

Rogoff, B., Correa-Chávez, M., & Cotuc, M. N. (2005). A cultural/historical view of schooling in human development. In D. B. Pillemer & S. H. White (Eds.), *Developmental psychology and social change: Research, history and policy* (pp. 225–263). New York, NY: Cambridge University Press.

Rohlen, T. P. (1983). *Japan's high schools.* Berkeley, CA: University of California Press.

Rolls, E. T. (2000). Memory systems in the brain. *Annual review of psychology, 51*(1), 599–630.

Roopnarine, J. L., Hossain, Z., Gill, P., & Brophy, H. (1994). Play in the East Indian context. In J. L. Roopnarine, J. E. Johnson, & F. H. Hooper (Eds.), *Children's play in diverse cultures* (pp. 9–30). Albany, NY: State University of New York Press.

Roscoe, B., Dian, M. S., & Brooks, R. H. (1987). Early, middle, and late adolescents' views on dating and factors influencing partner selection. *Adolescence, 22*, 59–68.

Rose, A. J., & Asher, S. R. (1999). Children's goals and strategies in response to conflicts within a friendship. *Developmental Psychology, 35*, 69–79.

Rose, P. (2004). The forest dweller and the beggar. *American Scholar, 73*, 5–11.

Rose, S. A., Feldman, J. F., Jankowski, J. J., & Van Rossem, R. (2005). Pathways from prematurity and infant abilities to later cognition. *Child Development, 76*, 1172–1184.

Rosenberg, M. (1979). *Conceiving the self.* New York, NY: Basic Books.

Rosenbloom, S. R., & Way, N. (2004). Experiences of discrimination among African American, Asian American, and Latino adolescents in an urban high school. *Youth & Society, 35*, 420–451.

Rosnow, R. L., & Rosenthal, R. L. (2005). *Beginning behavioral research* (5th ed.). Upper Saddle River, NJ: Prentice Hall.

Ross, H. S., & Lollis, S. P. (1989). A social relations analysis of toddler peer relationships. *Child Development, 60*, 1082–1091.

Rothbart, M. K. (2004). Emotion-related regulation: Sharpening the definition. *Child Development, 75*, 334–339.

Rothbart, M. K. (2011). *Becoming who we are: Temperament, personality and development.* New York, NY: Guilford Press.

Rothbart, M. K., & Bates, J. E. (2006). Temperament. In W. Damon & R. Lerner (Series Eds.), & N. Eisenberg (Vol. Ed.), *Handbook of child psychology: Vol. 3. Social, emotional, and personality development* (6th ed., pp. 99–166). New York, NY: Wiley.

Rothbart, M. K., Ahadi, S. A., & Evans, D. E. (2000). Temperament and personality: Origins and outcome. *Journal of Personality and Social Psychology, 78*, 122–135.

Rothbaum, F., Kakinuma, M., Nagaoka, R., & Azuma, H. (2007). Attachment and *amae*: Parent–child closeness in the United States & Japan. *Journal of Cross-Cultural Psychology, 38*, 465–486.

Rothbaum, F., & Morelli, G. (2005). Attachment and culture: Bridging relativism and universalism. In W. Friedlmeier, P. Chakkarath, & B. Schwarz (Eds.), *Culture and human development: The importance of cross-cultural research to the social sciences* (pp. 99–124). Lisse, The Netherlands: Swets & Zeitlinger.

Rothbaum, F., Weisz, J., Pott, M., Miyake, K., & Morelli, G. (2000). Attachment and culture: Security in the United States and Japan. *American Psychologist, 55*, 1093–1104.

Rothbaum, F., Weisz, J., Pott, M., Miyake, K., & Morelli, G. (2001). Deeper into attachment and culture. *American Psychologist, 56*, 827–829.

Rothenberger, A., Coghill, D., Dopfner, M., Falissard, B., & Stenhausen, H. C. (2006). Naturalistic observational studies in the framework of ADHD health care. *European Child and Adolescent Psychiatry, 15*(Suppl. 1), 1–3.

Rotheram-Borus, M. J. (1990). Adolescents' reference group choices, self-esteem, and adjustment. *Journal of Personality and Social Psychology, 59*, 1075–1081.

Rovee-Collier, C. K. (1999). The development of infant memory. *Current Directions in Psychological Science, 8*, 80–85.

Rowley, S. J., Kurtz-Costes, B., Mistry, R., & Feagans, L. (2007). Social status as a predictor of race and gender stereotypes in late childhood and early adolescence. *Social Development, 16*, 150–168.

Roy, A., & Wisnivesky, J. P. (2010). Comprehensive use of environmental control practices among adults with asthma. *Allergy and Asthma Proceedings, 31*, 72–77.

Rozin, P. (2006). Domain denigration and process preference in academic psychology. *Perspectives on Psychological Science, 1*, 365–376.

Rubin, K. H., & Pepler, D. J. (Eds.). (2013). *The development and treatment of childhood aggression*. New York, NY: Psychology Press.

Rubin, K. H., Bukowski, W., & Parker, J. G. (2006). Peer interactions, relationships and groups. In W. Damon & R. Lerner (Eds.), & N. Eisenberg (Vol. Ed.), *Handbook of child psychology: Vol. 3. Social, emotional and personality development* (6th ed., pp. 571–645). New York, NY: Wiley.

Rubin, K. H., Burgess, K. B., & Hastings, P. D. (2002). Stability and social-behavioral consequences of toddlers' inhibited temperament and parenting behaviors. *Child Development, 73*, 483–495.

Rubin, K., Fredstrom, B., & Bowker, J. (2008). Future directions in friendship in childhood and early adolescence. *Social Development, 17*, 1085–1096.

Ruble, D. N., Martin, C. L., & Berenbaum, S. (2006). Gender development. In W. Damon & R. M. Lerner (Series Eds.), & N. Eisenberg (Vol. Ed.), *Handbook of child psychology: Vol. 3. Social, emotional and personality development* (6th ed., pp. 858–932). Hoboken, NJ: Wiley.

Rucker, J. H., & McGuffin, P. (2010). Polygenic heterogeneity: A complex model of genetic inheritance in psychiatric disorders. *Biological Psychiatry, 68*, 312–313.

Rückinger, S., Beyerlein, A., Jacobsen, G., von Kries, R., & Vik, T. (2010a). Growth in utero and body mass index at age 5 years in children of smoking and non-smoking mothers. *Early Human Development, 86*, 773–777.

Rückinger, S., Rzehak, P., Chen, C. M., Sausenthaler, S., Koletzko, S., Bauer, C. P.,... GINI-plus Study Group. (2010b). Prenatal and postnatal tobacco exposure and behavioral problems in 10-year-old children: Results from the GINI-plus prospective birth cohort study. *Environmental Health Perspectives, 118*, 150–154.

Rudy, D., & Grusec, J. (2006). Authoritarian parenting in individualist and collectivist groups: Associations with maternal emotion and cognition and children's self esteem. *Journal of Family Psychology, 43*, 302–319.

Ruggeri, K., & Bird, C. E. (2014). *Single parents and employment in Europe*. Cambridge, England: Rand Europe.

Ruiz, S. A., & Silverstein, M. (2007). Relationships with grandparents and the emotional well-being of late adolescent and young adult grandchildren. *Journal of Social Issues, 63*, 793–808.

Russell, A., Hart, C. H., Robinson, C. C., & Olsen, S. F. (2003). Children's sociable and aggressive behavior with peers: A comparison of the U.S. and Australian, and contributions of temperament and parenting styles. *International Journal of Behavioral Development, 27*, 74–86.

Rutter, M. (1996). Maternal deprivation. In M. H. Bornstein (Ed.), *Handbook of parenting: Vol. 4. Applied and practical parenting* (pp. 3–31). Mahwah, NJ: Erlbaum.

Rutter, M. (2002). The interplay of nature, nurture, and developmental influences: The challenge ahead for mental health. *Archives of General Psychiatry, 59*(11): 996–1000.

Rutter, M., O'Connor, T. G., & the English and Romanian Adoptees Study Team. (2004). Are there biological programming effects for psychological development? Findings from a study of Romanian adoptees. *Developmental Psychology, 40*, 81–94.

Ryan, A. S., Zhou, W., & Arensberg, M. B. (2006). The effects of employment status on breastfeeding in the United States. *Women's Health Issues, 16*, 243–251.

Ryan, C., Huebner, D., Diaz, R. M., & Sanchez, J. (2009). Family rejection as a predictor of negative health outcomes in white and Latino lesbian, gay and bisexual young adults. *Pediatrics, 123*, 346–352.

Ryan, R. M., & Deci, E. L. (2000). Self-determination theory and the facilitation of intrinsic motivation, social development, and well-being. *American Psychologist, 55*(1), 68–78. http://doi.org/10.1037/0003-066X.55.1.68.

Ryan, R. M., & Weinstein, M. (2009). Undermining quality teaching and learning: A self-determination theory perspective on high-stakes testing. *Theory and Research in Education, 7*(2), 224–233. DOI: 10.1177/1477878509104327.

Rychlak, J. F. (2003). The self takes over. In J. F. Rychlak, *The human image in postmodern America* (pp. 69–82). Washington, DC: American Psychological Association.

Saarni, C. (1999). *The development of emotional competence*. New York, NY: Guilford.

Sadker, M., & Sadker, D. (1994). *Failing at fairness: How America's schools cheat girls*. New York, NY: Scribner.

Safe Kids Worldwide. (2009). *News and facts*. Retrieved from www.safekids.org.

Safe Kids Worldwide. (2013). *Unintentional childhood injury-related deaths*. Retrieved from http://www.safekidsgainesvillehall.org/unintentional-childhood-injury-related-deaths.

Saffran, J. R. (2003). Statistical language learning mechanisms and constraints. *Current Directions in Psychological Science, 12*(4), 110–114.

Saffran, J. R., Werker, J. F., & Werner, L. A. (2006). The infant's auditory world: Hearing, speech and the beginnings of language. In W. Damon & R. Lerner (Eds.), & D. Kuhn & R. Siegler (Vol. Eds.), *Handbook of child psychology: Vol. 2. Cognition, perception, and language* (6th ed., pp. 58–108). New York, NY: Wiley.

Saha, C., Riner, M. E., & Liu, G. (2005). Individual and neighborhood-level factors in predicting asthma. *Archives of Pediatrics and Adolescent Medicine, 159*, 759–763.

Salkind, N. (2011). *Exploring research*. Upper Saddle River, NJ: Pearson.

Salmivalli, C., & Voeten, M. (2004). Connections between attitudes, group norms, and behaviour in bullying situations. *International Journal of Behavioral Development, 28*, 246–258.

Sameroff, A. J., & Haith, M. M. (1996). *The five to seven year shift: The age of reason and responsibility*. Chicago, IL: University of Chicago Press.

Samuels, H. R. (1980). The effect of an older sibling on infant locomotor exploration of a new environment, *Child Development, 51*, 607–609.

Sandstrom, M. J., & Zakriski, A. L. (2004). Understanding the experience of peer rejection. In J. B. Kupersmidt & K. A. Dodge (Eds.), *Children's peer relations: From development to intervention*. (pp. 101–118). Washington, DC: American Psychological Association.

Sang, B., Miao, X., & Deng, C. (2002). The development of gifted and nongifted young children in metamemory knowledge. *Psychological Science (China), 25*, 406–424.

Sansavani, A., Bertoncini, J., & Giovanelli, G. (1997). Newborns discriminate the rhythm of multisyllabic stressed words. *Developmental Psychology, 33*, 3–11.

Sassler, S., Ciambrone, D., & Benway, G. (2008). Are they really mama's boys/ daddy's girls? The negotiation of adulthood upon returning to the parental home. *Sociological Forum, 23*, 670–698.

Savin-Williams, R. (2001). *Mom, Dad, I'm gay*. Washington, DC: American Psychological Association.

Savin-Williams, R. C. (2005). *The new gay teenager*. Cambridge, MA: Harvard University Press.

Savin-Williams, R. C., & Joyner, K. (2014). The dubious assessment of gay, lesbian, and bisexual adolescents of Add Health. *Archives of Sexual Behavior 43*(3), 413–422.

Saw, S. M., Carkeet, A., Chia, K. S., Stone, R. A., & Tan, D. T. (2002). Component dependent risk factors for ocular parameters in Singapore Chinese children. *Ophthalmology, 109*, 2065–2071.

Sawnani, H., Jackson, T., Murphy, T., Beckerman, R., & Simakajornboon, N. (2004). The effect of maternal smoking on respiratory and arousal patterns in preterm infants during sleep. *American Journal of Respiratory and Critical Care Medicine, 169*, 733–738.

Sax, L., & Kautz, K. J. (2003). Who first suggests the diagnosis of attention deficit/hyperactivity disorder? *Annals of Family Medicine, 1*, 171–174.

Saxe, G. B. (2002). Candy selling and math learning. In C. Desforges & R. Fox (Eds.), *Teaching and learning: The essential readings* (pp. 86–106). Malden, MA: Blackwell.

Saxe, G. B. (2008). Reflections on J.V. Wertsch's "From social interaction to higher psychological processes," Human Development, 1979. *Human Development, 51*(1), 80–89. http://doi.org/10.1159/000113157.

Saxe, G. B., & Esmonde, I. (2005). Studying cognition in flux: A historical treatment of fu in the shifting structure of Oksapmin mathematics. *Mind, Culture, and Activity, 12*(3–4), 171–225. http://doi.org/10.1207/s15327884mca123&4_2.

Sbarra, D. A., & Emery, R. E. (2008). Deeper into divorce: Using actor–partner analyses to explore systemic differences in coparenting conflict following custody dispute resolution. *Journal of Family Psychology, 22*, 144–152.

Scantlin, R. (2007). Educational television, effects of. In J. J. Arnett (Ed.), *Encyclopedia of children, adolescents, and the media* (pp. 255–258). Thousand Oaks, CA: Sage.

Scarr, S. (1993). Biological and cultural diversity: The legacy of Darwin for development. *Child Development, 54*, 424–435.

Scarr, S., & McCartney, K. (1983). How people make their own environments: A theory of genotype environment effects. *Child Development, 54*, 424–435.

Schaal, B., Marlier, L., & Soussignan, R. (2000). Human fetuses learn odours from their pregnant mother's diet. *Chemical Senses, 25*, 729–737.

Schachter, E. P. (2005). Erikson meets the postmodern: Can classic identity theory rise to the challenge? *Identity, 5*, 137–160.

Schachter, S. C., & Ransil, B. J. (1996). Handedness distributions in nine professional groups. *Perceptual and Motor Skills, 82*, 51–63.

Schaeffer, C., Petras, H., & Ialongo, B. (2003). Modeling growth in boys' aggressive behavior across elementary school: Links to later criminal involvement, conduct disorder, and antisocial personality disorder. *Developmental Psychology, 39*, 1020–1035.

Scheibe, C. (2007). Advertising on children's programs. In J. J. Arnett (Ed.), *Encyclopedia of children, adolescents, and the media* (pp. 59–60). Thousand Oaks, CA: Sage.

Schlegel, A. (2010). Adolescent ties to adult communities: The intersection of culture and development. In L. Jensen (Ed.), *Bridging cultural and developmental approaches to psychology* (pp. 138–159). New York, NY: Oxford University Press.

Schlegel, A. (2011). Adolescent ties to adult communities. In L. A. Jensen (Ed.), *Bridging cultural and developmental approaches to psychology: New syntheses in theory, research, and policy* (pp. 138–157). New York, NY: Oxford University Press.

Schlegel, A., & Barry, H. (1991). *Adolescence: An anthropological inquiry.* New York, NY: Free Press.

Schlegel, A., & Barry III, H. (2015). The nature and meaning of adolescent transition rituals. In L. A. Jensen (Ed.), *Oxford handbook of human development and culture: An interdisciplinary perspective.* New York, NY: Oxford University Press.

Schmidt, L., Holstein, B., Christensen, U., & Boivin, J. (2005). Does infertility cause marital benefit? An epidemiological study of 2250 men and women in fertility treatment. *Patient Education and Counseling, 59*, 244–251.

Schmidt, M. D., Freedson, P. S., Pekow, P., Roberts, D., Sternfeld, B., & Chasan-Taber, L. (2006). Validation of the Kaiser physical activity survey in pregnant women. *Medicine & Science in Sports & Exercise, 38*(1), 42–50.

Schmidt, M. E., Rich, M., Rifas-Shiman, S. L., Oken, E., & Taveras, E. M. (2009). Television viewing in infancy and child cognition at 3 years of age in a US cohort. *Pediatrics, 123*(3), e370–e375. doi:10.1542/peds.2008-3221.

Schmitow, C., & Stenberg, G. (2013). Social referencing in 10-month-old infants. *European Journal of Developmental Psychology, 10*, 533–545. doi: 10.1080/17405629.2013.763473.

Schneider, B. (2006). In the moment: The benefits of the Experience Sampling Method. In M. Pitt-Catsouphes, E. E. Kossek, & S. Sweet (Eds.), *The work and family handbook: Multi-disciplinary perspectives, methods, and approaches* (pp. 469–488). Mahwah, NJ: Erlbaum.

Schneider, B. (2009). Challenges of transitioning into adulthood. In I. Schoon & R. K. Silbereisen (Eds.), *Transitions from school to work: Globalization, individualization, and patterns of diversity* (pp. 265–290). New York, NY: Cambridge University Press.

Schneider, B., & Stevenson, D. (1999). *The ambitious generation: America's teenagers, motivated but directionless.* New Haven, CT: Yale University Press.

Schneider, W. (2002). Memory development in childhood. In U. Goswami (Ed.), *Blackwell handbook of childhood cognitive development* (pp. 236–256). Malden, MA: Blackwell.

Schneider, W. (2010). Metacognition and memory development in childhood and adolescence. In H. S. Waters & W. Schneider (Eds.), *Metacognition, strategy use, and instruction* (pp. 54–81). New York, NY: Guilford.

Schneider, W., & Bjorklund, D. F. (1992). Expertise, aptitude, and strategic remembering. *Child Development, 63*, 461–473.

Schneider, W., & Pressley, M. (1997). *Memory development between two and twenty* (2nd ed.). Mahwah, NJ: Erlbaum.

Schoenwald, S. K., Heiblum, N., Saldana, L., & Henggeler, S. W. (2008). The international implementation of multisystemic therapy. *Evaluation & the Health Professions, 31*, 211–225.

Schoolcraft, W. (2010). *If at first you don't conceive: A complete guide to infertility from one of the nation's leading clinics.* New York, NY: Rodale Books.

Schott, J. M., & Rossor, M. N. (2003). The grasp and other primitive reflexes. *Journal of Neurological and Neurosurgical Psychiatry, 74*, 558–560.

Schulz, R., & Curnow, C. (1988). Peak performance and age among superathletes: track and field, swimming, baseball, tennis, and golf. *Journal of Gerontology, 43*(5), P113–P120.

Schulze, P. A., & Carlisle, S. A. (2010). What research does and doesn't say about breastfeeding: A critical review. *Early Child Development and Care, 180*, 703–718.

Schum, T. R., McAuliffe, T. L., Simms, M. D., Walter, J. A., Lewis, M., & Pupp, R. (2001). Factors associated with toilet training in the 1990s. *Ambulatory Pediatrics, 1*, 79–86.

Shwalb, D. W., & Shwalb, B. J. (2015). Fathering diversity within societies. In L. A. Jensen (Ed.), *Oxford handbook of human development and culture.* New York, NY: Oxford University Press.

Schwartz, D., Proctor, L. J., & Chien, D. H. (2001). The aggressive victim of bullying: Emotional and behavioral dysregulation as a pathway to victimization by peers. In J. Juonen & S. Graham (Eds.), *Peer harassment in school: The plight of the vulnerable and victimized* (pp. 147–174). New York, NY: Guilford.

Schwartz, M., Share, D. L., Leikin, M., & Kozminsky, E. (2008). On the benefits of bi-literacy: Just a head start in reading or specific orthographic insights? *Reading and Writing, 21*, 905–927.

Schwartz, S. J. (2005). A new identity for identity research: Recommendations for expanding and refocusing the identity literature. *Journal of Adolescent Research, 20*, 293–308.

Schwartz, S. J. (2015). Identity development in emerging adulthood. In J. J. Arnett (Ed.), *Oxford handbook of emerging adulthood.* New York, NY: Oxford University Press.

Schwartz, S. J., Syed, M., Yip, T., Knight, G. P., Umaña-Taylor, A. J., Rivas-Drake, D., & Lee, R. M. (2014). Methodological issues in ethnic and racial identity research with ethnic minority populations: Theoretical precision, measurement issues, and research designs. *Child Development, 85*(1), 58–76.

Schweinle, A., & Wilcox, T. (2004). Intermodal perception and physical reasoning in young infants. *Infant Behavior & Development, 27,* 246–265.

Schweinhart, L. J., Montie, J., Xiang, Z., Barnett, W. S., & Belfield, C. R. (2004). *Lifetime effects: The High/Scope Perry Preschool Study through age 40.* Boston, MA: Strategies for Children. Retrieved from www.highscope.org/Research/PerryProject/perrymain.htm.

Scott, E., & Panksepp, J. (2003). Rough-and-tumble play in human children. *Aggressive Behavior, 29,* 539–551.

Seach, K. A., Dharmage, S. C., Lowe, A. J., & Dixon, J. B. (2010). Delayed introduction of solid feeding reduces child overweight and obesity at 10 years. *International Journal of Obesity, 34,* 1475–1479.

Sears, H. (2007). Canada. In J. J. Arnett (Ed.), *International encyclopedia of adolescence.* New York, NY: Routledge.

Sears, H. (2012). Canada. In J. J. Arnett (Ed.), *Adolescent psychology around the world.* New York, NY: Taylor & Francis.

Sedgh, G., Finer, L. B., Bankole, A., Eilers, M. A., & Singh, S. (2015). Adolescent pregnancy, birth, and abortion rates across countries: Levels and recent trends. *Journal of Adolescent Health, 56*(2), 223–230.

Segall, M. H., Dasen, P. R., Berry, J. W., & Poortinga, Y. H. (1999). *Human behavior in global perspective: An introduction to cross-cultural psychology.* Boston, MA: Allyn & Bacon.

Seiffge-Krenke, I. (2009). Leaving-home patterns in emerging adults: The impact of earlier parental support and developmental task progression. *European Psychologist, 14,* 238–248.

Selander, J. (2011). *Cultural beliefs honor placenta.* Retrieved from http://placentabenefits.info/culture.asp.

Sellen, D. W. (2001). Comparison of infant feeding patterns reported for nonindustrial populations with current recommendations. *Journal of Nutrition, 131,* 2707–2715.

Selwyn, N. (2008). An investigation of differences in undergraduates' academic use of the Internet. *Active Learning in Higher Education, 9,* 11–22.

Sembuya, R. (2010). Mother or nothing: The agony of infertility. *Bulletin of the World Health Organization, 88,* 881–882.

Sen, K., & Samad, A. Y. (Eds.). (2007). *Islam in the European Union: Transnationalism, youth, and the war on terror.* New York, NY: Oxford University Press.

Shafai, T., Mustafa, M., & Hild, T. (2014). Promotion of exclusive breastfeeding in low-income families by improving the WIC food package for breastfeeding mothers. *Breastfeeding Medicine, 9*(8), 375–376. http://doi.org/10.1089/bfm.2014.0062.

Shahaeian, A., Peterson, C. C., Slaughter, V., & Wellman, H. M. (2011). Culture and the sequence of steps in theory of mind development. *Developmental Psychology, 47*(5), 1239.

Shalatin, S., & Phillip, M. (2003). The role of obesity and leptin in the pubertal process and pubertal growth: A review. *International Journal of Obesity and Related Metabolic Disorders, 27,* 869–874.

Shanahan, L., McHale, S. M., Osgood, D. W., & Crouter, A. C. (2007). Conflict frequency with mothers and fathers from middle childhood to late adolescence: Within- and between-families comparisons. *Developmental Psychology, 43,* 539–550.

Shapiro, L. J., & Azuma, H. (2004). Intellectual, attitudinal, and interpersonal aspects of competence in the United States and Japan. In R. J. Sternberg & E. L. Grigorenko (Eds.), *Culture and competence: Contexts of life success* (pp. 187–206). Washington, DC: American Psychological Association.

Shapka, J. D., & Keating, D. P. (2005). Structure and change in self concept during adolescence. *Canadian Journal of Behavioural Science, 37,* 83–96.

Sharma, V., Sommerdyk, C., & Xie, B. (2015). Aripiprazole augmentation of antidepressants for postpartum depression: A preliminary report. *Archives of Women's Mental Health, 18*(1), 131–134. http://doi.org/10.1007/s00737-014-0462-3.

Shaughnessy, J., Zechmeister, E., & Zechmeister, J. (2011). *Research methods in psychology* (11th ed.). New York, NY: McGraw-Hill.

Shaw, P., Greenstein, D., Lerch, J., Clasen, L., Lenroot, R., Gogtay, N., & Evans, A. (2006). Intellectual ability and cortical development in children and adolescents. *Nature, 440,* 676–679.

Shaywitz, B. A., Shaywitz, S. E., Blachman, B. A., Pugh, K. R., Fulbright, R. K., Skudlarski, P., …Gore, J. C. (2004). Development of left occipitotemporal systems for skilled reading in children after a phonologically-based intervention. *Biological Psychiatry, 55,* 926–933.

Shields, L., Mamun, A. A., O'Callaghan, M., Williams, G. M., & Najman, J. M. (2010). Breastfeeding and obesity at 21 years: A cohort study. *Journal of Clinical Nursing, 19,* 1612–1617.

Shih, R. A., Miles, J. N., Tucker, J. S., Zhou, A. J., & D'Amico, E. J. (2010). Racial/ethnic differences in adolescent substance use: Mediation by individual, family, and school factors. *Journal of Studies on Alcohol and Drugs, 71*(5), 640.

Shipman, K. L., Zeman, J., Nesin, A. E., & Fitzgerald, M. (2003). Children's strategies for displaying anger and sadness: What works with whom? *Merrill-Palmer Quarterly, 49,* 100–122.

Shirtcliff, E. A., Dahl, R E., & Pollak, S. D. (2009). Pubertal development: Correspondence between hormonal and physical development. *Child Development, 80,* 327–337.

Shonkoff, J. P., & Phillips, D. A. (Eds.). (2000). *From neurons to neighborhoods: The science of early childhood development.* Washington, DC: National Academy Press.

Shope, J. T. (2007). Graduated driver licensing: Review of evaluation results since 2002. *Journal of Safety Research, 38,* 165–175.

Shope, J. T., & Bingham, C. R. (2008). Teen driving: Motor-vehicle crashes and factors that contribute. *American Journal of Preventative Medicine, 35*(3, Suppl. 1), S261–S271.

Shorten, A. (2010). Bridging the gap between mothers and medicine: "New insights" from the NIH Consensus Conference on VBAC. *Birth: Issues in Perinatal Care, Vol. 3,* 181–183.

Shreeve, J. (2010). The evolutionary road. *National Geographic,* 34–50.

Shulman, S., & Connolly, J. (2015). Romantic relationships in emerging adulthood. In J. J. Arnett (Ed.), *Oxford handbook of emerging adulthood.* New York, NY: Oxford University Press.

Shulman, S., Laursen, B., Kalman, Z., & Karpovsky, S. (1997). Adolescent intimacy revisited. *Journal of Youth & Adolescence, 26,* 597–617.

Shumaker, D. M., Miller, C., Ortiz, C., & Deutsch, R. (2011). The forgotten bonds: The assessment and contemplation of sibling attachment in divorce and parental separation. *Family Court Review, 49*(1), 46–58.

Shweder, R. A. (2003). *Why do men barbecue? Recipes for cultural psychology.* Cambridge, MA: Harvard University Press.

Shweder, R. A., Goodnow, J. J., Hatano, G., LeVine, R. A., Markus, H. R., & Miller, P. J. (2006). The cultural psychology of development: One mind, many mentalities. In W. Damon & R. Lerner (Eds.), & R. M. Lerner (Vol. Eds.), *Handbook of child psychology: Vol. 1. Theoretical models of human development* (6th ed., pp. 716–792). New York, NY: Wiley.

Shweder, R. A., Goodnow, J. J., Hatano, G., Levine, R. A., Markus, H., & Miller, P. (2011). The cultural psychology of development: One mind, many mentalities. In W. Damon (Ed.), *Handbook of child development* (6th ed.). New York, NY: Wiley.

Shweder, R. A., Mahapatra, M., & Miller, J. G. (1990). Culture and moral development. In J. W. Stigler, R. A. Shweder, & G. Herdt (Eds.), *Cultural psychology* (pp. 130–204). New York, NY: Cambridge University Press.

Shweder, R. A., Much, N. C., Mahapatra, M., & Park, L. (1997). The "big three" of morality (autonomy, community, divinity) and the "big three" explanations of suffering. In A. Brandt & D. Rozin (Eds.), *Morality and health* (pp. 119–169). New York, NY: Routledge.

Sidorowicz, L. S., & Lunney, G. S. (1980). Baby X revisited. *Sex Roles, 6,* 67–73.

Siegal, M. (2003). Cognitive development. In A. Slater & G. Bremner (Eds.), *An introduction to developmental psychology.* (Vol. xxv, pp. 189–210). Malden, MA: Blackwell Publishing.

Sigman, M. (1999). Developmental deficits in children with Down syndrome. In H. Tager-Flusberg (Ed.), *Neurodevelopmental disorders: Developmental cognitive neuroscience* (pp. 179–195). Cambridge, MA: MIT Press.

Silk, J. S., Morris, A. S., Kanaya, T., & Steinberg, L. (2003). Psychological control and autonomy granting: Opposite ends of a continuum or distinct constructs? *Journal of Research on Adolescence, 13,* 113–128.

Silva, C., & Martins, M. (2003). Relations between children's invented spelling and the development of phonological awareness. *Educational Psychology, 23,* 3–16.

Simkin, P. (2007). *The birth partner, Third edition: A complete guide to childbirth for dads, doulas, and all other labor companions.* Boston, MA: Harvard Common Press.

Simmons, C. A. (2014). Playing with popular culture–an ethnography of children's sociodramatic play in the classroom. *Ethnography and Education,* 1–14.

Simons, S. H. P., van Dijk, M., Anand, K. S., Roofhooft, D., van Lingen, R., & Tibboel, D. (2003). Do we still hurt newborn babies: A prospective study of procedural pain and analgesia in neonates. *Archives of Pediatrics & Adolescent Medicine, 157,* 1058–1064.

Simons-Morton, B. (2007). Parent involvement in novice teen driving: Rationale, evidence of effects, and potential for enhancing graduated driver licensing effectiveness. *Journal of Safety Research, 38,* 192–202.

Simons-Morton, B. G., Hartos, J. L., & Leaf, W. A. (2002). Promoting parental management of teen driving. *Injury Prevention, 8*(Suppl. 2), ii24–ii31.

Simons-Morton, B. G., Hartos, J. L., Leaf, W. A., & Preusser, D. F. (2006). Increasing parent limits on novice young drivers: Cognitive mediation of the effect of persuasive messages. *Journal of Adolescent Research, 21,* 83–105.

Simons-Morton, B. G., Ouimet, M. C., & Catalano, R. F. (2008). Parenting and the young driver problem. *American Journal of Preventative Medicine, 35*(3, Suppl. 1), S294–S303.

Singer, J. L., & Singer, D. G. (1998). *Barney & Friends* as entertainment and education: Evaluating the quality and effectiveness of a television series for preschool children. In J. K. Asamen & G. L. Berry (Eds.), *Research paradigms, television and social behavior* (pp. 305–367). Thousand Oaks, CA: Sage.

Singerman, J., & Lee, L. (2008). Consistency of the Babinski reflex and its variants. *European Journal of Neurology, 15,* 960–964.

Singh, L., Nestor, S., Parikh, C., & Yull, A. (2009). Influences of infant-directed speech on early word recognition. *Infancy, 14,* 654–666.

Sinha, S. P., & Goel, Y. (2012). Impulsivity and selective attention among adolescents. *Journal of Psychosocial Research, 7,* 61–67.

Sinnott, J. D. (2014). *Adult development: Cognitive aspects of thriving close relationships.* New York, NY: Oxford University Press.

Sippola, L. K., Buchanan, C. M., & Kehoe, S. (2007). Correlates of false self in adolescent romantic relationships. *Journal of Clinical Child and Adolescent Psychology, 36,* 515–521.

Sirsch, U., Dreher, E., Mayr, E., & Willinger, U. (2009). What does it take to be an adult in Austria? Views on adulthood in Austrian adolescents, emerging adults, and adults. *Journal of Adolescent Research, 24,* 275–292.

Skinner, B. F. (1953). *Science and human behavior.* Oxford, UK: Macmillan.

Slater, A., Field, T., & Hernandez-Reif, M. (2002). The development of the senses. In A. Slater & M. Lewis (Eds.), *Introduction to infant development.* New York, NY: Oxford University Press.

Slater, M. D., Henry, K. L., Swaim, R. C., & Anderson, L. L. (2003). Violent media content and aggressiveness in adolescents: A downward spiral model. *Communication Research, 30,* 713–736.

Sloat, E. A., Letourneau, N. L., Joschko, J. R., Schryer, E. A., & Colpitts, J. E. (2015). Parent-mediated reading interventions with children up to four years old: A systematic review. *Issues in Comprehensive Pediatric Nursing, 38*(1), 39–56.

Slobin, D. (1972). Children and language: They learn the same way around the world. *Psychology Today,* 71–76.

Slobin, D. I. (2014). The universal, the typological, and the particular in acquisition. In D. I. Slobin (Ed.), *The cross-linguistic study of language acquisition* (Vol. 5, pp. 1–40). New York, NY: Psychology Press.

Slonje, R., & Smith, P. K. (2008). Cyberbullying: Another main type of bullying? *Scandinavian Journal of Psychology, 49,* 147–154.

Small, M. (2001). *Kids: How biology and culture shape the way we raise young children.* New York, NY: Anchor.

Small, M. F. (1998). *Our babies, ourselves: How biology and culture shape the way we parent.* New York, NY: Anchor.

Small, M. F. (2005). The natural history of children. In Sharna Olfman (Ed.), *Childhood lost: How American culture is failing our kids* (pp. 3–17). Westport, CT: Praeger.

Smetana, J. G. (2005). Adolescent–parent conflict: Resistance and subversion as developmental processes. In L. Nucci (Ed.), *Conflict, contradiction, and contrarian elements in moral development and education* (pp. 69–91). Mahwah, NJ: Erlbaum.

Smink, F. R. E., van Hoeken, D., & Hoek, H. W. (2012). Epidemiology of eating disorders: Incidence, prevalence, and mortality rates. *Current Psychiatry Report, 14,* 404–414.

Smith, A., & Duggan, M. (n.d.). Online dating and relationships. Retrieved from http://www.pewinternet.org/2013/10/21/online-dating-relationships.

Smith, C., & Denton, M. L. (2005). *Soul searching: The religious and spiritual lives of American teenagers.* New York, NY: Oxford University Press.

Smith, C., & Snell, P. (2010). *Souls in transition: The religious lives of emerging adults in America.* New York, NY: Oxford University Press.

Smith, W. B. (2011). *Youth leaving foster care: A developmental, relationship-based approach to practice.* New York, NY: Oxford University Press.

Smylie, L., Maticka-Tyndale, E., & Boyd, D. (2008). Evaluation of a school-based sex education programme delivered to Grade Nine students in Canada. *Sex Education, 8*(1), 25–46.

Snarey, J. R. (1985). Cross-cultural universality of social moral development: A review of Kohlbergian research. *Psychological Bulletin, 97,* 202–232.

Snowling, M. J. (2004). Reading development and dyslexia. In U. Goswami (Ed.), *Blackwell handbook of childhood cognitive development.* Malden, MA: Blackwell.

Snyder, J., Cramer, A., & Afrank, J. (2005). The contributions of ineffective discipline and parental hostile attributions of child misbehavior to the development of conduct problems at home and school. *Developmental Psychology, 41,* 30–41.

Snyder, T. D., & Dillow, S. A. (2010). Digest of education statistics 2009 (NCES 2010–013), Washington, DC: National Center for Education Statistics, Institute of Education Sciences, U.S. Department of Education.

Society for Assisted Reproductive Technology (SART). (2014). *Clinic summary report.* Retrieved from https://www.sartcorsonline.com/rptCSR_PublicMultYear.aspx?ClinicPKID=0.

Soderstrom, M. (2007). Beyond babytalk: Re-evaluating the nature and content of speech input to preverbal infants. *Developmental Review, 27,* 501–532.

Soken, N. H., & Pick, A. D. (1992). Intermodal perception of happy and angry expressive behaviors by seven-month-old infants. *Child Development, 63,* 787–795.

Sokol, R. J., Delaney-Black, V., & Nordstrom, B. (2003). Fetal alcohol spectrum disorder. *Journal of the American Medical Association, 290,* 2996–2999.

Sorce, J. F., Emde, R. N., Campos, J. J., & Klinnert, M. D. (1985). Maternal emotional signaling: Its effect on the visual cliff behavior of 1-year-olds. *Developmental Psychology, 21*(1), 195–200.

Sørensen, K., Mouritsen, A., Aksglaede, L., Hagen, C. P., & Morgensen, S. S. (2012). Recent secular trends in pubertal timing: Implications for evaluation and diagnosis of precocious puberty. *Hormone research in pediatrics 77*(3), 137–145.

Sowell, E., Trauner, D., Ganst, A., & Jernigan, T. (2002). Development of cortical and subcortical brain structures in childhood and adolescence: A structural MRI study. *Developmental Medicine and Child Neurology, 44,* 4–16.

Spafford, C. S., & Grosser, G. S. (2005). *Dyslexia and reading difficulties* (2nd ed.). Boston, MA: Allyn & Bacon.

Spelke, E. S. (1979). Perceiving bimodally specified events in infancy. *Developmental Psychology, 5,* 626–636.

Spence, M. J., & DeCasper, A. J. (1987). Prenatal experience with low-frequency maternal voice sounds influences neonatal perception of maternal voice samples. *Infant Behavior and Development, 10,* 133–142.

Spencer, J. P., Verejiken, B., Diedrich, F. J., & Thelen, E. (2000). Posture and the emergence of manual skills. *Developmental Science, 3,* 216–233.

Spera, C. (2005). A review of the relationship among parenting practices, parenting styles, and adolescent school achievement. *Educational Psychology Review, 17,* 125–146.

Spock, B., & Needlman, R. (2004). *Dr. Spock's baby and child care* (8th ed.). New York, NY: Pocket.

Sprecher, S., & Regan, P. C. (1996). College virgins: How men and women perceive their sexual status. *Journal of Sex Research, 33,* 3–15.

Srinivas, A., White, M., & Omar, H. A. (2013). Teens texting and consequences: A brief review. In *Child and adolescent health yearbook, 2011* (pp. 371–376). Hauppauge, NY: Nova Biomedical Books.

Stafford, L. (2004). Communication competencies and sociocultural priorities of middle childhood. *Handbook of family communication,* 311–332.

Stanley, S. M., Rhoades, G. K., & Markman, H. J. (2006). Sliding versus deciding: Inertia and the premarital cohabitation effect. *Family Relations, 55,* 499–509.

Statistic Brain. (2014). Youth sports statistics. Retrieved from http://www.statisticbrain.com/youth-sports-statistics/.

Statistics Canada. (2012). Interjurisdictional cases of spousal and child support, 2010/2011. Juristat: Statistics Canada catalogue no. 85-002-X.

Sroufe, L. A., Egeland, B., Carlson, E. A., & Collins, W. A. (2005). *The development of the person: The Minnesota study of risk and adaptation from birth to adulthood.* New York, NY: Guilford.

St. James-Roberts, I., Bargn, J. G., Peter, B., Adams, D., & Hunt, S. (2003). Individual differences in responsivity to a neurobehavioural examination predict crying patterns of 1-week-old infants at home. *Developmental Medicine & Child Neurology, 45,* 400–407.

St. Louis, G. R., & Liem, J. H. (2005). Ego identity, ethnic identity, and psychosocial well-being of ethnic minority and majority college students. *Identity, 5,* 227–246.

Staff, J., Mortimer, J. T., & Uggen, C. (2004). Work and leisure in adolescence. In Lerner, R. M., and Steinberg, L. (Eds.), *Handbook of adolescent psychology (2nd ed.).* (pp. 429–450). Hoboken, NJ: John Wiley & Sons Inc.

Steele, J. (2006). Media practice model. In J. J. Arnett (Ed.), *Encyclopedia of children, adolescents, and the media.* Thousand Oaks, CA: Sage.

Steinberg, L. (2000, April). *We know some things: Parent–adolescent relations in retrospect and prospect.* [Presidential Address]. Presented at the biennial meeting of the Society for Research on Adolescence, Chicago, IL.

Steinberg, L. (2008). A social neuroscience perspective on adolescent risk-taking. *Developmental Review, 28*(1), 78–106. http://doi.org/10.1016/j.dr.2007.08.002.

Steinberg, L. (2010). A behavioral scientist looks at the science of adolescent brain development. *Brain and Cognition, 72*(1), 160–164.

Steinberg, L. (2011). Adolescent risk taking: A social neuroscience perspective. In E. Amsel & J. Smetana (Eds.), *Adolescent vulnerabilities and opportunities: Developmental and constructivist perspectives. Interdisciplinary perspectives on knowledge and development: The Jean Piaget Symposium series* (pp. 41–64). New York, NY: Cambridge University Press.

Steinberg, L., & Levine, A. (1997). *You and your adolescent: A parents' guide for ages 10 to 20* (rev. ed.). New York, NY: HarperCollins.

Steinberg, S. A. (2013). *America's 10 million unemployed youth spell danger for future economic growth.* Washington, DC: Center for American Progress.

Steinhausen, H.-C., Boyadjieva, S., Griogoroiu-Serbanescue, M., & Neumarker, K.-J. (2003). The outcome of adolescent eating disorders: Findings from an international collaborative study. *European Child & Adolescent Psychiatry, 12,* i91–i98.

Stenberg, C. R., Campos, J. J., & Emde, R. N. (1983). The facial expression of anger in seven-month-old infants. *Child Development,* 178–184.

Stephens, J. M., Young, M. F., & Calabrese, T. (2007). Does moral judgment go offline when students are online? A comparative analysis of undergraduates' belief of behaviors relates to conventional and digital cheating. *Ethics & Behavior, 17* (Special issue: Academic dishonesty), 233–254.

Steptoe, A., & Wardle, J. (2001). Health behavior, risk awareness, and emotional well-being in students from Eastern and Western Europe. *Social Science and Medicine, 53,* 1621–1630.

Sternberg, R. (1983). Components of human intelligence. *Cognition, 15,* 1–48.

Sternberg, R. (1988). *The triarchic mind: A new theory of human intelligence.* New York, NY: Viking Penguin.

Sternberg, R. J. (2002). Intelligence is not just inside the head: The theory of successful intelligence. In J. Aronson (Ed.), *Improving academic achievement* (pp. 227–244). San Diego, CA: Academic Press.

Sternberg, R. J. (2003). Our research program validating the triarchic theory of successful intelligence: Reply to Gottfredson. *Intelligence, 31,* 399–413.

Sternberg, R. J. (2004). Cultural and intelligence. *American Psychologist, 59,* 325–338.

Sternberg, R. J. (2005). The triarchic theory of successful intelligence. In D. P. Flanagan & P. L. Harrison (Eds.), *Contemporary Intellectual Assessment: Theories, Tests and Issues* (pp. 103–119). New York, NY: Guilford Press.

Sternberg, R. J. (2007). Intelligence and culture. In S. Kitayama & D. Cohen (Eds.), *Handbook of cultural psychology* (pp. 547–568). New York, NY: Guilford.

Steur, F. B., Applefield, J. M., & Smith, R. (1971). Televised aggression and interpersonal aggression of preschool children. *Journal of Experimental Child Psychology, 11*, 442–447.

Stevenson, H. W., & Lee, S. Y. (1990). Contexts of achievement: A study of American, Chinese, and Japanese children. *Monographs of the Society for Research in Child Development, 55,* (1–2, Serial No. 221).

Stevenson, H. W., Lee, S., & Mu, X. (2000). Successful achievement in mathematics: China and the United States. In C. F. M. van Lieshout & P. G. Heymans (Eds.), *Developing talent across the lifespan* (pp. 167–183). Philadelphia, PA: Psychology Press.

Stevenson, H. W., & Zusho, A. (2002). Adolescence in China and Japan: Adapting to a changing environment. In Brown, B. B., Larson, R. W., & Saraswathi, T. S. (Eds.), *The world's youth: Adolescence in eight regions of the globe.* (pp. 141–170). New York, NY: Cambridge University Press.

Stevens-Watkins, D., & Rostosky, S. (2010). Binge drinking in African American males from adolescence to young adulthood: The protective influence of religiosity, family connectedness, and close friends' substance use. *Substance Use & Misuse, 45*, 1435–1451.

Stigler, J. W., Shweder, R. A., & Herdt, G. (1990). *Cultural psychology: Essays on comparative human development.* New York, NY: Cambridge University Press.

Stipek, D. (2011). Classroom practices and children's motivation to learn. In E. Zigler, W. S. Gilliam, & W. S. Barnett (Eds.), *The pre-K debates: Current controversies and issues.* (Vol. xv, pp. 98–103). Baltimore, MD: Paul H Brookes Publishing.

Stoll, B., Hansen, N. I., Adams-Chapman, I., Fanaroff, A. A., Hintz, S. R., Vohr, B.,…Human Development Neonatal Research Network (2004). Neurodevelopmental and growth impairment among extremely low-birth-weight infants with neonatal infection. *Journal of the American Medical Association, 292*, 2357–2365.

Stones, M. J., & Kozma, A. (1996). Activity, exercise, and behavior. In J. E. Birren & K. W. Schaie (Eds.), *Handbook of psychology and aging* (4th ed., pp. 338–352). San Diego, CA: Academic Press.

Strang-Karlsson, S., Räikkönen, K., Pesonen, A.-K., Kajantie, E., Paavonen, J., Lahti, J.,…Andersson, S. (2008). Very low birth weight and behavioral symptoms of Attention Deficit Hyperactivity Disorder in young adulthood: The Helsinki Study of very-low-birth-weight adults. *American Journal of Psychiatry, 165*, 1345–1353.

Straus, M. A., & Donnelly, D. A. (1994). Beating the devil out of them: Corporal punishment in American families. New York, NY: Lexington Books.

Strauss, S. (2005). Teaching as a natural cognitive ability: Implications for classroom practice and teacher education. In D. B. Pillemer & S. H. White (Eds.), *Developmental psychology and social change: Research, history and policy.* (Vol. xii, pp. 368–388). New York, NY: Cambridge University Press.

Strauss, S., Ziv, M., & Stein, A. (2002). Teaching as a natural cognition and its relations to preschoolers' developing theory of mind. *Cognitive Development, 17*(3–4), 1473–1487.

Striegel-Moore, R. H., & Franko, D. L. (2006). Adolescent eating disorders. In C. A. Essau (Ed.), *Child and adolescent psychopathology: Theoretical and clinical implications* (pp. 160–183). New York, NY: Routledge.

Striegel-Moore, R. H., Seeley, J. R., & Lewinsohn, P. M. (2003). Psychosocial adjustment in young adulthood of women who experienced an eating disorder in adolescence. *Journal of the American Academy of Child & Adolescent Psychiatry, 42*, 587–593.

Stromquist, N. P. (2007). Gender equity education globally. In S. S. Klein, B. Richardson, D. A. Grayson, L. H. Fox, C. Kramarae, D. S. Pollard, & C. A. Dwyer (Eds.), *Handbook for achieving gender equity through education* (2nd ed., pp. 33–42). Mahwah, NJ: Lawrence Erlbaum.

Suarez-Orozco, C. (2015). Migration within and between countries: Implications for families and acculturation. In L. A. Jensen (Ed.), *Oxford handbook of human development and culture.* (pp. 43–60). New York, NY: Oxford University Press.

Suarez-Orozco, C., & Suarez-Orozco, M. (1996). *Transformations: Migration, family life and achievement motivation among Latino adolescents.* Palo Alto, CA: Stanford University Press.

Subrahmanyam, K., Reich, S. M., Waechter, N., & Espinoza, G. (2008). Online and offline social networks: Use of social networking sites by emerging adults. *Journal of Applied Developmental Psychology, 29*, 420–433.

Sullivan, C., & Cottone, R. R. (2010). Emergent characteristics of effective cross-cultural research: A review of the literature. *Journal of Counseling and Development, 88*, 357–362.

Sun, J., Dunne, M. P., Hou, X. Y., & Xu, A. Q. (2013). Educational stress among Chinese adolescents: Individual, family, school and peer influences. *Educational Review, 65*(3), 284–302.

Super, C. & Harkness, S. (2015). Charting infant development: Milestones along the way. In L. A. Jensen (Ed.), *The Oxford handbook of human development and culture: An interdisciplinary perspective. Oxford library of psychology,* (pp. 79–93). New York, NY: Oxford University Press.

Super, C. M., & Harkness, S. (1986). The developmental niche: A conceptualization at the interface of child and culture. *International Journal of Behavior Development, 9*, 545–569.

Super, C. M., & Harkness, S. (2009). The developmental niche of the newborn in rural Kenya. In K. J. Nugent, B. J. Petrauskas, & T. B. Brazelton (Eds.), *The newborn as a person: Enabling healthy infant development worldwide* (pp. 85–97). Hoboken, NJ: John Wiley & Sons.

Super, C. M., Harkness, S., van Tijen, N., van der Vlugt, E., Fintelman, M., & Dijkstra, J. (1996). The three R's of Dutch child-rearing and the socialization of infant arousal. In S. Harkness & C. M. Super (Eds.), *Parents' cultural belief systems: Their origins, expressions and consequences* (pp. 447–466). New York, NY: Guilford Press.

Susman, E. J., & Rogol, A. (2004). Puberty and psychological development. In R. M. Lerner & L. Steinberg (Eds.), *Handbook of adolescent psychology* (2nd ed., pp. 15–44). Hoboken, NJ: Wiley & Sons.

Sussman, S., Pokhrel, P., Ashmore, R. D., & Brown, B. B. (2007). Adolescent peer group identification and characteristics: A review of the literature. *Addictive Behaviors, 32*, 1602–1627.

Svetlova, M., Nichols, S. R., & Brownell, C. A. (2010). Toddlers' prosocial behavior: From instrumental to empathic to altruistic helping. *Child development, 81*(6), 1814–1827.

Swanson, H., Saez, L., & Gerber, M. (2004). Literacy and cognitive functioning in bilingual and nonbilingual children at or not at risk for reading disabilities. *Journal of Educational Psychology, 96*, 3–18.

Swanson, S. A., Crow, S. J., Le Grange, D., Swendsen, J., & Merikangas, K. R. (2011). Prevalence and correlates of eating disorders in adolescents: Results from the National Comorbidity Survey Replication—Adolescent Supplement. *Archives of General Psychiatry 68*(7), 714–723. doi:10.1001/archgenpsychiatry.2011.22.

Swinbourne, J. M., & Touyz, S. W. (2007). The comorbidity of eating disorders and anxiety disorders: A review. *European Eating Disorders Review, 15*, 253–274.

Swingley, D. (2010). Fast mapping and slow mapping in children's word learning. *Language Learning and Development, 6*, 179–183.

Syed, M., & Azmitia, M. (2010). Narrative and ethnic identity exploration: A longitudinal account of emerging adults' ethnicity–related experiences. *Developmental Psychology, 46*, 208–219.

Syed, M., & Mitchell, L. J. (2015). How race and ethnicity shape emerging adulthood. In J. J. Arnett (Ed.), *Oxford handbook of emerging adulthood.* New York, NY: Oxford University Press.

Syltevik, L. J. (2010). Sense and sensibility: Cohabitation in "cohabitation land." *The Sociological Review, 58,* 444–462.

Symons, D. K. (2001). A dyad-oriented approach to distress and mother–child relationship outcomes in the first 24 months. *Parenting: Science and Practice, 1,* 101–122.

Taber-Thomas, B., & Perez-Edgar, K. (2015). Emerging adulthood brain development. In J. J. Arnett (Ed.), *Oxford handbook of emerging adulthood.* New York, NY: Oxford University Press.

Taga, K. A., Markey, C. N., & Friedman, H. S. (2006). A longitudinal investigation of associations between boys' pubertal timing and adult behavioral health and well-being. *Journal of Youth and Adolescence, 35,* 401–411.

Takahashi, K., & Takeuchi, K. (2007). Japan. In J. J. Arnett (Ed.), *International encyclopedia of adolescence* (525–539). New York, NY: Routledge.

Takahashi, K. (1986). Examining the strange-situation procedure with Japanese mothers and 12-month-old infants. *Developmental Psychology, 22*(2), 265–270.

Talbani, A., & Hasanali, P. (2000). Adolescent females between tradition and modernity: Gender role socialization in south Asian immigrant families. *Journal of Adolescence, 23,* 615–627.

Talbot, M. (2015). The Talking Cure. *New Yorker.* http://www.newyorker.com/magazine/2015/01/12/talking-cure Retrieved online May 31, 2015.

Tamaru, S., Kikuchi, A., Takagi, K., Wakamatsu, M., Ono, K., Horikoshi, T., Kihara, H., & Nakamura, T. (2011). Neurodevelopmental outcomes of very low birth weight and extremely low birth weight infants at 18 months of corrected age associated with prenatal risk factors. *Early Human Development, 87,* 55–59.

Tamay, Z., Akcay, A., Ones, U., Guler, N., Kilie, G., & Zencir, M. (2007). Prevalence and risk factors for allergic rhinitis in primary school children. *International Journal of Pediatric Otorhinolaryngology, 71,* 463–471.

Tamis-LeMonda, C. S., Way, N., Hughes, D., Yoshikawa, H., Kalman, R. K., & Niwa, E. Y. (2008). Parents' goals for children: The dynamic coexistence of individualism and collectivism in cultures and individuals. *Social Development, 17,* 183–209.

Tanaka, H., & Seals, D. R. (2003). Dynamic exercise performance in master athletes: Insight into the effects of primary human aging on physiological functional capacity. *Journal of Applied Physiology, 95,* 2152–2162.

Tanaka, S. (2005). Parental leave and child health across OECD countries. *The Economic Journal, 115,* F7–F28.

Tanner, J. L. (2006). Recentering during emerging adulthood: A critical turning point in life span human development. In J. J. Arnett & J. L. Tanner (Eds.), *Emerging adults in America: Coming of age in the 21st century* (pp. 21–55). Washington, DC: American Psychological Association.

Tanner, J. L. (2015). Mental health in emerging adulthood. In J. J. Arnett (Ed.), *Oxford handbook of emerging adulthood.* New York, NY: Oxford University Press.

Tanon, F. (1994). *A cultural view on planning: The case of weaving in Ivory Coast.* Tilburg, Netherlands: Tilburg University Press.

Tardif, T., Fletcher, P., Liang, W., Zhang, Z., Kaciroti, N., & Marchman, V. A. (2008). Baby's first 10 words. *Developmental Psychology, 44* (4), 929–938.

Taylor, A. (2005). It's for the rest of your life: The pragmatics of youth career decision making. *Youth & Society, 36,* 471–503.

Taylor, M. J. (2006). Neural bases of cognitive development. In E. Bialystok & F. I. M. Craik (Eds.), *Lifespan cognition: Mechanisms of change* (pp. 15–26.) New York, NY: Oxford University Press.

Taylor, P., & Keeter, S. (2010). *Millennials: Confident. Connected. Open to change.* Retrieved from http://www.pewsocialtrends.org/files/2010/10/millennials-confident-connected-open-to-change.pdf.

Tedeschi, A., & Airaghi, L. (2006). Is affluence a risk factor for bronchial asthma and type 1 diabetes? *Pediatric Allergy and Immunology, 17,* 533–537.

Telama, R., Yang, X., Viikari, J., Välimäki, I., Wanne, O., & Raitakari, O. (2005). Physical activity from childhood to adulthood: A 21-year tracking study. *American Journal of Preventative Medicine, 28,* 267–273.

Terry, W. S. (2003). *Learning and memory* (2nd ed.). Boston, MA: Allyn & Bacon.

Teti, D. M., Sakin, K., Kucera, E., Corns, K. M., & Eiden, R. D. (1996). And baby makes four: Predictors of attachment security among preschool-aged first-borns during the transition to sibling-hood. *Child Development, 68,* 579–596.

Thach, B. T. (2009). Does swaddling decrease or increase the risk for Sudden Infant Death syndrome? *Journal of Pediatrics, 155,* 461–462.

Thacher, P. V. (2008). University students and the "all nighter": Correlates and patterns of students' engagement in a single night of total sleep deprivation. *Behavioral Sleep Medicine, 6,* 16–31.

Thacher, T. D., & Clarke, B. L. (2011). Vitamin D insufficiency. In *Mayo Clinic Proceedings, 86*(1), 50–60.

Thacker, S. B., & Stroup, D. E. (2003). Revisiting the use of the electronic fetal monitor. *Lancet, 361,* 445–446.

Thapar, A., Collishaw, S., Pine, D. S., & Thapar, A. K. (2012). Depression in adolescence. *The Lancet, 379*(9820), 1056–1067.

Tharpe, A. M., & Ashmead, D. H. (2001). A longitudinal investigation of infant auditory sensitivity. *American Journal of Audiology, 10,* 104–112.

Thelen, E. (2001). Dynamic mechanisms of change in early perceptual-motor development. In J. L. McClelland & R. S. Siegler (Eds.), *Mechanisms of cognitive development: Behavioral and neural perspectives* (pp. 161–184). Mahwah, NJ: Erlbaum.

Thiessen, E. D., Hill, E. A., & Saffran, J. R. (2005). Infant-directed speech facilitates word segmentation. *Infancy, 7,* 53–71.

Thomas, A., & Chess, S. (1977). *Temperament and development.* New York, NY: Brunner/Mazel.

Thomas, A., Chess, S., & Birch, H. G. (1968). *Temperament and behavior disorders in children.* New York, NY: New York University Press.

Thomas, T. L., Yarandi, H. N., Dalmida, S. G., Frados, A., & Klienert, K. (2015). Cross cultural differences and sexual risk behavior of emerging adults. *Journal of Transcultural Nursing, 26*(1), 64–72. http://doi.org/10.1177/1043659614524791.

Thompson, C. J. (2005). Consumer risk perceptions in a community of reflexive doubt. *The Journal of Consumer Research, 32,* 235–248.

Thompson, R. A. (1998). Early sociopersonality development. In W. Damon (Editor-in-Chief), & N. Eisenberg (Vol. Ed.), *Handbook of child psychology: Vol. 3. Social, emotional and personality development* (5th ed., pp. 25–104). New York, NY: Wiley.

Thompson, R. A. (2006). The development of the person: Social understanding, relationships, conscience, self. In W. Damon & R. Lerner (Eds.), & N. Eisenberg (Vol. Ed.), *Handbook of child psychology: Vol. 3. Social, emotional and personality development* (6th ed., pp. 24–98). New York, NY: Wiley.

Thompson, R. A. (2008). Measure twice, cut once: Attachment theory and the NICHD Study of early child care and youth development. *Attachment & Human Development, 10*(3), 287–297.

Thompson, R. A., & Goodvin, R. (2007). Taming the tempest in the teapot: Emotional regulation in toddlers. In C. A. Brownell & C. B. Kopp (Eds.), *Socioemotional development in the toddler years* (pp. 320–341). New York, NY: Guilford.

Thompson, R. A., & Nelson, C. A. (2001). Developmental science and the media. *American Psychologist, 56*, 5–15.

Thorne, B. (1993). *Gender play: Girls and boys in school.* New Brunswick, N.J.: Rutgers University Press.

Thurston, A., & Topping, K. J. (2007). Peer tutoring in schools: Cognitive models and organizational typography. *Journal of Cognitive Education and Psychology, 6*(3), 356–372.

Tierra, L., & Tierra, M. (1998). *Chinese traditional herbal medicine.* Twin Lakes, WI: Lotus Light.

Tiggemann, M., & Anesbury, T. (2000). Negative stereotyping of obesity in children: The role of controllability beliefs. *Journal of Applied Social Psychology, 30*, 1977–1993.

Tilton-Weaver, L. C., Burk, W. J., Kerr, M., & Stattin, H. (2013). Can parental monitoring and peer management reduce the selection or influence of delinquent peers? Testing the question using a dynamic social network approach. *Developmental Psychology, 49*(11), 2057–2070. http://doi.org/10.1037/a0031854.

Tobach, E. (2004). Development of sex and gender: Biochemistry, physiology, and experience. In A. M. Paludi (Ed.), *Praeger guide to the psychology of gender* (pp. 240–270). Westport, CT: Praeger.

Tobin, D. D., Menon, M., Menon, M., Spatta, B. C., Hodges, E. V. E., & Perry, D. G. (2010). The intrapsychics of gender: A model of self-socialization. *Psychological Review, 117*, 601–622.

Tobin, J., Hsueh, Y., & Karasawa, M. (2009). *Preschool in three cultures revisited: China, Japan, and the United States.* Chicago, IL: University of Chicago Press.

Tomasello, M., & Rakoczy, H. (2003). What makes human cognition unique? From individual to shared to collective intentionality. *Mind and Language, 18*, 121–147.

Tough, S., Clarke, M., & Cook, J. (2007). Fetal alcohol spectrum disorder prevention approaches among Canadian physicians by proportion of native/aboriginal patients: Practices during the preconception and prenatal periods. *Maternal and Child Health Journal, 11*, 385–393.

Tracy, J. L., & Robins, R. W. (2004). Putting the self into self-conscious emotions: A theoretical model. *Psychological Inquiry, 15*(2), 103–125. doi:10.1207/s15327965pli1502_01.

Trainor, L. J., Austin, C. M., & Desjardins, R. N. (2000). Is infant-directed speech prosody a result of the vocal expression of emotion? *Psychological Science, 11*, 188–195.

Treatment for Adolescents with Depression Study (TADS) team, U.S. (2004). Fluoxetine, cognitive-behavioral therapy, and their combination for adolescents with depression: Treatment for Adolescents with Depression Study (TADS) randomized controlled trial. *JAMA: Journal of the American Medical Association, 29*, 807–820.

Treatment for Adolescents with Depression Study Team. (2007). Long-term effectiveness and safety outcomes. *Archives of General Psychiatry, 64*, 1132–1143.

Trehub, S. E. (2001). Musical predispositions in infancy. *Annals of the New York Academy of Sciences, 930*, 1–16.

Trehub, S. E., Thorpe, L. A., & Morrongiello, B. A. (1985). Infants' perception of melodies: Changes in a single tone. *Infant Behavior and Development, 8*, 213–223.

Tremblay, R. E. (2000). The development of aggressive behaviour during childhood: What have we learned in the past century? *International Journal of Behavioral Development, 24*, 129–141.

Tremblay, R. E. (2002). Prevention of injury by early socialization of aggressive behavior. *Injury Prevention, 8*(Suppl. IV), 17–21.

Tremblay, R. E., & Nagin, D. S. (2005). Developmental origins of physical aggression in humans. In R. E. Tremblay, W. W. Hartup, & J. Archer (Eds.), *Developmental origins of aggression* (pp. 83–106). New York, NY: Guilford Press.

Triandis, H. C. (1995). *Individualism and collectivism.* Boulder, CO: Westview Press.

Tronick, E. (2007). *The neurobehavioral and social-emotional development of infants and children.* New York, NY: W. W. Norton.

Trost, K. (2012). Norway. In J. J. Arnett (Ed.), *Adolescent psychology around the world.* New York, NY: Taylor & Francis.

Truglio, R. T. (2007). Sesame Workshop. In J. J. Arnett (Ed.), *Encyclopedia of children, adolescents, and the media* (pp. 749–750). Thousand Oaks, CA: Sage.

Tseng, V. (2004). Family interdependence and academic adjustments in college: Youth from immigrant and U.S.-born families. *Child Development, 75*, 966–983.

Tsubokura, M., Komatsu, T., & Kami, M. (2008) The prevalence of high-risk human papillomavirus in women with different types of cervical cancer. *Annals Internal Medicine, 149*(4), 283.

Tudge, J. R. H., Doucet, F., Odero, D., Sperb, T. M., Piccinini, C. A., & Lopes, R. S. (2006). A window into different cultural worlds: Young children's everyday activities in the United States, Brazil, and Kenya. *Child Development, 77*, 1446–1469.

Turkheimer, E., Harden, K. P., D'Onofrio, B., & Gottesman, I. I. (2009). The Scarr-Rowe interaction between measured socioeconomic status and the heritability of cognitive ability. In K. McCartney & R. A. Weinberg (Eds.), *Experience and development: A festschrift in honor of Sandra Wood Scarr* (pp. 81–98). New York, NY: Psychology Press.

Twenge, J. M. (2006). *Generation me: Why today's young Americans are more confident, assertive, entitled—and more miserable than ever before.* New York, NY: Free Press.

Twisk, D. A. M., & Stacey, C. (2007). Trends in young driver risk and countermeasures in European countries. *Journal of Safety Research, 38*, 245–257.

Tyano, S., Keren, M., Herrman, H., & Cox, J. (2010). *The competent fetus.* New York, NY: Wiley.

U.S. Bureau of the Census. (2009). *Statistical abstracts of the United States.* Washington, DC: U.S. Government Printing Office.

U.S. Bureau of the Census. (2010). *Statistical abstracts of the United States.* Washington, DC: U.S. Government Printing Office.

U.S. Department of Education, Office of Special Education Programs. (2013). *Annual Report to Congress on the Implementation of the Individuals with Disabilities Education Act,* selected years, 1992 through 2006, and Individuals with Disabilities Education Act (IDEA) database, retrieved May 12, 2013, from http://tadnet.public.tadnet.org/pages/712. National Center for Education Statistics, Common Core of Data (CCD), "State Nonfiscal Survey of Public Elementary/Secondary Education," 2011-12.

U.S. Department of Health and Human Services. (2015). Health resources and services administration, maternal and child health. Retrieved March 7, 2015.

U.S. Department of Labor. (2012). Number of jobs held, labor market activity, and earnings growth among the youngest Baby Boomers: Results from a longitudinal survey summary. Economic News Release, Table 1. Retrieved from http://www.bls.gov/news.release/nlsoy.nro.htm.

U.S. Department of Transportation. (1995). *The economic costs of motor vehicle crashes, Technical report 1994.* Washington, DC: National Highway Traffic Safety Administration.

Umaña-Taylor, A. J. (2005). Self-esteem and ethnic identity among Latino adolescents. *Directions in Rehabilitation Counseling, 16*, 9–18.

Umrigar, A., Banijee, M., & Tsien, F. (2014). Down syndrome (Trisomy 21). LSUHSC School of Medicine. Retrieved from http://www.medschool.lsuhsc.edu/genetics/down_syndrome.aspx.

UNAIDS. (2010). UNAIDS report on the global AIDS epidemic. Available: http://www.unaids.org/globalreport/documents/20101123_GlobalReport_full_en.pdf.

Underwood, M. (2003). *Social-aggression among girls.* New York, NY: Guilford Press.

UNESCO. (2008). Regional overview: Sub-Saharan Africa. EFA Global Monitoring Report. en.unesco.org/gem-report/sites/gem-report/files/157229E.pdf Retrieved June 14, 2015.

UNESCO. (2014). Education: Total net enrollment, lower secondary school. Retrieved from http://data.uis.unesco.org/?ReportId=167.#

UNICEF. (2008). *State of the world's children*. New York, NY: Author.

UNICEF. (2011). *Breastfeeding Initiatives Exchange*. Retrieved from http://www.unicef.org/programme/breastfeeding/.

UNICEF. (2013). *Progress toward global immunization goals, 2012: Summary presentation of key indicators*. Retrieved from http://www.who.int/immunization/monitoring_surveillance/SlidesGlobalImmunization.pdf?ua=1.

UNICEF. (2014a). Four out of five unattended births worldwide take place in sub-Saharan Africa and South Asia. Retrieved from http://data.unicef.org/maternal-health/delivery-care.

UNICEF (2014b). *The state of the world's children in numbers*. New York, NY: Author.

United Nations Development Programme (UNDP). (2010). *Human development report*. New York, NY: Author.

United Nations Development Programme (UNDP). (2014). *Human development report*. New York, NY: Author.

United Nations Development Programme (UNDP). (2015). *Human development report*. New York, NY: Author.

Unsworth, G., Devilly, G. J., & Ward, T. (2007). The effect of playing violent video games on adolescents: Should parents be quaking in their boots? *Psychology, Crime, & Law, 13*, 383–394.

Updegraff, K. A., McHale, S. M., & Crouter, A. (2002). Adolescents' sibling relationship and friendship experiences: Developmental patterns and relationship linkages. *Social Development, 11*, 182–204.

Updegraff, K. A., Thayer, S. M., Whiteman, S. D., Denning, D. J., & McHale, S. M. (2005). Relational aggression in adolescents' sibling relationships: Links to sibling and parent–adolescent relationship quality. *Family Relations, 54*, 373–385.

Vaillancourt, T., & Hymel, S. (2006). Aggression and social status: The moderating roles of sex and peer-values characteristics. *Aggressive Behavior, 32*, 396–408.

Vaillancourt, T., Brendgen, M., Boivin, M., & Tremblay, R. E. (2003). A longitudinal confirmatory factor analysis of indirect and physical aggression: Evidence of two factors over time? *Child Development, 74*, 1628–1638.

Vainio, A. (2015). Finnish moral landscapes: A comparison of nonreligious, liberal religious, and conservative religious adolescents. In L. A. Jensen (Ed.), *Moral development in a global world: Research from a cultural-developmental perspective*. New York, NY: Cambridge University Press.

Valencia-Martín, J. L., Galan, I., & Rodríguez-Artalejo, F. (2007). Binge drinking in Madrid, Spain. *Alcoholism: Clinical and Experimental Research, 31*, 1723–1730.

Valentine, D., Williams, M., & Young, R. K. (2013). *Age-related factors in driving safety*. Austin, TX: Center for Transportation Research.

Valkenburg, P. M., & Buijzen, M. (2007). Advertising, purchase requests and. In J. J. Arnett (Ed.), *Encyclopedia of children, adolescents, and the media* (pp. 47–48). Thousand Oaks, CA: Sage.

Valkenberg, P. M., & Peter, J. (2011). Online communication among adolescents: An integrated model of its attractions, opportunities, and risks. *Journal of Adolescent Health 48*(2), 121–127.

Vallejo, M. C., Ramesh, V., Phelps, A. L., & Sah, N. (2007). Epidural labor analgesia: Continuous infusion versus patient–controlled epidural analgesia with background infusion versus without a background infusion. *The Journal of Pain, 8*, 970–975.

van Beinum, F. J. (2008). Frames and babbling in hearing and deaf infants. In B. L. Davis & K. Zajdó (Eds.), *The syllable in speech production* (pp. 225–241). New York, NY: Lawrence Erlbaum.

Van de Poel, E. V., Hosseinpoor, A. R., Speybroek, N., Van Ourti, T., & Vega, J. (2008). Socioeconomic inequality in malnutrition in developing countries. *Bulletin of the World Health Organization, 86*, 282–291.

Van Evra, J. (2007). School-age children, impact of media on. In J. J. Arnett (Ed.), *Encyclopedia of children, adolescents, and the media* (pp. 739–742). Thousand Oaks, CA: Sage.

Van Hecke, A. V., Mundy, P. C., Acra, C. F., Block, J. J., Delgado, C. E. F., Parlade, M. V., …Pomares, Y. B. (2007). Infant joint attention, temperament, and social competence in preschool children. *Child Development, 78*, 53–69.

Van Hoof, A. (1999). The identity status approach: In need of fundamental revision and qualitative change. *Developmental Review, 19*, 622–647.

Van Horn, K. R., & Cunegatto, M. J. (2000). Interpersonal relationships in Brazilian adolescents. *International Journal of Behavioral Development, 24*, 199–203.

van IJzendoorn, M. H., & Hubbard, F. O. A. (2000). Are infant crying and maternal responsiveness during the first year related to infant–mother attachment at 15 months? *Attachment and Human Development, 2*, 371–391.

van IJzendoorn, M. H., & Kroonenberg, P. M. (1988). Cross-cultural patterns of attachment: A meta-analysis of the Strange Situation. *Child Development, 59*, 147–156.

Van Ijzendoorn, M. H., & Sagi-Schwartz, A. (2008). Cross-cultural patterns of attachment: Universal and contextual dimensions. In J. Cassidy, Jude & P. Shaver (Eds.), *Handbook of attachment: Theory, research, and clinical applications* (2nd ed., pp. 880–905). New York: Guilford Press.

van IJzendoorn, M. H., Schuengel, C., & Bakermans-Kranenburg, M. J. (1999). Disorganized attachment in early childhood: Meta-analysis of precursors, concomitants and sequelae. *Development and Pscyhopathology, 11*, 225–249.

van IJzendoorn, M. H., Vereijken, C. M. J. L., Bakermans-Kraneburg, M. J., & Riksen-Walraven, J. M. (2004). Assessing attachment security with the Attachment Q Sort: Meta-analytic evidence for the validity of the Observer AQS. *Child Development, 75*, 1188–1213.

van Sleuwen, B. E., Engelberts, A. C., Boere-Boonekamp, M. M., Kuis, W., Schulpen, T. W. J., & L'Hoir, M. P. (2007). Swaddling: A systematic review. *Pediatrics, 120*, e1097–e1106.

Vandell, D. L., Burchinal, M. R., Belsky, J., Owen, M. T., Friedman, S. L., Clarke-Stewart, A., …Weinraub, M. (2005). Early child care and children's development in the primary grades: Follow-up results from the NICHD Study of Early Child Care. Paper presented at the biennial meeting of the Society for Research in Child Development, Atlanta, GA.

Vandereycken, W., & Van Deth, R. (1994). *From fasting saints to anorexic girls: The history of self-starvation*. New York, NY: New York University Press.

Varendi, H., Christensson, K., Porter, R. H., & Wineberg, J. (1998). Soothing effect of amniotic fluid smell in newborn infants. *Early Human Development, 51*, 47–55.

Vaughan, K. (2005). The pathways framework meets consumer culture: Young people, careers, and commitment. *Journal of Youth Studies, 8*, 173–186.

Vazsonyi, A. T., & Snider, J. B. (2008). Mentoring, competencies, and adjustment in adolescents: American part-time employment and European apprenticeships. *International Journal of Behavioral Development, 32*, 46–55.

Verkuyten, M. (2002). Multiculturalism among minority and majority adolescents in the Netherlands. *International Journal of Intercultural Relations, 26*, 91–108.

Verma, R. P., Shibli, S., Fang, H., & Komaroff, E. (2009). Clinical determinants and the utility of early postnatal maximum weight loss in fluid management of extremely low birth weight infants. *Early Human Development, 85*, 59–64.

Verma, S., & Larson, R. (1999). Are adolescents more emotional? A study of daily emotions of middle class Indian adolescents. *Psychology and Developing Societies, 11*, 179–194.

Vidyasagar, T. R. (2004). Neural underpinnings of dyslexia as a disorder of visuospatial attention. *Clinical and Experimental Optometry, 87*, 4–10.

Vig, S., Chinitz, S., & Shulman, L. (2005). Young children in foster care: Multiple vulnerabilities and complex service needs. *Infants and Young Children, 18*, 147–160.

Vilette, B. (2002). Do young children grasp the inverse relationship between addition and subtraction? Evidence against early arithmetic. *Cognitive Development, 17*, 1365–1383.

Vinanen, A., Munhbayarlah, S., Zevgee, T., Narantsetseg, L., Naidansuren, T. S., Koskenvuo, M.,...Terho, E. O. (2007). The protective effect of rural living against atopy in Mongolia. *Allergy, 62*, 272–280.

Vincent, L. (2008). "Boys will be boys": Traditional Xhosa male circumcision, HIV and sexual socialization in contemporary South Africa. *Culture, Health, and Sexuality, 10*, 431–446.

Visher, E. B., Visher, J. S., & Pasley, K. (2003). Remarriage families and step-parenting. In F. Walsh (Ed.), *Normal family processes* (pp. 153–175). New York, NY: Guilford.

Vlaardingerbroek, J., van Goudoever, J. B., & van den Akker, C. H. P. (2009). Initial nutritional management of the preterm infant. *Early Human Development, 85*, 691–695.

Volk, A., Craif, W., Bryce, W., & King, M. (2006). Adolescent risk correlates of bullying and different types of victimization. *International Journal of Adolescent Medicine and Health, 18*, 575–586.

Volling, B. L. (2003). Sibling relationships. In M. H. Bornstein, L. Davidson, C. L. M. Keyes, & K. A. Moore (Eds.), *Well-being: Positive development across the life course* (pp. 205–220). Mahwah, NJ: Erlbaum.

Vondra, J. L., & Barnett, D. (Eds.). (1999). Atypical attachment in infancy and early childhood among children at developmental risk. *Monographs of the Society for Research in Child Development, 64*(3, Serial No. 258).

Vouloumanos, A., & Werker, J. F. (2004). Tuned to the signal: The privileged status of speech for young infants. *Developmental Science, 7*, 270–276.

Vouloumanos, A., Hauser, M. D., Werker, J. F., & Martin, A. (2010). The tuning of human neonates' preference for speech. *Child Development, 81*, 517–527.

Vygotsky, L. S. (1978). *Mind in society.* Cambridge, MA: Harvard University Press.

Wagner, C. L., & Greer, F. R. (2008). Prevention of rickets and vitamin D deficiency in infants, children, and adolescents. *Pediatrics, 122*(5), 1142–1152.

Walcott, D. D., Pratt, H. D., & Patel, D. R. (2003). Adolescents and eating disorders: Gender, racial, ethnic, sociocultural and socioeconomic issues. *Journal of Adolescent Research, 18*, 223–243.

Walker-Andrews, A. S. (1997). Infants' perception of expressive behaviors: Differentiation of multimodal information. *Psychological Bulletin, 121*(3), 437–456. doi:10.1037/0033-2909.121.3.437.

Wallace, J. M., Yamaguchi, R., Bachman, J. G., O'Malley, P. M., Schulenberg, J. E., & Johnston, L. D. (2007). Religiosity and adolescent substance use: The role of individual and contextual influences. *Social Problems, 54*, 308–327.

Wallerstein, J. S., & Johnson-Reitz, K. (2004). Communication in divorced and single parent families. In A. L. Vangelisti (Ed.), *Handbook of family communication* (pp. 197–214). Mahwah, NJ: Erlbaum.

Walshaw, C.A. (2010). Are we getting the best from breastfeeding? *Acta Paediatria, 99*, 1292–1297.

Wang, Q., Conway, M. A., & Hou, Y. (2004). Infantile amnesia: A cross-cultural investigation. *Cognitive Sciences, 1*, 123–135.

Wang, S., & Tamis-LeMonda, C. (2003). Do childrearing values in Taiwan and the United States reflect cultural values of collectivism and individualism? *Journal of Cross-Cultural Psychology, 34*, 629–642.

Wang, S., Baillargeon, R., & Paterson, S. (2005). Detecting continuity violations in infancy: A new account and new evidence from covering and tube events. *Cognition, 95*, 129–173.

Wang, Y., & Fong, V. L. (2009). Little emperors and the 4:2:1 generation: China's singletons. *Journal of the American Academy of Child & Adolescent Psychiatry, 48*, 1137–1139.

Wang, Y., & Lobstein, T. (2006). Worldwide trends in childhood overweight and obesity. *International Journal of Pediatric Obesity, 1*, 11–25.

Wang, Y., Wang, X., Kong, Y., Zhang, J. H., & Zeng, Q. (2010). The Great Chinese Famine leads to shorter and overweight females in Chongqing Chinese population after 50 years. *Obesity, 18*, 588–592.

Warnock, F. F., Castral, T. C., Brant, R., Sekilian, M., Leite, A. M., De La Presa Owens, S., & Schochi, C. G. S. (2010). Brief report: Maternal Kangaroo Care for neonatal pain relief: A systematic narrative review. *Journal of Pediatric Psychology, 35*, 975–984.

Warnock, F., & Sandrin, D. (2004). Comprehensive description of newborn distress behavior in response to acute pain (newborn male circumcision). *Pain, 107*, 242–255.

Warren, R. (2007). Electronic media, children's use of. In J. J. Arnett (Ed.), *Encyclopedia of children, adolescents, and the media* (Vol. 1, pp. 286–288). Thousand Oaks, CA: Sage.

Warren, S. L., & Simmens, S. J. (2005). Predicting toddler anxiety/depressive symptoms: Effects of caregiver sensitivity of temperamentally vulnerable children. *Infant of Medical Health Journal, 26*, 40–55.

Wasik, B. A., & Hindman, A. H. (2015). Talk alone won't close the 30-million word gap. *Phi Delta Kappan, 96*(6), 50–54. http://doi.org/10.1177/0031721715575300.

Waterman, A. S. (1992). Identity as an aspect of optimal functioning. In G. R. Adams, T. P. Gullotta, & R. Montemayor (Eds.), *Adolescent identity formation* (Vol. 4, pp. 50–72). Newbury Park, CA: Sage.

Waterman, A. S. (1999). Issues of identity formation revisited: United States and the Netherlands. *Developmental Review, 19*, 462–479.

Waterman, A. S. (2007). Doing well: The relationship of identity status to three conceptions of well-being. *Identity, 7*, 289–307.

Waters, E., & Deane, K. E. (1987). Attachment Q-set. doi: http://dx.doi.org.eres.library.manoa.hawaii.edu/10.1037/t17841-000.

Waters, E., Vaughn, B. E., Posada, G., & Kondo-Ikemara, K. (1995). Caregiving, cultural, and cognitive perspectives on secure-base behavior and working models: New growing points of attachment theory and research. *Monographs of the Society for Research in Child Development, 60*(2–3).

Watkin, P. M. (2011). The value of the neonatal hearing screen. *Paediatrics and Child Health, 21*, 37–41.

Watson, J. B. (1924/1998). *Behaviorism.* New Brunswick, NJ: Transaction.

Watson, P. (2014). *The age of atheists: How we have sought to live since the death of God.* New York, NY: Simon and Schuster.

Waxman, S. R. (2003). Links between object categorization and naming: Origins and emergence in human infants. In D. H. Rakison & L. M. Oakes (Eds.), *Early category and concept development: Making sense of the blooming, buzzing confusion* (pp. 193–209). New York, NY: Oxford University Press.

Waxman, S. R., & Lidz, J. L. (2006). Early word learning. In W. Damon & R. Lerner (Eds.), & D. Kuhn & R. Siegler (Vol. Eds.), *Handbook of child psychology: Vol. 2. Cognition, perception and language* (6th ed., pp. 299–335). New York, NY: Wiley.

Way, N. (2004). Intimacy, desire, and distrust in the friendships of adolescent boys. In N. Way & J. Y. Chu (Eds.), *Adolescent boys: Exploring diverse cultures of boyhood* (pp. 167–196). New York, NY: New York University Press.

Way, N., Reddy, R., & Rhodes, J. (2007). Students' perceptions of school climate during the middle school years: Associations with trajectories of psychological and behavioral adjustment. *American Journal of Community Psychology, 40,* 194–213.

Weaver, S. E., & Coleman, M. (2010). Caught in the middle mothers in step-families. *Journal of Social and Personal Relationships, 27,* 305–326.

Weber, D. (2006). Media use by infants and toddlers: *A potential for play.* Oxford University Press, New York.

WebMD. (2011). *Vaginal birth after cesarean (VBAC)—Risks of VBAC and cesarean deliveries.* Retrieved from http://www.webmd.com/baby/tc/vaginal-birth-after-cesarean-vbac-risks-of-vbac-and-cesarean-deliveries.

Weglage, J., Fromm, J., van Teeffelen-Heithoff, A., Möller, H. E., Koletzko, B., Marquardt, T., ... Feldmann, R. (2013). Neurocognitive functioning in adults with phenylketonuria: results of a long term study. *Molecular Genetics and Metabolism, 110 Suppl,* S44–S48. http://doi.org/10.1016/j.ymgme.2013.08.013.

Weichold, K., Silbereisen, R. K., & Schmitt-Rodermund, E. (2003). Short-term and long-term consequences of early vs. late physical maturation in adolescents. In C. Haywood (Ed.), *Puberty and psychopathology* (pp. 241–276). Cambridge, MA: Cambridge University Press.

Weinberg, R. A. (2004). The infant and the family in the twenty-first century. *Journal of the American Academy of Child & Adolescent Psychiatry, 43,* 115–116.

Weiner, I. B. (1992). *Psychological disturbance in adolescence* (2nd ed.). New York, NY: Wiley.

Weinfeld, N. S., Whaley, G. J. L., & Egeland, B. (2004). Continuity, discontinuity, and coherence in attachment from infancy to late adolescence: Sequelae of organization and disorganization. *Attachment and Human Development, 6,* 73–97.

Weir, K. F., & Jose, P. E. (2010). The perception of false self scale for adolescents: Reliability, validity, and longitudinal relationships with depressive and anxious symptoms. *British Journal of Developmental Psychology, 28,* 393–411.

Weisgram, E. S., Bigler, R. S., & Liben, L. S. (2010). Gender, values, and occupational interests among children, adolescents, and adults. *Child Development, 81*(3), 778–796.

Weisleder, A., & Fernald, A. (2013). Talking to children matters early language experience strengthens processing and builds vocabulary. *Psychological science, 24*(11), 2143–2152.

Weisner, T. S. (1996). The 5 to 7 transition as an ecocultural project. In A. J. Sameroff & M. M. Haith. *The five to seven year shift: The age of reason and responsibility* (pp. 295–326). Chicago, IL: University of Chicago Press.

Weisner, T. S. (1997). The ecocultural project of human development: Why ethnography and its findings matter. *Ethos 25*(2), 177–190.

Weisner, T. (2008). Understanding new hope: A successful antipoverty program for working poor adults and their children. *Anthropology News, 49*(4), 19–20. doi:10.1525/an.2008.49.4.19.

Weisner, T. S. (1984). A cross-cultural perspective: Ecocultural niches of middle childhood. In A. Collins (Ed.). *The elementary school years: Understanding development during middle childhood* (pp. 335–369). Washington, DC: National Academy Press.

Wellman, H. M., & Liu, D. (2004). Scaling theory-of-mind tasks. *Child Development, 75,* 523–541. doi:10.1111/j.1467-8624.2004.00691.x.

Welti, C. (2002). Adolescents in Latin America: Facing the future with skepticism. In B. Brown, R. Larson, & T. S. Saraswathi (Eds.), *The world's youth: Adolescence in eight regions of the globe* (pp. 276–306). New York, NY: Cambridge University Press.

Wendland-Carro, J., Piccinini, C. A., & Millar, W. S. (1999). The role of an early intervention on enhancing the quality of mother–infant interaction. *Child Development, 70,* 713–731.

Wentzel, K. R. (2003). Sociometric status and adjustment in middle school: A longitudinal study. *The Journal of Early Adolescence, 23,* 5–38.

Werker, J. F., & Fennell, C. T. (2009). Infant speech perception and later language acquisition: Methodological underpinnings. In J. Colombo, P. McCardle, & L. Freund (Eds.), *Infant pathways to language: Methods, models, and research disorders* (pp. 85–98). New York, NY: Psychology Press.

Werker, J. F., & Byers-Heinlein, K. (2008). Bilingualism in infancy: first steps in perception and comprehension. *Trends in Cognitive Sciences, 12*(4), 144–151. doi:10.1016/j.tics.2008.01.008.

Werner, E. E., & Smith, R. S. (1982). *Vulnerable but invincible: A study of resilient children.* New York, NY: McGraw-Hill.

Werner, E. E., & Smith, R. S. (1992). *Overcoming the odds: High-risk children from birth to adulthood.* Ithaca, NY: Cornell University Press.

Werner, E. E., & Smith, R. S. (2001). *Journeys from childhood to midlife: Risk, resilience, and recovery.* Ithaca, NY: Cornell University Press.

Werner, E., Dawson, G., Osterling, J., & Dinno, N. (2000). Recognition of autism spectrum disorder before one year of age. A retrospective study based on home videotapes. *Journal of Autism & Developmental Disorders, 30,* 157–162.

Werner, L. A., & Marean, G. C. (1996). *Human auditory development.* Boulder, CO: Westview Press.

Westfall, R. E., & Benoit, C. (2004). The rhetoric of "natural" in natural childbirth: Childbearing women's perspectives on prolonged pregnancy and induction of labour. *Social Science & Medicine, 59,* 1397–1408.

Westling, E., Andrews, J. A., Hampson, S. E., & Peterson, M. (2008). Pubertal timing and substance use: The effects of gender, parental monitoring and deviant peers. *Journal of Adolescent Health, 42,* 555–563.

Westoff, C. F. (2003). *Trends in marriage and early childbearing in developing countries.* DHS Comparative Reports No. 5. Calverton, MD: ORC Macro.

Whaley, D. E. (2007). A life span developmental approach to studying sport and exercise behavior. In G. Tenenbaum & R. C. Eklund (Eds.), *Handbook of sport psychology* (3rd ed., pp. 645–661).

Whitaker, R. C., Wright, J. A., Pepe, M. S., Seidel, K. D., & Dietz, W. H. (1997). Predicting obesity in young adulthood from childhood and parental obesity. *The New England Journal of Medicine, 337,* 869–873.

White, M. J., & White, G. B. (2006). Implicit and explicit occupational gender stereotypes. *Sex Roles, 55,* 259–266.

Whiting, B. B. (1963). *Six cultures: Studies of child rearing.* Oxford, UK: Wiley.

Whiting, B. B., & Edwards, C. P. (1988). Children of different worlds: The formation of social behavior. Cambridge, MA: Harvard University Press. Whitman, J. S. (2010). Lesbians and gay men at midlife. In M. H. Guindon (Ed.), *Self-esteem across the lifespan: Issues and interventions* (pp. 235–248). New York, NY: Routledge.

Whiting, B. B., & Whiting, J. W. (1975). *Children of six cultures: A psychocultural analysis.* Oxford, England: Harvard University Press.

Whiting, J. W. M. (1966). *Field guide for a study of socialization* (Vol. 1). New York: J. Wiley.

Whitty, M. (2002). Possible selves: An exploration of utility of a narrative approach. *Identity, 2,* 211–228.

Wichstrom, L. (1999). The emergence of gender difference in depressed mood during adolescence: The role of intensified gender socialization. *Developmental Psychology, 35,* 232–245.

Wigfield, A., Eccles, J. S., Yoon, K. S., Harold, R. D., Arbreton, A. J., Freedman-Doan, C., & Blumenfeld, P. C. (1997). Changes in children's competence beliefs and subjective task values across the elementary school years: A three-year study. *Journal of Educational Psychology, 89*, 451–469.

Wilcox, A. J., Weinberg, C. R., & Baird, D. D. (1995). Timing of sexual intercourse in relation to ovulation: Effects on the probability of contraception, survival of the pregnancy, and sex of the baby. *New England Journal of Medicine, 333*, 1517–1519.

Wilcox, W. B. (2008). Focused on their families: Religion, parenting, and child well-being. In K. K. Kline (Ed.), *Authoritative communities: The scientific case for nurturing the whole child* (pp. 227–244). The Search Institute series on developmentally attentive community and society. New York, NY: Springer.

Willey, L. H. (2014). *Pretending to be normal: Living with Asperger's Syndrome (Autism Spectrum Disorder) Expanded Edition*. London, UK: Jessica Kingsley Publishers

Willford, Jennifer A., Richardson, G. A., Leech, S. L., & Day, N. L. (2004). Verbal and visuospatial learning and memory function in children with moderate prenatal alcohol exposure. *Alcoholism: Clinical and Experimental Research, 28*(3), 497–507.

Williams, A. F., & Ferguson, S. A. (2002). Rationale for graduated licensing and the risks it should address. *Injury Prevention, 8* (Suppl. II), ii9–ii16.

Williams, A. F., Tefft, B. C., & Grabowski, J. G. (2012). Graduated driver licensing research, 2010-present. *Journal of Safety Research, 43*(3), 195–203.

Williams, A. L., Khattak, A. Z., Garza, C. N., & Lasky, R. E. (2009). The behavioral pain response to heelstick in preterm neonates studied longitudinally: Description, development, determinants, and components. *Early Human Development, 85*, 369–374.

Williams, D. R. (2005). The health of U.S. racial and ethnic populations. *Journals of Gerontology, 60B*(Special Issue II), 53–62.

Willinger, M., Ko, C.-W., Hoffman, J. J., Kessler, R. C., & Corwin, M. J. (2003). Trends in infant bed sharing in the United States. *Archives of Pediatrics and Adolescent Medicine, 157*, 43–49.

Wilson, E. O. (2012). *The social conquest of earth*. New York, NY: W.W. Norton.

Wilson, J. Q., & Herrnstein, R. J. (1985). *Crime and human nature*. New York, NY: Simon and Schuster.

Wimer, C., & Bloom, D. (2014). *Boosting the life chances of young men of color: Evidence from promising programs* (SSRN Scholarly Paper No. ID 2466591). Rochester, NY: Social Science Research Network. Retrieved from http://papers.ssrn.com/abstract=2466591.

Winsler, A., Fernyhough, C., & Montero, I. (Eds.). (2009). *Private speech, executive functioning, and the development of verbal self-regulation*. Cambridge: Cambridge University Press.

Wolak, J., Mitchell, K. J., & Finkelhor, D. (2007). Does online harassment constitute bullying? An exploration of online harassment by known peers and online-only contacts. *Journal of Adolescent Health, 41*(Suppl. 6), S51–S58.

Wolf, J. B. (2007). Is breast really best? Risk and total motherhood in the national breastfeeding awareness campaign. *Journal of Health Politics, Policy and Law, 32*, 595–63.

Wong, S., Chan, K., Wong, V., & Wong, W. (2002). Use of chopsticks in Chinese children. *Child: Care, Health, & Development, 28*, 157–161.

Woodhall, S. C., Lehtinen, M., Verho, T., Huhtala, H., Hokkanen, M., & Kosunen, E. (2007). Anticipated acceptance of HPV vaccination at the baseline of implementation: A survey of parental and adolescent knowledge and attitudes in Finland. *Journal of Adolescent Health, 40*, 466–469.

Woodward, A. L., & Markman, E. M. (1998). Early word learning. In W. Damon (Ed.), & D. Kuhn & R. S. Siegler (Vol. Eds.), *Handbook of child psychology: Vol. 2. Cognition, perception and language* (5th ed., pp. 371–420). New York, NY: Wiley.

Woodward, E. H., & Gridina, N. (2000). *Media in the home, 2000: The fifth annual survey of parents and children*. Philadelphia, PA: The Annenberg Public Policy Center of the University of Pennsylvania. Available: http://www.appcpenn.org/mediainhome/survey/survey7.pdf.

World Bank. (2011). *India's undernourished children: A call for action*. Retrieved from http://web.worldbank.org/WBSITE/EXTERNAL/COUNTRIES/SOUTHASIAEXT/0,,contentMDK:20916955~pagePK:146736~pi PK:146830~theSitePK:223547,00.html.

World Health Organization (WHO). (2008a). *Significant caries index: Data for some selected countries*. Retrieved from www.whocollab.od.mah.se/sicdata.html.

World Health Organization (WHO). (2008b). *Worldwide prevalence of anaemia*. Geneva, Switzerland: Author.

World Health Organization (WHO). (2009). *Department of making pregnancy safer: Annual report*. Geneva, Switzerland: Author.

World Health Organization (WHO). (2011). *World health statistics*. Geneva, Switzerland: Author.

World Health Organization (WHO). (2013). *World malaria report*. Geneva, Switzerland: Author.

World Health Organization (WHO). (2015a). *Statement on Caesarean section rates*. Geneva, Switzerland: Author.

World Health Organization (WHO). (2015b). *World health statistics*. Geneva, Switzerland: Author.

World Health Organization, Multicentre Growth Reference Study Group (2006). *WHO child growth standards: Length/height-for-age, weight-for-age, weight-for-length, weight-for-height and body mass index-for-age*. Geneva, Switzerland: World Health Organization. Retrieved from http://www.who.int/childgrowth/standards/en/.

World Internet Project. (2013). *International report, Fifth edition*. Retrieved from http://www.worldinternetproject.net.

Worthman, C. M. (1987). Interactions of physical maturation and cultural practice in ontogeny: Kikuyu adolescents. *Cultural Anthropology, 2*, 29–38.

Worthman, C. M. (2010). The ecology of human development: Evolving models for cultural psychology. *Journal of Cross-Cultural Psychology, 41*(4), 546–562. doi:10.1177/0022022110362627.

Wrangham, R. (2009). *Catching fire: How cooking made us human*. New York, NY: Basic Books.

Wright, V. C., Schieve, L. A., Reynolds, M. A., Jeng, G., & Kissin, D. (2004). Assisted reproductive technology surveillance—United States 2001. *Morbidity and Mortality Weekly Report, 53*, 1–20.

Wu, C.-S., Jew, C. P., & Lu, H.-C. (2011). Lasting impacts of prenatal cannabis exposure and the role of endogenous cannabinoids in the developing brain. *Future Neurology, 6*(4), 459–480.

Wu, L., Schlenger, W., & Galvin, D. (2003). The relationship between employment and substance abuse among students aged 12 to 17. *Journal of Adolescent Health, 32*, 5–15.

Xue, Y., & Meisels, S. J. (2004). Early literacy instruction and learning in kindergarten: Evidence from the early childhood longitudinal study—kindergarten classes of 1998–1999. *American Educational Research Journal, 41*, 191–229.

Yang, Z., & Gaydos, L. M. (2010). Reasons for and challenges of recent increases in teen birth rates: A study of family planning service policies and demographic changes at the state level. *Journal of Adolescent Health, 46*(6), 517–524.

Yang, B., Ollendick, T. H., Dong, Q., Xia, Y., & Lin, L. (1995). Only children and children with siblings in the People's Republic of China: Levels of fear, anxiety, and depression. *Child Development, 66*, 1301–1311.

Yasui, M., Dorham, C. L., & Dishion, T. J. (2004). Ethnic identity and psychological adjustment: A validity analysis for European American and African American adolescents. *Journal of Adolescent Research, 19*, 807–825.

Yeung, D. Y. L., & Tang, C. S.-K., & Lee, A. (2005). Psychosocial and cultural factors influencing expectations of menarche: A study on Chinese premenarcheal teenage girls. *Journal of Adolescent Research, 20*, 118–135.

Yoos, H. L., Kitzman, H., Halterman, J. S., Henderson, C., Sidora-Arcoleo, K., & McMullen, A. (2006). Treatment regimens and health care utilization in children with persistent asthma symptoms. *Journal of Asthma, 43*, 385–391.

Young, K. S. (2008). Internet sex addiction risk factors, stages of development, and treatment. *American Behavioral Scientist, 52*, 21–37.

Young-Hyman, D., Schlundt, D. G., Herman-Wenderoth, L., & Bozylinski, K. (2003). Obesity, appearance, and psychosocial adaptation in young African American children. *Journal of Pediatric Psychology, 28*, 463–472.

Youniss, J., & Smollar, J. (1985). *Adolescent relations with mothers, fathers, and friends.* Chicago, IL: University of Chicago Press.

Youniss, J., McLellan, J. A., & Yates, M. (1999). Religion, community service, and identity in American youth. *Journal of Adolescence, 22*, 243–253.

Zach, T., Pramanik, A., & Ford, S. P. (2001). Multiple births. eMedicine. Retrieved from www.mypage.direct.ca/csamson/multiples/2twinningrates.html.

Zachrisson, H. D., Dearing, E., Lekhal, R., & Toppelberg, C. O. (2013). Little evidence that time in child care causes externalizing problems during early childhood in Norway. *Child Development, 84*, 1152–1170.

Zehle, K., Wen, L. M., Orr, N., & Rissel, C. (2007). "It's not an issue at the moment": A qualitative study of mothers about childhood obesity. *MCN: The American Journal of Maternal/Child Nursing, 32*, 36–41.

Zelazo, P. D., Müller, U., Frye, D., Marcovitch, S., Argitis, G., Boseovski, J., Chiang, J. K., Hongwanishkul, D., Schuster, B. V., Sutherland, A., & Carlson, S. M. (2003). The development of executive function in early childhood. *Monographs of the Society for Research in Child Development, 68*(3), i–151.

Zeskind, P. S., & Lester, B. M. (2001). Analysis of infant crying. In L. T. Singer & P. S. Zeskind (Eds.), *Biobehavioral assessment of the infant* (pp. 149–166). New York, NY: Guilford.

Zhang, W., & Fuligni, A. J. (2006). Authority, autonomy, and family relationships among adolescents in urban and rural China. *Journal of Research on Adolescence, 16*, 527–537.

Zhong, J., & Arnett, J. J. (2014). Conceptions of adulthood among migrant women workers in China. *International Journal of Behavioral Development, 38*, 255–265.

Zieber, N., Kangas, A., Hock, A., & Bhatt, R. S. (2014). The development of intermodal emotion perception from bodies and voices. *Journal of Experimental Child Psychology, 126*, 68–79.

Zielinski, D. S. (2009). Child maltreatment and adult socioeconomic well-being. *Child Abuse and Neglect, 33*, 666–678.

Zigler, E., & Styfco, S. J. (Eds.). (2004). *The Head Start debates.* Baltimore, MD: Brookes.

Zimmerman, F. J., Christakis, D. A., & Meltzoff, A. N. (2007). Associations between media viewing and language development in children under age 2 years. *The Journal of Pediatrics, 151*(4), 364–368. doi:10.1016/j.jpeds.2007.04.071.

Zimmermann, M. B., Pieter, L. J., & Chandrakant, S. P. (2008). Iodine-deficiency disorders. *The Lancet, 372*, 1251–1262.

Zumwalt, M. (2008). Effects of the menstrual cycle on the acquisition of peak bone mass. In J. J. Robert-McComb, R. Norman, & M. Zumwalt (Eds.), *The active female: Health issues throughout the lifespan* (pp. 141–151). Totowa, NJ: Humana Press.

Answers

Chapter 1

Research Focus (pp. 41–42)

1. c; 2. a

Chapter Quiz (p. 47)

1. b; 2. a; 3. d; 4. c;
5. b; 6. a; 7. a; 8. b;
9. d; 10. c; 11. a; 12. b;
13. a; 14. c; 15. d

Chapter 2

Research Focus (pp. 58–59)

1. d; 2. c

Chapter Quiz (pp. 82–83)

1. b; 2. b; 3. a; 4. c;
5. a; 6. d; 7. d; 8. c;
9. d; 10. d; 11. c; 12. b;
13. b; 14. b; 15. b; 16. d;
17. b

Chapter 3

Research Focus (pp. 115–116)

1. b; 2. c

Chapter Quiz (pp. 124–125)

1. c; 2. a; 3. d; 4. c;
5. a; 6. a; 7. b; 8. a;
9. b; 10. b; 11. c; 12. b;
13. c; 14. a; 15. d; 16. d;
17. b; 18. c

Chapter 4

Research Focus (pp. 164–165)

1. d; 2. b

Chapter Quiz (pp. 176–177)

1. b; 2. b; 3. a; 4. c;
5. d; 6. b; 7. d; 8. a;
9. c; 10. a; 11. c; 12. a;
13. c; 14. d; 15. a; 16. c;
17. c; 18. b; 19. b; 20. d;
21. b

Chapter 5

Research Focus (pp. 220–221)

1. b; 2. d

Chapter Quiz (pp. 226–227)

1. d; 2. b; 3. b; 4. d;
5. a; 6. b; 7. a; 8. c;
9. c; 10. a; 11. b; 12. d;
13. b; 14. c; 15. c; 16. b;
17. d; 18. b; 19. d; 20. b;
21. c

Chapter 6

Research Focus (pp. 277–278)

1. c

Chapter Quiz (pp. 284–285)

1. a; 2. d; 3. c; 4. d;
5. d; 6. a; 7. b; 8. c;
9. c; 10. a; 11. c; 12. b;
13. a; 14. c; 15. d; 16. a;
17. c; 18. c; 19. c; 20. b;
21. b; 22. a; 23. c; 24. a;
25. b

Chapter 7

Research Focus (pp. 340–341)

1. b

Chapter Quiz (pp. 343–345)

1. b; 2. b; 3. a; 4. d;
5. a; 6. b; 7. a; 8. a;
9. c; 10. b; 11. a; 12. d;
13. c; 14. a; 15. c; 16. a;
17. b; 18. b; 19. a; 20. c

Chapter 8

Research Focus (p. 385)

1. b

Chapter Quiz (pp. 403–405)

1. b; 2. b; 3. c; 4. a;
5. b; 6. a; 7. d; 8. b;
9. a; 10. c; 11. a; 12. c;
13. d; 14. b; 15. b; 16. c;
17. a; 18. b; 19. c; 20. a;
21. c; 22. d; 23. d; 24. c;
25. b

Chapter 9

Research Focus (p. 418)

1. b; 2. c

Chapter Quiz (pp. 454–455)

1. a; 2. b; 3. d; 4. c;
5. b; 6. d; 7. d; 8. d;
9. b; 10. c; 11. a; 12. b;
13. c; 14. c; 15. c; 16. c;
17. a; 18. c; 19. b

Credits

Text and Art

Chapter 1 Figure 1.2, p. 6: Source: Based on Kaiser Family Foundation (2013); **Extract, p. 17:** Source: Daniel J. Levinson, The Seasons of a man's life. Knopf, 1978; **Extract, p. 21:** Source: Watson, J. B. (1924/1998). Behaviorism. New Brunswick, NJ: Transaction, p. 82; **Figure 1.8, p. 30:** Source: Adapted from: Weisner, T. S. (1984). Ecocultural niches of middle childhood: A cross-cultural perspective. In A. Collins (Ed.), Development during middle childhood: The years from six to twelve. Washington, DC: National Academy Press; **Extract, p. 37:** Source: Based on Based on Fisher, C. B. (2003). A goodness-of-fit ethic for child assent to nonbeneficial research. The American Journal of Bioethics, 3, 27–28.; Rosnow, R. L., & Rosenthal, R. L. (2005). Beginning behavioral research (5th ed.). Upper Saddle River, NJ: Prentice Hall; **Extract, p. 40:** Source: Keegan, R.T. & Gruber, H.E. (1985) Charles Darwin's unpublished "Diary of an infant" An early phase in his psychological work. In G. Eckhardt, W.G. Bringmann & L. Spring (eds) Contributions to a history of developmental psychology. New York, Mouton, pp 127–145

Chapter 2 Extract, p. 80: Source: Righetti, P. L., Dell'Avanzo, M., Grigio, M., & Nicolini, U. (2005). Maternal/paternal antenatal attachment and fourth–dimensional ultrasound technique: A preliminary report. British Journal of Psychology, 96, 129–137

Chapter 3 Map 3.1, p. 89: Source: Based on WHO (2014); **Extract, p. 90:** Source: WedMD (2011). Vaginal birth after cesarean (VBAC)-Risks of VBAC and cesarean deliveries. Retrieved from http://www.webmd.com/baby/tc/vaginal-birth-after-cesaran-vbac-risks-of-vbac-and-cesarean-deliveries. Page 2; **Extract, p. 96:** Source: Mayo Clinic Staff (2011). Stages of Labor: Baby, it's time!; **Map 3.2, p. 101:** Source: Based on UNICEF (2014); **Figure 3.2, p. 117:** Source: Barr, R.G. (2009) The phenomena of early infant crying and colic, Paper presented at the Centre for Community and Child Health, Melbourne Australia, March 2. [see http://www.purplecrying.info/sections/index.php?sct=1&]; **Extract, p. 118:** Source: Data from Eisenberg et al., 2011; **Extract, p. 119:** Source: Barr, R.G. (2009) The phenomena of early infant crying and colic, Paper presented at the Centre for Community and Child Health, Melbourne Australia, March 2

Chapter 4 Figure 4.4, p. 133: Source: Based on Beckett, C., Maughan, B., Rutter, M., Castle, J., Colvert, E., Groothus, C, Sonuga-Barke, W.J.S. (2006) "Do the effects of early severe deprivation on cognition persist into early adolescence? Findings from the English and Romanian adoptees study", Child Development, 77, 696–711; **Extract, p. 135:** Source: DeLoache, J.S., & Gottlied, A. (2000). A world of babies: Imagined childcare guides for seven societies. New York, NY: Cambridge University Press; **Map 4.1, p. 139:** Source: Based on UNICEF (2014); **Figure 4.6, p. 140:** Source: Based on Pierre, Sabrina. "Vaccinations." Prezi.com. Prezi, 21 Nov. 2014. Web. 20 Oct. 2015; **Figure 4.10, p. 152:** Source: © Pearson Education, Inc.; **Extract, p. 155:** Source: Bayley, N. (2005). Bayley Scales of Infant and Toddler Development, Third Edition (Bayley-III). San Antonio, TX: Harcourt Assessment

Chapter 5 Figure 5.1, p. 181: Source: Based on World Health Organization (2006); **Extract, p. 193:** Source: Rogoff, B. (1995). Observing sociocultural activities on three planes: Participatory appropriation, guided participation, and apprenticeship. In J. V. Wertsch, P. del Rio, & A. Alvarez (Eds.) Sociocultural studies of the mind (pp. 273-294). New York: NY: Cambridge University Press. p .142; **Extract, p. 193:** Source: Leakey, R. (1994). The origins of humankind. New York, NY: Basic Books. p. 119; **Figure 5.3, p. 194:** Source: © Pearson Education, Inc.; **Extract, p. 204:** Source: Murkoff, H. E., Eisenberg, A., Mazel, S., & Hathaway, S.E. (2003). What to expect the first year (2nd ed). New York, NY: Workman; **Extract, p. 214:** Source: Ainsworth, M. S. (1977). Infant development and mother-infant interaction among Ganda and American families. In P.H. Leiderman, S. R. Tulkin, & A. Rosenfeld (Eds.), Culture and infancy: Variations in the human experience (pp. 119–149). New York, NY: Academic Press. p. 143; **Extract, p. 221:** Source: Donovan, J., & Zucker, C. (2010, October). Autism's first child. The Atlantic, pp. 78–90

Chapter 6 Figure 6.2, p. 233: Source: Based on Ogden CL, Carroll MD, Kit BK, & Flegal KM. (2014). Prevalence of childhood and adult obesity in the United States, 2011–2012. JAMA, 311(8), 806–814. http://doi.org/10.1001/jama.2014.732; **Figure 6.3, p. 235:** Source: Based on data from WHO; UN estimates; **Figure 6.6, p. 246:** Source: © Pearson Education, Inc.; **Extract, p. 256:** Source: Bem, S. L. (1981). Gender schema theory: A cognitive account of sex-typing. Psychological Review, 88, 354–364. p. 355

Chapter 7 Figure 7.3, p. 292: Source: Based on Fryar et al. (2012); **Extract, p. 298:** Source: Piaget, J. (1965) The moral judgment of the child. New York, NY: Free Press (Original work published 1932), p. 167; **Extract, p. 298:** Source: Adapted from Ginsburg. H.P. & Opper, S (1979) Piaget's Theory of Intellectual Development. Eaglewood cliffs, NJ: Prentice Hall. p. 123; **Extract, p. 322:** Source: Larson, R., & Richards, M. H. (1994, p. 85). Divergent realities: The emotional lives of mothers, fathers, and adolescents. New York, NY: Basic Books; **Figure 7.9, p. 339: Data** Source: Rideout (2013); **Extract, p. 376:** Source: Rousseau, Jean-Jacques Rousseau. Emilius and Sophia; or, The Solitaries. London: Printed by H. Baldwin, 1783

Chapter 8 Extract, p. 376: Source: Aristotle; **Extract, p. 376:** Source: Larson, R., & Richards, M. H. (1994, p. 85). Divergent realities: The emotional lives of mothers, fathers, and adolescents. New York, NY: Basic Books; **Extract, p. 390:** Source: Sussman, S., Pokhrel, P., Ashmore, R. D., & Brown, B. B. (2007). Adolescent peer group identification and characteristics: A review of the literature. Addictive Behaviors, 32, 1602–1627; **Extract, p. 401:** Source: Ann S. Masten, Ordinary magic. Resilience processes in development, American Psychologist, Vol. 56, No. 3, 227–238, 2001, p. 228

Chapter 9 Extract, p. 411: Source: Arnett, J.J., & Schwab, J. (2012). The Clark University Poll of Emerging Adults: Thriving, struggling, and hopeful. Worcester, MA: Clark University. Retrieved from http://www.clarku.edu/clark-poll-emerging-adults/; **Extract, p. 415:** Source: Brown, A. S., & Susser, E. S. (2002). In utero infection and adult schizophrenia. Mental Retardation and Developmental Disabilities Research Reviews, 8, 51–57; **Extract, p. 417:** Source: Arnett, J. J. (1996). Metalheads: Heavy metal music and adolescent alienation. Boulder, CO: Westview Press. p. 79; **Extract, p. 424:** Source: Rohlen, T. P. (1983). Japan's high schools. Berkeley: University of California Press; **Map 9.1, p. 425:** Source: Based on UNESCO (2013); **Extract, p. 435:** Source: Erikson, E. H. (1968). Identity: Youth and crisis. New York, NY: Norton. p. 156; **Extract, p. 443:** Source: Arnett, J. J. (2004). Emerging adulthood: The winding road from the late teens through the twenties. New York: Oxford University Press. p. 49; **Extract, p. 443:** Source: Arnett, J. J. (2004). Emerging adulthood: The winding road from the late teens through the twenties. New York: Oxford University Press. p. 54, 53; **Extract, p. 446:** Source: Popenoe, D., & Whitehead, B. D. (2001). The state of our unions, 2001: The social health of marriage in America. Report of the National Marriage Project, Rutgers, New Brunswick, NJ. Available: http://marriage.rutgers.edu; **Map 9.2, p. 449:** Source: Based on UNAIDS, GAP Report, 2014; **Extract, p. 451:** Source: Arnett, J.J., & Schwab, J. (2012). The Clark University Poll of Emerging Adults: Thriving, struggling, and hopeful. Worcester, MA: Clark University. Retrieved from http://www.clarku.edu/clark-poll-emerging-adults/

Photographs

Name Index

Dodge, K. A., 54, 167, 279, 280, 397
Doherty, I., 315
Dollahite, D. C., 383
Dolphin, T., 373
Domitrovich, C. E., 253
Domsch, H., 153
Donat, D., 315
Dondi, M., 168
Dong, Q., 275
Donnelly, D. A., 271
Donnelly, K., 157
D'Onofrio, B., 54, 305
Donovan, J., 221, 222, 223
Dooley, M. D., 329
Dopfner, M., 318
Döpfner, M., 318
Dorham, C. L., 438
Dorjee, T., 393
Dorn, L. D., 87, 351
Douglas-Palumberi, H., 273
Douglass, C. B., 409, 410, 412, 444, 446
Dove, H., 143
Doyle, L. W., 102
Doyle, R. E., 194
Drager, B., 238
Dratva, J., 115
Dreher, E., 411
Dreppner, J. M., 133
Driessen, R., 198
Dritsa, M., 122
Dronkers, N. F., 194
Dropik, P. I., 191
Drotar, D., 155
Du, J., 277
Duan, X., 293
Dubas, J. S., 443
DuBois, D., 378
DuBois, D. L., 401
DuCette, J., 271
Due, P., 391
Duggan, M., 396, 446, 450
Dumont-Driscoll, M., 356
Dunbar, C., 315
Duncan, G. J., 368
Dungan, J., 78
Dunn, D. M., 273
Dunn, J., 217, 218, 243, 275, 276, 315, 328, 331
Dunn, J. F., 274
Dunne, M. P., 312
Dupont, S., 438
Dupuis, G., 122
Durvasula, R., 392
Dustmann, C., 373
Dwokin, J., 389
Dworkin, J. B., 384
Dyer, S., 276, 277

E
Eaglesfield, D., 138
Eagly, A. H., 439
Ebbesen, E. B., 261

Eberhart-Phillips, J. E., 74
Eccles, J. S., 324
Eckenrode, J., 273
Eder, D., 378
Edgin, J., 78
Edmonds, L., 197
Edwards, C. P., 187, 199, 260, 270, 272, 274, 279, 326, 327, 333
Edwards, R. P., 270
Eftekhari, A., 328
Egeland, B., 212
Egerter, S., 414
Ehiri, J. E., 75
Ehrenberg, H. M., 70
Eidelman, A. I., 103, 104, 113
Eiden, R. D., 75, 100, 217
Eilers, M. A., 393
Eilers, R. E., 159
Eimas, P. D., 191
Eisenberg, A., 134, 144, 168, 185, 204
Eisenberg, N., 260, 262
Eisenstein, J., 271
Ekman, P., 166
Elben, C., 119
Eldin, A. S., 356
El harmi, J., 355
Eliasson, M., 92
Elkind, D., 364, 365, 366, 377
Elliott, G. C., 272
Ellison, N. C., 450
Ellison, R. C., 293
El-saleh, E., 355
Else-Quest, N., 252
Ember, C. R., 12
Ember, M., 12
Emde, R. N., 146, 167
Emery, R. E., 330, 331
Emory, E. K., 103
Emslie, G. J., 400
Engelberts, A. C., 118
Engelmann, J. B., 399
Englander, F., 450
Epperson, C. N., 121
Eppig, C., 305, 306
Erickson, J. D., 73, 74, 76
Erickson, P. I., 449
Ericsson, K. A., 414
Erikson, E. H., 19–21, 171, 173, 203, 260, 337, 408, 410, 433, 434, 435, 441
Eriksson, C., 92
Eriksson, K., 92
Erlandsson, K., 92
Eron, L. D., 340
Eslea, M., 336
Esmonde, I., 316
Espelage, D. L., 336
Espinosa, A., 438
Espinoza, G., 451
Espnes, G. A., 324
Espy, K. A., 75
Essex, M. J., 199
Estrada, S., 366

Estrada, S. M., 366
Eun, B. L., 353
Evans, D. E., 163
Evans, J., 121, 294
Evans, K., 357
Eveleth, P. B., 353
Everett, G. E., 270
Exner, N., 138
Ey, S., 400

F
Faber, B., 102
Fabes, R. A., 260, 277
Fabiano, G. A., 270
Facio, A., 411
Fackler, M., 424
Fagan, J. F., 156
Fagerlund, Å., 75
Fai, C. K., 394
Falissard, B., 318
Fanaroff, A. A., 102
Fang, H., 75, 98
Farber, H. J., 294
Farrington, D. P., 336
Farver, J. A., 438
Fast, P., 449
Fawcett, E., 170
Fay, K., 358
Fazzi, E., 109
Feagans, L., 379
Fearon, P., 102
Fedele, S. I. L. V. I. A., 209, 210, 212
Fefferman, N. H., 140
Feigenbaum, P., 192
Feigenson, L., 147
Fekkes, M., 336
Feldkamper, M., 289
Feldman, A., 439
Feldman, J. F., 153, 156
Feldman, R., 103, 104, 113
Feldman, S. D., 103
Feldmann, R., 80
Feldman-Savelsberg, P., 63
Felner, R., 378
Feng, J.-Y., 236
Fennell, C. T., 159
Ferber, S. G., 103
Ferguson, C. J., 271, 377
Ferguson, J., 315, 416
Ferguson, S. A., 417
Fergusson, D. M., 272
Fernald, A., 132, 150, 197, 199
Fernandez, M. I., 70
Fernyhough, C., 192
Feroleto, C. C., 194
Ferraro, V., 159
Ferrero, J., 354
Field, C. J., 234
Field, M. J., 235
field, T., 267
Field, T., 72, 103, 146
Field, T. M., 72, 103
Figueiredo, B., 120

Figueroa, Z., 103
Fildes, V., 112
Fincher, C. L., 305, 306
Fine, M., 331, 332
Fine, M. A., 329
Finer, L. B., 393
Fingerman, K. L., 433, 442
Finkel, M., 138
Finkelhor, D., 336, 391
Finkelstein, A. E., 295
Finley, G. E., 331
Finn, C. A., 60
Finnegan, L. P., 75
Finnegan, M., 75–76
Fintelman, M., 134
Finzi-Dottan, R., 389
Fisch, H., 78
Fischer, E. F., 392
Fischer, K. W., 151, 204, 206
Fisher, C. B., 37
Fisher, J. D., 448
Fisher, J. O., 233
Fisher, W. A., 448
Fitneva, S., 198, 199, 308
Fitzgerald, M., 322
Fitzgerald, P., 448
Fix, M., 368
Flament, M. F., 400
Flammer, A., 353
Flanagan, C., 440, 441
Flannery, K. A., 238
Flavell, J. H., 154, 196, 245, 300, 301, 363
Flegal, K. M., 233, 293, 294, 399
Fleming, T., 294
Fleming, T. P., 67
Fletcher, P., 159, 254
Floel, A., 238
Flood, M. F., 272
Flor, D. L., 401
Flower, D., 70
Flowers, P., 394
Floyd, F., 394
Floyd, L. R., 75
Flynn, J. R., 305
Foehr, U., 339
Foehr, U. G., 395, 396
Fogel, A., 168
Fomon, S. J., 128, 180
Fong, G. T., 449
Fong, V. L., 275
Foote, A., 75
Ford, C. S., 94, 392
Ford, G. W., 102
Ford, R. M., 301
Ford, S. P., 62
Forman, K. J., 103
Fortin, L., 400
Foss, R. D., 417
Foster, E. M., 157
Foster, P., 230
Foureur, M., 90
Fowler, F., 271

Subject Index

Boldface terms and page numbers indicate key terms. Page numbers followed by *f* indicate figures; those followed by *m* indicate maps; and those followed by *t* indicate tables.

A

Abortion, sex-selective, 52
Abstract thinking, 361
Abuse
  child, 272–273
  emotional, 272
  physical, 272
  substance, 358–360, 419–420
Academic performance, 312–313
  international comparisons in, 370–371
Accommodation, 23, 24
Achievement motivation in school, 314
Active genotype → environment effects, 57–58
Activity settings, 31
Actual self, 377
Addictive substance use in adolescence, 360
Adolescence, 346–403, 347
  cognitive development in, 361–374
    culture and cognition, 366–367
    information processing: selecting attention and advances in memory, 363–364
    Piaget's theory of formal operations, 361–363
    secondary education in United States, 367–368
    secondary education worldwide, 369–371
    social cognition, 364–366
    work, 371–373
  emotional and social development in, 375–403
    conflict with parents across cultures, 387
    crime and delinquency in, 397–399
    depression in, 399–401
    emotionality in, 376
    family relationships in, 384–388
    gender intensification in, 378–380
    media use in, 395–397
    moral development in, 380–383
    peers and friends in, 388–391
    pregnancy and contraceptive use in, 393
    religious beliefs in, 383
    resilience in, 401
    romantic relationships in, 391–392
    self-development in, 376–380
    sexuality in, 392–393
  physical development in, 348–360
    brain development in, 350–352
    changes of puberty in, 348–352
    eating disorders in, 356–358
    substance use in, 358–360
    timing of puberty in, 352–356
  as time of dramatic changes, 347
Adolescent egocentrism, 364
Adolescent-limited delinquent (ALD), 398
Adoption, intelligence quotient and, 304
Adult work, finding, in emerging adulthood, 428–430
Advertising, violence and, 280–281
African Americans
  asthma in children, 295
  infant mortality in, 103
Aggression
  bullying and, 336
  in early childhood, 278–280
  hostile, 279
  instrumental, 279
  media use and, 339–340
  physical, 279
  relational, 279
  verbal, 279, 280
Agility, 289
AIDS (acquired immune deficiency syndrome), 74
  transmission through breast milk, 114
Alcohol as teratogen, 75, 102
Allele, 51
Ambivalence, 322
American College of Obstetricians and Gynecologists (ACOG), 90
Amnesia, infantile, 232
Amniocentesis, 80–81
Amnion, 67
Amphetamine use in adolescence, 358
Anaclitic depression, 171
Anal stage, 19
Androgens, 349
Anemia, 234
  sickle-cell, 78–79
Anencephaly, 73
Animals, domestication of, 14
Animism, 25, 243
Anorexia nervosa, 356–358
A-not-B error, 150, 151
  toddlers avoidance of, 190
Anoxia, 99
Antidepressants
  in adolescence, 400

  in treating postpartum depression, 121–122
Apgar scale, 99–100, 99*t*, 106
Apprenticeship, 373
  in Europe, 373
Arab Spring, 442
Artificial insemination, 63
Asperger's syndrome, 221
Assessment in infant cognitive development, 155–157
Assimilation, 23, 24, 437
Assisted reproductive technologies (ART), 63
Asthma, 102, 294–295
Attachment in toddlers, 209–214
Attachment Q-Set (AQS), 214
Attachment theory, 171–172, 173, 209–212
  critiques of, 212–214
Attention, 153–154
Attention deficit/hyperactivity disorder (ADHD), 317–318
  in adolescence, 398
Attrition, 45
Authoritarian parents, 266–267
Authoritative parents, 266
Autism spectrum disorder (ASD), 221, 248
  in toddlers, 221–223
Autobiographical memory, 232
Automobile accidents, 295
Autonomy, 384
Autonomy versus shame and doubt, 20, 204
Axon, 130

B

Babbling, 158–159
"Baby Einstein" media, 156–157
Baby fat, loss of, 180
"BACK to Sleep" campaign, 134
Balance, 289
Barney and Friends (TV show), 224
Bayley Scales of Infant Development, 155
Behavior genetics, 54
  principles of, 54–55
Behaviorism, 21–22
Bicultural identity, 436
Biculturalism, 437
Bicycle accidents, 295
Bidirectional effects, 268
Bidirectional relation, 212